June 25–27, 2012
Pittsburgh, Pennsylvania, USA

**Association for
Computing Machinery**

Advancing Computing as a Science & Profession

SPAA'12

Proceedings of the

24th ACM Symposium on Parallelism in Algorithms and Architectures

Sponsored by:
ACM SIGACT & ACM SIGARCH

Supported by:
**Akamai, IBM Research, Intel, Oracle Labs
and Sandia National Laboratories**

Association for Computing Machinery

Advancing Computing as a Science & Profession

The Association for Computing Machinery
2 Penn Plaza, Suite 701
New York, New York 10121-0701

Copyright © 2012 by the Association for Computing Machinery, Inc. (ACM). Permission to make digital or hard copies of portions of this work for personal or classroom use is granted without fee provided that copies are not made or distributed for profit or commercial advantage and that copies bear this notice and the full citation on the first page. Copyright for components of this work owned by others than ACM must be honored. Abstracting with credit is permitted. To copy otherwise, to republish, to post on servers or to redistribute to lists, requires prior specific permission and/or a fee. Request permission to republish from: permissions@acm.org or Fax +1 (212) 869-0481.

For other copying of articles that carry a code at the bottom of the first or last page, copying is permitted provided that the per-copy fee indicated in the code is paid through www.copyright.com.

Notice to Past Authors of ACM-Published Articles
ACM intends to create a complete electronic archive of all articles and/or other material previously published by ACM. If you have written a work that has been previously published by ACM in any journal or conference proceedings prior to 1978, or any SIG Newsletter at any time, and you do NOT want this work to appear in the ACM Digital Library, please inform permissions@acm.org, stating the title of the work, the author(s), and where and when published.

ISBN: 978-1-4503-1213-4

Additional copies may be ordered prepaid from:

ACM Order Department
PO Box 30777
New York, NY 10087-0777, USA

Phone: 1-800-342-6626 (USA and Canada)
+1-212-626-0500 (Global)
Fax: +1-212-944-1318
E-mail: acmhelp@acm.org
Hours of Operation: 8:30 am – 4:30 pm ET

ACM Order Number: 417120

Printed in the USA

Foreword

This volume consists of papers that were presented at the 24th ACM Symposium on Parallelism in Algorithms and Architectures (SPAA 2012), held on 25–27 June 2012, in Pittsburgh, Pennsylvania, USA. It was sponsored by the ACM Special Interest Groups on Algorithms and Computation Theory (SIGACT) and Computer Architecture (SIGARCH) and organized in cooperation with the European Association for Theoretical Computer Science (EATCS). Financial support was provided by Akamai, IBM Research, and ACM SIGARCH.

The program committee selected the 31 SPAA 2012 regular presentations following electronic discussions. Of these papers, the paper *Memory-Mapping Support for Reducer Hyperobjects* by I-Ting Lee, Aamir Shafi, and Charles Leiserson was selected to receive the best paper award.

The regular presentations were selected out of 120 submitted abstracts. The mix of selected papers reflects the unique nature of SPAA in bringing together the theory and practice of parallel computing. SPAA defines parallelism very broadly to encompass any computational device or scheme that can perform multiple operations or tasks simultaneously or concurrently. The technical papers in this volume are to be considered preliminary versions, and authors are generally expected to publish polished and complete versions in archival scientific journals.

In addition to the regular presentations, this volume includes 8 brief announcements. The committee's decisions in accepting brief announcements were based on the perceived interest of these contributions, with the goal that they serve as bases for further significant advances in parallelism in computing. Extended versions of the SPAA brief announcements and posters may be published later in other conferences or journals. Finally, this year's program also included keynote addresses by Ravi Rajwar of Intel Corporation, and Doug Lea of the State University of New York at Oswego.

The program committee would like to thank all who submitted papers and who helped the committee in the review process. The names of these external reviewers appear later in the proceedings. We would very much like to thank the program committee for all of their hard work during the paper selection process. The authors, the external reviewers, and the program committee together made it possible to come up with a great collection of papers for the conference.

Guy Blelloch
Carnegie Mellon University
SPAA 2012 General Chair

Maurice Herlihy
Brown University
SPAA 2012 Program Chair

Table of Contents

Session 3: Parallel Algorithms
Session Chair: Phil Gibbons *(Intel Research)*

Session 4: Communication
Session Chair: Christian Scheideler *(University of Paderborn)*

Keynote Address II
Session Chair: Maurice Herlihy *(Brown University)*

Session 5: Concurrent Objects
Session Chair: Yehuda Afek *(Tel Aviv University)*

Brief Announcements II
Session Chair: David Bunde *(Knox College)*

Session 6: Parallel Algorithms II
Session Chair: Petra Berenbrink *(Simon Fraser University)*

Session 7: Scheduling
Session Chair: Yossi Lev *(Oracle Labs)*

Session 8: Games
Session Chair: David Bunde *(Knox College)*

Session 9: Parallel Algorithms and Data Structures

Session Chair: Yossi Lev *(Oracle Labs)*

Session 10: Networks

Session Chair: Rezaul Chowdhury *(SUNY Stony Brook)*

SPAA 2012 Symposium Organization

General Chair: Guy Blelloch *(Carnegie Mellon University, USA)*

Program Chair: Maurice Herlihy *(Brown University, USA)*

Program Committee: Yehuda Afek *(Tel Aviv University, Israel)*
Chen Avin *(Ben Gurion University of the Negev, Israel)*
Petra Berenbrink *(Simon Fraser University, Canada)*
Rezaul Chowdhury *(State University of New York at Stony Brook, USA)*
Benjamin Doerr *(MPI Saarbrücken, Germany)*
Jeremy Fineman *(Georgetown University, USA)*
Michael Goodrich *(University of California at Irvine, USA)*
Martin Höfer *(RWTH Aachen, Germany)*
Eric Koskinen *(New York University, USA)*
Christoph Lenzen *(Hebrew University of Jerusalem, Israel)*
Yossi Lev *(Oracle Labs, USA)*
Avi Mendelson *(Intel, USA)*
Binoy Ravindran *(Virginia Tech, USA)*
Boaz Patt-Shamir *(Tel Aviv University, Israel)*
Erez Petrank *(Technion, Israel)*
Giuseppe Persiano *(University of Salerno, Italy)*
Peter Sanders *(Karlsruhe Institute of Technology, Germany)*
Thomas Sauerwald *(MPI Saarbrücken, Germany)*

Publicity Chair: Jeremy Fineman *(Georgetown University, USA)*

Treasurer: David Bunde *(Knox College, USA)*

Secretary: Christian Scheideler *(University of Paderborn, Germany)*

Local Arrangements: Guy Blelloch *(Carnegie Mellon University, USA)*

Steering Committee: Guy Blelloch *(Carnegie Mellon University, USA)*
David Culler *(University of California at Berkeley, USA)*
Frank Dehne *(Carleton University, Canada)*
Pierre Fraigniaud *(University of Paris-Sud, France)*
Phil Gibbons *(Intel Research, USA)*
Maurice Herlihy *(Brown University, USA)*
Tom Leighton *(MIT and Akamai Technologies, USA)*
Charles Leiserson *(MIT, USA)*
Fabrizio Luccio *(University of Pisa, Italy)*
Friedhelm Meyer auf der Heide *(University of Paderborn, Germany)*
Gary Miller *(Carnegie Mellon University, USA)*
Burkhard Monien *(University of Paderborn, Germany)*
Franco Preparata *(Brown University, USA)*
Vijaya Ramachandran *(University of Texas at Austin, USA)*
Arnold Rosenberg *(Univ of Massachusetts Amherst & Colorado State Univ, USA)*
Paul Spirakis *(CTI, Greece)*
Uzi Vishkin *(University of Maryland, USA)*

Reviewers:

Fidaa Abed
Gul Agha
Hoda Akbari
Kamal Al-Bawani
Susanne Albers
Elliot Anshelevich
Vincenzo Auletta
Hillel Avni
Evripidis Bampis
Guy Blelloch
Markus Bläser
Richard Bornat
Michael Borokhovich
Matko Botincan
Anastasia Braginsky
Anat Bremler-Barr
Patrick Bridges
Karl Bringmann
Andre Brinkmann
David Bunde
Martin Burtscher
Keren Censor-Hillel
Shiri Chechik
Jian-Jia Chen
Asaf Cohen
Guojing Cong
Johannes Dams
Shantanu Das
Morgan Deters
Aditya Dhoke
David Dice
Michael Dinitz
Ran Duan
Omer Egecioglu
Robert Elsaesser
Matthias Englert
Leah Epstein
Funda Ergun
Yoav Etsion
Diego Fabregat-Traver
Diodato Ferraioli
Tom Friedetzky
Tobias Friedrich

Hiroshi Fujiwara
Leszek Gasieniec
Al Geist
George Giakkoupis
Garth Gibson
Joon-Min Gil
Olga Goussevskaia
Timothy Griffin
Samuel Guyer
Mika Göös
Yotam Harchol
Ahmed Hassan
Bingsheng He
Danny Hendler
Sachin Hirve
Torsten Hoefler
Chien-Chung Huang
Martina Hüllmann
Taisuke Izumi
Riko Jacob
Tomasz Jurkiewicz
Isaac Keslassy
Thomas Kesselheim
Junwhan Kim
Valerie King
Lasse Kliemann
Alex Kogan
Pascal Lenzner
Amir Levy
Aaron Lindsay
Thomas Locher
Zvi Lotker
Wei Lu
Victor Luchangco
Virendra Marathe
Conrado Martínez
Monaldo Mastrolilli
Moti Medina
Nicole Megow
Henning Meyerhenke

Additional reviewers (continued):

Mohamed Mohamedin
Mark Moir
Adam Morrison
Rene Mueller
Syed Rameez Naqvi
Adrian Neumann
Bobo Nick
Tim Nonner
Vitaly Osipov
Konstantinos Panagiotou
Gopal Pandurangan
Merav Parter
Kevin Pedretti
Shir Peled
Paolo Penna
Dmitry Perelman
Yvonne-Anne Pignolet
Christian Plessl
Dmitry Ponomarev
Ruediger Reischuk
Arch Robison
Liam Roditty
Samuel Rodrigo
Amir Ronen
Harald Räcke
Mohamed Saad
Gabriel Scalosub
Jörg Schad
Stefan Schmid
Warren Schudy

Benjamin Shelton
Peter Sibley
Christian Siebert
Francesco Silvestri
Harsha Vardhan Simhadri
Nodari Sitchinava
Michael Spear
Jochen Speck
Alexandre Stauffer
Dirk Sudholt
He Sun
Siddharth Suri
Sriram Swaminathan
Eno Thereska
Shahar Timnat
Jesmin Jahan Tithi
Sivan Toledo
Brian Towles
Jesper Larsson Träff
Alexandru Turcu
Rob van Stee
Sergei Vassilvitskii
Ashish Vulimiri
Lisa Wagner
Adam Welc
John Wickerson
Irad Yavneh
Greta Yorsh
Neal Young
Ayal Zaks
Bo Zhang

SPAA 2012 Sponsors & Supporters

Sponsors:

Supporters:

IBM Research

Oracle Labs

Time vs. Space Trade-offs for Rendezvous in Trees

Jurek Czyzowicz[*]
Département d'informatique
Univ. du Québec en Outaouais
Québec J8X 3X7, Canada
jurek@uqo.ca

Adrian Kosowski[†]
CEPAGE Project
Inria Bordeaux Sud-Ouest
LaBRI, 33400 Talence, France
adrian.kosowski@inria.fr

Andrzej Pelc[‡]
Département d'informatique
Univ. du Québec en Outaouais
Québec J8X 3X7, Canada
pelc@uqo.ca

ABSTRACT

Two identical (anonymous) mobile agents start from arbitrary nodes of an unknown tree and have to meet at some node. Agents move in synchronous rounds: in each round an agent can either stay at the current node or move to one of its neighbors. We consider deterministic algorithms for this rendezvous task. The main result of this paper is a tight trade-off between the optimal time of completing rendezvous and the size of memory of the agents. For agents with k memory bits, we show that optimal rendezvous time is $\Theta(n + n^2/k)$ in n-node trees. More precisely, if $k \geq c \log n$, for some constant c, we design agents accomplishing rendezvous in arbitrary trees of unknown size n in time $O(n + n^2/k)$, starting with arbitrary delay. We also show that no pair of agents can accomplish rendezvous in time $o(n + n^2/k)$, even in the class of lines of known length and even with simultaneous start. Finally, we prove that at least logarithmic memory is necessary for rendezvous, even for agents starting simultaneously in a n-node line.

Categories and Subject Descriptors

C.2.4 [**Computer-Communication Networks**]: Distributed Systems

Keywords

rendezvous, anonymous agents, time, memory space

[*]Supported in part by NSERC discovery grant.

[†]This research was done during the visit of Adrian Kosowski at the Research Chair in Distributed Computing of the Université du Québec en Outaouais. Research partially supported by the Polish National Research Center (DEC-2011/02/A/ST6/00201).

[‡]Supported in part by NSERC discovery grant and by the Research Chair in Distributed Computing of the Université du Québec en Outaouais.

Permission to make digital or hard copies of all or part of this work for personal or classroom use is granted without fee provided that copies are not made or distributed for profit or commercial advantage and that copies bear this notice and the full citation on the first page. To copy otherwise, to republish, to post on servers or to redistribute to lists, requires prior specific permission and/or a fee.
SPAA'12, June 25–27, 2012, Pittsburgh, Pennsylvania, USA.
Copyright 2012 ACM 978-1-4503-1213-4/12/06 ...$10.00.

1. INTRODUCTION

Two identical mobile agents, starting at two nodes of a network, have to meet in the same node at the same time. Agents move along links from node to node, in synchronous rounds: in each round an agent can either stay at the current node or move to one of its neighbors. This task is known as rendezvous [1, 4], and its various applications are discussed in [3]. These applications include the rendezvous of software agents, i.e., mobile pieces of software moving in a communication network in order to perform maintenance of its components or to collect data distributed in nodes of the network. Such software agents need to meet periodically, in order to exchange collected data and plan further moves.

The network is modeled as an undirected connected graph. We make three assumptions, standard in the literature on rendezvous in networks. The first is that nodes of the network are unlabeled. In other words, we seek rendezvous algorithms for agents that do not rely on the knowledge of node labels, and can work in anonymous graphs as well (cf. [3]). The importance of designing such algorithms is motivated by the fact that, even when nodes are equipped with distinct labels, agents may be unable to perceive them because of limited sensory capabilities, or nodes may refuse to reveal their labels, e.g., due to security or privacy reasons. The second assumption is that edges incident to a node v have distinct integer labels. Every undirected edge $\{u, v\}$ has two labels, which are called its *port numbers* at u and at v. The port numbering is *local*, i.e., there is no relation between port numbers at u and at v. Note that, in the absence of port numbers, the adversary could prevent rendezvous by always avoiding to direct an agent to some edge incident to the current node. The third assumption is that agents cannot leave any marks on visited nodes. While both this assumption [15, 30] and the opposite one, i.e., allowing agents to leave either tokens [10, 26] or larger messages on whiteboards at nodes [32], have been considered in the literature, the advantage of designing rendezvous algorithms not relying on marks is two-fold. On the one hand, nodes may not be equipped with such whiteboards designated to leave marks, and on the other hand, nodes need not be cooperative and may erase or alter the messages left by the agents after their visit.

In this paper we focus our attention on deterministic rendezvous in trees, establishing tight trade-offs between the optimal time of completing rendezvous and the size of memory of the agents. It should be noted that such a goal for arbitrary graphs seems to be presently out of reach, as even the optimal time of rendezvous with unlimited memory is not known, and the existing upper bounds on rendezvous time in arbitrary graphs [15, 24, 30] are large polynomials that seem far from optimal. Generalizing our result for trees (tight time-memory trade-offs) to arbitrary graphs would imply the solution of the above open problem.

It is well known that deterministic rendezvous with simultaneous start is impossible if the initial positions of the two agents are symmetric, i.e., if there is a port-preserving automorphism of the tree that carries one node on the other. (Indeed, in this case the positions of agents at each round will remain symmetric, thus precluding rendezvous.) Hence we always assume that the initial positions of agents are not symmetric.

1.1 Our results

The main result of this paper is a tight trade-off between optimal time of completing rendezvous and the size of memory of the agents. For agents with k memory bits, we show that optimal rendezvous time is $\Theta(n + n^2/k)$ in n-node trees. More precisely, if $k \geq c \log n$, for some constant c, we show agents accomplishing rendezvous in arbitrary trees of unknown size n in time $O(n + n^2/k)$, starting with arbitrary delay. We also show that no pair of agents can accomplish rendezvous in time $o(n + n^2/k)$, even in the class of lines and even with simultaneous start. Finally we prove that, contrary to an erroneous result established in [20], a logarithmic number of bits of memory are needed for rendezvous, even for agents starting simultaneously in a n-node line, for arbitrarily large n.[1]

1.2 Related work

The literature on rendezvous can be divided into two currents, significantly differing in the methodology and algorithm construction. The first concerns randomized rendezvous, where the initial positions of agents are random with some given distribution over the environment, and/or the rendezvous algorithm contains randomized inputs (coin tosses). An extensive survey of randomized rendezvous in various scenarios can be found in [3], cf. also [1, 2, 5, 9, 23]. Several authors considered randomized rendezvous time in the geometric scenario (rendezvous in an interval of the real line, see, e.g., [9, 10, 22], or in the plane, see, e.g., [6, 7]). Memory needed for randomized rendezvous in the ring is discussed, e.g., in [25].

For the deterministic setting a lot of effort has been dedicated to the study of the feasibility of rendezvous, and of the time required to achieve this task, when feasible. For instance, deterministic rendezvous with agents equipped with tokens used to mark nodes was considered, e.g., in [26]. Deterministic rendezvous of agents with unique labels was discussed in [14, 15, 24, 30]. (In the latter scenario, symmetry is broken by the use of the different labels of agents, and thus rendezvous is sometimes possible even for symmetric initial positions of the agents). Rendezvous time (both deterministic and randomized) of anonymous agents in trees without marking nodes has been studied in [17]. It was

shown that deterministic rendezvous in n-node trees can be always achieved in time $O(n)$, but only when the memory size of the agents is at least linear. Memory required by the agents to achieve deterministic rendezvous has been studied in [19, 20] for trees and in [12] for general graphs. In [12] it is shown that the minimum memory size for rendezvous in arbitrary n-node graphs is $\Theta(\log n)$. It should be noted that, unlike the present paper, papers [12, 19, 20] discussed only memory size without caring about time of rendezvous.

A natural extension of the rendezvous problem is that of gathering [18, 23, 27, 31], when more than two agents have to meet in one location. In [32] the authors considered rendezvous of many agents with unique labels.

Apart from the synchronous model used in this paper, several authors have investigated asynchronous rendezvous in the plane [11, 18] and in network environments [8, 13, 14]. In the latter scenario the agent chooses the edge which it decides to traverse but the adversary controls the speed of the agent. Under this assumption rendezvous in a node cannot be guaranteed even in very simple graphs, hence the rendezvous requirement is relaxed to permit the agents to meet inside an edge. In [8] the authors study the memory size needed for time-optimal asynchronous rendezvous in trees. (They do not allow rendezvous inside an edge, but for symmetric trees they allow that agents terminate not in one node but in two adjacent nodes.) They show that the minimum number of memory bits to achieve rendezvous in linear time is $\Theta(n)$.

2. FRAMEWORK AND PRELIMINARIES

We consider trees with unlabeled nodes and labeled ports. The port numbers at a node of degree d are $0, 1, \ldots, d - 1$. The number of nodes of a tree is called its *order*. An isomorphism between trees $T = (V, E)$ and $T' = (V', E')$ is a bijection $f : V \to V'$, such that for any $u, v \in V$, u is adjacent to v if and only if $f(u)$ is adjacent to $f(v)$. An isomorphism is said to *preserve port numbering* if for any $u, v \in V$, the port number corresponding to edge $\{u, v\}$ at node u is equal to the port number corresponding to edge $\{f(u), f(v)\}$ at node $f(u)$. An automorphism is an isomorphism of a tree on itself. A pair of distinct nodes u, v of a tree is called *symmetric*, if there exists an automorphism f preserving port numbering, and such that $f(u) = v$.

We consider identical mobile agents traveling in trees with locally labeled ports. Unless stated otherwise, the tree and its size are a priori unknown to the agents. We first define precisely an individual agent. An agent is an abstract state machine $\mathcal{A} = (S, \pi, \lambda, s_0)$, where S is a set of states among which there is a specified state s_0 called the *initial* state, $\pi : S \times \mathbb{Z}^2 \to S$, and $\lambda : S \to \mathbb{Z}$. Initially the agent is at some node u_0 in the initial state $s_0 \in S$. The agent performs actions in discrete rounds defined by its internal clock (which performs ticks, but has no integrated counter for measuring time). Each action can be either a move to an adjacent node or a null move resulting in remaining in the currently occupied node. State s_0 determines a natural number $\lambda(s_0)$. If $\lambda(s_0) = -1$ then the agent makes a null move (i.e., remains at u_0). If $\lambda(s_0) \geq 0$ then the agent leaves u_0 by port $\lambda(s_0)$ modulo the degree of u_0. When incoming to a node v in state $s \in S$, the behavior of the agent is as follows. It reads the number i of the port through which it entered v and the degree d of v. The pair $(i, d) \in \mathbb{Z}^2$ is an input symbol that causes the transition from state s to state $s' =$

---

[1] A result from [20] implies that rendezvous with simultaneous start from arbitrary non-symmetric initial positions in a n-node line is possible with $O(\log \log n)$ bits of memory. This result from [20] is untrue, although it may be applied in a different model which takes into account so-called topologically non-symmetric starting positions, cf. the corrected version of that paper [21].

$\pi(s, (i, d))$. If the previous move of the agent was null, (i.e., the agent stayed at node v in state s) then the pair $(-1, d) \in \mathbb{Z}^2$ is the input symbol read by the agent, that causes the transition from state s to state $s' = \pi(s, (-1, d))$. In both cases s' determines an integer $\lambda(s')$, which is either -1, in which case the agent makes a null move, or a non-negative integer indicating a port number by which the agent leaves v (this port is $\lambda(s') \bmod d$). The agent continues moving in this way, possibly infinitely. The memory of the agent is measured by the number of states of the corresponding state machine, or equivalently by the number of bits on which a state can be encoded. A state machine with K states requires $\Theta(\log K)$ bits of memory.

Since we consider the rendezvous problem for identical agents, we assume that agents are copies A_1 and A_2 of the same abstract state machine $\mathcal{A}$, starting at two distinct non-symmetric nodes v_1 and v_2, called the *initial positions*. We will refer to such identical machines as a *pair of agents*. Hence a pair of agents executes an identical algorithm. It is assumed that the internal clocks of a pair of agents tick at the same rate. The clock of each agent starts when the agent starts executing its actions. Agents start from their initial positions with *delay* $\theta \geq 0$ between their starting rounds, controlled by an adversary. This means that the later agent appears at its starting position and starts executing its actions θ rounds after the first agent. Agents do not know which of them is first and what is the value of θ. The time of a rendezvous algorithm is the number of rounds since the start of the later agent until rendezvous.

We say that a pair of agents using a deterministic algorithm solves the rendezvous problem *with arbitrary delay* (resp. *with simultaneous start*) in a class of trees, if, for any tree in this class and for any initial positions that are not symmetric, both agents are eventually in the same node of the tree in the same round, regardless of the starting rounds of the agents (resp. provided that they start in the same round).

Consider any tree T and the following sequence of trees constructed recursively: $T_0 = T$, and T_{i+1} is the tree obtained from T_i by removing all its leaves. We define $\hat{T}$ as T_j for the smallest j for which T_j has at most two nodes. If $\hat{T}$ has one node, then this node is called the *central node* of T. If $\hat{T}$ has two nodes, then the edge joining them is called the *central edge* of T. A tree T with port labels is called *symmetric*, if there exists a non-trivial automorphism f of the tree (i.e., an automorphism f such that $f(u) \neq u$, for some $u \in V$) which preserves port numbering. If a tree with port labels has a central node, then it cannot be symmetric. In a non-symmetric tree, every pair of nodes is non-symmetric, hence rendezvous is feasible for all initial positions of agents.

A *basic walk* in a n-node tree T, starting from node v is a traversal of all edges of the tree ending at the starting node v and defined as follows. Node v is left by port 0; whenever the walk enters a node by port i, it leaves it by port $(i+1) \bmod d$, where d is the degree of the node. We sometimes consider more than $2(n-1)$ steps of a basic walk, noting that this traversal is periodic with a period of length $2(n-1)$. The basic walk starting at a node v may be uniquely coded by the sequence (string of symbols) $BW(v) = (p_1(v), q_1(v), p_2(v), q_2(v), \ldots, p_{2(n-1)}(v), q_{2(n-1)}(v))$, where $p_1(v) = 0$, $p_i(v)$ is the port number by which the node is left in the i-th step of the walk, and $q_i(v)$ is the port number by which the node is entered in the i-th step

of the walk. A pair of nodes v_1 and v_2 of a tree T is not symmetric if and only if $BW(v_1) \neq BW(v_2)$. Thus an agent starting at node v can be uniquely identified in the tree using the string $BW(v)$, or using any string describing a longer traversal which has $BW(v)$ as its prefix. The definition of the string $BW(v)$ is independent on the upper bound N on n which is known to the agent.

A *reverse basic walk* starting from node w with port p is a traversal of all edges of the tree ending at the starting node w and defined as follows. Node v is left by port p; when the walk enters a node by port i, it leaves it by port $(i-1) \bmod d$, where d is the degree of the node.

For a string σ of length m, the rotation $rot_l(\sigma)$ is the string σ', such that $\sigma'[i] = \sigma[(i+l) \bmod m]$, for all indices $0 \leq i \leq m-1$. Any string σ can be uniquely encoded by its lexicographically minimal rotation $LMR(\sigma)$ and the smallest non-negative integer l such that $LMR(\sigma) = rot_l(\sigma)$.

3. THE RENDEZVOUS ALGORITHM

Our presentation of the rendezvous algorithm is divided into three stages. In the first stage we make two simplifying assumptions: (i) we assume that the maximum degree Δ of the tree is bounded by 3; (ii) we assume that the agents know *a priori* some upper bound N on the order n of the tree, such that $N \geq n \geq N/16$. (The reason for the choice of the constant 16 will become apparent in Section 3.3) In the second stage we remove assumption (i), still keeping (ii), and in the third stage we remove both assumptions, thus presenting the general algorithm.

3.1 Trees of approximately known size and bounded degrees

In this section we present the rendezvous algorithm for trees of maximum degree bounded by 3 and assuming that agents know an integer N, such that $N \geq n \geq N/16$. The overview of the algorithm is the following. In the first phase, whose time is $O(n + n^2/k)$, each agent computes an integer value $l \in \{0, 1, \ldots, n-1\}$ called its *signature*, such that agents with non-symmetric initial positions have different signatures. These signatures are used in the second phase to break symmetry and achieve rendezvous. The way in which this is done depends on the amount of memory available to the agents. If the agents have large memory (at least $\Omega(n/\log n)$ memory bits), then they can quickly locate either the central node or the central edge of a specifically chosen subtree of the tree in which they operate. In the first case they meet at its central node, in the second case they use the signatures to meet at one of the endpoints of its central edge. In the case of small memory ($o(n/\log n)$ memory bits), each agent uses a sequence of active and passive periods, each of length $4(N-1)$, determined by the successive bits of its signature: in an active period (bit 1 of the signature) an agent visits all nodes of the tree, in a passive period (bit 0 of the signature) it waits. This guarantees rendezvous in additional time at most $O(n \log n)$ which is dominated by $O(n^2/k)$, for small memory.

Procedure for computing agent signatures

Due to the periodic nature of tree traversal using the basic walk, all the strings $BW(v)$, for $v \in V$, are identical up to rotation, and hence have the same string describing their lexicographically minimal rotation. We define the signature $sig(v)$ of an agent with initial starting position v as the minimum l such that $LMR(BW(v)) = rot_l(BW(v))$. Hence, agents with non-symmetric initial positions have different signatures. Observe that $0 \leq sig(v) < 2(n-1)$, since $BW(v)$ is periodic with a period of length $2n-1$.

To compute the value of $sig(v)$, we apply the following procedure, called FINDSIGNATURE, which allows an agent starting at node v to detect the starting position of string $LMR(BW(v))$ as a rotation of $BW(v)$. To do this, in the pseudocode below we describe a variant of Duval's efficient maximum suffix algorithm [16] (cf. also [29] for an external I/O memory implementation), adapting it for the mobile agent computational model with limited memory. This is, to our knowledge, the first application of Duval's approach in mobile agent computing. Intuitively, the agent makes use of two pointers to symbols of $BW(v)$, represented by positions $left$ and $right$, which it sweeps from left to right. Index $left$ represents the starting position of the lexicographically minimal rotation which has been detected so far, while index $right$ represents the currently considered candidate for such a starting position. Our implementation of FINDSIGNATURE has two important features. Firstly, the comparison of characters of the string $BW(v)$ is encapsulated in subroutine COMPARESTRING ($left, right, maxLength$), which lexicographically compares the two substrings of $BW(v)$ having length $maxLength$ and starting at offsets $left$ and $right$, respectively. Secondly, the agent is not assumed to know the exact length $4(n-1)$ of sequence $BW(v)$; instead, the known upper bound of $4(N-1)$ is used, without affecting the correctness of the algorithm.

```
procedure FINDSIGNATURE ()
    left ← 1; right ← 2;
    repeat
        maxLength ← right − left;
        COMPARESTRING (left, right, maxLength);
        if 'left' string is greater { at some index } then
            left ← right;
            right ← right + 1;
        else if 'left' string is smaller at index i
            right ← right + i;
        else {strings are equal}
            right ← right + maxLength;
    until right > 4(N − 1);
    return left;
```

Procedure COMPARESTRING is most easily implemented by using a memory cache consisting of four memory blocks of the agent, called *views*, each of which can store a substring of μ successive symbols from the string $BW(v)$, where μ is some integer smaller than $k/4$ (recall that k is the number of bits of memory of the agent). By making use of these auxiliary memory blocks in the implementation of procedure COMPARESTRING, we can bound the time complexity of procedure FINDSIGNATURE.

COROLLARY 3.1. *For any upper bound N, such that $N \geq n \geq N/16$, and $k \geq c \log N$, where c is a constant, an agent starting at node v and equipped with k bits of memory can compute its signature $sig(v)$ in $O(n^2/k)$ rounds by following procedure FINDSIGNATURE for the value $\mu = k/8$.*

Due to space constraints, details of the implementation of procedure COMPARESTRING and the buffer updates, as well as proofs of all lemmas and corollaries, are omitted.

Rendezvous procedure for agents with small memory

The rendezvous procedure for an agent with an already computed signature $sig(v)$ depends on the relation between the number k of memory bits and the known upper bound N on the order of the tree. The first procedure, called SMALLMEMORYRV, guarantees rendezvous of agents with known signatures in $O(N \log N)$ rounds and using $\Theta(\log N)$ bits of memory. Consequently, the procedure will be applied in the case when $k < N/\log N$, since then $N \log N \in O(N^2/k)$ and the bound of $O(N^2/k)$ on execution time is achieved. A faster procedure for agents with larger memory will be presented further on.

Procedure SMALLMEMORYRV assigns each agent with a unique label defined as a string of $\lceil 2 \log N + 3 \rceil$ bits, encoding the binary representation of the integer $2sig(v) + 1$. The procedure is composed of phases such that in the i-th phase, depending on the value of the i-th bit of this label, the agent either visits all the nodes of the tree at least twice, or waits at its initial location for a number of rounds corresponding to such an exploration. This is iterated for all i, $1 \leq i \leq \lceil 2 \log N + 3 \rceil$, and then the whole process is repeated until rendezvous is achieved. The traversal of the tree, which needs to be performed as a subroutine, is implemented by $2(N-1)$ steps of the basic walk, and then returning to the starting node in $2(N-1)$ steps of the reverse basic walk.

```
procedure SMALLMEMORYRV ()
    sig ← FINDSIGNATURE ();
    repeat OSCILLATE (sig, 2(N − 1), 0);
    until rendezvous;

procedure OSCILLATE (sig, distance, firstPort)
    for i ← 1 .. ⌈2 log N + 3⌉ do
        for j ← 1, 2 do
            if i-th bit of (2sig + 1) is '1' then
                perform distance steps of the basic walk,
                    starting with port firstPort;
                perform distance steps of the reverse basic
                    walk, starting from the last port of entry;
            else remain idle for 2 · distance steps;
```

LEMMA 3.1. *For any upper bound N, such that $N \geq n \geq N/16$, and $k \geq c \log N$, where c is a constant, a pair of agents equipped with k bits of memory, starting at non-symmetric initial positions with arbitrary delay, can achieve rendezvous in time $O(n^2/k + n \log n)$ using procedure SMALLMEMORYRV.*

Rendezvous procedure for agents with large memory

Procedure LARGEMEMORYRV, which is applied when $k > N/\log N$, makes use of a more time-efficient approach to rendezvous by restricting the meeting location of the agents either to a specific node of the tree, or to one of the endpoints of a specific edge. Since the memory of the agent may be sublinear compared to the order of the tree T, we do not perform a structural (e.g., DFS-based) analysis of the entire tree to determine such a location. Instead, the agent attempts to determine a meeting point in the so called *trimmed tree* T', which is the port-labeled tree given by the following construction (provided for purposes of definition, only):

1. Initially, let $T' = T$.

2. *Trimming.* Let $z = \lceil 32N/k \rceil$. Remove from T' all edges e such that one of the connected components of

```
procedure TRIMMEDTREENEIGHBORHOOD () { at node u }
    O ← ∅;
    for outPort ∈ [0..deg(u) − 1] do
        perform 2z steps of the basic walk, starting with port outPort,
        memorizing all ports of this traversal;
        if the entire subtree rooted at u and containing edge with port outPort has not been
        explored then
            O ← O ∪ {outPort};
        move back to u by performing 2z rounds of the
        reverse basic walk;
    return O;
```

```
procedure TRAVERSECOMPRESSEDPATH (nextPort, [maxDistance])
    { the parameter maxDistance is optional and defaults to n }
    distance ← 0;
    repeat
        move along the edge with port nextPort;
        returnPort ← port by which new node is entered;
        O ← TRIMMEDTREENEIGHBORHOOD ();
        nextPort ← any element of set O \ {returnPort};
        distance ← distance + 1;
    until distance = maxDistance or |O| ≠ 2;
    return (returnPort, distance);
```

tree $T \setminus \{e\}$ has less than z nodes. Remove from T' all isolated nodes. Notice that, since $N < 16n$ and $k > \log n$, we have, in particular, $z < (n-1)/3$.

3. *Path contraction.* Remove from T' all nodes of degree 2 by contracting each path passing through such nodes into a single edge of the tree, preserving the port labeling at all the remaining nodes (of degree 1 or 3).

The above definition bears some resemblance to structures used in the parallel contraction algorithm from [28].

We remark that T' is a non-empty tree with at most $k/16$ nodes (see Lemma 3.2), which are by definition also nodes of tree T. The meeting node of the agents in procedure LARGE-MEMORYRV is selected as follows. If the trimmed tree has a central node v, then the agents will meet at v. Otherwise, the trimmed tree must have a central edge e which corresponds to a path $(v_0, v_1, \ldots, v_l)$ in T of some length $l \geq 1$. If l is even, then the agents meet at the node $v_{l/2}$. Otherwise, the agents meet at one of the endpoints of the edge $\{v_{\lfloor l/2 \rfloor}, v_{\lceil l/2 \rceil}\}$ of T. Observe that since T' is uniquely defined, the node or pair of nodes which will be selected for rendezvous is independent of the starting positions of the agents.

Our solution relies on two key subroutines which allow the agent to navigate in the tree T', called TRIMMEDTREENEIGHBORHOOD and TRAVERSECOMPRESSEDPATH.

Procedure TRIMMEDTREENEIGHBORHOOD, when called at a node u, computes the set of port numbers at node u which correspond to edges remaining after the trimming phase in the definition of T', i.e., edges of T leading from u to a subtree of at least z nodes. Testing if a port p at u leads to a sufficiently large subtree is implemented by performing $2z$ steps of the basic walk on T starting with port p at node u, memorizing the current tree-distance of the agent from u throughout this traversal. If the agent returns to u before completion of the last step of the walk, then the subtree has less than z nodes, and port p is not included in the output of the procedure.

Procedure TRAVERSECOMPRESSEDPATH, when called at a node $u \in T'$ with a single argument $nextPort$ (describ-

ing a port number at u in T') moves the agent using port number $nextPort$, to its neighbor w in T', following a contracted path in T. The values returned by the procedure are the port number by which w was entered when coming from u, and the length of the path in T connecting u and w. An optional second argument passed to TRAVERSECOMPRESSEDPATH allows the agent to move a specified number of steps along the path between u and w in T, e.g., in order to reach its center.

Procedure LARGEMEMORYRV consists of the following phases. First, the agent follows the basic walk on T, starting from its initial position, until it encounters the first node which is identified as a leaf of tree T', by using procedure TRIMMEDTREENEIGHBORHOOD. Next, the agent performs a basic walk in tree T', using procedures TRIMMEDTREENEIGHBORHOOD and TRAVERSECOMPRESSEDPATH to discover node neighborhoods and to navigate along edges of T', respectively. A basic walk in T' is defined as in tree T, with the additional condition that an agent leaving a leaf follows the only available port, regardless of its port number. The agent memorizes the entire port number sequence BW' used during this basic walk in T' and, by keeping track of the T' tree-distance from the starting node, detects the completion of the tour of the entire tree T'. Using local computations on the sequence BW', the agent now identifies the location of the central node or the central edge of tree T', expressed by the number of steps of the basic walk on T' required to reach this location from its initial position. If T' has a central node, then the agent reaches it, and stops, waiting for the other agent to arrive there. Otherwise, if T' has a central edge e, the agent proceeds to it and identifies the length l of the corresponding path $(v_0, v_1, \ldots, v_l)$ in T using procedure TRAVERSECOMPRESSEDPATH. If l is even, the agent moves to node $v_{l/2}$ by applying once more procedure TRAVERSECOMPRESSEDPATH, and stops. Otherwise, the agent reaches node $v_{\lfloor l/2 \rfloor}$ and applies procedure OSCILLATE. This is equivalent to performing SMALLMEMORYRV, but restricted to the two-node subtree (edge) $\{v_{\lfloor l/2 \rfloor}, v_{\lceil l/2 \rceil}\}$ of T.

LEMMA 3.2. *The tree T' is non-empty and has less than $k/16$ nodes.*

```
procedure LARGEMEMORYRV () { starting at v }
    sig ← FINDSIGNATURE ();
    { move the agent to a leaf of T' }
    while |TRIMMEDTREENEIGHBORHOOD()| ≠ 1 do
        move for one step of the basic walk on T;
    { perform the complete basic walk on the reduced tree T' by using the procedure
    TRIMMEDTREENEIGHBORHOOD to discover ports leading to neighbors in T' and pro-
    cedure TRAVERSECOMPRESSEDPATH to traverse edges of T' }
    BW' ← basic walk string for the reduced tree T' starting from the current location of
    the agent;
    { using string BW', locally compute whether T' has a central node or a central edge,
    and determine its location }
    i ← number of steps of basic walk on T' until the central node/edge of T';
    move for i steps of the basic walk on T';
    if T' has a central node then
        stop {at central node of T' }
    else {T' has a central edge, which has just been reached}
        (returnPort, l) ← traverse central edge of T' by using TRAVERSECOMPRESSEDPATH;
        { move to the center of the path in T corresponding to central edge of T' }
        (port, ·)←TRAVERSECOMPRESSEDPATH (returnPort, ⌈l/2⌉);
        if l is even then
            stop {in the middle of the central path of T' }
        else
            repeat
                OSCILLATE (sig, 1, port)
            until rendezvous;
```

LEMMA 3.3. *For any upper bound N, such that $N \geq n \geq N/16$, and $k \geq cN/\log N$, where c is a constant, a pair of agents equipped with k bits of memory, starting at non-symmetric initial positions with arbitrary delay, achieves rendezvous in time $O(n^2/k)$, using procedure* LARGEMEMORYRV.

By Lemmas 3.1 and 3.3, the following algorithm solves the rendezvous problem in time $O(n^2/k)$ for a known linear upper bound N on n and for trees of maximum degree 3.

Algorithm 1: Rendezvous for known linear upper bound $N \geq n$ and degree $\Delta \leq 3$.

```
if  k > N/log N  then
    LARGEMEMORYRV ();
else
    SMALLMEMORYRV ();
```

3.2 Trees of approximately known size and arbitrary degrees

When the maximum degree of the tree T is larger than 3, we consider the labeled tree T^* obtained from T by splitting each node v of degree $\deg(v) > 3$, and replacing it by a subpath consisting of $\deg(v)$ nodes, defined as follows:

- node v is replaced by nodes $\{v_0^*, v_1^*, \ldots, v_{\deg(v)-1}^*\}$,

- there is an edge $\{v_0^*, v_1^*\}$ with ports 0 at v_0^* and v_1^*,

- for $1 \leq i \leq \deg(v)-2$, there is an edge $\{v_i^*, v_{i+1}^*\}$ with port number 2 at v_i^* and number 0 at v_{i+1}^*,

- additionally, for each edge of T between a port p ($0 \leq p < \deg(v)$) at node v and a port q at node u, we add an edge to T^* leaving node v_p^* by port 1 and either

entering node u by port q (if $\deg(u) \leq 3$) or node u_q^* by port 1 (if $\deg(u) > 3$).

An agent can simulate a walk on tree T^* using only moves on tree T and local computations. As long as the visited nodes of T are of degree at most 3, the port labelings and moves on T^* correspond precisely to those on T. Upon entering a node v of T of degree larger than 3 by port q, the agent simulates arrival by port 1 at node v_q^* of tree T^*. While located at nodes v_i^*, the agent can easily compute the port of T^* by which it reached the current node, the degree of v_i^*, and the destinations of the edges of T^* incident to this node. For these computations, it only requires an additional $O(\log \Delta)$ bits of storage for two variables, describing the degree of the current node, and the index i of the agent's virtual location v_i^* in T^*. The values of these variables no longer need to be stored upon moving to another node of T.

Rendezvous in tree T may be achieved by applying all the procedures from the previous subsection, and replacing each step of the basic walk (or reverse basic walk) on T by a corresponding step on T^*. Indeed, a virtual rendezvous in T^* is a sufficient condition for rendezvous in T: agents which in their simulation arrive at the same location v_i^* in tree T^* will in fact meet at node v of tree T.

In all the computations, the agent needs to assume an upper bound N^* on the order of T^* in place of the upper bound N. Since each node v of T is replaced by at most $\deg(v)$ nodes of T^*, the number of nodes of T^* is bounded by $\sum_{v \in V}(\deg(v)) < 2n$. Hence, we can put $N^* = 2N$, and so all the asymptotic complexity results shown for trees of degree at most 3 are preserved in the case of trees with arbitrary maximum degree.

The above modification can also be applied when no upper bound on the order of the tree is known in advance. Consequently, in the next subsection we may assume that the maximum degree of the tree is at most 3.

3.3 The general algorithm

The algorithm for rendezvous in trees with no known upper bound $N \geq n$ is a refinement of Algorithm 1. The agent attempts to iterate a variant of Algorithm 1 for growing assumed values of N, starting from $N = k$, and increasing them by a multiplicative factor of 4 in subsequent iterations.

Within the range of values $N \geq k \geq N/\log N$, the agent attempts to execute procedure LARGEMEMORYRV, checking if the claim of Lemma 3.2 is not violated, i.e., if the trimmed tree T' has at most $k/16$ nodes. If this is the case, then the agent reaches rendezvous within the current call to procedure LARGEMEMORYRV, in view of Lemma 3.3. Otherwise, the agent returns to its initial position, and knowing the previously assumed upper bound of N to be insufficient, repeats the process for a 4 times larger value of N.

As soon as the condition $k < N/\log N$ is fulfilled, the agent applies a different approach, which is a variant of procedure SMALLMEMORYRV. In each iteration, for the assumed value of N, the agent first performs a synchronizing block of $8(N-1)$ rounds, consisting of $2(N-1)$ rounds of waiting, followed by $2(N-1)$ steps of the basic walk, another $2(N-1)$ rounds of waiting, and $2(N-1)$ steps of the reverse basic walk. This is intended to facilitate rendezvous if the other agent has already begun execution for a larger upper bound on n. If the agents do not meet during this block, the agent computes its signature using procedure FINDSIGNATURE, and synchronizes by waiting until the completion time of the slowest possible execution of FINDSIGNATURE for the given value of N. Finally, the agent repeatedly executes procedure OSCILLATE, so that the number of rounds spent within procedure OSCILLATE is at least equal to the number of rounds used when computing the agent's signature. If rendezvous is not achieved during these repetitions of procedure OSCILLATE, the entire process is repeated for a 4 times larger value of N. We will show that the algorithm will, at the very latest, reach rendezvous in the $(m+1)$-st repetition of the process, where m is the earliest repetition in which the value of N it assumes is larger than n. Consequently, the assumption $N < 16n$ is valid throughout the algorithm.

THEOREM 3.1. *For any $k \geq c \log N$, where c is a constant, a pair of agents equipped with k bits of memory, starting at non-symmetric initial positions with arbitrary delay, achieves rendezvous in time $O(n^2/k)$ using Algorithm 2.*

PROOF. Let $N_i = 4^i k$, and let l be the smallest non-negative integer such that the trimmed tree T' for parameter $N = N_l$ has at most $k/16$ nodes. The proof is split into two cases.

Case 1 ($k \geq N_l/\log N_l$). In this case, the agents successfully execute procedure LARGEMEMORYRV for $N = N_l$ without aborting (using at most k bits of memory), and either stop at the same node, or meet at one of the endpoints of the same edge of T, achieving rendezvous. To bound the time of execution, observe that since the tree T' for $N = N_{l-1} = N_l/4$ violates the claim of Lemma 3.2, we must have $N_l/4 < n$. Since the execution time of the i-th iteration of Phase 1 of Algorithm 2 is bounded by $O(N_i^2/k) = O(4^{2i}k)$, the overall execution time of the first $l + 1$ iterations of the loop is $O(4^{2l}k)$. Since $n > N_l/4 = 4^{l-1}k$, rendezvous is reached in $O(n^2/k)$ time.

Case 2 ($k < N_l/\log N_l$). In this case, both agents proceed to execute Phase 2 of Algorithm 2 after $O(n^2/k)$ rounds. Suppose w.l.o.g. that agent A_2 starts the execution of Phase 2 exactly $\theta' \geq 0$ rounds after agent A_1. Since the duration of any iteration of the loop is the same for both agents, agent A_1 will start the i-th iteration in some round t_i, while agent A_2 will start it in round $t_i + \theta'$. Let N_i' denote the value of N used by the agent in the i-th iteration of this loop. Observe that Phase 2 of the algorithm and all its subroutines are constructed so that throughout each interval of $2(N_i'-1)$ consecutive rounds of the form $[t_i + 2(N_i'-1)a, t_i + 2(N_i'-1)(a+1)) \subset [t_i, t_{i+1})$, where a is an integer, agent A_1 always performs one of the following three actions: it either remains motionless for $2(N_i'-1)$ rounds, or performs $2(N_i'-1)$ steps of the basic walk on T, or performs $2(N_i'-1)$ steps of the reverse basic walk.

Let m be the smallest integer such that $N_m' \geq n$. Consider the round $t_m + \theta'$ when agent A_2 starts the m-th iteration of the loop. Suppose that $t_m + \theta' \geq t_{m+1}$, i.e., agent A_1 has already started executing (at least) the $(m+1)$-st iteration of the loop at this time. Then, rendezvous will be achieved while agent A_2 is executing one of the lines (a), (b), (c), or (d) in its m-th iteration of the loop. To show this, we consider the following possibilities:

- Throughout all rounds in the interval $[t_m + \theta', t_m + \theta' + 4(N_m' - 1))$, agent A_1 is performing steps of the basic walk (resp., of the reverse basic walk). Then, during the time interval $[t_m + \theta', t_m + \theta' + 2(N_m' - 1))$, this agent visits all the nodes of the tree at least once, since $2(N_m' - 1) \geq 2(n - 1)$, which is the length of a single traversal of the tree using the basic walk. Hence, agent A_1 will meet agent A_2, which remains stationary throughout the considered time interval (line (a)).

- Throughout all rounds in the interval $[t_m + \theta', t_m + \theta' + 4(N_m' - 1))$, agent A_1 remains motionless. During the time interval $[t_m + \theta' + 2(N_m' - 1), t_m + \theta' + 4(N_m' - 1))$, agent A_2 visits all the nodes of the tree at least once (while performing the basic walk in line (b)), hence it meets the stationary agent A_1, achieving rendezvous.

- Agent A_1 performs at least two different actions during the interval $[t_m + \theta', t_m + \theta' + 4(N_m' - 1))$. Then, the agent will always perform the same action during the time interval $[t_m + \theta' + 4(N_m' - 1), t_m + \theta' + 8(N_m' - 1))$, since it can change the type of performed action after $2(N_{m+1}' - 1) > 8(N_m' - 1)$ steps at the earliest, by the construction of the algorithm. Depending on the type of action performed by agent A_1 in this time interval, it will meet agent A_2 while A_2 is performing either line (c) or line (d) of its m-th iteration of the loop; the details of the proof are the same as in the two cases above.

Thus, if the agents do not meet in the m-th iteration of the loop by A_1, then $t_m + \theta' < t_{m+1}$. From this, in view of $t_{i+1} - t_i \in \Theta(N_i'^2/k)$, we obtain: $\theta' < t_{m+1} - t_m < (t_{m+2} - t_{m+1})/4$. By the construction of the algorithm, in the $(m+1)$-st iteration of the loop agent A_2 performs its first call to procedure OSCILLATE exactly θ' rounds after agent A_1, and moreover the total duration of the calls to procedure OSCILLATE in this $(m+1)$-st iteration of the loop is at least $(t_{m+2} - t_{m+1})/2$. Consequently, for $(t_{m+2} - t_{m+1})/2 - \theta' >$

Algorithm 2: Rendezvous in arbitrary trees.

$N \leftarrow k$;

repeat { Phase 1: attempt rendezvous with large memory }

    try LARGEMEMORYRV (), aborting if tree T' has more than $k/16$ nodes;

    { the further steps are executed only if the assumed bound is too small ($N < n$) }

    return to the starting position;

    $N \leftarrow 4N$;

until $k < N/\log N$;

repeat { Phase 2: achieve rendezvous with small memory }

    $t \leftarrow$ current round number;

    wait for $2(N-1)$ rounds; { (a) }

    perform $2(N-1)$ steps of the basic walk; { (b) }

    wait for $2(N-1)$ rounds; { (c) }

    perform $2(N-1)$ steps of the reverse basic walk; { (d) }

    $\tau \leftarrow 8(N-1) +$ duration of the slowest possible execution of FINDSIGNATURE for current N;

    $sig \leftarrow$ FINDSIGNATURE ();

    wait until round number $t + \tau$;

    repeat

        OSCILLATE $(sig, 2(N-1), 0)$;

    until round number is larger than $t + 2\tau$;

    $N \leftarrow 4N$;

until rendezvous;

$(t_{m+2} - t_{m+1})/4$ rounds, the agents are concurrently repeating executions of procedure OSCILLATE with parameter $N = N'_{m+1} > n$. Since the execution time of procedure OSCILLATE is $O(N'_{m+1} \log N'_{m+1})$, this number of rounds is sufficient for agent A_2 to complete its first execution of procedure OSCILLATE. By the proof of Lemma 3.1, rendezvous will thus be achieved by the end of the first execution of procedure OSCILLATE by agent A_2.

To bound the time until rendezvous, note that the duration of the i-th loop of Phase 2 is $\Theta(N'^2_i/k)$ rounds, and moreover $N'_{m-1} < n$, thus $N'_{m+1} = 16N'_{m-1} < 16n$. Hence, the number of rounds required by agent A_2 to complete Phase 2 is $O(n^2/k)$. Since the same bound holds also for Phase 1, the entire algorithm is completed within $O(n^2/k)$ rounds. $\square$

4. LOWER BOUNDS

In this section we establish two lower bounds. The first is on the size of memory needed for rendezvous with simultaneous start, and the second is on rendezvous time with given memory. Theorem 4.1 from [20] says that rendezvous with simultaneous start from arbitrary non-symmetric initial positions in the class of trees with at most n nodes and at most l leaves is possible with agents equipped with $O(\log l + \log \log n)$ memory bits. In particular, it implies that rendezvous with simultaneous start from arbitrary non-symmetric initial positions in a n-node line can be achieved with $O(\log \log n)$ memory bits. Our first lower bound shows that this is not true and that the assumption of our rendezvous algorithm that the number of memory bits is at least logarithmic, cannot be removed, even for the class of lines. Our second lower bound concerns the trade-off between memory size and time of rendezvous. Again, it holds even for simultaneous start and even in the class of lines of known length, and shows that the time of our rendezvous algorithm is the best possible for any memory size for which rendezvous is feasible. Since a part of the proofs of both lower bounds is the same, we state them as one theorem.

THEOREM 4.1. *Consider a pair of agents equipped with k bits of memory and achieving rendezvous in any n-node line starting from arbitrary non-symmetric initial positions. Then:*

1. *For some constant c_1 and arbitrarily large n, we have $k \geq c_1 \log n$.*

2. *For some constant c_2 and arbitrarily large n, there exists a n-node line for which these agents use time at least $c_2(n + n^2/k)$ to accomplish rendezvous from some non-symmetric initial positions, even for simultaneous start.*

PROOF. Consider a n node line for even n. Let L be the part (segment) of the line with $\lceil n/3 \rceil + 1$ nodes starting from one end, let R be the part of the line with $\lceil n/3 \rceil + 1$ nodes starting from the other end, and let M be the remaining middle part of the line. Since ports at every node of degree 2 can be numbered in two different ways, there are at least $2^{n/3}$ possible port numberings for part L and for part R. The number of edges in part M is odd and it is at least $n/4$, for sufficiently large n. Fix the following port numbering of M: the central edge of M has ports 0 at both ends and all other edges in M have the same port numbers at both ends. Let u be the extremity of M adjacent to L and let v be the extremity of M adjacent to R. Let u' be the node in L adjacent to u and let v' be the node in R adjacent to v. Agents start simultaneously from initial positions u and v. Let $K = 2^k$ be the number of memory states of an agent. Let τ be the maximum rendezvous time for any rendezvous algorithm in such a line. Then $\tau \leq (nK)^2$. Indeed, if the agents do not meet after time $(nK)^2$, then by the pigeonhole principle there exist two rounds $t_1 < t_2 \leq (nK)^2 + 1$ such that the states and locations of both agents in round t_1 and in round t_2 are identical. From round t_2 on, the pair of agents must repeat infinitely the same loop, precluding the possibility of rendezvous.

Proof of Part 1. In this part of the proof we use an argument similar to that in [20] (Theorem 4.1). Fix an agent with the set S of states and fix a part L or R of the line.

Call this part P. (P is treated as a sequence of ports starting from the respective endpoint of the line.) We define the function $q : S \to S \times \{1, \ldots, \tau\}$, called the *behavior function*, by the formula $q(s) = (s', t)$, where s' is the state in which the agent entering part P (by node u' or v') in state s leaves this part, and t is the number of rounds to complete the visit of part P when starting in state s. The number of possible behavior functions is at most $F = (K\tau)^K$. A behavior function depends only on the part P for which it is constructed. Assume $k < \frac{1}{3}\log n$. For sufficiently large k we have:

$$\log K + \log\log(K\tau) \leq k + \log\log(n^2 K^3) \leq$$

$$< k + \log\log n + \log k + 3 < \frac{2}{3}\log n.$$

Hence $K\log(K\tau) < n^{2/3} < n/3$, and consequently $F = (K\tau)^K < 2^{n/3}$. Thus the number of possible behavior functions is strictly smaller than the total number of possible parts P. It follows that there are two such parts P_1 and P_2 for which the corresponding behavior functions are equal.

Consider two instances of the rendezvous problem in a n-node line. Within part M, both of them have the port labeling defined above. One instance has both parts L and R equal to P_1 and the second instance has $L = P_1$ and $R = P_2$. (In each case the sequence of ports of P_i has to be inserted starting from the endpoint of the line.) Rendezvous is impossible in the first instance because in this instance initial positions of the agents form a symmetric pair of nodes. Consider the second instance, in which the initial positions of the agents do not form a symmetric pair. Because of the symmetry of the port numbering of the part M, agents cannot meet inside any of the side parts. Indeed, when one of the agents is in L, the other one is in R. Since the behavior function associated with parts P_1 and P_2 is the same, the agents leave these parts always at the same time and in the same state. Hence they cannot meet in the part M, in view of the symmetry of their positions and states with respect to the central edge of M. This implies that they never meet, in spite of asymmetric initial positions. Hence rendezvous in the second instance requires at least $\frac{1}{3}\log n$ bits of memory.

Proof of Part 2. Fix an agent with the set S of states and fix a symmetric n-node line $\mathcal{L}$, i.e., a line with identical parts L and R. For $s \in S$ and for any round t, we say that the agent is in *configuration* (s, t) in node w, if it leaves node w in state s at time t. We define a *long trip* of the agent as a sequence of moves starting at an extremity of M, traversing only edges of M, traversing the central edge at least once, and ending at an extremity of M. The duration of a long trip is at least $n/4$. A *critical configuration* is a configuration of the agent at the beginning of a long trip. A *sequence of critical configurations* (SCC) is a sequence of consecutive critical configurations starting at time 0 at the initial position of the agent.

We may assume that $k \geq \frac{1}{3}\log n$; otherwise rendezvous is impossible by the proof of Part 1. Assume that $x = \lfloor cn/k \rfloor$, where $c = \frac{1}{28}$. Since there exist at most $K\tau$ different configurations, where $\tau \leq (nK)^2$, the number $(K\tau)^x$ of all SCC's of length x, taken over all symmetric n-node lines, is at most $(n^2 K^3)^x$. We have:

$$x\log(K\tau) \leq x\log(n^2 K^3) \leq \frac{cn}{k}\log(n^2 K^3) =$$

$$= \frac{cn}{k}(2\log n + 3k) \leq \frac{cn}{k}(9k) = 9cn < \frac{n}{3}.$$

Hence $(K\tau)^x < 2^{n/3}$. By the pigeonhole principle it follows that there exist at least two distinct symmetric lines $\mathcal{L}_1$ and $\mathcal{L}_2$ whose both side parts are, respectively, P_1 and P_2, for which the SCC of length x is the same. Let $(\gamma_1, \ldots, \gamma_x)$ be this common SCC.

Now consider the n-node line $\mathcal{L}_3$, for which $L = P_1$ and $R = P_2$. This line is not symmetric, hence the initial positions u and v of the agents in $\mathcal{L}_3$ are not a symmetric pair. We show that rendezvous of the agents cannot happen before each of them accomplishes at least x long trips. Call the agent starting at u the *left* agent, and the agent starting at v the *right* agent. The behavior of the left agent before the beginning of the first long trip is the same as that of the left agent in $\mathcal{L}_1$ and the behavior of the right agent before the beginning of the first long trip is the same as that of the right agent in $\mathcal{L}_2$. Hence both agents start their first long trip in configuration γ_1. Similarly, by induction on the long trip number, the agents start the i-th long trip in configuration γ_i, for $i \leq x$. During the periods between long trips, the agents are on different sides of the central edge, hence they cannot meet. During the long trips they cannot meet either, because these trips are executed inside the part M which is a symmetric line and configurations of agents at the beginning of each such trip are identical.

This shows that rendezvous cannot occur before each agent accomplishes at least x long trips. Since each long trip has duration at least $n/4$, the rendezvous time is at least $xn/4 \geq \frac{cn}{2k} \cdot \frac{n}{4} = \frac{1}{224}\frac{n^2}{k}$. The linear lower bound on rendezvous time is obvious, as the distance between initial positions of the agents is at least $n/4$. This completes the proof. $\square$

5. REFERENCES

[1] S. Alpern, The rendezvous search problem, SIAM J. on Control and Optimization 33 (1995), 673-683.

[2] S. Alpern, Rendezvous search on labelled networks, Naval Reasearch Logistics 49 (2002), 256-274.

[3] S. Alpern and S. Gal, The theory of search games and rendezvous. Int. Series in Operations research and Management Science, Kluwer Academic Publisher, 2002.

[4] J. Alpern, V. Baston, and S. Essegaier, Rendezvous search on a graph, Journal of Applied Probability 36 (1999), 223-231.

[5] E. Anderson and R. Weber, The rendezvous problem on discrete locations, Journal of Applied Probability 28 (1990), 839-851.

[6] E. Anderson and S. Fekete, Asymmetric rendezvous on the plane, Proc. 14th Annual ACM Symp. on Computational Geometry (1998), 365-373.

[7] E. Anderson and S. Fekete, Two-dimensional rendezvous search, Operations Research 49 (2001), 107-118.

[8] D. Baba, T. Izumi, F. Ooshita, H. Kakugawa, T. Masuzawa, Space-optimal rendezvous of mobile agents in asynchronous trees. Proc. 17th Int. Colloquium on Structural Information and Comm. Complexity, (SIROCCO 2010), Springer LNCS 6058, 86-100.

[9] V. Baston and S. Gal, Rendezvous on the line when the players' initial distance is given by an unknown probability distribution, SIAM J. on Control and Opt. 36 (1998), 1880-1889.

[10] V. Baston and S. Gal, Rendezvous search when marks are left at the starting points, Naval Reaserch Logistics 48 (2001), 722-731.

[11] M. Cieliebak, P. Flocchini, G. Prencipe, N. Santoro, Solving the robots gathering problem, Proc. 30th International Colloquium on Automata, Languages and Programming (ICALP 2003), 1181-1196.

[12] J. Czyzowicz, A. Kosowski, A. Pelc, How to meet when you forget: Log-space rendezvous in arbitrary graphs, Proc. 29th Annual ACM Symposium on Principles of Distributed Computing (PODC 2010), 450-459.

[13] J. Czyzowicz, A. Labourel, A. Pelc, How to meet asynchronously (almost) everywhere, Proc. 21st Annual ACM-SIAM Symposium on Discrete Algorithms (SODA 2010), 22-30.

[14] G. De Marco, L. Gargano, E. Kranakis, D. Krizanc, A. Pelc, U. Vaccaro, Asynchronous deterministic rendezvous in graphs, Theoretical Computer Science 355 (2006), 315-326.

[15] A. Dessmark, P. Fraigniaud, D. Kowalski, A. Pelc. Deterministic rendezvous in graphs. Algorithmica 46 (2006), 69-96.

[16] J.P. Duval, Factorizing words over an ordered alphabet, Journal of Algorithms 4 (1983), 363-381.

[17] S. Elouasbi, A. Pelc, Time of anonymous rendezvous in trees: Determinism vs. randomization, Proc. 19th International Colloquium on Structural Information and Communication Complexity (SIROCCO 2012).

[18] P. Flocchini, G. Prencipe, N. Santoro, P. Widmayer, Gathering of asynchronous oblivious robots with limited visibility, Proc. 18th Annual Symposium on Theoretical Aspects of Computer Science (STACS 2001), Springer LNCS 2010, 247-258.

[19] P. Fraigniaud, A. Pelc, Deterministic rendezvous in trees with little memory, Proc. 22nd International Symposium on Distributed Computing (DISC 2008), Springer LNCS 5218, 242-256.

[20] P. Fraigniaud, A. Pelc, Delays induce an exponential memory gap for rendezvous in trees, Proc. 22nd Ann. ACM Symposium on Parallel Algorithms and Architectures (SPAA 2010), 224-232.

[21] P. Fraigniaud, A. Pelc, Delays induce an exponential memory gap for rendezvous in trees, arXiv:1102.0467v1 [cs.DC].

[22] S. Gal, Rendezvous search on the line, Operations Research 47 (1999), 974-976.

[23] A. Israeli and M. Jalfon, Token management schemes and random walks yield self stabilizing mutual exclusion, Proc. 9th Annual ACM Symposium on Principles of Distributed Computing (PODC 1990), 119-131.

[24] D. Kowalski, A. Malinowski, How to meet in anonymous network, Proc. 13th Int. Colloquium on Structural Information and Comm. Complexity, (SIROCCO 2006), Springer LNCS 4056, 44-58.

[25] E. Kranakis, D. Krizanc, and P. Morin, Randomized Rendez-Vous with Limited Memory, Proc. 8th Latin American Theoretical Informatics (LATIN 2008), Springer LNCS 4957, 605-616.

[26] E. Kranakis, D. Krizanc, N. Santoro and C. Sawchuk, Mobile agent rendezvous in a ring, Proc. 23rd Int. Conference on Distributed Computing Systems (ICDCS 2003), IEEE, 592-599.

[27] W. Lim and S. Alpern, Minimax rendezvous on the line, SIAM J. on Control and Optimization 34 (1996), 1650-1665.

[28] G. Miller, J. Reif, Parallel Tree Contraction, Part 1: Fundamentals. Randomness and Computation (1989), JAI Press, 47-72.

[29] K. Roh, M. Crochemore, C.S. Iliopoulos, K. Park, External Memory Algorithms for String Problems, Fundamenta Informaticae 84 (2008), 17-32.

[30] A. Ta-Shma and U. Zwick. Deterministic rendezvous, treasure hunts and strongly universal exploration sequences. Proc. 18th ACM-SIAM Symposium on Discrete Algorithms (SODA 2007), 599-608.

[31] L. Thomas, Finding your kids when they are lost, Journal on Operational Res. Soc. 43 (1992), 637-639.

[32] X. Yu and M. Yung, Agent rendezvous: a dynamic symmetry-breaking problem, Proc. International Colloquium on Automata, Languages, and Programming (ICALP 1996), Springer LNCS 1099, 610-621.

Allowing Each Node to Communicate Only Once in a Distributed System: Shared Whiteboard Models

Florent Becker
LIFO, Université d'Orléans
florent.becker@univ-orleans.fr

Adrian Kosowski
LaBRI, INRIA
Bordeaux Sud-Ouest
kosowski@labri.fr

Nicolas Nisse
CNRS / Université Nice
Sophia-Antipolis
nicolas.nisse@sophia.inria.fr

Ivan Rapaport
DIM-CMM (UMI 2807 CNRS)
Universidad de Chile
rapaport@dim.uchile.cl

Karol Suchan
UAI (Chile) and U of Science
and Technology (Poland)
karol.suchan@uai.cl

ABSTRACT

In this paper we study distributed algorithms on massive graphs where links represent a particular relationship between nodes (for instance, nodes may represent phone numbers and links may indicate telephone calls). Since such graphs are massive they need to be processed in a distributed and streaming way. When computing graph-theoretic properties, nodes become natural units for distributed computation. Links do not necessarily represent communication channels between the computing units and therefore do not restrict the communication flow. Our goal is to model and analyze the computational power of such distributed systems where one computing unit is assigned to each node. Communication takes place on a whiteboard where each node is allowed to write at most one message. Every node can read the contents of the whiteboard and, when activated, can write one small message based on its local knowledge. When the protocol terminates its output is computed from the final contents of the whiteboard. We describe four synchronization models for accessing the whiteboard. We show that message size and synchronization power constitute two orthogonal hierarchies for these systems. We exhibit problems that *separate* these models, i.e., that can be solved in one model but not in a weaker one, even with increased message size. These problems are related to maximal independent set and connectivity. We also exhibit problems that require a given message size independently of the synchronization model.

Categories and Subject Descriptors

F.1.2 [**Computation by Abstract Devices**]: Modes of Computation—*Parallelism and Concurrency*

Permission to make digital or hard copies of all or part of this work for personal or classroom use is granted without fee provided that copies are not made or distributed for profit or commercial advantage and that copies bear this notice and the full citation on the first page. To copy otherwise, to republish, to post on servers or to redistribute to lists, requires prior specific permission and/or a fee.
SPAA'12, June 25–27, 2012, Pittsburgh, Pennsylvania, USA.
Copyright 2012 ACM 978-1-4503-1213-4/12/06 ...$10.00.

General Terms

Algorithms, Theory

Keywords

Distributed computing, local computation, graph properties, bounded communication

1. INTRODUCTION

A distributed system is typically represented by a graph where links correspond to a particular relationship between nodes. For instance, nodes may represent phone numbers and links may indicate telephone calls. A classical approach is to view each node as a processor. Since nodes lack global knowledge, new algorithmic and complexity notions arise. In contrast with classical algorithmic theory – where the Turing machine is the consensus formal model of algorithm – in distributed systems many different models are considered. Under the paradigm that communication is much slower and more costly than local computations, complexity analysis of distributed algorithms mainly focuses on message passing. That is, an important performance measure is the number and the size of messages that are sent by nodes for performing some computation. Theoretical models were conceived for studying particular aspects of protocols such as fault-tolerance, synchronism, locality, congestion, etc.

The particularity of this work lies in the fact that links between nodes do not necessarily represent communication channels between the computing units and therefore do not restrict the communication flow. In that sense our setting is similar to the "mud" (massive, unordered, distributed) model, where the authors tackle the problem of performing a computation when the data is distributed among many machines [4]. Roughly, in such mud algorithms, pieces of data are processed independently in parallel and pairs of messages are aggregated in any order. Only one message is created by each node because in truly massive database "a common approach for dealing with large datasets is to stream over the input in one pass" [4].

The problem we intend to model here is less general than the one addressed in [4]. In fact, in our setting *there exists an underlying graph and the information each node possesses is nothing but its neighborhood*. The computation the nodes need to perform collectively is related to some property of the graph. In [2] the first simple model for studying such scenario was introduced. In that model, the total amount of local information that each node was allowed to provide was bounded by $O(\log n)$ bits. Each node transmitted its message to a central authority, the referee, that collected and used them in order to give the correct output.

The main question was whether this small amount of local information provided by each node was sufficient for the referee to decide some basic structural properties of the graph G. For instance, simple questions like "Does G contain a square (cycle of length 4)?" or "Is the diameter of G at most 3?" cannot be solved. On the other hand, the referee can decode the messages in order to have full knowledge of G when G belongs to one of many graph classes such as planar graphs, bounded treewidth graphs and, more generally, bounded degeneracy graphs.

In this paper we define extensions of the model in [2] and investigate their computational power. It is interesting to point out that despite being extremely natural, these models of computation have never been studied before.

Communication using a shared whiteboard. The computational model in [2] can be stated equivalently in the following form. Given a question about the graph, every node writes *simultaneously* one message (computed from its local knowledge) on a global zone of shared memory, a *whiteboard*, and then one must be able to answer the question using only the contents of the whiteboard.

In this paper we intend to give more power to the initial model of [2]. For this purpose, we relax the simultaneity constraint in different ways. Roughly, messages may be written sequentially on the whiteboard. This allows nodes to compute their messages taking into account the contents of the whiteboard, i.e., the messages that have previously been written. In other words, in the new models we propose, nodes have more sophisticated ways to share information. Basically, the four models we now present aim at describing how the nodes can access the shared medium, in particular, differentiating synchronous and asynchronous networks.

We define a framework for synchronization without using a global clock. Instead, time is divided into *rounds* corresponding to observable events, i.e., whiteboard modifications. More precisely, a round terminates when a node writes a message on the whiteboard. Along the evolution of the system, the nodes may be in three states: *awake*, *active* or *terminated*. Initially, all nodes are awake. A node becoming active means that this node would like to write a message on the whiteboard. Metaphorically speaking, it "rises its hand to speak". To model the worst-case behavior, an *adversary* chooses, among the set of active nodes, the particular node which is going to write a message on the whiteboard. Afterwards, this node enters the terminated state. Therefore, a node is in state terminated when its message has been written on the whiteboard. In one round, several awake nodes may become active but exactly one active node becomes terminated. Note that a node may become active and terminated in one round. In our model, if a node is active in round i and it does not write a message then it must stay active in round $i+1$. In other words, once a node raises its hand it cannot "change its mind" later. After the last round, when all nodes are terminated, all of them must be able to answer the question by using *only* the information stored on the whiteboard.

In this setting, we propose several scenarios leading to the definition of four computational models. A computational model is *simultaneous* if all nodes become active (raise their hands) at the beginning of the process. On the other hand, the model is *free* if, in every round, any awake node may decide to become active based on its knowledge and on its own protocol. The other criterion we use to distinguish models is the state-transition during which a node creates the message it will eventually write on the whiteboard. In the *asynchronous* scenario, the nodes must create their message *as soon as they become active*. In the *synchronous* scenario, every node is allowed to create its message later, when the adversary chooses it to write the message on the whiteboard. Thus, in the asynchronous case, there may be some delay between the creation of a message and the step when it is written. In particular, the order in which the messages are created and the order in which they are actually available on the whiteboard may differ. In this way, we can model real-world asynchronous systems where there are no guarantees on the time of communications.

Our results. In this work we define four families of systems, namely $\textsc{SimAsync}[f(n)]$, $\textsc{SimSync}[f(n)]$, $\textsc{FreeAsync}[f(n)]$ and $\textsc{FreeSync}[f(n)]$, which correspond to the four possible free/simultaneous, asynchronous/synchronous scenarios, parametrized by the amount $f(n)$ of data (in bits) each node is allowed to write on the whiteboard. We show that these classes form a hierarchy from the point of view of message size as well as from the point of view of the synchronization mechanism. More precisely, for any $f(n) = o(n)$, we show that $\textsc{SimAsync}[f(n)] \subsetneq \textsc{SimSync}[f(n)] \subsetneq \textsc{FreeAsync}[f(n)] \subseteq \textsc{FreeSync}[f(n)]$; the strictness of the last inclusion is left as an open problem. On the other hand, we also prove that when $g(n) = o(f(n))$, $\textsc{FreeSync}[g(n)] \subsetneq \textsc{SimAsync}[f(n)]$. This means that message size and synchronization mechanisms are two orthogonal parameters with respect to the power of each instance of our model.

Connectivity problems in general, and breadth-first search (BFS) in particular, are classical problem in distributed computing, and we examine their positions in our hierarchy. We show that BFS is in the class $\textsc{FreeSync}[\log n]$ and that for the bipartite case it is in $\textsc{FreeAsync}[\log n]$. We also show that for all $f(n) = o(n)$, BFS is not in the class $\textsc{SimSync}[f(n)]$ even in the bipartite case.

Related work. The two main aspects of our approach, the *locality* and the fact that nodes are allowed to send *only one short message* have been addressed before. In the classical model $\mathcal{CONGEST}$ [8], where a network is represented by a graph whose nodes correspond to network processors and edges to inter-processor links, the n processors can send in each round a message of size $O(\log n)$ bits through each of its outgoing links. A restriction of the $\mathcal{CONGEST}$ model has been proposed by Grumbach and Wu to study *frugal* computation [5]. In this model, where the total amount of information traversing each link is bounded by $O(\log n)$ bits, they showed that any first order logic formula can be evaluated in any planar or bounded degree network [5]. Many variations to the $\mathcal{CONGEST}$ model have been proposed in order to focus on different aspects of distributed computing. In a seminal paper, Linial introduced the $\mathcal{LOCAL}$ model [7, 8]. In the $\mathcal{LOCAL}$ model, the restriction on the size of messages is removed so that every vertex is allowed to send unbounded size messages in every round. This model focuses on the issue of locality in distributed systems, and more precisely on the question "*What cannot be computed locally?*" [6]. Difficult problems like minimum vertex cover and minimum dominating set cannot be well approximated when processors can locally exchange arbitrary long messages during a bounded number of rounds [6].

The idea of abstracting away from the cost of *transmitting* data throughout the network and to look at *how much local information must be shared* in order to compute some property is present in the the Simultaneous Message Model defined in [1]. In such model the communication is *global*: n players must evaluate a function $f(x_1, \ldots, x_n)$ in which player i knows the whole input except x_i. Each player directly transmits *one message* to a central authority, the referee, that collects and uses them in order to compute $f(x_1, \ldots, x_n)$. The Simulateouus Message Model is a variant of the more general Multiparty Communication model, where the n players communicate by writing messages on a common whiteboard [3].

2. COMMUNICATION MODELS

Our protocols work on simple undirected connected n-node graphs. In $G = (V, E)$, each node $v \in V$ has a unique identifier $ID(v)$ between 1 and n. Typically, $V = \{v_1, \ldots, v_n\}$, where v_i is such that $ID(v_i) = i$. Throughout the paper, a graph should be understood as a labeled graph. At each node $v \in V$ there is an independent processing unit that knows its own identifier, the identifier of each of its neighbors and the total number of nodes n. Each node is in one of three *states*: awake, active or terminated. Initially, they are all awake.

All nodes execute the same algorithm. Roughly, if they are in the awake state, they must decide whether to become active, and if they are active, what to write on the whiteboard. Each node is allowed to write exactly one message on the whiteboard. Once they write the message they enter the terminated state. The size of these messages, in bits, is some $f(n) = o(n)$, typically $O(\log n)$.

Let $W_{n,s}$ be the set of possible configurations of the *whiteboard* with at most n messages of size at most s bits each.

We first define synchronous protocols, then asynchronous protocols. Synchronous protocols rely on some external synchronization primitives to ensure that messages are delivered one by one, whereas asynchronous protocols have to deal with concurrent messages, which means that messages are created as soon as the nodes become active. We also distinguish between simultaneous and free protocols. In simultaneous protocols, nodes must be ready to speak at any time, whereas in free protocols, they can decide when to become active. We get the following four family of models, with $f(n)$ representing the message size:

	message created when node becomes active
all nodes initially active	SimAsync[$f(n)$]
no node initially active	FreeAsync[$f(n)$]

	message created when node is chosen
all nodes initially active	SimSync[$f(n)$]
no node initially active	FreeSync[$f(n)$]

2.1 Synchronous protocols

DEFINITION 1. *Let n be a positive integer. Let $[1, n] = \{1, \ldots, n\}$. A synchronous protocol with output set O and message size $f(n)$ is a triplet $\mathcal{A} = (act_n, msg_n, out_n)$ where:*

- act_n: $[1, n] \times 2^{[1,n]} \times W_{n,f(n)} \to \{awake, active\}$ *is the activation function, which depending on the node's identifier, its neighborhood and the contents of the whiteboard decides whether to become active or stay awake.*

- msg_n: $[1, n] \times 2^{[1,n]} \times W_{n,f(n)} \to \{0, 1\}^{f(n)}$ *is the message function, which depending on the node's identifier, its neighborhood and the contents of the whiteboard decides what to write on the whiteboard.*

- out_n: $W_{n,f(n)} \to O$ *is the output function.*

Let FreeSync[$f(n)$] be the set of all synchronous protocols with message size at most $O(f(n))$. A *configuration* of a protocol corresponds to a configuration of the whiteboard in $W_{n,f(n)}$ together with a state in $\{awake, active, terminated\}^n$ (which must be interpreted as the state of each node). In the *initial configuration*, all nodes are awake and the whiteboard is empty.

A *round* corresponds to an observable transition of the protocol, which in practice occurs when a message is written on the whiteboard. In a round, awake nodes may decide to become active and one active node will write its message.

DEFINITION 2. *Consider the synchronous protocol $\mathcal{A} = (act_n, msg_n, out_n)$. Let $G = (V, E)$ be an n-node graph. A round goes from configuration C to configuration C' if:*

- *Any terminated node in C is also terminated in C'.*

- *For any node $v_i \in V$ which is awake in C, its state in C' is $act_n(i, N(v_i), W_C)$, where $N(v_i)$ is the set of identifiers of v_i's neighbors and W_C is the content of the whiteboard in configuration C.*

- *The configuration of the whiteboard $W_{C'}$ is the same as W_C but where the message $msg_n(j, N(v_j), W_C)$ is attached provided that there exists at least one active node v_j in C. In C' the node v_j enters the terminated state. Every other active node stays active.*

DEFINITION 3. *An execution of a protocol $\mathcal{A}$ is a (finite) sequence of configurations starting from the initial configuration where transitions are determined by rounds. The execution is successful if in the last configuration, all nodes are terminated. We say that the execution ends in a deadlock when we end up in a situation where there are no active nodes but the set of awake nodes is not empty. For a successful execution, where the last whiteboard configuration is W, we define the output to be $out_n(W)$.*

DEFINITION 4. *For a function F_n defined from the set of n-node graphs to an output set O, we say that $\mathcal{A}$ computes F_n if for all G, all maximal executions of $\mathcal{A}$ are successful and output $F_n(G)$. Therefore, we can assume that there is an adversary that chooses in each round which active node writes a message on the whiteboard.*

DEFINITION 5. *A protocol is simultaneous if all nodes are active from the beginning (the activation function is uniformly active). We note SimSync[$f(n)$] the set of simultaneous protocols. In this subclass of protocols there will never be deadlocks.*

2.2 Asynchronous protocols

In asynchronous protocols nodes create their messages as soon as they become active. Therefore, if two nodes become active simultaneously, then the first message written on the whiteboard does not affect the second message.

DEFINITION 6. *Let n be a positive integer. Let $[1, n] = \{1, \ldots, n\}$. An* asynchronous protocol *with output set O and message size $f(n)$ is a pair $\mathcal{A} = (act/msg_n, out_n)$ where:*

- *$act/msg_n \colon [1, n] \times 2^{[1,n]} \times W_{n, f(n)} \to \{awake, active\} \times \{0, 1\}^{f(n)}$ is the* activation/message function. *Note that this transition is such that a (nonempty) message is created only when the node enters the active state.*

- *$out_n \colon W_{n, f(n)} \to O$ is the* output function.

Let FREEASYNC$[f(n)]$ be the set of asynchronous protocols with message size $O(f(n))$.

The definition of configuration is similar to the synchronous case, except that since active nodes create their messages (following the act/msg function) before being chosen by the adversary for writing on the whiteboard (eventually), these messages are part of the configuration, despite the fact that they do not appear on the whiteboard.

We define rounds, executions, deadlocks, successful executions and computations as in the synchronous case. We also define the set SIMASYNC$[f(n)]$ of simultaneous asynchronous protocols.

This paper aims at deciding what kind of problems can be solved in each of these models. For instance, [2] proves that deciding if a graph has degeneracy k, $k \geq 1$, can be solved in SIMASYNC$[\log n]$. On the negative side, deciding whether a graph contains a triangle as a subgraph and deciding whether a graph has diameter at most 3 cannot be solved in SIMASYNC$[\log n]$ [2].

3. A COMPUTING POWER LATTICE

First of all, we prove the following lemma that extends a result of [2]. Let BUILD be the problem that consists in computing the adjacency matrix of a graph.

LEMMA 1. *Let $\mathcal{G}$ be a family of n-node graphs and $g(n)$ be the number of graphs in $\mathcal{G}$. Let $f(n) = o(n)$ and $\mathcal{C} \in \{$SIMASYNC, SIMSYNC, FREEASYNC, FREESYNC$\}$. If the problem BUILD, when the input graphs are restricted to the class $\mathcal{G}$, can be solved in the model $\mathcal{C}[f(n)]$, then $\log g(n) = O(n(f(n) + \log n))$.*

PROOF. Consider any algorithm in one of the four considered models. In any model, at the end of the communication process, n messages of size $O(f(n))$ bits are written on $\mathcal{B}$. Hence, at the end, accounting for the order of the messages, a total of $O(nf(n) + \log n)$ bits are available on the whiteboard. For the output function to distinguish two different graphs in $\mathcal{G}$, we must have $\log g(n) = O(n(f(n) + \log n))$. $\square$

For the ease of descriptions, in what follows we will not define explicitly the functions for activation, message creation and decision. Nevertheless, they always will be clear from the context.

In this section we intend to show that these models form a lattice in which the computational power grows strictly whenever either the syncronization model is enriched or the

message size is increased. On the other hand, when one resource is increased but the other restricted then the resulting class is incomparable with the original (neither is included in the other). The main result of this section is the following theorem:

THEOREM 1. *For all $\Omega(\log n) = f(n) = o(n)$, SIMASYNC$[f(n)] \subsetneq$ SIMSYNC$[f(n)] \subsetneq$ FREEASYNC$[f(n)] \subseteq$ FREESYNC$[f(n)]$.*

We start with the following weaker result:

LEMMA 2. *For all $f(n)$, SIMASYNC$[f(n)] \subseteq$ SIMSYNC$[f(n)] \subseteq$ FREEASYNC$[f(n)] \subseteq$ FREESYNC$[f(n)]$.*

PROOF. **SimAsync**$[f(n)] \subseteq$ **SimSync**$[f(n)]$. In the SIMSYNC model, any node applies directly the protocol of the SIMASYNC model. Nodes create their message initially, ignoring the messages present on the whiteboard when they write their own.

SimSync$[f(n)] \subseteq$ **FreeAsync**$[f(n)]$. Recall that a problem is solved in the SIMSYNC model if the nodes compute the output *no matter* the order chosen by the adversary. So we can translate a SIMSYNC protocol into a FREEASYNC one if we fix an order (for instance $v_1, \ldots, v_n$) and use this order for a sequential activation of the nodes.

FreeAsync$[f(n)] \subseteq$ **FreeSync**$[f(n)]$. The situation is that of the first inclusion. It suffices to force the protocols in FREESYNC to create their messages based only on what was known at the moment when they became active. $\square$

3.1 SIMASYNC vs. SIMSYNC

We consider here a "rooted" version of the INCLUSION MAXIMAL INDEPENDENT SET problem. This problem, denoted by MIS(X), takes as input an n-node graph $G = (V, E)$ together with an identifier $ID(x)$, $x \in V$, and the desired output is any maximal (by inclusion) independent set containing x.

THEOREM 2. *MIS(X) can be solved in the SIMSYNC$[\log n]$ model.*

PROOF. Recall that in the SIMSYNC model, all nodes are initially active and that the adversary chooses the ordering in which the nodes write their messages. Hence, an algorithm in this model must specify the message created by a node v, according to the local knowledge of v and the messages written on the whiteboard before v is chosen by the adversary.

The protocol is trivial (it is the greedy one). When node v is chosen by the adversary, the message of v is either its own ID (meaning that v belongs to the final independent set) or v writes "no" (otherwise). The choice of the message is done as follows. The message is $ID(v)$ either if $v = x$ or if $v \notin N(x)$ and $ID(y)$ does not appear on the whiteboard for any $y \in N(v)$. Otherwise, the message of v is "no".

Clearly, at the end, the set of vertices with their IDs on the whiteboard consists of an inclusion maximal independent set containing x. $\square$

THEOREM 3. *For any $f(n) = o(n)$, MIS(X) cannot be solved in the SIMASYNC$[f(n)]$ model.*

PROOF. Let $f(n) = o(n)$. We proceed by contradiction. Let us assume that there exists a protocol $\mathcal{A}$ for solving MIS(x) in the SIMASYNC$[f(n)]$ model. Then we show how to design an algorithm $\mathcal{A}'$ to solve the BUILD Problem for any graph in this model, contradicting Lemma 1.

Let $G = (V, E)$ be a graph with $V = \{v_1, \ldots, v_n\}$. For any $1 \leq i < j \leq n$, let $G_{i,j}^{(x)}$ be obtained from G by adding a vertex x adjacent to every vertex in V with the exception of v_i and v_j. Note that $\{x, v_i, v_j\}$ is the only inclusion maximal independent set containing x in $G_{i,j}^{(x)}$ if and only if $\{v_i, v_j\} \notin E$. Indeed, if $\{v_i, v_j\} \in E$, there are two inclusion maximal independent sets containing x: $\{x, v_i\}$ and $\{x, v_j\}$.

Recall that, in the SIMASYNC model, all nodes must create their message initially, i.e., while the whiteboard is still empty. Hence, the message created by a node only depends on its local knowledge

Notice that, for a given k, the node v_k only sees two different neighborhoods for all the possible $G_{i,j}^{(x)}$, depending on whether $k \in \{i, j\}$ or $k \notin \{i, j\}$. Therefore, we call m_k the message that v_k generates when $k \in \{i, j\}$ (i.e., x and v_k are not neighbors) and m_k' the message v_k generates when $k \notin \{i, j\}$ (i.e., x and v_k are neighbors).

From the previous protocol $\mathcal{A}$ we are going to define another protocol $\mathcal{A}'$ in the SIMASYNC$[f(n)]$ model which solves the BUILD problem for any graph. Protocol $\mathcal{A}'$ works as follows. Every node v_k generates the pair (m_k, m_k') of the two messages v_k would send in $\mathcal{A}$ when it is adjacent to x and when it is not. Clearly, this consists of $O(f(n))$ bits.

Now let us prove that any node can reconstruct $G = (V, E)$ from the messages generated by $\mathcal{A}'$. More precisely, for any $1 \leq s < t \leq n$, any node can decide whether $\{v_s, v_t\} \in E$ or not. It is enough for any node to simulate de decision function of $\mathcal{A}$ in $G_{s,t}^{(x)}$ by using messages m_s, m_t and $\{m_k' : k \in \{1, \cdots, n\} \setminus \{s, t\}\}$. Since the output of $\mathcal{A}$ is $\{x, v_s, v_t\}$ if and only if $\{v_s, v_t\} \notin E$, the results follows. This would mean that from $O(nf(n))$ bits we can solve BUILD in the class of all graphs, a contradiction. □

COROLLARY 1. For all $\Omega(\log n) = f(n) = o(n)$, SIMASYNC$[f(n)] \subsetneq$ SIMSYNC$[f(n)]$.

We discuss now another problem that could possibly separate the two models. Given an $(n-1)$-regular $2n$-node graph G, the 2-CLIQUES problem consists in deciding whether G is the disjoint union of two complete graphs with n vertices.

It is easy to show that 2-CLIQUES can be solved in the SIMSYNC$[\log n]$ model. Indeed, a trivial protocol can partition the vertices into two cliques numbered 0 and 1 if the input consists of two cliques, or otherwise indicate that it is not the case. The first vertex u to be chosen by the adversary writes $(ID(u), 0)$ on $\mathcal{B}$. Then, each time a vertex v is chosen, it writes $(ID(v), 0)$ if it "believes" to be in the same clique as u, and $(ID(v), 1)$ otherwise. More precisely, let S_v be the subset of neighbors of v that have already written a message on the whiteboard. If $S_v = \emptyset$ then v writes 1. If all nodes in S_v have written that they belong to the the same clique $c \in \{0, 1\}$ then v writes c, and v writes "no" otherwise. Clearly, G is the disjoint union of two cliques if and only if there is no message "no" on the whiteboard at the end of the communication process.

Proving that the problem 2-CLIQUES cannot be solved in the SIMASYNC$[f(n)]$ model (either for $f(n) = \log n$ or for any other $f(n)$) is an interesting question because it would

allow us to show that CONNECTIVITY (deciding whether a graph is connected or not) cannot be solved in the SIMASYNC model. Indeed, it is easy to show that an $(n-1)$ regular $2n$-node graph is the disjoint union of two cliques if and only if it is not connected. We leave this as an open question:

OPEN PROBLEM 1. *For which $f(n)$ can 2-CLIQUES be solved in the SIMASYNC$[f(n)]$ model?*

3.2 SIMSYNC vs. FREEASYNC

We say that a graph is *even-odd-bipartite* if there are no edges between nodes having identifiers with the same parity. For separating models SIMSYNC and FREEASYNC, the problem we are going to introduce is EOB-BFS. In this problem, the input is an arbitrary n-node graph G and the output is a BFS-tree (or BFS-forest) if G is even-odd bipartite, and a negative answer otherwise. The root of the BFS-tree in each connected component of G will be the node with the smallest identifier in the respective component.

THEOREM 4. *The problem EOB-BFS can be solved in the FREEASYNC$[\log n]$ model.*

PROOF. Let G be the input graph. All nodes detecting that they have a neighbor with the same parity become active and create a message saying that this is an "invalid" graph. So we are going to define our algorithm assuming that G is indeed even-odd-bipartite.

The protocol will activate the nodes layer by layer in the BFS-forest. The first node to become active is v_1, then all its neighbors, then all nodes at distance 2, and so on. When all nodes in layer k have written their messages, then the information appearing in the whiteboard will be sufficient to compute the number of edges crossing between layer k and layer $k+1$ (if such number is 0 then that would mean that another connected component must be activated).

Initially, only v_1 is active. Let N_v^* be the set of neighbors of v *that have already written a message* on the whiteboard. When node v becomes active it creates the message $(i(v), l(v), p(v), d_{-1}(v), d_{+1}(v))$ where:

$$
\begin{aligned}
i(v) \quad & \text{is its ID} \\
l(v) \quad & = min_{w \in N_v^*} l(w) + 1 \\
p(v) \quad & \text{is the node in } N_v^* \text{ with minimum ID, or} \\
& \text{ROOT if } N_v^* \text{ is empty} \\
d_{-1}(v) \quad & = |N_v^*| \\
d_{+1}(v) \quad & = d(v) - |N_v^*|, \text{ with } d(v) \text{ its degree}
\end{aligned}
$$

$l(v)$ represents the level of v, $d_{-1}(v)$ its degree towards the previous level, $d_{+1}(v)$ its degree towards the next level and $p(v)$ its parent in the BFS-forest. The message created by v_1 at the beginning is $(1, 0, \text{ROOT}, 0, d(v_1))$. Since v_1 is the only active node the adversary is forced to choose it and v_1 writes its message on the whiteboard. Then all the neighbors of v_1 become active and, since we want all nodes of the same layer to become active simultaneously, the protocol works as follows. An arbitrary node v becomes active (and computes its message) if the next two conditions are satisfied:

1. A neighbor w of v has already written its message on the whiteboard.

2. $\Sigma_{u \in L_{l(w)}} d_{-1}(u) = \Sigma_{u \in L_{l(w)-1}} d_{+1}(u)$, where L_k is the set of nodes in layer k that have already written a message.

The key argument is to see that the second condition for activation ensures that all edges from layer $k-1$ to layer k have written their messages before layer $k+1$ is activated.

Previous protocol works correctly if the graph has only one connected component. In order to avoid any deadlock we have to add another condition for becoming active. The idea is to verify that a component has already been covered. More precisely, v becomes active if the last message was written by a non-neighbor node w of v and the following three conditions are satisfied:

1. $\Sigma_{u \in L_{l(w)}} d_{+1}(u) = 0$.

2. $\Sigma_{u \in L_{l(w)}} d_{-1}(u) = \Sigma_{u \in L_{l(w)-1}} d_{+1}(u)$.

3. The ID of v is the minimum among the nodes that have not written a message yet.

These condition ensure that when the active connected component changes, exactly one node is activated. In the end, the output function corresponds to the forest indicated by the $p(v)$ of each message. $\square$

THEOREM 5. *For any $f(n) = o(n)$, EOB-BFS cannot be solved in the* SimSync$[f(n)]$ *model.*

PROOF. We proceed by contradiction. Let us assume that there exists a protocol $\mathcal{A}$ for solving EOB-BFS in SimSync$[f(n)]$ for some $f(n) = o(n)$. The idea is to construct a protocol $\mathcal{A}'$ for solving the BUILD problem for even-odd-bipartite graphs in SimAsync$[f(n)]$, in contradiction with Lemma 1. Note that there are $2^{O(n^2)}$ even-odd-bipartite graphs with n vertices.

Let $G = (V, E)$ be an even-odd-bipartite graph with $V = \{v_1, \ldots, v_{n-1}\}$. Assume (w.l.o.g) that n is odd, and renumber the vertices so that $V = \{v_2, \ldots, v_n\}$.

Let $V' = \{v_1, v_{n+1}, v_{n+2}, \ldots, v_{2n-1}\}$. Let $3 \leq i \leq n$ be odd. We are going to define the auxiliar even-odd-bipartite graph $G_i = (V \cup V', E \cup E_i)$ where the edges E_i are defined as follows: connect v_1 with v_{i+n-2}, v_j with v_{j+n-2} for every $3 \leq j \leq n$ odd and v_j with v_{j+n} for every $2 \leq j \leq n-1$ even.

Suppose now that we run $\mathcal{A}$ on G_i. A node v_j is at level 3 of the BFS-tree rooted in v_1 if and only if v_i and v_j are neighbors in G. Thus, if we simulate $\mathcal{A}$ on every G_i (i.e., for all $3 \leq i \leq n$ odd) at once, then we would solve BUILD in SimSync$[f(n)]$.

Note that if we run $\mathcal{A}$ on each of the G_i's with the nodes activated in order $(v_2, v_3, \ldots, v_{2n-1}, v_1)$ then the messages written by the nodes in $V = \{v_2, \ldots, v_n\}$ will not depend on the choice of i. In fact, the neighbourhood of all of these nodes is the same in every G_i, and their messages can only depend on such neighborhoods and the previous messages. We then define $\mathcal{A}'$ to be the protocol in which each node in G sends the message it would send in any of the G_i's when running $\mathcal{A}$. Once all these messages have been collected, $\mathcal{A}'$ simulates $\mathcal{A}$ for every G_i in order to compute the neighbourhood of v_i. Thus, EOB-BFS is not in FreeAsync$[f(n)]$. $\square$

COROLLARY 2. *For all $\Omega(\log n) = f(n) = o(n)$,* SimSync$[f(n)] \subsetneq$ FreeAsync$[f(n)]$.

3.3 Message size

Obviously, by increasing the size of the messages we make the system more powerful. What is more interesting is that this resource is orthogonal (independent) to the synchronization power. We have already seen in previous section that MIS(x) $\in$ SimSync$[\log n]$ but MIS(x) $\notin$ SimAsync$[o(n)]$. In other words, there are problems that can not be solved if we go down in the sinchronization hierarchy *no matter the extra length given to the size of the messages*. Now we are going to prove a more general result.

THEOREM 6. *Let $f(n) = o(n)$.* SUBGRAPH$_f$ *is the problem where the input is an n-node graph $G = (V, E)$ and the output is the subgraph obtained by removing all edges between nodes in $\{v_{f(n)+1}, \ldots, v_n\} \subseteq V$. Let $g(n) = o(f(n))$. It follows that* SUBGRAPH$_f \in$ SimAsync$[f(n)]$ *but* SUBGRAPH$_f \notin$ FreeSync$[g(n)]$.

PROOF. It is obvious that SUBGRAPH$_f \in$ SimAsync$[f(n)]$. In fact, each node sends a vector consisting of the $f(n)$ first bits of its line in the adjacency matrix of the graph. Let $g(n) = o(f(n))$. SUBGRAPH$_f$ cannot be in FreeSync$[g(n)]$, since that would allow us to solve BUILD for graphs of size n where $\{v_{f(n+1)}, \ldots, v_n\}$ are isolated nodes. This contradicts Lemma 1 because these graphs need $2^{O(nf(n))}$ bits to be defined. $\square$

4. CONNECTIVITY AND RELATED PROBLEMS

One of the main questions arising in distributed environments concerns connectivity. For instance, one important task in wireless networks consists in computing a connected spanning subgraph (i.e., a spanning tree) since the links of such subgraph are used for communication.

In Section 3 we proved that, in the FreeAsync$[\log n]$ model, it is possible to compute a BFS-forest for even-odd-bipartite graphs (i.e., bipartite graphs where the bipartition is *fully known* to every node). In such model it is in fact possible to get a protocol which outputs a BFS-forest *for all bipartite graphs without knowledge of the bipartition*. In the case of a non-bipartite graph though, running this protocol can result in a deadlock: at some point, no more nodes are activated. With synchronzation, as we are going to see in the next theorem, we do not need the graph to be bipartite and BFS *can be solved in the general case*, for arbitrary input graphs. Formally, the input of problem BFS is an arbitrary n-node graph G and the output is a BFS-tree (or BFS-forest). The root of the BFS-tree in each connected component of G will be the node with the smallest identifier in the respective component.

THEOREM 7. BFS *can be solved in the* FreeSync$[\log n]$ *model.*

PROOF. The protocol is very similar to the one we used for EOB-BFS, but we need to keep track of edges within a level (these edges do not exist in the bipartite case).

Initially, only v_1 is active. Let N_v^* be the set of neighbors of v *that have already written a message* on the whiteboard. When node v becomes active it creates the message $(i(v), l(v), p(v), d_{-1}(v), d_0(v), d_{+1}(v))$ where:

$i(v)$ is its ID

$l(v) = min_{w \in N_v^*} l(w) + 1$

$p(v)$ is the node in N_v^* with minimum ID, or
ROOT if N_v^* is empty

$d_{-1}(v) = |\{w \in N_v^* : l(w) = l(v) - 1\}|$

$d_0(v) = |\{w \in N_v^* : l(w) = l(v)\}|$

$d_{+1}(v) = d(v) - d_{-1}(v)$, with $d(v)$ its degree

Consider nodes v at distance at least 2 from the ROOT. These nodes v become active if the condition $(1 \wedge 2) \vee 3$ is satisfied, where

1. A neighbor w of v has already written its message on the whiteboard.

2.
$$\sum_{u \in L_{l(w)}} d_{-1}(u) = \sum_{u \in L_{l(w)-1}} d_{+1}(u) - 2 \sum_{u \in L_{l(w)-1}} d_0(u),$$

where L_k is the set of nodes in layer k that have already written a message on the whiteboard.

3. v is the node with the smallest ID that has not written a message on the whiteboard, the last message was written by a non-neighbor w,
$$\sum_{u \in L_{l(w)}} d_{-1}(u) = \sum_{u \in L_{l(w)-1}} d_{+1}(u) - 2 \sum_{u \in L_{l(w)-1}} d_0(u),$$
and
$$\sum_{u \in L_{l(w)}} d_{+1}(u) - 2 \sum_{u \in L_{l(w)}} d_0(u) = 0.$$

Condition 2, by counting the edges crossing from layer $l(v) - 1$ to layer $l(v) - 2$, ensures that all the nodes in layer $l(v) - 1$ have sent their messages and the nodes of layer $l(v)$ may become active. Condition 3 ensures that, when the active connected component changes (because there are no edges "going outside" the last layer), exactly one node is activated. $\square$

COROLLARY 3. *In* FREEASYNC[$\log n$] *there exists a protocol which, on any bipartite graph G, outputs a BFS-forest of G.*

PROOF. In a bipartite graph there are no edges between nodes in the same layer. In other words, we need to apply the protocol for the general case without computing $d_0(v)$. Thanks to this, all the information the nodes in layer k need to compute is available when layer k is activated. $\square$

OPEN PROBLEM 2. *Is it possible to solve* SPANNING-TREE *or even* CONNECTIVITY *in the* FREEASYNC[$f(n)$] *model? For which $f(n)$?*

OPEN PROBLEM 3. *Is it true that for all (or some) $f(n)$,* FREEASYNC[$f(n)$] $\subsetneq$ FREESYNC[$f(n)$]*? We conjecture that this is the case and that in fact BFS cannot be solved in the* FREEASYNC[$f(n)$] *model for $f = o(n)$.*

5. ACKNOWLEDGMENTS

Partially supported by programs Fondap and Basal-CMM (I.R., K.S.), Fondecyt 1090156 (I.R.), Anillo ACT88 (K.S.), Fondecyt 11090390 (K.S) and FP7 STREP EULER (N.N.).

6. REFERENCES

[1] L. Babai, A. Gál, P. G. Kimmel, and S. V. Lokam. Communication complexity of simultaneous messages. *SIAM J. Comput.*, 33:137–166, 2004.

[2] F. Becker, M. Matamala, N. Nisse, I. Rapaport, K. Suchan, and I. Todinca. Adding a referee to an interconnection network: What can(not) be computed in one round? In *International Parallel and Distributed Processing Symposium*, IPDPS '11, pages 508–514. IEEE Computer Society, 2011.

[3] A. K. Chandra, M. L. Furst, and R. J. Lipton. Multi-party protocols. In *Proceedings of the 15th Annual ACM Symposium on Theory of Computing*, STOC '83, pages 94–99. ACM, 1983.

[4] J. Feldman, S. Muthukrishnan, A. Sidiropoulos, C. Stein, and Z. Svitkina. On distributing symmetric streaming computations. *ACM Trans. Algorithms*, 6:66:1–66:19, 2010.

[5] S. Grumbach and Z. Wu. Logical locality entails frugal distributed computation over graphs. In *Proceedings of 35th International Workshop on Graph-Theoretic Concepts in Computer Science (WG)*, volume 5911 of *Lecture Notes in Computer Science*, pages 154–165, 2009.

[6] F. Kuhn, T. Moscibroda, and R. Wattenhofer. What cannot be computed locally! In *Proceedings of the 23rd Annual ACM Symposium on Principles of Distributed Computing (PODC)*, pages 300–309. ACM, 2004.

[7] N. Linial. Locality in distributed graph algorithms. *SIAM J. Comput.*, 21(1):193–201, 1992.

[8] D. Peleg. *Distributed computing: a locality-sensitive approach.* SIAM Monographs on Discrete Mathematics and Applications, 2000.

Optimal and Competitive Runtime Bounds for Continuous, Local Gathering of Mobile Robots

Barbara Kempkes
Heinz Nixdorf Institute &
Computer Science
Department
University of Paderborn
barbaras@upb.de

Peter Kling*
Heinz Nixdorf Institute &
Computer Science
Department
University of Paderborn
peter.kling@upb.de

Friedhelm Meyer auf der Heide
Heinz Nixdorf Institute &
Computer Science
Department
University of Paderborn
fmadh@upb.de

ABSTRACT

We consider a scenario in which n mobile robots with a limited viewing range are distributed arbitrarily in the plane, such that the visibility graph of the robots is connected. The goal is to gather the robots in one (not predefined) point. Each robot may base its decision where to move only on the current relative positions of the robots which are in its viewing range. That is, besides having a limited viewing range, the robots are oblivious (they do not use information from the past), they do not have IDs, and they do not have a common sense of direction. On the other hand side, we assume that they are points, i.e., have no extent.

Variants of this problem have been studied extensively in different discrete time models. In this paper, we study the gathering problem in a continuous time model. That is, the robots continuously sense the positions of their neighboring robots within their viewing range, and continuously adapt speed and direction, according to a *local rule*. We assume a speed limit normalized to 1, so that the maximum distance traveled by any robot is smaller or equal to the runtime. Gordon, Wagner and Bruckstein have proposed a simple and intuitive continuous algorithm in ANTS '04, and they showed that their algorithm gathers the robots in finite time. But the runtime of this algorithm has been open since then. We present a runtime analysis for their algorithm and show two runtime bounds. The first one is an optimal worst case bound $O(n)$, the second one shows the $\log(OPT)$-competitiveness in the sense that if OPT is the runtime of an optimal global algorithm, the local algorithm is at most by a factor of $\log(OPT)$ slower than the global algorithm. Best previous bounds on the distance traveled by the robots are obtained for discrete time models and are $O(n^2)$ in the worst case and only $O(n)$ competitive.

Categories and Subject Descriptors

F.1.2 [**Computation by Abstract Devices**]: Modes of Computation—*Parallelism and concurrency*; F.2.2 [**Analysis of Algorithms**

and Problem Complexity]: Nonnumerical Algorithms and Problems—*geometrical problems and computations*

Keywords

mobile robots, local algorithms, distributed algorithms, robot gathering

1. INTRODUCTION

Envision a scenario with n mobile robots which have a limited viewing range and are placed arbitrarily in the plane (assuming that the visibility graph of the robots is connected). The goal is to gather all these robots in one (not predefined) point. Each robot has to plan and perform its movement based solely on the positions of the other robots within its viewing range, which we normalize to 1 — no global view, communication or long term memory is provided.

Most algorithms for this *gathering problem* and similar formation problems base on one of different discrete round models. For example, in [1, 6] it is shown that gathering can be achieved with a very simple algorithm with robots with limited visibility in a synchronous discrete time model in $O(n^2)$ rounds. The authors of [4] analyze a simple algorithm for the same problem with an unlimited viewing range in several asynchronous time models. Further publications consider the gathering problem in similar time models [12, 15, 11, 14, 7, 10, 3]. All of these models have in common that they base on the so-called *Look-Compute-Move (LCM) model*. That is, the robots act in rounds, where each round consists of a look operation, in which the robot determines the positions of all visible robots, a compute operation, where the robot strategy is used to determine a target point based on the observed robot positions, and a move operation, where the robot finally moves towards the previously computed target point. The concrete models differ in whether these operations are executed synchronously or asynchronously (or something in between). [9] also uses such a model. It is shown that robots with a limited viewing range can scatter (that is, move to pairwise different positions in the plane) in $O(\min\{n, D^2 \log n\})$ rounds, where D is the diameter of the initial configuration.

A different approach is to use a continuous time model. This was first done in [8] for the gathering problem. The proposed model is not a classical round model, but rather all robots can perpetually and at the same time measure and adjust their movement paths, leading to curves as trajectories for the robots. A constant maximum speed is assumed. In this model, runtime cannot be defined as the number of rounds like in discrete time models. Instead, we can define it as the time needed by the robots to gather in one point. When assuming a constant maximum speed of 1, the runtime is therefore also an upper bound on the distance the robots can travel.

*Supported by the Graduate School on Applied Network Science (GSANS).

Permission to make digital or hard copies of all or part of this work for personal or classroom use is granted without fee provided that copies are not made or distributed for profit or commercial advantage and that copies bear this notice and the full citation on the first page. To copy otherwise, to republish, to post on servers or to redistribute to lists, requires prior specific permission and/or a fee.
SPAA'12, June 25–27, 2012, Pittsburgh, Pennsylvania, USA.
Copyright 2012 ACM 978-1-4503-1213-4/12/06 ...$10.00.

The authors of [8] propose a simple algorithm for the gathering problem in the continuous time model. They show that the robots gather in one point in finite time, but the time it takes the robots to gather is since then open. More recently, it was shown in [2] that similar processes in discrete time models may have an exponential behavior. In [5], the same continuous time model is used for the related robot chain problem. The robots, which initially form an arbitrarily winding chain between two stationary endpoints, need to move on the line between these points. It is shown that the robots reach this line, and a runtime bound of $\mathcal{O}(min\{n, (OPT + d) \log n\})$ is given, n denoting the number of robots, OPT the time needed by an optimal global algorithm and d the distance between the end points. With this result, the strategy is not only faster than similar strategies for the same problem working in a discrete synchronous time model, but its runtime can also be compared to that of an optimal global algorithm. Moreover, although the considered time model is unrealistic in the sense that it assumes the measurements and speed and direction adjustments to take zero time, it is close to real applications [13].

Therefore, we want to pursue this line of research and focus on the continuous time model. In this paper, we investigate the runtime of the simple algorithm from [8]. The strategy is rather intuitive: A robot determines whether it is a vertex on the boundary of the convex hull of the robot positions visible by him. If it is, it moves with maximum speed (which we normalize to 1) in direction of the angle bisector of the angle between its two neighboring vertices of the convex hull. If it is on a line of the convex hull, it stays on this line and moves with it. Otherwise, if it is strictly inside the convex hull, it does not move at all. Since the correctness of the strategy was already proven in [8], we analyze the strategy with respect to the runtime needed until all robots have gathered in one point.

In order to measure the quality of the strategy, we consider the worst-case time needed by the local strategy as such, but we also compare it to the time needed by an optimal global strategy. Therefore, we will show two runtime bounds. The first bound, which is $O(n)$, shows that the strategy is asymptotically optimal for worst-case instances: The robots can be placed in the plane such that two robots are in distance $\Theta(n)$ from each other. This instance cannot be solved faster than in time $\Omega(n)$, given a constant speed limit. Our second runtime bound of $O(OPT \log OPT)$ shows that even for instances which can be solved fast by an optimal global algorithm, the strategy is at most by a logarithmic factor slower than OPT, the time an optimal algorithm needs under global view.

Organization of the paper.

We begin the next section by formally introducing the model, the strategy, and an outline of the proof for the runtime bound. In particular, we describe how we measure "progress" of the gathering algorithm. Section 3 is dedicated to the analysis of the strategy. The analysis is divided into two parts: in Section 3.1 we show that the strategy gathers the robots in time $\mathcal{O}(n)$. In Section 3.2 we proceed to the main result of the paper. We show that input instances that are solved fast by an optimal global algorithm are also handled fast by the strategy in time $\mathcal{O}(OPT \log OPT)$. We conclude with some open questions.

2. PROBLEM DESCRIPTION

We consider a set of n autonomous mobile robots $v_1, v_1, \ldots, v_n$ placed in the two-dimensional Euclidean plane $\mathbb{R}^2$. Each robot has a viewing range of 1. We call the robots within a robot's viewing range its *neighbors*, and we assume that a robot can determine the positions of its neighbors accurately. The *unit disk graph* G_t of the robot positions at time t consists of a vertex for every robot,

and it has an edge between each pair of neighboring robots. The placement of the robots in the beginning may be arbitrary, under the constraint that the unit disk graph of the robots is connected. The goal is to gather the robots in one point.

The robots use only information from the current point of time (they are oblivious), they do not have a common coordinate system and do not share a common sense of direction, they do not have IDs and communicate only by observing the positions of their neighbors. We assume accuracy of the actors and sensors of the robots in several aspects: Measurements of the relative positions of the neighbors of a robot (the angle formed by a robot and its neighbors, distances to neighbors) are exact; The adjustment of speed and direction is accurate, and this adjustment is not delayed compared to the measurement.

The continuous time model.

In the continuous time model, which was introduced in [8], time passes in a continuous way and is not modeled by discrete time steps. Thus, robots are able to continuously measure the positions of their neighbors and adjust their trajectory and speed accordingly (keeping the speed limit of 1). The direction in which a robot moves as well as its speed can change in a non-continuous way, but with the considered strategy this occurs only at a finite number of points of time. Both direction and speed depend only on the positions of the neighboring robots. We assume that a robot can measure these positions *without delay*: the direction in which a robot moves depends only on the positions of its neighbors at the same time.

Note that this model can be seen as a continuous variant of the classical discrete Look-Compute-Move (LCM) model. At each point of time, each robot observes the positions of its neighbors, determines its movement direction and speed and moves in this direction. Therefore, assuming a speed limit of one, the continuous model arises from the discrete LCM model when fixing a maximum movement distance of δ per round and letting $\delta \to 0$.

The strategy.

At each point in time, each robot v_i observes all robot positions of those robots within distance 1 (the viewing range) of itself. Then it computes the convex hull $CH_i(t)$ of these positions including itself and performs one of the following actions.

- If v_i is strictly inside this convex hull, it does not move.
- If it is on a line of the border of the convex hull, it moves with this line, maintaining the ratio of distances between its two neighbors on the border.
- If it is a vertex of $CH_i(t)$, it moves with maximum speed 1 on the angle bisector towards the inner angle of $CH_i(t)$. We call this angle $\alpha_i^*(t)$. In the case that v_i has only one neighbor, $\alpha_i^*(t) = 0$ and v_i moves with maximum speed 1 towards its neighbor. See Figure 1 for an example.

Note that the trajectory of robots is continuous, but the direction in which a robot moves may change in a non-continuous way, when two robots come into viewing range of each other and one is a new neighbor in the local convex hull of the other. But since robots never lose visibility to a neighbor again [8] and therefore the number of changes of the unit disk graph is finite, this only occurs at a finite number of points of time. Note further that the $\alpha_i^*(t)$ are only defined for robots which move on an angle bisector.

Notation and progress measures.

Given a time $t \geq 0$, the position of robot v_i at this time is denoted by $v_i(t) \in \mathbb{R}^2$. The positions of the robots at time t defines the

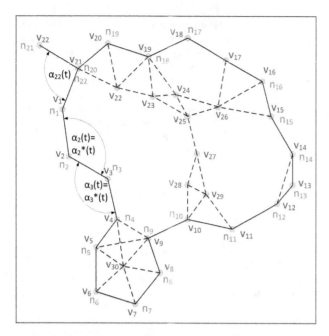

Figure 1: Example configuration. Lines (dashed or solid) between robots indicate that they are neighbors. The solid lines represent the outer border of $P(t)$.

configuration at time t. The configuration at time 0 is called *start configuration*. We will furthermore denote the scalar product of two vectors a and b simply by $a \cdot b$ and the length of a vector a by $||a||$.

For the analysis of the strategy, we will use two progress measures, which we will call the *length* $\mathfrak{l}(t)$ and the *height* $\mathfrak{h}(t)$ of a configuration at time t. For the definition of the height, note that the GATHERING-MOVE-ON-BISECTOR-strategy is deterministic. It thus exists a point M in which the robots will eventually gather. We will call M the *gathering point*.

Definition 1. The *height* $\mathfrak{h}(t)$ of a configuration at time t is the maximum distance between a robot and M at time t.

We define the *height-circle* $C_{\mathfrak{h}(t)}$ to be the circle around M with radius $\mathfrak{h}(t)$, which contains all robots. Moreover, we define $h := \mathfrak{h}(0)$ to be the height of the start configuration. Note that OPT is at least half of the diameter of the configuration, and h is at most the diameter. Therefore, $OPT \geq h/2$.

For the definition of the length, let G_t denote the unit disk graph of the robots at time t. G_t has a well-defined outer border, which has the form of a polygon, a line or in parts a polygon and in parts a line (see Fig. 1). Nevertheless, we can see the complete outer border as a polygon by using the edges of lines twice. For example, in Fig. 1, the vertices of the polygon are formed by the robots on the outer border in the order $v_1, v_2, \ldots, v_{21}, v_{22}, v_{21}, v_1$. The outer border of the unit disk graph is indicated by the solid line, edges of the unit disk graph which are not part of the outer border are indicated by dashed lines. We will call this polygon $P(t)$ from now on.

Let $B_G(t)$ denote the sequence of robots which are vertices of $P(t)$ starting at an arbitrary vertex and following $P(t)$ in counterclockwise order. Let $m(t)$ be the length of the sequence and therefore the number of vertices of $P(t)$. We rename the elements of $B_G(t)$ by n_1 to $n_{m(t)}$ and call them *outer nodes*. This way we get that n_i is a neighboring vertex of n_{i+1} and n_{i-1} in $P(t)$. In our example, we have started numbering the outer nodes at v_1. Note

that one robot can define several vertices and therefore outer nodes, as v_{21} in the example. Moreover, there can be robots on the outer border of the unit disk graph, which are on the line between their neighbors and therefore do not define a vertex of $P(t)$ (for example v_{17}). Finally, if several robots are at the same position, they define only one outer node. We denote the vector connecting two neighboring outer nodes n_{i-1} and n_i at time t by $w_i(t)$ for $i = 2, \ldots, m(t)$. $w_1(t)$ connects $n_{m(t)}$ and n_1, respectively.

Now we can define the length of a configuration.

Definition 2. The *length* $\mathfrak{l}(t)$ of a configuration at a fixed time t is defined as the sum of the distances between neighboring nodes of $P(t)$: $\mathfrak{l}(t) := \sum_{i=1}^{m(t)} ||w_i(t)||$.

Again, we define $l := \mathfrak{l}(0)$ as the length of the start configuration.

We now want to classify the outer nodes. Note first that, according to the strategy, not all of the robots which define an outer node move. In Fig. 1, for example the outer nodes n_{20}, n_{22} and n_4 do not move. But this can only be the case if the outer node forms a reflex angle of the polygon $P(t)$. If it forms a convex angle of $P(t)$, it moves on the angle bisector of this angle (for example n_2). It is also possible that a node which forms a reflex angle moves, like n_3 in Fig. 1.

We will see later that the speed with which the length decreases depends on the angles $\alpha_i^*(t)$ on whose bisector the outer nodes move. But since $\alpha_i^*(t)$ is only defined for nodes which move and not for all outer nodes, for the sake of description, we define an angle $\alpha_i(t)$ for each outer node n_i as the smaller of the two angles formed by $-w_i(t)$ and $w_{i+1}(t)$. It is defined such that if an outer node n_i moves, it moves in direction of the angle bisector of α_i. Therefore, if n_i is defined by robot v_k and v_k moves, $\alpha_k^*(t) = \alpha_i(t)$.

We know that all outer nodes n_i which form a convex angle of $P(t)$ move on the angle bisector of α_i, but whether or not outer nodes forming a reflex angle of $P(t)$ move depends on the current configuration. Therefore, we define an angle $\gamma_i(t)$ for each outer node, which will be used for the sake of notation instead of $\alpha_i(t)$ for bounding the speed with which the length decreases. Consider an outer node n_i. According to the algorithm, for each such outer node n_i at time t, exactly one of the following properties is true.

- n_i is a convex angle of $P(t)$. That is, n_i moves on the angle bisector of $\alpha_i(t)$. See for example robot v_2 in Fig. 1. In this case, we define the angle $\gamma_i(t)$ for the outer node n_i as $\gamma_i(t) := \alpha_i(t) < \pi$.

- n_i is a reflex angle of $P(t)$ (for example node n_3, n_4 or n_{22}). In this case, we cannot be sure whether n_i moves. Therefore, we define $\gamma_i(t) := \pi$, which will (according to Lemma 1) for this node result in a progress of 0 regarding the length of the outer border. Note that for robot v_{21}, this means that the angles γ of both outer nodes defined by it ($\gamma_{20}(t)$ and $\gamma_{22}(t)$) are set to π.

3. ANALYSIS

We start our runtime analysis with the worst-case upper bound of $O(n)$. This bound is asymptotically optimal for worst-case instances, since one can place a robot in distance $\Omega(n)$ from another robot and therefore a distance of $\Omega(n)$ has to be covered. In Section 3.2 we show our upper bound of $\mathcal{O}(OPT \log OPT)$, which means that the strategy is $\log OPT$-competitive.

3.1 The $O(n)$ upper bound

The idea of our first upper bound is to show that the length decreases with constant speed and therefore the robots gather in

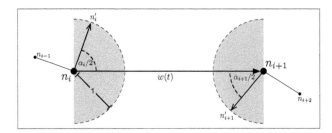

Figure 2: Illustration for the proof of Lemma 1

time $O(l)$. We will furthermore show that $l \leq 6n$, resulting in the desired upper bound.

Lemma 1 shows that the length decreases depending on the angles $\alpha_k^*(t)$ on whose bisector the outer nodes move. But as explained in Section 2, it is not guaranteed that all outer nodes move at all. Therefore, we have defined the angles $\gamma_i(t)$ in such a way that they are equal to the respective $\alpha_k^*(t)$, if a robot moves, and otherwise results in a progress of 0.

LEMMA 1. *Consider two neighboring outer nodes n_i and n_{i+1} at an arbitrary time t_0 and assume that the unit disk graph does not change at this time. Then, the distance between n_i and n_{i+1} decreases with speed at least $\cos\frac{\gamma_i(t_0)}{2} + \cos\frac{\gamma_{i+1}(t_0)}{2} \geq 0$.*

PROOF. We consider the vector $w_{i+1}(t)$ as a function of time mapping into $\mathbb{R}^2$. To simplify the notation, we furthermore drop the index in the following. That is, we consider the function $w : \mathbb{R}_{\geq 0} \to \mathbb{R}^2, t \mapsto w_{i+1}(t) = n_{i+1} - n_i$. Additionally, we consider the function $\mathsf{d} : \mathbb{R}_{\geq 0} \to \mathbb{R}_{\geq 0}, t \mapsto ||w(t)||$, the length of $w(t)$ at time t. Our goal is to show that $\mathsf{d}'(t_0) = -\left(\cos\frac{\gamma_i(t_0)}{2} + \cos\frac{\gamma_{i+1}(t_0)}{2}\right)$ for any $t_0 \in \mathbb{R}_{\geq 0}$. In the following, we refer to the x- and y-component of $w(t) \in \mathbb{R}^2$ by $w_x(t)$ and $w_y(t)$ respectively. Similarly, we denote the x-coordinate of the position of outer node n_i at time t by $n_{i,x}(t)$ and its derivation by $n'_{i,x}(t)$. By translating and rotating the coordinate system, we can w.l.o.g. assume $n_i(t_0) = (0, 0)$ and $n_{i+1}(t_0) = (\mathsf{d}(t_0), 0)$. See Fig. 2 for an illustration.

Let us first consider node n_i defined by robot v_k. We show that $n'_{i,x}(t_0) \geq \cos\frac{\gamma_i(t_0)}{2}$. Due to the classification of the outer nodes, we can distinguish the following cases:

1. Outer node n_i forms a convex angle of $P(t)$. Then n_i moves in direction of the angle bisector of $\alpha_i(t_0)$, and the velocity vector of n_i at time t_0 is given by

$$n'_i(t_0) = \left(+\cos\frac{\alpha_i(t_0)}{2}, \pm\sin\frac{\alpha_i(t_0)}{2}\right)$$

$$= \left(+\cos\frac{\gamma_i(t_0)}{2}, \pm\sin\frac{\gamma_i(t_0)}{2}\right).$$

2. Outer node n_i forms a reflex angle of $P(t)$. We do not know whether n_i moves or not. If it does, then $n'_{i,x}(t_0) = +\cos\frac{\alpha_i(t_0)}{2} \geq 0$ as in case 1. Otherwise, $n'_i(t_0) = (0, 0)$. In any case, $\gamma_i(t_0) = \pi$ (by definition). Thus, $n'_{i,x}(t_0) \geq 0 = \cos\frac{\gamma_i(t_0)}{2}$.

Analogously, we can show $n'_{i+1,x}(t_0) \leq -\cos\frac{\gamma_{i+1}(t_0)}{2}$. Basic analysis now gives us the following equation for the first derivation of d at a time $t \in \mathbb{R}_{\geq 0}$[1]:

$$\mathsf{d}'(t) = \left(\frac{w_x(t)}{\mathsf{d}(t)} \quad \frac{w_y(t)}{\mathsf{d}(t)}\right) \cdot \left(\begin{array}{c} w'_x(t) \\ w'_y(t) \end{array}\right).$$

---

[1]Note that $\mathsf{d}(t) \neq 0$, since several robots at a single position define only one outer node.

Using $w_y(t_0) = 0$ and $w_x(t_0) = \mathsf{d}(t_0)$, we finally get

$$\mathsf{d}'(t_0) = w'_x(t_0) = (n_{i+1} - n_i)'_x(t_0) = \left(n'_{i+1,x}(t_0) - n'_{i,x}(t_0)\right)$$

$$\leq \quad -\left(\cos\frac{\gamma_i(t_0)}{2} + \cos\frac{\gamma_{i+1}(t_0)}{2}\right).$$

Therefore, the distance between n_i and n_{i+1} reduces at time t with speed at least $\cos(\frac{\gamma_i(t_0)}{2}) + \cos(\frac{\gamma_{i+1}(t_0)}{2})$. Furthermore, since we have $\gamma_i(t) \in [0, \pi]$ for any $t \in \mathbb{R}_{\geq 0}$ and $i \in \{1, \ldots, m(t)\}$, this speed is not negative. $\square$

Thus we can give the speed with which the length decreases as the sum over all edges of the polygon:

COROLLARY 1. *At an arbitrary time t, in which the unit disk graph does not change, the length $\mathfrak{l}(t)$ of the outer border decreases with speed $2\sum_{i=1}^{m(t)}\cos(\frac{\gamma_i(t)}{2})$.*

The next lemma shows that this sum is lower bounded by 4.

LEMMA 2. *At an arbitrary time t, in which the unit disk graph does not change, $\mathfrak{l}(t)$ decreases with speed at least 4.*

PROOF. We can bound the sum of the angles $\gamma_i(t)$, since the outer nodes forms a polygon. If $m(t)$ is the number of vertices of the polygon $P(t)$, the sum of its inner angles is $(m(t) - 2)\pi$. Now $\gamma_i(t)$ is not always an inner angle of n_i of the polygon $P(t)$. Let us see when this can happen. If n_i forms a convex angle of $P(t)$, the inner angle of $P(t)$ at n_i is $\alpha_i(t) = \gamma_i(t)$. If n_i forms a reflex angle of $P(t)$, the inner angle of $P(t)$ at n_i is greater than $\pi = \gamma_i(t)$. Thus, we know that $\sum_{i=1}^{m(t)}\gamma_i \leq (m(t) - 2)\pi$.

The length decreases with speed $2\sum_{i=1}^{m(t)}\cos(\frac{\gamma_i(t)}{2})$ (cf. Corollary 1). Using that $\cos(x) \geq -2/\pi \cdot x + 1$ for $0 \leq x \leq \pi/2$, the length decreases with total speed

$$\sum_{i=1}^{m(t)} 2\cos(\frac{\gamma_i}{2}) \geq 2\sum_{i=1}^{m(t)}\left(-\frac{2}{\pi}\frac{\gamma_i}{2} + 1\right) = 2m(t) - \frac{2}{\pi}\sum_{i=1}^{m(t)}\gamma_i$$

$$\geq 2m(t) - \frac{2}{\pi}\pi(m(t) - 2) = 4.$$

$\square$

Lemma 2 shows that the length decreases with speed 4 as long as the unit disk graph does not change. The next lemma shows that at these (finite) points in time, the length does not increase.

LEMMA 3. *The length $\mathfrak{l}(t)$ decreases monotonically.*

PROOF. As we have seen in Lemma 1, the length of the chain decreases as long as the unit disk graph does not change. So let us now see how the border of the unit disk graph and therefore the polygon $P(t)$ can change topologically and what influence this has on the length. For this, note first that due to the definition of the algorithm, a robot which does not define an outer node in the beginning may move on a line of the border, which does not change the length, but it can never become a vertex of the border of the unit disk graph and therefore define an outer node. That is, there are only two possibilities how the border of the unit disk graph can change topologically:

- Robots can move in a way that they stop to define an outer node: when a robot v_k, which defines an outer node n_i, reaches the line between its two neighboring outer nodes. In this case, the distance between its neighbors n_{i-1} and n_{i+1} (which will then be n_{i-1} and n_i) is set to $d(n_{i-1}, n_i) + d(n_i, n_{i+1})$. Thus, the length of the outer border does not change.

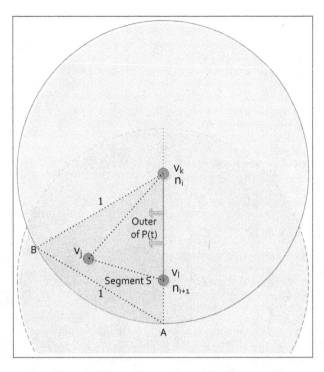

Figure 3: Illustration to the proof of Lemma 4

- Edges of the unit disk graph can never be deleted. But edges on the border can be replaced by another edge, when two robots on the border come into viewing range of each other (e.g., n_8 and n_{11} in Fig. 1). The robots in between (v_9, v_{10}) stop to define outer nodes, and the length $l(t)$ is decreased.

Thus, in both cases, the length is not increased. □

Note that the length decreases continuously during the open time intervals between two changes of the unit disk graph. In the moment of a change of the unit disk graph, the length may stay the same or even decrease non-continuously.

These lemmas show that the length decreases with speed 4, resulting in a runtime bound of $O(l)$. To derive an upper bound of $O(n)$, we need to show that a robot can define only a constant number of outer nodes (Lemma 4).

LEMMA 4. *For the length of the start configuration holds $l \leq 6n$.*

PROOF. We will show that each robot v_k can define at most 6 outer nodes. This is sufficient, since it follows that the polygon $P(0)$ can have at most $6n$ edges, each with a length of at most 1 (if there is an edge which is longer than 1, a robot must be on this line).

First note that if v_k defines x outer nodes, each of the outer nodes has a left and a right neighbor on the border of the polygon. These neighbors are either outer nodes themselves, or they are robots which are on the straight line between two outer nodes. Moreover, the x right neighbors of the x outer nodes are all distinct.

Now let n_i be an outer node defined by v_k, and n_{i+1} its right neighbor (w.l.o.g., let it also be an outer node, this simplifies the notation) which is defined by v_l. Let the outer of the polygon lie in clockwise direction of v_l when looking from v_k (see Fig. 3).

We will show that no robot can be in clockwise direction from v_l which is visible by both v_k and v_l. For the sake of contradiction, assume that there is such a robot v_j (see Fig. 3). Then the unit disk graph contains the edges (v_k, v_j) and (v_j, v_l). But then the

edge (v_k, v_l) cannot define the outer border of $P(t)$ in clockwise direction.

So we have found an area which cannot contain any robot. Consider the sector S of the visibility circle of v_k which is defined by two points A and B, where A is the point closest to v_l on the circle defining the visibility range of v_k, and B is the point on the circle defining v_k's visibility range in distance 1 in clockwise direction from A (see again Fig. 3). This sector is completely contained in the area which cannot contain any robot. The inner angle of the sector at v_k is $\pi/3$. Thus, v_l defines a sector with inner angle $\pi/3$ which cannot contain any robots.

Now consider another outer node defined by v_k, and its right neighbor. Call it v_s. Then the sectors defined by v_s and v_l cannot intersect, since otherwise v_s would be in v_l's sector or the other way round. Thus, all right neighbors of outer nodes defined by v_k define a sector of the visibility range of v_k which are mutually distinct. Since the inner angle of these sectors is $\pi/3$, there can be at most 6 such sectors and therefore also at most 6 right neighbors. It follows that v_k can define at most 6 outer nodes. □

Our runtime bound follows directly from the Lemmas 2 to 4.

THEOREM 1. *After time at most $1/4 \cdot l \leq 3/2 \cdot n$, the robots have gathered in one point.*

3.2 The $O(OPT \log OPT)$ upper bound

Assume we are given a configuration whose height is—relative to the length—very small. In this case, the upper bound of $\mathcal{O}(l)$ can be quite large compared to the time needed by an optimal global strategy (which can be as small as h). However, given a configuration with a long outer border and a small height, the outer border must be quite winding, yielding many relatively small angles α_i. The result is that the length decreases faster than in our worst-case bound, where we only use that the sum of the internal angles of the polygon is $(m(t) - 2)\pi$.

For the proof of the upper runtime bound $O(OPT \log OPT)$, we will divide the outer border into parts of length a bit greater than the diameter of the height-circle. We show that each part must contain some curves. In particular, in each part, the sum of the angles $\alpha_i(t)$ must be by a constant smaller than in a straight line (Lemma 5). Lemma 6 transfers this result for each part to the sum of the angles α_i of the whole outer border. But since the runtime according to Lemma 1 does not depend on the α_i, but on the γ_i, Lemma 7 transfers the result from Lemma 6 to the sum of the angles γ_i. Having that the sum of the angles γ_i in the whole chain cannot be arbitrarily large, Lemma 8 yields the speed by which the length of the chain decreases. Since the number of parts is dependent on the length of the chain, the speed is also dependent on it. Lemma 9 shows that $l \in \mathcal{O}(h^2)$, such that the speed is finally only dependent on h. Theorem 2 finally gives the upper bound of $\mathcal{O}(h \log h) = \mathcal{O}(OPT \log OPT)$.

LEMMA 5. *Let $\mathfrak{B}$ denote a circle containing the outer nodes $n_{a-1}, n_a, n_{a+1}, \ldots, n_b$ (for $a, b \in \{1, \ldots, m_t + 1\}$, $a < b$) at a given time $t \in \mathbb{R}_{>0}$ and let S be the diameter of the circle. Then we have:*

$$\sum_{i=a}^{b} ||w_i(t)|| \geq \sqrt{2} \cdot S \Rightarrow \sum_{i=a}^{b-1} \alpha_i(t) \leq (b-a)\pi - \frac{\pi}{3}$$

PROOF. We write α_i, n_i and w_i instead of $\alpha_i(t)$, $n_i(t)$ and $w_i(t)$. Furthermore, we assume w.l.o.g. that $a = 1$. Thus, we have to show $\sum_{i=1}^{b} ||w_i|| \geq \sqrt{2} \cdot S \Rightarrow \sum_{i=1}^{b-1} \alpha_i \leq (b-1)\pi - \frac{\pi}{3}$.

Consider the function $\angle : \mathbb{R}^2 \times \mathbb{R}^2 \to]-\pi, \pi]$ that maps two vectors (w_s, w_t) to the signed angle of absolute value $\leq \pi$ formed

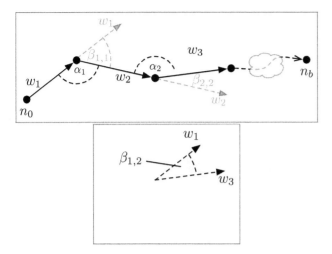

Figure 4: Note that the angles $\beta_{i,j}$ are signed: $\beta_{1,1} > 0$, $\beta_{2,2} < 0$, $\beta_{1,2} = \beta_{1,2} + \beta_{2,3} > 0$.

by them (it is not important which direction is used as positive angle, as long as it is equal for all pairs of vectors (w_s, w_t)). Note that we have $\alpha_i = \pi - |\angle(w_i, w_{i+1})|$ for all $i = 1, \dots, b-1$, for which α_i is defined. Let us define $\beta_{p,q} := \sum_{i=p}^{q} \angle(w_i, w_{i+1})$ and observe that $\angle(w_p, w_q) \equiv \beta_{p,q} \mod\ ]-\pi, \pi]$. See Figure 4 for an illustration.

Let us now assume $\sum_{i=1}^{b} \|w_i(t)\| \geq \sqrt{2} \cdot S$ and consider the following two cases:

Case 1: $\exists p, q, 1 \leq p < q \leq b : |\beta_{p,q}| \geq \frac{\pi}{3}$

Intuitively, if the angle between two vectors in the polygon is large, the sum of the angles α_i of the outer nodes in between cannot be arbitrarily large. More formally,

$$\sum_{i=1}^{b-1} \alpha_i \leq (s-1)\pi + \sum_{i=s}^{t} \alpha_i + (b-1-t)\pi$$

$$= (b+s-t-2)\pi + \sum_{i=s}^{t} (\pi - |\angle(w_i, w_{i+1})|)$$

$$= (b-1)\pi - \sum_{i=s}^{t} |\angle(w_i, w_{i+1})|$$

$$\leq (b-1)\pi - \left| \sum_{i=s}^{t} \angle(w_i, w_{i+1}) \right|$$

$$= (b-1)\pi - |\beta_{s,t}| \leq (b-1)\pi - \frac{\pi}{3}$$

Thus, the lemma holds in this case.

Case 2: $\forall p, q, 1 \leq p < q \leq b : |\beta_{p,q}| < \frac{\pi}{3}$

We will show that this case cannot occur by showing that the vector connecting n_0 and n_b, which is equal to $\sum_{i=1}^{b} w_i$, would have to be longer than S, which is a contradiction to n_0 and n_b both lying in $\mathfrak{B}$.

We have $\angle(w_p, w_q) = \beta_{p,q}$ and $|\beta_{p,q}| < \frac{\pi}{3}$ for all $1 \leq p < q \leq b$. In the following, we will use that the squared length

of a vector is equal to its scalar product with itself. Therefore:

$$\left\| \sum_{i=1}^{b} w_i \right\|^2 = \left(\sum_{i=1}^{b} w_i \right) \cdot \left(\sum_{i=1}^{b} w_i \right) = \sum_{1 \leq p,q \leq b} w_p \cdot w_q$$

$$= \sum_{1 \leq p,q \leq b} \|w_p\| \cdot \|w_q\| \cdot \cos(\beta_{p,q})$$

$$> \sum_{1 \leq p,q \leq b} \|w_p\| \cdot \|w_q\| \cdot \cos(\frac{\pi}{3})$$

$$= \cos(\frac{\pi}{3}) \sum_{1 \leq p,q \leq b} \|w_p\| \cdot \|w_q\|$$

$$= \frac{1}{2} \left(\sum_{i=1}^{b} \|w_i\| \right)^2 \geq \frac{1}{2} \cdot (\sqrt{2}S)^2 = S^2$$

This implies $\| \sum_{i=1}^{b} w_i \| > S$, leading to the desired contradiction.

$\square$

Dividing the outer border $P(t)$ in parts of length at least $\sqrt{2}$ times the diameter of the height-circle, Lemma 5 shows that each of the parts must contain some "small" angles. The robots at all of these angles which point inwards the polygon therefore shorten the length of the chain. For all angles which point outwards, we do not know whether the robots move or not. We will later see that this is nevertheless sufficient. The following lemma shows that using the technique of dividing the chain into parts yields an upper bound on the sum of the angles α_i of the chain.

LEMMA 6. *Let $S = 2\mathfrak{h}(t)$ denote the diameter of the robots' height-circle at a given time t. Then:*

$$\sum_{i=1}^{m(t)} \alpha_i(t) \leq n\pi - \frac{\pi}{3} \left\lfloor \frac{\mathfrak{l}(t)}{2\sqrt{2}S} \right\rfloor$$

PROOF. As in the proof for Lemma 5, we will omit the time parameter t in the following.

First note that we have $\|w_i\| \leq S$, because all robots lie inside the height-circle. This allows us to recursively define indices $1 = a_0 < a_1 < \dots < a_d \leq m(t) + 1$ by demanding $a_j \in \mathbb{N}$ to be minimal with $\sum_{i=a_{j-1}}^{a_j} \|w_i\| \in [\sqrt{2}S, (\sqrt{2}+1)S[$. That is, we divide the outer border at time t in d parts, where $n_{a_{j-1}}$ and n_{a_j} bound part j. n_{a_j} is the first robot in the chain such that the length of part j is at least $\sqrt{2}S$. Furthermore, since $\|w_{a_j}\| \leq S$, the length of part j is at most $\sqrt{2}S + S \leq 2\sqrt{2}S$, which implies $d \geq \left\lfloor \frac{\mathfrak{l}}{2\sqrt{2}S} \right\rfloor$. Since we have $\sum_{i=a_{j-1}}^{a_j} \|w_i\| \geq \sqrt{2}S$ for all $j = 1, \dots, d$, by Lemma 5 we get $\sum_{i=a_{j-1}}^{a_j-1} \alpha_i \leq (a_j - a_{j-1})\pi - \frac{\pi}{3}$. We now compute:

$$\sum_{i=1}^{a_d-1} \alpha_i = \sum_{j=1}^{d} \sum_{i=a_{j-1}}^{a_j-1} \alpha_i \leq \sum_{j=1}^{d} \left((a_j - a_{j-1})\pi - \frac{\pi}{3} \right)$$

$$= \pi \sum_{j=1}^{d} (a_j - a_{j-1}) - \frac{\pi}{3}d = (a_d - a_0)\pi - \frac{\pi}{3}d$$

$$= (a_d - 1)\pi - \frac{\pi}{3}d$$

This implies $\sum_{i=1}^{m(t)} \alpha_i \leq m(t)\pi - \frac{\pi}{3}d \leq n\pi - \frac{\pi}{3} \left\lfloor \frac{\mathfrak{l}}{2\sqrt{2}S} \right\rfloor$, as the lemma states. $\square$

Knowing that the sum of the angles α_i is bounded does not help us directly, since the speed with which the length decreases depends on the angles γ_i. The next lemma upper bounds the sum of the angles γ_i, using the bound on the sum of the angles α_i.

LEMMA 7. *Let $S = 2\mathfrak{h}(t)$ denote the diameter of the robots' height-circle at a given time t. Then:*

$$\sum_{i=1}^{m(t)} \gamma_i(t) \le n\pi - \frac{\pi}{6} \left\lfloor \frac{\mathfrak{l}(t)}{2\sqrt{2}S} \right\rfloor$$

PROOF. The intuition for this lemma is as follows. If α_i points outwards the polygon, its according γ_i is set to π. But if α_i points outwards the polygon, the according inner angle of the polygon is reflex, and in a polygon, the sum of convex inner angles is greater than the sum of reflex inner angles. Therefore, the sum of the γ_i's is at most $1/2$ times the sum of the α_i's plus $1/2 \cdot n\pi$.

For the formal proof, let β_i denote the inner angle of the polygon at outer node n_i. That is, $\beta_i = \alpha_i$ if α_i points inwards the polygon, and $\beta_i = 2\pi - \alpha_i$ if α_i points outwards the polygon. As the sum of the internal angles of a polygon with $m(t)$ vertices is $(m(t) - 2)\pi$, we have $\sum_{i=1}^{m(t)} \beta_i = \pi m(t) - 2\pi \le \pi n$. Let $[m(t)] := \{1, 2, ..., m(t)\}$. We get

$$\sum_{i=1}^{m(t)} \alpha_i = \sum_{i\in[m(t)]:\beta_i<\pi} \beta_i + \sum_{i\in[m(t)]:\beta_i>\pi} 2\pi - \beta_i$$

$$= \sum_{i\in[m(t)]:\beta_i<\pi} \beta_i - \sum_{i\in[m(t)]:\beta_i>\pi} \beta_i + \sum_{i\in[m(t)]:\beta_i>\pi} 2\pi.$$

Therefore,

$$-\sum_{i\in[m(t)]:\beta_i>\pi} \beta_i = \sum_{i=1}^{m(t)} \alpha_i - \sum_{i\in[m(t)]:\beta_i<\pi} \beta_i - \sum_{i\in[m(t)]:\beta_i>\pi} 2\pi.$$

Now consider the sum of the angles β_i. It can be subdivided into the sum of convex and reflex angles:

$$\sum_{i\in[m(t)]:\beta_i<\pi} \beta_i = \sum_{i=1}^{m(t)} \beta_i - \sum_{i\in[m(t)]:\beta_i>\pi} \beta_i$$

$$\le \pi n + \sum_{i=1}^{m(t)} \alpha_i - \sum_{i\in[m(t)]:\beta_i<\pi} \beta_i - \sum_{i\in[m(t)]:\beta_i>\pi} 2\pi.$$

The inequality follows from the bound on the internal angles, which is given in the introductory text, and from (1). Therefore,

$$2 \cdot \sum_{i\in[m(t)]:\beta_i<\pi} \beta_i \le \pi n + \sum_{i=1}^{m(t)} \alpha_i - \sum_{i\in[m(t)]:\beta_i>\pi} 2\pi.$$

Now the bound on the sum of the α_i's from Lemma 6 yields:

$$\sum_{i\in[m(t)]:\beta_i<\pi} \beta_i \le \pi n - \frac{\pi}{6}\left\lfloor \frac{\mathfrak{l}(t)}{2\sqrt{2}S} \right\rfloor - \sum_{i\in[m(t)]:\beta_i>\pi} \pi.$$

Finally, we use that $\gamma_i = \alpha_i = \beta_i$, iff $\beta_i < \pi$ and therefore α_i points inwards, and otherwise $\gamma_i = \pi$:

$$\sum_{i=1}^{m(t)} \gamma_i = \sum_{i\in[m(t)]:\beta_i<\pi} \beta_i + \sum_{i\in[m(t)]:\beta_i>\pi} \pi$$

$$\le \pi n - \frac{\pi}{6}\left\lfloor \frac{\mathfrak{l}(t)}{2\sqrt{2}S} \right\rfloor.$$

$\square$

Using that the sum of the angles γ_i is bounded, we can now give a lower bound for the speed by which the length decreases, which is linear in the current number of parts and therefore the current length of the outer border.

LEMMA 8. *The length of the outer border decreases at least with speed $\frac{1}{3}\left\lfloor \frac{\mathfrak{l}(t)}{2\sqrt{2}S} \right\rfloor$.*

PROOF. Fix a time $t \in \mathbb{R}_{\ge 0}$. By Corollary 1, the length decreases with a speed of $2\sum_{i=1}^n \cos\frac{\gamma_i(t)}{2}$. Using that $\cos(x)$ is lower bounded by $1 - \frac{2}{\pi}x$ for all $x \in [0, \pi/2]$ and by Lemma 7 we get:

$$\mathfrak{l}'(t) = -2\sum_{i=1}^n \cos\frac{\gamma_i(t)}{2} \le -2\sum_{i=1}^n \left(1 - \frac{\gamma_i(t)}{\pi}\right)$$

$$= -2n + \frac{2}{\pi}\sum_{i=1}^n \gamma_i(t)$$

$$\le -2n + \frac{2}{\pi}\left(n\pi - \frac{\pi}{3}\left\lfloor \frac{\mathfrak{l}(t)}{2\sqrt{2}S} \right\rfloor\right) = -\frac{1}{3}\left\lfloor \frac{\mathfrak{l}(t)}{2\sqrt{2}S} \right\rfloor.$$

$\square$

The speed with which the length decreases depends on the value $\mathfrak{l}(t)$, which is not directly comparable to the time an optimal global algorithm takes to gather the robots. But due to the nature of the outer border, the length can only be linear in the area in which the robots are positioned, as the next lemma shows.

LEMMA 9. $\mathfrak{l}(t) \in \mathcal{O}(\mathfrak{h}(t)^2)$.

PROOF. Let us consider the polygon $P(t)$. Since it is formed by the outer border of the unit disk graph of the robots, no robot can see any other robot outside $P(t)$. Thus, we can define an area $A(t)$ around $P(t)$, which contains all points outside $P(t)$ in distance at most $\frac{1}{4}$ from $P(t)$. This area cannot contain any robot, since it would be seen by at least one robot on the border of the unit disk graph. See Fig. 5 as an example. Moreover, $A(t)$ never intersects with itself, and thus for a length $\mathfrak{l}(t)$, $A(t)$ defines an area of size at least $\frac{1}{4}\mathfrak{l}(t)$ which does not contain any robots.

Now since the robots are all contained in the height-circle $C_{\mathfrak{h}(t)}$ (the circle around M with radius $\mathfrak{h}(t)$), the area of $A(t)$ is completely inside the circle $C_{\mathfrak{h}(t)+\frac{1}{4}}$ around M with radius $\mathfrak{h}(t) + 1/4$. This implies that the area of this circle must be at least the area of $A(t)$, which is at least $\frac{1}{4}\mathfrak{l}(t)$. Thus, we get

$$\frac{1}{4}\mathfrak{l}(t) \le \pi\left(\mathfrak{h}(t) + \frac{1}{4}\right)^2 = \pi\left(\mathfrak{h}(t)^2 + \frac{1}{2}\mathfrak{h}(t) + \frac{1}{16}\right)$$

and $\mathfrak{l}(t) \in \mathcal{O}(\mathfrak{h}(t)^2)$. $\square$

Now we can finally state our main result.

THEOREM 2. *The maximum distance traveled by any robot is $\mathcal{O}(h\log h) = \mathcal{O}(OPT\log OPT)$.*

PROOF. Set $m^* := \left\lfloor \frac{l}{2\sqrt{2}S} \right\rfloor$ and let us define m^* time-phases $\mathfrak{p}_i := [t_{i-1}, t_i]$ for $i = 1\ldots, m^*$ by setting $t_0 := 0$ and t_i for $i > 0$ to the time when we have $\mathfrak{l}(t_i) = (m^* - i + 1) \cdot 2\sqrt{2}S$. That is, during one phase $\mathfrak{p}_i$, the length is reduced by exactly $2\sqrt{2}S$ and thus in phase i, the chain must consist of at least m^* parts as defined in Lemma 6. Note that these t_i are well-defined, because by Lemma 8, in phase $\mathfrak{p}_i$ the chain length decreases with a speed of at least $\frac{1}{3}\left\lfloor \frac{\mathfrak{l}(t_i)}{2\sqrt{2}S} \right\rfloor = \frac{1}{3} \cdot (m^* - i + 1)$ (which is a constant for fixed

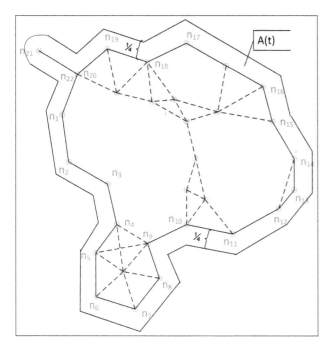

Figure 5: The area $A(t)$ is indicated for the example configuration

i). Furthermore, Lemma 8 gives us an upper bound on the length of each single phase p_i:

$$t_i - t_{i-1} \leq \frac{\mathfrak{l}(t_{i-1}) - \mathfrak{l}(t_i)}{\frac{2}{3}(m^* - i + 1)} \leq \frac{2\sqrt{2}S}{\frac{1}{3}(m^* - i + 1)}$$

This allows us to give an upper bound for the time when the last phase ends:

$$t_{m^*} = \sum_{i=1}^{m^*} (t_i - t_{i-1}) \leq 6\sqrt{2}S \sum_{i=1}^{m^*} \frac{1}{m^* - i + 1}$$

$$= 6\sqrt{2}S \sum_{i=1}^{m^*} i^{-1} < 6\sqrt{2}S \cdot (\ln m^* + 1)$$

Now consider the situation after time $t \geq t_{m^*}$. We have $\mathfrak{l}(t_{m^*}) = (m^* - m^* + 1)2\sqrt{2}S = 2\sqrt{2}S$. By Theorem 1, from now on it takes time at most $1/4 \cdot \mathfrak{l}(t_{m^*}) = \sqrt{2}/2 \cdot S$ for the robots to reach the optimal configuration. Together with the bound on t_{m^*} and with $S = \mathcal{O}(h)$ and $l = O(h^2)$ (Lemma 9), this yields a maximum time (and therefore traveled distance) of

$$6\sqrt{2} \cdot S \cdot (\ln m^* + 1) + \sqrt{2}/2 \cdot S$$

$$\leq 6\sqrt{2} \cdot S \cdot \left(\ln \left(\frac{l}{2\sqrt{2}S} \right) + 1 \right) + \sqrt{2}/2 \cdot S$$

$$= \mathcal{O}(S \cdot \ln l) = \mathcal{O}(h \ln h)$$

until the optimal configuration is reached. $\square$

4. OUTLOOK

We have shown an optimal runtime bound for worst-case instances and a competitive factor of $\mathcal{O}(\log OPT)$. It remains open whether this competitive factor is tight. In the future, we therefore want to investigate whether there exist lower bounds or a better competitive factor. In particular, the question is whether the strategy is c-competitive for some constant c. For this, a new technique of analysis would be required.

Furthermore, we want to apply the developed techniques for the continuous time model and the concept of comparing local algorithms to optimal global ones to further formation problems, such as building short two-dimensional communication infrastructures like trees.

Finally, we would like to investigate to which extend the strategy is robust under inaccuracies of sensors. How to formally model such inaccuracies? For which input instances is the strategy robust? Do we have to modify the strategy? We certainly have to assume that input instances have the property that neighboring robots have distance at most $1 - \gamma$, where $\gamma \in (0, 1)$ is chosen dependent on parameters describing the accuracy.

5. REFERENCES

[1] H. Ando, Y. Suzuki, and M. Yamashita. Formation and agreement problems for synchronous mobile robots with limited visibility. In *Proceedings of the 1995 IEEE International Symposium on Intelligent Control, ISIC 1995*, pages 453–460, Aug. 1995.

[2] B. Chazelle. Natural algorithms. In *Proceedings of the Twentieth Annual ACM-SIAM Symposium on Discrete Algorithms, SODA 2009*, pages 422–431, 2009.

[3] M. Cieliebak, P. Flocchini, G. Prencipe, and N. Santoro. Solving the Robots Gathering Problem. In *Automata, Languages and Programming: 30th International Colloquium, ICALP 2003*, pages 1181–1196, 2003.

[4] R. Cohen and D. Peleg. Convergence Properties of the Gravitational Algorithm in Asynchronous Robot Systems. *SIAM Journal on Computing*, 34(6):1516–1528, 2005.

[5] B. Degener, B. Kempkes, P. Kling, and F. Meyer auf der Heide. A continuous, local strategy for constructing a short chain of mobile robots. In *SIROCCO '10: Proceedings of the 17th International Colloquium on Structural Information and Communication Complexity*, pages 168–182, 2010.

[6] B. Degener, B. Kempkes, T. Langner, F. Meyer auf der Heide, P. Pietrzyk, and R. Wattenhofer. A tight runtime bound for synchronous gathering of autonomous robots with limited visibility. In *SPAA '11: Proceedings of the 23rd annual ACM symposium on parallel algorithms and architectures*, pages 139–147, 2011.

[7] Y. Dieudonné and F. Petit. Self-stabilizing Deterministic Gathering. In *Algorithmic Aspects of Wireless Sensor Networks, 5th International Workshop, ALGOSENSORS 2009*, pages 230–241, 2009.

[8] N. Gordon, I. A. Wagner, and A. M. Bruckstein. Gathering Multiple Robotic A(ge)nts with Limited Sensing Capabilities. In *Ant Colony Optimization and Swarm Intelligence, 4th International Workshop, ANTS 2004*, pages 142–153, 2004.

[9] T. Izumi, M. Gradinariu Potop-Butucaru, and S. Tixeuil. Connectivity-Preserving Scattering of Mobile Robots with Limited Visibility. In *Stabilization, Safety, and Security of Distributed Systems - 12th International Symposium, SSS 2010, Proceedings*, volume 6366 of *Lecture Notes in Computer Science*, pages 319–331, 2010.

[10] T. Izumi, Y. Katayama, N. Inuzuka, and K. Wada. Gathering Autonomous Mobile Robots with Dynamic Compasses: An Optimal Result. In *Distributed Computing, 21st International Symposium, DISC 2007*, pages 298–312, 2007.

[11] Y. Katayama, Y. Tomida, H. Imazu, N. Inuzuka, and K. Wada. Dynamic Compass Models and Gathering Algorithms for

Autonomous Mobile Robots. In *SIROCCO '07: Proceedings of the 14th International Colloquium on Structural Information and Communication Complexity*, volume 4474 of *Lecture Notes in Computer Science*, pages 274–288, 2007.

[12] B. Katreniak. Convergence with Limited Visibility by Asynchronous Mobile Robots. In A. Kosowski and M. Yamashita, editors, *SIROCCO '11: Proceedings of the 18th International Colloquium on Structural Information and Communication Complexity*, pages 125–137. LNCS 6796, 2011.

[13] H. G. Nguyen, N. Pezeshkian, S. M. Raymond, A. Gupta, and J. M. Spector. Autonomous communication relays for tactical robots. In *Proceedings of ICAR 2003: The International Conference on Advanced Robotics*, pages 35–40, 2003.

[14] G. Prencipe. Impossibility of gathering by a set of autonomous mobile robots. *Theoretical Computer Science*, 384(2-3):222–231, 2007.

[15] S. Souissi, X. Défago, and M. Yamashita. Gathering Asynchronous Mobile Robots with Inaccurate Compasses. In *Principles of Distributed Systems, 10th International Conference, OPODIS 2006*, pages 333–349, 2006.

Online Multi-Robot Exploration of Grid Graphs with Rectangular Obstacles

Christian Ortolf
University of Freiburg
Department of Computer Science
Georges-Koehler-Allee 51
79110 Freiburg, Germany
ortolf@informatik.uni-freiburg.de

Christian Schindelhauer
University of Freiburg
Department of Computer Science
Georges-Koehler-Allee 51
79110 Freiburg, Germany
schindel@informatik.uni-freiburg.de

ABSTRACT

We consider the multi-robot exploration problem of an unknown $n \times n$ grid graph with oriented disjoint rectangular obstacles. All robots start at a given node and have to visit all nodes of the graph. The robots are unrestricted in their computational power and storage. In the local communication model the robots can exchange any information if they meet at the same node. In the global communication model all robots share the same knowledge.

In this paper we present the first nontrivial upper and lower bounds. We show that k robots can explore the graph using only local communication in time $O(n \log^2(n) + (f \log n)/k)$, where f is the number of free nodes in the graph. This establishes a competitive upper bound of $O(\log^2 n)$.

For the lower bound we show a competitive factor of $\Omega\left(\frac{\log k}{\log \log k}\right)$ for deterministic exploration and $\Omega\left(\frac{\sqrt{\log k}}{\log \log k}\right)$ for randomized exploration strategies using global communication.

Categories and Subject Descriptors

G.2.2 [**Mathematics of Computing**]: DISCRETE MATHEMATIC-SGraph Theory[Graph algorithms, Trees]; F.2.2 [**Theory of Computation**]: ANALYSIS OF ALGORITHMS AND PROBLEM COMPLEXITY Nonnumerical Algorithms and Problems

General Terms

Algorithms,Theory

Keywords

competitive analysis, mobile agent, robot, collective graph exploration

1. INTRODUCTION

Recent advancements allow the usage of robots in everyday use. Today's consumers are buying robotic vacuum cleaners and in the future one might expect the use of larger quantities of such robots. This alone is ample motivation for the investigation of exploration strategies of unknown terrains. Instead of an euclidean plain with scattered objects, we concentrate on the two-dimensional grid graph with oriented disjoint rectangular obstacles as a discrete model for this. The task is to explore all nodes of the graph. For this, each robot can only identify the current node and its neighboring nodes of the graph. In each step a robot can move to an adjacent node. Robots have unlimited memory, computational power and know their positions. In the local communication model they are able to exchange their findings with all the other robots if they meet in the same node. In the global communication model they can exchange their findings immediately.

We measure the efficiency of the robot exploration strategy by the competitive ratio, i.e. the number of steps needed by the robots in parallel following an exploration strategy on an unknown graph divided by the number of steps the robots need using an optimal exploration strategy (with the knowledge of the graph). For the deterministic lower bound we consider an adversary who chooses the graph knowing the exploration algorithm. To lower bound randomized strategies the adversary chooses a graph without knowing the random guesses of the randomized strategy.

Related Work.

For the exploration problem many different variants exist differing in reliability of sensor data, the number of robots, computational power, memory, range of communication, different kinds of graphs and computational or energy limitations (for a survey we refer to [15]). Most work on exploration of undirected graphs only handles the single robot case.

Competitive analysis of the exploration problem has been done by Dessmark et al. in [8] with a single robot. Dessmark also distinguishes between anchored and unanchored maps reducing the maps' effectiveness.

The hardness of the multi-robot exploration problem for trees is shown in [11]. They prove a lower bound for deterministic strategies with a competitive factor of $2 + \frac{1}{k}$. Later this bound was improved in [9], where a special graph, called Jellyfish-Tree has led to a lower bound of $\Omega(\frac{\log k}{\log \log k})$ for the competitive factor of a deterministic online exploration algorithm. Our work is based on this approach. As a side result we can generalize this result for randomized algorithms in this paper. Fraigniaud et al. prove in [11] the best positive result for competitive exploration of a tree with a competitive factor of $O\left(\frac{k}{\log k}\right)$.

Permission to make digital or hard copies of all or part of this work for personal or classroom use is granted without fee provided that copies are not made or distributed for profit or commercial advantage and that copies bear this notice and the full citation on the first page. To copy otherwise, to republish, to post on servers or to redistribute to lists, requires prior specific permission and/or a fee.
SPAA'12, June 25–27, 2012, Pittsburgh, Pennsylvania, USA.
Copyright 2012 ACM 978-1-4503-1213-4/12/06 ...$10.00.

The grid model with oriented disjoint rectangular obstacles has been investigated for the online-shortest path problem [14] by Papadimitriou et al. Such graphs have been considered for a variant of the shortest path problem, where a robot tries to reach a line. They prove a tight upper and lower bound of a competitive factor of $O(\sqrt{n})$ [14]. For randomized strategies this bound can be improved to $O(n^{4/9}\log n)$ [6]. It is shown in [3] that a robot can move to a given point in time $O(n\log n)$ if the point is within a $n \times n$-grid with such obstacles. We will use this result to give the first polylogarithmic upper bound for multi-robot exploration.

Practical work has been done by Franchi et al. [12] using simulations to validate their algorithms. There is also a vast number of results for multi-robot exploration using real robots, e.g. a frontier based exploration by Yamauchi [16].

For a geometrical setting Albers et al. provide in [2] a lower bound on competitiveness. They allow one exploration robot to have unlimited optical vision and call the single robot exploration successful if the whole area has been seen by the robot. For directed graphs competitive analyses of single robot exploration have been presented by Albers et al. [1], Fleischer et al. [10] and Papadimitriou et al. [7]. Their results indicate that this is a harder problem than the exploration in undirected graphs. For unlabeled graphs exploration is unsolvable with a single robot but can be solved with a single pebble or another robot [4, 5]. Exploration of undirected graphs as considered here, is a variant of the online k-TSP and closely related to the exploration of a landscape.

Our Contribution.

In the next section we present the first multi-robot exploration algorithm for oriented rectangular disjoint obstacles in a $n \times n$-grid with a polylogarithmic competitive ratio. In particular we prove that k robots can explore such a grid in time $O(n\log^2 n + f/k\log n)$ where f is the number of (non-obstacle) nodes in the grid. Since the optimal strategy needs at least $\max\{2n-1, f/k\}$ steps we show a competitive bound of $O(\log^2 n)$. The algorithm is a divide-and-conquer algorithm which uses the single-robot-exploration strategy of [3].

In Section 3 we present the first nontrivial lower bound for deterministic multi-robot exploration for such grids. We show a lower bound for the competitive factor of $\Omega\left(\frac{\log k}{\log\log k}\right)$. The construction is based on the lower bound for multi-robot-exploration in trees presented in [9].

Then, in Section 4 we consider lower bounds for randomized exploration strategies and show a lower bound of $\Omega\left(\frac{\sqrt{\log k}}{\log\log k}\right)$ for grid graphs with rectangular disjoint obstacles. To prove this result, we first prove a new lower bound for randomized exploration strategies in trees of $\Omega\left(\frac{\log k}{\log\log k}\right)$.

2. EFFICIENT MULTI-ROBOT EXPLORATION

In [3] it is shown that in a $n \times m$-grid ($n \geq m$) with unknown oriented rectangular disjoint obstacles a robot can navigate to any point in time $O(n\log m)$ or to the obstacle in which the point lies. We use this result for a divide-and-conquer strategy. We use the following notations.

Let N, E, S, W denote the directions. A $\delta_1\delta_2$-path is a directed path which consists only of steps with directions δ_1 and δ_2. For neighbored directions $\delta_1, \delta_2 \in \{N, E, S, W\}$ a *greedy $\delta_1\delta_2$-path* is a path without obstacles where from the starting point the path goes

to direction δ_1. Each time an obstacle occurs, the path takes a turn in direction δ_2 and continues until the way is free again in direction δ_1, then it continues in direction δ_1. From every point in the grid every greedy $\delta_1\delta_2$-path exists and has a maximum length of $2n - 1$.

We need the notion of *surroundable regions*.

Definition 1. A *surroundable region* is a set of connected nodes which has a bounding path which is described by the concatenation of a greedy NW, WS, SE, and EN-path. Note that the complete $n \times m$-grid is such a surroundable region.

The continuous area $A(R)$ of a region R is the area of the region of R where the path and the region is interpreted geometrically.

Every surroundable region has a bordering path with a length of at most $4n - 2$. For our divide-and-conquer algorithm we successively partition such regions. We also consider a geometric version of the grid graph in the Euclidean plane bounded to $[0, n]^2$. Obstacles are obviously modeled by rectangles. For the paths of the robot we consider series of line segments connecting the middle points of the empty squares representing the nodes of the graph.

LEMMA 2.1. *There exists a point p such that*

1. $Q_1(p) = Q_3(p)$ *and* $Q_2(p) = Q_4(p)$

2. $Q_1(p) + Q_3(p) \geq A(R)/2$ *or* $Q_2(p) + Q_4(p) \geq A(R)/2$.

PROOF. Consider the function $f_{13}(x, y) = Q_1(x, y) - Q_3(x, y)$. If x is smaller than any x-coordinate of a point in R and y is smaller than any y-coordinate of a point in R then $f_{13}(p_x, p_y) = A(R)$. If x is larger than any x-coordinate of a point in R and y is larger than any y-coordinate of a point in R then $f_{13}(p_x, p_y) = -A(R)$. Further, the function is continuous and decreases with x and y. Therefore, for each x there exists a y such that $f_{13}(x, y) = 0$ and for all y there exists a x such that $f(x, y) = 0$.

For the function $f_{24}(x, y) = Q_2(x, y) - Q_4(x, y)$ we can deduce the equivalent observations.

Given a rectangle $(x_1, y_1), (x_2, y_2)$ where $f_{13}(x_1, y_1) \leq 0$, $f_{13}(x_2, y_2) \geq 0$, $f_{24}(x_2, y_1) \leq 0$ and $f_{24}(x_1, y_2) \geq 0$, we can conclude that in one of the four equal-sized sub-rectangles this condition is preserved. The choice of the rectangle depends on the signs of $f_{13}(\frac{1}{2}(x_1 + x_2), \frac{1}{2}(y_1 + y_2))$ and $f_{24}(\frac{1}{2}(x_1 + x_2), \frac{1}{2}(y_1 + y_2))$. This implies the existence of a point p where $f_{13}(p) = f_{24}(p) = 0$.

Since $f_{13}(p) = f_{24}(p)$ it follows $Q_1(p) = Q_3(p)$ and $Q_2(p) = Q_4(p)$. If $Q_1(p) + Q_3(p) \geq Q_2(p) + Q_4(p)$ then

$$2(Q_1(p) + Q_3(p)) \geq Q_1(p) + Q_3(p) + Q_2(p) + Q_4(p) = A(R).$$

Otherwise we have $Q_1(p) + Q_3(p) < Q_2(p) + Q_4(p)$ and therefore

$$2(Q_2(p) + Q_4(p)) > Q_1(p) + Q_3(p) + Q_2(p) + Q_4(p) = A(R).$$

□

LEMMA 2.2. *Each surroundable region R can be partitioned into two surroundable regions R_1, R_2 such that $R_1 \cup R_2 = R$ and $A(R_i) \leq \frac{3}{4}A(R)$ for $i \in \{1, 2\}$. This can be done in time $O(n\log n)$ with a single robot.*

PROOF. For a fixed region R consider a point $p = (p_x, p_y)$ in this Euclidean space. Then we define $Q_1(p)$ as the area of R in the NE-quadrant (including obstacles). Similarly, we define Q_2, Q_3, Q_4 as the areas of R in the NW, SW and SE-quadrant. Clearly, the sum of all $Q_i(R)$ equals the area $A(R)$ of R. As visualisation we refer to Fig. 6 in the appendix.

This point p can be efficiently computed, since the region R is defined by horizontal boundaries. Now we navigate a robot to this point p using the algorithm of [3]. If it lies within an obstacle, the algorithm will circle the obstacle, otherwise it will reach the node which is nearest to the point.

Assume that $Q_1(p) + Q_3(p) \geq A(R)/2$. Then, we will construct a path within the second and forth quadrant which divides R into R_1 and R_2. For this, we simply follow a greedy NW-path until we reach the boundary of R. Then, we follow a greedy SE-path starting from p until we reach the boundary of R. This path will not leave the second and forth quadrant and the sub-regions are again surroundable.

If p lies within an obstacle, we take the obstacle corner points in the second and forth quadrant with respect of p. Then, we construct NW-paths and SE-paths from these two points and combine them with two surrounding paths of the rectangular obstacles around p.

In both cases we have $A(R_1) \geq Q_1(p) \geq \frac{1}{4}A(R)$ and also $A(R_2) \geq \frac{1}{4}A(R)$.

If $Q_1(p) + Q_3(p) < A(R)/2$ then we have $Q_2(p) + Q_4(p) \geq A(R)/2$ and we make the symmetric construction within the first and third quadrant of p using greedy NE and SW-paths. Again, we get $A(R_1) \geq \frac{1}{4}A(R)$ and $A(R_2) \geq \frac{1}{4}A(R)$. Since $A(R_1) + A(R_2) = A(R)$ the claim follows. $\square$

Algorithm 1 uses this partitioning to explore the square.

Algorithm 1 $O(\log^2 n)$-competitive multi-robot exploration of the $n \times n$ grid with k robots

---

1: Start with the full square as a single surroundable region
2: All robots start in the upper left corner
3: **for** $i \leftarrow 1, 2, \ldots, \log k$ **do**
4:     Partition all 2^{i-1} regions in parallel using one robot per region
5: **end for**
6: **while** Unexplored regions exist **do**
7:     Explore all k regions with one robot each using depth-first-search
8:     If a robot finishes the DFS it returns to the upper left corner
9:     **if** at least $k/2$ robots have returned to the upper left corner **then**
10:         Stop the entire exploration
11:         Partition all $k/2$ unexplored regions
12:     **end if**
13: **end while**

THEOREM 2.3. *Algorithm 1 can explore the $n \times n$ grid with k robots in time $O(n \log^2 n + n \log n \log k + (f \log n)/k)$ where f is the number of nodes in the grid (without obstacles) using the global communication model.*

PROOF. First note that a single robot can explore a connected area with f (non-obstacle) nodes using depth-first-search in time $2f$, but such an area cannot be explored with less than f steps by a single robot.

It takes at most $2 \log_{4/3} n$ rounds of re-partitioning until all surroundable regions have size of at most 1, since the size of a region is reduced by at least a factor of $3/4$. Each partitioning takes $O(n \log n)$ steps for one robot. Moving to the left upper corner takes $2n - 1$ steps using a greedy NE-path. So, the time of the lines 3–5 can be estimated by $O(n \log n \log k)$ steps. The while-loop (line 6) is executed at most $O(\log n)$ times. All partitioning steps in line 11 take therefore $O(n \log^2 n)$ steps.

For the exploration time we consider the rounds of the while-loop (lines 6–13). Let f_j denote the number of unexplored (free) cells at the beginning of the j-th round. There are two cases.

In the first case the loop finishes in round j since less than $k/2$ robots have returned and all regions are explored. So, more than $k/2$ robots have explored f_j free cells in parallel. This has taken at most $4f_j/k$ steps, since $k/2$ robots have explored at most f_j cells in parallel with DFS. So, the time for this round can be estimated by $4f/k$.

In the second case the $k/2$ robots have returned in the j-th round, but $k/2$ unexplored regions will be again completely revisited in the round $j + 1$. Let R be an explored region with the largest number of free cells (given by F). All explored regions have been explored in at most $2F(R)$ steps. However, all $k/2$ unexplored regions must have had at least $\frac{1}{2}F(R)$ free cells since otherwise they would have been explored in this round by the DFS. Summarizing over the $k/2$ unexplored regions we have $\frac{1}{4}kF(R) \leq f$ and therefore $F(R) \leq 4f/k$ which results in an upper time bound for the exploration of $8f/k$ steps in this round.

Since there are at most $O(\log n)$ rounds in the while-loop there are at most $O((f \log n)/k)$ steps for the exploration. $\square$

The global communication model can be replaced with a local communication scheme, if all robots stop the algorithm every $8n$ steps, move to the left upper node, communicate, and then return to their work. This needs $4n$ steps and increases the run-time by a constant factor.

COROLLARY 2.4. *Using the local communication model the $n \times n$ grid can be explored with k robots in time $O(n \log^2 n + n \log n \log k + (f \log n)/k)$ where f is the number of nodes in the grid (without obstacles) using the global communication model.*

Every optimal exploration strategy where all k robots start in the left upper corner needs at least $2n - 1$ steps to reach the opposite corner. The other lower bound of f/k results from the optimal parallelization of the exploration of the f cells. Further note, that n^2 robots can explore the $n \times n$ grid in time $O(n \log n)$. For this, each robot navigates to its assigned node. This establishes a competitive factor of $O(\log n)$. For $k \leq n^2$ we have $\log k \leq 2 \log n$ and thus a run-time of $O(n \log^2 n + f(\log n)/k)$ compared to lower bound of $\Omega(n + f/k)$ resulting in the following corollary.

COROLLARY 2.5. *There is an exploration strategy to explore an $n \times n$-grid with oriented disjoint rectangular obstacles with a competitive run-time ratio of $O(\log^2 n)$ in the local communication model.*

3. LOWER BOUND FOR CONVEX GRID-GRAPH

Since we are interested in asymptotic behavior we assume the edge length n of the overall grid and the number of robots k to be powers of 2. For our construction we choose $n = k^2$. Our construction is inspired by the lower bound construction in [9], called the Jellyfish-Tree in Fig. 4. Our grid graph separates k rectangular grids, called poison areas, such that the paths between these areas have a length of at least $n/2$ and at most $O(n)$ (non obstacle) cells are located outside of these poison areas, see Fig. 1.

Given the paths of robots in a poison area visiting at most w nodes in total and each robot starting (or departing) at one of the four corners of an area of $n/2 \times n/k$ we construct the grid poison in the following way: For each $j \in \{1, \ldots, \log n - \log k\}$ consider

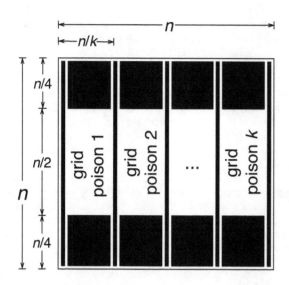

Figure 1: Separation of the grid poison areas

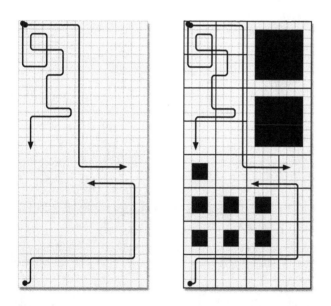

Figure 2: Deterministic construction of the grid poison based on the exploration paths of robots

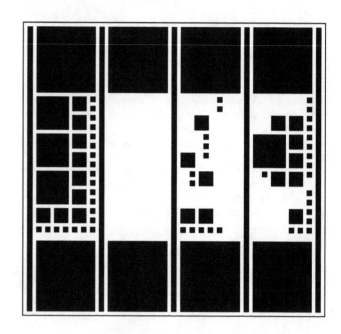

Figure 3: Example graph for the deterministic lower bound

a sub-grid of $2^j \times 2^j$-squares. If no robot has visited a square, then all cell nodes of this square but the border nodes (leftmost and rightmost column, lowermost uppermost row) will be removed. The border nodes are necessary to ensure that the square shaped obstacles remain disjoint and that the robot in the neighboring square does not learn anything. We call w the fooling size of the grid poison.

LEMMA 3.1. *Given a deterministic strategy of robots where the number of all traversed nodes of the robots is at most w in an $n \times m$ (with $n \geq m$) rectangle then the corresponding poison has at most size $O(n + w \log m)$. No visited cell is adjacent to a rectangle.*

PROOF. Clearly, the w traversed cells remain in the graph. When a subcell of dimension $2^j \times 2^j$ is removed, then $2^{j+2} - 2$ cells remain in the graph.

We estimate the number of such sub-grids which can be reached by any robots. Four cells can be reached without any traversal since the robots may start at the corners. The explored subcells are connected since they result from a set of paths starting in the corners. So, at most $4 + w2^{2-j}$ subcells of dimension $2^j \times 2^j$ can be reached.

We want to count all $2^j \times 2^j$ subcells which are replaced by an obstacle. Each such subcell has a neighbor cell (horizontal, vertical or diagonal) which has been visited by a robot or $m = 2^j$. Otherwise, the super-ordinate $2^{j+1} \times 2^{j+1}$ subcell would have been replaced by an obstacle. So the number of replaced subcells is at most $8(4 + w2^{2-j})$. In each of the $m \times m$ sub-squares of the $n \times m$ grid poison with at most w_i robot paths we observe at most the following number of free cells.

$$\sum_{j=2}^{\log m} 8(4 + w2^{2-j}) \cdot (2^{j+2} - 2) \leq 64m + 128w \log m$$

Summing over all such n/m squares we get at most $64n + 128w \log m = O(n + w \log m)$ free cells. $\square$

While w visited sub-cells are not enough to encounter any obstacle, we show that visiting $O(w \log m + n)$ cells suffice to visit all cells. An offline strategy with at most $k \leq n$ robots can do so in time $O(\frac{w}{k} \log m + n)$.

LEMMA 3.2. *A grid poison with fooling size w in a $n \times m$ rectangle ($n \geq m$) can be explored by k robots in time $O(n + \frac{w}{k} \log m)$ in the offline setting.*

PROOF. Partition the $p \leq 64n + 128w \log m$ empty cells of the grid poison in $b_i \times m$ rectangles such that $\sum_{i=1}^{k} b_i = n$ and that the number of empty cells in each rectangle is at most $\frac{p}{k} + m$. Each of the k robot explores one such rectangle. It needs n steps to reach the rectangle. For exploring such a rectangle, a robot may have to take a detour into neighbored rectangles because an obstacle hinders the direct path. Such detours have at most $4m$ cells. Furthermore, paths inside the rectangle may be traversed at most twice. This leads to an upper bound for $2b_i + 4m$ for the exploration within the rectangle. To reach the rectangle at most n steps are necessary. This results in an exploration time of at most $n + 6m + 2\frac{p}{k} = O(n + \frac{w \log m}{k})$. $\square$

The fooling size of the grid poisons is chosen according to the following distribution:

$$w_{\sigma(i)} = \left\lceil \frac{kn}{(\log k)^2} \cdot \frac{1}{i} \right\rceil$$

Where σ denotes a permutation depending on the deterministic exploration strategy.

LEMMA 3.3. *There is an offline strategy which explores this graph within $O(n)$ steps using k robots.*

PROOF. Remember that $n = k^2$ and $m = k$. Define $W := \sum_{i=1}^{k} w_{\sigma(i)} \log k$ and note that $W = O\left(k + \frac{kn}{\log k}\right)$. An offline exploration strategy sends one robot in each grid poison for time cn to explore the grid poison. After this round, it sends $\left\lfloor \frac{w_{\sigma(i)}}{W} k \right\rfloor$ robots in each unexplored grid poison for time cn as well.

All cells with fooling size of at most $n/\log k$ can be explored within the first round. If $w_{\sigma(i)} > \frac{W}{k} = O(1)$ then at least one robot will explore the grid poison after this round. This is the case for $i \leq c\frac{k}{\log k}$ for some constant $c > 0$. Exploring such a poison costs time linear in

$$n + \frac{w_{\sigma(i)}}{\left\lceil k \frac{w_{\sigma(i)}}{W} \right\rceil} \log m = O\left(n + \frac{W}{k} \log m\right) = O(n).$$

$\square$

THEOREM 3.4. *Any deterministic exploration strategy needs at least $\Omega\left(n \cdot \frac{\log k}{\log \log k}\right)$ steps to explore this graph with k robots.*

A proof is analogous to the lower bound in [9] and can be found in Appendix A.1.

This implies an online time for any deterministic algorithm of

$$\Omega\left(n \cdot \frac{\log k}{\log \log k}\right)$$

leading directly to a lower bound for the competitive ratio of

$$\Omega\left(\frac{\log k}{\log \log k}\right)$$

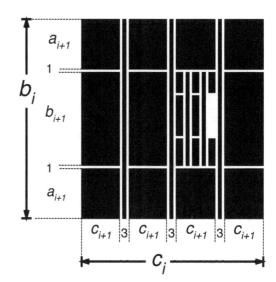

Figure 5: Recursive construction of poison areas for the randomized lower bound

4. LOWER BOUNDS FOR RANDOMIZED ALGORITHMS

Now we show that the lower bound given in [9] also applies for randomized algorithms. Consider the Jellyfish-Tree in Fig. 4. We use the same construction with k subtrees and a random permutation σ over $\{1, \ldots, k\}$. The i-th subtree consists of a path of length $t = k$ and a poison which is a tree of size $t \cdot s_{\sigma(i)}$ and depth $s_{\sigma(i)}$ where

$$s_{\sigma(i)} := \left\lceil \frac{k}{\log k} \cdot \frac{1}{i} \right\rceil$$

where in each level $k - 1$ leaves are connected to a parent and the graph continues at a random child, which we call the target child. The permutation σ is chosen uniformly at random. In [9] the following lemma has been shown regarding the offline exploration time.

LEMMA 4.1. *The Jellyfish-Tree can be explored in time $O(t)$ using k robots.*

Yao's principle [17] is used to show a lower bound for randomized strategies. We choose the randomized Jellyfish-Tree for a deterministic exploration strategy and show a lower bound on the expected time.

THEOREM 4.2. *For every randomized online exploration algorithm A, there is a graph such that the total time is at least $\Omega\left(\frac{\log k}{\log \log k}\right)$ times longer than the optimal time needed to explore this graph offline by k robots.*

Proof deferred to Appendix A.2.

4.1 Randomized Lower Bound for Grids

This theorem can be transferred to grids with rectangular bounds. Again we use a construction with poison areas like in the deterministic lower bound for the grid. It is clear that we cannot use the same construction, since it heavily depends on the knowledge of the deterministic strategy.

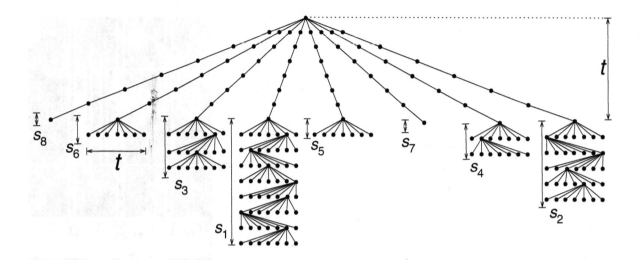

Figure 4: Jellyfish-Tree construction from [9].

Therefore, we use a randomized recursive construction where we place one poison within another. This "Matryoshka doll"-like construction has two features. First, it is hard to find the next enclosed grid poison. Second and most astonishingly, every next Matryoshka doll inside is twice as large as the outer one. This is possible, because of the fact that the outer poison has much fewer (yet longer) paths.

The outer grid construction is depicted in Fig. 2. We construct poison areas specifically designed for $k = \sqrt{n}$ randomized robots where the overall size of the grid is $n \times n$. The whole area is designed such that there is an offline strategy where k robots explore the graph in $O(n)$ steps.

We recursively define the poison areas as depicted in Fig. 5 starting with the uppermost layer which fits into the overall construction with $a_0 = \frac{1}{4}n - 2$, $b_0 = b = \frac{1}{2}n$ and $c_0 = c = \frac{n}{k+3}$ in the overall construction of Fig. 2. Further, define for $i \geq 0$

$$a_{i+1} = \frac{1}{4}b_i - 2 , \quad b_{i+1} = \frac{1}{2}b_i , \quad c_{i+1} = c_i \frac{1}{2^{2i}}$$

So, we have the closed form for $i \geq 0$:

$$a_i = n\, 2^{-i-2} - 2 , \quad b_i = n\, 2^{-i-1} , \quad c_i = \frac{n}{k 2^{i(i+1)}}$$

This recursive definition ends when $c_{r+1} \leq 1$ for some r. Therefore

$$\frac{n}{k 2^{(r+1)(r+2)}} \geq 1$$

which is implied by

$$\log n \geq \log k + (r+1)^2$$

And therefore:

$$r \leq \sqrt{\log n - \log k} - 1 = \frac{\sqrt{2}}{2}\sqrt{\log n} - 1$$

Note that the recursive constructions replace at most one of the inner rectangles with the next level. In this construction one of the inner obstacles is replaced by another element. In the lowest level this obstacle is a barrier. The following lemma describes the length of all paths in the fixed level i of the recursion.

LEMMA 4.3. *For a grid poison of level $i \geq 1$ the complete area to be explored is at most $n 2^i$.*

PROOF. We have at least $\lceil \frac{c_i}{c_{i+1}+3} \rceil$ vertical paths of length b_i which have an overall length of $b_i = n 2^{-i-1}$. Note that by definition

$$\frac{c_i}{c_{i+1}} = 2^{2i}$$

Therefore

$$\frac{c_i}{c_{i+1}+3} b_i \leq 2^{2i}\, n\, 2^{-i-1} = n 2^{i-1}$$

The length of all horizontal paths is bounded by $4c_i \leq n$. □

Define the workload of an exploration strategy in a poison as the sum of all paths of all robots.

LEMMA 4.4. *For all $p \in [0,1]$ in a grid poison of level $i \geq 1$ the next recursive grid poison has not been found with a workload of at most $\frac{1}{2}pn2^i$ with probability $1 - p$.*

PROOF. Consider the paths of a deterministic strategy of length $w = pn2^i$. The expected number of possible poisons that can be inspected with this workload is at most $\frac{1}{2}\frac{pn2^i}{b_i} = \frac{1}{2}\frac{pn2^i}{n2^{-i-1}} = p2^{2i}$. Clearly the probability is p for finding the correct target and therefore $1 - p$ for failing to do so. □

Now we choose the levels ℓ_j of the poisons $1, \ldots, k$ according to the following distribution where σ is a random permutation over $\{1, \ldots, k\}$.

$$s_{\sigma(i)} = \frac{tk}{\log k} \cdot \frac{1}{i}$$

and

$$\ell_j = \lfloor \log s_j \rfloor$$

The maximum size of such a grid poison is bounded by $t2^{O(\sqrt{\log k})}$. So, we replace our distribution of poison sizes with

$$s_{\sigma(i)} = \begin{cases} \dfrac{tk}{\log k} \cdot \dfrac{1}{i} & \text{if } \dfrac{k}{2^{O(\sqrt{\log k})\log k}} \leq i \\ n2^{O(\sqrt{\log k})} & \text{else} \end{cases}$$

where we round to the next power of two.

THEOREM 4.5. *For every randomized online exploration algorithm there is a grid graph with disjoint rectangular obstacles such that the total time is at least* $\Omega\left(\frac{\sqrt{\log k}}{\log\log k}\right)$ *times longer than the optimal time needed to explore this graph offline by k robots.*

The full proof can be found in Appendix A.3. The proof is analogous to the proof of the randomized lower bound for trees. One main difference is that we do not prove with high probability, but with probability $1 - \frac{1}{\log n}$. This probability for each poison is large enough since the expected number of unexplored poisons is considered.

Another main difference is that the number of rounds is now limited by $r = \frac{\sqrt{\log k}}{\log\log k}$. This is the reason for the worse lower bound.

The lower bounds can be easily generalized to robots with vision where each cell needs only to be seen by the robots (and not necessarily visited). This can be done by placing small view obstructing squares at all junctions in the lower bound construction presented here.

5. CONCLUSIONS

We consider multi-robot exploration where robots know their locations and are computationally well equipped. From the algorithmic perspective little is known. It turns out that even for trees the question how well an unknown graph can be explored is wide open between the lower bound for the competitive time ratio of $\Omega(\log k / \log\log k)$ and the upper bound of $O(k/\log k)$ for k robots. In this paper we have generalized the lower bound to random algorithms. But note that the trivial lower bound of 1 and the trivial upper bound of $O(k)$, where only one robot explores the tree, are not far from the known bounds.

Planar sceneries with disjoint oriented rectangular obstacles have been considered so far only for single robot exploration. We present an efficient online algorithm which explores such areas with time overhead of factor $O(\log^2 n)$ compared to the optimal solution in an $n \times n$ grid. As lower bounds we prove $\Omega(\log k / \log\log k)$ for deterministic strategies and $\Omega(\sqrt{\log k}/\log\log k)$ for random strategies with k robots. So, there is only a logarithmic gap between the upper and the lower bound.

For multi-robot exploration in general graphs little is known and finding efficient algorithms is a pressing research topic since the robotic exploration plays an increasing part in practical research.

6. REFERENCES

[1] S. Albers and M. R. Henzinger. Exploring Unknown Environments. *SIAM Journal on Computing*, 29(4):1164, 2000.

[2] S. Albers, K. Kursawe, and S. Schuierer. Exploring unknown environments with obstacles. In *Proceedings of the tenth annual ACM-SIAM symposium on Discrete algorithms*, SODA '99, pages 842–843, Philadelphia, PA, USA, 1999. Society for Industrial and Applied Mathematics.

[3] E. Bar-Eli, P. Berman, A. Fiat, and P. Yan. Online navigation in a room. *J. Algorithms*, 17:319–341, November 1994.

[4] M. A. Bender. The power of team exploration: Two robots can learn unlabeled directed graphs. In *In Proceedings of the Thirty Fifth Annual Symposium on Foundations of Computer Science*, pages 75–85, 1994.

[5] M. A. Bender, A. Fernández, D. Ron, A. Sahai, and S. Vadhan. The power of a pebble: Exploring and mapping directed graphs. *Information and Computation*, 176(1):1 – 21, 2002.

[6] P. Berman, A. Blum, A. Fiat, H. Karloff, A. Rosén, and M. Saks. Randomized robot navigation algorithms. In *Proceedings of the seventh annual ACM-SIAM symposium on Discrete algorithms*, SODA '96, pages 75–84, Philadelphia, PA, USA, 1996. Society for Industrial and Applied Mathematics.

[7] X. Deng and C. Papadimitriou. Exploring an unknown graph. In *Foundations of Computer Science, 1990. Proceedings., 31st Annual Symposium on*, pages 355 –361 vol. 1, oct 1990.

[8] A. Dessmark and A. Pelc. Optimal graph exploration without good maps. *Theor. Comput. Sci.*, 326:343–362, October 2004.

[9] M. Dynia, J. Lopuszanski, and C. Schindelhauer. Why robots need maps. In *Proceedings of the 14th international conference on Structural information and communication complexity*, SIROCCO'07, pages 41–50, Berlin, Heidelberg, 2007. Springer-Verlag.

[10] R. Fleischer and G. Trippen. Exploring an unknown graph efficiently. In G. Brodal and S. Leonardi, editors, *Algorithms – ESA 2005*, volume 3669 of *Lecture Notes in Computer Science*, pages 11–22. Springer Berlin / Heidelberg, 2005. 10.1007/11561071_4.

[11] P. Fraigniaud, L. Gąsieniec, D. R. Kowalski, and A. Pelc. Collective tree exploration. *Netw.*, 48:166–177, October 2006.

[12] A. Franchi, L. Freda, G. Oriolo, and M. Vendittelli. A randomized strategy for cooperative robot exploration. In *Robotics and Automation, 2007 IEEE International Conference on*, pages 768 –774, april 2007.

[13] W. Hoeffding. Probability inequalities for sums of bounded random variables. *Journal of the American Statistical Association*, 58:13–30, 1963.

[14] C. H. Papadimitriou and M. Yannakakis. Shortest paths without a map. *Theor. Comput. Sci.*, 84:127–150, July 1991.

[15] N. S. V. Rao, S. Kareti, W. Shi, and S. S. Iyengar. Robot navigation in unknown terrains: Introductory survey of non-heuristic algorithms. Technical Report ORNL/TM-12410:1–58, Oak Ridge National Laboratory, July 1993.

[16] B. Yamauchi. Frontier-based exploration using multiple robots. In *Proceedings of the second international conference on Autonomous agents*, AGENTS '98, pages 47–53, New York, NY, USA, 1998. ACM.

[17] A. C.-C. Yao. Probabilistic computations: Toward a unified measure of complexity. In *Foundations of Computer Science, 1977., 18th Annual Symposium on*, pages 222 –227, 31 1977-nov. 2 1977.

APPENDIX

A. OMITTED PROOFS

A.1 Proof for Lower Bound with Deterministic Exploration Strategy

PROOF. For the lower bound argument we consider rounds of length $n/2$. Note that in each round a robot can visit only one poison grid. Let $r_{t,i}$ denote the number of robots that visit poison i in round t. At the beginning of each round the adversary allows the robots to know the size of some of the poisons while a decreasing number of poisons remain of unknown size. As soon the robots learn the size of the poison the poison is lost and no more exploration costs are accounted for (since the overall offline exploration cost is $O(n)$).

Furthermore, we do not count the costs of replacement from one poison grid to another.

Let u_i be the number of unexplored poisons after the i-th round. Then, at least $\frac{u_i}{2}$ poisons are explored by at most $2\frac{k}{u_i}$ robots. By our construction we can ensure that

$$u_i \geq \frac{k}{2^i \log^{2i} k} \;.$$

For this we choose the permutation σ in the following way. All the poisons are sorted according to whether more than $2\frac{k}{u_i}$ robots visit a poison in the i-th round. For this we place the poison grids with larger number of robots in the first round at the beginning, then we continue within the set at the beginning by sorting poison grids according to the robots of the second round and so forth.

By induction before round i at least u_{i-1} poisons are unexplored. Now the search algorithm can place at most k robots among those poisons and at least $\frac{u_{i-1}}{2}$ poisons are explored by at most $2\frac{k}{u_{i-1}}$ robots in round i. So, the robots cannot explore those poisons where

$$s_{\sigma(i)} \geq n2^i \log^{2i-2} k \geq kn\left(\frac{1}{u_{i-1}} + \frac{1}{u_{i-2}} + \ldots + \frac{1}{u_0}\right)$$

(by induction) since the robots have only time $n/2$ to explore the poison area. The number of poisons u_i of this size can be evaluated by using the definition of the distribution.

$$\frac{kn}{u_i(\log k)^2} \leq n2^i \log^{2i-2} k$$

So, we have

$$u_i \geq \frac{k}{2^i \log^{2i} k}$$

which proves the number of unexplored poisons by induction.

Note that for $r = \frac{1}{4}\frac{\log k}{\log\log k}$ we have

$$u_r = \frac{k}{2^{2r}\log^{2r} k} \geq \frac{k}{k^{\frac{1}{2\log\log k}}2^{\frac{1}{2}\log k}} \geq \frac{k}{k^{\frac{1}{2}}k^{\frac{1}{2}}} = 1 \;.$$

By this construction we have at least $\Omega\left(\frac{\log k}{\log\log k}\right)$ rounds with unexplored poison grids where each of the rounds have a run-time of $\frac{n}{2}$. $\square$

A.2 Proof for Lower Bounds for Randomized Algorithms

PROOF. We consider rounds of length t. In each round a robot can visit only one poison. The deterministic exploration strategy knows the graph family. Therefore it has determined a poison if it has found all target children.

Now in each round of length t steps a different numbers of robots might explore a poison.

LEMMA A.1. *The probability that in a round a target child in depth ℓ is explored with $k' \leq t$ robots in less time than $\frac{1}{2}\frac{t}{k'}$ is at most $e^{-\frac{1}{8}\ell}$.*

PROOF. We assume that all k' robots test different children where each child is a target child with equal probability. Then, the probability to find the target child of the next level within i steps is $i \cdot \frac{k'}{t}$.

Define the random variable X which denotes the number of steps to find one target child with k' robots. Then $P[X = j] = \frac{k'}{t}$

for $j \in \{1, \ldots, \lceil t/k'\rceil - 1\}$ and $P[X = \lceil t/k'\rceil] = \frac{t - k' \bmod t}{t}$. Clearly, $\frac{1}{2}\lfloor t/k'\rfloor \leq E[X] \leq \frac{1}{2}t/k'$.

If $k' \geq t/2$ the target child may be found in each step. Otherwise if $k' \leq t_2$ we can bound the number of steps to find a series of ℓ target children using Hoeffding's tail inequality. Assume ℓ independent target children and let $S_\ell = \sum_{j=1}^{\ell} X_{j,i}$, where $X_{j,i}$ denotes the random variable above for k' robots. Then by the tail inequality in [13] we have for all $t \geq 0$ and $a_i = 1$ and $b_i = \lceil t/k'\rceil$

$$P[S_\ell - E[S_\ell] \leq -\delta] \leq e^{-2\delta^2/\sum_{i=1}^{\ell}(b_i - a_i)^2}$$

Since $b_i - a_i \leq t/k'$ we have

$$P[S_\ell - E[S_\ell] \leq -\delta] \leq e^{-2\delta^2 k'^2/(\ell t^2)}$$

We choose $\delta = \frac{1}{2}E[S_\ell] \geq \frac{1}{2}\ell \cdot \lfloor\frac{t}{k'}\rfloor$ and get for $k' \leq t/2$

$$P\left[S_\ell \leq \frac{1}{2}E[S_\ell]\right] \leq e^{-\frac{1}{2}\ell^2\lfloor t/k'\rfloor^2 k'^2/(\ell t^2)}$$
$$\leq e^{-\frac{1}{2}\ell(1-k'/t)^2} \leq e^{-\frac{1}{8}\ell}$$

Remember that for $k' > t/2$ we have

$$P\left[S_\ell \leq \frac{1}{2}E[S_\ell]\right] = 0$$

The probability that a target child in depth ℓ is explored with k' robots in less time than $\frac{1}{2}\frac{t}{k'}$ is at most $e^{-\frac{1}{8}\ell}$. $\square$

This implies the following corollary which shows that with high probability $1 - \frac{1}{n^2}$ that maximum speedup by randomization in a poison is a factor of $O(\log n)$.

COROLLARY A.2. *The probability that in a round of length t a target child in depth $16\ln n$ is explored with $k' \leq t = k$ robots in less time than $\frac{1}{2}\frac{t}{k'}$ is at most $\frac{1}{n^2}$.*

So, k' robots in a round of length t can only find all target children in depth of at most $32k'\ln n = (64\ln 2)k'\log k$ with probability $1 - \frac{1}{n^2}$.

Now in the first round we have k robots which are (deterministically) assigned to one poison each, but one necessarily each poisons receives the one robot. They have at most time t to explore each poison.

Consider poisons of depth of at least $c^j \log^j k$ for $c = 2^8$. There are $\frac{k}{c^j \log^{j+1} k}$ many such poisons. Such a poison cannot be explored with less than $\frac{c^j \log^{j-2} k}{2^6 \ln 2}$ robots with high probability. Then, only target children up to depth $c^j \log^{1-j} k$, i.e. a fraction of $\frac{1}{\log k}$ of the poison can be explored with high probability.

So, there at most $\frac{2^6(\ln 2)k}{c^j \log^{j-2} k}$ poisons which may have enough robots and these poisons are randomly distributed over the set of all poisons. The probability that more than $\frac{c^j \log^{j-2} k}{2^6 \ln 2}$ robots are assigned to a poison is at most $\frac{2^6(\ln 2)}{c^j \log^{j-2} k}$.

The expected number of explored poisons of this depth $c^j \log^j k$ after the first round is at most

$$r = \frac{k}{c^j \log^{j+1} k}\frac{2^6(\ln 2)}{c^j \log^{j-2} k} = \frac{2^6(\ln 2)k}{c^{2j}\log^{2j-1} k} \;.$$

We can apply a Chernoff bound since the explored poisons are negatively correlated: The exploration of a poison decreases the probability that another poison is explored. For $r \geq 8\ln n$ we get with high probability that at most $2r$ poisons are explored with high probability which is the case for $2 \leq j \leq \frac{1}{4} \log k / \log \log k$. Further, note that for $j \geq 2$

$$2r \leq \frac{k}{c^{j+1} \log^{j+1} k}$$

since

$$\frac{2^7 (\ln 2) k}{c^{2j} \log^{2j-1} k} \leq \frac{k}{c^{j+1} \log^{j+1} k}$$

and

$$c^j \log^j k \geq (2^7 \ln 2) c \log^2 k .$$

because $c \geq 2^7 \ln 2$.

Hence the number of unexplored poisons of depth at least $c^j \log^j k$ for $j \geq 2$ is at least

$$\left(1 - \frac{1}{c}\right) \frac{k}{c^j \log^{j+1} k}$$

after the first round with high probability.

By induction, at the beginning of the $(u+1)$-th round we have at least $(1 - \frac{1}{c})^u k c^{-j} \log^{-j-1} k$ unexplored poisons of depth at least $c^j \log^j k$ for $j \geq 2u$ and $j \leq \frac{1}{4} \log \log n / \log n$. We assume that these bounds are tight.

Again, for poisons of depth at least $c^j \log^j k$ a number of $\frac{c^j \log^{j-2} k}{2^6 \ln 2}$ of robots is not able to explore more than a fraction of $\frac{1}{\log k}$ of such poisons. So, there at most $\frac{2^6 (\ln 2) k}{c^j \log^{j-2} k}$ poisons which may have enough robots and these poisons are randomly distributed over the set of all unexplored poisons which is at least $(1 - \frac{1}{c})^u k c^{-2u} \log^{-2u-1} k$. The probability that enough robots are assigned to a poison is therefore at most

$$\frac{2^6 (\ln 2) k}{c^j \log^{j-2} k} \left(\left(1 - \frac{1}{c}\right)^u k c^{-2u} \log^{-2u-1} k \right)^{-1}$$
$$= 2^6 (\ln 2) c^{2u-j} \log^{2u-j+1} k$$

The expected number of explored poisons is at most

$$
\begin{aligned}
r &= \frac{\left(1 - \frac{1}{c}\right)^u k}{c^j \log^{j+1} k} \cdot 2^6 (\ln 2) c^{2u-j} \log^{2u-j+1} k \\
&= 2^6 (\ln 2) \left(1 - \frac{1}{c}\right)^u c^{2u-2j} k \log^{2u-2j-2} k
\end{aligned}
$$

Note that for $j \geq 2u + 2$

$$2r \leq \left(1 - \frac{1}{c}\right)^u \frac{k}{c^{j+1} \log^{j+1} k}$$

since

$$2^7 (\ln 2) \left(1 - \frac{1}{c}\right)^u c^{2u-2j} k \log^{2u-2j-2} k$$
$$\leq \left(1 - \frac{1}{c}\right)^u \frac{k}{c^{j+1} \log^{j+1} k}$$

and

$$c^{j-2u} \log^{j-2u} k \geq (2^7 \ln 2) c \log^2 k .$$

because $c \geq 2^7 \ln 2$. Again we can apply Hoeffding's bound since the explored poisons are negatively correlated. Applying Hoeffding's bound for $r \leq 8 \ln n$ we get with high probability that at most $2r$ poisons are explored with high probability which is the case for $2u \leq j \leq \frac{1}{4} \log k / \log \log k$.

So, the number of unexplored poisons of depth at least $c^j \log^j k$ for $j \geq 2u + 2$ is at least

$$\left(1 - \frac{1}{c}\right) \left(1 - \frac{1}{c}\right)^u \frac{k}{c^j \log^{j+1} k}$$

after the $(u+1)$-th round with high probability, which proves the induction.

Since for all $u \leq \frac{1}{4} \frac{\log k}{\log \log k}$ we can find unexplored poisons with high probability, the claim follows.

A.3 Proof for Randomized Lower Bound for Grids

PROOF. The proof is analogous to the proof of the randomized lower bound for graphs. The first difference is that we do not prove with high probability, but with probability $1 - \frac{1}{\log n}$. This probability for each poison is large enough since the expected number of unexplored poisons is considered.

The second difference is that the number of rounds is now limited by $r = \frac{\sqrt{\log k}}{\log \log k}$. This is the reason for the worse lower bound. We consider rounds of length $n/2$. In each round a robot can visit only one poison grid. We use Yao's principle [17] and consider a deterministic strategy on the random graphs.

Consider poison grids of level of at least $\log(c^j \log^j k)$ for $c = 2^8$. There are $\frac{k}{c^j \log^{j+1} k}$ many such poison grids. Not even a fraction of $\frac{1}{\log^2 k}$ of such a poison grid can be explored in a round of length $n/2$ with less than $c^j \log^{j-2} k$ robots with probability $1 - \frac{1}{\log^2 k}$. We can bound the number of poisons that are explored in the error case with Chernoff bounds. If $\frac{k}{c^j \log^{j-2} k} \geq 8 \ln n$ then the error probability that more than $2 \frac{k}{c^j \log^{j-2} k}$ such poison grids are explored is at most $\frac{1}{n^2}$.

So, there at most $3 \frac{k}{c^j \log^{j-2} k}$ poison grids which may have enough robots and these poisons are randomly distributed over the set of all poisons w.h.p. The probability that more than $c^j \log^{j-2} k$ robots are assigned to a poison is at most $c^{-j} \log^{2-j} k$.

The expected number of explored poisons of this level $\log(c^j \log^j k)$ after the first round is at most

$$r = \frac{k}{c^j \log^{j+1} k} \frac{3}{c^j \log^{j-2} k} = \frac{3}{c^{2j} \log^{2j-1} k}$$

We can apply a Chernoff bound since the explored poisons are negatively correlated: The exploration of a poison decreases the probability that another poison is explored. For $r \geq 8 \ln n$ we get with high probability that at most $2r$ poisons are explored with high probability which is the case for $2 \leq j \leq \sqrt{\log k} / \log \log k$.

Further, note that for $j \geq 2$

$$2r \leq \frac{k}{c^{j+1} \log^{j+1} k}$$

since

$$\frac{6k}{c^{2j} \log^{2j-1} k} \leq \frac{k}{c^{j+1} \log^{j+1} k}$$

and

$$c^j \log^j k \geq 6c \log^2 k .$$

if we choose $c \geq 6$.

Hence the number of unexplored poison grids of level at least $\log(c^j \log^j k)$ for $j \geq 2$ is at least

$$\left(1 - \frac{1}{c}\right) \frac{k}{c^j \log^{j+1} k}$$

after the first round with high probability.

After each round the robots may be placed on different poison grids. Although the robots need time $n/2$ to travel from one poison grid to another we do not use this feature, since we also have to deal with robots which do not travel to new poisons which complicates the analysis. It is easy to see that taking the travel time into account accounts only for a constant factor.

By induction, at the beginning of the $(u+1)$-th round we have at least $(1-\frac{1}{c})^u kc^{-j}\log^{-j-1} k$ unexplored poison grids of level at least $\log(c^j \log^j k)$ for $j \geq 2u$ and $j \leq \sqrt{\log\log n}/\log n$. We assume that these bounds are tight, i.e. we allow the robot strategy learn about the situation in the other poison grids.

Again, for poison grids of level at least $\log(c^j \log^j k)$ a number of $c^j \log^{j-2} k$ of robots is not able to explore more than a fraction of $\frac{1}{\log^2 k}$ of such poisons with probability $1 - \frac{1}{\log^2 k}$. Again we bound the error case by Chernoff bound if $\frac{k}{c^j \log^{j-2} k} \geq 8\ln n$ then the error probability that more than $2\frac{k}{c^j \log^{j-2} k}$ such poison grids are explored is at most $\frac{1}{n^2}$.

So, there at most $\frac{3k}{c^j \log^{j-2} k}$ poisons which may have enough robots and these poisons are randomly distributed over the set of all unexplored poisons which is at least $(1-\frac{1}{c})^u kc^{-2u}\log^{-2u-1} k$. The probability that enough robots are assigned to a poison is therefore at most

$$\frac{3}{c^j \log^{j-2} k}\left(\left(1-\frac{1}{c}\right)^u kc^{-2u}\log^{-2u-1} k\right)^{-1}$$
$$= 3c^{2u-j}\log^{2u-j+1} k$$

The expected number of explored poisons is at most

$$r = \frac{\left(1-\frac{1}{c}\right)^u k}{c^j \log^{j+1} k} \cdot 3c^{2u-j}\log^{2u-j+1} k$$
$$= 3\left(1-\frac{1}{c}\right)^u c^{2u-2j} k \log^{2u-2j-2} k$$

Note that for $j \geq 2u+2$

$$2r \leq \left(1-\frac{1}{c}\right)^u \frac{k}{c^{j+1} \log^{j+1} k}$$

since

$$6\left(1-\frac{1}{c}\right)^u c^{2u-2j} k \log^{2u-2j-2} k \leq \left(1-\frac{1}{c}\right)^u \frac{k}{c^{j+1} \log^{j+1} k}$$

and

$$c^{j-2u}\log^{j-2u} k \geq 6c\log^2 k .$$

because $c \geq 6$.

Again we can apply Hoeffding's bound since the explored poisons are negatively correlated. Applying Hoeffding's bound for $r \geq 8\ln n$ we get with high probability that at most $2r$ poisons are explored with high probability which is the case for $2u \leq j \leq \sqrt{\log k}/\log\log k$.

So, the number of unexplored poisons of depth at least $c^j \log^j k$ for $j \geq 2u+2$ is at least

$$\left(1-\frac{1}{c}\right)\left(1-\frac{1}{c}\right)^u \frac{k}{c^j \log^{j+1} k}$$

after the $(u+1)$-th round with high probability, which proves the induction.

So, for $\sqrt{\log n}/\log\log n$ rounds of length n there will be unexplored poisons with high probability. $\square$

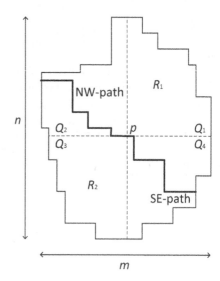

Figure 6: Partitioning an area for the efficient exploration

In Search of Parallel Dimensions

Ravi Rajwar
Intel Corporation

Abstract

Performance matters. But how we improve it is changing. Historically, transparent hardware improvements would mean software just ran faster. That may not necessarily be true in the future. To continue the pace of innovation, the future will need to be increasingly parallel—involving parallelism across data, threads, cores, and nodes. This talk will explore some of the dimensions of parallelism, and the opportunities and challenges they pose.

Categories & Subject Descriptors: C.1.4

Keywords: Parallelism; Performance; Synchronization; Vectors; Concurrency

Bio

Ravi Rajwar is a Microprocessor Architect in the Intel Architecture Group working on microarchitecture development, instruction set extensions, and performance analysis. He is one of the architects of Intel's next generation microprocessor codenamed Haswell. Most recently he was an architect on the Nehalem family of products.

Ravi has published research papers in the areas of high-performance microarchitectures, synchronization, and transactional memory. Ravi is also a co-author of a book on Transactional Memory, published by Morgan and Claypool in 2010. He received his M.S. and Ph.D. degrees in Computer Sciences from the University of Wisconsin-Madison.

boilerplate">
Copyright is held by the author/owner(s).
SPAA'12, June 25–27, 2012, Pittsburgh, Pennsylvania, USA.
ACM 978-1-4503-1213-4/12/06.

37

Delegation and Nesting in Best-effort Hardware Transactional Memory[*]

Yujie Liu
Lehigh University
yul510@cse.lehigh.edu

Stephan Diestelhorst
Advanced Micro Devices, Inc.
and Dresden University of
Technology
stephan.diestelhorst
@amd.com

Michael Spear
Lehigh University
spear@cse.lehigh.edu

ABSTRACT

The guiding design principle behind best-effort hardware transactional memory (BEHTM) is simplicity of implementation and verification. Only minimal modifications to the base processor architecture are allowed, thereby reducing the burden of verification and long-term support. In exchange, the hardware can support only relatively simple multiword atomic operations, and must fall back to a software run-time for any operation that exceeds the abilities of the hardware.

This paper demonstrates that BEHTM simplicity does not prohibit advanced and complex transactional behaviors. We exploit support for immediate non-transactional stores in the AMD Advanced Synchronization Facility to build a mechanism for communication among transactions. While our system allows arbitrary communication patterns, we focus on a design point where each transaction communicates with a system-wide manager thread. The API for the manager thread allows BEHTM transactions to delegate unsafe operations (such as system calls) to helper threads, and also enables the creation of nested parallel transactions. This paper also explores which forms of nesting are possible, and identifies constraints on nesting that are a consequence of how BEHTM is designed.

Categories and Subject Descriptors

D.1.3 [**Programming Techniques**]: Concurrent Programming—*Parallel programming*; C.1.4 [**Processor Architectures**]: Parallel Architectures

General Terms

Algorithms, Design

---

[*]At Lehigh University, this work was supported by the US National Science Foundation under grant CNS-1016828; and by financial support from Google.

Permission to make digital or hard copies of all or part of this work for personal or classroom use is granted without fee provided that copies are not made or distributed for profit or commercial advantage and that copies bear this notice and the full citation on the first page. To copy otherwise, to republish, to post on servers or to redistribute to lists, requires prior specific permission and/or a fee.
SPAA'12, June 25–27, 2012, Pittsburgh, Pennsylvania, USA.
Copyright 2012 ACM 978-1-4503-1213-4/12/06 ...$10.00.

Keywords

Transactional Memory, Nesting, Synchronization, Allocation

1 Introduction

The promise of transactional memory (TM) [24] lies in its simplicity: rather than reason about mutual exclusion, lock granularity, and deadlocks, with TM programmers simply annotate code regions that must execute atomically; a run-time system ensures correctness while finding as much parallelism as possible among these atomic blocks. Unfortunately, pure software TM (STM) incurs significant overhead due to per-access conflict detection overheads. Hardware TM (HTM) requires significant modification to processor implementations, possibly including the cache coherence protocol. The resulting verification requirements are considered too onerous for a technology that has not yet proven its merit.

An emerging approach is to minimally extend the hardware to provide limited support for TM. The resulting best-effort HTM (BEHTM) executes some transactions fully in hardware, and requires a fallback to a software system in all other cases. Example BEHTM systems include the Sun Rock prototype processor [13, 18], Intel's Transactional Synchronization Extensions (TSX) [27], and the AMD Advanced Synchronization Facility proposal (ASF)[1] [15]. BEHTM systems do not modify the cache coherence protocol, and they place hard constraints on the number of locations that can be read or written by a BEHTM transaction. They also forbid certain operations (e.g., system calls) within BEHTM transactions, and permit transactions to abort and restart due to low-level hardware events (such as TLB misses or page faults).

Recent efforts have shown that it is possible to exploit BEHTM to simplify algorithm design [17], make a locking STM non-blocking with minimal overhead [20], and even accelerate a general-purpose TM system by running small transactions entirely in hardware [16, 39]. In this last category, a key challenge is to minimize the number of transactions that must fall back to the software system to complete, because the existence of such transactions causes hardware transactions to incur greater overhead.

Surprisingly, many simple operations, such as memory allocation, require BEHTM transactions to fall back to software mode. In HTM publications, true allocation often is avoided artificially by having each thread pre-allocate object pools that are large enough to accommodate all possible allocations needed by a simulation. In STM, allocation is typically managed via *ad-hoc* open nesting [26]. While the details of why allocation within a hardware transaction

---

[1]ASF is an experimental feature and has not been announced for any future product.

is problematic are deferred to Appendix A, it suffices to note that any allocation might perform a system call to enlarge the heap, and that non-transactionally calling a lock-based allocator is dangerous because the parent transaction risks aborting while holding a lock.

In the AMD ASF proposal, a BEHTM transaction can perform *immediate* non-transactional loads and stores. These accesses are not intended for general use: if used incorrectly, they can violate failure atomicity and cause memory corruption. However, Riegel et al. demonstrated that careful use of non-transactional accesses can significantly enhance the usefulness of BEHTM [39].

In a similar vein, we show that the existing support for non-transactional accesses in ASF can be used to enable communication among transactions. In our system, transactions communicate with nontransactional helper threads, which can perform allocation and system calls on the transaction's behalf. In addition to supporting delegation, we show that helper threads can serve as nested transaction coordinators, and thus that it is possible to implement some forms of nested parallel transactions in ASF. We also identify nesting patterns that cannot be supported by BEHTM. These include unattainable patterns of sharing between a parent and its child, as well as limits on the number of closed-nested child BEHTM transactions that can exist in any parent/children relationship.

The remainder of this paper is organized as follows: We provide more background on BEHTM operation in Section 2. In Section 3, we discuss the abstract communication channel that we implement using non-transactional accesses. Sections 4 and 5 discuss how this communication channel can be used for delegation and nesting, respectively. Section 6 discusses relationships with prior work. In Section 7, we summarize our findings and suggest directions for future research.

2 BEHTM Background

Early HTM proposals aimed to provide strong performance without requiring a supporting software run-time system. To this end, they modified the processor cache [23,33] and included mechanisms for supporting "unbounded" transactions [2, 8, 32, 37]. Such transactions could speculatively access (for reading and writing) more data than could fit in their L1 cache, and could survive context switches.

While appealing, these proposals required significant changes to hard-to-verify components of the processor. A more pragmatic approach, embodied by best-effort TM designs, is to minimally change the hardware such that only a limited class of transactions are supported, and then delegate the execution of all other transactions to a software run-time.

The most prominent examples of BEHTM are the Sun Rock prototype processor [13, 18] and the AMD Advanced Synchronization Facility proposal (ASF) [15].[2] These systems share many characteristics. They both use a traditional invalidation cache protocol, resulting in an "attacker wins" conflict resolution policy [10], with conflicts detected at the granularity of cache lines. While this protocol allows for obstruction-free transactions, it is prone to livelock and false conflicts [10], and thus a software contention manager is recommended even for hardware transactions.

Both proposals place limits on the behavior of transactional code in terms of the absolute number of locations that can be read or written. In Rock, the L1 cache buffers transactional loads, with L1 capacity and dynamic associativity conflicts determining the total

number of loads a transaction can perform. Transactional stores stall in the store buffer until the transaction commits. Multiple stores to the same location are not likely to be coalesced. As an unimplemented proposal, ASF is less concrete. It allows for the L1 cache to bound the number of loads and stores, for a dedicated processor structure (the locked line buffer, or LLB) to manage all transactional accesses, or for a combination of the two (e.g., an LLB for stores and the L1 cache for loads) [14].

The most notable differences between Rock and ASF relate to non-transactional accesses. Both support non-transactional loads that happen "immediately." In ASF, immediate non-transactional stores are also allowed. These are presumably intended to prevent capacity from being wasted on stack writes in the register-limited x86 architecture. In Rock, non-transactional stores stall in the store buffer. Thus while they still "happen," they do so only when the transaction commits or aborts.

For completeness, we also note that Rock checkpoints the entire architectural state of the CPU when starting a transaction, whereas ASF checkpoints only the PC and stack pointer. Rock and ASF also forbid certain operations, possibly including floating-point operations, compare and swap, or TLB miss handlers. These points are immaterial to this paper.

In the absence of non-transactional stores, the correctness of code that uses BEHTM is easy to verify, due to a simple guarantee by the hardware: any violation of the BEHTM rules (e.g., capacity, TLB misses, unsupported instructions, etc) causes the transaction to abort and return a status code that can be used to resolve the problem (e.g., by manually filling the TLB or switching to software mode). Conflicting memory accesses (e.g., transactional or non-transactional operations by another thread) also cause aborts. Because BEHTM does not support escape actions [45], all aborts should be thought of as occurring "immediately;" put another way, an abort cannot be temporarily suppressed.

Non-transactional stores create many complications. First, because conflict detection occurs at cache-line granularity, the programmer must ensure that a line is not accessed both transactionally and non-transactionally; these accesses can cause immediate program termination. Second, if non-transactional stores are used to acquire and release locks in non-transactional code called from a transactional context, then the immediacy of aborts makes possible that a transaction will acquire a lock and then abort, rendering the lock permanently unavailable. Last, correct ordering of non-transactional stores relative to transactional and non-transactional loads may require the use of memory fences in some circumstances.

3 Extending BEHTM for Verifiable Communication

We now define methods and structures that can be used for communication involving BEHTM transactions, and then discuss an implementation using ASF's non-transactional stores. Note that while arbitrarily complex mechanisms can be built atop ASF's non-transactional load/store abilities, we limit our presentation to a simple design (a single bidirectional one-word communication channel per CPU core) that we believe could easily be added to Rock or TSX. We have not yet identified a situation in which this simple design sacrifices generality, though high performance implementations may wish to make more aggressive use of ASF's rich support for nontransactional accesses.

We define `TxChannel` as an unbuffered, bidirectional communication medium with exactly two endpoints. Communication is asynchronous and polling-based. The contents of `TxChannel`

---

[2]Details about the implementation of Intel's TSX hardware were not available at the time this paper was written, but available information suggests that apart from its lack of support for nontransactional loads and stores within transactions, TSX should behave like Rock and ASF.

consist of a fixed-size message (e.g., one memory word), which can be atomically read from either endpoint via the `LdTxChannel` method. Similarly, either endpoint can atomically overwrite the contents of `TxChannel` via the `StTxChannel` method.[3]

The `ConfigTxChannel` method binds a thread to a channel and returns a handle to the channel. We further constrain the `Tx-Channel` mechanism as follows: when thread T is executing a BEHTM transaction, it may not have more than one channel assigned to it, and it can neither bind to a channel, nor release its binding to a channel. Channel assignments are immutable for the duration of a transaction. Outside of a BEHTM transaction, a thread can change its channel configurations, and can communicate on multiple channels.

In the ASF specification, non-transactional loads and stores performed by a BEHTM transaction occur immediately, and do not incur transactional bookkeeping. The simplest implementation of `TxChannel` in ASF requires no hardware modifications: each `TxChannel` is simply a reserved memory region, `LdTxChannel` is a non-transactional load, and `StTxChannel` is a non-transactional store. For channels aligned on 8-byte boundaries, these loads and stores are naturally atomic using existing instructions in the x86 ISA. At application start, a pool of channels is created by allocating sufficient memory. `ConfigTxChannel` assigns an endpoint from this pool to its caller.

In ASF, no extra hardware is required for this `TxChannel` implementation. However, the overall correctness requires run-time software support. There are two main challenges. First, we must guarantee that endpoints are used correctly. Software must enforce the binding of a single thread to each channel endpoint (one approach can be found in the Singularity OS [19]). Second, the run-time system must ensure that a BEHTM transaction does not transactionally access the line on which its `TxChannel` is stored. This can be guaranteed by padding each channel to a cache line, and aligning the channel on a cache line boundary. To prevent false sharing, padding should take into consideration the size of L2 (and L3) cache lines, and whether the L2 prefetch unit always requests adjacent lines. In the worst case, modern machines might require each `TxChannel` to pad to four lines (256 bytes).

For well-structured communications, the atomicity of `LdTx-Channel` and `StTxChannel` can be relaxed to enable larger channel sizes. Consider a 64-byte (8-word) channel. If one word is reserved as a status field, then a message can be sent by using non-transactional stores to set the other seven words of the channel. Then the message can be marked ready by setting the status field via an eighth non-transactional store. For its part, `LdTxChannel` would begin by (non-transactionally) spinning on the status word, and would not read the remainder of the channel until the status word is set appropriately. As long as one endpoint cannot perform consecutive `StTxChannel` instructions without intervening acknowledgments, the illusion of atomicity is preserved.[4]

4 Delegation

By convention, a BEHTM transaction is connected to at most one `TxChannel`. While transactions could communicate directly, we propose that the most hardware-agnostic mechanism involves the use of a distinguished software thread (DT). In our system, DT serves as the remote endpoint for *every* transaction. The resulting topology is depicted in Figure 1. In multi-chip environments, the

---

[3]Given this definition, `TxChannel` can be thought of as an atomic register shared between exactly two threads.

[4]On architectures with relaxed memory consistency, one fence instruction would be required per channel access.

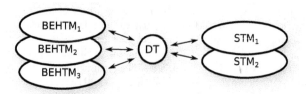

1: Multiple BEHTM and STM transactions using a single service thread DT.

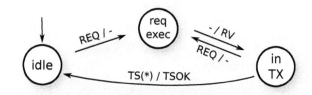

2: `TxChannel` state transitions, with messages sent to / by DT. If a transaction sends REQ to DT, it must send a TS on commit / abort. TS cannot be sent while DT is processing a request (reqexec).

number of DT threads could be dynamically adjusted (e.g., to ensure one per chip) without requiring the hardware to support multiple `TxChannel` interfaces, though the DT threads might need to synchronize with each other.

4.1 Communication Between Transactions and DT

Transactions communicate with DT via their unique `TxChannels`, using the `LdTxChannel` and `StTxChannel` commands. Because remote accesses to cache lines also accessed by a BEHTM transaction will cause it to abort, we suggest pass-by-value parameters whenever possible.

Assuming `TxChannel` is large enough to hold entire messages, the protocol for communication between a BEHTM thread and DT is as follows. There are two message types sent to DT: an operation request (REQ), containing an ID of the operation to be performed and the required operands; and transaction status (TS), signaling either abort (A) or commit (C). Communication is always initiated by the BEHTM thread through a REQ message. DT can send two message types: a return value packet (RV), also serving as ack of receipt of REQ; and ack on receipt of TS(*) (TSOK). The state machine governing the protocol is depicted in Figure 2. In addition, the following constraints apply: (1) TS(*) cannot be sent until after the transaction commits or aborts. (2) Before sending RV, DT must register onAbort and onCommit handlers for the requested operation. (3) Upon receipt of TS(A), DT calls all onAbort handlers registered on the `TxChannel`. (4) On receipt of a TS(C), DT calls all onCommit handlers registered on the `TxChannel`.

Lifting the size constraint on the exchanged messages can be accomplished easily by breaking send operations of larger messages into multiple short messages (REQ/RV) with the respective acknowledgment messages (REQOK/RVOK). We omit this for clarity and brevity of the presentation. More detail can be found in Appendix B.

In our description, a single DT listens to requests by all BEHTM transactions. If all requested actions are thread-safe, it is straightforward to use multiple service threads within DT, or to place a DT thread on each core. We leave this as future work.

A BEHTM thread can request execution of any instruction that is forbidden within its context. This includes requests for DT to perform floating-point operations, allocations, I/O and other system calls, and arbitrary library calls. The BEHTM transaction is free to continue executing in parallel with the service of its request by DT.

4.2 Handling Aborts During Delegation

We must expect that a BEHTM transaction B is vulnerable to abort at any time, including during communication with DT. To prevent races, B cannot notify DT of its abort unless it is sure that DT is not currently writing a message to B. Thus B must always be able to ascertain the channel state (e.g., by executing LdTxChannel).

With this guarantee, B can invoke arbitrary library code through DT. If B aborts while the library is running OS code or holds a lock, DT will simply complete, release locks, and send an RV. Only then will B send TS(A), at which time the delegated operation will be undone by DT. As an example, consider allocation: an allocated region must be returned to the heap if the transaction fails, and a deallocation must be deferred until the transaction commits [21, Ch. 5]. Bookkeeping this information in DT, and then finalizing or undoing operations in response to a commit/abort message, is straightforward.

4.3 Constraints

While our mechanism does not require general support for non-transactional stores within a BEHTM transaction, it must handle the possibility that the delegate and the BEHTM transaction share memory. ASF and Rock both provide strong atomicity [9], thus dangerous accesses will result in the BEHTM transaction aborting. If the correctness of the delegate depends on it reading a value written by the transaction, that value will not be available and arbitrary faults can ensue. Our prohibition on passing parameters by reference resolves this problem, and should not be a burden for the types of syscalls and library calls we aim to support.

A second concern is that polling for acks can lead to code that is difficult to analyze statically. While an adversary could easily create such code, we expect well-written code to encapsulate such control flow in objects that generate a few easily-recognizable instruction sequence patterns.

4.4 Overhead

When our mechanism is not used, a transaction must perform a single LdTxChannel on commit or abort. The call will return TSOK, indicating an idle channel (i.e., the transaction did not use the channel and need not send TS(*)). When delegation is used, overhead can be approximated by the number of round-trip cache communications that occur, with all but the last occurring before the transaction commits. This overhead can be reduced in two ways: First, when the delegate has no return value, polling for RV can be delayed until after the transaction commits. Second, in ASF it is technically possible to create parameter and return value packets for large messages in memory, and to transfer their ownership by passing pointers. While this technique obviates REQOK and RVOK messages, we do not recommend it: it is difficult to verify, requires strong store-store ordering, and would require a long-term commitment to broad hardware support for immediate non-transactional stores.

In practice, other sources of latency will arise. One example is the time to service the request and the time taken for DT to receive the request. If this delay is too great, it is possible to partition the transactions and employ multiple delegation threads.[5] Another is the overhead of commit and abort handlers. This cost is likely to be application-specific, though existing experience with allocation suggests that commit handlers should be inexpensive (e.g., resetting a log) in the common case.

5 Nesting

Our delegation mechanism is essentially an open-nested transaction, in which the parent uses BEHTM, and the child may or may not. It is further constrained in that the parent and child are assumed to share no memory. We now show how DT can serve as a transaction manager, enabling many interesting patterns of parallel nested child transactions.

Our goal is for a parent transaction to request that DT launches many child transactions on its behalf, and that children run in parallel. We assume an underlying TM similar to Hybrid NOrec [16,39]: STM and BEHTM transactions run concurrently, using the values stored in memory to detect conflicts. A single lock ensures atomicity when STM transactions commit, and BEHTM transactions incur extra overhead to commit when there are active STM transactions. STM transactions do not update memory until commit time. This contrasts with most nested STM proposals, which rely on in-place update [1, 5, 36, 43] to avoid overhead. However, in-place update appears incompatible with strong language-level memory consistency models [30].

We analyze both both open and closed nesting, to see how BE-HTM can be used in the parent and/or child transactions. We restrict our study to the case when a parent does not make progress while any children are running [35]. This assumption is common in prior explorations of nested parallel children, and removing this prohibition does not substantially affect our findings. Similarly, we do not consider deep nesting: the capacity limits of BEHTM make it unlikely that deep nesting would be practical.

We extend DT from the prior section to support nesting in a manner similar to the closed-nested transaction coordinator used by Ramadan et al. [38]. In that work, a transaction communicates with the manager to request that child transactions be assigned to idle threads, and then the children coordinate through the manager to commit "into" the parent. In Ramadan's work, children often would commit together, and thus DT would coordinate commit or unwind of children. We extend this system with support for both open nesting and BEHTM. We also add support for sandboxing child operations (the need for which is discussed below), and expose multiple mechanisms for merging child results into the parent. These mechanisms balance capacity constraints of a BEHTM transaction with run-time overhead and generality imposed by sharing constraints.

5.1 Sharing Data Between a Parent and its Nested Child

Most nested STM systems employ Agrawal et al.'s definition of conflicting transactions [1]. The definition permits maximal sharing among a parent and its children: a child transaction never conflicts with its parent, even if it reads or writes locations that its parent has accessed. This definition even holds when an open-nested transaction modifies a location its parent has also modified. Implementations that allow maximal sharing are necessarily complex [5].

At a high level, our system works by having parent transactions request that DT launch child transactions, and then relying on DT

---

[5]Note that concentrating certain operations on a single thread (e.g., system calls [12] or allocation [42]) may offer greater benefit than multiple DT threads.

41

ASA	RSO	SFF
$x \in C_{read} \Rightarrow x \notin P_{read} \bigcup P_{write}$	$x \in C_{read} \Rightarrow x \notin P_{write}$	$x \in C_{read} \Rightarrow x \notin P_{write}$
$x \in C_{write} \Rightarrow x \notin P_{read} \bigcup P_{write}$	$x \in C_{write} \Rightarrow x \notin P_{read} \bigcup P_{write}$	

3: Rules governing overlap between child (C) and parent (P) memory accesses.

to mediate the commit of those children. The parent-child relationship is invisible to the BEHTM hardware. Because BEHTM interprets any cache-level conflict as a cause for abort, we are unable to support the maximal model.

In more detail, suppose BEHTM transaction P has read location X and then requested that DT execute a nested child C. The cache line containing X will be tracked by the processor executing P, and thus if C fetches the cache line containing X into a writable state, the line will be evicted from P's processor's cache and P will abort. A similar condition occurs if P writes X and C attempts to read X. Consequently, we consider three weaker communication patterns for parents and children, shown in Figure 3:

- **Access set augmenting (ASA):** C is an ASA child of P if it does not access any cache line also accessed by P.
- **Read share only (RSO):** C is an RSO child of P if all overlapping accesses are reads by P and C.
- **Store forward forbidding (SFF):** C is an SFF child of P if it does not read a location written by P. C may write to locations read or written by P, and may read locations read by P.

5.2 Sandboxing

If C reads a location X written by its BEHTM parent P, P will abort and C will continue running, using the value of X that existed prior to P's write. This can lead to erroneous behavior: Suppose P writes $X = |X|$, and C computes $\sqrt{X}$. The programmer is likely to assume that $X \geq 0$ holds when C begins, and thus if the underlying TM run-time executing C is opaque [22], C should never fault. If P uses BEHTM, C's read will abort P and return the value of X from before P began; thus, C can execute with an inconsistent view of memory in which $X < 0$.

To address this problem, the TM runtime must ensure that C's inconsistent view of memory does not cause it to produce a visible fault, enter an infinite loop, execute a computed jump to non-transactional code, or corrupt the heap. If it cannot be statically proven that C does not read P's writes, the child must coordinate with DT to achieve a degree of run-time sandboxing: before any potentially unsafe operation, the child must query DT to check if P is still live. To prove P live, DT must communicate with P; it cannot simply read P's status, because P may be in its abort handler.

Our solution uses two new message types, CHKSTATE and LIVE. After a parent P sends REQ to invoke a set of child transactions, it executes a spin loop in which it reads from its channel, awaiting an RV or CHKSTATE message. As before, RV indicates that the child operations are complete, and P can resume. When CHKSTATE is received, P immediately sends LIVE. If P aborts, it must wait for a CHKSTATE or RV message, and then send TS(A). Failing to wait could result in its message racing with DT's next CHKSTATE or RV message.

The details of when sandboxing is needed have been explored elsewhere [40, 41]. Our contribution is discovering that sandboxing is needed even for an opaque TM if a child C of a BEHTM parent P can cause P to abort. Beyond the concerns raised in past work, we must ensure that if C computes an address and writes to it, the address computation was not based on inconsistent reads. This

requirement is outside of the sandboxing that BEHTM guarantees (i.e., that faults within a transaction cause it to abort), so a software child using in-place update must ensure its parent is live before it writes to a location that might not be protected by the TM. Otherwise, a subsequent undo action might participate in a data race. For the same reason, open-nested children (BEHTM and STM) must ensure their parents are live before committing. Sandboxing is also needed for some non-transactional stores performed by a BEHTM child (e.g., those that are not to the current stack frame) and by STM parents of closed-nested BEHTM children.

5.3 Findings

We now present our findings for all combinations of open and closed nesting, and BEHTM and STM transactions, in which at least one transaction uses BEHTM. A summary appears in Figure 4.

Open-nested BEHTM Child of BEHTM Parent: In our model, a BEHTM parent can have an unlimited number of open-nested BEHTM children. However, because the BEHTM parent cannot forward its speculative stores, these children must obey the ASA or RSO models.[6]

The algorithm is simple: P sends a REQ message to DT to request that the children run, and then DT assigns work to threads in its private pool. These threads' transactions communicate with DT via the TxChannel mechanism. Because P uses BEHTM, if child C attempts to read any location P has written, or to write any location P has read, P will abort. C will continue to run, but because it uses BEHTM, its effects are guarded until the commit point. Because an open-nested child C commits before its parent P, rather than atomically with P, child commit is straightforward: DT uses CHKSTATE to ensure that P is live, and then allows C to commit according to the Hybrid NOrec protocol. This is sufficient for correctness: because C is at its commit point, if P has not aborted, C's accesses must have been ASA or RSO. Should C abort at any time, DT restarts it only if P is still live. When C commits, it sends an RV to DT. The RV message includes the commit and abort handlers that must run when P completes, as well as any values to return to P. Because each open-nested child commits or aborts independently, no coordination is needed among children.

Open-nested STM Child of BEHTM Parent: An open-nested software child of a BEHTM parent runs in almost the same manner as just described. However, because BEHTM is not used in the child, it must sandbox more operations. Again, any number of children are possible, and these children must be ASA or RSO.

There is one additional restriction: because STM transactions in Hybrid NOrec use buffered writes, writes by C to locations read by P do not cause P to abort during C's execution. Instead, they cause P to abort during C's "redo" phase, after C has committed, which can lead to erroneous output. To prevent this, whenever C adds a location L to its write set, we require it to execute a write prefetch with L as the operand. If P has read L, the prefetch will cause P to abort before C's pre-commit check.

---

[6]In this and subsequent discussion, the parent can simulate a limited number of known child reads of parent writes by sending those speculatively written values as parameters to the child in the initial REQ message.

Parent	BEHTM	BEHTM	STM	BEHTM	STM	BEHTM
Child	BEHTM	STM	BEHTM	BEHTM	BEHTM	STM
Nesting	Open	Open	Open	Closed	Closed	Closed
Valid Access Patterns	ASA/RSO	ASA/RSO	ASA/RSO	None	ASA/RSO	ASA/RSO/SFF

4: Nesting and memory access patterns that can take advantage of BEHTM.

Open-nested BEHTM Child of STM Parent: In previous sections, we saw that the ability of a BEHTM parent to immediately detect conflicts with its children due to non-ASA/RSO sharing meant that little work was required by the parent when deciding whether a child could commit. The only cost was for the communication to ensure that the parent had not already aborted. When the parent is an STM transaction, more work is needed at this point: the parent must validate its read set and write-prefetch every location in its write set before sending LIVE.

Read-set validation serves two ends: it ensures P is still active (otherwise, C's commit could be erroneous) and causes C to abort if it has speculative writes to locations P has read. Note that validation does not cause C to abort due to read-read sharing in BEHTM. Similarly, write prefetching causes C to abort if it read from or stored to anything P had written. The net effect is that C can only commit if it is ASA or RSO.

If the language memory model allowed for in-place update, then child reads of parent writes could be forwarded to the BEHTM child. We leave explorations of this topic as future work.

Closed-nested BEHTM Child of BEHTM Parent: We are aware of two mechanisms for committing a closed-nested child. In STM, the more common approach is for C to merge its read and write sets into P. The other, which resembles distributed transactions, is for C to wait for P to reach its commit point, and then employ some protocol by which the two commit or abort together.

When a closed-nested child uses BEHTM, there is no software-accessible structure through which the child can communicate its accesses to its parent. Thus the first mechanism cannot be employed. In current BEHTM systems, the second approach cannot be achieved either. Thus a BEHTM parent cannot have a closed-nested BEHTM child.

To understand why the second approach cannot work, we show that it is impossible in current BEHTM systems to achieve a coordinated commit of two transactions. Recall that in BEHTM, a transaction executes a `commit` instruction to make all its effects visible (i.e., a one-phase commit protocol). Prior to issuing this command, the transaction is vulnerable to aborts (e.g., due to memory conflicts or context switches). After issuing the command, the transaction's updates are visible to other threads. Suppose we wish for BEHTM transactions A and B to commit as a single atomic event. By definition, A commits exactly when it executes its `commit` instruction. The same is true of B. If while A is issuing `commit`, B experiences a context switch, then A will commit while B aborts. A symmetric case covers B issuing `commit` before A. Even in the absence of additional threads, atomic group commit of two (or more) BEHTM transactions is not possible.

Closed-nested BEHTM Child of STM Parent: There is a slight difference between this and the prior pattern. The child BEHTM transaction still cannot communicate its read and write sets to the parent. However, a single closed-nested BEHTM child can commit atomically with its software parent, and thus this pattern can be supported in a limited sense.

Suppose that STM parent P invokes the closed-nested child C at the end of P's execution. In this case, once C finishes its compu-

tation, both it and P can commit. Our solution is for C to send its RV to DT, who then instructs P to "pre-commit." Once P completes this step, DT informs C to commit. If C succeeds, then P is instructed to finalize its commit. Otherwise, P aborts. Note that closed-nested STM children could also be involved in the commit; they would simply "commit into" P prior to the coordination between P and its BEHTM child.

Using Hybrid NOrec as an example, P's pre-commit consists of (a) acquiring the global commit lock, (b) validating its read set, and (c) write-prefetching all elements of the write set. These steps ensure that no other transaction will invalidate P, that P is valid, and that C will abort if it performed non-ASA/RSO accesses. Note, too, that C need not be the last step in P's computation. In that case, the ultimate commit follows the same protocol as already described. When C returns control to P, C has not committed and P must perform the write prefetch and validate steps (but not acquire the global lock), and then determine (through DT) that C is still live before continuing. Furthermore, P must be sandboxed from this point forward, so that any attempt to use a location written by C will not result in a fault. Sandboxing in this case entails P querying C to ensure C has not aborted because an abort by C could signify that P attempted to read one of C's writes.

Closed-nested STM Child of BEHTM Parent: The final pattern we consider is when P uses BEHTM but C does not. Naturally, C cannot read P's writes. All other sharing patterns are allowed, and thus ASA, RSO, and SFF children are possible.

Because the child is an STM transaction, it has precise logs of the address/value pairs it read and the address/value pairs it intends to write. Note that C does not perform write-prefetching. To commit, C simply passes all of this information to P in the RV message. Before P continues, it validates C's reads by checking that each address it received still holds the value that was sent. These checks use *transactional* reads, and thus merge C's reads into P's read set. P then re-executes C's writes using *transactional* stores, to add them to its write set.

There are three caveats. First, C must be sandboxed so attempts to read P's writes do not lead to erroneous behavior. Second, while writes to locations read or written by P are possible, overwrites of P's writes are not likely to succeed in practice because most writes are preceded by a read to the same location. Third, and most important, the size of C's read and write sets cannot be so large as to overflow the BEHTM capacity constraints imposed on P. Otherwise P will ultimately abort. While it is possible to communicate only C's writes in RV, and then require DT to validate C's reads before P commits, the resulting constraints on the behavior of P limit the technique's usefulness.

5.4 Relationship to Delegation

Delegation and nesting serve fundamentally different roles. Delegation addresses the use of orthogonal components that are forbidden within a BEHTM context, whereas nesting is a more general approach to achieving parallelism. Thus with delegation we assume that each delegate effectively operates on a private region of the heap, and there is no sharing between a delegate and the invoking transaction (though in reality there will be false conflicts, such as those arising when the allocator traverses metadata stored in the header of allocated objects). Because a parent abort cannot affect the delegate, delegation does not introduce the need for sandboxing, whereas nesting does.

The models also differ with respect to parallelism. With nesting, the parent does not execute in parallel with its children, because doing so can increase the likelihood of conflicts (particularly given BEHTM "attacker wins" conflict resolution). In contrast, delegation is naturally parallel, because delegate and transaction accesses are assumed to be disjoint.

In addition, we require nesting to employ the same transactional runtime as the parent, whereas delegate actions need not, and so a delegate could use locks, STM, or lock-free programming (perhaps assisted by ASF). The cost of this flexibility is that interactions with a delegate are pass-by-value.

6   Related Work

In the earliest (non-parallel) nested STM [36], several of the cases that BEHTM cannot handle were also problematic. The authors claimed that a child overwriting a parent's read should be rare in practice, which mitigates our inability to support the pattern in BEHTM. They also identified a child overwriting a parent's write as challenging. We can only support this pattern with closed-nested STM children, and our solution resembles theirs. Lastly, that work identified programming pitfalls such as deadlock in abort handlers; we expect their proposed solutions to apply to our work.

NePaLTM [43] used a mutex to run child transactions serially. Later, Barreto et al. implemented Agrawal's algorithm [5]. Since they used in-place update, their system was not compatible with strong language-level memory models. However, it supported more patterns of sharing than we can achieve when using BEHTM. They found that the time required to propagate updates to a parent increased the likelihood of false conflicts. This is likely to affect our closed-nested STM child transactions. Baek et al. implemented the first closed-nested STM (NeSTM) with buffered update [3]. Their implementation would experience "zombie" transactions in some cases. Our discovery of the need for sandboxing explains and prevents zombies.

Coordinated sibling transactions (CST) [38] are a closed-nested system supporting complex patterns of group commit for child transactions. Our use of a DT thread resembles CST's use of a master transaction coordinator to manage thread pools. We believe that our system could be used to implement the CST coordination patterns, with the caveats that a BEHTM parent can have only software CST children, a software parent can have at most one BEHTM child, and children must obey the access rules in Section 5.

Hardware Implementations of Nesting: Escape actions are a means of deferring aborts in HTM, which enable simple delegation operations such as time-related syscalls [45]. Moravan et al. [34] extended LogTM with (non-parallel) open-nested transactions, and FaNTM [4] accelerated NeSTM via hardware signatures. These techniques all required modifications to the pipeline or coherence protocol. FaNTM is also prone to complex deadlocks and livelocks as a result of partial rollback. Our use of livelock-free Hybrid NOrec avoids such problems.

Beyond Nesting: Our system can support many other patterns of communication, such as safe futures [44] and CST. Another promising direction is to implement communicators [28, 29], though the requirement that all participants in a communicator commit together necessitates that the communicator dynamically limits to one the number of BEHTM transactions bound to it.

7   Conclusions

This paper presented a system that supports delegation and nesting in best-effort hardware transactional memory. Our design is in keeping with the spirit of BEHTM, in that it requires minimal changes to existing hardware; in fact, the AMD ASF proposal requires no further extensions to implement our abstract communication channel, and we believe that a minimal implementation of our communication abstraction in the Rock prototype processor or forthcoming TSX platform would be straightforward.

Our system allows BEHTM transactions to invoke delegates to perform non-transactional actions on their behalf, such as system and library calls. As necessary, the transaction can register handlers to unwind or finalize the behavior of delegates on transaction commit or abort. We employ a dedicated helper thread to manage the relationship between a transaction and its delegates; ultimately, we showed that the mechanism can generalize to support open and closed-nested parallel transactions. While delegation prevents fallback to software mode for simple operations, such as time-related system calls and allocation, nesting allows for enhanced parallelism in workloads in which top-level transactions conflict with high frequency, but each possesses a significant amount of internal parallelism. Unfortunately, the promise of nested parallelism is tempered by the limitations we discovered, which appear to be intrinsic to BEHTM. When these limitations are encountered, the system will need to fall back to a pure software mode of execution.

We leave as future work a thorough performance evaluation of nesting in BEHTM because it requires more precise simulation support than is currently available. We are also investigating whether minimal hardware modifications could enable group commit, decrease the cost of sandboxing, or enable simple data forwarding among transactions. A further area of exploration relates to the performance tradeoff of supporting multiple TxChannels per transaction, or multiple DT threads.

8   References

[1] Kunal Agrawal, Jeremy Fineman, and Jim Sukha. Nested Parallelism in Transactional Memory. In *Proceedings of the 13th ACM Symposium on Principles and Practice of Parallel Programming*, Salt Lake City, Utah, February 2008.

[2] C. Scott Ananian, Krste Asanovic, Bradley C. Kuszmaul, Charles E. Leiserson, and Sean Lie. Unbounded Transactional Memory. In *Proceedings of the 11th International Symposium on High-Performance Computer Architecture*, February 2005.

[3] Woongki Baek, Nathan Bronson, Christos Kozyrakis, and Kunle Olukotun. Implementing and Evaluating Nested Parallel Transactions in Software Transactional Memory. In *Proceedings of the 22nd ACM Symposium on Parallelism in Algorithms and Architectures*, Santorini, Greece, June 2010.

[4] Woongki Baek, Nathan Bronson, Christos Kozyrakis, and Kunle Olukotun. Making Nested Parallel Transactions Practical using Lightweight Hardware Support . In *Proceedings of the 24th ACM International Conference on Supercomputing*, Tsukuba, Japan, June 2010.

[5] Joao Barreto, Aleksandar Dragojevic, Paulo Ferreira, Rachid Guerraoui, and Michal Kapalka. Leveraging Parallel Nesting in Transactional Memory. In *Proceedings of the 15th ACM Symposium on Principles and Practice of Parallel Programming*, Bangalore, India, January 2010.

[6] Andrew Baumann, Paul Barham, Pierre-Evariste Dagand, Tim Harris, Rebecca Isaacs, Simon Peter, Timothy Roscoe, Adrian Schupbach, and Akhilesh Singhania. The Multikernel: A New OS Architecture for Scalable Multicore Systems. In *Proceedings of the 22nd ACM Symposium on Operating Systems Principles*, Big Sky, Mont., October 2009.

[7] Emery Berger, Kathryn McKinley, Robert Blumofe, and Paul Wilson. Hoard: A Scalable Memory Allocator for Multithreaded Applications. In *Proceedings of the 9th International Conference on Architectural Support for Programming Languages and Operating Systems*, Cambridge, Mass., November 2000.

[8] Colin Blundell, Joe Devietti, E Christopher Lewis, and Milo Martin. Making the Fast Case Common and the Uncommon Case Simple in Unbounded Transactional Memory. In *Proceedings of the 34th International Symposium on Computer Architecture*, San Diego, Calif., June 2007.

[9] Colin Blundell, E Christopher Lewis, and Milo M. K. Martin. Subtleties of Transactional Memory Atomicity Semantics. *Computer Architecture Letters*, 5(2), November 2006.

[10] Jayaram Bobba, Kevin Moore, Haris Volos, Luke Yen, Mark Hill, Michael Swift, and David Wood. Performance Pathologies in Hardware Transactional Memory. In *Proceedings of the 34th International Symposium on Computer Architecture*, San Diego, Calif., June 2007.

[11] Silas Boyd-Wickizer, Haibo Chen, Rong Chen, Yandong Mao, M. Frans Kaashoek, Robert Morris, Aleksey Pesterev, Lex Stein, Ming Wu, Yue hua Dai, Yang Zhang, and Zheng Zhang. Corey: An operating system for many cores. In *Proceedings of the 8th USENIX Symposium on Operating Systems Design and Implementation*, San Diego, Calif., December 2008.

[12] Silas Boyd-Wickizer, Austin Clements, Yandong Mao, Aleksey Pesterev, M. Frans Kaashoek, Robert Morris, and Nickolai Zeldovich. An Analysis of Linux Scalability to Many Cores. In *Proceedings of the 9th USENIX Symposium on Operating Systems Design and Implementation*, Vancouver, B.C., Canada, October 2010.

[13] Shailender Chaudhry, Robert Cypher, Magnus Ekman, Martin Karlsson, Anders Landin, and Sherman Yip. Rock: A High-Performance Sparc CMT Processor. *IEEE Micro*, 29(2):6–16, March–April 2009.

[14] Dave Christie, Jae-Woong Chung, Stephan Diestelhorst, Michael Hohmuth, Martin Pohlack, Christof Fetzer, Martin Nowack, Torvald Riegel, Pascal Felber, Patrick Marlier, and Etienne Riviere. Evaluation of AMD's Advanced Synchronization Facility within a Complete Transactional Memory Stack. In *Proceedings of the EuroSys2010 Conference*, Paris, France, April 2010.

[15] Jaewoong Chung, Luke Yen, Stephan Diestelhorst, Martin Pohlack, Michael Hohmuth, Dan Grossman, and David Christie. ASF: AMD64 Extension for Lock-free Data Structures and Transactional Memory. In *Proceedings of the 43rd IEEE/ACM International Symposium on Microarchitecture*, Atlanta, Ga., December 2010.

[16] Luke Dalessandro, Francois Carouge, Sean White, Yossi Lev, Mark Moir, Michael Scott, and Michael Spear. Hybrid NOrec: A Case Study in the Effectiveness of Best Effort Hardware Transactional Memory. In *Proceedings of the 16th International Conference on Architectural Support for Programming Languages and Operating Systems*, Newport Beach, Calif., March 2011.

[17] Dave Dice, Yossi Lev, Virendra Marathe, Mark Moir, Marek Olszewski, and Dan Nussbaum. Simplifying Concurrent Algorithms by Exploiting Hardware TM. In *Proceedings of the 22nd ACM Symposium on Parallelism in Algorithms and Architectures*, Santorini, Greece, June 2010.

[18] David Dice, Yossi Lev, Mark Moir, and Daniel Nussbaum. Early Experience with a Commercial Hardware Transactional Memory Implementation. In *Proceedings of the 14th International Conference on Architectural Support for Programming Languages and Operating Systems*, Washington, D.C., March 2009.

[19] Manuel Fahndrich, Mark Aiken, Chris Hawblitzel, Orion Hodson, Galen Hunt, James Larus, and Steven Levi. Language Support for Fast and Reliable Message-based Communication in Singularity OS. In *Proceedings of the EuroSys2006 Conference*, Leuven, Belgium, April 2006.

[20] Francois Carouge and Michael Spear. A Scalable Lock-Free Universal Construction with Best Effort Transactional Hardware. In *Proceedings of the 24th International Symposium on Distributed Computing*, Cambridge, Mass., September 2010.

[21] Keir Fraser. *Practical Lock-Freedom*. PhD thesis, King's College, University of Cambridge, September 2003.

[22] Rachid Guerraoui and Michal Kapalka. On the Correctness of Transactional Memory. In *Proceedings of the 13th ACM Symposium on Principles and Practice of Parallel Programming*, Salt Lake City, Utah, February 2008.

[23] Lance Hammond, Vicky Wong, Mike Chen, Brian D. Carlstrom, John D. Davis, Ben Hertzberg, Manohar K. Prabju, Honggo Wijaya, Christos Kozyrakis, and Kunle Olukotun. Transactional Memory Coherence and Consistency. In *Proceedings of the 31st International Symposium on Computer Architecture*, Munich, Germany, June 2004.

[24] Tim Harris, James Larus, and Ravi Rajwar. *Transactional Memory, 2nd edition*. Synthesis Lectures on Computer Architecture. Morgan & Claypool, 2010.

[25] Danny Hendler, Itai Incze, Nir Shavit, and Moran Tzafrir. Flat Combining and the Synchronization-Parallelism Tradeoff. In *Proceedings of the 22nd ACM Symposium on Parallelism in Algorithms and Architectures*, Santorini, Greece, June 2010.

[26] Richard L. Hudson, Bratin Saha, Ali-Reza Adl-Tabatabai, and Benjamin Hertzberg. A Scalable Transactional Memory Allocator. In *Proceedings of the International Symposium on Memory Management*, Ottawa, Ont., Canada, June 2006.

[27] Intel Corp. *Intel Architecture Instruction Set Extensions Programming Reference*, 319433-012a edition, February 2012.

[28] Mohsen Lesani and Jens Palsberg. Communicating Memory Transactions. In *Proceedings of the 16th ACM Symposium on Principles and Practice of Parallel Programming*, San Antonio, Tex., February 2011.

[29] Victor Luchangco and Virendra Marathe. Transaction Communicators: Enabling Cooperation Among Concurrent Transactions. In *Proceedings of the 16th ACM Symposium on Principles and Practice of Parallel Programming*, San Antonio, Tex., February 2011.

[30] Vijay Menon, Steven Balensiefer, Tatiana Shpeisman, Ali-Reza Adl-Tabatabai, Richard Hudson, Bratin Saha, and Adam Welc. Practical Weak-Atomicity Semantics for Java STM. In *Proceedings of the 20th ACM Symposium on Parallelism in Algorithms and Architectures*, Munich, Germany, June 2008.

[31] Maged M. Michael. Scalable Lock-Free Dynamic Memory Allocation. In *Proceedings of the 25th ACM Conference on Programming Language Design and Implementation*, Washington, D.C., June 2004.

[32] Chi Cao Minh, Martin Trautmann, JaeWoong Chung, Austen McDonald, Nathan Bronson, Jared Casper, Christos Kozyrakis, and Kunle Olukotun. An Effective Hybrid Transactional Memory System with Strong Isolation Guarantees. In *Proceedings of the 34th International Symposium on Computer Architecture*, San Diego, Calif., June 2007.

[33] Kevin E. Moore, Jayaram Bobba, Michelle J. Moravan, Mark D. Hill, and David A. Wood. LogTM: Log-based Transactional Memory. In *Proceedings of the 12th International Symposium on High-Performance Computer Architecture*, February 2006.

[34] Michelle Moravan, Jayaram Bobba, Kevin Moore, Luke Yen, Mark Hill, Ben Liblit, Michael Swift, and David Wood. Supporting Nested Transactional Memory in LogTM. In *Proceedings of the 12th International Conference on Architectural Support for Programming Languages and Operating Systems*, San Jose, Calif., October 2006.

[35] Eliot Moss and Antony L. Hosking. Nested Transactional Memory: Model and Preliminary Architecture Sketches. In *Proceedings of the Workshop on Synchronization and Concurrency in Object-Oriented Languages*, San Diego, Calif., October 2005.

[36] Yang Ni, Vijay Menon, Ali-Reza Adl-Tabatabai, Antony Hosking, Rick Hudson, Eliot Moss, Bratin Saha, and Tatiana Shpeisman. Open Nesting in Software Transactional Memory. In *Proceedings of the 12th ACM Symposium on Principles and Practice of Parallel Programming*, San Jose, Calif., March 2007.

[37] Ravi Rajwar, Maurice Herlihy, and Konrad Lai. Virtualizing Transactional Memory. In *Proceedings of the 32nd International Symposium on Computer Architecture*, Madison, Wis., June 2005.

[38] Hany Ramadan and Emmett Witchel. The Xfork in the Road to Coordinated Sibling Transactions. In *Proceedings of the 4th ACM SIGPLAN Workshop on Transactional Computing*, Raleigh, N.C., February 2009.

[39] Torvald Riegel, Patrick Marlier, Martin Nowack, Pascal Felber, and Christof Fetzer. Optimizing Hybrid Transactional Memory: The Importance of Nonspeculative Operations. In *Proceedings of the 23rd ACM Symposium on Parallelism in Algorithms and Architectures*, June 2011.

[40] Bratin Saha, Ali-Reza Adl-Tabatabai, Richard L. Hudson, Chi Cao Minh, and Benjamin Hertzberg. McRT-STM: A High Performance Software Transactional Memory System For A Multi-Core Runtime. In *Proceedings of the 11th ACM Symposium on Principles and Practice of Parallel Programming*, New York, N.Y., March 2006.

[41] Michael F. Spear, Maged M. Michael, Michael L. Scott, and Peng Wu. Reducing Memory Ordering Overheads in Software Transactional Memory. In *Proceedings of the 2009 International Symposium on Code Generation and Optimization*, Seattle, Wash., March 2009.

[42] Devesh Tiwari, Sanghoon Lee, James Tuck, and Yan Solihin. MMT: Exploiting Fine-Grained Parallelism in Dynamic Memory Management. In *Proceedings of the 24th International Parallel and Distributed Processing Symposium*, Atlanta, Ga., April 2010.

[43] Haris Volos, Adam Welc, Ali-Reza Adl-Tabatabai, Tatiana Shpeisman, Xinmin Tian, and Ravi Narayanaswamy. NePaLTM: Design and Implementation of Nested Parallelism for Transactional Memory Systems. In *23rd European Conference on Object-Oriented Programming*, Genova, Italy, July 2009.

[44] Adam Welc, Suresh Jagannathan, and Antony Hosking. Safe Futures for Java. In *Proceedings of the 20th ACM Conference on Object-Oriented Programming, Systems, Languages, and Applications*, San Diego, Calif., October 2005.

[45] Craig Zilles and Lee Baugh. Extending Hardware Transactional Memory to Support Non-Busy Waiting and Non-Transactional Actions. In *Proceedings of the 1st ACM SIGPLAN Workshop on Languages, Compilers, and Hardware Support for Transactional Computing*, Ottawa, Ont., Canada, June 2006.

A   Use Case: Memory Allocation

TM makes it easy to express concurrent algorithms that operate on dynamic data structures. However, it is crucial that the allocation and reclamation of memory used to implement the data structure is handled correctly. While data structure microbenchmarks avoid the need to allocate from *within* a transaction by pre-allocating a single node before performing an insertion transaction, and by buffering a single deallocation in a removal transaction until the transaction commits, real code is not afforded this luxury. Once transactions are composed, it becomes impossible to predict the number and size of allocations, or the number of deallocations.

Most STM run-times provide a safe allocator interface [26] in which a transaction suspends when an allocation is requested, the allocator is invoked, and the transaction logs the result so the corresponding memory can be freed if the transaction aborts. These allocators also defer all deallocation until the transaction commits. This approach is not possible for BEHTM for several reasons. A rather trivial point is that the logging operations consume limited resources that should be used to write program data. More significantly, most allocators have some form of synchronization (e.g., locks). If the BEHTM transaction accesses this lock transactionally, it inherits a contention hotspot with all other allocations; if it accesses the lock non-transactionally, it risks aborting before releasing the lock, causing a deadlock. In addition, memory leaks are possible if the transaction aborts after allocating memory but before logging it. Finally, modern allocators [7,31] typically maintain a local heap that, if depleted, must be expanded by invoking the OS. Such an instruction would cause the BEHTM transaction to immediately abort, because context switches are unsupported.[7]

---

[7]This is a context switch in the broader sense: a change of the scope and privilege level of execution–not necessarily a switch to a different user-space application.

Even code that *might* perform such operations is not safe to call, and thus such simple operations as allocating or freeing memory usually require transactions to transition into software mode. Even if these operations were transaction-safe without locks, they would likely introduce aborts due to meta-data contention. A variety of approaches to reducing contention, varying from one-off solutions for allocation [42] and syscalls [11] to general lock-aggregating techniques like flat combining [25], all support the notion that aggregating certain computations on a single thread can effectively reduce latency by replacing meta-data contention and syscall overhead with the cost of a single round-trip communication.

A.1   Delegated Memory Allocation

These constraints on allocation within BEHTM transactions make it an ideal candidate for the delegation mechanism outlined in Section 4. The simplest implementation will begin with BEHTM transaction T sending an allocation request to DT, consisting of an identifier for the `malloc` operation and a size parameter. DT then performs the allocation, registers a corresponding undo action, and returns the obtained pointer through the channel. After making the request, T simply polls for a return value, using non-transactional loads. When T commits, it sends a message to DT indicating that the undo action can be unregistered; when T aborts, it informs DT that the undo action must be performed.

Deallocation can be achieved similarly: T sends a message consisting of an identifier for the `free` operation and the pointer to free. DT then logs the deallocation for replay at commit time, and sends an acknowledgment. T can run in parallel with DT, but cannot re-use the channel until it receives DT's (empty) response.

A.2   Performance Estimate

Delegated memory allocation incurs a communication overhead but prevents the cost associated with abort and restart of the hardware transaction. In addition, reduced synchronization through centralized execution can reduce the latency of the allocation operation.

If we ignore the gains that come from a simpler allocator design, we can estimate the worst-case overhead. First, we consider the raw cost of sending a message via shared memory, when the receiver is actively polling for a message. We conducted an experiment on a quad-core AMD Phenom[TM] II X4 945 Processor, running at 3.0 GHz, to measure round-trip time for communication between two cores. Using a single cache line for transfer and polling, the round-trip time was around 600 CPU cycles. Through careful placement of buffers, prefetching and polite polling, we could reduce the effective round-trip time to 300 cycles. This is in line with results from Baumann et al., where the authors report a round-trip time of 450 cycles for on-die communication for a similar AMD system [6]. The use of shallower cache hierarchies or write-through / inclusive caches could reduce this latency significantly.

This evaluation ignored the possibility that a transaction might wait while DT satisfies other requests. In general, this delay can be ignored: Tiwari et al. showed that under high load, centralized allocators can actually perform better, due to decreased meta-data contention [42]; under low load, the delay is already negligible.

B   Channel/Delegation Pseudocode

Listings 1 and 2 show an implementation of simple send and receive primitives for small and large messages, as discussed in Section 3. If used from within a BEHTM transaction, these functions use ASF non-transactional loads and stores; if used from outside, they use plain, atomic memory accesses.

Delegating the execution of unsafe operations from within a BE-HTM transaction to a service thread DT (Section 4) can be accomplished through the code in Listing 3 – while the corresponding handler in DT is shown in Listing 4. We present only code that handles a single, dedicated `TxChannel` in DT; however, the code remains similar if DT handles multiple `TxChannels`: the blocking receive operation would need to be replaced by a select-style operation, and abort and commit handlers would need to be per-channel. The BEHTM transaction would use the respective SIGNAL functions from Listing 3 when it aborts / commits.

If only a single-word channel were allowed, the mechanism of Listing 2 could suffice, with the REQ and RV messages sent 63 bits at a time (31 bits at a time in 32-bit mode). While this seems onerous, reserving a bit to identify the sender of the previous message in the `TxChannel` is necessary, so that a TS(A) message is not sent by a transaction's abort handler while DT is sending RV. We also note that in existing 64-bit systems, several high bits of pointers are unused. Thus, even with single-word channels, allocation and deallocation could be performed without introducing the need for REQOK/RVOK messages.

Listing 1 Sending and receiving small messages with ASF, using non-transactional accesses and relying on well-formed ping-pong communication.

---
procedure SENDMSGASF(src, dst, type, d[])
   $TxChannel[1\ldots7] \leftarrow d[0\ldots6]$ ▷ store the payload
   $TxChannel[0] \leftarrow (src, type)$
end procedure

procedure RCVMSGASF(src, dst, type, d[])
   repeat
      $(s, type) \leftarrow TxChannel[0]$ ▷ spin
   until $s = src$
   $d[0\ldots6] \leftarrow TxChannel[1\ldots7]$
end procedure

Listing 2 Sending long messages by chunking and acknowledging each chunk.

---
procedure SENDLONGMSGASF(src, dst, type, d[])
   $rem \leftarrow len(d)$
   while $rem > 0$ **do**   ▷ store operands in temporary
      $n \leftarrow max(rem, 7)$
      $tmp[0\ldots(n-1)] \leftarrow d[i\ldots(i+n-1)]$
      $(rem, i) \leftarrow (rem - n, i + n)$
      $sendMsgASF(src, (type, n, rem), tmp))$
      $rcvMsgASF(dst, t, ign)$ ▷ wait for ack
      $assert(t = (type, OK))$
   end while
end procedure

procedure RCVLONGMSGASF(src, dst, type, results[])
   $i \leftarrow 0$
   repeat   ▷ receive message in chunks
      $rcvMsgASF(src, t, d)$
      $(type, n, rem) \leftarrow t$
      $results[i\ldots(i+n-1)] \leftarrow d[0\ldots(n-1)]$
      $sendMsgASF(dst, (type, OK), \varnothing))$ ▷ ack
      $i \leftarrow i + n$
   until $rem = 0$
end procedure

Listing 3 Delegating an operation to DT, using the primitives from either Listing 1 or Listing 2.

---
procedure DELEGATESYNCTODT(id, operands[], res[])
   $sendMsg(TX, DT, REQ, (id, operands))$
   $rcvMsg(DT, TX, type, res)$
   $assert(type = RV)$
end procedure

procedure SIGNALABORTTODT
   $sendMsg(TX, DT, TS, A)$
   $rcvMsg(DT, TX, type, ign)$
   $assert(type = TSOK)$
end procedure

procedure SIGNALCOMMITTODT
   $sendMsg(TX, DT, TS, C)$
   $rcvMsg(DT, TX, type, ign)$
   $assert(type = TSOK)$
end procedure

Listing 4 Handling delegation requests inside DT.

---
procedure HANDLEDELEGATION
   $abortHnd \leftarrow \varnothing$
   $commitHnd \leftarrow \varnothing$
   repeat
      $rcvMsg(TX, DT, t, d)$
      if $t = REQ$ **then**
         $(id, op) \leftarrow d$
         if $abortHandler(id)$ **then**
            $abortHnd \leftarrow$
            $abortHnd \cup (abortHandler(id), op)$
         end if
         if $commitHandler(id)$ **then**
            $commitHnd \leftarrow$
            $commitHnd \cup (commitHandler(id), op)$
         end if
         $res[] \leftarrow handle(id, op)$
         $sendMsg(DT, TX, RV, res)$
      end if
   until $t = TS$
   if $d = C$ **then**
      $executeAll(commitHnd)$
   else if $d = A$ **then**
      $executeAll(abortHnd)$
   end if
   $sendMsg(DT, TX, TSOK, \varnothing)$
end procedure

Design, Verification and Applications of a New Read-Write Lock Algorithm

Jun Shirako
Rice University
6100 Main Street
Houston, Texas 77005
shirako@rice.edu

Nick Vrvilo
Rice University
6100 Main Street
Houston, Texas 77005
nick.vrvilo@rice.edu

Eric G. Mercer
Brigham Young University
3334 TMCB
Provo, Utah 84602
eric.mercer@byu.edu

Vivek Sarkar
Rice University
6100 Main Street
Houston, Texas 77005
vsarkar@rice.edu

ABSTRACT

Coordination and synchronization of parallel tasks is a major source of complexity in parallel programming. These constructs take many forms in practice including directed barrier and point-to-point synchronizations, termination detection of child tasks, and mutual exclusion in accesses to shared resources. A read-write lock is a synchronization primitive that supports mutual exclusion in cases when multiple reader threads are permitted to enter a critical section concurrently (read-lock), but only a single writer thread is permitted in the critical section (write-lock). Although support for reader threads increases ideal parallelism, the read-lock functionality typically requires additional mechanisms, including expensive atomic operations, to handle multiple readers. It is not uncommon to encounter cases in practice where the overhead to support read-lock operations overshadows the benefits of concurrent read accesses, especially for small critical sections.

In this paper, we introduce a new read-write lock algorithm that reduces this overhead compared to past work. The correctness of the algorithm, including deadlock freedom, is established by using the Java Pathfinder model checker. We also show how the read-write lock primitive can be used to support high-level language constructs such as object-level isolation in Habanero-Java (HJ) [6]. Experimental results for a read-write microbenchmark and a concurrent SortedLinkedList benchmark demonstrate that a Java-based implementation of the proposed read-write lock algorithm delivers higher scalability on multiple platforms than existing read-write lock implementations, including ReentrantReadWrite-Lock from the java.util.concurrent library.

Categories and Subject Descriptors

D.1.3 [**Programming Techniques**]: Concurrent Programming—
Parallel programming

Permission to make digital or hard copies of all or part of this work for personal or classroom use is granted without fee provided that copies are not made or distributed for profit or commercial advantage and that copies bear this notice and the full citation on the first page. To copy otherwise, to republish, to post on servers or to redistribute to lists, requires prior specific permission and/or a fee.
SPAA'12, June 25–27, 2012, Pittsburgh, Pennsylvania, USA.
Copyright 2012 ACM 978-1-4503-1213-4/12/06 ...$10.00.

Keywords

Read-write locks, mutual exclusion, model checking.

1. INTRODUCTION

It is widely recognized that computer systems anticipated in the 2020 timeframe will be qualitatively different from current and past computer systems. Specifically, they will be built using homogeneous and heterogeneous many-core processors with 100's of cores per chip, their performance will be driven by parallelism, and constrained by energy and data movement [15]. This trend towards ubiquitous parallelism has forced the need for improved productivity and scalability in parallel programming models. One of the major obstacles to improved productivity in parallel programming is the complexity of coordination and synchronization of parallel tasks. Coordination and synchronization constructs take many forms in practice and can be classified two types, *directed* and *undirected*. Directed synchronization, such as termination detection of child threads and tasks using join, sync [4], and finish [5] operations, collective synchronization using barriers and phasers [16], point-to-point synchronization using semaphores, and data-driven tasks [17] semantically define a "happens-before" execution order among portions of the parallel programs. Directed synchronization is most often used to enable deterministic parallelism. Undirected synchronization, such as operations on locks, actors, and transactional memory systems, is used to establish mutual exclusion in accesses to shared resources with strong or weak *atomicity* guarantees [9, 10]. Undirected synchronization is most often used to enable data-race-free nondeterministic parallelism.

Recent efforts to improve software productivity for atomicity are focused on declarative approaches that let the programmer demarcate blocks of codes to be atomically executed and defer the complexity of maintaining atomicity to the compiler and the runtime system. This approach aims to support higher programmability while delivering performance comparable to well-tuned implementations based on fine-grained locks. On the other hand, primitive fine-grained locks are still in demand for performance-critical software such as commonly used runtime libraries and system software rather than user programs. Further, fine-grained locks are easy to support across a wide range of languages and platforms, while the high-level declarative approaches are limited to specific languages and/or require special hardware support.

A *read-write lock* enforces a special kind of mutual exclusion, in which multiple reader threads are allowed to enter a critical section concurrently (read-lock), but only a single writer thread is permitted in the critical section (write-lock). Although support for reader threads increases ideal parallelism, the read-lock functionality usually requires additional mechanisms, including expensive atomic operations to handle multiple readers. It is not uncommon to find cases where the overhead of supporting read-lock operations overshadows the benefit of concurrent read accesses. As a result, the use of read-write locks can often degrade overall performance relative to standard fine-grained locks, due to the overheads involved.

In this paper, we introduce a new read-write lock algorithm that reduces the overhead of read-write locks compared to existing implementations. In practice, the additional overhead of our read-lock mechanism is equivalent to a pair of atomic increment and decrement operations invoked when a reader thread enters and leaves the critical section. As shown in our experimental results on a 64-thread Sun UltraSPARC T2 system and a 32-core IBM Power7 system, using efficient implementation of atomic increment operations, such as java.util.concurrent.AtomicInteger [13], achieves significant performance improvement over existing read-write lock approaches, including Java's ReentrantReadWriteLock. Although the implementation in this paper is based on atomic integers in Java, the underlying read-write lock algorithm is easily implemented in any language on any platform that includes an atomic compare-and-swap operation.

The correctness of the algorithm, including deadlock freedom, is established by using the Java Pathfinder model checker. We also show how the read-write lock primitive can be used to support high-level language constructs such as object-level isolation in Habanero-Java (HJ) [6]. Experimental results for a read-write micro-benchmark and a concurrent SortedLinkedList benchmark demonstrate that a Java-based implementation of the proposed read-write lock delivers higher scalability on multiple platforms than existing read-write lock implementations, including Java's ReentrantReadWriteLock.

The rest of the paper is organized as follows. Section 2 uses a sorted-list example as motivation for read-write locks by showing how they can be used directly in the example, or indirectly to support HJ's object-level isolation construct. Section 3 describes the details of our new read-write lock algorithm, and Section 4 proves the correctness of the proposed algorithm. Section 5 presents our experimental results, and Section 6 and Section 7 summarize related work and our conclusions.

2. USE OF READ-WRITE LOCKS IN A SORTED LIST ALGORITHM

2.1 Sorted Linked List Example with Explicit Locks

In this section, we use the Sorted Linked List example from [7] as a motivation for read-write locks, since it is representative of linked lists used in many applications. The nodes in the list are sorted in ascending order based on their integer key values (parameter v in Listing 1). There are four list operations: insert, remove, lookup, and sum. It is assumed that no lock is needed for lookup, fine-grained locking suffices for insert and remove, and a coarse-grained lock is needed for sum.

We implement this example by using a single read-write lock (globalRWLock), and multiple standard fine-grained locks (one per node). The assumption is that multiple calls to insert and remove can execute in parallel if they operate on disjoint nodes, but none of those calls can execute in parallel with a call to sum;

also, it is always safe for lookup to execute in parallel with any other operation. The inherent ordering in a linked list structure can be used to avoid deadlock when acquiring fine-grained locks on the nodes.

As shown in Listing 1, insert(v) atomically inserts a new node with value v into the list if no node in the list has value v. The role of globalRWLock is to manage the mutual exclusion rules for insert, remove, and sum operations. Specifically, insert and remove obtain read-locks on globalRWLock, thereby ensuring that they can all execute in parallel with each other. However, sum acquires a write-lock on globalRWLock to ensure that no instance of insert and remove can execute in parallel with it.

Since the new node corresponding to v must be atomically inserted between nodes prev and curr, insert operation obtains the locks corresponding to these nodes (lines 9–10 and 14–15) after obtaining a read-lock on globalRWLock . remove(v) (not shown in Listing 1) has a similar structure to insert, and atomically removes the node with value v if such a node exists in the list. Therefore, remove also obtains locks for the node with value v and its previous node. sum() computes the sum of all the values in the list, after obtaining the write-lock for globalRWLock.

2.2 Sorted Linked List Example with Object-Based Isolation in Habanero-Java

Section 2.1 showed how to implement the functionality required for insert/remove and sum, by using a global read-write lock and local locks for nodes. This two-level locking approach can also be used to enable higher levels of abstraction and safety, as described in this section. We briefly introduce Habanero-Java's *isolated* construct [6, 10] to support mutual exclusion with global and object-based (local) isolation, and show how a read-write lock can be employed to implement this extension.

- **Object-based isolation:** The isolated(⟨*obj-set*⟩) ⟨*stmt*⟩ construct supports mutual exclusion on ⟨*stmt*⟩ with respect to the objects specified in ⟨*obj-set*⟩. Mutual exclusion between two statements ⟨*stmt1*⟩ and ⟨*stmt2*⟩ is guaranteed if and only if ⟨*obj-set1*⟩ and ⟨*obj-set2*⟩ have a non-empty intersection. Further, while *isolated* statements may be nested, an inner *isolated* statement is not permitted to acquire an object that wasn't already acquired by an outer *isolated* statement.

- **Global isolation:** The isolated(*) ⟨*stmt*⟩ construct expands the scope to all objects and support global mutual exclusion on ⟨*stmt*⟩. This is the default semantics for HJ's *isolated* construct if no object set is provided

Unlike Java's *synchronized* construct, this definition of object-based isolation is guaranteed to be implemented with deadlock freedom. Further, no reference in the object set can trigger a NullPointerException as in Java's *synchronized* construct. Finally, Java does not have a *synchronized(*)* statement analogous to isolated(*).

To rewrite the insert method in Listing 1 with object-based isolation, lines 13–15 can be replaced by "isolated(lk1,lk2) {", and lines 22–24 can be replaced by "}". Likewise, the sum method can be rewritten using an isolated(*) construct. These rewrites result in much simpler code since the programmer does not have to worry about deadlock avoidance or null checks on the objects (a null entry is simply an empty contribution to the object set).

The actual implementation of object-based isolation relies on the use of a global read-write lock, as illustrated in Section 2.1. Deadlock avoidance is obtained by using some Comparable field so as to order the objects. Effectively, a program written using object-based isolation will be translated to code that is quite similar to the explicit lock version in Listing 1 .

```
1  public boolean insert(int v) {
2    while (true) {
3      INode curr, prev = null;
4      for (curr = first; curr != null; curr = curr.getNext()) {
5        if (curr.getValue() == v) return false;    // v already exists
6        else if (curr.getValue() > v) break;
7        prev = curr;
8      }
9      OrderedLock lk1 = getLocalLock(prev);        // Get local locks corresponding to nodes
10     OrderedLock lk2 = getLocalLock(curr);
11
12     boolean set = false;
13     globalRWLock.read_lock();                     // Obtain global read lock
14       if (lk1 != null) lk1.lock();                // Obtain local locks for nodes
15       if (lk2 != null) lk2.lock();
16       if (validate(prev, curr)) {
17         INode neo = new INode(v);
18         link(prev, neo, curr);
19         assignLocalLock(neo);                      // Assign a local lock to the new node
20         set = true;
21       }
22       if (lk2 != null) lk2.unlock();               // Release local locks for nodes
23       if (lk1 != null) lk1.unlock();
24     globalRWLock.read_unlock();                    // Release global read lock
25     if (set) return true;
26  } }
27
28  public int sum() {
29    int s = 0;
30    globalRWLock.write_lock();                       // Obtain global write lock
31    for (INode curr = first; curr != null; curr = curr.getNext())
32      s += curr.getValue();
33    globalRWLock.write_unlock();                     // Release global write lock
34    return s;
35  }
```

Listing 1: SortedLinkedList insert and sum methods

3. PROPOSED LOCK APPROACH AND ALGORITHM

This section first introduces an OrderedLock algorithm (Section 3.1) that is based on queue lock approaches such as Ticket Lock [11], Anderson's array-based queue lock [1], and Partitioned Ticket Lock [3]. We then introduce the OrderedReadWriteLock algorithm (Section 3.2), the primary focus of this paper. Although support for reader threads in read-write lock increases ideal parallelism, the read-lock functionality in current implementations typically requires additional mechanisms for managing multiple readers, which often overshadow the benefit of concurrent read accesses. In our approach, we focus on reducing the overhead of read-lock operations in OrderedReadWriteLock, while the overhead of write-lock operation is comparable to that of general queue lock operations such as OrderedLock. As described below, Ordered-Lock and OrderedReadWriteLock do not use atomic operations other than the atomic increment/decrement operation, which can be implemented with a compare-and-swap primitive.

3.1 OrderedLock

Our OrderedLock algorithm consists of two steps: 1) determine the synchronization order among critical sections on a first-come-first-served basis (as in Ticket Locks [11]) and 2) perform a point-to-point synchronization between two sections with continuous orders using arrays as in Anderson's array-based queue lock [1]. Figure 1 shows a sample lock-unlock sequence for four threads operating on a single OrderedLock. The first step needs an atomic increment operation to determine the synchronization order of each

section (1st to 5th in Figure 1), and the second step preserves the order by array-based point-to-point synchronization. This description of the OrderedLock is roughly equivalent to the Partitioned Ticket Lock [3], although we discuss some further performance tuning in Section 5.1.1. Listing 2 summarizes the OrderedLock interface. Note that the lock operation returns the order of the requester in the queue, and the unlock operation uses order. Our expectation is that the interface in Listing 2 will be used by library and language implementers, rather than application programmers who are not expected to see the internal details of the order values.

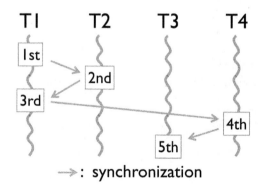

Figure 1: OrderedLock by four threads

```
1  class OrderedLock {
2    int lock();              // Acquire the lock and return order in queue
3    void unlock(int order);  // Use order when performing an unlock operation
4  }
```

Listing 2: Interface of queue lock

3.2 OrderedReadWriteLock

The write lock/unlock operation in OrderedReadWriteLock is equivalent to general lock/unlock, and the read lock/unlock operation consists of the following steps.

- **Read-lock**
  - First reader: Invoke general lock `OrderedLock.lock` to obtain lock
  - Other readers: Wait for the first reader to obtain lock

- **Read-unlock**
  - Last reader: Invoke general unlock `OrderedLock.unlock` to release lock
  - Other readers: No-op

There are several policy decisions on the priority for obtaining lock. In our approach, both a read-lock operation (reader) and a write-lock operation (writer) have the same priority when the write-lock is released (fair reader-writer policy), and once a read-lock is obtained, the subsequent readers can share the read lock regardless of the presence of waiting writers. Figure 2 shows an example for OrderedReadWriteLock by four threads T1, T2, T3, and T4. The writers, for example, W:1st and W:4th by T1, require general mutual exclusion and their own unique synchronization orders, while a synchronization order is assigned to several different readers, such as R:2nd (by T1 and T2), and R:3rd (by T2, T3, and T4). Here R:2nd by T1 is the last reader to releases the lock, and then R:3rd by T4 becomes the next first reader. As shown below, the key function of OrderedReadWriteLock is the management of the unlocking process among concurrent readers, whose efficiency directly affects the overall synchronization performance.

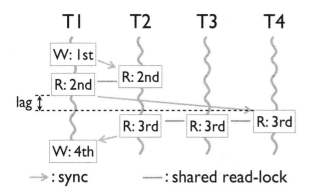

Figure 2: OrderedLock and OrderedReadWriteLock by four threads

Listing 3 describes OrderedReadWriteLock in written Java. Methods `write_lock` and `write_unlock` are equivalent to general `lock` and `unlock` of OrderedLock (lines 9 and 10). At the beginning of methods `read_lock` and `read_unlock`, atomic increment and decrement operations are respectively performed so as to detect the first reader and last reader (lines 13 and 28). For method `read_lock`, the first reader invokes `OrderedLock.lock` to obtain a synchronization order `readOrder`, which is shared by all readers (line 14) and set `readLocked = true` to notify that the order has been obtained (line 15), while non-first readers wait for the first reader to obtain the order (line 22). For method `read_unlock`, the last reader sets `readLocked = false` to notify that the current lock is released (line 32) and invokes `OrderedLock.unlock` to release the lock.

It is possible that `read_lock` is invoked by one thread while another is in the midst of the unlocking process in `read_unlock`. We refer to readers that invoke `read_lock` during an unlocking transition as *rapid readers*. In that case a first rapid reader will be blocked by `OrderedLock.lock` at line 14 as normal. In contrast, non-first rapid readers will reach line 17 and have two scenarios: 1) if flag `transit` is `true` (set at line 29), the rapid reader is blocked at line 19 until the last reader completes the unlocking process, or 2) if flag `transit` is `false`, the rapid reader passes the blocking operations (lines 19 and 22) and enters the critical section. The code at line 31 is to manage rapid readers encountering the second scenario so that the last reader waits for the rapid readers to leave the critical section. Section 4 discusses the correctness of OrderedReadWriteLock. Note that this transition process is a rare occurrence, at least in our benchmarks, and has almost no affect on performance as shown in Section 5.

The OrderedReadWriteLock provides no fairness or progress guarantees. Any number of readers can enter, exit, and re-enter their critical sections under the same lock as long as `numReaders` remains positive, thus enabling an infinite stream of repeated readers to starve a writer.

4. VERIFICATION OF LOCK ALGORITHM WITH MODEL CHECKING

We prove the correctness of our OrderedReadWriteLock implementation in three stages. We start by proving correctness for a four-thread model where each thread performs a single locking operation, assuming sequential consistency. We then prove a lack of data races for the same model, which guarantees sequential consistency. Finally, we show the results obtained from our four-thread model with single operations are sufficient to generalize to any number of threads and locking operations. The underlying OrderedLock is assumed correct throughout the proof due to its simplicity and basis in previous work (see Section 3.1).

For the first stage of our proof we use the Java Pathfinder (JPF) model checker, an automatic verification tool for concurrent Java programs [18]. JPF takes as input the Java program to verify, an environment to provide program input, and correctness conditions in the form of program assertions in the environment or model. JPF then uses state space exploration to enumerate all possible sequentially consistent executions allowed by the program and environment. The result is an exhaustive proof showing the absence of any execution that violates an assertion. JPF employs a partial order reduction to reduce the number of executions it must consider in the

```
 1  class OrderedReadWriteLock {
 2    OrderedLock olock = new OrderedLock();        // General lock
 3    int readOrder = 0;                            // Synchronization order shared by readers
 4    volatile boolean readLocked = false;          // True if first reader obtained lock
 5    AtomicInteger numReaders;                      // # readers at this moment (init by 0)
 6    volatile boolean transit = false;             // True if last reader is releasing lock
 7    AtomicInteger numBlockedInTransit;             // # blocked readers in transition (init by 0)
 8
 9    int write_lock() {  return olock.lock();  }
10    void write_unlock(int myOrder) {  olock.unlock(myOrder);  }
11
12    int read_lock() {
13      if (numReaders.addAndGet(1) == 1) {         // First reader
14        readOrder = olock.lock();                 // Get sync order to be shared by readers
15        readLocked = true;                        // Notify that lock has been obtained
16      } else {
17        if (transit) {                            // Transition of unlocking process (mostly false)
18          numBlockedInTransit.addAndGet(1);
19          while (transit);                        // Wait for last reader to release lock
20          numBlockedInTransit.addAndGet(-1);
21        }
22        while (!readLocked);                      // Wait for first reader to obtain lock
23      }
24      return readOrder;
25    }
26
27    void read_unlock(int myOrder) {
28      if (numReaders.addAndGet(-1) == 0) {        // Last reader
29        transit = true;                           // Start transition of unlocking process
30        if (numReaders.get() > 1)                 // Manage rapid readers (mostly false)
31          while (numBlockedInTransit.get()+1 < numReaders.get());
32        readLocked = false;                       // Notify that lock is released
33        transit = false;                          // End transition of unlocking process
34        olock.unlock(myOrder);                    // Actually release lock
35  } } }
```

Listing 3: OrderedReadWriteLock

proof construction and mitigate state space explosion in the verification [12]. The key aspects of the environment for checking our OrderedReadWriteLock are shown in Listing 4.

Each of the four threads in our model is an instance of EnvThread shown in Listing 4. The library call in the switch on line 9 tells JPF to explore the execution resulting for each value in the inclusive range 0 to 1, allowing our model to cover all possible combinations of readers and writers. We check for correct mutual exclusion using two assertions. Line 13 ensures that the shared-counter value does not change while under a read lock and that the readLocked is always set while a reader is in the critical section. Since readLocked is set immediately after a reader obtains the lock and unset immediately before the last reader releases the lock, this assertion guarantees that the lock is held by a reader, not a writer. Line 22 ensures that the final count reflects the actual number of writes to the shared counter. JPF checks these assertions for all possible thread orderings. Additionally, termination on all execution paths proves freedom from deadlock.

To prove data-race freedom we use Java Racefinder (JRF), a JPF module for detecting data races [8]. It is important to distinguish between a race condition and a data race. A race condition is anytime there are two concurrent accesses to a shared variable. A data race, however, is when those accesses conflict, such as a read and a write, and are not *happens-before ordered* [14]. Happens-before orderings are induced by synchronization primitives, such as atomic read-modify-write operations, access to variables declared volatile, explicit locks, etc. JRF tracks these synchronization primitives to construct the happens-before relation on-the-fly during state space exploration to prove a program is data-race free. For the data-race verification, we use the same model as with JPF, thus proving that there are no data races in the scenario or in the underlying lock. The Java memory model guarantees sequential consistency in the absence of data races [14]; therefore, the assumption in our JPF model of sequentially consistent executions is correct.

LEMMA 4.1. *The OrderedReadWriteLock is free of deadlock, implements mutual exclusion, and is free of data-race for up to four threads with each thread obtaining a lock.*

PROOF. Exhaustive proof via model checking with JPF and JRF using the environment described in Listing 4. The running time for each verification run is under 20 minutes on a standard desktop machine. Full details with all source and test harness files to recreate the proof are available online.[1] For completeness, we also mutated the lock and verified via JPF that the lock fails as expected. □

Lemma 4.1 proves correctness for our four-thread environment. We now prove that the model described in Listing 4 using four threads is sufficient to conclude correct behavior of the lock for any number of threads. We prove this by showing that any thread added in addition to the four used in our model will not result in exploring any interesting new states.

THEOREM 4.2. *The OrderedReadWriteLock is free of deadlock, implements mutual exclusion, and is free of data-race for any number of threads each obtaining any sequence of locks.*

[1] http://www.cs.rice.edu/~nv4/papers/spaa2012/ORWLockTest.tgz

52

```
1  volatile int sharedCounter = 0;
2  AtomicInteger envCounter = new AtomicInteger();
3  OrderedReadWriteLock instance = new OrderedReadWriteLock();
4  private java.util.Random generator = new java.util.Random();
5
6  class EnvThread extends Thread {
7      public void run() {
8          int next, mine;
9          switch(generator.nextInt(2)) {
10             case 0: // Reader thread
11                 next = instance.read_lock();
12                 mine = sharedCounter;
13                 assert(mine == sharedCounter && instance.readLocked);
14                 instance.read_unlock(next); break;
15             case 1: // Writer thread
16                 envCounter.getAndAdd(1);
17                 next = instance.write_lock();
18                 sharedCounter += 1;
19                 instance.write_unlock(next); break;
20 } } }
21
22 assert(sharedCounter == envCounter.get());
```

Listing 4: Generic environment for depth-bounded model check of the OrderedReadWriteLock using JPF.

PROOF. The underlying lock, `olock` in Listing 3, is assumed correct and orders requests to its lock interface accordingly. As such, it is sufficient to prove the case of a single writer with more than three readers because multiple writers are arbitrated by the `olock`, and anything less than four threads is covered by Lemma 4.1. All line numbers refer to Listing 3 in the proof.

Consider the case where the readers do not transfer ownership of `olock`. In such a scenario, either the writer or a single reader holds `olock` (line 9 and line 14). By Lemma 4.1, a single writer with three readers is correct as either the writer or readers will block until the other finishes. If the writer finishes first, then only the last reader enters line 28, does not enter the if-statement on line 30 as it is the last reader, and eventually releases `olock` on line 34. This case is no different than the all-readers case in Lemma 4.1.

Consider now the case where the readers transfer ownership of `olock`. As before, if the writer holds `olock`, then the readers block and the problem reduces to Lemma 4.1 with multiple readers. Let us then assume that the writer is queued up to obtain `olock`, which is currently held by a reader. Let us further assume that one reader takes the true branch on line 28 of Listing 3. We will refer to this thread as $reader_A$. Next, another reader takes the true branch on line 13 of `read_lock`, attempting to reacquire the lock. We will refer to this thread as $reader_B$. A final thread, which we will refer to as $reader_C$, is then forced to take the false branch on line 28 since `numReaders` is greater than 1. In this scenario, additional writer or reader threads do not affect the lock behavior, and the problem reduces to that of Lemma 4.1 with one writer and three readers.

To be specific, having `numReaders` > 1 means that $reader_C$ is now free to take any path through the remainder of the `read_lock` method. Since all remaining conditions in the method depend entirely on the current state of $reader_A$ in `read_unlock` and the state of `olock` (i.e., whether a writer or reader obtains `olock` next), we can conclude by Lemma 4.1 that all remaining control paths through `read_lock` are covered by $reader_C$, and no additional readers or writers are required to elicit new behavior. All additional threads added to the environment will continue to access the lock, read or increment the counters, and pass the assertions in our environment as in the four-thread scenario.

We have shown that we can obtain full coverage of the lock's behavior with the four threads in our counter scenario. Any threads interacting with the lock in excess of four will only duplicate behavior already observed in the four-thread model. Therefore, Theorem 4.2 is true via Lemma 4.1. These properties hold barring integer overflow in the internal lock state and improper client use of the lock. □

5. EXPERIMENTAL RESULTS

In this section, we present experimental results for the proposed OrderedReadWriteLock. All results in this paper were obtained on two platforms. The first platform is a 64-thread (8 cores × 8 threads/core) 1.2 GHz Sun UltraSPARC *T2* system with 32 GB main memory running Solaris 10. We conducted all experiments on this system by using the Java 2 Runtime Environment (build 1.5.0_12-b04) with Java HotSpot Server VM (build 1.5.0_12-b04, mixed mode). The second platform is a 32-core 3.55 GHz IBM *Power7* system with 256 GB main memory running Red Hat Enterprise Linux release 6.1. We used the IBM J9 VM (build 2.4, JRE 1.6.0) for all experiments on this platform. On both platforms, the main Java program was extended with a 10-iteration loop within the same process, and the best result was reported so as to reduce the impact of JIT compilation time and other JVM services in the performance comparisons.

5.1 Summary of implementation

In this section, we briefly summarize our preliminary Java-based implementations of OrderedLock and OrderedReadWriteLock.

5.1.1 OrderedLock

As described in Section 3.1, our general lock implementation is based on Ticket Lock [11] and has the same array-based extension as Partitioned Ticket Lock [3] so as to reduce memory and network contention. Ticket Lock consists of two counters, *request counter* to contain the number of requests to acquire the lock and *release counter* to contain the number of times the lock has been released. A thread requesting a lock is assigned a ticket (the value of the request counter) and waits until the release counter equals its ticket. In the implementation, the request counter must be an atomic vari-

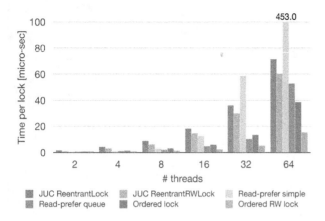

Figure 3: ReadWrite SyncBench (read rate = 90% on T2)

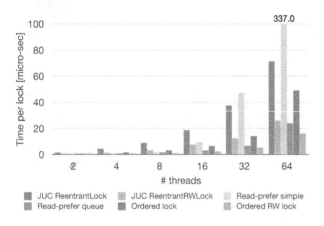

Figure 4: ReadWrite SyncBench (read rate = 99% on T2)

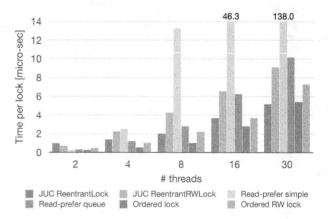

Figure 5: ReadWrite SyncBench (read rate = 90% on Power7)

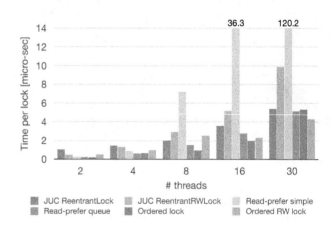

Figure 6: ReadWrite SyncBench (read rate = 99% on Power7)

able so that concurrent threads can get unique tickets, while the release counter can be a non-atomic variable since it is always updated by a thread that is releasing the lock. To avoid the contention on the single global release counter, Partitioned Ticket Lock and OrderedLock employ similar extensions to Anderson's array-based queue lock [1], which replaces the release counter variable by an array with cache line padding so that different threads can access different elements of the array. Appendix A includes a pseudo-code summary of our OrderedLock implementation in Java.

In an attempt to improve the scalability of atomic increments for the request counter, OrderedLock employs the idea of adding a delay to the atomic updating loop if the update fails [1]. By adding a delay, we reduce the contention and bus traffic for the update on the atomic variable. The delay function has various choices in the implementation, such as random, proportional, exponential, and constant. In this paper, we used a random function of the form, `delay * (1.0 + rand.nextDouble())`, where `delay` is a tunable parameter for each platform and `rand` is an instance of java.util.Random that returns a double value between 0 and 1.

5.1.2 OrderedReadWriteLock

The Java implementation for OrderedReadWriteLock was based on the design discussed earlier in Listing 3. We also employ the delay optimization for atomic increment operations discussed in Section 5.1.1.

5.2 Microbenchmark Performance

This section presents synchronization performance using a microbenchmark. We use the JGFSyncBench microbenchmark with the following extension to evaluate read-write lock functionality. Given an arbitrary number of parallel threads, each thread randomly invokes `readWork` with the probability of *reading_rate* or `writeWork`, whose probability is (1 - *reading_rate*). `readWork` and `writeWork` are guarded by read-lock and write-lock, respectively. Figures 3–6 show the synchronization performance (time per operation) on *T2* and *Power7* when *reading_rate* is 90% and 99%. The number of parallel threads ranges from 2 to 64 on *T2* and 2 to 30 on *Power7*. [2] There are six experimental variants:

- **JUC ReentrantLock** is the general lock implementation of java.util.concurrent (JUC).

- **JUC ReentrantRWLock** stands for ReentrantReadWriteLock, which is the read-write lock of JUC.

- **Read-prefer simple** is an implementation of the simple reader-preference lock approach [11]. [3]

---

[2] On *Power7*, two threads are reserved due to the possible system workload.

[3] We selected the read-preference policy because of the benchmarks that contain many read-locks and few write-locks.

Table 1: Rate of transitions over total critical sections executed

	read rate = 90%	read rate = 99%
T2 with 8 threads	7.5×10^{-5}	7.1×10^{-5}
T2 with 64 threads	9.7×10^{-5}	2.3×10^{-5}
Power7 with 8 threads	70.4×10^{-5}	22.6×10^{-5}
Power7 with 32 threads	4.4×10^{-5}	5.9×10^{-5}

- **Read-prefer queue** is an implementation of the scalable reader-preference queue-based lock [11].

- **OrderedLock / OrderedRWLock** is the proposed general / read-write lock approach.

Figure 3 shows the synchronization performance when the *reading_rate* = 90% on *T2*, which demonstrates that OrderedReadWriteLock gives much better efficiency than other lock approaches, by the factor of 4.67× for JUC ReentrantLock, 3.94× for JUC ReentrantReadWriteLock, 29.61× for simple reader-preference lock, 3.46× for scalable reader-preference queue-based lock, and 2.54× for OrderedLock. Figure 4 shows the case where the *reading_rate* is increased to 99% on *T2*. More concurrent reader threads improve the performance of other read-write lock approaches, although OrderedReadWriteLock wins in all experimental variants.

Figures 5 and 6 show the synchronization performance on *Power7* when the *reading_rate* = 90% and 99%, respectively. Due to faster clock frequency on *Power7*, the overlapping work in the readers' critical sections is relatively small compared to *T2*. Therefore, general lock implementations of ReentrantLock and OrderedLock attain better performance than read-write locks when the *reading_rate* = 90%. In the case where the *reading_rate* = 99%, however, OrderedReadWriteLock performs better by a factor of 1.25× than JUC ReentrantLock, 2.29× than JUC ReentrantReadWriteLock, 1.24× than OrderedLock, and 1.19× than scalable reader-preference queue-based lock.

Regarding the overhead due to the unlocking transition process discussed in Section 3.2, we measured the frequency of this process in *T2* and *Power7*. Specifically, we measured the ratio of the total number of last readers delayed by rapid readers (the condition at line 30 in Listing 3 becomes `true`) to the total number of critical sections executed under the lock. As shown in Table 1, the extremely low transition frequency indicates a negligible overhead.

5.3 Application Performance with Read-write Lock

We used SortedLinkedList to demonstrate the two-level lock approach shown in Section 2. We supported the `insert`, `remove` and `sum` operations using the following implementation variants.

- **Reentrant single** uses a JUC ReentrantLock as the single global lock to guarantee mutual exclusion of `insert`, `remove`, and `sum`.

- **Reentrant 2-lv** employs the two-level lock approach using JUC ReentrantReadWriteLock and JUC ReentrantLock.

- **Ordered single** uses a OrderedLock as the single global lock.

- **Ordered 2-lv** employs the two-level lock approach, using OrderedReadWriteLock and JUC ReentrantLock.

- **All ordered 2-lv** employs the two-level lock approach, using OrderedReadWriteLock and OrderedLock.

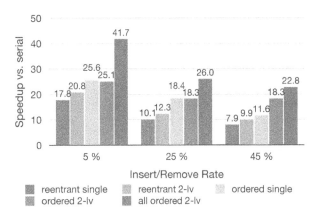

Figure 7: Speedup for SortedLinkedList 64-thread T2

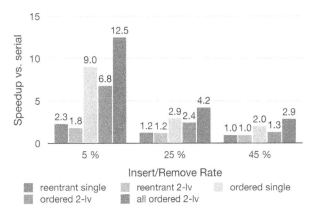

Figure 8: Speedup for SortedLinkedList 32-core Power7

Given an arbitrary number of parallel threads, each thread randomly invokes one of four list operations, `insert(v)`, `remove(v)`, `lookup(v)`, and `sum()`, where the value of `v` is a random number. The range of `v`, which determines the maximum list length, is 0 to 2048. There are 256 local locks to handle all nodes, and therefore up to 8 nodes are mapped into a local lock. We used a simple lock-assignment scheme for linked-list nodes based on a uniform sub-range partitioning of the node values. The probability of `insert` and `remove` is given by *insert_remove_rate*, the probability of `sum` is fixed as 1%, and `lookup` has the remaining possibility of (1 - *insert_remove_rate* × 2 - 0.01).

Figures 7 and 8 show the speedup ratio relative to the sequential execution on *T2* and *Power7*, respectively. The number of parallel threads is 64 on *T2* and 30 on *Power7*. Comparing **reentrant 2-lv** and **ordered 2-lv**, OrderedReadWriteLock performs better than ReentrantReadWriteLock for all cases by a factor of up to 3.78×, even though both implementations employ ReentrantLock as the local lock. Moreover, **all ordered 2-lv** shows that the combination of OrderedReadWriteLock and OrderedLock always performs the best, up to 41.7× speedup on *T2* and 12.5× speedup on *Power7*.

6. RELATED WORK

There is an extensive literature on general and read-write locks approaches. In this section, we focus on a few past contributions that are most closely related to this paper.

The FIFO queue-based lock is a simple and efficient approach to support mutual exclusion. Ticket Lock [11] is a queue-based lock that consists of two counters, one containing the number of requests to acquire the lock and the other the number of times the lock has been released. A thread requesting lock is assigned a ticket (the value of the request counter) and waits until the release counter equals its ticket.

Memory and network contentions can occur when all threads continuously check the same release counter. To reduce this contention and improve scalability, several array-based queue-lock approaches that allow threads to check different locations (different cache lines) have been proposed [1, 3]. List-based queue locks, such as MCS [11] and CLH [2] locks, also support scalable synchronizations in a similar manner and require a smaller space size.

Extending queue-based locks, several read-write lock algorithms with reader-preference, writer-preference, and fair reader-writer policies have been proposed [11]. Although these read-write locks employ efficient local-only spinning implementations, the processes to support read-write lock functionality require lots of atomic operations such as compare_and_store, fetch_and_add, fetch_and_and, fetch_and_or, and fetch_and_store because their algorithms strictly preserve the orders in their FIFO queues.

7. CONCLUSION

In this paper, we introduced a new read-write lock algorithm that supports concurrent reader threads and has lower overhead than existing implementations. The algorithm lowers overhead by tracking reader counts and only allowing the first and last reader threads to interact with the underlying lock that implements mutual exclusion between the readers and writers. The lower overhead is not free, however, as the new algorithm is considerably more complex than other existing algorithms. We demonstrated the correctness of this new algorithm, including deadlock freedom, via the Java Pathfinder model checker. To demonstrate the utility of this new lock, we described how the read-write lock primitive can support high-level language constructs, such as object-level isolation in Habanero-Java (HJ) [6]. We further implemented the proposed read-write lock algorithm as a Java library and demonstrated the efficiency of the approach on two platforms. The experimental results for a read-write microbenchmark show that our algorithm performs $3.94\times$ and $2.29\times$ better than java.util.concurrent.ReentrantReadWriteLock on a 64-thread Sun UltraSPARC T2 system and 32-core IBM POWER7 system, respectively. Performance measurements for a concurrent SortedLinkedList benchmark also demonstrate higher scalability for our algorithm on multiple platforms over the benchmark set. Opportunities for future research include scalability evaluations on a wider range of benchmark programs, support for additional high-level language constructs using the proposed read-write lock (*e.g.*, read/write permission regions), and experimenting with its implementation in non-Java language environments.

8. ACKNOWLEDGMENTS

We are grateful to John Mellor-Crummey and William Scherer at Rice University, and Doug Lea at SUNY Oswego, for their feedback on this work and its relationship to past work on read-write locks. The SortedList example used to obtain the results reported in this paper was derived from an earlier HJ version implemented by Rui Zhang and Jisheng Zhao. We would like to thank Jeff Bascom at Brigham Young University for developing the initial JPF model and generating early verification results, and Jill Delsigne at Rice University for her assistance with proof-reading the final version of this paper.

This work was supported in part by the U.S. National Science Foundation through awards 0926127 and 0964520. We would like to thank Doug Lea for providing access to the UltraSPARC T2 system used to obtain experimental results for this paper. The POWER7 system used to obtain experimental results for this paper was supported in part by NIH award NCRR S10RR02950 and an IBM Shared University Research (SUR) award in partnership with CISCO, Qlogic, and Adaptive Computing.

9. REFERENCES

[1] T. E. Anderson. The performance of spin lock alternatives for shared-memory multiprocessors. In *Proc. IEEE Int'l. Parallel and Distributed Processing Symp. (IPDPS)*, January 1990.

[2] T. Craig. Building FIFO and priority-queueing spin locks from atomic swap. In *Technical Report TR 93-02-02*. University of Washington, Dept. of Computer Science, 1993.

[3] D. Dice. Brief announcement: A partitioned ticket lock. In *SPAA '11: Proceedings of the 23rd annual ACM symposium on parallelism in algorithms and architectures*, New York, NY, USA, 2011. ACM.

[4] M. Frigo, C. E. Leiserson, and K. H. Randall. The implementation of the Cilk-5 multithreaded language. In *PLDI '98: Proceedings of the ACM SIGPLAN 1998 conference on Programming language design and implementation*, pages 212–223, New York, NY, USA, 1998. ACM.

[5] Y. Guo, R. Barik, R. Raman, and V. Sarkar. Work-first and help-first scheduling policies for async-finish task parallelism. In *IPDPS '09: Proceedings of the 2009 IEEE International Symposium on Parallel&Distributed Processing*, pages 1–12, Washington, DC, USA, May 2009. IEEE Computer Society.

[6] Habanero Java (HJ) Project. http://habanero.rice.edu/hj, 2009.

[7] M. Herlihy, V. Luchangco, M. Moir, and W. N. Scherer III. Software transactional memory for dynamic-sized data structures. In *PODC '03: Proceedings of the twenty-second annual symposium on Principles of distributed computing*, pages 92–101, New York, NY, USA, 2003. ACM Press.

[8] K. Kim, T. Yavuz-Kahveci, and B. A. Sanders. Precise data race detection in a relaxed memory model using heuristic-based model checking. In *Proceedings of the 2009 IEEE/ACM International Conference on Automated Software Engineering*, ASE '09, pages 495–499, Washington, DC, USA, 2009. IEEE Computer Society.

[9] J. R. Larus and R. Rajwar. *Transactional Memory*. Morgan & Claypool, 2006.

[10] R. Lublinerman, J. Zhao, Z. Budimlić, S. Chaudhuri, and V. Sarkar. Delegated Isolation. In *OOPSLA '11: Proceedings of the 26th ACM SIGPLAN conference on Object oriented programming, systems, languages, and applications*, 2011.

[11] J. Mellor-Crummey and M. Scott. Algorithms for Scalable Synchronization on Shared Memory Multiprocessors. *ACM Transactions on Computer Systems*, 9(1):21–65, February 1991.

[12] NASA Ames Research Center. JPF developer guide: On-the-fly partial order reduction. http://babelfish.arc.nasa.gov/trac/jpf/wiki/devel/partial _order_reduction, 2009.

[13] T. Peierls, J. Bloch, J. Bowbeer, D. Lea, and D. Holmes. *Java*

Concurrency in Practice. Addison-Wesley Professional, 2006.

[14] W. Pugh. JSR-133: Java memory model and thread specification. http://www.jcp.org/en/jsr/detail?id=133, August 2004.

[15] V. Sarkar, W. Harrod, and A. E. Snavely. Software Challenges in Extreme Scale Systems. January 2010. Special Issue on Advanced Computing: The Roadmap to Exascale.

[16] J. Shirako et al. Phasers: a unified deadlock-free construct for collective and point-to-point synchronization. In *ICS '08: Proceedings of the 22nd annual international conference on Supercomputing*, pages 277–288, New York, NY, USA, 2008. ACM.

[17] S. Taşırlar and V. Sarkar. Data-Driven Tasks and their Implementation. In *ICPP'11: Proceedings of the International Conference on Parallel Processing*, Sep 2011.

[18] W. Visser, K. Havelund, G. Brat, S. Park, and F. Lerda. Model checking programs. *Automated Software Engg.*, 10:203–232, April 2003.

APPENDIX

A. ORDEREDLOCK IMPLEMENTATION

```
1   class OrderedLock {
2     AtomicInteger order =new AtomicInteger(0);
3     // Array size (equal to HW threads)
4     int arraySize = getNumHardwareThreads();
5     VolatileInt[] syncVars = new VolatileInt[
        arraySize];
6
7     int lock() {
8       // Atomic increment
9       int myOrder = order.getAndAdd(1);
10      // Compute corresponding index
11      int idx = Math.abs(myOrder % arraySize);
12      VolatileInt sv = syncVars[idx];
13      // Spin-lock on myOrder
14      while (sv.val != myOrder);
15
16      return myOrder;
17    }
18
19    void unlock(int myOrder) {
20      int next = myOrder + 1;
21      // Compute corresponding index
22      int idx = Math.abs(next % arraySize);
23      VolatileInt sv = syncVars[idx];
24      // Release spin-lock on (myOrder+1)
25      sv.val = next;
26    }
27
28    class VolatileInt {
29      volatile int val;
30      // Avoid false sharing
31      int pad1, pad2, ..., padN;
32    }
33  }
```

Listing 5: OrderedLock

Listing 5 provides pseudo code for our Java-based implementation of OrderedLock. For method `lock`, an atomic increment operation determines the synchronization order `myOrder` (line 9), followed by a point-to-point waiting process on `myOrder` (lines 11–14). The waiting process first computes the index value `idx` to access array `syncVars` based on `myOrder` (line 11) and waits until the `val` field equals `myOrder` (line 14). The value of `myOrder` is returned since it is used for the unlocking process (line 16). Method `unlock` works as a point-to-point signal operation on `myOrder+1` so as to release the spin-lock of the following lock operation (lines 20–25). The signaling process also computes `idx` for `next = myOrder + 1` in the same manner (lines 20–22), and sets `next` to its `val` field (line 25). As shown at line 5, `syncVars` is an array of `VolatileInt` class that contains padding to avoid false sharing (line 31). By selecting a suitable array size for `syncVars` (equal to or larger than the number of hardware threads) we ensure that the hardware threads will concurrently access different elements of `syncVars` without unnecessary cache invalidation (line 4).

A Lock-Free B+tree *

Anastasia Braginsky
Dept. of Computer Science
Technion - Israel Institute of Technology
Haifa 32000, Israel
anastas@cs.technion.ac.il

Erez Petrank
Dept. of Computer Science
Technion - Israel Institute of Technology
Haifa 32000, Israel
erez@cs.technion.ac.il

ABSTRACT

Lock-free data structures provide a progress guarantee and are known for facilitating scalability, avoiding deadlocks and livelocks, and providing guaranteed system responsiveness. In this paper we present a design for a lock-free balanced tree, specifically, a B+tree. The B+tree data structure has an important practical applications, and is used in various storage-system products. As far as we know this is the first design of a lock-free, dynamic, and balanced tree, that employs standard compare-and-swap operations.

Categories and Subject Descriptors

E.1 [**Data**]: Data Structures—*trees, distributed data structures*; D.1.3 [**Software**]: Programming Techniques—*Concurrent Programming*

General Terms

Algorithms, Design, Theory

Keywords

Concurrent Data Structures, Progress Guarantee, Lock-Freedom, B+tree, Parallel Programming

1. INTRODUCTION

The growing popularity of parallel computing is accompanied by an acute need for data structures that execute efficiently and provide guaranteed progress on parallel platforms. Lock-free data structures provide a progress guarantee: if the program threads are run sufficiently long, then at least one of them must make progress. This ensures that the program as a whole progresses and is never blocked. Although lock-free algorithms exist for various data structures,

---

*Supported by THE ISRAEL SCIENCE FOUNDATION (grant No. 283/10).

Permission to make digital or hard copies of all or part of this work for personal or classroom use is granted without fee provided that copies are not made or distributed for profit or commercial advantage and that copies bear this notice and the full citation on the first page. To copy otherwise, to republish, to post on servers or to redistribute to lists, requires prior specific permission and/or a fee.
SPAA'12, June 25–27, 2012, Pittsburgh, Pennsylvania, USA.
Copyright 2012 ACM 978-1-4503-1213-4/12/06 ...$10.00.

lock-free balanced trees have been considered difficult to construct and as far as we know a construction for a lock-free balanced tree is not known.

In recent decades, the B-tree has been the data structure of choice for maintaining searchable, ordered data on disk. Traditional B-trees are effective in large part because they minimize the number of disk blocks accessed during a search. When using a B-tree on the computer memory, a reasonable choice is to keep a node on a single cache line. However, some studies show that a block size that is a (small) factor of the processor's cache line can deliver better performance if cache pre-fetching is employed by the hardware [14, 5]. Further details about the B-Tree structure and the B+tree variant appear in Subsection 2.1.

This paper presents the first lock-free, linearizable, dynamic B+tree implementation supporting searches, insertions, and deletions. It is dynamic in the sense that there is no (static) limit to the number of nodes that can be allocated and put in the tree. The construction employs only reads, writes, and (single-word) CAS instructions. Searches are not delayed by rebalancing operations. The construction employs the lock-free chunk mechanism proposed in [4]. The chunk mechanism provides a lock-free linked list that resides on a consecutive chunk of memory and maintains lower- and upper-bound on the number of elements. The chunks are split or joined with other chunks to maintain the bounds in the presence of insertions and deletions. This lock-free chunk mechanism fits naturally with a node of the B+tree that is split and joined, keeping the number of elements within given bounds, and thus maintaining the balance of the tree.

Our construction follows some basic design decisions that reduce the complexity of the algorithm. First, a node marked by the need to join or split is frozen, and no more operations are allowed on it. It is never resurrected, and one or two nodes are allocated to replace it. This eliminates much of the difficulty with threads waking up after a long idle period and encountering an old node that has been split or joined. In general, a node begins its lifespan as an infant, proceeds to become a normal node, and remains so until frozen for a split or a join, after which it is eventually reclaimed. This monotonic progress, reflected in the node's state, simplifies the design. The replacement of old nodes with new ones is challenging as data may be held in both the old and the new nodes simultaneously. To allow lock-freedom, we let the search operation dive into old nodes as well as new ones. But to ensure linearizability, we only allow new nodes to be modified after the replacement procedure is completed. Additionally, we take special care in the selection of a neighboring node to join with, to ensure that it cooperates correctly. Finally, we enforce the invariant that two join nodes always have the same parent. Our construction follows important lock-free techniques that have been previously used. In particular, we mark pointers to signify deletion following Harris [9], we assign nodes with states similarly to Ellen et al. [7]. We also propose new techniques that might be useful for future work, e.g., we use a gradual state transition for a node by gradually moving it from the *normal* to the *frozen* state, by marking its fields one by one as frozen.

This design of the lock-free B^+tree is meant to show the feasibility of a lock-free balanced tree. It is quite complex and we have not added (even straightforward) optimizations. We implemented the design (as is) in C and ran it against an implementation of a standard lock-based B^+tree [15]. The results show that the lock-based version wins when no contention exists or the contention is very low. However, as contention kicks in, the lock-free B^+tree behaves much better than the lock-based version. The lock-free tree is highly scalable and allows good progress even when many threads are executing concurrently. Similarly to the lock-free algorithm of the linked-list, a wait-free variant of the search method (denoted *contains*) can be defined here in the same manner. Again, to keep it simple, we do not spell it out.

In addition to implementing and measuring the algorithm, we also provide the full proof for the correctness of this design in the full version of this paper [3] with respect to linearizability [11] and (bounded) lock-freedom [10, 13]. Note that a balanced tree has a better worst-case behavior compared to regular trees. Ignoring concurrency, each operation has a worst-case complexity of $O(\log n)$ in contrast to a worst-case complexity of $O(n)$ for an imbalanced tree. Furthermore, in the presence of concurrent threads, we prove that progress must be made at worst-case within $O(T \log n + T^2)$ computational steps, where T is number of the concurrent running threads and n is number of keys in the B^+tree. (This means bounded lock-freedom with bound $O(T \log n + T^2)$.) Such guarantee can only be achieved with balanced trees, as computing a similar bound on the worst-case time to make progress in a non-balanced tree would yield $O(Tn)$[1].

Previous work on lock-free trees include Fraser's construction [8] of a lock-free balanced tree that builds on a transactional memory system. Our work does not require any special underlying system support. Fraser also presents a construction of a lock-free tree that uses multiple-word CAS [8], but this construction offers no balancing and at worst may require a linear complexity for the tree operations. Recently, Ellen *et al.* [7] presented a lock-free tree using a single-word CAS, but their tree offers no balancing. Bender *et al.* [2] described a lock-free implementation of a cache-oblivious B-tree from LL/SC operations. Our construction uses single-word CAS operations. Moreover, a packed-memory cache-oblivious B-tree is not equivalent to the traditional B^+tree data structure. First, it only guarantees amortized time complexity (even with no contention), as the data is kept in an array that needs to be extended occasionally by copying the entire data structure. Second, it does not keep the shallow structure and is thus not suitable for use with file

systems. Finally, a full version of [2] has not yet appeared and some details of lock-free implementation are not specified.

In Section 2 we set up some preliminaries and present the B^+tree representation in the memory together with the basic B^+tree algorithms. In Section 3 we describe the B^+tree node's states and recall the lock-free chunk functionality from [4]. Balancing functions are presented in Section 4, and the implementation and results are described in Section 5. In Section 6 we describe the linearization points. We conclude in Section 7. In the full version of this paper [3] more details and the entire pseudo-code can be found. In addition, the full correctness, linearizability and bounded lock-freedom proof is presented in [3] as well.

2. BACKGROUND AND DATA STRUCTURE

This section presents the underlying data structures used to implement the lock-free B^+tree, starting with a review of the lock-free chunk mechanism presented in [4].

A *chunk* is a (consecutive) block of memory that contains *entries*. Each entry contains a key and a data field, and the entries are stored in the chunk as a key-ordered linked list. A chunk consumes a fixed amount of space and has two parameters, determining the minimum and maximum entries that may reside in it. The chunk supports set operations such as *search*, *insert* and *delete*. When an insert of a new entry increases the number of entries above the maximum, a *split* is executed and two chunks are created from the original chunk. Similarly, when a deletion violates the minimum number of entries, the chunk mechanism *joins* this chunk and another chunk, obtained from the data structure using the chunks (in particular the B^+tree). Therefore, the B^+tree implements a method that the chunk can call to obtain a partner to join with. A different B^+tree method is called by the chunk mechanism when the split or join are completed to ask that the tree replaces the frozen nodes with new ones. The chunk also supports an additional *replace* operation that allows replacing the data of an entry with a new value atomically without modifying the entry's location in the list. This operation is useful for switching a descendant without modifying the key associated with it[2]. All operations are lock-free.

2.1 The B^+tree

A B^+tree [6] is a balanced tree used to maintain a set of *keys*, and a mapping from each key to its associated *data*. Each node of the tree holds entries; each entry has a key and an auxiliary data. In contrast to a B-tree, only the leaves in a B^+tree hold the keys and their associated data. The data of the keys in the internal nodes is used to allow navigating through the tree. Thus, data in an internal node of the tree contains pointers to descendants of the internal node. The B^+tree structure simplifies the tree insertions and deletions and is commonly used for concurrent access. In our variant of a B^+tree, key repetition is not allowed.

Each internal node consists of an ordered list of entries containing keys and their associated pointers. A tree search starts at the root and chooses a descendant according to the values of the keys, the convention being that the entry's key provides the upper bound on the set of keys in its subtree.

---

[1]Actually, we do not know how to show a lock-free bound which is lower than $O(T^2 n)$ for non-balanced concurrent trees.

[2]The replace operation did not appear in the short conference version of [4] and is described in [3].

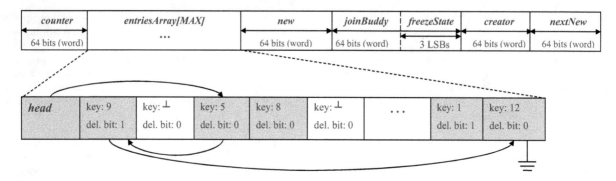

counter	entriesArray[MAX]	new	joinBuddy	freezeState	creator	nextNew
64 bits (word)	...	64 bits (word)	64 bits (word)	3 LSBs	64 bits (word)	64 bits (word)

Figure 1: The structure of a chunk. The allocated grey entries present the ordered linked list.

Each node has a minimum and maximum number of possible entries in it. In our B⁺tree the maximum is assumed to be even and is denoted d. The minimum is set to $d/2 - 3$. For $d \geq 10$ this ensures the balance of the tree, and specifically that the number of nodes to be read before reaching a leaf is bounded by a logarithm of the tree size. All insertions and deletions happen at leaves. When an insert violates the maximum allowed number of entries in the node, a split is performed on that node. When a deletion violates the minimum allowed number of entries, the algorithm attempts to join two nodes, resulting in borrowing entries from a neighboring node or merging the two nodes, if moving entries is not possible.

Splitting and joining leaves may, in turn, imply an insert or a delete to the parent, and such an update may roll up until the root. We ignore the minimum number of entries on the root, in order not to enforce a minimal number of entries in the tree. Note that splits and joins always create nodes with a legitimate number of entries. In practice, the minimum value is sometimes set to be smaller than $d/2 - 3$ to avoid frequent splits and joins.

2.2 The structure of the proposed B⁺tree

For simplicity, our construction assumes the key and the data fit into a single word. This is the assumption of the chunk mechanism and it makes the allocation of a new entry easier. In practice, this means a word of 64 bits, with a key of 32 bits and data of 32 bits.[3] An architecture that provides a double-word compare-and-swap would allow using a full word for each of the fields, removing the restrictions, and simplifying the construction. The key values are taken from a finite set, bounded from above by a value that we denote ∞. The tree is represented by a pointer to the root node, initially set to an empty root-leaf node.

Our B⁺tree node is built using the chunk structure of [4]. The chunk's maximum and minimum number of entries are set to d and $d/2 - 3$ to satisfy the B⁺tree node requirement (except for the zero minimum bound on the root). In addition to a chunk, the tree node contains two additional fields to support its management: a *height* field indicating the dis-

tance from the leaves and a *root* flag indicating whether the node is a root.

We briefly review the fields of a chunk (Figure 1). A detailed discussion appears in [4]. The main part of the chunk is an array that contains the entries. The *counter* field counts the number of entries in a chunk. It is accurate during sequential execution and is always guaranteed to hold a lower bound on the real count, even in the presence of concurrent executions. The pointers *new*, *joinBuddy*, *nextNew* and *creator* point to nodes involved in the rebalancing, to be described below in Section 4. The split and join of a chunk requires a *freeze* of all operations on it, which imposes the *freeze state* of a chunk to be declared using *freezeState* field. The freezing mechanism is explained later, in Section 3.

2.3 Memory Management

To avoid some of the ABA problems, lock-free algorithms typically rely on garbage collection or use the hazard pointer mechanism of Michael [12]. To simplify the current presentation, we assume the existence of garbage collection for the nodes. This means that nodes are never reused unless they become unreachable from all threads. An extension of the same scheme to a use of hazard pointers is possible.[4]

2.4 The Basic B⁺tree Operations

The B⁺tree interface methods: *SearchInBtree()*, *InsertToBtree()*, and *DeleteFromBtree()* are quite simple. The code of the basic B⁺tree operations appear in Algorithm 1. An insert, delete, or search operation first finds the leaf with the relevant key range, after which the appropriate chunk operation is run on the leaf's chunk. It either simply succeeds or a more complicated action of a split or a join begins. Some care is needed when the suitable leaf is a new one (an infant), whose insertion into the B⁺tree is not yet complete. In that case, we must help finish the insertion of the new node before continuing to perform the operation on it. Further explanations on the freezing of a node, on the infant state, etc. appear in Section 3.

Two important methods support the general use of the B⁺tree. The first one is the *FindLeaf()* method that is used for finding a leaf whose associated range of values contains a given key. The second widely used supporting method is *FindParent()*. When a split or a merge occurs, we may need to find the parent of the current node in order to modify its

---

[3]Since a data field cannot hold a full pointer, we assume a translation table, or some base pointer to which the 32-bit address is added to create the real memory address. In the first case, this limits the number of nodes to 2^{32} nodes, and in the second case, it limits the entire tree space to 4GB, which is not a harsh constraint.

[4]In the implementation we measured, we implemented hazard pointers inside the chunk and did not reclaim full nodes at all during the execution.

Algorithm 1 Search, Insert, and Delete – High Level Methods.

(a) Bool SearchInBtree (key, data) {
1: Node* node = FindLeaf(key);
2: **return** SearchInChunk(&(node→chunk), key, data);
}

(b) Bool InsertToBtree (key, data) {
1: Node* node = FindLeaf(key);
2: if (node→freezeState == INFANT)
3:   helpInfant(node);   // Help infant node
4: **return** InsertToChunk(&(node→chunk), key, data);
}

(c) Bool DeleteFromBtree (key, data) {
1: Node* node = FindLeaf(key);
2: if (node→freezeState == INFANT)
3:   helpInfant(node);   // Help infant node
4: **return** DeleteInChunk(&(node→chunk), key);
}

pointers.[5] Furthermore, we may need to find an adjacent node as a partner for a merge, when a node gets too sparse. The *FindLeaf()* and *FindParent()* methods are presented in detail in [3].

3. SPLITS AND JOINS WITH FREEZING

Before it is split or joined, a node's chunk must be frozen. The complete details appear in [4]. The freezing is executed by the chunk mechanism when its size limits are violated. This happens obliviously to the containing data structure, in this case, the B$^+$tree. Here we provide an overview on the chunk's freeze required to understand the B$^+$tree algorithm. To freeze a node, i.e., to freeze the chunk in it, all the chunk's entries are marked *frozen* (one by one) by setting a designated bit in each entry. After all the entries are marked frozen, no changes can occur on this node. A thread that discovers that a node needs to be frozen, or that a freeze has already begun, helps finish freezing the node. However, search operations do not need to help in freeze and can progress on the frozen nodes. Since changes may occur before all entries are marked frozen, the final state of the frozen node may not require a split or a join at the end of the freeze. Still a frozen node is never resurrected. After the freeze has been marked and the node can no longer be modified, a decision is made on whether it should be split, or joined with a neighboring node, or just copied into a single new node. If a join is required, then a neighboring node is found by the B$^+$tree. This communication between the chunk and the B$^+$tree is implemented using a predetermined method *FindJoinSlave()* that the tree supplies and the chunk mechanism uses. Then the neighboring chunk is frozen too. To recover from the node freeze, one or two nodes are allocated, and the live entries in the frozen node (or nodes) are copied into the new node (or nodes). Thereafter, a B$^+$tree method *CallForUpdate()* is called to let the tree replace the frozen nodes with the new ones. We focus in what follows on issues specific to the B$^+$tree, i.e., finding a neighbor, re-

placing the frozen nodes with the new ones in the B$^+$tree, and maybe rolling up more splits or joins.

Each tree node has a *freezeState* field, holding one of eight possible freeze states. Three bits are used to store the state. The freeze state is also a communication link between the B$^+$tree and the chunk mechanism, and so it can be read and updated both by the B$^+$tree and by the chunk. When a new node is created to replace a frozen node, and until it is properly inserted into the B$^+$tree, its freeze state is marked as INFANT. No insertions or deletions are allowed on an infant node until the node's freeze state becomes NORMAL. Any thread that attempts an operation on such a node must first help move this node from the INFANT to the NORMAL state. A node that is properly inserted into the B$^+$tree and can be used with no restrictions has a NORMAL freeze state. When an insert or a delete operation violates the maximum or minimum number of entries, a freeze of that node is initiated and its freeze state becomes FREEZE. After the freezing process stabilizes and the node can no longer be modified, a decision is reached about which action should be taken with this node. This decision is then marked in its freeze state as explained below.

When neither split nor join is required (because concurrent modifications have resulted in a legitimate number of entries), the freeze state of the node becomes COPY, and the node is simply copied into a newly allocated node. By the end of the copy, the parent's pointer into the old node is replaced (using the chunk's replace operation) with the pointer to the new node, and the new node becomes NORMAL. When a split is required, the node's frozen state changes to SPLIT and all its live entries are copied into two new INFANT nodes. These nodes are then inserted into the tree in place of the frozen node, after which they can become NORMAL. A join is more complicated since a neighbor must be found and *enslaved* for the purpose of the join. Since only three bits are required to store the freeze state, we can use the freeze state to also store a pointer to a join buddy and modify the state and the pointer together atomically.[6] The join process starts by looking for a neighbor that can be enslaved for the join and then the freeze state of the join initiator is changed into REQUEST_SLAVE together with a pointer to a potential join buddy in the *joinBuddy* word. Thus, the freeze state is actually modified into a pair ⟨REQUEST_SLAVE, *slave*⟩. At the enslaved node, its state is then modified from NORMAL into the pair ⟨SLAVE_FREEZE, *master*⟩, where *master* is a pointer to the node that initiated the join. (Upon failure, we try to resolve the contention and try again.) When the connection between the join initiator (the master) and the join slave is finalized, the freeze state of the master is modified into ⟨JOIN, *slave*⟩, where *slave* points to the determined join buddy node. The node that is typically chosen for a join is the immediate left sibling of the current node, except for the leftmost node, which chooses its immediate right sibling for the join. A special boundary condition appears when the two leftmost children of a node try to enslave each other. In order to break the symmetry in this case, we take special care to identify this situation and then choose the leftmost sibling among the two to be the slave. Figure 2 presents the state transition diagram for the *freezeState* field.

---

[5]Note that attempting to maintain a list of parent pointers is difficult for a B-Tree as each parent has a large number of children nodes that need to be simultaneously updated when the parent is modified via a split or a merge

[6]An 8-alignment of a node can be assumed in modern systems and the three redundant least-significant bits can hold the freeze state

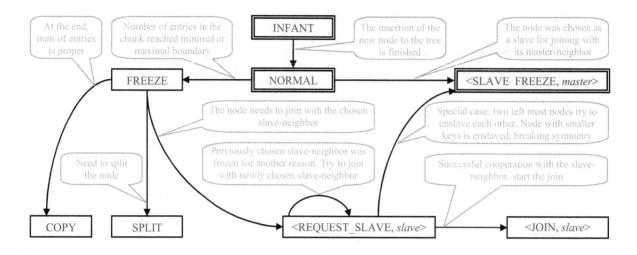

Figure 2: The state transitions of the freeze state of a node. The initial states are presented in the boxes with the double border.

4. BALANCING THE B⁺tree

The basic methods for the tree operations have been discussed in Section 2.4. We now give a description of how to rebalance the tree following a split or a join of a node, and discuss the interface between the chunk mechanism and the tree operations. As explained above, upon violation of the node size constraints, the chunk mechanism freezes the node to prevent it from being modified, and then determines the required rebalancing action (split, join, or copy). In case of a join, the chunk mechanism invokes the B⁺tree method *FindJoinSlave()*, which finds a join buddy. Later, the chunk mechanism creates new node(s) and copies the relevant information into them. When this part is completed, the chunk calls the B⁺tree method *CallForUpdate()*. This method lets the B⁺tree algorithm replace the frozen node (or nodes) with the newly created node(s) in the tree. The *CallForUpdate()* method actually redirects the calls according to whether a split, a copy, or a join occurred. We next examine each of these cases.

But before diving into the details, note that in general, upon creation of a node due to a split, a join, or a copy, the new node's freeze state is initiated to INFANT, its root flag is initiated to FALSE, its height value is copied from the original node's height value, and its counter is initiated to the exact number of entries copied into it. Also, the *creator* field of a new node is initiated to contain a pointer to the old node. the one that initiated the split, join, or copy operation.

4.1 Node Split

After the chunk mechanism executes a split, the original full node N is frozen, and N's *new* field points to the new node N_1 holding the lower half of the keys from the old node N. The field $N_1.nextNew$ points to the second new node N_2 holding the higher half of the keys from the old node N. The two new nodes' freeze states are initiated to INFANT so that no updates can occur on these nodes until they are inserted into the tree. When the chunk split is completed, the *CallForUpdate()* method is invoked and in this case it proceeds by invoking the *InsertSplitNodes()* method, the code of which appear in Algorithm 2.

The *InsertSplitNodes()* method receives a pointer to N

(n in the code), which is the frozen node whose split needs to be completed), and the *sepKey* parameter. The *sepKey* parameter holds the middle key that "separates" the two new nodes. The *sepKey* key and all lower keys have been placed in N_1 ($n1$ in the code), and all keys higher than *sepKey* have been placed in N_2 ($n2$ in the code).

Replacing the split node N starts by searching for its parent P in the tree, using *sepKey* for navigation in the tree. If the parent cannot be found, then the input node is no longer in the tree. This happens if the new node N_1 was properly inserted by some other thread, and the node N was disconnected in the process. In this case, the splitting process proceeds and attempts to insert N_2. Otherwise, and having found the parent, we modify it to point to the new node N_1. This is done by inserting a new entry to P (Line 6). The new entry contains the maximal key from N_1 as key and the pointer to N_1 as data. If the insert fails, it means that someone else has inserted this entry to the chunk and it is fine to continue. Therefore, we do not check if the insert succeeded. Note the possibility that the parent's chunk insert will create a split in the parent, which will recursively cause a split and roll it up the tree.

After the first new node is in place, we replace the pointer in the parent node, which points to the frozen node N, with the pointer to the second new node N_2 (Line 9). Again, this can only fail if another thread has done this earlier. The *ReplaceInChunk()* method finds the entry with key and data as in its third argument and replaces it with key and data as in its last argument. (The *combine()* method syntactically combines the key and the data values into a single word.) In order to invoke *ReplaceInChunk()* on the correct parent, we search for the parent (in the tree) of the split node, using the maximal key of that node for navigating in the tree. The second parent search may yield a different parent if the original parent was concurrently split or joined. After making the parent point to the two new nodes, it remains to set their state to NORMAL and return. The splitting process is complete.

If the original node N was determined to be the root, then a new root R with two new children N_1 and N_2 is created. Next, the B⁺tree's root pointer is swapped from pointing

Algorithm 2 The split of a non-root node

```
void InsertSplitNodes (Node* n, sepKey) {                        // sepKey is the highest key in the low-values new node
 1: Entry* nodeEnt;                                    // Pointer to the parent's entry pointing to the node about to be split
 2: Node* n1 = n→new;                                          // Pointer to the new node that holds the lower keys
 3: Node* n2 = n→new→nextNew;                                   // Pointer to the new node that holds the higher keys
 4: maxKey = getMaxKey(n);                                        // Get maximal key on the given frozen node
 5: if ((parent = FindParent(sepKey, n, &nodeEnt, NULL)) != NULL) {
 6:    InsertToChunk(parent→chunk, sepKey, n1);              // Can only fail if someone else completes it before we do
 7: }
 8: if ((parent = FindParent(maxKey, n, &nodeEnt, NULL)) != NULL) {
 9:    ReplaceInChunk(parent→chunk, nodeEnt→key,            // Can only fail if someone else completes it before we do
10:               combine(nodeEnt→key, n), combine(nodeEnt→key, n2));
11: }
12: CAS(&(n1→⟨freezeState, joinBuddy⟩), ⟨INFANT, NULL⟩, ⟨NORMAL, NULL⟩);     // Update the states of the new nodes
13: CAS(&(n2→⟨freezeState, joinBuddy⟩), ⟨INFANT, NULL⟩, ⟨NORMAL, NULL⟩);          // from INFANT to NORMAL
14: return;
}
```

Algorithm 3 The code of finding a node partner for a join in the lock-free B⁺tree.

```
Node* FindJoinSlave(Node* master) {
 1: Node* oldSlave = NULL;
 2: start: anyKey = master→chunk→head→next→key;                          // Obtain an arbitrary master key
 3: if ( (parent = FindParent(anyKey, master, &masterEnt, &slaveEnt)) == NULL) {   // If master is not in the B⁺tree;
 4:    return master→⟨*, joinBuddy⟩;                       // thus its slave was found and is written in the joinBuddy
 5: }
 6: slave=slaveEnt→data;                                             // Slave candidate found in the tree
 7: // Set master's freeze state to ⟨REQUEST_SLAVE, slave⟩; oldSlave is not NULL if the code is repeated
 8: if ( oldSlave == NULL ) expState = ⟨FREEZE, NULL⟩; else expState = ⟨REQUEST_SLAVE, oldSlave⟩;
 9: if ( !CAS(&(master→⟨freezeState, joinBuddy⟩), expState, ⟨REQUEST_SLAVE, slave⟩) ) {
10:    // Master's freeze state can be only REQUEST_SLAVE, JOIN or SLAVE_FREEZE if the roles were swapped
11:    if ( master→⟨freezeState,*⟩ == ⟨JOIN,*⟩ ) return master→⟨*, joinBuddy⟩;
12: }
13: slave = master→⟨*, joinBuddy⟩;                           // Current slave is the one pointed by joinBuddy
14: // Check that parent is not in a frozen state and help frozen parent if needed
15: if ( (parent→⟨freezeState,*⟩ != ⟨NORMAL,*⟩) && (oldSlave == NULL) ) {
16:    Freeze(parent, 0, 0, master, NONE, &result); oldSlave = slave; goto start;
17: }
18: // Set slave's freeze state from ⟨NORMAL, NULL⟩ to ⟨SLAVE_FREEZE, master⟩
19: if ( !SetSlave(master, slave, anyKey, slave→chunk→head→next→key) ) {oldSlave = slave; goto start;}
20: CAS(&(master→⟨freezeState, joinBuddy⟩),⟨REQUEST_SLAVE, slave⟩,⟨JOIN, slave⟩);     // We got the slave, update the master
21: if (master→⟨freezeState,*⟩ == ⟨JOIN,*⟩) return slave; else return NULL;
}
```

to N to point to R. The details of the root's split code are relegated to [3].

4.2 Nodes Join

Establishing the master-slave relationship: We assume that the join is initiated by a sparse node N, denoted *master*. The chunk mechanism has frozen the node N and it has determined that this node has too few entries. To complete the join, the chunk lets the B⁺tree find the *slave*. The B⁺tree establishes a master-slave relationship and later the chunk mechanism joins the entries of both nodes. The B⁺tree's *FindJoinSlave()* method is responsible for establishing the master-slave relationship and returning the slave for the given master. Its code is presented in Algorithm 3. The establishment of the master-slave relationship is described below.

The *FindJoinSlave()* method starts by calling the *Find-Parent()* method, which returns a pointer to the master's parent node together with the pointers to the master's and its potential slave's entries. The parent node search fails only if the node N has already been deleted from the tree,

in which case a slave has already been determined and can be retrieved from the *joinBuddy* field of N (Line 4). Otherwise, the parent and a potential slave node M were returned by *FindParent()*. The left-side neighbor is returned for all nodes except the left-most node, for which a right-side neighbor is returned. In order to establish the relationship we first change N's freeze state from ⟨FREEZE, NULL⟩ to ⟨REQUEST_SLAVE, M⟩. (Recall that the *joinBuddy* field and the freeze state field are located in a single word.) If this is not the first try, the field may hold a previous slave pointer (*oldSlave*) that we could not enslave. In this case, we change the value of N's freeze state from ⟨REQUEST_SLAVE, *oldSlave*⟩ to ⟨REQUEST_SLAVE, M⟩, where M is the new potential slave. The CAS operation in Line 9 may fail if N's freeze state has already been promoted to JOIN or it has become SLAVE_FREEZE due to swapping of master-slave roles as explained below. In these cases N's final slave was already set in the *joinBuddy* field of N. The CAS operation in Line 9 may also fail if another slave was already chosen due to delay of this CAS operation. In this case, we just use that slave (Line 13).

Algorithm 4 Setting the slave's freeze state for a join in the lock-free B$^+$tree.

```
Bool SetSlave(Node* master, Node* slave, masterKey, slaveKey) {
 1:  // Set slave's freeze state from ⟨NORMAL, NULL⟩ to ⟨SLAVE_FREEZE, master⟩
 2:  while (!CAS(&(slave→⟨freezeState,joinBuddy⟩),⟨NORMAL,NULL⟩,⟨SLAVE_FREEZE,master⟩))){
 3:      // Help slave, different helps for frozen slave and infant slave
 4:      if (slave→⟨freezeState, *⟩ == ⟨INFANT, *⟩) { helpInfant(slave); return FALSE; }
 5:      elseif (slave→⟨freezeState, *⟩ == ⟨SLAVE_FREEZE,master⟩) break;            // Completed by someone else
 6:      else {                                  // The slave is under some kind of freeze, help and look for new slave
 7:          // Check for a special case: two leftmost nodes try to enslave each other, break the symmetry
 8:          if ( slave→⟨freezeState, *⟩ == ⟨REQUEST_SLAVE, master⟩ ) {
 9:              if (masterKey < slaveKey) {         // Executing master node is left sibling and should become a slave
10:                  if ( (master→⟨freezeState,joinBuddy⟩ == ⟨SLAVE_FREEZE,slave⟩) || CAS(&(master→⟨freezeState,joinBuddy⟩),
11:                      ⟨REQUEST_SLAVE,slave⟩, ⟨SLAVE_FREEZE,slave⟩) ) return TRUE; else return FALSE;
12:              else                            // Current master node is right sibling and the other node should become a slave
13:                  if ( (slave→⟨freezeState,joinBuddy⟩ == ⟨SLAVE_FREEZE,master⟩) || CAS( &(slave→⟨freezeState,joinBuddy⟩),
14:                      ⟨REQUEST_SLAVE,master⟩, ⟨SLAVE_FREEZE,master⟩) ) return TRUE; else return FALSE;
15:          } // end case of two leftmost nodes trying to enslave each other
16:          Freeze(slave, 0, 0, master, ENSLAVE, &result);                    // Help an unrelated freeze activity
17:          return FALSE;
18:      } // end of investigating the enslaving failure
19:  } // end of while
20:  MarkChunkFrozen(slave→chunk); StabilizeChunk(slave→chunk);        // Slave enslaved successfully. Freeze the slave
21:  return TRUE;
}
```

Lines 15 and 16 are important for keeping the master and the slave descendants of the same parent This is further discussed in Subsection 4.3.

After finding a potential slave, we attempt to set its freeze state to ⟨SLAVE_FREEZE, N⟩ and freeze it. This is done in the *SetSlave()* method presented in Algorithm 4 and explained in the next paragraph. If this action is not successful, the *FindJoinSlave()* method is restarted from scratch. After succeeding in setting the slave's freeze state, we change the master's state from ⟨REQUEST_SLAVE, M⟩, to ⟨JOIN, M⟩ to enable the actual join attempts.

The *SetSlave()* method attempts to CAS the freeze state of the slave M from ⟨NORMAL, NULL⟩ to ⟨SLAVE_FREEZE, N⟩. If the CAS of the freeze state in the slave is successful, we may proceed with the join. But M's freeze state isn't necessarily NORMAL: if it is not, then M is either still an infant or it is already frozen for some other reason. In the first case, *SetSlave()* helps M to become NORMAL and retries to set M's freeze state. In the second case, it helps to complete M's freeze. After finishing the freeze on M, M is frozen and is not suitable to serve as a slave. Therefore, failure is returned by *SetSlave()* and another slave must be found. A special case occurs when the potential slave M has a master freeze-state as well and is concurrently attempting to enslave N for a join. This case can only happen with the two leftmost nodes and, if special care is not taken, an infinite run may result, in which each of the two nodes repeatedly tries to enslave the other. In order to break the symmetry, we check explicitly for this case, and let the leftmost node among the two give up and become the slave, with a SLAVE_FREEZE state and a pointer to its master (which was originally meant to be enslaved for it). The *FindJoinSlave()* checks for this case in its last line. If it is successful in turning the freeze state of the master into JOIN, then all is well. Otherwise, and given that *SetSlave()* completed successfully, then it must be the case that the master has become a slave. In this case, no slave is returned, and the returned NULL value tells the calling method (in the chunk mechanism) to treat the master as the slave.

Finally, the *SetSlave()* completes by freezing the slave in Line 20, so that the join can continue. Two methods of the chunking mechanism are used. The method *MarkChunkFrozen()* marks all entries of a node frozen by setting a designated bit in each entry. After the entries are marked frozen, the *StabilizeChunk()* method ensures that no changes occur on this node. At this point the slave has been enslaved and frozen.

Merge: If the number of entries on the master and the slave is less than d, the chunk mechanism creates a new single chunk to replace the master and the slave. It then invokes the *CallForUpdate()* method to insert the new node into the tree. We denote this operation as *merge*. In this situation, the *CallForUpdate()* method invokes *InsertMergeNode()* whose code is presented in Algorithm 5. At this point, a master-slave relationship has already been established, both M and N have been frozen, and a new node N_1 has been created with the keys of both M and N merged.

The *InsertMergeNode()* method's input parameter is a pointer to the master, this master's slave can be found in the *joinBuddy* field on the master. The *InsertMergeNode()* method starts by checking which of the original nodes (master and slave) has higher keys. Denote this node by *highNode*. Note that the master and the slave are frozen and thus immutable. Next, *FindParent()* is invoked on *highNode*. If the parent is not found, then *highNode* has already been deleted and we can proceed with handling the old node with the lower keys, *lowNode*. Otherwise, we modify the parent's reference to *highNode*, to point to the new node (Line 9). Next, we handle the pointer to *lowNode* at the parent by attempting to delete it. Finally, we turn the new node's freeze status from *infant* to *normal*.

Special care is given to the root. We must avoid a root with a single descendant, which can occur when the two descendants of a root are merged. In this case, we make the merged node become the new root. If merged node parent is found to be root, the *MergeRoot()* method is invoked from *InsertMergeNode()* instead of deleting the pointer to *lowNode* at the parent. This is so, because deleting an entry

Algorithm 5 The merge of two old nodes to one new node

```
void InsertMergeNode (Node* master) {
 1: Node* new = master→new;                                                      // Pointer to the new node.
 2: Node* slave = master→⟨*, joinBuddy⟩;
 3: maxMasterKey = getMaxKey(master); maxSlaveKey = getMaxKey(slave);                // Both nodes are frozen
 4: if ( maxSlaveKey < maxMasterKey ) {                        // Find low and high keys among master and slave
 5:    highKey = maxMasterKey; highNode = master; lowKey = maxSlaveKey; lowNode = slave;
 6: } else { highKey = maxSlaveKey; highNode = slave; lowKey = maxMasterKey; lowNode = master; }

 7: if ((parent = FindParent(highKey, highNode, &highEnt, NULL)) != NULL) {
 8:    highEntKey = highEnt→key;                                      // Change the highest key entry to point on new node
 9:    ReplaceInChunk(parent→chunk, highEntKey,                // If replacing fails, the parent chunk was updated by a helper
10:               combine(highEntKey, highNode), combine(highEntKey, new));            // continue anyway
11: } // If high node cannot be found continue to the low
12: if ((parent = FindParent(lowKey, lowNode, &lowEnt, NULL)) != NULL) {
13:    if (parent→root) MergeRoot(parent, new, lowNode, lowEnt→key);
14:    else DeleteInChunk(&(parent→chunk), lowEnt→key, lowNode);              // lowNode is the expected data
15: } // If also low node can no longer be found on the tree, then the merge was completed (by someone else).
16: CAS(&(new→⟨freezeState, joinBuddy⟩), ⟨INFANT, NULL⟩, ⟨NORMAL, NULL⟩); // Update the new node state from INFANT to NORMAL
17: return;
}
```

from the root may lead to having a single root descendant. (The *MergeRoot()* method is presented in [3].)

Borrow: If the keys of two join nodes cannot fit a single node, they are copied into two new nodes. This operation is called *borrow*. Due to lack of space, the details of the borrow operation are omitted here and can be found in the full version of this paper [3]. In a nutshell, the borrow case has four nodes involved: the master N, the slave M, the new node with the lower keys N_1 and the new node with the higher keys N_2. As in merge case, we start by finding the high and low keys' nodes, N_{high} and N_{low}, among the master and the slave. We then take the following steps: (1) Insert a reference to N_1 to the parent node (with the maximal key on the N_1 as the key); (2) Change the parent entry pointing to N_{high} to point to N_2; (3) Delete the parent entry pointing to N_{low}.

4.3 Two Invariants

Let us mention a couple of invariants that our algorithm maintains. These invariants may give some intuition on how the algorithm works and why it is correct.

Keys duplication. During the rebalancing operations described above, it sometimes happens that (for a short while) two duplicates of a key may become reachable from the root. However, at no point in the execution will a key be absent. For example, after the first new node is inserted to the parent as part of the split, there are keys that reside simultaneously in two different nodes: all keys in this first new node are also still available in the old split node, which is still in the tree. Similarly, as part of the merge, when an old frozen node with higher keys is replaced with the new node, there are keys that appear twice: all keys in the old frozen node with lower keys now also appear in the new node. Recall that a search in the B$^+$tree is allowed to navigate the tree and return the result, based on the data found on the frozen node.

This does not foil searches in the tree. When a key has duplicates available in two different reachable tree nodes the two nodes are immutable. One of these nodes must be frozen and the other must be an infant. Therefore, old searches may safely access keys in the old frozen node(s), and new searches

can access the new infant node(s). None of these nodes can be modified until the rebalance operation terminates.

We should also note that the tree doesn't grow too big because of duplication. Another invariant is that there can only be two copies of a key in the tree. Thus, even though we may increase the size of the tree during the rebalancing operations, the increase will be at most by a factor of two. The factor-two increase is theoretical. In practice, the increase in the tree size is negligible.

Master-slave bond. We take special care to guarantee that the master and the slave keep the same parent up to the end of their join. Initially, the master and the slave are siblings and children of the same node P. However, the parent node P may then be split and the master and slave may then have different parent nodes. This may subsequently lead to an inconsistent tree in which a key does not represent the highest key in its subtree. Therefore, we enforce an invariant that the master and slave nodes must remain on the same parent. Namely, we do not allow the parent entries that point to a master and to its slave to be separated into different nodes due to a parent's split or borrow, until new nodes replace the frozen master and slave. Ensuring this variant is taken care of both during the parent split as well as during the children join. On the split side, we check whether the break point between the keys has two descendants that form a master and a slave. In case they do, we enforce placement of both on the same new node. However, the descendants may get into a master-slave relationship only after we make this check at the parent node. Therefore, on the merge side, i.e., the descendants' side, after declaring the intent of a master to enslave its neighbor (setting the master's state to REQUEST_SLAVE), we check that the master's parent is not in a frozen state. If it is, the descendant master helps the parent recover before continuing the descendants' join (Lines 15, 16). This ensures that the parent split (and borrow, in a similar way) does not occur obliviously and concurrently with its descendants' join. More about correctness and progress guarantees can be found in [3].

4.4 Extensions to the Chunk Mechanism

The chunk interface requires some minor modifications over [4] to properly serve the B$^+$tree construction in this paper. Probably the most crucial modification arises from the need to deal with an ABA problem that arises during insertions and deletions of entries to the chunk of an internal node in the tree. The concern is that an insert or a delete may succeed twice due to a helper thread that remains idle for a while. Consider, for example, a merge and a subsequent delete of an entry at the parent node. Suppose that one thread executes the delete, but a second thread attempts this delete later, after the same key (with a different descendant) has been entered to the parent again. Thus, a delete should only succeed when the entry still points to the frozen node. As for inserts, we need to avoid reentering a pointer to a child node that has actually been frozen and deleted while the updating thread was stalled. To solve such problems, we add versioning to the *nextEntry* word in the chunk's linked-list. This eliminates the ABA problem, as a delayed CAS will fail and make us recheck the node that we attempt to insert or delete and discover that it has already been frozen. All extensions to the chunk mechanism are described in [3].

5. IMPLEMENTATION AND RESULTS

We have implemented the lock-free B$^+$tree presented in this paper as well as the lock-based B$^+$tree of [15] in the C programming language. The lock-free design in this paper can be optimized in many ways. However, we have implemented it as is with no further optimizations. The operations of the lock-based B$^+$tree progress in a top-down direction. During the descent through the tree, *lock-coupling* [1] is employed, i.e., a child is locked before its parent is unlocked. Exclusive locks on the nodes are used for insert and delete operations, and shared locks are used for search operations. Deadlock-freedom is guaranteed by a proactive approach to rebalancing that splits full nodes or joins sparse ones, while going down the path to the leaves.

We ran the experiments on the SUN FIRE machine with an UltraSPARC T1 8-core processor, each core running 4 hyper-threads, running Solaris 10. Overall, the eight cores, with quad hyper-threading simulates the concurrent execution of 32 threads. In both implementations the size of a B$^+$tree node was set to the machine's virtual page size, i.e., 8KB. In each test we start with a tree with N random keys in the range $[0, 2^{18}]$ already inserted to it, and during the test, we apply N operations on it. If the test runs T threads, then each executes N/T operations. The parameter N was varied among 10^4, 10^5 and 10^6. The operations consisted of insertions, deletions and searches in parallel, out of which 20% were insertions, 20% were deletions, and the remaining 60% were searches. All the threads start simultaneously at the beginning and we measure the time it takes to complete all operations by all threads.

The right graph of Figure 3 depicts the ratio between the time it took to complete the runs on the lock-free implementation as compared to the lock-based implementation. A result higher than 1 means that the lock-free implementation is slower. Clearly, the lock-free implementation outperforms the lock-based implementation when contention is not low. Note that contention increases as the tree gets smaller and as the number of threads increases. Also, the results show that the average cost of an operation increases as the tree gets larger, because rebalancing may ascend to higher levels. Such costs are heavier for the lock-free tree, but this overhead is offset by lock-freedom efficiency when contention kicks in. The right graph of Figure 3 depicts the speedup, which clearly shows that the lock-free algorithm is more scalable.

The weaker performance of the lock-free tree for low contention can be ameliorated by simple optimizations. For example, during the split, each thread helping the split copies the entries from the old node to a newly created private node and only one of these new nodes eventually replaces the old node and joins the tree. While threads can cooperate to perform copying, we decided to avoid it in this version because it complicates the design.

6. LINEARIZATION POINTS

When designing a concurrent data structure, it is important to spell out the linearization points for the different operations. This is done in this section. The B$^+$tree methods all have a similar pattern of operation: they traverse the B$^+$tree to find the relevant leaf node, and then call the appropriate chunking methods on the leaf's chunk. Thus the linearization points of the B$^+$tree are typically based on the linearization points defined for the chunk in [4].

Search linearization point: The linearization point of the search operation is exactly the linearization point of the leaf's chunk search, as in [4]. In particular, if the leaf is not frozen, then the linearization point follows that of the underlying linked-list in the leaf's chunk, and if the leaf is frozen then the linearization point is set to be the point in which the chunk became frozen. As the freezing mechanism is not instantaneous, we need to define a point in the freezing process more accurately for the linearization point. We follow [4] and set the linearization point to be the point in the freeze process by which all the frozen bits have been set and also the internal list of the freezing node has been stabilized. Define this point as the *freezing point*. The freezing process of a chunk is explained more thoroughly in [4]. Formally, consider the linearization point of the search of the linked-list that is inside the chunk of the leaf (as defined by Harris [9]). If the chunk's linked-list search linearization point occurs before the freezing point, then that is also the linearization point of the overall tree search. If the chunk's linked-list linearization point happens after the freezing point, then we define the overall tree search linearization point to be the later point between the freezing point and the point in which the search started. The latter maximum makes sure that the linearization point happens during the execution of the search.

Justifying this choice for non-frozen node is straightforward. As for frozen nodes, we note that the frozen node may be replaced with a new node during the search execution and various actions may be applied on the new node. But at the freezing point, we know that the values of the frozen node exist only in the frozen node and are properly represented by the view of the frozen node.

The delicate case is when the search starts after the freezing point and still gets to the frozen leaf and completes the search there. In this case, since the search ends up in this leaf, we know that a new node that replaces this leaf (following the end of the freeze) has not yet been modified while the search traversed the tree, because the rebalancing operation has not yet terminated at that point. Therefore the new node has definitely not been modified when the search started, and the frozen values represent correctly the state of the tree at that point in time.

Insert and delete linearization points: Unlike the

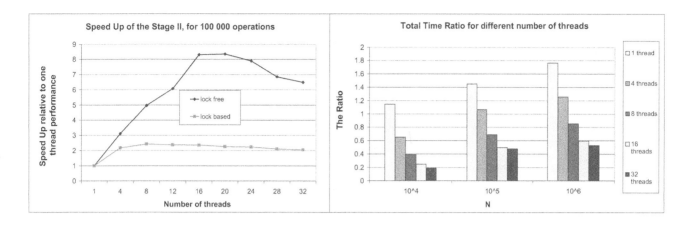

Figure 3: The empirical results.

analysis of the search operation, frozen nodes are not hazardous for the insert's and delete's initial tree traversing. If an insert or delete arrive at a frozen leaf, than the *Insert-ToChunk()* or the *DeleteInChunk()* methods will redirect the operation (after helping the frozen node) to a non-frozen leaf node. Intuitively, the insert operation is assumed to be finished when a leaf including the new key is reachable from the root via data pointers. Similarly, the delete operation is assumed to be finished when a leaf excluding an old key is reachable from the root via data pointers. In a worst-case, this may require more than just handling a freeze.

There are three cases possible here. First, if the insert or delete operation doesn't cause a rebalancing activity (split, merge, borrow, or copy), than the linearization point is simply determined to be the leaf's chunk linearization point. Second, if a rebalancing (by freezing) occurs and if the thread performing the insert or delete operation has its operation executed in the node that replaces the frozen node, then the linearization point of the operation becomes the linearization point of the insert operation of the new node to the parent of the frozen node (replacing the frozen node with the new one). Note that this definition may be recursive if the parent requires rebalancing for the insertion. The third case is when the result of this operation is not reflected in the node that replaces the frozen one. In this case, we again define the linearization point recursively, setting it to be the linearization point of the re-attempted operation on the new node that replaced the frozen one.

7. CONCLUSIONS

We presented a lock-free dynamic B^+tree, which builds on CAS synchronization. The construction is composed of a chunk mechanism that provides the low-level node implementation, including splitting and joining a node, and then a higher level mechanism which handles the operations at the tree level. The two mechanisms and their interface are lock-free. To the best of our knowledge, this is the first design of a lock-free balanced search tree for a general platform. Results indicate better handling of contention and higher scalability when compared to the lock-based version of the B^+tree. We have also proven the correctness (with respect to linearizability) of the algorithm and its lock-freedom property.

8. REFERENCES

[1] R. Bayer and M. Schkolnick. Concurrency of operations on b-trees. *Acta Informatica*, 9, 1977.
[2] M. A. Bender, J. T. Fineman, S. Gilbert, and B. C. Kuszmaul. Concurrent cache-oblivious b-tree. *SPAA*, 2005.
[3] A. Braginsky and E. Petrank. Lock-free B+tree (full version). http://www.cs.technion.ac.il/ erez/Papers/lfbtree-full.pdf.
[4] A. Braginsky and E. Petrank. Lock-free linked lists with improved locality. *ICDCN*, 2011.
[5] S. Chen, P. B. Gibbons, T. C. Mowry, and G. Valentin. Fractal prefetching b+-trees: Optimizing both cache and disk performance. *SIGMOD*, 2002.
[6] D. Comer. The ubiquitous b-tree. *ACM Computing Surverys*, 11(2), 1979.
[7] F. Ellen, P. Fatourou, E. Ruppert, and F. van Breugel. Non-blocking binary search tree. *PODC*, 2010.
[8] K. Fraser. Practical lock-freedom, 2004. Technical Report UCAM-CL-TR-579, University of Cambridge, Computer Laboratory.
[9] T. L. Harris. A pragmatic implementation of non-blocking linked-lists. *DISC*, 2001.
[10] M. Herlihy. Wait-free synchronization. *TOPLAS*, 13(1):124–149, 1991.
[11] M. Herlihy and J. Wing. Linearizability: a correctness condition for concurrent objects. *TOPLAS*, 12(3):463–492, 1990.
[12] M. M. Michael. Hazard pointers: Safe memory reclamation for lock-free objects. *TPDS*, 15(6):491–504, 2004.
[13] E. Petrank, M. Musuvathi, and B. Steensgaard. Progress guarantee for parallel programs via bounded lock-freedom. *PLDI*, pages 144–154, 2009.
[14] J. Rao and K. A. Ross. Cache conscious indexing for decision-support in main memory. *VLDB*, 1999.
[15] O. Rodeh. B-trees, shadowing, and clones. *ACM Transactions on Storage Journal*, 2008.

Brief Announcement:
The Problem Based Benchmark Suite

Julian Shun†   Guy E. Blelloch†   Jeremy T. Fineman*   Phillip B. Gibbons‡
Aapo Kyrola†   Harsha Vardhan Simhadri†   Kanat Tangwongsan†

†Carnegie Mellon University   *Georgetown University   ‡Intel Labs, Pittsburgh

{jshun,guyb,akyrola,harshas,ktangwon}@cs.cmu.edu
jfineman@cs.georgetown.edu, phillip.b.gibbons@intel.com

ABSTRACT

This announcement describes the problem based benchmark suite (PBBS). PBBS is a set of benchmarks designed for comparing parallel algorithmic approaches, parallel programming language styles, and machine architectures across a broad set of problems. Each benchmark is defined concretely in terms of a problem specification and a set of input distributions. No requirements are made in terms of algorithmic approach, programming language, or machine architecture. The goal of the benchmarks is not only to compare runtimes, but also to be able to compare code and other aspects of an implementation (e.g., portability, robustness, determinism, and generality). As such the code for an implementation of a benchmark is as important as its runtime, and the public PBBS repository will include both code and performance results.

The benchmarks are designed to make it easy for others to try their own implementations, or to add new benchmark problems. Each benchmark problem includes the problem specification, the specification of input and output file formats, default input generators, test codes that check the correctness of the output for a given input, driver code that can be linked with implementations, a baseline sequential implementation, a baseline multicore implementation, and scripts for running timings (and checks) and outputting the results in a standard format. The current suite includes the following problems: integer sort, comparison sort, remove duplicates, dictionary, breadth first search, spanning forest, minimum spanning forest, maximal independent set, maximal matching, K-nearest neighbors, Delaunay triangulation, convex hull, suffix arrays, n-body, and ray casting. For each problem, we report the performance of our baseline multicore implementation on a 40-core machine.

Categories and Subject Descriptors: F.2 [Analysis of Algorithms and Problem Complexity]: General

Keywords: Parallel Algorithms, Benchmarking, Algorithm Performance

1 Introduction

When writing parallel code for a particular problem, should one use transactions, race-free algorithms, nested parallelism, bulk synchronization, speculative parallelism, futures, data parallelism, threads, message passing, or other options? Should one use a GPU, a multicore, or a cluster? Despite decades of experience with parallelism,

Copyright is held by the author/owner(s).
SPAA'12, June 25–27, 2012, Pittsburgh, Pennsylvania, USA.
ACM 978-1-4503-1213-4/12/06.

there is still little guidance on what approach to use when writing parallel codes, especially for irregular, non-numeric applications.

To help address this challenge, we are developing a **problem-based benchmark suite** (PBBS) for a broad set of non-numeric problems (see http://www.cs.cmu.edu/~pbbs). Unlike most existing benchmarks, which are based on specific code, the benchmarks are defined in terms of the problem specifications—a concrete description of valid inputs and corresponding valid outputs, along with some specific inputs. Any algorithms, programming methodologies, specific programming languages, or machines can be used to solve the problems. The benchmark suite is designed to compare the benefits and shortcomings of different algorithmic and programming approaches, and to serve as a dynamically improving set of educational examples of how to parallelize applications. The nature of PBBS will encourage the community to submit open-source solutions that will be judged by not only its performance but also the quality of the code: its elegance, readability, extensibility, modularity, scalability, correctness guarantees, and the ability to formally analyze performance. We realize many of these measures are hard to quantify and ultimately the judgment will be in the eye of the reader. Thus, the main outcome should be the code itself (and its performance numbers).

Our benchmark problems are selected to have reasonably simple efficient solutions (our base implementations all use fewer than 500 lines of code), but represent realistic real-world problems covering a wide class of domains and potential solution approaches. These consist of many well-known problems that are already de facto standards for benchmarking, such as sorting, nearest-neighbor searching, breadth first search, Delaunay triangulation and ray tracing, as well as many others. In the suite, each benchmark consists of (1) the problem specification including specific input and output file formats, (2) input generators and specific input instances, (3) code for checking the correctness of output for the given input, (4) scripts for running tests, (5) a reasonably efficient sequential base implementation for the problem, and (6) a reasonably efficient parallel (multicore) base implementation for the problem.

2 Related Work

Many benchmark suites have been designed and are currently being used for many different purposes, but none match our goals for a problem-based suite. There are several broad-based performance-based suites such as SPEC, WorldBench, V8, and Da Capo [6]; and domain-specific benchmarks such as BioBench [2], the San Diego vision benchmarks [18], MediaBench [12] (multimedia), SATLIB [10] (satisfiability), MineBench [15] (data mining), and the TPC benchmarks (databases). Except for SATLIB and the TPC benchmarks,

Basic Building Blocks	Scan, Integer Sort, Comparison Sort, Remove Duplicates, Dictionary, Sparse matrix-vector multiply
Graph Algorithms	Breadth First Search, Spanning Forest, Minimum Spanning Forest, Maximal Independent Set, Maximal Matching, Graph Separators
Computational Geometry	Quad/Oct Tree, Delaunay Triangulation, Convex Hull, k-Nearest Neighbors
Text Processing	Tokenize, Suffix Array
Computational Biology	Multiple sequence alignment, Phylogenetic tree, N-body
Data Mining	Build Index, Edit Distance Graph
Graphics	Ray Casting, Micropolygon Rendering
Machine Learning	Sparse SVM, K-means, Gibbs Sampling in Graphical Models

Table 1. A (preliminary) set of 28 problem-based benchmarks covering a reasonably broad set of non-numerical applications.

these are code-based benchmarks. The TPC and SATLIB are problem based, but for specific domains.

For parallel machines, there have also been many benchmarks developed. Broad-based performance benchmarks include Splash-2 [19], PARSEC [5], and STAMP [8], which are designed for shared memory machines. Other benchmarks cover a more general class of machines but are meant to measure particular machine characteristics, such as the HPC Challenge Benchmarks [14] that put an emphasis on measuring communication throughput. There are benchmarks aimed at particular languages, such as the Java Grande Benchmark Suite [17]. There are also some domain-specific parallel benchmarks such as ALPBench [13] (multimedia) and BioParallel [11]. All these benchmarks are code-based. The Berkeley "dwarfs" define a set of 13 parallel computational patterns [3]. While sharing some of the same high-level goals as ours (e.g., evaluate parallel programming models), their benchmarks are in terms of patterns, not problems. The Galois benchmarks [16] are defined in terms of particular algorithmic approaches but are not problem based.

In terms of being defined with regards to a problem specification, perhaps the closest benchmarks to PBBS are the NAS benchmarks [4]. In the original form (NPB 1), these consisted of a set of eight problem-based benchmarks where one of the main goals was architecture neutrality. Indeed, several different programming styles (vector code, message passing, data parallel) were used to code the benchmarks on different machines. These benchmarks, however, did not focus on code quality and because vendors were not required to release their codes, some of the solutions were extremely messy. Also, the NAS benchmarks were focused on numerical computing.

Finally, there have also been various attempts to compare programming languages by defining a set of benchmarks. Probably the one that captures the broadest set of languages is the Computer Language Benchmarks Game [9], which compares over 25 programming languages on a set of 12 micro benchmarks. Benchmarks results are reported in terms of performance and size of the `gzip`-compressed source file (comments and redundant whitespace removed). The benchmarks, however, only consider small inputs—for example, their "n-body" benchmark consists of 5 bodies. Also, the benchmarks require that the program use the "same algorithm" as specified—returning the same result is not sufficient.

In summary, we know of no benchmark suite that matches our goals—i.e., defined in input/output terms, covers a broad set of non-numeric problems, scales to large problem sizes, and emphasizes code quality.

3 Benchmark Problems and Current Status

We selected benchmark problems with the following goals in mind. First, the set of problems should have a wide coverage from state-of-the-art real-world applications. Second, the problem must have a well-defined way to validate output correctness or quality. Third, the problem should have efficient solutions that can be implemented in a reasonably small program. Finally, the inputs to these problem should be scalable. Table 1 summarizes a set of problem-based benchmarks categorized by application domain or type of data. These 28 benchmarks represent our current list of what we believe would make a good mix of problems, though the list is flexible.

An important challenge with defining a benchmark in terms of a problem's input-output behaviors is picking a good and scalable set of test inputs. A good set of test inputs should withstand "tricks" that fail to work in the general case, should represent a realistic input, and should have varying sizes. We leverage the growing body of work on generating scalable synthetic data that models real data. There are many standard distributions used in computational geometry that are much more realistic than evenly distributed random data. Similarly, there has been considerable work in generating graphs that have characteristics similar to real-world graphs [1] and DNA data that represents a population.

We require the program to output the result to a file in a particular format. We provide test code that checks correctness and outputs any quality criteria (e.g. the size of a graph cut). The time for input and output is not included in the running time or code length—for some benchmarks it could dominate the cost.

It is important to have at least one base implementation of each benchmark so that results can be compared and as a proof of concept that the benchmarks fit within our parameters (e.g., have reasonably simple and efficient solutions). We are currently developing two base implementations for each benchmark, one serial and one parallel. Our parallel implementations are designed for multicores and use only parallel loops, nested fork-join, and compare-and-swap operations and are currently implemented in Intel Cilk Plus. We have implemented an initial set of base implementations for some of the benchmarks and have made initial timings. We ran our experiments on a 40-core (with hyper-threading) machine with 4×2.4GHZ Intel 10-core E7-8870 Xeon Processors, a 1066MHz bus, and 256GB of main memory. All programs were compiled with Intel's `icpc` compiler (version 12.1.0 with Cilk Plus support) with the $-O3$ flag.

Table 2 summarizes the results of these experiments. We report the weighted average of runtimes over various inputs. For example, for Comparison Sort, we use three sequences of doubles distributed according to uniform, exponential, and almost sorted distributions and two sequences of character strings from a trigram distribution. All sequences were of length 10^7. For the graph benchmarks, we used three types of graphs: random graphs, grid graphs, and rMat (power law) graphs. Each graph has either 10^7 or 2^{24} nodes. Descriptions of all the algorithms and further experimental results can

| Application | 1 | 40 | T_1/T_{40} | T_S/T_{40} |
Algorithm	thread	core		
Integer Sort				
serialRadixSort	0.48	–	–	–
parallelRadixSort	0.299	0.013	23.0	36.9
Comparison Sort				
serialSort	2.85	–	–	–
sampleSort	2.59	0.066	39.2	43.2
Remove Duplicates				
serialHash	0.689	–	–	–
parallelHash	0.867	0.027	32.1	25.5
Dictionary				
serialHash	0.574	–	–	–
parallelHash	0.748	0.025	29.9	23
Breadth First Search				
serialBFS	2.61	–	–	–
parallelBFS	5.54	0.247	22.4	10.6
Spanning Forest				
serialSF	1.733	–	–	–
parallelSF	5.12	0.254	20.1	6.81
Min Spanning Forest				
serialMSF	7.04	–	–	–
parallelKruskal	14.9	0.626	23.8	11.2
Maximal Ind. Set				
serialMIS	0.405	–	–	–
parallelMIS	0.733	0.047	14.1	8.27
Maximal Matching				
serialMatching	0.84	–	–	–
parallelMatching	2.02	0.108	18.7	7.78
K-Nearest Neighbors				
octTreeNeighbors	24.9	1.16	21.5	–
Delaunay Triangulation				
serialDelaunay	56.3	–	–	–
parallelDelaunay	76.6	2.6	29.5	21.7
Convex Hull				
serialHull	1.01	–	–	–
quickHull	1.655	0.093	17.8	10.9
Suffix Array				
serialKS	17.3	–	–	–
parallelKS	11.7	0.57	20.5	30.4
Ray Casting				
kdTree	7.32	0.334	21.9	–

Table 2. Weighted average of running times (seconds) over various inputs on a 40-core machine with hyper-threading (80 threads). Time of the parallel version on 40 cores (T_{40}) is shown relative to both (i) the time of the serial version (T_S) and (ii) the parallel version on one thread (T_1). In some cases our parallel version on one thread is faster than the baseline serial version.

be found in [7]. All code is available on the benchmark web page: http://www.cs.cmu.edu/~pbbs.

Acknowledgements. This work is partially funded by the National Science Foundation under Grant number 1019343 to the Computing Research Association for the CIFellows Project and Grant number CCF-1018188, and by Intel via the Intel Labs Academic Research Office for the Parallel Algorithms for Non-Numeric Computing Program and the Intel Science and Technology Center for Cloud Computing (ISTC-CC).

4 References

[1] L. Akoglu and C. Faloutsos. RTG: A recursive realistic graph generator using random typing. *Data Min. Knowl. Discov.*, 19(2), 2009.

[2] K. Albayraktaroglu, A. Jaleel, X. Wu, M. Franklin, B. Jacob, C.-W. Tseng, and D. Yeung. BioBench: A benchmark suite of bioinformatics applications. In *IEEE ISPASS*, 2005.

[3] K. Asanovic, R. Bodik, B. C. Catanzaro, J. J. Gebis, P. Husbands, K. Keutzer, D. A. Patterson, W. L. Plishker, J. Shalf, S. W. Williams, and K. A. Yelick. The landscape of parallel computing research: A view from Berkeley. Technical Report UCB/EECS-2006-183, EECS Department, UC Berkeley, 2006.

[4] D. H. Bailey, E. Barszcz, J. T. Barton, D. S. Browning, R. L. Carter, L. Dagum, R. Fatoohi, P. O. Frederickson, T. A. Lasinski, R. Schreiber, H. D. Simon, V. Venkatakrishnan, and S. Weeratunga. The NAS parallel benchmarks—summary and preliminary results. In *ACM/IEEE Supercomputing*, 1991.

[5] C. Bienia, S. Kumar, J. P. Singh, and K. Li. The PARSEC benchmark suite: Characterization and architectural implications. In *ACM PACT*, 2008.

[6] S. M. Blackburn et al. The DaCapo benchmarks: Java benchmarking development and analysis. In *ACM OOPSLA*, 2006.

[7] G. E. Blelloch, J. T. Fineman, P. B. Gibbons, and J. Shun. Internally deterministic parallel algorithms can be fast. In *ACM PPoPP*, 2012.

[8] C. Cao Minh, J. Chung, C. Kozyrakis, and K. Olukotun. STAMP: Stanford transactional applications for multi-processing. In *IISWC '08*, September 2008.

[9] B. Fulgham. The computer language benchmarks game. http://shootout.alioth.debian.org/, 2009.

[10] H. H. Hoos and T. Stützle. SATLIB: An online resource for research on SAT. In I. P. Gent, H. v. Maaren, and T. Walsh, editors, *SAT 2000*. IOS Press, 2000.

[11] A. Jaleel, M. Mattina, and B. Jacob. Last-level cache (LLC) performance of data-mining workloads on a CMP—A case study of parallel bioinformatics workloads. In *IEEE HPCA*, 2006.

[12] C. Lee, M. Potkonjak, and W. H. Mangione-Smith. MediaBench: A tool for evaluating and synthesizing multimedia and communications systems. In *IEEE/ACM MICRO*, 1997.

[13] M.-L. Li, R. Sasanka, S. V. Adve, Y.-K. Chen, and E. Debes. The ALPBench benchmark suite for complex multimedia applications. In *IEEE IISWC*, 2005.

[14] P. Luszczek, D. Bailey, J. Dongarra, J. Kepner, R. Lucas, R. Rabenseifner, and D. Takahashi. The HPC challenge (HPCC) benchmark suite. In *ACM/IEEE SC06 Conference Tutorial*, 2006.

[15] R. Narayanan, B. Ozisikyilmaz, J. Zambreno, G. Memik, and A. N. Choudhary. MineBench: A benchmark suite for data mining workloads. In *IEEE IISWC*, 2006.

[16] K. Pingali, D. Nguyen, M. Kulkarni, M. Burtscher, M. A. Hassaan, R. Kaleem, T.-H. Lee, A. Lenharth, R. Manevich, M. Méndez-Lojo, D. Prountzos, and X. Sui. The tao of parallelism in algorithms. In *ACM PLDI*, 2011.

[17] L. A. Smith, J. M. Bull, and J. Obdrzalek. A parallel Java Grande benchmark suite. In *ACM/IEEE SC2001*, 2001.

[18] S. K. Venkata, I. Ahn, D. Jeon, A. Gupta, C. Louie, S. Garcia, S. Belongie, and M. B. Taylor. SD-VBS: The San Diego vision benchmark suite. In *IEEE IISWC*, 2009.

[19] S. C. Woo, M. Ohara, E. Torrie, J. P. Singh, and A. Gupta. The SPLASH-2 programs: Characterization and methodological considerations. In *ACM ISCA*, 1995.

Brief Announcement: Subgraph Isomorphism on a Multithreaded Shared Memory Architecture

Claire C. Ralph
Baker Laboratory
Cornell University
Ithaca NY 14853
ccr53@cornell.edu

Vitus J. Leung
PO Box 5800
Sandia National Laboratory
Albuquerque NM 87185-1327
vjleung@sandia.gov

William McLendon III
PO Box 5800
Sandia National Laboratory
Albuquerque, NM 87185-1326
wmclen@sandia.gov

ABSTRACT

Graph algorithms tend to suffer poor performance due to the irregularity of access patterns within general graph data structures, arising from poor data locality, which translates to high memory latency. The result is that advances in high-performance solutions for graph algorithms are most likely to come through advances in both architectures and algorithms. Specialized MMT shared memory machines offer a potentially transformative environment in which to approach the problem. Here, we explore the challenges of implementing Subgraph Isomorphism (SI) algorithms based on the Ullmann and VF2 algorithms in the Cray XMT environment, where issues of memory contention, scheduling, and compiler parallelizability must be optimized.

Categories and Subject Descriptors

I.5.5 [**Implementation**]: Special architectures

Keywords

graphs, subgraph isomorphism, mutlithreading, cray xmt

1. INTRODUCTION

Graphs have proven to be a powerful data structure for representing large collections of interrelated data in disparate fields [4], [2]. The explosion of data in these fields means there is an urgent need for high performance computing (HPC) methods which can process and analyze this data. Unfortunately there are many challenges with adapting traditional HPC techniques to known graph algorithms, reviewed in depth here [1]. In graph problems, memory latency is the main bottleneck; processors sit idle without a high ratio of active threads to processors. Massively MultiThreaded (MMT) shared memory architectures, such as the Cray XMT [3], have hardware support allowing for tens of thousands of active threads. The XMT allows for single cycle context switching between threads, each of which can have up to ten outstanding memory requests. These features allow the XMT to *tolerate* rather than *hide* memory latency as is typical for other superscalar processors.

The high promise of MMT architectures for large scale graph processing applications means that it is imperative to develop and explore software implementations of graph algorithms on these systems. However, the development of

Copyright is held by the author/owner(s).
SPAA'12, June 25–27, 2012, Pittsburgh, Pennsylvania, USA.
ACM 978-1-4503-1213-4/12/06.

appropriate libraries cannot be achieved by simply porting and fine tuning extant parallel libraries for traditional architectures. Due to the unique characteristics of MMT machines, algorithms which perform well in other parallel environments may perform poorly on MMT platforms. The work reported here forms part of a larger effort to develop a set of high performance software components for graph algorithms on MMT architectures, namely the MultiThreaded Graph Library (MTGL) [1].

In this work we implement and assess exact subgraph isomorphism (SI) algorithms (matching a small graph G_A to a subgraph of a large graph, G_B), developed within the MTGL framework, on the Cray XMT. We take as our starting point the Ullmann [4] and VF2 algorithms [2] that can be considered as prototypical SI algorithms. In this context, we attempt to answer the following questions. Firstly, how can we write an efficient parallel SI implementation for an MMT architecture? This is a question which requires careful consideration of dynamic scheduling and memory contention. A further issue we had to consider, is the interaction with the programming environment, namely how to appropriately specifiy the algorithm to achieve efficient parallelization by the XMT compiler. Secondly, what is the importance of search space pruning in SI algorithms on a MMT architecture? Here, we find the unique memory access characteristics of a MMT environment, as compared to traditional parallel architectures, yields a different balance point between algorithms which aggressively prune the search space of candidate isomorphisms, and those which minimize memory contention.

2. THE ALGORITHMS

The difficulty in the general SI case lies in the size of the search space. We explore algorithms which attempt to prune this search space using *look ahead* rules which check the consistency of a partial mapping ϕ'. These rules define characteristics which must be true of any partial mapping contained in a SI mapping.

In order to prune the search space we define two phases: *Phase I:* Attempt elimination of matching vertex pairs that can not appear in any potential match. We define five elimination rules: The original rule proposed by Ullmann (U), Simplified Ullmann (SU) which solely relies upon the degree of the vertices in the graph, Extended Ullmann (EU) which extends (U) to Next Nearest Neighbors (NNN), and versions of (U) and (EU) such that for each vertex pair, every neighbor or NNN relationship is one to one. The latter two are referred to as (U+) and (EU+). *Phase II:* Traverse the remaining search space throwing away partial candidates which violate a look ahead rule. We define four rules, three of which are analogous to SU, U, and EU, and a fourth which is based upon the VF2 rule.

Phase II rules split neighbors of vertices included in the partial candidate into various classes, and take advantage of the fact that the neighbors in the smaller graph, G_A, must have a match in the larger graph, G_B. Ullmann based rules split the neighbors into two classes, those that have been matched and those that have not. VF2 based rules further split them into those that have a neighbor in the matching and those that do not. Please note we adapted the VF2 rules to solve SI rather than Induced SI.

3. IMPLEMENTATION

Phase II of the algorithm explores the truncated search space and makes up the bulk of the computation time. This phase must be implemented carefully as different implementations lead to very different performance characteristics on the XMT. We experimented with (i) recursion versus explicit looping, (ii) memory allocation patterns, and (iii) partial candidates loop scheduling.

Recursion versus explicit looping. Our initial algorithm explored the search space using a recursive method and a linked list data structure to keep track of the partial candidates. This is the algorithm and data structure that is responsible for the efficiency of the serial version of the VF2 algorithm. However, we achieved better parallelization reformulating the implementation as a set of three nested for loops as in Algorithm 1. Note v_i^A refers to a vertex in G_A; v_j^B refers to a vertex in G_B.

Algorithm 1 Phase II: Nested For Loop Formulation.

> **for** $v_i^A \in G_A$ **do**
>   **for** $c \in candidates[i-1]$ **do**
>   **if** c was kept **then**
>   **for** $v_j^B \in G_B$ **do**
> $c \leftarrow c + v_j^B$
>   **if** c is valid **then**
> $candidates[i] \leftarrow c$

Memory allocation. We observed poor parallelization while using dynamic memory allocation, thus we allocated all memory necessary to extend every candidate at the current depth, regardless of whether it was valid. This static approach is an order of magnitude faster than the dynamic approach.

Partial candidates loop scheduling. Scheduling of the inner two loops in Algorithm 1 requires knowledge of the number of kept partial candidates at the prior level. This computation, however, creates a significant bottleneck. To avoid this, we could schedule computation over all partial candidates and introduce a validity test between the second and third loops. The second and third loops should then both be parallelizable. In our tests, however, the third loop could not be parallelized by the XMT compiler, despite strong pragma directives. We therefore resorted to collapsing the loops by hand as in Algorithm 2, creating some additional work. In large graphs, however, the increase in parallelization more than makes up for this.

Algorithm 2 Collapsed For Loop with Static Array

> **for** $d = 1$ to $|G_A| - 1$ **do**
>   The next two loops can now be collapsed.
>   **for** $c \in candidates[d-1]$ **do**
>   **for** $v_B \in G_B$ **do**
>   **if** c was kept **then**
> $c \leftarrow c + v_B$
>   **if** lookAhead(c) **then**
>   compute j from c and v_B
> $candidates[d][j] \leftarrow c$
---

4. EXPERIMENTAL RESULTS

A central question in the evaluation of an SI algorithm regards the relative trade-off between strict look ahead-rules, which reduce the search space and more brute-force algorithms which have a larger search space, but which may be more parallelizable. The balance point is expected to be different on MMT architectures due to the large number of threads.

Table 1: Phase I Rules

Type of Graph		Small	Large
Erdos Renyi	$\mu = .01$	U+	U
	.05	SU	SU
	.10	SU	SU
Reg Mesh	$r = 2$	U+	U+
	4	U+	U+
	6	U+	U+
Irreg Mesh		U+	U+
Bounded Valence	$\nu = 3$	U	U+
	6	U	U
	9	U	U
Irreg Bound Valence	$\nu = 3$	U	U+
	6	U+	U+
	9	U+	U+

The look ahead rules were evaluated on a database of graphs previously developed for SI benchmarking [2]. This database contains 54,000 couples of graphs with a SI mapping among them. We used a subset of these graphs including: randomly connected graphs (ER), 2D regular and irregular meshes, bounded valence graphs, and irregular bounded

Table 2: Phase II Rules

Type of Graph		Small	Large
Erdos Renyi	$\mu = .01$	U	U
	.05	U	U
	.10	U	U
Reg Mesh	$r = 2$	U	U
	4	U	U
	6	U	U
Irreg Mesh		U	U
Bounded Valence	$\nu = 3$	SU	U
	6	SU	U
	9	SU	U
Irreg Bound Valence	$\nu = 3$	SU	U
	6	SU	U
	9	SU	U

Figure 1: Speedup plotted relative to the number of threads available for three types of graphs.

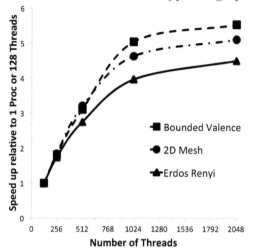

valence graphs. G_B ranged from 20 to 1000 vertices. We define "small" graphs as those with $|G_B| \leq 100$ and "large" graphs as those with $100 < |G_B| \leq 1000$. $|G_A|$ was about 20% of $|G_B|$. All experiments were run on a Cray XMT with 512 GB of memory, utilizing up to 32 processors.

In Phase I we find extending U to U+ is worthwhile. While this does significantly increase Phase I wall clock time by about a factor of 3, it does not increase the total time, as the potentially improved pruning can lead to significant savings in Phase II and Phase I only makes up about 10% of the total wall clock time. We thus used the Phase I Ullmann Plus rule for all our experiments with Phase II and would recommend its use in a general graph algorithm.

In Table 2 we compare the three variations of Ullmann's, as well as the VF2, Phase II look ahead rules. In this table we list the rule which led to the fastest solution of the SI problem as measured by wall-clock time. The best performing algorithm as measured by wall-clock time for the large graph instances (Ullmann) was also the most scalable as measured both by percentage machine utilization when using a fixed number of processors as well as by scaling studies where we varied the number of processors. The Ullmann algorithm showed about 50% parallel speedup in large graph computations involving more than 1000 threads. See Figure 1. Since candidate consistency checking in Phase II is all independent, the main limitation on scalability arises from memory contention.

5. CONCLUSIONS

The goal of this work was to explore various exact subgraph isomorphism (SI) algorithms in a MMT environment. Our study involved two components. Firstly, identify general implementation strategies adapted to the unique software environment and MMT hardware of the Cray XMT machine. Secondly, explore aspects of SI algorithms related to search space pruning and their influence on the algorithm performance. In particular, we expected the unique memory access characteristics of a MMT environment to yield a different balance point between algorithms which more aggressively prune the search space of candidate isomorphisms, and those which require fewer memory accesses.

We experimented with a variety of implementations in the

context of the XMT parallelizing environment, including the interaction with the unique compiler and programming environment. As opposed to minimizing FLOPS, we found that for an efficient implementation, three criteria had to be considered, namely minimizing dynamic scheduling, optimizing memory contention, and structuring the algorithm such that efficient parallelization could be recognized by the compiler. Due to the first two factors, the best implementation involved using a loop collapse with decreased memory contention and dynamic scheduling at the expense of higher levels of work. The third factor is important as despite strong directives, the compiler did not correctly choose the most efficient parallelization of the the three main loops, and thus required us to manually restructure code for increased parallelization.

Starting from our basic implementation, we explored the central algorithmic question of the benefits of stricter consistency criteria (increasing pruning) of the search tree in an MMT environment. We found the best performing algorithm for graphs of non-trivial size was the traditional Ullmann algorithm. This yielded both the highest scalability (over thousands of threads) and the maximum degree of processor utilization of 36%. The optimality of the Ullmann algorithm in our studies suggests that graph algorithms may need to be reassessed in new architectures such as the XMT. Indeed, as massively threaded architectures become more prevalent, the emphasis on optimal algorithms may need to focus less on search space size, and more on the complex issues of scheduling and memory contention.

Overall, we believe that the scalability of algorithms such as the Ullmann algorithm on the model problems in this work, support the notion that the global address space, large number of threads, and automated load balancing of the Cray XMT constitute a promising new architecture for graph problems. Consequently, as these MMT architectures mature, we expect to see significant breakthroughs in the application domain.

6. ACKNOWLEDGMENTS

Sandia National Laboratories is a multi-program laboratory managed and operated by Sandia Corporation, a wholly owned subsidiary of Lockheed-Martin Company, for the U.S. Department of Energy's National Nuclear Security Administration under contract DE-AC04-94AL85000. C. C. Ralph thanks DOE CSGF for funding.

7. REFERENCES

[1] J. W. Berry, B. Hendrickson, S. Kahan, and P. Konecny. Software and algorithms for graph queries on multithreaded architectures. In *IEEE International Parallel and Distributed Processing Symposium (IPDPS)*, pages 1–14, 2007.

[2] L. P. Cordella, P. Foggia, C. Sansone, and M. Vento. A (sub)graph isomorphism algorithm for matching large graphs. *IEEE Transactions on Pattern Analysis and Machine Intelligence*, 26(10):1367–1372, 2004.

[3] P. Konecny. Introducing the Cray XMT. In *Proc. Cray User Group meeting (CUG 2007)*, 2007.

[4] J. R. Ullmann. An algorithm for subgraph isomorphism. *Journal of the ACM*, 23(1):31–42, 1976.

Brief Announcement: Efficient Cache Oblivious Algorithms for Randomized Divide-and-Conquer in the Multicore Model

[Extended Abstract]

Neeraj Sharma
Mentor Graphics (INDIA) Pvt. Ltd.
Noida, UP 201301, India
neeraj_sharma@mentor.com

Sandeep Sen
Department of CSE, IIT Delhi
New Delhi 110016, India
ssen@cse.iitd.ernet.in

ABSTRACT

In this paper we present a cache-oblivious framework for randomized divide and conquer algorithms on the multicore model with private cache. We first derive an $O(\frac{n}{p} \log n + \log n \log \log n)$ expected parallel depth algorithm for sorting n numbers with expected $O(\frac{n}{B} \log_M n)$ cache misses where p, M and B respectively denote the number of processors, the size of an individual cache memory and the block size respectively. Although similar results have been obtained recently for sorting [4] , we feel that our approach is simpler and general and we apply it to obtain an algorithm for 3D convex hulls with similar bounds.

We also present a simple randomized processor allocation technique without the explicit knowledge of the number of processors that is likely to find additional applications in resource oblivious environments.

A longer version of this paper is available at [8].

Categories and Subject Descriptors

F.1 [**Computation by abstract devices**]: Models of computation

General Terms

Algorithms

Keywords

Parallel Algorithms, Randomization, Multicore, Cache-oblivious

1. INTRODUCTION

The private-cache multicore model and the closely related Parallel External Memory (PEM) model combines several features of parallel computing models like PRAM and the memory hierarchy issues captured by the External Memory Models. The goal is to capture the relevant aspects of a large scale multiprocessing environment, whose numerous parameters may be unknown to the algorithm designer. Although, it is not intuitive, this last requirement can be tackled using the strategy called *cache obliviousness* or more generally *resource obliviousness*.

These multiprocessing models consists of p processors (or cores) each having a private cache of size M. that commu-

nicate with each other through a shared memory - for full parallelism, $n \geq M \cdot p$. Initially, the input is present in the global memory stored in form of blocks of size B and all transfers are done in blocks of size B. We incur two types of cache related-cost in this model(previously defined in [4])

Cache misses : Whenever any core needs some data which is not present in its cache, that block is copied from the main memory into its cache and it is counted as one cache miss.

Block misses : When a block residing in multiple caches is modified, then every core containing the block incurs a block miss.

Both concurrent reads and concurrent writes are allowed in this model.

Concurrent Reads : If x cores are reading the same block, every core will incur one cache miss and the total cache cost will be x.

Concurrent Writes : If x cores write simultaneously to the same block, this block will migrate across these x cores to satisfy their write requests. Thus the ith core in sequence will have to wait for time equal to i cache misses before it can complete its write operation. So the total cache misses across all cores will be $\sum_{i=1}^{x-1} i = \Omega(x^2)$.

The performance of a multicore algorithm is characterized by two parameters - *Cache misses* (including block misses) and the *Critical path* length, which is the maximum time taken by any processor in the overall algorithm. Our goal is to design efficient *cache oblivious* algorithms where the parameters M, B cannot be used to customize the algorithm, yet, we would like to match the performance of Cache aware algorithms. Further, we would like to generate the parallel code without the knowledge of the the number of processors which is known as *resource obliviousness*.

1.1 Previous Related Work

For the external memory model, Aggarwal and Vitter [1] designed a version of merge sort, that uses a maximum $O(\frac{N}{B} \log_{M/B} N/B)$ I/O's and this is optimal. For the cache oblivious model, Frigo et al. [5] presented a sequential cache-oblivious sorting algorithm called Funnel sort which can sort n keys in $O(n \log n)$ time and $O(\frac{n}{B} \log_M n)$ cache misses.[1] Note that both time and cache misses achieved by this algorithm are optimal.

Arge et al. [2] formalized the PEM model and presented a cache-aware mergesort algorithm that runs in $O(\log n)$

Copyright is held by the author/owner(s).
SPAA'12, June 25–27, 2012, Pittsburgh, Pennsylvania, USA.
ACM 978-1-4503-1213-4/12/06.

---

[1]Using a slightly modified tall cache assumption - $M \geq B^{2.3}$, it follows that $\log_M n$ is $O(\log_{M/B} n/B)$.

time and has optimal cache misses. Blelloch et al. [3] presented a resource oblivious distribution sort algorithm that has expected $O(\log^{3/2} n)$ critical path-length and incurs suboptimal cache cost in the private-cache multicore model. Their distribution sort uses merging to divide the input which is the potential bottleneck for reducing the depth further. The algorithm given in [9] is designed for a BSP-style version of a cache aware, multi-level multicore which is difficult to compare it directly with the previous results. Recently Cole and Ramachandran [4] presented a new optimal merge sort algorithm (SPMS) for resource oblivious multicore model. This algorithm sorts n keys in $O(\frac{n}{p}\log n + \log n \log \log n)$ time using n processors with optimal number of cache misses on resource oblivious model assuming $n \geq Mp$ and $M \geq B^2 \log B \log \log B$. It works in $O(\log \log n)$ stages where each stage requires $O(\log n)$ time. The authors addressed a general computational paradigm called *Balanced Partitioning Trees* and designed a a resource-oblivious priority work scheduler based on work-stealing to attain the above bounds.

1.2 Our Work

In this paper, we have presented a randomized distributed sorting algorithm on cache-oblivious multicore model that is similar to Reischuk [7]. However, to bound the cache misses, we had to modify it significantly. First, we sample an appropriate number of elements from the input, sort them using a brute-force method, and use these elements to divide the input into disjoint buckets. To partition in a cache-oblivious fashion, we do it in two phases. Roughly speaking, we divide the n input keys into $\sqrt{n}$ buckets by successive partitioning into $n^{1/4}$ size buckets. This partitioning procedure, which is the crux of our distribution sort, in turn invokes an efficient merging procedure to attain the final bounds.

THEOREM 1.1. *Using p cores with tall cache, we can sort n keys in expected time $O(\frac{n}{p}\log n + \log n \log \log n)$ and expected cache misses $O(\frac{n}{B}\log_M n)$, using a cache oblivious algorithm.*

So the cache cost is optimal but time is optimal only for $p \leq (n/\log \log n)$. Since $n \geq Mp$, under a very weak condition, viz., $M \geq \log \log n$, it follows that $p \leq (n/\log \log n)$ and our algorithm matches both time and cache misses optimality. Our bounds for sorting match that of Cole and Ramachandran [4] in cache-misses and depth and we can obtain matching performance in the cache-oblivious PEM model. Further, our algorithm is based on a general framework for randomized divide-and-conquer that has other applications. In this work we exploit this to obtain an algorithm for constructing three dimensional convex hulls with bounds similar to sorting that is based on the approach of of Reif and Sen [6]. More specifically, we obtain the following result.

THEOREM 1.2. *Given n half-spaces in R^3 that contains the origin, we can find their intersection using p cores with tall cache in expected time $O(\frac{n}{p}\log n + \log n \log \log n)$ and expected $O(\frac{n}{B}\log_M n)$ cache misses using a cache oblivious algorithm.*

Since it is known that Voronoi diagrams can be reduced to three dimensional convex hulls, we obtain identical results for constructing 2D Voronoi diagrams.. We also present a

simple technique for processor-obliviousness where the algorithm need not have any prior knowledge of the number of processors and the processors can generate their ids on the fly. Our approach is fundamentally different from [4, 3] that design a scheduler to map tasks to processors in a resource-oblivious fashion.

2. AN OVERVIEW OF OUR ALGORITHM

The crux of our algorithm is an efficient cache-oblivious partitioning scheme that works as follows. Let $T(n, m)$ represent the total time to divide n keys into m buckets. Instead of dividing the n keys directly into m buckets, we first divide the n keys into $\sqrt{m}$ buckets and then every buckets is further split into $\sqrt{m}$ buckets.
1. Divide the n keys into $\sqrt{m}$ buckets. This is done in two steps.
(i) Divide n keys into $\sqrt{n}$ contiguous chunks of size $\sqrt{n}$ each. Now each chunk of size $\sqrt{n}$ is divided into $\sqrt{m}$ buckets recursively.
(ii) Now we have $\sqrt{n}$ lists, each divided into $\sqrt{m}$ buckets. We merge these lists and get a single list divided into $\sqrt{m}$ buckets. The merging procedure is summarized in Theorem 2.2.

$$T(n, \sqrt{m}) = \sqrt{n}T(\sqrt{n}, \sqrt{m}) + T_{merge}(\sqrt{n}, \sqrt{n}, \sqrt{m})$$

where $T_{merge}(\sqrt{n}, \sqrt{n}, \sqrt{m})$ represents the time needed to merge $\sqrt{n}$ lists, where each list is of size $\sqrt{n}$ and divided into $\sqrt{m}$ buckets.
2. Now we have $\sqrt{m}$ buckets $n_1, n_2, \ldots, n_{\sqrt{m}}$. We will divide each bucket again into $\sqrt{m}$ buckets.

$$T(n, m) = T(n, \sqrt{m}) + \sum_{i=1}^{m^{1/2}} T(n_i, \sqrt{m})$$

We follow the same approach as done in step 1 above with some modifications and subsequently merge the buckets.

Finally, we obtain the following recurrence for the parallel time $T''(n, m) = O(n/p + \log p) + 2T''(\sqrt{n}, \sqrt{m})..$ The analysis for cache misses is similar and is omitted from this abstract.

THEOREM 2.1. *Given an input array A of n elements and an ordered set $S = \{S_1, S_2 \ldots$ of $z - 1$ splitters, we can cache obliviously partition A into z contiguous sub-arrays B_1, B_2, ... , B_z such that for $i = 1, 2, \ldots z - 1$, we have $\max\{x | x \in B_i\} \leq S_i \leq \min\{x | x \in B_{i+1}\}$, using p processors with tall cache in time $O(\frac{n}{p}\log n + \log n \log \log n)$ incurring a total of $O(\frac{n}{B}\log_M n)$ cache misses, given $z \leq \sqrt{n}$.*

For merging x lists, each divided into t buckets, we assign the y keys equally to the p processors such that the first processor will write first $\frac{y}{p}$ keys, the second processor will write next $\frac{y}{p}$ keys and so on. For this, the input is partitioned using a prefix computation where the processors may have to read the keys from multiple lists, but while writing, they write contiguously. All the cores will read their corresponding keys sequentially unless one of the following events happen:
(i) The bucket that a core was reading, ends. It can increase the cache miss count by at most one compared to the sequential cache misses and this can happen at most xt times.
(ii) Processors may have to start or end reading in the middle of some block. This can increase cache miss count by at

most by one or two over sequential misses that is bounded by $O(p)$.

THEOREM 2.2. *Given x lists of total size y, that are indexed by t buckets, we can merge these lists into a single list partitioned into t contiguous buckets in time $O(\frac{y}{p} + \log p)$ using p processors with tall cache incurring $O(\frac{y}{B} + xt)$ cache misses in a cache-oblivious manner.*

Note that the above bounds are worst case deterministic. For the overall distribution sort, a random sample of size $n^{1/\alpha}$, $\alpha > 1$ is used to partition the problem, and the recurrence for the expected parallel running time can be written as

$$\bar{T}''(n,p) = \begin{cases} O\left(\frac{n}{p}\log n + \log n \log \log n\right) + & (1-r)\bar{T}''(n_i) \\ + r\bar{T}''(n) & \text{if } n \geq K \\ O(K \log K) & \text{otherwise} \end{cases} \quad (1)$$

where $K = N/P$ is the original problem size to processor ratio. For $n \geq 2^{18}$, we can choose α such that $n_i \leq n^{1-1/2\alpha}$ with probability $> 1 - 1/n$, i.e. $r < 1/n$. It follows that $\bar{T}''(n,p) = O(\alpha\frac{n}{p}\log n + \alpha \log n \log \log n)$. Using similar arguments, the expected number of cache misses $\bar{Q}(n)$ can be bounded by $O(\frac{n}{B}\log_M n)$.

$$\bar{Q}(n) = \begin{cases} O(\frac{n}{B}\log_M n) + \sum_{i=1}^{n^{1/\alpha}} \bar{Q}(n_i) & \text{if } n \geq K \\ O(\frac{K}{B}\log_M K) & \text{otherwise} \end{cases} \quad (2)$$

2.1 Processor oblivious load balancing

Traditionally, parallel programs are written assuming that there is a unique id (an integer in the range $1 \ldots p$) for each of the p processors. The processors id is used to designate a particular task to a specific processor. For example, for an input array of n numbers, a processor with id i may be allocated the task associated with the subarray $\frac{n}{p} \cdot i \ldots \frac{n}{p} \cdot (i+1)$. This is easy because p is known at the time the parallel code is generated. In our situation p is not known and the processors do not have any predefined unique id associated with them.

The basic idea is that each of the p processors simultaneously chooses a random number in the range $[1..n]$ and writes to the corresponding location in an array A. The expected number of processors writing to a specific location $A[i]$ $1 \leq i \leq n$, is p/n and no more than $O(\log n)$ w.h.p. - note that, from our earlier assumptions, $p \leq n/B$, so the expected number of elements writing into a B element block ≤ 1. Roughly speaking, a processor writing to a location i assumes responsibility for the block of n/p elements starting from $\lfloor \frac{i}{n/p} \rfloor$. However, because of conflicts caused by independent random choices, we have to do some limited redistribution and also *estimate* the value of p. It can be argued using Chernoff bounds that w.h.p. $\Theta(\log n)$ processors will choose a location in the range $[bi \ldots b(i+1))$ $i = 0, 1 \ldots$ where $b = (n/p) \cdot \log n$. If there are $c \log n$ processors for a block of size $n/p \log n$, then a processor has id $= <m', \ell'>$ where m' denotes the most significant $\log p - \log \log n$ bits, and ℓ' denotes the least significant bits. The processor is assigned locations $[\alpha \cdot m' + \beta \cdot \ell' \ldots \alpha \cdot m' + \beta(\ell' + 1)]$ where $\alpha = n/p \log n$ and $\beta = \frac{1}{c} \cdot (n/p)$. The ℓ' bits can be assigned using a counter when the processors write (concurrently) to

a common block. The details of computing m', ℓ' are omitted from this abstract.

In the above procedure, we have not accounted for the *block misses* when processors conflict in writing to a specific block. For instance, if j processors write to the same block, the *block misses* will be $\Omega(j^2)$. This could be as much as $\Omega(\log^2 n)$ since we can only bound $j \leq \log n$ with high probability. The overall block misses will be given by $\sum_{i=1}^{n'} n_i^2$ where $n' = n/B$ and n_i is the number of processors writing in block i. Note that $\sum_i n_i = p$. We can compute the expected *block misses* as follows. If n_j denotes the number of processors that chose block j, we are interested in the quantity $E[\sum_j n_j^2]$ that represents the total expected block misses. Let r.v. $X_i = 1$ if processor i writes to block 1 and 0 otherwise (we need concurrent write capability). Then $E[X_i] = 1/n'$ and moreover $E[X_i^2] = 1/n'$. From our earlier notation, $n_1 = \sum_{i=1}^{p} X_i$ and so $n_1^2 = \sum_{i=1}^{p} X_i^2$. Taking expectations,

$$E\left[\left(\sum_{i=1}^{p} X_i\right)^2\right] = p E[X_i^2] + \binom{p}{2} \cdot 2 E[X_i \cdot X_j]$$

$$= p \cdot \frac{1}{n'} + p(p-1) \cdot E[X_i] \cdot E[X_j] = p \cdot \frac{1}{n'} + p(p-1)\frac{1}{n'^2}$$

The first equality follows from linearity and the second from independence. Therefore, from symmetry, $E[n_1^2 + n_2^2 + \ldots] = n' \cdot (p/n' + p(p-1)/n'^2) = p(1 + (p-1)/n')$ which is $O(p)$ for $p \leq n' = n/B$.

At any time, if the above mentioned bounds are not satisfied during the processor allocation, we consider the overall algorithm to have failed and this probability can be bounded by ϵ for any fixed $\epsilon > 0$.

3. REFERENCES

[1] A. Aggarwal and J. S. Vitter. The input/output complexity of sorting and related problems. *Communications of the ACM*, pages 1116–1127, 1988.

[2] L. Arge, M. T. Goodrich, M. Nelson, and N. Sitchinava. Fundamental parallel algorithms for private-cache chip multiprocessors. In *SPAA*, pages 197–206, 2008.

[3] G. E. Blelloch, P. Gibbons, and H. V. Simhadri. Low depth cache-oblivious algorithms. In *SPAA*, pages 189–199, 2010.

[4] R. Cole and V. Ramachandran. Resource oblivious sorting on multicores. In *ICALP*, pages 226–237, 2010.

[5] M. Frigo, C. E. Leiserson, H. Prokop, and S. Ramachandran. Cache-oblivious algorithms. In *FOCS*, pages 285–298, 1999.

[6] J. H. Reif and S. Sen. Optimal parallel randomized algorithms for 3-d convex hulls and related problems. *SIAM Journal on Computing*, 21(3):466–485, 1992.

[7] R. Reischuk. A fast probabilistic parallel sorting algorithm. In *FOCS*, pages 212–219, 1981.

[8] N. Sharma and S. Sen. Efficient cache oblivious algorithms for randomized divide and conquer on the multicore model. *CoRR-abs/1204.6508*, available at http://arxiv.org/abs/1204.6508, 2012.

[9] L. G. Valiant. A bridging model for multi-core computing. In *ESA*, pages 13–28, 2008.

Brief Announcement:
Strong Scaling of Matrix Multiplication Algorithms and Memory-Independent Communication Lower Bounds

Grey Ballard[*]
UC Berkeley
ballard@cs.berkeley.edu

James Demmel[*][†]
UC Berkeley
demmel@cs.berkeley.edu

Olga Holtz[‡]
UC Berkeley and TU Berlin
holtz@math.berkeley.edu

Benjamin Lipshitz[*]
UC Berkeley
lipshitz@berkeley.edu

Oded Schwartz[§]
UC Berkeley
odedsc@cs.berkeley.edu

ABSTRACT

A parallel algorithm has perfect strong scaling if its running time on P processors is linear in $1/P$, including all communication costs. Distributed-memory parallel algorithms for matrix multiplication with perfect strong scaling have only recently been found. One is based on classical matrix multiplication (Solomonik and Demmel, 2011), and one is based on Strassen's fast matrix multiplication (Ballard, Demmel, Holtz, Lipshitz, and Schwartz, 2012). Both algorithms scale perfectly, but only up to some number of processors where the inter-processor communication no longer scales.

We obtain a memory-independent communication cost lower bound on classical and Strassen-based distributed-memory matrix multiplication algorithms. These bounds imply that no classical or Strassen-based parallel matrix multiplication algorithm can strongly scale perfectly beyond the ranges already attained by the two parallel algorithms mentioned above. The memory-independent bounds and the strong scaling bounds generalize to other algorithms.

ACM Classification Keywords: F.2.1

ACM General Terms: Algorithms, Design, Performance.

Keywords: Communication-avoiding algorithms, Strong scaling, Fast matrix multiplication

[*]Research supported by Microsoft (Award #024263) and Intel (Award #024894) funding and by matching funding by U.C. Discovery (Award #DIG07-10227). Additional support comes from Par Lab affiliates National Instruments, Nokia, NVIDIA, Oracle, and Samsung.

[†]Research is also supported by DOE grants DE-SC0003959, DE- SC0004938, and DE-AC02-05CH11231.

[‡]Research supported by the Sofja Kovalevskaja programme of Alexander von Humboldt Foundation and by the National Science Foundation under agreement DMS-0635607, while visiting the Institute for Advanced Study.

[§]Research supported by U.S. Department of Energy grants under Grant Numbers DE-SC0003959.

Copyright is held by the author/owner(s).
SPAA'12, June 25–27, 2012, Pittsburgh, Pennsylvania, USA.
ACM 978-1-4503-1213-4/12/06.

1. INTRODUCTION

In evaluating the recently proposed parallel algorithm based on Strassen's matrix multiplication [2] and comparing the communication costs to the known lower bounds [4], we found a gap between the upper and lower bounds for certain problem sizes. The main motivation of this work is to close this gap by tightening the lower bound for this case, proving that the algorithm is optimal in all cases, up to $O(\log P)$ factors. A similar scenario exists in the case of classical matrix multiplication; in this work we provide the analogous tightening of the existing lower bound [6] to show optimality of another recently proposed algorithm [8].

In addition to proving optimality of algorithms, the lower bounds in this paper yield another interesting conclusion regarding strong scaling. We say that an algorithm strongly scales perfectly if it attains running time on P processors which is linear in $1/P$, including all communication costs. While it is possible for classical and Strassen-based matrix multiplication algorithms to strongly scale perfectly, the communication costs restrict the strong scaling ranges much more than do the computation costs. These ranges depend on the problem size relative to the local memory size, and on the computational complexity of the algorithm.

Interestingly, in both cases the dominance of a memory-independent bound arises, and the strong scaling range ends, exactly when the memory-dependent latency lower bound becomes constant. This observation may provide a hint as to where to look for strong scaling ranges in other algorithms. Of course, since the latency cost cannot possibly drop below a constant, it is an immediate result of the memory-dependent bounds that the latency cost cannot continue to strongly scale perfectly. However the bandwidth cost typically dominates the cost, and it is the memory-independent bandwidth scaling bounds that limit the strong scaling of matrix multiplication in practice. For simplicity we omit discussions of latency cost, since the number of messages is always a factor of M below the bandwidth cost in the strong scaling range and always constant outside that range.

While the main arguments in this work focus on matrix multiplication, we present results in such a way that they can be generalized to other algorithms, including other $O(n^3)$-based dense and sparse algorithms as in [5] and other fast matrix multiplication algorithms as in [4].

Our paper is organized as follows. In Section 2.1 we prove a memory-independent communication lower bound for Strassen-based matrix multiplication algorithms, and we prove an analogous bound for classical matrix multiplication in Section 2.2. We discuss the implications of these bounds on strong scaling in Section 3 and compare the communication costs of Strassen and classical matrix multiplication as the number of processors increases. In Section 4 we discuss generalization of our bounds to other algorithms. The main results of this paper are summarized in Table 1.

2. COMMUNICATION LOWER BOUNDS

We use the distributed-memory communication model (see, *e.g.*, [5]), where the bandwidth cost of an algorithm is proportional to the number of words communicated and the latency cost is proportional to the number of messages communicated along the critical path. We will use the notation that n is the size of the matrices, P is the number of processors, M is the local memory size of each processor, and $\omega_0 = \log_2 7 \approx 2.81$ is the exponent of Strassen's matrix multiplication.

2.1 Strassen's Matrix Multiplication

In this section, we state a memory-independent lower bound for Strassen's matrix multiplication of $\Omega(n^2/P^{2/\omega_0})$ words, where $\omega_0 = \log_2 7$. The proof reuses notation and techniques from [5]. By prohibiting redundant computations we mean that each arithmetic operation is computed by exactly one processor. This is necessary for interpreting edge expansion as communication cost.

THEOREM 2.1. *Suppose a parallel algorithm performing Strassen's matrix multiplication minimizes computational costs in an asymptotic sense and performs no redundant computation. Then, for sufficiently large P,[1] some processor must send or receive at least $\Omega\left(\frac{n^2}{P^{2/w_0}}\right)$ words.*

Proof omitted. See technical report [3].

2.2 Classical Matrix Multiplication

In this section, we state a memory-independent lower bound for classical matrix multiplication of $\Omega(n^2/P^{2/3})$ words. The same result appears elsewhere in the literature, under slightly different assumptions: in the LPRAM model [1], where no data exists in the (unbounded) local memories at the start of the algorithm; in the distributed-memory model [6], where the local memory size is assumed to be $M = \Theta(n^2/P^{2/3})$; and in the distributed-memory model [8], where the algorithm is assumed to perform a certain amount of input replication. Our bound is for the distributed memory model, holds for any M, and assumes no specific communication pattern.

Recall the following special case of the Loomis-Whitney geometric bound:

LEMMA 2.2. [7] *Let V be a finite set of lattice points in $\mathbf{R}^3$, i.e., points (x, y, z) with integer coordinates. Let V_x be the projection of V in the x-direction, i.e., all points (y, z) such that there exists an x so that $(x, y, z) \in V$. Define V_y*

	Classical	Strassen
Memory-dependent lower bound	$\Omega\left(\frac{n^3}{P\sqrt{M}}\right)$	$\Omega\left(\frac{n^{\omega_0}}{PM^{\omega_0/2-1}}\right)$
Memory-independent lower bound	$\Omega\left(\frac{n^2}{P^{2/3}}\right)$	$\Omega\left(\frac{n^2}{P^{2/\omega_0}}\right)$
Perfect strong scaling range	$P = O\left(\frac{n^3}{M^{3/2}}\right)$	$P = O\left(\frac{n^{\omega_0}}{M^{\omega_0/2}}\right)$
Attaining algorithm	[8]	[2]

Table 1: **Bandwidth cost lower bounds for matrix multiplication and perfect strong scaling ranges. The classical memory dependent bound is due to [6], and the Strassen memory dependent bound is due to [4]. The memory-independent bounds are proved here, though variants of the classical bound appear in [1, 6, 8].**

and V_z similarly. Let $|\cdot|$ denote the cardinality of a set. Then $|V| \leq \sqrt{|V_x| \cdot |V_y| \cdot |V_z|}$.

Using Lemma 2.2 (in a similar way to [5, 6]), we can describe the ratio between the number of scalar multiplications a processor performs and the amount of data it must access.

LEMMA 2.3. *Suppose a processor has I words of initial data at the start of an algorithm, performs $\Theta(n^3/P)$ scalar multiplications within classical matrix multiplication, and then stores O words of output data at the end of the algorithm. Then the processor must send or receive at least $\Omega(n^2/P^{2/3}) - I - O$ words during the execution of the algorithm.*

Proof omitted. See technical report [3].

THEOREM 2.4. *Suppose a parallel algorithm performing classical dense matrix multiplication begins with one copy of the input matrices and minimizes computational costs in an asymptotic sense. Then, for sufficiently large P,[2] some processor must send or receive at least $\Omega\left(\frac{n^2}{P^{2/3}}\right)$ words.*

Proof omitted. See technical report [3].

3. LIMITS OF STRONG SCALING

In this section we present limits of strong scaling of matrix multiplication algorithms. These are immediate implications of the memory independent communication lower bounds proved in Section 2. Roughly speaking, the memory-dependent communication cost lower-bound is of the form $\Omega\left(f(n, M)/P\right)$ for both classical and Strassen matrix multiplication algorithms. However, the memory independent lower bounds are of the form $\Omega\left(f(n, M)/P^c\right)$ where $c < 1$ (see Table 1). This implies that strong scaling is not possible when the memory-independent bound dominates. We make this formal below.

COROLLARY 3.1. *Suppose a parallel algorithm performing Strassen's matrix multiplication minimizes bandwidth and computational costs in an asymptotic sense and performs no redundant computation. Then the algorithm can achieve perfect strong scaling only for $P = O\left(\frac{n^{\omega_0}}{M^{\omega_0/2}}\right)$.*

Proof omitted. See technical report [3].

---

[1] The theorem applies to any $P \geq 2$ with a strict enough assumption on the load balance among vertices in $Dec_{\lg n}C$ as defined in the proof.

[2] The theorem applies to any $P \geq 2$ with a strict enough assumption on the load balance.

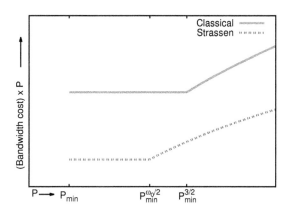

Figure 1: Bandwidth costs and strong scaling of matrix multiplication: classical vs. Strassen-based. Horizontal lines correspond to perfect strong scaling. $P_{\min}$ is the minimum number of processors required to store the input and output matrices.

COROLLARY 3.2. *Suppose a parallel algorithm performing classical dense matrix multiplication starts and ends with one copy of the data and minimizes bandwidth and computational costs in an asymptotic sense. Then the algorithm can achieve perfect strong scaling only for $P = O\left(\frac{n^3}{M^{3/2}}\right)$.*

Proof omitted. See technical report [3].

In Figure 1 we present the asymptotic communication costs of classical and Strassen-based algorithms for a fixed problem size as the number of processors increases. Both of the perfectly strong scaling algorithms stop scaling perfectly above some number of processors, which depends on the matrix size and the available local memory size.

Let $P_{\min} = \Theta\left(\frac{n^2}{M}\right)$ be the minimum number of processors required to store the input and output matrices. By Corollaries 3.1 and 3.2 the perfect strong scaling range is $P_{\min} \leq P \leq P_{\max}$ where $P_{\max} = \Theta(P_{\min}^{3/2})$ in the classical case and $P_{\max} = \Theta(P_{\min}^{\omega_0/2})$ in the Strassen case.

Note that the perfect strong scaling range is larger for the classical case, though the communication costs are higher.

4. EXTENSIONS AND OPEN PROBLEMS

The memory-independent bound and perfect strong scaling bound of Strassen's matrix multiplication (Theorem 2.1 and Corollary 3.1) apply to other Strassen-like algorithms, as defined in [5], with ω_0 being the exponent of the total arithmetic count, provided that $Dec_{\lg n}C$ is connected. The proof follows that of Theorem 2.1 and of Corollary 3.1, but uses Claim 18 of [4] instead of Fact 9 there, and replaces Lemma 10 there with its extension.

The memory-dependent bound of classical matrix multiplication of [6] was generalized in [5] to algorithms which perform computations of the form

$$\text{Mem}(c(i,j)) = f_{ij}(g_{ijk}(\text{Mem}(a(i,k)), \text{Mem}(b(k,j)))), \quad (1)$$

where $\text{Mem}(i)$ denotes the argument in memory location i and f_{ij} and g_{ijk} are functions which depend non-trivially on their arguments (see [5] for more detailed definitions).

The memory-independent bound of classical matrix multiplication (Theorem 2.4) applies to these other algorithms as well. If the algorithm begins with one copy of the input data and minimizes computational costs in an asymptotic sense, then, for sufficiently large P, some processor must send or receive at least $\Omega\left(\left(\frac{G}{P}\right)^{2/3} - \frac{D}{P}\right)$ words, where G is the total number of g_{ijk} computations and D is the number of non-zeros in the input and output. The proof follows that of Lemma 2.3 and Theorem 2.4, setting $|V| = G$ (instead of n^3), replacing n^3/P with G/P, and setting $I+O = O(D/P)$ (instead of $O(n^2/P)$).

Algorithms which fit the form of equation (1) include LU and Cholesky decompositions, sparse matrix-matrix multiplication, as well as algorithms for solving the all-pairs-shortest-paths problem. Only a few of these have parallel algorithms which attain the lower bounds in all cases. In several cases, it seems likely that one can prove better bounds than those presented here, thus obtaining a stricter bound on perfect strong scaling (see, *e.g.*, [8]).

We also believe that our bounds can be generalized to QR decomposition and other orthogonal transformations, fast linear algebra, fast Fourier transform, and other recursive algorithms.

5. REFERENCES

[1] AGGARWAL, A., CHANDRA, A. K., AND SNIR, M. Communication complexity of PRAMs. *Theoretical Computer Science 71*, 1 (1990), 3 – 28.

[2] BALLARD, G., DEMMEL, J., HOLTZ, O., LIPSHITZ, B., AND SCHWARTZ, O. Communication-optimal parallel algorithm for Strassen's matrix multiplication. In *SPAA '12: Proceedings of the 24th Annual Symposium on Parallelism in Algorithms and Architectures* (New York, NY, USA, 2012), ACM.

[3] BALLARD, G., DEMMEL, J., HOLTZ, O., LIPSHITZ, B., AND SCHWARTZ, O. Strong scaling of matrix multiplication algorithms and memory-independent communication lower bounds. EECS Technical Report EECS-2012-31, UC Berkeley, Mar. 2012.

[4] BALLARD, G., DEMMEL, J., HOLTZ, O., AND SCHWARTZ, O. Graph expansion and communication costs of fast matrix multiplication. In *SPAA '11: Proceedings of the 23rd Annual Symposium on Parallelism in Algorithms and Architectures* (New York, NY, USA, 2011), ACM, pp. 1–12.

[5] BALLARD, G., DEMMEL, J., HOLTZ, O., AND SCHWARTZ, O. Minimizing communication in numerical linear algebra. *SIAM J. Matrix Analysis Applications 32*, 3 (2011), 866–901.

[6] IRONY, D., TOLEDO, S., AND TISKIN, A. Communication lower bounds for distributed-memory matrix multiplication. *J. Parallel Distrib. Comput. 64*, 9 (2004), 1017–1026.

[7] LOOMIS, L. H., AND WHITNEY, H. An inequality related to the isoperimetric inequality. *Bulletin of the AMS 55* (1949), 961–962.

[8] SOLOMONIK, E., AND DEMMEL, J. Communication-optimal parallel 2.5D matrix multiplication and LU factorization algorithms. In *Euro-Par '11: Proceedings of the 17th International European Conference on Parallel and Distributed Computing* (2011), Springer.

Brief Announcement: On the Complexity of the Minimum Latency Scheduling Problem on the Euclidean Plane

Henry Lin
University of Maryland
3104E Biomolecular Sciences Bldg
College Park, MD 20742
henrylin@umiacs.umd.edu

Frans Schalekamp
The College of William and Mary
Department of Mathematics
Williamsburg, VA 23187
fms9@cornell.edu

ABSTRACT

We announce NP-hardness of the minimum latency scheduling (MLS) problem under the physical model of wireless networking. In this model a transmission is received successfully if the Signal to Interference-plus-Noise Ratio (SINR), is above a given threshold. In the MLS problem, the goal is to assign a time slot and power level to each transmission, so that all the messages are received successfully, and the number of distinct times slots is minimized.

Despite its seeming simplicity and several previous hardness results for various settings of the minimum latency scheduling problem, it has remained an open question whether or not the minimum latency scheduling problem is NP-hard, when the nodes are known to be placed in the Euclidean plane and arbitrary power levels can be chosen for the transmissions. We resolve this open question for all path loss exponent values $\alpha \geq 3$.

Categories and Subject Descriptors

F.2 [**Analysis of Algorithms and Problem Complexity**]: Miscellaneous; C.2.1 [**Network Architecture and Design**]: Wireless communication

Keywords

SINR model, NP-hardness, minimum latency scheduling problem, wireless networks, sensor networks

1. INTRODUCTION

In this announcement, we report NP-hardness for the minimum latency scheduling (MLS) problem in wireless networking, where we have nodes in a network, embedded in the Euclidean plane, seeking to send messages to each other in the physical model of wireless communication. For every message, a time slot and a power level has to be chosen. A message is received successfully if the transmission meets a Signal to Interference-plus-Noise Ratio (SINR) requirement. The objective of the problem is to minimize the number of time slots that are used to send all messages successfully. The hardness of the MLS problem with unrestricted power levels remained open since the work of [4], and was mentioned prominently in a survey paper by Locher, Rickenbach, and Wattenhofer [9]. We report that the MLS problem is NP-hard when arbitrary power levels can be chosen for the

Copyright is held by the author/owner(s).
SPAA'12, June 25–27, 2012, Pittsburgh, Pennsylvania, USA.
ACM 978-1-4503-1213-4/12/06.

transmissions, and the nodes are known to be placed in the Euclidean plane, for all path loss exponent values $\alpha \geq 3$. The path loss exponent controls how quickly the signal of each message decays over a distance, and in practice $\alpha \geq 2$ generally. Our hardness result also shows the MLS problem is NP-hard to approximate within a multiplicative factor better than $\frac{4}{3}$.

The physical model was first introduced in a seminal paper by Gupta and Kumar [5]. There has been much previous work on the problem of scheduling and choosing power levels to send messages in the physical model of wireless networking, and several hardness results [4, 1, 6, 3, 7] have been proven for this problem in various settings under differing assumptions. In this work, we consider the case when the nodes are known to be placed in the Euclidean plane, and the power levels can be chosen arbitrarily. This models practical situations in which sensors are deployed in a 2-dimensional area, such as in a field to monitor weather conditions, or along roads to monitor traffic conditions.

Katz, Völker, and Wagner [6] show that the MLS problem of scheduling and choosing transmission powers is NP-hard if the network is embedded in the Euclidean plane and there are known upper and lower bounds on the power levels that can be used. Their proof also shows that if there are only a finite set of transmission powers that can be chosen, then this problem is also NP-hard. However, it has remained an open question whether or not this problem is NP-hard when the nodes are in the Euclidean plane and arbitrary power levels can be chosen.

The distinction between the two problems can be thought of as follows. The work of Katz, Völker, and Wagner [6] is applicable in the setting in which we want to schedule messages on sensors that have already been built, as these sensors will naturally have an upper and lower bound on their allowable transmission powers due to hardware or software limitations. The setting we consider is more general and includes the case in which it is possible to design the sensors and choose arbitrary power levels at which they can transmit, so as to maximize the number of transmissions that can be sent in a given time period and minimize the total number of time periods that are needed to send a certain set of messages. Despite its seeming simplicity, the hardness of this problem has remained open and was featured prominently as an open question in [9].

The best algorithm for the MLS problem with arbitrary power levels is due to Kesselheim [8], who gives an $O(\log^2 n)$-approximation algorithm for the MLS problem in general metrics, and an $O(\log n)$-approximation for fading metrics.

2. HIGH LEVEL OVERVIEW OF THE REDUCTION

We show that the minimum latency scheduling problem is NP-hard, by reducing the 3-coloring problem of planar 4-regular graphs to it, which was shown to be NP-hard by Dailey [2]. In the 3-coloring problem on planar 4-regular graphs, we are given a planar graph $G = (V, E)$ of degree 4, and we want to determine whether there is a proper coloring of the nodes of G that uses only 3 colors. We can assume that the graph is given as an orthogonal grid graph, which is a graph drawn in the plane with all nodes placed at grid intersection points, and all edges drawn along grid lines without any edge crossings, but edges may bend at grid intersection points. This coloring problem on an orthogonal grid graph is also NP-hard because Shiloach [10] and Valiant [11] show that any planar G of degree at most 4 can be drawn as an orthogonal grid graph in an area of size at most $O(|V|^2)$.

In the reduction, we set the noise parameter $n_v = 0$ for all nodes v, thus proving that this problem is NP-hard for nodes placed in the Euclidean plane, *even if there is no background noise*. Note that this "no noise" assumption only makes the reduction *harder* as the MLS problem with noise is a more general problem with a noise parameter $n_v \geq 0$ for each node v. Thus, our result also shows the MLS problem with noise is NP-hard. Additionally, we will set the signal to noise threshold value $\beta_v = 1$ for each node v. When $n_v = 0$ and $\beta_v = 1$ for all nodes v, the SINR inequality simply requires that the signal be larger than the interference for a message to be successfully transmitted.

We construct an MLS instance whose transmissions can be completely scheduled in 3 rounds if and only if G is 3-colorable. The main difficulty to overcome in this reduction compared to previous hardness results is that we have no bounds on the power levels. This means that only the *layout* of the nodes can be used to make sure a feasible three-round schedule corresponds to a feasible solution of the problem we reduce from. The messages constructed in our reduction will correspond to coloring nodes certain colors in each round, and the key insight to making this idea work is ensuring that certain messages cannot be transmitted at the same time based only on the locations of their source and destination nodes. If an edge $\{u, v\}$ exists in the coloring instance, we ensure that the messages that correspond to coloring u red and coloring v red cannot be transmitted at the same time, so that a feasible 3 round solution for the MLS problem can be used to construct a solution for the 3 coloring problem. A careful analysis shows that our reduction works for all path loss exponents $\alpha \geq 3$.

3. OPEN QUESTIONS

It is an interesting open question to show NP-hardness for α arbitrary close to 2 and without any restrictions on the power levels used. For α arbitrarily close to 2, we are not sure whether our reduction can be used. We have an NP-hardness result for the case where the parameter α can have any arbitrary value, but then we need the additional assumption that there is a maximum power level for the transmissions, and in the reduction we make use of the noise parameter. This result is also stronger than what was known previously, since [6] for example, requires both an upper *and* lower bound on the power levels.

Another interesting open question is whether there ex-

ists an $O(1)$-approximation algorithm for this problem, or if the hardness result can be improved to show that the MLS problem is hard to approximate better than $O(\log n)$ to match the best known approximation algorithm. We also do not know whether it is harder to approximate this problem with or without power restrictions. Finally, we would like to note that the hardness result here holds for centralized algorithms, and therefore also for distributed algorithms. Another important problem is to find a good distributed algorithm for this problem. A full version of our paper is available at http://arxiv.org/abs/1203.2725 .

4. ACKNOWLEDGMENTS

Part of this work was done while both authors were at ITCS, Tsinghua University, Beijing. This work was supported in part by the National Natural Science Foundation of China Grant 60553001, and the National Basic Research Program of China Grant 2007CB807900, 2007CB807901.

5. REFERENCES

[1] M. Andrews and M. Dinitz. Maximizing capacity in arbitrary wireless networks in the SINR model: Complexity and game theory. *INFOCOM*, 2009.

[2] D. P. Dailey. Uniqueness of colorability and colorability of planar 4-regular graphs are NP-complete. *Discrete Mathematics*, 30(3):289 – 293, 1980.

[3] A. Fanghänel, T. Kesselheim, H. Räcke, and B. Vöcking. Oblivious interference scheduling. *PODC '09: Proceedings of the 28th ACM symposium on Principles of distributed computing*, pages 220–229, New York, NY, USA, 2009. ACM.

[4] O. Goussevskaia, Y. A. Oswald, and R. Wattenhofer. Complexity in geometric SINR. *Proc. of the 8th Intl. Symposium on Mobile Ad Hoc Networking and Computing (MobiHoc '07)*, 2007.

[5] P. Gupta and P. R. Kumar. The capacity of wireless networks. *IEEE Transactions on Information Theory*, 2000.

[6] B. Katz, M. Völker, and D. Wagner. Energy efficient scheduling with power control for wireless networks. *WiOpt*, pages 160–169, May 2010.

[7] T. Kesselheim. *Packet Scheduling with Interference*. PhD thesis, Rheinisch-Westfälische Technische Hochschule Aachen, 2009.

[8] T. Kesselheim. A constant-factor approximation for wireless capacity maximization with power control in the SINR model. *Symposium on Discrete Algorithms (SODA)*, 2011.

[9] T. Locher, P. von Rickenbach, and R. Wattenhofer. Sensor networks continue to puzzle: Selected open problems. S. Rao, M. Chatterjee, P. Jayanti, C. Murthy, and S. Saha, editors, *Distributed Computing and Networking*, volume 4904 of *Lecture Notes in Computer Science*, pages 25–38. Springer Berlin / Heidelberg, 2008.

[10] Y. Shiloach. *Arrangements of Planar Graphs on the Planar Lattice*. PhD thesis, Weizmann Institute of Science, Rehovot, Israel, 1976.

[11] L. Valiant. Universality considerations in VLSI circuits. *IEEE Transactions on Computers*, C-30:135–140, 1981.

Parallel and I/O Efficient Set Covering Algorithms

Guy E. Blelloch   Harsha Vardhan Simhadri   Kanat Tangwongsan

Carnegie Mellon University

{guyb, hsimhadr, ktangwon}@cs.cmu.edu

ABSTRACT

This paper presents the design, analysis, and implementation of parallel and sequential I/O-efficient algorithms for set cover, tying together the line of work on parallel set cover and the line of work on efficient set cover algorithms for large, disk-resident instances.

Our contributions are twofold: First, we design and analyze a parallel cache-oblivious set-cover algorithm that offers essentially the same approximation guarantees as the standard greedy algorithm, which has the optimal approximation. Our algorithm is the first efficient external-memory or cache-oblivious algorithm for when neither the sets nor the elements fit in memory, leading to I/O cost (cache complexity) equivalent to sorting in the Cache Oblivious or Parallel Cache Oblivious models. The algorithm also implies low cache misses on parallel hierarchical memories (again, equivalent to sorting). Second, building on this theory, we engineer variants of the theoretical algorithm optimized for different hardware setups. We provide experimental evaluation showing substantial speedups over existing algorithms without compromising the solution's quality.

Categories and Subject Descriptors: F.2 [Theory of Computation]: Analysis of Algorithms and Problem Complexity

General Terms: Algorithms, Theory

Keywords: Parallel algorithms, set cover, max k-cover, external memory algorithms, approximation algorithms.

1. INTRODUCTION

Set cover is one of the most fundamental and well-studied problems in optimization and approximation algorithms. For decades, this problem and its variants have found many applications, including locating warehouses, testing faults, scheduling crews on airlines, and allocating wavelength in wireless communication. These applications often have to

Permission to make digital or hard copies of all or part of this work for personal or classroom use is granted without fee provided that copies are not made or distributed for profit or commercial advantage and that copies bear this notice and the full citation on the first page. To copy otherwise, to republish, to post on servers or to redistribute to lists, requires prior specific permission and/or a fee.

SPAA'12, June 25–27, 2012, Pittsburgh, Pennsylvania, USA.

Copyright 2012 ACM 978-1-4503-1213-4/12/06 ...$10.00.

deal with massive data [14] and are well-suited for parallel and I/O efficient algorithms.

Let $\mathcal{U}$ be a set of n ground elements, $\mathcal{F}$ be a collection of subsets of $\mathcal{U}$ that together covers $\mathcal{U}$ (i.e., $\cup_{S \in \mathcal{F}} S = \mathcal{U}$), and $c : \mathcal{F} \to \mathbb{R}_+$ be a cost function. The *set cover problem* is to find the cheapest collection of sets $\mathcal{A} \subseteq \mathcal{F}$ that that covers $\mathcal{U}$ (i.e., $\cup_{S \in \mathcal{A}} S = \mathcal{U}$), where the cost of a solution $\mathcal{A}$ is specified by $c(\mathcal{A}) = \sum_{S \in \mathcal{A}} c(S)$. Unweighted set cover (all weights are equal) appeared as one of the 21 problems Karp identified as NP-complete in 1972 [21]. Two years later, Johnson [19] proved that the simple greedy method gives an approximation that is at most a factor $H_n = \sum_{k=1}^{n} \frac{1}{k}$ from optimal. Subsequently, Chvátal [13] proved the same approximation bounds for the weighted case. These results are complemented by a matching hardness result: Feige [16] showed that unless $\mathsf{NP} \subseteq \mathsf{DTIME}(n^{O(\log \log n)})$, set cover cannot be approximated in polynomial time with a ratio better than $(1 - o(1)) \ln n$. This essentially shows that the greedy algorithm is optimal. Furthermore, the greedy algorithm is particularly simple running in $O(W)$ time for the unweighted case and $O(W \log W)$ time for the weighted case. Here, $W \geq n$ is the sum of the sizes of the sets. In the bipartite graph view we will use later on, the quantity W is the number of edges in the graph.

The greedy algorithm seems hard to parallelize directly, but Berger, Rompel, and Shor [2] (BRS) showed that it can be "approximately" parallelized leading to an $O(\log^5 W)$-depth and $O(W \log^4 W)$-work randomized algorithm, giving a $(1 + \varepsilon) H_n$-approximation on a PRAM. Rajagopalan and Vazirani [24] later gave an improvement in both work and depth. More recently, this was improved to linear work and smaller depth [7]. In terms of I/O efficient algorithms, Cormode, Karloff, and Wirth recently developed an efficient algorithm for the case when the elements—but not necessarily the sets—fit in memory [14]. We know of *no* I/O efficient solutions for the general case (i.e. when neither the sets nor the elements fit in memory). Furthermore, the CKW algorithm is strictly sequential.

Our Contributions: This paper presents the design, analysis, and experimental evaluation of set-covering algorithms. First, we design and analyze approximation algorithms for set cover and related problems that are *both parallel and I/O efficient*. These are the first results we know of for I/O efficient set cover where neither the sets nor elements fit in memory. Building on this theory, we implemented slight variants of the theoretical algorithm optimized for two different hardware setups: one a high-end parallel workstation and the other a "wimpy" machine with small memory but a fast disk. We provide extensive experimental evaluation showing non-trivial speedups over existing algorithms without compromising the solution's quality.

Our theoretical results show how to implement recent results for parallel set cover [7] (BPT) in an I/O efficient manner. In the cache oblivious model [17] with cache size parameter M and block size B, our algorithm has cache complexity $O(\frac{W}{B} \log_{\frac{M}{B}} \frac{W}{B})$. This matches the complexity of sorting. Furthermore, we achieve polylogarithmic depth and the same cache complexity bounds in the more stringent parallel cache oblivious model [4]. Our results modify the BPT algorithm with appropriate data structures. The algorithms give an $(1 + \varepsilon)H_n$-approximation for arbitrary $\varepsilon > 0$ and hence are essentially optimal. In addition to set cover, as shown in [7], the same sequence of sets can be used as a solution to max cover and min-sum set cover. For max cover, this sequence is prefix optimal: for any prefix of length k, this prefix is a $(1 - 1/e - \varepsilon)$-approximation to the max k-cover problem.

We have implemented and experimented with two variants of our algorithm, one for shared-memory parallel machines and one for external memory. The main difference between the two variants is how we implement the communication steps. We experiment with the parallel variant on a modern 40-core machine and with the external memory variant on a more modest machine using a solid-state drive (SSD). We test the algorithms with several large instances with up to 5.5 billion edges. For the parallel version, we are able to achieve significant speedup over a fast sequential implementation. In particular, we compare to the CKW sequential algorithm which is already significantly faster than the greedy algorithm. For our largest graph with about 5.5 billion edges, the algorithm runs in around 10 seconds and is 13.5x faster than the CKW algorithm. In fact, it runs faster than optimized parallel sorting code [25] on the same sized data. For the max k-cover problem, we empirically show that it is often possible to speedup the computation by more than a factor of 2 by stopping the algorithm early when k is known and is small relative to the set cover's solution size. For the sequential I/O variant, we are able to achieve orders of magnitude speedups over the results of CKW when neither the sets nor elements fit in memory. When the elements fit in memory, the CKW algorithm is faster. With regards to quality of the results (number of sets returned), our algorithm returns about the same number of sets as the other algorithms.

2. PRELIMINARIES AND NOTATION

Let $[k]$ be the set $\{1, 2, \ldots, k\}$. For a graph G, we denote by $\deg_G(v)$ the degree of the vertex v in G. We denote by $N_G(v)$ the neighbor set of the node v and by $N_G(X)$ the neighbors of the vertex set X, i.e., $N_G(X) = \cup_{w \in X} N_G(w)$. We drop the subscript when the context is clear. Let $V(G)$ and $E(G)$ denote respectively the set of nodes and the set of edges. We also write $|G|$ to mean the number of edges of G. For an input of size W, we assume that every memory word has $O(\log W)$ bits.

Computation Model. We present algorithms in the nested parallel model, allowing arbitrary dynamic nesting of parallel loops and fork-join constructs but no other synchronizations. This corresponds to the class of algorithms with series-parallel dependence graphs (see Figure 1). Computations can be decomposed into "tasks", "parallel blocks" and

"strands" recursively: As a base case, a **strand** is a serial sequence of instructions not containing any parallel constructs or subtasks. A **task** is formed by serially composing $k \geq 1$ strands interleaved with $(k - 1)$ "parallel blocks" (denoted by $\mathsf{t} = \mathsf{s}_1; \mathsf{b}_1; \ldots; \mathsf{s}_k$). A **parallel block** is formed by composing in parallel one or more tasks with a fork point before all of them and a join point after (denoted by $\mathsf{b} = \mathsf{t}_1 \| \mathsf{t}_2 \| \ldots \| \mathsf{t}_k$). A parallel block can be, for example, a parallel loop or some constant number of recursive calls. The top-level computation is a task. The **span** (aka. **depth**) of a computation is the length of the longest path in the dependence graph.

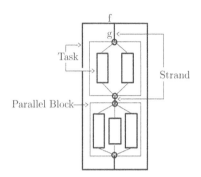

Figure 1. Decomposing the computation: tasks, strands and parallel blocks

Measuring Memory Access Costs. We will analyze algorithms in the Parallel Cache Oblivious (PCO) model [4], which is a parallel variant of the cache oblivious (CO) model and gives cache complexity costs that are always at least as large. Therefore any upper bounds on the PCO are also upper bounds on the CO model. The Cache Oblivious (CO) model [17] is a model for measuring cache misses of an algorithm, when run on a single processor machine with a two-level memory hierarchy—one level of finite cache and a memory of unbounded size. The cache complexity measure of an algorithm under this model $Q(n; M, B)$ counts the number of cache misses incurred by a problem instance of size n when run on a fully associative cache of size M and line size B using the optimal offline algorithm (i.e., the optimal cache replacement policy). Throughout the paper we assume that $M \geq B$ (the *tall cache assumption*).

Like the cache-oblivious model, in the **Parallel Cache-Oblivious (PCO) model**, there is a memory of unbounded size and a single cache with size M, line-size B (in words), and optimal replacement policy. The cache state κ consists of the set of cache lines resident in the cache at a given time. When a location in a non-resident line l is accessed and the cache is full, l replaces in κ the line accessed furthest into the future, incurring a *cache miss*. To extend the CO model to parallel computations, one needs to define how to analyze

> Task t forks subtasks t_1 and t_2, with $\kappa = \{l_1, l_2, l_3\}$
>
> t_1 accesses l_1, l_4, l_5 incurring 2 misses
> t_2 accesses l_2, l_4, l_6 incurring 2 misses
>
> At the join point: $\kappa' = \{l_1, l_2, l_3, l_4, l_5, l_6\}$

Figure 2. Applying the PCO model (Definition 2.1) to a parallel block. Here, $Q^*(\mathsf{t}; M, B; \kappa) = 4$.

the number of cache misses for the tasks that run in parallel in a parallel block. The PCO model approaches it by (i) ignoring any data reuse among the parallel subtasks and (ii) assuming the cache is flushed at each fork and join point of any task that does not fit within the cache.

More formally, let $loc(\mathsf{t}; B)$ denote the set of distinct cache lines accessed by task t, and $S(\mathsf{t}; B) = |loc(\mathsf{t}; B)| \cdot B$ denote its size (also let $s(\mathsf{t}; B) = |loc(\mathsf{t}; B)|$ denote the size in terms of number of cache lines). Let $Q(\mathsf{c}; M, B; \kappa)$ be the cache complexity of c in the sequential CO model when starting with cache state κ.

Definition 2.1 (Parallel Cache-Oblivious Model) *For cache parameters M and B the **cache complexity** of a strand, parallel block, and a task starting in cache state κ are defined recursively as follows (refer [4] for more details).*

- *For a strand, $Q^*(\mathsf{s}; M, B; \kappa) = Q(\mathsf{s}; M, B; \kappa)$.*
- *For a parallel block $\mathsf{b} = \mathsf{t}_1 \| \mathsf{t}_2 \| \dots \| \mathsf{t}_k$,*
  $Q^*(\mathsf{b}; M, B; \kappa) = \sum_{i=1}^{k} Q^*(\mathsf{t}_i; M, B; \kappa).$
- *For a task $\mathsf{t} = \mathsf{c}_1; \dots; \mathsf{c}_k$,*
  $Q^*(\mathsf{t}; M, B; \kappa) = \sum_{i=1}^{k} Q^*(\mathsf{c}_i; M, B; \kappa_{i-1}),$
  where $\kappa_i = \emptyset$ if $S(\mathsf{t}; B) > M$, and $\kappa_i = \kappa \cup_{j=1}^{i} loc(\mathsf{c}_j; B)$ if $S(\mathsf{t}; B) \leq M$.

We use $Q^*(\mathsf{c}; M, B)$ to denote a computation c starting with an empty cache, $Q^*(n; M, B)$ when n is a parameter of the computation. We note that $Q^*(\mathsf{c}; M, B) \geq Q(\mathsf{c}; M, B)$. When applied to a parallel machine, Q^* is a "work-like" measure and represents the total number of cache misses across all processors. An appropriate scheduler is used to evenly balance them across the processors.

Primitives. We need primitives such as sorting, prefix sums, merge, filter, map for the set cover algorithm. Parallel algorithms with optimal cache complexity in the PCO model and polylogarithmic depth can be constructed for these problems (for details, see [5, 4]). The cache complexity of sorting on an input instance n in the PCO model is $\mathrm{sort}(n; M, B) = O(\frac{n}{B} \log_{M/B} \frac{n}{B})$, while the complexity of the other primitives is $O(n/B)$. We use $\mathrm{sort}(n)$ as shorthand. All these primitives have $O(\log^2 n)$ depth.

3. ALGORITHM DESIGN

This section describes an efficient implementation of the BPT set cover algorithm [7] in the PCO model, implying good I/O complexity in other related models. We begin by reviewing the BPT algorithm and describing how to achieve an I/O efficient algorithm that satisfies Theorem 3.1. In the following section, we discuss optimizations we made to the theoretical algorithm to achieve good performance on different hardware setups.

We state the complexity of the set cover algorithm in terms of W, which, as defined previously, is the sum of the set sizes:

Theorem 3.1 (Parallel and I/O Efficient Set Cover) *The I/O (cache) complexity of the randomized approximate set cover algorithm on an instance of size W is expected $O(\mathrm{sort}(W))$ and the depth is $O(\mathrm{polylog}(W))$ **whp**. Furthermore, this implies an algorithm for prefix-optimal max cover and min-sum set cover in the same complexity bounds.*

Consider the BPT algorithm in Algorithm 3.1. At the core of it are the following 3 ingredients—prebucketing, maximal

---

Algorithm 3.1 SetCover — Blelloch et al. parallel greedy set cover.

Input: a set cover instance $(\mathcal{U}, \mathcal{F}, c)$ and a parameter $\varepsilon > 0$.
Output: a *ordered* collection of sets covering the ground elements.

  i. Let $\gamma = \max_{e \in \mathcal{U}} \min_{S \in \mathcal{F}} c(S)$, $W = \sum_{S \in \mathcal{F}} |S|$, $T = \log_{1/(1-\varepsilon)}(W^3/\varepsilon)$, and $\beta = \frac{W^2}{\varepsilon \cdot \gamma}$.

  ii. Let $(\mathcal{A}; A_0, \dots, A_T) = \mathtt{Prebucket}(\mathcal{U}, \mathcal{F}, c)$ and $\mathcal{U}_0 = \mathcal{U} \setminus (\cup_{S \in \mathcal{A}} S)$.

  iii. For $t = 0, \dots, T$, perform the following steps:

    1. Remove deleted elements from sets in this bucket: $A'_t = \{S \cap \mathcal{U}_t : S \in A_t\}$

    2. Only keep sets that still belong in this bucket: $A''_t = \{S \in A'_t : c(S)/|S| > \beta \cdot (1 - \varepsilon)^{t+1}\}$.

    3. Select a maximal nearly independent set from the bucket: $J_t = \mathtt{MaNIS}_{(\varepsilon, 3\varepsilon)}(A''_t)$.

    4. Remove elements covered by J_t: $\mathcal{U}_{t+1} = \mathcal{U}_t \setminus X_t$ where $X_t = \cup_{S \in J_t} S$

    5. Move remaining sets to the next bucket: $A_{t+1} = A_{t+1} \cup (A'_t \setminus J_t)$

  iv. Finally, return $\mathcal{A} \cup J_0 \cup \dots \cup J_T$.

---

near-independent set (MANIS), and bucket management—which we discuss in turn:

— *Prebucketing:* This component (Step ii of the algorithm) buckets the sets based on their cost. To ensure that the ratio between the costliest set and cheapest set is polynomially bounded so that the total number of buckets is kept logarithmic, as described in Lemma 4.2 of [7], sets that cost more than a threshold are discarded, and all sets cheaper than a certain threshold ($\mathcal{A}$) are included in the solution and the elements in these included sets marked as covered. Then $\mathcal{U}_0$ consists of the uncovered elements. The remaining sets are placed into $O(\log W)$ buckets $(A_0, A_1, \dots, A_T)$ by their normalized cost (cost per element).

The algorithm then enters the main loop (step iii.), iterating over the buckets from the least to the most expensive and invoking MANIS once in each iteration.

— *MANIS:* Invoked in Step iii(3) of the set cover algorithm, MANIS finds a subcollection of the sets in a bucket that are almost non-overlapping with the goal of closely mimicking the greedy behavior. Algorithm 3.2 shows the MANIS algorithm, reproduced from [7]. (The annotations on the side indicate which primitives in the PCO model we will use to implement them.) Conceptually, the input to MANIS is a bipartite graph with left vertices representing the sets and the right vertices representing the elements. The procedure starts with each left vertex picking random priorities (step 2). Then, each element identifies itself with the highest priority set containing it (step 3). If "enough" elements identify themselves with a set, the set selects itself (step 4). All selected sets and the elements they cover are eliminated (steps 5(1), 5(2)), and the cost of remaining sets is re-evaluated based on the uncovered elements. Only sets (A') with costs low enough to belong to the correct bucket (which invoked this MANIS) are selected in step 5(3) and the procedure continues with another level of recursion in step 6. The net result is that we choose nearly non-overlapping sets, and the sets that are not chosen are "shrunk" by a constant factor.

— *Bucket Movement:* The remaining steps in Algorithm 3.1 are devoted to moving sets between buckets, ensuring the contents of the least-costly bucket contain only sets in a specific cost range. Step iii(4) removes elements covered by the sets returned by MaNIS; step iii(5) transfers the sets not selected in MaNIS to the next bucket; and step iii(2) selects only those sets with costs in the current bucket's range for passing to MaNIS.

3.1   I/O Efficient Algorithm

We now discuss the right set of data structures and primitives to make the above algorithm both parallel and I/O efficient. In both the set cover and MaNIS algorithms, the set-element instance is represented as a bipartite graph with sets on the left. A list of sets as well as a compact and contiguous adjacency list for each set is stored. The universe of elements $\mathcal{U}$ is represented as a bitmap indexed by an element identifier which is updated to indicate when element has been covered. Since we only need one bit of information per element to indicate whether it is covered or not, this can be stored in $O(\frac{|\mathcal{U}|}{\log W})$ words. Unlike in [6], we do not maintain back pointers from the elements to the sets.

— *Prebucketing:* This phase involves sorting sets based on their cost and a filter to remove the costliest and the cheapest set. Sets can then be partitioned into buckets with a merge operation. All operations have less than sort(W) I/O complexity and $O(\log^2 n)$ depth in the PCO model.

— MaNIS: We invoke MaNIS in step 3 of the set cover algorithm. Inside MaNIS, we store the remaining elements of $\mathcal{U}$ (right vertices) as a sequence of element identifiers. To implement MaNIS, in Step 3, for each left vertex, we copy its value x_a to all the edges incident on it, then sort the edges based on the right vertex so that the edges incident on the same right vertex are contiguous. For each right vertex, we can now use a prefix "sum" using maximum to find the neighbor a with the maximum x_a. In step 4, the "winning" edges (an edge connecting a right vertex with it's chosen left vertex) are marked on the edge list for each right vertex we computed in step 3. The edge list is then sorted based on the left vertex. Prefix sum can then be used to compute the number of elements each set has "won". A compact representation for J and its adjacency list can be computed with a filter operation. In step 5(1), the combined adjacency list of elements in J is sorted and duplicates removed to get $\overline{B}$. For step 5(2), we first evaluate the list $A \setminus J$. Then, we sort the edges incident on $A \setminus J$ based on their right vertices; merge with the remaining elements to identify which is contained in $\overline{B}$, marking these edges accordingly. After sorting these edges based on their left vertices, for each left vertex $a \in A \setminus J$, we filter and pack the "live edges" to compute $N'_G(a)$. Steps 5(3) and 5(4) involve simple filter and sum operations. The most I/O intensive operation (as well as the operation with maximum depth) in each round of MaNIS is sorting, which requires at most $O(\text{sort}(|G|))$ I/O complexity and $O(\log^2 |G|)$ depth in the PCO model. As analyzed in [7], for a bucket with W_t edges to start with, MaNIS runs for at most $O(\log W_t)$ rounds—and after each round, the number of edges drops by a constant factor; therefore, we have the following bounds:

Lemma 3.2 *The cache (I/O) complexity in the PCO model of running MaNIS on a bucket with W_t edges is $O(\text{sort}(W_t))$, and the depth is $O(D_{sort}(W_t) \log W_t)$.*

— *Bucket Movement:* We assume the A_t, A'_t and A''_t are stored in the same format as the input for MaNIS (see 3.1).

The right set of vertices of the bipartite graph is now a bitmap corresponding to the elements indicating whether an element is alive or dead. Step iii(1) is similar to Step 3 of MaNIS. We first sort $S \in A_t$ to order the edges by element index, then merge this representation (with a vector of length $O(|\mathcal{U}| / \log W)$) to match them with the elements bitmap, do a filter to remove deleted edges, and perform another sort to get them back ordered by set. Step iii(2) is simply a filter. The append operation in Step iii.5 is no more expensive than a scan. In the PCO models, these primitives have I/O complexity at most $O(\text{sort}(W_t) + \text{scan}(|\mathcal{U}| / \log W))$ for a bucket with W_t edges. They all have $O(D_{sort}(W))$ depth.

To show the final cache (I/O) complexity bounds, we make use of the following claim:

Claim 3.3 ([7]) *Let W_t be the number of edges in bucket t at the beginning of the iteration which processes this bucket. Then, $\sum W_t = O(W)$.*

Therefore, we have $O(\text{sort}(W))$ from prebucketing, $O(\text{sort}(W))$ from MaNIS combined, and $O(\text{sort}(W) + \text{scan}(\mathcal{U}))$ from bucket management combined (since there are $\log(W)$ rounds). This simplifies to an I/O (cache) complexity of $Q^*(W; M, B) = O(\text{sort}(W; M, B))$ since $U \le W$. The depth is $O(\log^4 W)$, since set cover has $O(\log W)$ iterations to go through buckets, each and invoking a MaNIS which has $O(\log W)$ rounds (w.h.p.) and each round is dominated by the sort that has a maximum depth of $O(\log^2 W)$. of recursion.

4.   IMPLEMENTATION

We highlight a number of design decisions that we made for the two versions of the MaNIS-based set cover algorithm: one optimized for the multicore architecture and the other for the external-memory setting. In both implementations, we represent the set system (i.e., the sets and their elements) as a contiguous array of integers listing the elements belonging to the sets; we also keep a pointer to the starting point of each set. This is essentially the compressed sparse row (CSR) format for sparse matrices. Furthermore, in both implementations, we maintain a "bitmap" vector that indicates whether or not an element has been covered by a set already; however, as detailed below, how we keep this vector depends on the particular implementation.

Parallel Implementation. This implementation targets modern machines with many cores and sufficient RAM to fit and process the dataset if sufficient care is taken to manage the memory. The goal of this implementation is therefore to take advantage of available parallelism and locality, and strike a balance between the computation cost and memory-access cost. We chose to implement the "bitmap" as a vector of integers of length $|\mathcal{U}|$. On the surface, this may seem like a waste of space, but we made this decision so that MaNIS can be efficiently implemented in-place using priority writes. Initially, we apply bucket sort and standard prefix computations to classify the input sets into the buckets they belong. To implement MaNIS, we notice that each round of MaNIS involves two major phases: (1) deciding for each element the "winning" set—the set with the highest priority that covers it and (2) subsequently, counting for each set that the elements on which it has won. The former phase can be done using concurrent priority writes, and the latter

---

Algorithm 3.2 $\mathtt{MaNIS}_{(\varepsilon, 3\varepsilon)}(G)$

Input: A bipartite graph $G = (A, N_G(a))$
    A is a sequence of left vertices (the sets), and $N_G(a), a \in A$ are the neighbors of each left vertex on the right.
    These are represented as contiguous arrays. The right vertices are represented implicitly as $B = N_G(A)$.
Output: $J \subseteq A$ of chosen sets.

---

1. If A is empty, return the empty set.
2. For $a \in A$, randomly pick $x_a \in_R \{0, \dots, |G|^7 - 1\}$.   *//map*
3. For $b \in B$, let φ be b's neighbor with maximum x_a *// sort and prefix sum*
4. Pick vertices of A "chosen" by sufficiently many in B: *// sort, prefix sum, sort and filter*

$$J = \{a \in A | \#\{b : \varphi(b) = a\} \geq (1 - 4\varepsilon)D(a)\}.$$

5. Update the graph by removing J and its neighbors, and elements of A with too few remaining neighbors:
    (1) $\overline{B} = N_G(J)$ (elements to remove)   *// sort*
    (2) $N'_G = \{\{b \in N_G(a) | b \notin \overline{B}\} : a \in A \setminus J\}$ *// sort, merge, sort and filter*
    (3) $A' = \{a \in A \setminus J : |N'_G(a)| \geq (1 - \varepsilon)D(a)\}$ *// filter*
    (4) $N''_G = \{\{b \in N'_G(a)\} : a \in A'\}$ *// filter*
6. Recurse on reduced graph: $J_R = \mathtt{MaNIS}_{(\varepsilon, 3\varepsilon)}((A', N''_G))$
7. return $J \cup J_R$

---

phase involves random-accesses to the "bitmap" vector and resetting the values in the bitmap as necessary.

Our experiments show that simulating priority writes using compare and swap (CAS) on these sets in a standard way does not produce high contention—and is in fact faster than running sort a few times (like what was described previously). By doing so, we are able to implement MaNIS in-place, which helps reduce the memory footprint of our implementation. For performance, we also made efforts to minimize the number of passes over the bitmap and the data.

Extra care is given to how the MaNIS steps are implemented. To reduce the number of times a set needs to be processed within MaNIS, we use an approach which only processes the higher priority sets on each parallel round, using ideas similar to what is described in [3]. More specifically, we pre-order the sets by the (psuedo)-random priorities, and, on each round, process a prefix of this ordering. Since the prefix has high priorities, the sets are less likely to be forced to another round saving some work. In the limit, the prefix size would be one, effectively giving the CKW algorithm. In our experiments, we use a prefix containing about one fourth the original number of sets for all of the buckets except for the buckets with the largest sets. For the buckets with large sets, we specialize MaNIS to run with a prefix of size one (we term this `serialManis`). This leads to a light-weight implementation which can still take advantage of parallelism on the edges without the bulkiness of the full-fledged MaNIS.

Disk-optimized Implementation. At the other end of the spectrum, we target a single-core machine with so little fast memory that not even the bitmap—the bit indicator array for the elements—can fit in main memory, but this machine has relatively fast disk (e.g., a solid-state drive). In this case, random-accessing an array is in general very costly. Our implementation in this case follows the theoretical description rather closely: The "bitmap" vector is kept as a bit array—this most-obvious optimization yields substantially better performance than the alternative of using 1 byte per element. Initially, like in the parallel case, we apply bucket sort and standard prefix computations to classify the input sets into the buckets they belong. Each round of MaNIS, then, is implemented as a series of external-memory sorts and scans. We resort to STXXL, a C++

reimplementation of the Standard Template Library (STL) to perform external-memory (out-of-core) computations and disk-resident data management [15, 25]. STXXL hides from the users the intricate optimizations done at the low-level (e.g., asynchronous/bulk I/O).

5. EVALUATION

We empirically investigate the performance of the proposed algorithms. We implemented two variants of the algorithm, one optimized for the multicore architecture and the other optimized for disk-based computation. For a setting of ε, all implementations are guaranteed to produce a solution that is no worse than $(1 + \varepsilon)H_n$ times the optimal solution, where $H_n = 1 + \frac{1}{2} + \cdots + \frac{1}{n}$ denotes the n-th Harmonic number.

5.1 Experimental Setup

Datasets. Our study uses a diverse collection of instances derived from various sources of popular graphs. Many of the datasets here are obtained from the datasets made publicly available by the Laboratory for Web Algorithmics at Università degli studi di Milano [8, 10]. These datasets are derived from directed graphs of various kinds in a natural way: each node v gives rise to a set and all nodes that v points to are members of the set corresponding to v. We assign unit weight to all the sets. Since the graphs are directed, some nodes may have nonzero out-degree but have in-degree 0. For the experiments, we consider such a node a set but not an element (it will never be covered). This asymmetry is the reason that the number of sets is not the same as the number of elements. We give a detailed description of each instance below and present a summary of these instances in Table 1.

—*livejournal-2008* is derived from user-user relationships on the LiveJournal blogging and virtual community site. Our dataset is a snapshot taken by Chierichetti et al. [11], where each set S is a user of the site and covers all users that are listed as S's friends.

— *webdocs* is a collection of web pages with directed links between them [18]. We derive a set system from this graph as described earlier.

Dataset	# of sets	# of elts.	# of edges	avg $|S|$	max $|S|$	Δ
webdocs	1,692,082	5,267,656	299,887,139	177.2	71,472	1,429,525
livejournal-2008	4,817,634	5,363,260	79,023,142	16.4	2,469	19,409
twitter-2010	40,103,281	41,652,230	1,468,365,182	36.6	2,997,469	770,155
twitter-2009	54,127,587	62,539,895	1,837,645,451	34.0	2,968,120	748,285
uk-union	121,503,286	133,633,040	5,507,679,822	45.3	22,429	6,010,077
altavista-2002-nd	532,261,574	1,413,511,386	4,226,882,364	7.9	2,064	299,007

Table 1. A summary of the datasets used in our experiments, showing for every dataset the number of sets, the number of elements, the number of edges, the average set size (avg $|S|$), the maximum set size (max $|S|$), and the maximum number of sets containing an element ($\Delta := \max|\{S \ni e\}|$).

— *twitter-2010* is derived from a snapshot taken in 2010 of the follower relationship graph on the popular Twitter network, where there is an edge from x to y if y "follows" x [22]. The set system is derived as described earlier.
— *twitter-2009* is an older, but larger, Twitter snapshot taken in 2009 by a different research group [20].
— *altavista-2002-nd* is the AltaVista web links dataset from 2002 provided by Yahoo! WebScope. The dataset has been preprocessed to remove dangling nodes, as suggested by experts familiar with this dataset[1].
— *uk-union* combines snapshots of webpages in the .uk domain taken over a 12-month period between June 2006 and May 2007 [9].

While coincidentally the real-world data sets we consider in this paper have about the same number of sets as the number of elements, our algorithms are not optimized to take advantage of this characteristic in any way.

5.2 Parallel Performance

The first set of experiments is concerned with the performance of our multicore-optimized program in comparison to existing sequential algorithms. These experiments are designed to test our implementation on the following important metrics:

1. **Solution's Quality.** The parallel algorithm should deliver solutions with no significant loss in quality when compared to the sequential counterpart;
2. **Parallel Overhead.** The parallel algorithm running on a single core should not take much longer than its sequential counterpart, showing empirically that it is work efficient; and
3. **Parallel Speedup.** The parallel algorithm should achieve good speedup[2], indicating that the algorithm can successfully take advantage of parallelism.

The baseline for the experiments is our own implementation of Cormode et al.'s disk-friendly greedy (DFG) algorithm [14]. DFG is a good baseline for this experiment because it achieves significant performance improvements over the standard greedy algorithm by making a geometric-scale bucketing approximation similar to ours. As previously shown, this approximation does not harm the solutions' quality in practice but makes it run much faster on both disk- and RAM- based environments. Our implementation of DFG closely follows the description in their paper but is further optimized for performance. Because of the fine tuning we made to the code, our implementation runs significantly

faster than the numbers reported in Cormode et al. when all the data fits in RAM, taking in account the differences between machines. For this reason, we believe our DFG code is a reasonable baseline. We also implemented the standard greedy algorithm for comparison.

Evaluation Setup. Our parallel experiments were performed on a 40-core (with hyperthreading) Intel machine, consisting of *four* 2.4GHz 10-core E7-8870 Xeon processors, a 1066MHz bus, and 256GB of main memory. The machine is running Linux 3.2.0 (Red Hat). We compiled our programs with Intel Cilk++ build 8503 using the optimization flag `-O3`. The Cilk++ platform [23], in which the runtime system relies on a work-stealing scheduler, is known to impose only little overhead on both parallel and sequential code.

Results. Table 2 shows the performance of the three aforementioned RAM-based algorithms when run with $\varepsilon = 0.01$ (for DFG and parallel MANIS). Several things are clear. *First, parallel MANIS achieves essentially the same solutions' quality as both DFG and the baseline algorithm.* In fact, with ε set to 0.01 for both DFG and parallel MANIS, all algorithms produce solutions of roughly the same quality—within about 1% of each other. We will note that, despite doing the most work, the standard greedy algorithm does not always yield the best solution. Our experience has been that the additional randomness that parallel MANIS adds to the greedy algorithm often helps gain better solutions. In a number of datasets above, parallel MANIS *does* yield the best-quality solutions.

Second, the parallel overhead in running MANIS is small. This means that parallel MANIS is likely to be faster than DFG even on a modest number of processors. As the numbers show, in all cases, parallel MANIS is at most 1.8x slower than DFG when running on 1 core, and in 3 out of the 6 cases it runs in approximately the same time.

Third but perhaps most importantly, parallel MANIS shows substantial speedups on all but the small datasets. The experiments show that MANIS achieves upto 23.4x speedup with the speedup numbers ranging between 9x and 23.4x—except for the smallest dataset *webdocs* which obtains 6.9x speedup. This shows that the algorithm is able to effectively utilize available cores except when the datasets are too small to fully utilize parallelism (see discussion below).

To further understand the effects of the number of cores, we study the performance of parallel MANIS on the *uk-union* dataset as the number of threads used is varied between 1 and 80 (all available threads). As Figure 3 shows, the running time performance of our algorithm scales well with the number of cores until at least 24 cores. After that, even though the performance continues to improve, the marginal

---

[1]See, e.g., http://law.dsi.unimi.it/webdata/altavista-2002-nd/
[2]This measures how much faster it is running on many cores than running sequentially.

Dataset	Standard Greedy		DFG		Parallel MaNIS		
	T_1 (sec)	# sets	T_1 (sec)	# sets	T_1 (sec)	T_{40h} (sec)	# sets
webdocs	24.2	406,399	6.46	406,340	6.66	0.96	406,343
livejournal-2008	9.80	1,120,594	4.53	1,120,543	5.58	0.62	1,120,599
twitter-2010	365	3,846,209	65.5	3,845,345	64.4	6.47	3,845,089
twitter-2009	689	5,518,039	97.3	5,516,959	87.6	7.63	5,517,864
uk-union	263	18,416,670	161	18,388,007	278	11.9	18,379,547
altavista-2002-nd	467	33,173,320	241	33,103,284	429	22.6	33,090,726

Table 2. Performance with $\varepsilon = 0.01$ of RAM-based algorithms: the standard greedy implementation, the disk-friendly greedy (DFG) algorithm of Cormode et al., and our MaNIS-based parallel implementation. We show the running time (**in seconds**) one core T_1 and on 40 cores with hyperthreading T_{40h} (80 threads), and the number of sets in the solutions.

benefit diminishes. Figure 4 demonstrates the break down of sequential running time into components and the speedup of these components on 40 cores. While most components in the *uk-union* dataset have near linear speedup, the bucket movement (i.e., filter) step, which takes 36.4% of the running time, is bandwidth constrained and achieves a speedup of only 17, limiting the overall speed up. Further experiments with filter and other microbenchmarks confirm this bottleneck.

For the smaller datasets, the parallel performance is additionally constrained by the speedup of the MaNIS and the `serialMaNIS` operations. The speedup of MaNIS and `serialMaNIS` depends on the size of the bucket on which they are executed. On large buckets of size exceeding 10^5, the speedup is limited by the bandwidth. On smaller buckets, the speedup is limited by the overhead of running multiple `cilk_for` operations. This overhead is increasingly prominent in the smaller datasets such as *webdocs*, in which case MaNIS achieves a speed up of only 5.5x compared to 25.6x on *uk-union*.

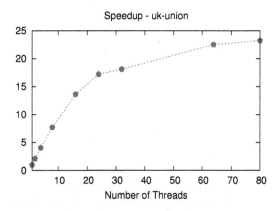

Figure 3. Speedup of the parallel MaNIS algorithm (i.e., how much faster is running the algorithm on n threads over running it sequentially) as the number of cores used is varied.

Max Cover. In the sequential setting, stopping the standard greedy set cover algorithm when it has found k sets gives the optimal $(1 - 1/e)$-approximation to max k-cover. An important feature of the parallel MaNIS algorithm is that it can be stopped early in the same way. To see how one might benefit from stopping the algorithm when the algorithm has found enough sets, we record the fraction of the total time when k sets are discovered. Presented in Figure 5 are plots from our 3 largest datasets (by the num-

ber of edges), *altavista-2002-nd*, *uk-union*, and *twitter-2009*. This experiment shows that although the rate varies between datasets, it is clear that most of the sets are added late in the algorithm; therefore, if the value of k of interest is small relative to the set cover solution's size, we can benefit from stopping early, which can often halve the running time. Chierichetti et. al. [12] present results for max k cover on map-reduce, however do not report any times so we were not able to compare.

5.3 Sequential Disk-based Performance

The second set of experiments deals with the performance of our disk-optimized implementation in comparison with existing disk-based algorithms. We are interested in evaluating the algorithms on the following metrics: (1) solutions' quality and (2) running time. Since the disk-optimized versions of both DFG and MaNIS implement the same algorithms as their parallel counterparts, their relative performance in terms of solutions' quality will be identical to the study conducted earlier for the parallel case. In the remainder of this section, we focus on investigating the running time as well as other performance characteristics of the disk-optimized MaNIS implementation.

Evaluation Setup. Our disk experiments were performed on a 4-core Intel machine although we only make use of a single core running at 2.66 Ghz. The machine is equipped with 8 GBytes of RAM and an Intel X25-M 160 GBytes SSD disk[3] (used both for input and as scratch space). There is a separate magnetic disk which we keep the OS Linux 2.6.38 (Ubuntu 11.04) and other system files. We compiled our programs with `g++` 4.5.2 using the optimization flag `-O3`.

We artificially limited the RAM size available to the set cover process to 512 MBytes and carefully control all disk-access buffers to use only these 512 MBytes. This may seem unrealistic at first, but this controlled setup models the types of machines available as embedded devices and computing nodes in low-power clusters (e.g., [1]) and provides a testbed for understanding the performance of these algorithms on such devices.

Table 3 reports the performance of the disk-based algorithms when run with $\varepsilon = 0.01$. On the larger graphs, the DFG algorithm did not complete within 40 hours. On the smaller sets, the disk based MaNIS is substantially faster (about 4x for *webdocs* and 39.6x for *livejournal-2008*). The

---

[3]Per Intel's specification, it has sustained sequential read and write bandwidths of 250 MB/s and 100 MB/s, resp.

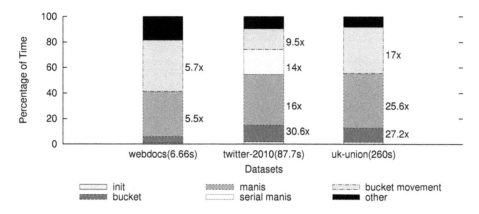

Figure 4. Timings and speedups of different components of the parallel set cover algorithms on `webdocs`, `twitter-2009`, `uk-union`. The sequential running time is shown next to the dataset's label, and the speedup of each major component is given next to the corresponding segment in the plot.

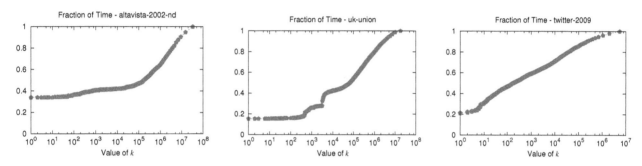

Figure 5. Max k-cover performance: The fraction of time spent to find the first k sets as the value of k is varied.

timing numbers may appear to be irregular, but a closer look at the results reveals patterns worthwhile mentioning:

When the bitmap representing the elements does not fully stay in fast memory (i.e., cache or RAM), the number of passes over the bitmap and the bitmap size crucially determine the performance of both algorithms. In DFG, which consults the bitmap every time it considers a set, this is lower-bounded by the number of sets in the output, whereas in disk MANIS, which batches "requests" to look up the bitmap and reduces them to one pass over it per MANIS round, this number is the total number of MANIS rounds summed across all buckets. This explains the difference in running-time patterns between the two algorithms on *webdocs* and *livejournal-2008*. For this reason also, the two Twitter datasets take roughly the same time to run disk MANIS despite significant differences in the number of sets in the solutions produced.

5.4 Effects of The Accuracy Parameter

In theory, the dependence on ε in the work bound is inversely proportional to $\log^3(1 + \varepsilon)$, which, for small ε, is roughly $O(1/\varepsilon^3)$. This seems alarming because as we decrease ε (i.e., increase accuracy), $\frac{1}{\varepsilon^3}$ grows rather rapidly, rendering the algorithm unusable in no time; however, in practice, the situation is much better. As we decrease ε, we will observe more buckets but an even larger fraction of these buckets will be empty, reducing the efforts needed to run MANIS to process them and counteracting the increase in the number

Algorithm	$\varepsilon = 0.1$	0.05	0.01	0.001
Disk MANIS	271	310	481	891
Parallel MANIS	0.36	0.47	0.96	2.06
# of sets	406,406	406,359	406,343	406,338

Table 4. Performance of MANIS-based algorithms on *webdocs* (**in seconds**) as ε is varied.

of buckets. Table 4 shows the effects of ε on *webdocs* for both the disk-optimized and parallel versions.

The numbers show that increasing the accuracy from $\varepsilon = 0.1$ to 0.001 (2 more digits of accuracy) increases the running time by less than 3x for the disk version and 6x for the parallel version. This trend seems to generalize across the datasets we have. More interesting, however, is the observation that ε only has small effect on the solutions' quality. Our experience on the datasets we have used is that we benefit more from spending computation time on different random priority orderings than adjusting ε to increase accuracy.

6. CONCLUSION

We presented a parallel cache-oblivious set-cover algorithm that has essentially the same approximation guarantees as the standard greedy algorithm. We implemented slight variants of the theoretical algorithm optimized for different hardware setups and provided experimental evaluation showing nontrivial speedups over existing algorithms while yielding the same solution's quality.

Dataset	DFG		Disk MANIS	
	Time	# of sets	Time	# of sets
webdocs	32m50s	406,340	481s	406,367
livejournal-2008	3h5m	1,120,543	280s	1,120,599
twitter-2010	> 40 hrs	-	55m2s	3,845,089
twitter-2009	> 40 hrs	-	1h11m	5,517,864
uk-union	> 40 hrs	-	6h49m	18,379,547
altavista-2002-nd	> 40 hrs	-	13h27m	33,090,726

Table 3. Performance with $\varepsilon = 0.01$ of disk-based algorithms: the disk-friendly greedy (DFG) algorithm of Cormode et al., and our disk-based MANIS implementation. We show the running time and the number of sets in the solutions.

Acknowledgments. This work is partially supported by the National Science Foundation under grant number CCF-1018188 and by generous gifts from IBM and Intel Labs Academic Research Office for Parallel Algorithms for Non-Numeric Computing. We thank the SPAA reviewers for their comments that helped improve this paper.

7. REFERENCES

[1] David G. Andersen, Jason Franklin, Michael Kaminsky, Amar Phanishayee, Lawrence Tan, and Vijay Vasudevan. FAWN: A fast array of wimpy nodes. In *Proc. 22nd ACM Symposium on Operating Systems Principles (SOSP)*, Big Sky, MT, October 2009.

[2] Bonnie Berger, John Rompel, and Peter W. Shor. Efficient *NC* algorithms for set cover with applications to learning and geometry. *J. Comput. Syst. Sci.*, 49(3):454–477, 1994.

[3] Guy E. Blelloch, Jeremy T. Fineman, Phillip B. Gibbons, and Julian Shun. Internally deterministic parallel algorithms can be fast. In *PPOPP*, pages 181–192, 2012.

[4] Guy E. Blelloch, Jeremy T. Fineman, Phillip B. Gibbons, and Harsha Vardhan Simhadri. Scheduling irregular parallel computations on hierarchical caches. In *SPAA*, pages 355–366, 2011.

[5] Guy E. Blelloch, Phillip B. Gibbons, and Harsha Vardhan Simhadri. Low-depth cache oblivious algorithms. In *SPAA*, 2010.

[6] Guy E. Blelloch, Anupam Gupta, Ioannis Koutis, Gary L. Miller, Richard Peng, and Kanat Tangwongsan. Near linear-work parallel SDD solvers, low-diameter decomposition, and low-stretch subgraphs. In *SPAA*, pages 13–22, 2011.

[7] Guy E. Blelloch, Richard Peng, and Kanat Tangwongsan. Linear-work greedy parallel approximate set cover and variants. In *SPAA*, pages 23–32, 2011.

[8] Paolo Boldi, Marco Rosa, Massimo Santini, and Sebastiano Vigna. Layered label propagation: A multiresolution coordinate-free ordering for compressing social networks. In *Proceedings of the 20th international conference on World Wide Web*. ACM Press, 2011.

[9] Paolo Boldi, Massimo Santini, and Sebastiano Vigna. A large time-aware graph. *SIGIR Forum*, 42(2):33–38, 2008.

[10] Paolo Boldi and Sebastiano Vigna. The WebGraph framework I: Compression techniques. In *Proc. of the Thirteenth International World Wide Web Conference (WWW 2004)*, pages 595–601, Manhattan, USA, 2004. ACM Press.

[11] Flavio Chierichetti, Ravi Kumar, Silvio Lattanzi, Michael Mitzenmacher, Alessandro Panconesi, and Prabhakar Raghavan. On compressing social networks. In *KDD*, pages 219–228, 2009.

[12] Flavio Chierichetti, Ravi Kumar, and Andrew Tomkins. Max-cover in map-reduce. In *Proceedings of the 19th international conference on World wide web*, WWW '10, pages 231–240, New York, NY, USA, 2010. ACM.

[13] V. Chvatal. A greedy heuristic for the set-covering problem. *Mathematics of Operations Research*, 4(3):pp. 233–235, 1979.

[14] Graham Cormode, Howard J. Karloff, and Anthony Wirth. Set cover algorithms for very large datasets. In *CIKM*, pages 479–488, 2010.

[15] R. Dementiev, L. Kettner, and P. Sanders. STXXL: standard template library for XXL data sets. *Software: Practice and Experience*, 38(6):589–637, 2008.

[16] Uriel Feige. A threshold of $\ln n$ for approximating set cover. *J. ACM*, 45(4):634–652, 1998.

[17] Matteo Frigo, Charles E. Leiserson, Harald Prokop, and Sridhar Ramachandran. Cache-oblivious algorithms. In *FOCS*, 1999.

[18] B. Goethals. Frequent itemset mining dataset repository. http://fimi.ua.ac.be/data/.

[19] David S. Johnson. Approximation algorithms for combinatorial problems. *J. Comput. System Sci.*, 9:256–278, 1974.

[20] U. Kang, Brendan Meeder, and Christos Faloutsos. Spectral analysis for billion-scale graphs: Discoveries and implementation. In *PAKDD (2)*, pages 13–25, 2011.

[21] R. M. Karp. Reducibility Among Combinatorial Problems. In R. E. Miller and J. W. Thatcher, editors, *Complexity of Computer Computations*, pages 85–103. Plenum Press, 1972.

[22] Haewoon Kwak, Changhyun Lee, Hosung Park, and Sue B. Moon. What is Twitter, a social network or a news media? In *WWW*, pages 591–600, 2010.

[23] Charles E. Leiserson. The Cilk++ concurrency platform. *J. Supercomputing*, 51(3), 2010. Springer.

[24] Sridhar Rajagopalan and Vijay V. Vazirani. Primal-dual *RNC* approximation algorithms for set cover and covering integer programs. *SIAM J. Comput.*, 28(2):525–540, 1998.

[25] Johannes Singler, Peter Sanders, and Felix Putze. The multi-core standard template library. In *Euro-Par*, pages 682–694, 2007.

A Scalable Framework for Heterogeneous GPU-Based Clusters *

Fengguang Song
Innovative Computing Laboratory
University of Tennessee
Knoxville, TN, USA
song@eecs.utk.edu

Jack Dongarra
University of Tennessee, USA
Oak Ridge National Laboratory, USA
University of Manchester, UK
dongarra@eecs.utk.edu

ABSTRACT

GPU-based heterogeneous clusters continue to draw attention from vendors and HPC users due to their high energy efficiency and much improved single-node computational performance, however, there is little parallel software available
that can utilize all CPU cores and all GPUs on the heterogeneous system efficiently. On a heterogeneous cluster, the
performance of a GPU (or a compute node) increases in a
much faster rate than the performance of the PCI-Express
connection (or the interconnection network) such that communication eventually becomes the bottleneck of the entire
system. To overcome the bottleneck, we developed a multi-
level partitioning and distribution method that guarantees
a near-optimal communication volume. We have also extended heterogeneous tile algorithms to work on distributed-
memory GPU clusters. Our main idea is to execute a serial program and generate hybrid-size tasks, and follow a
dataflow programming model to fire the tasks on different
compute nodes. We then devised a distributed dynamic
scheduling runtime system to schedule tasks, and transfer
data between hybrid CPU-GPU compute nodes transparently. The runtime system employs a novel distributed task-
assignment protocol to solve data dependencies between tasks
without coordination between processing units. The runtime system on each node consists of a number of CPU
compute threads, a number of GPU compute threads, a
task generation thread, an MPI communication thread, and
a CUDA communication thread. By overlapping computation and communication through dynamic scheduling, we are
able to attain a high performance of 75 TFlops for Cholesky
factorization on the heterogeneous Keeneland system [25] using 100 nodes, each with twelve CPU cores and three GPUs.
Moreover, our framework is able to attain high performance
on distributed-memory clusters without GPUs, and shared-
system multiGPUs.

*This material is based upon work supported by the NSF
grants CCF-0811642, OCI-0910735, by the DOE grant DE-
FC02-06ER25761, by Nvidia, and by Microsoft Research.

Permission to make digital or hard copies of all or part of this work for
personal or classroom use is granted without fee provided that copies are
not made or distributed for profit or commercial advantage and that copies
bear this notice and the full citation on the first page. To copy otherwise, to
republish, to post on servers or to redistribute to lists, requires prior specific
permission and/or a fee.
SPAA'12, June 25–27, 2012, Pittsburgh, Pennsylvania, USA.
Copyright 2012 ACM 978-1-4503-1213-4/12/06 ...$10.00.

Categories and Subject Descriptors

D.1.3 [**Programming Techniques**]: Concurrent Programming—*Parallel programming*; C.1.2 [**Processor Architectures**]: Multiple Data Stream Architectures (Multiprocessors)—*SIMD*

General Terms

Design, Performance

Keywords

Distributed runtime, manycore scheduling, hybrid CPU-GPU
architectures, heterogeneous clusters, linear algebra

1. INTRODUCTION

Based on the November 2011 Green500 list [22], twenty-
three out of the top thirty greenest supercomputers are GPU-
based. However, there is little software that can take advantage of the large-scale heterogeneous systems efficiently,
especially to utilize all CPU cores and all GPUs. Considering many operations of scientific computing applications are
carried out through numerical linear algebra libraries, we focus on providing fundamental linear algebra operations on
the new heterogeneous architectures.

A great amount of effort has gone into the implementation
of linear algebra libraries. LAPACK [5], Intel MKL, AMD
ACML, and PLASMA [4] are mainly designed for shared-
memory multicore machines. ScaLAPACK [10] is intended
for distributed memory CPU-based machines. CUBLAS
[19], MAGMA [24], and CULA [16] provide a subset of the
LAPACK subroutines but work on a single GPU. So far
these libraries do not support computations using multiple
CPU cores and multiple GPUs on a single node, not to mention distributed GPU-based clusters. Moreover, with an increasing number of cores on the host whose performance
continues to keep up with the GPU performance, new parallel software should not ignore either GPUs or CPUs.

Our work aims to provide a unified framework to solve linear algebra problems on any number of CPU cores, any number of GPUs, and for either shared-memory or distributed-
memory systems. Our solution consists of three essential
components: (1) a static multi-level data distribution method,
(2) heterogeneous tile algorithms, and (3) a distributed dynamic scheduling runtime system. The solution works as
follows. Given a matrix input, we first split it into tiles of
hybrid sizes. Then we distribute the tiles to the hosts' main
memories and the GPU device memories on a cluster with a

static method. Each compute node runs a runtime system (launched as an MPI process) that schedules tasks within the node dynamically. Different nodes communicate with each other by means of MPI messages. Our runtime system follows the data-flow programming model and builds a partial directed acyclic graph (DAG) dynamically, where a completed task will trigger a set of new tasks in the DAG.

We use a static multi-level distribution method to allocate data to different hosts and GPUs. Each compute node is heterogeneous since it has both CPUs and GPUs, but different nodes have the same performance. Therefore, we design a multi-level distribution method. On the top (i.e., inter-node) level, we use a 2-D block cyclic distribution method. On the second (i.e., intra-node between different GPUs) level, we allocate a node's local blocks to merely GPUs with a 1-D or 2-D block cyclic method. On the third (i.e., intra-node between CPUs and GPUs) level, we cut a slice from each GPU's local block and put it to the host. The output of the multi-level distribution method is that each matrix block is uniquely assigned to the host or a GPU on a specific node.

We also use heterogeneous tile algorithms to handle the difference between CPUs and GPUs. In the algorithms, there are a great number of small tasks for CPU cores, and a great number of large tasks for GPUs, to compute concurrently at any time. A heterogeneous tile algorithm is based on two types of tiles: small ones for CPU cores, and large ones for GPUs. Our work combines the heterogenous tile algorithms and the multi-level distribution method together so that the algorithms are applicable to heterogeneous clusters with hybrid CPUs and GPUs.

We design a distributed scheduling runtime system for heterogeneous clusters. Each compute node is executing a runtime system that can solve data dependencies dynamically, and transfer data from a parent task to its children transparently. All runtime systems (one per node) proceed in parallel, and execute a task-assignment protocol to build subsets (or partitions) of a DAG dynamically. There is no communication required when building the DAG. The protocol guarantees that all runtime systems make a unanimous decision without coordinating with each other such that every task is computed by one and only one processing unit (on a host or a GPU).

Our experiments with double-precision Cholesky and QR factorizations, on the heterogeneous Keeneland system [25] at the Oak Ridge National Laboratory, demonstrate great scalability from one to 100 nodes using all CPUs and GPUs. In addition, we apply our framework to the other two possible environments: clusters without GPUs, and shared systems with multiple CPUs and multiple GPUs. Compared with vendor-optimized and open source libraries (i.e., Intel MKL 10.3.5, and StarPU 0.9.1 [6]), our framework is able to provide better performance thank Intel MKL by up to 75% on clusters without GPUs, and up to 250% better performance than StarPU on shared-system multiGPUs.

2. BACKGROUND

We place greater emphasis on communications in the design of our framework. On a host that is attached with multiple GPUs through PCI-Express connections, the ratio of computation to communication on the GPUs keeps increasing. Eventually the communication time on a PCI-Express connection will become the bottleneck of the entire system.

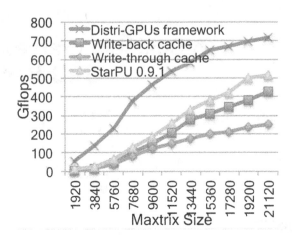

Figure 1: A comparison between dynamic scheduling systems and our distributed-GPU framework.

Researchers often use dynamic scheduling methods to support heterogeneous systems, where each CPU core or GPU picks up a ready task from task queues independently whenever a processing unit becomes idle. At the beginning of our design, we have also implemented a dynamic scheduling runtime system. In the implementation of our dynamic runtime system, all the CPU cores and GPUs share a global ready task queue, and each GPU owns a software cache on its device memory. Whenever a GPU reads a block of data from the host, it stores the data to its software cache. All the data in the GPUs' software caches are also backed up by the main memory on the host. We have used two cache writing policies: write-through and write-back. With the write-through policy, every modification to the software cache must be updated to the host main memory immediately. With the write-back policy, a modification to the software cache is updated to the host main memory only when a different device wants to access the modified data. To achieve the best performance, our software cache size on each GPU is configured as large as the input matrix size to eliminate the capacity cache misses.

Figure 1 shows our experiments with the double-precision Cholesky factorization on a single node of the Keeneland system using 12 cores and 3 Nvidia Fermi GPUs. In the figure, we compare our software-cache based dynamic scheduling runtime system, the generic dynamic scheduling runtime system of StarPU [6], and our distributed-GPUs framework that builds upon a static data distribution method. By changing from the write-through policy to the write-back policy, we can improve the program performance greatly due to reduced communications.

Differently, StarPU consists of profiling, performance modeling, and sophisticated scheduling policies to achieve load balancing and to reduce data transfers. However, since our static data distribution method can guarantee a near lower-bound communication cost and has less scheduling overhead, it is faster than StarPU by up to 250% for small to medium matrix sizes. This has inspired us to employ a static data distribution method on GPU-based clusters. Here we emphasize that despite its better performance, our framework is intended for solving dense linear algebra problems, while StarPU is more generic and can support other applications.

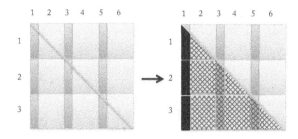

Figure 2: An example of the heterogeneous tile algorithm for Cholesky factorization.

3. HETEROGENEOUS TILE ALGORITHMS

Our previous work has designed a class of heterogeneous tile algorithm and applied them to shared-system multiGPUs [23]. Here we mention it briefly for completeness. In the algorithm, each task takes several individual tiles as input and output. Also on a heterogeneous system with CPUs and GPUs, there are two different types of tiles.

Figure 2 shows a matrix that is stored in a tile data layout with two types of tiles. All the tasks that modify small tiles are to be executed by CPU cores, and those that modify large tiles are to be executed by GPUs. Given a matrix with three tile rows and six tile columns, Cholesky factorization can be computed recursively as follows. At the first iteration, (1) we solve Cholesky factorizations on tiles A_{11}, A_{21}, and A_{31} in the first column. That is, $L_{11} \leftarrow Cholesky(A_{11})$, and $L_{ij} \leftarrow A_{ij}(L_{11}^T)^{-1}$; (2) then we update the trailing submatrix located between the second and the last sixth column. That is, $A_{ij} \leftarrow A_{ij} - L_{i1}L_{j1}$. The Cholesky factorization can be completed by recursively applying the above two steps to the trailing submatrix that starts from the j-th tile column. If a matrix has n tile columns, the factorization takes n iterations to complete. The same idea can be applied to other matrix factorizations (e.g., QR and LU factorizations). For more details, please refer to our paper [23] for the exact algorithms of Cholesky and QR factorizations.

3.1 Multi-Level Block Cyclic Distribution

This section presents a new multi-level partitioning scheme to create small and large tiles on distributed-memory heterogeneous clusters. (1) At the top level, we divide a matrix into $p \times p$ large tiles, each of which is of size $B \times B$. (2) We distribute the $p \times p$ large tiles to a process grid of P_r rows $\times P_c$ columns using a 2-D block cyclic method. There is one process per node. (3) At the bottom level (i.e., within each node), we vertically cut every large tile of size $B \times B$ on each node into a number of $(s-1)$ small tiles of size $B \times b$, and one remaining large tile of size $B \times (B - (s-1) \cdot b)$. We allocate the small tiles to the entire set of CPU cores on the host, while allocate the remaining large tiles to GPUs using a 1-D or 2-D block cyclic method. So far we use a 1-D block cyclic method because of the small number of GPUs (i.e., ≤ 4) on each compute node.

After the multi-level block cyclic distribution, each node is assigned to a number of $\frac{p}{P_r} \times \frac{p \cdot s}{P_c}$ rectangular tiles. Given a tile indexed by [I, J], we first map it to node N_{id} then to device D_j, where D_0 denotes the host, and $D_{j \geq 1}$ denotes the j-th GPU located on node N_{id}. Assuming each node has a number of G GPUs, we can calculate node N_{id} (i.e.,

$0 \leq id \leq P_r P_c$-1), and device D_j as follows:

$$N_{id} = (I \mod P_r) \cdot P_c + (\frac{J}{s} \mod P_c),$$

$$D_j = \begin{cases} 0 & : (J \mod s) < s-1 \\ (\frac{J/s}{P_c} \mod G) + 1 : (J \mod s) = s-1 \end{cases}$$

In other words, Step (2) distributes the large tiles across $P_r \times P_c$ nodes (*for N_{id}*). Next, within each node, the tile columns whose indices are multiples of $(s-1)$ are mapped to the node's G GPUs in a 1-D cyclic way, and the rest of the columns are mapped to all CPUs on the host (*for D_j*). Although small tasks are assigned to all the CPUs, each CPU core can pick up any small task independently (i.e., not in a fork-join manner). We also tune the tile sizes of B and b to achieve the highest performance. The following Section 3.2 describes how we choose the best tile sizes.

3.2 Tile Size Auto-Tuning

We adjust the ratio of the small tiles on the host to the large tiles on GPUs to keep load balancing between CPUs and GPUs within each node. Meanwhile the load balancing between nodes is attained automatically by the 2-D block cyclic distribution method.

Given a tile of size $B \times B$, we partition it into two parts: $B \times B_h$ and $B \times B_g$, where $B_h + B_g = B$. We also suppose $B_h = b(s-1)$, where b is a sub-tile size. The left partition of size $B \times B_h$ is allocated to the host, and the right partition of size $B \times B_g$ is allocated to a GPU. We let $T(m \times n)$ denote the number of floating operations to compute a matrix of size $m \times n$. f_{core} and f_{gpu} denote the speed (i.e., flop/s) on a CPU core and a GPU, respectively.

In a block cyclic data distribution (either 1-D or 2-D), a number of G tiles are allocated to a number of G GPUs such that each GPU has one tile and it takes $T(B \times B_g)/f_{gpu}$ time for a GPU to compute. Differently, the CPU cores on the host receive G small partitions (each is of size $B \times B_h$) from the G tiles, and it takes $G \times T(B \times B_h)/(f_{core} \times NumCores)$ time to compute. To achieve load balancing, we determine B_h by the following formula:

$$\frac{T(B \times B_g)}{f_{gpu}} = \frac{G \times T(B \times B_h)}{f_{core} \times NumCores}$$

$$\Rightarrow \frac{T(B \times B_h)}{T(B \times B_g)} = \frac{f_{core} \times NumCores}{f_{gpu} \times G}$$

$$\Rightarrow B_h = B \times \frac{f_{core} \times NumCores}{f_{core} \times NumCores + f_{gpu} \times G}$$

In practice, f_{core} or f_{gpu} denotes the maximum performance of the dominant computational kernel in an algorithm. We also fine-tune the value of B_h automatically. We start from the estimated size B_h and search for an optimal B_h^* near B_h. We wrote a script to execute a matrix factorization with an input of size $N = c_0 \cdot B \cdot G$, where we set $c_0 = 3$ to reduce the tuning time. The script adjusts the value of B_h to search for the minimum difference between the CPU and the GPU computation time. Note that B_h is dependent only on the number of CPU cores and the number of GPUs, assuming the machine and the implementation of the computational kernels have not changed.

The large tile size B is critical for the GPU performance. To determine the best B, we search for the minimal matrix size that provides the best performance for the dominant GPU kernel in an algorithm (e.g., GEMM for Cholesky factorization). Our search ranges from 256 to 2048, and is performed only once for every new computational library and every new GPU architecture.

4. OUR FRAMEWORK OVERVIEW

We design a distributed dynamic scheduling runtime system for the heterogeneous GPU-based clusters. Given a cluster with P nodes, we launch P MPI processes (one process per node), each of which executes an instance of the runtime system. We also assume a matrix is stored in the hybrid tile data layout that uses two different tile sizes.

Not only do we distribute data to hosts and GPUs on different nodes statically, but also we distribute tasks to hosts and GPUs statically. We require that the location of a task be the same as the location of the task's output. Although a task's allocation is static, we schedule tasks dynamically within a host or GPU in order to reduce synchronization points and overlap computation with communication.

Our runtime system follows a dataflow programming model and is essentially data-availability driven. Whenever a parent task completes, it triggers its child tasks immediately. The runtime system can identify data dependencies between tasks and unroll a Directed Acyclic Graph (DAG) dynamically. Note that a DAG has never been created and stored in our runtime system explicitly. A parallel program starts with an entry task and finishes with an exit task of the DAG, respectively. The runtime system is also responsible for transferring data from a parent task to its children transparently.

Each runtime system instance is multi-threaded. It creates five types of threads: a task-generation thread, a set of CPU compute threads for CPU cores, a set of GPU management threads for GPUs, an inter-node MPI communication thread, and an intra-node CUDA communication thread. If a machine is not distributed, the MPI communication thread is not created. Similarly, if there is no GPU, the CUDA communication thread is not created.

A task-generation thread creates tasks (similar to a CPU issuing instructions) and drives the execution of a user program. There are actually P task-generation threads running on P compute nodes. All the task-generation threads execute the same serial program independently and create task instances for the program without communication. They execute a distributed task-assignment protocol. Based on the common knowledge of the static multi-level distribution, each task-generation thread is able to decide by itself which task it should compute and where the task's children are located without exchanging any messages.

5. THE FRAMEWORK IMPLEMENTATION

As shown in Fig. 3, our runtime system consists of seven components that are listed as follows. (1) Task window: a fixed-size task queue that stores all the generated but not finished tasks. (2) Ready task queues: a number of ready task lists. (3) Task-generation thread: a single thread that executes a serial program and generates new tasks. (4) CPU compute threads: there is a compute thread running on each CPU core. (5) GPU management (or compute) threads: there is a GPU management thread for each GPU. (6) MPI communication thread: a single thread that transfers data

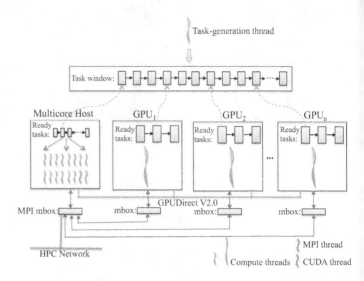

Figure 3: The runtime system architecture on each hybrid CPU-GPU compute node.

between different nodes. (7) CUDA communication thread: a single thread that transfers data among the host and multiple GPUs within the same node using cudaMemcpyAsync.

5.1 Different Task Queues

A *task window* stores generated tasks in a single-linked list. It also keeps the original sequential order between tasks. Each task consists of the information of a task's input and output. Based on the input and output information, when a task modifies its output, the runtime system can scan the list to search for the tasks who are waiting for the output. However, a global task list is often too long to search and can result in severe contention between threads.

To make accesses to the task window faster, we use 2-D task lists to implement the task window. As illustrated in Fig. 4, each tile in a matrix has its own task list. If a task's input or output is tile [I, J], the runtime system will add an instance of the task to [I, J]'s task list. When a matrix is distributed to different compute nodes, we partition the 2-D task lists into different nodes according to the location of the tiles. That is, if tile [I, J] is allocated to node P_k, tile [I, J]'s task list is also assigned to node P_k.

A *ready task queue* stores "ready-to-go" tasks whose inputs are all available. If a task writes to a tile that belongs to the

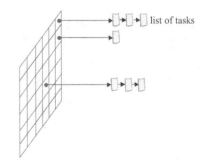

Figure 4: The 2-D task window implementation. Each tile has its own task list whose tasks either read or write the tile.

host or a GPU, it is added to that host or GPU's ready task queue correspondingly. Task stealing has not been implemented to avoid unnecessary data transfers and to increase data reuse. In addition, a ready task in our implementation is simply a pointer that points to a task stored in the task window.

5.2 Solving Data Dependencies

A tile's task list keeps the serial semantic order between tasks that either read or write the tile. Whenever two tasks access the same tile and one of them is write, the runtime system detects a data dependency and stalls the successor till the predecessor is finished. Here we only consider the true dependency RAW (read after write), and use renaming to eliminate the WAR (write after read) and WAW (write after write) dependencies. Figure 5 shows an example of a task list that is used for tile A[i, j], where tasks 1-3 are waiting for task 0's output.

Figure 5: Solving data dependencies for a set of tasks that read or write tile A[i, j]. The completion of Task 0 will FIRE Tasks 1-3 that want to read A[i,j].

There are two operations to access a task list: FIRE and APPEND. After a task completes and modifies its output tile [I, J], the FIRE operation searches [I, J]'s task list for those tasks that want to read [I, J]. It scans the list from the just completed task to find which tasks are waiting for [I, J]. The scan process will exit when confronting a task that wants to write to [I, J]. If a task is visited before the scan process exits, the FIRE operation marks the task's input as "ready". When all the inputs of a task become ready, the task evolves into a ready task.

The APPEND operation is invoked by the task-generation thread. After generating a new task, the generation thread inspects every input and output of the task. Given an input that reads tile [I, J], before actually appending the input task instance, APPEND scans [I, J]'s task list from the list head to find if there exists a task that writes to tile [I, J]. If none of them writes to [I, J], the input task instance is marked as "ready". Otherwise, it is "unready". By contrast, given an output [I, J], APPEND puts an output task instance to the end of [I, J]'s task list immediately.

5.3 Computation Component

A CPU core runs a CPU compute thread. Whenever a CPU compute thread becomes idle, it picks up a ready task from the host's shared ready task queue and computes it on its own. After finishing the task, it invokes the FIRE operation to determine which tasks are the children of the finished task, and moves them to a ready task queue if possible.

Every GPU has a GPU compute thread. A GPU compute thread is essentially a GPU management thread, which is running on the host but can start GPU kernels quickly. For convenience, we think of the GPU management thread as a powerful compute thread. If a node has g GPUs and n CPU cores, our runtime system will launch g GPU compute

```
wait4send = wait4recv = 0;
while(!is_done || wait4send) {
  if(!is_done && !wait4recv) {
    call MPI_Irecv(recv_buf, MPI_ANY_SOURCE, &recv_req);
    wait4recv = 1;
  }
  if(!wait4send) {
    msg = get_msg(host's out_mbox);
    call MPI_Isend(msg->data, msg->dst_pid, &send_req);
    wait4send = 1;
  }
  if(wait4send) {
    call MPI_Test(&send_req);
    if(success) wait4send = 0;
  }
  if(wait4recv) {
    call MPI_Test(&recv_req);
    if(success) {
      store recv_buf to the host memory;
      wait4recv = 0;
    }
  }
}
```

Figure 6: Pseudocode of the MPI communication thread in our distributed runtime system.

threads to represent (or manage) the g GPUs, and $(n - g - 2)$ CPU compute threads to represent the remaining CPU cores. The remaining number of CPU cores is not equal to $(n - g)$ since we use one CPU core for MPI communication and another one for CUDA memory copies.

5.4 Communication Component

There are two types of communications on a GPU-based cluster: communication between nodes, and communication within a node. On each node, we launch a thread to perform MPI operations to transfer data between different nodes, and another thread to copy memories among the host and different GPUs within the same node.

The technique of CUDADirect V2.0 supports direct memory copies between GPUs on the same node. It may also send or receive GPU buffers on different nodes directly if an MPI library supports CUDADirect. To make our framework more portable, we choose to move data from GPU to the host on the source node first, then send it to a destination node. After the destination host receives the data, it copies the data from its host to one or more of its GPUs.

An MPI communication thread runs on a dedicated CPU core. It calls nonblocking MPI point-to-point operations to send and receive messages. At the beginning, the thread posts an MPI_Irecv operation and an MPI_Isend operation. Next, it checks whether the pending receive or send operation has finished with busy-polling. Whenever an operation is finished, it posts a new operation to replace the finished one so that there are always two operations (one receive and one send) ongoing at the same time. Figure 6 shows our pseudocode to implement the MPI communication thread. In the code, wait4send and wait4recv indicate if there exists a pending send or receive operation. The flag is_done is a global variable that shows whether the computation is completed or not.

A CUDA communication thread also uses a dedicated CPU core on the host. Each GPU has two mail boxes: out_mbox and in_mbox. The messages in an out_mbox are intended from the GPU to other devices, and the messages in an in_mbox are intended from other devices to the GPU itself. We create two streams for each GPU: one for outgoing traffic and the other for incoming traffic. Similar to the MPI communication thread, the CUDA communication thread tries to start one incoming memory copy and one outgoing memory copy for each GPU simultaneously. If there are a number of g GPUs, there will be $2g$ `cudaMemcpyAsync` operations happening concurrently in which each GPU has two operations. To implement the CUDA communication thread, `wait4send` and `wait4recv` have been changed to bitsets, where the i-th bit denotes the status of the i-th GPU. We have also implemented `select_GPU_streams` to substitute `MPI_Test` so that we can test in which GPU streams the asynchronous cudaMemcpy operations have finished.

5.5 Data Storage and Management

The host and each GPU have an indirect data structure to store matrices. Given a matrix with $p \times q$ tiles, the indirect structure consists of $p \times q$ pointers each pointing to a tile. A pointer is null if the corresponding tile is not stored in the host or GPU. We store a GPU's indirect data structure to the host memory, but the pointers in the GPU's indirect structure actually point to GPU device memories. By using the indirect data structure, a GPU compute thread can simply look up the structure and pass correct arguments (i.e. GPU device pointers) to launch GPU kernels.

Our runtime system can transfer data from a parent task to its children automatically, however, it does not know how long the data should persist in the destination device. We provide programmers with a special function of `Release_Tile()` to free data. Release_Tile does not free any memory, but sets up a marker in the task window. The marker tells the runtime system that the tile will not be needed by any future tasks (i.e., tasks after the marker), and it is safe to free the tile whenever possible. When a programmer writes a sequential program, he or she can add Release_Tile() to the program just like calling the ANSI C function `free`. The task-generation thread keeps track of the expected number of visits for each tile. Meanwhile the compute threads count the actual number of visits for each tile. The runtime system will free a tile if and only if: i) Release_Tile has been called to mark the tile, and ii) the actual number is equal to the expected number of visits to the tile. In essence, this is an asynchronous deallocation method with which a dynamic runtime system can decide when it is safe to free data.

6. DISTRIBUTED TASK ASSIGNMENT PROTOCOL

Numerous runtime systems (one runtime per node) execute the same code and generate the same set of tasks so that a task may be duplicated on each node. We design a protocol to guarantee that a task is computed by one and only one processing unit (a CPU core or a GPU), and an input is always sent to the waiting task exactly once.

Given a task with k_1 inputs, all the runtime systems across the cluster will generate k_1 input task instances in total. It is exactly k_1 instances because each input belongs to exactly one node and only that node will claim ownership of the input. Also we define that the first output of a task is the *main* output, and the rest outputs are *minor* outputs. We use *main* and *minor* merely to distinguish a task's multiple outputs.

Our runtime system generates eight types of task instances using a set of rules. The rational behind the rules is that when all runtime systems look at the same input or output, they should make a unanimous decision merely based on a predefined distribution (i.e., the multi-level block cyclic distribution) without any communication. Note that the following rules of 1, 2-4 and 5-8 are used to generate a task's main output, inputs, and minor-outputs, respectively.

1. *Owner.* Each runtime system looks at a newly generated task's main output. If the main output is assigned to the host or a GPU on $node_i$ based upon a static data distribution, only $node_i$'s runtime system will create an owner task instance. An owner task instance stores the complete information of the task (i.e., input, output, the ready status of each input).

2. *Native input.* Each input of a new task will be checked by every runtime system. If the input and the task's main output are assigned to the same host or GPU (e.g., on $node_i$), only $node_i$'s runtime system will create a native-input task instance. The native-input instance stores a pointer pointing to the task's owner instance.

3. *Intra-node alien input.* Unlike Rule 2, if the input and the task's main output belong to the same node (e.g., on $node_i$) but on different devices, the runtime system on $node_i$ will create an intra-node alien-input task instance. The intra-node alien-input instance also stores a pointer pointing to the task's owner instance.

4. *Inter-node alien input.* Unlike Rule 3, if the input and the task's main output belong to different nodes, and suppose the input belongs to $node_i$, the runtime system on $node_i$ will create an inter-node alien-input task instance. The inter-node alien-input instance stores the location of the task's main output.

5. *Native minor-output.* Every runtime system looks at each minor output of a newly generated task. If the minor output and the task's main output belong to the same host or GPU (e.g., on $node_i$), the runtime system on $node_i$ will create a native minor-output task instance. The task's owner instance stores a pointer pointing to the native minor-output instance.

6. *Sink minor-output.* Unlike Rule 5, if the minor output and the main output belong to different devices (regardless of nodes), and suppose the minor output is assigned to $node_j$, the runtime system on $node_j$ will create a sink minor-output task instance. The sink instance is expecting its corresponding source to send data to it.

7. *Intra-node source minor-output.* If the minor output and the main output belong to different devices but on the same node (e.g., $node_i$), the runtime system on $node_i$ will create an intra-node source minor-output task instance. The intra-node source minor-output stores a pointer pointing to its corresponding sink instance (generated by Rule 6) on the same node.

8. *Inter-node source minor-output.* If the minor output and the main output belong to different nodes, and

suppose the main output is assigned to $node_i$, the runtime system on $node_i$ will create an inter-node source minor-output task instance. The inter-node source minor-output stores the location of its corresponding sink instance on a remote node.

Since we require the location of an owner task instance be where the task computation occurs, our runtime system is designed to support linking a task's input instances, minor-output instances, and owner instance together so that the availability of an input triggers the owner. In our runtime system, the linking information is either a pointer or the location of the owner task instance. Also by distinguishing *intra-node* from *inter-node*, the runtime system can decide if it needs to copy data to a different device, or even send an MPI message to a different node in order to fire a child task.

A distinctive feature of the protocol is that all the runtime systems can follow the same rules to generate tasks and solve data dependencies in an embarrassingly parallel manner without any communication (except for the actual data transfers). We believe the same principle can be applied to other distributed computing problems with minor changes.

7. PERFORMANCE EVALUATION

We conducted experiments with the Cholesky factorization and QR factorization in double precision on the heterogeneous Keeneland system [25] at the Oak Ridge National Laboratory. The Keeneland system has 120 nodes and is connected by a Qlogic QDR InfiniBand network. Each node on the system runs CentOS 5.5, and has two Intel Xeon 2.8 GHz 6-core processors and three Nvidia Fermi 1.15 GHz M2070 GPUs. The host on each node has 24 GB memories, and each GPU has 6 GB device memories. There is a full PCI-Express bandwidth to every GPU on the system. All the nodes have installed CUDA 4.0, Intel Compilers 12.0, Intel MKL 10.3.5, and OpenMPI 1.5.1.

In the following experiments, we perform weak scalability experiments to measure the capability of our programs to solve potentially larger problems if there are more computing resources. While we are focused on clusters with distributed GPUs, our framework is also able to achieve high performance in the other two environments: multicore clusters without GPUs, and shared-system multiGPUs (i.e., a node with both CPUs and GPUs).

7.1 Distributed GPUs

We did experiments on Keeneland using all twelve CPU cores and all three GPUs on each node. Figure 7 shows how our distributed-GPU framework scales as we increase the number of nodes and the matrix size simultaneously. Although there are 120 nodes on Keeneland, its batch scheduler only allows a job to use 110 nodes in maximum. Since one or two nodes are unavailable sometimes, we use a number of nodes from one to 100. As the number of nodes is increased by k, we increase the matrix size by $\sqrt{k}$. The single-node experiment takes an input matrix of size 34,560.

We measure the total number of TeraFlops to solve the Cholesky factorization and the QR factorization, shown in Fig. 7 (a) and (b), respectively. To display the possible maximum performance (i.e., upper bound) of our programs, we also depict the curves of *DGEMM* and *DSSRFB* that are the dominant computational kernels of Cholesky factorization and QR factorization, respectively. We calculate the upper bound with the following formula: `kernel UB` = serial_cpu_kernel_perf $\times$ #cores + gpu_kernel_perf $\times$ #gpus. To show the benefits of using GPUs, we also present the performance of the Intel MKL 10.3.5 ScaLAPACK library which uses CPUs only. In (a), the overall performance of our distributed-GPU Cholesky factorization reaches 75 TFlops on 100 nodes, while MKL ScaLAPACK reaches 6.3 TFlops. In (b), the overall performance of our distributed-GPU QR factorization reaches 40 TFlops on 100 nodes, while MKL ScaLAPACK reaches 9.2 TFlops.

Figure 7 (c) and (d) show another view (i.e., Performance Per Node) for the same experiments as displayed in (a) and (b). That is, TFlops-Per-Node = $\frac{Overall\ TFlops}{NumberNodes}$ on a given number of nodes. Ideally, the performance-per-node is a constance number in a weak scalability experiment. From (c), we can see that our distributed-GPU Cholesky factorization does not lose any performance from one node to 100 nodes. In (d), our distributed-GPU QR factorization scales well again from four nodes to 100 nodes. The performance-per-node on four nodes drops from 0.44 TFlops to 0.41 TFlops because the four-node experiment uses a 2×2 process grid and has a larger communication overhead than a process grid with $P_r = 1$ (Appendix A analyzes the related communication cost).

7.2 Clusters without GPUs

We did another set of experiments to test whether our framework can deliver high performance on a conventional cluster without GPUs. We only use the 12 CPU cores on each Keeneland node to do the experiments, and compare our Cholesky and QR factorizations with the Intel MKL 10.3.5 ScaLAPACK library.

We perform weak scalability experiments again, where the input size increases by $\sqrt{2}$ whenever we double the number of nodes. In Fig. 8 (a), the overall performance of our Cholesky factorization is faster than the ScaLAPACK Cholesky factorization by 75% on 100 nodes. In (b), our QR factorization and the ScaLAPACK QR factorization have comparable overall performance. Figure 8 (c) and (d) show the performance per node. In (c), our CPU-only Cholesky factorization scales well from 2 to 100 nodes. Its curve has a dip from one to two nodes since our runtime system on each node uses a dedicated core to do MPI communication (i.e., $\frac{1}{12}$ less computing power) if there are more than one node. Similar to Cholesky factorization, in (d), our QR factorization scales well from 4 to 100 nodes. Because of its good scalability, our QR program eventually outperforms the Intel MKL ScaLAPACK QR factorization by 5% when the number of nodes is greater than 32. Note that we use 11 out of 12 cores on each node to do the real computation, while ScaLAPACK uses all 12 cores, however we are still 5% faster.

7.3 Shared-System MultiGPUs

To evaluate our framework on a shared-system with multicore CPUs and multiple GPUs, we compare our Cholesky factorization to StarPU 0.9.1 [6] on a single node of the Keeneland system.

StarPU uses a dynamic scheduling runtime system to assign tasks to CPUs and GPUs to keep load balancing and reduce data transfers. The StarPU implementation of Cholesky factorization uses the same computational kernels as ours,

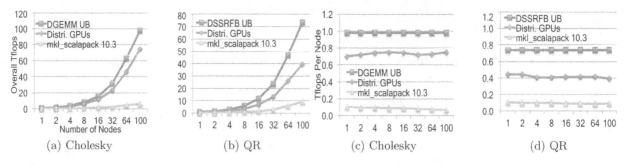

Figure 7: Weak scalability on distributed GPUs. (a) and (b) show the overall performance, while (c) and (d) show the performance-per-node for the Cholesky and QR factorizations (in double precision), respectively. Every experiment uses all 12 CPU cores and 3 GPUs on each node.

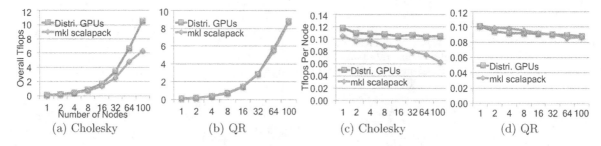

Figure 8: Weak scalability on clusters with CPUs only. Every experiment uses 12 CPU cores on each node.

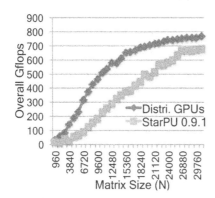

Figure 9: Cholesky factorization (in double precision) on a shared-system with 12 cores and 3 GPUs.

which calls subroutines from the Intel MKL 10.3.5, CUBLAS 4.0, and MAGMA 1.0 libraries. With the help from one of the StarPU developers, we ported the StarPU Cholesky factorization to Keeneland and also tuned its performance thoroughly. Porting the StarPU QR factorization to Nvidia Fermi GPUs is not successful so far due to numerical errors in the result.

Figure 9 shows the overall performance of our framework and StarPU 0.9.1 to solve double-precision Cholesky factorizations. All the StarPU experiments use 9 CPU cores and 3 GPUs to do the real computation, and use the remaining three cores to manage the three GPUs. By contrast, our implementation uses 8 CPU cores and 3 GPUs to do the real computation since we also use an additional core to do CUDA communications. The performance data shows that our framework can rise to high performance more quickly than the StarPU program. When the input size is not too large, our framework is faster than StarPU (i.e., 250% faster

when $N \leq 7680$, and 100% faster when $N \leq 12480$). When the input size is sufficiently large (i.e., $N \geq 26{,}880$), StarPU starts to be close to our framework.

8. RELATED WORK

There are a number of runtime systems developed to support multiple GPU devices on a shared-memory system. StarPU develops a dynamic scheduling runtime system to execute a sequential code on the host CPUs and GPUs in parallel [6], and has been applied to the Cholesky, QR, and LU factorizations [3, 2, 1]. SuperMatrix is another runtime system that supports shared-memory systems with multiple GPUs [20]. It uses several software-cache schemes to maintain the coherence between the host RAM and the GPU memories. While SuperMatrix requires that GPUs take most of the computations, our framework utilizes all CPU cores and all GPUs on both shared-memory and distributed-memory systems.

StarSs is a programming model that uses directives to annotate a sequential source code to execute on various architectures such as SMP, CUDA, and Cell [7]. A programmer is responsible for specifying which piece of code should be executed on a GPU. It is also possible to use the hybrid MPI/SMPSs approach to support clusters with multi-core CPUs [18]. PTask provides a set of OS abstractions to manage and schedule compute tasks on GPUs by using a data-flow programming model [21].

There is research work that supports scientific computations on distributed GPUs. Fatica [14] uses CUDA to accelerate the LINPACK Benchmark [13] on heterogeneous clusters by modifying the original source code slightly. The revised code intercepts every DTRSM or DGEMM, and splits it into two calls to execute on both CPUs and GPUs, respectively. Those calls to CPUs rely on setting `OMP_NUM_THREADS` to utilize all CPU cores on the host. Differently, our framework allows every CPU core to compute tasks independently. On the other hand, we use one MPI process per node, instead of one MPI process per GPU.

Fogué et al. ported the PLAPACK library to GPU accelerated clusters [15]. They require that CPUs compute the diagonal block factorizations while GPUs compute all the remaining operations. They also store all data in GPU memories to reduce communication. In our method, we distribute a matrix across the host and GPUs, and can utilize all CPU cores and all GPUs. Note that it is possible that the computational power of a host may be greater than that of a GPU such that the host needs to compute most of the work.

Many researchers have studied the static data distribution strategies on heterogeneous distributed memory systems. Dongarra et al. designed an algorithm to map a set of uniform tiles to a 1-D collection of heterogeneous processors [11]. Robert et al. proposed a heuristic 2-D block data allocation to extend ScaLAPACK to work on heterogeneous clusters [9]. Lastovetsky et al. developed a static data distribution strategy that takes into account both processor heterogeneity and memory heterogeneity for dense matrix factorizations [17]. Our work targets clusters of nodes that consist of multicore CPUs and multiple GPUs, and uses a novel static multi-level block cyclic strategy.

9. CONCLUSION AND FUTURE WORK

As the trend of adding more GPUs to each node to deliver high performance continues, it is important to start to design new parallel software on the heterogeneous architectures. We present a new framework to solve dense linear algebra problems on large-scale GPU-based clusters. To attain scalable performance, we focus our design on minimizing communication, maximizing the degree of task parallelism, accommodating processor heterogeneity, hiding communication, and keeping load balance. The framework essentially consists of a static multi-level partitioning and distribution method, heterogeneous tile algorithms, and a distributed scheduling runtime system.

Our experiments with the Cholesky and QR factorizations on the heterogeneous Keeneland system demonstrate great scalability in various environments: clusters with or without GPUs, and shared-systems with multi-GPUs. Our future work along this line is to apply the approach to two-sided factorizations and sparse matrices. Another future work is to add NUMA support to our runtime system to improve performance on each node that has hundreds or even thousands of CPU cores as well as a great number of NUMA memory nodes.

10. REFERENCES

[1] E. Agullo, C. Augonnet, J. Dongarra, M. Faverge, J. Langou, H. Ltaief, and S. Tomov. LU factorization for accelerator-based systems. ICL Technical Report ICL-UT-10-05, Innovative Computing Laboratory, University of Tennessee, 2010.

[2] E. Agullo, C. Augonnet, J. Dongarra, M. Faverge, H. Ltaief, S. Thibault, and S. Tomov. QR factorization on a multicore node enhanced with multiple GPU accelerators. In *IPDPS 2011*, Alaska, USA, 2011.

[3] E. Agullo, C. Augonnet, J. Dongarra, H. Ltaief, R. Namyst, J. Roman, S. Thibault, and S. Tomov. Dynamically scheduled Cholesky factorization on multicore architectures with GPU accelerators. In *Symposium on Application Accelerators in High Performance Computing (SAAHPC)*, Knoxville, USA, 2010.

[4] E. Agullo, J. Dongarra, B. Hadri, J. Kurzak, J. Langou, J. Langou, H. Ltaief, P. Luszczek, and A. YarKhan. PLASMA Users' Guide. Technical report, ICL, UTK, 2011.

[5] E. Anderson, Z. Bai, C. Bischof, L. Blackford, J. Demmel, J. Dongarra, J. D. Croz, A. Greenbaum, S. Hammarling, A. McKenney, and D. Sorensen. *LAPACK Users' Guide*. SIAM, 1992.

[6] C. Augonnet, S. Thibault, R. Namyst, and P.-A. Wacrenier. StarPU: A unified platform for task scheduling on heterogeneous multicore architectures. *Concurr. Comput. : Pract. Exper., Special Issue: Euro-Par 2009*, 23:187–198, Feb. 2011.

[7] E. Ayguadé, R. M. Badia, F. D. Igual, J. Labarta, R. Mayo, and E. S. Quintana-Ortí. An extension of the StarSs programming model for platforms with multiple GPUs. In *Proceedings of the 15th International Euro-Par Conference on Parallel Processing*, Euro-Par '09, pages 851–862. Springer-Verlag, 2009.

[8] G. Ballard, J. Demmel, O. Holtz, and O. Schwartz. Communication-optimal parallel and sequential Cholesky decomposition. In *Proceedings of the twenty-first annual symposium on Parallelism in algorithms and architectures*, SPAA '09, pages 245–252. ACM, 2009.

[9] O. Beaumont, V. Boudet, A. Petitet, F. Rastello, and Y. Robert. A proposal for a heterogeneous cluster ScaLAPACK (dense linear solvers). *IEEE Transactions on Computers*, 50:1052–1070, 2001.

[10] L. S. Blackford, J. Choi, A. Cleary, E. D'Azevedo, J. Demmel, I. Dhillon, J. Dongarra, S. Hammarling, G. Henry, A. Petitet, K. Stanley, D. Walker, and R. Whaley. *ScaLAPACK Users' Guide*. SIAM, 1997.

[11] P. Boulet, J. Dongarra, Y. Robert, and F. Vivien. Static tiling for heterogeneous computing platforms. *Parallel Computing*, 25(5):547 – 568, 1999.

[12] J. W. Demmel, L. Grigori, M. F. Hoemmen, and J. Langou. Communication-optimal parallel and sequential QR and LU factorizations. LAPACK Working Note 204, UTK, August 2008.

[13] J. J. Dongarra, P. Luszczek, and A. Petitet. The LINPACK Benchmark: past, present, and future. *Concurrency and Computation: Practice and Experience*, 15:803–820, 2003.

[14] M. Fatica. Accelerating Linpack with CUDA on heterogenous clusters. In *Proceedings of 2nd Workshop on General Purpose Processing on Graphics Processing Units*, GPGPU-2, pages 46–51. ACM, 2009.

[15] M. Fogué, F. D. Igual, E. S. Quintana-ortŠ, and R. V. D. Geijn. Retargeting PLAPACK to clusters with hardware accelerators. FLAME Working Note 42, 2010.

[16] J. R. Humphrey, D. K. Price, K. E. Spagnoli, A. L. Paolini, and E. J. Kelmelis. CULA: Hybrid GPU accelerated linear algebra routines. In *SPIE Defense and Security Symposium (DSS)*, April 2010.

[17] A. Lastovetsky and R. Reddy. Data distribution for dense factorization on computers with memory heterogeneity. *Parallel Comput.*, 33:757–779, December 2007.

[18] V. Marjanović, J. Labarta, E. Ayguadé, and M. Valero. Overlapping communication and computation by using a hybrid MPI/SMPSs approach. In *Proceedings of the 24th ACM International Conference on Supercomputing*, ICS '10, pages 5–16. ACM, 2010.

[19] NVIDIA. CUDA Toolkit 4.0 CUBLAS Library, 2011.

[20] G. Quintana-Ortí, F. D. Igual, E. S. Quintana-Ortí, and R. A. van de Geijn. Solving dense linear systems on platforms with multiple hardware accelerators. In *Proceedings of the 14th ACM SIGPLAN symposium on Principles and practice of parallel programming*, PPoPP '09, pages 121–130. ACM, 2009.

[21] C. J. Rossbach, J. Currey, M. Silberstein, B. Ray, and E. Witchel. PTask: Operating system abstractions to manage GPUs as compute devices. In *Proceedings of the Twenty-Third ACM Symposium on Operating Systems Principles*, SOSP '11, pages 233–248. ACM, 2011.

[22] S. Sharma, C.-H. Hsu, and W. chun Feng. Making a case for a Green500 list. In *IEEE International Parallel and Distributed Processing Symposium (IPDPS 2006)/ Workshop on High Performance - Power Aware Computing*, 2006.

[23] F. Song, S. Tomov, and J. Dongarra. Efficient support for matrix computations on heterogeneous multi-core and multi-GPU architectures. LAPACK Working Note 250, UTK, June 2011.

[24] S. Tomov, R. Nath, P. Du, and J. Dongarra. MAGMA Users' Guide. Technical report, ICL, UTK, 2011.

[25] J. Vetter, R. Glassbrook, J. Dongarra, K. Schwan, B. Loftis, S. McNally, J. Meredith, J. Rogers, P. Roth, K. Spafford, and S. Yalamanchili. Keeneland: Bringing heterogeneous GPU computing to the computational science community. *Computing in Science Engineering*, 13(5):90 –95, sept.-oct. 2011.

APPENDIX

A. COMMUNICATION COST ANALYSIS

We count the number of messages and the number of words communicated by a process that has the most communication among all processes. Assume there are P processes (one process per node), and the broadcast between processes is implemented by a tree topology. We use P_r and P_c to denote a $P_r \times P_c$ process grid, where $P = P_r \cdot P_c$. In a multi-level block cyclic data distribution, we use n, B, s to denote the matrix size, the top-level tile size, and the number of partitions of each top-level tile, respectively.

A.1 Distributed Heterogeneous Tile Cholesky

For each iteration, we first broadcast the diagonal block down the panel (i.e. $\log P_r$ messages), next each process that owns data on the panel broadcasts to $P_c + P_r$ processes that are waiting for the panel data (i.e. $\frac{\#rows}{BP_r} \log(P_c + P_r)$ messages, where $\#rows = n - \lfloor \frac{i}{s} \rfloor B$ at the j-th iteration).

The number of messages and words are expressed as follows:

$$
\begin{aligned}
\text{msg}_{chol} &= \sum_{j=0}^{\frac{n}{B}s-1} \log P_r + \frac{n - \lfloor \frac{i}{s} \rfloor B}{BP_r} \log(P_c + P_r) \\
&= \frac{ns}{2B} \log P + \frac{n^2 s}{4B^2 \sqrt{P}} \log P + \frac{n^2 s}{2B^2 \sqrt{P}}
\end{aligned}
$$

$$
\text{word}_{chol} = \frac{nB}{4} \log P + \frac{n^2}{4\sqrt{P}} \log P + \frac{n^2}{2\sqrt{P}}
$$

A.2 Distributed Heterogeneous Tile QR

In the tile QR factorization, we can stack up v adjacent tiles to form a virtual tile, which is always allocated to the same host or GPU. At the j-th iteration, each process has $\frac{n - \lfloor \frac{i}{s} \rfloor B}{(vB)P_r} \times \frac{n - \lfloor \frac{i}{s} \rfloor B}{BP_c}$ virtual tiles of size $(vB) \times B$. Since one $B \times B$ tile out of every virtual tile will be sent down to its below process as a message (there is no message if $P_r = 1$), and every tile on the panel will be broadcast right to P_c processes, the number of messages and words are expressed as follows:

$$
\begin{aligned}
\text{msg}_{qr} &= \sum_{j=0}^{\frac{n}{B}s-1} \frac{n - \lfloor \frac{i}{s} \rfloor B}{vBP_r} \cdot \frac{n - \lfloor \frac{i}{s} \rfloor B}{BP_c} + \frac{n - \lfloor \frac{i}{s} \rfloor B}{BP_r} \log P_c \\
&= \frac{n^3 s}{3vB^3 P} + \frac{n^2 s}{4B^2 \sqrt{P}} \log P
\end{aligned}
$$

$$
\text{word}_{qr} = \frac{n^3}{3vBP} + \frac{n^2}{4\sqrt{P}} \log P = (\frac{n}{3vB\sqrt{P}\log P} + \frac{1}{4}) \frac{n^2}{\sqrt{P}} \log
$$

If we set the virtual tile size v as $n/B/P_r$, $(vB\sqrt{P})$ is equal to n. Therefore, $\text{msg}_{qr} = \frac{n^2 s}{3B^2 \sqrt{P}} + \frac{n^2 s}{4B^2 \sqrt{P}} \log P$, and $\text{word}_{qr} = (\frac{1}{3\log P} + \frac{1}{4}) \frac{n^2}{\sqrt{P}} \log P$.

A.3 Comparison with ScaLAPACK

Table 1 compares our distributed-version heterogeneous tile algorithms with the communication lower bound (LB), and the ScaLAPACK subroutines regarding the number of words (i.e., communication volume) and the number of messages. From the table, we can see that the heterogeneous Cholesky factorization has attained the communication volume lower bound to within a logarithmic factor. The communication volume of the heterogeneous QR factorization is greater than its lower bound, but we could increase v to minimize its communication volume to reach the lower bound to within a factor of $(\frac{1}{3} + \frac{1}{4} \log P)$.

Table 1: Communication cost.

	#words	#messages
Cholesky LB [[8]]	$\Omega(\frac{n^2}{\sqrt{P}})$	$\Omega(\sqrt{P})$
PDPOTRF [[8]]	$(\frac{nb}{4} + \frac{n^2}{\sqrt{P}}) \log P$	$\frac{3n}{2b} \log P$
Hetero. Cholesky	$(\frac{1}{4} \log P + \frac{1}{2}) \frac{n^2}{\sqrt{P}}$	$\frac{n^2 s}{4B^2 \sqrt{P}} (\log P + 2)$
QR LB [[12]]	$\Omega(\frac{n^2}{\sqrt{P}})$	$\Omega(\sqrt{P})$
PDGEQRF [[12]]	$(\frac{3}{4} \frac{n^2}{\sqrt{P}} + \frac{3}{4} nb) \log P$	$(\frac{3}{2} + \frac{5}{2b}) n \log P$
Hetero. QR	$(\frac{n}{3vB\sqrt{P}\log P} + \frac{1}{4}) \frac{n^2}{\sqrt{P}} \log P$	$\frac{n^3 s}{3vB^3 P} + \frac{n^2 s}{4B^2 \sqrt{P}} \log P$

Faster and Simpler Width-Independent Parallel Algorithms for Positive Semidefinite Programming

Richard Peng   Kanat Tangwongsan

Carnegie Mellon University

{yangp, ktangwon}@cs.cmu.edu

ABSTRACT

This paper studies the problem of finding a $(1+\varepsilon)$-approximate solution to positive semidefinite programs. These are semidefinite programs in which all matrices in the constraints and objective are positive semidefinite and all scalars are non-negative. At *FOCS'11*, Jain and Yao gave an NC algorithm that requires $O(\frac{1}{\varepsilon^{13}} \log^{13} m \log n)$ iterations on input n constraint matrices of dimension m-by-m, where each iteration performs at least $\Omega(m^{\omega})$ work since it involves computing the spectral decomposition.

We present a simpler NC parallel algorithm that on input with n constraint matrices, requires $O(\frac{1}{\varepsilon^4} \log^4 n \log(\frac{1}{\varepsilon}))$ iterations, each of which involves only simple matrix operations and computing the trace of the product of a matrix exponential and a positive semidefinite matrix. Further, given a positive SDP in a factorized form, the total work of our algorithm is nearly-linear in the number of non-zero entries in the factorization. Our algorithm can be viewed as a generalization of Young's algorithm and analysis techniques for positive linear programs (Young, *FOCS'01*) to the semidefinite programming setting.

Categories and Subject Descriptors: F.2 [Theory of Computation]: Analysis of Algorithms and Problem Complexity

General Terms: Algorithms, Theory

Keywords: Parallel algorithms, semidefinite programming, covering semidefinite programs, approximation algorithms

1. INTRODUCTION

Semidefinite programming (SDP), alongside linear programming (LP), has been an important tool in approximation algorithms, optimization, and discrete mathematics. In the context of approximation algorithms alone, it has emerged as a key technique which underlies a number of impressive results that substantially improve the approximation ratios.

Permission to make digital or hard copies of all or part of this work for personal or classroom use is granted without fee provided that copies are not made or distributed for profit or commercial advantage and that copies bear this notice and the full citation on the first page. To copy otherwise, to republish, to post on servers or to redistribute to lists, requires prior specific permission and/or a fee.
SPAA'12, June 25–27, 2012, Pittsburgh, Pennsylvania, USA.
Copyright 2012 ACM 978-1-4503-1213-4/12/06 ...$10.00.

In order to solve a semidefinite program, algorithms from the linear programming literature such as Ellipsoid or interior-point algorithms [GLS93] can be applied to derive near exact solutions. But this can be very costly. As a result, finding efficient approximations to such problems is a critical step in bringing these results closer to practice.

From a parallel algorithms standpoint, both LPs and SDPs are P-complete to even approximate to any constant accuracy, suggesting that it is unlikely that they have a polylogarithmic depth algorithm. For linear programs, however, the special case of positive linear programs, first studied by Luby and Nisan [LN93], has an algorithm that finds a $(1 + \varepsilon)$-approximate solution in $O(\text{poly}(\frac{1}{\varepsilon} \log n))$ iterations. This weaker approximation guarantee is still sufficient for approximation algorithms (e.g., solutions to vertex cover and set cover via randomized rounding), spurring interest in studying these problems in both sequential and parallel contexts (see, e.g., [LN93, PST95, GK98, You01, KY07, KY09]).

The importance of problems such as MaxCut and Sparsest Cut has led to the identification and study of positive SDPs. The first definition of positive SDPs was due to Klein and Lu [KL96], who used it to characterize the MaxCut SDP. The MaxCut SDP can be viewed as a direct generalization of positive (packing) LPs. More recent work defines the notion of positive packing SDPs [IPS11], which captures problems such as MaxCut, sparse PCA, and coloring; and the notion of covering SDPs [IPS10], which captures the ARV relaxation of Sparsest Cut among others. The bulk of work in this area tends to focus on developing fast sequential algorithms for finding a $(1 + \varepsilon)$-approximation, leading to a series of nice sequential algorithms (e.g., [AHK05, AK07, IPS11, IPS10]). The iteration count for these algorithms, however, depends on the so-called "width" parameter of the input program or some parameter of the spectrum of the input program. In some instances, the width parameter can be as large as $\Omega(n)$, making it a bottleneck in the depth of direct parallelization. Most recently, Jain and Yao [JY11] studied a particular class of positive SDPs and gave the first positive SDP algorithm whose work and depth are independent of the width parameter (commonly known as width-independent algorithms).

Our Work. We present a simple algorithm that offers the same approximation guarantee as [JY11] but has less work-depth complexity. Each iteration of our algorithm involves only simple matrix operations and computing the trace of the product of a matrix exponential and a positive semidefinite matrix. Furthermore, our proof only uses elementary linear-algebraic techniques and the now-standard Golden-Thompson inequality.

The input consists of an accuracy parameter $\varepsilon > 0$ and a positive semidefinite program (PSDP) in the following standard primal form:

$$\begin{aligned}
\text{Minimize} \quad & \mathbf{C} \bullet \mathbf{Y} \\
\text{Subject to:} \quad & \mathbf{A}_i \bullet \mathbf{Y} \geq b_i \quad \text{for } i = 1, \ldots, n \\
& \mathbf{Y} \succeq \mathbf{0},
\end{aligned} \quad (1.1)$$

where the matrices $\mathbf{C}, \mathbf{A}_1, \ldots, \mathbf{A}_n$ are m-by-m symmetric positive semidefinite matrices, $\bullet$ denotes the pointwise dot product between matrices (see Section 2), and the scalars $b_1, \ldots, b_n$ are non-negative reals. This is a subclass of SDPs where the matrices and scalars are "positive" in their respective settings. We also make the now-standard assumption that the SDP has strong duality. Our main result is as follows:

Theorem 1.1 (Main Theorem) *Given a primal positive SDP involving $m \times m$ matrices with n constraints and an accuracy parameter $\varepsilon > 0$, there is an algorithm* approxPSDP *that produces a $(1 + \varepsilon)$-approximation in $O(\frac{1}{\varepsilon^4} \log^4 n \log(\frac{1}{\varepsilon}))$ iterations, where each iteration involves computing matrix sums and a special primitive that computes $\exp(\boldsymbol{\Phi}) \bullet \mathbf{A}$ in the case when $\boldsymbol{\Phi}$ and $\mathbf{A}$ are both positive semidefinite.*

The theorem quantifies the cost of our algorithm in terms of the number of iterations. The work and depth bounds implied by this theorem vary with the format of the input and how the matrix exponential is computed in each iteration. As we will discuss in Section 4, with input given in a suitable form, our algorithm runs in nearly-linear work and polylogarithmic depth. For comparison, the algorithm given in [JY11] requires $O(\frac{1}{\varepsilon^{13}} \log^{13} m \log n)$ iterations, each of which involves computing spectral decompositions using least $\Omega(m^\omega)$ work.

Recently, in an independent work, Jain and Yao [JY12] gave a similar algorithm for positive SDPs that is also based on Young's algorithm. Their algorithm solves a class of SDPs which contains both packing and diagonal covering constraints. Since matrix packing conditions between diagonal matrices are equivalent to point-wise conditions of the diagonal entries, these constraints are closer to a generalization of positive covering LP constraints. We believe that removing this restriction on diagonal packing matrices would greatly widen the class of problems included in this class of SDPs and discuss possibilities in this direction in Section 5.

1.1 Overview

All the parallel positive SDP algorithms to date can be seen as generalizations of previous works on positive linear programs (positive LPs). In the positive LPs literature, Luby and Nisan (LN) were the first to give a parallel algorithm for approximately solving a positive LP [LN93]. This algorithm provided the foundations for the algorithm given in [JY11], which like the LN algorithm, also works directly on the primal program. Using the dual as guide, the update step is intricate as their analysis is based on carefully analyzing the eigenspaces of a particular matrix before and after each update. Each of these iterations involves computing the spectral decomposition.

Our algorithm follows a different approach, based on the algorithm of Young [You01] for positive LPs. At the core of our algorithm is an algorithm for solving the decision version of the dual program. We derive this core routine by generalizing the algorithm and analysis techniques of Young [You01], using the matrix multiplicative weights update (MMWU) mechanism in place of Young's "soft" min and max. This leads to a simple algorithm: besides standard operations on (sparse) matrix, the only special primitive needed is the matrix dot product $\exp(\boldsymbol{\Phi}) \bullet \mathbf{A}$, where $\boldsymbol{\Phi}$ and $\mathbf{A}$ are both positive semidefinite.

More specifically, our algorithm works with normalized primal/dual programs shown in Figure 1.1. This is without loss of generality because any input program can be transformed into the normalized form by "dividing through" by $\mathbf{C}$ (see Appendix A). We solve a normalized SDP by resorting to an algorithm for its decision version and binary search. In particular, we design an algorithm with the property that given a goal value $\hat{o}$, either find a dual solution $x \in \mathbb{R}_n^+$ to (1.2-D) with objective at least $(1 - \varepsilon)\hat{o}$, or a primal solution $\mathbf{Y}$ to (1.2-P) with objective at most $\hat{o}$. Furthermore, by scaling the $\mathbf{A}_i$'s, it suffices to only consider the case where $\hat{o} = 1$. With this algorithm, the optimization version can be solved by binary searching on the objective a total of at most $O(\log(\frac{n}{\varepsilon}))$ iterations.

Intuitions. For intuition about packing SDPs and the matrix multiplicative weights update method for finding approximate solutions, a useful analogy of the decision problem is that of packing a (fractional) amount of ellipses into the unit ball. Figure 2 provides an example involving 3 matrices (ellipses) in 2 dimensions. Note that $\mathbf{A}_1$ and $\mathbf{A}_2$ are axis-aligned, so their sum is also an axis-aligned sum in this case. In fact, positive linear programs in the broader context corresponds exactly to the restriction of all ellipsoids being axis-aligned. In this setting, the algorithm of [You01] can be viewed as creating a penalty function by weighting the length of the axises using an exponential function. Then, ellipsoids with sufficiently small penalty subject to this function have their weights increased. However, once we allow general ellipsoids such as $\mathbf{A}_3$, the resulting sum will no longer be axis-aligned. In this setting, a natural extension is to take the exponential of the semi-major axises of the resulting ellipsoid instead. As we will see in later sections, the rest of Young's technique for achieving width-independence can also be adapted to this more general setting.

Work and Depth. We now discuss the work and depth bounds of our algorithm. The main cost of each iteration of our algorithm comes from computing the dot product between a matrix exponential and a PSD matrix. Like in the sequential setting [AHK05, AK07], we need to compute for each iteration the product $\mathbf{A}_i \bullet \exp(\boldsymbol{\Phi})$, where $\boldsymbol{\Phi}$ is some PSD matrix. The cost of our algorithm therefore depends on how the input is specified. When the input is given prefactored—that is, the m-by-m matrices $\mathbf{A}_i$'s are given as $\mathbf{A}_i = \mathbf{Q}_i \mathbf{Q}_i^\top$ and the matrix $\mathbf{C}^{-1/2}$ is given, then Theorem 4.1 can be used to compute matrix exponential in $O(\frac{1}{\varepsilon^3}(m + q) \log n \log q \log(1/\varepsilon))$ work and $O(\frac{1}{\varepsilon} \log n \log q \log(1/\varepsilon))$ depth, where q is the number of nonzero entries across $\mathbf{Q}_i$'s and $\mathbf{C}^{-1/2}$. This is because the matrix $\boldsymbol{\Phi}$ that we exponentiate has $\|\boldsymbol{\Phi}\|_2 \leq O(\frac{1}{\varepsilon} \log n)$, as shown in Lemma 3.8. Therefore, as a corollary to the main theorem, we have the following cost bounds:

	Primal				*Dual*	

$$
\begin{array}{llll}
\text{Minimize} & \mathsf{Tr}\,[\mathbf{Y}] \\
\text{Subject to:} & \mathbf{A}_i' \bullet \mathbf{Y} \geq 1 & \text{for } i=1,\dots,n \\
& \mathbf{Y} \succcurlyeq 0
\end{array}
\qquad
\begin{array}{ll}
\text{Maximize} & \mathbf{1}^\top x \\
\text{Subject to:} & \sum_{i=1}^n x_i \mathbf{A}_i' \preccurlyeq \mathbf{I} \\
& x \geq \mathbf{0}.
\end{array}
\qquad (1.2)
$$

Figure 1. Normalized primal/dual positive SDPs. The symbol $\mathbf{I}$ represents the identity matrix.

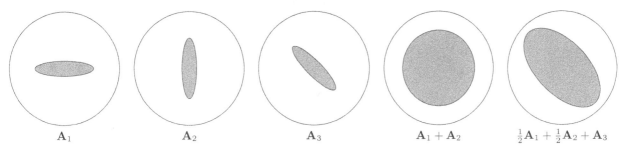

$\mathbf{A}_1$	$\mathbf{A}_2$	$\mathbf{A}_3$	$\mathbf{A}_1 + \mathbf{A}_2$	$\frac{1}{2}\mathbf{A}_1 + \frac{1}{2}\mathbf{A}_2 + \mathbf{A}_3$

Figure 2. An instance of a packing SDP in 2 dimensions.

Corollary 1.2 *The algorithm* approxPSDP *has in* $\widetilde{O}(n+m+q)$ *work and* $O(\log^{O(1)}(n+m+q))$ *depth.*

If, however, the input program is not given in this form, we can add a preprocessing step that factors each $\mathbf{A}_i$ into $\mathbf{Q}_i \mathbf{Q}_i^\top$ since $\mathbf{A}_i$ is positive semidefinite. In general, this preprocessing requires at most $O(m^4)$ work and $O(\log^3 m)$ depth using standard parallel QR factorization [JáJ92]. Furthermore, these matrices often have certain structure that makes them easier to factor. Similarly, we can factor and invert $\mathbf{C}$ with the same cost bound, and can do better if it also has specialized structure.

2. BACKGROUND AND NOTATION

We review notation and facts that will prove useful later in the paper. Throughout this paper, we use the notation $\widetilde{O}(f(n))$ to mean $O(f(n)\,\mathrm{polylog}(f(n)))$.

Matrices and Positive Semidefiniteness. Unless otherwise stated, we will deal with real symmetric matrices in $\mathbb{R}^{m \times m}$. A symmetric matrix $\mathbf{A}$ is positive semidefinite, denoted by $\mathbf{A} \succcurlyeq 0$ or $0 \preccurlyeq \mathbf{A}$, if for all $\mathbf{z} \in \mathbb{R}^m$, $\mathbf{z}^\top \mathbf{A} \mathbf{z} \geq 0$. Equivalently, this means that all eigenvalues of $\mathbf{A}$ are nonnegative and the matrix $\mathbf{A}$ can be written as

$$
\mathbf{A} = \sum_i \lambda_i \mathbf{v}_i \mathbf{v}_i^\top,
$$

where $\mathbf{v}_1, \mathbf{v}_2, \dots, \mathbf{v}_m$ are the eigenvectors of $\mathbf{A}$ with eigenvalues $\lambda_1 \geq \cdots \geq \lambda_m$ respectively. We will use $\lambda_1(\mathbf{A})$, $\lambda_2(\mathbf{A}), \dots, \lambda_m(\mathbf{A})$ to represent the eigenvalues of $\mathbf{A}$ in decreasing order and also use $\lambda_{\max}(\mathbf{A})$ to denote $\lambda_1(\mathbf{A})$. Notice that positive semidefiniteness induces a partial ordering on matrices. We write $\mathbf{A} \preccurlyeq \mathbf{B}$ if $\mathbf{B} - \mathbf{A} \succcurlyeq 0$.

The trace of a matrix $\mathbf{A}$, denoted $\mathsf{Tr}\,[\mathbf{A}]$, is the sum of the matrix's diagonal entries: $\mathsf{Tr}\,[\mathbf{A}] = \sum_i A_{i,i}$. Alternatively, the trace of a matrix can be expressed as the sum of its eigenvalues, so $\mathsf{Tr}\,[\mathbf{A}] = \sum_i \lambda_i(\mathbf{A})$. Furthermore, we define

$$
\mathbf{A} \bullet \mathbf{B} = \sum_{i,j} A_{i,j} B_{i,j} = \mathsf{Tr}\,[\mathbf{A}\mathbf{B}].
$$

It follows that $\mathbf{A}$ is positive semidefinite if and only if $\mathbf{A} \bullet \mathbf{B} \geq 0$ for all PSD $\mathbf{B}$.

Matrix Exponential. Given an $m \times m$ symmetric positive semidefinite matrix $\mathbf{A}$ and a function $f \colon \mathbb{R} \to \mathbb{R}$, we define

$$
f(\mathbf{A}) = \sum_{i=1}^m f(\lambda_i) \mathbf{v}_i \mathbf{v}_i^\top,
$$

where, again, $\mathbf{v}_i$ is the eigenvector corresponding to the eigenvalue λ_i. It is not difficult to check that for $\exp(\mathbf{A})$, this definition coincides with $\exp(\mathbf{A}) = \sum_{i \geq 0} \frac{1}{i!} \mathbf{A}^i$.

Our algorithm relies on a matrix multiplicative weights (MMW) algorithm, which can be summarized as follows. For a fixed $\varepsilon_0 \leq \frac{1}{2}$ and $\mathbf{W}^{(1)} = \mathbf{I}$, we play a "game" a number of times, where in iteration $t = 1, 2, \dots$, the following steps are performed:

1. Produce a probability matrix $\mathbf{P}^{(t)} = \mathbf{W}^{(t)} / \mathsf{Tr}\left[\mathbf{W}^{(t)}\right]$;

2. Incur a gain matrix $\mathbf{M}^{(t)}$; and

3. Update the weight matrix as

$$
\mathbf{W}^{(t+1)} = \exp(\varepsilon_0 \sum_{t' \leq t} \mathbf{M}^{(t')}).
$$

Like in the standard setting of multiplicative weight algorithms, the gain matrix is chosen by an external party, possibly adversarially. In our algorithm, the gain matrix is chosen to reflect the step we make in the iteration. Arora and Kale [AK07] shows that the MMW algorithm has the following guarantees (restated for our setting):

Theorem 2.1 ([AK07]) *For* $\varepsilon_0 \leq \frac{1}{2}$, *if* $\mathbf{M}^{(t)}$'s *are all PSD and* $\mathbf{M}^{(t)} \preccurlyeq \mathbf{I}$, *then after* T *iterations,*

$$
(1+\varepsilon_0) \sum_{t=1}^T \mathbf{M}^{(t)} \bullet \mathbf{P}^{(t)} \geq \lambda_{\max}\left(\sum_{t=1}^T \mathbf{M}^{(t)}\right) - \frac{\ln n}{\varepsilon_0}. \quad (2.1)
$$

3. SOLVING POSITIVE SDPS

In this section, we describe a parallel algorithm for solving positive packing SDPs, inspired by Young's algorithm for positive LPs. As described earlier, by using binary search and appropriately scaling the input program, a positive packing SDP can be solved assuming an algorithm for the following decision problem:

Decision Problem: Find either an $\boldsymbol{x} \in \mathbb{R}_n^+$ (a dual solution) such that

$$\|\boldsymbol{x}\|_1 \geq 1 - \varepsilon \quad \text{and} \quad \sum_{i=1}^n x_i \mathbf{A}_i \preccurlyeq \mathbf{I}$$

or a PSD matrix $\mathbf{Y}$ (a primal solution) such that

$$\mathsf{Tr}\left[\mathbf{Y}\right] \leq 1 \text{ and } \forall i, \mathbf{A}_i \bullet \mathbf{Y} \geq 1.$$

The following theorem provides a solution to this problem:

Theorem 3.1 *Let* $0 < \varepsilon \leq 1$. *There is an algorithm* `decisionPSDP` *that given a positive SDP, in* $O\left(\frac{\log^3 n}{\varepsilon^4}\right)$ *iterations solves the Decision Problem.*

Presented in Algorithm 3.1 is an algorithm that satisfies the theorem. But before we go about proving it, let us take a closer look at the algorithm. Fix an accuracy parameter $\varepsilon > 0$. We set K to $\frac{1}{\varepsilon}(1 + \ln n)$. The reason for choosing this value is technical, but the motivation was so that we can absorb the $\ln n$ term in Theorem 2.1 and account for the contribution of the starting solution $\boldsymbol{x}^{(0)}$.

The algorithm is a multiplicative weight updates algorithm, which proceeds in rounds. Initially, we work with the starting solution $x_i^{(0)} = \frac{1}{n \, \mathsf{Tr}[\mathbf{A}_i]}$. This solution is chosen to be small so that $\sum_i x_i^{(0)} \mathbf{A}_i \preccurlyeq \mathbf{I}$, hence respecting the dual constraint, and it contains enough mass that subsequent updates (each update is a multiple of the current solution) are guaranteed to make rapid progress. In each iteration, we compute $\mathbf{W}^{(t)} = \exp(\boldsymbol{\Psi}^{(t-1)})$, where $\boldsymbol{\Psi}^{(t-1)} = \sum_i x_i^{(t-1)} \mathbf{A}_i$. (For some intuitions for the $\mathbf{W}^{(t)}$ matrix, we refer the reader to [AK07, Kal07].)

The next two steps (Steps 3–4) of the algorithm are responsible for identifying which coordinates of $\boldsymbol{x}$ to update. For starters, it may help to think of them as follows: let $\mathbf{P}^{(t)} = \mathbf{W}^{(t)} / \mathsf{Tr}\left[\mathbf{W}^{(t)}\right]$—and $B^{(t)}$ be $\{i \in [n] : \mathbf{P}^{(t)} \bullet \mathbf{A}_i \leq 1 + \varepsilon\}$. The actual algorithm discretizes $\mathsf{Tr}\left[\mathbf{W}^{(t)}\right]$ to ensure certain monotonicity properties on $B^{(t)}$. As we show later on in Lemma 3.2, the set $B^{(t)}$ cannot be empty unless the system is infeasible. The final steps of the algorithm increment each coordinate $i \in B^{(t)}$ of the solution by the amount $\alpha \cdot x_i^{(t)}$.

The choice of α may seem mysterious at this point; it is chosen to ensure that (1) $\sum_i \delta_i^{(t)} \mathbf{A}_i \preccurlyeq \varepsilon \mathbf{I}$ and (2) $\mathbf{1}^\top \delta^{(t)} \leq \varepsilon$. Intuitively, these bounds prevent us from taking too big a step from the current solution. At a more technical level, the first requirement is needed to satisfy the MMW algorithm's condition, and the second requirement makes sure when we cannot overshoot by much when exiting from the while loop.

3.1 Analysis

We will bound the approximation guarantees and analyze the cost of the algorithm. Before we start, we will need some notation and definitions. An easy induction gives that the

---

Algorithm 3.1 Parallel Packing SDP algorithm

Let $K = \frac{1}{\varepsilon}(1 + \ln n)$.
Let $x_i^{(0)} = \frac{1}{n \cdot \mathsf{Tr}[\mathbf{A}_i]}$.
Initialize $\boldsymbol{\Psi}^{(0)} = \sum_{i=1}^n x_i^{(0)} \mathbf{A}_i$, $t = 0$.
While $\|\boldsymbol{x}^{(t)}\|_1 \leq K$

1. $t = t + 1$.
2. Let $\mathbf{W}^{(t)} = \exp(\boldsymbol{\Psi}^{(t-1)})$.
3. Let p be such that $(1+\varepsilon)^{p-1} < \mathsf{Tr}\left[\mathbf{W}^{(t)}\right] \leq (1+\varepsilon)^p$.
4. Let $B^{(t)} = \{i \in [n] : \mathbf{W}^{(t)} \bullet \mathbf{A}_i \leq (1+\varepsilon)^{p+1}\}$.
5. If $B^{(t)}$ is empty, return $\mathbf{Y}^* = \mathbf{W}^{(t)} / \mathsf{Tr}\left[\mathbf{W}^{(t)}\right]$ as a primal solution.
6. Let $\delta^{(t)} = \alpha \cdot \boldsymbol{x}_B^{(t-1)}$, where

$$\alpha = \min\{\varepsilon/\|\boldsymbol{x}_B^{(t-1)}\|_1, \varepsilon/(1+10\varepsilon)K\}.$$

7. Update $\boldsymbol{x}^{(t)} = \boldsymbol{x}^{(t-1)} + \delta^{(t)}$ and $\boldsymbol{\Psi}^{(t)} = \boldsymbol{\Psi}^{(t-1)} + \sum_{i=1}^n \delta^{(t)} \mathbf{A}_i$

Return $\boldsymbol{x}^* = \frac{1}{K(1+10\varepsilon)} \boldsymbol{x}^{(t)}$ as a dual solution.

---

quantities that we track across the iterations of Algorithm 3.1 satisfy the following relationships:

$$\boldsymbol{x}^{(t)} = \boldsymbol{x}^{(0)} + \sum_{\tau=1}^t \delta^{(\tau)} \tag{3.1}$$

$$\mathbf{W}^{(t)} = \exp(\boldsymbol{\Psi}^{(t-1)}) \tag{3.2}$$

$$\mathbf{P}^{(t)} \overset{\mathsf{def}}{=} \mathbf{W}^{(t)} / \mathsf{Tr}\left[\mathbf{W}^{(t)}\right] \tag{3.3}$$

$$\mathsf{Tr}\left[\mathbf{P}^{(t)}\right] = \mathsf{Tr}\left[\mathbf{W}^{(t)} / \mathsf{Tr}\left[\mathbf{W}^{(t)}\right]\right]$$
$$= \mathsf{Tr}\left[\mathbf{W}^{(t)}\right] / \mathsf{Tr}\left[\mathbf{W}^{(t)}\right] = 1 \tag{3.4}$$

$$\mathbf{M}^{(t)} \overset{\mathsf{def}}{=} \frac{1}{\varepsilon} \sum_{i=1}^n \delta_i^{(t)} \mathbf{A}_i \qquad \text{when } t \geq 1 \tag{3.5}$$

$$\boldsymbol{\Psi}^{(t)} = \sum_{i=1}^n x_i^{(t)} \mathbf{A}_i = \varepsilon \sum_{\tau=0}^t \mathbf{M}^{(\tau)} \tag{3.6}$$

To bound the approximation guarantees and the cost of this algorithm, we reason about the spectrum of $\boldsymbol{\Psi}^{(t)}$ and the ℓ_1 norm of the vector $\boldsymbol{x}^{(t)}$ as the algorithm executes. Since the coordinates of our vector $\boldsymbol{x}^{(t)}$ are always non-negative, we note that $\|\boldsymbol{x}^{(t)}\|_1 = \mathbf{1}^\top \boldsymbol{x}^{(t)}$ and we use either notation as convenient. We begin the analysis by showing that $B^{(t)}$ can never be empty unless the system is infeasible:

Lemma 3.2 (Feasibility) *If there is an iteration t such that $B^{(t)}$ is empty, then $\mathbf{P}^{(t)} = \mathbf{W}^{(t)} / \mathsf{Tr}\left[\mathbf{W}^{(t)}\right]$ is a valid primal solution with objective value 1. Furthermore, by duality theory, there exists no dual solution $\boldsymbol{x} \in \mathbb{R}_+^n$ with objective value at least 1.*

PROOF. The fact that $B^{(t)}$ is empty means that for all $i = 1, \ldots, n$, $\mathbf{W}^{(t)} \bullet \mathbf{A}_i \geq (1+\varepsilon)^{p+1}$. But we know that $\mathsf{Tr}\left[\mathbf{W}^{(t)}\right] > (1+\varepsilon)^{p-1}$, so

$$\mathbf{P}^{(t)} \bullet \mathbf{A}_i = \frac{\mathbf{W}^{(t)}}{\mathsf{Tr}\left[\mathbf{W}^{(t)}\right]} \bullet \mathbf{A}_i \geq (1+\varepsilon)^2 \geq 1,$$

As noted above, $\mathsf{Tr}\left[\mathbf{P}^{(t)}\right] = 1$, so $\mathbf{P}^{(t)}$ is a valid primal solution with objective at most 1, so no dual solution with objective more than 1 exists. □

We proceed to analyze the vector $\boldsymbol{x}^{(t)}$ in the case that $B^{(t)}$ never becomes empty. The main loop in Algorithm 3.1 terminates only if $\|\boldsymbol{x}^{(t)}\|_1 > K$, so the solution we produce satisfies

$$\|\boldsymbol{x}^*\|_1 = \frac{1}{(1+10\varepsilon)K}\|\boldsymbol{x}^{(t)}\|_1 \geq \frac{K}{(1+10\varepsilon)K} \geq 1-10\varepsilon \quad (3.7)$$

In order for this to be a dual solution, we still need to show that it satisfies $\sum_i x_i^* \mathbf{A}_i \preccurlyeq \mathbf{I}$. In particular, it suffices to show that $\frac{1}{(1+10\varepsilon)K}\boldsymbol{\Psi}^{(T)} \preccurlyeq \mathbf{I}$, where T is the final iteration.

Spectrum Bounds. The rest of the analysis hinges on bounding the spectrum of $\boldsymbol{\Psi}^{(t)}$. More specifically, we prove the following lemma, which shows that the spectrum of all intermediate $\boldsymbol{\Psi}^{(t)}$'s is bounded by $(1 + O(\varepsilon))K$:

Lemma 3.3 (Spectrum Bound) *For $t = 0, \ldots, T$, where T is the final iteration,*

$$\boldsymbol{\Psi}^{(t)} = \sum_{i=1}^{n} x_i^{(t)} \mathbf{A}_i \preccurlyeq (1+10\varepsilon)K\mathbf{I}. \quad (3.8)$$

We prove this lemma by resorting to properties of the MMW algorithm (Theorem 2.1), which relates the final spectral values to the "gain" derived at each intermediate step. For this, we will show a claim (Claim 3.5) that quantifies the gain we get in each step as a function of the ℓ_1-norm of the change we make in that step. But first, we analyze the initial matrix:

Claim 3.4

$$\lambda_{\max}\left(\boldsymbol{\Psi}^{(0)}\right) = \lambda_{\max}\left(\sum_{i=1}^{n} x_i^{(0)} \mathbf{A}_i\right) \leq 1$$

PROOF. Our choice of $\boldsymbol{x}^{(0)}$ guarantees that for all $i = 1, \ldots, n$,

$$x_i^{(0)} \mathbf{A}_i = \frac{1}{n\,\mathsf{Tr}\,[\mathbf{A}_i]}\mathbf{A}_i \preccurlyeq \frac{1}{n}\mathbf{I}.$$

Summing across $i = 1, \ldots, n$ gives the desired bound. □

The following claim bounds the value of $\mathbf{M}^{(t)} \bullet \mathbf{P}^{(t)}$ in terms of the ℓ_1 norm of the change to the dual solution vector. This is precisely the quantity we track in Theorem 2.1:

Claim 3.5 *For all $t = 1, \ldots, T$,*

$$\mathbf{M}^{(t)} \bullet \mathbf{P}^{(t)} \leq \frac{(1+\varepsilon)^2}{\varepsilon} \cdot \|\delta^{(t)}\|_1. \quad (3.9)$$

PROOF. Consider that

$$\mathbf{M}^{(t)} \bullet \mathbf{P}^{(t)} = \frac{1}{\varepsilon}\left(\sum_{i=1}^{n} \delta_i^{(t)} \mathbf{A}_i\right) \bullet \mathbf{P}^{(t)}$$

$$= \frac{1}{\varepsilon}\left(\sum_{i\in B} \delta_i^{(t)} \mathbf{A}_i \bullet \mathbf{P}^{(t)}\right)$$

Every $i \in B^{(t)}$ has the property that

$$\mathbf{A}_i \bullet \mathbf{W}^{(t)} \leq (1+\varepsilon)^{p+1}$$

So then, since

$$\mathbf{P}^{(t)} = \frac{\mathbf{W}^{(t)}}{\mathsf{Tr}\,[\mathbf{W}^{(t)}]} \preccurlyeq \frac{\mathbf{W}^{(t)}}{(1+\varepsilon)^{p-1}},$$

we have

$$\mathbf{A}_i \bullet \mathbf{P}^{(t)} \leq (1+\varepsilon)^2$$

and thus

$$\mathbf{M}^{(t)} \bullet \mathbf{P}^{(t)} \leq \frac{1}{\varepsilon}\left(\sum_{i\in B} \delta_i^{(t)}(1+\varepsilon)^2\right)$$

$$\leq \frac{(1+\varepsilon)^2}{\varepsilon}\|\delta^{(t)}\|_1,$$

which proves the claim. □

We can then bound the total ℓ_1 norm of the change to the dual solution by bounding the ℓ_1 norm of $\boldsymbol{x}^{(t)}$. Specifically we show that unless the algorithm terminates at the first iteration, $\boldsymbol{x}^{(T)}$ does not exceed $K + \varepsilon$ in ℓ_1 norm.

Claim 3.6 *For $t = 1, \ldots, T$,*

$$\|\boldsymbol{x}^{(t)}\|_1 \leq (1+\varepsilon)K$$

PROOF. Since T is the iteration when the algorithm terminate and for all $t \geq 0$, $\delta^{(t)} \in \mathbb{R}_+^n$, we have

$$\|\boldsymbol{x}^{(t)}\|_1 \leq \|\boldsymbol{x}^{(t-1)}\|_1 + \|\delta^{(t)}\|_1$$

$$\leq K + \|\delta^{(t)}\|_1$$

By our choice of α, we know that $\alpha \leq \varepsilon/\|\boldsymbol{x}_B^{(t-1)}\|_1$ and therefore $\|\delta^{(T)}\|_1 = \alpha\|\boldsymbol{x}_B^{(t-1)}\|_1 \leq \varepsilon$. Substituting this into the equation above gives $\|\boldsymbol{x}^{(t)}\|_1 \leq K + \varepsilon$ and the claim follows from $K \geq 1$. □

We are now ready to complete the proof of the spectrum bound lemma (Lemma 3.3):

PROOF OF LEMMA 3.3. We can rewrite $\boldsymbol{\Psi}^{(t)}$ as

$$\boldsymbol{\Psi}^{(t)} = \sum_{i=1}^{n} x_i^{(0)} \mathbf{A}_i + \sum_{\tau=1}^{t}\sum_{i=1}^{n} \delta_i^{(\tau)} \mathbf{A}_i = \sum_{i=1}^{n} x_i^{(0)} \mathbf{A}_i + \varepsilon \sum_{\tau=1}^{t} \mathbf{M}^{(\tau)},$$

so

$$\lambda_{\max}(\boldsymbol{\Psi}^{(t)}) \leq \lambda_{\max}\left(\sum_{i=1}^{n} x_i^{(0)} \mathbf{A}_i\right) + \varepsilon \cdot \lambda_{\max}\left(\sum_{\tau=1}^{t} \mathbf{M}^{(\tau)}\right)$$

since both sums yield positive semidefinite matrices.

By Claim 3.4, we know that the first term is at most 1. To bound the second term, we again apply Theorem 2.1, which we restate below:

$$(1+\varepsilon)\sum_{\tau=1}^{t} \mathbf{M}^{(\tau)} \bullet \mathbf{P}^{(\tau)} \geq \lambda_{\max}\left(\sum_{\tau=1}^{t} \mathbf{M}^{(t)}\right) - \frac{\ln n}{\varepsilon}$$

Rearranging terms, we have

$$\lambda_{\max}\left(\sum_{\tau=1}^{t} \mathbf{M}^{(\tau)}\right) \leq (1+\varepsilon)\sum_{\tau=1}^{t} \mathbf{M}^{(\tau)} \bullet \mathbf{P}^{(\tau)} + \frac{\ln n}{\varepsilon}.$$

We also want to make sure that each $\mathbf{M}^{(\tau)}$ satisfies $\mathbf{M}^{(\tau)} \preccurlyeq \mathbf{I}$. With an easy induction on t, we can show that (3.8) holds for all $\tau \leq t - 1$. This means that for $\tau = 1, \ldots, t$, each $\mathbf{M}^{(\tau)}$ satisfies

$$\mathbf{M}^{(\tau)} = \frac{1}{\varepsilon} \sum_{i=1}^{n} \delta_i^{(\tau)} \mathbf{A}_i$$

$$\preccurlyeq \frac{\alpha}{\varepsilon} \sum_{i=1}^{n} x_i^{(\tau)} \mathbf{A}_i$$

$$\preccurlyeq \frac{\varepsilon/(1+10\varepsilon)K}{\varepsilon} \sum_{i=1}^{n} x_i^{(\tau)} \mathbf{A}_i$$

$$\preccurlyeq \frac{\varepsilon/(1+10\varepsilon)K}{\varepsilon} (1 + 10\varepsilon) K \mathbf{I} \preccurlyeq \mathbf{I},$$

since $\alpha \leq \varepsilon/(1+10\varepsilon)K$. It then follow from Claim 3.5 that

$$\varepsilon \cdot \lambda_{\max} \left(\sum_{\tau=1}^{t} \mathbf{M}^{(\tau)} \right) \leq (1 + \varepsilon) \sum_{\tau=1}^{t} (1 + \varepsilon)^2 \cdot \|\delta^{(\tau)}\|_1 + \ln n$$

$$= \ln n + (1 + \varepsilon)^3 \|\boldsymbol{x}^{(t)}\|_1$$

Where the last step follows from $\boldsymbol{x}^{(t)} = \boldsymbol{x}^{(0)} + \sum_{\tau=1}^{t} \delta^{(\tau)}$ and each entry of $\boldsymbol{x}^{(0)}$ and $\delta^{(\tau)}$ being non-negative. Applying the bound on $\|\boldsymbol{x}^{(t)}\|_1$ from Claim 3.6 then gives:

$$\varepsilon \cdot \lambda_{\max} \left(\sum_{\tau=1}^{t} \mathbf{M}^{(\tau)} \right) \leq \ln n + (1 + \varepsilon)^4 K$$

Putting these together, we get:

$$\lambda_{\max}(\boldsymbol{\Psi}^{(t)}) \leq 1 + \ln n + (1 + \varepsilon)^4 K \leq \varepsilon K + (1 + \varepsilon)^4 K,$$

which allows us to conclude that $\boldsymbol{\Psi}^{(t)} \preccurlyeq (1 + 10\varepsilon)K\mathbf{I}$. $\qquad \square$

The spectrum bound lemma says that at any point in the algorithm, the solution vector $\boldsymbol{x}^{(t)}$ satisfies $\sum_i x_i^{(t)} \mathbf{A}_i \preccurlyeq (1 + 10\varepsilon)K\mathbf{I}$. Together with Equation (3.7), we know that if the algorithm completes the **while** loop, the solution $\boldsymbol{x}^*$ that we return satisfies $\|\boldsymbol{x}^*\|_1 \geq 1 - 10\varepsilon$ and

$$\sum_i x_i^* \mathbf{A}_i = \frac{1}{(1+10\varepsilon)K} \sum_i x_i^{(t)} \mathbf{A}_i \preccurlyeq \mathbf{I}.$$

Thus, $\boldsymbol{x}^*$ is indeed a dual solution with value at least $1 - 10\varepsilon$.

To piece everything together, we set ε to $\varepsilon/10$, so if there is an iteration in which $B^{(t)}$ is empty, we produce a primal solution with value at most 1; otherwise, we return a dual solution with value at least $1 - \varepsilon$. Hence, the algorithm has the promised approximation bounds. Next we will analyze its cost.

Cost Analysis. Similar to Young's analysis, our analysis relies on the notion of phases, grouping together iterations with similar $\mathbf{W}^{(t)}$ matrices into a phase in a way that ensures the existence of a coordinate i with the property that this coordinate is incremented (i.e., $\delta_i^{(t)} > 0$) by a significant amount in every iteration of this phase. To this end, we say that an iteration t belongs to *phase* p if and only if $(1 + \varepsilon)^{p-1} < \mathsf{Tr}\left[\mathbf{W}^{(t)}\right] \leq (1 + \varepsilon)^p$. A phase ends when the algorithm terminates or the next iteration belongs to a different phase.

Almost immediate from this definition is a bound on the number of phases:

Lemma 3.7 *The total number of phases is at most $O(K/\varepsilon)$.*

PROOF. On the one hand, we have $\mathbf{0} \preccurlyeq \boldsymbol{\Psi}^{(0)}$, so

$$\mathsf{Tr}\left[\mathbf{W}^{(0)}\right] \geq n \cdot e^0 = n.$$

On the other hand, we know that $\boldsymbol{\Psi}^{(T)} \preccurlyeq (1 + O(\varepsilon))K$, so $\mathsf{Tr}\left[\mathbf{W}^{(t)}\right] \leq n \exp\left((1 + O(\varepsilon))K\right)$. This means that the total of number is phases is at most

$$\log_{1+\varepsilon} \frac{\mathsf{Tr}\left[\mathbf{W}^{(T)}\right]}{\mathsf{Tr}\left[\mathbf{W}^{(0)}\right]} \leq \log_{1+\varepsilon} \exp\left((1 + O(\varepsilon))K\right) \quad (3.10)$$

$$\leq \frac{1}{\varepsilon}(1 + O(\varepsilon))K = O\left(\frac{K}{\varepsilon}\right) \quad (3.11)$$

$\qquad \square$

To bound the total number of steps, we'll analyze the number of iterations within a phase. For this, we'll need a couple of claims. The first claim shows that if a coordinate is incremented at the end of a phase, it must have been incremented at every iteration of this phase.

Claim 3.8 *If $i \in B^{(t)}$, then for all $t' < t$ belonging to the same phase as t, $i \in B^{(t')}$.*

PROOF. Suppose t belongs to phase p. As $i \in B^{(t)}$, we know that $\mathbf{W}^{(t)} \bullet \mathbf{A}_i \leq (1 + \varepsilon)^{p+1}$. Since $t' < t$ we have

$$\boldsymbol{\Psi}^{(t)} - \boldsymbol{\Psi}^{(t')} = \sum_{t' \leq \tau < t} \mathbf{M}^{(\tau)} \quad (3.12)$$

$$= \sum_{t' \leq \tau < t} \sum_i \delta_i^{(\tau)} \mathbf{A}_i \succeq 0 \quad (3.13)$$

Therefore $\mathbf{W}^{(t')} \preccurlyeq \mathbf{W}^{(t)}$ and that

$$\mathbf{W}^{(t')} \bullet \mathbf{A}_i \leq \mathbf{W}^{(t)} \bullet \mathbf{A}_i \leq (1 + \varepsilon)^{p+1}, \quad (3.14)$$

which means that $i \in B^{(t')}$, as desired. $\qquad \square$

In the second claim, we'll place a bounding box around each coordinate $x_i^{(t)}$ of our solution vectors. This turns out to be an important machinery in bounding the number of iterations required by the algorithm.

Claim 3.9 (Bounding Box) *For all index i, at any iteration t,*

$$x_i^{(t)} \leq (1 + O(\varepsilon))n^2 K / \mathsf{Tr}\left[\mathbf{A}_i\right] x_i^{(0)}$$

PROOF. Recall that $x_i^{(0)} = 1/(n \mathsf{Tr}\left[\mathbf{A}_i\right])$. To argue an upper bound on $x_i^{(t)}$, note that Lemma 3.3 gives

$$\boldsymbol{\Psi}^{(t)} \preccurlyeq (1 + O(\varepsilon))\mathbf{I}K \quad (3.15)$$

Since $\sum_{j=1}^n x_j^{(t)} \mathbf{A}_i = \boldsymbol{\Psi}^{(t)}$ and each $\mathbf{A}_i$ is positive semidefinite, we have

$$\mathsf{Tr}\left[x_i^{(t)} \mathbf{A}_i\right] \leq \mathsf{Tr}\left[\boldsymbol{\Psi}^{(t)}\right] \leq (1 + O(\varepsilon))nK \quad (3.16)$$

We conclude that $x_i^{(t)} \leq (1 + O(\varepsilon))n^2 K / \mathsf{Tr}\left[\mathbf{A}_i\right] x_i^{(0)}$, as claimed. $\qquad \square$

The final claim shows that each iteration makes significant progress in incrementing the solution.

Claim 3.10 *In each iteration, either $\|\delta^{(t)}\|_1 = \varepsilon$ or $\alpha \geq \Omega(\varepsilon/K)$.*

PROOF. We chose α to be $\min\{\varepsilon/\|\boldsymbol{x}_B^{(t-1)}\|_1, \varepsilon/(1+10\varepsilon)K\}$. If $\alpha = \varepsilon/\|\boldsymbol{x}_B^{(t-1)}\|_1$, then $\|\delta^{(t)}\|_1 = \varepsilon$ and we are done. Otherwise, we have $\alpha = \varepsilon/(1+10\varepsilon)K$, which is $\Omega(\varepsilon/K)$. $\square$

Combining these claims, we have the following bounds on the number of iterations:

Corollary 3.11 *The number of iterations per phase is at most*

$$O\left(\frac{K}{\varepsilon}\ln(nK)\right).$$

and the total number of iterations is at most:

$$O\left(\frac{\log^3 n}{\varepsilon^4}\right)$$

PROOF. Consider a phase of the algorithm, and let f be the final iteration of this phase. By Claim 3.10, each iteration t satisfies $\|\delta^{(t)}\|_1 = \varepsilon$ or $\alpha \geq \Omega(\varepsilon/K)$. Since $\|\boldsymbol{x}^{(t)}\|_1 \leq K + \varepsilon$ for all $t \leq T$, the number of iterations in which $\|\delta^{(t)}\|_1 = \varepsilon$ can be at most $O(K/\varepsilon)$. Now, let $i \in B^{(f)}$ be a coordinate that got incremented in the final iteration of this phase. By Claim 3.8, this coordinate got incremented in every iteration of this phase. Therefore, the number of iterations within this phase where $\alpha \geq \Omega(\varepsilon/K)$ is at most

$$\log_{1+\Omega(\varepsilon/K)}(x_i^{(f)}/x^{(0)}) \leq \log_{1+\Omega(\varepsilon/K)}\left((1+O(\varepsilon)n^2K\right)$$
$$= O\left(\frac{K}{\varepsilon}\ln\left((1+O(\varepsilon))K\right)\right).$$

Combining with Lemma 3.7 and the setting of $K = O\left(\frac{\log n}{\varepsilon}\right)$ gives the overall bound. $\square$

4. MATRIX EXPONENTIAL EVALUATION

We describe a fast algorithm for computing the matrix dot product of a positive semidefinite matrix and the matrix exponential of another positive semidefinite matrix.

Theorem 4.1 *There is an algorithm* `bigDotExp` *that when given a m-by-m matrix $\boldsymbol{\Phi}$ with p non-zero entries, $\kappa \geq \max\{1, \|\boldsymbol{\Phi}\|_2\}$, and m-by-m matrices $\mathbf{A}_i$ in factorized form $\mathbf{A}_i = \mathbf{Q}_i\mathbf{Q}_i^\top$ where the total number of nonzeros across all $\mathbf{Q}_i$ is q;* `bigDotExp`$(\boldsymbol{\Phi}, \{\mathbf{A}_i = \mathbf{Q}_i\mathbf{Q}_i^\top\}_{i=1}^n)$ *computes $(1 \pm \varepsilon)$ approximations to all $\exp(\boldsymbol{\Phi}) \bullet \mathbf{A}_i$ in $O(\kappa \log m \log(1/\varepsilon))$ depth and $O(\frac{1}{\varepsilon^2}(\kappa \log(1/\epsilon)p + q)\log m)$ work.*

The idea behind Theorem 4.1 is to approximate the matrix exponential using a low-degree polynomial because evaluating matrix exponentials exactly is costly. For this, we will apply the following lemma, reproduced from Lemma 6 in [AK07]:

Lemma 4.2 ([AK07]) *If $\mathbf{B}$ is a PSD matrix such that $\|\mathbf{B}\|_2 \leq \kappa$, then the operator*

$$\widehat{\mathbf{B}} = \sum_{0 \leq i < k} \frac{1}{i!}\mathbf{B}^i \qquad \text{where } k = \max\{e^2\kappa, \ln(2\varepsilon^{-1})\}$$

satisfies

$$(1 - \varepsilon)\exp(\mathbf{B}) \preceq \widehat{\mathbf{B}} \preceq \exp(\mathbf{B}).$$

PROOF OF THEOREM 4.1. The given factorization of each $\mathbf{A}_i$ allows us to write $\exp(\boldsymbol{\Phi}) \bullet \mathbf{A}_i$ as the 2-norm of a vector:

$$\exp(\boldsymbol{\Phi}) \bullet \mathbf{A}_i = \mathsf{Tr}\left[\exp(\boldsymbol{\Phi})\mathbf{Q}_i\mathbf{Q}_i^\top\right]$$
$$= \mathsf{Tr}\left[\mathbf{Q}_i^\top \exp(\tfrac{1}{2}\boldsymbol{\Phi})\exp(\tfrac{1}{2}\boldsymbol{\Phi})\mathbf{Q}_i\right]$$
$$= \|\exp(\tfrac{1}{2}\boldsymbol{\Phi})\mathbf{Q}_i\|_2$$

By Lemma 4.2, it suffices to evaluate $\widehat{\mathbf{B}} \bullet \mathbf{A}_i$ where $\widehat{\mathbf{B}}$ is an approximation to $\mathbf{B} = \exp(\tfrac{1}{2}\boldsymbol{\Phi})$. To further reduce the work, we can apply the Johnson-Lindenstrauss transformation [DG03, IM98] to reduce the length of the vectors to $O(\log m)$; specifically, we find a $O(\frac{1}{\varepsilon^2}\log m) \times m$ Gaussian matrix $\boldsymbol{\Pi}$ and evaluate

$$\|\boldsymbol{\Pi}\widehat{\mathbf{B}}\mathbf{Q}_i\|_2$$

Since $\boldsymbol{\Pi}$ only has $O(\frac{1}{\varepsilon^2}\log m)$ rows, we can compute $\boldsymbol{\Pi}\widehat{\mathbf{B}}$ using $O(\log m)$ evaluations of $\widehat{\mathbf{B}}$. The work/depth bounds follow from doing each of the evaluations of $\widehat{\mathbf{B}}\boldsymbol{\Pi}_i$, where $\boldsymbol{\Pi}_i$ denotes the i-th column of $\boldsymbol{\Pi}$, and matrix-vector multiplies involving $\boldsymbol{\Phi}$ in parallel. $\square$

5. CONCLUSION

We presented a simple NC parallel algorithm for packing SDPs that requires $O(\frac{1}{\varepsilon^4}\log^4 n \log(\frac{1}{\varepsilon}))$ iterations, where each iteration involves only simple matrix operations and computing the trace of the product of a matrix exponential and a positive semidefinite matrix. When a positive SDP is given in a factorized form, we showed how the dot product with matrix exponential can be implemented in nearly-linear work, leading to an algorithm with $\widetilde{O}(m + n + q)$ work, where n is the number of constraint matrices, m is the dimension of these matrices, and q is the total number of nonzero entries in the factorization.

Compared to the situation with positive LPs, the classification of positive SDPs is much richer because packing/covering constraints can take many forms, either as matrices (e.g. $\sum_{i=1}^n x_i\mathbf{A}_i \preccurlyeq \mathbf{I}$ for packing, $\sum_{i=1}^n x_i\mathbf{A}_i \succcurlyeq \mathbf{I}$ for covering) or as dot products between matrices (e.g. $\mathbf{A}_i \bullet \mathbf{Y} \leq 1$ for packing, $\mathbf{A}_i \bullet \mathbf{Y} \geq 1$ for covering). The positive SDPs studied in [JY11] and our paper should be compared with the closely related notion of covering SDPs studied by Iyengar et al [IPS10]; however, among the applications they examine, only the beamforming SDP relaxation discussed in Section 2.2 of [IPS10] falls completely within the framework of packing SDPs as defined in 1.2. Problems such as MaxCut and SparsestCut require additional matrix-based packing constraints. We believe extending these algorithms to solve mixed packing/covering SDPs is an interesting direction for future work.

Acknowledgments

This work is partially supported by the National Science Foundation under grant numbers CCF-1018463, CCF-1018188, and CCF-1016799 and by generous gifts from IBM, Intel, and Microsoft. Richard Peng is supported by a Microsoft Fellowship. We thank the SPAA reviewers for suggestions that helped improve this paper.

References

[AHK05] Sanjeev Arora, Elad Hazan, and Satyen Kale. Fast algorithms for approximate semide.nite programming using the multiplicative weights update method. In *FOCS*, pages 339–348, 2005.

[AK07] Sanjeev Arora and Satyen Kale. A combinatorial, primal-dual approach to semidefinite programs. In *STOC*, pages 227–236, 2007.

[DG03] Sanjoy Dasgupta and Anupam Gupta. An elementary proof of a theorem of johnson and lindenstrauss. *Random Struct. Algorithms*, 22(1):60–65, 2003.

[GK98] Naveen Garg and Jochen Könemann. Faster and simpler algorithms for multicommodity flow and other fractional packing problems. In *Proceedings of the 39th Symposium on the Foundations of Computer Science (FOCS)*, pages 300–309, 1998.

[GLS93] Martin Grötschel, László Lovász, and Alexander Schrijver. *Geometric Algorithms and Combinatorial Optimization*. Springer-Verlag, New York, 2nd edition, 1993.

[IM98] Piotr Indyk and Rajeev Motwani. Approximate nearest neighbors: Towards removing the curse of dimensionality. In *Proceedings of the 30th ACM Symposium on the Theory of Computing (STOC)*, pages 604–613, 1998.

[IPS10] Garud Iyengar, David J. Phillips, and Clifford Stein. Feasible and accurate algorithms for covering semidefinite programs. In *SWAT*, pages 150–162, 2010.

[IPS11] Garud Iyengar, David J. Phillips, and Clifford Stein. Approximating semidefinite packing programs. *SIAM Journal on Optimization*, 21(1):231–268, 2011.

[JáJ92] Joseph JáJá. *An Introduction to Parallel Algorithms*. Addison-Wesley, 1992.

[JY11] Rahul Jain and Penghui Yao. A parallel approximation algorithm for positive semidefinite programming. In *FOCS*, pages 463–471, 2011.

[JY12] Rahul Jain and Penghui Yao. A parallel approximation algorithm for mixed packing and covering semidefinite programs. *CoRR*, abs/1201.6090, 2012.

[Kal07] Satyen Kale. *Efficient Algorithms using the Multiplicative Weights Update Method*. PhD thesis, Princeton University, August 2007. Princeton Tech Report TR-804-07.

[KL96] Philip N. Klein and Hsueh-I Lu. Efficient approximation algorithms for semidefinite programs arising from MAX CUT and COLORING. In *STOC*, pages 338–347, 1996.

[KY07] Christos Koufogiannakis and Neal E. Young. Beating simplex for fractional packing and covering linear programs. In *FOCS*, pages 494–504, 2007.

[KY09] Christos Koufogiannakis and Neal E. Young. Distributed and parallel algorithms for weighted vertex cover and other covering problems. In *PODC*, pages 171–179, 2009.

[LN93] Michael Luby and Noam Nisan. A parallel approximation algorithm for positive linear programming. In *STOC'93*, pages 448–457, New York, NY, USA, 1993.

[PST95] Serge A. Plotkin, David B. Shmoys, and Éva Tardos. Fast approximation algorithms for fractional packing and covering problems. *Math. Oper. Res.*, 20(2):257–301, 1995.

[You01] Neal E. Young. Sequential and parallel algorithms for mixed packing and covering. In *FOCS*, pages 538–546, 2001.

APPENDIX

A. NORMALIZED POSITIVE SDPS

This is the same transformation that Jain and Yao presented [JY11]; we only present it here for easy reference.

Consider the primal program in (1.1). It suffices to show that it can be transformed into the following program without changing the optimal value:

$$
\begin{aligned}
\text{Minimize} \quad & \mathsf{Tr}\,[\mathbf{Z}] \\
\text{Subject to:} \quad & \mathbf{B}_i \bullet \mathbf{Z} \geq 1 \quad \text{for } i = 1, \ldots, m \qquad \text{(A.1)} \\
& \mathbf{Z} \succeq 0,
\end{aligned}
$$

We can make the following assumptions without loss of generality: First, $b_i > 0$ for all $i = 1, \ldots, m$ because if b_i were 0, we could have thrown it away. Second, all $\mathbf{A}_i$'s are the support of $\mathbf{C}$, or otherwise we know that the corresponding dual variable must be set to 0 and therefore can be removed right away. Therefore, we will treat C as having a full-rank, allowing us to define

$$
\mathbf{B}_i \overset{\text{def}}{=} \frac{1}{b_i} \mathbf{C}^{-1/2} \mathbf{A}_i \mathbf{C}^{-1/2}
$$

It is not hard to verify that the normalized program (A.1) has the same optimal value as the original SDP (1.1).

Note that if we're given factorization of $\mathbf{A}_i$ into $\mathbf{Q}_i \mathbf{Q}_i^{\top}$, then $\mathbf{B}_i$ can also be factorized as:

$$
\mathbf{B}_i = \frac{1}{b_i} (\mathbf{C}^{-1/2} \mathbf{Q}_i)(\mathbf{C}^{-1/2} \mathbf{Q}_i)^{\top}
$$

Furthermore, it can be checked that the dual of the normalized program is the same as the dual in Equation 1.2.

Deterministic Multi-Channel Information Exchange

Stephan Holzer
Distributed Computing Group
ETH Zurich, Switzerland
stholzer@ethz.ch

Thomas Locher
ABB Corporate Research
Baden-Dättwil, Switzerland
thomas.locher@ch.abb.com

Yvonne-Anne Pignolet
ABB Corporate Research
Baden-Dättwil, Switzerland
yvonne-anne.pignolet@ch.abb.com

Roger Wattenhofer
Distributed Computing Group
ETH Zurich, Switzerland
wattenhofer@ethz.ch

ABSTRACT

In this paper, we study the information exchange problem on a set of multiple access channels: k arbitrary nodes have information they want to distribute to the entire network via a shared medium partitioned into channels. We present algorithms and lower bounds on the time and channel complexity for disseminating these k information items in a single-hop network of n nodes. More precisely, we devise a deterministic algorithm running in asymptotically optimal time $\mathcal{O}(k)$ using $\mathcal{O}(n^{\log(k)/k})$ channels if $k \leq \frac{1}{6} \log n$ and $\mathcal{O}(\log^{1+\rho}(n/k))$ channels otherwise, where $\rho > 0$ is an arbitrarily small constant. In addition, we show that $\Omega(n^{\Omega(1/k)} + \log_k n)$ channels are necessary to achieve this time complexity.

Categories and Subject Descriptors

F.2.3. [**Theory of Computation**]: Analysis of Algorithms and Problem Complexity—*Tradeoffs among Complexity Measures*

General Terms

Algorithms, Theory

Keywords

Information Dissemination, Wireless Networks, Single-Hop, Multi-Channel, No Collision Detection.

1. INTRODUCTION

A fundamental problem of many communication systems that rely on a shared communication medium, e.g., wireless and bus networks, is (co-channel) interference, which occurs when more than one network entity tries to transmit a message over the same communication channel at the same time. Such simultaneous (or interleaved) transmissions of two or more messages over the same channel are commonly

referred to as *collisions*. Typically, a collision distorts all transmitted messages significantly, which entails that none of the messages can be decoded successfully at the receivers. Hence, there is a need for mechanisms scheduling the message transmissions appropriately in order to enable an efficient exchange of messages over the communication medium. There are various techniques to address or simplify this basic scheduling problem: By introducing a notion of time, the network entities can transmit in synchronized *time slots*, which reduces the potential for collisions. Another common trick is to use randomization, as in, e.g., the Aloha protocol. If the network entities further have the ability to detect collisions, which allows the entities to learn that other entities strive to transmit as well, back-off mechanisms can be applied to ensure an eventual transmission of all messages.

Moreover, in various communication systems several non-conflicting communication channels are available, which can be leveraged to disseminate information. While there is a lot of work on scheduling message transmissions for various models of communication channels, surprisingly little is known about the benefits and limits of using multiple channels for the purpose of information dissemination. This is the focus of this paper, which addresses the question of how many communication channels are required in order to solve an information exchange problem as quickly as possible. More generally, we study the power of having additional channels at one's disposal when trying to disseminate information. We believe that this is an important missing piece in the study of communication over shared channels. Before giving a more formal definition of the considered information exchange problem, we present the communication model used throughout this paper.

1.1 Model

In this paper, we consider a simple network topology, the complete (single-hop) communication network in which every node can communicate with every other node. There are n nodes in total, each with a given, unique identifier in the range $[n] := \{1, \ldots, n\}$ (when using an initialization algorithm that assigns identifiers to nodes, e.g., [17, 18], this assumption can be dropped). We assume that multiple channels are available for communication and that local computations require zero time (since we focus on communication complexity). Additionally, we make the simplifying assumption that time is divided into synchronized time slots, i.e., we study slotted protocols: In any time slot, each node v may choose a channel i and perform exactly one of two operations, **send**, which means that v *broadcasts* a message

Permission to make digital or hard copies of all or part of this work for personal or classroom use is granted without fee provided that copies are not made or distributed for profit or commercial advantage and that copies bear this notice and the full citation on the first page. To copy otherwise, to republish, to post on servers or to redistribute to lists, requires prior specific permission and/or a fee.
SPAA'12, June 25–27, 2012, Pittsburgh, Pennsylvania, USA.
Copyright 2012 ACM 978-1-4503-1213-4/12/06 ...$10.00.

on channel i or `receive`, in which case v *listens* on channel i.[1] A transmission is *successful* if and only if exactly one node transmits its message on a given channel in a specific time slot. A node listening on a particular channel i only receives a message in a given time slot if there is a successful transmission on this channel. Messages are of bounded size, i.e., we assume that each message can only contain one information item (e.g., a node identifier). We further assume that there is no *collision detection*, i.e., if a node v does not receive a message when listening on a channel i, node v cannot determine whether there was a collision or no message was sent. This is a reasonable assumption as, e.g., simple wireless devices often do not have a reliable collision detection mechanism. Moreover, solutions in this model can be applied in settings with collision detection but not vice versa. We study the following problem in this communication model without collision detection.

Definition 1. (Information Exchange Problem.) There is an arbitrary subset of $k \leq n$ nodes (called *reporter nodes* or simply *reporters*) where each of the k nodes is given a distinct piece of information. This subset is determined by an adversary before the first time slot. The objective is to disseminate these k information items to every node in the network. The subset of reporters is not known initially. The number n of nodes and the number k of reporters may or may not be known.

This problem lies between two fundamental information dissemination problems: broadcasting (one-to-all communication) and gossiping (total information exchange). In other words, we generalize the *Information Exchange Problem* [12] (also known as *k-Selection* [15] and *Many-to-All Communication* [8]) for networks with several communication channels. In order to measure the quality of a solution to the *Information Exchange Problem*, we must define adequate complexity measures. Clearly, it takes a certain number of time slots to distribute all information items. As mentioned before, the goal is to disseminate all information items as quickly as possible. Therefore, the primary objective pursued in this paper is to find an algorithm $\mathcal{A}$ with an optimal *time complexity*, which is defined as the maximum number of synchronous time slots that $\mathcal{A}$ requires to disseminate all k items for a worst-case selection of reporters. Since only one information item can be transmitted in any message, i.e., items cannot be bundled, and each node can only listen on one channel per time slot, it follows that the time complexity of any algorithm is at least $\Omega(k)$. The key question thus becomes how many channels does an algorithm for the *Information Exchange Problem* require in order to achieve an asymptotically optimal time complexity of $\Theta(k)$? Chlebus and Kowalski [7] prove that it is not possible to disseminate all information items in time $\mathcal{O}(k)$ with only one communication channel by giving a lower bound of $\Omega(k + \log n)$. If more channels are available, the lower bound $\Omega(k)$ can be matched using *randomized* algorithms [14]. However, these algorithms need a large number of channels and there is a (small) probability that these algorithms fail.

1.2 Contributions

In this paper, we propose *deterministic* algorithms for the *Information Exchange Problem* when n and k are known. In particular, we introduce two algorithms both exhibiting an

asymptotically optimal time complexity of $\Theta(k)$, which are appropriate for different values of k, and give bounds on the number of channels that each algorithm requires for a given interval of k. The first algorithm, called Algorithm $\mathcal{A}_S$, is useful for small values of k, that is for $k \leq \frac{1}{6} \log n$,[2] and requires $\mathcal{O}(n^{\log(k)/k})$ channels. For larger values of k we apply Algorithm $\mathcal{A}_L$ using $\mathcal{O}(\log^{1+\rho}(n))$ channels for some constant $\rho > 0$ when $k \in (\frac{1}{6} \log n, \log(n) \cdot \log \log(n))$ and $\mathcal{O}(\log(n/k))$ channels for larger k up to $n - 2\lceil \log n \rceil$. Note that for $k > n - 2\lceil \log n \rceil$ we can simply iterate over all nodes to find the reporters in time $\mathcal{O}(k) = \mathcal{O}(n)$, therefore we ignore this case in the remainder of this paper.

We complement these results with a lower bound on the number of channels that any deterministic algorithm needs in order to achieve an optimal time complexity: Any deterministic algorithm with a time complexity of $\mathcal{O}(k)$ must use at least $\Omega(n^{\Omega(1/k)} + \log_k n)$ channels (Theorem 5). The following table summarizes these results.

Range of k	$[1, \frac{1}{6} \log n]$	$(\frac{1}{6} \log n, \log(n) \log \log n)$
Algorithm	$\mathcal{A}_S$ (Thm. 3)	$\mathcal{A}_L$ (Thm. 4)
Channels	$\mathcal{O}\left(n^{\log(k)/k}\right)$	$\mathcal{O}\left(\log^{1+\rho}(n)\right)$
Lower Bound	$\Omega\left(n^{\Omega(1/k)}\right)$	$\Omega\left(\log(n)/\log \log(n)\right)$

R.	$[\log(n) \cdot \log \log(n), n - 2\lceil \log n \rceil)$	$[n - 2\lceil \log n \rceil, n]$
A.	$\mathcal{A}_L$ (Thm. 4)	Text above
C.	$\mathcal{O}(\log(n/k))$	1
L.	$\Omega(\log_k n)$	1

We derive the lower bound on the number of channels by first proving a lower bound on the time complexity when the (maximum) number of channels c is given. The lower bounds for a given number c of channels are of interest since in reality the number of available channels is often limited to a number c and does not grow with n or k. If c channels are available, the lower bound on the time complexity of deterministic algorithms is $\Omega(\log_c(n/k) + k)$ (see proof of Theorem 5 combined with $\Omega(k)$). This lower bound holds even in a less restrictive model where nodes can detect collisions and listen on all channels simultaneously. In light of this, it is surprising that the proposed algorithms are almost able to match the given lower bounds for certain values of k and n.

1.3 Related Work

Several papers study the information exchange problem for single-channel and multi-channel networks without collision detection. Kowalski [15] proves the existence of an oblivious deterministic algorithm without collision detection that distributes k information items on a single channel in time $\mathcal{O}(k \log(n/k))$ based on selectors as well as a matching lower bound. Moreover, he presents an explicit polynomial-time construction with time complexity $\mathcal{O}(k \operatorname{polylog} n)$ to solve this problem deterministically. Later these results have been improved and extended by Chlebus et al. [7] to multi-hop networks and the authors provide bounds for centralized and distributed algorithms. In contrast to our assumptions, they assume that all k information items fit into one message. When restricted to single hop networks, they present

---

[1] Naturally, a node may also choose not to perform any operation in a given time slot.

[2] Note that the base of the logarithm is 2 throughout the paper.

a randomized algorithm for one channel that disseminates all information items in time $\mathcal{O}(\log(k) \cdot (\log^2 n + k))$ whp$_k$, i.e., with probability at least $1 - 1/k^\lambda$, where $\lambda \geq 1$ is a parameter in the algorithm or in the analysis.

Kushilevitz and Mansour [16] proved a lower bound of $\Omega(k + \log n)$ on the expected time of randomized algorithms. The average time complexity in directed networks is addressed by Chlebus et al. [8] who present an upper and a lower bound of $\mathcal{O}(\min\{k \log(n/k), n \log n\})$ and $\Omega(k/\log n + \log n)$, respectively. Moreover, they devised a protocol for the case when information items have to be delivered separately as in our model within time $\mathcal{O}(k \log(n/k) \cdot \log n)$ and a lower bound of $\Omega(k \log n)$.

Recently, Fernandez et al. [1] presented a randomized algorithm for single-channel, single-hop networks that works without information on the number of contenders and of the size of the network in time $\mathcal{O}(k)$ whp$_k$. The authors of [14] showed that better bounds can be achieved by exploiting the availability of multiple channels: the dissemination problem can be solved with an asymptotically optimal time complexity of $\Theta(k)$. However, the randomized algorithms provided in their paper require $\sqrt{n}$ channels for $k < \sqrt{\log n}$ and $n^{\log(k)/k}$ channels for $\sqrt{\log n} < k < \log n$. Moreover, their deterministic algorithm uses n channels.

The information exchange problem in networks suffering from adversarial interference has been studied in [10, 11] where n nodes inform each other about $n - t$ values and an adversary can disturb communication on t channels by jamming.

In a recent paper by Gilbert and Kowalski [12] upper and lower bounds are given for the information exchange problem in single-channel networks where some of the nodes exhibit Byzantine behavior.

The closely related problems of consensus and mutual exclusion have lately been studied in [3, 9] for single-channel networks with and without a global clock, collision detection, and knowledge of the number of nodes in the network. Some parts of our algorithms are inspired by the algorithms presented in [6]. In this paper, Chlebus and Kowalski propose algorithms based on lossless expander graphs for the *renaming problem* [2]. In the renaming problem, each of n processes initially has a unique identifier in the range $[n] := \{1, \ldots, n\}$. The goal is to assign new unique names[3] from a smaller range to a subset of k processes using r shared registers. The algorithm must be correct for every selection of k processes. The renaming problem has been studied in a variety of communication models, mainly in shared memory and message passing models (see [5] for a recent survey). The time complexity of renaming algorithms depends on the communication model, the (un)known parameters, the number of reporters relative to the network size, and the range of the output names.

We adapt the compete operation of [6] for MAC models and introduce a new class of bipartite graphs as a base for our renaming algorithms. The special nature of the communication medium and the fact that no external devices (such as registers) can be used requires new ideas. We prove the existence of graphs with different properties leading to better results for our model. To the best of our knowledge, this paper is the first to provide renaming algorithms for MAC.

---

[3]We refer to the identifiers in the old namespace as "identifiers" while the identifiers in the new namespace are simply called "names".

2. BUILDING BLOCKS

While the algorithms introduced in the subsequent section are based on different techniques, they still share certain basic algorithmic ideas, which are discussed in this section. Note that throughout the paper we assume that $k \geq 2$ as the information exchange problem is trivial for $k \leq 1$.

2.1 Matching Graphs

A core concept used in our algorithms is a special class of bipartite expander graphs $G = (V \cup W, E)$, where the edges in E connect the nodes in the two disjoint node sets V and W, which we refer to as *matching graphs*. In these graphs each node is provided with a fixed ordering of its incident edges. Using this order, a *weak unique-neighbor* property is satisfied in matching graphs: for any subset $X \subseteq V$ of a certain maximum size and an arbitrarily small but fixed constant parameter $\varepsilon \in (0, 1)$, there is an edge index i such that at least $\lceil \varepsilon |X| \rceil$ nodes in W are adjacent to exactly one (and thus a unique) neighbor $v \in X$ when we consider the subgraph G_i induced by the ith edges of each node $v \in X$. Therefore, a matching between $\lceil \varepsilon |X| \rceil$ nodes in X and nodes in W can be found by iterating over the edges according to the fixed edge order of the nodes in X. These graphs have certain expansion properties that are implied by their unique-neighbor property. Note that matching graphs are inspired by lossless expanders (see, e.g., [4]) used in the context of asynchronous exclusive selection [6]. While lossless expanders are well suited for asynchronous exclusive selection, the less restrictive matching graphs yield better results in our wireless setting.[4] Formally, matching graphs are defined as follows.

Definition 2. ((K, Δ, ε)-matching Graphs.) Let $G = (V \cup W, E)$ be a bipartite graph, where V and W are the disjoint node sets and $E \subseteq V \times W$ is the edge set. For each $v \in V$, there is an edge ordering and $\Gamma(v, i)$ denotes the ith neighbor of v. G is a (K, Δ, ε)-*matching* graph if each $v \in V$ has Δ neighbors, and for each subset $X \subseteq V$ of size at most K, there is an index $1 \leq i \leq \Delta$ such that at least $\lceil \varepsilon |X| \rceil$ nodes in X have a unique i-neighbor. For each node $v \in X$ and index i, node $\Gamma(v, i)$ is a unique i-neighbor if $\Gamma(v, i) \neq \Gamma(w, i)$ for all $w \in X \setminus \{v\}$.

We would like to have a matching graph with a small node set W and a small degree Δ while keeping ϵ as large as possible. It is not hard to see that the minimum cardinality of W depends not only on Δ, K, and ε, but also on the size of V. Given these parameters, we prove that matching graphs exist if the following restriction on the minimum size of the node set W holds.

THEOREM 1. *For any* $\varepsilon \in (0, 1)$, $\alpha > \frac{2}{1-\varepsilon}$, $K \geq 2$, *and* $\Delta \geq 1$, *a* (K, Δ, ε)-*matching graph* $G = (V \cup W, E)$ *exists if the following two conditions are satisfied:*

$$|W| \geq |V|^{\frac{\alpha}{\Delta}} \tag{1}$$

$$|W| \geq e^{\frac{(1+\varepsilon)\alpha}{(1-\varepsilon)\alpha-2}} \left(\frac{1+\varepsilon}{2}\right)^{\frac{(1-\varepsilon)\alpha}{(1-\varepsilon)\alpha-2}} \cdot K^{\frac{(2-\varepsilon)\alpha}{(1-\varepsilon)\alpha-2}} \tag{2}$$

PROOF. We use the probabilistic method to prove this statement. Specifically, we show that letting each node $v \in V$ choose Δ neighbors $\Gamma(v, 1), \Gamma(v, 2), \ldots, \Gamma(v, \Delta)$ in W uniformly at random results in a (K, Δ, ε)-matching graph

---

[4]All lossless expanders are also matching graphs.

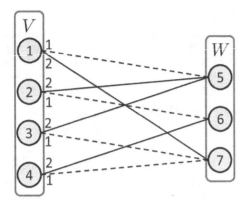

Figure 1: An example of a $(4, 2, 1/2)$-matching graph with $|V| = 4$ and $|W| = 3$ is shown. The index numbers on the edges define the order of the neighbors. Edges with index 1 are dashed, edges with index 2 are full lines. If we consider, e.g., the set $X = \{1, 3, 4\}$, the edges with index 1 do not provide a sufficiently large matching since two out of the three nodes share the same 1-neighbor (nodes 3 and 4). However, index 2 delivers a sufficiently large matching since all nodes (and thus at least half of the nodes in X) have a unique 2-neighbor. For $X = \{2, 3\}$ index 1 can be used, while index 2 cannot. For $X = \{1, 2\}$ both indices can be chosen. For any other subset $X \subseteq V$, there is always at least one index that works.

with positive probability if Condition (1) and Condition (2) are satisfied.

Given such a randomly constructed graph, consider any subset $X \subset V$ of cardinality $x \leq K$. Let the random variable N_i denote the number of nodes in W that are neighbors of the nodes in X if we only consider the ith edge of each node $v \in X$. Formally, $N_i = |\{w \in W \mid \exists v \in X : \Gamma(v, i) = w\}|$. We now prove that the probability that N_i is at least $\lceil \frac{1+\varepsilon}{2}x \rceil$ is large. For this purpose, we need the following inequality:

$$
|W|^{\left(\frac{1-\varepsilon}{2} - \frac{1}{\alpha}\right)x}
$$

$$
\overset{(2)}{\geq} \left(e^{\frac{(1+\varepsilon)\alpha}{(1-\varepsilon)\alpha - 2}} \left(\frac{1+\varepsilon}{2} \right)^{\frac{(1-\varepsilon)\alpha}{(1-\varepsilon)\alpha - 2}} \cdot K^{\frac{(2-\varepsilon)\alpha}{(1-\varepsilon)\alpha - 2}} \right)^{\left(\frac{1-\varepsilon}{2} - \frac{1}{\alpha}\right)x}
$$

$$
= e^{\frac{1+\varepsilon}{2}x} \left(\frac{1+\varepsilon}{2} \right)^{\frac{1-\varepsilon}{2}x} \cdot K^{\frac{1-\varepsilon}{2}x + \frac{x}{2}}
$$

$$
\overset{K \geq x \geq 2}{\geq} e^{\frac{1+\varepsilon}{2}x} \left(\frac{1+\varepsilon}{2} \right)^{\frac{1-\varepsilon}{2}x} \cdot x^{\frac{1-\varepsilon}{2}x + 1}
$$

$$
> e^{\frac{1+\varepsilon}{2}x} \left(\frac{1+\varepsilon}{2}x \right)^{\frac{1-\varepsilon}{2}x + 1}. \tag{3}
$$

Since there are $\binom{|W|}{j}$ ways to choose j nodes in W and there are at most j^x ways to choose neighbors for the nodes in X in such a way that all j nodes are chosen at least once, we get that $\mathbb{P}[N_i = j] \leq \binom{|W|}{j} \frac{j^x}{|W|^x}$. The probability that N_i is

smaller than $\lceil \frac{1+\varepsilon}{2}x \rceil$ is upper bounded by

$$
\mathbb{P}\left[N_i < \left\lceil \frac{1+\varepsilon}{2}x \right\rceil \right] = \sum_{j=1}^{\lceil \frac{1+\varepsilon}{2}x \rceil - 1} \mathbb{P}[N_i = j]
$$

$$
\leq \sum_{j=1}^{\lceil \frac{1+\varepsilon}{2}x \rceil - 1} \binom{|W|}{j} \frac{j^x}{|W|^x} < \sum_{j=1}^{\lceil \frac{1+\varepsilon}{2}x \rceil - 1} \left(\frac{|W|e}{j} \right)^j \frac{j^x}{|W|^x}.
$$

We observe that when we consider $\left(\frac{|W|e}{j} \right)^j$ as a function of $j \in \mathbb{R}$ it is strictly monotonically increasing in the range $j \in \mathbb{R} \cap [|W|]$, which implies that the above probability is upper bounded by

$$
\left(\left\lceil \frac{1+\varepsilon}{2}x \right\rceil - 1 \right) \left(\frac{|W|e}{\lceil \frac{1+\varepsilon}{2}x \rceil - 1} \right)^{\lceil \frac{1+\varepsilon}{2}x \rceil - 1} \frac{\left(\lceil \frac{1+\varepsilon}{2}x \rceil - 1 \right)^x}{|W|^x}
$$

$$
< \left(\frac{1+\varepsilon}{2}x \right) \left(\frac{|W|e}{\frac{1+\varepsilon}{2}x} \right)^{\frac{1+\varepsilon}{2}x} \frac{\left(\frac{1+\varepsilon}{2}x \right)^x}{|W|^x}
$$

$$
= \frac{e^{\frac{1+\varepsilon}{2}x} \left(\frac{1+\varepsilon}{2}x \right)^{\frac{1-\varepsilon}{2}x + 1}}{|W|^{\frac{1-\varepsilon}{2}x}} \overset{(3)}{<} \frac{1}{|W|^{\frac{x}{\alpha}}} \overset{(1)}{\leq} \frac{1}{|V|^{\frac{x}{\Delta}}} < 1.
$$

If there are at least $\lceil \frac{1+\varepsilon}{2}x \rceil$ neighbors in W, then there are at least $\lceil \varepsilon x \rceil$ unique i-neighbors. Therefore, the probability that fewer than $\lceil \varepsilon x \rceil$ nodes in X have a unique i-neighbor for a certain i is strictly smaller than 1.

For any subset of size x, let the random variable F_x denote the event that there are fewer than $\lceil \varepsilon x \rceil$ unique i-neighbors for all $i \in [\Delta]$. Since the random variables $N_1, N_2, \ldots, N_\Delta$ are independent, we immediately get that $\mathbb{P}[F_x] < |V|^{-x}$. Let the random variable F be the event that F_x occurs for any subset of size x for any size $x \in \{2, \ldots, K\}$. The probability of this event is upper bounded by

$$
\mathbb{P}[F] \leq \sum_{x=2}^{K} \binom{|V|}{x} \mathbb{P}[F_x] < \sum_{x=2}^{\infty} \binom{|V|}{x} |V|^{-x} = e - 2 < 1.
$$

Hence, there is a positive probability that such a randomly chosen graph is a (K, Δ, ε)-matching graph, which proves that such a graph must exist. $\square$

In the remainder of this paper, we use matching graphs with $\varepsilon = 1/8$, which are guaranteed to exist if

$$
|W| \geq |V|^{8/\Delta} \quad \text{and} \quad |W| \geq 3K^3. \tag{4}
$$

Note that the constants in the exponents can be reduced with a more elaborate analysis.

2.2 Reporter-Free Set

A *reporter-free set* is, as the name implies, a set of nodes that are not reporters. Depending on k, different techniques can be employed to compute such a set. A procedure that finds such a set of cardinality x in $\mathcal{O}(k)$ time using one channel has been described in the literature [14]. We now discuss an extension of this procedure, which we call $FindRFS(x)$.

Case 1: If k is in the same order of magnitude as x or larger, there exists a constant $c > 0$ such that $x \leq c \cdot k$. Finding a reporter-free set of size x can be accomplished by letting the nodes with identifiers $1, 2, \ldots, k + x$ transmit (on the single channel) if they are reporters or not. This procedure stops after x non-reporters have been found, or the k reporters have been detected and the information exchange problem is solved (and the reporter-free set is thus not needed anymore).

Case 2: Alternatively, we can compute a reporter-free set of size $x \leq n/(k+1)$, which is more suitable for smaller values of k, as follows. The first two nodes (with identifier 1 and 2) are assigned the roles of *leader* and *guard*. All nodes are partitioned into $k+1$ groups based on their identifiers, each containing roughly $n/(k+1)$ nodes. In the first time step, the reporters in the first group (if any) transmit a message on a single predefined channel while the leader is listening unless it is a reporter itself. The guard node also transmits a message containing its identifier if it is not a reporter, otherwise it remains silent. As a consequence, if the leader receives the guard's message, none of the other nodes in the first group are reporters. The leader can then (depending on the guard's message and its own status) announce in the next time step whether the first group is reporter-free and the algorithm terminates. Otherwise, the leader instructs the nodes to continue, in which case all reporters in the second group and also the guard node send a message in the next time step. Again, if the leader only receives the guard's message, it has found a reporter-free set of size $n/(k+1)$, otherwise the same steps are repeated with the third group, fourth group, etc. until a reporter-free group is found. The first x nodes of this group are then assigned to the reporter-free set.

LEMMA 1 (EXTENSION OF LEMMA 5.1 OF [14]).
Procedure FindRFS(x) ensures deterministically that after its completion all nodes know the identifiers of a reporter-free set of size x after $\mathcal{O}(k)$ time steps using one channel if (i) $x \leq c \cdot k$ for some constant c or (ii) $x \leq n/(k+1)$.

PROOF. Case 1: The correctness of the algorithm is immediate. The number of time steps required is at most $\min\{(c+1)k, n\} \in \mathcal{O}(k)$.

Case 2: For all groups it holds that receiving the guard's message implies that the group does not contain any reporters: For the first group, the guard only transmits if it is not a reporter, and due to possible collisions the leader only receives this message if all other nodes in the first group remain silent, i.e., no node is a reporter. For any group $2, \ldots, k+1$, the guard always sends, and the leader receives this message if there are no reporters in the corresponding group. Since there are $k+1$ groups, there is at least one group that does not contain reporters. Hence, a reporter-free set of size $x \leq n/(k+1)$ is always found. It takes 2 time steps to determine whether a group is reporter-free and to broadcast this information. As there are $k+1$ groups, the number of time steps is upper bounded by $2(k+1) \in \mathcal{O}(k)$. □

COROLLARY 1. *Lemma 1 implies that a reporter-free set of size $\Omega(k+n/k) = \Omega(\sqrt{n})$ can be found in $\mathcal{O}(k)$ time slots.*

As we will see in Section 3, our algorithms start by computing such a set. After this computation, in order to simplify the notation, we assume that each node that is not part of the reporter-free set chooses a (potentially) new unique name in the range $1, \ldots, n'$, where n' is the number of nodes not in the reporter-free set minus the number of reporters that have already been detected while computing the reporter-free set. This renaming does not require any communication because the set of nodes in the reporter-free set is globally known.

2.3 Renaming

Renaming is an important concept that is used repeatedly in our algorithms. Initially, the identifiers of the k reporters are in the range $[n] = \{1, \ldots, n\}$. The goal of renaming is to assign new names to the reporters in order to reduce the size of the possible range with reporters so that the reporters can be determined quickly by examining this smaller range. In this section, we describe Procedure $BasicRename(k, n)$, which uses matching graphs for efficient renaming.

Let W denote the target namespace, i.e., once $BasicRename(k, n)$ terminates, each reporter has a new unique name in W, and let the names in this set be $1, \ldots, |W|$. A prerequisite for $BasicRename(k, n)$ is a reporter-free set of size $|W|$, which we assume to be given. As we will see, the namespace W can be chosen to be small enough for all our purposes such that a reporter-free set of size $|W|$ can be computed in $\mathcal{O}(k)$ time using procedure $FindRFS(x)$ (Corollary 1). The nodes in the reporter-free set are called *guard nodes*. Moreover, we assume that there are $|W|$ channels $1, \ldots, |W|$. Procedure $BasicRename(k, n)$ itself consists of two phases: a *competition phase* and a *conflict resolution phase*.

The goal of the competition phase is to assign a new name in W to each reporter. It is possible that several reporters obtain the same name in this phase. A reporter v competes for a name $i \in W$ by sending its own identifier on channel i. The ith guard node g_i in the reporter-free set listens on channel i. If it receives an identifier, we say that the reporter v that sent this message *won* the competition for name $i \in W$. In this case, g_i adds v's identifier to the list of identifiers that acquired this name. In the subsequent time step, g_i transmits v's identifier on channel i and v listens. This way v is informed that it has won the competition. Each reporter remains *active* until it wins its first competition, i.e., it continues to compete for a name by sending its identifier on the corresponding channel and listen for the retransmission in the subsequent time slot until it succeeds. Once a reporter wins, it becomes *inactive*, which means that it remains silent until the end of the competition phase. The sequence of names that each individual reporter v competes for is determined using a (shared) (K, Δ, ε)-matching graph $G = (V \cup W, E)$, where $K \geq k$. The set V represents the original $n = |V|$ node identifiers, and W represents the target namespace (the new temporary node "names"). Reporter v first competes for its 1-neighbor $\Gamma(v, 1)$, and then for its 2-neighbor $\Gamma(v, 2)$, etc. If it loses the competition for $\Gamma(v, \Delta)$, it starts again with $\Gamma(v, 1)$, i.e., a reporter cycles through its neighbors until it wins. After $\Delta \cdot \lceil \log k / \log(1/(1-\varepsilon)) \rceil$ competitions, the competition phase is over. We show in the proof of Theorem 2 that this number of competitions suffices to guarantee that each reporter indeed wins one of the competitions.

The goal of the conflict resolution phase is to ensure that each reporter obtains a unique name in W. For this purpose, the reporter-free set is partitioned into $\lceil |W|/k \rceil$ groups, each consisting of at most k guard nodes based on their identifiers. Since the identifiers of the nodes in the reporter-free set are known, no communication is necessary for this partitioning. Consider the jth such guard group. The guard node with the smallest identifier starts transmitting the identifiers of the reporters that won a competition for its name on channel j. Once it has transmitted all winning identifiers, the guard node with the next larger identifier starts transmitting on channel j and so on until all guards have transmitted their winners. Each reporter v that won the competition for a name i listens to the communication in the group to which the guard of i belongs and records the identifiers of all reporters that won a competition in this group (includ-

Algorithm 1 Procedure $BasicRename(k,n)$: Guard node g_i assigned to channel i

```
   // ** competition phase starts
1: winnerList := ∅
2: for t := 1,...,9Δ⌈log k⌉ do
3:     receive message on channel i
4:     if identifier id received then
5:         send id on channel i
6:         winnerList := winnerList ∪ {id}
7:     else
8:         send ⊥ on channel i
9:     end if
10: end for
11: nextGuard := 1; winnerId := ⊥

   // ** conflict resolution phase starts
12: for t := 1,...,2k − 1 do
13:     if nextGuard = i mod k then
14:         if winnerList = ∅ then
15:             nextGuard := nextGuard + 1
16:         else
17:             winnerId := min{id | id ∈ winnerList}
18:             winnerList := winnerList \ {winnerId}
19:         end if
20:         send [nextGuard, winnerId] on channel ⌈i/k⌉
21:     else
22:         receive message [guard, id] on channel ⌈i/k⌉
23:         nextGuard := guard
24:     end if
25: end for
```

Algorithm 2 Procedure $BasicRename(k,n)$: Reporter v

```
   // ** competition phase starts
1: for t := 1,...,9Δ⌈log k⌉ do
2:     send id_v on channel Γ(v, (t mod Δ) + 1)
3:     receive message on channel Γ(v, (t mod Δ) + 1)
4:     if id_v received then
5:         winningChannel := Γ(v, (t mod Δ) + 1)
6:         sleep 2(9Δ⌈log k⌉ − t) time slots
7:         break for-loop
8:     end if
9: end for
10: winnerList := ∅

   // ** conflict resolution phase starts
11: for i := 1,...,2k − 1 do
12:     receive message [guard, id] on
                channel ⌈winningChannel/k⌉
13:     winnerList := winnerList ∪ {id}
14: end for
15: pos := v's position in winnerList
16: rename to (⌈winningChannel/k⌉ − 1) · k + pos
```

ing its own). If v listens to the communication in group j and v's identifier is at position $pos \in [k]$ in the ordered list of all received identifiers, node v renames itself using name $(j-1) \cdot k + pos$. After the execution of this algorithm all reporters know their own new name. Note that they know nothing about the new names of the other reporters; what knowledge the other nodes have gained is not considered.

The actions of the guard nodes and the reporters are summarized in Algorithm 1 and Algorithm 2, respectively. Throughout the entire paper, we use the convention that time only passes in the pseudo code if the node *waits* until a certain time or if it sends or receives a message. More precisely, if a node sends/receives a message at time t, the time is $t + 1$ *after* this operation, i.e., receiving is non-blocking (in the sense that the operation lasts exactly one time step). If a node *waits* until time t, it is exactly time t after this operation. The following theorem summarizes the properties of procedure $BasicRename(k,n)$.

THEOREM 2. *Given a $(K, \Delta, 1/8)$-matching graph $G(V \cup W, E)$, where $|V| = n$ and $K \geq k$, and a reporter-free set of size $|W|$, $BasicRename(k,n)$ assigns a unique name in $[|W|]$ to all k reporters in time $\mathcal{O}(\Delta \cdot \log(k) + k)$ using $|W|$ channels.*

PROOF. The time complexity follows from the description of the algorithm: The competition phase takes $O(\Delta \cdot \log k)$ time steps and the conflict resolution phase takes $2k − 1$ time steps, i.e., the overall time complexity is $\mathcal{O}(\Delta \cdot \log(k) + k)$ as claimed. While the competition phase requires $|W|$ channels, $\lceil W/k \rceil$ channels suffice for the conflict resolution phase. Thus, $|W|$ channels are used in total.

It remains to prove the correctness of the algorithm. For each competition it holds that if there is exactly one con-

tending node v for channel i, then v wins the competition for name i; otherwise, all competitors lose. This property holds due to the synchronous nature of our model and the fact that the guard node only receives a message if exactly one node competes for the channel at a given point in time.

Since the nodes use a $(K, \Delta, 1/8)$-matching graph, it holds that for some $i \leq \Delta$ at least $1/8$ of the $k \leq K$ reporters have a unique i-neighbor and thus have competed for a channel successfully after Δ competitions. Hence, at most $\lfloor 7k/8 \rfloor$ reporters are active after Δ competitions, $1/8$ of which win in the next Δ competitions and so on, i.e, after $i\Delta$ competitions at most $\lfloor (7/8)^i \cdot k \rfloor$ reporters are left. Consequently, there are no active reporters left after $\Delta \cdot \lceil (\log k / \log(8/7)) \rceil < 6\Delta \cdot \log k$ competitions as required. At the end of the competition phase, all reporters listening to the same group j choose distinct names in the range $[(j-1)k, jk]$. Assume that v listening to group j and v' listening to group $j' \neq j$ choose the same name. Without loss of generality, assume that $j > j'$. In this case, reporter v chooses the name $(j-1)k + p \geq j'k + p = (j'-1)k + (k+p)$ for some p, implying that the position in the ordered list of all received identifiers for v' is at least $k + p \notin [k]$, a contradiction. □

Note that the nodes are not required to store a matching graph for all possible values of k and Δ. As we will see in the subsequent sections, we only use matching graphs if k is polylogarithmic in n. Since we do not optimize constants, it hence suffices to store $\mathcal{O}(\log \log n)$ matching-graphs for $k = 2, 4, 8, 16$ and so on. The right choice of Δ for these graphs is discussed in Section 3.

2.4 Information Propagation on Trees

This building block is a procedure that disseminates information over a binary tree. This technique is used in our algorithms for two different purposes: In one algorithm, it is used to inform one node, the root of the tree, about all k reporters, and in the other algorithm, the tree is used to disseminate information about the number of collisions recorded at the leaves. We consider trees containing $N \leq n$ nodes of the network whose identifiers are known to all other nodes participating in the tree-algorithm such that each node can determine its positions in the tree accordingly.

LEMMA 2. *The time complexity of disseminating b items on a balanced binary tree of N nodes is $\mathcal{O}(b + \log N)$ using $\mathcal{O}(N)$ channels.*

PROOF. In the standard synchronous message-passing model, a straightforward algorithm to gather information at the root is to forward each information item to the parent, and potentially receive information items from the children, in every time step. The time complexity of this algorithm when forwarding b items to the root in a tree of height h is $b + h - 1$. Unfortunately, this simple scheme does not work in our setting because a) a node cannot send and receive simultaneously and b) it cannot listen to different nodes at the same time. However, these problems can be solved by splitting each round into four sub-rounds and ordering the actions in these sub-rounds according to the level in the tree: Every node v_i in the tree has its own channel i. If a node is at an even (or odd) level and it is the left child of its parent, it sends on channel i in the first sub-round. If it is the right child, it sends in the second sub-round. In the third and fourth sub-round, it listens to transmissions from its left and right child on their channels, respectively. If a node is at an odd (or even) level, it first listens to its children on their channels and transmits either in the third or fourth sub-round on its own channel depending on whether it is its parent's left or right child. It is not hard to see that the four sub-rounds simulate a single round in the message passing model and that there are no conflicts.

Note that the same bound on the time complexity holds if information is disseminated from the root to the leaves of the tree. If the nodes are required to forward an aggregate of the information in their subtree, such as, e.g., the sum of nodes in its subtrees, every node only needs to send a message to its parent once (upon receiving the necessary information from its children). The structure of the tree is based on the participating node identifiers, i.e., it is known a-priori; hence, all nodes in the tree can compute their schedule locally without any communication. As the height of a binary tree with N nodes is $\mathcal{O}(\log N)$ and every node uses its own channel for communication, the statement of the lemma follows. □

3. ALGORITHMS

Having discussed the basic building blocks, we now describe our information exchange algorithms. The algorithms presented in this paper are composed of two phases, a *scheduling phase* and a *broadcast phase*. In the scheduling phase, the reporter nodes (and some of the other nodes) exchange messages on the available channels in order to derive a schedule for the broadcast phase. This schedule defines an injective function from the set of reporters to the $\mathcal{O}(k)$ time slots of the broadcast phase. In other words, assuming that the first time slot of the broadcast phase occurs at the logical time 1, every reporter is assigned a unique time slot in the range $[C \cdot k]$ for some constant $C > 1$ after the scheduling phase. In the broadcast phase, each reporter transmits its information in its assigned time slot on channel 1 while all other nodes listen. The time complexity of the broadcast phase is thus $\mathcal{O}(k)$, and it guarantees that all nodes know all information items in the end using only one channel. Hence, the time complexity of an algorithm and the number of channels used depend on the scheduling phase

only. Moreover, since the broadcast phase always works the same way, it suffices to discuss the scheduling phase of each algorithm. In order to guarantee that the time complexity of the scheduling phase is always $\mathcal{O}(k)$ we apply different techniques for different values of k.

3.1 Algorithm $\mathcal{A}_S$ for $k \leq \frac{1}{6} \log n$

For small values of k, we propose an information exchange algorithm, denoted by $\mathcal{A}_S$, that uses matching graphs and the procedures described in the previous section.

The algorithm works as follows. First, we determine a reporter-free set of size $n/(k + 1)$ using *FindRFS* (in time $O(k)$, see Corollary 1). Subsequently, *BasicRename(k, n)* is executed using a $(k, \Delta, 1/8)$-matching graph for which $\Delta := \lfloor 10k/\log k \rfloor$ and $|W| := \lceil |V|^{8/\Delta} \rceil$. In the proof of Theorem 3, we show that such a graph exists. In the next step, a case distinction is required.

Case 1: If $|W| \leq 2^{6k}$, we use a binary tree containing $|W|$ nodes from the reporter-free set that have been computed with *FindRFS*. The tree is built up layer by layer based on the nodes' identifiers: The node with the smallest identifier is the root, the node with the second smallest identifier is its left child, the node with the third smallest is its right child, etc. Note that no communication is necessary to build this tree as the nodes in the reporter-free set and their identifiers are known to all nodes in the network. The identifiers of the k reporters are forwarded to the root as described in Section 2.4. The root can then distribute all identifiers of reporters in the next k communication rounds.

Case 2: If $|W| > 2^{6k}$, *BasicRename(k, n)* is executed again using the new names as the "input-identifiers". We refer to the new set of names as V' (which is identical to W). The same number Δ of neighbors is used, and $|W'| := \lceil |V'|^{8/\Delta} \rceil$. Again, the existence of such a graph is shown in the proof. Afterwards, all distinct k-element subsets of W' are assigned to distinct nodes in the reporter-free set. This assignment can be computed locally as all nodes in the reporter-free set are known. Each reporter-free node that is assigned at least one subset is called a *listener* (we will get back to this assignment in more detail later). A listener may be assigned at most two distinct subsets.

In the next step, each reporter transmits its identifier on the channel that corresponds to its unique name in W', during the next $2k$ time slots. Simultaneously, each listener listens for one time slot on each of the channels in its first assigned subset during the first k time slots, and then, if it is assigned a second subset, it listens on each channel in the second assigned subset for one time slot.

Finally, the listener receiving identifiers in each of the k communication rounds for a given assigned subset informs the remaining nodes on channel 1 about the reporters in the next k communication rounds. In the proof of Theorem 3 we show that there is one unique listener broadcasting this. Therefore no collisions occur and all nodes know the identifiers of all reporters. Thus the information items can easily be disseminated in the broadcast phase. We get the following result.

THEOREM 3. *Algorithm $\mathcal{A}_S$ solves the information exchange problem for $k \leq \frac{1}{6} \log n$ in time $\mathcal{O}(k)$ using $\mathcal{O}(n^{\log(k)/k})$ channels.*

PROOF. We start by proving the existence of the matching graph used in the first step. Since

$\Delta \leq 10k/\log k$ and $k \leq \frac{1}{6}\log n$, we have that $|V|^{8/\Delta} \geq n^{\frac{4}{5}\frac{\log k}{k}} \geq n^{24/5\frac{\log k}{\log n}} = k^{24/5} \overset{k\geq 2}{>} 3k^3$. This bound together with Theorem 1 implies that such a graph indeed exists. According to Theorem 2, the time required for this renaming is bounded by $\mathcal{O}(\Delta \log k + k) = \mathcal{O}(k)$.

Case 1: Corollary 2 states that $|W| - 1 \in \mathcal{O}(n^{\log(k)/k})$ channels are required, i.e., the same number as for the renaming. The bound $|W| \leq 2^{6k}$ entails that the time complexity is bounded by $4(k+h-1) \leq 4(k+\log|W|-1) < 28k \in \mathcal{O}(k)$. Since the renaming also takes $\mathcal{O}(k)$ time, the total time complexity is $\mathcal{O}(k)$ as claimed. The correctness follows from the correctness of the renaming and the propagation protocol on trees.

Case 2: Since $|W| > 2^{6k}$, we get that $|V'|^{8/\Delta} = |W|^{8/\Delta} > 2^{48k/\Delta} \geq 2^{24\log(k)/5} = k^{24/5} \overset{k\geq 2}{>} 3k^3$. Thus, Theorem 1 again implies that there is a matching graph where $|W'| = \lceil |V'|^{8/\Delta}\rceil$.

We now show an upper bound on $|W'|$. As $|W'| > 3k^3 \geq 24$, we have that $|W'| < |V'|^{8/\Delta} + 1 < |V'|^{8/\Delta} + \frac{1}{24}|W'|$ and thus

a) $\quad |W'| < \frac{24}{23}|V'|^{8/\Delta}, \qquad$ b) $\quad |V'| < \frac{24}{23}n^{8/\Delta}$

c) $\quad \Delta > \frac{10k}{\log k} - 1 > \frac{28}{3}\frac{k}{\log k} \qquad\qquad (5)$

since $|V'| > 3k^3 \geq 24$, with a similar argument as above, and the fact that $k/\log k$ is larger than $3/2$ for all k implies the third inequality. If we combine these bounds, we get that

$$|W'| \overset{(5a,b)}{<} \left(\frac{24}{23}\right)^{1+8/\Delta} n^{(8/\Delta)^2}$$

$$\overset{(5c)}{<} \left(\frac{24}{23}\right)^{1+\frac{6\log k}{7k}} n^{\left(\frac{6\log k}{7k}\right)^2} < \left(\frac{24}{23}\right)^{\frac{11}{7}} n^{\frac{1}{k}}. (6)$$

Hence, the number of k-element subsets of W' is upper bounded by $\binom{|W'|}{k} < \frac{|W'|^k}{k!} \overset{(6)}{<} \frac{\left(\frac{24}{23}\right)^{\frac{11}{7}k} n}{k!} \overset{k\geq 2}{<} 2\frac{n}{k+1}$. Thus, the subsets can be assigned in such a way that each node in the reporter-free set is assigned at most two subsets. Therefore, a unique listener determines the identifiers of the k reporters within $2k$ time slots, which proves the correctness of the algorithm in this case. Since both the second renaming and the computation of the correct k-element subset need fewer channels than the first renaming, the number of channels required is $|W| = |V'| \in \mathcal{O}(n^{\log(k)/k})$. The second renaming also takes $\mathcal{O}(\Delta \log k + k) = \mathcal{O}(k)$ time, and the computation of the subset requires $2k$ time slots. Hence, Algorithm $\mathcal{A}_S$ needs $\mathcal{O}(k)$ time slots in total for Case 2 as well. $\square$

3.2 Algorithm $\mathcal{A}_L$ for $k \in \left(\frac{1}{6}\log n, n - 2\lceil\log(n)\rceil\right)$

For $k \in \left(\frac{1}{6}\log n, n - 2\lceil\log(n)\rceil\right)$ we use a different approach than in Algorithm $\mathcal{A}_S$. We start with a high-level descriptions of Algorithm $\mathcal{A}_L$ and its main building block called an *epoch* which is discussed in more detail in Section 3.2.1 and Section 3.2.2.

High-level description of Algorithm $\mathcal{A}_L$: After some preprocessing, Algorithm $\mathcal{A}_L$ executes a sequence of *epochs*. The goal of an epoch is to identify some previously unknown reporters. The number of epochs that need to be carried out depends on the number k of reporters. If k is smaller than $\log(n) \cdot \log\log(n)$ (Case 1), we run a procedure called *DetectFraction* several times, to reduce the number of unknown reporters. During the execution of *DetectFraction*, temporary names are assigned to the reporters using matching graphs. The range of these temporary names is smaller than the range of the identifiers of the nodes. Subsequently, multiple epochs are executed using these temporary names. Due to the smaller range of temporary names, not all temporary names are unique and thus an epoch might detect only a few reporters because the messages of reporters with the same temporary names collide. Procedure *DetectFraction* executes Δ epochs, one for each neighbor index of the used matching graph, which will be specified later. This allows us to guarantee that in at least one of these epochs the number of unknown reporters is reduced significantly. Otherwise (Case 2), one epoch is sufficient to detect all reporters. After $\mathcal{O}(k)$ time slots all reporters are known in both cases.

High-level description of an epoch: Given k' reporters with temporary names in a temporary namespace $[n']$ that were not detected in a previous epoch, an epoch finds and broadcasts the identifiers (in $[n]$) of reporters with a unique temporary name in $[n']$. This is achieved as follows. First, the temporary namespace is partitioned into groups. The assignment of temporary names to the groups is then refined in a number of phases. At the beginning of a phase, each group comprises a range of temporary names and each reporter's temporary name belongs to exactly one group. After a phase, the number of groups is the same but the temporary names belonging to a group change. Moreover, each group contains fewer temporary names than before and it still holds that each reporter's temporary name belongs to exactly one group.

Since the number of temporary names per group decreases in each phase, the number of temporary names in each group is one after a certain number of phases. If this left-over temporary name belongs to exactly one reporter, we can determine whether this node is a reporter and broadcast its identifier to the whole network. Multiple channels are used to ensure that the time complexity of each epoch is small enough.

3.2.1 Description of Algorithm $\mathcal{A}_L$

Algorithm $\mathcal{A}_L$ uses $2c := 2\tau \cdot \lceil\log(n/k)\rceil$ channels, for some τ defined later, and a reporter-free set of $2c$ nodes. Among these $2c$ nodes, c nodes are *master nodes* denoted by $\{m_1, \ldots, m_c\}$, the other c nodes are *helper nodes* $\{h_1, \ldots, h_c\}$. Master m_j communicates on channel j unless stated otherwise. As mentioned in the high-level description, $\mathcal{A}_L$ executes one or more epochs to detect unknown reporters with unique temporary names in $[n']$. We distinguish between two cases.

Case 1: If $k < \log(n) \cdot \log\log(n)$, we set $\tau := \lceil\log^\rho n\rceil$ for some constant $\rho > 0$. Next, we run Procedure *DetectFraction* (Line 9) multiple times. This procedure comprises several epochs and detects a constant fraction of the k' remaining unknown reporters. We repeatedly execute *DetectFraction* until at most $\frac{1}{6}\log n$ reporters are unknown (Lines 8–10). Once $k' \leq \frac{1}{6}\log n$, Algorithm $\mathcal{A}_S$ is called to detect the remaining unknown reporters (Line 11).

Procedure *DetectFraction* uses a (k, Δ, ε)-matching graph G with $\Delta = \lceil\log\log n\rceil$, $\varepsilon = 1/8$, $|V| = n$, $|W| = n' := \lceil n^{8/\Delta}\rceil$ (Line 13). Theorem 1 proves the existence of such a graph. This graph is utilized to compute the temporary names that are used throughout one of the Δ epochs

Algorithm 3 Sketch of Algorithm $\mathcal{A}_L$

1: **if** $k < \log(n) \cdot \log\log n$ **then**
    // ** Case 1:
2:    $\tau := \lceil \log^\rho n \rceil$; $c := \tau \cdot \lceil \log(n/k) \rceil$; $k' := k$
3:    **compute** c master and c helper nodes
4:    **while** $k' > \frac{1}{6}\log n$ **do**
5:        **run** $DetectFraction()$
6:    **end while**
7:    **run** Algorithm $\mathcal{A}_S$ for remaining reporters
8: **else**
    // ** Case 2:
9:    $\tau := 2$; $c := \tau \cdot \lceil \log(n/k) \rceil$
10:    **compute** c master and c helper nodes
11:    **run** epoch on temporary namespace $[n'] := [n]$
12: **end if**

Procedure $DetectFraction$:
13: $G := (k, \lceil \log\log n \rceil, 1/8)$-matching graph
            with $|W| = n' = \lceil n^{8/\lceil \log\log n \rceil} \rceil$
14: **for** $i := 1, \ldots, \lceil \log\log n \rceil$ **do**
15:    temporary names according to i^{th} neighbor in G
16:    **run** epoch with these temporary names in $[n']$
17:    $k' := k' - \#$reporters detected in epoch
18: **end for**

---

of $DetectFraction$; in the ith epoch, the unknown reporters use temporary names according to their i^{th} neighbor in the (k, Δ, ε)-matching graph. In each of the epochs, a few reporters are able to tell their original identifiers to the rest of the nodes. The temporary name l in $[n']$ of a node v (called v_l) may not always be unique. Although there can be several nodes with the same temporary name, we write v_l when we refer to one of these nodes.

Case 2: If $k \geq \log(n) \cdot \log\log(n)$ (Lines 2–4 in Algorithm 3), only one epoch with temporary namespace $[n'] := [n]$ and $\tau := 2$ is used (Line 2). Before executing this epoch (Line 4), Algorithm $\mathcal{A}_L$ starts the preprocessing by computing a reporter-free set of size $2c$, and assigns master and helper nodes accordingly (Line 3).

In Section 3.2.3 we prove that Algorithm $\mathcal{A}_L$ successfully identifies the k reporters in $\mathcal{O}(k)$ time.

3.2.2 Description of an Epoch

Throughout the entire execution of an epoch, each unknown reporter v_i is a member of exactly one out of at most $\tau \cdot k'$ disjoint groups. Observe that we defined groups to contain temporary names. For simplicity we also treat them as if they contained nodes: a node is a member of a group if its temporary name is contained in this group.

As mentioned earlier, an epoch consists of several phases. Group membership of a name/node remains the same throughout the course of a phase but it may change at the end of each phase. Therefore we introduce a *group number* $g(i)$ for each temporary name i, which indicates to which group node v_i belongs due to its temporary name i in the current time slot. I.e., $g(i) = j$ indicates that v_i is in the jth group, where $j \in \{1, \ldots, \tau \cdot k'\}$. In phase 1, a node v_i belongs to group $g(i) = \lceil i \cdot \tau \cdot k'/n' \rceil$, i.e., any reporter with a temporary name less than $\lceil n'/(\tau \cdot k') \rceil$ belongs to group number 1, reporters among the next $\lceil n'/(\tau \cdot k') \rceil$ nodes to group number 2 and so on. In other words, at the beginning of an epoch the temporary namespace $[n']$ is partitioned into

disjoint ranges of length at most $\lceil n'/(\tau \cdot k') \rceil$, each associated with one group.

In every phase, reporter v_i also stores the range $r(i) := [l, r]$ of temporary names lying in its group's range, i.e., l is the lowest temporary name such that $g(l) = g(i)$ and r is the largest temporary name such that $g(r) = g(i)$. This range is updated each time v_i's group changes.

The algorithm ensures that at the end of an epoch, if v_i has a unique temporary name i, it is the only reporter in the group with identifier $g(i)$. Otherwise, group $g(i)$ contains either no reporters or more than one reporter.

Now we specify how reporters and masters communicate. Each master communicates with reporters belonging to at most $s := \lceil \tau \cdot k'/c \rceil = \lceil k'/\lceil \log(n/k) \rceil \rceil$ distinct groups: m_1 communicates on channel 1 with reporters in the first s groups, m_2 communicates on channel 2 with reporters in the next s groups, and so on, i.e., master m_j communicates on channel j with reporters in the group ℓ if $j = \lceil \ell/s \rceil$. We say that these groups *belong* to master m_j. In each phase, reporter v_i only communicates with the master $m_{\lceil g(i)/s \rceil}$ to which the group number $g(i)$ belongs, i.e., it uses channel $\lceil g(i)/s \rceil$ for communication. Furthermore, each reporter v_i stores its group's position $p(i) := g(i) \bmod s$ in the sorted list of all groups that belong to its group's master. The position is used to determine the communication time slot between the nodes in a specific group and its master. Note that a master m_j always communicates with the same groups, but these might contain different reporters in each phase.

Since every phase is identical, it suffices to study the operation of a single phase to understand an epoch. The goal of a phase is to reduce the number of nodes contained in each group. Recall that at the beginning of a phase, each group contains a certain number of temporary names. Each reporter is contained in some group due to its temporary name. After a phase, the number of groups is the same, the temporary names contained in a group might differ, but each group contains a smaller temporary namespace than before. It still holds that each reporter is contained in some group via its temporary name.

A phase consists of three parts. Since the helper nodes only operate in the first part of any given phase and act at the same times on the same channels as their masters, pseudo code for the helpers is omitted. The execution of a phase is described for masters in Algorithm 4 and for reporters in Algorithm 5. As every phase takes the same number of time steps, we can assume for ease of notation that every phase starts at a (logical) time $t = 0$. Note that master, helper and reporter nodes execute their specific code at the same time in synchronized time slots.

We now proceed to describe the steps of a phase in greater detail. The three parts of a phase work as follows.

Part 1 of a phase: Detect all groups that contain at least one reporter. See Lines 1–7 in Algorithm 4 and Lines 1–4 in Algorithm 5. We denote the set of groups in which m_j detects a reporter by $\mathcal{C}_j$. To compute $\mathcal{C}_j$, each master m_j checks each of its $s = \lceil \tau \cdot k'/c \rceil$ groups for reporters one after another. Any master m_j listens and its helper h_j sends an arbitrary message on channel j for s time steps, while each reporter v_i sends a message on channel $\lceil g(i)/s \rceil$ to its master at time $p(i)$. Remember that v_i is in the $p(i)^{th}$ group that belongs to $m_{\lceil g(i)/s \rceil}$ at that time. Thus, we can conclude that if a master m_j receives a message at a time $t + q$, $q \in \{1, \ldots, c\}$, on channel j, it must be the message sent by helper h_j, i.e., m_j learns that there are no reporters

Algorithm 4 Code executed by master m_j during a phase within Algorithm $\mathcal{A}_L$.

```
// ** Part 1:
1:  C_j := ∅
2:  for t := 0 … s − 1 do
3:      receive message on channel j
4:      if no message received then
5:          C_j := C_j ∪ {t};   // ** collision in the t^th group
6:      end if
7:  end for
    // ** Part 2:
8:  coll_{j−1} := sumOfCollisionsAtMasters(m_1, …, m_{j−1}, |C_j|)
9:  wait until t = s − 1 + 8⌈log c⌉
    // ** Part 3:
10: for γ := 0 … s − 1 do
11:     if γ ∈ C_j then
12:         send coll_{j−1} on channel γ
13:         coll_{j−1} := coll_{j−1} + 1
14:     end if
15: end for
```

Algorithm 5 Code executed by reporter v_i in group $g(i)$ with range $r(i) = [l, r]$ during a phase within Algorithm $\mathcal{A}_L$.

```
// ** Part 1:
1:  c(i) := ⌈g(i)/s⌉ // ** channel of this group
2:  t := 0 // ** beginning of phase
3:  wait until t = p(i) // ** position of this group
4:  send "message" on channel c(i)
    // ** Part 2: reporters sleep
    // ** Part 3:
5:  wait until t = s − 1 + 8⌈log c⌉ + p(i)
    // ** The master of v_i's group is m_j with j := ⌈g(i)/s⌉
6:  receive coll_{j−1} on channel c(i)
7:  compute j, s.t., v_i ∈ [l + j(r − l)/τ, l + (j + 1)(r − l)/τ)
8:  g(i) := τ · coll_{j−1} + j
9:  r(i) := [l + j(r − l)/τ, l + (j + 1)(r − l)/τ]
10: p(i) := g(i)  mod s // ** update position of this
                              group in the list of its (new) master
```

in its qth group. On the other hand, if no message is received, a collision must have occurred due to some node v_i with $\lceil g(i)/s \rceil = j$ and $p(i) = q$, implying that the qth group contains at least one reporter. Thus, each masters m_j knows its set C_j after Part 1.

Part 2 of a phase: Redefine groups. Each master m_j computes for each group it is responsible the range of temporary names that m_j will assign in Part 3 to the (new) groups that result from splitting any group in which m_j detected a collision in Part 1. See Line 8 in Algorithm 4. First, each master m_j (with $j > 1$) has to learn the number $coll_{j−1} := \sum_{p=1}^{j−1} |C_p|$ of all collisions that occurred at the masters $m_1, \ldots, m_{j−1}$ (thus $coll_{j−1}$ is at most $(j − 1) \cdot s$). This is achieved by calling the function *sumOfCollisionsAtMasters*, which uses a balanced binary tree (see Section 2.4) of depth $\log c$ to compute $coll_{j−1}$ for master m_j (for all $j \in \{1, c − 1\}$ simultaneously.) In this tree, the c masters are the leaves and $c − 1$ helpers are used as the inner nodes. By aggregating the number of collisions $|C_1|, \ldots, |C_{c−1}|$ from the leaves, each inner node h knows the number of collisions that occurred at the masters in its left and right subtree. Let ℓ_h denote the number of collisions in its left subtree. Aggregating the total sum of collisions at the root (e.g., h_1) takes at most $4\lceil \log c \rceil$ time steps and at most c channels as discussed in Section 2.4. The number of collisions at the leaves (masters) in the left subtree of the root is then computed as follows: The root sends 0 to its left child and the number ℓ_{h_1} of collisions in its left tree to its right child. Any inner node h that receives x from its parent sends x to its left child and $x + \ell_h$ to its right child. It is easy to verify that each master m_j receives exactly the number of collisions $\sum_{p=1}^{j−1} |C_p|$ that were reported by the masters $m_1, \ldots, m_{j−1}$ since these are positioned to m_j's left in the tree. This is exactly $coll_{j−1}$. Propagating this information from the root to the leaves takes at most $4\lceil \log c \rceil$ time steps as shown in Section 2.4.

Part 3 of a phase: Each group that contains at least one reporter is split into τ (new) groups. Group identifiers are reassigned to these (new) groups. See Lines 9–15 in Algorithm 4 and Lines 5–12 in Algorithm 5. First, each master m_j creates $\tau \cdot |C_j|$ new groups: τ new groups for each of the $|C_j|$ groups in which it detected a

collision. Since node m_j knows that the total number of collisions that occurred at the masters $\{m_1, \ldots, m_{j−1}\}$ is $coll_{j−1}$, it can assign the group numbers from $\tau \cdot coll_{j−1}$ to $\tau \cdot (coll_{j−1} + |C_j|) − 1$ to these new groups.

The reporters are informed about their new group numbers by executing a code sequence similar to Part 1 again, in which the roles of sender and receiver are switched, and the helper nodes remain silent. That is, the masters broadcast group identifiers and the reporters receive them. Afterwards, temporary names are reassigned to the new groups: Each new group with group number in $[\tau \cdot coll_{j−1}, \tau \cdot (coll_{j−1} + |C_j|) − 1]$ receives a $1/\tau$ fraction of the temporary names of an original group that is split. A reporter v_i changes its group membership $g(i)$ to $\tau \cdot coll_{(\lceil g(i)/s \rceil)−1} + \ell$ if its temporary name i lies in the range of the ℓth new group that its master $m_{\lceil g(i)/s \rceil}$ created. Each reporter knows what to change by listening to the corresponding channel as indicated in the pseudocode of Algorithm 5. Each reporter is able to determine which master its group belongs to in the next phase by performing the computations described earlier.

3.2.3 Analysis of Algorithm $\mathcal{A}_L$

First, we study the time and channel complexity of an epoch.

LEMMA 3. *Given a reporter-free set of size $2c$, one epoch of Algorithm $\mathcal{A}_L$ for k' unknown reporters detects all reporters with unique temporary names in the temporary namespace $[n']$ using $2c = 2\tau \cdot \lceil \log(n/k) \rceil$ channels in time*
$$\mathcal{O}\left(\left(\frac{k'}{\log(n/k)} + \log c \right) \cdot \left(\frac{\log \frac{n'}{\tau \cdot k'}}{\log \tau} \right) \right).$$

PROOF. *Correctness:* Since every master has its own channel to communicate with its groups, there are no collisions between the masters. Consider master m_j and its groups. According to the description, only the reporters of the same group send at the same time together with the helper h_j, i.e., collisions among reporters with distinct temporary names can only occur if two or more reporters are in the same group, which proves that the groups with reporters with distinct temporary names are detected correctly. The information propagation on the tree is correct as discussed in Section 2.4, and thus the masters can successfully narrow down the ranges of the temporary names that belong to at least one reporter in each phase and inform the reporters about their new group memberships.

Time complexity: The execution of the tree algorithm in each phase depends on the height of the tree, which is logarithmic in the number of masters and thus takes time $\mathcal{O}(\log c)$. Hence, the time complexity of a single phase is

$$\mathcal{O}(s + \log c) = \mathcal{O}\left(\frac{k'}{\log(n/k)} + \log c\right),$$

taking the length of the **for** and the **while** loops into account. Since the maximum number of temporary names contained in a group in phase 0 is $\lceil n'/(\tau \cdot k')\rceil$, which is divided by τ in each phase, one epoch consists of at most $\left\lceil \log_\tau \left\lceil \frac{n'}{\tau \cdot k'}\right\rceil\right\rceil \in \mathcal{O}\left(\frac{\log \frac{n'}{\tau \cdot k'}}{\log \tau}\right)$ phases. Hence the time complexity of one epoch is $\mathcal{O}\left(\left(\frac{k'}{\log(n/k)} + \log c\right)\cdot\left(\frac{\log \frac{n'}{\tau \cdot k'}}{\log \tau}\right)\right)$. $\square$

THEOREM 4. *Algorithm $\mathcal{A}_L$ solves the information exchange problem in time $\mathcal{O}(k)$ using*

Case 1: $\mathcal{O}(\log^{1+\rho} n)$ channels for some constant $\rho > 0$ if $k \in (\frac{1}{6}\log n, \log(n) \cdot \log\log n)$.

Case 2: $\mathcal{O}(\log(n/k))$ channels if $k \geq \log(n) \cdot \log\log n$.

PROOF. Note that for both cases a reporter-free set of size $2c$ can be found in time $\mathcal{O}(k)$ as shown in Lemma 1, which is a prerequisite for the correctness and the time complexity.

Case 1: Correctness: Note that messages sent by reporters with the same temporary name in $[n']$ always collide and their groups are detected, and therefore their identifiers cannot be detected at the end of an epoch. However, their participation does not disturb the course of the algorithm. Due to the property of the $(k, \Delta, 1/8)$-matching graphs used, at least $1/8$ of the unknown reporters have unique temporary names during some epoch, and will be detected in this epoch. We conclude that the number of unknown reporters is reduced in each call of the Procedure $DetectFraction$ and only an $(1 - 1/8) = 7/8$-fraction of the reporters that were unknown before calling $DetectFraction$ remain unknown. At some point, all but $\frac{1}{6}\log n$ reporters have been detected. These remaining reporters are then determined by Algorithm $\mathcal{A}_S$, and it follows that Algorithm $\mathcal{A}_L$ correctly identifies all reporters.

Complexity: It holds that at least $\frac{1}{8}k'_{old}$ of the k'_{old} reporters that were unknown before executing $DetectFraction$ are detected during Procedure $DetectFraction$. Procedure $DetectFraction$ is called again if the new number k'_{new} of still unknown nodes is $k'_{new} > \frac{1}{6}\log n$.

CLAIM 1. *If there are k' reporters, $DetectFraction$ needs time $\mathcal{O}(k')$ and $\mathcal{O}(\log^{1+\rho} n)$ channels.*

PROOF. By applying Lemma 3 with $n' := \lceil n^{8/\lceil \log\log n\rceil}\rceil$ and $\tau := \lceil \log^\rho n\rceil$, we can deduce that $2c = 2\tau \cdot \lceil \log(n/k)\rceil \in \mathcal{O}\left(\log^{1+\rho} n\right)$ channels suffice and the time complexity of one epoch is

$$\mathcal{O}\left(\left(\frac{k'}{\log(n/k)} + \log c\right)\cdot\left(\frac{\log \frac{n'}{\tau \cdot k'}}{\log \tau}\right)\right)$$
$$= \mathcal{O}\left(\frac{k'}{\log(\log n)\cdot \log\tau} + \frac{\log(c)\cdot \log n}{\log(\log n)\cdot \log\tau}\right)$$
$$= \mathcal{O}\left(\frac{k'}{(\log\log n)^2} + \frac{\log n}{\log\log n}\right),$$

which is $\mathcal{O}\left(\frac{k'}{\log\log n}\right)$ due to the range of k that we consider in this case. In total, $\Delta = \log\log n$ epochs are executed and the claim follows. $\square$

When starting with $k' := k$, in each call of Procedure $DetectFraction$ at least $1/8$ of the remaining reporters are detected. After i calls, k' is reduced to at most $(7/8)^i k$. Claim 1 proves that k' is less than $\frac{1}{6}\log n$ after at most $\sum_{i=0}^{\log_{7/8}(k-\frac{1}{6}\log n)}\mathcal{O}((7/8)^i k) = \mathcal{O}(k)$ time slots and we can apply Algorithm $\mathcal{A}_S$.

Case 2: The correctness of Algorithm $\mathcal{A}_L$ for the second range of k follows directly from Lemma 3. Analogously, both the channel and the time complexity can be derived by applying Lemma 3 with $n' = n$, $\tau = 2$ and $k' = k$: We get a bound on the channel complexity of $\mathcal{O}(\log(n/k))$, and a time complexity of $\mathcal{O}\left(\left(\frac{k}{\log(n/k)} + \log c\right)\cdot \log(n/k)\right) = \mathcal{O}(k)$. $\square$

4. LOWER BOUND

In this section, we prove a lower bound on the number of channels required to achieve a time complexity of $\mathcal{O}(k)$ in a deterministic setting. Again, we assume that $k > 1$ as the information exchange problem is trivial for $k \leq 1$. Throughout this section, the nodes are allowed to send and listen on all c channels *at the same time*; moreover, the nodes can detect collisions, i.e., they have the ability to distinguish between a collision and a transmission-free channel. Thus, the lower bound holds in a stronger model than the algorithms we described.

We proceed by first showing that for any deterministic algorithm $\mathcal{A}$ there is an assignment of the k reporters such that it takes at least a certain number of communication rounds to detect them given a specific number of channels c. As we will see, this result directly implies a lower bound on the number of channels required to guarantee a time complexity of $\mathcal{O}(k)$. In order to prove that there is such an assignment, we introduce the notion of *potential reporters*, which are all the nodes that may be reporters after a certain number of communication rounds. In particular, this means that an "adversary" may still decide for each node among the potential reporters whether or not it is a reporter subject to the constraint that k nodes must be reporters. Formally, let R^ℓ denote the set of all potential reporters after $\ell \geq 0$ rounds of communication. Naturally, we have that $R^0 = V$. The following lemma, which states that there is an assignment of reporters for which the number of potential reporters is reduced by at most a factor of $(c+1)^2$ per communication round, is key for the arguments used later.

LEMMA 4. *Assume that all nodes only know that the k reporters are in R^ℓ, where $|R^\ell| \geq (c+1)^2 \cdot (k+2)$, after $\ell \geq 0$ rounds of communication. The reporters can be assigned in such a way that after $\ell + 1$ rounds of communication all nodes only know that the k reporters are in $R^{\ell+1}$, where $|R^{\ell+1}| \geq \lfloor |R^\ell|/(c+1)^2\rfloor$.*

PROOF. Consider the actions of the nodes when executing round $\ell+1$ of algorithm $\mathcal{A}$. Let $R^\ell_{(i,j)}$ denote the set of nodes that would send on channel $i \in \{0, 1, \ldots, c\}$ if they were a *reporter* and send on channel $j \in \{0, 1, \ldots, c\}$ if they were a *non-reporter*, where sending on channel 0 simply means that the node remains silent. Thus, there are exactly $(c+1)^2$ possible actions. Consequently, there must be a set $R^\ell_{(i',j')} \subseteq R^\ell$ of size $|R^\ell_{(i',j')}| \geq \lfloor |R^\ell|/(c+1)^2\rfloor \geq k + 2$. We now argue that we can set $R^{\ell+1} := R^\ell_{(i',j')}$ and that all nodes do not know anything about the reporters except that they are in $R^{\ell+1}$. Note that by definition, the k reporters all send on channel i' and the 2 or more non-reporters send on channel j', causing collisions on these channels. Of course, it is possible that $i' = j'$, in which case they only cause one collision, or even no collision if $i' = j' = 0$. Either way, no message is transmitted, and all nodes may at best learn that the reporters are in $R^\ell_{(i',j')} \cup R^\ell_{(j',i')} \supseteq R^\ell_{(i',j')}$. If the nodes in $V \setminus R^\ell_{(i',j')}$ cause additional collisions, the set of potential reporters may only become larger. It is possible that some of these nodes successfully transmit messages. However, since they do not possess any information that the other nodes do not already know from always listening on all channels, these transmissions cannot reduce the size of the set of potential reporters, which proves the claim. $\square$

While Lemma 4 is used in the proof of Theorem 5 for small k, the next lemma strengthens our bound for large k.

LEMMA 5. *Any deterministic information exchange algorithm with time complexity $\mathcal{O}(k)$ needs $\Omega(\log_k n)$ channels.*

PROOF. A time complexity lower bound of $\Omega(k \log_k n)$ has been proven in the same model for one channel [13]. Any algorithm that is restricted to using one channel can simulate an algorithm that uses c channels by splitting each round into c sub-rounds and sending the messages that would be transmitted on channel $i \in \{1, \ldots, c\}$ in the ith sub-round. Thus, simulating an algorithm on up to c channels takes at most c times longer, implying a time complexity of at least $\Omega(k \frac{\log_k n}{c})$ for any algorithm on up to c channels. Restricting the time to $\mathcal{O}(k)$ communication rounds, implies that the number of channels must be at least $\Omega(\log_k n)$. $\square$

We can now prove the following theorem.

THEOREM 5. *If $1 < k < n^{1-\varepsilon}$ for some constant $\varepsilon > 0$ and n is sufficiently large, any deterministic information exchange algorithm whose time complexity is $\mathcal{O}(k)$ needs $\Omega(n^{\Omega(1/k)} + \log_k n)$ channels.*

PROOF. Lemma 4 states that there is an assignment of reporters such that the set of potential reporters shrinks at most by a factor of $(c+1)^2$ in each communication round, which entails that the set of potential reporters is larger than k after $\ell < \frac{1}{2} \log_{(c+1)} \left(\frac{n}{k}\right)$ rounds. Thus, the time complexity is at least $\Omega(\log_c \frac{n}{k})$. In order to achieve an upper bound of $\mathcal{O}(k)$, it must therefore hold that $c \in \Omega((n/k)^{\Omega(1/k)}) = \Omega(n^{\Omega(1/k)})$, where we use that $k < n^{1-\varepsilon}$. Hence the number of channels is at least $\Omega(\log_k n)$ according to Lemma 5. $\square$

5. REFERENCES

[1] A. F. Anta, M. A. Mosteiro, and J. R. Muñoz. Unbounded Contention Resolution in Multiple-access Channels. In *Proc. 25th International Symposium on Distributed Computing (DISC)*, pages 225–236, 2011.

[2] H. Attiya, A. Bar-Noy, D. Dolev, D. Peleg, and R. Reischuk. Renaming in an Asynchronous Environment. *Journal of the ACM (JACM)*, 37(3):524–548, 1990.

[3] M. Bienkowski, M. Klonowski, M. Korzeniowski, and D. R. Kowalski. Dynamic Sharing of a Multiple Access Channel. In *Proc. 27th International Symposium on Theoretical Aspects of Computer Science (STACS)*, pages 83–94, 2010.

[4] M. Capalbo, O. Reingold, S. Vadhan, and A. Wigderson. Randomness Conductors and Constant-degree Lossless Expanders. In *Proc. 34th Annual ACM Symposium on Theory of Computing (STOC)*, pages 659–668, 2002.

[5] A. Castañeda, S. Rajsbaum, and M. Raynal. The Renaming Problem in Shared Memory Systems: an Introduction. Technical report, INRIA, 2010.

[6] B. Chlebus and D. Kowalski. Asynchronous Exclusive Selection. In *Proc. 27th Annual ACM SIGACT-SIGOPS Symposium on Principles of Distributed Computing (PODC)*, pages 375–384, 2008.

[7] B. Chlebus, D. Kowalski, and T. Radzik. Many-to-Many Communication in Radio Networks. *Algorithmica*, 54(1):118–139, 2009.

[8] B. Chlebus, D. Kowalski, and M. Rokicki. Average-time Complexity of Gossiping in Radio Networks. In *Proc. 13th International Colloquium in Structural Information and Communication Complexity (SIROCCO)*, pages 253–267, 2006.

[9] J. Czyzowicz, L. Gasieniec, D. R. Kowalski, and A. Pelc. Consensus and Mutual Exclusion in a Multiple Access Channel. In *Proc. 23rd International Conference on Distributed Computing (DISC)*, pages 512–526, 2009.

[10] S. Dolev, S. Gilbert, R. Guerraoui, and C. Newport. Secure Communication Over Radio Channels. In *Proc. 27th Annual ACM SIGACT-SIGOPS Symposium on Principles of Distributed Computing (PODC)*, pages 105–114, 2008.

[11] S. Gilbert, R. Guerraoui, D. Kowalski, and C. Newport. Interference-resilient Information Exchange. In *Proc. 28th IEEE Conference on Computer Communications (INFOCOM)*, 2009.

[12] S. Gilbert and D. Kowalski. Trusted Computing for Fault-Prone Wireless Networks. In *Proc. 24th International Symposium on Distributed Computing (DISC)*, pages 359–373, 2010.

[13] A. Greenberg and S. Winograd. A Lower Bbound on the Time Needed in the Worst Case to Resolve Conflicts Deterministically in Multiple Access Channels. *Journal of the ACM (JACM)*, 32(3):589–596, 1985.

[14] S. Holzer, Y. Pignolet, J. Smula, and R. Wattenhofer. Time-Optimal Information Exchange on Multiple Channels. In *Proc. 7th ACM SIGACT-SIGMOBILE International Workshop on Foundations of Mobile Computing (FOMC)*, 2011.

[15] D. Kowalski. On Selection Problem in Radio Networks. In *Proc 24th Annual ACM SIGACT-SIGOPS Symposium on Principles of Distributed Computing (PODC)*, pages 158–166, 2005.

[16] E. Kushilevitz and Y. Mansour. An $\Omega(D \log(N/D))$ Lower Bound for Broadcast in Radio Networks. *SIAM Journal on Computing (SICOMP)*, 27(3):702–712, 1998.

[17] K. Nakano and S. Olariu. Randomized Initialization Protocols for Ad Hoc Networks. *IEEE Transactions on Parallel and Distributed Systems (TPDS)*, 11(7):749–759, 2000.

[18] D. E. Willard. Log-logarithmic Selection Resolution Protocols in a Multiple Access Channel. *SIAM Journal on Computing (SICOMP)*, 15(2):468–477, 1986.

High-Performance RMA-Based Broadcast on the Intel SCC

[Extended Abstract] [*]

Darko Petrović, Omid Shahmirzadi, Thomas Ropars, André Schiper
Ecole Polytechnique Fédérale de Lausanne (EPFL)
Lausanne, Switzerland
firstname.lastname@epfl.ch

ABSTRACT

Many-core chips with more than 1000 cores are expected by the end of the decade. To overcome scalability issues related to cache coherence at such a scale, one of the main research directions is to leverage the message-passing programming model. The Intel Single-Chip Cloud Computer (SCC) is a prototype of a message-passing many-core chip. It offers the ability to move data between on-chip Message Passing Buffers (MPB) using Remote Memory Access (RMA). Performance of message-passing applications is directly affected by efficiency of collective operations, such as broadcast. In this paper, we study how to make use of the MPBs to implement an efficient broadcast algorithm for the SCC. We propose *OC-Bcast* (*On-Chip Broadcast*), a pipelined k-ary tree algorithm tailored to exploit the parallelism provided by on-chip RMA. Using a LogP-based model, we present an analytical evaluation that compares our algorithm to the state-of-the-art broadcast algorithms implemented for the SCC. As predicted by the model, experimental results show that OC-Bcast attains almost three times better throughput, and improves latency by at least 27%. Furthermore, the analytical evaluation highlights the benefits of our approach: OC-Bcast takes direct advantage of RMA, unlike the other considered broadcast algorithms, which are based on a higher-level send/receive interface. This leads us to the conclusion that RMA-based collective operations are needed to take full advantage of hardware features of future message-passing many-core architectures.

Categories and Subject Descriptors

D.1.3 [**Programming Techniques**]: Concurrent Programming—*parallel programming*

Keywords

Broadcast, Message Passing, Many-Core Chips, RMA, HPC

---

[*] A full version of this paper is available at
`http://infoscience.epfl.ch/record/176499`

Permission to make digital or hard copies of all or part of this work for personal or classroom use is granted without fee provided that copies are not made or distributed for profit or commercial advantage and that copies bear this notice and the full citation on the first page. To copy otherwise, to republish, to post on servers or to redistribute to lists, requires prior specific permission and/or a fee.
SPAA'12, June 25–27, 2012, Pittsburgh, Pennsylvania, USA.
Copyright 2012 ACM 978-1-4503-1213-4/12/06 ...$10.00.

1. INTRODUCTION

Studies on future Exascale High-Performance Computing (HPC) systems point out energy efficiency as the main concern [16]. An Exascale system should have the same power consumption as the existing Petascale systems while providing thousand times more computational power. A direct consequence of this observation is that the number of *flops per watt* provided by a single chip should dramatically increase compared to the current situation [27]. The solution is to increase the level of parallelism on a single chip by moving from multi-core to many-core chips [5]. A many-core chip integrates a large number of cores connected using a powerful Network-on-Chip (NoC). Soon, chips with hundreds if not thousands of cores will be available.

Taking the usual shared memory approach for many-core chips raises scalability issues related to the overhead of hardware cache coherence [20]. To avoid relying on hardware cache coherence, two main alternatives are proposed: (i) sticking to the shared memory paradigm, but managing data coherence in software [27], or (ii) adopting message passing as the new communication paradigm [20]. Indeed, a large set of cores connected through a highly efficient NoC can be viewed as a parallel message-passing system.

The Intel Single-Chip Cloud Computer (SCC) is an example of a message-passing many-core chip [14]. The SCC integrates 24 2-core tiles on a single chip connected by a 2D-mesh NoC. It is provided with on-chip low-latency memory buffers, called *Message Passing Buffers* (MPB), physically distributed across the tiles. *Remote Memory Access* (RMA) to these MPBs allows fast inter-core communication.

The natural choice to program a high-performance message-passing system is to use Single Program Multiple Data (SPMD) algorithms. The Message Passing Interface (MPI) [21] is the *de facto* standard for programming SPMD HPC applications. MPI defines a set of primitives for point-to-point communication, and also defines a set of collective operations, i.e., operations involving a group of processes. Several works study implementation of point-to-point communications on the Intel SCC [30, 23, 22], but only little attention has been paid to implementation of collective operations. This paper studies implementation of collective operations for the Intel SCC. It focuses on the broadcast primitive (*one-to-all*), with the aim of understanding how to efficiently leverage on-chip RMA-based communication. Note that the need for efficient collective operations for many-core systems, especially the need for efficient broadcast, goes far beyond the scope of MPI applications, and is of general interest in these systems [27].

1.1 Related work

A message-passing many-core chip, such as the SCC, is very similar to many existing HPC systems since it gathers a large number of processing units connected through a high-performance RMA-based network. Broadcast has been extensively studied in these systems. Algorithms based on a k-ary tree have been proposed [4]. In MPI libraries, binomial trees and *scatter-allgather* [24] algorithms are mainly considered [11, 26]. A binomial tree is usually selected to provide better latency for small messages, while the *scatter-allgather* algorithm is used to optimize throughput for large messages. These solutions are implemented on top of send/receive point-to-point functions and do not take topology issues into account. This is not an issue for small to medium scale systems like the SCC. However, it has been shown that for mesh or torus topologies, these solutions are not optimal at large scale: non-overlapping spanning trees can provide better performance [1].

As already mentioned, MPI libraries usually implement collective operations on top of classical *two-sided* send/receive communication[1]. To take advantage of the RMA capabilities of high-performance network interconnects such as InfiniBand [2], *one-sided put* and *get* operations, have been introduced [21]. In one-sided communication, only one party (sender or receiver) is involved in the data transfer and specifies the source and destination buffers. One-sided operations increase the design space for communication algorithms, and can provide better performance by overlapping communication and computation. On the SCC, RMA operations on the MPBs allow the implementation of efficient one-sided communication [19].

Two-sided communication can be implemented on top of one-sided communication [18]. This way, collective operations based on two-sided communication can benefit from efficient one-sided communication. Currently available SCC communication libraries adopt this solution. The RCCE library [19] provides efficient one-sided *put/get* operations and uses them to implement two-sided send/receive communication. The RCCE_comm library implements collective operations on top of two-sided communication [7]: the RCCE_comm broadcast algorithm is based on a binomial tree or on *scatter-allgather* depending on the message size. The same algorithms are used in the RCKMPI library [28].

Most high-performance networks provide *Remote Direct Memory Access* (RDMA) [1, 2], *i.e.*, the RMA operations are offloaded to the network devices. Some works try to directly take advantage of these RDMA capabilities to improve collective operations [12, 13, 17, 25]. However, it is hard to reuse the results presented in these works in the context of the SCC for two main reasons: (i) they leverage hardware specific features not available on the SCC, i.e., hardware multicast [13, 17], and (ii) they make use of large RDMA buffers [12, 25], whereas the on-chip MPBs have a very limited size (8 KB per core). Note also that accesses to the MPBs are not RDMA operations since message copying is performed by the core issuing the operation.

1.2 Contributions

We are investigating the implementation of an efficient broadcast algorithm for a message-passing many-core chip,

---

[1] In a classical two-sided communication, a matching operation is required by both parties: *send* by the sender, *receive* by the receiver.

such as the Intel SCC. The broadcast operation allows one process to send a message to all processes in the application. As specified by MPI, the collective operation is executed by having all processes in the application call the communication function with matching arguments: the sender calls the *broadcast* function with the message to broadcast, while the receiver processes call it to specify the reception buffer.

To take advantage of on-chip RMA, we propose OC-Bcast (*On-Chip Broadcast*), a pipelined k-ary tree algorithm based on one-sided communication: k processes get the message in parallel from their parent to obtain a high degree of parallelism. The degree of the tree is chosen to avoid contention on the MPBs. To provide efficient synchronization between a process and its children in the tree, we introduce an additional binary notification tree. Double buffering is used to further improve the throughput.

We evaluate OC-Bcast analytically using a LogP-based performance model [9]. The evaluation shows that our algorithm based on one-sided communication outperforms existing broadcast algorithms based on two-sided communication. The main reason is that OC-Bcast reduces the amount of data moved between the off-chip memory and the MPBs on the critical path.

Finally, we confirm the analytical results through experiments. The comparison of OC-Bcast with the RCCE_comm binomial tree and *scatter-allgather* algorithms based on two-sided communication shows that: (i) our algorithm has at least 27% lower latency than the binomial tree algorithm; (ii) it has almost 3 times higher peak throughput than the *scatter-allgather* algorithm. These results clearly show that collective operations for message-passing many-core chips should be based on one-sided communication in order to fully exploit the hardware resources.

The paper is structured as follows. In Section 2 we describe the architecture and the communication features of the Intel SCC. Section 3 presents our inter-core communication model. Section 4 is devoted to our RMA-based broadcast algorithm. Analytical and experimental evaluations are presented in Sections 5 and 6 respectively. Finally, Section 7 concludes the paper.

2. THE INTEL SCC

The SCC is a general-purpose many-core prototype developed by Intel Labs. In this section we describe the SCC architecture and inter-core communication.

2.1 Architecture

The cores and the NoC of the SCC are depicted in Figure 1. There are 48 Pentium P54C cores, grouped into 24 tiles (2 cores per tile) and connected through a 2D mesh NoC. Tiles are numbered from (0,0) to (5,3). Each tile is connected to a router. The NoC uses high-throughput, low-latency links and deterministic virtual cut-through X-Y routing [15]. Memory components are divided into (i) message passing buffers (MPB), (ii) L1 and L2 caches, as well as (iii) off-chip private memories. Each tile has a small (16KB) on-chip MPB equally divided between the two cores. The MPBs allow on-chip inter-core communication using RMA: each core is able to read and write in the MPB of all other cores. There is no hardware cache coherence for the L1 and L2 caches. By default, each core has access to a private off-chip memory through one of the four memory controllers, denoted by MC in Figure 1. The off-chip memory is phys-

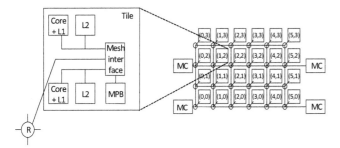

Figure 1: SCC Architecture

ically shared, so it is possible to provide portions of shared memory by changing the default configuration.

2.2 Inter-core communication

To leverage on-chip RMA, cores can transfer data using the one-sided *put* and *get* primitives provided by the RCCE library [29]. Using *put*, a core (a) reads a certain amount of data from its own MPB or its private off-chip memory and (b) writes it to some MPB. Using *get*, a core (a) reads a certain amount of data from some MPB and (b) writes it to its own MPB or its private off-chip memory. The unit of data transmission is the cache line, equal to 32 bytes. If the data is larger than one cache line, it is sequentially transferred in cache-line-sized packets. During a remote read/write operation, each packet traverses all routers on the way from the source to the destination. The local MPB is accessed directly or through the local router[2].

3. MODELING *PUT* AND *GET* PRIMITIVES

In this section we propose a model for RMA *put* and *get* primitives. Our model is based on the LogP model [9] and the Intel SCC specifications [14]. We experimentally validate our model and assess its domain of validity.

3.1 The model

The LogP model [9] characterizes a message passing parallel system using the number of processors (P), the time interval or *gap* between consecutive message transmissions (g), the maximum communication latency of a single-word-sized message (L), and the overhead of sending or receiving a message (o). This basic model assumes small messages. To deal with messages of arbitrary size, it can be extended to express L, o and g as a function of the message size [10].

We adapt the LogP model to the SCC communication characteristics. The LogP model assumes that the latency is the same between all processes. However, the SCC mesh communication latency is a function of the number of routers traversed on the path from the source to the destination. In our model, the number of routers traversed by one packet is defined by the parameter d. Communication on the SCC mesh is done at the packet granularity. A packet can carry one cache line (32 Bytes). We use the number of cache lines (CL) as unit for message size. Note that the SCC cores, network and memory controllers are not required to work at the same frequency. For that reason, time is chosen as the common unit for all model parameters.

---

[2]Direct access to the local MPB is discouraged because of a bug in the SCC hardware.

For each operation, we model (i) the completion time, i.e., the time for the operation to return, and (ii) the latency, i.e., the time for the message to be available at the destination. We start by modeling read/write on the MPBs and on the off-chip private memory. Then we model put/get operations based on read/write. The read operation, executed by some core c, brings one cache line from an MPB, or from the off-chip private memory of core c, to its internal registers[3]. The write operation, executed by some core c, copies one cache line from some internal registers of core c to an MPB, or the off-chip private memory of core c. The formulas representing our model are given in Figure 2.

3.1.1 MPB read/write

Any read or write operation of a single cache line includes some core overhead o^{mpb}, as well as some mesh overhead which depends on d (the distance between the core and the MPB). We define L^{hop} as the time needed for one packet to traverse one router; it is independent of the packet size. Therefore, the latency of writing one cache line to an MPB is given by Formula 1 in Figure 2. The write completes when the acknowledgment from the MPB is received, which adds $d \cdot L^{hop}$ (Formula 2).

To read one cache line from an MPB, a request has to be sent to this MPB; the cache line is received as a response. Therefore the latency and the completion time are equal (Formula 3).

3.1.2 Off-chip read/write

By o_r^{mem} and o_w^{mem}, we represent the constant overhead of reading and writing one cache line from/to the off-chip memory. Note that in the LogP model, an overhead o is supposed to represent the time during which the processor is involved in the communication. We choose to include memory read and write overheads in o_r^{mem} and o_w^{mem} for the sake of simplicity. The latency and the completion time of off-chip memory read/write correpond to Formulas 4-6, where d represents the distance between the core that executes the read/write operation and the memory controller.

3.1.3 Operation put

To model *put* (and later *get*) from MPB to MPB, we introduce o_{put}^{mpb} (respt. o_{get}^{mpb}) to define the core overhead of the *put* (respt. *get*) function apart from the time spent moving data. The corresponding o_{put}^{mem} and o_{get}^{mem} are used for operations involving private off-chip memory. A *put* operation executed by core c reads data from some source and writes it to some destination: the source is either c's local MPB (Formula 7) or private off-chip memory (Formula 8), and the destination is an MPB. We denote by d^{src} the distance between the data and core c executing the operation, and by d^{dst} the distance between c and the MPB to which the data is written. If c moves data from its local MPB then $d^{src} = 1$. Otherwise, d^{src} is the distance between c and the memory controller. Note also that the P54C cores can only

---

[3]The read operation, as defined here, should not be interpreted as a single instruction. Indeed, it is implemented as a sequence of instructions, which read an aligned cached line word by word. The first instruction causes a cache miss, and the corresponding cache line is moved to the L1 cache of the calling core. The subsequent instructions hit the L1 cache. Analogous holds for write operations, except that L1 prefetching is implemented in software.

$$L_w^{mpb}(d) = o^{mpb} + d \cdot L^{hop} \qquad (1)$$

$$C_w^{mpb}(d) = o^{mpb} + 2d \cdot L^{hop} \qquad (2)$$

$$L_r^{mpb}(d) = C_r^{mpb}(d) = o^{mpb} + 2d \cdot L^{hop} \qquad (3)$$

$$L_w^{mem}(d) = o_w^{mem} + d \cdot L^{hop} \qquad (4)$$

$$C_w^{mem}(d) = o_w^{mem} + 2d \cdot L^{hop} \qquad (5)$$

$$L_r^{mem}(d) = C_r^{mem}(d) = o_r^{mem} + 2d \cdot L^{hop} \qquad (6)$$

$$C_{put}^{mpb}(m, d^{dst}) = o_{put}^{mpb} + m \cdot C_r^{mpb}(1) + m \cdot C_w^{mpb}(d^{dst}) \qquad (7)$$

$$C_{put}^{mem}(m, d^{src}, d^{dst}) = o_{put}^{mem} + m \cdot C_r^{mem}(d^{src}) + m \cdot C_w^{mpb}(d^{dst}) \qquad (8)$$

$$L_{put}^{mpb}(m, d^{dst}) = o_{put}^{mpb} + m \cdot C_r^{mpb}(1) + (m-1) \cdot C_w^{mpb}(d^{dst}) + L_w^{mpb}(d^{dst}) \qquad (9)$$

$$L_{put}^{mem}(m, d^{src}, d^{dst}) = o_{put}^{mem} + m \cdot C_r^{mem}(d^{src}) + (m-1) \cdot C_w^{mpb}(d^{dst}) + L_w^{mpb}(d^{dst}) \qquad (10)$$

$$L_{get}^{mpb}(m, d^{src}) = C_{get}^{mpb}(m, d^{src}) = o_{get}^{mpb} + m \cdot C_r^{mpb}(d^{src}) + m \cdot C_w^{mpb}(1) \qquad (11)$$

$$L_{get}^{mem}(m, d^{src}, d^{dst}) = C_{get}^{mem}(m, d^{src}, d^{dst}) = o_{get}^{mem} + m \cdot C_r^{mpb}(d^{src}) + m \cdot C_w^{mem}(d^{dst}) \qquad (12)$$

Figure 2: Communication Model

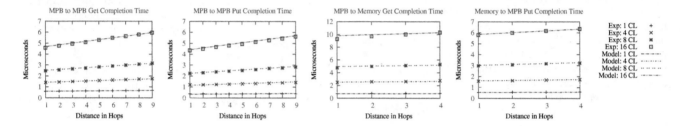

Figure 3: *get* and *put* performance (CL = Cache Line)

execute one memory transaction at a time: moving a message of m cache lines takes m times the time needed to move one cache line[4]. The latency is a bit lower, since it does not include the acknowledgment of the last cache line written to the remote MPB (Formulas 9 and 10).

3.1.4 Operation get

A *get* operation executed by core c reads data from some source and writes it to some destination: the source is an MPB, and destination is c's local MPB (Formula 11) or private off-chip memory (Formula 12). We denote by d^{src} the distance between the data and core c executing the operation, and by d^{dst} the distance between c and the MPB to which the data is written. If c moves data to its local MPB, then $d^{dst} = 1$. Otherwise, d^{dst} is the distance between c and the memory controller. In the case of a get operation, latency and completion time are equal.

3.2 Model validation

We perform a set of experiments to determine the value of the parameters we introduced and to validate our model. Experimental settings are detailed in Section 6. Figure 3 presents with dots the completion time of *put* and *get* operations from MPB to MPB or to private memory as a function of the distance for different message sizes. The parameter values obtained are presented in Table 1. The performance obtained from the model is represented by lines in Figure 3. It shows that our model precisely estimates the communication performance. Note that, for a given message size, the

performance difference between the 1-hop distance (which means accessing the MPB of the other core on the same tile) and the 9-hop distance (maximum distance) is only 30%.

3.3 Contention issues

The proposed model assumes a contention-free execution. Bearing that in mind, we study contention on the SCC, to assess the validity domain of the model. We identify two possible sources of contention related to RMA communication: the NoC mesh and the MPBs. Generally speaking, concurrent accesses to the off-chip private memory could be another source of contention. However, in the configuration without shared memory, assumed throughout this paper, each core has one memory rank for itself and there is no measurable performance degradation even when the 48 cores are accessing their private portion of the off-chip memory at the same time [30].

To understand if the mesh could be subject to contention, we have run an experiment that highly loads one link. We selected the link between tile $(2, 2)$ and tile $(3, 2)$. To put a maximum stress on this link, all cores except the ones located on these two tiles are repeatedly getting 128 cache lines from one core in the third row of the mesh, but on the opposite side of the mesh compared to their own location. For instance, a core located on tile $(5, 1)$ gets data from tile $(0, 2)$. Because of X-Y routing, all data packets go through the link between tile $(2, 2)$ and tile $(3, 2)$. The measurement of a MPB-to-MPB *get* latency between tile $(2, 2)$ and tile $(3, 2)$ with the heavily loaded link did not show any performance drop, compared to the load-free *get* performance. This shows that, at the current scale, the network cannot be a source of contention.

---

[4]For this reason, we do not need to use the parameter g of the LogP model.

parameter	L^{hop}	o^{mpb}	o_w^{mem}	o_r^{mem}	o_{put}^{mpb}	o_{get}^{mpb}	o_{put}^{mem}	o_{get}^{mem}
value	$0.005~\mu s$	$0.126~\mu s$	$0.461~\mu s$	$0.208~\mu s$	$0.069~\mu s$	$0.33~\mu s$	$0.19~\mu s$	$0.095~\mu s$

Table 1: Parameters of our model

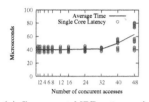
(a) Concurrent MPB *get* completion time (128 cache lines)

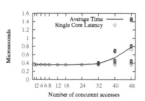
(b) Concurrent MPB *put* completion time (1 cache line)

Figure 4: MPB contention evaluation

Contention could also arise from multiple cores concurrently accessing the same MPB. To evaluate this, we have run a test where cores are getting data from the MPB of core 0 (on tile (0,0)), and another test where cores are putting data into the MPB of core 0. For these tests, we select two representative scenarios of the access patterns in our broadcast algorithm presented in Section 4: parallel *gets* of 128 cache lines and parallel *puts* of 1 cache line. Note that having parallel *puts* of a large number of cache lines is not a realistic scenario since it would result in several cores writing to the same location. Figure 4a shows the impact on latency when increasing the number of cores executing *get* in parallel. Figure 4b shows the same results for parallel *put* operations. The x axis represents the number of cores executing *get* or *put* at the same time. The results are the average values over millions of iterations. In addition to the average latency, the performance of each core is displayed to better highlight the impact of contention (small circles in Figure 4). When all 48 cores are executing *get* or *put* in parallel, contention can be clearly noticed. In this case, the slowest core is more than two times slower than the fastest one for *get*, and more than four times slower for a *put* operation. Moreover we observed non-deterministic overhead after the contention threshold, by running the same experiment on other cores than core 0. It can be noticed that contention does not equally affect all cores, which makes it hard to model.

These experiments indicate that MPB contention has to be taken into account in the design of algorithms for collective operations. They show that up to 24 cores accessing the same MPB do not create any measurable contention. Next we present a broadcast algorithm that takes advantage of this property.

4. RMA-BASED BROADCAST

This section describes the main principles of OC-Bcast, our algorithm for on-chip broadcast. The full description of the algorithm, including the pseudocode, is provided in the full version of the paper.

4.1 Principle of the broadcast algorithm

To simplify the presentation, we assume first that messages to be broadcast fit in the MPB. This assumption is later removed. The core idea of the algorithm is to take advantage of the parallelism that can be provided by the RMA operations. When a core c wants to send message *msg* to a set of cores *cSet*, it *puts msg* in its local MPB, so that all the cores in *cSet* can *get* the data from there. If all *gets* are issued in parallel, this can dramatically reduce the latency of the operation compared to a solution where, for instance, the sender c would *put msg* sequentially in the MPB of each core in *cSet*. However, having all cores in *cSet* executing *get* in parallel may lead to contention, as observed in Section 3.3. To avoid contention, we limit the number of parallel *get* operations to some number k, and base our broadcast algorithm on a k-ary tree; the core broadcasting a message is the root of this tree. In the tree, each core is in charge of providing the data to its k children: the k children *get* the data in parallel from the MPB of their parent.

Note that the k children need to be notified that a message is available in their parent's MPB. This is done using a flag in the MPB of each of the k children. The flag, called *notifyFlag*, is set by the parent using *put* once the message is available in the parent's MPB. Setting a flag involves writing a very small amount of data to remote MPBs, but nevertheless sequential notification could impair performance especially if k is large. Thus, instead of having a parent setting the flag of its k children sequentially, we introduce a binary tree for notification to increase the parallelism. This choice is not arbitrary: It can be shown analytically that a binary tree provides the lowest notification latency, when compared to trees of higher output degrees. Figure 5 illustrates the k-ary tree used for message propagation, and the binary trees used for notification. C_0 is the root of the message propagation tree; the subtree with root C_1 is shown. Node C_0 notifies its children using the binary notification tree shown at the right of Figure 5. Node C_1 notifies its children using the binary notification tree, as depicted at the bottom of Figure 5.

Apart from the *notifyFlag* used to inform the children about message availability in their parent's MPB, another flag is needed to notify the parent that the children have got the message (in order to free the MPB). For this we use k flags in the parent MPB, called *doneFlag*, each set by one of the k children.

To summarize, considering the general case of an intermediate core, *i.e.*, the core that is neither the root nor a leaf, a core is performing the following steps. Once it has been notified that a new chunk is available in the MPB of its parent C_s: (i) it notifies its children, if any, in the notification tree of C_s; (ii) it gets the chunk in its own MPB; (iii) it sets its *doneFlag* in the MPB of C_s; (iv) it notifies its children in its own notification tree, if any; (v) it gets the chunk from its MPB to its off-chip private memory.

Finding an efficient k-ary tree taking into account the topology of the NoC is a complex problem [4] and it is orthogonal to the design of OC-Bcast. It is outside the scope of this paper since our goal is to show the advantage of using RMA to implement broadcast. In the rest of this paper,

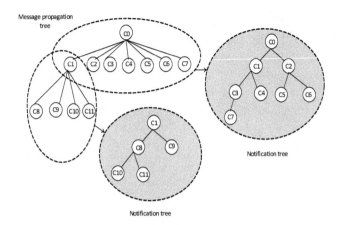

Figure 5: k-ary message propagation tree ($k = 7$) **and binary notification trees.**

we assume that the tree is built using a simple algorithm based on the core ids: Assuming that s is the id of the root and P the total number of processes, the children of core i are the cores with ids ranging from $(s + ik + 1)\,mod\,P$ to $(s + (i+1)k)\,mod\,P$. Figure 5 shows the tree obtained for $s = 0$, $P = 12$ and $k = 7$.

4.2 Handling large messages

Broadcasting a message larger than an MPB can easily be handled by decomposing the large message in chunks of MPB size, and broadcasting these chunks one after the other. This can be done using pipelining along the propagation tree, from the root to the leaves.

We can further improve the efficiency of the algorithm (throughput and latency) by using a double-buffering technique, similar to the one used for point-to-point communication in the iRCCE library [8]. Up to now, we have considered messages split into chunks of MPB size,[5] which allows an MPB buffer to store only one message chunk. With double-buffering, messages are split into chunks of half the MPB size, which allows an MPB buffer to store two message chunks. The benefit of double-buffering is easy to understand. Consider message msg split into chunks ck_1 to ck_n being copied from the MPB buffer of core c to the MPB buffer of core c'. Without double buffering, core c copies ck_i to its MPB in a step r; core c' gets ck_i in step $r + 1$; core c copies to its MPB ck_{i+1} in step $r + 2$; etc. If each of these steps takes δ time units, the total time to transfer the message is roughly $2n\delta$. With double buffering, the message chunks are two times smaller and so, message msg is split into chunks ck_1 to ck_{2n}. In a step r, core c can copy ck_{i+1} to the MPB while core c' gets ck_i. If each of these steps takes $\delta/2$ time units, the total time is roughly only $n\delta$.

5. ANALYTICAL EVALUATION

We analytically compare OC-Bcast with two state-of-the-art algorithms based on two-sided communication: binomial tree and *scatter-allgather*. We consider their implementations from the RCCE_comm library [7]. RCKMPI [28] uses the same algorithms, but still keeps their original MPICH2

---

[5]Of course, some MPB space needs to be allocated to the flags.

---

implementation, not optimized for the SCC. Also, our experiments have confirmed that RCCE_comm currently performs better than RCKMPI. Thus, we have chosen to conduct the analysis using RCCE_comm, as the fastest available implementation of collectives on the SCC, to the best of our knowledge.

To highlight the most important properties, we divide the analysis into two parts: latency of small messages (OC-Bcast vs. binomial tree) and throughput for large messages (OC-Bcast vs. *scatter-allgather*). The analysis is based on the model introduced in Section 3. For a better understanding of the presented results, first we give some necessary implementation details.

5.1 Implementation details

Both OC-Bcast and the *RCCE_comm* library use flags allocated in the MPBs to implement synchronization between the cores. SCC guarantees read/write atomicity on 32B cache lines. So, allocating one cache line per flag is enough to ensure atomicity (no additional mechanism such as locks is needed). In the modeling of the algorithms we assume that no time elapses between setting the flag (by one core) and checking that the flag is set (by the other core). OC-Bcast requires $k + 1$ flags per core. The rest of the MPB can be used for the message payload. For this, OC-Bcast uses two buffers of $M_{oc} = 96$ cache lines each. RCCE_comm, which is based on RCCE, uses a payload buffer of $M_{rcce} = 251$ cache lines. Since topology issues are not discussed in the paper, we simply consider an average distance $d^{mpb} = 1$ for accessing remote MPBs, and an average distance $d^{mem} = 1$ for accessing the off-chip memory.

5.2 Latency of short messages

We define the latency of the broadcast primitive as the time elapsed between the call of the broadcast function by the source, and the time at which the message is available at all cores (including the source), i.e., when the last core returns from the function. The analytically computed latency for small messages on the SCC is shown in Figure 6. For OC-Bcast, different values of k are given ($k = 2$, $k = 7$, $k = 47$). Note that OC-Bcast with $k = 7$ provides the best trade-off between latency and throughput according to our analysis. Although the characteristics of the SCC allow us to increase k up to 24 without experiencing measurable contention (as discussed in Section 3), the same tree depth is reached already with $k = 7$. As we can see, OC-Bcast significantly outperforms the binomial tree algorithm. The difference increases as the message size increases.

The improvement of OC-Bcast over the binomial tree algorithm is a direct consequence of using RMA. To clarify this, we now derive the formulas used to obtain the data in Figure 6. For the sake of simplicity, we ignore notification costs here and concentrate only on the critical path of data movement in the algorithms. Figure 7 summarizes the simplified formulas, whereas the complete formulas are given in the full version of the paper.

5.2.1 Latency of OC-Bcast

For OC-Bcast, the critical path of data movement is expressed as follows. Consider a message of size $m \le M_{oc}$ to be broadcast by some core c. Core c first puts the message in its MPB, which takes $C_{put}^{mem}(m)$ time to complete. Then, depending on k, there might be multiple intermediate nodes

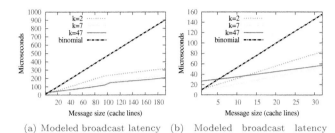

(a) Modeled broadcast latency   (b) Modeled broadcast latency (zoom-in)

Figure 6: Broadcast algorithms: analytical latency comparison. Legend: k=x, OC-Bcast with the corresponding k; binomial, RCCE_comm binomial.

before the message reaches the leaves. For P cores and a k-ary tree, there are $O(log_k P)$ levels of intermediate nodes. At each intermediate level, the cores copy the message from their parent's MPB to their own MPB in parallel, which takes $C_{get}^{mpb}(m)$ time to complete. Note that after copying, each node has to get the message to its private memory, but this operation is not on the critical path. Finally, the leaves copy the message, first to their MPB ($C_{get}^{mpb}(m)$) and then to the off-chip private memory ($C_{get}^{mem}(m)$). Therefore, the total latency is given by Formula 13 in Figure 7.

5.2.2 Latency of the two-sided binomial tree

The binomial tree broadcast algorithm is based on a binary recursive tree. The set of nodes is divided into two subsets of $\lfloor \frac{P}{2} \rfloor$ and $\lceil \frac{P}{2} \rceil$ nodes. The root, belonging to one of the subsets, sends the message to one node from the other subset. Then, broadcast is recursively called on both subsets. Obviously, the formed tree has $O(log_2 P)$ levels and in each of them the whole message is sent between the pairs of nodes. A send/receive operation pair involves a *put* by the sender and a *get* by the receiver, so the total latency of the algorithm is $O(log_2 P) \cdot (C_{put}^{mem}(m) + C_{get}^{mem}(m))$. However, note that after receiving the broadcast message, a node keeps sending it to other nodes in every subsequent iteration. Therefore, if the message is small, we can assume that it will be available in the core's L1 cache, which reduces the cost of the *put* operation. We approximate reading from the L1 cache with zero cost. With this, we get Formula 14.

5.2.3 Latency comparison

Now we can directly compare the analytical expressions for the two broadcast algorithms. In Formula 13, which represents the latency of OC-Bcast, there are only two off-chip memory operations ($C_{r/w}^{mem}$) on the critical path for one chunk, regardless of the number of cores P. This is not the case for the binomial algorithm, represented by Formula 14. Moreover, as k increases, the number of MPB-to-MPB copy operations reduces for OC-Bcast.

The gain of OC-Bcast increases further when increasing the message size because of double buffering and pipelining. It can be observed in Figure 6a that the slope changes for messages larger than $M_{OC-Bcast}$ (96 cache lines). In Figure 6b, we can notice that OC-Bcast-47 is the slowest for very small message in spite of having only two levels in the data propagation tree (the root and its 47 children). The reason is that a large value of k increases the cost of polling. For

$k = 47$, the root has 47 flags to poll before it can free its MPB.

5.3 Throughput for large messages

Now we consider messages large enough to fill the propagation tree pipeline used by OC-Bcast. For such messages, every core executes a loop, where one chunk is processed in each iteration. We compare OC-Bcast with the RCCE_comm *scatter-allgather* algorithm.

Table 2 gives the throughput based on the analytical model. The same values of k are considered for OC-Bcast as in the latency analysis. Regardless of the choice of k, the throughput is almost three times better than the one provided by two-sided *scatter-allgather*. To understand this gain, we again compute the critical path of the message payload. As in the latency analysis, we derive simplified formulas (Figure 7), and provide complete formulas in the full version of the paper. To simplify the modeling, we assume a message of size $P \cdot M_{oc}$. With OC-Bcast, such a message is transferred in P chunks of size M_{oc}. *Scatter-allgather* transfers the same message by dividing it into P slices of size M_{oc}.

5.3.1 Throughput of OC-Bcast

To express the critical path of data movement of OC-Bcast, we need to distinguish between the root and the other nodes (intermediate nodes and leaves). The root repeatedly moves new chunks from its private off-chip memory to its MPB, which takes $C_{put}^{mem}(M_{oc})$ for each chunk. The other nodes repeat two operations: First, they copy a chunk from the parent's MPB to their own MPB, and then copy the same chunk from the MPB to their private memory, which gives the completion time of $C_{get}^{mpb}(M_{oc}) + C_{get}^{mem}(M_{oc})$. The throughput is determined by the throughput of the slowest node. For the parameter values valid on the SCC, the root is always faster than the other nodes, so the throughput of OC-Bcast (in cache lines per second) is expressed by Formula 15. Note that the peak throughput is not a function of k. This is because we assume that the message is large enough to fill the whole pipeline.

5.3.2 Throughput of two-sided scatter-allgether

Scatter-allgather has two phases. During the *scatter* phase, the message is divided into P equal slices of size M_{oc} (recall that the message size is fixed to $P \cdot M_{oc}$). Each core then receives one slice of the original message. The second phase of the algorithm is *allgather*, during which a node should obtain the remaining $P - 1$ slices of the message. To implement *allgather*, the Bruck algorithm [6] is used: At each step, core i sends to core $i - 1$ the slices it received in the previous step.

Now we consider the completion time of the two phases of the *scatter-allgather* algorithm. The *scatter* phase is done using a binary recursive tree, similar to the one used by the binomial algorithm. The difference is that in this case we transfer only a part of the message in each step. In the end, the root has to send out each of the P slices but its own, so the critical path of this step consists of $P - 1$ send/receive operations, which gives the completion time of $(P - 1)(C_{put}^{mem}(M_{oc}) + C_{get}^{mem}(M_{oc}))$. The allgather phase consists of $P - 1$ exchange rounds. In each round, core i sends one slice to core $i - 1$ and receives one slice from core $i + 1$. Thus, there are two send/receive operations between pairs of processes in each round, so this phase takes $2(P -$

$$L_{OC-Bcast}^{critical}(P,m,k) = C_{put}^{mem}(m) + O(log_k P) \cdot C_{get}^{mpb}(m) + C_{get}^{mem}(m)$$

$$= m \cdot \left(O(log_k P) \cdot (C_r^{mpb} + C_w^{mpb}) + C_r^{mem} + C_w^{mem} \right) \quad (13)$$

$$L_{binomial}^{critical}(P,m) = O(log_2 P) \cdot (m \cdot C_w^{mpb} + C_{get}^{mem}(m))$$

$$= m \cdot \left(O(log_2 P) \cdot (C_r^{mpb} + C_w^{mpb} + C_w^{mem}) + C_r^{mem} \right) \quad (14)$$

$$B_{OC-Bcast} = \frac{M_{oc}}{C_{get}^{mpb}(M_{oc}) + C_{get}^{mem}(M_{oc})} = \frac{1}{2C_r^{mpb} + C_w^{mpb} + C^{mem}} \quad (15)$$

$$B_{scatter\_allgather} = \frac{P \cdot M_{oc}}{P \cdot (C_{put}^{mem}(M_{oc}) + C_{get}^{mem}(M_{oc})) + (2P-3)(M_{oc} \cdot C_w^{mpb} + C_{get}^{mem}(M_{oc}))}$$

$$\approx \frac{1}{3C_r^{mpb} + 3C_w^{mpb} + C_r^{mem} + 3C_w^{mem}} \quad (16)$$

Figure 7: Latency and Throughput Model for Broadcast Operations

1)$(C_{put}^{mem}(M_{oc}) + C_{get}^{mem}(M_{oc}))$ to complete. As with the binomial tree, taking the existance of the caches into account gives a more accurate model. Note, however, that this holds only for the allgather phase. Finally, the completion times of the two phases are added up. There is no pipelining in this algorithm, so the throughput can be easily expressed as a reciprocial value of the computed completion time on the root. Formula 16 presents the modeled throughput of the two-sided *scatter-allgather* algorithm (in cache lines per second).

5.3.3 Throughput comparison

The additional terms in Formula 16 compared to Formula 15 explain the performance difference in Table 2, and show the advantage of designing a broadcast protocol based on one-sided operations: The number of write accesses to the MPBs and to the off-chip memory (C_w^{mpb} and C_w^{mem}) with OC-Bcast is three times lower than that of the *scatter-allgather* algorithm based on two-sided communication. The number of read accesses is also reduced.

5.4 Discussion

The presented analysis shows that our broadcast implementation based on one-sided operations brings considerable performance benefits, in terms of both latency and throughput. Note, however, that OC-Bcast is not the only possible design of RMA-based broadcast. Our goal in this paper is not to find the most efficient algorithm and prove its optimality, but to highlight the potential for exploiting parallelism using RMA-based approach. Indeed, a good example of another possible broadcast implementation is adapting the two-sided *scatter-allgather* algorithm to use the one-sided primitives available on the SCC.

Furthermore, some simple, yet effective optimizations can be applied to OC-Bcast to make it even faster. For instance, a leaf in a broadcast tree does not need to copy the data to its MPB, but directly to the off-chip private memory. Similarly, we could take advantage of the fact that there are two cores accessing the same physical MPB, to have less data copying. However, we have chosen not to include these optimizations because they would result in having to deal with many special cases, which would likely obfuscate the main point of the presented work.

6. EXPERIMENTAL EVALUATION

In this section we evaluate the performance of OC-Bcast on Intel SCC and compare it with both the binomial and the *scatter-allgather* broadcast of RCCE_comm [7].

6.1 Setup

The experiments have been done using the default settings for the SCC: 533 MHz tile frequency, 800 MHz mesh and DRAM frequency and the standard LUT entries. We use the sccKit version 1.4.1.3, running a custom version of sccLinux, based on Linux 2.6.32.24-generic. As already mentioned in the previous section, we fix the chunk size used by OC-Bcast to 96 cache lines, which leaves enough space for flags (for any choice of k). The presented experiments use core 0 as the source. Selecting another core as the source gives similar results. A message is broadcast from the private memory of core 0 to the private memory of all other cores. The results are the average values over 10'000 broadcasts, discarding the first 1'000 results. For time measurement, we use global counters accessible by all cores on the SCC, which means that the timestamps obtained by different cores are directly comparable. The latency is defined as in Section 5. To avoid cache effects in repeated broadcasts, we preallocate a large array and in every broadcast we operate on a different (currently uncached) offset inside the array.

6.2 Evaluation results

We have tested the algorithms with message sizes ranging from 1 cache line (32 bytes) to 32'768 cache lines (1 MiB). As in Section 5, we first focus on the latency of short messages, and then analyze the throughput of large messages. Regarding the binomial tree and *scatter-allgather* algorithms, our experiments have confirmed that the former performs better with small messages, whereas the latter is a better fit for large messages. Therefore, we compare OC-Bcast only with the better one for a given message size.

6.2.1 Latency of small messages

Figure 8a shows the latency of messages of size $m \leq 2M_{OC-Bcast}$. Comparing the results with Figure 6a shows the accuracy of our analytical evaluation, and confirms the performance increase. Even for messages of one cache line, OC-Bcast with $k = 7$ provides 27% improvement compared

Algorithm	OC-Bcast, k=2	OC-Bcast, k=7	OC-Bcast, k=47	scatter-allgather
Throughput (MB/s)	35.22	34.30	35.88	13.38

Table 2: Broadcast algorithms: analytical comparison of throughput

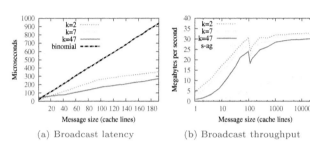

(a) Broadcast latency   (b) Broadcast throughput

Figure 8: Experimental comparison of broadcast algorithms. Legend: k=x, OC-Bcast with the corresponding value of k; binomial, RCCE_comm binomial; s-ag, RCCE_comm scatter-allgather.

to the binomial tree ($16.6\mu s$ vs. $21.6\mu s$). As expected, the difference grows with the message size, since a larger message implies more off-chip memory accesses in the RCCE_comm algorithms, but not in OC-Bcast. It can also be noticed that large values of k help improving the latency in OC-Bcast by reducing the depth of the tree. For message size between 96 and 192 cache lines, the latency of OC-Bcast with $k = 7$ is around 25% better than with $k = 2$.

Another result worth mentioning is the relation between the curves representing $k = 7$ and $k = 47$. Namely, we can see that they almost completely overlap in Figure 8a, whereas there is a more significant difference indicated by the analytical evaluation (Figure 6a). This can be attributed to MPB contention – recall that too many parallel accesses to the same MPB can impair the performance, as pointed out in Section 3.

6.2.2 Throughput for large messages

The results of the throughput evaluation are given in Figure 8b (note that the x-axis is logarithmic). The peak performance is very close to the results presented in Table 2: OC-Bcast gives an almost threefold throughput increase compared to the two-sided *scatter-allgather* algorithm. The OC-Bcast performance drop for a message of 97 cache lines is due to the chunk size. Recall that the size of a chunk in OC-Bcast is 96 cache lines. A message of 97 cache lines is divided into a 96 cache lines chunk and 1 cache line chunk. The second chunk is then limiting the throughput. For large messages, this effect becomes negligible since there is always at most one non-full chunk.

It can be noticed that the only significant difference with respect to the analytical predictions is for OC-Bcast with $k = 47$ (the throughput is about 16% lower than predicted). Once again, MPB contention is one of the sources of the observed performance degradation. This confirms that large values of k might be inappropriate, especially at large scale, since the linear gain in parallelism could be paid by an exponential loss related to contention.

6.3 Discussion

The expected performance based on the model is slightly better than the results we obtain through the experiments. The main reason is that in the analytical evaluation, we assumed a distance of one hop for all *put* and *get* operations: This is physically not possible on the SCC no matter what tree generation strategy is used. However, note that the measured values are still very close to the computed ones.

7. CONCLUSION

OC-Bcast is a pipelined k-ary tree broadcast algorithm based on one-sided communication. It is designed to leverage the inherent parallelism of on-chip RMA in many-cores. Experiments on the SCC show that it outperforms the state-of-the-art broadcast algorithms on this platform. OC-Bcast provides around 3 times better peak throughput and improves latency by at least 27%. An analysis using a LogP-based model shows that this performance gain is mainly due to a limited number of off-chip data movements on the critical path of the operation: one-sided operations allow to take full advantage of the on-chip MPBs. These results show that hardware-specific features should be taken into account to design efficient collective operations for message-passing many-core chips, such as the Intel SCC.

The work presented in this paper considers the SPMD programming model. Our ongoing work includes extending OC-Bcast to handle the MPMD programming model by leveraging parallel inter-core interrupts. Many-core operating systems [3] are an interesting use-case for such a primitive. We also plan to extend our approach to other collective operations and integrate them in an MPI library, so we can analyze the overall performance gain in parallel applications.

8. ACKNOWLEDGEMENTS

We would like to thank Martin Biely, Žarko Milošević and Nuno Santos for their useful comments. Thanks also to Ciprian Seiculescu for helping us understand the behaviour of the SCC NoC. We are also thankful for the help provided by the Intel MARC Community.

9. REFERENCES

[1] G. Almási, P. Heidelberger, C. J. Archer, X. Martorell, C. C. Erway, J. E. Moreira, B. Steinmacher-Burow, and Y. Zheng. Optimization of MPI collective communication on BlueGene/L systems. In *Proceedings of the 19th annual international conference on Supercomputing*, ICS '05, pages 253–262, 2005.

[2] I. T. Association. *InfiniBand Architecture Specification: Release 1.0*. InfiniBand Trade Association, 2000.

[3] A. Baumann, P. Barham, P.-E. Dagand, T. Harris, R. Isaacs, S. Peter, T. Roscoe, A. Schüpbach, and A. Singhania. The multikernel: a new OS architecture for scalable multicore systems. In *Proceedings of the*

ACM SIGOPS 22nd symposium on Operating systems principles, SOSP '09, pages 29–44, 2009.

[4] O. Beaumont, L. Marchal, and Y. Robert. Broadcast Trees for Heterogeneous Platforms. In *Proceedings of the 19th IEEE International Parallel and Distributed Processing Symposium*, IPDPS '05, pages 80–92, 2005.

[5] S. Borkar. Thousand core chips: a technology perspective. In *Proceedings of the 44th annual Design Automation Conference*, DAC '07, pages 746–749, 2007.

[6] J. Bruck, C.-T. Ho, E. Upfal, S. Kipnis, and D. Weathersby. Efficient Algorithms for All-to-All Communications in Multiport Message-Passing Systems. *IEEE Transactions on Parallel and Distributed Systems*, 8:1143–1156, November 1997.

[7] E. Chan. RCCE comm: A Collective Communication Library for the Intel Single-chip Cloud Computer. http://communities.intel.com/docs/DOC-5663, 2010.

[8] C. Clauss, S. Lankes, J. Galowicz, and T. Bemmerl. iRCCE: a non-blocking communication extension to the RCCE communication library for the Intel Single-chip Cloud Computer. http://communities. intel. com/docs/DOC-6003, 2011.

[9] D. Culler, R. Karp, D. Patterson, A. Sahay, K. E. Schauser, E. Santos, R. Subramonian, and T. von Eicken. LogP: Towards a Realistic Model of Parallel Computation. In *Proceedings of the fourth ACM SIGPLAN symposium on Principles and practice of parallel programming*, PPOPP '93, pages 1–12, 1993.

[10] D. E. Culler, L. T. Liu, R. P. Martin, and C. O. Yoshikawa. Assessing Fast Network Interfaces. In *IEEE Micro*, pages 35–43, Feb. 1996.

[11] E. Gabriel, G. E. Fagg, G. Bosilca, T. Angskun, J. J. Dongarra, J. M. Squyres, V. Sahay, P. Kambadur, B. Barrett, A. Lumsdaine, R. H. Castain, D. J. Daniel, R. L. Graham, and T. S. Woodall. Open MPI: Goals, concept, and design of a next generation MPI implementation. In *Proceedings, 11th European PVM/MPI Users' Group Meeting*, pages 97–104, Budapest, Hungary, September 2004.

[12] R. Gupta, P. Balaji, D. K. Panda, and J. Nieplocha. Efficient Collective Operations Using Remote Memory Operations on VIA-Based Clusters. In *Proceedings of the 17th International Symposium on Parallel and Distributed Processing*, IPDPS '03, pages 46–62, 2003.

[13] T. Hoefler, C. Siebert, and W. Rehm. A practically constant-time MPI Broadcast Algorithm for large-scale InfiniBand Clusters with Multicast. In *Proceedings of the 21st IEEE International Parallel & Distributed Processing Symposium*, IPDPS '07, page 232, 2007.

[14] J. Howard, S. Dighe, Y. Hoskote, S. Vangal, D. Finan, G. Ruhl, D. Jenkins, H. Wilson, N. Borkar, G. Schrom, and et al. A 48-Core IA-32 message-passing processor with DVFS in 45nm CMOS. In *2010 IEEE International SolidState Circuits Conference*, pages 108–109. IEEE, 2010.

[15] P. Kermani and L. Kleinrock. Virtual cut-through: A new computer communication switching technique. *Computer Networks*, 3(4):267–286, 1979.

[16] P. Kogge et al. Exascale Computing Study: Technology Challenges in Achieving Exascale Systems. Technical report, DARPA, 2008.

[17] J. Liu, A. R. Mamidala, and D. K. Panda. Fast and Scalable MPI-Level Broadcast Using InfiniBand's Hardware Multicast Supportsch. In *Proceedings of the 18th International Symposium on Parallel and Distributed Processing*, IPDPS '04, page 10, 2004.

[18] J. Liu, J. Wu, S. P. Kini, P. Wyckoff, and D. K. Panda. High performance RDMA-based MPI implementation over InfiniBand. In *Proceedings of the 17th annual international conference on Supercomputing*, ICS '03, pages 295–304, 2003.

[19] T. Mattson and R. Van Der Wijngaart. RCCE: a Small Library for Many-Core Communication. http://techresearch.intel.com, 2010.

[20] T. G. Mattson, R. Van der Wijngaart, and M. Frumkin. Programming the Intel 80-core network-on-a-chip terascale processor. In *Proceedings of the 2008 ACM/IEEE conference on Supercomputing*, SC '08, pages 38:1–38:11, 2008.

[21] MPI Forum. MPI2: Extensions to the Message-Passing Interface. www.mpi-forum.org, 1997.

[22] T. Preud'homme, J. Sopena, G. Thomas, and B. Folliot. BatchQueue: Fast and Memory-Thrifty Core to Core Communication. In *Proceedings of the 2010 22nd International Symposium on Computer Architecture and High Performance Computing*, SBAC-PAD '10, pages 215–222, 2010.

[23] R. Rotta. On efficient message passing on the intel scc. In *Proceedings of the 3rd MARC Symposium*, pages 53–58, 2011.

[24] M. Shroff and R. Van De Geijn. CollMark: MPI collective communication benchmark. In *International Conference on Supercomputing 2000*, page 10, 1999.

[25] S. Sur, U. K. R. Bondhugula, A. Mamidala, H. W. Jin, and D. K. Panda. High performance RDMA based all-to-all broadcast for infiniband clusters. In *Proceedings of the 12th international conference on High Performance Computing*, HiPC'05, pages 148–157, 2005.

[26] R. Thakur, R. Rabenseifner, and W. Gropp. Optimization of Collective Communication Operations in MPICH. *IJHPCA*, 19(1):49–66, 2005.

[27] J. Torrellas. Architectures for Extreme-Scale Computing. *Computer*, 42(11):28–35, Nov. 2009.

[28] I. A. C. Ureña, M. Riepen, and M. Konow. RCKMPI - lightweight MPI implementation for intel's single-chip cloud computer (SCC). In *Proceedings of the 18th European MPI Users' Group conference on Recent advances in the message passing interface*, EuroMPI'11, pages 208–217, 2011.

[29] R. F. van der Wijngaart, T. G. Mattson, and W. Haas. Light-weight communications on Intel's single-chip cloud computer processor. *ACM SIGOPS Operating Systems Review*, 45(1):73–83, Feb. 2011.

[30] M. W. van Tol, R. Bakker, M. Verstraaten, C. Grelck, and C. R. Jesshope. Efficient Memory Copy Operations on the 48-core Intel SCC Processor. In *Proceedings of the 3rd MARC Symposium*, pages 13–18, 2011.

The Impact of the Power Law Exponent on the Behavior of a Dynamic Epidemic Type Process

Robert Elsässer
University of Paderborn
Institute for Computer Science
Fürstenallee 11
33102 Paderborn, Germany
elsa@upb.de

Adrian Ogierman
University of Paderborn
Institute for Computer Science
Fürstenallee 11
33102 Paderborn, Germany
adriano@upb.de

ABSTRACT

Epidemic processes are widely used to design efficient distributed algorithms with applications in various research fields. In this paper, we consider a dynamic epidemic process in a certain (idealistic) urban environment modeled by a complete graph. The epidemic is spread among n agents, which move from one node to another according to a power law distribution that describes the so called attractiveness of the corresponding locations in the urban environment. If two agents meet at some node, then a possible infection may be transmitted from one agent to the other.

We analyze two different scenarios. In the first case we assume that the attractiveness of the nodes follows a power law distribution with some exponent less than 3, as observed in real world examples. Then, we show that even if each agent may spread the disease for $f(n)$ time steps, where $f(n) = o(\log n)$ is a (slowly) growing function, at least a small (but still polynomial) number of agents remains uninfected and the epidemic is stopped after a logarithmic number of rounds. In the second scenario we assume that the power law exponent increases to some large constant, which can be seen as an implication of certain countermeasures against the spreading process. Then, we show that if each agent is allowed to spread the disease for a constant number of time steps, the epidemic will only affect a polylogarithmic number of agents and the disease is stopped after $(\log \log n)^{\mathcal{O}(1)}$ steps. Our results explain possible courses of a disease, and point out why cost-efficient countermeasures may reduce the number of total infections from a high percentage of the population to a negligible fraction.

Categories and Subject Descriptors

F.0 [**Theory of Computation**]: General; F.2.2 [**Nonnumerical Algorithms and Problems**]: Computations on discrete structures; G.3 [**Mathematics of Computing**]: Probability and statistics; C.2.0 [**Computer-communication networks**]: General

Permission to make digital or hard copies of all or part of this work for personal or classroom use is granted without fee provided that copies are not made or distributed for profit or commercial advantage and that copies bear this notice and the full citation on the first page. To copy otherwise, to republish, to post on servers or to redistribute to lists, requires prior specific permission and/or a fee.
SPAA'12, June 25–27, 2012, Pittsburgh, Pennsylvania, USA.
Copyright 2012 ACM 978-1-4503-1213-4/12/06 ...$10.00.

General Terms

Algorithms, Human Factors, Theory

Keywords

Epidemic algorithms, power law, disease spreading

1. INTRODUCTION

In distributed computing epidemic processes are one of the most powerful paradigms with various applications in e.g. replicated data-bases [10], peer-to-peer communication [23], or wireless sensor networks [35]. A fundamental problem in this context is the dissemination of information in large networks. Here, the goal is to optimize the speed of the process, the amount of informed nodes, and the number of message transmissions on the edges of the network [24]. However, if we assume that a malicious piece of information spreads among the participants of a network, such as a computer virus or an epidemic disease, then the goal is to stop the spreading process before a certain fraction of the nodes becomes informed. In this paper, we examine a natural dissemination process of a malicious piece of information in a simple dynamic environment. In particular, we analyze the impact of certain parameters on the spreading behavior, and show that slight changes in the behavior of the network participants imply huge changes w.r.t. the final size of informed nodes.

Formally, we consider an epidemic disseminated by a number of agents which move around on a fixed network. A so called infected agent forwards the disease to all neighbors in his vicinity. Since in each step all agents move from a node to another, the set of neighbors of an agent changes over time. The nodes of the network are called cells, which model so called locations/targets for the agents. Then, the neighbors of an agent at some time step are the agents situated at his current location. Clearly, different movement patterns result in different dissemination characteristics. In order to determine the impact of these parameter settings on the spread of the epidemic, we mainly consider two distinct models w.r.t. the agents' movement behavior.

1.1 Motivation: Social Behavior vs. Disease Spreading

For our motivation we refer to the widely studied field of epidemic diseases in an urban area, and consider two different society models which we call the *fearless* and the *hypochondriacal society*, respectively. In the fearless society, the individuals do not change their behavior if an epidemic outbreak occurs. The question is whether this implies that the disease infects the whole population. In the hypochondriacal society, if an epidemic outbreak occurs, then the individuals are willing to spend time and money to protect themselves. Here, the question is whether certain changes in the individuals' behavior can significantly reduce the spread of the disease among the population.

How can I protect myself if an epidemic outbreak occurs? This question concerns us all. Individuals protect themselves by avoiding contacts to infected people, companies exploit all possibilities to keep their employees viable, and governments try to ensure the public health and safety. However, in all these cases one must take into account that we live in a mobile society, and prohibiting personal contacts between individuals - which define a so called *social interaction network* - is not desirable.

Mobility seems to be one of the major reasons for the spread of epidemics. Nowadays, even the mobility within a single city is extremely high [15]. However, in such a dynamic environment mechanisms that are able to control the spread of epidemics are quite expensive. Protection systems and an enormous amount of mostly expensive antidotes are needed, which may not be available when a yet unknown disease appears. Moreover, the immunization of the majority of the population is most likely not feasible.

Another source of protection may be the use of media to change the individuals' behavior. One can assume that in a modern city, individuals are well connected to various types of information sources such as newspaper, television, and the Internet. Since these powerful and effective tools are already established and often used, a government can easily warn the population. From this time on (for the duration of the epidemic) the majority of the informed people will act more carefully.

In the following we start by considering the fearless society model. Therefore we assume that no countermeasures are taken when an epidemic outbreak occurs. Then, the question is whether it is possible for the population of a large city to survive despite these circumstances. In the hypochondriacal society model we assume that certain (limited) countermeasures can be taken. First, the government is able to cure a certain number of individuals simultaneously. Furthermore, the health care system is capable of taking people into quarantine to protect the rest of the population, and the media is also omnipresent. Thus, a message communicated via newspaper, television, or the Internet will be received by the whole population within a short time. We include these countermeasures in our model, and analyze whether we obtain a positive impact on the embankment of an epidemic.

1.2 Related Work

In this subsection we provide an overview of the results which are closely related to our topic. For simplicity, we stick to the context of our motivation and the original terminology of the presented papers. However, these results can also be viewed in the general context of epidemic processes and algorithms.

The structure of this subsection is as follows. At the beginning we present a simple model which is used to describe an epidemic. Since movement is a key feature for us, this topic is described subsequently. Afterwards, we present some results considering countermeasures and awareness.

Then, we conclude by covering the importance of some parameters for the theoretical point of view as well as giving a brief overview regarding simulations in this field.

There is plenty of work considering epidemiological processes in different scenarios and on various networks. The simplest model of mathematical disease spreading is the so called SIR model (see e.g. [21, 32]). The population is divided into three categories: susceptible (S), i.e., all individuals which do not have the disease yet but can become infected, infective (I), i.e., the individuals which have the disease and can infect others, and recovered (R), i.e., all individuals which recovered and have permanent immunity (or have been removed from the system). Most papers model the spread of epidemics using a differential equation based on the assumption that any susceptible individual has uniform probability β to become infected from any infective individual. Furthermore, any infected player recovers at some stochastically constant rate γ.

This traditional (fully mixed) model can easily be generalized to a network. It has been observed that such a case can be modeled by bond percolation on the underlying graph [19, 31]. Callaway et al. [7] considered this model on graph classes constructed by the so called configuration model (i.e., a random graph with a given degree distribution). The SIR model has also been analyzed in some other scenarios, including various kinds of correlations between the rates of infection or the infectivity times, in networks with a more complex structure containing different types of vertices [31], or in graphs with correlations between the degrees of the vertices [29]. Interestingly, for certain graphs with a power law degree distribution, there is no constant threshold for the epidemic outbreak as long as the power law exponent is less than 3 [32] (which is the case in most real world networks, e.g. [14, 1, 3, 34]). If the network is embedded into a low dimensional space, or has high transitivity, then there might exist a non-zero threshold for certain types of correlations between vertices. However, none of the papers above considered the dynamic movement of individuals, which seems to be the main source of the spread of diseases in urban areas [13].

In [13], Eubank et al. modeled physical contact patterns, which result from movement of individuals between specific locations, by a dynamic bipartite graph. The graph is partitioned into two parts. The first part contains the people who carry out their daily activities moving between different locations. The other part represents the various locations in a certain city. There is an edge between two nodes, if the corresponding individual visits a certain location at a given time. Certainly, the graph changes dynamically at every time step.

Eubank et al. [13, 9] analyzed the corresponding network for Portland, Oregon. According to their study, the degrees of the nodes describing different locations follow a power law distribution with exponent around 2.8[1]. For many epidemics, transmission occurs between individuals being simultaneously at the same place, and then people's movement is mainly responsible for the spread of the disease.

The authors of [13] also considered different countermeasures in order to avoid an epidemic outbreak. They stated that early detection combined with targeted vaccination are effective ways of defense compared to mass vaccination of

---

[1]In [13] the degree represents the number of individuals visiting these places over a time period of 24 hours.

a population. However, it is often not possible to find the individuals having many acquaintances, and in many cases vaccinations cannot even be applied (e.g., SARS, or swine flu in its early stages).

Borgs et al. [6] focused on how to distribute antidote to control epidemics. The authors analyzed a variant of the contact process in the *susceptible-infected-susceptible (SIS) model* on a finite graph in which the cure rate is allowed to vary among the vertices. That is, the rate ρ_v at which an infected node v becomes healthy is proportional to the amount of antidote it receives, given a fixed amount of antidote $R = \sum_{x \in V} \rho_x$ for the whole network. The authors state that using contact tracing on a star would require a total amount of antidote which is super-linear in the number of vertices. Here, contact tracing on a graph means that the cure rate is adjusted to $\rho_v = \rho + \rho' d_v^*(t)$ at every time t, where $d_v^*(t)$ denotes the number of infected neighbors of v at time t and $\rho, \rho' > 0$ are some constants. However, setting ρ_v proportional to the degree requires an amount of antidote that scales only linearly with the number of vertices, even on general graphs, provided the average degree is bounded. On the other side, even if the underlying graph is an expander, curing proportional to the degree cannot reduce the needed amount of antidote by more than a constant factor.

However, in realistic scenarios one does not only consider the spreading process itself. In reality, we are influenced by many factors, e.g. the awareness about an epidemic. In [16], Funk et al. analyzed the spread of awareness on epidemic outbreaks. That is, the information about a disease is also spread in the network and has its own dynamic. In [16] the authors described the two spreading scenarios (awareness vs. disease) by the following model. Each individual has a level of awareness which depends on the number of hops the information has passed before arriving to this individual. This was combined with the traditional SIR model. It has been shown that in a well mixed population, the spread of awareness can result in a slower size of outbreak, however, it will not affect the epidemic threshold. Nevertheless, if the spread of information about a disease is considered as a local effect in the proximity of an outbreak, then awareness can completely stop the epidemic. Moreover, the impact of spreading awareness is even intensified if the social network of infections and informations overlap.

In [27] Liu et al. examined the influence of two parameters - the decay rate of the disease and the range a person can be infected in - on the spread of an epidemic in the urban environment of the Haizhu district of Guangzhou. The results imply the importance of both parameters. Especially the results of the distance parameter, which is influenced by peoples behavior, imply significant impact on the disease spreading if manipulated wisely.

Concerning mobility in a 2D field, Valler et al. [36] analyzed the epidemic threshold for a mobile ad-hoc network. They showed that if the connections between devices are given by a sequence of matrices $A_1, \ldots A_T$, then for $\lambda_S < 1$ no epidemic outbreak occurs, with high probability, where λ_S is the first eigenvalue of $\Pi_{i=1}^T (1 - \delta) I + \beta A_i$ with β and δ being the virus transmission probability and the virus death probability, respectively. They also approximated the epidemic threshold for different mobility models in a predefined 2D area, such as random walk, Levy flight, and random waypoint.

In addition to the papers described above, plenty of empirical work has also been done [4, 25, 26, 2, 5]. Two of the most popular approaches are the so called agent-based and structured meta-population-based, respectively (cf. [2, 22]). To combine the advantages of both systems, hybrid environments were implemented (e.g. [5]). Many of the models used in such simulations integrate different locations like schools, theaters, etc... An agent may or may not be infected depending on his own choices and the ones made by agents in his vicinity. Such agents may be defined very precisely, including e.g., race, gender, educational level, nutritional status, age, priority groups, participant class, etc. [25, 26]. Thus they may provide a huge amount of very detailed data. With such systems one was able to confirm the positive impact of non-pharmaceutical countermeasures [18], which is underpinned by examinations on real data (e.g. [28]).

1.3 Our Results

In our model we integrate the results of [13], and assume that every agent chooses a location in a step independently and uniformly at random according to a power law degree distribution. This is the first analytical result on an epidemic process in a dynamic scenario, where the impact of the power law distribution describing the attractiveness of the locations is considered. We present two main results.

First, we show that in the fearless society model a polynomial fraction of the agents remains uninfected even if they are allowed to transmit the infection for $o(\log n)$ time steps. That is, it is very unlikely for a (deadly) epidemic to wipe out the whole population. This holds due to the decreasing number of survivors and infected people over time. That is, the remaining population size is decreasing over time while the available space for such an individual is increasing. This implies an increasing probability for a healthy individual to avoid the infected ones (cf. Section 3.1). Additionally, this provides an analytical evidence for a conjecture expressed in a historical documentation about the plague in the mid ages [17].

Second, we show that in the *hypochondriacal society model* only $\log^{O(1)} n$ agents will be infected until the epidemic process is stopped. This is achieved within $\mathcal{O}((\log \log n)^4)$ time steps with probability $1 - o(1)$. Here, the agents are allowed to transmit the infection only for a constant number of time steps. Additionally, the power law exponent describing the attractiveness of all target places increases up to a large constant. In the context of our motivating example this can be interpreted as follows. The use of news services combined with an appropriate health care budget limits the number of infected persons to a negligible fraction. Due to the warnings, the population will act more carefully and thus the corresponding power law exponent increases. That is, a noticeable number of people avoid locations with plenty of individuals. Simultaneously, the number of accommodated persons in these locations decreases.

The main disadvantage of our model is that we do not take into account the personal preferences of different people, and we ignore any dependency between certain choices (e.g., a married couple is in many cases together at the same place). Nevertheless, since most of the above dependencies in the real world are positively correlated[2], the results should even

---

[2]That is, persons who meet at some place will more likely meet at (other) places too. On the other side, it is not very likely that persons who have not met within a certain time frame, will meet each other afterwards.

be stronger in more realistic scenarios. This also seems to hold for periodic mobility [36]. It would also be interesting to integrate the Levy flight model to some extent, although this in general does not hold in urban environments [15].

We should note that the obtained results are only a first step in an idealistic dynamic model. Nevertheless, even the simple mobility model analyzed in this paper provides evidence for the positive impact of non-pharmaceutical interventions (e.g. school closures) and cautious behavior (public gathering bans as well as public warnings), which has already been observed in real world studies [28].

2. MODEL AND ANNOTATION

Environment. To model the environment we use a *complete graph* (also called network) with κn nodes, which are called *cells* in the rest of the paper. These cells represent locations an agent can visit. Each cell may contain agents (also called nodes or individuals), depending on the cells so called *attractiveness*. The *attractiveness* d of a cell v is chosen randomly with probability proportional to $1/d^{\alpha}$, where α is a constant larger than 2 (according to [13], $\alpha \approx 2.8$ for locations in Philadelphia). We bind the highest attractiveness to $\sqrt[\alpha]{\kappa n}$. Since the agents move randomly, the expected number of nodes contained in a specific cell with attractiveness d is given by $n \cdot d / \sum_{i=2}^{\sqrt[\alpha]{\kappa n}} c \frac{\kappa n}{i^{\alpha}} i$, where c is some normalizing constant such that $\sum_{i=2}^{\sqrt[\alpha]{\kappa n}} c \frac{\kappa n}{i^{\alpha}} = \kappa n$. This scenario describes e.g. a city with different locations, in which the individuals visit these locations according to their attractiveness.

Moving agents. In the structure described above there are n agents (also called nodes or individuals), which move in each step from one cell to another. Each node chooses the target location in some step independently and with probability proportional to its attractiveness. Now, assume that an infection starts to spread among these nodes. To model the spreading process, we use three different states, which partition the set of nodes in three groups; $\mathcal{I}(j)$ contains the infected nodes in step j, $\mathcal{U}(j)$ contains the uninfected (susceptible) nodes in step j, and $\mathcal{R}(j)$ contains the resistant nodes in step j. Whenever it is clear from the context, we simply write $\mathcal{I}$, $\mathcal{U}$, and $\mathcal{R}$, respectively. If at some step j an uninfected node i visits a cell which also contains a node of $\mathcal{I}(j)$, then i becomes infected and carries the disease further[3].

Possible variations. In our model, there are only three variables which can vary. One is α, which governs the probability distribution of the attractiveness of different locations. Another is κ, which, as a multiplicative factor, manipulates the total number of cells, i.e., the locations the agents may visit. Additionally, the time until an infected individual is cured again can also vary. That is, a time period τ is assigned to the epidemic, which means that an individual is infective for τ consecutive steps. With τ very large (i.e., $\omega(\log n)$) we obtain the model without any recovery.

---

[3]This model can easily be extended to the case, in which the disease is spread with a given probability.

Parameters. In the fearless society model we assume $\alpha \in (2, 3)$, $\kappa = 1$, and $\tau = o(\log n)$. Due to the countermeasures, in the hypochondriacal society model we assume that α, κ, and τ are suitable (large) constants. We refer to this when needed. In both models an uninfected node becomes infected (with probability 1) if it meets an infected one.

The model of this paper differs from most of the models considered in Subsection 1.2. In many of these papers, the authors used the well known mean field theory to model the spread of epidemics in urban areas (e.g. census areas around airports [4] or within different mixing groups [18]). Then, with a certain probability, infected individuals may pass the disease to every other member of their community. In our model, the infection is only transmitted between individuals being in the same cell at a certain time step, which implies different results depending on the distribution of individuals among the cells. Concerning the geographic mobility models (e.g. [36]), several interesting results w.r.t. different mobility patterns have been derived, such as Levy flight or random waypoint. In all these cases, free movement in a 2D simulation field is considered, where the spacial distribution of the random walk or Levy flight are uniform, and the distribution of nodes in the neighborhood of an infected node is Gaussian.

3. ANALYSIS

For the sake of simplicity we stick to the terminology of our motivating example. We start our analysis with a basic observation. As we will see, the number of cells with a high attractiveness decreases with an increasing α. On the other side, while κ increases, the area in which infected nodes may infect other nodes decreases.

OBSERVATION 1. *The expected number of nodes choosing a specific and an arbitrary cell with attractiveness d is proportional to d and $d^{-\alpha+1}$, respectively.*

3.1 Fearless Society Model

Let us assume a non curable course of disease, in which the infected individuals decease after some time period. At some time, there is only a small fraction of the population which is still alive, and some of them still carry the infection further. We model this situation (at some time step j) by assuming that $|\mathcal{I}(j)| \cdot |\mathcal{U}(j)| \leq n^{2\epsilon}$, for some small constant $\epsilon \leq 1/4$. The most interesting question is whether this epidemic process manages to infect the healthy individuals, and exterminate the whole population.

LEMMA 1. *Let $|\mathcal{I}(j)| \cdot |\mathcal{U}(j)| \leq n^{2\epsilon}$, where $\epsilon \leq 1/4$ is an arbitrarily small constant, κ is a constant and τ is a slowly growing function in n (i.e., $\tau = o(\log n)$). Then, in a round there is no newly infected node with probability $1 - n^{-\Omega(1)}$.*

Proof. Let a pairing of two nodes $i \in \mathcal{I}(j)$, $i' \in \mathcal{U}(j)$ describe the event that i and i' choose the same cell. Let $x_{i,i',d}$ be the event that nodes i and i', where $i \neq i'$, choose the same (specific) cell with attractiveness d. Then, the probability $Pr(x_{i,i',d})$ is bounded by

$$Pr(x_{i,i',d}) = \left(\frac{d}{\sum_{l=2}^{\sqrt[\alpha]{n}} c \frac{n}{l^{\alpha}} l} \right)^2 \leq \left(\frac{d}{cn \frac{1}{\alpha-2} \left(\frac{1}{2^{\alpha-2}} - o(1) \right)} \right)^2$$

$$\leq \left(\frac{d(\alpha-2)2^{3-\alpha}}{cn} \right)^2.$$

Further, let $x_{i,i'}$ be the event that node i and i' meet in an arbitrary cell. Then, $Pr(x_{i,i'}) \leq \sum_{d=2}^{\sqrt[\alpha]{n}} c\frac{\kappa n}{d^\alpha} Pr(x_{i,i',d})$, and we obtain

$$Pr(x_{i,i'}) \leq \left(\frac{(\alpha-2)2^{3-\alpha}}{c}\right)^2 \sum_{l=2}^{\sqrt[\alpha]{n}} \frac{c\kappa n}{l^\alpha} \frac{l}{n} \frac{\sqrt[\alpha]{n}}{n}$$

$$= \frac{\kappa\left((\alpha-2)2^{3-\alpha}\right)^2}{cn^{1-1/\alpha}} \sum_{i=2}^{\sqrt[\alpha]{n}} \frac{1}{i^{\alpha-1}}$$

$$\leq \frac{\kappa(\alpha-2)\left(2^{3-\alpha}\right)^2}{cn^{1-1/\alpha}}(1+o(1)).$$

Now, a fixed uninfected node i' becomes infected with probability at most $|\mathcal{I}(j)|Pr(x_{i,i'})$ and the expected number of newly infected nodes is bounded by

$$\mu \leq |\mathcal{U}(j)||\mathcal{I}(j)|Pr(x_{i,i'}) \leq \frac{\kappa(\alpha-2)\left(2^{3-\alpha}\right)^2}{cn^{1-1/\alpha-2\epsilon}}(1+o(1)).$$

Since the nodes of $\mathcal{U}(j)$ are assigned to the cells independently, we use Chernoff bounds [8] to obtain the desired result. With $(1+\delta)\mu = 1$ and X being the random variable describing the number of newly infected nodes, we obtain

$$Pr[X \geq (1+\delta)\mu] \leq \left[\frac{e^\delta}{(1+\delta)^{(1+\delta)}}\right]^\mu \leq \left(\frac{e^{1/\mu-1}}{(1/\mu)^{1/\mu}}\right)^\mu$$

$$= \mu \cdot \frac{e}{e^\mu} = n^{-\Omega(1)}.$$

$\square$

In the next theorem, we show that at least a polynomial fraction of the population remains uninfected, even if no countermeasures are taken.

THEOREM 1. *Let $\kappa = 1$ and let τ be a slowly growing function in n (i.e., $\tau = o(\log n)$). Then, a polynomial fraction of the population remains uninfected when the spreading process runs out.*

Proof. We analyze the process in three phases. The first phase contains only the increase in the number of infected nodes. However, we will ensure that a sufficient number of uninfected nodes will still be present, whereby this number may be very small compared to the size of the population. In the second phase we show that either the spreading process runs out at some time when the number of uninfected nodes is polynomial in n, or we will have a situation where the assumptions of Lemma 1 are fulfilled. Consequently, we apply Lemma 1 in the third phase. Let i denote the current time step, and let t_1, t_2 describe the step *after* the corresponding phases 1 and 2 have ended.

Phase 1.

For this phase we assume that no node gets cured. Thus, all infected nodes remain infected during this phase, and carry the disease to all nodes they meet. According to the power law distribution of the attractiveness, a constant fraction of cells will have attractiveness $d = 2$. Remember that $\kappa = 1$, and hence the number of all cells is n in total[4]. The

---
[4]The result can easily be extended to arbitrary constant κ.

number of cells not hosting any infected node can be modeled by a simple balls into bins game and we obtain that the number of such cells is $\Theta(n)$ [33]. Then, the probability that an uninfected node remains uninfected in one step is also constant. Since the uninfected nodes are assigned to the cells independently, we apply Chernoff bounds to conclude that, as long as $|\mathcal{U}(i)| = n^{\Theta(1)}$, a constant fraction of $\mathcal{U}(i)$ remains uninfected after step i, with probability $1 - n^{-\Omega(1)}$.

Phase 2.

We now add the curing procedure to our analysis. Thus, $|\mathcal{R}(t_1 + i)|$ will increase in each step. However, from the first phase we know that $|\mathcal{U}(j+1)| = \Theta(|\mathcal{U}(j)|)$ for any j. Then, the number of uninfected nodes will not decrease below some polynomial in n, or there is some step j such that $|\mathcal{I}(j) \cup \mathcal{R}(j)| = n - n^{\epsilon'}$ and $|\mathcal{U}(j)| = n^{\epsilon'}$ for some $\epsilon' > 0$ small enough. Assuming that $\tau = o(\log n)$, after τ steps it holds that $\mathcal{R}(i+\tau) = \mathcal{I}(i) \cup \mathcal{R}(i)$ and $|\mathcal{U}(i+\tau)| = |\mathcal{U}(i)|/n^{o(1)}$. Thus,

$$|\mathcal{I}(i+\tau)| \cdot |\mathcal{U}(i+\tau)| \in \left(\frac{n^{\epsilon'}}{n^{o(1)}}, n^{2\epsilon'}\right),$$

where we assumed that $\mathcal{I}(i+\tau) \neq \emptyset$. Thus, there is some constant $\epsilon > 0$ small enough, such that $|\mathcal{I}(i+\tau)| \cdot |\mathcal{U}(i+\tau)| = n^{2\epsilon}$.

Phase 3.

Since at this point $|\mathcal{I}(t_2)| \cdot |\mathcal{U}(t_2)| \leq n^{2\epsilon}$, applying Lemma 1 for τ steps gives the theorem. $\square$

Theorem 1 implies that if $\tau = o(\log n)$, the disease will run out, and a polynomial fraction of the population survives. This is surprising, given the fact that an aggressive virus with a long time frame for transmitting the infection (i.e., τ unbounded) is spread among the individuals of a population. Theorem 1 seems to explain the behavior of certain epidemics known from the history. We know that some of these epidemics exterminated a large fraction of the population of various cities. However, a fraction of the citizens always managed to survive (e.g. the plague [17]).

3.2 Hypochondriacal Society Model

In this case, we assume that after an individual becomes infected, it starts spreading the disease until the symptoms become visible. Then, the infected individual is isolated. We assume that the disease has an incubation time not larger than a constant $\mathfrak{s}$, and model this by setting $\tau = \mathfrak{s}$. Now it remains to include the warnings communicated through the media into our model. A warning basically affects the constants α and κ, since the individuals will most likely avoid places with a large number of persons, waive needless tours, and be more careful when meeting other people. Although one of these modifications alone is most likely not sufficient [28], we show that a combination of these strategies, which is able to sufficiently influence the constants α and κ, is enough to stop the spread of the disease. Therefore, we assume that α and κ are suitable (large) constants.

LEMMA 2. *Let the set G_k contain all cells with attractiveness 2^k up to $2^{k+1} - 1$ and let $|\mathcal{I}(j)| = f^q(n)$ for a specific step j, where $f(n)$ is some function with $\lim_{n\to\infty} f(n) = \infty$*

and $q > 3$ is a constant. If $k \leq \frac{1}{(\alpha-2)} \cdot \log\left(\frac{|\mathcal{I}(j)|}{f^3(n)}\right)$, then the number of newly infected nodes in G_k is bounded by $\mathcal{O}\left(\frac{|\mathcal{I}(j)|}{(2^k-1)^{\alpha-3}}\right)$ with probability $1 - \frac{1}{e^{\Omega(f(n))}}$.

Proof. According to our assumption, the expected number of infected nodes at the beginning of step j, which choose cells in group G_k with $k \leq \frac{1}{(\alpha-2)} \cdot \log\left(\frac{|\mathcal{I}(j)|}{f^3(n)}\right)$, is

$$\sum_{d=2^k}^{2^{k+1}-1} \frac{|\mathcal{I}(j)|d}{\sum_{i=2}^{\sqrt[\alpha]{\kappa n}} c\frac{\kappa n}{i^\alpha}i} = \Theta\left(\frac{|\mathcal{I}(j)|}{(2^k-1)^{\alpha-2}}\right) = \Omega(f^3(n)).$$

To prove the lemma, we formulate the problem as a vertex exposure martingale [30]. Let $z_{a,b}$ be the event that node a and b choose the same cell. We define a graph $G = (V, E)$ by setting $V = \mathcal{I}(j) \cup L$, where $L = \{1, ..., n - |\mathcal{I}(j)|\}$ and $\mathcal{I}(j) \cap L = \emptyset$. The set of edges is $E = \{(x_i, l) \mid x_i \in \mathcal{I}(j) \wedge l \in L \wedge z_{x_i,l}\}$. Let the vertex exposure sequence be given by $x_1, ..., x_{|\mathcal{I}(j)|} \in \mathcal{I}(j)$. Thus, each x_i represents an infected node which may establish edges connecting itself to the set L. By standard Chernoff bounds [8, 20] it follows that if α is large enough, i.e., $2^k = 2^{1/(\alpha-2)\cdot\log(\mathcal{I}(j)/f^3(n))} = o(f(n))$, then an infected node has $\mathcal{O}(f(n))$ edges with probability $1 - 1/e^{\Omega(f(n))}$. By using the union bound, we may conclude that with probability $1 - \frac{f^q(n)}{e^{\Omega(f(n))}}$ all infected nodes placed in cells of the group G_k have $\mathcal{O}(f(n))$ edges.

Now we restrict the probability space to the events, in which $\mathcal{O}\left(\frac{|\mathcal{I}(j)|}{(2^k-1)^{\alpha-2}}\right)$ infected nodes choose cells in G_k, and each of these nodes has $\mathcal{O}(f(n))$ edges. We obtain such an event with probability $1 - e^{-\Omega(f(n))}$. Let $X_0, X_1, ...$ be the vertex exposure martingale, where X_i is the expectation on the number of edges incident to $V \cap \mathcal{I}_{G_k}(j)$, conditioned by the knowledge of the edges incident to $x_1, ..., x_i$, where $\mathcal{I}_{G_k}(j)$ is the set of infected nodes choosing cells in G_k. Note that we only expose the infected vertices lying in G_k. Given the assumption above, for any $k \leq \frac{1}{(\alpha-2)} \cdot \log\left(\frac{|\mathcal{I}(j)|}{f^3(n)}\right)$ we have $|X_k - E[X_k]| \leq \mathcal{O}(f(n))$. Then,

$$Pr(|X_{|\mathcal{I}_{G_k}(j)|} - X_0| \geq \lambda) \leq 2 \cdot e^{-\frac{\lambda^2}{2\sum_{k=1}^t f(n)^2}}$$

$$\leq \exp\left(-\frac{1}{\kappa}\frac{f^3(n)}{\mathcal{O}(f^2(n))}\right),$$

with $\lambda = \frac{|\mathcal{I}(j)|}{\kappa(2^k-1)^{\alpha-2}} \geq \frac{f^3(n)}{\kappa}$. Since the expected number of uninfected nodes in a cell of G_k is less than $2^{k+1} - 1$, we obtain $X_0 = \mathcal{O}\left(\frac{|\mathcal{I}(j)|}{(2^k-1)^{\alpha-2}}\right) \cdot (2^{k+1} - 1) = \mathcal{O}\left(\frac{|\mathcal{I}(j)|}{(2^k-1)^{\alpha-3}}\right)$, and the lemma follows. $\square$

Theorem 2. *Let an epidemic disease be spread in a κn network as described in Section 2. Then, for all fixed τ there exist suitable κ and α, such that the network is healthy again after $\mathcal{O}((\log\log n)^4)$ steps, with probability $1 - o(1)$. Moreover, when $\mathcal{I} = \emptyset$, the set $\mathcal{R}$ has size $\log^{O(1)} n$.*

Proof. The proof consists of three parts. In the first part we show that the number of infected nodes decreases after $\mathfrak{s}$ steps by at least a constant factor, with probability $1 - 2\mathfrak{s}|\mathcal{I}(j)|^{-1/q}$, where q is a constant and $\tau = \mathfrak{s}$. The second part states a result about the oscillating behavior (w.r.t. the number of infected nodes) during the whole process. Finally, the third part shows that if the number of informed nodes is

just small enough (although dependent on n), it is sufficient to consider $\mathcal{O}((\log\log n)^4)$ additional steps to eliminate the remaining infected nodes, with probability $1 - \log^{-\Omega(1)}(n)$. All parts combined imply the validity of the theorem.

Part 1.

Let ν be a proper upper bound on the number of newly infected nodes in the network. This bound holds with probability $1 - \mathcal{O}(|\mathcal{I}(j)|^{-1/q})$ at step j and will be computed later. By setting $\tau = \mathfrak{s}$ the infected nodes will carry the infection further only for a constant time $\mathfrak{s}$. Let a super-step be a sequence of $\mathfrak{s}$ consecutive steps. We know that after a super-step the nodes which were infected at the beginning of this super-step get cured (i.e., they are moved to the set $\mathcal{R}$). Let $j \geq \mathfrak{s}$ be an arbitrary time step. Then,

$$|\mathcal{I}(j)| \leq |\mathcal{I}(j-\mathfrak{s})|(1+\nu)^{\mathfrak{s}} - |\mathcal{I}(j-\mathfrak{s})|$$
$$\leq |\mathcal{I}(j-\mathfrak{s})|\left((1+\nu)^{\mathfrak{s}} - 1\right). \quad (1)$$

To obtain a value for ν we need to compute an upper bound for the amount of different cells that become occupied by infected nodes. Therefore, we group the cells with respect to their attractiveness. The group G_k contains all cells with attractiveness 2^k up to $2^{k+1} - 1$. Let x_{ij} describe the number of nodes which are infected by $i \in \mathcal{I}(j)$ in step j, and let $X_j := \sum_{\forall i \in \mathcal{I}(j)} x_{ij}$. Further, we assume that $|\mathcal{I}(j)| = \log^q n$. Note that if α is large enough (cf. Lemma 2) the expected number of infected nodes contained in all the cells of attractiveness at least $2^{\frac{1}{\alpha-2}\log\left(\frac{|\mathcal{I}(j)|}{\log^3 n}\right)}$ is bounded by $\mathcal{O}(\log^3 n)$, with probability $1 - \rho^{-\log(n)}$, where ρ is some proper constant. If the attractiveness is larger than $l = 2^{\frac{1}{\alpha-2}\log(|\mathcal{I}(j)|\log^{1+\Theta(1)} n)}$, then the expected number of infected nodes in all these cells together is $o(\log^{-3} n)$.

Let $E_{k,n}$ be the expected number of infected nodes contained in G_k. Note that $E_{k,n}$ decreases with the number of overall infected nodes. According to Lemma 2, if $f(n) = \log n$, then the number of newly infected nodes in G_k in some step j is $\mathcal{O}\left(\frac{|\mathcal{I}(j)|}{(2^k-1)^{\alpha-3}}\right)$, with probability $1 - n^{-\Omega(1)}$. Thus, we obtain

$$X_j \leq \sum_{k=2}^{\frac{1}{\alpha-2}\log\left(\frac{|\mathcal{I}(j)|}{\log^3 n}\right)} \mathcal{O}\left(\frac{|\mathcal{I}(j)|}{(2^k-1)^{\alpha-3}}\right)$$
$$+ \mathcal{O}(\log^3 n) \cdot (2 \cdot l - 1)$$
$$\leq c' \cdot |\mathcal{I}(j)| \left(1 + \frac{\mathcal{O}(\log^{1+\Theta(1)} n)}{|\mathcal{I}(j)|^{1-\frac{1}{\alpha-2}}}\right)$$
$$= c' \cdot |\mathcal{I}(j)| (1 + o(1)), \quad (2)$$

with probability $1 - o(\log^{-1} n)$. Note that considering the attractiveness up to l only is crucial here, since no infected node is in some cell with attractiveness larger than l with probability $1 - o(\log^{-1} n)$. In this context c' is a small constant depending on α and κ. For decreasing $|\mathcal{I}(j)|$ we obtain the general formulas where $\log(n)$ is replaced by $f(n)$ in the statements above. Note that at this point one can represent $|\mathcal{I}(j)|$ as $f^q(n)$. Then inequality (2) holds with probability $1 - |\mathcal{I}(j)|^{-1/q}$. Thus, $\nu = c'$ with the probability given above. Then, it holds that

$$((1+\nu)^{\mathfrak{s}}-1) = \sum_{k=0}^{\mathfrak{s}}\left(\binom{\mathfrak{s}}{k}1^{\mathfrak{s}-k}\nu^{k}\right) - 1$$

$$= \sum_{k=1}^{\mathfrak{s}}\binom{\mathfrak{s}}{k}1^{\mathfrak{s}-k}\nu^{k} \le \frac{(\nu\mathfrak{s})\frac{(1-\nu)^{\mathfrak{s}-1}}{(1-1/\mathfrak{s})^{\mathfrak{s}-1}}}{(1-\nu)^{\mathfrak{s}-1}}$$

$$\le \nu\mathfrak{s}e^{\frac{\mathfrak{s}-1}{\mathfrak{s}}} \ll 1, \tag{3}$$

if $c'\mathfrak{s} \ll 1/e$. Here, the first inequality in (3) can be obtained using the following estimation from [20]

$$\sum_{k=1}^{\mathfrak{s}}\binom{\mathfrak{s}}{k}1^{\mathfrak{s}-k}\nu^{k}(1-\nu)^{\mathfrak{s}-1} \le \left(\frac{\nu}{1/\mathfrak{s}}\right)^{\frac{1}{\mathfrak{s}}\mathfrak{s}}\left(\frac{1-\nu}{1-1/\mathfrak{s}}\right)^{(1-1/\mathfrak{s})\mathfrak{s}}.$$

Then (1), (2) and (3) imply a decreasing number of infected nodes after each super-step by a factor of $\nu\mathfrak{s}e$, with probability at least $1 - 2\mathfrak{s}|\mathcal{I}(j)|^{-1/q}$.

Part 2.

The results so far imply an oscillating behavior of the number of infected nodes. That is, the set $\mathcal{I}$ will mainly decrease (cf. Part 1). However, the number of infected nodes may also increase in some time steps. If one infected node chooses a destination with plenty of nodes from $\mathcal{U}$, then $\mathcal{I}$ increases drastically. Thus, it remains to compute the probability for such an event.

Now we divide the whole process into *phases*. Lets consider each phase separately, and assume that a specific phase begins at time step j. A phase consists usually of $\mathfrak{s}$ steps, and a step is divided into two substeps. In the first substep of a step j', we allow each infected node to transmit the disease to every other node being in the same cell. In the second substep, all nodes which were infected in step $j' - \mathfrak{s}$ are moved to $\mathcal{R}$, and stop transmitting the disease in the subsequent steps.

Now, a phase starting at some time step j ends after $\mathfrak{s}$ steps, if in all these steps $j' \le \mathfrak{s}$ it holds that $|\mathcal{I}(j + j') \setminus \mathcal{I}(j)| \le \nu\mathfrak{s}e|\mathcal{I}(j)|$. This holds with probability at least $1 - 2\mathfrak{s}|\mathcal{I}(j)|^{-1/q}$ (see above). If in some step $j' \le \mathfrak{s}$ $|\mathcal{I}(j + j') \setminus \mathcal{I}(j)| > \nu\mathfrak{s}e|\mathcal{I}(j)|$, then this phase ends, and in the next step we start with a new phase.

Now we model the process as a special random walk (cf. Figure 1). For this, let $G' = (V', E')$ be a directed graph, where $V' = \{\log\log\log\log n, \ldots, \log^q n\}$. A node $v \in V'$ corresponds to the case $|\mathcal{I}| = v$. From each v, there is a transition to $\max\{v_{\min}, \nu\mathfrak{s}ev\}$ with probability $1 - 2\mathfrak{s}v^{-1/q}$, where $v_{\min} = \log\log\log\log n$ (all the other transitions are not relevant and can be arbitrary). In order to show that within $\mathcal{O}((\log\log n)^4)$ steps the vertex $v_{\min}$ is visited $(\log\log n)^2$ steps, we state the following lemma.

LEMMA 3. *Let* $(X_t)_{t=1}^{\infty}$ *be a Markov chain using space* $\{1, \ldots, m\}$ *and fulfilling the following property:*

- *there are constants* $c_1, c_2 < 1$ *such that for any* $t \in \mathbb{N}$, $Pr[X_{t+1} \le c_1 X_t] \ge 1 - X_t^{-c_2}$.

Let $T = \min\{t \in \mathbb{N} \mid X_t = 1\}$. *Then,* $Pr[T = \mathcal{O}(\log^2 m)] \ge 1 - m^{-4}$.

Proof. Note that this lemma has certain similarities to the multiplicative drift theorem of [12]. There, it is assumed that $E[X_t - X_{t+1} \mid X_t] = \Omega(X_t)$, and then a result

w.r.t. $E[T]$ is derived. The proof of our lemma uses some of the arguments of Claim 2.9 from [11]. However, there are two main differences. First, the probability of not moving toward the target (which is m in their case and 1 in our case) is in [11] exponentially small w.r.t. the current state $-X_t$, while we only have some polynomial probability in X_t^{-1}. Second, in their case the failure in moving toward the target most likely occurs at the other end of the graph (close to 1), while in our case a failure mainly occurs at some state close to the target.

We define a step to be decreasing, if $X_{t+1} \le c_1 X_t$. Furthermore, a decreasing step is successful, if $X_{t+1} = 1$ after some $X_t > 1$. Let Y be a random variable which denotes the number of consecutive decreasing steps without reaching a successful step. Note that $t = \log_{1/c_1} m$ is an upper bound on Y since $X_t \le c_1^{\log_{1/c_1} m}m = 1$.

Now we divide the Markovian process X_t into consecutive epochs. Every time we fail to have a decreasing step, we start a new epoch. Furthermore, if a step is successful, we stop. Now we show that an epoch is successful with some constant probability. Let P_i be the probability that some epoch i contains a successful step. Then,

$$P_i \ge \prod_{j=0}^{\log_{1/c_1} m - 1}\left(1 - (c_1^j m)^{-c_2}\right)$$

$$\ge \prod_{j=0}^{\log_{1/c_1} m - 1}\rho^{-(c_1^j m)^{-c_2}} = \rho^{-a}$$

where ρ is a proper constant with $1 < \rho \le (1 - c_1^{c_2})^{-c_1^{-c_2}}$. Then for the exponent a we have

$$a = \sum_{j=0}^{\log_{1/c_1} m - 1}(c_1^j m)^{-c_2} = \sum_{j=0}^{\log_{1/c_1} m - 1}\frac{(1/c_1^{c_2})^j}{m^{c_2}}$$

$$= \frac{1 - (1/c_1^{c_2})^{\log_{1/c_1} m}}{(1 - 1/c_1^{c_2})m^{c_2}} = \frac{m^{c_2} - 1}{(1/c_1^{c_2} - 1)m^{c_2}} = \Theta(1).$$

Let T' be the first epoch in which we reach a successful step. As in [11], we know that an epoch has such a step with constant probability, and hence (as in [11]) $Pr[T' = \mathcal{O}(\log m)] \ge 1 - m^{-4}$. Since an epoch can only last for $\mathcal{O}(\log m)$ steps, we obtain that a successful step is reached within $\mathcal{O}(\log^2 m)$ steps, with probability $1 - m^{-4}$. $\square$

According to the lemma above, in the graph G', node $v_{\min}$ is visited at least once within $\mathcal{O}((\log\log n)^2)$ phases, with probability at least $1 - \log^{-4q} n$. Furthermore, if $|\mathcal{I}(j)| = \log^q n$ for some j, then $|\mathcal{I}(j + \mathfrak{s})| = \nu\mathfrak{s}e|\mathcal{I}(j)|$ with probability $1 - 2\mathfrak{s}\log^{-1} n$. Therefore, using the union bound we conclude that $v_{\min}$ is visited $(\log\log n)^2$ times by the random walk within $\mathcal{O}((\log\log n)^4)$ phases, without visiting $\log^q n$ twice in any two consecutive phases, with probability $1 - o(\log^{-0.99} n)$.

Part 3.

In order to conclude, we observe that within one step, $|\mathcal{I}|$ does not increase to some value larger than $\log^q n$ with probability $1 - o(\log^{-1} n)$ (cf. inequality (2)). Furthermore, given that $|\mathcal{I}|$ is always smaller than $\log^q n$, we know that within $\mathcal{O}((\log\log n)^4)$ steps, with probability $1 - o(\log^{-0.99} n)$ there are $\Theta(\log^2\log n)$ time steps, in which the number of infected

Figure 1: Model of the random walk for part 2 of Theorem 2, with $c = (\nu s e)^{-1}$, and partially plotted edges for node i.

nodes is at most $\log\log\log\log n$. To show that the disease becomes eliminated from the system, we consider the probability for these nodes not to meet any other node for τ consecutive time steps.

For this, we only consider time steps in which the number of infected nodes is at most $\log\log\log\log n$. First, we assign the uninfected nodes to the cells. As in Observation 1, the probability for a node to choose a specific cell with constant attractiveness is proportional to $\frac{\mathcal{O}(1)}{\kappa n}$. Thus, at least a constant fraction of the cells will remain empty, since the probability for a cell with constant attractiveness to be empty is $(1 - \mathcal{O}(1)/\kappa n)^n = e^{-\Theta(1)}$. Let $t = \log^2 \log n$ be the number of so called phases, where each phase consists of τ steps. Then, an (infected) node chooses an empty cell for τ consecutive steps with probability $e^{-\Theta(\tau)}$ and all nodes of $\mathcal{I}$ choose empty cells in τ consecutive steps with probability $e^{-\Theta(\tau|\mathcal{I}(j)|)}$. Then, in all t phases there is at least one node $v \in \mathcal{I}$ which does not choose an empty cell in at least one of the steps with probability

$$\left(1 - \frac{1}{e^{\Theta(\tau|\mathcal{I}(j)|)}}\right)^t \le \exp\left(-\frac{t}{e^{\Omega(|\mathcal{I}(j)|)}}\right) \le \log^{-\Omega(1)} n. \quad (4)$$

Hence, after $\mathcal{O}(\log^4 \log n)$ steps there is at least one phase in which all nodes of $\mathcal{I}$ spend τ consecutive steps alone in some cells with probability $1 - \log^{-\Omega(1)} n$.

Thus, the network becomes completely healthy again after $\mathcal{O}((\log\log n)^4)$ steps with probability $1 - o(1)$. □

4. CONCLUSION

We presented a model, which describes a simple movement behavior of individuals as well as the impact of the power law exponent on the spread of epidemics in a dynamic environment. Two different parameter settings were used for the analysis. In the first case the epidemic can spread nearly unhindered. The obtained result for this case implies that w.r.t. our model a part of the population will survive with probability $1 - o(1)$. In the second case the epidemic is combated by public warnings, isolation and (limited) medications, which lead to an increase of the corresponding power law exponent. One can observe that in this case the epidemic is embanked after a short time with probability $1 - o(1)$. Furthermore, the number of total infections decreases from a high percentage of the population to a negligible fraction.

Nevertheless, several open questions remain. In our model, we assumed that every node chooses a cell with attractiveness d with probability proportional to $d^{-\alpha+1}$. However, different individuals may have different preferences which are not included in our analysis. Furthermore, different types of movement models are conceivable like Levy flight, periodic mobility model, and grid like movement. Although all these characteristics are not considered in this paper, our methods and techniques might be useful to analyze more realistic movement models in the future.

References

[1] L. A. Adamic and B. A. Huberman. Power-law distribution of the world wide web. *Science*, 287(5461):2115, 2000.

[2] M. Ajelli, B. Goncalves, D. Balcan, V. Colizza, H. Hu, J. Ramasco, S. Merler, and A. Vespignani. Comparing large-scale computational approaches to epidemic modeling: Agent-based versus structured metapopulation models. *BMC Infectious Diseases*, 10(190), 2010.

[3] L. A. Amaral, A. Scala, M. Barthelemy, and H. E. Stanley. Classes of small-world networks. *PNAS*, 97(21):11149–11152, 2000.

[4] D. Balcan, H. Hu, B. Goncalves, P. Bajardi, C. Poletto, J. J. Ramasco, D. Paolotti, N. Perra, M. Tizzoni, W. V. den Broeck, V. Colizza, and A. Vespignani. Seasonal transmission potential and activity peaks of the new influenza A(H1N1): a Monte Carlo likelihood analysis based on human mobility. *BMC Medicine*, 7:45, 2009.

[5] G. V. Bobashev, D. M. Goedecke, F. Yu, and J. M. Epstein. A hybrid epidemic model: combining the advantages of agent-based and equation-based approaches. In *Proc. of WSC '07*, pages 1532–1537, Piscataway, NJ, USA, 2007. IEEE Press.

[6] C. Borgs, J. Chayes, A. Ganesh, and A. Saberi. How to distribute antidote to control epidemics. *Random Struct. Algorithms*, 37:204–222, September 2010.

[7] D. S. Callaway, M. E. J. Newman, S. H. Strogatz, and D. J. Watts. Network robustness and fragility: Percolation on random graphs. *Physical Review Letters*, 85(25):5468–5471, 2000.

[8] H. Chernoff. A measure of asymptotic efficiency for tests of a hypothesis based on the sum of observations. *Annals of Math. Stat.*, 23(4):493–509, 1952.

[9] G. Chowell, J. M. Hyman, S. Eubank, and C. Castillo-Chavez. Scaling laws for the movement of people between locations in a large city. *Physical Review E*, 68(6):661021–661027, Dec. 2003.

[10] A. Demers, D. Greene, C. Hauser, W. Irish, J. Larson, S. Shenker, H. Sturgis, D. Swinehart, and D. Terry. Epidemic algorithms for replicated database maintenance. In *Proc. of PODC '87*, pages 1–12, New York, NY, USA, 1987. ACM Press.

[11] B. Doerr, L. A. Goldberg, L. Minder, T. Sauerwald, and C. Scheideler. Stabilizing consensus with the power of two choices. In *Proc. of SPAA '11*, pages 149–158, New York, NY, USA, 2011. ACM.

[12] B. Doerr, D. Johannsen, and C. Winzen. Multiplicative drift analysis. In *Proc. of GECCO'10*, pages 1449–1456, 2010.

[13] S. Eubank, H. Guclu, V. Kumar, M. Marathe, A. Srinivasan, Z. Toroczkai, and N. Wang. Modelling disease outbreaks in realistic urban social networks. *Nature*, 429(6988):180–184, 2004.

[14] M. Faloutsos, P. Faloutsos, and C. Faloutsos. On power-law relationships of the internet topology. In *Proc. of SIGCOMM '99*, pages 251–262, 1999.

[15] W. Frey. Suburb population growth slows, July 2009.

[16] S. Funk, E. Gilad, C. Watkins, and V. A. A. Jansen. The spread of awareness and its impact on epidemic outbreaks. *PNAS*, 106(16):6872–6877, 2009.

[17] R. Gardner. The Plague. DVD/TV, 2005. Produced for the History Channel.

[18] T. C. Germann, K. Kadau, I. M. Longini, and C. A. Macken. Mitigation strategies for pandemic influenza in the United States. *PNAS*, 103(15):5935–5940, 2006.

[19] P. Grassberger. On the critical behavior of the general epidemic process and dynamical percolation. *Mathematical Biosciences*, 63(2):157 – 172, 1983.

[20] T. Hagerup and C. Rüb. A guided tour of Chernoff bounds. *Inf. Process. Lett.*, 33(6):305–308, 1990.

[21] H. W. Hethcote. The mathematics of infectious diseases. *SIAM Review*, 42(4):599–653, 2000.

[22] S. W. Jaffry and J. Treur. Agent-Based and Population-Based Simulation: A Comparative Case Study for Epidemics. In *Proc. of ECMS'08*, pages 123–130, 2008.

[23] M. Jelasity, S. Voulgaris, R. Guerraoui, A.-M. Kermar-rec, and M. van Steen. Gossip-based peer sampling. *ACM Trans. Comput. Syst.*, 25(3), 2007.

[24] R. Karp, C. Schindelhauer, S. Shenker, and B. Vocking. Randomized rumor spreading. In *Proc. of FOCS '00*, page 565, Washington, DC, USA, 2000. IEEE Computer Society.

[25] B. Y. Lee, V. L. Bedford, M. S. Roberts, and K. M. Carley. Virtual epidemic in a virtual city: simulating the spread of influenza in a us metropolitan area. *Translational Research*, 151(6):275 – 287, 2008.

[26] B. Y. Lee, S. T. Brown, P. C. Cooley, R. K. Zimmerman, W. D. Wheaton, S. M. Zimmer, J. J. Grefenstette, T.-M. Assi, T. J. Furphy, D. K. Wagener, and D. S. Burke. A computer simulation of employee vaccination to mitigate an influenza epidemic. *American Journal of Preventive Medicine*, 38(3):247 – 257, 2010.

[27] T. Liu, X. Li, B. Ai, J. Fu, and X. Zhang. Multi-agent simulation of epidemic spatio-temporal transmission. In *Proc. of ICNC '08*, volume 7, pages 357–361, 2008.

[28] H. Markel, H. B. Lipman, J. A. Navarro, A. Sloan, J. R. Michalsen, A. M. Stern, and M. S. Cetron. Nonpharmaceutical Interventions Implemented by US Cities During the 1918-1919 Influenza Pandemic. *JAMA : The Journal of the American Medical Association*, 298(6):644–654, Aug. 2007.

[29] Y. Moreno and A. Vázquez. Disease spreading in structured scale-free networks. *European Physical Journal B*, 31(2):265–271, 2003.

[30] R. Motwani and P. Raghavan. *Randomized Algorithms*. Cambridge University Press, 1995.

[31] M. E. J. Newman. Spread of epidemic disease on networks. *Phys. Rev. E*, 66(1):016128, 2002.

[32] M. E. J. Newman. The structure and function of complex networks. *SIAM Review*, 45(2):167–256, 2003.

[33] M. Raab and A. Steger. Balls into bins - a simple and tight analysis. In *Proc. of RANDOM '98*, volume 1518, pages 159–170, 1998.

[34] M. Ripeanu, I. Foster, and A. Iamnitchi. Mapping the gnutella network: Properties of large-scale peer-to-peer systems and implications for system. *IEEE Internet Computing Journal*, 6(1):50–57, 2002.

[35] S. Rührup, C. Schindelhauer, K. Volbert, and M. Grünewald. Performance of distributed algorithms for topology control in wireless networks. In *Proc. of IPDPS'03*, page 28, 2003.

[36] N. Valler, B. A. Prakash, H. Tong, M. Faloutsos, and C. Faloutsos. Epidemic spread in mobile ad hoc networks: Determining the tipping point. In *Proc. of NETWORKING '11*, pages 266–280, 2011.

Discovery through Gossip *

Bernhard Haeupler
MIT, USA
haeupler@mit.edu

Gopal Pandurangan
NTU, Singapore, and
Brown University, USA
gopalpandurangan@gmail.com

David Peleg
Weizmann Institute, Israel
david.peleg@weizmann.ac.il

Rajmohan Rajaraman
Northeastern University, USA
rraj@ccs.neu.edu

Zhifeng Sun
Northeastern University, USA
austin@ccs.neu.edu

ABSTRACT

We study randomized gossip-based processes in dynamic networks that are motivated by information discovery in large-scale distributed networks such as peer-to-peer and social networks. A well-studied problem in peer-to-peer networks is *resource discovery*, where the goal for nodes (hosts with IP addresses) is to discover the IP addresses of all other hosts. Also, some of the recent work on self-stabilization algorithms for P2P/overlay networks proceed via discovery of the complete network. In social networks, nodes (people) discover new nodes through exchanging contacts with their neighbors (friends). In both cases the discovery of new nodes changes the underlying network — new edges are added to the network — and the process continues in the changed network. Rigorously analyzing such dynamic (stochastic) processes in a continuously changing topology remains a challenging problem with obvious applications.

This paper studies and analyzes two natural gossip-based discovery processes. In the *push discovery* or *triangulation* process, each node repeatedly chooses two random neighbors and connects them (i.e., "pushes" their mutual information to each other). In the *pull discovery* process or the *two-hop walk*, each node repeatedly requests or "pulls" a random contact from a random neighbor and connects itself to this two-hop neighbor. Both processes are lightweight in the sense that the amortized work done per node is constant per round, local, and naturally robust due to the inherent randomized nature of gossip.

Our main result is an almost-tight analysis of the time taken for these two randomized processes to converge. We show that in any undirected n-node graph both processes take $O(n \log^2 n)$ rounds to connect every node to all other nodes with high probability, whereas $\Omega(n \log n)$ is a lower bound. We also study the two-hop walk in directed graphs, and show that it takes $O(n^2 \log n)$ time with high probability, and that the worst-case bound is tight for arbitrary directed graphs, whereas $\Omega(n^2)$ is a lower bound for strongly connected directed graphs. A key technical challenge that we overcome in our work is the analysis of a randomized process that itself results in a constantly changing network leading to complicated dependencies in every round. We discuss implications of our results and their analysis to discovery problems in P2P networks as well as to evolution in social networks.

Categories and Subject Descriptors

F.2.2 [**Theory of Computation**]: Analysis of Algorithms and Problem Complexity—*Nonnumerical Algorithms and Problems*

General Terms

Algorithms, Theory

Keywords

Resource discovery, Social networks, Gossip-based algorithm, Distributed algorithm, Probabilistic analysis

1. INTRODUCTION

Many large-scale, real-world networks such as peer-to-peer networks, the Web, and social networks are highly dynamic with continuously changing topologies. The evolution of the network as a whole is typically determined by the decentralized behavior of nodes, i.e., the local topological changes made by the individual nodes (e.g., adding edges between neighbors). Understanding the dynamics of such local processes is critical for both analyzing the underlying stochastic phenomena, e.g., in the emergence of structures in social networks, the Web and other real-world networks [6, 28, 29], and designing practical algorithms for associated algorithmic problems, e.g., in resource discovery in distributed networks [17, 25] or in the analysis of algorithms for the Web [8, 11]. In this paper, we study the dynamics of network evolution that result from *local* gossip-style processes. Gossip-based processes have recently received significant attention because of their simplicity of implementation, scalability to large network size, and robustness to frequent network topology changes; see, e.g., [12, 22, 23, 9, 21, 20, 27, 7, 19, 4] and

---

*GP was supported in part by the following grants: Nanyang Technological University grant M58110000, Singapore Ministry of Education (MOE) Academic Research Fund (AcRF) Tier 2 grant MOE2010-T2-2-082, and US NSF grant CCF-1023166. GP and DP were supported in part by a grant from the US-Israel Binational Science Foundation (BSF). RR and ZS were supported in part by NSF grant CNS-0915985.

Permission to make digital or hard copies of all or part of this work for personal or classroom use is granted without fee provided that copies are not made or distributed for profit or commercial advantage and that copies bear this notice and the full citation on the first page. To copy otherwise, to republish, to post on servers or to redistribute to lists, requires prior specific permission and/or a fee.
SPAA'12, June 25–27, 2012, Pittsburgh, Pennsylvania, USA.
Copyright 2012 ACM 978-1-4503-1213-4/12/06 ...$10.00.

the references therein. In particular, gossip-based protocols have been used to efficiently and robustly construct various overlay topologies dynamically in a fully decentralized manner [19]. In a local gossip-based algorithm (e.g., [9]), each node exchanges information with a small number of randomly chosen neighbors in each round.[1] The randomness inherent in the gossip-based protocols naturally provides robustness, simplicity, and scalability. While many of the recent theoretical gossip-based work (including those on rumor spreading), especially, the *push-pull* type algorithms ([20, 21, 9, 14, 10, 15]) focus on analyzing various gossip-based tasks (e.g., computing aggregates or spreading a rumor) on *static* graphs, a key feature of this work is rigorously analyzing a gossip-based process in a *dynamically changing* graph.

We present two illustrative application domains for our study. First, consider a P2P network, where nodes (computers or end-hosts with IDs/IP addresses) can communicate only with nodes whose IP address are known to them. A basic building block of such a dynamic distributed network is to efficiently discover the IP addresses of all nodes that currently exist in the network. This task, called *resource discovery* [17], is a vital mechanism in a dynamic distributed network with many applications [17, 1]: when many nodes in the system want to interact and cooperate they need a mechanism to discover the existence of one another. Resource discovery is typically done using a local mechanism [17]; in each *round* nodes discover other nodes and this changes the resulting network — new edges are added between the nodes that discovered each other. As the process proceeds, the graph becomes denser and denser and will finally result in a complete graph. Such a process was first studied in [17] which showed that a simple randomized process is enough to guarantee almost-optimal time bounds for the time taken for the entire graph to become complete (i.e., for all nodes to discover all other nodes). Their randomized *Name Dropper* algorithm operates as follows: in each round, each node chooses a random neighbor and sends *all* the IP addresses it knows. Note that while this process is also gossip-based the information sent by a node to its neighbor can be extremely large (i.e., of size $\Omega(n)$). More recently, self-stabilization protocols have been designed for constructing and maintaining P2P overlay networks e.g, [5, 18]. These protocols guarantee convergence to a desired overlay topology (e.g., the SKIP+ graph) starting from any arbitrary topology via local checking and repair. For example, the self-stabilizing protocol of [5] proceeds by continuously discovering new neighbors (via transitive closure) till a complete graph is formed. Then the repair process is initiated. This can also be considered as a local gossip-based process in an underlying virtual graph with changing (added) edges.   In both the above examples, the assumption is that the starting graph is arbitrary but (at least) weakly connected. The gossip-based processes that we study also have the same goal — starting from an arbitrary connected graph, each node discovers all nodes as

quickly as possible – in a setting where individual message sizes are small ($O(\log n)$ bits).

Second, in social networks, nodes (people) discover new nodes through exchanging contacts with their neighbors (friends). Discovery of new nodes changes the underlying network — new edges are added to the network — and the process continues in the changed network. For example, consider the *LinkedIn* network[2], a large social network of professionals on the Web. The nodes of the network represent people and edges are added between people who directly know each other — between direct contacts. Edges are generally undirected, but LinkedIn also allows directed edges, where only one node is in the contact list of another node. LinkedIn allows two mechanisms to discover new contacts. The first can be thought of as a *triangulation* process (see Figure 1(a)): A person can introduce two of his friends that could benefit from knowing each other — he can mutually introduce them by giving their contacts. The second can be thought of as a *two-hop* process (see Figure 1(b)): If *you* want to acquire a new contact then you can use a shared (mutual) neighbor to introduce yourself to this contact; i.e., the new contact has to be a two-hop neighbor of yours. Both the processes can be modeled via gossip in a natural way (as we do shortly below) and the resulting evolution of the network can be studied: e.g., how and when do clusters emerge? how does the diameter change with time? In the social network context, our study focuses on the following question: how long does it take for all the nodes in a connected induced subgraph of the network to discover all the nodes in the subgraph? This is useful in scenarios where members of a social group, e.g., alumni of a school, members of a club, discover all members of the group through local gossip operations.

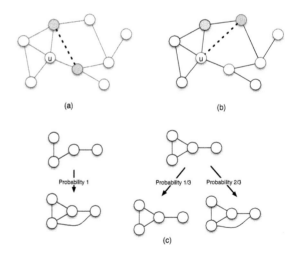

Figure 1: (a) Push discovery or triangulation process. (b) Pull discovery or two-hop walk process. (c) Non-monotonicity of the triangulation process – the expected convergence time for the 4-edge graph exceeds that for the 3-edge subgraph.

Gossip-based discovery. Motivated directly by the above applications, we analyze two lightweight, randomized gossip-based discovery processes. We assume that we start with an

---

[1]Gossip, in some contexts (see e.g., [20, 21]), has been used to denote communication with a random node in the network, as opposed to only a directly connected neighbor. The former model essentially assumes that the underlying graph is complete, whereas the latter (as assumed here) is more general and applies even to arbitrary graphs. The local gossip process is typically more difficult to analyze due to the dependences that arise as the network evolves.

[2]http://www.linkedin.com.

arbitrary undirected connected graph and the process proceeds in synchronous rounds. Communication among nodes occurs only through edges in the network. We further assume that the size of each message sent by a node in a round is at most $O(\log n)$ bits, i.e., the size of an ID.

1. Push discovery (triangulation): In each round, each node chooses two random neighbors and connects them by "pushing" their mutual information to each other. In other words, each node adds an undirected edge between two of its random neighbors; if the two neighbors are already connected, then this does not create any new edge. Note that this process, which is illustrated in Figure 1(a), is completely local. To execute the process, a node only needs to know its neighbors; in particular, no two-hop information is needed. Note that this is similar in spirit to the *triangulation* procedure of Linkedin described earlier, i.e., a node completes a triangle with two of its chosen neighbors. [3]

2. Pull discovery (two-hop walk): In each round, each node connects itself to a random neighbor of a neighbor chosen uniformly at random, by "pulling" a random neighboring ID from a random neighbor. Alternatively, one can think of each node doing a two-hop random walk and connecting to its destination. This process, illustrated in Figure 1(b), can also be executed locally: a node asks a neighbor v for an ID of one of v's neighbors and then adds an undirected edge to the received contact. Note that this is similar in spirit to the *two-hop* procedure of LinkedIn described earlier [4].

Both the above processes are local in the sense that each node only communicates with its neighbors in any round, and lightweight in the sense that the amortized work done per node is a constant per round. Both processes are also easy to implement and generally oblivious to the current topology structure, changes or failures. It is interesting also to consider variants of the processes in directed graphs. In particular, we study the two-hop walk process which naturally generalizes in directed graphs: each node does a two-hop directed random walk and adds a *directed* edge to its destination. We are mainly interested in the time taken by the process to converge to the *transitive closure* of the initial graph, i.e., till no more new edges can be added.

Our results. Our main contribution is an analysis of the above gossip-based discovery processes in both undirected and directed graphs. In particular, we show the following results (the precise theorems are in the respective sections.)

- **Undirected graphs:** In Sections 3 and 4, we show that for *any* undirected n-node graph, both the push and the pull discovery processes converge in $O(n \log^2 n)$ rounds with high probability. We also show that $\Omega(n \log n)$ is a lower bound on the number of rounds needed for almost any n-node graph. Hence our analysis is tight to within a logarithmic factor. Our results also apply when we require only a subset of nodes to converge. In particular, consider a subset of k nodes that induce a

connected subgraph and run the gossip-based process *restricted to this subgraph*. Then by just applying our results to this subgraph, we immediately obtain that it will take $O(k \log^2 k)$ rounds, with high probability (in terms of k), for all the nodes in the subset to converge to a complete subgraph. As discussed above, such a result is applicable in social network scenarios where all nodes in a subset of network nodes discover one another through gossip-based processes.

- **Directed graphs:** In Section 5, we show that the pull process takes $O(n^2 \log n)$ time for any n-node directed graph, with high probability. We show a matching lower bound for weakly connected graphs, and an $\Omega(n^2)$ lower bound for strongly connected directed graphs. Our analysis indicates that the directionality of edges can greatly impede the resource discovery process.

Applications. The gossip-based discovery processes we study are directly motivated by the two scenarios outlined above, namely algorithms for resource discovery in distributed networks and analyzing how discovery process affects the evolution of social networks. Since our processes are simple, lightweight, and easy to implement, they can be used for resource discovery in distributed networks. The *Name Dropper* discovery algorithm has been applied to content delivery systems[17]. As mentioned earlier, *Name Dropper* and other prior algorithms for the discovery problem [17, 25, 24, 1] complete in polylogarithmic number of rounds ($O(\log^2 n)$ or $O(\log n)$), but may transfer $\Theta(n)$ bits per edge per round. As a result, they may not be scalable for bandwidth and resource-constrained networks (e.g., peer-to-peer, mobile, or sensor networks). One approach to use these algorithms in a bandwidth-limited setting ($O(\log n)$-bits per message) is to spread the transfer of long messages over a linear number of rounds, but this requires coordination and maintaining state. In contrast, the "stateless" nature of the gossip processes we study and the fact that the results apply to any initial graph make the process attractive in unpredictable environments. Our analyses can also give insight into the growth of real-social networks such as LinkedIn, Twitter, or Facebook, that grow in a decentralized way by the local actions of the individual nodes. In addition to the application of discovering all members of a group, analyses of the processes such as the ones we study can help analyze both short-term and long-term evolution of social networks. In particular, it can help in predicting the sizes of the immediate neighbors as well as the sizes of the second and third-degree neighbors (these are listed for every node in LinkedIn). An estimate of these can help in designing efficient algorithms and data structures to search and navigate the social network.

Technical contributions. Our main technical contribution is a probabilistic analysis of localized gossip-based discovery in arbitrary networks. While our processes can be viewed as graph-based coupon collection processes, one significant distinction with past work in this area [2, 3, 13] is that the graphs in our processes are constantly changing. The dynamics and locality inherent in our process introduces nontrivial dependencies, which makes it difficult to characterize the network as it evolves. A further challenge is posed by the fact that the expected convergence time for the two processes is *not monotonic*; that is, the processes may *take longer* to converge starting from a graph G than

---

[3] However, we note that in our process the two neighbors are chosen randomly, unlike in LinkedIn.

[4] Again, one difference is that in the process we analyze the particular each node in the two-hop walk is chosen uniformly at random from the appropriate neighborhood.

starting from a subgraph H of G. Figure 1(c) presents a small example illustrating this phenomenon. This seemingly counterintuitive phenomenon is, however, not surprising considering the fact that the cover time of random walks also share a similar property. One consequence of these hurdles is that analyzing the convergence time for even highly specialized or regular graphs is challenging since the probability distributions of the intermediate graphs are hard to specify. Our lower bound analysis for a specific strongly connected directed graph in Theorem 15 illustrates some of the challenges. In our main upper bound results (Theorems 8 and 12), we overcome these technical difficulties by presenting a uniform analysis for all graphs, in which we study different local neighborhood structures and show how each leads to rapid growth in the minimum degree of the graph.

2. PRELIMINARIES

In this section, we define the notations used in our proofs, and state some common lemmas for Section 3 and Section 4. Let G denote a connected graph, $d(u)$ denote the degree of node u, and $N^i(u)$ denote the set of nodes that are at distance i from u. Let δ denote the minimum degree of G. We note that G, $d(u)$, and $N^i(u)$ all change with time and are, in fact, random variables. For any nonnegative integer t, we use subscript t to denote the random variable at the start of round t; for example G_t refers to the graph at the start of round t. We list the notation in Table 1.

Table 1: Notation table

Notation	description
δ_t	minimum degree of graph G_t
$N_t^i(u)$	set of nodes that are at distance i from u in G_t
$\left\vert N_t^i(u) \right\vert$	number of nodes in $N_t^i(u)$
$d_t(u)$	degree of node u in G_t
$d_t\left(u, N_t^i(v)\right)$	number of edges from u to nodes in $N_t^i(v)$, i.e., degree induced on $N_t^i(v)$

We state two lemmas that are used in the proofs in Section 3 and Section 4. Lemma 1 gives a lower bound on the number of neighbors within distance 4 for any node u in G_t while Lemma 2 is a standard analysis of a sequence of Bernoulli experiments and can be proved by a direct coupon collector argument or using a Chernoff bound. We defer the proofs to the full paper [16].

LEMMA 1. $\left\vert \cup_{i=1}^4 N_t^i(u) \right\vert \geq \min\{2\delta_t, n-1\}$ for $u \in G_t$.

LEMMA 2. Consider k Bernoulli experiments, in which the success probability of the ith experiment is at least i/m where $m \geq k$. If X_i denotes the number of trials needed for experiment i to output a success and $X = \sum_{i=1}^k X_i$, then $\Pr[X > (c+1)m \ln m]$ is less than $1/m^c$.

3. TRIANGULATION: PULL DISCOVERY

In this section, we analyze the triangulation process on undirected connected graphs, which is described by the following iteration: In each round, for each node u, we add edge (v, w) where v and w are drawn uniformly at random from $N_t^1(u)$. The triangulation process yields the following push-based resource discovery protocol. In each round, each node u introduces two random neighbors v and w to one another. The main result of this section is that the triangulation process transforms an arbitrary connected n-node graph to a complete graph in $O(n \log^2 n)$ rounds with high probability. We also establish an $\Omega(n \log n)$ lower bound on the triangulation process for almost all n-node graphs.

3.1 Upper bound

We obtain the $O(n \log^2 n)$ upper bound by proving that the minimum degree of the graph increases by a constant factor (or equals $n-1$) in $O(n \log n)$ steps. Towards this objective, we study how the neighbors of a given node connect to the two-hop neighbors of the node. We say that a node v is **weakly tied** to a set of nodes S if v has less than $\delta_0/2$ edges to S (i.e., $d_t(v, S) < \delta_0/2$), and **strongly tied** to S if v has at least $\delta_0/2$ edges to S (i.e., $d_t(v, S) \geq \delta_0/2$). (Recall that δ_0 is the minimum degree at start of round 0.)

LEMMA 3. If $\delta_0 \leq d_t(u) < (1 + 1/4)\delta_0$ and $w \in N_t^1(u)$ is strongly tied to $N_t^2(u)$, then the probability that u connects to a node in $N_t^2(u)$ through w in round t is at least $2/(7n)$.

PROOF. Since w is strongly tied to $N_t^2(u)$, $d_t\left(w, N_t^2(u)\right) \geq \delta_0/2$. Therefore, the probability that u connects to a node in $N_t^2(u)$ through w in round t is

$$
\begin{aligned}
&= \frac{d_t\left(w, N_t^2(u)\right)}{d_t(w)} \cdot \frac{1}{d_t(w)} \geq \frac{d_t\left(w, N_t^2(u)\right)}{d_t(w)} \cdot \frac{1}{n} \\
&\geq \frac{d_t\left(w, N_t^2(u)\right)}{\left\vert N_t^1(u) \right\vert + d_t\left(w, N_t^2(u)\right)} \cdot \frac{1}{n} \\
&\geq \frac{d_t\left(w, N_t^2(u)\right)}{(1 + 1/4)\delta_0 + d_t\left(w, N_t^2(u)\right)} \cdot \frac{1}{n} \\
&\geq \frac{\delta_0/2}{(1 + 1/4)\delta_0 + \delta_0/2} \cdot \frac{1}{n} = \frac{2}{7n}.
\end{aligned}
$$
$\square$

LEMMA 4. If $\delta_0 \leq d_t(u) < (1 + 1/4)\delta_0$, $w \in N_0^1(u)$ is weakly tied to $N_t^2(u)$, and $v \in N_0^2(u) \cap N_0^1(w)$, then the probability that u connects to v through w in round t is at least $1/(4\delta_0^2)$.

PROOF. Since w is weakly tied to $N_t^2(u)$ and $d_t(w)$, is at most $\left\vert N_t^1(u) \right\vert + d_t\left(w, N_t^2(u)\right)$, we obtain that $d_t(w)$ is at most $(1 + 1/4)\delta_0 + \delta_0/2$. Therefore, the probability that u connects to v through w in round t is

$$
= \frac{1}{d_t(w)^2} \geq \frac{1}{((1 + 1/4)\delta_0 + \delta_0/2)^2} \geq \frac{1}{(7\delta_0/4)^2} \geq \frac{1}{4\delta_0^2}.
$$
$\square$

For analyzing the degree growth of a node u, we consider two overlapping cases. The first is when more than $\delta_0/4$ nodes of $N_t^1(u)$ are strongly tied to $N_t^2(u)$, and the second is when less than $\delta_0/3$ nodes of $N_t^1(u)$ are strongly tied to $N_t^2(u)$. The analysis for the first case is relatively straightforward: when several neighbors of a node u are strongly tied to u's two-hop neighbors, then their triangulation steps connect u to a large fraction of these two-hop neighbors.

LEMMA 5. [**When several neighbors are strongly tied to two-hop neighbors**] There exists $T = O(n \log n)$ such that if more than $\delta_0/4$ nodes in $N_t^1(u)$ are strongly tied to $N_t^2(u)$ for all $t < T$, then $d_T(u) \geq (1 + 1/4)\delta_0$ with probability at least $1 - 1/n^2$.

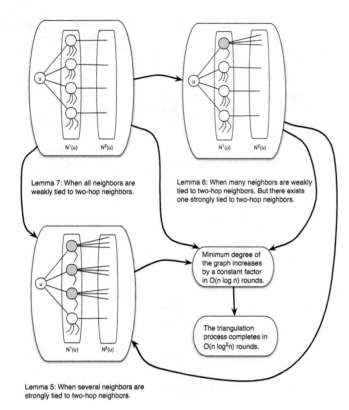

Figure 2: This figure illustrates the different cases and relations between lemmas used in the proof of Theorem 8. The shaded nodes in $N_t^1(u)$ are strongly tied to $N_t^2(u)$. Others are weakly tied to $N_t^2(u)$.

PROOF. If at any round $t < T$, $d_t(u) \geq (1 + 1/4)\delta_0$, then the desired claim holds. In the remainder of this proof, we assume $d_t(u) < (1 + 1/4)\delta_0$ for all $t < T$. Let $w \in N_t^1(u)$ be a node that is strongly tied to $N_t^2(u)$. By Lemma 3 we know that the probability that u connects to a node in $N_t^2(u)$ through w in round t is at least $2/(7n) > 1/(6n)$.

We have more than $\delta_0/4$ such w's in $N_t^1(u)$, each of which independently executes a triangulation step in any given round. Consider a run of $T_1 = 72n \ln n/\delta_0$ rounds. This implies at least $18n \ln n$ attempts to add an edge between u and a node in $N_t^2(u)$. Thus,

$$\Pr\left[u \text{ connects to a node in } N_t^2(u) \text{ after } T_1 \text{ rounds}\right]$$
$$\geq 1 - \left(1 - \frac{1}{6n}\right)^{18n \ln n} \geq 1 - e^{-3 \ln n} = 1 - \frac{1}{n^3}.$$

If a node that is two hops away from u becomes a neighbor of u by round t, it is no longer in $N_t^2(u)$. Therefore, in $T = T_1 \delta_0/4 = O(n \log n)$ rounds, u will connect to at least $\delta_0/4$ new nodes with probability at least $1 - 1/n^2$, i.e., $d_T(u) \geq (1 + 1/4)\delta_0$. $\square$

We next consider the second case where less than $\delta_0/3$ neighbors of a given node u are strongly tied to the two-hop neighborhood of u. This case is more challenging since the neighbors of u that are weakly tied may not contribute many new edges to u. We break the analysis of this part into two subcases based on whether there is at least one neighbor of

u that is strongly tied to $N_0^2(u)$. Figure 2 illustrates the different cases and lemmas used in the proof of Theorem 8.

LEMMA 6. [**When few neighbors are strongly tied to two-hop neighbors**] *There exists $T = O(n \log n)$ such that if less than $\delta_0/3$ nodes in $N_t^1(u)$ are strongly tied to $N_t^2(u)$ for all $t < T$, and there exists a node $v_0 \in N_0^1(u)$ that is strongly tied to $N_0^2(u)$, then $d_T(u) \geq (1 + 1/8)\delta_0$ with probability at least $1 - 1/n^2$.*

PROOF. If at any point $t < T$, $d_T(u) \geq (1 + 1/8)\delta_0$, then the claim of the lemma holds. In the remainder of this proof, we assume $d_T(u) < (1 + 1/8)\delta_0$ for all $t < T$. Let S_t^0 denote the set of v_0's neighbors in $N_t^2(u)$ which are strongly tied to $N_t^1(u)$ at round t, W_t^0 denote the set of v_0's neighbors in $N_t^2(u)$ which are weakly tied to $N_t^1(u)$ at round t.

Consider any node v in S_t^0. Less than $\delta_0/3$ nodes in $N_t^1(u)$ are strongly tied to $N_t^2(u)$, thus more than $\delta_0/2 - \delta_0/3 = \delta_0/6$ neighbors of v in $N_t^1(u)$ are weakly tied to $N_t^2(u)$. Let w be one such weakly tied node. By Lemma 4, the probability that u connects to v through w in round t is at least $1/(4\delta_0^2)$. We have at least $\delta_0/6$ such w's, each of which executes a triangulation step each round. Consider $T = 72\delta_0 \ln n$ rounds of the process. Then the probability that u connects to v in T rounds is at least

$$1 - \left(1 - \frac{1}{4\delta_0^2}\right)^{12\delta_0^2 \ln n} \geq 1 - e^{-3 \ln n} = 1 - \frac{1}{n^3}.$$

Thus, if $|S_t^0| \geq \delta_0/8$, in an additional $O(n \log n)$ rounds, $d_T(u) \geq (1 + 1/8)\delta_0$ with probability at least $1 - 1/n^2$.

Therefore, in the remainder of the proof we consider the case where $|S_t^0| < \delta_0/8$. Define $R_t^0 = R_{t-1}^0 \cup W_t^0$, $R_0^0 = W_0^0$. If at least $\delta_0/8$ nodes in R_t^0 are connected to u at any time, then the claim of the lemma holds. Thus, in the following we consider the case where $|R_t^0 \cap N_t^1(u)| < \delta_0/8$. From the definition of R_t^0, we can derive

$$|R_t^0| \geq |W_t^0| = d_t(v_0, N_t^2(u)) - |S_t^0| \geq d_t(v_0, N_t^2(u)) - \delta_0/8$$

At round 0, v_0 is strongly tied to $N_0^2(u)$, i.e., $d_0(v_0, N_0^2(u)) \geq \delta_0/2$. Since $\delta_0 \leq d_t(u) < (1 + 1/8)\delta_0$, we have

$$d_t(v_0, N_t^2(u)) \geq d_t(v_0, N_0^2(u)) - \delta_0/8 \geq 3\delta_0/8$$

Let e_1 denote the event $\{u$ connects to a node in $R_t^0 \setminus N_t^1(u)$ through v_0 in round $t\}$.

$$\begin{aligned}
\Pr[e_1] &= \frac{|R_t^0 \setminus N_t^1(u)|}{d_t(v_0)} \cdot \frac{1}{d_t(v_0)} \\
&= \frac{|R_t^0| - |R_t^0 \cap N_t^1(u)|}{d_t(v_0)} \cdot \frac{1}{d_t(v_0)} \\
&\geq \frac{|R_t^0| - |R_t^0 \cap N_t^1(u)|}{d_t(v_0)} \cdot \frac{1}{n} \\
&= \frac{|R_t^0| - |R_t^0 \cap N_t^1(u)|}{|N_t^1(u)| + d_t(v_0, N_t^2(u))} \cdot \frac{1}{n} \\
&\geq \frac{|R_t^0| - \delta_0/8}{|N_t^1(u)| + d_t(v_0, N_t^2(u))} \cdot \frac{1}{n} \\
&\geq \frac{d_t(v_0, N_t^2(u)) - \delta_0/8 - \delta_0/8}{|N_t^1(u)| + d_t(v_0, N_t^2(u))} \cdot \frac{1}{n} \\
&\geq \frac{3\delta_0/8 - \delta_0/8 - \delta_0/8}{|N_t^1(u)| + 3\delta_0/8} \cdot \frac{1}{n} \\
&\geq \frac{3\delta_0/8 - \delta_0/8 - \delta_0/8}{(1 + 1/8)\delta_0 + 3\delta_0/8} \cdot \frac{1}{n} = \frac{1}{12n}
\end{aligned}$$

Let X_1 be the number of rounds it takes for e_1 to occur. When e_1 occurs, let v_1 denote a witness for e_1; i.e., if we use X_1 to denote the round at which e_1 occurs, then let v_1 denote a node in $R_{X_1}^0 \setminus N_{X_1}^1(u)$ to which u connects through v_0 in round X_1. Since v_1 is in $R_{X_1}^0$, it is also in $W_{t_1}^0$ for some $t_1 \leq X_1$; therefore, v_1 is strongly tied to $N_t^2(u) \cap N_t^3(u)$. If $d_t(v_1, N_t^2(u)) < 3\delta_0/8$ at any point t, then $d_t(u) \geq (1 + 1/8)\delta_0$. Thus, in the remainder of the proof, we consider the case where $d_t(v_1, N_t^2(u)) \geq 3\delta_0/8$. Let S_t^1 (resp., W_t^1) denote the set of v_1's neighbors in $N_t^2(u)$ that are strongly tied (resp., weakly tied) to $N_t^1(u)$. If $|S_t^1| \geq \delta_0/8$, then as we did for the case $|S_t^0| \geq \delta_0/8$, we argue that in $O(n \log n)$ rounds, the degree of u is at least $(1+1/8)\delta_0$ with probability at least $1 - 1/n^2$.

Thus, in the remainder, we assume that $|S_t^1| < \delta_0/8$. Define $R_t^1 = R_{t-1}^1 \cup W_t^1$, $R_{t_1}^1 = W_{t_1}^1$. Let e_2 denote the event $\{u$ connects to a node in $R_t^0 \setminus N_t^1(u)$ (or $R_t^1 \setminus N_t^1(u)$) through v_0(or v_1) in round $t\}$. By the same calculation as for v_0, we have $\Pr[e_2] \geq 1/6n$. Similarly, we can define $e_3, X_3, e_4, X_4, \ldots, e_{\delta_0/4}, X_{\delta_0/4}$, and obtain $\Pr[e_i] \geq i/(12n)$. The total number of rounds for u to gain $\delta_0/4$ edges is bounded by $T = \sum_i X_i$. By Lemma 2, $T \leq 36 n \ln n$ with probability at least $1 - 1/n^2$, completing the proof. $\square$

LEMMA 7. [**When all neighbors are weakly tied to two-hop neighbors**] *There exists $T = O(n \log n)$ such that if all nodes in $N_t^1(u)$ are weakly tied to $N_t^2(u)$ for all $t < T$, then $d_T(u) \geq \min\{(1+1/8)\delta_0, n-1\}$ with probability at least $1 - 1/n^2$.*

PROOF. If $d_t(u) \geq \min\{(1 + 1/8)\delta_0, n - 1\}$ at any point $t < T$, then the claim of this lemma holds. In the remainder of this proof, we assume $d_t(u) < \min\{(1+1/8)\delta_0, n-1\}$ for all $t < T$. In the following, we first show, any node $v \in N_0^2(u)$ will have at least $\delta_0/4$ edges to $N_{T_1}^1(u)$, where $T_1 = O(n \log n)$. After that, v will connect to u in $T_2 = O(n \log n)$ rounds. Therefore, the total number of rounds used for v to connect to u is $T_3 = T_1 + T_2 = O(n \log n)$.

Node v at least connects to one node in $N_0^1(u)$. Call it w_1. Because all nodes in $N_t^1(u)$ are weakly tied to $N_t^2(u)$, we have $d_t(w_1, N_t^1(u)) \geq \delta_0 - \delta_0/2 = \delta_0/2$. In the case that $d_t(w_1, N_t^1(u) \setminus N_t^1(v))$ is less than $\delta_0/4$ then v already has $\delta_0/4$ edges to $N_t^1(u)$. Thus, in the following we consider the opposite case; that is, we assume $d_t(w_1, N_t^1(u) \setminus N_t^1(v)) \geq \delta_0/4$. Let e_1 denote the event $\{v$ connects to a node in $N_t^1(u) \setminus N_t^1(v)$ through $w_1\}$.

$$
\begin{aligned}
\Pr[e_1] &= \frac{d_t(w_1, N_t^1(u) \setminus N_t^1(v))}{d_t(w_1)} \cdot \frac{1}{d_t(w_1)} \\
&\geq \frac{d_t(w_1, N_t^1(u) \setminus N_t^1(v))}{|N_t^1(u)| + d_t(w_1, N_t^2(u))} \cdot \frac{1}{d_t(w_1)} \\
&\geq \frac{\delta_0/4}{(1+1/8)\delta_0 + \delta_0/2} \cdot \frac{1}{d_t(w_1)} \\
&\geq \frac{2}{13} \cdot \frac{1}{n} > \frac{1}{7n}
\end{aligned}
$$

Let X_1 be the number of rounds needed for e_1 to occur. When e_1 occurs, let w_2 denote a witness for e_1; i.e., let w_2 denote a vertex in $N_t^1(u) \setminus N_t^1(v)$ to which v connects. Note that here the value of t is the round at which the event occurs. By our choice, w_2 is also weakly tied to $N_t^2(u)$. By an argument similar to the one in the above paragraph, we have $d_t(w_2, N_t^1(u) \setminus N_t^1(v)) \geq \delta_0/4$. Let e_2 denote the event

$\{v$ connects to a node in $N_t^1(u)$ through w_1 or $w_2\}$. We have $\Pr[e_2] \geq 2/(7n)$. Let X_2 be the number of rounds needed for e_2 to occur. Similarly, we can define $e_3, X_3, \ldots, e_{\delta_0/4}, X_{\delta_0/4}$ and show $\Pr[e_i] \geq i/(7n)$. Set $T_1 = \sum_i X_i$, which is the bound on the number of rounds needed for v to have at least $\delta_0/4$ neighbors in $N_t^1(u)$. By Lemma 2, $T_2 \leq 28 n \ln n$ with probability at least $1 - 1/n^3$. Now we show v will connect to u in T_2 rounds after this. Notice that, all w_i's are still weakly tied to $N_t^2(u)$. By Lemma 4, the probability that u connects to v through w_i in round t is at least $1/(4\delta_0^2)$. We have $w_1, w_2, \ldots, w_{\delta_0/4}$ independently executing a triangulation step each round. Consider $T_2 = 48\delta_0 \ln n$ rounds of the process. Then,

$$
\begin{aligned}
&\Pr[u \text{ connects to } v \text{ in } T_2 \text{ rounds}] \\
&\geq 1 - \left(1 - \frac{1}{4\delta_0^2}\right)^{12\delta_0^2 \ln n} \geq 1 - \frac{1}{n^3}.
\end{aligned}
$$

We have shown for any node $v \in N_0^2(u)$, it will connect to u in round $T_3 = T_1 + T_2$ with probability at least $1 - 1/n^3$. This implies in round T_3, u will connect to all nodes in $N_0^2(u)$ with probability at least $1 - |N_0^2(u)|/n^3$. Then, $N_0^2(u) \subseteq N_{T_3}^1(u)$, $N_0^3(u) \subseteq N_{T_3}^1(u) \cup N_{T_3}^2(u)$, $N_0^4(u) \subseteq N_{T_3}^1(u) \cup N_{T_3}^2(u) \cup N_{T_3}^3(u)$. We apply the above analysis twice, and obtain that in round $T = 3T_3 = O(n \log n)$, $N_0^2(u) \cup N_0^3(u) \cup N_0^4(u) \subseteq N_T^1(u)$ with probability at least $1 - |N_0^2(u) \cup N_0^3(u) \cup N_0^4(u)|/n^3 \geq 1 - 1/n^2$. By Lemma 1, $|N_0^2(u) \cup N_0^3(u) \cup N_0^4(u)| \geq \min\{2\delta_0, n-1\}$, thus completing the proof. $\square$

THEOREM 8. [**Upper bound for triangulation process**] *For any connected undirected graph, the triangulation process converges to a complete graph in $O(n \log^2 n)$ rounds with high probability.*

PROOF. We first show that in $O(n \log n)$ rounds, either the graph becomes complete or its minimum degree increases by a factor of at least $1/12$. Then we apply this argument $O(\log n)$ times to complete the proof.

For each u where $d_0(u) < \min\{(1+1/8)\delta_0, n-1\}$, we consider the following 2 cases. The first case is if more than $\delta_0/3$ nodes in $N_0^1(u)$ are strongly tied to $N_0^2(u)$. By Lemma 5, there exists $T = O(n \log n)$ such that if at least $\delta_0/4$ nodes in $N_t^1(u)$ are strongly tied to $N_t^2(u)$ for $t < T$, then $d_T(u) \geq (1 + 1/8)\delta_0$ with probability at least $1 - 1/n^2$. Whenever the condition is not satisfied, i.e., less than $\delta_0/4$ nodes in $N_t^1(u)$ are strongly tied to $N_t^2(u)$, it means more than $\delta_0/3 - \delta_0/4 = \delta_0/12$ strongly tied nodes became weakly tied. By the definitions of strongly tied and weakly tied, this implies $d_T(u) \geq (1 + 1/12)\delta_0$.

The second case is if less than $\delta_0/3$ nodes in $N_0^1(u)$ are strongly tied to $N_0^2(u)$. By Lemmas 6 and 7, we know that there exists $T = O(n \log n)$ such that if we remain in this case for T rounds, then $d_T(u) \geq \min\{(1+1/8)\delta_0, n-1\}$ with probability at least $1 - 1/n^2$. Whenever the condition is not satisfied, i.e., more than $\delta_0/3$ nodes in $N_t^1(u)$ are strongly tied to $N_t^2(u)$, we move to the analysis in the first case, and $d_T(u) \geq (1 + 1/8)\delta_0$ in $T = O(n \log n)$ rounds with probability at least $1 - 1/n^2$.

Combining the above 2 cases and applying a union bound, we obtain $\delta_T \geq \min\{(1+1/8)\delta_0, n-1\}$ in $T = O(n \log n)$ rounds with probability at least $1 - 1/n$. We now apply the above argument $O(\log n)$ times to obtain the desired $O(n \log^2 n)$ upper bound. $\square$

3.2 Lower bound

THEOREM 9. [**Lower bound for triangulation process**] *For any connected undirected graph G that has $k \geq 1$ edges less than the complete graph the triangulation process takes $\Omega(n \log k)$ steps to complete with probability at least $1 - O\left(e^{-k^{1/4}}\right)$.*

PROOF. We first observe that during the triangulation process there is a time t when the number of missing edges is at least $m = O(\sqrt{k})$ and the minimum degree is at least $n/3$. If $k < \frac{2}{3}n$ then this is true initially and for larger k this is true at the first time t the minimum degree is large enough. The second case follows since the degree of a node (and thus also the minimum degree) can at most double in each step guaranteeing that the minimum degree is not larger than $\frac{2}{3}n$ at time t also implying that at least $\frac{n}{3} = \Omega(\sqrt{k})$ edges are still missing.

Given the bound on the minimum degree any missing edge $\{u, v\}$ is added by a fixed node w with probability at most $\frac{9}{2n^2}$. Since there are at most $n-2$ such nodes the probability that a missing edge gets added is at most $\frac{9}{2n}$. To analyze the time needed for all missing edges to be added we denote with X_i the random variable counting the number of steps needed until the ith of the m missing edges is added. We would like to analyze $\Pr[X_1 \leq T, X_2 \leq T, \ldots, X_m \leq T]$ for an appropriately chosen number of steps T. Note that the events $X_i < T$ and $X_j < T$ are not independent and indeed can be positively or negatively correlated. Nevertheless, independent of the conditioning onto any of the events $X_j < T$, we have that $\Pr[X_1 \leq T] \leq 1 - (1 - \frac{9}{2n})^T \leq 1 - \frac{1}{\sqrt{m}}$ for an appropriately chosen $T = \Omega(n \log m)$, where m is again the number of missing edges at time t. Thus,

$$\Pr[X_1 \leq T, X_2 \leq T, \ldots, X_m \leq T]$$
$$= \Pr[X_1 \leq T | X_2 \leq T, \ldots, X_m \leq T] \cdot$$
$$\Pr[X_2 \leq T | X_3, \ldots, X_m \leq T] \cdot \ldots \cdot \Pr[X_m \leq T]$$
$$\leq \left(1 - \frac{1}{\sqrt{m}}\right)^m = O\left(e^{-\sqrt{m}}\right) = O\left(e^{-k^{1/4}}\right)$$

This shows that the triangulation process takes with probability at least $1 - O\left(e^{-k^{1/4}}\right)$ at least $\Omega(n \log m) = O(n \log k)$ steps to complete. □

4. TWO-HOP WALK: PULL DISCOVERY

In this section, we analyze the two-hop walk process on undirected connected graphs, which is described by the following simple iteration: In each round, for each node u, we add edge (u, w) where w is drawn uniformly at random from $N_t^1(v)$, where v is drawn uniformly at random from $N_t^1(u)$. The two-hop walk yields the following pull-based resource discovery protocol. In each round, each node u contacts a random neighbor v, receives the identity of a random neighbor w of v, and sends its identity to w. The main result of this section is that the two-hop walk process transforms an arbitrary connected n-node graph to a complete graph in $O(n \log^2 n)$ rounds with high probability. We also establish an $\Omega(n \log n)$ lower bound on the two-hop walk for almost all n-node graphs.

As for the two-hop walk process, we establish the $O(n \log^2 n)$ upper bound by showing that the minimum degree of the graph increases by a constant factor (or equals $n-1$) in

$O(n \log n)$ rounds with high probability. For analyzing the growth in the degree of a node u, we consider two overlapping cases. The first case is when the two-hop neighborhood of u is not too large, i.e., $|N_t^2(u)| < \delta_0/2$, and the second is when the two-hop neighborhood of u is not too small, i.e., $|N_t^2(u)| \geq \delta_0/4$.

LEMMA 10. [**When the two-hop neighborhood is not too large**] *There exists $T = O(n \log n)$ such that either $|N_T^2(u)| \geq \delta_0/2$ or $d_T(u) \geq \min\{2\delta_0, n-1\}$ with probability at least $1 - 1/n^2$.*

PROOF. By the definition of δ_0, $d_0(w) \geq \delta_0$ for all w in $N_0^1(u)$. Let X be the first round at which $|N_X^2(u)| \geq \delta_0/2$. We consider two cases. If X is at most $cn \log n$ for a constant c to be specified later, then the claim of the lemma holds. In the remainder of this proof we consider the case where X is greater than $cn \log n$; thus, for $0 \leq t \leq cn \log n$, $|N_t^2(u)| < \delta_0/2$.

Consider any node w in $N_0^1(u)$. Since $d_0(w) \geq \delta_0$ and $|N_t^2(u)| < \delta_0/2$, w has at least $\delta_0/2$ edges to nodes in $N_0^1(u)$. Fix a node v in $N_0^2(u)$. In the following, we first show that in $O(n \log n)$ rounds, v is strongly tied to the neighbors of u with probability at least $1 - 1/n^3$. Let T_1 denote the first round at which v has is strongly tied to $N_{T_1}^1(u)$, i.e., when $|N_{T_1}^1(v) \cap N_{T_1}^1(u)| \geq \delta_0/4$. We know that v has at least one neighbor, say w_1, in $N_0^1(u)$. Consider any $t < T_1$. Since v is weakly tied to $N_0^1(u)$ at time t, w_1 has at least $\delta_0/4$ neighbors in $N_0^1(u)$ which do not have an edge to v at time t. This implies that the probability that v connects to a node in $N_0^1(u)$ through w_1 in round t is at least $1/(4n)$.

Let e_1 denote the event $\{v$ connects to a node in $N_0^1(u)\}$, and X_1 be the number of rounds for e_1 to occur. When e_1 occurs, let w_2 denote a witness for e_1; i.e., w_2 is a node in $N_0^1(u)$ to which v connects in round X_1. We note that $w_1, w_2 \in N_0^1(u) \subseteq N_{X_1}^1(u)$. If v is weakly tied to $N_{X_1}^1(u)$, both w_1 and w_2 have at least $\delta_0/4$ neighbors in $N_{X_1}^1(u)$ that do not have an edge to v yet. Let e_2 denote the event $\{v$ connects to a node in $N_{X_1}^1(u)\}$, and X_2 be the number of rounds for e_2 to occur. Then $\Pr[e_2] = 2\Pr[e_1] \geq 1/2n$. Similarly, we define $e_3, X_3, \ldots, e_{\delta_0/4}, X_{\delta_0/4}$ and we obtain $\Pr[e_i] \geq i/(4n)$. We now apply Lemma 2 to obtain that $X_1 + X_2 + \ldots X_{\delta_0/4}$ is at most $16n \ln n$ with probability at least $1 - 1/n^3$. Thus, with probability at least $1 - |N_0^2(u)|/n^3$, $T_1 \leq 16n \ln n$. After T_1 rounds, we obtain that for any $v \in N_0^1(u)$,

$$\Pr[u \text{ connects to } v \text{ in a single round}] \geq \frac{\delta_0/4}{2\delta_0} \cdot \frac{1}{n} = \frac{1}{8n}.$$

which implies that with probability at least $1 - 1/n^3$, u has an edge to every node in $N_0^2(u)$ in another $T_2 \leq 24n \ln n$ rounds.

Let T_3 equal $T_1 + T_2$; we set c to be at least $120 \ln 2$ so that $X > 3T_3$. We thus have $N_0^2(u) \subseteq N_{T_3}^1(u)$, $N_0^3(u) \subseteq N_{T_3}^1(u) \cup N_{T_3}^2(u)$, and $N_0^4(u) \subseteq N_{T_3}^1(u) \cup N_{T_3}^2(u) \cup N_{T_3}^3(u)$. We now repeat the above analysis again twice and obtain that at time $T = 3T_3$, $N_0^2(u) \cup N_0^3(u) \cup N_0^4(u) \subseteq N_T^1(u)$ with probability at least $1 - |N_0^2(u) \cup N_0^3(u) \cup N_0^4(u)|/n^3 \geq 1 - 1/n^2$. By Lemma 1, we have $|N_T^1(u)| \geq \min\{2\delta_0, n-1\}$, thus completing the proof of the lemma. □

LEMMA 11. [**When the two-hop neighborhood is not too small**] *There exists $T = O(n \log n)$ such that either*

$\left|N_T^2(u)\right| < \delta_0/4$ *or* $d_T(u) \geq \min\left\{(1+1/8)\delta_0, n-1\right\}$, *with probability at least* $1 - 1/n^2$.

PROOF. Let X be the first round at which $N_X^2(u) < \delta_0/4$. We consider two cases. If X is at most $cn \log n$ for a constant c to be specified later, then the claim of the lemma holds. In the remainder of this proof we consider the case where X is greater than $cn \log n$; thus, for $0 \leq t \leq cn \log n$, $\left|N_t^2(u)\right| \geq \delta_0/4$. If $v \in N_0^2(u)$ is strongly tied to $N_0^1(u)$, then

$$\Pr\left[u \text{ connects to } v \text{ in a single round}\right]$$
$$\geq \quad \frac{d_t\left(v, N_0^1(u)\right)}{|N_t^1(u)|} \cdot \frac{1}{n} \geq \frac{\delta_0/4}{(1+1/8)\delta_0} \cdot \frac{1}{n} = \frac{2}{9n}$$

Thus, in $T = 13.5n \ln n$ rounds, u will add an edge to v with probability at least $1 - 1/n^3$. If there are at least $\delta_0/8$ nodes in $N_0^2(u)$ that are strongly tied to $N_0^1(u)$, then u will add edges to all these nodes in T rounds with probability at least $1 - 1/n^2$.

In the remainder of this proof, we focus on the case where the number of nodes in $N_0^2(u)$ that are strongly tied to $N_0^1(u)$ at the start of round 0 is less than $\delta_0/8$. In this case, because $\left|N_t^2(u)\right| \geq \delta_0/4$, more than $\delta_0/8$ nodes in $N_0^2(u)$ are weakly tied to $N_0^1(u)$, and, thus, have at least $3\delta_0/4$ edges to nodes in $N_0^2(u) \cup N_0^3(u)$.

In the following we show u will connect to $\delta_0/8$ nodes in $O(n \log n)$ rounds with probability at least $1 - 1/n^2$. For any round t, let W_t denote the set of nodes in $N_t^2(u)$ that are weakly tied to $N_t^1(u)$. We refer to a length-2 path from u to a node two hops away as an *out-path*. Let P_0 denote the set of out-paths to W_0. Since we have at least $\delta_0/8$ nodes in $N_0^2(u)$ that are weakly tied to $N_0^1(u)$, $|P_0|$ is at least $\delta_0/8$ at time $t = 0$. Define $e_1 = \{u$ picks an out-path in P_0 and connects to node v_1 in $N_0^2(u)\}$, and X_1 to be the number of rounds for e_1 to occur. When $0 \leq t \leq X_1$, for each $w_i \in N_t^1(u)$, let f_i be the number of edges from w_i to nodes in $N_t^1(u) \cup N_t^2(u)$, and p_i be the number of edges from w_i to nodes in $N_0^2(u)$ that are weakly tied to $N_0^1(u)$.

$$\Pr\left[e_1\right] = \sum_i \frac{1}{d_t(u)} \cdot \frac{p_i}{f_i} \geq \sum_i \frac{1}{d_t(u)} \cdot \frac{p_i}{n-1}$$
$$= \frac{\sum_i p_i}{(1+1/8)\delta_0(n-1)} = \frac{|S|}{(1+1/8)\delta_0(n-1)}$$
$$\geq \frac{\delta_0/8}{(1+1/8)\delta_0(n-1)} \geq \frac{1}{9n}.$$

After X_1 rounds, u will pick an out-path in P_0 and connect such a v_1. Define P_1 to be a set of out-paths from u to W_{X_1}. We now place a lower bound on $|P_1 \setminus P_0|$. Since $v_1 \in N_0^2(u)$ is added to $N_{X_1}^1(u)$, those out-paths in P_0 consisting of edges from v_1 to nodes in $N_0^1(u)$ are not in P_1. The number of out-paths we lose because of this is at most $\delta_0/4$. But v_1 also has at least $3\delta_0/4$ edges to $N_0^2(u) \cup N_0^3(u)$. The end points of these edges are in $N_{X_1}^1(u) \cup N_{X_1}^2(u)$. If more than $\delta_0/8$ of them are in $N_{X_1}^1(u)$, then $d_{X_1}(u) \geq (1+1/8)\delta_0$. Now let's consider the case that less than $\delta_0/8$ such end points are in $N_{X_1}^1(u)$. This means the number of edges from v_1 to $N_{X_1}^2(u)$ is at least $3\delta_0/4 - \delta_0/4 - \delta_0/8 = 3\delta_0/8$. Among the end points of these edges, if more than $\delta_0/8$ of them are strongly tied to $N_{X_1}^1(u)$, then the degree of u will become at least $(1+1/8)\delta_0$ in $O(n \log n)$ rounds with probability $1 - 1/n^2$ by our earlier argument. If not, we know that more than $\delta_0/4$ newly added edges are pointing to nodes that are weakly tied to $N_{X_1}^1(u)$.

Thus, $|P_1 \setminus P_0|$ is by at least $\delta_0/4$. $|S| \geq 2 \cdot \delta_0/8$. Define $e_2 = \{u$ picks an out-path in P_1 and connects to node $v_2\}$, and X_2 to be the number of rounds for e_2 to occur. During time $X_1 \leq t \leq X_2$, $\Pr[e_2]$ is at least $2 \cdot \frac{1}{9n}$. Similarly, we define $e_3, X_3, \ldots, e_{\delta_0/8}, X_{\delta_0/8}$ and derive $\Pr[e_i] \geq i/(9n)$. By Lemma 2, the number of rounds for $d_t(u) \geq (1+1/8)\delta_0$ is bounded by

$$T = X_1 + X_2 + \cdots + X_{\delta_0/8} \leq (2+1)9n \ln n = 27n \ln n$$

with probability at least $1 - 1/n^2$, completing the proof of this lemma. $\square$

THEOREM 12. [**Upper bound for two-hop walk process**] *For connected undirected graphs, the two-hop walk process completes in* $O(n \log^2 n)$ *rounds with high probability.*

The proof of the above theorem is deferred to the full paper [16]. The proof of Theorem 13 is similar to that for Theorem 9, and is omitted.

THEOREM 13. [**Lower bound for two-hop walk process**] *For any connected undirected graph G that has $k \geq 1$ edges less than the complete graph the two-hop process takes $\Omega(n \log k)$ steps to complete with probability at least* $1 - O\left(e^{-k^{1/4}}\right)$.

5. TWO-HOP WALK IN DIRECTED GRAPHS

In this section, we analyze the two-hop walk process in directed graphs. We say that the process terminates at time t if for every node u and every node v, G_t contains the edge (u, v) whenever u has a path to v in G_0.

THEOREM 14. *On any n-node directed graph, the two-hop walk terminates in $O(n^2 \log n)$ rounds with high probability. There exists a (weakly connected) directed graph for which the process takes $\Omega(n^2 \log n)$ rounds to terminate.*

The lower bound in the above theorem, whose proof is deferred to full paper [16], takes advantage of the fact that the initial graph is not strongly connected. Extending the above analysis for strongly connected graphs appears to be much more difficult since the events corresponding to the addition of new edges interact in significant ways. We present an $\Omega(n^2)$ lower bound for a strongly connected graph by a careful analysis that tracks the event probabilities with time and takes dependencies into account. The graph G_0, depicted in Figure 3, is similar to the example in [17] used to establish an $\Omega(n)$ lower bound on the Random Pointer Jump algorithm, in which each node gets to know all the neighbors of a random neighbor in each step. Since the graphs are constantly changing over time in both the processes, the dynamic edge distributions differ significantly in the two cases, and we need a substantially different analysis.

THEOREM 15. *There exists a strongly connected directed graph for which the expected number of rounds taken by the two-hop process is $\Omega(n^2)$.*

PROOF. The graph $G_0 = (V, E)$ is depicted in Figure 3 and formally defined as $G_0 = (V, E)$ where $V = \{1, 2, \ldots, n\}$ with n being even, and

$$E = \{(i, j) : 1 \leq i, j \leq n/2\} \cup \{(i, i+1) : n/2 \leq i < n\}$$
$$\cup \{(i, j) : i > j, i > n/2, i, j \in V\}.$$

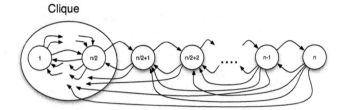

Clique

Figure 3: Lower bound example for two-hop walk process in directed graphs

We first establish an upper bound on the probability that edge $(i, i+h)$ is added by the start of round t, for given i, $1 \le i \le n-h$. Let $p_{h,t}$ denote this probability. The following base cases are immediate: $p_{h,0}$ is 1 for $h=1$ and $h<0$, and 0 otherwise. Next, the edge $(i, i+h)$ is in G_{t+1} if and only if $(i, i+h)$ is either in G_{t-1} or added in round t. In the latter case, $(i, i+h)$ is added by a two-hop walk $i \to i+k \to i+h$, where $-i < k \le n - i$. Since the out-degree of every node is at least $n/2$, for any k the probability that i takes such a walk is at most $4/n^2$.

$$
\begin{aligned}
p_{h,t+1} &\le p_{h,t} + \frac{4}{n^2} \sum_{k>-i}^{n-i} p_{k,t} p_{h-k,t} \\
&= p_{h,t} + \frac{4}{n^2}\Big(\sum_{k=1}^{i-1} p_{h+k,t} + \sum_{k=1}^{h-1} p_{k,t} p_{h-k,t} + \\
&\qquad \sum_{k=h+1}^{n-i} p_{k,t}\Big)
\end{aligned}
\tag{1}
$$

We show by induction on t that

$$
p_{h,t} \le \left(\frac{\alpha t}{n^2}\right)^{h-1}, \quad \text{for all } t \le \epsilon n^2
\tag{2}
$$

where α and ϵ are positive constants that are specified later.

The induction base is immediate. For the induction step, we use the induction hypothesis for t and Equation 1 and bound $p_{h,t+1}$ as follows.

$$
\begin{aligned}
p_{h,t+1} &\le \left(\frac{\alpha t}{n^2}\right)^{h-1} + \frac{4}{n^2}\Big(\sum_{k=1}^{i-1}\left(\frac{\alpha t}{n^2}\right)^{h+k-1} + \\
&\quad \sum_{k=1}^{h-1}\left(\frac{\alpha t}{n^2}\right)^{k-1}\left(\frac{\alpha t}{n^2}\right)^{h-k-1} + \sum_{k=h+1}^{n-i}\left(\frac{\alpha t}{n^2}\right)^{k-1}\Big) \\
&\le \left(\frac{\alpha t}{n^2}\right)^{h-1} + \\
&\quad \frac{4}{n^2}\left((h-1)\left(\frac{\alpha t}{n^2}\right)^{h-2} + \left(\frac{\alpha t}{n^2}\right)^{h}\frac{2}{1-\alpha t/n^2}\right) \\
&\le \left(\frac{\alpha t}{n^2}\right)^{h-1} + (h-1)\left(\frac{\alpha t}{n^2}\right)^{h-2}\frac{1}{n^2}\left(4+\frac{4\epsilon^2}{(1-\alpha\epsilon)}\right) \\
&\le \left(\frac{\alpha t}{n^2}\right)^{h-1} + (h-1)\left(\frac{\alpha t}{n^2}\right)^{h-2}\frac{\alpha}{n^2} \\
&\le \left(\frac{\alpha(t+1)}{n^2}\right)^{h-1} .
\end{aligned}
$$

(In the second inequality, we combine the first and third

summations and bound them by their infinite sums. In the third inequality, we use $t \le \epsilon n^2$. For the fourth inequality, we set α sufficiently large so that $\alpha \ge 4 + 4/(1-\alpha\epsilon)$. The final inequality follows from Taylor series expansion.)

For an integer x, let C_x denote the cut $(\{u : u \le x\}, \{v, v > x\})$. We say that a cut C_x is *untouched* at the start of round t if the only edge in G_t crossing the cut C_x is the edge $(x, x+1)$; otherwise, we say C_x is *touched*. Let X denote the smallest integer such that C_X is untouched. We note that X is a random variable that also varies with time. Initially, $X = n/2$.

We divide the analysis into several phases, numbered from 0. A phase ends when X changes. Let X_i denote the value of X at the start of phase i; thus $X_0 = n/2$. Let T_i denote the number of rounds in phase i. A new edge is added to the cut C_{X_i} only if either X_i selects edge (X_i, X_i+1) as its first hop or a node $u < X_i$ selects $u \to X_i \to X_i+1$. Since the degree of every node is at least $n/2$, the probability that a new edge is added to the cut C_i is at most $2/n + n(4/n^2) = 6/n$, implying that $E[T_i] \ge n/6$.

We now place a bound on X_{i+1}. Fix a round $t \le \epsilon n^2$, and let E_x denote the event that C_x is touched by round t. We first place an upper bound on the probability of E_x for arbitrary x using Equation 2.

$$
\Pr[E_x] \le \sum_{h\ge 2} h\left(\frac{\alpha t}{n^2}\right)^{h-1} \le \frac{\alpha t(4 - 3(\alpha t)/n^2 + (\alpha t)^2/n^4)}{n^2(1 - (\alpha t)/n^2)^3},
$$

for $t \le \epsilon n^2$, where we use the inequality $\sum_{h\ge 2} h^2 \delta^h = \delta(4 - 3\delta + \delta^2)/(1-\delta)^3$ for $0 < \delta < 1$. We set ϵ sufficiently small so that $(4 - 3\epsilon + \epsilon^2)/(1-\epsilon)^3 \le 5$, implying that the above probability is at most 5ϵ.

If E_x were independent from E_y for $x \ne y$, then we can invoke a straightforward analysis using a geometric probability distribution to argue that $E[X_{i+1} - X_i]$ is at most $1/(1 - 5\epsilon) = O(1)$; to see this, observe that $X_{i+1} - X_i$ is stochastically dominated by the number of tosses of a biased coin needed to get one head, where the probability of tail is 5ϵ. The preceding independence does not hold, however; in fact, for $y > x$, $\Pr[E_y \mod E_x] > \Pr[E_y]$. In the full paper [16], we show that the impact of this correlation is very small when x and y are sufficiently far apart. In particular, we consider a sequence of cuts $C_{x_1}, C_{x_2}, \ldots, C_{x_\ell}, \ldots$ where $x_\ell = x_{\ell-1} + c\ell$, for a constant c chosen sufficiently large, and $x_0 = X_i + 2$, and show that

$$
\Pr[E_{x_\ell} | E_{x_{\ell-1}} \cap E_{x_{\ell-2}} \cdots E_{x_1}] \le 6\epsilon.
$$

Since X_{i+1} is at most the smallest x_ℓ such that C_{x_ℓ} is untouched, we obtain that

$$
E[X_{i+1} - X_i] \le 2 + \sum_{\ell \ge 2} (6\epsilon)^\ell c\ell^2 \le c',
$$

for a constant c' chosen sufficiently large. We thus obtain that after $\epsilon' n$ phases, $E[X]$ is at most $\epsilon' c' n$, where ϵ' is chosen sufficiently small so that $n - E[X]$ is $\Omega(n)$. Since the expected length of each phase is at least $n/6$, it follows that the expected number of rounds it takes for the two-hop process to complete is $\Omega(n^2)$ rounds. $\quad\square$

6. CONCLUSION

We have analyzed two natural gossip-based discovery processes in networks and showed almost-tight bounds on their convergence in arbitrary networks. Our processes are motivated by the resource discovery problem in distributed networks as well as by the evolution of social networks. We would like to study variants of the processes that take into account failures associated with forming connections, the joining and leaving of nodes, or having only a subset of nodes to participate in forming connections. We believe our techniques can be extended to analyze such situations as well. From a technical standpoint, the main problem left open by our work is to resolve the logarithmic factor gap between the upper and lower bounds. It is not hard to show that from the perspective of increasing the minimum degree by a constant factor, our analysis is tight up to constant factors. It is conceivable, however, that a sharper upper bound can be obtained by an alternative analysis that uses a "smoother" measure of progress.

7. REFERENCES

[1] I. Abraham and D. Dolev. Asynchronous resource discovery. *Computer Networks*, 50:1616–1629, July 2006.

[2] M. Adler, E. Halperin, R. M. Karp, and V. V. Vazirani. A stochastic process on the hypercube with applications to peer-to-peer networks. In *STOC*, pages 575–584, 2003.

[3] N. Alon. Problems and results in extremal combinatorics – II. *Discrete Mathematics*, 2003.

[4] O. Babaoglu and M. Jelasity. Self-* properties through gossiping. *Philosophical Transactions of the Royal Society A*, 366:3747–3757, 2008.

[5] A. Berns, S. Ghosh, and S. Pemmaraju. A framework for building self-stabilizing overlay networks. In *PODC*, pages 398–399, 2010. Brief Announcement.

[6] S. Bornholdt and H. Schuster (Editors). *Handbook of Graphs and Networks*. Wiley-VCH, 2003.

[7] S. Boyd, A. Ghosh, B. Prabhakar, and D. Shah. Randomized gossip algorithms. *IEEE Trans. on Infor. Theory*, 52(6):2508–2530, 2006.

[8] S. Chakrabarti, A. Frieze, and J. Vera. The influence of search engines on preferential attachment. In *SODA*, 2005.

[9] J. Chen and G. Pandurangan. Optimal gossip-based aggregate computation. In *SPAA*, pages 124–133, 2010.

[10] F. Chierichetti, S. Lattanzi, and A. Panconesi. Almost tight bounds on rumor spreading and conductance. In *STOC*, 2010.

[11] C. Cooper and A. Frieze. Crawling on web graphs. In *STOC*, 2002.

[12] A. Demers, D. Greene, C. Hauser, W. Irish, J. Larson, S. Shenker, H. Sturgis, D. Swinehart, and D. Terry. Epidemic algorithms for replicated database maintenance. In *PODC*, pages 1–12, 1987.

[13] N. B. Dimitrov and C. Greg Plaxton. Optimal cover time for a graph-based coupon collector process. In *ICALP*, pages 702–716, 2005.

[14] B. Doerr, T. Friedrich, and T. Sauerwald. Quasi-random rumor spreading. In *SODA*, pages 773–781, 2008.

[15] Giakkoupis. Tight bounds for rumor spreading in graphs of a given conductance. In *STACS*, pages 57–68, 2011.

[16] B. Haeupler, G. Pandurangan, D. Peleg, R. Rajaraman, and Z. Sun. Discovery through Gossip arXiv:1202.2092v1 [cs.DC]

[17] M. Harchol-Balter, T. Leighton, and D. Lewin. Resource discovery in distributed networks. In *PODC*, pages 229–237, 1999.

[18] R. Jacob, A. Richa, C. Scheideler, S. Schmid, and H. Taubig. A distributed polylogarithmic time algorithm for self-stabilizing skip graphs. In *PODC*, pages 131–140, 2009.

[19] M. Jelasity, A. Montresor, and O. Babaoglu. T-man: Gossip-based fast overlay topology construction. *Computer networks*, 53:2321–2339, 2009.

[20] R. M. Karp, C. Schindelhauer, S. Shenker, and B. Vöcking. Randomized rumor spreading. In *FOCS*, pages 565–574, 2000.

[21] D. Kempe, A. Dobra, and J. Gehrke. Gossip-based computation of aggregate information. In *FOCS*, pages 482–491, 2003.

[22] D. Kempe and J. Kleinberg. Protocols and impossibility results for gossip-based communication mechanisms. In *FOCS*, 2002.

[23] D. Kempe, J. Kleinberg, and A. Demers. Spatial gossip and resource location protocols. In *STOC*, 2001.

[24] S. Kutten, D. Peleg, and U. Vishkin. Deterministic resource discovery in distributed networks. In *SPAA*, 2001.

[25] C. Law and K. Siu. An $O(\log n)$ randomized resource discovery algorithm. In *DISC*, pages 5–8, 2000. Brief Announcement.

[26] M. Mitzenmacher and E. Upfal. *Probability and Computing: Randomized Algorithms and Probabilistic Analysis*. Cambridge University Press, 2004.

[27] D. Mosk-Aoyama and D. Shah. Computing separable functions via gossip. In *PODC*, pages 113–122, 2006.

[28] M. J. Newman, A. Barabasi, and D. J. Watts. *Structure and Dynamics of Networks*. Princeton University Press, 2006.

[29] F. Vega-Redondo. *Complex Social Networks*. Cambridge University Press, 2007.

Keynote Talk

Abstraction Failures in Concurrent Programming

Doug Lea
State University of New York at Oswego
Oswego, NY, USA
dl@cs.oswego.edu

Abstract

Creating components based on concurrent and parallel algorithms and data structures often requires more attention to "engineering" issues not seen with most other libraries. Components created in the "obvious" way sometimes turn out to be wrong, to perform poorly, or are unusable in most applications, because the abstractions in which they are expressed are leaky, imprecise, or incorrectly specified. While many of these issues are encountered in other aspects of concurrent programming, the impact is accentuated when they continue to leak through to APIs provided by library components.

This presentation surveys some examples and lessons learned from the design, implementation, and applications of the java.util.concurrent library, including those surrounding memory models, resource management and garbage collection, thread management, optimization, and code generation.

Categories & Subject Descriptors: D.1.3 Concurrent Programming

Author Keywords: Concurrent library design;

Bio

Doug Lea is a professor of Computer Science at the State University of New York at Oswego. He is an author of books, articles, reports, and standardization efforts on object oriented software development including those on specification, design and implementation techniques, distributed, concurrent, and parallel object systems, and software reusability; and has served as chair, organizer, or program committee member for many conferences and workshops in these areas. He is the primary author of several widely used software packages and components.

Copyright is held by the author/owner(s).
SPAA'12, June 25–27, 2012, Pittsburgh, Pennsylvania, USA.
ACM 978-1-4503-1213-4/12/06.

SALSA: Scalable and Low Synchronization NUMA-aware Algorithm for Producer-Consumer Pools

Elad Gidron
CS Department
Technion, Haifa, Israel
eladgi@cs.technion.ac.il

Idit Keidar
EE Department
Technion, Haifa, Israel
idish@ee.technion.ac.il

Dmitri Perelman*
EE Department
Technion, Haifa, Israel
dima39@tx.technion.ac.il

Yonathan Perez
EE Department
Technion, Haifa, Israel
yonathan0210@gmail.com

ABSTRACT

We present a highly-scalable non-blocking producer-consumer task pool, designed with a special emphasis on lightweight synchronization and data locality. The core building block of our pool is *SALSA, Scalable And Low Synchronization Algorithm* for a single-consumer container with task stealing support. Each consumer operates on its own SALSA container, stealing tasks from other containers if necessary. We implement an elegant self-tuning policy for task insertion, which does not push tasks to overloaded SALSA containers, thus decreasing the likelihood of stealing.

SALSA manages large chunks of tasks, which improves locality and facilitates stealing. SALSA uses a novel approach for coordination among consumers, without strong atomic operations or memory barriers in the fast path. It invokes only two CAS operations during a chunk steal.

Our evaluation demonstrates that a pool built using SALSA containers scales *linearly* with the number of threads and significantly outperforms other FIFO and non-FIFO alternatives.

Categories and Subject Descriptors

D.1.3 [**Software**]: Concurrent Programming

General Terms

Algorithms, Performance

Keywords

Multi-core, concurrent data structures

---

*This work was partially supported by Hasso Plattner Institute.

Permission to make digital or hard copies of all or part of this work for personal or classroom use is granted without fee provided that copies are not made or distributed for profit or commercial advantage and that copies bear this notice and the full citation on the first page. To copy otherwise, to republish, to post on servers or to redistribute to lists, requires prior specific permission and/or a fee.
SPAA'12, June 25–27, 2012, Pittsburgh, Pennsylvania, USA.
Copyright 2012 ACM 978-1-4503-1213-4/12/06 ...$10.00.

1. INTRODUCTION

Emerging computer architectures pose many new challenges for software development. First, as the number of computing elements constantly increases, the importance of *scalability* of parallel programs becomes paramount. Second, accessing memory has become the principal bottleneck, while multi-CPU systems are based on NUMA architectures, where memory access from different chips is asymmetric. Therefore, it is instrumental to design software with *local data access, cache-friendliness,* and *reduced contention* on shared memory locations, especially across chips. Furthermore, as systems get larger, their behavior becomes less predictable, underscoring the importance of *robust* programs that can overcome unexpected thread stalls.

Our overarching goal is to devise a methodology for developing parallel algorithms addressing these challenges. In this paper, we focus on one of the fundamental building blocks of highly parallel software, namely a producer-consumer task pool. Specifically, we present a scalable and highly-efficient non-blocking pool, with lightweight synchronization-free operations in the common case. Its data allocation scheme is cache-friendly and highly suitable for NUMA environments. Moreover, our pool is robust in the face of imbalanced loads and unexpected thread stalls.

Our system is composed of two independent logical entities: 1) *SALSA, Scalable and Low Synchronization Algorithm,* a single-consumer pool that exports a stealing operation, and 2) a work stealing framework implementing a management policy that operates multiple SALSA pools.

In order to improve locality and facilitate stealing, SALSA keeps tasks in chunks, organized in per-producer chunk lists. Only the producer mapped to a given list can insert tasks to chunks in this list, which eliminates the need for synchronization among producers.

Though each consumer has its own task pool, inter-consumer synchronization is required in order to allow stealing. The challenge is to do so without resorting to costly atomic operations (such as CAS or memory fences) upon each task retrieval. We address this challenge via a novel chunk-based stealing algorithm that allows consume operations to be synchronization-free in the common case, when no stealing occurs, which we call the *fast path*. Moreover, SALSA reduces the stealing rate by moving entire chunks of tasks in one steal operation, which requires only two CAS operations.

In order to achieve locality of memory access on a NUMA architecture, SALSA chunks are kept in the consumer's local memory. The management policy matches producers and consumers according to their proximity, which allows most task transfers to occur within a NUMA node.

In many-core machines running multiple applications, system behavior becomes less predictable. Unexpected thread stalls may lead to an asymmetric load on consumers, which may in turn lead to high stealing rates, hampering performance. SALSA employs a novel auto-balancing mechanism that has producers insert tasks to less loaded consumers, and is thus robust to spurious load fluctuations.

We have implemented SALSA in C++, and tested its performance on a 32-core NUMA machine. Our experiments show that the SALSA-based work stealing pool *scales linearly* with the number of threads; it is 20 times faster than other work-stealing alternatives, and shows a significant improvement over state-of-the-art non-FIFO alternatives. SALSA-based pools scale well even in unbalanced scenarios.

This paper proceeds as follows. Section 2 describes related work. We give the system overview in Section 3. The SALSA single-consumer algorithm is described in Section 4 and its correctness is discussed in Section 5. We discuss our implementation and experimental results in Section 6, and finally conclude in Section 7.

2. RELATED WORK

Task pools.

There is a large body of work on lock-free unbounded FIFO queues and LIFO stacks [12, 16, 17, 21, 22]. However, due to the inherent need for ordering all operations, such algorithms generally have high contention and do not scale, and are therefore less appealing for use as task pools.

A number of previous works have recognized this limitation, and observed that strict FIFO order is seldom needed in multi-core systems [3, 4, 7, 24]. To the best of our knowledge, all previous solutions use strong atomic operations (like CAS), at least in every consume operation. Moreover, most of them [3, 4, 7] do not partition the pool among processors, and therefore do not achieve good locality and cache-friendliness, which has been shown to limit their scalability on NUMA systems [6].

The closest non-FIFO pool to our work is the Concurrent Bags of Sundell et al. [24], which, like SALSA, uses per-producer chunk lists. This work is optimized for the case that the same threads are both consumers and producers, and typically consume from themselves, while SALSA improves the performance of such a task pool in NUMA environments where producers and consumers are separate threads. Unlike our pool, the Concurrent Bags algorithm uses strong atomic operations upon each consume. In addition, steals are performed in the granularity of single tasks and not whole chunks as in SALSA. Overall, their throughput does not scale linearly with the number of participating threads, as shown in [24] and in Section 6 of this paper.

Techniques.

Variations of techniques we employ were previously used in various contexts. Work-stealing [9] is a standard way to reduce contention by using individual per-consumer pools, where tasks may be stolen from one pool to another. We improve the efficiency of stealing by transferring a chunk of tasks upon every steal operation. Hendler et al. [15] have proposed stealing of multiple items by copying a range of tasks from one dequeue to another, but this approach requires costly CAS operations on the fast-path and introduces non-negligible overhead for item copying. In contrast, our approach of chunk-based stealing coincides with our synchronization-free fast-path, and steals whole chunks in O(1) steps. Furthermore, our use of page-size chunks allows for data migration in NUMA architectures to improve locality, as done in [8].

The principle of keeping NUMA-local data structures was previously used by Dice et al. for constructing scalable NUMA locks [11]. Similarly to their work, our algorithm's data allocation scheme is designed to reduce inter-chip communication.

The concept of a synchronization-free fast-path previously appeared in works on scheduling queues, e.g., [5, 14]. However, these works assume that the same process is both the producer and the consumer, and hence the synchronization-free fast-path is actually used only when a process transfers data to *itself*. On the other hand, our pool is synchronization-free even when tasks are transfered among multiple threads; our synchronization-free fast-path is used also when multiple producers produce data for a single consumer. We do not know of any other work that supports synchronization-free data transfer among different threads.

The idea of organizing data in chunks to preserve locality in dynamically-sized data structures was previously used in [10, 12, 14, 24]. SALSA extends on the idea of chunk-based data structures by using chunks also for efficient stealing.

3. SYSTEM OVERVIEW

In the current section we present our framework for scalable and NUMA-aware producer-consumer data exchange. Our system follows the principle of separating mechanism and policy. We therefore consider two independent logical entities:

1. *A single consumer pool (SCPool)* mechanism manages the tasks arriving to a given consumer and allows tasks stealing by other consumers.

2. A management policy operates SCPools: it routes producer requests to the appropriate consumers and initiates stealing between the pools. This way, the policy controls the system's behavior according to considerations of load-distribution, throughput, fairness, locality, etc. We are especially interested in a management policy suitable for NUMA architectures (see Figure 1), where each CPU has its own memory, and memories of other CPUs are accessed over an interconnect. As a high rate of remote memory accesses can decrease the performance, it is desirable for the SCPool of a consumer to reside close to its own CPU.

SCPool abstraction.

The SCPool API provides the abstraction of a single-consumer task pool with stealing support, see Algorithm 1. A producer invokes two operations: **produce()**, which attempts to insert a task to the given pool and fails if the pool

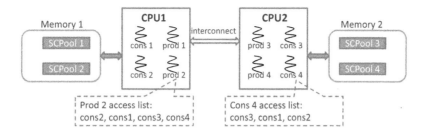

Figure 1: Producer-consumer framework overview. In this example, there are two processors connected to two memory banks (NUMA architecture). Two producers and two consumers running on each processor, and the data of each consumer is allocated at the closest physical memory. A producer (consumer) has a sorted access list of consumers for task insertion (respectively stealing).

Algorithm 1 API for a Single Consumer Pool with stealing support.

1: boolean: produce(Task, SCPool) ▷ Tries to insert the task to the pool, returns false if no space is available.
2: void: produceForce(Task, SCPool) ▷ Insert the task to the pool, expanding the pool if necessary.
3: {Task ∪⊥}: consume()   ▷ Retrieve a task from the pool, returns ⊥ if no tasks in the pool are detected.
4: {Task ∪⊥}: steal(SCPool from)   ▷ Try to steal a number of tasks from the given pool and move them to the current pool. Return some stolen task or ⊥.

---

is full, and **produceForce()**, which always succeeds by expanding the pool on demand. There are also two ways to retrieve a task from the pool: the owner of the pool (only) can call the **consume()** function; while any other thread can invoke **steal()**, which tries to transfer a number of tasks between two pools and return one of the stolen tasks.

A straightforward way to implement the above API is using dynamic-size multi-producer multi-consumer FIFO queue (e.g., Michael-Scott queue [21]). In this case, **produce()** enqueues a new task, while **consume()** and **steal()** dequeue a task. In the next section we present SALSA, a much more efficient SCPool.

Management policy.

A management policy defines the way in which: 1) a producer chooses an SCPool for task insertion; and 2) a consumer decides when to retrieve a task from its own pool or steal from other pools. Note that the policy is independent of the underlying SCPool implementation. We believe that the policy is a subject for engineering optimizations, based on specific workloads and demands.

In the current work, we present a NUMA-aware policy. If the individual SCPools themselves are lock-free, then our policy preserves lock-freedom at the system level. Our policy is as follows:

- **Access lists.** Each process in the system (producer or consumer) is provided with an *access list*, an ordered list of all the consumers in the system, sorted according to their distance from that process (see Figure 1). Intuitively, our intention is to have a producer mostly interact with the closest consumer, while stealing mainly happens inside the same processor node.

- **Producer's policy.** The producer policy is implemented in the **put()** function in Algorithm 2. The op-

---

Algorithm 2 Work stealing framework pseudo-code.

5: **Local variables:**
6:    SCPool myPool ▷ The consumer's pool
7:    SCPool[] accessList

8: **Function get():**
9:    **while**(true)
10:        ▷ First try to get a task from the local pool
11:        t ← **myPool.consume()**
12:        **if** (t ≠ ⊥) **return** t
13:        ▷ Failed to get a task from the local pool – steal
14:        **foreach** SCPool p in *accessList* in order do:
15:            t ← **p.steal()**
16:            **if** (t ≠ ⊥) **return** t
17:        ▷ No tasks found – validate emptiness
18:        **if** (**checkEmpty()**) **return** ⊥

19: **Function put(Task t):**
20:    ▷ Produce to the pools by the order of the *access list*
21:    **foreach** SCPool p in *accessList* in order do:
22:        **if** (p.**produce**(t)) **return**
23:    firstp ← the first entry in *accessList*
24:    ▷ If all pools are full, expand the closest pool
25:    **produceForce**(t,firstp)
26:    **return**

---

eration first calls the **produce()** of the first SCPool in its access list. Note that this operation might fail if the pool is full, (which can be seen as evidence of that the corresponding consumer is overloaded). In this case, the producer tries to insert the task into other pools, in the order defined by its access list. If all insertions fail, the producer invokes **produceForce()** on the closest SCPool, which always succeeds (expanding the pool if needed).

- **Consumer's policy.** The consumer policy is implemented in the **get()** function in Algorithm 2. A consumer takes tasks from its own SCPool. If its SCPool is empty, then the consumer tries to steal tasks from other pools in the order defined by its access list. The **checkEmpty()** operation handles the issue of when a consumer gives up and returns ⊥. This is subtle issue, and we discuss it in Section 5. Stealing serves two purposes: first, it is important for distributing the load among all available consumers. Second, it ensures that tasks are not lost in case they are inserted into the SCPool of a crashed (or very slow) consumer.

4. ALGORITHM DESCRIPTION

In the current section we present the SALSA SCPool. We first show the data structures of SALSA in Section 4.1, and then present the basic algorithm without stealing support in Section 4.2. The stealing procedure is described in Section 4.3, finally, the role of chunk pools is presented in Section 4.4. For the simplicity of presentation, in this section we assume that the the memory accesses satisfy sequential consistency [19], we describe the ways to solve memory reordering issues in Section 6.1.

4.1 SALSA Structure

Algorithm 3 SALSA implementation of SCPool: Data Structures.

27: **Chunk type**
28:　　Task[CHUNK_SIZE] tasks
29:　　int owner ▷ owner's consumer id
30: **Node type**
31:　　Chunk c; initially ⊥
32:　　int idx; initially -1
33:　　Node next;
34: **SALSA per consumer data structure**:
35:　　int consumerId
36:　　List⟨Node⟩[] chunkLists ▷ one list per producer + extra list for stealing (every list is single-writer multi-reader)
37:　　Queue⟨Chunk⟩ chunkPool ▷ pool of spare chunks
38:　　Node currentNode, initially ⊥ ▷ current node to work with

---

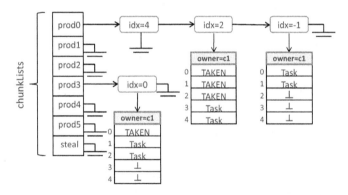

Figure 2: Chunk lists in SALSA single consumer pool implementation. Tasks are kept in chunks, which are organized in per-producer lists; an additional list is reserved for stealing. Each list can be modified by the corresponding producer only. The only process that is allowed to retrieve tasks from a chunk is the owner of that chunk (defined by the ownership flag). A Node's index corresponds to the latest task taken from the chunk or the task that is about to be taken by the current chunk owner.

The SALSA data structure of a consumer c_i is described in Algorithm 3 and partially depicted in Figure 2. The tasks inserted to SALSA are kept in chunks, which are organized in per-producer chunk lists. Only the producer mapped to a given list can insert a task to any chunk in that list. Every chunk is owned by a single consumer whose id is kept in the

owner field of the chunk. The owner is the only process that is allowed to take tasks from the chunk; if another process wants to take a task from the chunk, it should first steal the chunk and change its ownership. A task entry in a chunk is used at most once. Its value is ⊥ before the task is inserted, and TAKEN after it has been consumed.

The per-producer chunk lists are kept in the array *chunkLists* (see Figure 2), where *chunkLists[j]* keeps a list of chunks with tasks inserted by producer p_j. In addition, the array has a special entry *chunkLists[steal]*, holding chunks stolen by c_i. Every list has a single writer who can modify the list structure (add or remove nodes): *chunkLists[j]*'s modifier is the producer p_j, while *chunkLists[steal]*'s modifier is the SCPool's owner. The nodes of the used chunks are lazily reclaimed and removed by the list's owner. For brevity, we omit the linked list manipulation functions from the pseudo-code bellow. Our single-writer lists can be implemented without synchronization primitives, similarly to the single-writer linked-list in [20]. In addition to holding the chunk, a node keeps the index of the latest taken task in that chunk, this index is then used for chunk stealing as we show in Section 4.3.

Safe memory reclamation is provided by using hazard pointers [20] both for nodes and for chunks. The free (reclaimed) chunks in SALSA are kept at per-consumer *chunkPools* implemented by lock-free Michael-Scott queues [21]. As we show in Section 4.4, the chunk pools serve two purposes: 1) efficient memory reuse and 2) producer-based load balancing.

4.2 Basic Algorithm

4.2.1 SALSA producer

The description of SALSA producer functions is presented in Algorithm 4. The insertion of a new task consists of two stages: 1) finding a chunk for task insertion (if necessary), and 2) adding a task to the chunk.

Finding a chunk.

The chunk for task insertions is kept in the local producer variable *chunk* (line 41 in Algorithm 4). Once a producer starts working with a chunk c, it continues inserting tasks to c until c is full – the producer is oblivious to chunk stealing. If the *chunk*'s value is ⊥, then the producer should start a new chunk (function *getChunk*). In this case, it tries to retrieve a chunk from the chunk pool and to append it to the appropriate chunk list. If the chunk pool is empty then the producer either returns ⊥ (if force=false), or allocates a new chunk by itself (otherwise) (lines 56–58).

Inserting a task to the chunk.

As previously described in Section 4.1, different producers insert tasks to different chunks, which removes the need for synchronization among producers. The producer local variable *prodIdx* indicates the next free slot in the chunk. All that is left for the insertion function to do, is to put a task in that slot and to increment *prodIdx* (line 48). Once the index reaches the maximal value, the *chunk* variable is set to ⊥, indicating that the next insertion operation should start a new chunk.

4.2.2 SALSA consumer without stealing

The consumer's algorithm without stealing is given in the

Algorithm 4 SALSA implementation of SCPool: Producer Functions.

39: **Producer local variables:**	52: **Function produceForce**(Task t, SCPool scPool):
40: int producerId	53: **insert**(t, scPool, true)
41: Chunk chunk; initially $\perp$ ▷ the chunk to insert to	
42: int prodIdx; initially 0 ▷ the prefix of inserted tasks	54: **Function getChunk**(SALSA scPool, bool force)
	55: newChunk ← dequeue chunk from scPool.chunkPool
43: **Function produce**(Task t, SCPool scPool):	56: **if** (chunk = $\perp$) ▷ no available chunks in this pool
44: **return insert**(t, scPool, false)	57: **if** (force = false) **then return false**
	58: newChunk ← allocate a new chunk
45: **Function insert**(Task t, SCPool scPool, bool force):	59: newChunk.owner ← scPool.consumerId
46: **if** (chunk = $\perp$) **then** ▷ allocate new chunk	60: node ← new node with idx = −1 and c = newChunk
47: **if** (**getChunk**(scPool, force) = **false**) **then return false**	61: scPool.chunkLists[producerId].**append**(node)
48: chunk.tasks[prodIdx] ← t; prodIdx++	62: chunk ← newChunk; prodIdx ← 0
49: **if**(prodIdx = CHUNK_SIZE) **then**	63: **return true**
50: chunk ← $\perp$ ▷ the chunk is full	
51: **return true**	

---

left column of Algorithm 5. The consumer first finds a nonempty chunk it owns and then invokes **takeTask()** to retrieve a task.

Unlike producers, which have exclusive access to insertions in a given chunk, a consumer must take into account the possibility of stealing. Therefore, it should notify other processes which task it is about to take.

To this end, each node in the chunk list keeps an index of the taken prefix of its chunk in the idx variable, which is initiated to −1. A consumer that wants to take a task T, first increments the index, then checks the chunk's ownership, and finally changes the chunk entry from T to $TAKEN$ (lines 78–80). By doing so, a consumer guarantees that idx always points to the last taken task or to a task that is about to be taken. Hence, a process that is stealing a chunk from a node with $idx = i$ can assume that the tasks in the range $[0 \ldots i)$ have already been taken. The logic for dealing with stolen chunks is described in the next section.

4.3 Stealing

The stealing algorithm is given in the function **steal()** in Algorithm 5. We refer to the stealing consumer as c_s, the victim process whose chunk is being stolen as c_v, and the stolen chunk as ch.

The idea is to turn c_s to the exclusive owner of ch, such that c_s will be able to take tasks from the chunk without synchronization. In order to do that, c_s changes the ownership of ch from c_v to c_s using CAS (line 96) and removes the chunk from c_v's list (line 104). Once c_v notices the change in the ownership it can take at most one more task from ch (lines 83–86).

When the **steal()** operation of c_s occurs simultaneously with the **takeTask()** operation of c_v, both c_s and c_v might try to retrieve the same task. We now explain why this might happen. Recall that c_v notifies potential stealers of the task it is about to take by incrementing the idx value in ch's node (line 78). This value is copied by c_s in line 99 when creating a copy of ch's node for its steal list.

Consider, for example, a scenario in which the idx is incremented by c_v from 10 to 11. If c_v checks ch's ownership before it is changed by c_s, then c_v takes the task at index 11 *without synchronization* (line 80). Therefore, c_s cannot be allowed to take the task pointed by idx. Hence, c_v has to take the task at index 11 even if it does observe the ownership change. After stealing the chunk, c_s will eventually try

to take the task pointed by $idx + 1$. However, if c_s copies the node before idx is incremented by c_v, c_s might think that the value of $idx + 1$ is 11. In this case, both c_s and c_v will try to retrieve the task at index 11. To ensure that the task is not retrieved twice, both invoke CAS in order to retrieve this task (line 108 for c_s, line 83 for c_v).

The above algorithm works correctly as long as the stealing consumer can observe the node with the updated index value. This might not be the case if the same chunk is concurrently stolen by another consumer rendering the idx of the original node obsolete. In order to prevent this situation, stealing a chunk from the pool of consumer c_v is allowed only if c_v is the owner of this chunk (line 96). This approach is prone to the ABA problem: consider a scenario where consumer c_a is trying to steal from c_b, but before the execution of the CAS in line 96, the chunk is stolen by c_c and then stolen back by c_b. In this case, c_a's CAS succeeds but c_a has an old value of idx. To prevent this ABA problem, the owner field contains a "tag", which is incremented on every CAS operation. For brevity, tags are omitted from the pseudo-code.

A naïve way for c_s to steal the chunk from c_v would be first to change the ownership and then to move the chunk to the steal list. However, this approach may cause the chunk to "disappear" if c_s is stalled, because the chunk becomes inaccessible via the lists of c_s and yet c_s is its owner. Therefore, SALSA first adds the original node to the steal list of c_s, then change the ownership, and only then replaces the original node with a new one (lines 95–104).

4.4 Chunk Pools

As described in Section 4.1, each consumer keeps a pool of free chunks. When a producer needs a new chunk for adding a task to consumer c_i, it tries to get a chunk from c_i's chunk pool – if no free chunks are available, the **produce()** operation fails.

As described in Section 3, our system-wide policy defines that if an insertion operation fails, then the producer tries to insert a task to other pools. Thus, the producer avoids adding tasks to overloaded consumers, which in turn decreases the amount of costly steal operations. We further refer to this technique as producer-based balancing.

Another SALSA property is that a chunk is returned to the pool of a consumer that retrieves the latest task of this chunk. Therefore, the size of the chunk pool of consumer c_i

Algorithm 5 SALSA implementation of SCPool: Consumer Functions.

```
64: Function consume():
65:    if (currentNode ≠ ⊥) then ▷ common case
66:       t ← takeTask(currentNode)
67:       if (t ≠ ⊥) then return t
68:    foreach Node n in ChunkLists do: ▷ fair traversal
69:       if (n.c ≠ ⊥ ∧ n.c.owner = consumerId) then
70:          t ← takeTask(n)
71:          if (t ≠ ⊥) then currentNode ← n; return t
72:    currentNode ← ⊥; return ⊥

73: Function takeTask(Node n):
74:    chunk ← n.c
75:    if (chunk = ⊥) then return ⊥ ▷ stolen chunk
76:    task ← chunk.tasks[n.idx + 1]
77:    if (task = ⊥) then return ⊥ ▷ no inserted tasks
       ▷ tell the world you're going to take a task from idx
78:    n.idx++
79:    if (chunk.owner = consumerId) then ▷ common case
80:       chunk.tasks[n.idx] ← TAKEN
81:       checkLast(n)
82:       return task
       ▷ the chunk has been stolen, CAS the last task and
       go away
83:    success ← (task ≠ TAKEN ∧
          CAS(chunk.tasks[n.idx], task, TAKEN))
84:    if(success) then checkLast(n)
85:    currentNode ← ⊥
86:    return (success) ? task : ⊥

87: Function checkLast(Node n):
88:    if(n.idx + 1 = CHUNK_SIZE) then
89:       n.c ← ⊥; return chunk to chunkPool
90:       currentNode ← ⊥
```

```
91: Function steal(SCPool p):
92:    prevNode ← a node holding tasks, whose owner is p,
       from some list in p's pool ▷ different policies possible

93:    if (prevNode = ⊥) return ⊥ ▷ No Chunk found
94:    c ← prevNode.c; if (c = ⊥) then return ⊥
       ▷ make it restealable
95:    chunkLists[steal].append(prevNode)
96:    if (CAS(c.owner,p.consumerId,consumerId)=false)
97:       chunkLists[steal].remove(prevNode)
98:       return ⊥ ▷ failed to steal
99:    newNode ← copy of prevNode
100:   if (newNode.idx+1 = CHUNK_SIZE)
101:      chunkLists[steal].remove(prevNode)
102:      return ⊥
103:   replace prevNode with newNode in chunkLists[steal]
104:   prevNode.c ← ⊥
       ▷ done stealing the chunk, take one task from it
105:   idx ← newNode.idx
106:   task ← c.tasks[idx+1]
107:   if (task = ⊥) then return ⊥ ▷ still no task at idx+1

108:   if (task = TAKEN ∨
          !CAS(c.tasks[idx+1], task, TAKEN)) then
109:      task ← ⊥
110:   if (task ≠ ⊥) then checkLast(newNode)
111:   newNode.idx ← newNode.idx+1
112:   if (c.owner = consumerId) currentNode ← newNode
113:   return task
```

is proportional to the rate of c_i's task consumption. This property is especially appealing for heterogeneous systems – a faster consumer c_i, (e.g., one running on a stronger or less loaded core), will have a larger chunk pool, and so more **produce()** operations will insert tasks to c_i, automatically balancing the overall system load.

5. CORRECTNESS

Linearizability.

In the full version of the paper [13], we prove that SALSA does not return the same task twice. However, for our system to be linearizable, we must ensure that SALSA's **get()** operation returns ⊥ only if the pool contains no tasks at some point during the consume operation. We describe a policy for doing so in a lock-free manner.

Let us examine why a naïve approach, of simply traversing all task pools and returning ⊥ if no task is found, violates correctness. First, a consumer might "miss" one task added during its traversal, and another removed during the same traversal, as illustrated in Figure 3. In this case, a single traversal would have returned ⊥ although the pool was not empty at any point during the consume operation. Second, a consumer may miss a task that is moved from one pool to another due to stealing. In order to identify these two cases, we add to each pool a special *emptyIndicator*, a bit array with a bit per-consumer, which is cleared every time the

pool *may* become empty. In SALSA, this occurs when the last task in a chunk is taken or when a chunk is stolen. In addition, we implement a new function, **checkEmpty()** (full pseudo-code shown in [13]), which is called by the framework whenever a consumer fails to retrieve tasks from its pool and all other pools. This function return true only if there is a time during its execution when there are no tasks in the system. If **checkEmpty()** returns false, the consumer simply restarts its operation.

Denote by c the number of consumers in the system. The **checkEmpty()** function works as follows: the consumer traverses all SCPools, to make sure that no tasks are present. After checking a pool, the consumer sets its bit in *emptyIndicator* using CAS. The consumer repeats this traversal c times, where in all traversals except the first, it checks that its bit in *emptyIndicator* is set, i.e., that no chunks were emptied or removed during the traversal. The c traversals are needed in order to account for the case that other consumers have already stolen or removed tasks, but did not yet update *emptyIndicator*, and thus their operations were not detected by the consumer. Since up to $c - 1$ pending operations by other consumers may empty pools before any *emptyIndicator* changes, it is guaranteed that among c traversals in which no chunks were seen and the *emptyIndicator* did not change, there is one during which the system indeed contains no tasks, and therefore it is safe to return

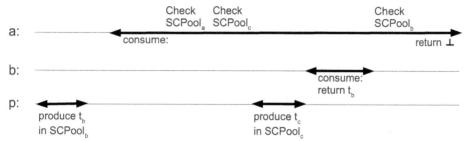

Figure 3: An example where a single traversal may violate linearizability: consumer a is trying to get a task. It fails to take a task from its own pool, and starts looking for chunks to steal in other pools. At this time there is a single non-empty chunk in the system, which is in b's pool; a checks c's pool and finds it empty. At this point, a producer adds a task to c's pool and then b takes the last task from its pool before a checks it. Thus, a finds b's pool empty, and returns $\perp$. There is no way to linearize this execution, because throughout the execution of a's operation, the system contains at least one task.

$\perp$. This method is similar to the one used in Concurrent Bags [24].

Lock-freedom.

The operations of every individual SALSA SCPool are trivially wait-free, since they always return. However, a **get**() operation is restarted whenever **checkEmpty**() returns false, and therefore the algorithm does not guarantee that a consumer will finish every operation. Nevertheless, as shown in the full version of the paper [13], the system is lock-free, i.e., there always exists some consumer that makes progress.

6. IMPLEMENTATION AND EVALUATION

In this section we evaluate the performance of our work-stealing framework built on SALSA pools. We first present the implementation details on dealing with memory reordering issues in Section 6.1. The experiment setup is described in Section 6.2, we show the overall system performance in Section 6.3, study the influence of various SALSA techniques in Section 6.4 and check the impact of memory placement and thread scheduling in Section 6.5.

6.1 Dealing with Memory Reordering

The presentation of the SALSA algorithm in Section 4 assumes sequential consistency [19] as the memory model. However, most existing systems relax sequential consistency to achieve better performance. Specifically, according to x86-TSO [23], memory loads can be reordered with respect to older stores to different locations. In SALSA, this reordering can cause an index increment to occur after the ownership validation (lines 78, 79 in Algorithm 5), which violates correctness as it may cause the same task to be taken twice, by both the original consumer and the stealing thread.

The conventional way to ensure a correct execution in such cases is to use memory fences to force a specific memory ordering. For example, adding an `mfence` instruction between lines 78 and 79 guarantees SALSA's correctness. However, memory fences are costly and their use in the common path degrades performance. Therefore, we prefer to employ a synchronization technique that does not add substantial overhead to the frequently used **takeTask**() operation. One example for such a technique is location-based memory fences, recently proposed by Ladan-Mozes et al. [18], which is unfortunately not implemented in current hardware.

In our implementation, we adopt the synchronization technique described by Dice et al. [1], where the slow thread (namely, the stealer) binds directly to the processor on which the fast thread (namely, the consumer) is currently running, preempting it from the processor, and then returns to run on its own processor. Thread displacement serves as a full memory fence, hence, a stealer that invokes the displacement binding right after updating the ownership (before the line 99 in Algorithm 5) observes the updated consumer's index. On the other hand, the steal-free fast path is not affected by this change.

6.2 Experiment Setup

We compare the following task pool implementations:

- **SALSA** – our work-stealing framework with SCPools implemented by SALSA.

- **SALSA+CAS** – our work-stealing framework with SCPools implemented by a simplistic SALSA variation, in which every **consume**() and **steal**() operation tries to take a single task using CAS. In essence, SALSA+CAS removes the effects of SALSA's low synchronization fast-path and per-chunk stealing. Note that disabling per-chunk stealing in SALSA annuls the idea of chunk ownership, hence, disables its low synchronization fast-path as well.

- **ConcBag** – an algorithm similar to the lock-free Concurrent Bags algorithm [24]. It is worth noting that the original algorithm was optimized for the scenario where the same process is both a producer and a consumer (in essence producing tasks to itself), which we do not consider in this paper; in our system no thread acts as both a producer and a consumer, therefore every consume operation steals a task from some producer. We did not have access to the original code, and therefore reimplemented the algorithm in our framework. Our implementation is faithful to the algorithm in the paper, except in using a simpler and faster underlined linked list algorithm. All engineering decisions were made to maximize performance.

- **WS-MSQ** – our work-stealing framework with SCPools implemented by Michael-Scott non-blocking queue [21]. Both **consume**() and **steal**() operations invoke the **dequeue**() function.

- **WS-LIFO** – our work-stealing framework with SCPool implemented by Michael's LIFO stack [20].

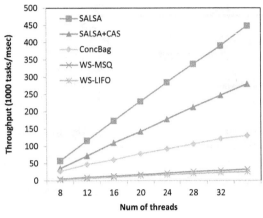

(a) System throughput – N producers, N consumers.

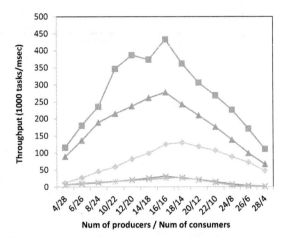

(b) System throughput – variable producers-consumers ratio.

Figure 4: System throughput for various ratios of producers and consumers. SALSA scales linearly with the number of threads – in the 16/16 workload, it is ×20 faster than WS-MSQ and WS-LIFO, and ×3.5 faster than Concurrent Bags. In tests with equal numbers of producers and consumers, the differences among work-stealing alternatives are mainly explained by the consume operation efficiency, since stealing rate is low and hardly influences performance.

We did not experiment with additional FIFO and LIFO queue implementations, because, as shown in [24], their performance is of the same order of magnitude as the Michael-Scott queue. Similarly, we did not evaluate CAFÉ [7] pools because their performance is similar to that of WS-MSQ [6], or ED-Pools [3], which have been shown to scale poorly in multi-processor architectures [6, 24].

All the pools are implemented in C++ and compiled with `-O2` optimization level. In order to minimize scalability issues related to allocations, we use `jemalloc` allocator, which has been shown to be highly scalable in multi-threaded environments [2]. Chunks of SALSA and SALSA+CAS contain 1000 tasks, and chunks of ConcBag contain 128 tasks, which were the respective optimal values for each algorithm (see the full version of the paper [13]).

We use a synthetic benchmark where 1) each producer works in a loop of inserting dummy items; 2) each consumer works in a loop of retrieving dummy items. Each data point shown is an average of 5 runs, each with a duration of 20 seconds. The tests are run on a dedicated shared memory NUMA server with 8 Quad Core AMD 2.3GHz processors and 16GB of memory attached to each processor.

6.3 System Throughput

Figure 4(a) shows system throughput for workloads with equal number of producers and consumers. SALSA *scales linearly* as the number of threads grows to 32 (the number of physical cores in the system), and it clearly outperforms all other competitors. In the 16/16 workload, SALSA is ×20 faster than WS-MSQ and WS-LIFO, and more than ×3.5 faster than Concurrent Bags.

We note that the performance trend of ConcBags in our measurements differs from the results presented by Sundell et al. [24]. While in the original paper, their throughput *drops* by a factor of 3 when the number of threads increases from 4 to 24, in our tests, the performance of ConcBags *increases* with the number of threads. The reasons for the better scalability of our implementation can be related to the

use of different memory allocators, hardware architectures, and engineering optimizations.

All systems implemented by our work-stealing framework scale linearly because of the low contention between consumers. Their performance differences are therefore due to the efficiency of the **consume()** operation – for example, SALSA is ×1.7 faster than SALSA+CAS thanks to its fast-path consumption technique.

In ConcBags, which is not based on per-consumer pools, every **consume()** operation implies stealing, which causes contention among consumers, leading to sub-linear scalability. The stealing policy of ConcBags algorithm plays an important role. The stealing policy described in the original paper [24] proposes to iterate over the lists using round robin. We found out that the approach in which each stealer initiates stealing attempts from the predefined consumer improves ConcBags' results by 53% in a balanced workload.

Figure 4(b) shows system throughput of the algorithms for various ratios of producers and consumers. SALSA outperforms other alternatives in all scenarios, achieving its maximal throughput with equal number of producers and consumers, because neither of them is a system bottleneck.

We next evaluate the behavior of the pools in scenarios with a single producer and multiple consumers. Figure 5(a) shows that the performance of both SALSA and SALSA+CAS does not drop as more consumers are added, while the throughput of other algorithms degrades by the factor of 10. The degradation can be explained by high contention among stealing consumers, as evident from Figure 5(b), which shows the average number of CAS operations per task transfer.

6.4 Evaluating SALSA techniques

In this section we study the influence of two of the techniques used in SALSA: 1) chunk-based-stealing with a low-synchronization fast path (Section 4.3), and 2) producer-based balancing (Section 4.4). To this end, we compare SALSA and SALSA+CAS both with and without producer-

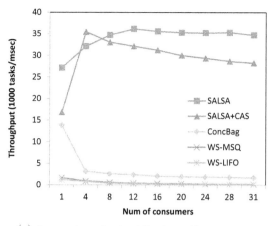

(a) System throughput – 1 Producer, N consumers.

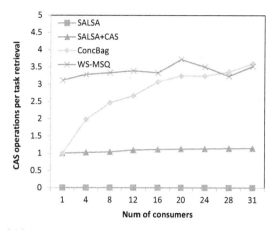

(b) CAS operations per task retrieval – 1 Producer, N consumers.

Figure 5: System behavior in workloads with a single producer and multiple consumers. Both SALSA and SALSA+CAS efficiency balance the load in this scenario. The throughput of other algorithms drops by a factor of 10 due to increased contention among consumers trying to steal tasks from the same pool.

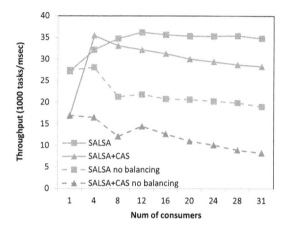

Figure 6: System throughput – 1 Producer, N consumers. Producer-based balancing contributes to the robustness of the framework by reducing stealing. With no balancing, chunk-based stealing becomes important.

based balancing (in the latter a producer always inserts tasks to the same consumer's pool).

Figure 6 depicts the behavior of the four alternatives in single producer / multiple consumers workloads. We see that producer-based balancing is instrumental in redistributing the load: neither SALSA nor SALSA+CAS suffers any degradation as the load increases. When producer-based balancing is disabled, stealing becomes prevalent, and hence the stealing granularity becomes more important: SALSA's chunk based stealing clearly outperforms the naïve task-based approach of SALSA+CAS.

6.5   Impact of Scheduling and Allocation

We now evaluate the impact of scheduling and allocation in our NUMA system. To this end, we compare the following three alternatives: 1) the original SALSA algorithm; 2) SALSA with no affinity enforcement for the threads s.t. producers do not necessarily work with the closest consumers;

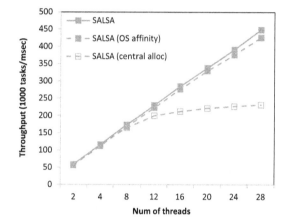

Figure 7: Impact of scheduling and allocation (equal number of producers and consumers). Performance decreases once the interconnect becomes saturated.

3) SALSA with all the memory pools preallocated on a single NUMA node.

Figure 7 depicts the behavior of all the variants in the balanced workload. The performance of SALSA with no predefined affinities is almost identical to the performance of the standard SALSA, while the central allocation alternative looses its scalability after 12 threads.

The main reason for performance degradation in NUMA systems is bandwidth saturation of the interconnect. If all chunks are placed on a single node, every remote memory access is transfered via the interconnect of that node, which causes severe performance degradation. In case of random affinities, remote memory accesses are distributed among different memory nodes, hence their rate remains below the maximum available bandwidth of each individual channel, and the program does not reach the scalability limit.

7.   CONCLUSIONS

We presented a highly-scalable task pool framework, built upon our novel SALSA single-consumer pools and work stealing. Our work has employed a number of novel techniques for improving performance: 1) lightweight and synchronization-free produce and consume operations in the common case; 2) NUMA-aware memory management, which keeps most data accesses inside NUMA nodes; 3) a chunk-based stealing approach that decreases the stealing cost and suits NUMA migration schemes; and 4) elegant producer-based balancing for decreasing the likelihood of stealing.

We have shown that our solution scales linearly with the number of threads. It outperforms other work-stealing techniques by a factor of 20, and state-of-the art non-FIFO pools by a factor of 3.5. We have further shown that it is highly robust to imbalances and unexpected thread stalls.

We believe that our general approach of partitioning data structures among threads, along with chunk-based migration and an efficient synchronization-free fast-path, can be of benefit in building additional scalable high-performance services in the future.

8. REFERENCES

[1] http://home.comcast.net/~pjbishop/Dave/Asymmetric-Dekker-Synchronization.txt.

[2] www.facebook.com/notes/facebook-engineering/scalable-memory-allocation-using-jemalloc/480222803919.

[3] Y. Afek, G. Korland, M. Natanzon, and N. Shavit. Scalable producer-consumer pools based on elimination-diffraction trees. In *Proceedings of the 16th international Euro-Par conference on Parallel processing: Part II*, Euro-Par'10, pages 151–162, 2010.

[4] Y. Afek, G. Korland, and E. Yanovsky. Quasi-linearizability: Relaxed consistency for improved concurrency. In *Principles of Distributed Systems*, Lecture Notes in Computer Science, pages 395–410.

[5] N. S. Arora, R. D. Blumofe, and C. G. Plaxton. Thread scheduling for multiprogrammed multiprocessors. In *Proceedings of the tenth annual ACM symposium on Parallel algorithms and architectures*, SPAA '98, pages 119–129, 1998.

[6] D. Basin. Café: Scalable task pools with adjustable fairness and contention. Master's thesis, Technion, 2011.

[7] D. Basin, R. Fan, I. Keidar, O. Kiselov, and D. Perelman. Café: scalable task pools with adjustable fairness and contention. In *Proceedings of the 25th international conference on Distributed computing*, DISC'11, pages 475–488, 2011.

[8] S. Blagodurov, S. Zhuravlev, M. Dashti, and A. Fedorova. A case for numa-aware contention management on multicore systems. In *Proceedings of the 2011 USENIX conference on USENIX annual technical conference*, USENIXATC'11, 2011.

[9] R. D. Blumofe and C. E. Leiserson. Scheduling multithreaded computations by work stealing. *J. ACM*, 46:720–748, September 1999.

[10] A. Braginsky and E. Petrank. Locality-conscious lock-free linked lists. In *Proceedings of the 12th international conference on Distributed computing and networking*, ICDCN'11, pages 107–118, 2011.

[11] D. Dice, V. J. Marathe, and N. Shavit. Flat-combining numa locks. In *Proceedings of the 23rd ACM*

[12] A. Gidenstam, H. Sundell, and P. Tsigas. Cache-aware lock-free queues for multiple producers/consumers and weak memory consistency. In *Proceedings of the 14th international conference on Principles of distributed systems*, OPODIS'10, pages 302–317, 2010.

[13] E. Gidron, I. Keidar, D. Perelman, and Y. Perez. SALSA: Scalable and Low Synchronization NUMA-aware Algorithm for Producer-Consumer Pools. Technical report, Technion, 2012.

[14] D. Hendler, Y. Lev, M. Moir, and N. Shavit. A dynamic-sized nonblocking work stealing deque. *Distrib. Comput.*, 18:189–207, February 2006.

[15] D. Hendler and N. Shavit. Non-blocking steal-half work queues. In *Proceedings of the twenty-first annual symposium on Principles of distributed computing*, PODC '02, pages 280–289, 2002.

[16] D. Hendler, N. Shavit, and L. Yerushalmi. A scalable lock-free stack algorithm. In *Proceedings of the sixteenth annual ACM symposium on Parallelism in algorithms and architectures*, SPAA '04, pages 206–215, 2004.

[17] M. Hoffman, O. Shalev, and N. Shavit. The baskets queue. In *Proceedings of the 11th international conference on Principles of distributed systems*, OPODIS'07, pages 401–414, 2007.

[18] E. Ladan-Mozes, I.-T. A. Lee, and D. Vyukov. Location-based memory fences. In *Proceedings of the 23rd ACM symposium on Parallelism in algorithms and architectures*, SPAA '11, pages 75–84, 2011.

[19] L. Lamport. How to make a multiprocessor computer that correctly executes multiprocess programs. *IEEE Trans. Comput.*, pages 690–691, 1979.

[20] M. M. Michael. Hazard pointers: Safe memory reclamation for lock-free objects. *IEEE Trans. Parallel Distrib. Syst.*, 15:491–504, June 2004.

[21] M. M. Michael and M. L. Scott. Simple, fast, and practical non-blocking and blocking concurrent queue algorithms. In *Proceedings of the fifteenth annual ACM symposium on Principles of distributed computing*, PODC '96, pages 267–275, 1996.

[22] M. Moir, D. Nussbaum, O. Shalev, and N. Shavit. Using elimination to implement scalable and lock-free fifo queues. In *Proceedings of the seventeenth annual ACM symposium on Parallelism in algorithms and architectures*, SPAA '05, pages 253–262, 2005.

[23] P. Sewell, S. Sarkar, S. Owens, F. Z. Nardelli, and M. O. Myreen. x86-tso: a rigorous and usable programmer's model for x86 multiprocessors. *Commun. ACM*, pages 89–97, 2010.

[24] H. Sundell, A. Gidenstam, M. Papatriantafilou, and P. Tsigas. A lock-free algorithm for concurrent bags. In *Proceedings of the 23rd ACM symposium on Parallelism in algorithms and architectures*, SPAA '11, pages 335–344, 2011.

A Non-Blocking Internal Binary Search Tree

Shane V. Howley and Jeremy Jones
School of Computer Science and Statistics
Trinity College Dublin, Ireland
{howleysv, jones}@scss.tcd.ie

ABSTRACT

Recent work on concurrent search trees has yielded solutions which either rely on locking parts of the data structure or exhibit suboptimal memory use. Trees are typically non-trivial to parallelise due to having multiple mutable fields per node but their average search time relative to simpler structures like linked-lists makes them desirable. We present a parallel binary search tree algorithm built using single-word reads, writes, and compare-and-swap. In this algorithm, operations will only contend if concurrent updates affect the same node(s). Updates are non-blocking as threads can complete each other's operations if necessary and each operation is linearisable. Experimental evidence shows it to be fast when compared with alternative solutions and scalable to large numbers of concurrently executing threads. It outperforms concurrent skip lists in the majority of scenarios tested; showing 65% more throughput when the performance difference of every experiment is averaged, and its memory footprint is significantly smaller than that of the other structures tested.

Categories and Subject Descriptors

D.1.3 [**Programming Techniques**]: Concurrent Programming—*Parallel Programming*; E.1 [**Data Structures**]: Trees

Keywords

data structures, concurrency, multi-processing

1. INTRODUCTION

Modern CPU designs have reached a relative stagnation in terms of single-threaded throughput, with each new generation of chips only providing small increases. Hardware architects have instead focussed on raising the number of processing cores per CPU package. Algorithms that can effectively use these extra processing resources are therefore required in order achieve higher performance from computer applications.

Multiple threads working cooperatively must communicate and synchronise through data structures stored in shared memory. The efficiency of these data structures can be crucial to performance,

Permission to make digital or hard copies of all or part of this work for personal or classroom use is granted without fee provided that copies are not made or distributed for profit or commercial advantage and that copies bear this notice and the full citation on the first page. To copy otherwise, to republish, to post on servers or to redistribute to lists, requires prior specific permission and/or a fee.
SPAA'12, June 25–27, 2012, Pittsburgh, Pennsylvania, USA.
Copyright 2012 ACM 978-1-4503-1213-4/12/06 ...$10.00.

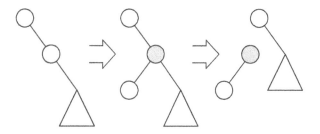

Figure 1: An example of using pointer marking on a BST resulting in a malformed structure. At the second step, the right child of the central node is marked and a concurrent insert happens at the left child. When the node is unlinked as in the final step, the added node is no longer accessible.

but their design is generally considered quite difficult. Often, the potentially huge number of possible thread interleavings that can occur makes such algorithms difficult to prove correct.

An efficient, non-blocking (also called lock-free) implementation of a shared object is desirable for its capability to deal with contentious access. It provides a guarantee that in the case of one or multiple thread failures, the system can still achieve overall progress. This means that access to the shared object is protected from lock-related drawbacks such as priority inversion, deadlock and convoying.

We present an algorithm for a non-blocking internal binary search tree (BST). It is compatible with a wide range of systems due to its reliance on the commonly available operations: single word reads, writes and compare-and-swap (CAS). Traversing the tree can be performed in a read only manner and does not interfere with concurrent updates. Most updates to the internal structure of the tree can be tolerated without triggering a restart.

A description of our algorithm is provided, starting with a high-level overview of its operation (section 3.1) followed by a detailed examination of a C++ style implementation (section 3.2). Memory management issues and solutions are discussed in section 3.3. A proof sketch for its non-blocking and linearisability properties is provided in section 4. We show that it achieves good throughput when compared with the best known concurrent set algorithms and it scales well for increasing numbers of threads (section 5).

2. RELATED WORK

Many of the list-based data structures such as linked lists, queues, and skip lists have been successfully adapted into concurrent, non-blocking forms [14, 6, 11]. The basis for all of these algorithms lies in the method of a two-stage deletion of nodes in the list by using compare-and-swap (CAS) to 'mark' a pointer, as proposed by Harris [7]. This method lends itself well to structures for which the consistency of the key set can be managed using a singly linked list. For tree-based data structures, nodes contain multiple links to successor nodes in the search path and updating the tree is not always as straightforward as modifying a single link. This means that a concurrent tree algorithm which applies Harris' method directly is not possible.

Software Transactional Memory (STM) offers a general solution to parallelising a data structure by making updates to multiple memory locations appear atomic. This is done by tracking all reads and only making tentative changes to locations which must be written, the changes then committed providing no conflicts with another transaction were detected. A contention management algorithm must be used to deal with conflicts, deciding which transaction will succeed and which will abort and retry. STM performance has been examined when applied to a number of data structures and it has been shown to outperform solutions which use a simple lock to protect the data structure [10]. The downside to STM is that its throughput tends to lag behind that of algorithms optimised toward a specific data structure [3].

Binary search tree algorithms are typically divided into either external trees or internal trees. An external tree only stores keys in leaf nodes as opposed to an internal tree which stores a key in every node. The higher up nodes in an external tree also contain keys but these are only used for comparison and routing, a key contained in a routing node is not necessarily an element in the tree's set. The main advantage to using an external tree is that it simplifies node removal. To remove a node with two children from an internal tree, that node's must be replaced by the node with the next largest or next smallest key. This makes concurrent implementations difficult as the replacement node may be many links away which could make a large part of the tree inaccessible if locks are used. Removing a leaf from an external tree can be done by simply removing the parent routing node and replacing it with the sibling of the removed leaf. External trees offer suboptimal memory use, however, due to the fact that a tree containing n keys must have n leaves and n - 1 routing nodes.

Fraser, in his Ph.D thesis [6], described a lock-free implementation of an internal BST which uses multiple CAS (MCAS) to update multiple parts of the tree structure atomically. An implementation of MCAS built using CAS is described, which uses descriptors to acquire the set of memory locations to be updated. If all the locations are acquired, they can be updated with the new values, otherwise the operation must be rolled back. Removing a node with two children requires up to eight memory locations to be updated atomically, which adds an appreciable overhead to the BST algorithm.

Ellen et al. [4] have developed the first practical non-blocking external BST. Changes to the routing nodes are performed by applying Barnes' [2] method of cooperative updates. A link to a structure containing all the information necessary to complete an update is copied into each node which is to be modified, and any thread which is obstructed by the ongoing update can attempt to complete the operation on behalf of the creating thread. The use of an external tree means that the worst case scenario is just two consecutive routing nodes being obstructed in this way.

The concurrent relaxed balance AVL tree designed by Bronson et al. [3] uses per-node locks to manage updates, but avoids the issue of locking large parts of the tree during a remove-and-replace operation by leaving removed nodes with two children in the tree to act as routing nodes. Local improvements (such as removing routing nodes or performing a rotation) are made after an update is

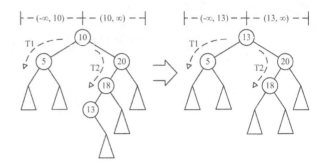

Figure 2: Key replacement in a BST. The first state shows two threads, T1 searching for key 3 in the left subtree of the root node and T2 searching for key 11 in right subtree. The range of keys allowed in each subtree is shown above the root. The second state occurs after a concurrent removal on the root node, which has its key replaced by the node with the next largest key, 13. At this point, T1 is safe to continue its search because its search range has expanded but T2 must detect its contracted search range and restart.

performed in order to approximately balance the tree. This partially external tree design was experimentally shown to have a negligible increase (0-20%) on the total number of nodes.

Skip lists were first presented by Pugh [15] as an alternative to balanced trees. At the base level, they consist of a linked list, but the base nodes can contain extra levels of links to nodes which are further down the list. This allows searches to use these extra links to 'skip' over large chunks of the list during a traversal. The optimal structure provides an $O(log\ n)$ time complexity for locating a node so they are often used in place of BSTs. Lock-free skip list algorithms using CAS have been presented by Fraser [6] and Formitchev and Ruppert [5].

3. ALGORITHM DESCRIPTION

3.1 High-level Overview

This algorithm implements the set abstract data structure interface. A set comprises a collection of unique key values with methods: add(k) to add the key k to the set if it is not already a member of the set; remove(k) to remove the key k from the set if it is a member of the set; and contains(k) to test for membership in the set. The underlying data structure is a binary search tree (BST). A BST is a type of binary tree which guarantees an ordering such that for any node N in the BST, its left subtree contains only nodes with keys less than N's key and its right subtree contains only nodes with keys greater than N's key. A BST takes $O(log\ n)$ time for add, remove and contains and $O(n)$ only in its worst case. This gives it an advantage over sorted linked lists which require $O(n)$ time. The algorithm is non-blocking which guarantees that there is system-wide throughput even if individual threads starve. It is also linearisable [12] - meaning that each operation has a single point at which it seems to take effect. For any concurrent execution, the ordering of these linearisation points represents a sequential history which adheres to the expected response for the implemented object.

Typically a problem with implementing a tree based structure using CAS is the inability to make changes to multiple child pointers atomically. This complicates the use of algorithms such as Harris' pointer marking [7] as one child pointer could become marked while a node is added to a different child pointer (fig. 1).

The structure of our tree closely mirrors that of a sequential BST,

162

with the addition of an operation field in each node. This field is used to store details about an ongoing update to the node and precludes updates by a competing operation until after it has completed. An insert is performed by including all the data needed for another thread to complete the operation into a structure, then copying a pointer to the structure into the operation field of the node gaining the new child. Once the operation field has been updated, the operation cannot fail so the key can be considered logically inserted at this point. The operation field will only be modified with CAS and can only have operations placed into it if it is clear. This stops contending operations interfering with each other.

Removing a node with less than two children is similarly straightforward. A key is logically removed by marking the operation field of the node containing the key. Once marked, there is no way the removal can be undone. An operation similar to insertion can then be applied to the parent of this node, completing the physical removal.

A major barrier to parallelisation of BSTs relates to removing a node from the tree which has two children. In the sequential BST algorithm, once the node to be removed *A* is found, a search is performed to locate the node with the next largest or next smallest key *B*. *A*'s key is then substituted with *B*'s and *B* is removed from the tree. Doing this in a concurrent BST presents two main problems: the first is making updates to both *A* and *B* appear atomic and the second is detecting if a search has been invalidated due to keys moving higher in the tree.

The updates are performed by copying the data necessary to make the changes to *A* into a structure and placing a reference to it in *B*'s operation field. This prevents any changes to *B* during the operation. Then an attempt to place the same reference into *A*'s operation field is made. If this succeeds, *A*'s key is updated, its operation field is cleared and *B*'s operation field is marked.

If a node's key is replaced as a result of a removal, this affects the range of keys that can be possibly contained in each of its subtrees. Replacing with a larger key causes the range to the left subtree to expand and the range of the right subtree to reduce. The opposite is true for replacing with a smaller key. This has implications for ongoing searches traversing the subtrees of this node. Expanding the range will have no effect on a search, as the key being searched for must still be contained in that subtree, but reducing the range may require a search in that subtree to restart (fig. 2).

An instance of the tree can support either replacing with the next largest or next smallest key but not both. It could be modified to support either simultaneously but some ABA prevention mechanism must be employed to protect the key field of a node. The listed implementation always replaces a key with the next largest key. This means that we need only check the last node for which the right child link was followed for changes.

3.2 Detailed Implementation

3.2.1 Structures

The declarations for the various classes used are listed in fig. 3. The Node class closely resembles that of a sequential BST but with the addition of the op field which is used to signify if changes are being made which affect the node. Memory allocations on a 32-bit system will normally only return addresses which are aligned on a 4-byte boundary which effectively means that the two least significant bits of a pointer can be used to store auxiliary data. This is considered to be a widely used technique when using CAS on pointer values [7, 5, 4, 6]. This technique is used to store which of four different states of change a node can be in: NONE - no ongoing operation; MARK - the node's key is no longer in the set and the node should be physically removed; CHILDCAS - one of

```
1   class Node {
2     int volatile key;
3     Operation* volatile op;
4     Node* volatile left;
5     Node* volatile right;
6   }

8   class Operation {}

10  class ChildCASOp : Operation {
11    bool isLeft;
12    Node* expected;
13    Node* update;
14  }

16  class RelocateOp : Operation {
17    int volatile state = ONGOING;
18    Node* dest;
19    Operation* destOp;
20    int removeKey;
21    int replaceKey;
22  }
```

Figure 3: Structures declared

the node's child pointers is being modified; RELOCATE - the node is one of two affected by a key relocation.

The following macros are also defined to aid in modifying this data: FLAG(ptr, state) - sets the state of the Operation pointer ptr to one of the above states, GETFLAG(ptr) - strips away the pointer data to leave just the state information, UNFLAG(ptr) - strips away the state bits leaving the pointer intact.

The left and right child pointers use special values to denote a null pointer. This is done to avoid the ABA problem occurring when a child pointer is null, is then set to point to a valid node, that node is removed and the pointer is set back to null again. The mechanism that is used to store null values is to retain the pointer data but set an unused low order bit to signify if a pointer is null. This guarantees that every null pointer is unique for that field. The macros SETNULL(ptr) and ISNULL(ptr) are used to set the null bit of a node pointer and to check if a pointer is null respectively. A node is initialized with null left and right pointers. All the fields of a node are mutable but key, right, and left can only be modified if the corresponding operation has already been written to the op field first.

A ChildCASOp object contains enough information for another thread to complete an operation which modifies one of a node's child pointers. The following information is required: whether the change is to be made to the left or right child pointer, the expected data at that location, and the updated value it should be changed to. There is no need to store the destination node in the structure because the destination is the same node where the reference to the operation object was found. An active ChildCASOp operation is flagged with the CHILDCAS state in a node's op field.

A RelocateOp object contains enough information for another thread to attempt to complete an operation which removes the key of a node with two children and replaces it with the next largest key. The following information is required: A pointer to the node whose key is to be removed, the data stored in that node's op field, the key being removed, and the key to attempt replacement with. The destination must be stored in this descriptor because a pointer to the structure is stored in op field of both the node whose key would be removed and the node whose key will be relocated. An active RelocateOp operation is flagged with the RELOCATE state in a node's op field. The purpose of the state field is covered in the explanation of the remove operation in section 3.2.4.

```
23  bool contains(int k) {
24    Node* pred, * curr;
25    Operation* predOp, * currOp;
26    return find(k, pred, predOp, curr, currOp, &root) ==
          FOUND;
27  }

29  int find(int k, Node*& pred, Operation*& predOp, Node*&
        curr, Operation*& currOp, Node* auxRoot) {
30    int result, currKey;
31    Node* next, * lastRight;
32    Operation* lastRightOp;
33  retry:
34    result = NOTFOUND_R;
35    curr = auxRoot;
36    currOp = curr->op;
37    if (GETFLAG(currOp) != NONE) {
38      if (auxRoot == &root) {
39        helpChildCAS(UNFLAG(currOp), curr);
40        goto retry;
41      } else return ABORT;
42    }
43    next = curr->right;
44    lastRight = curr;
45    lastRightOp = currOp;
46    while (!ISNULL(next)) {
47      pred = curr;
48      predOp = currOp;
49      curr = next;
50      currOp = curr->op;
51      if (GETFLAG(currOp) != NONE) {
52        help(pred, predOp, curr, currOp);
53        goto retry;
54      }
55      currKey = curr->key;
56      if (k < currKey) {
57        result = NOTFOUND_L;
58        next = curr->left;
59      } else if (k > currKey) {
60        result = NOTFOUND_R;
61        next = curr->right;
62        lastRight = curr;
63        lastRightOp = currOp;
64      } else {
65        result = FOUND;
66        break;
67      }
68    }
69    if ((result != FOUND) && (lastRightOp != lastRight->op)
        ) goto retry;
70    if (curr->op != currOp) goto retry;
71    return result;
72  }
```

Figure 4: contains and find functions.

The tree class is unlisted but it contains a Node object, root, whose right child field points to the logical root of the tree or is a null value if the tree is empty. This is done to simplify the implementation of various functions.

The CAS operation takes three parameters: the memory location that will be accessed, the expected value at that location, and the value to write to the location if what is read matches the expected value. It returns a Boolean true or false based on whether it was successful or not. We also make use of a VCAS or 'Value CAS' operation which returns instead, the value stored in the memory location before the operation was attempted. If not available, it is sufficient for our uses to replace VCAS with a CAS followed by a read.

3.2.2 contains(k)

The code listing for the contains operation can be seen in fig. 4. It calls the find method which is used by all operations to locate the position or potential position of a key from a specified start point

```
73  bool add(int k) {
74    Node* pred, * curr, * newNode;
75    Operation* predOp, * currOp, * casOp;
76    int result;
77    while (true) {
78      result = find(k, pred, predOp, curr, currOp, &root);
79      if (result == FOUND) return false;
80      newNode = new Node(k);
81      bool isLeft = (result == NOTFOUND_L);
82      Node* old = isLeft ? curr->left : curr->right;
83      casOp = new ChildCASOp(isLeft, old, newNode);
84      if (CAS(&curr->op, currOp, FLAG(casOp, CHILDCAS))) {
85        helpChildCAS(casOp, curr);
86        return true;
87      }
88    }
89  }

91  void helpChildCAS(ChildCASOp* op, Node* dest) {
92    Node** address = op->isLeft ? &dest->left : &dest->
        right;
93    CAS(address, op->expect, op->update);
94    CAS(&dest->op, FLAG(op, CASCHILD), FLAG(op, NONE));
95  }
```

Figure 5: add function.

auxRoot in the tree. The position is returned in the variables pred & curr and the values of their op fields when traversed are returned in variables predOp & currOp. The result of the search can be one of four values: FOUND - if k is a member of the set, NOTFOUND_L if k is not in the set but would be positioned at the left child of curr if it were inserted, NOTFOUND_R similar to NOTFOUND_L but for the right child, ABORT if the search of a subtree can't return a usable result. ABORT is only seen when searching for the next largest key during a remove operation.

The search begins by initialising the search variables curr, currOp, next, lastRight & lastRightOp before the traversing loop starts. next is used to point to the next node along the search path, after curr. lastRight & lastRightOp are used to keep a record of the last node (and its op) for which the right child path was taken. The check at lines 37-38 is done to catch the special case when the root has an ongoing operation to either add to the empty tree or remove the logical root.

The search loop traverses nodes one at a time until either the key is found or a null node is reached. The check at line 51 represents a simplified version of the code which attempts to help complete any ongoing operations seen during the traverse and then restarts the search. This is presented here purely as a means to reduce code complexity and the number of special cases which must be dealt with. An optimised version of find with the ability to pass seen operations is outlined in section 3.2.5. When the traversal has completed, the check on line 69 is done to verify that having searched lastRight's right subtree, k cannot have been added to lastRight's left subtree. This is done by confirming that no operation has been performed on lastRight. The final check at line 70 is done to ensure that curr had not been modified between reading its op field and reading its key.

3.2.3 add(k)

The method for adding a key to the set is included in fig. 5. Once the key is verified not to be in the tree and the insertion point is found, a new node and a ChildCASOp object are created with the information necessary to perform the insertion. CAS is used to insert the operation into curr's op field at which point k can be considered logically inserted. The CAS succeeding means that curr's op field hasn't been modified since it was first read. This

```
96  bool remove(int k) {
97    Node* pred, * curr, * replace;
98    Operation* predOp, * currOp, * replaceOp, * relocOp;
99    while (true) {
100     if (find(k, pred, predOp, curr, currOp, &root) != FOUND) return false;
101     if (ISNULL(curr->right) || ISNULL(curr->left)) {
102       // Node has < 2 children
103       if (CAS(&curr->op, currOp, FLAG(currOp, MARK))) {
104         helpMarked(pred, predOp, curr);
105         return true;
106       }
107     } else {
108       // Node has 2 children
109       if ((find(k, pred, predOp, replace, replaceOp, curr) == ABORT) || (curr->op != currOp)) continue;
110       relocOp = new RelocateOp(curr, currOp, k, replace->key);
111       if (CAS(&replace->op, replaceOp, FLAG(relocOp, RELOCATE))) {
112         if (helpRelocate(relocOp, pred, predOp, replace)) return true;
113       }
114     }
115   }
116 }

118 bool helpRelocate(RelocateOp* op, Node* pred, Operation* predOp, Node* curr) {
119   int seenState = op->state;
120   if (seenState == ONGOING) {
121     Operation* seenOp = VCAS(&op->dest->op, op->destOp, FLAG(op, RELOCATE));
122     if ((seenOp == op->destOp) || (seenOp == FLAG(op, RELOCATE))) {
123       CAS(&op->state, ONGOING, SUCCESSFUL);
124       seenState = SUCCESSFUL;
125     } else {
126       seenState = VCAS(&op->state, ONGOING, FAILED);
127     }
128   }
129   if (seenState == SUCCESSFUL) {
130     CAS(&op->dest->key, removeKey, replaceKey);
131     CAS(&op->dest->op, FLAG(op, RELOCATE), FLAG(op, NONE));
132   }
133   bool result = (seenState == SUCCESSFUL);
134   if (op->dest == curr) return result;
135   CAS(&curr->op, FLAG(op, RELOCATE), FLAG(op, result ? MARK : NONE));
136   if (result) {
137     if (op->dest == pred) predOp = FLAG(op, NONE);
138     helpMarked(pred, predOp, curr);
139   }
140   return result;
141 }
```

Figure 6: remove function.

in turn means that all of curr's other fields are also unchanged, so the operation to CAS one of curr's child pointers cannot fail to complete - whether performed by the operation thread or another. The helpChildCAS method does the main work of physically adding the new node to the tree, and cleaning up after the operation. This can be called by any thread that encounters the ongoing operation in curr's op field. Executing either of the two CAS's performed by helpChildCAS at any time after the operation has been completed is safe because they will be guaranteed to fail at that point. This is because curr's child pointer and op pointer can never return to their original values.

3.2.4 remove(k)

The code for remove is listed in fig. 6 and its associated helper functions in fig. 7. Once the node containing k has been found, one of two paths is taken. The path starting line 102 is taken if the node has less than two children or the path starting line 108 is taken otherwise. The case with less than two children is much simpler to deal with as the node can be simply excised from the tree. CAS is used to change curr's operation state from NONE to MARK at which point k can be considered logically removed from the set. helpMarked is used to perform the physical removal. It uses a ChildCASOp operation to replace pred's child pointer to

curr with either a null pointer if curr is a leaf node, or a pointer to curr's only child. Note that predOp may have changed since it was read inside find, so removing the marked node may fail. If a guarantee is required that a marked node is excised before the marking operation returns, another call to find(k) can be made if the CAS at line 152 fails which will ensure removal.

If the initial search finds the key in a node with two children, an additional search must be done to locate the node with the next largest key. This is done by searching for the same key in curr's right subtree. The result is deemed invalid if the search aborts by finding curr's op field has been modified since the first search (line 41), in which case the entire remove operation must be restarted. If the search succeeds, a RelocateOp object is created to attempt to replace curr's key with the key of the node returned, replace. This operation is inserted into replace's op field to ensure that replace's key cannot be removed while this operation is in progress. The first step in helpRelocate is the CAS to insert the RelocateOp into the node with key k's op field, on line 121. A successful CAS means the relocate operation cannot fail and at this point, k can be considered logically removed from the set. Because any thread has the potential to determine the success or failure of the operation, a mechanism is required to relay the result back to the thread conducting the removal. This is im-

```
142  void helpMarked(Node* pred, Operation* predOp, Node* curr
          ) {
143    Node* newRef;
144    if (ISNULL(curr->left)) {
145      if (ISNULL(curr->right))
146        newRef = SETNULL(curr);
147      else
148        newRef = curr->right;
149    } else
150      newRef = curr->left;
151    Operation* casOp = new ChildCASOp(curr == pred->left,
          curr, newRef);
152    if (CAS(&pred->op, predOp, FLAG(casOp, CHILDCAS)))
153      helpChildCAS(casOp, pred);
154  }

156  void help(Node* pred, Operation* predOp, Node* curr,
          Operation* currOp) {
157    if (GETFLAG(currOp) == CHILDCAS)
158      helpChildCAS(UNFLAG(currOp), curr);
159    else if (GETFLAG(currOp) == RELOCATE)
160      helpRelocate(UNFLAG(currOp), pred, predOp, curr);
161    else if (GETFLAG(currOp) == MARK)
162      helpMarked(pred, predOp, curr);
163  }
```

Figure 7: Other helper functions.

plemented in a similar fashion to the MCAS descriptor of Harris et al. [8] operating on a single memory location. The initial state is set to ONGOING until the result of the operation is known. If any thread either completes the CAS, or observes the completed CAS, it will set the operation state to SUCCESSFUL, or if any other value is seen it will attempt to CAS the state from ONGOING to FAILED. Note the use of VCAS in line 123 to return the actual value of state even if the thread determined the operation has failed because if the operation has succeeded, the node may have had further operations applied to it since success was determined. If successful, a CAS is performed on the key to update it to the new value, and a second CAS is used to remove the ongoing RelocateOp from the same node. Note that the CAS to replace the key can't suffer from the ABA problem because it can only be replaced with a larger key. The second part of helpRelocate (from line 133 onward) performs cleanup on replace by either marking and excising it, if the relocation was successful, or clearing its op field if it failed. The check in line 134 is first done to ensure that curr is the node which potentially had its key relocated and not the node whose key was to be removed, which can be the case if helpRelocate is called from find. If the operation was successful and curr is marked, curr is excised from the list using helpMarked as above. The code in line 137 takes into account the special case where the node whose key was removed is the parent of curr and so, predOp must be updated to the value it was changed to in line 131.

3.2.5 Optimising traversal

The optimised version of find ignores ongoing operations during its search but still must adhere to the requirement that it return a node without an operation attached to it. This is done by performing a help and retry only if the node found at the end of a traverse contains an active operation. Because help requires that pred has no ongoing operation, it is necessary for progress to back track to the last node seen during the traversal which had no operation attached and perform the help from that point in the tree. This back track point will have been explicitly stored during the traversal. It is at least possible that during a traversal, chains of logically deleted nodes could be traversed - so depending on how the

memory management system handles physically removed nodes, it may be necessary to verify physical deletion has not yet occurred at each traversal step over logically deleted nodes. This can be done safely because the physical removal of a chain of marked nodes only happens at the highest unmarked node in the tree, which can be checked for updates. The optimisations violate the guarantee that when find returns, pred was observed without an operation. While this would affect a remove operation excising a node, it does not stop the remove from successfully linearising. If there is a requirement to not leave marked nodes in the tree, a subsequent call to find can be made. contains can be made completely read-only by using a specialised version of the optimised find. If an ongoing operation is detected at the end point of the traversal, instead of helping to update the tree, it is possible to determine if the searched key is in the set by examining the state and contents of the seen operation.

A search which passes a single marked node or a ChildCASOp is naturally safe because they can't affect the validity of a search result. Furthermore, care must be taken when passing multiple sequential marked nodes as mentioned in the previous paragraph. What is not immediately clear is the correctness of ignoring a key relocation. In the case where a RelocateOp has been observed and passed before the key change has occurred, a search can only be affected by this if this was the last node for which the right child path was taken. The danger would be that the node which was used for replacement could be removed before any changes to lastRightOp are made but helpRelocate guarantees that this can never be the case by ensuring lastRight's operation is cleared before this node is marked. This would then be detected at the end of a search, triggering a restart.

3.3 Memory Management

The algorithm avoids the ABA problem occurring at the child or operation fields by using bit flags (NULL flag for children or NONE flag for operations) to essentially create unique null pointers, as also used by the BST of Ellen et al. [4]. In order to ensure the uniqueness of these pointers and avoid the ABA problem, the memory they reference cannot be reused until the null pointer has been replaced. The consequences of this is that the memory usage of the algorithm increases as the majority of nodes will contain a unique null operation pointer and nodes at the edge of the tree can contain up to two unique null child pointers. Once the unique null is removed, the reuse of these objects could be handled by a garbage collector or a memory reclamation system such as hazard pointers [13].

This situation is not ideal as we would like to be able to reuse or free these defunct objects as soon as they are removed from the logical tree. If the system supports a double-width CAS (DWCAS), which allows two sequential memory locations to be CASed simultaneously, the problem can be solved by adding a tag value adjacent to each pointer which is in danger from the ABA problem. If the tag is incremented each time the pointer is modified, it ensures that the ABA problem cannot occur even if the pointers being DWCASed are the same. Unfortunately, DWCAS doesn't have wide support across modern architectures (Intel x86_64 is the only 64-bit architecture known to support it) so a solution that uses single word CAS would be more desirable. Such a solution has been implemented which uses unique null pointers that don't depend on object references, with no impact to performance, and it is currently being evaluated by the authors. These memory management implementations require no extra memory per node or otherwise, and in the specific case of hazard pointers: five protected object pointers per thread are required.

4. CORRECTNESS

4.1 Non-blocking

The non-blocking property of the algorithm is proved by describing the interactions that can occur between reading and writing threads. A thread traversing the tree will eventually either locate the key it is searching for or stop on a leaf node, assuming nodes are not repeatedly added in its path ad infinitum. A retry can be triggered in a few cases: if an ongoing operation is encountered `help` is called in an attempt to complete it, if `lastRight` has been updated since its `op` field was read, or if `curr` was updated since its `op` field was read. In each of these cases, the `find` has been restarted due to a node on the search path being updated. If these `op` fields contain a `CHILDCAS` or `MARK` flag, this means another thread has applied an update to the tree so system-wide throughput was achieved. For a `RELOCATE` flag, if the node encountered is the node being replaced, this implies a successful remove operation. Otherwise there is potential for the relocate operation to be rolled back which means the thread performing the removal did not achieve progress. Finally, if the modified `op` field has the `NONE` flag, a successful `ChildCAS`, relocation or rollback relocation must have occurred.

A relocation being forced to roll back still implies the progress of another thread, as follows. The `find`s which are part of a remove are governed by the same properties as previously mentioned, but the second `find` can abort and trigger a retry at line 41 if the node to be removed is seen to have an ongoing operation. The change can also be detected by a failure of the CAS which installs the `RelocateOp` link into the node whose key is to be removed (line 121). Because this node has two children, this can only either be a `ChildCAS`; if one of the child nodes is being excised or a relocate; if another thread is removing the same key - in either case, another thread has successfully performed an operation on the node.

An add is always performed on a leaf node so if a valid insertion point is returned by `find`, a retry will only occur if the leaf's `op` field has been modified. This can only occur if another thread has successfully added a new child to the node, has marked the node, or is using the node as a replacement for a removal higher up in the tree. In each of these cases we have previously demonstrated that system-wide progress was achieved.

4.2 Linearisability

We prove that our algorithm is linearisable by defining the linearisation points of the add, remove and contains operations. These linearisation points were proved by creating a model of the tree algorithm using the SPIN model checker [1]. Due to the limitations on the size of a simulation in SPIN, this could not be proved exhaustively but a small number of cases that should result in a variation of every concurrent interaction were chosen.

The contains operation has two possible outcomes, that the key was found in the tree or not. The linearization point for finding a key is the point at which an atomic read of the key has occurred at line 55. However, this result will only be linearised providing the check at line 70 passes. This is done to verify that the node didn't change between its `op` field being read and the linearisation point. Failure to find will either linearise when the end of a search path is reached by reading a null link at line 58 or line 61. Again, this result is subject to checks which verify the result. The `lastRight` node must be unmodified or the subtree's key range may have been modified during the search, this is confirmed in line 69. Node `curr` must also be verified at this point to ensure the node didn't undergo a change (such as adding a `ChildCASOp` operation) between reading its `op` field and the linearisation point. In the special case that

the tree is empty, the contains operation linearises at line 43 when `next` is assigned a null value.

The optimised version of the `find` function (described in section 3.2.5) has the same linearisation points as the simplified version - providing that at the end of the search, `curr` was observed to have no ongoing operation. Most of the cases for the read-only contains are similar to this with the following exceptions: If the traversal ends on a marked node, the failure to find linearises when the marked node is verified not to have been excised, again subject to verification by checking `lastRight` hasn't been modified; If the key is found in a node being used for relocation, a successful search will linearise if the key exchange is verified not to have completed yet; If the key is not found but a `ChildCASOp` is seen, the search will linearise once the key of the node to be added is read and subject to a subsequent verification that the `ChildCASOp` is still ongoing.

An insert fails if it is determined that the key is already contained in the set, and therefore has the same linearization point as a successful contains. A successful insertion occurs when the `ChildCASOp` operation is inserted into the node `curr`, returned by `find`. This is true because if any other thread were to search for `k` at this point, they would encounter the `CHILDCAS` flag in `curr`'s `op` field and must either help complete the operation or, in the case of read-only searches, must conclude that the key is in the set based on the `ChildCASOp` contents.

A remove will fail, similarly to insert, if `find` determines that the key is not in the set and as before has the same linearization point as an unsuccessful contains. The removal of a node with less than two children will linearise when the node is set as marked in line 103. Removing a node with two children requires two CASs to succeed, one on the node which has the next largest key, and one on the node containing the key to be removed. A failure of either CAS will cause changes to be rolled back and the creating thread will retry its search. A successful remove can be linearised by a thread other than the one which created the operation as it occurs once the `RelocateOp` is installed in the second node which is performed in the `helpRelocate` method, line 121.

5. RESULTS

5.1 Experimental Setup

Four concurrent ordered set algorithms were compared:

- **Howley tree** - Our lock-free internal binary search tree;

- **Ellen tree** - The lock-free external binary seach tree of Ellen et al. [4];

- **Opt tree** - The optimistic relaxed balance AVL tree of Bronson et al. [3];

- **Skip list** - The Java library's `ConcurrentSkipListMap`, written by Doug Lea and based on the work of Fraser and Harris [6].

All the algorithms were implemented in C++ and benchmarked using a common test harness. The pseudocode provided for the Ellen tree translated to C++ relatively easily, except the type identification of Node subclasses needed in the tree traversal. This was made possible by adding a field to the Node class to store the derived object type. The code for both the Opt tree and Skip list implemented the `java.util.Map` interface, and these were simplified to work as a set instead while maintaining their linearisability. The Opt tree rebalancing methods which were absent from the original paper were adapted from code in a software repository listed by the authors. In the original algorithm, updates are only made to the Opt tree after entering java synchronized blocks which are implemented in current versions of java using a mutex field in every object. These blocks were translated to C++ using mutexes available from the POSIX threads (pthread) API. The Skip list was tuned as per the Java implementation such that each node in the base level had a ¼ probability of having higher level indexing nodes, and each level of indexing had a ½ probability of having higher level indices. The maximum height of the Skip list was statically set to an optimal level given the structure size, in each experiment.

The benchmarked version of our algorithm optimised the contains operation to be read-only by passing over ongoing operations or interpreting their contents if necessary. This resulted in 0-25% increased throughput across the benchmark configurations tested. The add and remove operations used the find function as defined in section 3.2.2 as there was a negligible effect on performance by allowing finds to pass ongoing operations.

Experiments were run on a dual processor system with two six-core Intel Xeon E5645 CPUs and 64GB of RAM. Each CPU has a 12MB shared L3 cache and 12 hardware thread contexts available. The operating system was the x86_64 version of Ubuntu 11.04, with Linux kernel 2.6.38-13-generic. The benchmarks were compiled using gcc 4.5.2 with optimisation level O2.

A pseudo random number generator instance for each thread was used to generate key values and operation types. The generators were seeded with unique values for each benchmark run. Due to the random nature of the key and operation selection, the number of keys contained in the sets during a run tended toward the total number of keys in the key range multiplied by the ratio of adds to removes. In order to get more consistent results, especially at larger key ranges, a 'steady-state' number of random keys were added to the set before results were gathered for each run. All threads were started simultaneously and allowed to run for 15 seconds, periodically checking their own run time after every 10,000 operations. When the last thread finished, the total time taken for all threads was divided into the total number of operations completed to yield the total throughput for that experiment. Each experiment was run a minimum of 30 times, and the average throughput was reported.

In order to eliminate any contention caused by requesting memory from the operating system, each thread was allowed to allocate itself a pool of memory for each experiment before timing measurements were taken. This memory pool was allocated to be large enough to service all memory allocations required by the thread for the duration of the experiment. Objects created by threads were aligned to cache line boundaries (64-byte boundaries for the CPU tested) in order to eliminate the effects of 'false sharing' where writes to two separate objects can contend if they happen to reside in the same cache line. Memory was not reused by operations or freed to the operating system until the benchmark completed.

Experimental parameters that were varied were: the number of threads concurrently executing operations on the structure; the range of keys that could be selected for operations (and hence controlling the total number of nodes in the structure); and the ratio of add, remove and contains operations. The selection of these parameters is influenced by the experiments performed in previous literature comparing concurrent sets [9, 3]. The thread numbers were chosen to be a wide scale starting with 1, 2, 4 & 6 threads running on a single CPU and then increasing in powers of two up to 192 (or 8 threads per hardware thread context available). Four different key ranges, from 2,000 to 2,000,000 increasing in powers of 10, were used to illustrate performance for varying contention levels and data structure sizes. The workloads were varied from being write dominated (50% add, 50% remove, 0% contains) to read

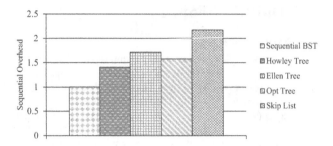

Figure 8: Single-threaded overhead versus a sequential BST algorithm.

dominated (9% add, 1% remove, 90% contains) with a balanced workload (20% add, 10% remove, 70% contains) in between.

5.2 Throughput

The single threaded performance of each concurrent algorithm was compared with that of a sequential BST in fig. 8. This was done to investigate the overhead associated with parallelising the data structure and also gives insight into the numbers of concurrently operating threads required to match sequential throughput. This was tested for a write heavy workload and averaged across all key ranges. Of the four concurrent algorithms, Howley tree has the lowest sequential overhead with a 39% increase in execution complexity. The throughput of Ellen tree and Opt tree were lower with overheads of 72% and 58% respectively. The Skip list was the poorest showing here (117% overhead) despite having a similar $O(log\ n)$ search time because it must read the contents of many more objects during a search.

The graph array in fig. 9 shows the throughput of the various algorithms in millions of operations per second on the y axes and number of concurrently executing threads on the x axes. Each row of graphs represents a different key range and each column represents a different access pattern. Performance was compared for highly-threaded experiments (averaged using results from experiments with $\geq$24 threads) by normalising throughput to that of Howley tree and averaging across the various key ranges (fig. 10(a)) and across the various access patterns (fig. 10(b)).

Overall, our algorithm scales very well - showing a linear increase in throughput as more execution resources are made available. It does not appear to be particularly negatively affected by high contention scenarios and offers the best all-round throughput of the algorithms tested when all the results are considered.

Howley tree and Opt tree, both being internal trees, have a consistent performance profile when an access pattern is compared across the different key ranges, with the exception of the smallest. Performance at heavily threaded workloads show Howley tree having a constant 15-30% higher throughput for the 50-50-0 workload and a 5-15% lead for 20-10-70. Similar performance is exhibited under the read dominated 9-1-90 access pattern which is expected given the read-only contains method and structural similarity of each set. The inconsistent results for the 2,000 key range are attributable to Opt tree's per-thread mutexes inhibiting progress of other threads.

The simpler traversal loop of the Ellen tree means that its performance is good compared with Howley tree for small key ranges despite the larger number of nodes which must be traversed to find a key. Ellen tree also tends to have more competitive performance for write dominated workloads given its much simpler remove routine. It performed on average 5% better for the 2,000 key range

Key range

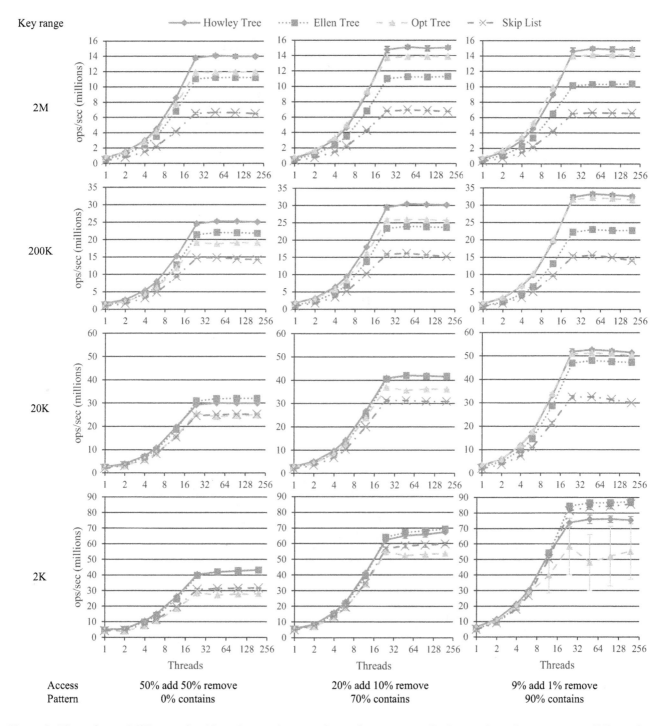

| Access | 50% add 50% remove | 20% add 10% remove | 9% add 1% remove |
| Pattern | 0% contains | 70% contains | 90% contains |

Figure 9: Throughput of different algorithms for varying experimental parameters. Each row of graphs represents a different key range, and each column represents a different access pattern. Each graph plots throughput in millions of operations per second against the number of threads concurrently executing. Error bars show one standard deviation.

for highly threaded workloads when compared with Howley tree. However, it is let down by its external tree structure when the other results are considered. Its average search time is longer than an internal tree as each search must traverse all the way to the leaf nodes - this is reflected in the results for the read dominated workloads. Larger key ranges compound this effect because the height of the tree is greater. The 2,000,000 key range showed Howley tree to perform on average 34% better and the 9-1-90 workload showed it

16% better. The peak average performance differential for a benchmark was tied between the 200,000 and 2,000,000 key ranges with a 9-1-90 workload in which Howley tree outperformed Ellen tree by 45%.

The Skip list shows very competitive performance for the smallest key range tested and even displayed 10% higher throughput than Howley tree for a heavily-threaded read-dominated workload. As the key ranges increase, however, it is not able to keep up with

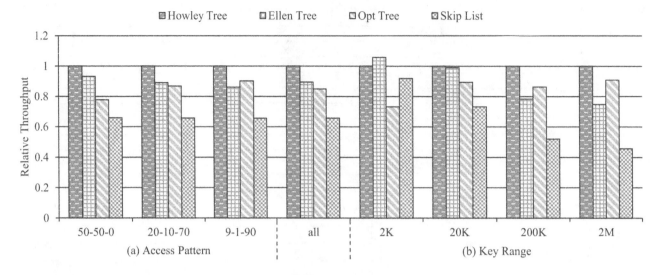

Figure 10: Throughput ratio to Howley tree averaged across common experimental parameters with ≥24 threads.

the tree-based structures due to its longer traversal (in terms of objects visited). The performance begins to plateau across the various workloads sooner than the other algorithms as the key ranges increase, which would suggest that the search uses a bigger proportion of CPU time in an operation than the other algorithms. The largest key range tested shows Howley tree having a consistent doubling of throughput or better and the trend would suggest that this gap would widen if structure size was even further increased.

5.3 Memory efficiency

The memory usage of each algorithm was also compared. Results were gathered using the same benchmark as for the throughput results with a 2,000 key range and a 50-50-0 workload. Fig. 11(a) shows the steady state memory footprint per key of the four algorithms tested. The theoretical memory footprint was calculated by counting the number of objects used by each structure at the end of a run to contain the key set. The `sizeof` operator was used to total the minimum packed size of these objects. Because a memory allocator will generally not allocate memory for these objects in the most efficiently sized blocks, we also totalled what is a more realistic memory usage figure by calculating the memory footprint based on the assumption that all objects are aligned on 64-byte blocks - as in our benchmark.

We also considered the dynamic memory consumption of each algorithm (fig. 11(b)) which is the amount of memory allocated during an operation averaged across all operations. For the 50-50-0 workload, the completed operations will consist 25% successful add, 25% unsuccessful add, 25% successful remove and 25% unsuccessful remove. This does not factor into the steady-state size of the data structure but represents the load imparted on the memory allocator or memory management subsystem.

Despite only requiring a single node object per key, Opt tree has significantly higher memory usage per key than the other algorithms. This is down to the extra fields in its node class combined with the `pthread_mutex_t` structure which itself amounts to 40 bytes. Ellen tree and Skip list have a good theoretical memory footprint because of Ellen tree's small Leaf object and Skip list's small node and index objects, but they suffer from relatively poor real memory efficiency because they both require more objects per key. The tuning factor used for skip list meant that there should be roughly half as many index objects as there were nodes but vary-

ing this would increase or decrease it's memory efficiency while also affecting performance [15]. Opt tree also suffers an overhead beyond the memory use for a single node here because the 50-50-0 workload causes it to retain an extra 20% superfluous routing nodes. This means that its real memory footprint is the least efficient at 144% higher than that of Howley tree along with Ellen tree and Skip list being 100% and 52% higher respectively.

The memory consumption rates experimentally determined can be accounted for by adding up the amount of memory allocated for each of the possible operations. Taking Ellen tree as an example, an unsuccessful add or remove will just perform a read-only search, a successful add requires the creation of a four objects and a successful remove requires the creation of one object. There is also a small overhead of wasted memory if the objects are created but then the operation is ultimately unsuccessful. Opt tree's memory consumption is quite low here because it only allocates memory for an add operation and it is guaranteed not to go to waste because the insertion point is locked at that point. It also has the ability to 'reactivate' routing nodes, therefore requiring no memory allocation for those particular add operations. Howley tree and Ellen tree allocate more memory per operation than the two others here because they both use operation structures to allow helping, but with Ellen tree using 49% more than Howley tree. Opt tree and Skip list are more efficient here, only needing 50% and 45%, respectively, of the requirement of Howley tree. In real-world terms, higher figures here could result in reduced performance if the memory allocator, garbage collector or similar is causing a bottleneck.

6. CONCLUSIONS AND FUTURE WORK

In this paper, we have presented a non-blocking internal binary search tree and have informally proved it to be linearisable. Replacing an internal node is performed without preventing access to all nodes between the node to be removed and the replacement node. Searches can detect concurrent updates which may affect the validity of their results by simply monitoring the one or two nodes which govern the range of keys in a subtree. Our results show its concurrent performance to be very good compared with other ordered set algorithms, even when scaled to multi-CPU systems.

We found our algorithm to be very memory efficient, requiring only a fraction of the memory footprint of the other algorithms

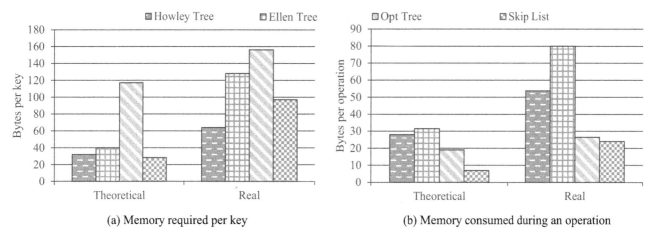

(a) Memory required per key

(b) Memory consumed during an operation

Figure 11: Memory usage of the tested algorithms for a 2,000 key range and a 50% add 50% remove 0% contains workload

tested - when very large data structures are considered, this could result in a significant memory saving. When compared with a lock-free external binary search tree, our algorithm outperformed it in almost every metric. A concurrent AVL tree does hold the advantage of being self-balanced, but at the cost of structure size and its lack of immunity to thread stalls or failures due to its use of locks. Lock-free skip lists were found to lose competitiveness at larger structure sizes when compared with the tree based structures, with our algorithm showing 65% more throughput when all the performance differentials are averaged. However, the nature of skip lists means that nodes are probabilistically balanced which is an advantage for workloads that perform poorly on unbalanced trees.

The experiments in the paper were all run using randomly generated keys. This would typically have the effect of keeping trees approximately balanced. In the worst case scenario, with all keys inserted in ascending order, a tree would resemble a linked list and it is expected that the balanced data structures would have a significant advantage. We would like to extend our algorithm to include an approximate and low overhead balancing algorithm in a lock-free manner to ensure performance cannot be degraded in this way.

We have successfully applied a number of lock-free memory management systems to our tree. We have described a method using tagged pointers which allows arbitrary memory reuse, and we are currently evaluating a method which can be implemented using a single-word CAS and requires no extra memory per node.

7. REFERENCES

[1] SPIN model checker. http://spinroot.com.
[2] G. Barnes. A method for implementing lock-free shared-data structures. In *Proceedings of the 5th ACM Symposium on Parallel Algorithms and Architectures*, SPAA '93, pages 261–270, Velen, Germany, June 1993. ACM.
[3] N. G. Bronson, J. Casper, H. Chafi, and K. Olukotun. A practical concurrent binary search tree. In *Proceedings of the 15th ACM SIGPLAN Symposium on Principles and Practice of Parallel Programming*, PPoPP '10, pages 257–268, Bangalore, India, January 2010. ACM.
[4] F. Ellen, P. Fatourou, E. Ruppert, and F. van Breugel. Non-blocking binary search trees. In *Proceedings of the 29th ACM SIGACT-SIGOPS Symposium on Principles of Distributed Computing*, PODC '10, pages 131–140, Zurich, Switzerland, July 2010. ACM.
[5] M. Fomitchev and E. Ruppert. Lock-free linked lists and skip lists. In *Proceedings of the 23nd ACM Symposium on Principles of Distributed Computing*, PODC '04, pages 50–59, St. John's, Newfoundland, Canada, July 2004. ACM.
[6] K. Fraser. *Practical lock-freedom*. PhD thesis, Computer Laboratory, University of Cambridge, UK. Also available as Technical Report UCAM-CL-TR-579, September 2003.
[7] T. L. Harris. A pragmatic implementation of non-blocking linked-lists. In *Proceedings of the 15th International Conference on Distributed Computing*, DISC '01, pages 300–314, Lisbon, Portugal, October 2001. Springer-Verlag.
[8] T. L. Harris, K. Fraser, and I. A. Pratt. A practical multi-word compare-and-swap operation. In *Proceedings of the 16th International Conference on Distributed Computing*, DISC '02, pages 265–279, Toulouse, France, October 2002. Springer-Verlag.
[9] M. Herlihy, Y. Lev, V. Luchangco, and N. Shavit. A provably correct scalable concurrent skip list. In *Proceedings of the 10th International Conference On Principles of Distributed Systems*, OPODIS '06, Bordeaux, France, December 2006.
[10] M. Herlihy, V. Luchangco, M. Moir, and W. N. Scherer, III. Software transactional memory for dynamic-sized data structures. In *Proceedings of the 22nd ACM Symposium on Principles of Distributed Computing*, PODC '03, pages 92–101, Boston, Massachusetts, July 2003. ACM.
[11] M. Herlihy and N. Shavit. *The Art of Multiprocessor Programming*. Morgan Kaufmann, 2008.
[12] M. P. Herlihy and J. M. Wing. Linearizability: a correctness condition for concurrent objects. *ACM Transactions on Programming Languages and Systems*, 12:463–492, July 1990.
[13] M. Michael. Hazard pointers: safe memory reclamation for lock-free objects. *Parallel and Distributed Systems, IEEE Transactions on*, 15(6):491–504, june 2004.
[14] M. M. Michael. High performance dynamic lock-free hash tables and list-based sets. In *Proceedings of the 14th ACM Symposium on Parallel Algorithms and Architectures*, SPAA '02, pages 73–82, Winnipeg, MB, Canada, August 2002. ACM.
[15] W. Pugh. Skip lists: a probabilistic alternative to balanced trees. *Communications of ACM*, 33(6):668–676, June 1990.

Lower Bounds for Restricted-Use Objects

Extended Abstract

James Aspnes
Department of Computer
Science, Yale University
aspnes@cs.yale.edu

Hagit Attiya[*]
Department of Computer
Science, Technion
hagit@cs.technion.ac.il

Keren Censor-Hillel[†]
Computer Science and
Artificial Intelligence
Laboratory, MIT
ckeren@csail.mit.edu

Danny Hendler[‡]
Department of Computer
Science, Ben-Gurion
university of the Negev
hendlerd@cs.bgu.ac.il

ABSTRACT

Concurrent objects play a key role in the design of applications for multi-core architectures, making it imperative to precisely understand their complexity requirements. For some objects, it is known that implementations can be significantly more efficient when their usage is restricted. However, apart from the specific restriction of one-shot implementations, where each process may apply only a single operation to the object, very little is known about the complexities of objects under general restrictions.

This paper draws a more complete picture by defining a large class of objects for which an operation applied to the object can be "perturbed" L consecutive times, and proving lower bounds on the time and space complexity of deterministic implementations of such objects. This class includes bounded-value max registers, limited-use approximate and exact counters, and limited-use collect and compare-and-swap objects; L depends on the number of times the object can be accessed or the maximum value it supports.

For implementations that use only historyless primitives, we prove lower bounds of $\Omega(\min(\log L, n))$ on the worst-case step complexity of an operation, where n is the number of processes; we also prove lower bounds of $\Omega(\min(L, n))$ on the space complexity of these objects. When arbitrary primitives can be used, we prove that either some operation incurs $\Omega(\min(\log L, n))$ memory stalls or some operation performs $\Omega(\min(\log L, n))$ steps.

[*]Supported in part by the *Israel Science Foundation* (grant number 1227/10).

[†]Supported by the Simons Postdoctoral Fellows Program

[‡]Supported in part by the *Israel Science Foundation* (grant number 1227/10).

Permission to make digital or hard copies of all or part of this work for personal or classroom use is granted without fee provided that copies are not made or distributed for profit or commercial advantage and that copies bear this notice and the full citation on the first page. To copy otherwise, to republish, to post on servers or to redistribute to lists, requires prior specific permission and/or a fee.
SPAA'12, June 25–27, 2012, Pittsburgh, Pennsylvania, USA.
Copyright 2012 ACM 978-1-4503-1213-4/12/06 ...$10.00.

In addition to these deterministic lower bounds, the paper establishes a lower bound on the expected step complexity of restricted-use randomized approximate counting in a weak oblivious adversary model.

Categories and Subject Descriptors

D.1.3 [**Programming Techniques**]: Concurrent Programming—*Distributed programming*; F.2.2 [**Analysis of Algorithms and Problem Complexity**]: Nonnumerical Algorithms and Problems

General Terms

Theory, Algorithms

Keywords

Concurrent objects, lower bounds, restricted-use objects, perturbable objects

1. INTRODUCTION

With multi-core and multi-processor systems now prevalent, there is growing need to gain better understanding of concurrent objects and, specifically, to establish lower bounds on the cost of implementing them. An important general class of concurrent objects, defined by Jayanti, Tan and Toueg [15], are *perturbable* objects, including widely-used objects, such as *counters*, *max registers*, *compare-and-swap*, *single-writer snapshot* and *fetch-and-add*.

Lower bounds are known for *long-lived* implementations of perturbable objects, where processes apply an unbounded number of operations to the object. For example, Jayanti *et al.* [15] consider obstruction-free implementations of perturbable objects from *historyless* primitives, such as *read*, *write*, *test-and-set* and *swap*. They prove that such implementations require $\Omega(n)$ space and that the worst-case step-complexity of the operations they support is $\Omega(n)$, where n is the number of processes sharing the object.

In some applications, however, objects are used in a restricted manner. For example, there might be a bound on the total number of operations applied on the object, or a bound on the values that the object needs to support. When an object is designed to allow only restricted use, it is sometimes possible to construct more efficient implementations than for the general case.

Indeed, Aspnes, Attiya and Censor-Hillel [3] showed that at least some restricted-use perturbable objects admit implementations that "beat" the lower bound of [15]. For example, a max register can do a write of v in $O(\min(\log v, n))$ steps, while a counter limited to m increments can do each increment in $O(\min(\log^2 m, n))$ steps. Such a restricted-use counter leads to a randomized consensus algorithm with $O(n)$ individual step complexity [4], while restricted-use counters and max registers are used in a mutual exclusion algorithm with sub-logarithmic amortized work [7].

This raises the natural question of determining lower bounds on the complexity of restricted-use objects. The proof of Jayanti *et al.* [15] breaks for restricted-use objects because the executions constructed by this proof exceed the restrictions on these objects.

For the specific restriction of *one-time* object implementations, where each process applies exactly one operation to the object, there are lower bounds which are logarithmic in the number of processes, for specific objects [2, 1, 6] and generic perturbable objects [14]. Yet, these techniques yield bounds that are far from the upper bounds, e.g., when the object can be perturbed a super-polynomial number of times.

This paper draws a more complete picture of the cost of implementing restricted-use objects by studying the middle ground. We give time and space lower bounds for implementations of objects that are only required to work under restricted usage, for general families of restrictions.

We define the notion of *L-perturbable objects* that strictly generalizes classical perturbability; specific examples are bounded-value max registers, limited-use approximate and exact counters, and limited-use compare-and-swap and collect objects.[1] L, the perturbation bound, depends on the number of times the object can be accessed or the maximum value it can support (see Table 1).

For L-perturbable objects, we show lower bounds on the step and space complexity of obstruction-free deterministic implementations from historyless primitives. The step complexity lower bound is $\Omega(\min(\log L, n))$, and its proof uses a technique that we call *backtracking covering*, which is a quantified version of a technique introduced by Fich, Hendler and Shavit in [11] and later used in [5]. The space complexity lower bound is $\Omega(\min(L, n))$.

We also consider implementations that can apply *arbitrary* primitives not just historyless primitives, and use the *memory stalls* measure [8] to quantify the contention incurred by such implementations. We extend backtracking covering to prove that either an implementation's worst-case operation step complexity is $\Omega(\min(\log L, n))$ or some operation incurs $\Omega(\min(\log L, n))$ stalls.

In addition to our deterministic lower bounds, we establish a lower bound of $\Omega\left(\frac{\log \log m - \log \log c}{\log \log \log m}\right)$ on the expected step complexity of randomized *m*-valued *c-multiplicative-accurate counters*, a particularly weak class of counters that allow a multiplicative error of factor at most c. Our lower

---

[1] A single-writer snapshot object is also a collect object (the converse is, in general, false). Therefore, our lower bounds for the collect object also hold for the single-writer snapshot object.

bound employs Yao's Principle [16] and assumes a weak oblivious adversary. Table 1 summarizes the lower bounds for specific L-perturbable objects.

Aspnes *et al.* [3] prove lower bounds on obstruction-free implementations of max registers and approximate counters from historyless primitives: an $\Omega(\min(\log m, n))$ step lower bound for deterministic implementations and a $\Omega(\log m / \log \log m)$ lower bound, when $m \leq n$, on the expected step complexity of randomized implementations. These bounds, however, use a different proof technique, which is specifically tailored for the semantics of the particular objects, and does not seem to generalize to the restricted-use versions of *arbitrary* perturbable objects. Moreover, they neither prove space-complexity lower bounds nor consider implementations from arbitrary primitives.

2. MODEL AND DEFINITIONS

A shared-memory system consists of n *asynchronous* processes $p_1, \ldots, p_n$ communicating by applying primitive operations (*primitives*) on shared *base objects*. An application of each such primitive is a shared memory *event*. A *step* taken by a process consists of local computation followed by one shared memory event.

A primitive is *nontrivial* if it may change the value of the base object to which it is applied, e.g., a *write* or a *read-modify-write*, and *trivial* otherwise, e.g., a *read*. Let o be a base object that is accessed with two primitives f and f'; f *overwrites* f' on o [10], if starting from any value v of o, applying f' and then f results in the same value as applying just f, using the same input parameters (if any) in both cases. A set of primitives is *historyless* if all the nontrivial primitives in the set overwrite each other; we also require that each such primitive overwrites itself. A set that includes the write and swap primitives is an example of a historyless set of primitives.

2.1 Executions and Operations

An *execution fragment* is a sequence of shared memory events applied by processes. An execution fragment is p_i-free if it contains no steps of process p_i. An *execution* is an execution fragment that starts from an initial configuration (in which all shared variables and processes' local states assume their initial values). For execution fragments α and β, we let $\alpha\beta$ denote the execution fragment which results when the events of β are concatenated to those of α.

An *operation instance* of an operation Op on an implemented object is a subsequence of an execution, in which some process p_i performs the operation Op on the object. The primitives applied by the operation instance may depend on the values of the shared base objects before this operation instance starts and during its execution (p_i's steps may be interleaved with steps of other processes).

An execution is *well-defined* if it may result when processes each perform a sequence of operation instances according to their algorithms. All the executions we consider are well-defined.

An implementation is *obstruction-free* [12] if a process terminates its operation instance if it runs in isolation long enough.

A process p is *active* after execution α if p is in the middle of performing an operation instance, i.e., p has applied at least one event of the operation instance in α, but the instance is not complete in α. Let *active(α)* denote the set

	perturbation bound (L)	step complexity	max(steps, stalls)	space complexity	rand. step complexity
compare & swap	$\sqrt[3]{m}-1$	$\Omega(\min(\log m, n))$	$\Omega(\min(\log m, n))$	$\Omega(\min(\sqrt[3]{m}, n))$	—
collect	$m-1$	$\Omega(\min(\log m, n))$	$\Omega(\min(\log m, n))$	$\Omega(\min(m, n))$	—
max register	$m-1$	$\Omega(\min(\log m, n))$ (also [3])	$\Omega(\min(\log m, n))$	$\Omega(\min(m, n))$	$\Omega(\frac{\log\log m}{\log\log\log m})$ (for $m \le n$, [3])
k-additive counter	$\sqrt{\frac{m}{k}}-1$	$\Omega(\min(\log m - \log k, n))$ (also [3])	$\Omega(\min(\log m - \log k, n))$	$\Omega(\min(\sqrt{\frac{m}{k}}, n))$	$\Omega(\frac{\log\log m}{\log\log\log m})$ (for $m \le n$)

Table 1: **Summary of lower bounds for restricted-use objects; where m is the maximum value assumed by the object or the bound on the number of operations applied to it. All the bounds are derived in this paper, except when stated otherwise.**

of processes that are active after α. If p is not active after α, we say that p is *idle* after α.

A base object o is *covered after* an execution α if there is a process p in the configuration resulting from α that has a nontrivial event about to access o; we say that p *covers* o after α.

2.2 Restricted-Use Objects

Our main focus in this paper is on objects that support restricted usage. One example of such objects are objects that have a limit on the number of operation instances that can be performed on them, as captured by the following definition. An *m-limited-use* object is an object that allows at most m operation instances; m is the *limit* of the object.

Another type of objects with restricted usage are objects that have a value associated with their state which cannot exceed some bound. Examples are bounded max-registers and bounded counters [3], whose definitions we now provide.

A *max-register* is a linearizable [13] object that supports a `Write` (v) operation, which writes the value v to the object, and a `ReadMax` operation, which returns the maximum value written by a `Write` operation instance linearized before it. In the bounded version of these objects, the object is only required to satisfy its specification if its associated value does not exceed a certain threshold.

A *counter* is a linearizable object that supports a `CounterIncrement` operation and a `CounterRead` operation, which returns the number of `CounterIncrement` operation instances linearized before it. In a *k-additive-accurate counter*, every `CounterRead` operation returns a value within $\pm k$ of the number of `CounterIncrement` operation instances linearized before it. A *c-multiplicative-accurate counter* is a counter for which any `CounterRead` operation returns a value x with $v/c \le x \le vc$, where v is the number of `CounterIncrement` operation instances linearized before it.

A *b-bounded max register* takes values in $\{0, \dots, b-1\}$. A *b-bounded counter* is a counter that takes values in $\{0, \dots, b-1\}$.

For a *b-bounded* object $\mathcal{O}$, b is the *bound* of $\mathcal{O}$.

We also consider collect and compare-and-swap objects.

A *collect* object provides two operations: a *store(val)* by process p_i sets *val* to the latest value for p_i. A *collect* operation *cop* returns a *view*, $\langle v_1, \dots, v_n \rangle$, satisfying the following properties: 1) if $v_j = \perp$, then no *store* operation by p_j completes before *cop* starts, and 2) if $v_j \ne \perp$, then v_j is the operand of a *store* operation *sop* by p_j that starts before *cop* completes and there is no store operation by p_j that starts after *sop* completes and completes before *cop* starts.

A linearizable *b*-valued *compare-and-swap* object has a value in $\{1, \dots, b\}$ and supports the operations *read* and *CAS(u,v)*, for all $u, v \in \{1, \dots, b\}$. When the object's value is u (as determined by the sequence of operation instances on the object that were linearized), *CAS(u,v)* changes its value to v and returns *true*; when the object's value differs from u, *CAS(u,v)* returns *false* and does not change the object's value.

3. LOWER BOUNDS FOR DETERMINISTIC RESTRICTED-USE OBJECTS

In this section, we prove lower bounds for obstruction-free implementations of some restricted-use objects. Our starting point is the definition of *perturbable* objects by Jayanti *et al.* [15]. Roughly speaking, an object is perturbable if in some class of executions, events applied by an operation of one process influence the response of an operation of another process. The flavor of the argument used by Jayanti *et al.* to obtain their linear lower bound is that since the perturbed operation needs to return different responses with each perturbation, it must be able to distinguish between perturbed executions, implying that it must perform an increasing number of accesses to base objects.

The formal definition of perturbable objects is as follows.

DEFINITION 1. *(See Figure 1.)* An object $\mathcal{O}$ is *perturbable if there is an operation instance op_n by process p_n, such that for every p_n-free execution $\alpha\lambda$ where no process applies more than a single event in λ and for some process $p_\ell \ne p_n$ that applies no event in λ, there is an extension of α, γ, consisting of events by p_ℓ, such that p_n returns different responses when performing op_n by itself after $\alpha\lambda$ and after $\alpha\gamma\lambda$.*

We observe that $\alpha\gamma\lambda$ in the above definition is a well-defined execution if $\alpha\lambda$ is well-defined. This is because no process applies more than a single event in λ and p_ℓ applies no events in λ, hence no process can distinguish between the two executions before it applies its last event.

The linear lower bounds [15] on the space and step complexity of obstruction-free implementations on perturbable objects (as defined in Definition 1 above) are obtained by constructing executions of unbounded length, hence they do not apply in general for restricted-use objects.

To prove lower bounds for restricted-use objects, we define a class of *L-perturbable* objects. As opposed to the definition of a perturbable object, we do not require every execution of an *L-perturbable* object to be perturbable, since this requirement is in general not satisfied by restricted-use

174

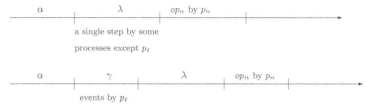

Figure 1: A perturbable object: op_n returns different responses in the two executions.

objects. For such objects, some executions already reach the limit or bound of the object, not allowing any further operation to affect the object, which rules out a perturbation of these executions. To achieve our lower bounds we only need to show the existence of a special perturbing sequence of executions rather than attempting to perturb every execution. The longer the sequence, the higher the lower bound, since the perturbed operation will have to access more base objects in order to distinguish between executions in the sequence and be able to return different responses.

DEFINITION 2. *An object O is L-perturbable if there exists an operation instance op_n by p_n such that an L-perturbing execution of O can be constructed as follows: The empty execution is 0-perturbing. Assume the object has a $(k-1)$-perturbing execution $\alpha_{k-1}\lambda_{k-1}$, where no process applies more than a single event in λ_{k-1}.*

1. *If $|\lambda_{k-1}| = n-1$, then we say that $\alpha_{k-1}\lambda_{k-1}$ is saturated, and the execution $\alpha_k\lambda_k$ with $\alpha_k = \alpha_{k-1}$, $\lambda_k = \lambda_{k-1}$ is k-perturbing.*

2. *Otherwise, if there exists a process $p_\ell \neq p_n$ that applies no event in λ_{k-1} and an extension of α_{k-1}, γ, consisting of events by p_ℓ, such that p_n returns different responses when performing op_n by itself after $\alpha_{k-1}\lambda_{k-1}$ and after $\alpha_{k-1}\gamma\lambda_{k-1}$, then we define a k-perturbing execution as follows. Let $\gamma = \gamma'e\gamma''$, where e is the first event of γ such that op_n returns different responses after $\alpha_{k-1}\lambda_{k-1}$ and after $\alpha_{k-1}\gamma'e\lambda_{k-1}$. Let λ be a permutation of the events in λ_{k-1} and the event e, and let λ', λ'' be any two sequences of events such that $\lambda = \lambda'\lambda''$. The execution $\alpha_k\lambda_k$ is k-perturbing, where $\alpha_k = \alpha_{k-1}\gamma'\lambda'$ and $\lambda_k = \lambda''$.*

If an object is L-perturbable, then, starting from the initial configuration, we may construct a sequence of $L+1$ perturbing executions, $\alpha_k\lambda_k$, for $0 \leq k \leq L$, each of which extending its predecessor perturbing execution. If for some i, $\alpha_i\lambda_i$ is saturated, then we cannot further extend the sequence of perturbing executions since we do not have available processes to perform the perturbation. However, in this case we have lower bounds that are linear in n. For presentation simplicity, we assume in this case that the rest of the sequence's perturbing executions are identical to $\alpha_i\lambda_i$.

Definition 2 allows flexibility in determining which of the events of λ_{k-1} are contained in λ_k and which are contained in α_k. We use this flexibility to prove lower bounds on the step, space and stall-complexity of L-perturbable objects.

The definition implies that every perturbable object is L-perturbable for every integer $L \geq 0$; hence, the class of L-perturbable objects generalizes the class of perturbable objects. On the other hand, there are L-perturbable objects that are not perturbable; for example, a b-bounded n-process max register, for $b \in \text{poly}(n)$, is not perturbable in general,

by the algorithm of [3]. That is, the class of perturbable objects is a proper subset of the class of L-perturbable objects.

The next lemma establishes that several common restricted-use objects are L-perturbable, where L is a function of the limit on the number of different operations that may be applied to them. The challenge in the proof is in increasing L, which later translates to higher lower bounds.

LEMMA 1. *1. An obstruction-free implementation of a b-bounded-value max register is $(b-1)$-perturbable.*

2. *An obstruction-free implementation of an m-limited-use max register is $(m-1)$-perturbable.*

3. *An obstruction-free implementation of an m-limited-use counter is $(\sqrt{m}-1)$-perturbable.*

4. *An obstruction-free implementation of a k-additive-accurate m-limited-use counter is $(\sqrt{\frac{m}{k}}-1)$-perturbable.*

5. *An obstruction-free implementation of an m-limited-use b-valued compare-and-swap object is $(\sqrt[3]{m}-1)$-perturbable (if $b \geq n$).*

6. *An obstruction-free implementation of an m-limited-use collect object is $(m-1)$-perturbable.*

PROOF. We present the proofs for representative objects; proofs for other objects appear in the full paper.

1. Let $\mathcal{O}$ be a b-bounded-value max register and consider an obstruction-free implementation of $\mathcal{O}$. We show that $\mathcal{O}$ is $(b-1)$-perturbable for a `ReadMax` operation instance op_n of p_n, by induction, where the base case for $r=0$ is immediate for all objects. We perturb the executions by writing values that increase by one to the max register. This guarantees that op_n has to return different values each time, while getting closer to the limit of the object as slowly as possible.

   Formally, let $r < b$ and let $\alpha_{r-1}\lambda_{r-1}$ be an $(r-1)$-perturbing execution of $\mathcal{O}$. If $\alpha_{r-1}\lambda_{r-1}$ is saturated, then, by case (1) of Definition 2, it is also an r-perturbing execution.

   Otherwise, our induction hypothesis is that op_n returns $r-1$ when run after $\alpha_{r-1}\lambda_{r-1}$. For the induction step, we build an r-perturbing execution after which the value returned by op_n is r. Since $\alpha_{r-1}\lambda_{r-1}$ is not saturated, there is a process $p_\ell \neq p_n$ that does not take steps in λ_{r-1}. Let γ be the execution fragment by p_ℓ where it first finishes any incomplete operation in α and then performs a `Write` operation to the max register with the value $r \leq b-1$. Then op_n returns the value r when run after $\alpha_{r-1}\gamma\lambda_{r-1}$, and $r-1$ when run after the $(r-1)$-perturbing execution $\alpha_{r-1}\lambda_{r-1}$. It follows that r-perturbing executions may be constructed from $\alpha_{r-1}\lambda_{r-1}$ and γ as specified by Definition 2.

2. The proof for an m-limited-use max register appears in the full paper.

3. When $\mathcal{O}$ is an m-limited-use counter, we use a proof similar to the one we used for a limited-use max register, where we perturb a `CounterRead` operation op_n by applying `CounterIncrement` operations. The subtlety in the case of a counter comes from the fact that a single perturbing operation may not be sufficient for guaranteeing that op_n returns a different value after $\alpha_{r-1}\lambda_{r-1}$ and after $\alpha_{r-1}\gamma\lambda_{r-1}$, since we do not know how many of the `CounterIncrement` operations by processes that are active after α_{r-1} were linearized. As there are at most $r - 1$ such operations, in order to ensure that different values are returned by p_n after these two executions, we construct γ by letting the process p_ℓ apply r `CounterIncrement` operations after finishing any incomplete operation in α_{r-1}. This can be done as long as $r \leq \sqrt{m}$ in order not to pass the limit on the number of operations allowed, which will be $1 + \sum_{r=1}^{\sqrt{m}} r = 1 + \frac{(\sqrt{m}-1)\sqrt{m}}{2} \leq m$.

4. For a k-additive-accurate m-limited-use counter, the proof is similar to that of a counter, except that p_ℓ needs to perform an even larger number of `Counter-Increment` operations in γ, because of the inaccuracy allowed in the returned value of the `CounterRead` operation op_n. The details appear in the full paper.

5. Let $\mathcal{O}$ be an m-limited-use b-bounded *compare-and-swap* object, $b \geq n$. We show that it is $(\sqrt[3]{m} - 1)$-perturbable for a *read* operation instance by p_n, by induction, where the base case for $r = 0$ is immediate for all objects. In our construction, all processes except for p_n perform only CAS operation instances.

Let $r < \sqrt[3]{m} - 1$ and let $\alpha_{r-1}\lambda_{r-1}$ be an $(r - 1)$-perturbing execution of $\mathcal{O}$. If $\alpha_{r-1}\lambda_{r-1}$ is saturated, then, by case (1) of Definition 2, it is also an r-perturbing execution.

Otherwise, our induction hypothesis is that $\alpha_{r-1}\lambda_{r-1}$ includes at most $\sum_{i=1}^{r-1} i^2$ CAS operation instances. Let u be the value returned by op_n after $\alpha_{r-1}\lambda_{r-1}$, and let j denote the number of processes that apply events in λ_{r-1} and let $p_{r-1}^1, \ldots, p_{r-1}^j$ be these processes. Let ξ be an execution fragment that follows α_{r-1} in which all active processes other than $p_{r-1}^1, \ldots, p_{r-1}^j$ finish any incomplete operation instances they started in α_{r-1}. For $k \in \{1, \ldots, j\}$, let (u_k, v_k) denote the operands of the last CAS operation instance started by p_{r-1}^k in α_{r-1}. Since $\alpha_{r-1}\lambda_{r-1}$ is not saturated and since $r - 1 < \sqrt[3]{m} - 1$, there is a process $p_\ell \notin \{p_{r-1}^1, \ldots, p_{r-1}^j\} \cup \{p_n\}$ and, moreover, there is a value $v \in \{1, \ldots, n\} \setminus \{u, u_1, \ldots, u_j\}$.

Denote by β the sequence of operation instances $CAS(u, v)CAS(v_1, v)\ldots CAS(v_j, v)$, denote by β^r the sequence of operation instances resulting from concatenating r copies of β and let $\gamma = \xi\beta^r$.

We claim that $\mathcal{O}$'s value after $\alpha_{r-1}\gamma\lambda_{r-1}$ is v. Consider $\mathcal{O}$'s value after p_ℓ executes β once after $\alpha_{r-1}\xi$. There are two possibilities: either $\mathcal{O}$'s value is v (in which case it remains v also after $\alpha\gamma$), or, otherwise, all the CAS instances in β failed, implying that one or more of the operation instances performed by

$p_{r-1}^1, \ldots, p_{r-1}^j$ are linearized when execution fragment γ is performed. In the latter case, consider $\mathcal{O}$'s value after p_ℓ executes β twice after $\alpha_{r-1}\xi$. Once again, either $\mathcal{O}$'s value is v (and remains v also after $\alpha_{r-1}\gamma$), or, otherwise, additional operation instances performed by $p_{r-1}^1, \ldots, p_{r-1}^j$ are linearized when the second instance of execution fragment β is performed. Applying this argument iteratively and noting that $j \leq r - 1$, by construction, establishes our claim.

Consider the execution $\alpha_{r-1}\gamma\lambda_{r-1}\phi$, where ϕ is an execution of *read* by p_n. Then ϕ must return v, whereas an execution of *read* by p_n after $\alpha_{r-1}\lambda_{r-1}$ returns $u \neq v$. Execution $\alpha_r\lambda_r$ can now be constructed as in the proofs for limited use max registers and counters. The number of operation instances applied by p_ℓ in γ is $(j + 1) \cdot r \leq r^2$. Since $\mathcal{O}$ allows only m operation instances, this implies that the sequence can have length $\sqrt[3]{m} - 1$, because the total number of operation instances will be $1 + \sum_{r=1}^{\sqrt[3]{m}-1} r^2 < m$.

6. Let $\mathcal{O}$ be an m-limited-use collect object and consider an obstruction-free implementation of $\mathcal{O}$. We show that $\mathcal{O}$ is $(m - 1)$-perturbable for a *collect* operation instance op_n of p_n, by induction, where the base case for $r = 0$ is immediate for all objects. We perturb the executions by having processes store values that change their collect component. This guarantees that op_n has to return different values each time, while getting closer to the limit of the object as slowly as possible.

Formally, let $r < m$ and let $\alpha_{r-1}\lambda_{r-1}$ be an $(r - 1)$-perturbing execution of $\mathcal{O}$. If $\alpha_{r-1}\lambda_{r-1}$ is saturated, then, by case (1) of Definition 2, it is also an r-perturbing execution.

Otherwise, Let $V = < v_1, \ldots, v_n >$ denote the value that is returned by a *collect* operation by p_n after $\alpha_{r-1}\lambda_{r-1}$. Since $\alpha_{r-1}\lambda_{r-1}$ is not saturated, there is a process $p_\ell \neq p_n$ that does not take steps in λ_{r-1}. Let γ be the execution fragment by p_ℓ where it first finishes any incomplete operation in α and then applies an $update(v'_\ell)$ operation operation to $\mathcal{O}$, for some $v'_\ell \neq v_\ell$. Then op_n must return different values when run after $\alpha_{r-1}\gamma\lambda_{r-1}$ and after the $(r - 1)$-perturbing execution $\alpha_{r-1}\lambda_{r-1}$. It follows that r-perturbing executions may be constructed from $\alpha_{r-1}\lambda_{r-1}$ and γ as specified by Definition 2. $\square$

3.1 Lower bounds for implementations using historyless objects

We define the concept of an access-perturbation sequence, and prove a step-complexity lower bound for objects that admit such a sequence.

DEFINITION 3. *(See Figure 2.)* *An access-perturbation sequence of length L of an operation instance op_n by process p_n on an object $\mathcal{O}$ is a sequence of executions $\{\alpha_r\lambda_r\phi_r\}_{r=0}^L$, such that $\alpha_0\lambda_0$ is empty, ϕ_0 is an execution of op_n by p_n starting from the initial configuration, and for every r, $1 \leq r \leq L$, the following properties hold:*

  1. The execution $\alpha_r\lambda_r$ is p_n-free.

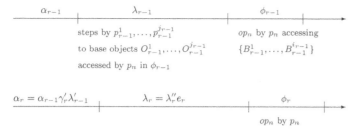

Figure 2: An access-perturbation sequence of length L: the above describes the executions for every r, $1 \le r \le L$. Notice that $\alpha_r \lambda_r$ is p_n-free for every r.

2. In ϕ_r, process p_n runs solo after $\alpha_r \lambda_r$ until it completes the operation instance op_n, in the course of which it accesses the base objects $B_r^1, \ldots, B_r^{i_r}$.

3. λ_r consists of $j_r \ge 0$ nontrivial events applied by j_r distinct processes, $p_r^1, \ldots, p_r^{j_r}$ to distinct base objects $O_r^1, \ldots, O_r^{j_r}$, respectively, all of which are accessed by p_n in ϕ_r. If $j_r = n - 1$, we say that $\alpha_r \lambda_r \phi_r$ is saturated.

4. (a) If $\alpha_{r-1} \lambda_{r-1} \phi_{r-1}$ is saturated, then we let $\alpha_r = \alpha_{r-1}$, $\lambda_r = \lambda_{r-1}$ and $\phi_r = \phi_{r-1}$.

   (b) Otherwise, we let $\alpha_r = \alpha_{r-1} \gamma_r' \lambda_{r-1}'$, and $\lambda_r = \lambda_{r-1}'' e_r$, where λ_{r-1}' is the subset of λ_{r-1} containing all events to base objects that are not accessed by p_n in ϕ_r, λ_{r-1}'' is the subset of λ_{r-1} containing all events to base objects that are accessed by p_n in ϕ_r, and $\gamma_r' e_r$ is an execution fragment by a process p_{ℓ_r} not taking steps in λ_{r-1}, where e_r is its first nontrivial event to a base object in $\{B_{r-1}^1, \ldots, B_{r-1}^{i_{r-1}}\} \setminus \{O_{r-1}^1, \ldots, O_{r-1}^{j_{r-1}}\}$.

We now prove that every L-perturbable objects has an access-perturbation sequence of length L.

LEMMA 2. *An L-perturbable object implementation from historyless primitives has an access-perturbation sequence of length L.*

PROOF. Let $\mathcal{O}$ be an L-perturbable object implementation from historyless primitives. We show that it has an access-perturbation sequence of length L, for the operation op_n as defined in Definition 3. The proof is by induction, where we prove the existence of the execution $\alpha_r \lambda_r \phi_r$, for every r, $0 \le r \le L$. To allow the proof to go through, in addition to proving that the execution $\alpha_r \lambda_r \phi_r$ satisfies the four conditions of Definition 3, we will prove that $\alpha_r \lambda_r$ is r-perturbing.

For the base case, $r = 0$, $\alpha_0 \lambda_0$ is empty and ϕ_0 is an execution of op_n starting from the initial configuration. Moreover, the empty execution is 0-perturbing. We next assume the construction of the sequence up to $r - 1 < L$ and construct the next execution $\alpha_r \lambda_r \phi_r$ as follows.

By the induction hypothesis, the execution $\alpha_{r-1} \lambda_{r-1}$ is $(r-1)$-perturbing. If $\alpha_{r-1} \lambda_{r-1}$ is saturated, then, by case (1) of Definition 2, $\alpha_r = \alpha_{r-1}$, $\lambda_r = \lambda_{r-1}$ and $\alpha_r \lambda_r$ is r-perturbing. Moreover, by property 4(a) of Definition 3, $\alpha_r \lambda_r \phi_r$ is the r'th access-perturbation execution, where $\phi_r = \phi_{r-1}$.

Assume otherwise. Then, by property 2 of Definition 2, there is a process $p_{\ell_r} \ne p_n$ that does not take steps in λ_{r-1}, for which there is an extension of α_{r-1}, γ_r, consisting of events by p_{ℓ_r}, such that p_n returns different responses when performing op_n by itself after $\alpha_{r-1} \lambda_{r-1}$ and

after $\alpha_{r-1} \gamma_r \lambda_{r-1}$. As per Definition 2, let $\gamma_r = \gamma_r' e_r \gamma_r''$, where e_r is the first event of γ such that op_n returns different responses after $\alpha_{r-1} \lambda_{r-1}$ and after $\alpha_{r-1} \gamma_r' e_r \lambda_{r-1}$. Clearly e_r is a nontrivial event.

Denote by ϕ_r the execution of op_n by p_n after $\alpha_{r-1} \gamma_r' e_r \lambda_{r-1}$. Since op_n returns different values after $\alpha_{r-1} \lambda_{r-1}$ and after $\alpha_{r-1} \gamma_r' e_r \lambda_{r-1}$, and since the implementation uses only historyless primitives, this implies that e_r is applied to some base object B not in $\{O_{r-1}^1, \ldots, O_{r-1}^{j_{r-1}}\}$ that is accessed by p_n in ϕ_r.

We define λ_{r-1}' to be the subsequence of λ_{r-1} containing all events to base objects that are not accessed by p_n in ϕ_r, and λ_{r-1}'' to be the subsequence of λ_{r-1} containing all events to base objects that are accessed by p_n in ϕ_r. We then define $\alpha_r = \alpha_{r-1} \gamma_r' \lambda_{r-1}'$, $\lambda_r = \lambda_{r-1}'' e_r$ and show that $\alpha_r \lambda_r \phi_r$ satisfies the properties of Definition 3.

We first observe that $\alpha_r \lambda_r \phi_r$ is a well-defined execution, since the execution fragment γ_r' by p_{ℓ_r} is performed after α_{r-1}, and all operations in λ_{r-1} are nontrivial events to distinct base objects none of which is by p_{ℓ_r}. It follows that $\alpha_r \lambda_r$ and $\alpha_{r-1} \gamma_r' e_r \lambda_{r-1}$ are indistinguishable to p_n, hence ϕ_r is a solo execution of op_n by p_n after both executions.

Property 1 holds since $\alpha_r \lambda_r$ is p_n-free by construction, and ϕ_r is a solo execution fragment by p_n in which it performs op_n, so Property 2 holds. To show Property 3, we observe that $\alpha_r \lambda_r$ is indistinguishable to p_n from $\alpha_{r-1} \gamma_r' e_r \lambda_{r-1}$ and hence p_n accesses the base object B in ϕ_r. Finally, Property 4 follows by construction.

We conclude the proof by claiming that $\alpha_r \lambda_r$ is r-perturbing, which follows from its construction and Definition 2. $\square$

Next, we prove a step lower bound for implementations that have an access-perturbation sequence. If the sequence is saturated, then the lower bound is linear in the number of processes, otherwise it is logarithmic in the length of the sequence. Our goal is to prove that p_n has to access a large number of base objects as it runs solo while performing an instance op_n of Op in one of the executions of op_n's access-perturbation sequence. Let π_r denote the sequence of base objects accessed by p_n in ϕ_r, in the order of their first access in ϕ_r; π_r is p_n's *solo path* in ϕ_r. If all the objects accessed in π_r are also in λ_r, i.e., p_n accesses them also in ϕ_r, then $\lambda_r = \lambda_{r-1} e_r$. However, the application of e_r may have the undesirable effect (from the perspective of an adversary) of making π_r shorter than π_{r-1}: p_n may read the information written by p_{ℓ_r} and avoid accessing some other objects that were previously in π_{r-1}.

To overcome this difficulty, we employ the *backtracking covering* technique, which is a quantitative version of a technique previous used in [5, 11]. The observation underlying this technique is that objects that are in π_{r-1} will be absent from π_r only if the additional object to which p_{ℓ_r} applies the nontrivial event e_r precedes them in π_{r-1}. Thus the set of objects along π_r that are covered after $\alpha_r\lambda_r$ is 'closer', in a sense, to the beginning of p_n's solo path in ϕ_{r-1}. It follows that if there are many access-perturbation sequence executions r for which $|\pi_r| < |\pi_{r-1}|$, then one of the solo paths π_r must be 'long'.

To capture this intuition, we define Ψ, a monotonically-increasing progress function of r. Ψ_r is a $(\log L)$-digit binary number defined as follows. Bit 0 (the most significant bit) of Ψ_r is 1 if and only if the first object in π_r is covered after α_r (by one of the events of λ_r); bit 1 of Ψ_r is 1 if and only if the second object in π_r exists and is covered after α_r, and so on. Note that we do not need to consider paths that are longer than $\log L$. If such a path exists, the lower bound clearly holds.

To construct the r'th access-perturbation sequence execution, we deploy a free process, p_{ℓ_r} and let it run solo until it is about to write to an uncovered object, O, along π_r. (Since the sequence is not saturated, it follows from Property 4(b) of Definition 3 that such p_{ℓ_r} and O exist.) In terms of Ψ, this implies that the covering event e_r might flip some of the digits of Ψ_{r-1} from 1 to 0. But O corresponds to a more significant digit, and this digit is flipped from 0 to 1, hence $\Psi_r > \Psi_{r-1}$ must hold. Thus we can construct executions $\alpha_r\lambda_r\phi_r$, for $1 \le r \le L$, in each of which Ψ_r increases. It follows that $\Psi_r = L-1$ must eventually hold, implying that π_r's length is $\Omega(\log L)$.

THEOREM 3. *Let A be an n-process obstruction-free implementation of an L-perturbable object $\mathcal{O}$ from historyless primitives. Then A has an execution in which some process accesses $\Omega(\min(\log L, n))$ distinct base objects during a single operation instance.*

PROOF. Lemma 2 establishes that every implementation of $\mathcal{O}$ from historyless primitives has an access-perturbation sequence of length $L \ge 1$, $\{\alpha_r\lambda_r\phi_r\}_{r=0}^{L}$. If the sequence is saturated, then Definition 3 immediately implies that p_n accesses $n-1$ distinct base objects in the course of performing ϕ_r, and the lower bound holds. Otherwise, we show that op_n accesses $\Omega(\log L)$ distinct base objects in one of these executions.

Let $\pi_r = B_r^1 \ldots B_r^{i_r}$ denote the sequence of all distinct base objects accessed by p_n in ϕ_r (after $\alpha_r\lambda_r$) according to Property 2 of Definition 3, and let S_{π_r} denote the set of these base objects. Let $S_r^C = \{O_r^1, \ldots, O_r^{j_r}\}$ be the set of base objects defined in Property 3 of Definition 3. Observe that, by Property 3, $S_r^C \subseteq S_{\pi_r}$ holds. Without loss of generality, assume that $O_r^1, \ldots, O_r^{j_r}$ occur in π_r in the order of their superscripts.

In the execution $\alpha_r\lambda_r\phi_r$, p_n accesses i_r distinct base objects. Thus, it suffices to show that some i_r is in $\Omega(\log L)$. For $j \in \{1, \ldots, i_r\}$, let b_r^j be the indicator variable whose value is 1 if $B_r^j \in S_r^C$ and 0 otherwise. We associate an integral progress parameter, Ψ_r, with each $r \ge 0$, defined as follows:

$$\Psi_r = \sum_{j=1}^{i_r} b_r^j \cdot \frac{L}{2^j} \ .$$

For simplicity of presentation, and without loss of generality, assume that $L = 2^s$ for some integer $s > 0$, so $s = \log L$. If $i_r > s$ for some r then we are done. Assume otherwise, then Ψ_r can be viewed as a binary number with s digits

whose j'th most significant bit is 1 if the j'th base object in π_r exists and is in S_r^C, or 0 otherwise. This implies that the number of 1-bits in Ψ_r equals $|S_r^C|$. Our execution is constructed so that Ψ_r is monotonically increasing in r and eventually, for some r', $\Psi_{r'}$ equals $L-1 = L\sum_{j=1}^s \frac{1}{2^j}$. This would imply that p_n accesses exactly s base objects during $\phi_{r'}$ (after $\alpha_{r'}\lambda_{r'}$).

We next show that $\Psi_r > \Psi_{r-1}$, for every $0 < r \le L$. Since $\alpha_{r-1}\lambda_{r-1}\phi_{r-1}$ is not saturated, by Property 4(b) of Definition 3, there is a process p_{ℓ_r} that takes no steps in λ_{r-1}, and an execution fragment $\gamma_r'e_r$ of p_{ℓ_r} after α_{r-1}, such that e_r is the first nontrivial event of p_{ℓ_r} in $\gamma_r'e_r$ to a base object in $\{B_{r-1}^1, \ldots, B_{r-1}^{i_{r-1}}\} \setminus \{O_{r-1}^1, \ldots, O_{r-1}^{j_{r-1}}\}$. By Property 2 of that definition, this object is accessed by p_n in ϕ_r. Let k be the index of the object among the objects accessed in ϕ_{r-1}, i.e., it is B_{r-1}^k. This implies that $B_{r-1}^k \in S_{\pi_{r-1}} \setminus S_{r-1}^C$.

As $B_{r-1}^k \notin S_{r-1}^C$, we have $b_{r-1}^k = 0$. Since e_r is the first nontrivial event of p_{ℓ_r} in $\gamma_r'e_r$ to a base object in $S_{\pi_{r-1}} \setminus S_{r-1}^C$, we have that the values of objects $B_{r-1}^1 \cdots B_{r-1}^{k-1}$ are the same after $\alpha_{r-1}\lambda_{r-1}$ and $\alpha_r\lambda_r$. It follows that $b_{r-1}^j = b_r^j$ for $j \in \{1, \ldots, k-1\}$. This implies, in turn, that $B_{r-1}^k = B_r^k$. As $B_r^k \in S_r^C$, we have $b_r^k = 1$. We get:

$$\begin{aligned}
\Psi_r &= \sum_{j=1}^{i_r} b_r^j \cdot \frac{L}{2^j} \\
&= \sum_{j=1}^{k-1} b_r^j \cdot \frac{L}{2^j} + b_r^k \cdot \frac{L}{2^k} + \sum_{j=k+1}^{i_r} b_r^j \cdot \frac{L}{2^j} \\
&= \sum_{j=1}^{k-1} b_{r-1}^j \cdot \frac{L}{2^j} + \frac{L}{2^k} + \sum_{j=k+1}^{i_r} b_r^j \cdot \frac{L}{2^j} \\
&\ge \sum_{j=1}^{k-1} b_{r-1}^j \cdot \frac{L}{2^j} + \frac{L}{2^k} \\
&> \sum_{j=1}^{k-1} b_{r-1}^j \cdot \frac{L}{2^j} + \sum_{j=k+1}^{i_{r-1}} b_{r-1}^j \frac{L}{2^j} \\
&= \Psi_{r-1},
\end{aligned}$$

where the last equality is based on the observation that $b_{r-1}^k = 0$.

As $\Psi_0 = 0$ and since Ψ_r strictly grows with r and can never exceed $L-1$, it follows that $\Psi_L = L-1$, which concludes the proof. $\square$

Lemmas 1, 2 and Theorem 3 imply the following.

THEOREM 4. *An n-process obstruction-free implementation of an m-limited-use max register, m-limited-use counter, m-limited-use b-valued compare-and-swap object or an m-limited-use collect object from historyless primitives has an operation instance requiring $\Omega(\min(\log m, n))$ steps. An obstruction-free implementation of a b-bounded max register from historyless primitives has an operation instance requiring $\Omega(\min(\log b, n))$ steps. An obstruction-free implementation of a k-additive-accurate m-limited-use counter from historyless primitives has an operation instance requiring $\Omega(\min(\log m - \log k, n))$ steps.*

To prove space-complexity lower bounds on L-perturbable objects, we construct perturbing sequences in which many objects are covered; not all of them are necessarily accessed by the reader, but, nevertheless, they must be distinct, giving a lower bound on the number of base objects. The proof of the next theorem appears in the full paper.

THEOREM 5. *The space complexity of an obstruction-free implementation of an m-limited-use max register or an m-limited-use collect object from historyless primitives is $\Omega(\min(m, n))$.*

The space complexity of an obstruction-free implementation of an m-limited-use b-valued compare-and-swap object from historyless primitives is $\Omega(\min(\sqrt[3]{m}, n))$.

The space complexity of an obstruction-free implementation of a b-bounded max register from historyless primitives is $\Omega(\min(b, n))$.

The space complexity of an obstruction-free implementation of a k-additive-accurate m-limited-use counter from historyless primitives is $\Omega(\min(\sqrt{\frac{m}{k}}, n))$.

3.2 Lower bounds for implementations using arbitrary primitives

The number of steps performed by an operation, as we have measured for implementations using only historyless objects, is not the only factor influencing the performance of an operation. The performance of a concurrent object implementation is also influenced by the extent to which multiple processes *simultaneously* access widely-shared memory locations. Dwork *et al.* [8] introduced a formal model to capture such contention, taking into consideration both the number of steps taken by a process and the number of *stalls* it incurs as a result of memory contention with other processes. More formally, an event e applied by a process p to object O in an execution α *incurs k memory stalls* if it is immediately preceded by k events by distinct processes different from p that apply nontrivial primitives to O.

Our next result shows a lower bound on implementations using *arbitrary* read-modify-write primitives. Its proof employs an extension of the backtracking covering technique that uses a "bins-and-balls" argument. The proof of Theorem 3 uses access-perturbable sequence of executions, in which each new execution deploys a process to cover an object that is not covered in the preceding execution. Such a series of executions cannot, in general, be constructed for algorithms that may use arbitrary primitives. Instead, the proof constructs a series of executions in which each new execution deploys a process that covers *some* object along p_n's path.

DEFINITION 4. *An access-stall perturbation sequence of length L of an operation instance op_n by process p_n on an object $\mathcal{O}$ is a sequence of executions $\alpha_r \sigma_{r,1} \cdots \sigma_{r,j_r} \rho_r$, such that α_0 is empty, $j_0 = 0$, ρ_0 is an execution of op_n by p_n starting from the initial configuration, and for every r, $1 \leq r \leq L$, the following properties hold:*

1. *α_r is p_n-free,*

2. *in ρ_r process p_n runs solo until it completes the operation instance op_n; in this instance, p_n accesses the base objects $B_r^1, \ldots, B_r^{i_r}$,*

3. *there is a subsequence $O_r^1, \ldots O_r^{j_r}$ of disjoint objects in $B_r^1, \ldots B_r^{i_r}$ and disjoint nonempty sets of processes $S_r^1, \ldots, S_r^{j_r}$ such that, for $j = 1, \ldots, j_r$,*

- *each process in S_r^j covers O_r^j after α_r, and*

- *in $\sigma_{r,j}$, process p_n applies events until it is about to access O_r^j for the first time, then each of the processes in S_r^j accesses O_r^j, and, finally, p_n accesses O_r^j.*

4. *let λ_{r-1} be the subsequence of events by the processes in $S_{r-1}^1 \cup \cdots S_{r-1}^{j_{r-1}}$ that are applied in $\sigma_{r-1,1} \cdots \sigma_{r-1,j_{r-1}}$, then $\alpha_{r-1} \lambda_{r-1}$ is an $r-1$-perturbing execution; if $\alpha_{r-1} \lambda_{r-1}$ is saturated, then we say that $\alpha_{r-1} \sigma_{r-1,1} \cdots \sigma_{r-1,j_{r-1}} \rho_{r-1}$ is saturated,*

5. *If $\alpha_{r-1} \sigma_{r-1,1} \cdots \sigma_{r-1,j_{r-1}} \rho_{r-1}$ is saturated, then the r'th execution in the access-stall perturbation sequence is defined as identical to it. Otherwise, the following holds: $O_r^{j_r} = B_{r-1}^k$, for some $1 \leq k \leq i_{r-1}$; $B_r^i = B_{r-1}^i$, for all $i \in \{1, \ldots k\}$; $O_{r-1}^i = O_r^i$ and $S_{r-1}^i = S_r^i$ for all objects O_{r-1}^i that precede B_{r-1}^k in the sequence $B_{r-1}^1, \ldots, B_{r-1}^{i_r}$; and either $B_{r-1}^k \notin \{O_{r-1}^1, \ldots, O_{r-1}^{j_{r-1}}\}$ or $O_r^{j_r} = O_{r-1}^{j_r}$ and $|S_r^{j_r}| = |S_{r-1}^{j_r}| + 1$.*

The proof of the following lemma appears in the full paper.

LEMMA 6. *An L-perturbable object implementation has an access-stall perturbation sequence of length L.*

THEOREM 7. *Let A be an n-process obstruction-free implementation of an L-perturbable object $\mathcal{O}$ from read-modify-write primitives. Then A has an execution in which some process either accesses $\Omega(\min(\log L, n))$ distinct base objects or incurs $\Omega(\min(\log L, n))$ memory stalls, during a single operation instance.*

PROOF. For simplicity and without loss of generality, assume that $L = 2^{2s}$ for some integer s. If A has an execution in which some process accesses s distinct base objects during a single operation instance, then the theorem holds. Otherwise, Lemma 6 establishes that A has an access-stall perturbation sequence of length L. If one of these executions, $\alpha_r \sigma_{r,1} \cdots \sigma_{r,j_r} \rho_r$, for some $r \leq L$, is saturated, then it follows from Definition 4 that p_n incurs $n - 1$ memory stalls in the course of $\sigma_{r,1} \cdots \sigma_{r,j_r}$ and the theorem holds. We therefore assume in the following that none of the executions in A's access-stall perturbation sequence is saturated. We will prove that p_n incurs $\Omega(s)$ memory stalls in one of these executions.

For $i \in \{1, \ldots, i_r\}$, let variable n_r^i be defined as follows:

$$n_r^i = \begin{cases} |S_r^m|, & \text{if } \exists m \in \{1, \ldots, j_r\} : B_r^i = O_r^m, \\ 0, & \text{otherwise.} \end{cases}$$

Let $N_r = \sum_{i=1}^{i_r} n_r^i$. Thus, it suffices for the proof to show that one of these executions has $N_r = \Omega(s)$. We associate the following integral progress parameter, Φ_r, with each execution $r \geq 0$:

$$\Phi_r = \sum_{i=1}^{i_r} n_r^i \cdot s^{s-i}.$$

If $n_r^i \geq s - 1$ for some $0 \leq r \leq L$ and $i \in \{1, \ldots, i_r\}$, then we are done, since clearly $N_r \geq s - 1$ holds in this case. Assume otherwise, then Φ_r can be viewed as an s-digit number in base s whose i'th most significant digit is 0 if $i > i_r$ or equals the number of processes in $S_r^1, \ldots, S_r^{j_r}$ covering B_r^i after α_r, otherwise.

From the last property of Definition 4, $O_{r+1}^{j_{r+1}} = B_r^k$, for some $1 \leq k \leq i_r$ and, moreover, $B_{r+1}^i = B_r^i$ for $i \in \{1, \ldots k\}$, $n_{r+1}^i = n_r^i$ for $i \in \{1, \ldots, k-1\}$, $n_{r+1}^k = n_r^k + 1$, and $n_{r+1}^i = 0$ for $i \in \{k+1, \ldots, i_r\}$. We get:

$$
\begin{aligned}
\Phi_{r+1} &= \sum_{i=1}^{i_{r+1}} n_{r+1}^i \cdot s^{s-i} \\
&= \sum_{i=1}^{k} n_{r+1}^i \cdot s^{s-i} \\
&= \sum_{i=1}^{k-1} n_r^i \cdot s^{s-i} + (n_r^k + 1) \cdot s^{s-k} \\
&> \sum_{i=1}^{k} n_r^i \cdot s^{s-i} + \sum_{i=k+1}^{s} (s-1) \cdot s^{s-i} \\
&\geq \sum_{i=1}^{i_r} n_r^i \cdot s^{s-i} \\
&= \Phi_r
\end{aligned}
$$

Since the sequence $\Phi_1, \ldots \Phi_L$ is strictly growing, each Φ_r is unique. By the definition of Φ, each value Φ_r corresponds to a different partitioning of integer N_r to the values of the s digits of Φ_r. What is the maximum number $\mathcal{N}$ of different executions r for which $N_r \leq s$ holds? $\mathcal{N}$ is at most the number of distinguishable partitions of up to s identical balls into s bins. Let $A_{b,c}$ be the number of distinguishable partitions of b identical balls into c bins, then:

$$
\begin{aligned}
\mathcal{N} &\leq \sum_{j=0}^{s} A_{j,s} \\
&= A_{s,s+1} \\
&= \binom{2s}{s} \\
&= \binom{\log L}{\log L/2} \\
&= \Theta\left(\frac{4^{\log L/2}}{\sqrt{\pi \log L/2}} \right) \\
&= \Theta\left(\frac{L}{\sqrt{\pi \log L/2}} \right) \\
&< L.
\end{aligned}
$$

Where the penultimate equality above follows from Stirling's approximation and the fact that the error of the approximation ratio $\binom{\log L}{\log L/2} / \frac{4^{\log L/2}}{\sqrt{\pi \log L/2}}$ is inversely proportional to s [9, page 75]. Thus, for all $L \geq 4$, there is an execution $\alpha_{r'} \sigma_{r',1} \cdots \sigma_{r',j_{r'}} \rho_{r'}$ such that $N_{r'} > s$ holds. $\quad\square$

Lemma 1 and Theorem 7 yield the following specific bounds.

THEOREM 8. *An n-process obstruction-free implementation of an m-limited-use max register, m-limited-use counter, an m-limited-use b-valued compare-and-swap object or an an m-limited-use collect object from read-modify-write primitives has an operation instance that either requires $\Omega(\min(\log m, n))$ steps or incurs $\Omega(\min(\log m, n))$ stalls.*

An obstruction-free implementation of a b-bounded max register from read-modify-write primitives has an operation instance that either requires $\Omega(\min(\log b, n))$ steps or incurs $\Omega(\min(\log b, n))$ stalls.

An obstruction-free implementation of a k-additive-accurate m-limited-use counter from read-modify-write primitives has an operation instance that either requires $\Omega(\min(\log m - \log k, n))$ steps or incurs $\Omega(\min(\log m - \log k, n))$ stalls.

4. LOWER BOUND FOR RANDOMIZED APPROXIMATE COUNTERS

Proving lower bounds for *randomized* implementations of concurrent objects is more difficult, due to the extra flexibility these implementations have. We were not able to prove general lower bounds for a class of objects, but we take a first step in this direction by proving a lower bound for a specific, but very useful, object, namely an approximate counter. This object allows some error in the operations applied to them. We consider two variants, depending on whether the error is additive or multiplicative.

We assume an *oblivious adversary*, which fixes the sequence of process steps in advance, without being able to predict the coin-flips of the processes or the progress of the execution; in fact, our adversary does not even require knowledge of the implementation, allowing us to prove the lower bound using Yao's Principle [16]. We consider *deterministic algorithms*, since a randomized algorithm can be seen as a weighted average of deterministic ones. A distribution over schedules that gives a high cost on average for any fixed deterministic algorithm, also gives a high cost on average for any randomized algorithm, which also implies that there exists some specific schedule that does so. We will describe an (oblivious) adversary strategy achieving the next lower bound:

THEOREM 9. *For a randomized implementation of an m-valued c-multiplicative-accurate counter using historyless primitives for $n \geq m$ processes, a fixed $\epsilon > 0$, and $w > 0$, there is an oblivious adversary strategy that yields, with probability at least $1 - \epsilon$, an execution consisting of at most $m - 1$ concurrent `CounterIncrement` operation instances, some of which may be incomplete, followed by a `CounterRead` operation instance, in which one of the following conditions holds: (a) a constant fraction of the `CounterIncrement` instances take more than w operations; (b) the value returned by the `CounterRead` operation instance is not consistent with any linearization of the completed operation instances; or (c) the `CounterRead` operation instance takes $\Omega\left(\frac{\log\log m - \log\log c}{\log w} \right)$ operations.*

We first consider a schedule constructed as follows. Process p_1 carries out an operation β_1 for at most w steps. With probability p for each step, p_1 is stopped early and is suspended before it can carry the step out; if the step is not a read operation, this means that the target register is now covered by a pending operation that can be delivered later to overwrite any subsequent work by other processes. Whether p_1 completes its operation or not, process p_2 is next scheduled to carry out at most w steps, each of which causes p_2 to be suspended with probability p as before, and this process is repeated for the remaining processes up through p_{n-1}. In this way we assemble a schedule $\Gamma = \beta_1' \beta_2' \ldots \beta_{n-1}'$, where each β_i' is an initial prefix of some high-level operation β_i.

Let r be chosen arbitrarily. From Γ, we construct a family of schedules $\{\Xi_k\}_{k\geq 0}$, where each Ξ_k consists of an initial prefix of Γ of length k (i.e., consisting of k steps), followed by the delivery of all delayed operations from Γ, and in turn followed by the first r steps of a single operation α executed by p_n. Thus each Ξ_k is of the form $\beta_1'\beta_2'\ldots\beta_{m-1}'\beta_m''\delta_m\delta_{m-1}\ldots\delta_1\alpha$, where δ_i is either the delayed operation of i or the empty sequence if there is no such operation, α is the single operation of p_n, and β_m'' is a prefix of β_m of length $k - |\beta_1'\beta_2'\cdots\beta_{m-1}'|$.

The proof is based first on bounding the number of distinct values returned by the reader across all the schedules Ξ_k as a function of p and r, and then showing that we can select a subset of these schedules that must either violate the restriction to short increment and read operations or return significantly more distinct values. This implies that choosing one of these schedules uniformly at random is likely to hit one of the bad outcomes. The next lemma bounds the number of distinct return values, and its proof appears in the full paper.

LEMMA 10. *Among the schedules Ξ_k above, α returns at most $(1+1/p)^r$ distinct values on average, where the average is taken over the random choices of the adversary for when to delay operations.*

The key idea is that because α is deterministic, the value it returns can depend only on the values of the at most r registers it reads, and that each register will get at most $1 + 1/p$ values on average in all the Ξ_k before it becomes covered by some δ_i. This is essentially the same idea as used in [3] for max registers, except that we provide a more careful analysis of the dependence between the number of values found in each registers, because the union bound used in [3] reduces the lower bound by a $\Theta(\log\log m)$ factor that in our case would eliminate the lower bound completely.

Lemma 10 holds for arbitrary sequences of operations. To prove Theorem 9, we show that for the specific case where $p = 1/4w$ and each β_i is a `CounterIncrement` and α is a `CounterRead` for a c-multiplicative-accurate counter, we can pick out a subfamily of executions $\Xi_{k_0}, \Xi_{k_1}, \ldots \Xi_{k_{\ell-1}}$, where $\ell - 1 = \lfloor\frac{1}{2}\log_{2c}\sqrt{m}\rfloor - 1 = \Theta(\log m/\log c)$, such that, on average, a constant fraction of the executions Ξ_{k_i} satisfies one of the conditions in Theorem 9. A detailed proof appears in the full paper.

If we choose w to match the lower bound on `Counter-Read`, we get a lower bound on the worst-case cost of a c-multiplicative-accurate counter operation for fixed c of $\Omega\left(\frac{\log\log m - \log\log c}{\log\log\log m}\right)$. This is much smaller than Jayanti's lower bound of $\Omega(\log n)$ on randomized n-bounded counters [14], which also allows much stronger primitives in the implementation. But the smaller bound is not surprising if one considers that, for any constant c, a c-multiplicative-accurate counter effectively provides only $\Theta(\log\log m)$ bits of information about the number of increments, compared with $\Theta(\log m)$ for standard counter.

5. SUMMARY

This paper presents lower bounds for concurrent obstruction-free implementations of objects that are used in a restricted manner. (See Table 1 in the introduction.)

The step lower-bound on max registers is tight [3] and the step lower bound on randomized counters is almost tight, as there is an $O(\log\log m)$ upper bound [7], under the same adversary model. It is unclear whether the other lower bounds are tight.

Another interesting research direction is to devise generic implementations for L-perturbable objects. This is of particular interest in the case of randomized implementations, where there is also an important issue of the type of adversary tolerated.

6. REFERENCES

[1] D. Alistarh, J. Aspnes, K. Censor-Hillel, S. Gilbert, and M. Zadimoghaddam. Optimal-time adaptive tight renaming, with applications to counting. In *PODC*, pages 239–248, 2011.

[2] D. Alistarh, J. Aspnes, S. Gilbert, and R. Guerraoui. The complexity of renaming. In *FOCS*, pages 718–727, 2011.

[3] J. Aspnes, H. Attiya, and K. Censor. Polylogarithmic concurrent data structures from monotone circuits. *J. ACM*, 59(1), Feb. 2012. Previous version in *PODC*, pages 36–45, 2009.

[4] J. Aspnes and K. Censor. Approximate shared-memory counting despite a strong adversary. *ACM Transactions on Algorithms*, 6(2), 2010.

[5] H. Attiya, R. Guerraoui, D. Hendler, and P. Kuznetsov. The complexity of obstruction-free implementations. *J. ACM*, 56(4), 2009.

[6] H. Attiya and D. Hendler. Time and space lower bounds for implementations using k-cas. *IEEE Trans. Parallel Distrib. Syst.*, 21(2):162–173, 2010.

[7] M. A. Bender and S. Gilbert. Mutual exclusion with $O(\log\log n)$ amortized work. In *FOCS*, pages 728–737, 2011.

[8] C. Dwork, M. Herlihy, and O. Waarts. Contention in shared memory algorithms. *J. ACM*, 44(6):779–805, 1997.

[9] W. Feller. *An Introduction to Probability Theory and Its Applications, Vol. 1*. Wiley, 1968.

[10] F. Fich, M. Herlihy, and N. Shavit. On the space complexity of randomized synchronization. *J. ACM*, 45(5):843–862, 1998.

[11] F. E. Fich, D. Hendler, and N. Shavit. Linear lower bounds on real-world implementations of concurrent objects. In *FOCS*, pages 165–173, 2005.

[12] M. Herlihy, V. Luchangco, and M. Moir. Obstruction-free synchronization: Double-ended queues as an example. In *ICDCS*, pages 522–529, 2003.

[13] M. Herlihy and J. M. Wing. Linearizability: a correctness condition for concurrent objects. *ACM Trans. Prog. Lang. Syst.*, 12(3):463–492, June 1990.

[14] P. Jayanti. A time complexity lower bound for randomized implementations of some shared objects. In *PODC*, pages 201–210, 1998.

[15] P. Jayanti, K. Tan, and S. Toueg. Time and space lower bounds for nonblocking implementations. *SIAM J. Comput.*, 30(2):438–456, 2000.

[16] A. C.-C. Yao. Probabilistic computations: Toward a unified measure of complexity. In *FOCS*, pages 222–227, 1977.

Brief Announcement:
Towards a Communication Optimal Fast Multipole Method and its Implications at Exascale

Aparna Chandramowlishwaran
Georgia Institute of
Technology
aparna@gatech.edu

Jee Whan Choi
Georgia Institute of
Technology
jee@gatech.edu

Kamesh Madduri
The Pennsylvania State
University
madduri@cse.psu.edu

Richard Vuduc
Georgia Institute of
Technology
richie@cc.gatech.edu

ABSTRACT

This paper presents the first in-depth models for compute and memory costs of the kernel-independent Fast Multipole Method (KIFMM). The Fast Multiple Method (FMM) has asymptotically linear time complexity with a guaranteed approximation accuracy, making it an attractive candidate for a wide variety of particle system simulations on future exascale systems. This paper reports on three key advances. First, we present lower bounds on cache complexity for key phases of the FMM and use these bounds to derive analytical performance models. Secondly, using these models, we present results for choosing the optimal algorithmic tuning parameter. Lastly, we use these performance models to make predictions about FMM's scalability on possible exascale system configurations, based on current technology trends. Looking forward to exascale, we suggest that the FMM, though highly compute-bound on today's systems, could in fact become memory-bound by 2020.

Categories and Subject Descriptors

F.2 [**Analysis of Algorithms and Problem Complexity**]: Numerical Algorithms and Problems

Keywords

Fast Multipole Method; Cache Complexity Analysis; Performance Modeling; Exascale

1. INTRODUCTION

We report on a new analysis of memory hierarchy communication for the Fast Multipole Method (FMM) [6], which is widely regarded as one of the most significant algorithms in scientific computing [3]. For a particle simulation involving n interacting particles, which naïvely is a $\mathcal{O}\left(n^2\right)$ computation, the FMM performs a work-optimal $\mathcal{O}\left(n\right)$ operations with user-selectable accuracy guarantee.

Our analysis refines the estimates of the constants, normally ignored in traditional asymptotic analyses of the FMM, with calibration against our state-of-the-art implementation [4, 5]. The re-

Copyright is held by the author/owner(s).
SPAA'12, June 25–27, 2012, Pittsburgh, Pennsylvania, USA.
ACM 978-1-4503-1213-4/12/06.

sult is an analytical performance model with two important properties. First, the model predicts the optimal setting of one of the FMM's tuning parameters, which in practice had previously required manual experimentation to set. Secondly, since the analysis includes important high-level architectural parameters, such as last-level cache capacity, the resulting models can be used to estimate whether the FMM will scale or not on future architectural designs.

In fact, our model suggests a new kind of high-level analytical *co-design* of the algorithm and architecture. For instance, classical analyses of *balance* relate algorithmic properties, such as intensity (intrinsic ratio of useful operations to bytes transferred), to a processor's balance (its peak ops/sec divided by peak bandwidth). The total time T is given by the sum of the times taken by the different phases of FMM. Based on the analytical execution time estimates for the most expensive phases of FMM, we derive analytically an optimal value for an algorithmic tuning parameter, denoted by q (see Section 2), which practitioners had previously thought could only be determined experimentally.

$$q = \frac{\gamma^{3/2}}{C_1} \sqrt{C_2 + C_3 \frac{C_0}{\beta_{mem}}} \qquad (1)$$

The constants C_1, C_2, and C_3 can be estimated given a kernel and an implementation. The fraction $\frac{C_0}{\beta_{mem}}$ is the processor's balance and γ is the number of digits of precision required. For our current state-of-the-art multicore implementation, $\frac{C_2}{C_3} \approx 50$ and on a single socket Intel Westmere node $\frac{C_0}{\beta_{mem}} = 2.6$ resulting in the optimal $q \approx 250$ which exactly matches our experimental value.

If we further assume that $q = \mathcal{O}(\gamma^{\frac{3}{2}})$, then T can be simplified as the expression below.

$$T = \frac{N\gamma^{3/2}}{C_0}(C' + C'' \frac{C_0}{\beta_{mem}}) \qquad (2)$$

C' and C'' are constants defined in terms of prior constants.

One corollary of our analysis is that the accuracy of the FMM and one of its algorithmic tuning parameters can be used to compensate for processor imbalance, which is an unavoidable technology trend. However, we also find that although the FMM is today compute-bound and therefore highly scalable in practice, the current trajectory of processor architecture design could cause the FMM to become communication-bound as early as the year 2020.

2. FAST MULTIPOLE METHOD

Given a system of N *source* particles, with positions given by $\{y_1, \ldots, y_N\}$, and N *targets* with positions $\{x_1, \ldots, x_N\}$, we wish to compute the N sums, $f(x_i) = \sum_{j=1}^{N} K(x_i, y_i) \cdot s(y_j)$, where $f(x)$ is the desired *potential* at target point x; $s(y)$ is the *density* at source point y; and $K(x, y)$ is an *interaction kernel* that specifies "the physics" of the problem. The FMM can *approximate* of all of these sums in an optimal $O(N)$ time with a guaranteed user-specified accuracy ϵ [6]. This acceleration is based on two key ideas: (i) organizing the points spatially in a *tree representation*, such as an octree in three dimensions or a quadtree in 2D; and (ii) *fast approximate evaluation*, in which we compute summaries at each node using a constant number of tree traversals with constant work per node.

The tree is constructed so that the leaves contain no more than q points each, where q is a tuning parameter chosen by the user. We also associate with each node of the tree one or more neighbor *lists*. Each list has bounded constant length and contains (logical) pointers to a subset of other tree nodes. These are canonically known as the U, V, W, and X lists. Given the tree T, evaluating the sums consists of six distinct computational phases: one per U, V, W, and X lists (which are all neighborhood iterations), as well as *upward* (up) and *downward* (down) phases.

We model and implement the *kernel-independent variant* of the FMM, or KIFMM [11]. Our analysis uses our own recent implementation for multicore and GPU systems [4, 5, 7, 9].

3. ANALYTICAL PERFORMANCE MODEL FOR FMM

In this section, we present the lower bounds for the two key phases of FMM. We assume a uniform random distribution of source and target points for the rest of the analysis.

We assume a simple two-level memory hierarchy, consisting of an infinite memory and a cache of size Z. Data is transferred between the memory and cache in cache lines of size L.

3.1 Near field Interactions (U list step)

For each target leaf box, this phase of the FMM algorithm performs a direct summation of potentials due the source boxes in its immediate neighborhood. The neighborhood of a box B is defined to be the set of all the source leaf boxes adjacent to B, and contains B as well. This list of boxes L_U^B is called the U list, and we refer to this near field interactions evaluation phase as the U list step.

For each target-source pair, a dense matrix of kernel evaluations is created, and the target potential vector is updated with a dense matrix and vector multiplication. Given b leaf boxes and assuming q points per leaf box, the computational complexity of the near field interaction phase is $O(bq^2)$. In 3D, the operation count is more precisely $27bq^2$. This estimate can be further refined to account for boundary boxes, and we have $(3b^{1/3} - 2)^3 q^2$.

The time spent performing floating-point operations in the U list step is the total number of floating point operations, divided by the peak computation throughput (C_0) in floating-point operations per unit time.

$$T_{comp,u} = \frac{C_u^1 \cdot (3b^{1/3} - 2)^3 \cdot q^2}{C_0} \qquad (3)$$

C_u^1 is a kernel- and implementation-dependent constant.

To account for memory costs in accessing the source and target box data structures, we observe that the outer loops of the computation can be modeled as a sparse matrix vector multiply (SpMV).

Each source box contains q points on an average. For each point, the position (x, y, and z coordinates) and density are maintained, resulting in a cumulative size of $4q$ machine words per source or target box.

Blelloch et al. [1, 2] present a cache-oblivious algorithm for SpMV that is based on a separator-based reordering of the matrix. They show that if the support graph of a matrix satisfies the n^ϵ edge-separator theorem [8], then such a matrix, when laid out in row-major format after reordering, would incur at most $O\left(\frac{m}{L} + \frac{n}{Z^{1-\epsilon}}\right)$ (where m is the number of non-zeros in the matrix) cache misses for SpMV. The U list implicit dependency matrix is indeed structured, and this is a result of the spatial sorting of the boxes during tree construction. The source boxes are also stored contiguously in row-major format, and so we can adapt the SpMV bounds for near interaction computation.

The memory access costs for this step are comprised of read accesses to the source boxes, the U lists for each target box, and updates to the target leaf box potentials. The rows of the kernel matrix K are constructed on-the-fly for each source-target pair prior to matrix vector multiplication, and so we do not consider accesses to this matrix. The U list upper bounds for the number of cache lines fetched are as follows:

$$Q_u = Q_{u\_src} + Q_{u\_trg} + Q_{u\_lists}$$

$$Q_{u\_src} \leq k_u \cdot \frac{N}{q} \cdot \frac{4q}{L} = \frac{4k_u N}{L}$$

$$Q_{u\_trg} \leq \frac{N}{q} \cdot \frac{4q}{L} = \frac{4N}{L}$$

$$Q_{u\_lists} \leq \frac{k_u \frac{N}{q}}{L}$$

Here, k_u is the average number of source boxes in the U list of a target leaf box. The above bound for Q_{u_src} assumes that there is no reuse of source boxes. The cache complexity for U list is thus dominated by the time to read source boxes.

Utilizing the SpMV bounds from [1] and assuming $\epsilon = 2/3$ for 3D, we get a tighter bound on Q_{u_src}, and thus the overall cache complexity. Since each non-zero in the matrix corresponds to a source box of size $4q$, we scale the fast memory capacity Z by a factor of $4q$.

$$Q_u \leq \frac{4N}{L} + \frac{k_u \frac{N}{q}}{L} + \frac{4N}{L} + \frac{\frac{N}{q}}{\left(\frac{Z}{4q}\right)^{\frac{1}{3}}} \qquad (4)$$

The dominant memory access time in this step is modeled as the total data fetched into fast memory, divided by the peak rate at which data is fetched into memory (i.e., memory bandwidth β_{mem}).

$$T_{mem,u} = \frac{C_u^2 N}{\beta_{mem}} + \frac{C_u^3 N L}{\beta_{mem}(Z^{\frac{1}{3}} q^{\frac{2}{3}})} \qquad (5)$$

C_u^2 and C_u^3 are implementation- and machine-dependent constants that we determine empirically by fitting the execution times to the model.

3.2 Far field Interactions (V list step)

For each target box in the tree, this phase accumulates the multipole expansions of the source boxes in its V list into a local expansion. This step is also called multipole to local (M2L) translation.

The V list of a box B is defined to be the set of all source boxes that are children of the neighbors of box B's parent, but not adjacent to B itself. The computation performed in the V list is 3D convolution. We implement this in 3 steps, namely, (a) 3D FFT, (b) complex pointwise multiplication in the frequency domain, and (c) 3D inverse FFT. Assuming b_s source boxes, the computational complexity of the FFT phase is $\mathcal{O}(b_s \cdot p^{\frac{3}{2}} \log p)$ where p is a constant determined by the desired accuracy ($p = \mathcal{O}(\gamma^2)$). The inverse FFT's are done once for each target box, resulting in a complexity of $\mathcal{O}(b_t \cdot p^{\frac{3}{2}} \log p)$, assuming b_t target boxes. Each target box performs k_v pointwise multiplications ($k_v = 189$ for an interior box for an uniform distribution), and has an asymptotic complexity of $\mathcal{O}(b_t \cdot k_v \cdot p^{\frac{3}{2}})$.

Refining these estimates, the computational time for V list if given by

$$T_{comp,v} = \frac{C_v^1 \ (b_s + b_t + 343) \ p^{\frac{3}{2}} \log p}{C_0} + \frac{C_v^2 \ b_t \ k_v \ p^{\frac{3}{2}}}{C_0} \quad (6)$$

C_v^1 and C_v^2 are implementation-dependent constants.

The number of translation operators (316) is fixed and hence we assume they fit in the shared cache Z. Hence, the effective cache size becomes $Z' = Z - 316p^{\frac{3}{2}}$. The V-list implicit dependency matrix between target boxes, source boxes, and translation operators is also structured and similar to U list, re-applying the SpMV bounds from [2], we get an upper bound on the cache complexity for this phase:

$$Q_v \leq \frac{(b_t + b_s) \ p^{\frac{3}{2}}}{L} + \frac{k_v \ b_t}{L} + \frac{b_t}{\left(\frac{Z'}{p^{\frac{3}{2}}}\right)^{\frac{1}{3}}} \quad (7)$$

Considering the higher order terms, the memory access time of V list can be approximated by,

$$T_{mem,v} = \frac{C_v^3 N p^{\frac{3}{2}}}{q\beta_{mem}} + \frac{C_v^4 N p^{\frac{1}{2}} L}{(Z'^{\frac{1}{3}} q)\beta_{mem}} \quad (8)$$

4. EXASCALE PROJECTIONS

Using the above analytic expression for execution time and the optimal choice of q, we predict the execution time for large-scale problem instances on possible future CPU-based exascale systems. The machine characteristics of the exascale system are based on extrapolating historical technology trends [10]. Figure 1 shows the execution time split into computational and memory access time. We observe that the crossover point when the memory access time T_{mem} matches the compute time T_{comp} would occur around 2020. We are currently extending our KIFMM performance model and analysis to GPU-based systems.

5. REFERENCES

[1] G. E. Blelloch, R. A. Chowdhury, P. B. Gibbons, V. Ramachandran, S. Chen, and M. Kozuch. Provably good multicore cache performance for divide-and-conquer algorithms. In *Proc. 19th Annual ACM-SIAM Symposium on Discrete Algorithms (SODA '08)*, pages 501–510, Philadelphia, PA, USA, 2008. SIAM.

[2] G. E. Blelloch, P. B. Gibbons, and H. V. Simhadri. Low depth cache-oblivious algorithms. In *Proc. ACM Symposium*

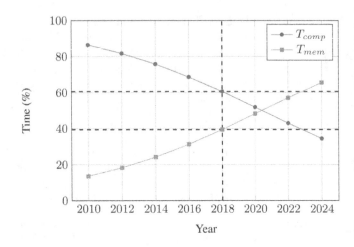

Figure 1: A depiction of the KIFMM computational and memory costs for parallel execution on extrapolated CPU-like multicore systems. The problem size N starts at 4 million points in 2010, and is scaled at the same rate as the cache size Z.

on Parallel Algorithms and Architectures (SPAA), Thira, Santorini, Greece, July 2010.

[3] J. Board and K. Schulten. The fast multipole algorithm. *Computing in Science and Engineering*, 2(1):76–79, January/February 2000.

[4] A. Chandramowlishwaran, K. Madduri, and R. Vuduc. Diagnosis, tuning, and redesign for multicore performance: A case study of the Fast Multipole Method. In *Proc. ACM/IEEE Conf. Supercomputing (SC)*, New Orleans, LA, USA, November 2010.

[5] A. Chandramowlishwaran, S. Williams, L. Oliker, I. Lashuk, G. Biros, and R. Vuduc. Optimizing and tuning the Fast Multipole Method for state-of-the-art multicore architectures. In *Proc. IEEE Int'l. Parallel and Distributed Processing Symp. (IPDPS)*, Atlanta, GA, USA, April 2010.

[6] L. Greengard and V. Rokhlin. A fast algorithm for particle simulations. *J. Comp. Phys.*, 73:325–348, 1987.

[7] I. Lashuk, A. Chandramowlishwaran, H. Langston, T.-A. Nguyen, R. Sampath, A. Shringarpure, R. Vuduc, L. Ying, D. Zorin, and G. Biros. A massively parallel adaptive Fast Multipole Method on heterogeneous architectures. In *Proc. ACM/IEEE Conf. Supercomputing (SC)*, Portland, OR, USA, November 2009.

[8] R. Lipton and R. Tarjan. A separator theorem for planar graphs. *SIAM Journal on Applied Mathematics*, 36(2), 1979.

[9] A. Rahimian, I. Lashuk, D. Malhotra, A. Chandramowlishwaran, L. Moon, R. Sampath, A. Shringarpure, S. Veerapaneni, J. Vetter, R. Vuduc, D. Zorin, and G. Biros. Petascale direct numerical simulation of blood flow on 200k cores and heterogeneous architectures. In *Proc. ACM/IEEE Conf. Supercomputing (SC)*, New Orleans, LA, USA, November 2010.

[10] R. Vuduc and K. Czechowski. What GPU computing means for high-end systems. *IEEE Micro*, 31(4):74–78, July/August 2011.

[11] L. Ying, D. Zorin, and G. Biros. A kernel-independent adaptive Fast Multipole Method in two and three dimensions. *J. Comp. Phys.*, 196:591–626, May 2004.

Brief Announcement: Application-Sensitive QoS Scheduling in Storage Servers

Ahmed Elnably
Rice University
6100 Main St.
Houston, Texas 77005
ahmed.elnably@rice.edu

Peter Varman
Rice University
6100 Main St.
Houston, TX 77005
pjv@rice.edu

ABSTRACT

The growing popularity of multi-tenant, cloud-based computing platforms is driving research into new QoS models that permit flexible sharing of the underlying infrastructure. In this paper, we re-examine the use of the popular proportional-share model for resource allocation, in the context of modern heterogeneous, multi-tiered storage systems. We highlight the limitations of the conventional proportional sharing approach to resource allocation, and describe a new allocation model that provides strong isolation between clients. This improves the performance characteristics from the viewpoints of both the clients and the service provider.

Categories and Subject Descriptors

D.4.2 [**Software**]: OPERATING SYSTEMS—*Allocation/deallocation strategies*

General Terms

ALGORITHMS, PERFORMANCE

Keywords

Resource Allocation, Tiered Storage, QoS, Cloud, Scheduling, IO

1. INTRODUCTION

This paper presents a new resource allocation policy and scheduling mechanism for modern shared storage architectures. Two major trends motivated this work. The first is the growing use of virtualized data centers hosted on shared physical infrastructure, which support paying customers who expect performance comparable to running on dedicated resources. The second is the popularity of tiered storage systems that combine traditional hard disks (HD) and fast flash-based storage (SSD). The performance of an application heavily depends on its mix of SSD and HD accesses. However, traditional proportional sharing (PS) resource allocation policies are insensitive to this behavior, resulting in lower system utilization and weak isolation between clients. We propose a storage QoS performance model that more closely reflects the performance of applications on a dedicated server. The idea is to reward applications that make more efficient use of the resources as they would in a dedicated environment, rather than using the gains from one application to subsidize the performance of less-well-performing applications. The subsidy model exemplified by PS is currently the most common approach for resource allocation in storage systems [4, 5, 9]. However such solutions implicitly assume homoge-

Copyright is held by the author/owner(s).
SPAA'12, June 25–27, 2012, Pittsburgh, Pennsylvania, USA.
ACM 978-1-4503-1213-4/12/06.

neous resources, and are less acceptable when server performance can fluctuate. Models providing stronger isolation in periodic-real time multi-media scheduling were proposed in [7, 1]. Time slicing for extracting higher disk utilization for sequential stream access was addressed in [8, 6]. These works deal with only a single sequentially-accessed device.

2. OVERVIEW AND MODEL

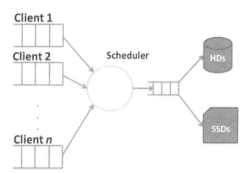

Figure 1: System Model

The model in Figure 1 shows several clients accessing a tiered storage system composed of hard disks (HD) and solid-state disk (SSD). The storage system has a queue to buffer pending requests from where they are dispatched to the device when idle. IO requests that can be served from the SSD are *hits*; the remaining *misses* are served from the HD. The *hit ratio* of client $i's$ workload (h_i) is the fraction of its IO requests that are hits. The *miss ratio* $m_i = 1-h_i$. Clients may also have a *static weight* w_i that represents its relative importance. The service times of the HD and SSD are Γ and τ respectively.

We motivate our scheduling algorithm using an extended example. Suppose we have two clients of equal weight sharing a storage system with Γ=10ms and τ=5ms. Let $(a_1, a_2, \cdots)$ and $(b_1, b_2, \cdots)$ denote the accesses of the two clients, and h_1=h_2=0. The aggregate system throughput of 100 IOs/sec (IOPS) is equally shared between the two clients. Now consider what happens if h_2 increases to 0.5, so that one in two requests of client 2 is a hit. Figure 2(a) shows the service profile of the 1:1 interleaved sequence $(a_1, b_1, a_2, b_2, \cdots)$. For simplicity, the HD and SSD accesses of client 2 are assumed to be perfectly interleaved. Notice that the system throughput increases from 100 IOPS to 133.3 IOPS, since 4 requests are done every 30ms. Each client receives 66.6 IOPS.

We argue that proportional sharing as described above is not ideal for either the client or the system. With PS, the throughputs of both clients increases when the hit ratio of client 2 improves.

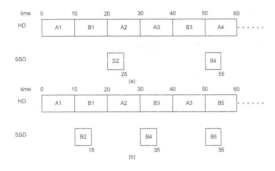

Figure 2: Scheduling in 1:1 and 1:2 ratios

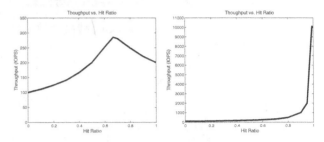

Figure 3: $\alpha = 2, h^T = 0.67$ **Figure 4:** $\alpha = 100, h^T = 0.99$

This appears to be a win-win situation since both clients benefit and the system utilization also improves. However, this is debatable. Notice that client 2 experiences a smaller increase in IOPS than it would have on a dedicated infrastructure. If run in isolation, its IOPS will *double* when its hit ratio increases to $1/2$, while in the shared system it increased by only 33%. With additional shared clients the performance improvement will be even smaller. Secondly, in a pay-for-services situation, the fact that client 2 is subsidizing the improved performance of client 1 may be considered unfair (for instance, it may be paying for SSD use, or may have incurred costs for application tuning). Interestingly, client 1 may also object to receiving additional IOPS if they cost extra.

In this paper, we propose a *reward based resource allocation model* that provides strict isolation between clients, and thereby emulates a client's performance when running on a dedicated infrastructure. In this example, the increase in IOPS resulting from client 2's better hit ratio will all be directed to it, while client 1's allocation will remain unchanged. Also, since the extra resources go to the more efficient client, the system utilization will increase even further. In Figure 2(b) we change the ratio in which clients 1 and 2 are served, from $1:1$ to $1:2$. The interleaved request sequence in this case is $(a_1, b_1, b_2, a_2, b_3, b_4, \cdots)$. As can be seen, the aggregate system throughput increases to 3 requests every 20ms, or 150 IOPS (up from the 133.3 IOPS with $1:1$ weight ratio). More importantly, client 1 continues to receives 50 IOPS, while client 2 *doubles* its throughput to 100 IOPS.

3.   STRONG ISOLATION POLICY

We begin by considering how the throughput of client i running in isolation varies with its hit ratio h_i. Let $\alpha = \Gamma/\tau > 1$ be the ratio of the disk and SSD service times. Denote the *threshold hit ratio* $h^T = \alpha/(\alpha + 1)$. We define the *entitlement* of client i to be the maximum throughput it would receive if it were running in isolation. The entitlement depends only on the hit ratio h_i of the client and the device speeds.

Lemma: The entitlement of client i is given by $1/(m_i \times \Gamma)$ for $h_i \in [0, h^T]$ and $1/(h_i \times \tau)$ for $h_i \in [h^T, 1]$.

To see this, note that if N requests have been serviced, the elapsed time is at least the maximum of the disk service time ($Nm_i\Gamma$), and the SSD service time ($Nh_i\tau$). In the range $[0, h^T]$, $m_i\Gamma \geq h_i\tau$ (HD is the bottleneck) and so the maximum throughput is $N/(Nm_i\Gamma)$. A symmetrical argument holds in the other range. The throughput increases till the threshold h^T and then falls.

The behavior is confirmed by simulation results shown in Figures 3 and 4, for the two cases $\alpha = 2$ and $\alpha = 100$. In the figures, service times are exponentially distributed with means of $\Gamma = 10ms$ and τ equal to $5ms$ and $0.1ms$ respectively. Each request is independently classified as a hit (miss) with probability h_i (respectively, $1 - h_i$).

Now consider the case where multiple clients are sharing the server. The aim is to provide clients with capacity allocations that reflect their efficiency in a dedicated system. We propose the following allocation policy to model this behavior.

Strong Isolation Policy (SIP): Allocate the capacity among the clients in the *ratio of their entitlements*. If the clients have static weights then allocate capacity in the ratio of weighted entitlements.

Unless explicitly stated we will assume that all clients have the same weight. Under SIP, if the system has enough capacity then each client (with sufficient demand) will receive its entitlement. If the capacity is insufficient, the allocation will reward the clients with higher entitlements in preference to those that have lower throughputs in a dedicated system. For example, consider two clients with $h_i = 1/2$ and $h_j = 2/3$ when run in isolation on a system with $\Gamma = 10ms$ and $\tau = 5ms$. The entitlements of i and j are 200 IOPS and 300 IOPS respectively. Under SIP, they would receive allocations in the ratio $2:3$ when consolidated on the server. The system throughput will be 250 IOPS, allocated as 100 and 150 IOPS respectively.

Scheduler: To implement SIP, the scheduler must monitor each client workload to estimate its current miss ratio over a small window of requests. We assume that the scheduler is able to determine whether an access is a hit or a miss either directly from its address, or is informed by the storage system after servicing the request. Approaches to inferring the miss ratio using black-box measurements are considered in [3]. Using the hit ratios, the entitlements can be computed and used as weights of the clients in a standard proportional scheduler. This will allocate capacity in the ratio of the entitlements as required by SIP. However directly computing the entitlements requires knowledge of the device speeds, which is difficult in practice. To work around this issue, note that if the hit ratios of two clients are both is in the range $[0, h^T]$, the ratio of their entitlements depends only on their miss ratios and does not depend on the device speeds. The speed ratio between SSDs and hard disks is typically around 50-100, so that h^T is in the range 0.98-0.99. Hence the vast majority of workloads will have hit ratios less than h^T; in other cases it can be clamped at h^T with very little performance impact. Our scheduler sets the hit ratio h_i of client i to be the smaller of its measured hit ratio and h^T. It then assigns client i a weight of $1/(1 - h_i)$ and allocates the capacity in proportion to these weights.

We state the following properties of SIP without proof (see [2]).
Lemma: Let w_i to denote the static weight of client i, $\sum_i w_i = 1$, and $h_i \leq h^T$. The *system throughput* is given by $\frac{1}{\Gamma}\sum_i (w_i/m_i)$. The *throughput of client i* is given by $\frac{1}{\Gamma}(w_i/m_i)$.

Experimental Results: We performed simulation experiments to show the behavior of SIP, with exponentially distributed HD and SSD service times with means Γ=10ms and τ=1ms respectively.

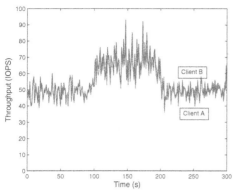

(a) Proportional Share Scheduling

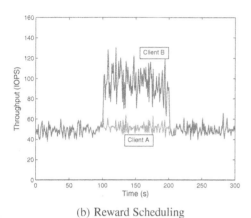

(b) Reward Scheduling

Figure 5: Comparison of Allocation in PS and SIP Schedulers

(a) A and B weight ratio: 1:1

Q	Client A	Client B	HD Util	SSD Util	Sys Cap
2	126 IOPS	700 IOPS	64%	77%	826
20	149 IOPS	915 IOPS	75%	100%	1064
50	148 IOPS	915 IOPS	75%	100%	1063

(b) A and B weight ratio: 1:2

Q	Client A	Client B	HD Util	SSD Util	Sys Cap
2	80 IOPS	881 IOPS	40%	93%	961
20	81 IOPS	952 IOPS	40%	100%	1033
50	80 IOPS	948 IOPS	40%	100%	1028

(c) A and B weight ratio: 2:1

Q	Client A	Client B	HD Util	SSD Util	Sys Cap
2	164 IOPS	457 IOPS	83%	55%	621
20	195 IOPS	571 IOPS	100%	68%	766
50	199 IOPS	582 IOPS	100%	69%	781

Table 1: Throughputs and Utilizations

The scheduler monitors the hit ratio of each workload over a moving window of 100 requests, and allocates service in proportion to $1/m_i$. Figure 5 shows the results for PS and SIP based scheduling algorithms. We show two clients A and B with equal weights and initial hit ratios of 0. During the interval $[100, 200]$ the hit ratio of B's workload increases to 0.5. With PS, both A and B increased their throughput to roughly 67 IOPS between 100-200s. However under SIP, A is not affected by the changes in B's hit ratio, and maintains a constant 50 IOPS. B increases its throughput from 50 to roughly 100 IOPS as predicted.

In the second experiment, clients A and B had hit ratios of 0.5 and 1.0 respectively. Note that h_B is capped at h^T by the scheduler in this case. Table 1 shows the throughputs and device utilizations as the static weights and size of the storage queue changes. The allocations are close to the ratio w_i/m_i as predicted. When the weights change, client A (B) is throttled to meet the preferential allocation of B (respectively A), which saturates the SSD (HD).

4. ACKNOWLEDGMENTS

The support of the National Science Foundation under NSF Grants CNS 0917157 and CCF 0541369 is gratefully acknowledged.

5. REFERENCES

[1] L. L. Abeni, G., and G. Buttazzo. Constant Bandwidth vs. Proportional Share Resource Allocation. In *IEEE International Conference on Multimedia Computing and Systems*, volume 2, pages 107–111, 1999.

[2] A. Elnably. Reward Scheduling for QoS in Cloud Applications. Master's thesis, Rice University, 2012.

[3] A. Elnably, H. Wang, A. Gulati, and P. Varman. Efficient QoS for Multi-Tiered Storage Systems. In *4th USENIX Workshop on Hot Topics in Storage and File Systems*, 2012 (to appear).

[4] A. Gulati, I. Ahmad, and C. Waldspurger. PARDA: Proportional Allocation of Resources for Distributed Storage Access. In *In FAST '09: Proceedings of the 7th Usenix Conference on File and Storage Technologies*, pages 85–98, 2009.

[5] A. Gulati, A. Merchant, and P. J. Varman. mClock: Handling Throughput Variability for Hypervisor IO Scheduling. In *USENIX OSDI*, pages 1–7, 2010.

[6] C. R. Lumb, J. Schindler, G. R. Ganger, D. F. Nagle, and E. Riedel. Towards Higher Disk Head Utilization: Extracting Free Bandwidth From Busy Disk Drives. In *Proceedings of the 4th Conference on Symposium on Operating System Design & Implementation*, page 7, 2000.

[7] A. Povzner, T. Kaldewey, S. Brandt, R. Golding, T. M. Wong, and C. Maltzahn. Efficient Guaranteed Disk Request Scheduling with Fahrrad. In *Proceedings of the 3rd ACM SIGOPS/EuroSys European Conference on Computer Systems*, pages 13–25, 2008.

[8] M. Wachs, M. Abd-El-Malek, E. Thereska, and G. Ganger. Argon: Performance Insulation for Shared Storage Servers. In *In FAST '07: Proceedings of the 5th Usenix Conference on File and Storage Technologies*, pages 61–76, 2007.

[9] C. A. Waldspurger and W. E. Weihl. Lottery Scheduling: Flexible Proportional-Share Resource Management. In *Proceedings of the 1st USENIX Conference on Operating Systems Design and Implementation*, 1994.

Brief Announcement: A GPU Accelerated Iterated Local Search TSP Solver

Kamil Rocki
Department of Computer Science
Graduate School of Information Science and
Technology
The University of Tokyo, CREST, JST
7-3-1, Hongo, Bunkyo-ku
113-8656 Tokyo
kamil.rocki@is.s.u-tokyo.ac.jp

Reiji Suda
Department of Computer Science
Graduate School of Information Science and
Technology
The University of Tokyo, CREST, JST
7-3-1, Hongo, Bunkyo-ku
113-8656 Tokyo
reiji@is.s.u-tokyo.ac.jp

ABSTRACT

In this paper we are presenting high performance GPU implementations of the 2-opt and 3-opt local search algorithms used to solve the Traveling Salesman Problem. This type of local search optimization is a very effective and fast method in case of small problem instances. However, the time spent on comparing the graph edges grows significantly with the problem size growing. They are usually a part of global search algorithms such as Iterated Local Search (ILS). Our results showed, that at least 90% of the time during a single ILS run is spent on the local search itself. Therefore we utilized GPU to parallelize the local search and that greatly improved the overall speed of the algorithm. Our results show that the GPU accelerated algorithm finds the optimal swaps approximately 3 to 26 times compared to parallel CPU code using 32 cores, operating at the speed of over 1.5 TFLOPS on a single GeForce GTX 680 GPU. The preliminary experimental studies show that the optimization algorithm using the GPU local search converges 10 to 50 times faster on average compared to the sequential CPU version, depending on the problem size.

Categories and Subject Descriptors

I.2.8 [**Artificial Intelligence**]: Problem Solving, Control Methods, and Search

General Terms

Algorithms

Keywords

Optimization, GPU, TSP, Iterated Local Search

1. INTRODUCTION

The traveling salesman problem (TSP)[1] is one of the most widely studied combinatorial optimization problems and it has become a testbed for new algorithms. This problem is classified as NP-hard[4], with a pure brute force algorithm requiring factorial time. A large number of heuristics

Copyright is held by the author/owner(s).
SPAA'12, June 25–27, 2012, Pittsburgh, Pennsylvania, USA.
ACM 978-1-4503-1213-4/12/06.

have been developed that give reasonably good approximations to the optimal tour in polynomial time. One of the most well known methods of solving the problem (approximately) is repeating a series of steps called 2-opt or 3-opt exchanges [2]. The ILS algorithm[3] uses this type of local search and a random perturbation after finding local minima to avoid being stuck and leading to the global solution, given search time is infinite. Our results show that at least 90% of the time during a single ILS run is spent on the local search itself and that number increases with the problem size growing. Recently the use of graphics processing units (GPUs) as general-purpose computing devices has risen significantly, accelerating many non-graphics programs that exhibit a lot of parallelism with low synchronization requirements. Moreover, the current trend in modern supercomputer architectures is to use GPUs as low-power consumption devices. Therefore, for us it is important to analyze possible application of CUDA as a GPU programming language to speedup optimization and provide a basis for future similar applications using massively parallel systems. The generic ILS algorithm comprises 4 parts: *Generating an initial solution*, *Local search* (here, 2-opt or 3-opt local search), *Perturbation* and *Acceptance Criterion*. ILS escapes from local optima by applying perturbations to the current local minimum. The way of choosing a worsening move relies on so called neighborhood of the current solutions. There are several ways to define such a neighborhood and choose one of the routes from it. Our perturbation algorithm is very simple, we just perform a random double 2-opt move to worsen the solution and escape from the local miminum.

2. METHODOLOGY

Assuming that there are N cities in a route, the number of distinct pairs of edges can be approximated by $\frac{n*(n-1)}{2}$, which means that i.e. in case of kroE100 problem from TSPLIB[5], there are 4851 swaps to be checked. In order to calculate the effect of the edge exchange, the distance between the cities needs to be known. It can be obtained in two ways. The first one involves calculating the distance based on the points' coordinates. The second way, uses Look-Up Table (LUT) with pre-calculated distances. The main disadvantage of the latter one is the memory usage (n^2 or $\frac{n^2}{2}$). In case of 3-opt local search, the number of the exchanges to be checked increases to $\frac{n*(n-1)*(n-2)}{6}$.

Table 1: 2-opt and 3-opt time needed for a single run, GPU and 1 CPU core, LUT - Look-Up Table

Problem (TSPLIB)	Number of cities (points)	GPU kernel time 2-opt	GPU kernel time 3-opt	Host to device copy time	Device to host copy time	GPU total time 2-opt	GPU total time 3-opt	CPU time 2-opt	CPU time LUT 2-opt	CPU time 3-opt	CPU time LUT 3-opt
kroE100	100	31 μs	56 μs	7 μs	12 μs	50 μs	75 μs	343 μs	182 μs	12.6 ms	4.43 ms
pr439	439	36 μs	1.42 ms	8 μs	12 μs	56 μs	1.44 ms	3.4 ms	1.3 ms	632.8 ms	190 ms
vm1084	1084	79 μs	16.95 ms	8 μs	12 μs	99 μs	16.96 ms	14.3 ms	8.3 ms	9.65 s	3.06 s
pr2392	2392	267 μs	159.9 ms	10 μs	12 μs	289 μs	160 ms	57.7 ms	63 ms	104.4 s	59.28 s
fnl4461	4461	855 μs	925.8 ms	11 μs	12 μs	878 μs	925.3 ms	188 ms	262 ms	682.9 s	533.2 s

Thousands of threads can run on a GPU simultaneously and best results are achieved when GPU is fully *loaded* to hide memory latency. Since the large off-chip GPU memory has high latency and the fast on-chip memory is very limited, we knew that accessing pre-calculated data is not a good idea. Additionally, GPU has very high peak computational power compared to CPUs. Therefore we decided to store only the coordinates of the points in the fast on-chip 48kB of shared memory and calculate the distance each time when it is needed. First, we calculate the number of checks performed by each thread: $\frac{n*(n-1)}{2*blocks*threads}$. Then each thread checks assigned pair number and then jumps *blocks*threads* distance *iter* times. This allows us to avoid using global memory as it is accessed only one time at the beginning of the execution. I.e. For a 28 x 1024 CUDA kernel configuration and pr2392 problem, $(2857245/(28*1024)) = 100$ iterations will be necessary for each thread. This way we can reuse previously stored data in the shared memory without having to access the slow global memory many times.

3. RESULTS AND CONCLUSION

We tested our algorithms using GeForce GTX 680 GPU (PCIe 3.0), AMD Opteron 6276 CPU and CUDA 4.2. The table (Table 1) shows a comparison of time needed to perform a single 2-opt and 3-opt search using different TSPLIB instances and methods. In case of small problem sizes the CPU LUT method is quite effective, but at some point accessing the coordinates only and calculation become faster (possibly due to the memory throughput limitation). GPU implementations are much faster even after including the time needed for the data transfer. It can be explained by the very fast on-chip shared memory which can be treated as user-managable cache and GPU's much higher peak memory throughput. Additionally, in case of a bigger problem instances the advantage of using LUT is diminished, since much more memory is needed to store the data which is accessed randomly (cache efficiency is decreased drastically). We recorded the peak GPU performance of 1.53 TFLOPS (single precision) in 3-opt and 407 GFLOPS in 2-opt. We would expect even higher numbers for local search like 4-opt as the computation/memory load ratio would increase. As expected, the GPU algorithm provides much better solutions after the same time period when compared to the CPU alternative in terms of convergence (full ILS algorithm), showing that GPU is capable of fast optimization even in case of such large number of cities. The speed difference increases to approximately 20 for the vm1084 (Figure 1) and 50 for the pr2392 problem. The results may be preliminary, but in our opinion, this shows that many of the problems can be

optimized well basically in *real-time*. Especially, when we consider starting points which are very far from the global solutions. To summarize, our results show that by using our algorithm for GPU, the search time can be decreased up to 26 times compared to a 32-core CPU (not presented here) or over 500 times when the sequential algorithm is considered. The whole algorithm converges up to 50 times faster depending on the problem size. One of our main observations is the changing programming scheme needed to take advantage of modern, highly parallel architectures. The number of processing units constantly increases, but the memory limitations remain almost the same. Therefore, in order to achieve good results with GPU or multi-core CPU, we needed to take utilize computational resources as much as possible, treating memory as a scarce resource. We believe that this approach will be proper for the upcoming new hardware as well.

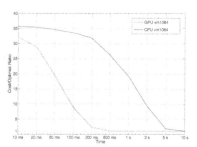

Figure 1: vm1084.tsp - convergence speed

4. REFERENCES

[1] Lawler, E.L., Lenstra, J.K., Rinnooy Kan, A.H.G., Shmoys, D.B.: The Traveling Salesman Problem: A Guided Tour of Combinatorial Optimization. Wiley, Chichester, 1985

[2] Croes G. A.;A Method for Solving Traveling-Salesman Problems, Operations Research November/December 1958 6: pages 791–812

[3] Lourenco, H. R. Martin, O. C. Stutzle, T.: Iterated Local Search, International series in operations research and management science, 2003, ISSU 57, pages 321–354

[4] Garey, M.R. and Johnson, D.S. Computers and Intractability: A Guide to the Theory of NP-Completeness. San Francisco: W.H. Freeman, 1979

[5] Reinelt, G.: TSPLIB - A Traveling Salesman Problem Library. ORSA Journal on Computing, Vol. 3, No. 4, 1991, pages 376–384

Brief Announcement: Speedups for Parallel Graph Triconnectivity

James A. Edwards
University of Maryland
College Park, Maryland
jedward5@umd.edu

Uzi Vishkin
University of Maryland
College Park, Maryland
vishkin@umd.edu

ABSTRACT

We present a parallel solution to the problem of determining the triconnected components of an undirected graph. We obtain significant speedups over the only published optimal (linear-time) serial implementation of a triconnected components algorithm running on a modern CPU. This is accomplished on the PRAM-inspired XMT many-core architecture. To our knowledge, no other parallel implementation of a triconnected components algorithm has been published for any platform.

Categories and Subject Descriptors

D.1.3 [**Programming Techniques**]: Concurrent Programming—Parallel programming; C.1.4 [**Processor Architectures**]: Parallel Architectures

Keywords

graph algorithm, triconnected components, many-core, PRAM

1. INTRODUCTION

A k-(*vertex-*)*cut* of an undirected graph is a set of k vertices whose removal results in the graph being disconnected. An undirected graph is k-(*vertex-*)*connected* if it has no cut of size $k-1$ or less. A 1-connected graph is said to be *connected*, a 2-connected graph *biconnected*, and a 3-connected graph *triconnected*. A *biconnected component* of a graph G is a maximal biconnected subgraph of G.

The triconnected components of a graph G are defined in [10]. A 2-cut is also called a *separation pair*. Briefly, assuming that G is biconnected, it is repeatedly *split* into two subgraphs with respect to one of its separation pairs. Each time G is split using a pair $\{u, v\}$, an edge (u, v), called a *virtual edge*, is added to both subgraphs. When no more splitting is possible, the resulting graphs (called *split components*) are of one of three types: triconnected graphs, triangles (rings of 3 vertices), and triple bonds (multigraphs consisting of 3 parallel edges). Then, split components of the same type that share a common virtual edge are *merged* (the inverse of splitting); triangles are merged to (recursively) form polygons (rings), and triple bonds are merged to (recursively) form n-bonds (with n parallel edges). The (unique) graphs that result are called the *triconnected components of G*. If all the triconnected components of a graph are merged together, the result is the original graph. The triconnected components of a general graph G are the triconnected components of its biconnected components.

Copyright is held by the author/owner(s).
SPAA'12, June 25–27, 2012, Pittsburgh, Pennsylvania, USA.
ACM 978-1-4503-1213-4/12/06.

The triconnected components of a graph provide useful information about the graph, such as the resilience of an underlying network to defects. The *SPQR-tree* of a graph G, with a vertex for every triconnected component of G and an edge between any two components that share a virtual edge, can be used to represent the planar embeddings of a graph; this can be used, for instance, to test whether a graph would remain planar after adding a given edge [1].

In this paper, we evaluate an implementation of an efficient PRAM triconnectivity algorithm on the experimental Explicit Multi-Threading (XMT) architecture, developed at the University of Maryland to efficiently support PRAM-like programming and shown [2, 5] to support some advanced graph algorithms. Nevertheless, the current work represents the most complex algorithm that has been tested on XMT, and uses quite a few building blocks, which are simpler PRAM algorithms. The speedups obtained (up to 129x) and their scalability provide points of reference for comparing XMT to other approaches beyond that of a simple benchmark kernel. The importance of going beyond simple kernels and toy problems for comparing architectures has long been recognized in the SPEC benchmarks and in the standard text [8]. The source code for our implementation is available at http://www.umiacs.umd.edu/users/vishkin/XMT/OPEN_SOURCE_GRAPH_ALGS/.

2. TRICONNECTIVITY ALGORITHMS

For a graph with n vertices and m edges, an efficient $O(n + m)$-time **serial algorithm** to determine its triconnected components based on depth-first search is given by Hopcroft and Tarjan [10]. This algorithm was implemented and tested by Gutwenger and Mutzel [7] and was made available as part of [4]. Neither we nor the authors of [7] are aware of any other publicly-available implementation of a linear- (or near-linear-) work triconnected components algorithm, either serial or parallel.

Several **parallel triconnectivity algorithms** have been described. Miller and Ramachandran (MR) [14] proposed an efficient algorithm that runs in $O(\log^2 n)$ time while performing $O(m \log^2 n)$ work on a CRCW PRAM and is based on finding an open ear decomposition [13] of the input graph. Their algorithm has two parts, one to find the nontrivial candidate sets of the input graph (sets of vertices such that any two vertices in a set are a separation pair) and one to split the graph into its triconnected components based on its nontrivial candidate sets. An earlier algorithm for finding nontrivial candidate sets by Ramachandran and Vishkin (RV) [15] required only $O(\log n)$ time while still performing $O(m \log^2 n)$ work.

Our **implementation on XMT** uses the RV algorithm to find the nontrivial candidate sets and the MR algorithm to split the graph into its triconnected components. The most significant contributor to its runtime is the need to make $O(\log n)$ calls to a connected components routine. We use the Shiloach-Vishkin (SV) [16] connectivity algorithm, which runs in $O(\log n)$ time and $O(m \log n)$ work on a CRCW PRAM. Each call to SV actually computes the connected components of multiple subgraphs derived from the input graph. This combining of inputs is done to permit flattening of memory allocation and parallelism to improve performance. Some care is required to keep the subgraphs from interacting; details are omitted due to space limitations.

3. THE XMT MANY-CORE PLATFORM

The Explicit Multi-Threading (XMT) general-purpose computer architecture [17] is designed to improve single-task completion time. It does so by supporting programs based on Parallel Random-Access Machine (PRAM) algorithms but relaxing the synchrony required by the PRAM model. A key enhancement of XMT is providing hardware support for things that are done in software in other architectures.

The XMT architecture consists of the following: a number of lightweight cores (thread control units or TCUs) grouped into clusters, a single core (master TCU or MTCU) with its own local cache, a number of mutually-exclusive cache modules shared by the TCUs and MTCU, an interconnection network connecting the TCUs to the cache modules, and a number of DRAM controllers connecting the cache modules to off-chip memory. Each TCU has a register file, a program counter, an execution pipeline, a lightweight ALU, and prefetch buffers. Each cluster has one or more multiply/divide units (MDUs) and a compiler-managed read-only cache, all of which are shared by the TCUs within the cluster. When a parallel section of code is reached, the MTCU broadcasts the instructions in that section to all of the TCUs, and each TCU stores the instructions in a buffer. Virtual threads are dynamically assigned to TCUs using a dedicated prefix-sum network. A more detailed overview of XMT can be found in [3].

4. EXPERIMENTAL RESULTS

We measured the speedups of our parallel triconnectivity implementation by comparing it to the best available serial implementation [4] running on an Intel Core i7 920 CPU. We used three types of graphs in our comparison.

- Random graphs are generated by randomly selecting $|E|$ edges with uniform probability.

- Planar3 graphs are planar graphs generated level by level. The first level is a triangle of three vertices. Each succeeding level consists of three vertices, an edge between each pair of vertices in that level, and an edge from each vertex in that level to a distinct vertex in the previous level.

- Ladder graphs are similar to planar3 graphs, but with only two vertices per level (they are also planar).

The random graphs are used as representatives of dense graphs, in contrast to the sparse planar3 and ladder graphs. The input graphs we used are listed in Table 1.

We ran our parallel code on two versions of the XMT architecture: (i) a 64-core FPGA prototype whose cycle counts reflect those of an 800-MHz ASIC [18] and (ii) a 1024-core configuration simulated on the cycle-accurate XMTSim simulator. The results are shown in Figure 1.

It is shown in [3] that the latter configuration would use about the same area as an NVIDIA GTX 280 GPU; [11] showed similar power using a similar clock speed. Parameters such as the number and sizes of cache modules, number of clusters, and latencies of pipelines were calibrated according to the number of TCUs.

Data set	Vertices (n)	Edges (m)	Sep. pairs (s)
Random-10K	10K	3000K	0
Random-20K	20K	5000K	0
Planar3-1000K	1000K	3000K	0
Ladder-20K	20K	30K	10K
Ladder-100K	100K	150K	50K
Ladder-1000K	1000K	1500K	500K

Table 1: Properties of the graphs used in the experiments.

Next, we discuss the relationship between the FPGA results and a simulated 64-TCU configuration of XMT. As [12] notes, currently, only on-chip components are simulated in a cycle-accurate manner, but DRAM is modeled as simple latency with controlled rate of memory requests. However, we expect the simulator results to be the correct representative of the capability of XMT as its assumed bandwidth is realistic for state-of-the-art industry-grade processors. The DRAM controller used in the FPGA is not representative of controllers that would be used in an industry-grade implementation of XMT. Also, DRAM bandwidth has increased since the FPGA prototype was built (e.g., transition from DDR2 to DDR3); this is in line with [8] that reports a trend of drastic improvement in bandwidth over latency (by a factor of 300 over three decades). Specifically, the simulator ran between 14% and 52% faster than the FPGA, with the larger gaps for larger input graphs. The graph with the highest speedup, Random-20K, ran 16% faster. These gaps are due to the behavior of the DRAM controller in the FPGA and in the simulator, as can be shown by reducing the clock frequency of the simulated DRAM controller, and thus its peak bandwidth, by 33%. In this case, the situation is reversed, and the simulator becomes between 10% slower and 5% faster than the FPGA, with a 20% to 31% drop in performance relative to the original configuration. Intuitively, this makes sense because larger graphs are less likely to have a working set that fits in cache, and bandwidth to DRAM becomes a dominant factor. The transition from DDR2 to DDR3 itself would double this bandwidth [8], eliminating the gaps.

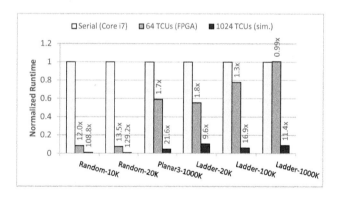

Figure 1: Performance of the parallel triconnectivity algorithm; numbers above bars represent speedup relative to serial (Core i7).

The parallel algorithm scales well, with a 9x to 13x improvement in speedup in all but one case when moving from 64 TCUs to 1024 TCUs. The weaker improvement (5x) for the Ladder-20K graph is because it is too small, providing insufficient parallelism to take full advantage of the additional TCUs.

The lower speedups on sparse graphs (Planar3- and Ladder-) are due to the parallel algorithm performing more work than the se-

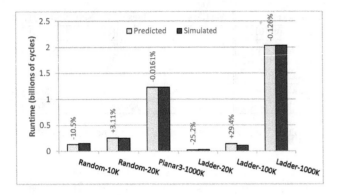

Figure 2: Predicted vs. observed runtime for the 1024-TCU configuration using Equation 1; numbers above bars represent percent error of prediction relative to simulation.

rial algorithm. Unlike the serial algorithm, which revisits the input graph a constant number of times, the parallel algorithm revisits the input $O(\log^2 n)$ times, with the coefficient in the final (splitting) stage of the algorithm depending on the number of separation pairs in the input graph. The runtime of the parallel triconnectivity algorithm running under the 1024-TCU configuration of XMT, in cycles, for a graph with n vertices, m edges, and s separation pairs can be approximated by

$$T(n, m, s) = (2.38n + 0.238m + 4.75s) \log^2 n \qquad (1)$$

where the base of the logarithm is 2 and lower-order terms have been neglected; see Figure 2. Note that there are only 3 degrees of freedom (# data points - # constants in equation), so more data points will be required to verify that the equation holds in general; this is work in progress.

5. FUTURE WORK

An alternate algorithm to the one tested here is the algorithm of [6]. It runs in $O(\log n)$ time using $O(m \log \log n)$ work ($O(m \log n)$ work if implemented using the SV connected components algorithm) and is based on finding the biconnected components of a "local replacement graph" derived from the st-numbering of the input graph. It would be worthwhile to see if this algorithm provides better performance on large graphs. However, we have not yet implemented it because the implementation is more involved and builds upon the work presented here.

6. CONCLUSION

The XMT architecture provides good performance and scalability on triconnectivity, which relies on subroutines such as connected components. The fact that XMT performs well on this complex problem demonstrates that (i) the previously demonstrated advantages of XMT are not limited to small kernels and (ii) the advantage of XMT on small kernels extends to larger problems that rely on those kernels. [2] demonstrated strong XMT speedups of up to 108x for max-flow (versus the best serial implementation). The recent paper [5] reported XMT speedups of up to 33x, and the question this raised was whether connectivity problems are less amenable to parallel speedups than other graph problems, such as max-flow. The strong speedups of up to 129x for triconnectivity reported here suggests it was perhaps the compactness of the serial biconnectivity algorithm of [9] that needs only a single visit of the

vertices and edges that limited speedups, rather than a more general problem.

7. REFERENCES

[1] G. D. Battista and R. Tamassia. Incremental planarity testing. In *Proc. FOCS*, pages 436–441, 1989.

[2] G. Caragea and U. Vishkin. Better speedups for parallel max-flow. In *Proc. SPAA*, 2011.

[3] G. C. Caragea, F. Keceli, A. Tzannes, and U. Vishkin. General-purpose vs. GPU: Comparison of many-cores on irregular workloads. In *Proc. HotPar*, 2010.

[4] M. Chimani, C. Gutwenger, M. Jünger, K. Klein, P. Mutzel, and M. Schulz. The open graph drawing framework. Technische Universität Dortmund and University of Cologne, http://ogdf.net/, 2010.

[5] J. A. Edwards and U. Vishkin. Better speedups using simpler parallel programming for graph connectivity and biconnectivity. In *Proc. PMAM,* held in conjunction with *PPoPP*, 2012.

[6] D. Fussell, V. Ramachandran, and R. Thurimella. Finding triconnected components by local replacement. *SIAM J. Computing*, 22(3):587–616, 1993.

[7] C. Gutwenger and P. Mutzel. A linear time implementation of SPQR-trees. In J. Marks, editor, *Graph Drawing*, volume 1984 of *Lecture Notes in Computer Science*, pages 77–90. Springer Berlin / Heidelberg, 2001.

[8] J. L. Hennessy and D. A. Patterson. *Computer Architecture: A Quantitative Approach*. Fifth edition, 1990-2012.

[9] J. Hopcroft and R. Tarjan. Algorithm 447: efficient algorithms for graph manipulation. *Commun. ACM*, 16(6):372–378, 1973.

[10] J. E. Hopcroft and R. E. Tarjan. Dividing a graph into triconnected components. *SIAM J. Computing*, 2(3):135–158, 1973.

[11] F. Keceli, T. Moreshet, and U. Vishkin. Power-performance comparison of single-task driven many-cores. In *Proc. ICPADS*, 2011.

[12] F. Keceli, A. Tzannes, G. Caragea, R. Barua, and U. Vishkin. Toolchain for programming, simulating and studying the XMT many-core architecture. In *Proc. IPDPSW*, pages 1282–1291, 2011.

[13] Y. Maon, B. Schieber, and U. Vishkin. Parallel ear decomposition search (EDS) and st-numbering in graphs. *Theor. Comput. Sci.*, 47:277–298, 1986.

[14] G. L. Miller and V. Ramachandran. A new graph triconnectivity algorithm and its parallelization. *Combinatorica*, 12(1):53–76, 1992.

[15] V. Ramachandran and U. Vishkin. Efficient parallel triconnectivity in logarithmic time. In *Proc. AWOC*, pages 33–42, 1988.

[16] Y. Shiloach and U. Vishkin. An $O(\log n)$ parallel connectivity algorithm. *J. Algorithms*, 3(1):57–67, 1982.

[17] U. Vishkin. Using simple abstraction to reinvent computing for parallelism. *Commun. ACM*, 54:75–85, 2011.

[18] X. Wen and U. Vishkin. FPGA-based prototype of a PRAM-on-chip processor. In *Proc. CF*, pages 55–66, 2008.

Communication-Optimal Parallel Algorithm for Strassen's Matrix Multiplication

Grey Ballard[*]
EECS Department
UC Berkeley
Berkeley, CA 94720
ballard@cs.berkeley.edu

James Demmel[*][†]
Mathematics Department
and CS Division, UC Berkeley
Berkeley, CA 94720
demmel@cs.berkeley.edu

Olga Holtz[‡]
Mathematics Departments
UC Berkeley and TU Berlin
Berkeley, CA 94720
holtz@math.berkeley.edu

Benjamin Lipshitz[*]
EECS Department
UC Berkeley
Berkeley, CA 94720
lipshitz@cs.berkeley.edu

Oded Schwartz[§]
EECS Department
UC Berkeley
Berkeley, CA 94720
odedsc@cs.berkeley.edu

ABSTRACT

Parallel matrix multiplication is one of the most studied fundamental problems in distributed and high performance computing. We obtain a new parallel algorithm that is based on Strassen's fast matrix multiplication and minimizes communication. The algorithm outperforms all known parallel matrix multiplication algorithms, classical and Strassen-based, both asymptotically and in practice.

A critical bottleneck in parallelizing Strassen's algorithm is the communication between the processors. Ballard, Demmel, Holtz, and Schwartz (SPAA '11) prove lower bounds on these communication costs, using expansion properties of the underlying computation graph. Our algorithm matches these lower bounds, and so is communication-optimal. It exhibits perfect strong scaling within the maximum possible range.

Benchmarking our implementation on a Cray XT4, we obtain speedups over classical and Strassen-based algorithms ranging from 24% to 184% for a fixed matrix dimension $n = 94080$, where the number of processors ranges from 49 to 7203.

Our parallelization approach generalizes to other fast matrix multiplication algorithms.

Categories and Subject Descriptors: F.2.1 [Analysis of Algorithms and Problem Complexity]: Numerical Algorithms and Problems: Computations on matrices

ACM General Terms: algorithms

Keywords: parallel algorithms, communication-avoiding algorithms, fast matrix multiplication

1. INTRODUCTION

Matrix multiplication is one of the most fundamental algorithmic problems in numerical linear algebra, distributed computing, scientific computing, and high-performance computing. Parallelization of matrix multiplication has been extensively studied (e.g., [10, 6, 12, 1, 26, 21, 36, 11, 24, 31, 4, 3]). It has been addressed using many theoretical approaches, algorithmic tools, and software engineering methods in order to optimize performance and obtain faster and more efficient parallel algorithms and implementations.

We obtain a new parallel algorithm based on Strassen's fast matrix multiplication.[1] It is more efficient than any other parallel matrix multiplication algorithm of which we are aware, including those that are based on classical ($\Theta(n^3)$) multiplication, and those that are based on Strassen's and other Strassen-like matrix multiplications. We compare the efficiency of the new algorithm with previous algorithms, and provide both asymptotic analysis (Sections 3 and 4) and benchmarking data (Section 5).

1.1 The communication bottleneck

To design efficient parallel algorithms, it is necessary not only to load balance the computation, but also to minimize the time spent communicating between processors. The inter-processor communication costs are in many cases significantly higher than the computational costs. Moreover, hardware trends predict that more problems will become

[*]Research supported by Microsoft (Award #024263) and Intel (Award #024894) funding and by matching funding by U.C. Discovery (Award #DIG07-10227). Additional support comes from Par Lab affiliates National Instruments, Nokia, NVIDIA, Oracle, and Samsung.

[†]Research is also supported by DOE grants DE-SC0003959, DE-SC0004938, and DE-AC02-05CH11231.

[‡]Research supported by the Sofja Kovalevskaja programme of Alexander von Humboldt Foundation and by the National Science Foundation under agreement DMS-0635607, while visiting the Institute for Advanced Study.

[§]Research supported by U.S. Department of Energy grants under Grant Numbers DE-SC0003959.

Permission to make digital or hard copies of all or part of this work for personal or classroom use is granted without fee provided that copies are not made or distributed for profit or commercial advantage and that copies bear this notice and the full citation on the first page. To copy otherwise, to republish, to post on servers or to redistribute to lists, requires prior specific permission and/or a fee.
SPAA'12, June 25–27, 2012, Pittsburgh, Pennsylvania, USA.
Copyright 2012 ACM 978-1-4503-1213-4/12/06 ...$10.00.

[1]Our actual implementation uses the Winograd variant [38]; see Section 2.3 for details.

communication-bound in the future [20, 19]. Even matrix multiplication becomes communication-bound when run on sufficiently many processors. Given the importance of communication costs, it is preferable to match the performance of an algorithm to a communication lower bound, obtaining a communication-optimal algorithm.

1.2 Communication costs of matrix multiplication

We consider a distributed-memory parallel machine model as described in Section 2.1. The communication costs are measured as a function of the number of processors P, the local memory size M in words, and the matrix dimension n. Irony, Toledo, and Tiskin [24] proved that in the distributed memory parallel model, the bandwidth cost of classical n-by-n matrix multiplication is bounded below by $\Omega\left(\frac{n^3}{PM^{1/2}}\right)$. Using their technique one can also deduce a memory-independent bandwidth cost lower bound of $\Omega\left(\frac{n^2}{P^{2/3}}\right)$[3] and generalize it to other classes of algorithms [5]. For a shared-memory model similar bounds were shown in [2]. Until recently, parallel classical matrix multiplication algorithms (e.g., "2D" [10, 36], and "3D" [6, 1]) have minimized communication only for specific values of M. The first algorithm that minimizes the communication costs for the entire range of M has recently been obtained by Solomonik and Demmel [31]. See Section 4.1 for more details.

None of these techniques for obtaining lower bounds or parallel algorithms generalizes to fast matrix multiplication, such as [33, 27, 7, 30, 29, 14, 34, 15, 13, 37]. A communication cost lower bound for fast matrix multiplication algorithms has only recently been obtained [4]: Strassen's algorithm run on a distributed-memory parallel machine has bandwidth cost $\Omega\left(\left(\frac{n}{M^{1/2}}\right)^{\omega_0} \cdot \frac{M}{P}\right)$ and latency cost $\Omega\left(\left(\frac{n}{M^{1/2}}\right)^{\omega_0} \cdot \frac{1}{P}\right)$, where $\omega_0 = \log_2 7$ (see Section 2.5). These bounds generalize to other, but not all, fast matrix multiplication algorithms, with ω_0 being the exponent of the computational complexity.

In the sequential case,[2] the lower bounds are attained by the natural recursive implementation [33] which is thus optimal. However, a communication-optimal parallel Strassen algorithm was not previously known. Previous parallel algorithms that use Strassen (e.g., [21, 26, 18]) decrease the computational costs at the expense of higher communication costs. The factors by which these algorithms exceed the Strassen lower bounds are typically small powers of P and M, as discussed in Section 4. However both P and M can be large (e.g. on a modern supercomputer, one may have $P \sim 10^5$ and $M \sim 10^9$).

1.3 Parallelizing Strassen's matrix multiplication in a communication efficient way

The main impetus for this work was the observation of the asymptotic gap between the communication costs of existing parallel Strassen-based algorithms and the communication lower bounds for Strassen. Because of the attainability of the lower bounds in the sequential case, we hypothesized that the gap could be closed by finding a new algorithm rather than by tightening the lower bounds.

We made three observations from the lower bound results of [4] that led to the new algorithm. First, the lower bounds for Strassen are lower than those for classical matrix multiplica-

---

[2]See [4] for a discussion of the sequential memory model.

tion. This implies that in order to obtain an optimal parallel Strassen algorithm, the communication pattern cannot be that of a classical algorithm but must reflect the properties of Strassen's algorithm. Second, the factor $M^{\omega_0/2-1}$ that appears in the denominator of the communication cost lower bound implies that an optimal algorithm must use as much local memory as possible. That is, there is a tradeoff between memory usage and communication (the same is true in the classical case). Third, the proof of the lower bounds shows that in order to minimize communication costs relative to computation, it is necessary to perform each sub-matrix multiplication of size $\Theta(\sqrt{M}) \times \Theta(\sqrt{M})$ on a single processor.

With these observations and assisted by techniques from previous approaches to parallelizing Strassen, we developed a new parallel algorithm which achieves perfect load balance, minimizes communication costs, and in particular performs asymptotically less computation and communication than is possible using classical matrix multiplication.

1.4 Our contributions and paper organization

Our main contribution is a new algorithm we call Communication-Avoiding Parallel Strassen, or *CAPS*.

THEOREM 1.1. *CAPS asymptotically minimizes computational and bandwidth costs over all parallel Strassen algorithms. It also minimizes latency cost up to a logarithmic factor in the number of processors.*

CAPS performs asymptotically better than any previous previous classical or Strassen-based parallel algorithm. It also runs faster in practice. The algorithm and its computational and communication cost analyses are presented in Section 3. There we show it matches the communication lower bounds.

We provide a review and analysis of previous algorithms in Section 4. We also consider two natural combinations of previously known algorithms (Sections 4.4 and 4.5). One of these new algorithms that we call "2.5D-Strassen" communicates less than all previous algorithms, but still more than CAPS.

We discuss our implementations of the new algorithms and compare their performance with previous ones in Section 5 to show that our new CAPS algorithm outperforms previous algorithms not just asymptotically, but also in practice. Benchmarking our implementation on a Cray XT4, we obtain speedups over classical and Strassen-based algorithms ranging from 24% to 184% for a fixed matrix dimension $n = 94080$, where the number of (quad-core) processors ranges from 49 to 7203.

In Section 6 we show that our parallelization method applies to other fast matrix multiplication algorithms. It also applies to classical recursive matrix multiplication, thus obtaining a new optimal classical algorithm that matches the 2.5D algorithm of Solomonik and Demmel [31]. In Section 6, we also discuss its numerical stability, generalizations, and future work.

2. PRELIMINARIES

2.1 Communication model

We model communication of distributed-memory parallel architectures as follows. We assume the machine has P processors, each with local memory of size M words, which are connected via a network. Processors communicate via messages, and we assume that a message of w words can be communicated in time $\alpha + \beta w$. The bandwidth cost of the algorithm is given by the word count and denoted by $BW(\cdot)$, and the latency cost is given by the message count and denoted by $L(\cdot)$. Similarly the computational cost is given by the number of floating point operations and denoted by $F(\cdot)$. We call the time per floating point operation γ.[3]

We count the number of words, messages and floating point operations along the *critical path* as defined in [39]. That is, two messages that are communicated between separate pairs of processors simultaneously are counted only once, as are two floating point operations performed in parallel on different processors. This metric is closely related to the total running time of the algorithm, which we model as

$$\alpha L(\cdot) + \beta BW(\cdot) + \gamma F(\cdot).$$

We assume that (1) the architecture is homogeneous (that is, γ is the same on all processors and α and β are the same between each pair of processors), (2) processors can send/receive only one message to/from one processor at a time and they cannot overlap computation with communication (this latter assumption can be dropped, affecting the running time by a factor of at most two), and (3) there is no communication resource contention among processors. That is, we assume that there is a link in the network between each pair of processors. Thus lower bounds derived in this model are valid for any network, but attainability of the lower bounds depends on the details of the network.

2.2 Strassen's algorithm

Strassen showed that 2×2 matrix multiplication can be performed using 7 multiplications and 18 additions, instead of the classical algorithm that does 8 multiplications and 4 additions [33]. By recursive application this yields an algorithm which multiplies two $n \times n$ matrices with $O(n^{\omega_0})$ flops, where $\omega_0 = \log_2 7 \approx 2.81$. Winograd improved the algorithm to use 7 multiplications and 15 additions in the base case, thus decreasing the hidden constant in the O notation [38]. Further reduction in the number of additions is not possible [28, 9]. We review the Strassen-Winograd algorithm in Section 2.3.

In this paper, we use the term *parallel Strassen algorithm* for a parallel algorithm that performs exactly the same arithmetic operations as any variant[4] of Strassen's (sequential) algorithm. We use the broader term *parallel Strassen-based algorithm* for a parallel matrix multiplication algorithm that is a hybrid of any variant of Strassen's and the classical algorithm. Examples of such hybrids are given in the next section. Note that Theorems 2.1 and 2.2 below apply to parallel Strassen algorithms, but not to all Strassen-based algorithms.

2.3 Strassen-Winograd Algorithm

The Strassen-Winograd algorithm is usually preferred to Strassen's algorithm in practice since it requires fewer additions. We use it for our implementation of CAPS. Divide the

input matrices A, B and output matrix C into 4 submatrices:

$$A = \begin{bmatrix} A_{11} & A_{12} \\ A_{21} & A_{22} \end{bmatrix} \quad B = \begin{bmatrix} B_{11} & B_{12} \\ B_{21} & B_{22} \end{bmatrix} \quad C = \begin{bmatrix} C_{11} & C_{12} \\ C_{21} & C_{22} \end{bmatrix}$$

Then form 7 linear combinations of the submatrices of each of A and B, call these T_i and S_i, respectively; multiply them pairwise; then form the submatrices of C as linear combinations of these products:

$T_0 = A_{11}$	$S_0 = B_{11}$	$Q_0 = T_0 \cdot S_0$	$U_1 = Q_0 + Q_3$
$T_1 = A_{12}$	$S_1 = B_{21}$	$Q_1 = T_1 \cdot S_1$	$U_2 = U_1 + Q_4$
$T_2 = A_{21} + A_{22}$	$S_2 = B_{12} + B_{11}$	$Q_2 = T_2 \cdot S_2$	$U_3 = U_1 + Q_2$
$T_3 = T_2 - A_{12}$	$S_3 = B_{22} - S_2$	$Q_3 = T_3 \cdot S_3$	$C_{11} = Q_0 + Q_1$
$T_4 = A_{11} - A_{21}$	$S_4 = B_{22} - B_{12}$	$Q_4 = T_4 \cdot S_4$	$C_{12} = U_3 + Q_5$
$T_5 = A_{12} + T_3$	$S_5 = B_{22}$	$Q_5 = T_5 \cdot S_5$	$C_{21} = U_2 - Q_6$
$T_6 = A_{22}$	$S_6 = S_3 - B_{21}$	$Q_6 = T_6 \cdot S_6$	$C_{22} = U_2 + Q_2$

This is one step of Strassen-Winograd. The algorithm is recursive since it can be used for each of the 7 smaller matrix multiplications. In practice, one often uses only a few steps of Strassen-Winograd, although to attain $O(n^{\omega_0})$ computational cost, it is necessary to recursively apply it all the way down to matrices of size $O(1) \times O(1)$. The precise computational cost of Strassen-Winograd is

$$F(n) = c_s n^{\omega_0} - 5n^2. \tag{1}$$

Here c_s is a constant depending on the cutoff point at which one switches to the classical algorithm. For a cutoff size of n_0, the constant is $c_s = (2n_0 + 4)/n_0^{\omega_0 - 2}$ which is minimized at $n_0 = 8$ yielding a computational cost of approximately $3.73n^{\omega_0} - 5n^2$. As with Strassen's algorithm, Equation (1) applies only if the ratio n/n_0 is a power of 2.

2.4 Previous work on parallel Strassen

In this section we briefly describe previous efforts to parallelize Strassen. More details, including communication analyses, are in Section 4. A summary appears in Table 1.

Luo and Drake [26] explored Strassen-based parallel algorithms that use the communication patterns known for classical matrix multiplication. They considered using a classical 2D parallel algorithm and using Strassen locally, which corresponds to what we call the "2D-Strassen" approach (see Section 4.2). They also consider using Strassen at the highest level and performing a classical parallel algorithm for each subproblem generated, which corresponds to what we call the "Strassen-2D" approach. The size of the subproblems depends on the number of Strassen steps taken (see Section 4.3). Luo and Drake also analyzed the communication costs for these two approaches.

Soon after, Grayson, Shah, and van de Geijn [21] improved on the Strassen-2D approach of [26] by using a better classical parallel matrix multiplication algorithm and running on a more communication-efficient machine. They obtained better performance results compared to a purely classical algorithm for up to three levels of Strassen's recursion.

Kumar, Huang, Johnson, and Sadayappan [25] implemented Strassen's algorithm on a shared-memory machine. They identified the tradeoff between available parallelism and total memory footprint by differentiating between "partial" and "complete" evaluation of the algorithm, which corresponds to what we call depth-first and breadth-first traversal of the recursion tree (see Section 3.1). They show that by using ℓ DFS steps before using BFS steps, the memory footprint is reduced by a factor of $(7/4)^\ell$ compared to using all

---

[3]This parallel model resembles the BSP model of Valiant [35], however we do not require the communication to be bulk synchronous. Note that both the CAPS algorithm and the lower bounds of [4, 3] hold under the more restrictive BSP model.

[4]A *variant* of Strassen's algorithm is any algorithm based on 2×2 matrix multiplication using 7 scalar multiplications.

BFS steps. They did not consider communication costs in their work.

Other parallel approaches [18, 23, 32] have used more complex parallel schemes and communication patterns. However, they restrict attention to only one or two steps of Strassen and obtain modest performance improvements over classical algorithms.

2.5 Strassen lower bounds

For parallel Strassen algorithms, the bandwidth cost lower bound has been proved using expansion arguments on the computation graph, and the latency cost lower bound is an immediate corollary.

THEOREM 2.1. *(Memory-dependent lower bound) [4] Consider a parallel Strassen algorithm running on P processors each with local memory size M. Let $BW(n, P, M)$ be the bandwidth cost and $L(n, P, M)$ be the latency cost of the algorithm. Assume that no intermediate values are computed twice. Then*

$$BW(n, P, M) = \Omega\left(\left(\frac{n}{\sqrt{M}}\right)^{\omega_0} \cdot \frac{M}{P}\right),$$

$$L(n, P, M) = \Omega\left(\left(\frac{n}{\sqrt{M}}\right)^{\omega_0} \cdot \frac{1}{P}\right).$$

A memory-independent lower bound has recently been proved using the same expansion approach:

THEOREM 2.2. *(Memory-independent lower bound) [3] Consider a parallel Strassen algorithm running on P processors. Let $BW(n, P)$ be the bandwidth cost and $L(n, P)$ be the latency cost of the algorithm. Assume that no intermediate values are computed twice. Assume only one copy of the input data is stored at the start of the algorithm and the computation is load-balanced in an asymptotic sense. Then*

$$BW(n, P) = \Omega\left(\frac{n^2}{P^{2/\omega_0}}\right),$$

and the latency cost is $L(n, P) = \Omega(1)$.

Note that when $M = O(n^2/P^{2/\omega_0})$, the memory-dependent lower bound dominates, and when $M = \Omega(n^2/P^{2/\omega_0})$, the memory-independent lower bound dominates.

3. COMMUNICATION-AVOIDING PARALLEL STRASSEN

In this section we present the CAPS algorithm, and prove it is communication-optimal. See Algorithm 1 for a concise presentation and Algorithm 2 for a more detailed description.

THEOREM 3.1. *CAPS has computational cost $\Theta\left(\frac{n^{\omega_0}}{P}\right)$, bandwidth cost $\Theta\left(\max\left\{\frac{n^{\omega_0}}{PM^{\omega_0/2-1}}, \frac{n^2}{P^{2/\omega_0}}\right\}\right)$, and latency cost $\Theta\left(\max\left\{\frac{n^{\omega_0}}{PM^{\omega_0/2}}\log P, \log P\right\}\right)$.*

By Theorems 2.1 and 2.2, we see that CAPS has optimal computational and bandwidth costs, and that its latency cost is at most $\log P$ away from optimal. Thus Theorem 1.1 follows. We prove Theorem 3.1 in Section 3.5.

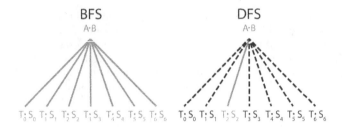

Figure 1: Representation of BFS and DFS steps. In a BFS step, all seven subproblems are computed at once, each on 1/7 of the processors. In a DFS step, the seven subproblems are computed in sequence, each using all the processors. The notation follows that of Section 2.3.

3.1 Overview of CAPS

Consider the recursion tree of Strassen's sequential algorithm. CAPS traverses it in parallel as follows. At each level of the tree, the algorithm proceeds in one of two ways. A "breadth-first-step" *(BFS)* divides the 7 subproblems among the processors, so that $\frac{1}{7}$ of the processors work on each subproblem independently and in parallel. A "depth-first-step" *(DFS)* uses all the processors on each subproblem, solving each one in sequence. See Figure 1.

In short, a BFS step requires more memory but reduces communication costs while a DFS step requires little extra memory but is less communication-efficient. In order to minimize communication costs, the algorithm must choose an ordering of BFS and DFS steps that uses as much memory as possible.

Let $k = \log_7 P$ and $s \geq k$ be the number of distributed Strassen steps the algorithm will take. In this section, we assume that n is a multiple of $2^s 7^{\lceil k/2 \rceil}$. If k is even, the restriction simplifies to n being a multiple of $2^s\sqrt{P}$. Since P is a power of 7, it is sometimes convenient to think of the processors as numbered in base 7. CAPS performs s steps of Strassen's algorithm and finishes the calculation with local matrix multiplication. The algorithm can easily be generalized to other values of n by padding or dynamic peeling.

We consider two simple schemes of traversing the recursion tree with BFS and DFS steps. The first scheme, which we call the Unlimited Memory *(UM)* scheme, is to take k BFS steps in a row. This approach is possible only if there is sufficient available memory. The second scheme, which we call the Limited Memory *(LM)* scheme is to take ℓ DFS steps in a row followed by k BFS steps in a row, where ℓ is minimized subject to the memory constraints.

It is possible to use a more complicated scheme that interleaves BFS and DFS steps to reduce communication. We show that the LM scheme is optimal up to a constant factor, and hence no more than a constant factor improvement can be attained from interleaving.

3.2 Data layout

We require that the data layout of the matrices satisfies the following two properties:

1. At each of the s Strassen recursion steps, the data layouts of the four sub-matrices of each of A, B, and C must match so that the weighted additions of these

Algorithm 1 CAPS, in brief. For more details, see Algorithm 2.

Input: A, B, n, where A and B are $n \times n$ matrices
 P = number of processors
Output: $C = A \cdot B$
 ▷ The dependence of the S_i's on A, the T_i's on B and C
 on the Q_i's follows the Strassen or Strassen-Winograd
 algorithm. See Section 2.3.
1: **procedure** C = CAPS(A, B, n, P)
2: $\quad$ **if** enough memory **then** $\qquad$ ▷ Do a BFS step
3: $\quad\quad$ locally compute the S_i's and T_i's from A and B
4: $\quad\quad$ **parallel for** $i = 1 \dots 7$ **do**
5: $\quad\quad\quad$ redistribute S_i and T_i
6: $\quad\quad\quad$ $Q_i = \text{CAPS}(S_i, T_i, n/2, P/7)$
7: $\quad\quad\quad$ redistribute Q_i
8: $\quad\quad$ locally compute C from all the Q_i's
9: $\quad$ **else** $\qquad\qquad\qquad\qquad$ ▷ Do a DFS step
10: $\quad\quad$ **for** $i = 1 \dots 7$ **do**
11: $\quad\quad\quad$ locally compute S_i and T_i from A and B
12: $\quad\quad\quad$ $Q_i = \text{CAPS}(S_i, T_i, n/2, P)$
13: $\quad\quad\quad$ locally compute contribution of Q_i to C

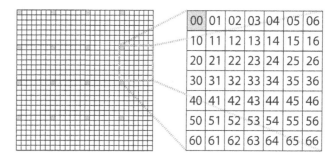

Figure 2: An example matrix layout for CAPS. Each of the 16 submatrices as shown on the left has exactly the same layout. The colored blocks are the ones owned by processor 00. On the right is a zoomed-in view of one submatrix, showing which processor, numbered base 7, owns each block. This is block-cyclic layout with some blocksize b, and matches our layout requirements with parameters $(n = 4 \cdot 7 \cdot b, P = 49, s = 2)$.

sub-matrices can be performed locally. This technique follows [26] and allows communication-free DFS steps.

2. Each of these submatrices must be equally distributed among the P processors for load balancing.

There are many data layouts that satisfy these properties, perhaps the simplest being block-cyclic layout with a processor grid of size $7^{\lfloor k/2 \rfloor} \times 7^{\lceil k/2 \rceil}$ and block size $\frac{n}{2^s 7^{\lfloor k/2 \rfloor}} \times \frac{n}{2^s 7^{\lceil k/2 \rceil}}$. (When $k = \log_7 P$ is even these expressions simplify to a processor grid of size $\sqrt{P} \times \sqrt{P}$ and block size $\frac{n}{2^s \sqrt{P}}$.) See Figure 2.

Any layout that we use is specified by three parameters, (n, P, s), and intermediate stages of the computation use the same layout with smaller values of the parameters. A BFS step reduces a multiplication problem with layout parameters (n, P, s) to seven subproblems with layout parameters $(n/2, P/7, s-1)$. A DFS step reduces a multiplication problem with layout parameters (n, P, s) to seven subproblems with layout parameters $(n/2, P, s-1)$.

Note that if the input data is initially load-balanced but distributed using a different layout, we can rearrange it to the above layout using no more than $O\left(\frac{n^2}{P}\right)$ words and $O(P)$ messages. This has no asymptotic effect on the bandwidth cost but may significantly increase the latency cost.

3.3 Unlimited Memory (UM) scheme

In the UM scheme, we take $k = \log_7 P$ BFS steps in a row. Since a BFS step reduces the number of processors involved in each subproblem by a factor of 7, after k BFS steps each subproblem is assigned to a single processor, and so is computed locally with no further communication costs. We first describe a BFS step in more detail.

The matrices A and B are initially distributed as described in Section 3.2. In order to take a recursive step, the 14 matrices $S_1, \dots S_7, T_1, \dots, T_7$ must be computed. Each processor allocates space for all 14 matrices and performs local additions and subtractions to compute its portion of the matrices. Recall that the submatrices are distributed identically, so this step requires no communication. If the layouts of A

and B have parameters (n, P, s), the S_i and the T_i now have layout parameters $(n/2, P, s-1)$.

The next step is to redistribute these 14 matrices so that the 7 pairs of matrices (S_i, T_i) exist on disjoint sets of $P/7$ processors. This requires disjoint sets of 7 processors performing an all-to-all communication step (each processor must send and receieve a message from each of the other 6). To see this, consider the numbering of the processors base-7. On the mth BFS step, the communication is between the seven processors whose numbers agree on all digits except the mth (counting from the right). After the mth BFS step, the set of processors working on a given subproblem share the same m-digit suffix. After the above communication is performed, the layout of S_i and T_i has parameters $(n/2, P/7, s-1)$, and the sets of processors that own the T_i and S_i are disjoint for different values of i. Since each all-to-all communication only involves seven processors no matter how large P is, this algorithm does not have the scalability issues that typically come from an all-to-all communication pattern.

3.3.1 Memory requirements

The extra memory required to take one BFS step is the space to store all 7 triples S_j, T_j, Q_j. Since each of those matrices is $\frac{1}{4}$ the size of A, B, and C, the extra space required at a given step is 7/4 the extra space required for the previous step. We assume that no extra memory is required for the local multiplications.[5] Thus, the total local memory requirement for taking k BFS steps is given by

$$\text{Mem}_{\text{UM}}(n, P) = \frac{3n^2}{P} \sum_{i=0}^{k} \left(\frac{7}{4}\right)^i = \frac{7n^2}{P^{2/\omega_0}} - \frac{4n^2}{P}$$
$$= \Theta\left(\frac{n^2}{P^{2/\omega_0}}\right).$$

3.3.2 Computational costs

The computation required at a given BFS step is that of the local additions and subtractions associated with computing

---

[5]If one does not overwrite the input, it is impossible to run Strassen in place; however using a few temporary matrices affects the analysis here by a constant factor only.

Algorithm 2 CAPS, in detail

Input: A, B, are $n \times n$ matrices
    P = number of processors
    rank = processor number base-7 as an array
    M = local memory size
Output: $C = A \cdot B$

1: **procedure** C = CAPS(A, B, P, rank, M)
2:     $\ell = \left\lceil \log_2 \frac{4n}{P^{1/\omega_0} M^{1/2}} \right\rceil$
               ▷ ℓ is number of DFS steps to fit in memory
3:     $k = \log_7 P$
4:     **call** DFS(A, B, C, k, ℓ, rank)

1: **procedure** DFS(A, B, C, k, ℓ, rank)
            ▷ Do $C = A \cdot B$ by ℓ DFS, then k BFS steps
2:     **if** $\ell \leq 0$ **then call** BFS(A, B, C, k, rank); **return**
3:     **for** $i = 1 \ldots 7$ **do**
4:         locally compute S_i and T_i from A and B
               ▷ following Strassen's algorithm
5:         **call** DFS(S_i, T_i, Q_i, k, $\ell - 1$, rank)
6:         locally compute contribution of Q_i to C
               ▷ following Strassen's algorithm

1: **procedure** BFS(A, B, C, k, rank)
            ▷ Do $C = A \cdot B$ by k BFS steps, then local Strassen
2:     **if** $k == 0$ **then call** localStrassen(A, B, C); **return**
3:     **for** $i = 1 \ldots 7$ **do**
4:         locally compute S_i and T_i from A and B
               ▷ following Strassen's algorithm
5:     **for** $i = 1 \ldots 7$ **do**
6:         target = rank
7:         target[k] = i
8:         send S_i to target
9:         receive into L
               ▷ One part of L comes from each of 7 processors
10:        send T_i to target
11:        receive into R
               ▷ One part of R comes from each of 7 processors
12:     **call** BFS(L, R, V, $k - 1$, rank)
13:     **for** $i = 1 \ldots 7$ **do**
14:        target = rank
15:        target[k] = i
16:        send i^{th} part of V to target
17:        receive from target into Q_i
18:     locally compute C from Q_i
               ▷ following Strassen's algorithm

---

the S_i and T_i and updating the output matrix C with the Q_i. Since Strassen-Winograd performs 15 additions and subtractions, the computational cost recurrence is

$$F_{\text{UM}}(n, P) = 15 \left(\frac{n^2}{4P} \right) + F_{\text{UM}} \left(\frac{n}{2}, \frac{P}{7} \right)$$

with base case $F_{\text{UM}}(n, 1) = c_s n^{\omega_0} - 5n^2$, where c_s is the constant of Strassen-Winograd. See Section 2.3 for more details. The solution to this recurrence is

$$F_{\text{UM}}(n, P) = \frac{c_s n^{\omega_0} - 5n^2}{P} = \Theta \left(\frac{n^{\omega_0}}{P} \right).$$

3.3.3 Communication costs

Consider the communication costs associated with the UM scheme. Given that the redistribution within a BFS step is performed by an all-to-all communication step among sets of 7 processors, each processor sends 6 messages and receives 6 messages to redistribute $S_1, \ldots, S_7$, and the same for $T_1, \ldots, T_7$. After the products $Q_i = S_i T_i$ are computed, each processor sends 6 messages and receives 6 messages to redistribute $Q_1, \ldots, Q_7$. The size of each message varies according to the recursion depth, and is the number of words a processor owns of any S_i, T_i, or Q_i, namely $\frac{n^2}{4P}$ words.

As each of the Q_i is computed simultaneously on disjoint sets of $P/7$ processors, we obtain a cost recurrence for the entire UM scheme:

$$BW_{\text{UM}}(n, P) = 36 \frac{n^2}{4P} + BW_{\text{UM}} \left(\frac{n}{2}, \frac{P}{7} \right)$$

$$L_{\text{UM}}(n, P) = 36 + L_{\text{UM}} \left(\frac{n}{2}, \frac{P}{7} \right)$$

with base case $L_{\text{UM}}(n, 1) = BW_{\text{UM}}(n, 1) = 0$. Thus

$$BW_{\text{UM}}(n, P) = \frac{12n^2}{P^{2/\omega_0}} - \frac{12n^2}{P} = \Theta \left(\frac{n^2}{P^{2/\omega_0}} \right)$$

$$L_{\text{UM}}(n, P) = 36 \log_7 P = \Theta (\log P). \qquad (2)$$

3.4   Limited Memory (LM) scheme

In this section we discuss a scheme for traversing Strassen's recursion tree in the context of limited memory. In the LM scheme, we take ℓ DFS steps in a row followed by k BFS steps in a row, where ℓ is minimized subject to the memory constraints. That is, we use a sequence of DFS steps to reduce the problem size so that we can use the UM scheme on each subproblem without exceeding the available memory.

Consider taking a single DFS step. Rather than allocating space for and computing all 14 matrices $S_1, T_1, \ldots, S_7, T_7$ at once, the DFS step requires allocation of only one subproblem, and each of the Q_i will be computed in sequence.

Consider the ith subproblem: as before, both S_i and T_i can be computed locally. After Q_i is computed, it is used to update the corresponding quadrants of C and then discarded so that its space in memory (as well as the space for S_i and T_i) can be re-used for the next subproblem. In a DFS step, no redistribution occurs. After S_i and T_i are computed, all processors participate in the computation of Q_i.

We assume that some extra memory is available. To be precise, assume the matrices A, B, and C require only $\frac{1}{3}$ of the available memory:

$$\frac{3n^2}{P} \leq \frac{1}{3} M. \qquad (3)$$

In the LM scheme, we set

$$\ell = \max \left\{ 0, \left\lceil \log_2 \frac{4n}{P^{1/\omega_0} M^{1/2}} \right\rceil \right\}. \qquad (4)$$

The following subsection shows that this choice of ℓ is sufficient not to exceed the memory capacity.

3.4.1   Memory requirements

The extra memory requirement for a DFS step is the space to store one subproblem. Thus, the extra space required at this step is $1/4$ the space required to store A, B, and C. The local memory requirements for the LM scheme is given by

$$\text{Mem}_{\text{LM}}(n, P) = \frac{3n^2}{P} \sum_{i=0}^{\ell-1} \left(\frac{1}{4}\right)^i + \text{Mem}_{\text{UM}}\left(\frac{n}{2^\ell}, P\right)$$

$$\leq \frac{M}{3} \sum_{i=0}^{\ell-1} \left(\frac{1}{4}\right)^i + \frac{7\left(\frac{n}{2^\ell}\right)^2}{P^{2/\omega_0}}$$

$$\leq \frac{127}{144} M < M,$$

where the last line follows from (4) and (3). Thus, the limited memory scheme does not exceed the available memory.

3.4.2 Computational costs

As in the UM case, the computation required at a given DFS step is that of the local additions and subtractions associated with computing each S_i and T_i and updating the output matrix C with the Q_i. However, since all processors participate in each subproblem and the subproblems are computed in sequence, the recurrence is given by

$$F_{\text{LM}}(n, P) = 15\left(\frac{n^2}{4P}\right) + 7 \cdot F_{\text{LM}}\left(\frac{n}{2}, P\right).$$

After ℓ steps of DFS, the size of a subproblems is $\frac{n}{2^\ell} \times \frac{n}{2^\ell}$, and there are P processors involved. We take k BFS steps to compute each of these 7^ℓ subproblems. Thus

$$F_{\text{LM}}\left(\frac{n}{2^\ell}, P\right) = F_{\text{UM}}\left(\frac{n}{2^\ell}, P\right),$$

and

$$F_{\text{LM}}(n, P) = \frac{15n^2}{4P} \sum_{i=0}^{\ell-1} \left(\frac{7}{4}\right)^i + 7^\ell \cdot F_{\text{UM}}\left(\frac{n}{2^\ell}, P\right)$$

$$= \frac{c_s n^{\omega_0} - 5n^2}{P} = \Theta\left(\frac{n_0^\omega}{P}\right).$$

3.4.3 Communication costs

Since there are no communication costs associated with a DFS step, the recurrence is simply

$$BW_{\text{LM}}(n, P) = 7 \cdot BW_{\text{LM}}\left(\frac{n}{2}, P\right)$$

$$L_{\text{LM}}(n, P) = 7 \cdot L_{\text{LM}}\left(\frac{n}{2}, P\right)$$

with base cases

$$BW_{\text{LM}}\left(\frac{n}{2^\ell}, P\right) = BW_{\text{UM}}\left(\frac{n}{2^\ell}, P\right)$$

$$L_{\text{LM}}\left(\frac{n}{2^\ell}, P\right) = L_{\text{UM}}\left(\frac{n}{2^\ell}, P\right).$$

Thus the total communication costs are given by

$$BW_{\text{LM}}(n, P) = 7^\ell \cdot BW_{\text{UM}}\left(\frac{n}{2^\ell}, P\right)$$

$$\leq \frac{12 \cdot 4^{\omega_0-2} n^{\omega_0}}{P M^{\omega_0/2-1}}$$

$$= \Theta\left(\frac{n^{\omega_0}}{P M^{\omega_0/2-1}}\right).$$

$$L_{\text{LM}}(n, P) = 7^\ell \cdot L_{\text{UM}}\left(\frac{n}{2^\ell}, P\right)$$

$$\leq \frac{(4n)^{\omega_0}}{P M^{\omega_0/2}} 36 \log_7 P$$

$$= \Theta\left(\frac{n^{\omega_0}}{P M^{\omega_0/2}} \log P\right). \tag{5}$$

3.5 Communication optimality

PROOF. (of Theorem 3.1). In the case that $M \geq$ $\text{Mem}_{\text{UM}}(n, P) = \Omega\left(\frac{n^2}{P^{2/\omega_0}}\right)$ the UM scheme is possible. Then the communication costs are given by (2) which matches the lower bound of Theorem 2.2. Thus the UM scheme is communication-optimal (up to a logarithmic factor in the latency cost and assuming that the data is initially distributed as described in Section 3.2). For smaller values of M, the LM scheme must be used. Then the communication costs are given by (5) and match the lower bound of Theorem 2.1, so the LM scheme is also communication-optimal. □

We note that for the LM scheme, since both the computational and communication costs are proportional to $\frac{1}{P}$, we can expect *perfect strong scaling*: given a fixed problem size, increasing the number of processors by some factor will decrease each cost by the same factor. However, this strong scaling property has a limited range. For any fixed M and n, increasing P increases the global memory size PM. The limit of perfect strong scaling is exactly when there is enough memory for the UM scheme. See [3] for details.

4. ANALYSIS OF OTHER ALGORITHMS

In this section we detail the asymptotic communication costs of other matrix multiplication algorithms, both classical and Strassen-based. These communication costs and the corresponding lower bounds are summarized in Table 1.

Many of the algorithms described in this section are hybrids of two different algorithms. We use the convention that the names of the hybrid algorithms are composed of the names of the two component algorithms, hyphenated. The first name describes the algorithm used at the top level, on the largest problems, and the second describes the algorithm used at the base level on smaller problems.

4.1 Classical Algorithms

Any classical algorithm must communicate asymptotically more than an optimal parallel Strassen algorithm. To compare the lower bounds, it is necessary to consider three cases for the memory size: when the memory-dependent bounds dominate for both classical and Strassen, when the memory-dependent bound dominates for classical, but the memory-independent bound dominates for Strassen, and when the memory-independent bounds dominate for both classical and Strassen. This analysis is detailed in Appendix A. Briefly, the factor by which the classical bandwidth cost exceeds the Strassen bandwidth cost is P^a where a ranges from $\frac{2}{\omega_0} - \frac{2}{3} \approx 0.046$ to $\frac{3-\omega_0}{2} \approx 0.10$ depending on the relative problem size. The same sort of analysis is used throughout Section 4 to compare each algorithm with the parallel Strassen lower bounds.

Various parallel classical matrix multiplication algorithms minimize communication relative to the classical lower bounds for certain amounts of local memory M. For example, Cannon's algorithm [10] minimizes communication for $M = O(n^2/P)$. Several more practical algorithms exist (such as SUMMA [36]) which use the same amount of local memory and have the same asymptotic communication costs. We call this class of algorithms "2D" because the communication patterns follow a two-dimensional processor grid.

		Flops	Bandwidth	Latency
Classical	Lower Bound [3, 24]	$\frac{n^3}{P}$	$\max\left\{\frac{n^3}{PM^{1/2}}, \frac{n^2}{P^{2/3}}\right\}$	$\max\left\{\frac{n^3}{PM^{3/2}}, 1\right\}$
	2D [10, 36]	$\frac{n^3}{P}$	$\frac{n^2}{P^{1/2}}$	$P^{1/2}$
	3D [1, 6]	$\frac{n^3}{P}$	$\frac{n^2}{P^{2/3}}$	$\log P$
	2.5D [31]	$\frac{n^3}{P}$	$\max\left\{\frac{n^3}{PM^{1/2}}, \frac{n^2}{P^{2/3}}\right\}$	$\frac{n^3}{PM^{3/2}} + \log P$
Strassen	Lower Bound [3, 4]	$\frac{n^{\omega_0}}{P}$	$\max\left\{\frac{n^{\omega_0}}{PM^{\omega_0/2-1}}, \frac{n^2}{P^{2/\omega_0}}\right\}$	$\max\left\{\frac{n^{\omega_0}}{PM^{\omega_0/2}}, 1\right\}$
	2D-Strassen [26]	$\frac{n^{\omega_0}}{P^{(\omega_0-1)/2}}$	$\frac{n^2}{P^{1/2}}$	$P^{1/2}$
	Strassen-2D [21, 26]	$\left(\frac{7}{8}\right)^\ell \frac{n^3}{P}$	$\left(\frac{7}{4}\right)^\ell \frac{n^2}{P^{1/2}}$	$7^\ell P^{1/2}$
	2.5D-Strassen	$\max\left\{\frac{n^3}{PM^{3/2-\omega_0/2}}, \frac{n^{\omega_0}}{P^{\omega_0/3}}\right\}$	$\max\left\{\frac{n^3}{PM^{1/2}}, \frac{n^2}{P^{2/3}}\right\}$	$\frac{n^3}{PM^{3/2}} + \log P$
	Strassen-2.5D	$\left(\frac{7}{8}\right)^\ell \frac{n^3}{P}$	$\max\left\{\left(\frac{7}{8}\right)^\ell \frac{n^3}{PM^{1/2}}, \left(\frac{7}{4}\right)^\ell \frac{n^2}{P^{2/3}}\right\}$	$\left(\frac{7}{8}\right)^\ell \frac{n^3}{PM^{3/2}} + 7^\ell \log P$
	CAPS	$\frac{n^{\omega_0}}{P}$	$\max\left\{\frac{n^{\omega_0}}{PM^{\omega_0/2-1}}, \frac{n^2}{P^{2/\omega_0}}\right\}$	$\max\left\{\frac{n^{\omega_0}}{PM^{\omega_0/2}} \log P, \log P\right\}$

Table 1: **Asymptotic computational and communication costs of matrix multiplication algorithms and corresponding lower bounds. Here $\omega_0 = \log_2 7 \approx 2.81$ is the exponent of Strassen; ℓ is the number of Strassen steps taken. The CAPS algorithm attains the lower bounds of Section 2.5, and thus is optimal. All of the other Strassen-based algorithms have asymptotically higher communication costs; see Section 4 for details.**

Another class of algorithms, known as "3D" [6, 1] because the communication pattern maps to a three-dimensional processor grid, uses more local memory and reduces communication relative to 2D algorithms. This class of algorithms minimizes communication relative to the classical lower bounds for $M = \Omega(n^2/P^{2/3})$. As shown in [3], it is not possible to use more memory than $M = \Theta(n^2/P^{2/3})$ to reduce communication.

Recently, a more general algorithm has been developed which minimizes communication in all cases. Because it reduces to a 2D and 3D for the extreme values of M but interpolates for the values between, it is known as the "2.5D" algorithm [31].

4.2 2D-Strassen

One idea to construct a parallel Strassen-based algorithm is to use a 2D classical algorithm for the inter-processor communication, and use the fast matrix multiplication algorithm locally [26]. We call such an algorithm "2D-Strassen". It is straightforward to implement, but cannot attain all the computational speedup from Strassen since it uses a classical algorithm for part of the computation. In particular, it does not use Strassen for the largest matrices, when Strassen provides the greatest reduction in computation. As a result, the computational cost exceeds $\Theta(n^{\omega_0}/P)$ by a factor of $P^{(3-\omega_0)/2} \approx P^{0.10}$. The 2D-Strassen algorithm has the same communication cost as 2D algorithms, and hence does not match the communication costs of CAPS. In comparing the 2D-Strassen bandwidth cost, $\Theta(n^2/P^{1/2})$, to the CAPS bandwidth cost in Section 3, note that for the problem to fit in memory we always have $M = \Omega(n^2/P)$. The bandwidth cost exceeds that of CAPS by a factor of P^a, where a ranges from $(3-\omega_0)/2 \approx .10$ to $2/\omega_0 - 1/2 \approx .21$, depending on the relative problem size. Similarly, the latency cost, $\Theta(P^{1/2})$,

exceeds that of CAPS by a factor of P^a where a ranges from $(3-\omega_0)/2 \approx .10$ to $1/2 = .5$.

4.3 Strassen-2D

The "Strassen-2D" algorithm applies ℓ DFS steps of Strassen's algorithm at the top level, and performs the 7^ℓ smaller matrix multiplications using a 2D algorithm. By choosing certain data layouts as in Section 3.2, it is possible to do the additions and subtractions for Strassen's algorithm without any communication [26]. However, Strassen-2D is also unable to match the communication costs of CAPS. Moreover, the speedup of Strassen-2D in computation comes at the expense of extra communication. For large numbers of Strassen steps ℓ, Strassen-2D can approach the computational lower bound of Strassen, but each step increases the bandwidth cost by a factor of $\frac{7}{4}$ and the latency cost by a factor of 7. Thus the bandwidth cost of Strassen-2D is a factor of $\left(\frac{7}{4}\right)^\ell$ higher than 2D-Strassen, which is already higher than that of CAPS. The latency cost is even worse: Strassen-2D is a factor of 7^ℓ higher than 2D-Strassen.

One can reduce the latency cost of Strassen-2D at the expense of a larger memory footprint. Since Strassen-2D runs a 2D algorithm 7^ℓ times on the same set of processors, it is possible to pack together messages from independent matrix multiplications. In the best case, the latency cost is reduced to the cost of 2D-Strassen, which is still above that of CAPS, at the expense of using a factor of $\left(\frac{7}{4}\right)^\ell$ more memory.

4.4 2.5D-Strassen

A natural idea is to replace a 2D classical algorithm in 2D-Strassen with the superior 2.5D classical algorithm to obtain an algorithm we call 2.5D-Strassen. This algorithm uses the 2.5D algorithm for the inter-processor communication, and then uses Strassen for the local computation.

When $M = \Theta(n^2/P)$, 2.5D-Strassen is exactly the same as 2D-Strassen, but when there is extra memory it both decreases the communication cost and decreases the computational cost since the local matrix multiplications are performed (using Strassen) on larger matrices. To be precise, the computational cost exceeds the lower bound by a factor of P^a where a ranges from $1 - \frac{\omega_0}{3} \approx 0.064$ to $\frac{3-\omega_0}{2} \approx 0.10$ depending on the relative problem size. The bandwidth cost exceeds the bandwidth cost of CAPS by a factor of P^a where a ranges from $\frac{2}{\omega_0} - \frac{2}{3} \approx 0.046$ to $\frac{3-\omega_0}{2} \approx 0.10$. In terms of latency, the cost of $\frac{n^3}{PM^{3/2}} + \log P$ exceeds the latency cost of CAPS by a factor ranging from $\log P$ to $P^{(3-\omega_0)/2} \approx P^{0.10}$, depending on the relative problem size.

4.5 Strassen-2.5D

Similarly, by replacing a 2D algorithm with 2.5D in Strassen-2D, one obtains the new algorithm we call Strassen-2.5D. First one takes ℓ DFS steps of Strassen, which can be done without communication, and then one applies the 2.5D algorithm to each of the 7^ℓ subproblems. The computational cost is exactly the same as Strassen-2D, but the communication cost will typically be lower. Each of the 7^ℓ subproblems is multiplication of $n/2^\ell \times n/2^\ell$ matrices. Each subproblem uses only $1/4^\ell$ as much memory as the original problem. Thus there may be a large amount of extra memory available for each subproblem, and the lower communication costs of the 2.5D algorithm help. The choice of ℓ that minimizes the bandwidth cost is

$$\ell_{\text{opt}} = \max \left\{ 0, \left\lceil \log_2 \frac{n}{M^{1/2}P^{1/3}} \right\rceil \right\}.$$

The same choice minimizes the latency cost. Note that when $M \geq \frac{n^2}{P^{2/3}}$, taking zero Strassen steps minimizes the communication within the constraints of the Strassen-2.5D algorithm. With $\ell = \ell_{\text{opt}}$, the bandwidth cost is a factor of $P^{1-\omega_0/3} \approx P^{0.064}$ above that of CAPS. Additionally, the computational cost is not optimal, and using $\ell = \ell_{\text{opt}}$, the computational cost exceeds the optimal by a factor of $P^{1-\omega_0/3}M^{3/2-\omega_0/2} \approx P^{0.064}M^{0.096}$.

It is also possible to take $\ell > \ell_{\text{opt}}$ steps of Strassen to decrease the comptutational cost further. However the decreased computational cost comes at the expense of higher communication cost, as in the case of Strassen-2D. In particular, each extra step over ℓ_{opt} increases the bandwidth cost by a factor of $\frac{7}{4}$ and the latency cost by a factor of 7. As with Strassen-2D, it is possible to use extra memory to pack together messages from several subproblems and decrease the latency cost, but not the bandwidth cost.

5. PERFORMANCE RESULTS

We have implemented CAPS using MPI on a Cray XT4 ("Franklin" at the National Energy Research Scientific Computing Center), and compared it to various previous classical and Strassen-based algorithms. The benchmarking data is shown in Figure 3.

5.1 Experimental setup

Each node of the Cray XT4 has 8GB of memory and a quad-core AMD "Budapest" processor running at 2.3GHz. We treat the entire node as a single processor, and when we use the classical algorithm we call the optimized threaded BLAS in Cray's LibSci to provide parallelism between the four cores in a node. The peak flop rate is 9.2 GFLOPS per

core, or 36.8 GFLOPS per node. The machine consists of 9,572 nodes. All the data in Figure 3 is for multiplying two square matrices with $n = 94080$.

5.2 Performance

Note that the vertical scale of Figure 3 is "effective GFLOPS", which is a useful measure for comparing classical and fast matrix multiplication algorithms. It is calculated as

$$\text{Effective GFLOPS} = \frac{2n^3}{(\text{Execution time in seconds})10^9}.$$
(6)

For classical algorithms, which perform $2n^3$ floating point operations, this gives the actual GFLOPS. For fast matrix multiplication algorithms it gives the performance relative to classical algorithms, but does not accurately represent the number of floating point operations performed.

Our algorithm outperforms all previous algorithms, and attains performance as high as 49.1 effective GFLOPS/node, which is 33% above the theoretical maximum for all classical algorithms. Compared with the best classical implementation, our speedup ranges from 51% for small values of P up to 94% when using most of the machine. Compared with the best previous parallel Strassen algorithms, our speedup ranges from 24% up to 184%. Unlike previous Strassen algorithms, we are able to attain substantial speedups over the entire range of processors.

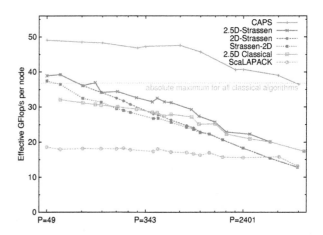

Figure 3: **Strong scaling performance of various matrix multiplication algorithms on Cray XT4 for fixed problem size $n = 94080$. The top line is CAPS as described in Section 3, and substantially outperforms all the other classical and Strassen-based algorithms. The horizontal axis is the number of nodes in log-scale. The vertical axis is effective GFLOPS, which are a performance measure rather than a flop rate, as discussed in Section 5.2. See Section 5.4 for a description of each implementation.**

5.3 Strong scaling

Figure 3 is a strong scaling plot: the problem size is fixed and each algorithm is run with P ranging from the minimum that provides enough memory up to the largest allowed value of P smaller than the size of the machine. Perfect strong scaling corresponds to a horizontal line in the plot. As the communication analysis predicts, CAPS exhibits better strong scaling than any of the other algorithms (with the exception of ScaLAPACK, which obtains very good strong scaling by having poor performance for small values of P).

5.4 Details of the implementations

5.4.1 CAPS

This implementation is the CAPS algorithm, with a few modifications from the presentation in Section 3. First, when computing locally it switches to classical matrix multiplication below some size n_0. Second, it is generalized to run on $P = c7^k$ processors for $c \in \{1, 2, 3, 6\}$ rather than just 7^k processors. As a result, the base-case classical matrix multiplication is done on c processors rather than 1. Finally, the implementation uses the Winograd variant of Strassen; see Section 2.3 for more details. Every point in the plot is tuned to use the best interleaving pattern of BFS and DFS steps, and the best total number of Strassen steps. For points in the figure, the optimal total number of Strassen steps is always 5 or 6.

5.4.2 ScaLAPACK

We use ScaLAPACK [8] as optimized by Cray in LibSci. This is an implementation of the SUMMA algorithm, and can run on an arbitrary number of processors. It should give the best performance if P is a perfect square so the processors can be placed on a square 2D grid. All the runs shown in Figure 3 are with P a perfect square.

5.4.3 2.5D classical

This is the code of [31]. It places the P processors in a grid of size $\sqrt{P/c} \times \sqrt{P/c} \times c$, and requires that $\sqrt{P/c}$ and c are integers with $1 \leq c \leq P^{1/3}$, and c divides $\sqrt{P/c}$. Additionally, it gets the best performance if c is as large as possible, given the constraint that c copies of the input and output matrices fit in memory. In the case that $c = 1$ this code is an optimized implementation of SUMMA. The values of P and c for the runs in Figure 3 are chosen to get the best performance.

5.4.4 Strassen-2D

Following the algorithm of [21, 26], this implementation uses the DFS code from the implementation of CAPS at the top level, and then uses the optimized SUMMA code from the 2.5D implementation with $c = 1$. Since the classical code requires that P is a perfect square, this requirement applies here as well. The number of Strassen steps taken is tuned to give the best performance for each P value, and the optimal number varies from 0 to 2.

5.4.5 2D-Strassen

Following the algorithm of [26], the 2D-Strassen implementation is analagous to the Strassen-2D implementation, but with the classical algorithm run before taking local Strassen steps. Similarly the same code is used for local Strassen steps here and in our implementation of CAPS. This code also requires that P is a perfect square. The number of Strassen steps is tuned for each P value, and the optimal number varies from 0 to 3.

5.4.6 2.5D-Strassen

This implementation uses the 2.5D implementation to reduce the problem to one processor, then takes several Strassen steps. The processor requirements are the same as for the 2.5D implementation. The number of Strassen steps is tuned for each number of processors, and the optimal number varies from 0 to 3. We also tested the Strassen-2.5D algorithm, but its performance was always lower than 2.5D-Strassen in our experiments.

6. DISCUSSION AND FUTURE WORK

6.1 Stability of fast matrix multiplication

CAPS has the same stability properties as sequential versions of Strassen. For a complete discussion of the stability of fast matrix multiplication algorithms, see [22, 17]. We highlight a few main points here. The tightest error bounds for classical matrix multiplication are component-wise: $|C - \hat{C}| \leq n\epsilon |A| \cdot |B|$, where $\hat{C}$ is the computed result and ϵ is the machine precision. Strassen and other fast algorithms do not satisfy component-wise bounds but do satisfy the slightly weaker norm-wise bounds: $\|C - \hat{C}\| \leq f(n)\epsilon \|A\| \|B\|$, where $\|A\| = \max_{i,j} A_{ij}$ and f is polynomial in n [22]. Accuracy can be improved with the use of diagonal scaling matrices: $D_1 C D_3 = D_1 A D_2 \cdot D_2^{-1} B D_3$. It is possible to choose D_1, D_2, D_3 so that the error bounds satisfy either $|C_{ij} - \hat{C}_{ij}| \leq f(n)\epsilon \|A(i, :)\| \|B(:, j)\|$ or $\|C - \hat{C}\| \leq f(n)\epsilon \||A| \cdot |B|\|$. By scaling, the error bounds on Strassen become comparable to those of many other dense linear algebra algorithms, such as LU and QR decomposition [16]. Thus using Strassen for the matrix multiplications in a larger computation will often not harm the stability at all.

6.2 Testing on various architectures

We have implemented and benchmarked CAPS on only one architecture, a Cray XT4. It remains to check that it outperforms other matrix multiplication algorithms on a variety of architectures. On some architectures it may be more important to consider the topology of the network and redesign the algorithm to minimize contention, which we have not done.

6.3 Improvements to the algorithm

CAPS as presented in Section 3 requires P to be a power of seven. To be practically useful, it is important to generalize the number of processors on which CAPS can run. Of course, CAPS can then be run on any number of processors by simply ignoring no more than $\frac{6}{7}$ of them and incurring a constant factor overhead. Thus we can run on arbitrary P and attain the communication and computation lower bounds up to a constant factor. However the computation time is still dominant in most cases, and it is preferable to attain the computation lower bound exactly. It is an open question whether any algorithm can run on arbitrary P, attain the computation lower bound exactly, and attain the communication lower bound up to a constant factor.

Moreover, although the communication costs of this algorithm match the lower bound up to a constant factor in bandwidth, and up to a $\log P$ factor in latency, it is an open question to determine the optimal constant in the lower bound and perhaps provide a new algorithm that matches it exactly. Note that in the analysis of CAPS in Section 3, the constants could be slightly improved.

6.4 Parallelizing other algorithms

6.4.1 Another optimal classical algorithm

We can apply our parallelization approach to recursive classical matrix multiplication to obtain a communication-optimal algorithm. This algorithm has the same asymptotic communication costs as the 2.5D algorithm [31]. We observed comparable performance to the 2.5D algorithm on our experimental platform. As with CAPS, this algorithm has not been optimized for contention, whereas the 2.5D algorithm is very well optimized for contention on torus networks.

6.4.2 Other fast matrix multiplication algorithms

Our approach of executing a recursive algorithm in parallel by traversing the recursion tree in DFS or BFS manner is not limited to Strassen's algorithm. Recursive matrix multiplication algorithms are typically built out of ways to multiply $n_0 \times n_0$ matrices using $q < n_0^3$ multiplications. As with Strassen and Strassen-Winograd, they compute q linear combinations of entries of each of A and B, multiply these pairwise, then compute the entries of C as linear combinations of these. CAPS can be easily generalized to any such multiplication, with the following modifications:

- The number of processors P is a power of q.

- The data layout must be such that all n_0^2 blocks of A, B, and C are distributed equally among the P processors with the same layout.

- The BFS and DFS determine whether the q multiplications are performed simultaneously or in sequence.

The communication costs are then exactly as above, but with $\omega_0 = \log_{n_0} q$.

Using the techniques from Theorem 3.3 of [17], one can convert any fast matrix multiplication algorithm into one that is nearly as fast and is of the form above. Using the CAPS parallelization approach this gives a communication-avoiding parallel algorithm corresponding to any fast matrix multiplication algorithm. We conjecture that there is a matching lower bound, making these algorithms optimal.

7. REFERENCES

[1] AGARWAL, R. C., BALLE, S. M., GUSTAVSON, F. G., JOSHI, M., AND PALKAR, P. A three-dimensional approach to parallel matrix multiplication. *IBM Journal of Research and Development 39* (1995), 39–5.

[2] AGGARWAL, A., CHANDRA, A. K., AND SNIR, M. Communication complexity of PRAMs. *Theor. Comput. Sci. 71* (March 1990), 3–28.

[3] BALLARD, G., DEMMEL, J., HOLTZ, O., LIPSHITZ, B., AND SCHWARTZ, O. Strong scaling of matrix multiplication algorithms and memory-independent communication lower bounds, 2012. Manuscript, submitted to SPAA 2012.

[4] BALLARD, G., DEMMEL, J., HOLTZ, O., AND SCHWARTZ, O. Graph expansion and communication costs of fast matrix multiplication. In *SPAA '11: Proceedings of the 23rd annual symposium on parallelism in algorithms and architectures* (New York, NY, USA, 2011), ACM, pp. 1–12.

[5] BALLARD, G., DEMMEL, J., HOLTZ, O., AND SCHWARTZ, O. Minimizing communication in numerical linear algebra. *SIAM J. Matrix Analysis Applications 32*, 3 (2011), 866–901.

[6] BERNTSEN, J. Communication efficient matrix multiplication on hypercubes. *Parallel Computing 12*, 3 (1989), 335 – 342.

[7] BINI, D. Relations between exact and approximate bilinear algorithms. applications. *Calcolo 17* (1980), 87–97. 10.1007/BF02575865.

[8] BLACKFORD, L. S., CHOI, J., CLEARY, A., D'AZEVEDO, E., DEMMEL, J., DHILLON, I., DONGARRA, J., HAMMARLING, S., HENRY, G., PETITET, A., STANLEY, K., WALKER, D., AND WHALEY, R. C. *ScaLAPACK Users' Guide*. SIAM, Philadelphia, PA, USA, May 1997. Also available from http://www.netlib.org/scalapack/.

[9] BSHOUTY, N. H. On the additive complexity of 2×2 matrix multiplication. *Information Processing Letters 56*, 6 (1995), 329 – 335.

[10] CANNON, L. *A cellular computer to implement the Kalman filter algorithm*. PhD thesis, Montana State University, Bozeman, MN, 1969.

[11] CHOI, J. A new parallel matrix multiplication algorithm on distributed-memory concurrent computers. *Concurrency: Practice and Experience 10*, 8 (1998), 655–670.

[12] CHOI, J., WALKER, D. W., AND DONGARRA, J. J. PUMMA: Parallel universal matrix multiplication algorithms on distributed memory concurrent computers. *Concurrency: Practice and Experience 6*, 7 (1994), 543–570.

[13] COHN, H., KLEINBERG, R. D., SZEGEDY, B., AND UMANS, C. Group-theoretic algorithms for matrix multiplication. In *FOCS* (2005), pp. 379–388.

[14] COPPERSMITH, D., AND WINOGRAD, S. On the asymptotic complexity of matrix multiplication. *SIAM Journal on Computing 11*, 3 (1982), 472–492.

[15] COPPERSMITH, D., AND WINOGRAD, S. Matrix multiplication via arithmetic progressions. In *Proceedings of the Nineteenth Annual ACM Symposium on Theory of Computing* (New York, NY, USA, 1987), STOC '87, ACM, pp. 1–6.

[16] DEMMEL, J., DUMITRIU, I., AND HOLTZ, O. Fast linear algebra is stable. *Numerische Mathematik 108*, 1 (2007), 59–91.

[17] DEMMEL, J., DUMITRIU, I., HOLTZ, O., AND KLEINBERG, R. Fast matrix multiplication is stable. *Numerische Mathematik 106*, 2 (2007), 199–224.

[18] DESPREZ, F., AND SUTER, F. Impact of mixed-parallelism on parallel implementations of the Strassen and Winograd matrix multiplication algorithms: Research articles. *Concurr. Comput. : Pract. Exper. 16* (July 2004), 771–797.

[19] FULLER, S. H., AND MILLETT, L. I., Eds. *The Future of Computing Performance: Game Over or Next Level?* The National Academies Press, Washington, D.C., 2011. 200 pages, http://www.nap.edu.

[20] GRAHAM, S. L., SNIR, M., AND PATTERSON, C. A., Eds. *Getting up to Speed: The Future of Supercomputing*. Report of National Research Council of the National Academies Sciences. The National

Academies Press, Washington, D.C., 2004. 289 pages, http://www.nap.edu.

[21] GRAYSON, B., SHAH, A., AND VAN DE GEIJN, R. A high performance parallel Strassen implementation. In *Parallel Processing Letters* (1995), vol. 6, pp. 3–12.

[22] HIGHAM, N. J. *Accuracy and Stability of Numerical Algorithms*, 2nd ed. SIAM, Philadelphia, PA, 2002.

[23] HUNOLD, S., RAUBER, T., AND RÜNGER, G. Combining building blocks for parallel multi-level matrix multiplication. *Parallel Computing 34* (July 2008), 411–426.

[24] IRONY, D., TOLEDO, S., AND TISKIN, A. Communication lower bounds for distributed-memory matrix multiplication. *J. Parallel Distrib. Comput. 64*, 9 (2004), 1017–1026.

[25] KUMAR, B., HUANG, C.-H., JOHNSON, R., AND SADAYAPPAN, P. A tensor product formulation of Strassen's matrix multiplication algorithm with memory reduction. In *Proceedings of Seventh International Parallel Processing Symposium* (apr 1993), pp. 582 –588.

[26] LUO, Q., AND DRAKE, J. A scalable parallel Strassen's matrix multiplication algorithm for distributed-memory computers. In *Proceedings of the 1995 ACM symposium on Applied computing* (New York, NY, USA, 1995), SAC '95, ACM, pp. 221–226.

[27] PAN, V. Y. New fast algorithms for matrix operations. *SIAM Journal on Computing 9*, 2 (1980), 321–342.

[28] PROBERT, R. L. On the additive complexity of matrix multiplication. *SIAM Journal on Computing 5*, 2 (1976), 187–203.

[29] ROMANI, F. Some properties of disjoint sums of tensors related to matrix multiplication. *SIAM Journal on Computing 11*, 2 (1982), 263–267.

[30] SCHÖNHAGE, A. Partial and total matrix multiplication. *SIAM Journal on Computing 10*, 3 (1981), 434–455.

[31] SOLOMONIK, E., AND DEMMEL, J. Communication-optimal parallel 2.5D matrix multiplication and LU factorization algorithms. In *Euro-Par '11: Proceedings of the 17th International European Conference on Parallel and Distributed Computing* (2011), Springer.

[32] SONG, F., DONGARRA, J., AND MOORE, S. Experiments with Strassen's algorithm: From sequential to parallel. In *Proceedings of Parallel and Distributed Computing and Systems (PDCS)* (Nov. 2006), ACTA.

[33] STRASSEN, V. Gaussian elimination is not optimal. *Numer. Math. 13* (1969), 354–356.

[34] STRASSEN, V. Relative bilinear complexity and matrix multiplication. *Journal für die reine und angewandte Mathematik (Crelles Journal) 1987*, 375–376 (1987), 406–443.

[35] VALIANT, L. G. A bridging model for parallel computation. *Commun. ACM 33*, 8 (Aug. 1990), 103–111.

[36] VAN DE GEIJN, R. A., AND WATTS, J. SUMMA: scalable universal matrix multiplication algorithm. *Concurrency - Practice and Experience 9*, 4 (1997), 255–274.

[37] WILLIAMS, V. V. Breaking the Coppersmith-Winograd barrier, 2012. Manuscript.

[38] WINOGRAD, S. On the multiplication of 2 × 2 matrices. *Linear Algebra Appl. 4*, 4 (October 1971), 381–388.

[39] YANG, C.-Q., AND MILLER, B. Critical path analysis for the execution of parallel and distributed programs. In *Proceedings of the 8th International Conference on Distributed Computing Systems* (Jun. 1988), pp. 366–373.

APPENDIX

A. COMMUNICATION-COST RATIOS

In this section we derive the ratio R of classical to parallel Strassen bandwidth cost lower bounds that appear in the beginning of Section 4. Note that both classical and Strassen lower bounds are attained by optimal algorithms. Similar derivations apply to the other ratios quoted in that section. Because the bandwidth cost lower bounds are different in the memory-dependent and the memory-independent cases, and the threshold between these is different for the classical and Strassen bounds, it is necessary to consider three cases.

Case 1. $M = \Omega(n^2/P)$ and $M = O(n^2/P^{2/\omega_0})$. The first condition is necessary for there to be enough memory to hold the input and output matrices; the second condition puts both classical and Strassen algorithms in the memory-dependent case. Then the ratio of the bandwidth costs is:

$$R = \Theta\left(\frac{n^3}{PM^{1/2}} \Big/ \frac{n^{\omega_0}}{PM^{\omega_0/2-1}}\right) = \Theta\left(\left(\frac{n^2}{M}\right)^{(3-\omega_0)/2}\right).$$

Using the two bounds that define this case, we obtain $R = O(P^{(3-\omega_0)/2})$ and $R = \Omega(P^{3/\omega_0-1})$.

Case 2. $M = \Omega(n^2/P^{2/\omega_0})$ and $M = O(n^2/P^{2/3})$. This means that in the classical case the memory-dependent lower bound dominates, but in the Strassen case the memory-independent lower bound dominates. Then the ratio is:

$$R = \Theta\left(\frac{n^3}{PM^{1/2}} \Big/ \frac{n^2}{P^{2/\omega_0}}\right) = \Theta\left(\left(\frac{n^2}{M}\right)^{1/2} P^{2/\omega_0-1}\right).$$

Using the two bounds that define this case, we obtain $R = O(P^{3/\omega_0-1})$ and $R = \Omega(P^{2/\omega_0-2/3})$.

Case 3. $M = O(P^{2/3})$. This means that both the classical and Strassen lower bounds are dominated by the memory-independent cases. Then the ratio is:

$$R = \Theta\left(\frac{n^2}{P^{2/3}} \Big/ \frac{n^2}{P^{2/\omega_0}}\right) = \Theta\left(P^{2/\omega_0-2/3}\right).$$

Overall, depending on the ratio of the problem size to the available memory, the factor by which the classical bandwidth costs exceed the Strassen bandwidth costs is between $\Theta(P^{2/\omega_0-2/3})$ and $\Theta(P^{(3-\omega_0)/2})$.

Parallel Probabilistic Tree Embeddings, k-Median, and Buy-at-Bulk Network Design

Guy E. Blelloch   Anupam Gupta   Kanat Tangwongsan

Carnegie Mellon University

{guyb, anupamg, ktangwon}@cs.cmu.edu

ABSTRACT

This paper presents parallel algorithms for embedding an arbitrary n-point metric space into a distribution of dominating trees with $O(\log n)$ expected stretch. Such embedding has proved useful in the design of many approximation algorithms in the sequential setting. We give a parallel algorithm that runs in $O(n^2 \log n)$ work and $O(\log^2 n)$ depth—these bounds are independent of $\Delta = \frac{\max_{x,y} d(x,y)}{\min_{x \neq y} d(x,y)}$, the ratio of the largest to smallest distance. Moreover, when Δ is exponentially bounded ($\Delta \leq 2^{O(n)}$), our algorithm can be improved to $O(n^2)$ work and $O(\log^2 n)$ depth.

Using these results, we give an RNC $O(\log k)$-approximation algorithm for k-median and an RNC $O(\log n)$-approximation for buy-at-bulk network design. The k-median algorithm is the first RNC algorithm with non-trivial guarantees for arbitrary values of k, and the buy-at-bulk result is the first parallel algorithm for the problem.

Categories and Subject Descriptors: F.2 [Theory of Computation]: Analysis of Algorithms and Problem Complexity

General Terms: Algorithms, Theory

Keywords: Parallel algorithms, probabilistic tree embedding, k-median, buy-at-bulk network design

1. INTRODUCTION

The idea of embedding a finite metric into a distribution of "simpler" metrics has proved to be a useful and versatile technique in the algorithmic study of metric spaces, with far-reaching consequences to understanding finite metrics and developing approximation algorithms. An important line of work in this pursuit is concerned with embedding a finite metric space into a distribution of dominating trees [Bar98] that minimizes distance distortion: Given an n-point metric space (X, d), the goal is to find a distribution $\mathcal{D}$ of trees to minimize β such that

(1) *Non-contracting:* for all $T \in \mathcal{D}$, $d(x,y) \leq d_T(x,y)$ for all $x, y \in X$; and

(2) *Small Distortion:* $\mathbf{E}_{T \sim \mathcal{D}}[d_T(x,y)] \leq \beta \cdot d(x,y)$ for all $x, y \in X$,

where $d_T(\cdot, \cdot)$ denotes the distance in the tree T, and $\mathbf{E}_{T \sim \mathcal{D}}$ draws a tree T from the distribution $\mathcal{D}$. The series work on this problem (e.g., [Bar98, Bar96, AKPW95]) culminated in the result of Fakcharoenphol, Rao, and Talwar (FRT) [FRT04], who gave an elegant optimal algorithm with $\beta = O(\log n)$. This has proved to be instrumental in many approximation algorithms (see, e.g., [FRT04] and the references therein). For example, the first polylogarithmic approximation algorithm for the k-median problem was given using this embedding technique. Remarkably, all these algorithms only require pairwise expected stretch, so their approximation guarantees are expected approximation bounds and the technique is only applicable to problems whose objectives are linear in the distances.

In this paper, motivated by getting a parallel algorithm for the k-median problem, we consider the problem of computing such tree embeddings in parallel. None of the previous low-depth parallel approximation algorithms for k-median worked for all ranges of k; all previous algorithms giving non-trivial approximations either had more than polylogarithmic depth, or could only handle k smaller than polylog(n) [BT10]. Using the parallel tree-embedding results in this paper, we give parallel approximation algorithms for k-median. Moreover, we use these embeddings to give parallel approximation algorithms for the *buy-at-bulk network design* problem.

A crucial design constraint is to ensure that the parallel work of our algorithms remains close to that of the sequential counterparts (aka. *work efficiency*) while achieving small, preferably polylogarithmic, depth (parallel time). Work efficiency is important since it allows an algorithm to be applied efficiently to both a modest number of processors (*one* being the most modest) and a larger number. Even with a larger number of processors, work-efficient algorithms limit the amount of resources used and hence presumably the cost of the computation (e.g. in terms of the energy used, or the rental cost of a machine in the "cloud"). We will be less concerned with polylogarithmic factors in the depth since such a measure is typically not robust across models.

Our Results. We give a parallel algorithm to embed any n-point metric into a distribution of hierarchically well-separated trees (HSTs)[1] with $O(n^2 \log n)$ (randomized) work and $O(\log^2 n)$ depth that offers the same distance-preserving guarantees as FRT [FRT04]. When the ratio between the largest and smallest distance $\Delta = \frac{\max_{x,y} d(x,y)}{\min_{x \neq y} d(x,y)}$ is exponentially bounded (i.e., $\Delta \leq 2^{O(n)}$), our algorithm can be improved to $O(n^2)$ work and $O(\log^2 n)$ depth. The main challenge arises in ensuring the depth of the computation is polylogarithmic even when the resulting tree is highly imbalanced—the FRT algorithm, as stated, works level by level, and a naïve

---
[1] A definition of HSTs is given in Section 2.

Permission to make digital or hard copies of all or part of this work for personal or classroom use is granted without fee provided that copies are not made or distributed for profit or commercial advantage and that copies bear this notice and the full citation on the first page. To copy otherwise, to republish, to post on servers or to redistribute to lists, requires prior specific permission and/or a fee.
SPAA'12, June 25–27, 2012, Pittsburgh, Pennsylvania, USA.
Copyright 2012 ACM 978-1-4503-1213-4/12/06 ...$10.00.

implementation incurs $O(\log \Delta)$ depth, which is undesirable when Δ is more than polynomial in n. Our contribution lies in recognizing an alternative view of the FRT algorithm and developing an efficient algorithm to exploit it. Our analysis also implies probabilistic embeddings into trees without Steiner nodes of height $O(\log n)$ whp. (though not HSTs).

Using these embedding algorithms, in Section 4, we give an RNC $O(\log k)$-approximation for k-median—see Theorem 4.4. This is the first RNC algorithm that gives non-trivial approximation for arbitrary values of k. (There is an RNC algorithm that give a $(5+\varepsilon)$-approximation for $k \leq \text{polylog}(n)$ [BT10].) Furthermore, the algorithm is work-efficient relative to previously described sequential techniques. It remains an intriguing open problem to give an RNC algorithm for k-median with a constant-factor approximation.

Finally, in Section 5, we give an RNC $O(\log n)$-approximation algorithm for buy-at-bulk network design—see Theorem 5.1. This algorithm for buy-at-bulk network design is within an $O(\log n)$ factor of being work efficient if the input contains all-pairs shortest paths distances of the graph. All our algorithms are randomized and all our guarantees are expected approximation bounds.

2. PRELIMINARIES AND NOTATION

Throughout the paper, let $[n] = \{1, 2, \ldots, n\}$. For alphabet Σ and a sequence $\alpha \in \Sigma^*$, we denote by $|\alpha|$ the length of α and by α_i (or alternatively $\alpha(i)$) the i-th element of α. Given sequences α and β, we say that $\alpha \sqsubseteq \beta$ if α is a prefix of β. Furthermore, we denote by $\text{LCP}(\alpha, \beta)$ the *longest common prefix* of α and β. Let $\text{prefix}(\alpha, i)$ be the first i elements of α.

Let $G = (V, E)$ be a graph with edge lengths $\ell : E \to \mathbb{R}_+$. Let $d_G(u, v)$ or simply $d(u, v)$ denote the shortest-path distance in G between u and v. We write $V(G)$ and $E(G)$ to mean the vertex set and the edge set of G. We represent graphs and trees in a form of adjacency array, where the vertices and the edges are each stored contiguously, and each vertex has a pointer to a contiguous array of pointers to its incident edges. A *hierarchically well-separated tree* (HST) is a rooted tree where the edges from each node to its children have the same length, and the lengths of consecutive edges on any root-leaf path decrease by some factor $\alpha > 1$.

An event happens with high probability (**whp.**) if it happens with probability at least $1 - n^{-\Omega(1)}$. We analyze the algorithms in the PRAM model and use both the EREW (Exclusive Read Exclusive Write) and CRCW (Concurrent Read Concurrent Write), assuming for the CRCW that an arbitrary value is written. By *work*, we mean the total operation count, and by *depth*, we mean the longest chain of dependencies (i.e., parallel time).

A *trie* (also known as a prefix tree) is an ordered tree where each tree edge is marked with a symbol from (constant-sized) Σ and a node v corresponds to the sequence given by the symbols on the root-to-v path, in that order. In this work, we only deal with non-empty sequences $s_1, s_2, \ldots, s_k$ of equal length. The trie corresponding to these sequences is one in which there are k leaf nodes, each corresponding uniquely to one of the sequences. If these sequences have long common prefixes, its trie has many long paths (i.e., a line of non-branching nodes). This can be compressed. Contracting all non-root degree-2 nodes by concatenating the symbols on the incident edges results in a *Patricia tree* (also known as a radix tree), in which by definition, all internal node except the root has degree at least 3. Using a (multiway-)Cartesian tree algorithm of Blelloch and Shun and a known reduction [BS11], the Patricia tree of a lexicographically ordered sequence of strings $s_1, \ldots, s_n$ can be constructed in $O(n)$ work and $O(\log^2 n)$ depth assuming the following as input: (1) the sequences s_i's themselves, (2) $|s_i|$ the

length of each s_i for $i \in [n]$, and (3) $|\text{LCP}(s_i, s_{i+1})|$ the length of the longest common prefix between s_i and s_{i+1} for $i \in [n-1]$.

We also rely on the following primitives on trees. Given a commutative semigroup $(U, *)$, and a rooted tree T (not necessarily balanced) where every node $v \in V(T)$ is tagged with a value $\text{val}(v) \in U$, there is an algorithm $\texttt{treeAgg}$ that computes the aggregate value for each subtree of T (i.e., for each $v \in V(T)$, compute the result of applying $*$ to all $\text{val}(\cdot)$ inside that subtree) in $O(n)$ work and $O(\log n)$ depth, assuming the binary operator $*$ is a constant-time operation [MRK88, JáJ92]. In the same work-depth bounds, the lowest common ancestor (LCA) of a pair of vertices u and v, denoted by $\text{LCA}(u, v)$, can be determined (via the tree primitive just mentioned or otherwise) [SV88, BV93].

Finally, we recall a useful fact about random permutations:

Lemma 2.1 ([Sei92]) *Let* $\pi \colon [n] \to [n]$ *be a random permutation on* $[n]$, *and let* $y_i = \min\{\pi(j) : j = 1, \ldots, i\}$. *Then,* y_i's *form a non-increasing sequence. Moreover, the number of times* y_i's *change to a smaller value is expected* $O(\log n)$. *In fact, it is* $O(\log n)$ *with high probability.*

3. PARALLEL FRT EMBEDDING

An input instance is a finite metric space (X, d), where $|X| = n$ and the symmetric distance function $d(\cdot, \cdot)$ is specified by an n-by-n matrix, normalized so that for all $x \neq y$, $1 \leq d(x, y) \leq \Delta$, where Δ is a power of two (i.e., $\Delta = 2^\delta$). As is standard, we assume that $d(x, x) = 0$.

In the sequential case, FRT [FRT04] developed an elegant algorithm that preserves the distances up to $O(\log n)$ in expectation. Their algorithm can be described as a top-down recursive *low-diameter decomposition* (LDD) of the metric. In broad strokes, the algorithm is given a metric space (X, d) with diameter Δ and it applies an LDD procedure to partition the points into clusters of diameter roughly $\Delta/2$, then each cluster into smaller clusters diameter of $\Delta/4$, etc. This construction produces a laminar family of clusters that we connect up based on set-inclusion, yielding a so-called FRT tree. The algorithm gives an optimal distance-preserving guarantee and as described it can be implemented in $O(n^2 \log n)$ sequential time if $\Delta \leq 2^{O(n)}$.

While the low-diameter decomposition step is readily parallelizable, there is potentially a long chain of dependencies in the tree construction: for each i, determining the clusters with diameter 2^i requires knowing the clusters of diameter 2^{i+1}. This $O(\log \Delta)$ chain is undesirable for large Δ. Our algorithms get rid of this dependence. The main theorem of this section is the following:

Theorem 3.1 (Parallel FRT Embedding) *There is a randomized algorithm that on input a finite metric space* (X, d) *with* $|X| = n$, *produces a tree* T *such that for all* $x, y \in X$, $d(x, y) \leq d_T(x, y)$ *(with probability 1) and* $\mathbf{E}[d_T(x, y)] \leq O(\log n)\, d(x, y)$. *The algorithm runs in* $O(n^2 \log n)$ *work and* $O(\log^2 n)$ *depth* **whp**. *Furthermore, if* $\Delta \leq 2^{O(n)}$, *the algorithm can be improved to run in* $O(n^2)$ *work and* $O(\log^2 n)$ *depth* **whp**.

Remarks. When $\Delta \leq 2^{O(n)}$, the improvement comes from replacing comparison-based sort with parallel radix sort; we describe this in more detail in the algorithm's description.

3.1 FRT Tree as Sequences

To achieve this parallelization, we take a different, though equivalent, view of the FRT algorithm. The main conceptual difference is as follows. Instead of adopting a cluster-centric view which maintains

Algorithm 3.1 Implicit simultaneous low-diameter decompositions

1. Pick a permutation $\pi : X \to [n]$ uniformly at random.
2. Pick $\beta \in [1, 2]$ with the distribution $f_\beta(x) = 1/(x \ln 2)$.
3. For all $v \in X$, compute the partition sequence $\chi_{\pi,\beta}^{(v)}$.

---

a set of clusters that are refined over time, we explore a point-centric view which tracks the movement of each point across clusters but without explicitly representing the clusters. This view can also be seen as representing an FRT tree by the root-to-leaf paths of all external nodes (corresponding to points in the metric space). We formalize this idea in the following definition:

Definition 3.2 ((π, β)-Partition Sequence) *For $v \in X$, the partition sequence of v with respect to a permutation $\pi : X \to [n]$ and a parameter $\beta > 0$, denoted by $\chi_{\pi,\beta}^{(v)}$, is a length-$(\delta + 1)$ sequence such that $\chi_{\pi,\beta}^{(v)}(0) = 1$ and*

$$\chi_{\pi,\beta}^{(v)}(i) = \min\{\pi(w) \mid w \in X, \ d(v,w) \le \beta \cdot 2^{\delta-i-1}\}$$

for $i = 1, \ldots, \delta = \log_2 \Delta$.

For each combination of π and β, each $\chi_{\pi,\beta}^{(v)}$ is the sequence of the lowest-numbered vertices (where the numbering is given by the random permutation π) that the node v can "see" as it reduces its range-of-vision geometrically from Δ down to 0. Thus, these numbers keep increasing from $1 = \min_{w \in X} \pi(w)$ to $\pi(v)$. Hence, the first step in generating an FRT tree is to pick a random permutation π on the nodes and a value β, and compute the partition sequence $\chi_{\beta,\pi}^{(v)}$ for each node $v \in X$, as shown in Algorithm 3.1. These partition sequences encode all the information we need to construct an FRT tree T, which can be done as follows:

Vertices: For $i = 0, \ldots, \delta$, let $L_i = \{\text{prefix}(\chi_{\pi,\beta}^{(v)}, i+1) \mid v \in X\}$ be the i-th level in the tree. The vertices of T are exactly $V(T) = \cup_i L_i$, where each $v \in X$ corresponds to the node identified by the sequence $\chi_{\pi,\beta}^{(v)}$.
Edges: Edges only go between L_i and L_{i+1} for $i \ge 1$. In particular, a node $x \in L_i$ has an edge with length $2^{\delta-i}$ to $y \in L_{i+1}$ if $x \sqsubseteq y$.

This construction yields a tree because edges are between adjacent levels and defined by the subsequence relation. Note that the full $\chi_{\pi,\beta}^{(v)}$ are the leaves of T.

We will show in the following two lemmas distance-preserving properties of the tree T. The first lemma shows that d_T is an upper bound for d; the second shows that d_T preserves the distance d up to a $O(\log n)$ factor in expectation.

Lemma 3.3 *For all $u, v \in X$, for all β, π,*

$$d(u, v) \le d_T(\chi_{\pi,\beta}^{(u)}, \chi_{\pi,\beta}^{(v)}).$$

PROOF. The proof is straightforward and is given for completeness. Let $u, v \in X$ such that $u \ne v$ be given. These nodes are "separated" at a vertex y that is the longest common prefix (LCP) of $\chi^{(u)}$ and $\chi^{(v)}$. Let $i^* = |\text{LCP}(\chi^{(u)}, \chi^{(v)})|$. This means there is a vertex w at distance at most $\beta \cdot 2^{\delta-i^*-1}$ from both u and v, so $d(u, v) \le 2^{\delta-i^*+1}$. On the other hand, both $\chi^{(u)}$ and $\chi^{(v)}$ are in the subtree rooted at y; therefore, $d_T(\chi^{(u)}, \chi^{(v)}) \ge 2 \cdot 2^{\delta-i^*} \ge 2^{\delta-i^*+1}$, which concludes the proof. $\square$

Lemma 3.4 *For all $u, v \in X$,*

$$\mathbf{E}\left[d_T(\chi_{\pi,\beta}^{(u)}, \chi_{\pi,\beta}^{(v)})\right] \le O(\log n) \cdot d(u, v).$$

This process is equivalent to that of [FRT04]. Here, we adapt their proof to our setting. Before beginning the analysis, we state a useful fact: Because β is picked from $[1, 2]$ with the probability density function (pdf.) $\frac{1}{x \ln 2}$, we have

$$\mathbf{Pr}\left[\exists i \ge 1, \beta \cdot 2^{i-1} \in [x, x+dx]\right] \le \frac{dx}{x \ln 2}. \quad (3.1)$$

PROOF. Let distinct $u, v \in X$ be given. In the tree constructed, $\chi^{(u)}$ and $\chi^{(v)}$ will be separated at the least common ancestor (LCA) of the two nodes. At the split point, the two sequences differ for the first time. For the analysis, we will need two definitions: First, we say that $\chi^{(u)}$ and $\chi^{(v)}$ are *split* by $w \in X$ if $\pi(w)$ is the smaller of the two values at the first position where $\chi^{(u)}$ and $\chi^{(v)}$ differ. Second, we say that $w \in X$ is a *lead* of a vertex u if $\pi(w) = \min\{\pi(z) \mid d(u, z) \le d(u, w)\}$ (i.e., w has the smallest π number among points in the ball of radius $d(u, w)$ centered at u).

The crux of the argument is in noticing that u and v are necessarily split by some w, and when this happens, the following must be true:

1. There exists a level i such that $d(w, u) \le \beta \cdot 2^{\delta-i-1} < d(w, v)$ —we assume without loss of generality that $d(w, u) \le d(w, v)$.
2. w is a lead of u or v. (Note that w must be a lead since it is the smaller of the two values at the position where the sequences first differ.)

For each node w, define $\texttt{contrib}_w$ to be the distance in the tree between $\chi^{(u)}$ and $\chi^{(v)}$ assuming w splits u and v. The following claim bounds $\texttt{contrib}_w$ conditioned on w being a lead of u or v:

Claim 3.5 *For any $w \ne u, v$,*

$$\mathbf{E}[\texttt{contrib}_w \mid w \textit{ is a lead of } u \textit{ or } v] \le 8d(u, v).$$

Using this claim, which will be proved below, we can express $\mathbf{E}\left[d_T(\chi^{(u)}, \chi^{(v)})\right]$ as follows: Because we know $d_T(\chi^{(u)}, \chi^{(v)}) \le \sum_w \texttt{contrib}_w$, we have

$$\mathbf{E}\left[d_T(\chi^{(u)}, \chi^{(v)})\right] \le \sum_w \mathbf{E}[\texttt{contrib}_w \mid w \text{ is a lead of } u, v]$$
$$\times \mathbf{Pr}\left[w \text{ is a lead of } u, v\right]$$
$$\le 8d(u, v) \mathbf{E}\left[\sum_w \mathbf{1}_{\{w \text{ is a lead of } u,v\}}\right].$$

To complete the proof, we know from Lemma 2.1 that the number of vertices that could be a lead of u or v is $O(\log n)$ in expectation. Therefore, we conclude that $\mathbf{E}\left[d_T(\chi^{(u)}, \chi^{(v)})\right] \le O(\log n)d(u, v)$. $\square$

PROOF OF CLAIM 3.5. Assume WLOG that $d(w, u) < d(w, v)$. By (3.1), for a particular x between $d(w, u)$ and $d(w, v)$, we know

$$\mathbf{Pr}\left[\exists i \ge 1, \beta \cdot 2^{\delta-i-1} \in [x, x+dx]\right] \le \frac{dx}{x \ln 2}.$$

Furthermore, if u is separated from v at level i, then

$$\texttt{contrib}_w \le 2 \cdot \sum_{i' \ge i} 2^{\delta-i'} = 2^{\delta-i+2} \le 8\beta 2^{\delta-i-1}.$$

This means that the claimed expectation is at most

$$\int_{d(w,u)}^{d(w,v)} \frac{1}{x \ln 2} 8x \, dx \le 8(d(w,v) - d(w,u)) \le 8d(u,v),$$

which concludes the proof. □

3.2 A Simple Parallel FRT Algorithm

We now present a naïve parallelization of the above construction. This naïve version still has the $\log \Delta$ dependence. Notice that a parallel algorithm with such parameters can be inferred directly from [FRT04]; however, the presentation here is instructive: it relies on computing partition sequences and building the tree using them, which will be useful for the improved parallel algorithm in the section that follows.

Lemma 3.6 *Given π and β, each $\chi_{\pi,\beta}^{(v)}$ can be computed in (worst-case) $O((n + \log \Delta) \log n)$ work and $O(\log n)$ depth.*

PROOF. Let $v \in X$, together with π and β, be given. We can sort the vertices by the distance from v so that $v = v_n$ and $d(v,v_1) \ge d(v,v_2) \ge \cdots \ge d(v,v_n) = 0$, where $v_1, \ldots, v_n$ are distinct vertices. This requires $O(n \log n)$ work and $O(\log n)$ depth. Then, we compute $\ell_i = \min\{\pi(v_j) \mid j \ge i\}$ for $i = 1, \ldots, n$. This quantity indicates that by going to distance at least $d(v,v_i)$, the point v could reach a number as low as ℓ_i. This step requires $O(n)$ work and $O(\log n)$ depth (using a prefix computation). Finally, for each $k = 1, \ldots, \delta$, use a binary search to determine the smallest index i (i.e., largest distance) such that $d(v,v_i) \le \beta \cdot 2^{\delta-k-1}$—and $\chi^{(v)}(k)$ is simply ℓ_i. There are $O(\log \Delta)$ such k values, each independently running in $O(\log n)$ depth and work, so this last step requires $O(\log \Delta \log n)$ work and $O(\log n)$ depth, which completes the proof. □

Using this algorithm, we can compute all partition sequences independently in parallel, leading to a total of $O(n(n + \log \Delta) \log n)$ work and $O(\log n)$ depth for computing $\chi^{(v)}$ for all $v \in X$. The next step is to derive an embedding tree from these partition sequences. From the description in the previous section, to compute the set of level-i vertices, we examine all length-i prefixes prefix$(\chi_{\pi,\beta}^{(v)}, i)$ for $v \in X$ and remove duplicates. The edges are easy to derive from the description. Each level i can be done in expected $O(i^2)$ work and $O(\log n)$ depth, so in total we need $O(\log^3 \Delta)$ work and $O(\log n \log \Delta)$ depth in expectation to build the tree from these sequences, proving the following theorem:

Theorem 3.7 *There is an algorithm* simpleParFRT *that computes an FRT tree in expected $O(n^2 \log n + n \log \Delta \log n + \log^3 \Delta)$ work and $O(\log n \log \Delta)$ depth.*

Notice that the naïve algorithm has Δ dependence in both work and depth. While this is fine for small Δ, the depth term can be undesirable for large Δ. For example, when Δ is $2^{O(n)}$, the algorithm has $O(n \log n)$ depth. In the section that follows, we present an algorithm that removes this Δ dependence.

3.3 An Improved Algorithm

The simple algorithm in the preceding section had a $\log \Delta$ dependence in both work and depth. We now show the power of the partition sequence view and derive an algorithm whose work and depth bounds are independent of Δ. Moreover, the algorithm performs the same amount of work as the sequential algorithm.

At first glance, the $\log \Delta$ dependence in the generation of partition sequences in our previous algorithm seems necessary, and the

reason is simple: the length of each partition sequence is $O(\log \Delta)$. To remove this dependence, we work with a different representation of partition sequences, one which has length at most n in the worst case but with high probability, has length $O(\log n)$. This representation is based on the observation that any partition sequence is non-decreasing and its entries are numbers between 1 and n. Consequently, the sequence cannot change values more than n times and we only have to remember where it changes values. Furthermore, by Lemma 2.1, we know that this sequence changes values at most $O(\log n)$ times **whp.** This inspires the following definition:

Definition 3.8 (Compressed Partition Sequence) *For $v \in X$, the compressed partition sequence of v, denoted by $\sigma_{\pi,\beta}^{(v)}$, is the unique sequence $\langle (s_i, p_i) \rangle_{i=1}^k$ such that $1 = s_1 < \cdots < s_k < s_{k+1} = \delta + 1$, $p_1 < p_2 < \cdots < p_k$, and for all $i \le k$ and $j \in \{s_i, s_i + 1, \ldots, s_{i+1} - 1\}$, $\chi_{\pi,\beta}^{(v)}(j) = p_i$, where $\chi_{\pi,\beta}^{(v)}$ is the partition sequence of v.*

In words, if we view π as assigning priority values to X, then the compressed partition sequence of v tracks the distance scales at which the lowest-valued vertex within reach from v changes. As an example, at distances $\beta \cdot 2^{\delta-s_1+1}, \beta \cdot 2^{\delta-(s_1+1)+1}, \ldots, \beta \cdot 2^{\delta-(s_2-1)+1}$, the lowest-valued vertex within reach of v is p_1—and $\beta \cdot 2^{\delta-s_2+1}$ is the first distance scale at which p_1 cannot be reached and $p_2 > p_1$ becomes the new lowest-valued node. The following lemma shows how to efficiently compute the compressed partition sequence of a given vertex.

Lemma 3.9 *Given π and β, each compressed partition sequence $\sigma_{\pi,\beta}^{(v)}$ can be computed in (worst-case) $O(n \log n)$ work and $O(\log n)$ depth. Furthermore, if $\Delta \le 2^{O(n)}$, this can be improved to $O(n)$ work and $O(\log n)$ depth **whp.***

PROOF. The idea is similar to that of the partition sequence, except for how we derive the sequence at the end. Let $v \in X$, together with π and β, be given. Sort the vertices by the distance from v so that $v = v_n$ and $d(v,v_1) \ge d(v,v_2) \ge \cdots \ge d(v,v_n)$, where $v_1, \ldots, v_n$ are distinct vertices. This has $O(n \log n)$ work and $O(\log n)$ depth—or, if $\Delta \le 2^{O(n)}$, this can be done in $O(n)$ work and $O(\log n)$ depth since the distance scales then can be identified by numbers between 0 and $O(n)$, which can be efficiently sorted using parallel radix sort [RR89]. Again, compute $\ell_i = \min\{\pi(v_j) \mid j \ge i\}$ for $i = 1, \ldots, n$. Furthermore, let $b_i = \max\{j \ge 1 \mid \beta \cdot 2^{\delta-j-1} \ge d(v,v_i)\}$ for all $i = 1, \ldots, n$. This index b_i represents the smallest distance scale that v can still see v_i. Then, we compute $\rho_i = \min\{\ell_j \mid b_j = b_i\}$. Because the b_i's are non-decreasing, computing ρ_i's amounts to identifying where b_i's change values and performing a prefix computation. Thus, the sequences ℓ_i's, b_i's, and ρ_i's can be computed in $O(n)$ work and $O(\log n)$ depth.

To derive the compressed partition sequence, we look for all indices i such that $\rho_{i-1} \ne \rho_i$ and $b_{i-1} \ne b_i$—these are precisely the distance scales at which the current lowest-numbered vertex becomes unreachable from v. These indices can be found in $O(n)$ work and $O(1)$ depth, and using standard techniques involving prefix sums, we put them next to each other in the desired format. □

We will now construct an FRT tree from these compressed partition sequences. Notice that to keep the work term independent of $\log \Delta$, we cannot, for example, explicitly write out all the nodes. The FRT tree has to be in a specific "compressed" format for the construction to be efficient. For this reason, we will store the resulting FRT tree in a compressed format. A *compacted FRT tree* is obtained by contracting all degree-2 internal nodes of an FRT tree, so that every internal node except for the root has degree at least 3 (a single parent and at least 2 children). By adding the weights of merged edges, the compacting preserves the distance between every pair of leaves. Equivalently, an FRT tree as described earlier is in fact a trie with the partition sequences as its input—and a compacted FRT tree is a *Patricia (or radix) tree on these partition sequences*.

Our task is therefore to construct a Patricia tree given compressed partition sequences. As discussed in Section 2, the Patricia tree of a *lexicographically ordered* sequence of strings $s_1, \ldots, s_n$ can be constructed in $O(n)$ work and $O(\log^2 n)$ depth if we have the following as input: (1) $|s_i|$ the length of each s_i for $i \in [n]$, and (2) $\text{LCP}(s_i, s_{i+1})$ the length of the longest common prefix between s_i and s_{i+1} for $i \in [n-1]$. These sequences can be lexicographically ordered in no more than $O(n \log^2 n)$ work[2] and $O(\log^2 n)$ depth **whp.** and the LCP between all adjacent pairs can be computed in $O(n^2)$ work and $O(\log n)$ depth. Combining this with the Patricia tree algorithm [BS11] gives the promised bounds, concluding the proof of Theorem 3.1.

3.4 FRT Tree Without Steiner Vertices

Some applications call for a tree embedding solution that consists of only the original input vertices. To this end, we describe how to convert a compacted FRT tree from the previous section into a tree that contains no Steiner vertices. As a byproduct, the resulting non-Steiner tree has $O(\log n)$ depth with high probability.

Theorem 3.10 *There is an algorithm* FRTNoSteiner *running in* $O(n^2 \log n)$ *work and* $O(\log^2 n)$ *depth* **whp.** *that on input an n-point metric space (X, d), produces a tree T such that (1) $V(T) = X$; (2) T has $O(\log n)$ depth* **whp.**; *and (3) for all $x, y \in X$, $d(x, y) \le d_T(x, y)$ and $\mathbf{E}\left[d_T(x, y)\right] \le O(\log n)\, d(x, y)$. Furthermore, the bounds can be improved to $O(n^2)$ work and $O(\log^2 n)$ depth* **whp.** *if $\Delta \le 2^{O(n)}$.*

We begin by recalling that each leaf of an FRT tree corresponds to a node in the original metric space, so there is a bijection $f : L_\delta \to X$. Now consider an FRT tree T on which we will perform the following transformation: (1) obtain T' by multiply all the edge lengths of T by 2, (2) for each node $x \in V(T')$, label it with $\text{label}(x) = \min\{\pi(f(y)) \mid y \in \text{leaves}(T'_x)\}$, where $\text{leaves}(T'_x)$ is the set of leaf nodes in the subtree of T' rooted at x, and (3) construct T'' from T' by setting an edge to length 0 if the endpoints are given the same label—but retaining the length otherwise. The following lemma bounds the depth of the resulting tree T'' (the proof appears in the appendix).

Lemma 3.11 *The depth of T'' is $O(\log n)$ with high probability.*

Several things are clear from this transformation: First, for all $u, v \in X$, $d(u, v) \le d_{T'}(\chi^{(u)}, \chi^{(v)})$ and

$$\mathbf{E}\left[d_{T'}(\chi^{(u)}, \chi^{(v)})\right] \le O(\log n)\, d(u, v)$$

(of course, with worse constants than d_T). Second, T'' is no longer an HST, but $d_{T''}$ is a lowerbound on $d_{T'}$ (i.e., for all $u, v \in X$, $d_{T''}(\chi^{(u)}, \chi^{(v)}) \le d_{T'}(\chi^{(u)}, \chi^{(v)})$). Therefore, to prove distance-preserving guarantees similar to Theorem 3.1, we only have to show that $d_{T''}$ dominates d (the proof appears in Appendix A).

Lemma 3.12 *For all $u, v \in X$, $d(u, v) \le d_{T''}(\chi^{(u)}, \chi^{(v)})$.*

---

[2] The length of the compressed partition sequence of v is upperbounded by the number of times the sequence $y_i = \min\{\pi(v_j) \mid n - 1 \ge j \ge i\}$ changes value. By Lemma 2.1, this is at most $O(\log n)$ **whp.**

On a compacted FRT tree, this transformation is easy to perform. First, we identify all leaves with their corresponding original nodes. Computing the label for all nodes can be done in $O(n)$ work and $O(\log n)$ depth using treeAgg (Section 2), which is a variant of tree contraction. Finally, we just have to contract zero-length edges, which again, can be done in $O(n)$ work and $O(\log n)$ depth using standard tree-contraction techniques [JáJ92]. Notice that we only have to compute the minimum on the nodes of a compacted tree, because the label (i.e., the minimum value) never changes unless the tree branches.

4. THE K-MEDIAN PROBLEM

The k-median problem is a standard clustering problem, which has received considerable attention from various research communities. The input to this problem is a set of vertices $V \subseteq X$, where (X, d) is a (finite) metric space, and the goal is to find a set of at most k centers $F_S \subseteq V$ that minimizes the objective

$$\Phi(F_S) = \sum_{j \in V} d(j, F_S).$$

Since we will be working with multiple metric spaces, we will write $\Phi_D(F_S) = \sum_{j \in V} D(j, F_S)$ to emphasize which distance function is being used. In the sequential setting, several approximation algorithms are known, including $O(1)$-approximations (see [AGK+04] and the references therein) and approximation via tree embeddings [Bar98, FRT04]. In the parallel setting, these algorithms seem hard to parallelize directly: to our knowledge, the only RNC algorithm for k-median gives a $(5 + \varepsilon)$-approximation but only achieves polylogarithmic depth when k is at most $\text{polylog}(n)$ [BT10].

Our goal is to obtain an $O(\log k)$-approximation that *has polylogarithmic depth for all k* and has essentially the same work bound as the sequential counterpart. The basic idea is to apply bottom-up dynamic programming to solve k-median on a tree, like in Bartal's paper [Bar98]. Later, we describe a sampling procedure to improve the approximation guarantee from $O(\log n)$ to $O(\log k)$. While dynamic programming was relatively straightforward to apply in the sequential setting, more care is needed in the parallel case: the height of a compacted FRT tree can be large, and since the dynamic program essentially considers tree vertices level by level, the total depth could be much larger than $\text{polylog}(n)$.

Rather than working with compacted FRT trees, we will be using FRT trees that contain no Steiner node, constructed by the algorithm FRTNoSteiner in Theorem 3.10. This type of trees is shown to have the same distance-preserving properties as an FRT tree but has $O(\log n)$ depth with high probability. Alternatively, we give an algorithm that reduces the depth of a compacted FRT tree to $O(\log n)$; this construction, which assumes the HST property, is presented in Appendix B and may be of independent interest.

4.1 Solving k-Median on Trees

Our second ingredient is a parallel algorithm for solving k-median when the distance metric is the shortest-path distance in a (shallow) tree. For this, we will parallelize a dynamic programming (DP) algorithm of Tamir [Tam96], which we now sketch. Tamir presented a $O(kn^2)$ algorithm for a slight generalization of k-median on trees, where in his setting, each node $i \in V$ is associated with a cost c_i if it were to be chosen; every node i also comes equipped with a nondecreasing function f_i; and the goal becomes to find a set $A \subseteq V$ of size at most k to minimize

$$\sum_{i \in A} c_i + \sum_{j \in V} \min_{i \in A} f_j(d(v_j, v_i)).$$

This generalization (which also generalizes the facility-location problem) provides a convenient way of taking care of Steiner nodes in an FRT tree. For our purpose, these f_i's will simply be the identity function[3] $x \mapsto x$, and c_i's are set so that it is 0 if i is a real node from the original instance and ∞ if i is a Steiner node (to prevent it from being chosen).

Tamir's algorithm is a DP which solves the problem exactly, but it requires the input tree to be binary. While Tamir also gave an algorithm that converts any tree into a binary tree, his approach can significantly increase the depth of the tree. For our setting, *we need a different algorithm that ensures not only that the tree is binary but also that the depth does not grow substantially.* The simplest solution is to replace each node that has outdegree d with a perfect binary tree with d leaves; this can increase the depth of the tree from $O(\log n)$ to $O(\log^2 n)$ in the worst case. But this increase can be avoided. We give a parallel algorithm based on the Shannon-Fano code construction [Sha48], as detailed in Section 4.2 below, which outputs a binary tree whose depth is an additive $\log n$ larger than the original depth. Then, we set edge lengths as follows: The new edges will have length 0 except for the edges incident to the original v_i's: the parent edge incident to v_i will inherit the edge length from $v_i v$. Also, the added nodes have cost ∞. As a result of this transformation, the depth of the new tree is at most $O(\log n)$ and the number of nodes will at most double.

The main body of Tamir's algorithm begins by producing for each node v a sequence of vertices that orders all vertices by their distances from v with ties appropriately broken. His algorithm for generating these sequences are readily parallelizable because the sequence for a vertex v involves merging the sequences of its children in a manner similar to the merge step in merge sort. The work for this step, as originally analyzed, is $O(n^2)$. Each merge can be done in $O(\log n)$ depth and there are at most $O(\log n)$ levels; this step has depth $O(\log^2 n)$.

4.2 Making Trees Binary

Given a tree T with n nodes and depth h but of arbitrary fanout, we give a construction that yields a tree with depth $O(h + \log n)$. In contrast, the simpler alternative that replaces each node that has fanout d with a perfect binary tree with d leaves produces a tree with depth $O(h \log n)$ in the worst case. Instead, our algorithm makes use of a well-known idea, which goes back to a construction of Shannon and Fano [Sha48]: For each original tree node v with children $v_1, \ldots, v_k$, we assign to v_i the "probability"

$$p_i = \frac{|V(T_{v_i})|}{|V(T_v)|},$$

where T_u denotes the subtree of T rooted at u. Shannon and Fano's result implies that there is a binary tree whose external nodes are exactly these $v_1, \ldots, v_k$, and the path from v to v_i in this binary tree has length at most $1 + \log(1/p_i)$. Applying this construction on all nodes with degree more than 2 gives the following lemma:

Lemma 4.1 *Given a tree T with n nodes and depth h but of arbitrary fanout, there is an algorithm* treeBinarize *producing a binary tree with depth at most $h + \log n$.*

PROOF. Let w be a leaf node in T and consider the path from the root node to w. Suppose on this path, the subtrees have sizes $n = n_1 > n_2 > \cdots > n_{d'} = 1$, where $d' \leq h$. Applying the aforementioned construction, this path expands to a path of length

[3]In the weighted case, we will use $f_i(x) = w_i \cdot x$ to reflect the weight on node i.

at most

$$1 + \sum_{i=1}^{d'-1} \left(1 + \log(\tfrac{1}{p_i}) \right) = 1 + \sum_{i=1}^{d'-1} \left(1 + \log(\tfrac{n_i}{n_{i+1}}) \right)$$
$$\leq d' + \log n$$
$$\leq h + \log n,$$

which proves the lemma. □

This construction is also directly parallelizable as all that is needed is sorting the probabilities in decreasing order (so that $p_1 \geq p_2 \geq \cdots p_k$), computing the cumulative probabilities (i.e., $P_i = \sum_{i' \leq i} p_i$), finding the point where the cumulative probability splits in (roughly) half, and recursively applying the algorithm on the two sides. Since each call involves a sort and a prefix computation, and the total number of children is $O(n)$, the transformation on the whole tree will take $O(n \log n)$ work and $O(\log^2 n)$ depth.

4.3 Paralellizing the DP Step

Armed with this, the actual DP is straightforward to parallelize. Tamir's algorithm maintains two tables F and G, both indexed by a tuple (i, q, r) where $i \in [n]$ represents a node, $q \leq k$ counts the number of centers inside the subtree rooted at i, and r indicates roughly the distance from i to the closest selected center outside of the subtree rooted at i. As such, for each i and q, there can be at most n different values for r. Now Tamir's DP is amendable to parallelization because the rules of the DP compute an entry using *only* the values of its immediate children. Further, each rule is essentially taking the minimum over a combination of parameters and can be parallelized using standard algorithms for finding the minimum and prefix sums. Therefore, we can compute the table entries for each level of the tree and move on to a higher level. It is easy to show that each level can be accomplished in $O(\log n)$ depth, and as analyzed in Tamir's paper, the total work is bounded by $O(kn^2)$.

4.4 Parallel Successive Sampling

Our algorithm thus far gives an $O(\log n)$-approximation on input consisting of n points. To improve it to $O(\log k)$, we devise a parallel version of Mettu and Plaxton's successive sampling (shown in Algorithm 4.1) [MP04]. We then describe how to apply it to our problem. Since the parallel version produces an identical output to the sequential one, guarantees about the output follow directly from the results of Mettu and Plaxton. Specifically, they showed that there are suitable settings of α and β such that by using $K = \max\{k, \log n\}$, the algorithm SuccSampling$_{\alpha, \beta}(V, K)$ runs for $O(\log(n/K))$ rounds and produces Q of size at most $O(K \cdot \log(n/K))$ with the following properties:

Theorem 4.2 (Mettu and Plaxton [MP04]) *There exists an absolute constant C_{SS} such that if $Q = $ SuccSampling (V, K), then with high probability, Q satisfies $\Phi(Q) \leq C_{SS} \cdot \Phi(OPT_k)$, where OPT_k is an optimal k-median solution on the instance V.*

In other words, the theorem says that Q is a bicriteria approximation which uses $O(K \log(n/K))$ centers and obtains a C_{SS}-approximation to k-median. To obtain a parallel implementation of successive sampling (Algorithm 4.1), we will make steps 1–3 parallel. We have the following runtime bounds:

Lemma 4.3 *For $|V| = n$ and $K \leq n$, SuccSampling(V, K) has $O(nK)$ work and $O(\log^2 n)$ depth **whp**.*

Algorithm 4.1 `SuccSampling`$_{\alpha,\beta}(V, K)$—successive sampling

---
Let $U_0 = V$, $i = 0$
while $(|U_i| > \alpha K)$
1. Sample from U_i u.a.r. (with replacement) $\lfloor \alpha K \rfloor$ times—call the chosen points S_i.
2. Compute the smallest r_i such that $|B_{U_i}(S_i, r_i)| \geq \beta \cdot |U_i|$ and let $C_i = B_{U_i}(S_i, r_i)$, where $B_U(S, r) = \{w \in U \mid d(w, S) \leq r\}$.
3. Let $U_{i+1} = U_i \setminus C_i$ and $i = i + 1$.
Output $Q = S_0 \cup S_1 \cup \cdots \cup S_{i-1} \cup U_i$

PROOF. First, by the choice of C_i, we remove at least a β fraction of U_i and since α and β are constants, we know that the number of iterations of the **while** loop is $O(\log(n/K))$. Now step 1 of the algorithm can be done in $O(nK)$ work and $O(1)$ depth (assuming concurrent writes). To perform Step 2, first, we compute for each $p \in U_i$, the distance to the nearest point in S_i. This takes $O(|U_i|K)$ work and $O(\log K)$ depth. Then, using a linear-work selection algorithm, we can find the set C_i and r_i in $O(|U_i|)$ work and $O(\log |U_i|)$ depth. Since each time $|U_i|$ shrinks by a factor β, the total work is $O(nK)$ and the total depth is $O(\log^2 n)$. $\square$

Piecing together the components developed so far, we obtain an expected $O(\log k)$-approximation. The following theorem summarizes our main result for the k-median problem:

Theorem 4.4 *For $k \geq \log n$, there is a randomized algorithm for the k-median problem that produces an expected $O(\log k)$-approximate solution running in $O(nk + k(k\log(\frac{n}{k}))^2) \leq O(kn^2)$ work and $O(\log^2 n)$ depth **whp**. For $k < \log n$, the problem admits an expected $O(1)$-approximation with $O(n\log n + k^2 \log^5 n)$ work and $O(\log^2 n)$ depth **whp**.*

Here is a proof sketch, see Appendix A.1 for more details: we first apply Algorithm 4.1 to get the set Q (in $O(nK)$ work and $O(\log^2 n)$ depth, Lemma 4.3). Then, we "snap" the clients to their closest centers in Q (paying at most $C_{SS}\,\Phi(\mathrm{OPT}_k)$ for this), and depending on the range of k, either use an existing parallel k-median algorithm for $k < \log n$ [BT10] or use the FRT-based algorithm on these "moved" clients to get the $O(\log q)$-approximation (in $O(kq^2)$ work and $O(\log^2 q)$ depth, where $q = O(K\log(n/K))$, because we are running the algorithm only on $O(K\log(n/K))$ points). Note that we now need a version of the k-median algorithm on trees (Section 4.1) where clients also have weights, but this is easy to do (by changing the f_i's to reflect the weights).

5. BUY-AT-BULK NETWORK DESIGN

In this section, we explore another application of our parallel probabilistic tree embedding algorithm. Let $G = (V, E)$ be an undirected graph with n nodes; edge lengths $\ell : E \to \mathbb{R}_+$; a set of k demand pairs $\{\mathsf{dem}_{s_i,t_i}\}_{i=1}^k$; and a set of cables, where cable of type i has capacity u_i and costs c_i per unit length. The goal of the problem is to find the cheapest set of cables that satisfy the capacity requirements and connect each pair of demands by a path. Awerbuch and Azar [AA97] gave a $O(\log n)$-approximation algorithm in the sequential setting. Their algorithm essentially finds an embedding of the shortest-path metric on G into a distribution of trees *with no Steiner nodes*, a property which they exploit when assigning each tree edge to a path in the input graph. For an edge with net demand dem, the algorithm chooses the cable type that

minimizes $c_i \lceil \mathsf{dem}/u_i \rceil$. This is shown to be an expected $O(\log n)$-approximation. From a closer inspection, their algorithm can be parallelized by developing parallel algorithms for the following:

1. Given a graph G with edge lengths $\ell : E(G) \to \mathbb{R}_+$, compute a dominating tree T with no Steiner node such that T $O(\log n)$-probabilistically approximate d in expectation.
2. For each $(u, v) \in E(T)$, derive the shortest path between u and v in G.
3. For each $e \in E(T)$, compute the net demand that uses this edge, i.e., $f_e = \sum_{i : e \in P_T(s_i, t_i)} \mathsf{dem}_{s_i, t_i}$, where $P_T(u, v)$ denotes the unique path between u and v in T.

We consider these in turn. First, the shortest-path metric d can be computed using a standard all-pair shortest paths algorithm in $O(n^3 \log n)$ work and $O(\log^2 n)$ depth. With this, we apply the algorithm in Section 3.4 to produce a dominating tree T in which d_T $O(\log n)$-probabilistically approximates d. Furthermore, for each tree edge $e = (u, v)$, the shortest path between u and v can be obtained from the calculation performed to derive d at no extra cost.

Next we describe how to calculate the net demand on every tree edge. We give a simple parallel algorithm using the `treeAgg` primitive discussed in Section 2. As a first step, we identify for each pair of demands its least common ancestor (LCA), where we let $\mathrm{LCA}(u, v)$ be the LCA of u and v. This can be done in $O(n)$ work and $O(\log n)$ depth for each pair. Thus, we can compute the LCA for all demand pairs in $O(n + k\log n)$ work and $O(\log n)$ depth. As input to the second round, we maintain a variable $\mathrm{up}(w)$ for each node w of the tree. Then, for every demand pair $\mathsf{dem}_{u,v}$, we add to both $\mathrm{up}(u)$ and $\mathrm{up}(v)$ the amount of $\mathsf{dem}_{u,v}$—and to $\mathrm{up}(\mathrm{LCA}(u, v))$ the *negative* amount $-2\mathsf{dem}_{u,v}$. As such, the sum of all the values up inside a subtree rooted at u is the amount of "upward" flow on the edge out of u toward the root. This is also the net demand on this edge. Therefore, the demand f_e's for all $e \in E(T)$ can be computed in $O(n + k\log n)$ work and $O(\log n)$ depth. Finally, mapping these back to G and figuring out the cable type (i.e., computing $\min_i c_i \lceil \mathsf{dem}/u_i \rceil$) are straightforward and no more expensive than computing the all-pair shortest paths. Hence, we have the following theorem with the cost broken down by components:

Theorem 5.1 *If the all-pairs shortest path problem on G can be solved in W_{APSP} work and D_{APSP} depth and an FRT tree with no steiner node can be computed in W_{FRT} work and D_{FRT}, then there is a randomized algorithm for the buy-at-bulk network design problem with k demand pairs on an n-node graph that runs in $O(W_{\text{APSP}} + W_{\text{FRT}} + n + k\log n)$ work and $O(D_{\text{APSP}} + D_{\text{FRT}} + \log n)$ depth and produces an expected $O(\log n)$-approximation.*

This means that using the standard $O(n^3 \log n)$-work, $O(\log^2 n)$-depth algorithm for the all-pairs shortest path computation, and using our FRT algorithm, we have an expected $O(\log n)$-approximation for the buy-at-bulk network design problem that runs in $O(n^3 \log n)$ work and $O(\log^2 n)$ depth **whp**. If, on the other hand, the input already contains the all-pairs shortest paths distances, our algorithm runs in $O(n^2 \log n)$ work and and $O(\log^2 n)$ depth **whp**.

6. CONCLUSION

We gave an efficient parallel algorithm for tree embedding with $O(\log n)$ expected stretch. Our contribution is in making these bounds independent of the ratio of the smallest to largest distance, by recognizing an alternative view of the FRT algorithm and developing an efficient algorithm to exploit it. Using the embedding algorithms, we developed the first RNC $O(\log k)$-approximation algorithm for k-median and an RNC $O(\log n)$-approximation for buy-at-bulk network design.

Acknowledgments

This work is partially supported by the National Science Foundation under grant numbers CCF-0964474, CCF-1016799, and CCF-1018188 and by generous gifts from IBM and Intel Labs Academic Research Office for Parallel Algorithms for Non-Numeric Computing. We thank the SPAA reviewers for their comments that helped improve this paper.

References

[AA97]   Baruch Awerbuch and Yossi Azar. Buy-at-bulk network design. In *Proceedings of the 38thFOCS*, pages 542–547, 1997.

[AGK+04] Vijay Arya, Naveen Garg, Rohit Khandekar, Adam Meyerson, Kamesh Munagala, and Vinayaka Pandit. Local search heuristics for k-median and facility location problems. *SIAM J. Comput.*, 33(3):544–562, 2004.

[AKPW95] Noga Alon, Richard M. Karp, David Peleg, and Douglas West. A graph-theoretic game and its application to the k-server problem. *SIAM J. Comput.*, 24(1):78–100, 1995.

[Bar96]   Yair Bartal. Probabilistic approximations of metric spaces and its algorithmic applications. In *Proceedings of the 37thFOCS*, pages 184–193, 1996.

[Bar98]   Yair Bartal. On approximating arbitrary metrics by tree metrics. In *Proceedings of the 30th ACM Symposium on the Theory of Computing (STOC)*, pages 161–168, 1998.

[BS11]   Guy E. Blelloch and Julian Shun. A simple parallel cartesian tree algorithm and its application to suffix tree construction. In *ALENEX*, pages 48–58, 2011.

[BT10]   Guy E. Blelloch and Kanat Tangwongsan. Parallel approximation algorithms for facility-location problems. In *SPAA*, pages 315–324, 2010.

[BV93]   Omer Berkman and Uzi Vishkin. Recursive star-tree parallel data structure. *SIAM J. Comput.*, 22(2):221–242, 1993.

[FRT04]   Jittat Fakcharoenphol, Satish Rao, and Kunal Talwar. A tight bound on approximating arbitrary metrics by tree metrics. *J. Comput. System Sci.*, 69(3):485–497, 2004.

[JáJ92]   Joseph JáJá. *An Introduction to Parallel Algorithms*. Addison-Wesley, 1992.

[MP04]   Ramgopal R. Mettu and C. Greg Plaxton. Optimal time bounds for approximate clustering. *Machine Learning*, 56(1-3):35–60, 2004.

[MRK88]   Gary L. Miller, Vijaya Ramachandran, and Erich Kaltofen. Efficient parallel evaluation of straight-line code and arithmetic circuits. *SIAM J. Comput.*, 17(4):687–695, 1988.

[RR89]   Sanguthevar Rajasekaran and John H. Reif. Optimal and sublogarithmic time randomized parallel sorting algorithms. *SIAM J. Comput.*, 18(3):594–607, 1989.

[Sei92]   Raimund Seidel. Backwards analysis of randomized geometric algorithms. In *Trends in Discrete and Computational Geometry, volume 10 of Algorithms and Combinatorics*, pages 37–68. Springer-Verlag, 1992.

[Sha48]   C. E. Shannon. A Mathematical Theory of Communication. *Bell System Technical Journal*, 27, 1948.

[SV88]   Baruch Schieber and Uzi Vishkin. On finding lowest common ancestors: Simplification and parallelization. *SIAM J. Comput.*, 17(6):1253–1262, 1988.

[Tam96]   Arie Tamir. An $O(pn^2)$ algorithm for the p-median and related problems on tree graphs. *Operations Research Letters*, 19(2):59–64, 1996.

APPENDIX

A. VARIOUS PROOFS

PROOF OF LEMMA 3.12. Let $u \neq v \in X$ be given and let $y = \text{LCP}(\chi^{(u)}, \chi^{(v)})$. In T'' (also T and T'), y is the lowest common ancestor of $\chi^{(u)}$ and $\chi^{(v)}$. Let $i^* = |\text{LCP}(\chi^{(u)}, \chi^{(v)})|$. This means there is a vertex w at distance at most $\beta \cdot 2^{\delta - i^* - 1}$ from both u and v, so $d(u, v) \leq 2^{\delta - i^* + 1}$. Now let a (resp. b) be the child of y such that T_a (resp. T_b) contains $\chi^{(u)}$ (resp. $\chi^{(v)}$). So then, we argue that $d_{T''}(\chi^{(u)}, \chi^{(v)}) \geq 2 \cdot 2^{\delta - i^*}$ because label(y) must differ from at least one of the labels label(a) and label(b)— and such non-zero edges have length $2^{\delta - i^* + 1}$ since we doubled its length in Step (1). This establishes the stated bound. □

PROOF OF LEMMA 3.11. The depth of T'' is upperbounded by the length of the longest compressed partition sequence. Consider a vertex $v \in X$ and let $v_1, \ldots, v_{n-1} \in X$ be such that $d(v, v_1) > d(v, v_2) > \cdots > d(v, v_{n-1}) > 0$. The length of the compressed partition sequence of v is upperbounded by the number of times the sequence $y_i = \min\{\pi(v_j) \mid n - 1 \geq j \geq i\}$ changes value. By Lemma 2.1, this is at most $O(\log n)$ **whp**. Taking union bounds gives the desired lemma. □

A.1 Piecing Together the k-median Algorithm

A.1.1 Case I: $k \geq \log n$:

Let $Q = \{q_1, \ldots, q_K\} = \text{SuccSampling}(V, K)$, where $K = \max\{k, \log n\}$ and $\varphi : V \to Q$ be the mapping that sends each $v \in V$ to the closest point in Q (breaking ties arbitrarily). Thus, $\varphi^{-1}(q_1), \varphi^{-1}(q_2), \ldots, \varphi^{-1}(q_K)$ form a collection of K non-intersecting clusters that partition V. For $i = 1, \ldots, K$, we define $w(q_i) = |\varphi^{-1}(q_i)|$. We prove a lemma that relates a solution's cost in Q to the cost in the original space (V, d).

Lemma A.1 *Let $A \subseteq Q \subseteq V$ be a set of k centers satisfying*

$$\sum_{i=1}^{K} w(q_i) \cdot d(q_i, A) \leq \beta \cdot \min_{\substack{X \subseteq Q \\ |X| \leq k}} \sum_{i=1}^{K} w(q_i) \cdot d(q_i, X)$$

for some $\beta \geq 1$. Then,

$$\Phi(A) = \sum_{x \in V} d(x, A) \leq O(\beta \cdot c_{SS}) \cdot \Phi(OPT_k),$$

where OPT_k, as defined earlier, is an optimal k-median solution on V.

PROOF. For convenience, let

$$\lambda = \sum_{x \in V} d(x, Q) = \sum_{x \in V} d(x, \varphi(x)),$$

and so $\lambda \le c_{SS} \cdot \Phi(\text{OPT}_k)$. We establish the following:

$$
\begin{aligned}
\sum_{x \in V} d(x, A) &\le \lambda + \sum_{i=1}^{K} w(q_i) \cdot d(q_i, A) \\
&\le \lambda + \beta \cdot \min_{\substack{X \subseteq Q \\ |X| \le k}} \sum_{i=1}^{K} w(q_i) \cdot d(q_i, X) \\
&\le \lambda + \beta \sum_{i=1}^{K} w(q_i) \cdot d(q_i, \varphi(\text{OPT}_k)) \\
&\le \lambda + 2\beta \sum_{i=1}^{K} w(q_i) \cdot d(q_i, \text{OPT}_k) \\
&\le \lambda + 2\beta \sum_{i=1}^{K} \sum_{x \in \varphi^{-1}(q_i)} \Big(d(q_i, x) + d(x, \text{OPT}_k) \Big) \\
&\le \lambda + 2\beta\lambda + 2\beta\Phi(\text{OPT}_k) \\
&= O(\beta \cdot c_{SS}) \cdot \Phi(\text{OPT}_k),
\end{aligned}
$$

which proves the lemma. $\qquad\square$

By this lemma, the fact that the k-median on tree gives a $O(\log |Q|)$-approximation, and the observation that $|Q| \le k^2$ (because $k \ge \log n$), we have that our approximation is $O(\log k)$.

A.1.2 Case II: $k < \log n$:

We run successive sampling as before, but this time, we will use the parallel local-search algorithm [BT10] instead. On input consisting of n points, the BT algorithm has $O(k^2 n^2 \log n)$ work and $O(\log^2 n)$ depth. Since $k < \log n$, we have $K = \log n$ and the successive sampling algorithm would give $|Q| \le \log^2 n$. This means we have an algorithm with total work $O(n \log n + k^2 \log^5 n)$ and depth $O(\log^2 n)$.

B. TREE TRIMMING FOR K-MEDIAN

Another way to control the height of the tree is by taking advantage of a cruder solution (which can be computed inexpensively) to prune the tree. The first observation is that if $A \subseteq V$ is a ρ-approximation to k-center, then A is a ρn-approximation to k-median. Using a parallel k-center algorithm [BT10], we can find a 2-approximation to k-center in $O(n \log^2 n)$ work and $O(\log^2 n)$ depth. This means that we can compute a value β such that if OPT is an optimal k-median solution, then $\Phi(\text{OPT}) \le \beta \le 2n \cdot \Phi(\text{OPT})$.

Following this observation, two things are immediate when we consider an *uncompacted* FRT tree:

1. If we are aiming for a $C \cdot \log n$ approximation, no clients could go to distance more than than $C \cdot \log n \cdot \Phi(\text{OPT}) \le C \cdot n\beta$. This shows twe can remove the top portion of the tree where the edge lengths are more than $Cn\beta$.
2. If a tree edge is shorter than $\tau = \frac{\beta}{8n^2}$, we could set its length to 0 without significantly affecting the solution's quality. These 0-length edges can be contracted together. Because an FRT tree as constructed in Theorem 3.1 is a 2-HST, it can be shown that if T' is obtained from an FRT tree T by the contraction process described, then for all $x \ne y$, $d_T(x, y) \le d_{T'}(x, y) + 4\tau$.

Both transformations can be performed on compacted trees in $O(n)$ work and $O(\log n)$ depth, and the resulting tree will have height at most $O(\log(8n^3)) = O(\log n)$. Furthermore, if $A \subseteq V$ is any k-median solution, then

$$
\begin{aligned}
\Phi_d(A) \le \Phi_{d_T}(A) &= \sum_{x \in V} d_T(x, A) \\
&\le \sum_{x \in V} \Big(d_{T'}(x, A) + 4t \Big) \\
&\le \Phi_{d_{T'}}(A) + n \cdot \frac{\beta}{2n^2} \\
&\le \Phi_{d_{T'}}(A) + \Phi_d(\text{OPT}).
\end{aligned}
$$

A Parallel Buffer Tree

Nodari Sitchinava
Institite for Theoretical Informatics
Karlsruhe Institute of Technology
nodari@ira.uka.de

Norbert Zeh[*]
Faculty of Computer Science
Dalhousie University
nzeh@cs.dal.ca

ABSTRACT

We present the *parallel buffer tree*, a parallel external memory (PEM) data structure for batched search problems. This data structure is a non-trivial extension of Arge's sequential buffer tree to a private-cache multiprocessor environment and reduces the number of I/O operations by the number of available processor cores compared to its sequential counterpart, thereby taking full advantage of multicore parallelism.

The parallel buffer tree is a search tree data structure that supports the batched parallel processing of a sequence of N insertions, deletions, membership queries, and range queries in the optimal $O(\text{sort}_P(N) + K/PB)$ parallel I/O complexity, where K is the size of the output reported in the process and $\text{sort}_P(N)$ is the parallel I/O complexity of sorting N elements using P processors.

Categories and Subject Descriptors

E.1 [**Data Structures**]: Trees; F.1.2 [**Computation by Abstract Devices**]: Modes of Computation—*Parallelism and Concurrency*

General Terms

Algorithms, Theory

Keywords

Parallel external memory model, PEM model, buffer tree, batched data structures, parallel data structures, parallel buffer tree, parallel buffered range tree

1. INTRODUCTION

Parallel (multicore) processors have become the standard even for desktop systems. This spawned a renewed focus on parallel algorithms, with a particular focus on multicore systems. The main difference between modern multicore processors and previous models for parallel computing is the combination of a shared memory, much like in the PRAM model, and private caches of the cores that cannot be accessed by any other core. The cache architectures of current multicore chips vary. Some provide a flat model where each processor has its private cache and all processors have access to a shared memory. Others provide a hierarchical cache structure where intermediate cache levels are added and subsets of processors share access to caches at these levels.

Several models have been proposed to capture the hierarchical memory design of modern parallel architectures to a varying degree [6, 10, 11, 14, 21]. Private-cache models are the simplest among them and assume a 2-level memory hierarchy: a fast *private cache* for each processor and a slow *shared memory*. While these models may not accurately represent the full memory hierarchy of most multicores, every multicore architecture has private caches at some level of the memory hierarchy, as well as RAM shared by all processors, which is typically much slower. Thus, private-cache models focus on the common denominator of multicore processors and are useful for the development of techniques to utilize the private caches on such processors.

In this paper, we work in one such private-cache model: the *parallel external memory (PEM) model* [6,19]. The PEM model is a natural extension of the widely accepted *I/O model* [1] to multiple processors/processor cores. In this model, the computer has P processors, each with its own private *cache* of size M. Each processor can access only its own cache. At the same time, all processors have access to a *shared memory* of conceptually unlimited size. All computation steps carried out by a processor have to happen on data present in its cache. Data is transferred between shared memory and the processors' caches using (parallel) *I/O operations* (I/Os). In one I/O operation, each processor can transfer one block of B consecutive data items between its cache and shared memory. The complexity of an algorithm in the PEM model is the number of such parallel I/O operations it performs. Throughout this paper, we assume *block-level concurrent read, exclusive write* access, that is, multiple processors may read the same block of data simultaneously, but a block written by one processor during an I/O operation may not be accessed (read or written) by another processor during the same I/O operation, even if the two processors access different addresses within the block.

[*]Supported by NSERC and the Canada Research Chairs programme.

Permission to make digital or hard copies of all or part of this work for personal or classroom use is granted without fee provided that copies are not made or distributed for profit or commercial advantage and that copies bear this notice and the full citation on the first page. To copy otherwise, to republish, to post on servers or to redistribute to lists, requires prior specific permission and/or a fee.
SPAA'12, June 25–27, 2012, Pittsburgh, Pennsylvania, USA.
Copyright 2012 ACM 978-1-4503-1213-4/12/06 ...$10.00.

1.1 Our Results

We present the *parallel buffer tree*, a batched data structure that is able to process a sequence of N INSERT, DELETE, FIND, and RANGEQUERY operations in the optimal number of $O(\text{sort}_P(N) + K/PB)$ parallel I/Os, where K is the total output size produced by all queries. This structure is an extension of the sequential buffer tree [5] to the PEM model. The sequential buffer tree has been used as a basis for a wide range of sequential I/O-efficient algorithms (see, for example, Arge's survey [4]). By extending this data structure to the PEM model, we provide an important first step towards enabling analogous solutions to these problems in the PEM model.

1.2 Previous Work

The first problems studied in the PEM model were fundamental problems such as sorting, scanning, and computing prefix sums. Sorting in the PEM model takes $\text{sort}_P(N) = O\left(\frac{N}{PB}\log_{M/B}\frac{N}{B}\right)$ I/Os, provided $P \le N/B^2$ and $M = B^{O(1)}$ [6,19]. Scanning a sequence of N elements and computing prefix sums take $O(\log P + N/PB)$ I/Os, which equals $O(N/PB)$ whenever $N \ge P\log P$. Subsequent papers in this model studied graph algorithms [7] and some geometric problems [2,3]. Other related papers explored the connection between cache-oblivious algorithms and private-cache architectures and proposed general techniques for translating cache-oblivious algorithms into algorithms for private- and mixed-cache architectures [10,11,13,14]. None of these results immediately leads to a buffer tree for private cache models because no cache-oblivious equivalent of the buffer tree is known.

Sequential search structures are ubiquitous in computer science. The B-tree [8] is widely used in database systems for fast searching of data stored on disk. The proliferation of parallelism particularly through multicore processors has led to a recognition in the research community that strictly sequential data structures quickly become a bottleneck in applications that can otherwise benefit greatly from multicore parallelism, including database systems. One approach to alleviate this bottleneck is the support of *concurrency*, where multiple processors are allowed to access and manipulate the data structure simultaneously. The support of concurrency in B-trees has been investigated extensively in the database community (for example, see [20] and references therein). More recently, cache-oblivious concurrent B-trees were proposed in [9].

While certainly related and motivated by the same trend in modern computer architectures, these results do not address the problem studied in this paper: how to process a *sequence* of operations, as opposed to individual operations, as quickly as possible. Just as the sequential buffer tree [5], the parallel buffer tree may delay the answering of queries but ensures that queries produce the same answer as if they had been answered immediately. This is crucial for achieving the I/O bound stated in Section 1.1 because processing each query immediately requires at least one I/O per query, even if it produces very little output. The structures discussed in the previous paragraph and even structures designed to efficiently support batched updates [18] answer queries immediately and, thus, cannot achieve an optimal I/O complexity for processing a sequence of operations.

Concurrency also provides much looser support for paral-

lel processing than explicitly *parallel* data structures, such as the parallel buffer tree presented in this paper. Concurrency only allows multiple processors to operate simultaneously *and independently* on the data structure. In a parallel data structure, on the other hand, processors *cooperate* to speed up the processing of updates and queries. In the PRAM model, several parallel search tree data structures were proposed [12,16,17]. However, these structures are not I/O-efficient, as they makes use of random access to the shared memory provided by the PRAM model.

2. PRIMITIVES

Two primitives we use extensively in our algorithms are the merging of two sorted sequences and the distribution of a sorted sequence of elements into buckets. The next two lemmas state the complexities of these operations.

LEMMA 1. *Two sorted sequences S_1 and S_2 can be merged using* $O\left(\left\lceil\frac{|S_1|+|S_2|}{PB}\right\rceil + \log P\right)$ *I/Os.*

PROOF. The algorithm is shown in Figure 1. Choosing the subsequences S_1' and S_2' in Step 1 takes $O(1)$ I/Os, and merging these subsequences to obtain S' takes $O(\log P)$ I/Os. Each subsequence $S_{(a,b)}$ to be produced by a processor in Step 2 is contained in the union of two subsequences of S_1 and S_2 bounded by consecutive elements in S_1' and S_2'. Thus, a single processor can produce $S_{(a,b)}$ using $O\left(\left\lceil\frac{|S_1|+|S_2|}{PB}\right\rceil\right)$ I/Os, and each processor has to produce only two such sequences. This leaves the issue of concatenating these sequences to obtain the final merged sequence S. Using a prefix sum computation on the lengths of these sequences $S_{(a,b)}$, we can compute the position of each subsequence $S_{(a,b)}$ in S. This takes $O(\log P)$ I/Os. Given these positions, each processor can write $S_{(a,b)}$ to the correct blocks in S. The only issue to be resolved is when multiple processors try to write to the same block. in this case, at most P processors try to write to the same block, and the portions of S to be written to this block by different processors can be merged using $O(\log P)$ I/Os. □

LEMMA 2. *A sorted sequence of N elements can be distributed to k buckets delimited by a sorted sequence R of $k-1$ pivot elements using* $O\left(\left\lceil\frac{N+k}{PB}\right\rceil + \lceil k/P\rceil + \log P\right)$ *I/Os.*

PROOF. The algorithm is shown in Figure 2. By Lemma 1, the I/O complexity of the first step is $O\left(\left\lceil\frac{N+k}{PB}\right\rceil + \log P\right)$. Step 2 can be accomplished by using a prefix sum computation to annotate each element of S with the index of the last pivot that precedes it. The same prefix sum computation can be used to count the number of elements of S between every pair of consecutive pivot elements in the merged list (Step 3). Using a similar technique, we can separate the elements of S into two lists, one containing full blocks of B elements to be sent to the same bucket, and the second one containing one block per bucket, which stores the remaining less than B elements to be sent to this bucket. Step 4 distributes the blocks of the first list to the buckets. Step 5 distributes the elements of the non-full blocks to the buckets. In each step, we allocate the same number of blocks from the respective lists to each processor. Since there are at most k non-full blocks, the last three steps take $O((N/PB) + \lceil k/P\rceil + \log P)$ I/Os. The lemma follows. □

MERGE(S_1, S_2):
1. Choose P evenly spaced elements from each of S_1 and S_2 and merge the resulting two subsequences S_1' and S_2' to obtain a sequence S'.
2. Assign two pairs of consecutive elements in S' to each processor. Each such pair (a, b) delimits a subsequence $S_{(a,b)}$ of the merged sequence $S = S_1 \cup S_2$ that contains all elements $x \in S$ with $a \leq x < b$. The processor that is assigned the pair (a, b) produces the subsequence $S_{(a,b)}$ of the output sequence S.

Figure 1: Merging two sorted sequences S_1 and S_2

DISTRIBUTE(S, R):
1. Merge the sets S and $\{r_0\} \cup R$ using Lemma 1, where $r_0 = -\infty$.
2. Annotate each element in S with the bucket i where it should be sent.
3. Compute the number of items to be sent to each bucket.
4. Distribute full blocks of B items.
5. Distribute the non-full blocks (at most one per bucket).

Figure 2: Distributing a sorted sequence S of N items to a set of k buckets defined by pivots $R = \{r_1, \cdots, r_{k-1}\}$

3. THE PARALLEL BUFFER TREE

In this section, we describe the basic structure of the parallel buffer tree and show how to support INSERT, DELETE, and FIND operations. In Section 4, we show how to extend the structure to support RANGEQUERY operations. The input is a sequence of N INSERT, DELETE, and FIND operations. An INSERT(x) operation inserts element x into the buffer tree, a DELETE(x) operation removes it, and a FIND(x) operation needs to decide whether x is in the buffer tree at the time of the query.[1] All these operations may be delayed—in particular, the answers to FIND queries may be produced much later than the queries are asked—but the results of all queries must be the same as if all operations were carried out immediately. More precisely, a FIND(x) query answers yes if and only if the last operation affecting x and preceding this FIND(x) query in the input sequence is an INSERT(x) operation.

We show how to process any sequence of N such operations using O($\text{sort}_P(N)$) parallel I/Os. Note that we could achieve this simply by sorting the operations in the sequence primarily by the elements they affect and secondarily by their positions in the sequence of operations (time stamps) and then applying a parallel prefix sum computation to the resulting sequence of operations. This is indeed what we do at each node of the buffer tree. However, we use the buffer tree to answer range queries in Section 4, a problem that cannot be solved in this naïve manner.

The parallel buffer tree is an (a, b)-tree with parameters $a = f/4$ and $b = f$, for some branching parameter $f \geq PB$, that is, all leaves are at the same distance from the root, every non-root internal node has between $f/4$ and f children, and the root r has between 2 and f children. Each leaf of the tree stores $\Theta(B)$ elements, so the height of the tree is O($\log_f(N/B)$). Each non-leaf node v has an associated buffer $\mathcal{B}_v$ of size $\Theta(g)$, where $g = fB$, which is stored in shared memory. We call an internal (i.e., non-leaf) node a *fringe node* if its children are leaves of the tree. As in a standard (a, b)-tree, every internal node v with children $w_1, w_2, \ldots, w_k$ stores $k - 1$ *routing elements*

$r_1, r_2, \ldots, r_{k-1}$, which separate the children of v: each routing element r_i is no less than the elements stored in w_i's descendant leaves and no greater than the elements in w_{i+1}'s descendant leaves.

We assume the sequence of operations is provided to the buffer tree in batches of PB operations.[2] Each operation is annotated with a time stamp indicating its position in the sequence of operations. We do not require the operations in each batch to be sorted by their time stamps, which potentially makes the parallel generation of these batches of operations easier, but we do require that any operation in a batch has a greater time stamp than any operation in a preceding batch. For each batch $\mathcal{O}$ of PB operations, we assign one processor to each block of B operations in $\mathcal{O}$, and the processor inserts this block into the root buffer $\mathcal{B}_r$. If $\mathcal{B}_r$ contains more than g operations, we apply the buffer emptying procedure NONFRINGEEMPTY (Figure 3) to r, to distribute the operations in $\mathcal{B}_r$ to the buffers of r's children. For each child v whose buffer overflows as a result of receiving additional operations, we invoke NONFRINGEEMPTY(v) recursively unless v is a fringe node. Every fringe node whose buffer overflows is added to a list $\mathcal{F}$ of full fringe nodes. Once the recursive application of the buffer emptying procedure for non-fringe nodes finishes, we apply the buffer emptying procedure FRINGEEMPTY (Figure 4) to the nodes in $\mathcal{F}$, one at a time. Part of the work done by this procedure is rebalancing the tree to reflect the creation/destruction of leaves as a result of the insertion/deletion of data items.

This general approach of propagating operations down the tree in a batched fashion is identical to the approach used in the sequential buffer tree [5]. The difference lies in the implementation of the steps of the two buffer emptying procedures, which need to distribute the work across processors. Next we discuss these two procedures in more detail.

3.1 Emptying Non-Fringe Buffers

The buffer emptying procedure for non-fringe internal nodes is shown in Figure 3. The goal of Step 1 is to sort $\mathcal{B}_v$. This can be done as described in the algorithm because all but the first at most g elements in $\mathcal{B}_v$ were inserted into $\mathcal{B}_v$

---

[1] Alternatively, we could require a FIND(x) operation to report information associated with x in the tree. Either of these variants of the FIND operation are equally easy/hard to support.

[2] We cannot control how the sequence of operations is produced by an application using the buffer tree. If the entire sequence of operations is given up front, it is easy to divide this sequence into batches of size PB.

NONFRINGEEMPTY(v):

1. Divide $\mathcal{B}_v$ into two parts $\mathcal{B}'_v$ and $\mathcal{B}''_v$. $\mathcal{B}'_v$ contains the first g elements in $\mathcal{B}_v$, $\mathcal{B}''_v$ the remaining elements. Sort the elements in $\mathcal{B}'_v$ primarily by their keys and secondarily by their time stamps and merge the resulting list with $\mathcal{B}''_v$ by running MERGE($\mathcal{B}'_v, \mathcal{B}''_v$) (Figure 1).
2. Answer and eliminate FIND queries with matching INSERT or DELETE operations in $\mathcal{B}_v$ and eliminate matching INSERT and DELETE operations in $\mathcal{B}_v$.
3. Distribute the remaining elements in $\mathcal{B}_v$ to the buffers of v's children by running DISTRIBUTE($\mathcal{B}_v, R_v$) (Figure 2), where R_v is the set of routing elements at node v.
4. For every child w of v whose buffer $\mathcal{B}_w$ now contains more than g operations, invoke NONFRINGEEMPTY(w) recursively unless w is a fringe node. If $\mathcal{B}_w$ contains more than g elements and w is a fringe node, append w to the list $\mathcal{F}$ of full fringe nodes.

Figure 3: The buffer emptying procedure for non-fringe internal nodes

FRINGEEMPTY(v):

1. Sort the operations in $\mathcal{B}_v$.
2. Merge the operations in $\mathcal{B}_v$ with the elements stored in v's children, treating each such element as an INSERT operation with time stamp $-\infty$. Then remove matching INSERT and DELETE operations and answer FIND queries. Finally, replace every INSERT operation in the list without a matching DELETE operation with the element it inserts. The resulting list is the list of elements E_v to be stored in v's children.
3. Populate v's children:
   3.1. If $g/4 \leq |E_v| \leq g$, store the elements of E_v in $f/4 \leq \lceil E_v/B \rceil \leq f$ leaves and make them the new children of v.
   3.2. If $|E_v| \leq g/4$, store the elements of E_v in $\lceil E_v/B \rceil$ leaves, make these leaves the new children of v, and add v to a list $\mathcal{U}$ of underfull fringe nodes.
   3.3. If $|E_v| > g$, partition E_v into groups of $g/2$ elements. If the last group has less than $g/4$ elements, merge it with the previous group to obtain a group with between $g/2$ and $3g/4$ elements. The $f/2$ blocks in the first group become the new children of v. For each subsequent group, one at a time, create a new fringe node w, make the blocks in the group w's children, make w a sibling of v, and rebalance the tree using node splits as necessary.

Figure 4: The buffer emptying procedure for fringe nodes

by a single buffer emptying operation applied to v's parent and, hence, are already sorted. The elimination of matching INSERT and DELETE operations in Step 2 takes a single prefix sum computation on the sorted sequence of elements in $\mathcal{B}_v$. We can answer a FIND(x) operation in $\mathcal{B}_v$ without propagating it further down the tree if it is preceded by an INSERT(x) or DELETE(x) operation in $\mathcal{B}_v$. In the former case, x is in the tree at the time of the FIND(x) operation; in the latter, it is not. This condition can be checked and the FIND(x) operation eliminated in the same prefix sum computation used to eliminate matching INSERT and DELETE operations. If there is no INSERT(x) or DELETE(x) operation in $\mathcal{B}_v$ preceding the FIND(x) operation, the FIND(x) operation needs to be propagated to the appropriate child.

LEMMA 3. *Emptying the buffer $\mathcal{B}_v$ of a non-fringe internal node and placing these operations into the buffers of v's children takes $O(\lceil X/g \rceil \cdot \mathrm{sort}_P(g))$ I/Os, where X is the number of operations in $\mathcal{B}_v$.*

PROOF. It takes $O(\mathrm{sort}_P(g))$ I/Os to sort the first g elements in $\mathcal{B}_v$. By Lemmas 1 and 2 and because $f = g/B \leq X/B$, the remainder of the procedure takes $O(X/PB + \log P) = O(\lceil X/g \rceil \cdot \mathrm{sort}_P(g))$ I/Os. □

3.2 Emptying Fringe Buffers

After recursively emptying the buffers of non-fringe internal nodes as discussed in Section 3.1, we now process the full fringe nodes in $\mathcal{F}$ one at a time. For each such node v, it is guaranteed that the buffers of its ancestors in the tree are empty, a fact we use when performing node splits or fusions to rebalance the tree.

To empty the buffer of a fringe node v, we invoke the buffer emptying procedure in Figure 4. As in the sequential buffer tree, we first compute the set of elements to be stored in v's children. If this requires fewer or more children than the node currently has, we add or remove children. When adding leaves makes it necessary to rebalance the tree, we do so immediately. When deleting leaves decreases the degree of a fringe node v to less than $f/4$, on the other hand, we add v to a list $\mathcal{U}$ of underful fringe nodes to be rebalanced after the buffers of all fringe nodes in $\mathcal{F}$ have been emptied. The main difference to the sequential buffer tree is that we cannot perform these leaf additions/deletions one leaf at a time.

The sorting of $\mathcal{B}_v$ in Step 1 and the merging of $\mathcal{B}_v$ with the elements in v's children in Step 2 can be implemented as when emptying the buffer of a non-fringe node. In Step 3, making the blocks in a partition of E_v the children of v or of a new fringe node w requires the construction of a list of pointers to these nodes to be stored with v or w. This can be done using a prefix sum computation on the elements in each such group of blocks and thus takes $O(g/(PB) + \log P) = O(\mathrm{sort}_P(g))$ I/Os. Every node split necessary to rebalance the tree can be implemented using $O(\mathrm{sort}_P(g))$ I/Os in a similar fashion.

Once we have applied procedure FRINGEEMPTY to all nodes in $\mathcal{F}$, we process the underfull fringe nodes in $\mathcal{U}$, i.e., nodes that have fewer than $f/4$ children. For each such node v, we traverse the path from v to the root and perform node fusions until we reach a node that is no longer underfull. For a node w to be fused with a sibling, we first empty the buffers of its two immediate siblings. If this triggers recursive buffer emptying steps and adds new overfull fringe nodes to $\mathcal{F}$, we first process these nodes before continuing the processing of w. Then we choose an immediate sibling w' of w and replace w and w' with a single node that has the children of w and w' as its children. If this new node now has more than f children, we split it into two nodes again. Similarly to node splits, a node fusion takes $O(\text{sort}_P(g))$ I/Os, as it involves emptying two buffers with less than g elements in them and concatenating the $O(f)$ routing elements and child pointers of two nodes. (Note that if emptying the siblings' buffers triggers recursive buffer emptying operations, this is the result of these buffers overflowing and thus can be charged to the elements in these buffers that are pushed one level down the tree.)

THEOREM 1. *The parallel buffer tree can process a sequence of N INSERT, DELETE, and FIND operations using $O(\text{sort}_P(N))$ parallel I/Os.*

PROOF. By Lemma 3, emptying each non-fringe buffer containing $X \geq g$ elements takes $O((X/g) \cdot \text{sort}_P(g))$ I/Os. A similar analysis proves the same bound for emptying a fringe buffer. Since each element is involved in one such buffer emptying procedure per level and the height of the tree is $O(\log_f(N/B))$, the total cost of emptying buffers is $O((N/g) \cdot \text{sort}_P(g) \cdot \log_f(N/B)) = O(\text{sort}_P(N))$ I/Os.

Since every new fringe node we create has at least $g/2$ and at most $3g/4$ elements in its children, and we split/fuse such a node only when its children store more than g or less than $g/4$ elements, the total number of fringe nodes we create/destroy during a sequence of N updates is $O(N/g)$. Using the analysis of (a,b)-trees from [15], this implies that the total number of node splits/fusions is $O(N/g)$. Since each such rebalancing operation costs $O(\text{sort}_P(g))$ I/Os, the total rebalancing cost is also $O(\text{sort}_P(N))$ I/Os.

Finally, after inserting the last batch of operations into the root buffer, some operations may remain in buffers of internal nodes without being pushed down the tree because the buffers containing them have not overflowed. We force a buffer emptying procedure on each node of the tree in a top-down fashion. This causes at most one buffer emptying operation per node that cannot be charged to an overflowing buffer and hence to the elements in the buffer. Since there are $O(N/g)$ internal nodes in the tree, the cost of these forced buffer emptying operations is also $O(\text{sort}_P(N))$. $\square$

4. SUPPORTING RANGE QUERIES

In this section, we show how to support range queries on the parallel buffer tree. Each such RANGEQUERY(x_1, x_2) operation is represented by its query range $[x_1, x_2]$ and is to report all elements that have been inserted before the time of the query, fall within the query range $[x_1, x_2]$, and have not been deleted before the time of the query. As in [5], we assume the sequence of operations to be applied to the buffer tree is *well-formed* in the sense that every INSERT operation inserts an element that *is not* in the buffer tree at the time of the operation, and every DELETE operation deletes an element that *is* in the buffer tree at the time of the operation.

To answer range queries, we again follow the framework of the sequential buffer tree [5], modifying the buffer emptying processes for internal nodes to utilize all available processors. As in [5], the output of each query may be reported in parts, during different buffer emptying operations. In other words, the result of processing a sequence of INSERT, DELETE, and RANGEQUERY operations is an unordered sequence of query-element pairs (q, x), where x is part of the output of query q as defined at the beginning of this section.

We associate a range $\mathcal{R}_v$ with every node v in the buffer tree. For the root r, we define $\mathcal{R}_r := (-\infty, +\infty)$. For each child w_i of a node v with range $\mathcal{R}_v = [x_1, x_2]$, with children $w_1, w_2, \ldots, w_k$, and with routing elements $r_1, r_2, \ldots, r_{k-1}$, we define $\mathcal{R}_{w_i} := [r_{i-1}, r_i]$, where $r_0 := x_1$ and $r_k := x_2$. When emptying the buffer $\mathcal{B}_v$ of a node v with children $w_1, w_2, \ldots, w_k$, we consider all range queries $[x_1, x_2]$ in $\mathcal{B}_v$ and all children w_i of v such that $\mathcal{R}_{w_i} \subseteq [x_1, x_2]$. We output the elements in each such node w_i's subtree that are alive at the time of the query and then forward the query to the buffers of the two children w_h and w_j such that $x_1 \in \mathcal{R}_{w_h}$ and $x_2 \in \mathcal{R}_{w_j}$. One of the endpoints of the query may be outside the range $\mathcal{R}_v$, in which case only one of the nodes w_h and w_j exists.

4.1 Time Order Representation

To support range queries, the sequential buffer tree introduced a *time order representation* of a sequence S' of INSERT, DELETE, and RANGEQUERY operations. We employ the same representation here. In this representation, all DELETE operations are "older" (have an earlier time stamp) than all RANGEQUERY operations, which in turn are older than all INSERT operations. The elements in each of these three groups are ordered by their keys (by their left endpoints in the case of RANGEQUERY operations). The main property of this representation is that the RANGEQUERY operations in S' cannot report any elements affected by INSERT or DELETE operations in S', which follows from the well-formedness of the sequence of operations given to the buffer tree. In general, of course, the input sequence S of the buffer tree is not in time order representation—otherwise range queries would never produce any output. The central operation needed to support range queries on the buffer tree is to transform various subsequences of S into time order representation and report matching query-element pairs in the process. A single sorting step suffices to bring the elements in such a subsequence S' into time order representation. To report the necessary query-element pairs, the sequential buffer tree implements this sorting step using pairwise element swaps, employing the following rules to report matching query-element pairs and eliminate matching pairs of INSERT and DELETE operations. Let o_1 and o_2 be two adjacent operations in S' to be swapped, with o_1 preceding o_2.

- If o_1 is an INSERT operation and o_2 is a DELETE operation affecting the same element, all range queries precede the insertion or succeed the deletion. Thus, o_1 and o_2 can be discarded.

- If o_1 is an INSERT(x) operation and o_2 is a RANGEQUERY(x_1, x_2) operation with $x \in [x_1, x_2]$, then the deletion of x succeeds the range query. Thus, we report x as part of the query's output and then swap the two operations.

- If o_1 is a RANGEQUERY(x_1, x_2) operation and o_2 is a DELETE(x) operation with $x \in [x_1, x_2]$, then the insertion of x precedes the range query. Thus, we report x as part of the query's output and then swap the two operations.

- Any other pair of operations o_1 and o_2 is swapped without any special action being taken.

This construction of a time order representation is inherently sequential. Our first step towards supporting range queries on a parallel buffer tree is to show how to construct a time order representation efficiently in parallel.

LEMMA 4. *Provided $g \geq PB^2 \log^2 P$, a sequence of g operations can be brought into time order representation using $O(\text{sort}_P(g) + K'/PB)$ I/Os and $O(g + K')$ space, while also reporting all K' elements that need to be reported according to the swapping rules just discussed.*

PROOF. As already discussed, once all pairs of matching INSERT and DELETE operations have been eliminated, a single sorting step suffices to transform the sequence into time order representation. This takes $O(\text{sort}_P(g))$ I/Os. Thus, it suffices to discuss how to eliminate these matching pairs of INSERT and DELETE operations and how to report matching query-element pairs before sorting the sequence.

To do the latter, we use the connection between range queries and orthogonal line segment intersection. We map every range query q with query interval $[x_1, x_2]$ and time stamp t to the horizontal segment with endpoints (x_1, t) and (x_2, t). Similarly, we map every element x inserted at time t_1 and deleted at time t_2 to the vertical segment with endpoints (x, t_1) and (x, t_2). Element x is to be reported by query q if and only if the two segments intersect. Thus, to report all matching query-element pairs in the current sequence, we construct this set of horizontal and vertical segments and apply the PEM orthogonal line segment intersection algorithm of [3] to report their intersections using $O(\text{sort}_P(g) + K'/PB)$ I/Os and $O(g + K')$ space, where K' is the number of intersections found. Constructing the horizontal segments corresponding to range queries is trivial. To construct the vertical segments corresponding to input elements, we sort the operations so that range queries succeed insertions and deletions and so that insertions and deletions are sorted primarily by the elements they affect and secondarily by their time stamps. Let S be the resulting sequence. We turn every matching pair of consecutive INSERT and DELETE operations into a vertical segment. Every DELETE(x) operation at time t not preceded by an INSERT(x) operation is represented as a segment with top endpoint (x, t) and bottom endpoint $(x, -\infty)$. Every INSERT(x) operation at time t not succeeded by a DELETE(x) operation is represented as a segment with bottom endpoint (x, t) and top endpoint $(x, +\infty)$. We apply a parallel prefix sum computation to S to eliminate matching INSERT and DELETE operations immediately prior to sorting the remaining operations in time order. $\square$

LEMMA 5. *Let S_1 and S_2 be two operation sequences in time order representation, with all elements in S_2 older than all elements in S_1. The time order representation of $S_1 \cup S_2$ can be constructed using $O\left(\frac{|S_1| + |S_2|}{g} \cdot \text{sort}_P(g) + K/PB\right)$ I/Os and $O(g + K)$ space, where K is the number of elements reported in the process.*

PROOF. We "merge" S_1 and S_2 using the algorithm in Figure 5. The correctness proof of this procedure is straightforward and therefore omitted. By Lemma 1, Steps 1 and 4 take $O\left(\frac{|S_1| + |S_2|}{PB} + \log P\right) = O\left(\frac{|S_1| + |S_2|}{g} \cdot \text{sort}_P(g)\right)$ I/Os.

Step 3 is identical to Step 2. Thus, it suffices to analyze Step 2. The total cost of splitting list L in Step 2.2.1 is $O((N + K)/PB)$ I/Os because every element in L either becomes part of L' or of L''. In the former case, it adds at least one element to the output. In the latter case, this is the last iteration it is part of L. Every invocation of the line segment intersection algorithm on $2g$ elements in Step 2.2.2 can be charged either to g queries in L'' or to the g deletions in D'. Hence, the total cost of Step 2.2.2 is $O\left(\frac{|S_1| + |S_2|}{g} \cdot \text{sort}_P(g) + K/PB\right)$ I/Os. In Step 2.2.3, we report at least one query-element pair per deletion in D'. Since D' contains $g \geq PB$ deletions unless this is the last batch, it is trivial to report the query-element pairs in this step using $O(K/PB)$ I/Os. Every iteration of Step 2.2.4 except the last can be charged to g queries retrieved from Q_2. Hence, the total cost of this step is also $O\left(\frac{|S_1| + |S_2|}{g} \cdot \text{sort}_P(g) + K/PB\right)$ I/Os. $\square$

LEMMA 6. *Let $\mathcal{T}$ be a parallel buffered range tree with N/B leaves and at most g elements in each buffer. Emptying all buffers of $\mathcal{T}$ and collecting their operations in time order representation takes $O\left(\text{sort}_P(g) \sum_{x \in \mathcal{T}} h_x + (N + K)/PB\right)$ I/Os, where the sum is over all operations x in buffers of $\mathcal{T}$, h_x is the distance of the buffer storing operation x from the leaf level, and K is the number of elements reported in the process.*

PROOF. The algorithm is almost the same as for the sequential buffer tree, except that we use Lemmas 1, 4, and 5 to implement its basic steps efficiently in parallel.

First we collect the buffer contents of the nodes on each level in a single sequence. This takes $O(N/PB)$ I/Os. Since each buffer contains at most g operations, we can divide the sequence representing each level into subsequences of $\Theta(g)$ elements such that each buffer content is contained in one such subsequence. By Lemma 4, we can transform all of these subsequences into time order representation using $O((X/g)\text{sort}_P(g) + K/PB)$ I/Os, where X is the total number of operations in $\mathcal{T}$'s buffers. Next we concatenate the deletion, range query, and insertion sequences of the time order representations at each level to obtain a single time order representation of all operations at this level. This takes $O(X/(PB) + \log P) = O((X/g)\text{sort}_P(g))$ I/Os. Let $S_1, S_2, \ldots, S_k$ be the resulting time order sequences of all levels, sorted from the fringe nodes to the root. The operations in S_{i+1} are younger than the operations in S_i, for all $1 \leq i < k$. Thus, we can apply Lemma 5 to merge S_{i+1} into S_i, for $i = k - 1, k - 2, \ldots, 1$. Each such merge step has cost $O\left(\frac{|S_i| + |S_{i+1}|}{g} \cdot \text{sort}_P(g) + K'/PB\right)$ I/Os, where K' is the size of the output it produces. Since each operation in a sequence S_i participates in i such merge steps, the lemma follows. $\square$

4.2 Emptying Buffers

The buffer emptying process is similar to the one in the sequential buffer tree. The main difference is that we use the results from Section 4.1 to construct time order representations as needed and that we need to ensure the reporting of output elements during each buffer emptying process is distributed evenly across processors. As in Section 3, the buffer emptying processes for non-fringe and fringe nodes differ. These procedures are shown in Figures 6 and 7.

TIMEORDERMERGE(S_1, S_2):

1. Merge the subsequences D_1 and I_2 of deletions in S_1 and insertions in S_2 using Lemma 1, delete matching INSERT and DELETE operations, and arrange the remaining insertions and deletions in time order $D_1'I_2'$ using a parallel scan of the merged list to split it into two output streams D_1' and I_2'.

2. Swap the sequences D_1' and Q_2 and report all pairs ($[x_1, x_2], x$) such that Q_2 contains a range query with interval $[x_1, x_2]$ and D_1' contains a DELETE(x) operation with $x \in [x_1, x_2]$. The swapping of D_1' and Q_2 is easily achieved using a parallel scan. We report the query answers as follows:

   2.1. Create a list L of "long" queries. Initially, this list is empty.

   2.2. Divide D_1' into batches of g deletions. For each batch D', do the following:

      2.2.1. Using a parallel scan of L, divide L into two lists L' and L'' such that all queries in L' have their right endpoints to the right of the last element in D' and the queries in L'' do not.

      2.2.2. Divide L'' into batches of size g and, for each batch, report the queries in the batch containing each element in D' using orthogonal line segment intersection as in Lemma 4. After processing all elements in L'' in this fashion, discard L''.

      2.2.3. Every query in L' contains all elements in D'. Distribute the elements in D' evenly across processors. Then let each processor report the query-element pairs defined by its assigned deletions and the queries in L'. After processing L' in this fashion, set $L := L'$.

      2.2.4. While the next element in Q_2 has a left boundary no greater than the rightmost deletion in D', read the next batch Q' of queries from Q_2. Run the line segment intersection algorithm on D' and Q' to report all matches between queries in Q' and deletions in D'. Then apply a parallel scan to Q' to identify all queries whose right endpoints are to the right of the rightmost deletion in D'. Append these queries to L.

3. Swap the sequences I_2' and Q_2 and report all pairs ($[x_1, x_2], x$) such that Q_1 contains a range query with interval $[x_1, x_2]$ and I_2' contains an INSERT(x) operation with $x \in [x_1, x_2]$. This is analogous to Step 2.

4. Merge D_1' with D_2, Q_1 with Q_2, and I_1 with I_2' using Lemma 1.

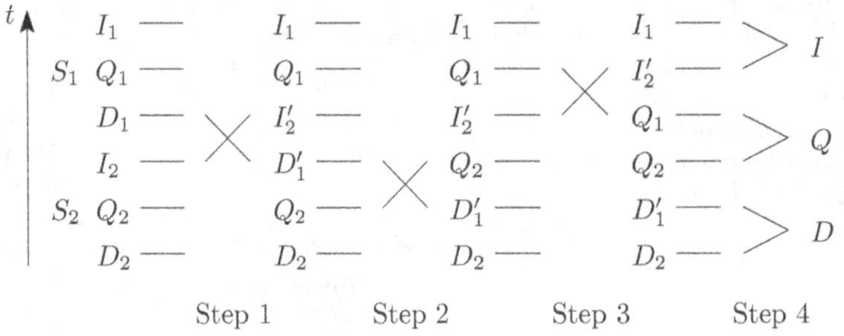

Figure 5: Merging two sequences $S_1 = D_1 Q_1 I_1$ and $S_2 = D_2 Q_2 I_2$ in time order representation

To empty the buffer $\mathcal{B}_v$ of a non-fringe node v, we first compute its time order representation (Step 1) and distribute the DELETE operations in the resulting sequence to the children of v (Step 2). Then we inspect the range queries in $\mathcal{B}_v$ and identify all children w_i of v that are spanned by at least one range query in $\mathcal{B}_v$ (Step 3). We do this by merging the set of range queries in $\mathcal{B}_v$ with the set of children of v, each represented by its range $\mathcal{R}_{w_i}$. In the resulting list, the range queries and children of v are sorted by the left endpoints of their ranges. A prefix sum computation now suffices to label each child w_i of v with the rightmost right boundary of any range query preceding $\mathcal{R}_{w_i}$ in the merged list. $\mathcal{B}_v$ contains a range query spanning w_i if and only if this rightmost right boundary is to the right of the right boundary of $\mathcal{R}_{w_i}$. An analogous procedure allows us to mark every range query in $\mathcal{B}_v$ that spans at least one child of v, and a prefix sum over the list of range queries followed by a parallel scan suffices to extract the subset Q' of all marked queries.

In Step 4, we compute the lists of elements to be reported from the subtrees of all marked children of v and answer range queries pending in each such subtree $\mathcal{T}_{w_i}$. The correctness of this procedure is not difficult to see. The reason for first excluding the set of deletions just sent to such a child w_i in Step 4.1 and then, in Step 4.3, merging them with the time order representation constructed in Step 4.2 is that Lemma 6 requires that each buffer in $\mathcal{T}_{w_i}$ contains at most g operations. Similar to Section 3, we postpone the emptying of fringe buffers in $\mathcal{T}_{w_i}$ because emptying these buffers might trigger rebalancing operations that could interfere with buffer emptying procedures still pending at non-fringe nodes. A difference to Section 3 is that we schedule even non-full fringe buffers of $\mathcal{T}_{w_i}$ to be emptied once we are done emptying non-fringe buffers (Step 4.8) if these buffers contain more than $g/16$ operations or the leaves below the corresponding nodes store fewer than $g/8$ elements after Step 4.5. This is necessary to ensure that we can charge the cost of merging L_{w_i} with the contents of the leaves of $\mathcal{T}_{w_i}$ to elements deleted from $\mathcal{T}_{w_i}$ or reported by range queries in $\mathcal{B}_v$ that span $\mathcal{R}_{w_i}$.

In Step 5, we report all the elements in subtrees spanned by range queries in $\mathcal{B}_v$, for all queries spanning these subtrees. The key in this step is to balance the work of reporting output elements among the processors. We process the queries spanning the ranges of children of v in batches of g

RangeNonFringeEmpty(v):

1. Compute the time order representation $S = DQI$ of $\mathcal{B}_v$. The first g operations can be brought into time order representation using Lemma 4. The remaining operations are already in time order representation because they were added to $\mathcal{B}_v$ during a single buffer emptying process at v's parent. Thus, they can be merged with the time order representation of the first g operations using Lemma 5.

2. Distribute the DELETE operations in D to the buffers of the relevant children of v using Lemma 2.

3. Mark all children of v that are spanned by at least one range query in Q and compute the subset $Q' \subseteq Q$ of range queries that span at least one child of v.

4. For each marked child w_i of v, do the following, where $\mathcal{T}_{w_i}$ denotes the subtree with root w_i:

   4.1. Set aside the set $D_{w_i} \subseteq D$ of all DELETE operations distributed to $\mathcal{B}_{w_i}$ in Step 2.

   4.2. Using Lemma 6, empty all buffers of internal nodes of $\mathcal{T}_{w_i}$ and compute a time order representation L_{w_i} of the operations in these buffers.

   4.3. Merge the deletions in D_{w_i} into L_{w_i} using Lemma 5.

   4.4. Distribute copies of the operations in L_{w_i} to the buffers of the fringe nodes of $\mathcal{T}_{w_i}$ according to the routing elements stored in $\mathcal{T}_{w_i}$. (Range queries are sent to the leaves containing their endpoints.) This can be done using Lemma 1 by merging L_{w_i} with the sequence of routing elements of the fringe nodes after creating copies of the RANGEQUERY operations, sorting these copies by their right endpoints, and merging them into L_{w_i}.

   4.5. Mark all fringe nodes spanned by at least one range query in L_{w_i} and construct the list Q'_{w_i} of all range queries in L_{w_i} that span at least one fringe node. This can be done similarly to Step 3. For each marked fringe node u, apply the deletions in its buffer $\mathcal{B}_u$ to the leaves below it and remove the deletions from $\mathcal{B}_u$. Now answer the range queries in Q'_{w_i} in a manner similar to Step 5 below.

   4.6. Remove all RANGEQUERY operations from L_{w_i}. Merge the list of elements stored in the leaves of $\mathcal{T}_{w_i}$ into L_{w_i} using Lemma 1 and eliminate matching INSERT and DELETE operations using a prefix sum computation.

   4.7. Store the value of $|L_{w_i}|$ with node v.

   4.8. Add each fringe node of $\mathcal{T}_{w_i}$ whose buffer contains at least $g/16$ operations or whose leaves store less than $g/8$ elements to the list $\mathcal{F}$ of fringe nodes to be emptied after we are done emptying non-fringe nodes.

5. Divide Q' into batches of g RANGEQUERY operations. For each such batch Q'', do the following:

   5.1. For each range query $q = [x_1, x_2] \in Q''$, determine the range $w_h, w_{h+1}, \ldots, w_j$ of children of v such that $\mathcal{R}_{w_i} \subseteq [x_1, x_2]$, for all $h \leq i \leq j$, and create copies $q_{w_h}, q_{w_{h+1}}, \ldots, q_{w_j}$ of q. Let $wt(q_{w_i}) = |L_{w_i}|$ be the weight of q_{w_i}, for all $h \leq i \leq j$.

   5.2. For each query $q_{w_i} \in Q''$, report the elements in L_{w_i}. Distribute the load of reporting the output of all queries evenly among the processors.

6. Distribute all range queries in Q to the children of v so that each query $q = [x_1, x_2] \in Q$ is sent to children w_h and w_j satisfying $x_1 \in \mathcal{R}_{w_h}$ and $x_2 \in \mathcal{R}_{w_j}$, if these children exist. When sending query $[x_1, x_2]$ to a child w_i, replace the query range with $[x_1, x_2] \cap \mathcal{R}_{w_i}$.

7. Distribute the insertions in I to the buffers of the appropriate children of v. For each marked child w_i, distribute the operations sent to w_i in Steps 6 and 7 to the fringe buffers of $\mathcal{T}_{w_i}$. This can be done in a way similar to Step 4.4.

8. If the buffer of any child node w_i is now full, and w_i is not a fringe node, recursively empty w_i's buffer. If w_i's buffer is full and w_i is a fringe node, add w_i to the list $\mathcal{F}$ of fringe nodes to be emptied after we are done emptying non-fringe nodes.

Figure 6: Emptying the buffer of a non-fringe node of the parallel buffered range tree

queries. For each batch Q'' and each query $q \in Q''$, we first create a separate copy q_{w_i} of q for each subtree $\mathcal{T}_{w_i}$ such that q spans $\mathcal{R}_{w_i}$ (Step 5.1). We do this as follows: A single prefix sum computation similar to Step 3 suffices to label every query in Q'' with the leftmost child of v it spans. We sort the queries in Q'' by their right endpoints and repeat this procedure to label each query with the rightmost child of v it spans. Then we return the queries to their original order. Using a prefix sum computation, we can count the total number of copies of queries in Q'' to be created. Next we distribute the creation of these copies evenly among the processors: If C is the total number of copies to be created, we use a parallel scan to divide Q'' into two subsequences, those queries with no more than C/P copies to be created and those queries with more than C/P copies to be created. Using a prefix sum computation, we partition the first sequence of queries into P subsequences, one per processor, so that no processor has to create a total of more than $2C/P$ copies. Each processor then produces the copies of its assigned queries. Using a second prefix sum computation, we

assign processors to each query in the second sequence so that each query q with $C_q > C/P$ copies to be created is assigned at least $\lceil PC_q/C \rceil$ processors and each processor is assigned to at most two queries. We divide the creation of copies of each such query evenly among its assigned processors, which ensures that no processor creates more than $2C/P$ copies. The load balancing in Step 5.2 is achieved analogously, based on the weights assigned to the copies of the queries. Steps 6–8 are analogous to the buffer emptying process for non-fringe nodes in Section 3.

After we have emptied the buffers of all full non-fringe nodes, we need to empty the buffers of all fringe nodes in $\mathcal{F}$. When emptying the buffer of a fringe node v (Figure 7), the merging of the buffer $\mathcal{B}_v$ with the elements in the leaves below v answers all range queries in $\mathcal{B}_v$. Thus, after the merge, we can remove the RANGEQUERY operations from $\mathcal{B}_v$ and construct the new leaf contents from the current leaf contents and the INSERT and DELETE operations remaining in the fringe buffer, followed by rebalancing the tree as in Section 3.

RANGEFRINGEEMPTY(v):
1. Construct the time order representation of $\mathcal{B}_v$ as in Step 1 of Figure 6.
2. Merge the elements in the children of v into $\mathcal{B}_v$ using Lemma 5.
3. Remove all range queries from $\mathcal{B}_v$.
4. Empty the buffer $\mathcal{B}_v$ (and rebalance the tree) using algorithm FRINGEEMPTY in Figure 4.

Figure 7: Emptying the buffer of a fringe node of the parallel buffered range tree

THEOREM 2. *The total cost of an arbitrary sequence of N* INSERT, DELETE, *and* RANGEQUERY *operations performed on an initially empty buffered range tree is* $O(\mathrm{sort}_P(N) + K/PB)$ *I/Os, where K is the number of reported elements. The data structure uses* $O(N + K)$ *space.*

PROOF. The correctness of the algorithm is easy to see because all range queries are answered correctly during the construction of the appropriate time order representations (Lemmas 4 and 5) and by reporting the elements in subtrees completely spanned by these queries (Steps 4 and 5 of Figure 6).

To prove the I/O bound, we assign $\Theta(\frac{1}{PB} \log_{M/B} N/B) = \Theta(\frac{1}{PB} \cdot \log_{g/B} N/B \cdot \log_{M/B} g/B)$ credits to each operation when inserting it into the root buffer of the buffer tree and maintain the invariant that each operation in the buffer $\mathcal{B}_v$ of a node v that is the root of a subtree of height h has $\Theta(\frac{h}{PB} \cdot \log_{M/B} g/B)$ credits remaining. We show that we can use these credits plus $O(1/PB)$ credits per output element to pay for the cost of all buffer emptying operations, excluding the cost of rebalancing operations triggered by the emptying of fringe buffers. Since the rebalancing cost is the same as in the basic parallel buffer tree discussed in Section 3, and the proof of Theorem 1 bounds this cost by $O(\mathrm{sort}_P(N))$ I/Os, the I/O bound follows.

Consider the emptying of a non-fringe buffer $\mathcal{B}_v$. The cost of Steps 1, 2, 3, 6, and 7 is $O((|\mathcal{B}_v|/g)\mathrm{sort}_P(g) + K'/PB)$ I/Os, where K' is the number of output elements produced by these steps. For Steps 1, 2, 6, and 7, this follows from Lemmas 2, 4, and 5. For Step 3, this follows because this step involves only merging two sequences of total size $O(|\mathcal{B}_v|)$ (Lemma 1), followed by a prefix sum and parallel scan of the merged list. Since all operations in $\mathcal{B}_v$ are either eliminated or moved to v's children, the credits of these operations and the produced output elements can pay for the cost of these steps.

In Step 4, consider a single subtree $\mathcal{T}_{w_i}$ with N'/B leaves. By Lemma 6, Step 4.2 takes $O\left(\mathrm{sort}_P(g) \sum_{x \in \mathcal{T}_{w_i}} h_x + (N' + K')/PB\right)$ I/Os, where K' is the number of elements reported in this step. Steps 4.1 and 4.3 take $O((X/g)\mathrm{sort}_P(g) + K'/PB)$ I/Os, where X is the total number of operations in $\mathcal{T}_{w_i}$'s buffers and K' is again the number of elements reported by this step. Step 4.4 takes $O(N'/PB + \log P)$ I/Os, by Lemma 1. Step 4.5 takes $O\left(\frac{N'+K'}{PB} + \log P\right)$ I/Os, by the same analysis as for Steps 3 and 5 (below). Steps 4.6–4.8, finally, take $O\left(\frac{N'+X}{PB} + \log P\right)$ I/Os, by Lemma 1. The $O(K'/PB)$ terms can be paid for by the reported elements. The remaining cost is dominated by the cost of Step 4.2. The $O\left(\mathrm{sort}_P(g) \sum_{x \in \mathcal{T}_{w_i}} h_x\right)$ term can be paid for by the credits of the operations in $\mathcal{T}_{w_i}$'s buffers because these operations are moved to fringe buffers. The $O(N'/(PB))$ term can be paid for by the elements in the leaves of $\mathcal{T}_{w_i}$ because

a constant fraction of these elements either get deleted or become part of the output of at least one range query in $\mathcal{B}_v$ that spans $\mathcal{R}_{w_i}$.

The cost of Step 5 is bounded by $O(f/P + K'/(PB)) = O\left(\frac{g+K'}{PB}\right)$ I/Os because we ensure that each processor creates roughly the same number of copies of queries and reports roughly the same number of output elements, and the number of copies of queries we create is $O(K')$ because we only copy queries that span the ranges of children of v.

The analysis of the cost of emptying fringe buffers is analogous once we observe that each such buffer emptying operation can be charged to $\Omega(g)$ operations: either the emptied buffer contains at least $g/16$ operations or the leaves below the corresponding node must have lost at least $3g/8$ elements since their creation, which can only happen as a result of DELETE operations.

The space bound follows because all steps in our algorithms use linear space. The only exception is the orthogonal line segment intersection algorithm of [3], which requires $O(N + K)$ space in order to achieve the optimal I/O complexity. □

5. REFERENCES

[1] A. Aggarwal and J. S. Vitter. The input/output complexity of sorting and related problems. *Communications of the ACM*, 31(9):1116–1127, 1988.

[2] D. Ajwani, N. Sitchinava, and N. Zeh. Geometric algorithms for private-cache chip multiprocessors. In *Proceedings of the 18th European Symposium on Algorithms, Part II*, volume 6347 of *Lecture Notes in Computer Science*, pages 75–86. Springer-Verlag, 2010.

[3] D. Ajwani, N. Sitchinava, and N. Zeh. I/O-optimal distribution sweeping on private-cache chip multiprocessors. In *Proceedings of the 26th IEEE International Parallel and Distributed Processing Symposium*, pages 1114–1123, 2011.

[4] L. Arge. External memory data structures. In J. Abello, P. M. Pardalos, and M. G. C. Resende, editors, *Handbook of Massive Data Sets*, pages 313–357. Kluwer Academic Publishers, Norwell, MA, USA, 2002.

[5] L. Arge. The buffer tree: A technique for designing batched external data structures. *Algorithmica*, 37(1):1–24, 2003.

[6] L. Arge, M. T. Goodrich, M. J. Nelson, and N. Sitchinava. Fundamental parallel algorithms for private-cache chip multiprocessors. In *Proceedings of the 20th ACM Symposium on Parallelism in Algorithms and Architectures*, pages 197–206, 2008.

[7] L. Arge, M. T. Goodrich, and N. Sitchinava. Parallel external memory graph algorithms. In *Proceedings of the 24th IEEE International Parallel and Distributed Processing Symposium*, pages 1–11, 2010.

[8] R. Bayer and E. M. McCreight. Organization and maintenance of large ordered indexes. *Acta Informatica*, 1:173–189, 1972.

[9] M. A. Bender, J. T. Fineman, S. Gilbert, and B. C. Kuszmaul. Concurrent cache-oblivious B-trees. In *Proceedings of the 17th ACM Symposium on Parallelism in Algorithms and Architectures*, pages 228–237, 2005.

[10] G. Blelloch, P. Gibbons, and H. Simhadri. Low depth cache-oblivious algorithms. In *Proceedings of the 22nd ACM Symposium on Parallelism in Algorithms and Architectures*, pages 189–199, 2010.

[11] G. E. Blelloch, R. A. Chowdhury, P. B. Gibbons, V. Ramachandran, S. Chen, and M. Kozuch. Provably good multicore cache performance for divide-and-conquer algorithms. In *Proceedings of the 19th ACM-SIAM Symposium on Discrete Algorithms*, pages 501–510, 2008.

[12] M. Carey and C. Thompson. An efficient implementation of search trees on [lg n + 1] processors. *IEEE Transactions on Computers*, C-33(11):1038–1041, 1984.

[13] R. A. Chowdhury and V. Ramachandran. Cache-efficient dynamic programming for multicores. In *Proceedings of the 20th ACM Symposium on Parallelism in Algorithms and Architectures*, pages 207–216, 2008.

[14] R. Cole and V. Ramachandran. Resource-oblivious sorting on multicores. In *Proceedings of the 37th International Colloquium on Automata, Languages and Programming, Part I*, volume 6198 of *Lecture Notes in Computer Science*, pages 226–237. Springer-Verlag, 2010.

[15] S. Huddleston and K. Mehlhorn. A new data structure for representing sorted lists. *Acta Informatica*, 17:157–184, 1982.

[16] H. Park and K. Park. Parallel algorithms for red-black trees. *Theoretical Computer Science*, 262(1-2):415–435, 2001.

[17] W. Paul, U. Vishkin, and H. Wagener. Parallel dictionaries on 2-3 trees. In *Proceedings of the 10th International Colloquium on Automata, Languages and Programming*, volume 154 of *Lecture Notes in Computer Science*, pages 597–609. Springer-Verlag, 1983.

[18] K. Pollari-Malmi, E. Soisalon-Soininen, and T. Ylonen. Concurrency control in B-trees with batch updates. *IEEE Transactions on Knowledge and Data Engineering*, 8(6):975–984, 1996.

[19] N. Sitchinava. *Parallel External Memory Model — A Parallel Model for Multi-Core Architectures*. PhD thesis, University of California, Irvine, 2009.

[20] V. Srinivasan and M. J. Carey. Performance of B+ tree concurrency control algorithms. *The VLDB Journal*, 2(4):361–406, 1993.

[21] L. G. Valiant. A bridging model for parallel computation. In *Proceedings of the 16th European Symposium on Algorithms*, volume 5193 of *Lecture Notes in Computer Science*, pages 13–28. Springer-Verlag, 2008.

A $(3/2 + \epsilon)$ Approximation Algorithm for Scheduling Moldable and Non-Moldable Parallel Tasks *

Klaus Jansen
Institut für Informatik, Universität zu Kiel
Olshausenstr. 40, D - 24098 Kiel, Germany.
kj@informatik.uni-kiel.de

ABSTRACT

In this paper we study a scheduling problem with moldable and non-moldable parallel tasks on m processors. A non-moldable parallel task is one that runs in parallel on a specific given number of processors. The goal is to find a non-preemptive schedule on the m processors which minimizes the makespan, or the latest task completion time. The previous best result is the list scheduling algorithm with an absolute approximation ratio of 2. On the other hand, there does not exist an approximation algorithm for scheduling non-moldable parallel tasks with ratio smaller than 1.5, unless $P = NP$. In this paper we show that a schedule with length $(1.5 + \epsilon)OPT$ can be computed for the scheduling problem in time $O(n \log n) + f(1/\epsilon)$. Furthermore we present an $(1.5 + \epsilon)$ approximation algorithm for scheduling moldable parallel tasks.

Categories and Subject Descriptors

F.2 [**Theory of Computation**]: Analysis of Algorithms and Problem Complexity; G.2 [**Mathematics of Computing**]: Discrete Mathematics

Keywords

Scheduling Theory, Approximation Algorithms

1. INTRODUCTION

Problem Definition. In this paper we study the following scheduling problem with non-moldable parallel tasks (sometimes also called rigid tasks). Suppose a set $\mathcal{J} = \{J_1, \ldots, J_n\}$ of n jobs and a set $M = \{1, \ldots, m\}$ of m identical processors are given. Each job J_j has a processing time $p_j \in \mathbb{Z}^+$ and requires the simultaneous use of $q_j \leq m$ processors during its execution. A schedule $S =$

---

*Supported in part by DFG Project, Approximative Algorithmen für zwei- und dreidimensionale Packungsprobleme und verwandte Schedulingprobleme, JA 612/12-2.

Permission to make digital or hard copies of all or part of this work for personal or classroom use is granted without fee provided that copies are not made or distributed for profit or commercial advantage and that copies bear this notice and the full citation on the first page. To copy otherwise, to republish, to post on servers or to redistribute to lists, requires prior specific permission and/or a fee.
SPAA'12, June 25–27, 2012, Pittsburgh, Pennsylvania, USA.
Copyright 2012 ACM 978-1-4503-1213-4/12/06 ...$10.00.

$((S_1, M_1), \ldots, (S_n, M_n))$ is a sequence of starting times $S_j \geq 0$ together with a set $M_j \subset M$ of assigned processors of cardinality $|M_j| = q_j$ for $j = 1, \ldots, n$. A schedule is feasible if each processor executes at most one job at any given time. The objective of the problem denoted by $P|size_j|C_{max}$ is to find a feasible schedule with minimum length $OPT = \max_{j=1,\ldots,n}(S_j + p_j)$.

Results. The problem $P|size_j|C_{max}$ is strongly NP-hard even for a constant number $m \geq 5$ of processors [6]. Therefore, we are interested in approximation algorithms. An α-approximation algorithm for a minimization problem is a polynomial-time algorithm A that constructs for each instance I a solution of value at most α times the optimum value $OPT(I)$ (i.e. algorithm A generates a solution of length $A(I) \leq \alpha OPT(I)$); α is called the absolute approximation ratio of the algorithm. Using a reduction from the partition problem it can be shown that there is no approximation algorithm for $P|size_j|C_{max}$ with ratio better than 1.5, unless $P = NP$. Furthermore, there is no asymptotic approximation algorithm with $A(I) \leq \alpha OPT(I) + \beta$, where $\alpha < 1.5$ and β is a polynomial in n [19]. The best known approximation algorithm (the list scheduling algorithm), which has absolute ratio 2, was given implicity by Garey and Graham [10] as pointed out by Turek et al. [28] and Ludwig and Tiwari [25]. Feldmann, Sgall and Teng [8] observed that the length of a non-preemptive schedule produced by the list scheduling algorithm is actually at most $(2 - 1/m)$ times the optimum preemptive makespan.

A polynomial time approximation scheme (PTAS) for the case when the number m of processors is constant, denoted by $Pm|size_j|C_{max}$, was presented in [1, 14]. A polynomial time approximation scheme is a family of algorithms that compute for any fixed $\epsilon > 0$ and instance I a schedule with length at most $(1 + \epsilon)OPT(I)$. Recently, Jansen and Thöle [17] found a PTAS for the case where the number of processors is polynomially bounded in the number of jobs. For the general problem without any restrictions on the instance, the best known approximation algorithm is the list scheduling algorithm with ratio 2. The following property is important for our approach. Let S_j be the starting time of the job $J_j \in \mathcal{J}$. Suppose that for each time step t the set $\mathcal{J}_t$ of jobs executed at time t uses at most m processors (i.e. for $\mathcal{J}_t = \{J_j | t \in [S_j, S_j + p_j)\}$ we have $\sum_{J_j \in \mathcal{J}_t} q_j \leq m$ for all time steps $t \in [0, max_j S_j + p_j)$). A sufficient condition for the existence of a feasible schedule is that the above property holds for all starting times of the jobs. If this property is satisfied for all starting times we can generate a feasible (canonical) schedule [19, 17] by assigning jobs to processors at each starting time, starting with time $t = 0$. Furthermore, the number of processor intervals used by jobs and idle intervals at each time step can be bounded by $n + 1$ [19], where n is the number of jobs. Here a processor interval is a set of consecutive processors of maximal cardinality such that all processors in this set are processing the same job. Formally, a processor interval is completely specified by the index of its first and last processor. Therefore, we can obtain a compact way of encoding the output with polynomial size.

In the case with release dates $r_j \geq 0$, the starting time S_j of a job J_j must be larger than or equal to r_j. For this problem, denoted by $P|size_j, r_j|C_{max}$, the list scheduling algorithm produces a schedule with makespan at most twice the makespan of an optimum preemptive schedule [19]. This leads to a 2-approximation algorithm for $P|size_j, r_j|C_{max}$. Naroska and Schwiegelshohn [27] independently showed that list scheduling gives a 2-approximation for the problem. Furthermore, no list scheduling [19] can achieve a better performance guarantee than 2 for the problem $P|size_j, r_j|C_{max}$. For an overview of other multiprocessor scheduling problems and results we refer to [3, 5]. Finding an improved approximation algorithm to reduce the gap between the best known ratio 2 and the lower bound of $3/2$ (with and without release dates) is known as an open problem in the research area (see for example [19, 24]). We present the following new result in this paper:

THEOREM 1.1. *For every fixed $\epsilon > 0$, there is an algorithm A such that $A(I) \leq (1.5+\epsilon)OPT(I)$ for every instance I of $P|size_j|C_{max}$, where $A(I)$ is the length of the schedule generated by algorithm A and $OPT(I)$ is the length of an optimum schedule. The running time (number of elementary arithmetic operations) of algorithm A is $O(n \log n) + f(1/\epsilon)$. All arithmetic operations are performed on numbers whose encoding length is bounded by a polynomial in $\log(n)$, $\log(m)$, and $\log(p_{max})$.*

This result narrows the gap between the best known approximation algorithm with ratio 2 and the lower bound of 1.5. It can be generalized to the case with additional release dates. Note that the input length $|I| \leq O(\log(n) + \log(m) + \sum_{j=1}^{n}(\log(q_j) + \log(p_j))) \leq O(n(\log(m) + \log(p_{max})))$ and $|I| \geq n + \log(m) + \log(p_{max})$.

Problem Definition. A related problem is scheduling moldable parallel jobs, denoted by $P|fctn_j|C_{max}$, where the number of processors per job is not known a priori. Here the execution time of a job depends on the number of allotted processors. Instead of one pair (p_j, q_j) for each job J_j we have a function $p_j : D_j \to \mathbb{Z}^+$ that gives the execution time $p_j(a)$ of each job J_j in terms of the number $a \in D_j$ of processors that are assigned to J_j (where M is the set of processors and $D_j \subset M$ is a subset of possible processor numbers for job J_j; e.g. $D_j = \{1, 2, 4, 8, \ldots\}$). The goal is to find a feasible schedule S with minimum length $C_{max}^* = \max_{j=1,\ldots,n}(S_j + p_j(m_j))$, where $m_j \in D_j$ is the chosen number of processors for job J_j. Here moldable means that the degree of parallelism (the number of processors) can be chosen when a jobs starts but is fixed afterwards. Furthermore, preemptions are not allowed. Notice that in several papers moldable tasks are called malleable tasks [4, 25, 26, 14, 17], but recent papers [5, 7] use malleable for jobs where the number of processors can be changed anytime during their execution and preemptions are allowed.

Results. Belkhale and Banerjee [2] gave an algorithm with approximation ratio $2/(1 + 1/m)$ for monotone moldable jobs. Moldable jobs are called monotone, if their processing times and work are monotone; i.e. allocating more machines to a job decreases the running time and increases the work: if $\ell \leq \ell'$, then $p_j(\ell) \geq p_j(\ell')$ and $\ell p_j(\ell) \leq \ell' p_j(\ell')$. Turek et al. [28] improved this result, using no assumptions, and showed an approximation ratio of 2. Ludwig and Tiwari [25] also presented an approximation algorithm for moldable tasks with ratio 2, but with an improved running time. For monotone moldable jobs, Mounie, Rapine and Trystram [26] presented an approximation algorithm for the scheduling problem with ratio $1.5 + \epsilon$. Decker, Lücker, and Monien [4] presented an 1.25 approximation algorithm for scheduling n identical moldable jobs on m processors. Jobs are called identical, if the execution time on any number of processors is the same for all jobs (i.e. $p_j(\ell) = p_{j'}(\ell)$ for all pairs $J_j, J_{j'} \in \mathcal{J}$ and all numbers $\ell \in \{1, \ldots, m\}$).

Jansen and Porkolab [14] also presented a PTAS for the scheduling problem $Pm|fctn_j|C_{max}$ with running time $O(n) + f(1/\epsilon)$ for the case when the number m of processors is constant. Recently, Jansen and Thöle [17] gave a PTAS for scheduling moldable jobs for the case when the number of processors is polynomially bounded by the number of jobs. The best previous result without additional assumptions (on the processing times and work) are algorithms with approximation ratio 2. Since the scheduling problem with parallel tasks is a special case of scheduling moldable tasks (with $D_j = \{q_j\}$ for each job J_j), there is no approximation algorithm for $P|fctn_j|C_{max}$ with ratio < 1.5, unless $P = NP$. In this paper we prove the following new result.

THEOREM 1.2. *For every $\epsilon > 0$, there is an algorithm A such that $A(I) \leq (1.5 + \epsilon)OPT(I)$ for every instance I of $P|fctn_j|C_{max}$, where $A(I)$ is the length of the schedule generated by algorithm A and $OPT(I)$ is the length of an optimum schedule. The running time of algorithm A is polynomial in n, $\max_j |D_j|$ and $\log(m + p_{max})$; i.e. polynomial in the input length for any $\epsilon > 0$.*

The algorithm can also be generalized to the variant with release dates; for details we refer to our full version [18].

Techniques. We use a rounding and elimination technique for the jobs (with large or medium processing times) by Jansen and Solis-Oba [16] and a delay technique for the huge jobs (with very large execution times) by Jansen and Thöle [17] to obtain structural results for an approximate schedule. A variant of the AFPTAS for 2D strip packing by Kenyon and Rémila [21] is used to schedule the small jobs into horizontal layers. The main difficulty is to avoid that the running time of our algorithm depends on the number m of processors (since $|I| \leq O(n(\log(m) + \log(p_{max})))$. To obtain a polynomial running time, we use two interesting new techniques. First we create a gap in the schedule of height $1/2 + \delta$ and width $(1/8)\delta^4 m$ (where δ depends on ϵ) by analyzing the structure of the approximate schedule. Second we round the width of each large narrow job down to a multiple of αm (where α also depends on ϵ) and use a dynamic program to calculate the starting times of these jobs. To get the desired faster parameterized running time, we use another approach for the large narrow jobs. Here we guess an approximate load vector for these jobs and solve a linear program (LP) approximately to compute a schedule for almost all large narrow jobs. The remaining non-scheduled large jobs are placed into the constructed gap.

For moldable tasks the scheduling problem gets more complicated, because we do not know the processor numbers in advance. Here we set up a linear program (LP) to select the number of allotted processors for the jobs. One problem is how to combine the small jobs with other jobs in the linear program. To do this we guess at the beginning the approximate structure of the small jobs in an optimum schedule and include this information into the LP. Interestingly, a basic LP solution has only a constant number of fractional variables. Fractional small and medium jobs can be executed at the end of the schedule, and fractional large jobs can be placed as above into a gap. The main difficulty here are the fractional huge jobs. To handle these jobs, we pre-assign a constant number of huge jobs (depending on the number of fractional jobs in the LP) with largest widths for each rounded starting and execution time. This helps us to select an integral processor number for each fractional huge job and to compute a feasible approximate schedule for all jobs.

Organization of the paper. First we discuss the approximation algorithm for parallel tasks. Next we discuss the generalization of our approximation algorithm to moldable tasks. The variant with additional release dates is discussed in the full version of the paper [18].

2. SCHEDULING PARALLEL TASKS

2.1 Structural Results

First we determine a constant $\delta \in (0, \epsilon/15]$ depending on the accuracy $\epsilon > 0$ such that $1/\delta$ is an even integer and the total load $\sum_{j:p_j \in (\delta^5, \delta]} p_j q_j \leq \delta \sum_{j=1}^{n} p_j q_j$. Note that we may suppose that $\epsilon \leq 1$ (otherwise simply reduce ϵ to 1). Such a choice of a constant δ has been used by Jansen and Solis-Oba [16]. Suppose from now on that the number of processors m is larger than a polynomial in $1/\delta$; the exact bound is specified later. The case $m \leq poly(1/\delta)$ is easier and discussed at the end of Subsection 2.5. By computing an 2-approximate solution with makespan $LS(I) \leq 2OPT(I)$, we know that the optimum makespan $OPT(I) \in [LS(I)/2, LS(I)]$. By scaling (i.e. dividing all processing times by $LS(I)$) the optimum makespan $OPT(I) \in [1/2, 1]$. We run the algorithm described below for several discrete values $T(i) = 1/2 + i\delta$, where $i = 0, \ldots, 1/(2\delta)$. Clearly, there is one value i^* such that $T(i^*) \leq OPT(I) < T(i^* + 1)$. By dividing the processing times by $T(i^*)$, for this choice we obtain $1 \leq OPT(I) < T(i^* + 1)/T(i^*) \leq 1 + 2\delta$.

The goal is now to find a packing or schedule of the jobs into a big rectangle of width m and height $1 + 2\delta$. It is allowed to cut jobs of width q_j into vertical slices with integral widths. The vertical slices corresponding to a job have to be placed into the big rectangle on the same level to start them at the same time. We divide now the schedule (or the big rectangle) into horizontal layers of height δ^2. Notice that there is only a constant number $(1 + 2\delta)/\delta^2$ of horizontal layers. Next we partition the jobs into four classes:

(a) huge jobs with running time $p_j > 1/2 + \delta$,

(b) large jobs with running time $p_j \in (\delta, 1/2 + \delta]$,

(c) medium jobs with running time $p_j \in (\delta^5, \delta]$, and

(d) small jobs with running time $p_j \leq \delta^5$.

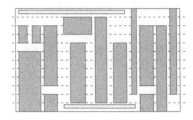

Figure 1: Approximate schedule after rounding the execution times

By a modification of the schedule we obtain the following result (for the proof we refer to our full version).

LEMMA 2.1. *If there is a schedule for the job set $\mathcal{J}$ with length $OPT(I) \leq 1 + 2\delta$ (where δ satisfies the load constraint above and $\delta \leq 1/10$), then there is also an approximate schedule for a subset $\mathcal{J}' \subset \mathcal{J}$ with length at most $1 + 5\delta$ such that*

(1) *huge and large jobs have processing time which are multiples of δ^2,*

(2) *huge and large jobs start and finish at multiples of δ^2,*

(3) *there are no medium jobs in $\mathcal{J}'$,*

(4) *small jobs lie completely in horizontal layers of height δ^2.*

The remaining jobs in $\mathcal{J} \setminus \mathcal{J}'$ are all medium and can be placed at the end of the schedule with length $\leq 2.5\delta$.

We need an additional structure for an approximate schedule. Notice that jobs are in general not executed on consecutive processors. This complicates the structure of the solution. On the other hand, we can repack configurations or sets of huge and large jobs on processors such that most of the consecutive processors have the same pattern of starting times and execution times for these jobs. One important step is to exchange processors such that configurations with the same execution time (and same starting time) of a huge job (with $p_j > 1/2 + \delta$) are executed on consecutive processors. In the same way we can modify the schedule such that vertical slices of the same huge job are packed on consecutive processors (for an illustration see Figure 2). This is possible, since each processor contains at most one huge job.

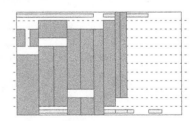

Figure 2: Approximate schedule after vertical exchange steps

2.2 Dynamic Program for Large Jobs

Let us now consider the large jobs. Using the property stated in the introduction to obtain a canonical schedule, it is sufficient to assign the starting times to the jobs. By the modification of the schedule for the large jobs, the starting times are multiples $a\delta^2$ where $a \in \{0, \ldots, (1+4\delta)/\delta^2 - 1\}$. Notice that large jobs cannot be started at time $1 + 4\delta$ or afterwards. Therefore, each schedule can be described as a vector $(m_0, \ldots, m_{(1+4\delta)/\delta^2-1})$, where m_a is the number of processors used at time $a\delta^2$ for each a. Since the total number of different vectors is too large (i.e. polynomial in m), we first assign starting times to large jobs with width larger than $\lfloor \alpha m \rfloor$ (where α is a constant depending on δ or ϵ specified later). The number of different assignments for all large wide jobs can be bounded by a function $f(\alpha, \delta) = O(1)$, since the area of each large wide job is at least $\delta \lfloor \alpha m \rfloor$ and there are at most $\frac{(1+5\delta)m}{\delta \lfloor \alpha m \rfloor} = \frac{(1+5\delta)}{\delta} \frac{m}{\lfloor \alpha m \rfloor} \leq \frac{2(1+5\delta)}{\alpha \delta}$ of these jobs in the solution. Here we suppose that $m \geq 2/\alpha$ and obtain $\frac{m}{\lfloor \alpha m \rfloor} \leq \frac{2}{\alpha}$. To avoid the dependence on m in the running time, we round the width of each remaining large narrow job down to a multiple of $(\alpha m/n)$ (i.e. a fractional value); this can be done in time polynomial in $\log(n/\alpha)$ and $\log(m)$ for each job. Then, using dynamic programming, we assign a set of jobs with total rounded (fractional) width $b(\alpha m/n)$ (where $b \in \{0, 1, \ldots, n/\alpha\}$) to each possible rounded starting time $a\delta^2$ and each rounded processing time $h\delta^2 \in \{\delta + \delta^2, \ldots, 1/2 + \delta\}$. Notice there are at most $1/(2\delta^2) - 1/\delta \leq 1/(2\delta^2)$ many different rounded large processing times. Each assignment can be described by a vector $v = (v_{a,h})$ where $v_{a,h}$ is the total rounded number of processors used by jobs with starting time $a\delta^2$ and execution time $h\delta^2$. The number of assignments or vectors can be bounded by the polynomial $(n/\alpha + 1)^{O(1/\delta^4)}$ (i.e. independent of m) for each constant δ. All possible vectors can be computed via a dynamic program. Notice that for each approximate schedule S for $\mathcal{J}'$ there exists a vector $v = (v_{a,h})$ where the distance between the value $v_{a,h}$ and the number of processors used in S is at most $n_{a,h}(\alpha m/n)$, where $n_{a,h}$ is the number of large narrow jobs with starting time $a\delta^2$ and rounded execution time $h\delta^2$.

LEMMA 2.2. *There exists a vector v with rounded numbers of processors used by large jobs corresponding to an approximate schedule for $\mathcal{J}'$ with length $1 + 5\delta$ such that all large jobs with original processor numbers can be finished until time $1 + 5\delta$ with exception of a subset of large jobs with total width $\leq \lceil (1/\delta^4)\alpha m \rceil$.*

For the proof of the lemma above we refer to our full version. The next step is to delay all huge jobs by at most $1/2 + 4\delta$ such that all huge jobs are finished at the same horizontal level (i.e. they finish all at time $1 + 5\delta$). To avoid an overlap, all other jobs that lie completely above the horizontal line $1/2 + \delta$ are delayed by exactly $1/2 + 4\delta$. Notice that each large job J_j with starting time $a_j\delta^2 \geq 1/2 + \delta$ will be moved up by $1/2 + 4\delta$; i.e. the starting of J_j is delayed by $1/2 + 4\delta$. Therefore, these jobs are started now after time $1 + 5\delta$. This increases the total length of the schedule by at most $1/2 + 4\delta$, but now the structure of the enlarged schedule is easier. The huge jobs can be packed on consecutive processors one by one on the same level. The modified solution for our example is given in Figure 3. A computed vector v in the dynamic program for the large jobs

is feasible, if after the transformation of the schedule above for each time step t there are at most m processors used by huge and large jobs. If the vector v is infeasible, then v can be discarded. We obtain the following intermediate result.

LEMMA 2.3. *If there is an approximate schedule for $\mathcal{J}'$ of length at most $1 + 5\delta$, then there exists an approximate schedule of length $3/2 + 9\delta$ for $\mathcal{J}'$ such that all huge jobs finish at time $1 + 5\delta$.*

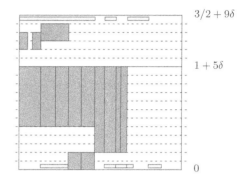

Figure 3: Modified approximate solution after vertical movements

2.3 Construction of the Gap

In order to reschedule a set of large jobs with total width at most $\lceil (1/\delta^4)\alpha m \rceil$, we need a gap of height $1/2 + \delta$ and width $\geq \lceil (1/\delta^4)\alpha m \rceil$ in our solution.

LEMMA 2.4. *For each optimum schedule of $\mathcal{J}$ with length at most $1 + 2\delta$, there exists an approximate schedule of the non-medium job set $\mathcal{J}'$ with length $3/2 + 9\delta$ such that*

(1) *all huge jobs finish at time $1 + 5\delta$,*

(2) *all huge and large jobs have processing times and starting times that are multiples of δ^2, and*

(3) *there exists a gap of width $\geq \lfloor (1/8)\delta^4 m \rfloor$ and height $1/2 + \delta$ in the schedule.*

Furthermore, we can guess the position of the gap by constant many choices.

PROOF. Depending on the structure of the optimum solution, there are four possible places for such a gap.

Case 1: The total width of all jobs with height $> 1/2 + \delta$ is at most $m/2$.

Case 1.1: The total width of all jobs with height $\in (\delta, 1/2 + \delta]$ that intersect the horizontal line at height $1/2 + (5/2)\delta$ is at most $m/4$. In this case we have a gap of width $\geq m/4$ and height $1/2 + (5/2)\delta$ after the vertical movements. We may suppose that the gap lies exactly between the horizontal lines at $1/2 + (5/2)\delta$ and $1 + 5\delta$ (see also Figure 4).

Case 1.2: The total width of all jobs with height $\in (\delta, 1/2 + \delta]$ that intersect the horizontal line at height $1/2 + (5/2)\delta$ is larger than $m/4$. Notice that there are at most $(1 + 5\delta)/(2\delta^2)$ many levels (or different rounded finishing times) of large jobs that cross the horizontal line at $1/2 + (5/2)\delta$. One of these levels at time $\ell\delta^2$ contains large jobs with total width at least $\frac{(m/4)}{(1+5\delta)/(2\delta^2)} \geq (1/4)\delta^2 m$ for $\delta \leq 1/5$. The movement

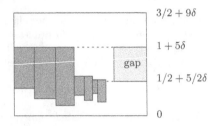

Figure 4: Gap for large jobs in case 1.1

of the jobs above the level generates a gap after time $\ell\delta^2$ of width $\geq (1/4)\delta^2 m$ and height $\geq 1/2+(5/2)\delta$. Then, the gap can be allocated from time $\ell\delta^2$ to $\ell\delta^2+1/2+(5/2)\delta$ (see also Figure 5). Notice that we can guess the place of the gap in this case (by enumerating at most $(1+5\delta)/(2\delta^2) = O(1/\delta^2)$ choices).

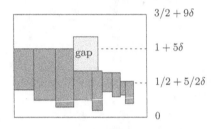

Figure 5: Gap for large jobs in case 1.2

Case 2: The total width of all jobs with height $> 1/2+\delta$ is larger than $m/2$.

Case 2.1 If there is a huge job J_{j*} of width $\geq (1/8)\delta^4 m$, then we simply take this job J_{j*} and guess the starting time of J_{j*}. In this case we fix the position of J_{j*} and only move the other huge jobs upwards. This generates a gap of height $\geq 1/2+(5/2)\delta$ and width $(1/8)\delta^4 m$ above J_{j*} (for an illustration of this case see Figure 6).

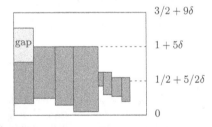

Figure 6: Gap for large jobs in case 2.1

Case 2.2 There is no huge job of width $\geq (1/8)\delta^4 m$. In the optimum solution there are at most $(1+5\delta)/\delta^2$ many levels or finishing times of huge jobs with the same height or execution time. Furthermore, the number of different huge rounded execution times is at most $(1/2+\delta)/\delta^2$. This implies that there are at most $(1+5\delta)(1/2+\delta)/\delta^4$ many blocks of jobs with the same execution and finishing time. Therefore, there is at least one block with width at least $\frac{m/2}{(1+5\delta)(1/2+\delta)/\delta^4} \geq (1/4)\delta^4 m$. If we do not move this block in the modification of the schedule above, then we have a gap of height $1/2+(5/2)\delta$ and width at least $1/4\delta^4 m$ above

the block. Actually we can calculate the position of the gap by guessing the starting time $s\delta^2$ of the block and the execution time $h\delta^2$ of the corresponding jobs.

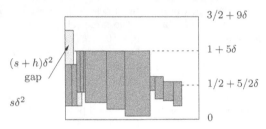

Figure 7: Gaps for large jobs in case 2.2

Now we greedily take a set $\mathcal{J}'$ of jobs, each with processing time $h\delta^2$, and width $< (1/8)\delta^4 m$ until the total width $w(\mathcal{J}') \in [(1/8)\delta^4 m, (1/4)\delta^4 m]$. If the total width of all jobs with execution time $h\delta^2$ is smaller than $(1/8)\delta^4 m$, then the guess $h\delta^2$ is not correct and can be discarded. Otherwise, all jobs in $\mathcal{J}'$ are started at time $s\delta^2$ and the remaining huge jobs (with the same execution time) are delayed as described above. In this case we have a gap of height $1/2+(5/2)\delta$ and width at least $(1/8)\delta^4 m$ just above set $\mathcal{J}'$. To be on the safe side, we only use the width $(1/8)\delta^4 m$ for the gap. Furthermore, for the other calculations, we suppose that a block of width $(1/4)\delta^4 m$ is occupied from time $s\delta^2$ to $1+5\delta-h\delta^2$. This is possible, since the optimum schedule has a block of jobs with total width at least $(1/4)\delta^4 m$ starting at time $s\delta^2$ with execution time $h\delta^2$. For an illustration of this interesting case we refer to Figure 7. □

Now, depending on the guesses, including the position and structure of the gap, the positions for the large wide jobs, the vector with the rounded widths of large narrow jobs and the total widths of huge jobs for each rounded execution times, we can compute the total number of free processors for each horizonal layer. Notice that it is sufficient to use the horizontal layers between 0 and $1/2+\delta$ and between $1+5\delta$ and $3/2+9\delta$ for the small jobs (see also Figure 8). The transformation of the schedule (i.e. moving jobs upwards and enlarging the schedule to length $3/2+9\delta$)) generates more space in the corresponding layers.

Choice of α. We have to reschedule large jobs with total width at most $\lceil(1/\delta^4)\alpha m\rceil$. On the other hand, we have generated a gap of width $\geq \lfloor(1/8)\delta^4 m\rfloor$ above. Notice that $\lceil(1/\delta^4)\alpha m\rceil \leq \lfloor(1/8)\delta^4 m\rfloor$ holds if $(1/\delta^4)\alpha m + 2 \leq (1/8)\delta^4 m$. This inequality holds for $\alpha = (1/16)\delta^8$ and $m \geq 32(1/\delta)^4$. In Subsection 2.2 we supposed that $m \geq 2/\alpha$ (to bound the number of large wide jobs). This implies that m should be larger than $32/\delta^8$.

2.4 How to place the Small Jobs?

After the placement of the large and huge jobs there are m_ℓ free processors in layer ℓ that can be used for small jobs. Since we do not use the layers between $1/2+\delta$ and $1+5\delta$ and the total number of layers is $(3/2+9\delta)/\delta^2$, the number L of layers for small jobs is equal to $(1+5\delta)/\delta^2$. To simplify the notation, we suppose that m_ℓ is the number of free processors for layer $\ell = 0,\ldots,(1+5\delta)/\delta^2 - 1$ (see also Figure 8 for an illustration). First we check whether the total area of all small jobs is larger than the space left; in this case we discard the corresponding guess for the large jobs and the gap. Otherwise we round the widths of the small wide jobs with widths $> \gamma m$ (where γ depends on δ specified later) up, using a method for 2-dimensional strip packing by Kenyon and Rémila [21]. It generates $G \leq 1/\gamma^2$ different rounded widths $w_1 > \ldots > w_G > \gamma m$. Furthermore, the total area of all jobs after this rounding is at most $(1 + 5\delta)m(1 + \gamma)$.

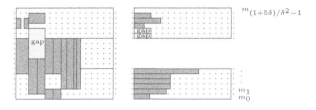

Figure 8: Free Processors for small jobs after locating the gap

Next we set up a linear program for the rounded wide small jobs. First we remove a set $\bar{\mathcal{J}}$ of small wide jobs with the largest numbers of processors required and total execution time within $[\gamma^2 P(\mathcal{J}_{sw}), \gamma^2 P(\mathcal{J}_{sw}) + \delta^5)$, where $\mathcal{J}_{sw}$ is the set of all small wide jobs and $P(\mathcal{J}_{sw}) = \sum_{J_j \in \mathcal{J}_{sw}} p_j$. Then we know that the set $\mathcal{J}_{sw} \setminus \bar{\mathcal{J}}$ of remaining rounded small wide jobs fractionally fits into the horizontal layers (if the guess above corresponds to an approximate schedule). This follows from the rounding technique, since the rounded remaining small wide jobs can be fractionally inserted into the packing for the original small wide jobs [21]. Let n_i be the total execution time of all jobs in $\mathcal{J}_{sw} \setminus \bar{\mathcal{J}}$ with rounded width w_i. Furthermore, let $C_j^{(\ell)}$ be a multiset with rounded wide jobs of total width m_ℓ for layer $\ell = 0, \ldots, L - 1$; i.e. $C_j^{(\ell)} = \{a_{j,1}^{(\ell)} : w_1, \ldots, a_{j,G}^{(\ell)} : w_G\}$ such that $\sum_i a_{j,i}^{(\ell)} w_i \leq m_\ell$. Here $a_{j,i}^{(\ell)}$ denotes the number of jobs of width w_i in $C_j^{(\ell)}$. We use a variable $x_j^{(\ell)}$ to indicate the height of the multiset $C_j^{(\ell)}$ in the solution. Suppose that the empty multiset is also allowed. With $\mathcal{C}^{(\ell)}$ we denote the set of all configurations for layer ℓ. Then, the linear program $LP(m_1, \ldots, m_L)$ for a list of n_i jobs of width w_i has the following form:

$$
\begin{array}{rcll}
\sum_j x_j^{(\ell)} & = & \delta^2 & \ell = 0, \ldots, L-1 \\
\sum_\ell \sum_j x_j^{(\ell)} a_{j,i}^{(\ell)} & \geq & n_i & i = 1, \ldots, G \\
x_j^{(\ell)} & \geq & 0 & \ell = 0, \ldots, L-1, \\
& & & j = 1, \ldots, |\mathcal{C}^{(\ell)}|
\end{array}
$$

Let ρ be a constant that depends on δ; the exact value is specified later. An ρ-approximate solution of this linear program covering $n_i(1 - \rho)$ execution time of width w_i can be computed using the algorithm by Grigoriadis et al. [12], if there is a feasible solution of the LP. The algorithm by Grigoriadis et al. needs $O(G(\log G + 1/\rho^2))$ iterations with $O(1/\delta^2)$ block optimization steps. Each block optimization consists of an $(1 - \rho/6)$ approximation algorithm for a knapsack problem. Since there is an FPTAS for the knapsack problem, the linear program can be solved approximately in time polynomial in $1/\rho$ and G. If the linear program has no feasible approximate solution, then we discard the corresponding guess for the large jobs and the gap. In this case the small wide jobs do not fractionally fit into the horizontal layers.

The number of variables $x_j^{(\ell)} > 0$ in the generated solution is at most $O(1/\delta^2 1/\gamma^2 (\log 1/\gamma + \log 1/\rho))$ and can be reduced to $\bar{G} \leq 1/\gamma^2 + (1 + 5\delta)/\delta^2 \leq 1/\gamma^2 + 2/\delta^2$ by solving a sequence of systems of equalities. Finally we set $\tilde{x}_j^{(\ell)} = x_j^{(\ell)}(1 + 2\rho)$ for each variable. This implies that $\sum_\ell \sum_j \tilde{x}_j^{(\ell)} a_{j,i}^{(\ell)} \geq (1 + 2\rho)(1 - \rho)n_i \geq n_i$ for $\rho \leq 1/2$. For each layer ℓ we obtain $\sum_j \tilde{x}_j^{(\ell)} = (1 + 2\rho)\delta^2$. Summing over all layers, the length of the schedule is at most $(3/2 + (15/2)\delta)(1 + 2\rho)$. Similar to the AFPTAS by Kenyon and Rémila [21], the wide small jobs can be placed into the space generated by the solution $\tilde{x}_j^{(\ell)}$ of the LP for the multisets $C_j^{(\ell)}$. The additional height to pack these jobs integrally into a layer ℓ can be bounded by the number of positive variables corresponding to layer ℓ times the maximum height $h_{max} \leq \delta^5$ of a small job. The total increase over all layers is at most $2\bar{G}h_{max} \leq 2\bar{G}\delta^5 \leq 2(1/\gamma^2 + 2/\delta^2)\delta^5$ where $\bar{G} \leq (1/\gamma^2 + 2/\delta^2)$ (generating a nice integral packing; see also [15]). The total area $Area(\bar{\mathcal{J}}) = \sum_{J_j \in \bar{\mathcal{J}}} p_j q_j$ can be bounded by $(\gamma^2 P(\mathcal{J}_{sw}) + \delta^5)m \leq (\gamma^2 \frac{Area(\mathcal{J}_{sw})}{\gamma m} + \delta^5)m \leq \gamma Area(\mathcal{J}_{sw}) + \delta^5 m \leq \gamma(1 + 5\delta)m + \delta^5 m$ (using $Area(\mathcal{J}_{sw}) \geq \gamma m P(\mathcal{J}_{sw})$). These jobs can be executed at the end of the schedule with total length $\leq 2\max[(1+5\delta)\gamma + \delta^5, \delta^5] = 2(1 + 5\delta)\gamma + 2\delta^5$. Then, the total height of the packing of all jobs (excluding the small narrow ones) is at most $h' \leq (3/2 + 9\delta)(1 + 2\rho) + 2(1 + 5\delta)\gamma + (2\bar{G} + 2)\delta^5 \leq (3/2 + 9\delta)(1 + 3\gamma) + (2\bar{G} + 2)\delta^5$, where $\bar{G} \leq (1/\gamma^2 + 2/\delta^2)$, and $\rho = \gamma/2$. The small narrow jobs with widths $\leq \gamma m$ can be placed greedily with NFDH at the side, leaving only $\leq \gamma m$ processors idle. Suppose that the height h'' after packing the small narrow jobs is larger than h' and that the guess corresponds to an approximate solution. Then we obtain $h'' \leq Area(L_{aux})/(m - \gamma m) + (4\bar{G} + 1)h_{max}$, where $h_{max} \leq \delta^5$ and L_{aux} consists of the rounded huge, large and small wide jobs and the original small narrow jobs (see also [15, 21]). Since $Area(L_{aux}) \leq (1 + 5\delta)m(1 + \gamma)$, $h'' \leq \frac{(1+5\delta)(1+\gamma)m}{(1-\gamma)m} + (4\bar{G}+1)\delta^5 \leq (1+5\delta)(1+3\gamma) + (4\bar{G}+1)\delta^5$ using $\gamma \leq 1/3$. Therefore, the total height $\max\{h', h''\}$ of the packing for $\mathcal{J}'$ is at most $(3/2 + 9\delta)(1 + 3\gamma) + (4\bar{G} + 1)\delta^5$. Including the medium jobs, the total height h_{final} can be bounded by $(3/2 + 9\delta)(1 + 3\gamma) + (4\bar{G} + 1)\delta^5 + 2.5\delta \leq (3/2 + 11.5\delta) + \delta + 2.5\delta \leq 3/2 + 15\delta$ using $\gamma = \delta/3$ and $\delta \leq 1/10$. Using $\delta \leq \epsilon/15$, the final height $h_{final} \leq 3/2 + \epsilon \leq (3/2 + \epsilon)OPT(I)$. This gives an approximation algorithm with ratio $1.5 + \epsilon$ for scheduling parallel tasks.

2.5 Faster Solution for Large Jobs

The approach presented above results in an algorithm with running time $n^{f(1/\epsilon)}$ for each $\epsilon > 0$. In this subsection we show how to improve this running time to $f(1/\epsilon) + poly(n)$. All large jobs with width $> \lfloor \alpha m \rfloor$ are placed again via enumeration. Instead of using a dynamic program for the large narrow jobs, we guess the total load of these large jobs assigned to each rounded start time $s\delta^2$ and execution time $h\delta^2$. Let $\Pi_{s,h}^*$ be the total load of large narrow jobs corresponding to the optimum solution. We can guess the vector $\Pi^* = (\Pi_{s,h}^*)$ up to an additional error of $\lfloor \alpha m \rfloor$ in each component. To do this we guess all load vectors $\Pi = (\Pi_{s,h})$ where $\Pi_{s,h} = a_{s,h}\lfloor \alpha m \rfloor$ with $a_{s,h} \in \{0, \ldots, 2/\alpha\}$. To ensure that $(2/\alpha)(\alpha m - 1) \geq m$, we use here again the property that $m \geq 2/\alpha$. Notice that the numbers of different rounded starting times and processing times are bounded by $1/(2\delta^2)$ and $(1+4\delta)/\delta^2$, respectively. The number of all such vectors is bounded by $(2/\alpha+1)^{(1+4\delta)/\delta^2 1/(2\delta^2)} = g(1/\delta)$ for a positive function g using $1/\alpha = p(1/\delta)$, where p is a polynomial. Then, there is a vector Π such that $\Pi_{s,h} \leq \Pi^*_{s,h} \leq \Pi_{s,h} + \lfloor \alpha m \rfloor$ for all s, h. Instead of using Π^*, we use Π for the space reserved for the set $\mathcal{J}_{\ell n}$ of large narrow jobs. Moreover, we set up the following linear program for $\Pi' = \Pi + (\lfloor \alpha m \rfloor, \ldots, \lfloor \alpha m \rfloor)^T$ to determine the positions for most of the large narrow jobs. The linear program uses a variable $y_{j,s}$ for each large narrow job $J_j \in \mathcal{J}_{\ell n}$ and each possible starting time $s\delta^2$.

$$
\begin{aligned}
\sum_{j:p_j=h\delta^2} y_{j,s} q_j &\leq \Pi'_{s,h} && h=1/\delta+1,\ldots,(1/2+\delta)/\delta^2, \\
& && s=0,\ldots,(1+4\delta)/\delta^2-1 \\
\sum_{s:s\delta^2+p_j\leq(1+5\delta)} y_{j,s} &= 1 && J_j\in\mathcal{J}_{ln} \\
y_{j,s} &\geq 0 && J_j\in\mathcal{J}_{ln}, \\
& && s=0,\ldots,(1+4\delta)/\delta^2-1
\end{aligned}
$$

If $\Pi_{s,h} \leq \Pi^*_{s,h} \leq \Pi_{s,h} + \lfloor \alpha m \rfloor$ for all s, h, then there is a fractional (and also integral) solution of the LP corresponding to Π'. The LP for the large narrow jobs can be interpreted as a scheduling problem on a constant number $O(1/\delta^4)$ of unrelated processors [22]. This problem can be solved approximately with ratio $(1+\alpha/2)$ in time $O(n) + g(1/\delta)$, where $1/\alpha = poly(1/\delta)$ and g is exponential in $1/\delta$ [9]. Each approximate solution of the scheduling problem determines positions for large narrow jobs with load bounded by $\Pi_{s,h} + \lfloor \alpha m \rfloor + \alpha m/2 \leq \Pi_{s,h} + 2\lfloor \alpha m \rfloor$ (using $m \geq 2/\alpha$). If we remove for each starting time $s\delta^2$ and execution time $h\delta^2$ a set of large narrow jobs of total load between $2\lfloor \alpha m \rfloor$ and $3\lfloor \alpha m \rfloor$, the remaining jobs fit into the space reserved for the large narrow jobs given by Π. All other jobs have a total load of $(3\lfloor \alpha m \rfloor)[(1+4\delta)/\delta^2][1/(2\delta^2)] \leq 3\lfloor \alpha m \rfloor/\delta^4$, using $\delta \leq 1/4$. If again α is small enough (i.e. if $3\lfloor \alpha m \rfloor/\delta^4 \leq \lfloor (1/8)\delta^4 m \rfloor$ or $3(\alpha m + 1)/\delta^4 \leq (1/8)\delta^4 m - 1$), then all of them can be packed into a gap of height $1/2 + (5/2)\delta$ and width $(1/8)\delta^4 m$. The inequality above holds for $\alpha = (1/48)\delta^8$ and $m \geq 48/\delta^8 + 16/\delta^4$. Therefore, instead of using the dynamic program we can guess the approximate load vector Π and solve the corresponding scheduling program approximately for Π'. If the linear program has an integral solution, then most of the large narrow jobs can be packed according to Π. The remaining jobs can be packed into the gap as described in Subsection 2.3. This step helps us to reduce the running time. The main algorithm works as follows:

(1) compute a 2-approximate solution for $P|size_j|C_{max}$ and scale the instance such that $OPT(I) \in [1/2, 1]$.

(2) determine the constant δ to partition the jobs into four classes and to discard the medium jobs. Then round the processing times of large and huge jobs to obtain a simplified approximate schedule (see Subsection 2.1).

(3) for each value $T(i) = 1/2 + i\delta$, $i \in \{0, 1, \ldots, 1/(2\delta)\}$ scale the instance again by $T(i)$ and try to find an approximate schedule as follows:

(3.1) guess the starting times for the large jobs with width $> \lfloor \alpha m \rfloor$, an approximate load vector Π for large narrow jobs (see Subsection 2.5) and a position of the gap of height $1/2 + (5/2)\delta$ and width $\lfloor (1/8)\delta^4 m \rfloor$ (and in case 2 the position of a huge

wide job J_j^* or the position and height of a subset of huge jobs with large width as described in Subsection 2.3).

(3.2) for each possible guess

(3.2.1) if there is a time step with more than m processors used by large and huge jobs (after the transformation of the schedule), then discard the guess above. Otherwise calculate the number of free processors in the layers for the small jobs as described in Subsection 2.4. If the total area of all small jobs is larger than the free space in the layers, then discard the guess, too.

(3.2.2) solve the linear program to the enlarged load vector Π' for large narrow jobs and solve the linear program for the small wide jobs as described in Subsection 2.4 and 2.5. If both linear programs have a feasible solution, then store the guessed starting times, the approximate load vector, the position of the gap and both feasible solutions. Otherwise discard the guess, too.

(4) for the smallest $T(i)$ where we obtain in step (3.2) a feasible guess, we assign the large jobs according to the load vector and place the remaining non-packed large jobs into the gap. Next we place the huge jobs such that most of them finish at time $1 + 5\delta$; in case 2 either job J_j^* or a subset $\mathcal{J}'$ is placed depending on the guessed starting time.

(5) The small wide jobs are packed into the layers according to the LP solution and the small narrow jobs are packed greedily into the layers (as described in Subsection 2.4). Finally we pack the remaining non-packed jobs at the end of the schedule.

The list scheduling algorithm in step (1) can be implemented in time $O(n \log n)$ by sorting the jobs in non-increasing order of their widths. The running time of our algorithm is dominated by the number of guessing steps (i.e. exponential in $1/\delta$) and the running time to solve the corresponding scheduling problem approximately for each approximate load vector. By merging large narrow jobs together with the same profile, the number of large narrow jobs can be reduced in a pre-processing step to $\min[n, (\log(1/\delta)/\alpha)^{O(1/\delta^4)}]$ [9]. This enables us to solve step (3) of our algorithm in time $O(n) + g'(1/\delta)$. Since the small jobs can be packed into the layers in time $O(n \log n) + poly(1/\delta)$, the total running time of our algorithm for $m \geq 2/\alpha = poly(1/\delta)$ (where δ depends on ϵ [16]) is at most $O(n \log n) + f(1/\epsilon)$.

For $m \leq poly(1/\delta)$, the situation is much easier. First we compute an exact assignment of rounded starting times $s\delta^2$ to all large and huge jobs via dynamic programming in time $m^{O(1/\delta^4)} = 2^{O(1/\delta^4 \log(1/\delta))}$ (as described in [17]). This implies that we can avoid the construction of the gap for the large jobs and the delays for the huge jobs. For each feasible assignment above we calculate the number of free processor in each horizontal layer of height δ^2 and solve the linear program for the small jobs as described in Section 2.4 approximately in $poly(1/\delta)$ time. As above we insert the small jobs into the horizontal layers in $O(n \log n) + poly(1/\delta)$ time. Therefore, in this case we compute all starting times for the jobs in time $O(n \log n) + f(1/\epsilon)$, where the schedule length is at most $(1 + \epsilon)OPT(I)$. Furthermore, the total number of processor intervals in the canonical schedule can be bounded by $O(nf'(1/\epsilon))$.

3. SCHEDULING MOLDABLE TASKS

3.1 Guessing Steps

First we guess the value of $\delta \in (0, \epsilon/25]$ such that the load of the medium jobs in the optimum solution is small compared to all jobs and $1/\delta$ is integral. This is still possible although we do not know the optimum solution or δ in advance (see also [17]). For simplicity let us suppose that we know δ; in the algorithm similar to [17] we test a constant number of choices for δ. Again we suppose that the number of processors m is larger than a polynomial; the exact bound is specified later. For $m \leq poly(1/\delta)$ we can use the PTAS for $Pm|fctn_j|C_{max}$ [14]. As in the case with parallel tasks, we can scale the instance such that the optimum makespan $OPT(I) \in [1/2, 1]$. To do this we first compute a 2-approximate solution using the algorithm by Turek et al. [28] with value $MOL(I) \leq 2OPT(I)$ and divide all processing times by $MOL(I)$. Notice that the input length of a problem instance I satisfies $|I| \leq O(\sum_j ||D_j|(\log(m) + \log(p_{max})))$ and $|I| \geq n + \log(m) + \max_j |D_j| + \log(p_{max})$.

In the first phase we guess the structure of the small wide jobs in an optimum solution. Let γ be a constant that depends polynomially on δ. We guess $1/\gamma^2$ many different small wide jobs with height $\leq \delta^5$ and width $> \lfloor \gamma m \rfloor$. Clearly there is only a polynomial number n^{1/γ^2} of choices. For these chosen jobs J_j we also guess the number of used processors $\ell_j \in D_j \subset M$. Notice that there is only a polynomial number $(\max_j |D_j|)^{1/\gamma^2}$ of possible choices. If there are less than $1/\gamma^2$ small wide jobs in the solution, we simply remove them from the solution and execute them at the end of the schedule. This increases the length of the schedule by at most $1/\gamma^2 \delta^5 \leq \delta$ using $\delta^2 \leq \gamma$.

Otherwise the $1/\gamma^2$ jobs play the role of the rounded values; if we put all small wide jobs ordered by their widths on a stack (see Figure 9), then the $1/\gamma^2$ jobs form so called threshold rectangles. The corresponding rounding idea was used by Kenyon and Rémila [21] to obtain an AFPTAS for 2D strip packing. We sort the widths of the chosen jobs such that $w_1 \geq w_2 \geq \ldots \geq w_{1/\gamma^2}$. Let H be the total height of all small wide jobs in an optimum solution. We guess the approximate total height H_{app} up to a multiple of γ^2; i.e. $H_{app} = c\gamma^2 \in [H - \gamma^2, H]$. Since the optimum makespan $OPT(I) \in [1/2, 1]$ and each small wide job has width $> \lfloor \gamma m \rfloor$, the total height H of all small wide jobs corresponding to an optimum solution is bounded by $m/\gamma m \leq 1/\gamma$. This implies that the number of choices for c is at most $1 + 1/\gamma^3$. Removing the widest small jobs with total height at most $\gamma^2 + \delta^5 \leq \delta$ from the optimum solution generates a solution where the total height of the small wide jobs is at most H_{app}. By removing also the guessed small wide jobs, we obtain $1/\gamma^2 - 1$ groups of jobs with each group of total height $\leq \gamma^2 H_{app}$. The removed jobs have total height at most $1/\gamma^2 \delta^5 \leq \delta$. Considering only different widths, we obtain a sequence $w_1' > w_2' > \ldots > w_G'$ with $G \leq 1/\gamma^2 - 1$, where each rounded width w_i' occurs with total height $c_i \gamma^2 H_{app}$ in our solution where $c_i \in \{1, \ldots, 1/\gamma^2 - 1\}$. For simplicity, let w_0' be the maximum original guessed width w_1. An example

with the stack for the original small wide jobs and the stack for the rounded small wide jobs is given in Figure 9.

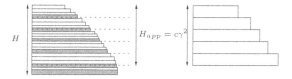

Figure 9: Stack with small wide jobs corresponding to an optimal solution

Now we guess for each horizontal layer ℓ of height δ^2 in our solution the approximate number $\beta^{(\ell)}$ of processors or approximate width used by small jobs. Since small jobs are packed into the layers fractionally, it is sufficient to consider here a relaxation of the solution and to allow that small jobs are divided into horizontal slices and packed into the layers. The underlying idea here is a linear program relaxation for the small jobs. The width of a layer for small jobs is determined by the maximum width $maxwidth^{(\ell)}$ of a configuration with small wide jobs (i.e. given by a subset of small wide jobs) in it plus an integral multiple of γm (i.e. a fractional value) to reserve approximately some additional space for small narrow jobs. For each horizontal layer, the number of guesses is at most $n^{1/\gamma}(1/\gamma + 1)$. Therefore, the total number of guesses here is polynomial in n.

LEMMA 3.1. *Suppose that there is an approximate schedule for $\mathcal{J}'$ (with rounded processing and starting times for huge and large jobs, but without medium jobs) with length $\leq 1 + 5\delta$. Furthermore, let $\beta_{org}^{(\ell)}$ be the original number of processors used by small jobs in layer $\ell = 0, \ldots, (1 + 5\delta)/\delta^2 - 1$.*

Then there exists also an approximate schedule for almost all jobs in $\mathcal{J}'$ with length $\leq (1 + 5\delta)$ that only uses $\beta^{(\ell)}$ processors for small jobs in layer ℓ where $\beta^{(\ell)} = maxwidth^{(\ell)} + \alpha_\ell \gamma m \in [\beta_{org}^{(\ell)} - \gamma m, \beta_{org}^{(\ell)}]$ and $\alpha_\ell \in \mathbb{Z}^+$. The non-scheduled jobs are all small narrow and have total area $\leq 2\gamma m(1 + 5\delta)$.

For the proof of this lemma we refer to our full version. If we additionally remove the widest group of rounded small wide jobs with height $\gamma^2 H_{app}$ (i.e. we set $\bar{c}_1 = c_1 - 1$ and $\bar{c}_i = c_i$ for $i \geq 2$), then this generates an approximate solution for the remaining original small wide jobs that fit fractionally into the layers. Let $\beta^{(\ell)}$ be the guessed width for layer ℓ. Via a linear program (similar to Subsection 2.4)

$$
\begin{aligned}
\sum_j x_j^{(\ell)} &= \delta^2 & \ell &= 0, \ldots, (1 + 5\delta)/\delta^2 - 1 \\
\sum_\ell \sum_j x_j^{(\ell)} a_{j,i}^{(\ell)} &\geq \bar{c}_i \gamma^2 H_{app} & i &= 1, \ldots, G \\
x_j^{(\ell)} &\geq 0 & \ell &= 0, \ldots, (1 + 5\delta)/\delta^2 - 1 \\
& & j &= 1, \ldots, |\mathcal{C}^{(\ell)}|
\end{aligned}
$$

with variables $x_j^{(\ell)}$ for configurations $C_j^{(\ell)}$ with total width at most $\beta^{(\ell)}$ (i.e. a multiset $\{a_{j,1} : w_1', \ldots, a_{j,G} : w_G'\}$ with $\sum_i a_{j,i}^{(\ell)} w_i' \leq \beta^{(\ell)}$) we can test whether the rounded small wide jobs fit fractionally into the horizontal layers of widths $\beta^{(0)}, \ldots, \beta^{(\frac{1+5\delta}{\delta^2}-1)}$. The linear program has a constant number of variables and constraints, where the number of variables is exponential in $1/\gamma$ and the number of constraints is polynomial in $1/\delta + 1/\gamma$. Moreover, the coefficients $a_{j,i}^{(\ell)}$ in the LP are bounded by the constant $1/\gamma$ (using $w'_i \geq \gamma m$ and $\beta^{(\ell)} \leq m$). The linear program can be solved exactly in time polynomial in the number of variables and constraints (e.g. using the algorithm by Vaidya [29]). Notice that we here do not select which jobs are small, we only test whether rounded small wide jobs of width w'_i and total height $\bar{c}_i \gamma^2 H_{app}$ fit into the horizontal layers fractionally.

Next we guess all jobs and their rounded starting and execution time in our solution with height $\in (\delta, 1 + 2\delta)$ and width $> \lfloor \alpha m \rfloor$. For each guessed job J_j with rounded execution time $a\delta^2$ we choose the minimum number of processors $\ell \in D_j$ such that $p_j(\ell) \in ((a-1)\delta^2, a\delta^2]$; if there is no such ℓ then this guess is infeasible and can be discarded. We guess also which jobs are scheduled as medium jobs with large width $> \lfloor \alpha m \rfloor$ (here we choose as width a number of processors $\ell \in D_j$ such that $p_j(\ell) \in (\delta^5, \delta]$ with minimum area $\ell p_j(\ell)$; if there is no such ℓ the guess can be discarded). Since we have at most $\leq (1 + 5\delta)/(\delta^5 \alpha)$ many such jobs, this can be done in polynomial time. If the total area of all guessed medium wide jobs is larger than $\delta(1 + 2\delta)m$, then we also discard the corresponding guess. Finally, we guess for each rounded huge execution time $h\delta^2 \in (1/2 + \delta, 1 + 5\delta]$ and each rounded starting time $s\delta^2$ a constant number $K = 3\bar{K} \leq 6(1/\delta^2 + 1/\gamma^2)$ of jobs with the largest width (the width is determined as the minimum number of processors used as above). Here $\bar{K} = (1 + 5\delta)/\delta^2 + 1/\gamma^2 + 2$ is an upper bound for the number of fractional variables in a linear program described in the next subsection. All other jobs assigned to the same rounded execution time h and starting time s need a width smaller than or equal to the smallest guessed width $\bar{w}_{h,s}$. If the total number of processors in a layer used by large and huge jobs is larger than m, then we also discard the guess.

Similar to the case with parallel jobs, we could also guess the total approximate load of all large jobs for each rounded execution time and rounded starting time. But as we see below, this does not help us to determine the free space for the huge jobs. In fact, it is not possible to determine the exact structure consisting of the total width for each rounded huge processing time and each rounded starting time. This is one of the main difficulties here. There could be different possible scenarios corresponding to the same load values (see also Figure 10).

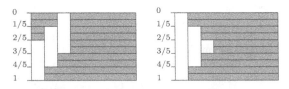

Figure 10: Different scenarios for the same remaining processor numbers

3.2 Linear Program Formulation

We solve this difficulty via a linear program that implicitly determines the corresponding best possible scenario. We use variables $x^{(huge)}_{j,i}$, $x^{(large)}_{j,i}$, $x^{(sw)}_{j,i}$, $x^{(sn)}_j$, and $x^{(m)}_j$ to indicate whether a job J_j is executed as huge, large, small wide, small narrow or medium job (here index i indicates either the rounded execution time $i\delta^2$ for huge and large jobs or the rounded width w'_i). Furthermore, we use a variable $y_{j,i,k}$

to indicate the starting time $k\delta^2$ of a large or huge job J_j with running time $i\delta^2$.

For each job J_j executed as a huge or large job with rounded execution time $i\delta^2 \in (\delta, 1 + 5\delta]$, let $A_{j,i}$ be the minimum number of processors $a \in D_j$ used by J_j with running time $p_j(a) \in ((i-1)\delta^2, i\delta^2]$ (this gives the smallest number of processors with such a rounded processing time). If there is no such $a \in D_j$ with this property, then we set the corresponding variable $x^{(h)}_{j,i} = 0$ or $x^{(\ell)}_{j,i} = 0$. For each job J_j executed as a small wide job with rounded processor number w'_i for $i \in \{1, \dots, G\}$, let $B_{j,i}$ be the minimum processing time $p_j(a)$ over all processor numbers $a \in (w'_{i+1}, w'_i] \cap D_j$ (this gives the smallest execution time or height in the stack for the 2-dimensional strip packing). Again, if there is no such a then we set $x^{(sw)}_{j,i} = 0$.

In addition we allow that some jobs are small and very wide (these are the jobs in the last group of the original stack). For a job J_j in this group, let $B_{j,0}$ be the minimum processing time $p_j(a)$ over all processor numbers $a \in D_j \cap [w'_1, m]$ (for $D_j \cap [w'_1, m] = \emptyset$ we set $x^{(sw)}_{j,0} = 0$). For J_j executed as a medium (with processing time in $(\delta^5, \delta]$) or small narrow job (with number of processors $\leq \lfloor \gamma m \rfloor$ and processing time $\leq \delta^5$), let $C_{j,m}$ (and $C_{j,sn}$) be the smallest area $ap_j(a)$ over all possible feasible choices of $a \in D_j$ such that $p_j(a)$ is medium and ($p_j(a)$ is small and a is narrow), respectively. Again, if there is no such $a \in D_j$ then we set $x^{(m)}_j = 0$ or $x^{(sn)}_j = 0$.

Let Π_ℓ be the number of processors used by all pre-placed large and huge jobs in the horizontal layer ℓ plus the approximate value $\beta^{(\ell)}$ for the small wide jobs. The remaining $m - \Pi_\ell$ processors can be used for other large and huge jobs. Finally, let $\mathcal{J}''$ be the set of jobs which are not pre-placed in our guessing steps. The guessed small wide jobs are not considered in the LP below; they are packed at the end of the schedule.

The linear program for the moldable jobs has the following form.

$$\sum_{k:(k+i)\delta^2 \leq 1 + 5\delta} y_{j,i,k} = x^{(huge)}_{j,i} \qquad \forall J_j \in \mathcal{J}'' \forall i$$
$$\sum_{k:(k+i)\delta^2 \leq 1 + 5\delta} y_{j,i,k} = x^{(large)}_{j,i} \qquad \forall J_j \in \mathcal{J}'' \forall i$$
$$\sum_{j,i,k:k \leq \ell < k+i} y_{j,i,k} A_{j,i} \leq m - \Pi_\ell \ \forall \ell = 0, \dots, \tfrac{1+5\delta}{\delta^2} - 1$$
$$\sum_j x^{(sw)}_{j,i} B_{j,i} \leq c_i \gamma^2 H_{app} \qquad \forall i = 1, \dots, G$$
$$\sum_j x^{(sw)}_{j,0} B_{j,0} \leq \gamma^2$$
$$\sum_j x^{(m)}_j C_{j,m} \leq \lceil \delta(1+2\delta)m \rceil$$
$$\sum_{j,i} x^{(sw)}_{j,i} B_{j,i} w'_i + \sum_j x^{(sn)}_j C_{j,sn} \leq \sum_\ell \beta^{(\ell)} \delta^2 + 4\gamma m$$
$$\sum_i x^{(huge)}_{j,i} + \sum_i x^{(large)}_{j,i} + \sum_i x^{(sw)}_{j,i} + x^{(sn)}_j + x^{(m)}_j = 1$$
$$\forall J_j \in \mathcal{J}''$$
$$x^{(huge)}_{j,i}, x^{(large)}_{j,i}, x^{(sw)}_{j,i}, x^{(sn)}_j, x^{(m)}_j \geq 0 \qquad \forall J_j \in \mathcal{J}'' \forall i$$
$$y_{j,i,k} \geq 0 \qquad \forall J_j \in \mathcal{J}'' \forall i, k$$

In addition we set a variable $y_{j,i,k} = 0$, if the width $A_{j,i}$ of job J_j with rounded processing time $i\delta^2$ and starting time $k\delta^2$ is larger than the smallest pre-assigned width $\bar{w}_{i\delta^2, k\delta^2}$. Furthermore, we set $y_{j,i,k} = 0$ for $i\delta^2 \leq \delta$. If a job J_j is chosen as a medium wide job in the guessing step above, we set $x^{(m)}_j = 1$. The additive term in the last inequality is given by the additional space that we need to place all small jobs.

LEMMA 3.2. *Suppose that there is an approximate schedule $\mathcal{S}$ for $\mathcal{J}'$ (with rounded processing and starting times for* *huge and large jobs, but without medium jobs) with length $\leq 1 + 5\delta$ where the medium jobs in $(\mathcal{J} \setminus \mathcal{J}')$ have total area at most $\delta(1 + 2\delta)m$. Furthermore, let $\beta^{(\ell)}$ be the approximate number of processors in $\mathcal{S}$ used by small jobs in layer ℓ, for $\ell = 0, \ldots, (1 + 5\delta)/\delta^2 - 1$.*

Then there also exists a feasible solution of the linear program for the non-guessed jobs in $\mathcal{J}''$ (including medium jobs).

The proof of the lemma above can be found in the full paper [18].

3.3 How to handle the Fractional Jobs?

In total we here have a linear program with $\leq \bar{K} = (1 + 5\delta)/\delta^2 + 1/\gamma^2 + 2 \leq 2(1/\delta^2 + 1/\gamma^2) = O(1/\delta^2 + 1/\gamma^2)$ (using $\delta \leq 1/5$ and $\gamma \leq 1/2$) inequalities (not counting the non-negativity constraints) plus one equality for each non-preassigned job. Actually we can replace the variables $x_{j,i}^{(huge)}$, $x_{j,i}^{(large)}$ in the equalities with the sum of the corresponding variables $y_{j,i,k}$. Let n' be the number of non-preassigned jobs. A basic feasible solution of the LP has at most $n' + \bar{K}$ variables with strict positive value. Since we need at least one positive variable for each job, the number of fractional variables can be bounded by $\bar{K} \leq O(1/\delta^2 + 1/\gamma^2)$. The jobs with integral values can be placed according to the LP values. Jobs that have a fractional amount $x_j^{(sn)} \in (0, 1)$ or $x_{j,i}^{(sw)} \in (0, 1)$ (like small jobs) can be eliminated and scheduled at the end. This gives $\leq 2(1/\delta^2 + 1/\gamma^2)\delta^5 \leq 4(1/\delta^4)\delta^5 \leq 4\delta$ as additional height. Jobs that have a fractional amount $x_j^{(m)} \in (0, 1)$ (e.g. a fractional medium job) have a total area $\leq \alpha m \delta 2(1/\delta^2 + 1/\gamma^2) \leq \delta m$ if $\alpha \leq (1/4)\delta^4$ is small enough. Here αm is the largest width and δ is the largest execution time of a medium job, respectively. The list scheduling algorithm generates a schedule for these jobs with height $\leq 2\max[\delta m/m, \delta] = 2\delta$. Here we use the assumption that medium jobs of large width are guessed before.

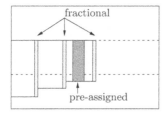

Figure 11: Placement of pre-assigned and fractional huge jobs

Jobs that have a fractional amount $x_{j,i}^{(large)} \in (0, 1)$ with $i\delta^2 \leq 1/2 + \delta$ (i.e. fractional large jobs) can be grouped into a block of height $1/2 + \delta$ and width $\leq 2(1/\delta^2 + 1/\gamma^2) \cdot \lfloor \alpha m \rfloor \leq \delta^5 m$ for $\alpha \leq (1/4)\delta^9$ and $\delta^2 \leq \gamma$. Since the total width is integral, the width of the block can be bounded by $\lfloor \delta^5 m \rfloor$. These jobs can be packed into a gap similar to our approach for parallel jobs. The main difficulty now are the remaining fractional huge jobs (i.e. jobs with $x_{j,i}^{(huge)} \in (0, 1)$ and $i\delta^2 > 1/2 + \delta$). All other jobs have either integral corresponding variables or are removed in the step above. By vertical exchanges of processors and corresponding configurations and moving all huge jobs up similar to the variant

with parallel jobs, all huge jobs or their fractional parts finish at the same time $1 + 5\delta$ (see Figure 11). In Figure 11 we have three fractional parts of a huge job with different execution times and one indicated pre-assigned job.

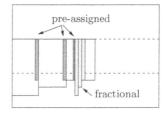

Figure 12: The solution after exchanging fractional and pre-assigned huge jobs

Huge jobs with fractional amounts for different rounded execution times have to be grouped together. We have to choose one of the corresponding processor numbers and to modify the generated schedule. For each such job J_j, we choose the smallest width m_j (i.e. the number of processors) used among its fractional parts. Let k_j be the corresponding rounded processing time with width m_j and let b_j be the smallest processing time among all fractional parts for J_j. By exchanging with a part of a pre-assigned job J^* of larger width (but with the smallest possible one) in the group corresponding to b_j, all fractional parts of J_j can be placed together into the group with processing time b_j. The exchanged parts of J^* are placed instead of the fractional parts into the other groups all finishing at time $1 + 5\delta$ (see Figure 12 for an illustration of our example above; fractional parts of the huge job and parts of the pre-assigned huge job are exchanged).

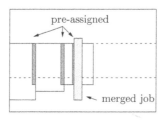

Figure 13: Solution after merging the fractional parts of a huge job

The fractional parts of J_j are merged together as one job with processing time k_j; that results in a width smaller than or equal to the sum of the fractional parts. But now the height of this job could be larger than the processing time b_j. Since J^* was pre-assigned, we can move J_j downwards to the starting time of J^* (see also Figure 13 where the merged job is moved downwards). Since we have a free space of height at least $1 + 5\delta$ just above the starting time of J^*, the merged job J_j fits into this gap. Since K is larger than the number of fractional variables, we can do this exchange step for all fractional jobs one by one. Notice that J^* is now fractionally assigned to different groups. On the other hand, we do not change the starting or finishing time of J^*. Furthermore, we do not increase the number of processors used for J_j before we merge the parts of J_j together. This implies that the starting times still satisfy the sufficient condition to have a feasible schedule. Therefore, we are still able to generate a canonical schedule.

3.4 How to generate the Gap?

Similar to the scheduling problem with parallel tasks we consider different cases to locate the gap for the fractional large jobs of height $1/2 + (5/2)\delta$ and total width at most $\delta^5 m$. We consider the situation before we delay some jobs.

Case 1: The total width of all huge jobs is at most $m/2$.

Case 1.1: The total width of all large jobs intersecting with the horizontal line at $1/2 + (5/2)\delta$ is at most $m/4$. In this case we have a gap of width $m/4$ as before.

Case 1.2: The total width of all large jobs intersecting with the horizontal line at $1/2 + (5/2)\delta$ is larger than $m/4$. Then, there is again at least one level with width $\geq \frac{m/4}{(1+5\delta)/(2\delta^2)} \geq (1/4)\delta^2 m$ for $\delta \leq 1/5$. This generates a gap of width $(1/4)\delta^2 m$ just above one group of large jobs finishing at the same level.

Case 2: The total width of all huge jobs with height $> 1/2 + \delta$ is larger than $m/2$.

Case 2.1 There is a huge job J_{j*} of height $> 1/2 + \delta$ and width $\geq (1/8)\delta^4 m$ (if there are several such jobs we take the widest one). Such a job is pre-assigned if $(1/8)\delta^4 m > \alpha m$ or equivalently $\alpha < (1/8)\delta^4$. We have chosen α small enough such that this is fulfilled. Since K is large enough, the job J_{j*} is not touched in the exchange step before (since we use there jobs with the smallest width). Then we simply take this job J_{j*} and do not modify the starting time of J_{j*} given by the pre-assignment. After moving the other jobs above J_{j*} by $1/2 + (5/2)\delta$, we obtain a gap of height $1/2 + (5/2)\delta$ and width $(1/8)\delta^4 m$ just above J_{j*}.

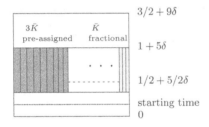

Figure 14: A level with $3\bar{K}$ pre-assigned wide jobs and some fractional jobs

Case 2.2: There is no huge job of width $\geq (1/8)\delta^4 m$. In this case there is at least one finishing time or level with jobs of the same height and total width $\geq \frac{m/2}{(1+5\delta)(1/2+\delta)/\delta^4} \geq (1/4)\delta^4 m$.

Consider this level of jobs with the same finishing time and same height in more detail. For an illustration with $3\bar{K}$ pre-assigned wide jobs and some fractional jobs on such a level we refer to Figure 14. Notice that it contains at least 3 times the number of fractional variables (i.e. $K = 3\bar{K}$ and $\bar{K} = (1+5\delta)/\delta^2 + 1/\gamma^2 + 2 \leq O(1/\delta^2 + 1/\gamma^2)$) of pre-assigned jobs with larger width than the other assigned jobs. And suppose that we only choose pre-assigned jobs (at most $\bar{K}$ many) with the smallest width in the exchange step. These jobs or parts of them are replaced by other maybe longer merged jobs. In addition there are $\leq \bar{K}$ fractional jobs in this block. Some of them stay here and are merged later with other fractional ones and some of them are replaced by pieces

of pre-assigned jobs of other blocks. The total width of these $\leq 2\bar{K}$ exchanged jobs after the replacement is at most the width of the $2\bar{K}$ wider jobs. Therefore, the largest $2\bar{K}$ pre-assigned jobs plus the jobs with corresponding integral LP values cover at least $1/2$ of the entire width of the block. This gives a block of width $\geq \lfloor (1/8)\delta^4 m \rfloor$. We can move this block and the corresponding jobs to the starting time given by the LP. This gives us a gap of $1/2 + (5/2)\delta$ and width $\geq \lfloor (1/8)\delta^4 m \rfloor$ just above this block (see also Figure 15). If $\delta \leq 1/8$ then $\delta^5 m \leq (1/8)\delta^4 m$. This implies that $\lfloor \delta^5 m \rfloor \leq \lfloor (1/8)\delta^4 m \rfloor$. Therefore, this gap can be used to insert the block with all fractional large jobs.

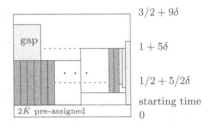

Figure 15: Using a wide level to locate the gap

The guessed small wide jobs, the fractional small narrow and small wide and the fractional and integral medium jobs generate an additional height of at most $\delta + 4\delta + 4.5\delta \leq 10\delta$. Notice that the height for the integral medium jobs $2 \max\left[\frac{\lceil \delta(1+2\delta)m \rceil}{m}, \delta\right]$ is at most 2.5δ using $m \geq 1/\delta^2$ and $\delta \leq 1/25$. Furthermore, the approximate guess of the stack height (including one additional small job), rounding of the widths of the small wide jobs and modifying the total width for small jobs in each layer gives an additional area of at most $\gamma^2 m + \delta^5 m + \gamma^2 H_{app} m + 2\gamma m(1 + 5\delta) \leq 5\delta^2 m$ using $H_{app} \leq 1/\gamma$, $\gamma = \delta^2$ and $\delta \leq 1/25$. List scheduling gives us here an additional height of at most $10\delta^2 \leq \delta$ using $\delta \leq 1/25$. Similar to the variant with parallel tasks almost all small wide and narrow jobs can be inserted into the horizontal layers. This step costs an additional height of $(4\bar{G} + 1)\delta^5 \leq 5\delta$ where $\bar{G} \leq 1/\gamma 2 + 2/\delta^2$ (see also Section 2.4).

Therefore, the final length of our schedule can be bounded by $(3/2 + 9\delta) + 16\delta \leq 3/2 + 25\delta \leq 3/2 + \epsilon$ using $\delta \leq (1/25)\epsilon$. The running time of the algorithm is dominated by the number of guesses multiplied with the running time to solve the linear program above. The number of variables and constraints are both bounded by $O(n(1/\delta^4 + 1/\gamma^2)) = O(n^2)$. Furthermore, the coefficients of the (in-)equalities are at most $O(mp_{max}/\gamma^5)$ (in order to get integral coefficients some of the inequalities are multiplied by $1/\gamma^4$, $1/\gamma^2$ or $1/\gamma$). Since a linear program with N variables and M constraints can be solved in time $O(((M + N)N^2 + (M + N)^{1.5}N)L)$ [29], where L is the length of the input, the running time to solve our LP can be bounded by $O(n^5(\log(m + p_{max})))$. Notice that L can be bounded by $O(n^2/\delta^8 \log(mp_{max}/\gamma)) = O(n^2 \log(m + p_{max}))$. In addition, the number of guesses is polynomial in $\max |D_j|$ and n for any fixed $\delta > 0$. Therefore, the total running time is polynomial in n, $\max |D_j|$ and $\log(p_{max} + m)$ (i.e. polynomial in the input length of the instance).

4. CONCLUSION

In this paper, we have presented an approximation algorithm with running time $O(n \log n) + f(1/\epsilon)$ which computes a schedule for parallel tasks of length at most $(1.5 + \epsilon)OPT(I)$. This narrows the gap between the lower bound of 1.5 and the previous upper bound of 2. Furthermore we have generalized our approximation algorithm to moldable tasks. Of course, faster approximation algorithms for the scheduling problem are interesting. An interesting open problem is the question whether there is an approximation algorithm for (non-moldable or moldable) parallel tasks with ratio exactly 1.5 (i.e. avoiding the additional $\epsilon > 0$) or not. We believe that the proposed techniques in this paper can also be used for other scheduling problems.

5. REFERENCES

[1] A.K. Amoura, E. Bampis, C. Kenyon, and Y. Manoussakis. Scheduling independent multiprocessor tasks. *Algorithmica*, 32(2):247–261, 2007.

[2] K.P. Belkhale and P. Banerjee. Approximate algorithms for the partitionable independent task scheduling problem. *Proc. of International Conference on Parallel Processing (ICPP)*, pages 72–75, 1990.

[3] J. Blazewicz, K.H. Ecker, E. Pesch, G. Schmidt, and J. Weglarz. *Handbook on Scheduling: From Theory to Applications*. Springer, 2007.

[4] T. Decker, T. Lücking, and B. Monien. A 5/4 - approximation algorithm for scheduling identical malleable tasks. *Theoretical Computer Science*, 361(2):226–240, 2006.

[5] M. Drozdowski. *Scheduling for Parallel Processing*. Computer Communications and Networks, Springer, 2009.

[6] J. Du and J.Y.T. Leung. Complexity of scheduling parallel task systems. *SIAM Journal on Discrete Mathematics*, 2(4):473–487, 1989.

[7] P.-F. Dutot, G. Mounie, and D. Trystram. Scheduling parallel tasks: approximation algorithms, *Handbook of Scheduling*, CRC Press, Ch. 26, 2004.

[8] A. Feldmann, J. Sgall, and S.-H. Teng. Dynamic scheduling on parallel machines. *Theoretical Computer Science*, 130:49–72, 1994.

[9] A. Fishkin, K. Jansen, and M. Mastrolilli. Grouping techniques for scheduling problems: faster and simpler. *Algorithmica*, 51:183-199, 2008.

[10] M.R. Garey and R.L. Graham. Bounds for multiprocessor scheduling with resource constraints, *SIAM Journal on Computing*, 4:187-200, 1975.

[11] M.R. Garey and D.S. Johnson. *Computers and Intractability: A Guide to the Theory of NP-Completeness*. W. H. Freeman and Company, 1979.

[12] M.D. Grigoriadis, L.G. Khachiyan, L. Porkolab, and J. Villavicencio: Approximate max-min resource sharing for structured concave optimization, *SIAM Journal on Optimization*, 41: 1081–1091, 2001.

[13] L. Hall and D. Shmoys. Approximation schemes for constrained scheduling problems. *Proc. of IEEE Symposium on Foundations of Computer Science (FOCS)*, pages 134–140, 1989.

[14] K. Jansen and L. Porkolab. Linear-time approximation schemes for scheduling malleable parallel tasks. *Algorithmica*, 32(3):507–520, 2002.

[15] K. Jansen. Approximation algorithms for min-max and max-min resource sharing problems, and applications. In *Efficient Approximation and Online Algorithms*, LNCS 3484, pages 156–202, 2006.

[16] K. Jansen and R. Solis-Oba. New approximability results for 2-dimensional packing problems. *Proc. of Mathematical Foundations of Computer Science (MFCS)*, pages 103–114, 2007.

[17] K. Jansen and R. Thöle. Approximation algorithms for scheduling parallel jobs. *SIAM Journal on Computing*, 39, 3571–3615, 2010.

[18] K. Jansen. A $(3/2 + \epsilon)$ approximation algorithm for scheduling malleable and non-malleable parallel tasks. *Technical Report* TR-12-03, Department of Computer Science, University of Kiel.

[19] B. Johannes. Scheduling parallel jobs to minimize the makespan. *Journal of Scheduling*, 9(5):433–452, 2006.

[20] R. Kannan. Minkowski's convex body theorem and integer programming. *Mathematics of Operations Research*, 12:415–440, 1987.

[21] C. Kenyon and E. Rémila. A near optimal solution to a two-dimensional cutting stock problem. *Mathematics of Operations Research*, 25:645–656, 2000.

[22] J.K. Lenstra, D.B. Shmoys, and E. Tardos. Approximation algorithms for scheduling unrelated parallel machines. *Mathematical Programming*, 46:269-271, 1990.

[23] J.Y.T. Leung, editor. *Handbook of Scheduling: Algorithms, Models, and Performance Analysis*. Chapman and Hall/CRC, 2004.

[24] W.T. Ludwig. Algorithms for scheduling malleable and non-malleable parallel tasks. PhD thesis, University if Wisconsin-Madison, 1995.

[25] W.T. Ludwig and P. Tiwari. Scheduling malleable and nonmalleable parallel tasks. *Proc. of ACM-SIAM Symposium on Discrete Algorithms (SODA)*, pages 167–176, 1994.

[26] G. Mounie, C. Rapine, and D. Trystram. A $\frac{3}{2}$ - approximation algorithm for scheduling independent monotonic malleable tasks. *SIAM Journal on Computing*, 37(2):401–412, 2007.

[27] E. Naroska and U. Schwiegelshohn. On an on-line scheduling problem for parallel jobs. *Information Processing Letters*, 81: 297–304, 2002.

[28] J. Turek, J.L. Wolf, and P.S. Yu. Approximate algorithms for scheduling parallelizable tasks. *Proc. of ACM Symposium on Parallel Algorithms and Architectures (SPAA)*, pages 323–332, 1992.

[29] P.M. Vaidya. An algorithm for linear programming which requires $O(((m + n)n^2 + (m + n)^{1.5}n)L)$ arithmetic operations. *Mathematical Programming*, 47: 175–201, 1990.

Cache-Conscious Scheduling of Streaming Applications

Kunal Agrawal
Washington University in
St. Louis
kunal@wustl.edu

Jeremy T. Fineman
Georgetown University
jfineman@cs.georgetown.edu

Jordan Krage
Washington University in
St. Louis
jordan.krage@wustl.edu

Charles E. Leiserson
Massachusetts Institute of
Technology
cel@mit.edu

Sivan Toledo
Tel-Aviv University
stoledo@tau.ac.il

ABSTRACT

This paper considers the problem of scheduling streaming applications on uniprocessors in order to minimize the number of cache-misses. Streaming applications are represented as a directed graph (or multigraph), where nodes are *computation modules* and edges are *channels*. When a module fires, it consumes some data-items from its input channels and produces some items on its output channels. In addition, each module may have some state (either code or data) which represents the memory locations that must be loaded into cache in order to execute the module. We consider *synchronous dataflow graphs* where the input and output rates of modules are known in advance and do not change during execution. We also assume that the state size of modules is known in advance.

Our main contribution is to show that for a large and important class of streaming computations, cache-efficient scheduling is essentially equivalent to solving a constrained graph partitioning problem. A streaming computation from this class has a cache-efficient schedule if and only if its graph has a low-bandwidth partition of the modules into components (subgraphs) whose total state fits within the cache, where the *bandwidth* of the partition is the number of data items that cross intercomponent channels per data item that enters the graph.

Given a good partition, we describe a runtime strategy for scheduling two classes of streaming graphs: pipelines, where the graph consists of a single directed chain, and a fairly general class of directed acyclic graphs (dags) with some additional restrictions. The runtime scheduling strategy consists of adding large external buffers at the input and output edges of each component, allowing each component to be executed many times. Partitioning enables a reduction in cache misses in two ways. First, any items that are generated on edges internal to subgraphs are never written

out to memory, but remain in cache. Second, each subgraph is executed many times, allowing the state to be reused.

We prove the optimality of this runtime scheduling for all pipelines and for dags that meet certain conditions on buffer-size requirements. Specifically, we show that with constant-factor memory augmentation, partitioning on these graphs guarantees the optimal number of cache misses to within a constant factor. For the pipeline case, we also prove that such a partition can be found in polynomial time. For the dags we prove optimality if a good partition is provided; the partitioning problem itself is NP-complete.

Categories and Subject Descriptors

F.2 [**Analysis of Algorithms and Problem Complexity**]: General

General Terms

Algorithms, Performance, Theory

Keywords

Caching, dag, graph, partitioning, pipelining, scheduling, streaming, synchronous dataflow.

1. INTRODUCTION

Streaming programming models have received enormous attention in recent years, mostly because they are perceived as enablers of high-performance computing and because of the continuing shift from signal processing by analog hardware to digital signal processing. Examples include academic projects like StreamIt [27] and StreamC/KernelC [12], community-based open-source projects like GNU Radio [9], and commercial products including Simulink® [20] and LabVIEW [16].

Naturally, there has been extensive research on how to map these programming models to hardware and on how to schedule them so as to maximize various objective functions, often subject to constraints. Much of the research has focused on maximizing *throughput*, defined as the number of data items processed per unit time, and on minimizing delay or latency (the period between the time an input data item enters the computation and the time it affects an output

Permission to make digital or hard copies of all or part of this work for personal or classroom use is granted without fee provided that copies are not made or distributed for profit or commercial advantage and that copies bear this notice and the full citation on the first page. To copy otherwise, to republish, to post on servers or to redistribute to lists, requires prior specific permission and/or a fee.
SPAA'12, June 25–27, 2012, Pittsburgh, Pennsylvania, USA.
Copyright 2012 ACM 978-1-4503-1213-4/12/06 ...$10.00.

data item) [6, 13]. More recently, additional metrics have been considered, such as power consumption [29], memory usage [4, 23], and cache efficiency [15, 21, 25].

Because streaming computational models are restricted, it is possible to map and schedule them efficiently. A streaming application can be represented as a graph (or multigraph) where nodes are *computation modules* and the edges are *channels* connecting the modules. Channels have buffers associated with them. The modules send data in the form of *tokens* (also called *messages* or *items*),[1] to each other via these channels. When a module *fires*, it consumes some tokens from its incoming channels, performs some computation, and produces some tokens on its outgoing channels. A module is *ready* to fire each time each of its input channels contains sufficient tokens to enable it to compute. Each module accesses some associated state, almost always of static size (but not identical across modules), when it fires. Designated channels stream (a possibly infinite number of) tokens into and out of the application.

This paper focuses on cache-efficient scheduling of streaming computations on a single processor. Because cache efficiency is such an important determinant of performance, there is a rich history of algorithms and data structures designed to minimize the number of cache misses incurred by a program (see [1, 3, 5, 7, 11, 24] for a sample). Cache efficiency is often overlooked in streaming models, since data items in channels are written exactly once and read exactly once, and they are not reused. Streaming applications exhibit two kinds of cache misses, however, that can be controlled using intelligent scheduling. First, since modules access their state when they fire, it may be advantageous to execute the same module many times once its state has been brought into the cache. Second, consider a module A which outputs some data item on a channel between itself and a module B. If modules A and B are scheduled in a quick succession, then this data item remains in cache. If they are not, then this data item may be spilled out to main memory, leading to a cache miss when module B eventually reads it. Therefore, it is advantageous to execute consecutive modules one after the other whenever possible. Minimizing one of these two kinds of cache misses may compete with the objective of minimizing the other, however, and we must balance the concerns intelligently while scheduling streaming applications.

The algorithms in this paper for minimizing the number of cache misses are based on the idea of partitioning. The streaming graph is divided into subgraphs, each of which fits in cache. That is, given a cache of size M, the sum of the state size in any single subgraph does not exceed M. Within subgraphs, we use small buffers (the minimum required on that edge), whereas on channels between subgraphs, we use large buffers. This approach reduces cache misses in two ways. After a particular subgraph is cached, it can be executed any number of times — as long as sufficient input data is available — without causing any cache misses to load or spill state. Additionally, each module of the subgraph is executed so that the data moving through the subgraph remains cached, with the exception of the initial input and final output. The key to minimizing cache misses using this method is to partition the modules to minimize the amount of data transferred though the channels that cross between subgraphs.

We assume that each time a module fires, the number of items it produces and consumes from each of its input and output channels is known in advance and that this value does not change during execution. Such computations are called *synchronous dataflow* graphs. Without loss of generality, we also assume that all data items are unit sized. Finally, we assume that the state size of each module is known in advance. These assumptions are satisfied by a wide range of streaming computations.[2]

This paper makes the following contributions:

- A theoretical argument that provides a lower bound for the cost of scheduling a directed acyclic graph (dag). Specifically, consider an optimal "well-ordered" partition $\mathcal{P}$ into subgraphs each with $O(M)$ total state, where "well-ordered" means that the graph induced by contracting each component is acyclic. An optimal partition is one with minimum "bandwidth," which is the total number of messages that must cross partition boundaries for each input item consumed. Then *every* schedule incurs an amortized cost of at least $\Omega((1/B) \, bandwidth(\mathcal{P}))$ cache misses per input item, where M is the cache size, B is the block size.

- An upper bound for certain dags. Specifically, suppose that we are given a well-ordered partition $\mathcal{P}$ subject to certain additional restrictions. We show how to schedule the dag on a machine with cache size $O(M)$ and block size B with $O((1/B) \, bandwidth(\mathcal{P}))$ amortized cache misses per input item. If $\mathcal{P}$ is optimal, the upper and lower bound match to within constant factors. Therefore, the partitioned scheduler incurs at most a constant factor more cache misses than the optimal scheduler if given a constant-factor larger cache.

- We also show how to find a good partition for the case of *pipelines*, where the streaming graph consists of a single directed chain of modules. For more general dag topologies, finding the minimum bandwidth well-ordered partition is NP-complete [8, ND15: Acyclic Partition].

The additional restrictions for the upper bound require the partition to have $O(M/B)$ edges leaving each subgraph, and each component to be schedulable with internal buffers having a total of $O(M)$ size. The latter condition holds when all modules have uniform input and output rates, and both conditions always hold for the pipeline even without uniform rates. Both conditions also hold for a wide class of dags without uniform rates.

2. MODEL AND DEFINITIONS

This section describes the analysis and streaming models. We discuss assumptions about the streaming graphs used throughout the paper and define needed terminology.

Analysis model

To analyze the cost of a schedule for a streaming application, we use the *external-memory model* or *I/O model* [1], sometimes also called the *disk-access model* (DAM). The

---

[1]These terms are used interchangeably.

[2]Some streaming applications satisfy our assumptions except for very few modules, such as modules that extract symbols or packets from a waveform, modules that produce television frames from a compressed stream, and so on. Our techniques can still be used to schedule these computations, perhaps suboptimally, by forcing these models to the boundaries of subgraphs.

I/O model is a two-level memory hierarchy consisting of a fast internal memory (cache) of size M and a slow, arbitrarily large external memory (disk), organized into contiguous **blocks** of size B. An algorithm may only operate on data that resides in the cache — requesting data that is not in cache causes a **cache miss**, wherein the block containing the data must first be moved from disk to cache (likely causing other data to be evicted from the bounded cache). The cost in this model is the number of cache misses.

Streaming model

We model a streaming computation as a directed acyclic graph (dag) $G = (V, E)$. Each vertex $v \in V$ corresponds to a module, which has a predefined **state size** denoted by $s(v)$. Each edge corresponds to a directed channel between modules, with **buffers** (implementing FIFO queues) along each edge to store messages that have not yet been consumed by the receiving module. A module has (integral) parameters $in(u, v)$ and $out(v, w)$ specifying, respectively, the number of messages that must be consumed from the incoming edge (u, v)'s buffer each time v executes and the number of messages produced into outgoing edge (v, w) when v executes. When each module has at most 1 input and output (as in the pipeline case), we use $in(v)$ and $out(v)$ as a shorthand for the inputs/outputs consumed by that module. A streaming dag is **homogeneous** if $in(u, v) = out(u, v) = 1$ for every edge (u, v), that is, each module consumes exactly one message from each of its input channels and produces exactly one message to each of its output channels.

In order to execute, or **fire** a module v, the entire state of that module must be loaded into the cache. Moreover, the module may only fire if all of its input buffers contain at least the requisite minimum number of messages.

Assumptions

Throughout the paper, we make the following assumptions about the streaming graph. Except for the last one, these assumptions are all either without loss of generality (and made only to simplify the exposition) or necessary to admit any reasonable solution.

We assume that all messages are unit size and that the state of size each module is at most M. The former assumption is without loss of generality given the arbitrary input and output rates. The latter is necessary to allow a module to be fully loaded into cache when fired.

We assume that the streaming graph contains a single source node s with no incoming edges that produces an infinite stream of input data. Similarly, the graph contains a single sink node t with no outgoing edges that consumes all terminal outputs. This assumption is without loss of generality, as a multisource or multisink dag can be transformed into one with a single source and sink.

We assume that the streaming dag is **rate matched**, by which we mean that the value $\prod_{(u,v) \in p}(out(u, v)/in(u, v))$ is identical for all directed paths p between a fixed pair of vertices. This property is necessary and sufficient to allow the dag to be scheduled without deadlocks with bounded buffers on all channels.

Finally, let $minBuf(e)$ denote the minimum buffer size required by channel e, which can be computed for rate-matched dags using the procedure described in [17]. We assume that for any subgraph $G_i = (V_i, E_i)$ induced by a subset of vertices $V_i \subseteq V$, we have $\sum_{e \in E_i} minBuf(e) =$ $O(\sum_{v \in V_i} s(v))$. In other words, for any subset of modules, the state size of the modules exceeds the minimum buffer size of channels connecting those modules. This assumption allows us to amortize the cost of reading/writing the buffers for modules against loading the module. For a large class of applications, such as pipelines and homogeneous dags, $minBuf(e) = in(e) + out(e)$, making this condition hold without loss of generality, since a module must regardless load this much of its input and output each time it fires.

Additional definitions

Finally, we define some terms and notation used throughout the paper. When there exists a directed path from u to v in the dag, we say that u **precedes** v, denoted by $u \prec v$. When referring to a particular execution of a module v, the **progeny** of this execution are those messages that may (eventually) appear later in the dag as a result of this execution. In other words, the progeny of a particular execution of v are those messages that may be produced only after v is fired, but before the next time v is fired. We similarly define the progeny of a particular message m along channel (u, v) as the progeny of the execution of v that consumes message m.

We use the term "gain," defined as follows, to describe the rate of amplification of messages along paths through the dag. Gain is only well defined for rate-matched dags.

DEFINITION 1. *For a vertex v, the **gain** of the module is the number of times v fires for each time the source s fires. That is, for any path $p : s = x_0 \to x_1 \to x_2 \to \cdots \to x_{|p|} = v$, we define*

$$gain(v) = \prod_{i=1}^{|p|} (out(x_{i-1}, x_i)/in(x_{i-1}, x_i)) .$$

*For an edge (u, v), the **gain** of the edge is defined as the number of messages produced along the edge for each time the source s fires, denoted by $gain(u, v) = gain(u) \, out(u, v)$.*

3. SCHEDULING AND EXECUTION

In this paper, we concentrate on schedules induced by a "partition" of the dag. Sections 4 and 5 shows that partitioning is a good strategy for scheduling streaming dags of various topologies if the goal is to minimize the number of cache misses. This section describes partition scheduling and the execution model that ensues when streaming applications are scheduled using partition scheduling.

A **partition** of a streaming dag V is a collection of disjoint subsets of vertices $\{V_i\}$ such that $\bigcup_i V_i = V$. We call each of the sets V_i in the partition a **component** of the partition. The edges that are internal to a particular component are called **internal edges** and the edges that cross from one component to another are called **cross edges**. We are interested in "well-ordered" partitions:

DEFINITION 2. *Consider a partition $\mathcal{P} = \{V_1, V_2, \ldots, V_k\}$ of a streaming dag V. The partition $\mathcal{P}$ is **well ordered** if the multigraph induced by contracting each component V_i to a single vertex is a dag.*

In addition, we want the partition to have the property that each component V_i "fits" in cache. That is, the state of all the modules in the subset, as well as the buffers on internal edges, all fit in cache at the same time. We call a partition of modules $\{V_1, V_2, \ldots, V_k\}$ a **c-bounded partition** if the total state size $\sum_{u \in V_i} s(u)$ of all modules within each subset is at most cM. The quality of a partition depends on its "bandwidth":

DEFINITION 3. *Consider a partition $\mathcal{P} = \{V_1, V_2, \ldots, V_k\}$ of a streaming dag V, and let C be the set of cross edges. The **bandwidth** of $\mathcal{P}$ is the sum of the gains of the cross edges:*

$$bandwidth(\mathcal{P}) = \sum_{(x,y) \in C} gain(x,y) \ .$$

Thus, for homogeneous applications, the bandwidth is simply the total number of crossing edges.

We say that a well-ordered c-bounded partition is an **optimal c-bounded partition** if there is no other well-ordered c-bounded partition of smaller bandwidth. We denote the bandwidth of an optimal c-bounded partition of the graph G by $minBW_c(G)$.

Partition scheduling begins by finding a c-bounded partition with small bandwidth. The scheduling of a partitioned dag is now considered at two levels: the higher level corresponds coarsely to scheduling components, and the lower level corresponds to scheduling modules within each component.

At the lower level, once a component is brought into cache, the modules within it must be scheduled. Each internal edge e is allocated a buffer with size $minBuf(e)$, which is the minimum buffer size required by e to avoid deadlocks. Since we have

$$\sum_{e \text{ incident on } v} minBuf(e) = O(s(v))$$

for all v, the sum of internal buffers sizes of a component V_i is $O(s(V_i)) = O(M)$. Therefore, these internal buffers fit in cache. Since a component is a rate-matched dag, one can always schedule at the lower level without overflowing these buffers [17].

For the higher level, the main idea is that once a component is loaded into the cache, it may be executed many times without incurring any additional cache misses, except when reading from or writing to those cross edges leaving the component. Two properties of the scheduler and partition enable this approach: the addition of large buffers along cross edges, and the fact that the partition is well ordered.[3]

Since the component is executed many times, we can amortize the cost of loading the component's state against the number of reads/writes to cross edges (the bandwidth of the partition). We say that a component is **schedulable** whenever (1) "enough" inputs exist, and (2) "enough" space remains in the output buffers. In particular, the component is schedulable if it can be executed continuously until it consumes a total of at least $\Omega(M)$ inputs (or produces at least $\Omega(M)$ outputs) along cross edges to pay for loading the $O(M)$ state. The buffers on the cross edges must be large enough to ensure that, at all times, some component is schedulable. By enforcing this condition, we not only guarantee that the scheduling algorithm is deadlock free, but we allow dynamic schedules to be computed easily. The sizes of

buffers on cross edges to satisfy this schedulability constraint is different for different stream topologies.

Scheduling inhomogeneous graphs

Inhomogeneous graphs may require large buffers on cross edges. How to improve the buffer sizes for inhomogeneous graphs is an interesting problem, but since the size of the cross-edge buffers does not affect our cache bounds, we leave this problem open. To design a schedule for this case, first compute any value T such that for every edge (u, v), the value $T \, gain(u, v)$ is integral, is divisible by $out(u, v)$ and by $in(u, v)$, and is at least M. Under these conditions, all progeny of the T executions of the source node s can pass through the entire dag and be consumed by the sink t without requiring any future inputs at any node in the dag. We thus schedule at a granularity of T inputs. For each cross edge (u, v), allocate a buffer with size $T \, gain(u, v)$. For each internal edge, as already stated, allocate a buffer of size $minBuf(u, v)$. At the higher level, execute the components in a topological-sort order, loading each component V_i exactly once per T inputs. For the lower level, execute the modules within the component V_i until all relevant progeny of the T source-node executions have been consumed and no items are buffered by this component except in the outgoing cross edges. The low-level scheduling can be accomplished by repeatedly choosing any module that can be fired without exceeding output buffer size.

Note that at the high level, once a component V_i is loaded, it is executed fully before proceeding to a different component. Moreover, it is never executed again until the next batch of T inputs. In contrast, at the lower level, many different modules may be interleaved with a successive executions of a particular module due to the tighter size restrictions on internal buffers.

Scheduling homogeneous graphs

For stream graphs where every module reads and writes exactly one item from its input and output channels, the scheduling is simpler. In this case, setting $T = M$ and proceeding as above suffices, but the lower level also becomes even more straightforward as $minBuf(e) = 1$ along all edges. In particular, at the higher level, each time the component is loaded, it is fired repeatedly until consuming M inputs along all incoming cross edges and producing M outputs along all outgoing cross edges. At the lower level, the modules are topologically sorted and are each fired just once in order; this lower-level schedule repeats M times.

In this case, one can extend this approach to an asynchronous or parallel dynamic schedule. (Throughout the remainder of this paper, however, our analyses are performed assuming the uniprocessor case.) To schedule components, choose any component(s) with M data items on all incoming cross edges and empty outgoing cross edges. Then schedule each internal module M times as above until the incoming buffers are empty and the outgoing buffers are full. The homogeneity of the graph ensures that it is always possible to find a schedulable component.

Scheduling pipelines

In the case of **pipelines**, where modules form of a chain (single directed path) but can have nonunit input and output rates, it is again possible to reduce the buffer sizes on cross edges. Each cross edge is assigned a buffer size of $\Theta(M)$. The

---

[3]If the partition were not well ordered, then a single component could not necessarily be scheduled repeatedly in isolation: some other module might need to be scheduled in between modules of the component.

schedule works a little differently, however. A component is schedulable whenever its input buffer is at least half full and its output buffer is at most half full. It is then executed until either the input buffer becomes empty or the output buffer becomes full. Thus, either $\Omega(M)$ inputs are read, or $\Omega(M)$ outputs are written. A continuity argument now suffices to show that some component can always be scheduled. Scan the cross edges in topological-sort order until the first cross edge that is at most half full is encountered. The preceding component has a more-than-half-full input buffer by construction, and so it is schedulable. (The sink of the graph is treated as though its output buffer is always empty.) This schedule also readily generalizes to the asynchronous or parallel case as with the homogeneous graphs.

4. STREAMING PIPELINES

This section proves that a good partitioning schedule is nearly optimal for the problem of scheduling a pipeline with arbitrary input and output rates. More precisely, a good partitioning schedule has $O(Q)$ cache misses when run on a cache of size $O(M)$, where Q is the minimum possible number of cache misses of any schedule on a size-M cache. In other words, this schedule is $O(1)$-competitive when given $O(1)$ cache augmentation. Moreover, this schedule can be found in polynomial time. Proving the optimality of the schedule hinges on a strong lower bound, which is a substantial part of the technical content of this section.

The crux of the lower bound is to show that any schedule must "pay" for messages to pass certain edges in the pipeline, essentially showing that the bandwidth of the best partition provides a lower bound on the cost of any schedule. We later present a more general lower bound (Theorem 10 of Section 5), which extends this partitioning lower bound to the more general case of dags. Theorem 10 thus subsumes the lower bound of this section, albeit with different constant factors. Nevertheless, we include both, as the lower bound here is less complicated and provides different intuition. Moreover, although finding the optimal partition for general dags is NP-complete, and we are not aware of any approximation algorithms, the pipeline lower bound immediately suggests a polynomial algorithm for finding an asymptotically optimal schedule for minimizing cache misses on pipelines.

For a pipeline, the well-ordered partitions can be represented compactly as a collection of segments. A **u-v segment**, denoted by $\langle u, v \rangle$, corresponds to the set of all modules x with $u \preceq x \preceq v$. We define the **gain-minimizing edge** $gainMin(u, v)$ to be an edge with minimum gain in the segment $\langle u, v \rangle$.

The following lemma states that if the first node u in a segment $\langle u, v \rangle$ is fired enough times, then at least one of two things happens: (1) many messages are buffered within the segment, or (2) some output is produced from v. In either case, a certain number of cache misses occur, either due to the buffered messages in the case of (1) or due to the loading of state of the entire segment in the case of (2). One subtle point about the proof is that although the lemma is stated with respect to the number of times the module u is fired, we shall in fact charge against the gain-minimizing edge. Specifically, the eventual lower-bound theorem does not charge for reading the inputs to u — cache misses are assessed only for loading the state of $\langle u, v \rangle$ or buffering inside $\langle u, v \rangle$.

LEMMA 1. *Consider a segment $\langle u, v \rangle$ of a pipeline graph with gain-minimizing edge (x, y). Then module u may be fired at most $2M(gain(u)/gain(x, y))$ times before either*

- *some progeny of one of these executions of u is output from module v, or*
- *at least $2M$ progeny of these executions of u are stored in buffers between modules u and v.*

PROOF. If any progeny is output from the segment, the claim holds trivially. Consider the case where no progeny are output from module v. Then the progeny of u must be buffered somewhere between u and v. The term $gain(z_1, z_2)/gain(u)$ is by definition the number of messages that (eventually) pass through edge (z_1, z_2) each time u is fired. These messages may be buffered or they may be passed to the next module. The number of messages buffered is thus minimized when $gain(z_1, z_2)$ is minimized, implying that at least $gain(x, y)/gain(u)$ messages must be buffered each time u fires. Hence if u fires at least $2M(gain(u)/gain(x, y))$ times, then at least $2M$ messages must be buffered. $\square$

If we apply Lemma 1 to a large enough segment, we see that if u is fired enough times, then either $\Omega(M)$ messages must be buffered, or $\Omega(M)$ state must be loaded, thereby incurring $\Omega(M/B)$ cache misses implying a lower bound on the number of cache misses. The following corollary formalizes this observation.

COROLLARY 2. *Consider any segment $\langle u, v \rangle$ of a pipeline graph satisfying the constraint $\sum_{z \in \langle u, v \rangle} s(z) \geq 2M$, and suppose that (x, y) is the gain-minimizing edge for this segment. Then any (sub)schedule that fires module u at least $2M(gain(u)/gain(x, y))$ times must incur at least $\Omega(M/B)$ cache misses. In other words, $\Omega((1/B) gain(x, y)/gain(u))$ is a lower bound on the amortized cost of firing u. This bound holds even if u's inputs and v's outputs are not counted towards cache misses.*

PROOF. Between the time a new message enters the segment and some progeny of that message leaves the segment, each of the modules in the segment must be in cache. Since the total state of these modules is at least $2M$ and can only initially hold at most M of this state, there must be at least M/B cache misses.

Similarly, if $2M$ new messages are buffered, they must be buffered in different memory locations, at most M of which already reside in cache. Thus, there must be at least M/B cache misses.

Applying Lemma 1, we see that the maximum number of times u can be fired before either of these events occurs is $2M(gain(u)/gain(x, y))$, and each event causes $\Omega(M/B)$ cache misses. To calculate the amortized cost, divide the $\Omega(M/B)$ cache misses by the number of executions of u. $\square$

We conclude by showing that the total bandwidth of the gain-minimizing edges provide a lower bound on the schedule cost. In this theorem, we consider any schedule that fires the sink t of the graph, which is the latest node in the pipeline, at least $T \cdot gain(t)$ times, for T a large-enough integer. In other words, we consider schedules that produce a large-enough number of outputs from the pipeline. Note that in order for the sink node to fire at least $T \cdot gain(t)$ times, the source node s must also fire at least T times. The reason to consider outputs here is to avoid any accounting ambiguity due to buffered items throughout the rest of the pipeline.

THEOREM 3. *Consider a pipeline graph in which $S = \{\langle u_i, v_i \rangle\}$ is any collection of disjoint segments such that each segment has total size at least $2M$. Then any schedule of the graph that fires the sink node t at least $T \cdot gain(t)$ times must incur at least $\Omega((T/B) \sum_{s \in S} gain(gainMin(s)))$ cache misses, as long as T is sufficiently large.*

PROOF. If each segment can be considered separately, this theorem follows directly from Corollary 2, since firing t at least $T \cdot gain(t)$ times implies that module u_i must be fired at least $T \cdot gain(u_i)$ times.

To see that each $\langle u_i, v_i \rangle$ can be considered separately, notice that the only shared state across different segments is on the cross edges shared between two segments. Since Corollary 2 does not count those edges towards the number of cache misses, there is no double-counting of state/buffer cache misses. □

To provide an upper bound, we show constructively that there indeed exists a partitioning schedule that has cost asymptotically matching the lower bound. The following lemma shows that the number of cache misses of a partitioned schedule is related to the bandwidth of a partition. This lemma uses unbounded buffers on cross edges, but this issue is resolved at the end of the section.

LEMMA 4. *Consider any partition $\mathcal{P} = \{V_i\}$ of a pipeline graph into segments such that each segment contains at most M total state. Then on a machine with cache size $O(M)$, it is possible to schedule the pipeline such that the sink t fires $\lceil T \cdot gain(t) \rceil$ times with $O((T/B) \cdot bandwidth(\mathcal{P}))$ cache misses in total, as long as T is sufficiently large.*

PROOF. Let C be the set of cross edges induced by partition $\mathcal{P}$. Consider the segments $V_1, V_2, \ldots$ in topologically sorted order, where $V_i = \langle u_i, v_i \rangle$ and the edge $(v_i, u_{i+1}) \in C$. In sorted order, fire u_i a total of $O(T \cdot gain(u_i))$ times using a local schedule for V_i that has small bounded buffers on internal edges as described in Section 3. Since each V_i fits in $O(M)$ space including the internal buffers, we can repeatedly execute the loaded modules while only paying for reading and writing to external buffers. The total cost is therefore $O(M/B)$ to load V_i's state plus $O((1/B)T(gain(v_{i-1}, u_i) + gain(v_i, u_{i+1})))$ to read inputs for u_i and to write outputs from v_i. For sufficiently large $T = \Omega(M/ gain(v_{i-1}, u_i))$, the number of items read by V_i is $\Omega(M)$, costing $\Omega(M/B)$ cache misses, which dominates the cost. (The value T must also be large enough that t can be fired $\lceil T \cdot gain(t) \rceil$ times after firing s at most $O(T)$ times, which occurs when T is at least as large as the gain of every edge in the graph.) Summing across all V_i completes the proof. □

The following theorem concludes that our lower bound is tight, modulo constant factors in both the number of cache misses and cache augmentation. Specifically, if Q is the optimal cache cost provided by any schedule (partitioned or not) on a machine with M cache, then there exists a partitioned schedule with cost $O(Q)$ cache cost on a machine with $O(M)$ cache. The upper-bound schedule is exhibited constructively.

THEOREM 5. *There exists a partition $\mathcal{P} = \{V_i\}$ of any pipeline graph into segments such that for sufficiently large integer T,*

- *every schedule (not necessarily a partitioned schedule) that fires t at least $T \cdot gain(t)$ times must cost $\Omega((T/B) \cdot bandwidth(\mathcal{P}))$ cache misses in total for a machine with a size-M cache, and*
- *there exists a partitioned schedule (based on $\mathcal{P}$) that fires t a total of $\lceil T \cdot gain(t) \rceil$ times and costs $O((T/B) \cdot bandwidth(\mathcal{P}))$ cache misses in total for a machine with a size-$O(M)$ cache.*

Moreover, such a partition can be found in polynomial time.

PROOF. Construct segments W_i as follows. These segments will be used to build V_i later. Start at the beginning of the pipeline, with the current segment initially being W_1, and consider all modules in topologically sorted order. Add modules to the current segment W_i until the total state size of W_i exceeds $2M$. If there is more than $2M$ state remaining, finish with W_i and proceed with initially empty W_{i+1} as the current segment. If, on the other hand, less than $2M$ state remains, add all remaining modules to the current segment. By construction, each W_i has total state at least $2M$. Moreover, since all modules have state size at most M, each W_i contains at most $5M$ state. (In fact, only the last segment can be this large, as all preceding segments have state between $2M$ and $3M$.)

For each W_i produced through this process, let $(x_i, y_i) = gainMin(W_i)$ be the gain-minimizing edge for the segment. Then let $C = \bigcup_i \{(x_i, y_i)\}$ be the set of cross edges. These cross edges induce a partition $\mathcal{P} = \{V_i\}$, that is, with $V_0 = \langle s, x_i \rangle$, $V_i = \langle y_i, x_{i+1} \rangle$ for $1 \leq i < |C|$, and $V_{|C|} = \langle y_{|C|}, t \rangle$, where s and t are the source and sink of the pipeline, respectively. Since each W_i contains at most $5M$ state, and each V_i spans at most 2 segments W_i and W_{i+1}, it follows that each V_i contains at most $10M$ state. In fact, this bound may be tightened to $8M$, since only the last segment can be so large. Therefore, for $c = 8$, this partition has the property that each segment is of size at most cM.

To achieve the lower bound, apply Theorem 3 with $S = \{W_i\}$. To achieve the upper bound, apply Lemma 4 with partition $\{V_i\}$. □

COROLLARY 6. *For a given pipeline graph and a sufficiently large number of outputs to produce, one can construct a schedule that incurs at most $O(1)$ times as many cache misses as the optimal schedule, as long as the schedule is allowed to use a constant factor more cache than the optimal schedule.* □

Although the partition described in Theorem 5 provides an asymptotically optimal upper bound on the number of cache misses (modulo memory augmentation), this partition is not the minimum bandwidth c-bounded partition. As it turns out, one can find the minimum bandwidth c-bounded partition for pipelines using a simple dynamic program. This (minimum bandwidth) partition provides no more cache misses than the partition described in Theorem 5, but not asymptotically fewer. Moreover, this optimal partition does not guarantee optimal cache performance. It still only guarantees *asymptotically* optimal cache performance.

Producing an optimal dynamic schedule

Lemma 4 (and Theorem 5) give schedules for the pipeline that rely on the number of outputs to produce. In particular, as specified, each segment V_i in the partition is considered in order and fired repeatedly until enough outputs are produced. For the pipeline case, these schedules can be easily transformed into dynamic schedules, where the number $T \cdot gain(T)$ of times the sink must be fired is not specified *a priori*. Specifically, Lemma 4 requires only that each V_i consume $\Omega(M)$ inputs or produce $\Omega(M)$ outputs each time it is loaded. Thus, the segments can be scheduled as described in Section 3 in order to get the same bounds.

5. STREAMING DAGS

This section considers the case when the stream graph is a general directed acyclic graph (dag). A natural generalization of the pipeline schedule is the following: partition the dag into regions that fit in cache while minimizing the total gain of edges crossing the partitions. The key to showing that this type of strategy yields an asymptotically optimal cache bound is to provide a lower bound on the cache complexity of any schedule, showing that any schedule must incur at least as many misses (asymptotically) as some partition-based schedule. We first prove this claim for the homogeneous dataflow case (all gains are 1), and then we generalize to nonunit gains later in the section.

Proving a lower bound for the cache complexity of scheduling a streaming dag is significantly more complicated than for a pipeline. The following theorem shows that the bandwidth of an optimal c-bounded partition does indeed provide such a lower bound for the case of homogeneous dataflow. Recall that the term $minBW_3(G)$ used in the statement of the next theorem denotes the minimum possible bandwidth of a well-ordered partition into components such that each component has total state size at most $3M$. Without loss of generality, we assume a single input node (source) and a single output node (sink) to simplify exposition of the proof.

THEOREM 7. *Any schedule for a homogeneous dataflow dag that fires the sink node at least $T \geq B$ times must incur at least $\Omega((T/B) \cdot minBW_3(G))$ cache misses, where B is the block size.*

PROOF. The main idea of this proof is to look at (the progeny of) a single message passing through the entire dag from the source to the sink. We will argue that any schedule of this dag must pay at least $\Omega(1/B)$ block transfers for each edge crossing some 3-bounded partition (in particular, an optimal 3-bounded partition). Since modules may be executed more than once each time they are loaded, we must be careful about the way we count the block transfers incurred by loading the state of a module. It is not obvious that we can analyze a single message in isolation, although the proof will essentially do just this.

Consider any schedule π of modules that fires the sink T times. A schedule π is a list of module executions $\pi = u_1, u_2, \ldots, u_m$ for some m. The same module can occur many times in the list (i.e., $u_i = u_j$ for some $j \neq i$). In particular, with all gains equal to 1, every module occurs at least T times in any schedule that produces T outputs. This interpretation of a schedule ignores whether messages are stored in intermodule buffers or not, but the proof charges for buffering where necessary.

Starting at the beginning of the schedule π, partition the schedule into contiguous subschedules $\pi = \pi_1, \ldots, \pi_r$, each containing between $2M$ and $3M$ distinct state (except for the last subschedule which may be smaller). Such a partition is possible because each module has size at most M.

We first claim that beginning each subschedule π_i with an empty cache does not increase the overall cost of the schedule π by more than a constant factor. This fact follows because each π_i contains at least $2M$ state, and thus it must incur $\Omega(M/B)$ cache misses regardless of what is in the cache at the beginning of that subschedule. We can therefore afford to pay $O(M/B)$ to load any arbitrary initial cache state at the beginning of each subschedule without asymptotically increasing the cost.

Now look at any subschedule π_i. Let K_i be the total number of outputs produced by modules in π_i that are not consumed as input by another module within π_i. Each of these outputs must be written to cache or memory, taking a total of K_i space. Since we can assume that the cache is flushed at the end of each subschedule, the cost of executing π_i becomes $\Omega(K_i/B)$.

Showing that $\sum_i K_i \geq T \cdot minBW_3(G)$ will complete the proof. We do so by arguing that the progeny of a single source-node firing must contribute at least $minBW_3(G)$ edges to $\sum_i K_i$ (and hence the total for T firings is at least T times more). Proving this fact has two components. We first show that π can be reduced to a schedule π', tracking only the progeny of one firing, such that every edge crossing a subschedule boundary in π' also crosses the same boundary in π. Then we argue that π' is a well-ordered, 3-bounded partition. If both of these claims hold, then the number of edges that a single firing contributes to $\sum_i K_i$ is at least the number of edges crossing some well-ordered 3-bounded partition, and hence at least $minBW_3(G)$.

To reduce π to π', consider a single source-node execution and all of its progeny throughout the dag, and consider the schedule $\pi' = \pi'_1, \ldots, \pi'_r$ induced by removing all but the corresponding modules from π. This schedule corresponds to every module firing exactly once within π'. All edges in π' also occur in π. Thus, each edge crossing subschedule boundaries in π' also crosses subschedule boundaries in π and contribute to some K_i.

To show that π' is a well-ordered 3-bounded partition, observe that since each π_i (and hence π'_i) contains at most $3M$ state, π' corresponds to a 3-bounded partition. Moreover, since every module is included just once in the schedule and the schedule obeys precedence constraints, it follows that modules $\pi'_1, \ldots, \pi'_k$ have no edges pointing to earlier modules. Hence each contracted π'_i has no edges pointing to the earlier components, and the contracted graph is a dag, meaning that it is well-ordered. □

We now prove the upper bound, that is, if a good partition exists, then it is possible to schedule the pipeline with asymptotically optimal cache performance on a machine with $O(1)$ cache-size augmentation. In order to schedule a dag using partitioning, we need the partition to be **degree-limited**, meaning each component of the partition has degree $O(M/B)$, for the following reason. When a component is loaded into cache and executed, the cache should also be large enough to accommodate at least one block from the buffers on cross edges that are incident on this component. For a wide class of graphs, all $O(1)$-bounded partitions are degree limited. For example, if every module u contains at least $\Omega(Bd_u)$ state, where d_u is its degree, then all $O(1)$-bounded partitions are degree limited. The following lemma shows that the bandwidth of the partition determines the number of cache misses by a partitioned schedule.

LEMMA 8. *Consider any degree-limited $O(1)$-bounded partition $\mathcal{P} = \{V_i\}$ of a homogeneous dataflow dag. Then on a machine with $O(M)$ cache size and for sufficiently large T, there exists a schedule of the dag that fires the sink node T times with $O((T/B) \cdot bandwidth(\mathcal{P}))$ cache misses in total.*

PROOF. As mentioned in Section 3, we add (large) buffers of size $\Theta(M)$ to each cross edge and then load each component into cache one at a time, executing each $O(M)$ times once loaded. Since each V_i fits in $O(M)$ space including the internal buffers, we can repeatedly execute the loaded modules while only paying for reading all the inputs from and writing all the outputs to external buffers. The total cost is then $O(M/B)$ to load V_i's state plus the cost of reading the inputs from the incoming edges and writing outputs to outgoing edges. For large enough T, i.e., $T > M$, the number of inputs read is $\Theta(M)$ from each input edge (similarly for outputs) each time a component is scheduled. Since the degree of each partition is $O(M/B)$, we can afford to keep at least 1 block for each external buffer in cache at the same time, and thus reading/writing these external messages has cost $\Theta(1/B)$ times the number of message read or written. Therefore, reading the inputs and writing the outputs costs $\Theta(M/B)$ per cross edge, which dominates the cost of reading the state. Summing across all V_i and repeating T/M times completes the proof. $\square$

The following corollary (which follows directly from Theorem 7 and Lemma 8) says that a partitioned schedule is asymptotically optimal given $O(1)$-memory augmentation. More generally, since finding the optimal well-ordered partition is NP-complete [8], we show that if we have an α-approximation for the partitioning problem, then we have an $O(\alpha)$-competitive schedule.

COROLLARY 9. *Let $\mathcal{P}_{OPT}$ be an optimal 3-bounded partition of a homogeneous streaming dag G, and let $\mathcal{P}$ be any 3-bounded degree-limited partition of G. Suppose that we have $bandwidth(\mathcal{P}) \leq \alpha \cdot bandwidth(\mathcal{P}_{OPT})$ for some $\alpha \geq 1$. Then for any sufficiently large number of outputs produced, the partition schedule using $\mathcal{P}$ incurs at most $O(\alpha)$ times as many cache misses as the optimal schedule, as long as the partitioning schedule is allowed to use a constant times larger cache than the optimal schedule uses.* $\square$

Notes on the upper bound

Corollary 9 is most useful for those dags with the following property: there exists a degree-limited 3-bounded partition with similar bandwidth to the optimal (not necessarily degree-limited) 3-bounded partition. When this property does not hold, the cost of the upper-bound partition may be worse by a factor of B (every read and write to cross-edge buffers may cause a cache miss), implying only that our schedule is $O(\alpha B)$-competitive. The cost of a naive schedule, however, may be much worse, since only the messages moving along cross edges are charged. Moreover, we have not discussed how to find such a partition. Like most partitioning problems, finding an optimal well-formed 3-bounded partition is NP-hard. Since the partitioning occurs at compile time, however, and the streaming application is intended to be longer running, it may be reasonable to use an exponential-time algorithm for constructing a good partition. In any event, we have reduced the problem of scheduling to that of partitioning.

Generalizing to inhomogeneous streaming dags

Theorem 7 generalizes to the inhomogeneous case, but the reduction is not immediately obvious. Our approach is based on tracking fractional progeny through the dag and charging corresponding fractional costs to each edge crossing a subschedule boundary. The most natural fractional transformation is to treat a module v as though each time it fires, it consumes $in(u_i, v) \, gain(v)$ inputs on each input edge (u_i, v) and produces $out(v, w_j) \, gain(v)$ outputs on each output edge (v, w_j). The problem with this transformation is that modification may *restrict* the optimal schedule, since for $gain(v) > 1$, the "fractional" module is forced to consume more inputs than the original module. Therefore, these obvious fractional amounts do not work. This approach of using fractional items is sound only if working with fractional messages makes the lower bound looser, that is, we give more power to the optimal schedule.

Instead, we track a tiny fractional message, with size $1/\gamma$, where γ is the product of all output rates in the entire dag. (This value γ is much larger than it needs be, but since this value is only employed for a proof and not in an algorithm, there is no need to reduce it.) A fractional module v then fires $gain(v)/\gamma$ times for each fractional firing of the source node of the dag.

THEOREM 10. *Any schedule for a dataflow dag that fires the sink node at least $T \cdot gain(t) \geq B$ times must incur at least $\Omega((T/B) \cdot minBW_3(G))$ cache misses, where B is the block size.*

PROOF SKETCH. The proof is nearly identical to that of Theorem 7, except that we track the $1/\gamma$ fractional progeny through the network, where γ is the product of all output rates in the dag. When nonunit outputs are produced, they contribute to some K_i in the same way, but they only contribute according to the size of the message written, which is $1/\gamma$ times the gain along the edge. When reducing π to π', we consider each module firing once as described above, consuming inputs and producing outputs proportional to gains times $1/\gamma$. Thus, π' still contains each module once.

The one additional point in this proof is to argue that a fractional schedule is more powerful than every feasible nonfractional schedule, which follows from the fact that each module can be fired an integral number of times to simulate the nonfractional schedule. In particular, firing the fractional module v a total of $\gamma/gain(v)$ times is equivalent to firing the original module once. Since $1/gain(v)$ is the product of input rates divided by output rates, and γ is the product of all output rates, the resulting number is the product of the remaining integral output rates and some integral input rates. Thus, $\gamma/gain(v)$ is integral. $\square$

6. RELATED WORK

Most of the work on scheduling streaming applications aims to maximize throughput and/or maximize latency [2, 6, 18], minimize buffer sizes [4, 23, 28], or to optimize both while avoiding deadlocks [13, 19]. A few papers address other issues, such as power consumption [29]. None of these relates directly to our results.

Heuristic cache-aware scheduling of streaming programs on both single processors and multiprocessors has been studied by several research groups [15, 21, 25], but the proposed heuristics are all evaluated empirically. To the best of our knowledge, no previous work provides any theoretical guarantees comparable to ours. Kohli [15] proposes a greedy scheduling heuristic for streaming dags that have a unique topological ordering (this class is a minor generalization of pipelines). The heuristic makes local decisions as to whether to continue to execute one module or to move on to its successor in the topological ordering based on an estimate of the number of cache misses that either decision will generate. Since this heuristic makes only local decisions, it does not provide an asymptotically optimal number of cache misses. Another difference from our work is that Kohli considers data-cache and instruction-cache misses separately, while we assume either that instruction cache is not an important bottleneck or that instructions are part of the state of the module. Sermulins et al. [25] also try to heuristically optimize for both the data cache and the instruction cache. Their schedule-optimization method starts from some given steady-state schedule that maintains bounded buffer sizes. Their optimizer takes this schedule and produces a new schedule which replaces each module invocation in the steady-state schedule by s back-to-back invocations. This scaling leads to state reuse, but it may cause spilling of buffers into main memory. Their method computes the largest s that avoids catastrophic spills. Since this method generates a small range of schedules, all of which are derived from the given steady-state schedule, it is suboptimal in many cases. Sermulins et al. also propose a module-fusion heuristic that can also reduce cache misses. This heuristic can be viewed as a special case of our partitioning method. Moonen et al. [21] also scale a given schedule in the same way, but in a more general setup that includes multiple processors and computational graphs that allow module to change their gains in a cyclic fashion. They do not provide any theoretical guarantees (it is unlikely that any can be proved for the method), but they do show convincing empirical results, demonstrating a cache-miss reduction of over a factor of 4 on a real-world application. Taken together, the empirical results strongly support our fundamental claim that effective scheduling can dramatically improve the performance of streaming applications.

Graph partitioning has also been used to improve cache efficiency under computational models other than streaming models. Examples include mesh processing for visualization [26], which provides theoretical guarantees, and repeated sparse matrix-vector multiplication [30], which employs an empirical heuristic methodology.

7. CONCLUSIONS

We have shown that in many cases the problem of cache-efficient scheduling of streaming applications can be reduced to the problem of partitioning the computational graph into components that have a small boundary and have a small-enough state to fit within the cache. On some classes of graphs, such as pipelines, solving the resulting partitioning problem is computationally easy. For more complex applications where the streaming graph is a synchronous dag, we can still show that the scheduling problem reduces to a partitioning problem. The problem of finding the optimal well-ordered partition for general dags is NP-complete [8], however. This situation is common to many mapping and scheduling problems in high-performance computing.

There are a few ways way to address this difficulty. One practical approach is to use an exact integer-programming

graph partitioner when the dag is relatively small. This strategy has proved effective in scheduling streaming computations on distributed memory-limited systems [22], for example. Another approach is to use a heuristic graph partitioner (see, for example, [10, 14]). Heuristic strategies are widely used to map and schedule large-scale parallel applications. Alternatively, since our results are approximation preserving, one can try to find a provably good approximation algorithm for the partitioning problem. We plan to address this issue in future work.

Another direction for future research is to study the cache-efficient scheduling of streaming computations on multiprocessors. If the number of cache misses is the only criterion, then the optimal uniprocessor schedule is trivially the optimal multiprocessor schedule. When considering multiprocessors, however, we must consider both load balancing and the number cache misses simultaneously.

Our work has also delineated the tougher theoretical problems in scheduling streaming applications. These include, not surprisingly, feedback (cycles in the graph) and modules whose output rates are not simple functions of their input rates (such as modules that sift through data and produce an output when they find something interesting, modules that make routing decisions, etc.). These computational structures also raise theoretical and practical difficulties unrelated to caching, such as the possibility of deadlocks due to insufficient buffer space. These issues, some of which are clearly online-scheduling problems, represent good opportunities for future research.

Acknowledgments

We would like to thank Fanny Dufossé of ENS Lyon for helpful discussions. This research was supported in part by NSF grants CCF-1150036, CNS-1017058, and CCF-0937860, by grant 1045/09 from the Israel Science Foundation (founded by the Israel Academy of Sciences and Humanities), and by grant 2010231 from the United-States-Israel Binational Science Foundation.

8. REFERENCES

[1] Alok Aggarwal and Jeffrey Scott Vitter. The input/output complexity of sorting and related problems. *Communications of the ACM*, 31(9):1116–1127, September 1988.

[2] Kunal Agrawal, Anne Benoit, Fanny Dufossé, and Yves Robert. Mapping filtering streaming applications. *Algorithmica*, pages 1 –51, September 2010.

[3] D. H. Bailey. FFTs in external or hierarchical memory. *Journal of Supercomputing*, 4(1):23–35, May 1990.

[4] Mohamed Benazouz, Olivier Marchetti, Alix Munier-kordon, and Thierry Michel. A new method for minimizing buffer sizes for cyclo-static dataflow graphs. In *Proceedings of the 8th IEEE Workshop on Embedded Systems for Real-Time Multimedia (ESTIMedia)*, pages 11–20, 2010.

[5] M. A. Bender, E. Demaine, and M. Farach-Colton. Cache-oblivious B-trees. In *41st Annual Symposium on Foundations of Computer Science (FOCS)*, pages 399–409, 2000.

[6] Sardar M. Farhad, Yousun Ko, Bernd Burgstaller, and Bernhard Scholz. Orchestration by approximation mapping stream programs onto multicore

architectures. *ACM SIGPLAN Notices*, 46:357–368, 2011.

[7] Matteo Frigo, Charles E. Leiserson, Harald Prokop, and Sridhar Ramachandran. Cache-oblivious algorithms. *ACM Transactions on Algorithms*, January 2012.

[8] Michael R. Garey and David S. Johnson. *Computers and Intractability: A Guide to the Theory of NP-Completeness*. W. H. Freeman & Co., New York, NY, USA, 1979.

[9] GNU Radio, 2001. Software, `gnuradio.org`.

[10] Bruce Hendrickson and Robert Leland. A multilevel algorithm for partitioning graphs. In *Proceedings of the 1995 ACM/IEEE conference on Supercomputing*, page 14 pages on CDROM, 1995.

[11] Jia-Wei Hong and H. T. Kung. I/O complexity: the red-blue pebbling game. In *Proceedings of the 13th Annual ACM Symposium on Theory of Computing (STOC)*, pages 326–333, Milwaukee, 1981.

[12] Ujval J. Kapasi, Peter Mattson, William J. Dally, John D. Owens, and Brian Towles. Stream scheduling. Concurrent VLSI Architecture Tech Report 122, Stanford University, Computer Systems Laboratory, March 2002.

[13] Michal Karczmarek, William Thies, and Saman Amarasinghe. Phased scheduling of stream programs. *ACM SIGPLAN Notices*, 38(7):103–112, 2003.

[14] George Karypis and Vipin Kumar. A fast and high quality multilevel scheme for partitioning irregular graphs. *SIAM Journal on Scientific Computing*, 20:359–392, 1998.

[15] Sanjeev Kohli. Cache aware scheduling for synchronous dataflow programs. Technical Report UCB/ERL M04/3, EECS Department, University of California, Berkeley, 2004.

[16] LabVIEW, 2011. Software, `www.ni.com/labview`.

[17] E.A. Lee and D.G. Messerschmitt. Synchronous data flow. *Proceedings of the IEEE*, 75(9):1235–1245, 1987.

[18] Edward Ashford Lee and David G Messerschmitt. Static scheduling of synchronous data flow programs for digital signal processing. *IEEE Transactions on Computers*, C-36:24–35, 1987.

[19] Peng Li, Kunal Agrawal, Jeremy Buhler, and Roger D. Chamberlain. Deadlock avoidance for streaming computations with filtering. In *Proceedings of the 22nd ACM symposium on Parallelism in algorithms and architectures*, SPAA '10, pages 243–252, New York, NY, USA, 2010. ACM.

[20] Mathworks. *Simulink User's Guide*, 2011. Release 2011b.

[21] Arno Moonen, Marco Bekooij, Rene Van Den Berg, and Jef Van Meerbergen. Cache aware mapping of streaming applications on a multiprocessor system-on-chip. In *Proceeings of the conference on Design, Automation and Test in Europe (DATE '08)*, pages 300–305, 2008.

[22] Ryan Newton, Sivan Toledo, Lewis Girod, Hari Balakrishnan, and Samuel Madden. Wishbone: Profile-based partitioning for sensornet applications. In *Proceedings of the ACM SIGCOMM Conference on Networked Systems Design and Implementaion (NSDI 2009)*, April 2009.

[23] Jongsoo Park and William J Dally. Buffer-space efficient and deadlock-free scheduling of stream applications on multi-core architectures. In *Proceedings of the 22nd ACM symposium on Parallelism in Algorithms and Architectures (SPAA '10)*, pages 1–10, 2010.

[24] J. E. Savage. Extending the Hong-Kung model to memory hierarchies. In Ding-Zhu Du and Ming Li, editors, *Computing and Combinatorics*, volume 959 of *Lecture Notes in Computer Science*, pages 270–281. Springer Verlag, 1995.

[25] Janis Sermulins, William Thies, Rodric Rabbah, and Saman Amarasinghe. Cache aware optimization of stream programs. *ACM SIGPLAN Notices*, 40(7):115–126, 2005.

[26] M. Tchiboukdjian, V. Danjean, and B. Raffin. Binary mesh partitioning for cache-efficient visualization. *IEEE Transactions on Visualization and Computer Graphics*, 16:815–828, 2010.

[27] William Thies, Michal Karczmarek, and Saman P. Amarasinghe. Streamit: A language for streaming applications. In *Proceedings of the 11th International Conference on Compiler Construction*, CC '02, pages 179–196, London, UK, 2002. Springer-Verlag.

[28] Maarten H Wiggers, Marco J G Bekooij, and Gerard J M Smit. Efficient computation of buffer capacities for cyclo-static dataflow graphs. In *Proceedings of the 44th ACM/IEEE Design Automation Conference*, pages 658–663, 2007.

[29] Ruibin Xu. *Energy-aware scheduling for streaming applications*. PhD thesis, University of Pitsburgh, 2010.

[30] A. N. Yzelman and Rob H. Bisseling. Cache-oblivious sparse matrix-vector multiplication by using sparse matrix partitioning methods. *SIAM Journal on Scientific Computing*, 31:3128–3154, 2009.

Non-clairvoyant Weighted Flow Time Scheduling with Rejection Penalty

Ho-Leung Chan[*]
University of Hong Kong,
Hong Kong
hlchan@cs.hku.hk

Sze-Hang Chan
University of Hong Kong,
Hong Kong
shchan@cs.hku.hk

Tak-Wah Lam[†]
University of Hong Kong,
Hong Kong
twlam@cs.hku.hk

Lap-Kei Lee[‡]
University of Hong Kong,
Hong Kong
lklee@cs.hku.hk

Jianqiao Zhu
University of Hong Kong,
Hong Kong
jqzhu@cs.hku.hk

ABSTRACT

This paper initiates the study of online scheduling with rejection penalty in the non-clairvoyant setting, i.e., the size (processing time) of a job is not assumed to be known at its release time. In the rejection penalty model, jobs can be rejected with a penalty, and the user cost of a job is defined as the weighted flow time of the job plus the penalty if it is rejected before completion. Previous work on minimizing the total user cost focused on the clairvoyant single-processor setting [2, 8] and has produced $O(1)$-competitive online algorithm for jobs with arbitrary weights and penalties. This paper gives the first non-clairvoyant algorithms that are $O(1)$-competitive for minimizing the total user cost on a single processor and multi-processors, when using slightly faster (i.e., $(1 + \epsilon)$-speed for any $\epsilon > 0$) processors. Note that if no extra speed is allowed, no online algorithm can be $O(1)$-competitive even for minimizing (unweighted) flow time alone. The new user cost results can also be regarded as a generalization of previous non-clairvoyant results on minimizing weighted flow time alone (WSETF [4] for a single processor; WLAPS [14] for multi-processors).

The above results assume a processor running at a fixed speed. This paper shows more interesting results on extending the above study to the dynamic speed scaling model, where the processor can vary the speed dynamically and the rate of energy consumption is an arbitrary increasing function of speed. A scheduling algo-

[*]The research of Ho-Leung Chan was partially supported by GRF Grant HKU710210E.

[†]The research of Tak-Wah Lam was partially supported by HKU Grant 201109176197.

[‡]Part of the work was done when Lap-Kei Lee was working in MADALGO (Center for Massive Data Algorithmics, a Center of the Danish National Research Foundation), Aarhus University, Denmark.

Permission to make digital or hard copies of all or part of this work for personal or classroom use is granted without fee provided that copies are not made or distributed for profit or commercial advantage and that copies bear this notice and the full citation on the first page. To copy otherwise, to republish, to post on servers or to redistribute to lists, requires prior specific permission and/or a fee.
SPAA'12, June 25–27, 2012, Pittsburgh, Pennsylvania, USA.
Copyright 2012 ACM 978-1-4503-1213-4/12/06 ...$10.00.

rithm has to decide job rejection and determine the order and speed of job execution. It is interesting to study the tradeoff between the above-mentioned user cost and energy. This paper gives two $O(1)$-competitive non-clairvoyant algorithms for minimizing the user cost plus energy on a single processor and multi-processors, respectively.

Categories and Subject Descriptors

C.4 [**Performance of Systems**]: Performance Attributes; F.2.0 [**Analysis of Algorithms and Problem Complexity**]: General

Keywords

Online scheduling, competitive analysis, weighted flow time, non-clairvoyant scheduling, rejection penalty

1. INTRODUCTION

It is common that servers prioritize their jobs and reject some low-priority jobs during peak load to meet the performance guarantee. Serving too many jobs prolongs their individual response time, yet rejecting jobs would cause users' inconvenience and waste the processing power already spent on them. To study the tradeoff between response time and rejection penalty, Bansal et al. [2] and Chan et al. [8] considered flow-time scheduling on a single processor when jobs can be rejected at some penalty. Jobs arrive online with arbitrary sizes, weights and penalties, and a scheduler may reject some jobs before completion. Each job defines a *user cost* equal to its weighted flow time plus the penalty if it is rejected, where the flow time (or simply flow) of a job is the time elapsed since the job is released until it is completed or rejected. The objective is to minimize the total user cost of all jobs.

Bansal et al. [2] showed that any online algorithm is $\Omega(\max\{n^{\frac{1}{4}}, C^{\frac{1}{2}}\})$-competitive, where n is the number of jobs and C is the max-min ratio of job penalties. In view of the lower bound, they consider giving the online algorithm a slightly faster processor. Using a $(1 + \epsilon)$-speed processor for any $\epsilon > 0$, they gave an $O(\frac{1}{\epsilon}(\log W + \log C)^2)$-competitive algorithm where W is the max-min ratio of job weights. Recently, Chan et al. [8] improved the competitive ratio to $O((1 + \frac{1}{\epsilon})^2)$ when using a $(1 + \epsilon)^2$-speed processor, which is independent of W and C. These two results are based on job rejection policies that know the size of a job at its re-

	Weighted flow	User cost	Weighted flow + energy	User cost + energy
Single processor	$1 + \frac{1}{\epsilon}$ [4]	$12(1 + \frac{1}{\epsilon})^2$ [†]	$8(1 + \frac{1}{\epsilon})^2$ [7]	$36(1 + \frac{1}{\epsilon})^2$ [†]
$m > 1$ processors	$8(1 + \frac{1}{\epsilon})^2$ [14]	$20(1 + \frac{1}{\epsilon})^2$ [†]	$12(\log m + 2)(1 + \frac{1}{\epsilon})^2$ [†] (using $2(1 + \epsilon)$-speed processors)	

Table 1: Competitive ratios of non-clairvoyant scheduling for different objectives involving weighted flow time. Recall that user cost equals weighted flow plus penalty. All results assume using a faster processor and, unless specified otherwise, are using $(1 + \epsilon)$-speed processors. Our new results are marked with [†].

lease time and its remaining size at any time, i.e., they only work in the clairvoyant setting. In this paper, we extend the study of rejection penalty to the *non-clairvoyant* setting, where the size of a released job is not known until the job is completed. Such a setting is natural from the viewpoint of operating systems.

Non-clairvoyant flow-time scheduling on a single processor. For the special case when each job has infinite penalty, no jobs would be rejected and the problem reduces to the classic problem of minimizing weighted flow time only. In the non-clairvoyant setting, even for unweighted jobs, any algorithm is $\Omega(n^{1/3})$-competitive [12] for minimizing the total flow, where n is the number of jobs. Using a slightly faster processor, Kalyanasundaram and Pruhs [11] analyzed a non-clairvoyant algorithm SETF (Shortest Elapsed Time First, which prefers jobs that have been processed the least) for a single processor, and they showed that it is $(1 + \epsilon)$-speed $(1 + \frac{1}{\epsilon})$-competitive for (unweighted) flow. Later, Bansal and Dhamdhere [4] generalized this result for weighted jobs, and showed that the algorithm WSETF is $(1 + \epsilon)$-speed $(1 + \frac{1}{\epsilon})$-competitive for weighted flow.

Multi-processor scheduling with arbitrary parallelizability. On a multi-core chip that provides $m \geq 1$ identical processors, some jobs might be processed faster when using several processors in parallel, while others might be inherently sequential. In the literature, the degree of parallelizability of a job was modeled as follows (e.g., [9, 10, 14]): A job consists of a number of phases, each with an arbitrary size and arbitrary speedup function that specifies the amount of speedup when running the job on a given number of processors. A non-clairvoyant scheduler has no information about the phases in advance. For minimizing (unweighted) flow in such a multi-processor model, Edmonds [9] gave a $(2 + \epsilon)$-speed $O(\frac{1}{\epsilon})$-competitive algorithm, and Edmonds and Pruhs [10] later showed that another algorithm LAPS (Latest Arrival Processor Sharing, which shares the processing power equally among a constant fraction of latest-arrival jobs) is $(1 + \beta + \epsilon)$-speed $O(\frac{1 + \beta + \epsilon}{\beta \epsilon})$-competitive, for any $\epsilon > 0$ and $0 < \beta \leq 1$ [10]. Very recently, Zhu et al. [14] extended the latter result to weighted jobs and gave an algorithm WLAPS (Weighted LAPS) that is $(1 + \epsilon)$-speed $8(1 + \frac{1}{\epsilon})^2$-competitive for weighted flow.

New results on flow plus penalty. In this paper, we extend the non-clairvoyant results on flow-time scheduling to the rejection penalty model. In particular, we propose a simple job rejection policy RWE (Reject When weighted flow Equals penalty), which rejects an unfinished job when the weighted flow incurred equals the job penalty. Unlike previous job rejection policies [2, 8], RWE does not require any information on job size, and it can be used in different settings. We develop a rather general technique for analyzing RWE. In the single-processor setting, we show that WLAPS coupled with RWE is $(1 + \epsilon)$-speed $12(1 + \frac{1}{\epsilon})^2$-competitive for minimizing total user cost; in the multi-processor setting, the competitive ratio becomes $20(1 + \frac{1}{\epsilon})^2$. For the special case when jobs must all be completed (i.e., with infinite penalty), our new algorithm behaves exactly as WLAPS. The first two columns of Table 1

summarize the results on weighted flow and user cost (weighted flow plus penalty).

Dynamic speed scaling and energy. The above results assume that processors are running at a fixed speed. We show that RWE also works well in the dynamic speed scaling model, in which the scheduler can manage the energy consumption by scaling the processor speed dynamically (see [1] for a survey). Specifically, the processor speed can vary between 0 and a maximum speed T, and its rate of energy consumption (i.e., power) P increases with the speed s according to a certain given power function, say, $P(s) = s^3$. In this model, a scheduler has to determine dynamically which job and at what speed to execute.

Tradeoff between user cost and energy. The past few years have witnessed several online results on optimizing the tradeoff between flow and energy under the dynamic speed scaling model (see [1] for survey). Chan et al. [8] have also extended the study of rejection penalty to the dynamic speed scaling model and considered the tradeoff between user cost and energy consumption, but their result is limited to the clairvoyant setting. In particular, they gave a clairvoyant algorithm that is $(1 + \epsilon)^2$-speed $O((1 + \frac{1}{\epsilon})^2)$-competitive for minimizing total user cost plus energy on a single processor [8]. In this context, a λ-speed processor (where $\lambda > 1$) means that, given power $P(s)$, it can run at speed $\lambda \cdot s$. In this paper, we use RWE to obtain a non-clairvoyant algorithm RAW which is $(1 + \epsilon)$-speed $36(1 + \frac{1}{\epsilon})^2$-competitive for minimizing total user cost plus energy (see Table 1).

Multi-processor result. We further show that RWE also leads to a new non-clairvoyant algorithm for minimizing user cost plus energy on $m > 1$ processors, where each processor can scale its speed independently and jobs comprise phases with different degrees of parallelizability. The only past relevant work was done by Chan, Edmonds and Pruhs [6], who considered scheduling unweighted jobs non-clairvoyantly on processors with power function $P(s) = s^\alpha$ for any $\alpha > 1$, and maximum speed $T = \infty$. The objective is to minimize total flow plus energy, and jobs must be all completed. They showed a strong lower bound of $\Omega(m^{(\alpha-1)/\alpha^2})$ on the competitive ratio. In view of this lower bound, they assume that jobs satisfy two properties: (1) They do not have side effect, i.e., the execution of a job does not affect anything external to itself, so multiple copies of a job can run simultaneously. (2) They are checkpointable, i.e., each copy can save its state periodically and then restart each copy from the point of execution of the copy that made the most progress. Then Chan, Edmonds and Pruhs [6] were able to extend LAPS to a new algorithm Multi-LAPS which is $O(2^\alpha \log m \frac{\alpha^2}{\log \alpha})$-competitive for minimizing (unweighted) flow plus energy, and showed that any algorithm for such checkpointable jobs is $\Omega(\log^{1/\alpha} m)$-competitive. Roughly speaking, previous speed scaling work scales the speed such that flow and energy are incurred at the same rate, yet MultiLAPS needs to run two times faster, leading to the multiplicative factor of 2^α in the competitive ratio.

We extend the above result to the rejection penalty model, and more interestingly, allowing weighted jobs and arbitrary power function $P(s)$. We give an algorithm MultiRAW which uses RWE as job rejection policy and is $2(1+\epsilon)$-speed $12(\log m + 2)(1 + \frac{1}{\epsilon})^2$-competitive for minimizing total user cost plus energy. To analyze MultiRAW, we need to restrict the total processor speed of the optimal offline algorithm to follow some function depending on total weight of unfinished jobs, and show that such a restriction does not increase the competitive ratio by a constant factor. To this end, we generalize the offline transformation algorithm LLB (Latest Lag Behind) first given in [7] for single processor, and allow it to transform an offline algorithm that would run multiple different jobs simultaneously on multiple processors. The transformed offline algorithm may also run different jobs at the same time using time sharing and always has the processor speed following the required function, and we show that its weighted flow is at most the weighted flow plus energy of the original algorithm.

Organization of the paper. The following discussion focuses on the results in the dynamic speed scaling model. Note that the results in the fixed speed model would be shown as special cases. Section 2 defines the models, problems and notations formally. Results on single processor and multi-processors are given in Sections 3 and 4, respectively.

2. FORMAL PROBLEM DEFINITIONS AND NOTATIONS

We study job scheduling on a chip containing $m \geq 1$ identical processors. Jobs are arriving online, where each job j has a release time $r(j)$, a size $p(j)$, a weight $w(j)$ and a rejection penalty $c(j)$. Jobs are *non-clairvoyant*, meaning that the size of a job is unknown until it is completed. Preemption and migration are allowed and free.

Each processor can run independently at any speed $s \in [0, T]$ (where T is the maximum speed of the processor which may be ∞). The rate of energy usage is given by an arbitrary power function $P(s)$. Similar to [3], we assume that $P(0) = 0$, and P at all speeds in $[0, T]$ is defined, strictly increasing, nonnegative, continuous, strictly convex and differentiable. As shown in [3], it is possible to use such a power function P to emulate any arbitrary power function with an arbitrarily small increase in the competitive ratio. Let $Q(y) = \min\{P^{-1}(y), T\}$. Note that Q is monotonically increasing and concave. E.g., if $P(s) = s^\alpha$ for some $\alpha > 1$, then $Q(x) = x^{1/\alpha}$.

In the single processor setting, each job is processed by at most one processor and its processing rate is always the speed of the processor times the fraction of the processor assigned to this job. The processing rate is more complicated in the multi-processor setting due to the varying parallelizability of the job. In particular, we consider each job as a sequence of $q(j)$ phases $\langle j^1, j^2, \ldots, j^{q(j)} \rangle$. Each phase j^k is an ordered pair $\langle p(j^k), \Gamma_{j^k} \rangle$, where $p(j^k)$ is the amount of work in the phase and Γ_{j^k} is a *speed-up function* specifying the degree of parallelism of the phase. More precisely, $\Gamma_{j^k}(y)$ represents the rate at which work in the phase j^k is processed when using y processors running at speed 1. If the y processors are running at speed s, then the work is processed at rate $\Gamma_{j^k}(y) \cdot s$. Following the previous work (e.g., [6, 9, 10]), we assume that each speedup function Γ is non-negative, monotonically increasing and sublinear, i.e., $\frac{\Gamma(y)}{y} \geq \frac{\Gamma(y')}{y'}$ for any $y \leq y'$. We assume that for any phase, its speed-up function Γ satisfies that $\Gamma(y) = y$ for $y \in [0, 1]$. This assumption corresponds to the fact that when a phase is processed by time-sharing on a $y \leq 1$ fraction of a processor, its processing rate should be y times the speed of the processor.

In the non-clairvoyant setting, we assume that the size and speedup function of each phase is not known to the online algorithm.

In the speed scaling model, the objective is to minimize the sum of the total weighted flow time, total rejection penalty and total energy usage. We call it the *cost* of a schedule. Let OPT be the optimal offline algorithm that always minimizes the cost. We analyze our algorithms when they are given faster processors. Precisely, a y-speed processor runs at speed sy when the rate of energy usage is $P(s)$.

Previous definitions. Our results make use of previous work like WLAPS and AJW (e.g., [7]). We review the necessary definitions. We say that a job is *active* at time t if it has arrived but has not yet finished or rejected by time t. Throughout this paper, we denote $n_a(t)$ as the number of active job in the online algorithm at time t and $w_a(t)$ be their total weight.

DEFINITION 1 (β-ADJUSTED WEIGHT). *Let $\beta \in (0, 1]$ be a parameter. Consider any time t. Let $j_1, j_2, \ldots, j_{n_a(t)}$ be the active jobs in the online algorithm ordered in increasing order of arrival times. Let τ be the largest integer such that the latest arrived jobs $\{j_\tau, j_{\tau+1}, \ldots, j_{n_a(t)}\}$ have total weight at least $\beta w_a(t)$. Then, the β-adjusted weight of j_i at time t, denoted $w'_\beta(j_i, t)$ (or simply $w'(j_i, t)$) when β is clear in context), is defined as follows:*

$$w'_\beta(j_i, t) = \begin{cases} 0 & \text{if } i < \tau \\ \beta w_a(t) - \sum_{i=\tau+1}^{n_a(t)} w(j_i) & \text{if } i = \tau \\ w(j_i) & \text{if } i > \tau \end{cases}$$

DEFINITION 2 (JOB ASSIGNMENT POLICY WLAPS). *WLAPS(β) is parameterized by a constant $\beta \in (0, 1]$. It assumes all processors are running at the same speed. At any time t, WLAPS shares the processors among all active jobs proportional to their adjusted weights at time t, i.e., each job j is assigned a fraction $\frac{w'(j,t)}{\beta w_a(t)}$ of the processors.*

DEFINITION 3 (SPEED SCALING POLICY AJW). *At any time t, AJW sets the speed of each processor to $s(t) = Q(\frac{w_a(t)}{m})$. Intuitively, the speed $s(t)$ ensures that the total rate of energy usage equals $w_a(t)$, or $s(t) = T$ if $mP(T) < w_a(t)$.*

3. SINGLE PROCESSOR RESULTS

In this section, we propose a simple job rejection policy RWE (Reject When weighted flow Equals penalty). Combining RWE with WLAPS, we can obtain an O(1)-competitive algorithm for minimizing weighted flow plus penalty on a fixed-speed processor. Below we show a more general result on combining RWE with WLAPS and AJW to obtain an O(1)-competitive algorithm for minimizing weighted flow plus penalty plus energy under the dynamic speed scaling model. RWE is defined as follows.

DEFINITION 4 (JOB REJECTION POLICY RWE). *RWE rejects a job j if it is not completed by time $r(j) + \frac{c(j)}{w(j)}$.*

Algorithm RAW. Let $\beta \in (0, 1]$ be a constant. RAW assumes a $(1+\epsilon)$-speed processor where $\epsilon > 0$ can be any real. RAW assigns jobs to the processor by WLAPS, i.e., sharing the processor among all active jobs proportional to their adjusted weights. RAW scales the processor speed to $(1+\epsilon) \cdot Q(w_a(t))$ (so the rate of energy usage is $w_a(t)$). RAW rejects jobs according to RWE.

We call the algorithm RAW to stand for RWE-AJW-WLAPS. Our main result is the following.

THEOREM 1. *Let* $\beta = \frac{\epsilon}{2(1+\epsilon)}$. *RAW is* $(1+\epsilon)$-*speed* $36(1 + \frac{1}{\epsilon})^2$-*competitive for minimizing weighted flow plus penalty plus energy.*

To prove Theorem 1, let OFF be the offline algorithm that minimizes the cost under the condition that OFF scales the processor speed by AJW, and OFF rejects a job j at time $r(j)$ if OPT rejects j. It is known that the cost of OFF is at most twice of OPT when they do not reject jobs [7]. Below we show that this relationship remains valid even if they reject jobs.

LEMMA 2. *The cost of* OFF *is at most twice the cost of* OPT.

PROOF. For each job j, recall that OFF rejects j when j arrives if OPT rejects j. Then, OFF schedules the remaining jobs by the algorithm LLB [7], which uses AJW to scale the processor speed. [7] shows that the total weighted flow time plus energy usage of LLB is at most twice that of OPT. Since the total penalty of OFF is the same as that of OPT, the cost of OFF is at most twice that of OPT. □

Hence, it suffices to analyze RAW against OFF, which would incur an extra factor of two in the competitive ratio. At any time t, let $q_a(j,t)$ be the remaining work of j in RAW and let $q_o(j,t)$ be that in OFF. Note that $q_a(j,t)$ (resp., $q_o(j,t)$) becomes 0 once RAW (resp., OFF) rejects j. We are interested in the progress of the jobs that are not rejected by OFF.

DEFINITION 5 (LAGGING WORK). *At any time t, for any job j, the amount of* lagging work *of j is defined as*

$$x(j,t) = \begin{cases} 0 & \text{if OFF rejects } j \text{ at } r(j) \\ \max\{q_a(j,t) - q_o(j,t), 0\} & \text{otherwise} \end{cases}$$

Intuitively, $x(j,t)$ is the amount of "useful" work that RAW is lagging behind OFF. In particular, if j is already rejected by OFF, then all work remaining in RAW is not useful.

At any time t, let $R(t)$ be the set of jobs being processed by RAW. Recall that the total adjusted weight of jobs in $R(t)$ is $\beta w_a(t)$, where $w_a(t)$ is the total weight of all active jobs. Let $L(t) \subseteq R(t)$ be those jobs in $R(t)$ such that $x(j,t) > 0$. We call $L(t)$ the lagging jobs. We denote $\phi(t) = \sum_{j \in L(t)} w'(j,t)$. Then Theorem 1 follows from the following two lemmas.

LEMMA 3 (LOWER BOUND OF OFF). $\int_0^\infty (\beta w_a(t) - \phi(t))dt$ $\leq W_o + C_o$, *where W_o and C_o are the total weighted flow and the total rejection penalty of* OFF, *respectively.*

LEMMA 4 (UPPER BOUND OF RAW). $\int_0^\infty w_a(t)\ dt \leq$ $\frac{1}{\beta^2}\int_0^\infty ((\beta w_a(t) - \phi(t)) + \beta w_o(t))dt$, *where $w_o(t)$ is the total weight of active jobs in* OFF *at time t.*

Before proving Lemmas 3 and 4, we show how to use these two lemmas to prove Theorem 1.

PROOF. (*Proof of Theorem 1*) Recall that that $\beta < 1/2$. By Lemmas 3 and 4, the total weighted flow time of RAW is at most $\frac{1}{\beta^2}(W_o + C_o + \int_0^\infty \beta w_o(t)dt) = (2(1+\frac{1}{\epsilon}))^2((1+\beta)W_o + C_o) \leq 6(1+\frac{1}{\epsilon})^2 \cdot (W_o + C_o)$. Note that for each job j rejected by RWE, the weighted flow time incurred is $\frac{c(j)}{w(j)} \cdot w(j) = c(j)$. Hence, the total penalty of RAW is at most its total weighted flow time. Furthermore, by running AJW, RAW has energy usage at most its weighted flow time. In summary, the cost of RAW is at most $18(1+\frac{1}{\epsilon})^2$ times the cost of OFF. The latter is at most twice the cost of OPT (by Lemma 2). Theorem 1 follows. □

PROOF. (*Proof of Lemma 3*) Consider any time t. Note that $\beta w_a(t) - \phi(t)$ is the total weight of jobs in $R(t) \setminus L(t)$, which are the jobs j being processed by RAW with $x(j,t) = 0$. Note that $x(j,t) = 0$ only if j is rejected by OFF at $r(j)$ or $q_a(j,t) \leq q_o(j,t)$ at time t. Let C be the set of jobs rejected by OFF. Let $C(t) = C \cap R(t) \setminus L(t)$ be those jobs in C that are still active in RAW at time t and let $N(t) \subseteq R(t) \setminus L(t)$ be those jobs j not rejected by OFF but $q_a(j,t) \leq q_o(j,t)$ at time t. Then,

$$\int_0^\infty (\beta w_a(t) - \phi(t))dt = \int_0^\infty \sum_{j \in C(t)} w(j)dt + \int_0^\infty \sum_{j \in N(t)} w(j)dt.$$

Note that for each job j, j remains in RAW for at most $\frac{c(j)}{w(j)}$ units of time and incurs a weighted flow time of at most $c(j)$. Hence, $\int_0^\infty \sum_{j \in C(t)} w(j)dt \leq \sum_{j \in C} c(j) = C_o$.

For each job j in $N(t)$, j is not completed by OFF at time t. Hence, $\int_0^\infty \sum_{j \in N(t)} w(j)dt \leq \int_0^\infty w_o(t)dt \leq W_o$, where $w_o(t)$ is the total weight of jobs in OFF at time t. □

PROOF. (*Proof of Lemma 4*) We use a potential function analysis. Let $j_1, j_2, \ldots, j_{n_a(t)}$ be the active jobs in RAW at time t arranged in increasing order of arrival times. We denote $h(j_i) = \sum_{k=1}^i w(j_i)$ as the total weight of active jobs arrived no later than j_i. Recall that $x(j,t)$ is the lagging work of j at time t. Then, we define

$$\Phi(t) = \gamma \sum_{i=1}^{n_a(t)} f(h(j_i)) \cdot x(j_i, t),$$

where $\gamma = \frac{1}{\beta(1+\epsilon)}$ and $f(h) = h/Q(h)$. Note that $f(h)$ is non-decreasing.[1] We will show that Φ satisfies the following three conditions.

- *Boundary condition*: $\Phi = 0$ before the first job arrives and after all jobs are finished.
- *Discrete event condition*: Φ does not increase at job arrival, completion or rejection.
- *Running condition*: At any other time t,

$$w_a(t) + \frac{d\Phi(t)}{dt} \leq \frac{1}{\beta^2}((\beta w_a(t) - \phi(t)) + \beta w_o(t)).$$

Then, by integrating these conditions over time, the lemma follows. The boundary condition is true as $n_a(t) = 0$ before any job is released and after all jobs are finished. When a job j arrives, no matter whether OFF rejects j, $x(j,t) = 0$, so Φ does not increase. When j is completed by OFF, $x(j,t)$ and Φ do not change. When j is completed or rejected by RAW, the term corresponding to j disappears and other terms may only decrease, so Φ does not increase. Thus, the discrete event condition is true. For the running condition, Lemma 5 below shows that $\frac{d\Phi}{dt} \leq \frac{1-2\beta}{\beta} \max\{w_a(t), w_o(t)\} - \frac{1}{\beta^2}(1-\beta)\phi(t)$. Note that $\frac{1-2\beta}{\beta} \max\{w_a(t), w_o(t)\}$ is no greater than $\frac{1}{\beta} \max\{w_a(t), w_o(t)\} - 2w_a(t)$, and $\frac{1}{\beta}\phi(t) \leq \frac{1}{\beta}\beta w_a(t) \leq w_a(t)$. Therefore,

$$w_a(t) + \frac{d\Phi(t)}{dt}$$
$$\leq w_a(t) + \frac{1-2\beta}{\beta} \max\{w_a(t), w_o(t)\} - \frac{1}{\beta^2}(1-\beta)\phi(t)$$
$$\leq w_a(t) + \frac{1}{\beta} \max\{w_a(t), w_o(t)\} - 2w_a(t) - \frac{1}{\beta^2}\phi(t) + w_a(t)$$
$$\leq \frac{1}{\beta^2}[\beta \max\{w_a(t), w_o(t)\} - \phi(t)]$$
$$\leq \frac{1}{\beta^2}((\beta w_a(t) - \phi(t)) + \beta w_o(t)).$$

□

---

[1] Since Q is concave, for any $\lambda \in [0, 1]$ and $h \geq 0$, $(1 - \lambda)Q(0) + \lambda Q(h) \leq Q((1 - \lambda)0 + \lambda h)$, i.e., $\lambda Q(h) \leq Q(\lambda h)$. Hence, $f(\lambda h) = \frac{\lambda h}{Q(\lambda h)} \leq \frac{h}{Q(h)} = f(h)$.

LEMMA 5. *At any time t without discrete events, $\frac{d\Phi}{dt} \le \frac{1-2\beta}{\beta} \cdot \max\{w_a(t), w_o(t)\} - \frac{1}{\beta^2}(1-\beta)\phi(t)$.*

PROOF. We consider $\frac{d\Phi}{dt}$ as a combined effect due to the action of RAW and OFF. Let $\frac{d\Phi_a}{dt}$ and $\frac{d\Phi_o}{dt}$ be the rate of change of Φ due to RAW and OFF, respectively. Then $\frac{d\Phi}{dt} = \frac{d\Phi_a}{dt} + \frac{d\Phi_o}{dt}$.

For each active job j in RAW, if $j \in L(t)$, $x(j,t) > 0$ and $h(j) \ge (1-\beta)w_a(t)$. RAW processes j at a speed $(1+\epsilon)\frac{w'(j,t)}{\beta w_a(t)} \cdot Q(w_a(t))$. Hence, for each term $\gamma \cdot f(h(j)) \cdot x(j,t)$ where $j \in L(t)$, the term is decreasing at a rate at least

$$\gamma \cdot \frac{h(j)}{Q(h(j))} \cdot (1+\epsilon)\frac{w'(j,t)}{\beta w_a(t)}Q(w_a(t))$$
$$\ge \quad \gamma \cdot \frac{(1-\beta)w_a(t)}{Q((1-\beta)w_a(t))} \cdot (1+\epsilon)\frac{w'(j,t)}{\beta w_a(t)}Q(w_a(t))$$
$$\ge \quad \gamma\frac{1-\beta}{\beta}(1+\epsilon)w'(j,t) = \frac{1-\beta}{\beta^2}w'(j,t)$$

where the first inequality comes from that $f(h) = h/Q(h)$ is non-decreasing with h, and the second inequality comes from that Q is increasing. For each job $j \notin L(t)$, the term $\gamma \cdot f(h(j)) \cdot x(j,t)$ is non-increasing. Hence, $\frac{d\Phi_a}{dt} \le -\frac{1}{\beta^2}\sum_{j\in L(t)} w'(j,t) = -\frac{1-\beta}{\beta^2}\phi(t)$.

For OFF, the worst case (in which $\frac{d\Phi_o}{dt}$ is the largest) occurs when it processes the job with maximum $h(j)$, which equals $w_a(t)$, using all its speed $s_o = Q(w_o(t))$. Then $\frac{d\Phi_o}{dt} \le \gamma \cdot f(w_a(t)) \cdot s_o = \gamma\frac{w_a(t)}{Q(w_a(t))} \cdot Q(w_o(t))$. If $w_a(t) \ge w_o(t)$, $Q(w_a(t)) \ge Q(w_o(t))$ and $\frac{d\Phi_o}{dt} \le \gamma w_a(t)$. Otherwise, $w_a(t) < w_o(t)$. Since f is non-decreasing, $f(w_a(t)) \le f(w_o(t))$. Hence, $\frac{d\Phi_o}{dt} \le \gamma f(w_o(t)) \cdot s_o = \gamma w_o(t)$. Combining the two cases, we have $\frac{d\Phi_o}{dt} \le \gamma \cdot \max\{w_a(t), w_o(t)\}$. Notice that $\beta = \frac{\epsilon}{2(1+\epsilon)}$ and $\frac{1}{1+\epsilon} = 1-2\beta$. Hence, $\gamma\max\{w_a(t), w_o(t)\} = \frac{1}{\beta(1+\epsilon)} \cdot \max\{w_a(t), w_o(t)\} = \frac{1-2\beta}{\beta}\max\{w_a(t), w_o(t)\}$ and the lemma follows. $\square$

Remarks on fixed speed setting. Since the fixed speed setting is a special case of the arbitrary power function setting (where energy usage of any algorithm is zero), the previous result immediately implies that RAW is $36(1 + \frac{1}{\epsilon})^2$-competitive using a $(1+\epsilon)$-speed processor. Yet we can tighten the analysis to achieve a better competitive ratio. In particular, we can directly compare RAW and OPT and show lemmas similar to Lemma 3 and 4, which can upper bound the total weighted flow of RAW to be at most $6(1 + \frac{1}{\epsilon})^2$ times the cost of OPT. The total rejection penalty of RAW is at most its weighted flow. The following theorem follows.

THEOREM 6. *For the fixed speed setting, RAW is $(1 + \epsilon)$-speed $12(1 + \frac{1}{\epsilon})^2$-competitive for minimizing weighted flow plus penalty.*

4. MULTI-PROCESSOR RESULTS

We consider scheduling on $m > 1$ processors in the speed scaling model. We give an algorithm MultiRAW which is $2(1 + \epsilon)$-speed $12(1+\frac{1}{\epsilon})^2(\log m+2)$-competitive for minimizing weighted flow plus penalty plus energy. Note that MultiRAW follows the job rejection policy RWE given in Section 3. The fixed speed model is treated as a special case; we can modify the result of MultiRAW to get an $(1+\epsilon)$-speed $20(1+\frac{1}{\epsilon})^2$-competitive algorithm for weighted flow plus penalty. For simplicity, we first assume that the number of processors m is a power of two. We will explain how to remove this assumption later.

Our algorithm is built on MultiLAPS proposed by [6], in which they consider unweighted jobs that cannot be rejected and the power function is $P(s) = s^\alpha$ without maximum speed bound. Their objective is to minimize the total flow time plus energy usage.

Algorithm MultiLAPS [6]. Let $\beta \in (0, 1]$ be a constant and $n_a(t)$ be the number of active jobs in MultiLAPS at time t. MultiLAPS divides the m processors into $\log m$ groups such that for $\ell = 1, \ldots, \log m$, the ℓ-th group consists of $m_\ell = 2^{-\ell}m$ processors each running at speed $2(\frac{n_a(t)}{m_\ell})^{1/\alpha}$. Each group runs independently and processes the $\lceil\beta n_a(t)\rceil$ jobs with the latest arrival times by sharing the processors within the group equally among the jobs. Note that each of these jobs is duplicated into $\log m$ copies and processed simultaneously by the $\log m$ groups. Since the jobs are checkpointable, at any time, the processing rate of a job is the maximum processing rate among all the copies of the job in the $\log m$ groups.

Algorithm MultiRAW. To handle weighted jobs, rejection penalty, and arbitrary power functions, we extend the algorithm MultiLAPS as follows.

- For the ℓ-th group, we set the speed of each processor to $s_\ell = 2(1+\epsilon)Q(\frac{w_a(t)}{m_\ell})$; recall that $Q(y) = \min\{P^{-1}(y), T\}$, and $w_a(t)$ is the total weight of the active jobs at time t.
- We share the processors within a group proportional to the adjusted weight of the jobs. Hence, a job j is processed by $\frac{w'(j,t)}{\beta w_a(t)} \cdot m_\ell$ processors in the ℓ-th group.
- (Job rejection policy RWE) We reject a job j if it is not finished by time $r(j) + \frac{c(j)}{w(j)}$.

Our main result is the following theorem. Sections 4.1 to 4.5 are devoted to proving this theorem.

THEOREM 7. *Let $\epsilon > 0$ be any real and $\beta = \frac{\epsilon}{2(1+\epsilon)}$. MultiRAW is $2(1+\epsilon)$-speed $12(1+\frac{1}{\epsilon})^2(\log m+2)$-competitive for minimizing weighted flow plus penalty plus energy.*

4.1 Restricting input instances and offline algorithm

Canonical instances. We first show that it suffices to consider some specific input instances. Recall that jobs may have varying parallelizability and the parallelizability of a phase is given by a speedup function Γ. We call Γ *parallel up to σ processors* if $\Gamma(y) = y$ for all $y \le \sigma$ and $\Gamma(y) = \sigma$ for $y > \sigma$. We call an instance *canonical* if each job phase is parallel up to σ processors for some $\sigma \in [1, m]$, where σ may be different for different phases.

LEMMA 8. *For any input instance I, we can transform I into a canonical instance such that the cost of MultiRAW does not change and the cost of OPT may only decrease.*

Canonical instances were first introduced in [6,14], and Lemma 8 can be proven in a similar way as in [6, 14]. In the following, we consider canonical instances only.

Restricted offline algorithm. To prove Theorem 7, we need to compare MultiRAW against the optimal offline algorithm OPT. Without loss of generality, OPT rejects jobs at their release time. It is sometimes easier to compare MultiRAW against an offline algorithm that rejects the same set of jobs as OPT but works on a single processor with maximum speed $m \cdot T$. Let OFF be such an offline algorithm that minimizes the weighted flow alone under the condition that the single processor always runs at speed $m \cdot Q(\frac{w_o(t)}{m})$, where $w_o(t)$ is the total weight of active jobs in OFF. Note that OFF does not have energy concern in its objective.

LEMMA 9. *The weighted flow of OFF is at most the weighted flow plus energy of OPT.*

To prove Lemma 9, we generalize the algorithm LLB (Latest Lag Behind) given in [7] to transform OPT (which minimizes weighted flow plus energy of the jobs not rejected on m processors) to an offline algorithm LLB$'$ on a single processor with maximum speed $m \cdot T$ that at any time t, follows the speed $m \cdot Q(\frac{w_b(t)}{m})$, where $w_b(t)$ is the total weight of active jobs in LLB$'$. A new feature of LLB$'$ is the ability to handle the case that OPT can run multiple jobs by time sharing at the same time.

Algorithm LL $'$. Consider any time t. Let $n_b(t)$ be the number of active jobs in LLB$'$. For any job j, let $p_b(j,t)$ and $p_o(j,t)$ be the work done on j up to time t by LLB$'$ and OPT, respectively. Furthermore, let $d(j,t) = p_o(j,t) - p_b(j,t)$. We say a job j is *lagging* at time t if $d(j,t) > 0$. Let $y(j)$ be the latest time when j has become lagging; if j is non-lagging, let $y(j) = t$. We denote the active jobs in LLB$'$ at time t as $j_1, j_2, \ldots, j_{n_b(t)}$, arranged in increasing order of $y(j_i)$, i.e., $y(j_1) \leq y(j_2) \leq \cdots \leq y(j_{n_b(t)})$. Let ℓ be the number of lagging jobs ($0 \leq \ell \leq n_b(t)$). Let s_o be the total speed of the m processors in OPT at time t. Let $s_x \leq s_o$ be the total speed OPT assigns to all jobs j with $d(j,t) = 0$. LLB$'$ sets its speed $s_b = m \cdot Q(\frac{w_b(t)}{m})$, and focuses on the job j_a defined to be j_ℓ if $\ell > 0$, and $j_{n_b(t)}$ otherwise. Details are as follows:

- If OPT is not running any job j_i with $d(j_i,t) = 0$, then LLB$'$ runs j_a with speed s_b.
- If OPT is processing some jobs j_i with $d(j_i,t) = 0$, but $s_x \leq s_b$ (i.e., LLB$'$ has enough speed to prevent all of them from becoming lagging), then LLB$'$ follows OPT's speed on each of those jobs and runs j_a with the remaining speed $s_b - s_x$.
- Otherwise ($s_b < s_x$), LLB$'$ follows OPT's speed for each of those jobs j_i, in descending order of the index i, until there is some job j which LLB$'$ cannot follow OPT's total speed on j. LLB$'$ then assigns all of its remaining speed to j.

Roughly speaking, LLB$'$ attempts to catch up with the progress of OPT; it gives priority to the job that has become lagging most recently, while trying to avoid creating more new lagging jobs. We can show that the weighted flow of LLB$'$ is at most the weighted flow plus energy of OPT. Its proof is given in Appendix B. Since OFF minimizes weighted flow, Lemma 9 follows.

4.2 Lower bound on processing of MultiRAW

At any time t, consider any active job j in MultiRAW. We define $\sigma(j,t)$ such that the next available work of j belongs to a phase that is parallel up to $\sigma(j,t)$ processors. We call $\sigma(j,t)$ the *saturated number* of j at time t. Intuitively, any processor allocated to j beyond $\sigma(j,t)$ is wasted and cannot further increase the processing rate.

At any time t, let $R(t)$ be the set of jobs j with positive adjusted weight, i.e., $w'(j,t) > 0$. Note that $R(t)$ is the set of jobs being processed by MultiRAW and the processing rate of a job $j \in R(t)$ is the maximum of its processing rate in the $\log m$ groups. We classify the work of j into two types as follows. We label the work as *unsaturated* if it is processed by no more processors than its saturation number in *all* groups; and label the work as *saturated* otherwise. We call a job $j \in R(t)$ saturated at time t if MultiRAW is processing its saturated work, and call j unsaturated otherwise. Intuitively, by running j on $\log m$ groups, MultiRAW guarantees at least one group has a sufficient processing rate on j.

LEMMA 10. *At any time t, consider any job $j \in R(t)$. If j is unsaturated, the processing rate on j is at least $(1+\epsilon)\frac{w'(j,t)}{\beta w_a(t)} \cdot m \cdot Q(\frac{w_a(t)}{m})$. If j is saturated, the processing rate on j is at least $(1+\epsilon) \cdot \sigma(j,t) \cdot Q(\frac{w'(j,t)}{\sigma(j,t)})$.*

PROOF. If j is unsaturated, consider the processing rate of j by the first group, which has $m/2$ processors each running at speed $2(1+\epsilon)Q(\frac{w_a(t)}{m/2})$. The job j receives $\frac{w'(j,t)}{\beta w_a(t)}$ fraction of the processors. Since j is unsaturated, the processing rate on j equals $m/2 \cdot \frac{w'(j,t)}{\beta w_a(t)} \cdot 2(1+\epsilon)Q(\frac{w_a(t)}{m/2})$. Since Q is non-decreasing and $\frac{w_a(t)}{m/2} \geq \frac{w_a(t)}{m}$, we obtain the desired bound.

If j is saturated, we let the k-th group be the group such that $m_k \frac{w'(j,t)}{\beta w_a(t)} \leq \sigma(j,t) < 2m_k \frac{w'(j,t)}{\beta w_a(t)}$, where m_k is the number of processors in the group. Note that k must exist since $\sigma(j,t) \geq 1 = m_{\log m} \geq m_{\log m} \frac{w'(j,t)}{\beta w_a(t)}$. The processing rate on j by this group equals $m_k \frac{w'(j,t)}{\beta w_a(t)} \cdot 2(1+\epsilon)Q(\frac{w_a(t)}{m_k}) \geq (1+\epsilon)\sigma(j,t)Q(\frac{w_a(t)}{m_k})$. Since $\frac{w_a(t)}{m_k} \geq \frac{w'(j,t)}{\beta\sigma(j,t)} \geq \frac{w'(j,t)}{\sigma(j,t)}$, we obtain the desired bound. □

4.3 Bounding weighted flow of MultiRAW

To bound the weighted flow of MultiRAW, we identify a subset of jobs such that the weighted flow of MultiRAW is at most a constant times the total weighted flow of these jobs in MultiRAW. Then, we upper bound this cost by the weighted flow of OFF and the cost of OPT in Section 4.4, and the desired result follows.

Now, we compare MultiRAW against OFF. For any job j and time t, let $q_a(j,t)$ and $q_o(j,t)$ be the remaining amount of *unsaturated* work of j in MultiRAW and OFF, respectively. In particular, $q_a(j,t)$ (resp., $q_o(j,t)$) is zero if j has been rejected by MultiRAW (resp., OFF) by time t. Recall that OFF only rejects j at $r(j)$. We define the amount of lagging work of a job j, denoted $x(j,t)$, in the same way as in Definition 5 in Section 3.

Consider any time t. It is useful to have a detailed breakdown of the set $R(t)$ of jobs being processed by MultiRAW. We divide $R(t)$ into two sets $S(t)$ and $U(t)$ containing the saturated and unsaturated jobs, respectively. We further divide $U(t)$ into $L(t)$ and $N(t)$ which contain jobs with $x(j,t) > 0$ and $x(j,t) = 0$, respectively. We call $L(t)$ the lagging jobs and $N(t)$ the non-lagging jobs. Recall that the total adjusted weight of jobs in $R(t)$ is $\beta w_a(t)$. Let $\phi(t) = \sum_{j \in L(t)} w'(j,t)$. Similar to Lemma 4 in the single processor setting, we try to bound the total weighted flow time of MultiRAW by weighted flow time incurred due to jobs in $R(t) \setminus L(t)$.

LEMMA 11 (WEIGHTED FLOW OF MULTIRAW).

$$\int_0^\infty w_a(t)dt \leq \frac{1}{\beta^2} \int_0^\infty ((\beta w_a(t) - \phi(t)) + \beta w_o(t))\, dt,$$

where $w_o(t)$ is the total weight of active jobs in OFF at time t.

The proof is similar to that of Lemma 4. In particular, by Lemma 10, the processing rate of each unsaturated job j in MultiRAW is at least $(1+\epsilon)\frac{w'(j,t)}{\beta w_a(t)} \cdot m \cdot Q(\frac{w_a(t)}{m})$. On the other hand, the processing rate of an unsaturated job j in OFF is at most $m \cdot Q(\frac{w_o(t)}{m})$. Hence, by redefining the potential function $\Phi(t)$ to $\gamma \sum_{i=1}^{n_a(t)} f(\frac{h(j_i)}{m}) \cdot x(j_i,t)$, we can prove a lemma identical to Lemma 5 (see Appendix A). Then we can prove Lemma 11 in the same way as Lemma 4.

4.4 Bounding non-lagging jobs and saturated jobs

In the following, we show that $\int_0^\infty (\beta w_a(t) - \phi(t))dt$ can be bounded by the weighted flow of OFF and the cost of OPT. Let C be set of jobs rejected by OPT, which is also the set of jobs rejected by OFF. Let $C(t) = C \cap (S(t) \cup N(t))$. Then, $\beta w_a(t) - \phi(t) = \sum_{j \in C(t)} w'(j,t) + \sum_{j \in N(t) \setminus C(t)} w'(j,t) + \sum_{j \in S(t) \setminus C(t)} w'(j,t)$.

We further break down the proof into two parts. Let W^*, E^* and C^* be the weighted flow, energy and penalty of OPT, respectively. Let W_o be the weighted flow of OFF.

LEMMA 12.
$$\int_0^\infty \sum_{j \in C(t)} w'(j,t) + \sum_{j \in N(t)\setminus C(t)} w'(j,t)dt \le W_o + C^*$$

PROOF. For each $j \in C(t)$, j remains in MultiRAW for at most $c(j)/w(j)$ units of time, incurring a weighted flow of at most $c(j)$. Hence, $\int_0^\infty \sum_{j \in C(t)} w(j)dt \le \sum_{j \in C} c(j) = C^*$. For each $j \in N(t) \setminus C(t)$, j is unfinished by OFF at time t. Hence, $\int_0^\infty \sum_{j \in N(t)\setminus C(t)} w(j)dt \le \int_0^\infty w_o(t)dt = W_o$, where $w_o(t)$ is the total weight of active jobs in OFF at time t. The lemma follows by observing that $w'(j,t) \le w(j)$ for any job j at any time t. □

LEMMA 13. $\int_0^\infty \sum_{j \in S(t)\setminus C(t)} w'(j,t)dt \le W^* + E^*$.

PROOF. Consider any job j not rejected by OPT. Let $\Delta(j)$ be the union of all saturated work in j. We divide the saturated work $\Delta(j)$ into infinitesimal pieces $\{x_1, x_2, \dots\}$ such that (1) within a piece of work, the saturation number remains the same; and (2) MultiRAW processes each piece continuously at a fixed rate, and so as OPT; and (3) there is no job arrival, rejection or completion during the processing of a piece. Each piece is infinitesimal. For any piece $x \in \Delta(j)$, we let $\sigma(x)$ be its saturation number. Let $s(x)$ and $s^*(x)$ be the processing rate on x by MultiRAW and OPT, respectively. Let $w'(x)$ be the adjusted weight of j when x is being processed by MultiRAW. Let $p(x)$ be the size of x. Let S^* be the set of jobs that are not rejected by OPT. Then,

$$\int_0^\infty \sum_{j \in S(t)\setminus C(t)} w'(j,t)dt = \sum_{j \in S^*} \sum_{x \in \Delta(j)} \frac{p(x)}{s(x)} w'(x)$$

Since x is a piece of saturated work, by Lemma 10, $s(x) \ge (1+\epsilon)\sigma(x)Q(\frac{w'(x)}{\sigma(x)}) > \sigma(x)Q(\frac{w'(x)}{\sigma(x)})$. Hence, $\frac{p(x)}{s(x)}w'(x) \le p(x)\frac{w'(x)/\sigma(x)}{Q(w'(x)/\sigma(x))} \le p(x)\frac{w(j)/\sigma(x)}{Q(w(j)/\sigma(x))}$. The last inequality comes from the fact that $\frac{y}{Q(y)}$ is increasing with y (as Q is nonnegative and concave) and $w'(x) \le w(j)$.

Consider the same piece of work x. The weighted flow incurred by x in OPT is $\frac{p(x)}{s^*(x)}w(j)$. OPT processes x at the rate $s^*(x)$; the most energy efficient way is to use $\sigma(x)$ processors each running at speed $\frac{s^*(x)}{\sigma(x)}$. The rate of energy usage is $\sigma(x) \cdot P(s^*(x)/\sigma(x))$. Considering the cost in OPT, we have

$$W^* + E^* \ge \sum_{j \in S^*} \sum_{x \in \Delta(j)} \left(\frac{p(x)}{s^*(x)}w(j) + \frac{p(x)}{s^*(x)} \cdot \sigma(x) \cdot P(\frac{s^*(x)}{\sigma(x)}) \right)$$

It remains to show $\frac{w(j)}{s^*(x)} + \frac{\sigma(x)}{s^*(x)} \cdot P(\frac{s^*(x)}{\sigma(x)}) \ge \frac{w(j)/\sigma(x)}{Q(w(j)/\sigma(x))}$. To this end, we consider two cases. If $s^*(x) \le \sigma(x)Q(w(j)/\sigma(x))$, then $\frac{w(j)}{s^*(x)} \ge \frac{w(j)/\sigma(x)}{Q(w(j)/\sigma(x))}$; otherwise, we note that $\frac{P(y)}{y}$ is increasing with y.

$$\frac{\sigma(x)}{s^*(x)} \cdot P(\frac{s^*(x)}{\sigma(x)}) = \frac{P(s^*(x)/\sigma(x))}{s^*(x)/\sigma(x)} \ge \frac{P(Q(w(j)/\sigma(x)))}{Q(w(j)/\sigma(x))}$$
$$= \frac{w(j)/\sigma(x)}{Q(w(j)/\sigma(x))}$$

The last equality follows from the fact that $\sigma(x)T \ge s^*(x) > \sigma(x)Q(w(j)/\sigma(x))$. Therefore, $T > Q(w(j)/\sigma(x))$ and we have $P(Q(w(j)/\sigma(x))) = w(j)/\sigma(x)$. □

4.5 Conclusion — Proof of Theorem 7

We are ready to prove Theorem 7.

PROOF. (Proof of Theorem 7) By Lemmas 12 and 13, we have $\int_0^\infty (\beta w_a(t) - \phi(t))dt \le W_o + W^* + E^* + C^*$. Together with Lemma 11 and that $\beta < \frac{1}{2}$, the weighted flow of MultiRAW is at most $\frac{1}{\beta^2}((1+\beta)W_o + W^* + E^* + C^*) \le \frac{1}{\beta^2}(1.5W_o + W^* + E^* + C^*)$, which by Lemma 9, is at most $\frac{2.5}{\beta^2}$ times the cost of OPT. The total energy usage of MultiRAW is at most $\log m$ times its weighted flow time. The rejection penalty of MultiRAW is at most its weighted flow time. Hence, MultiRAW is at most $(\frac{2.5}{\beta^2}(\log m + 2))$-competitive against OPT. Finally, putting $\beta = \frac{\epsilon}{2(1+\epsilon)}$, we conclude that MultiRAW is $10(1 + \frac{1}{\epsilon})^2(\log m + 2)$-competitive.

So far, we have assumed that m is a power of two. If m is not a power of two, let $m_1 = \lceil m/2 \rceil$ and $m_i = \left\lceil (m - \sum_{j=1}^{i-1} m_j)/2 \right\rceil$, where m_i is the number of processors in the i-th group. We can show that $m_i \le 3m_{i+1}$. Repeating the argument of Lemma 10, we can show that each saturated job j has a processing rate at least $\frac{2}{3}(1+\epsilon) \cdot \sigma(j,t) \cdot Q(\frac{w'(j,t)}{\sigma(j,t)})$. The only consequence is that the right-hand-side of Lemma 13 is weakened to $1.5(W^* + E^*)$. The competitive ratio of MultiRAW is increased by a factor of $\frac{3}{2.5}$ and becomes $12(1 + \frac{1}{\epsilon})^2(\log m + 2)$. □

Remarks on fixed speed setting. If all the processors have speed one and energy is not a concern, we can largely simplify the algorithm by running a single group with all the m processors. We assume that the online algorithm is given $(1 + \epsilon)$-speed processors and we share the processors to the active jobs proportional to the adjusted weight $w'(j,t)$. Then, similar to Lemma 10, we can show that each unsaturated job is processed at a rate at least $\frac{w'(j,t)}{\beta w_a(t)}m(1+\epsilon)$ and each saturated job is processed at a rate at least $(1+\epsilon)\sigma(j,t)$. We can check that Lemmas 11, 12 and 13 remain true, where $E^* = 0$. Hence, the total weighted flow is at most $\frac{2.5}{\beta^2}$ times the cost of OPT. The rejection penalty of the online algorithm is at most its total weighted flow time. Note that $\beta = \frac{\epsilon}{2(1+\epsilon)}$. Hence, we have the following theorem.

THEOREM 14. For the fixed speed setting, there is a $(1 + \epsilon)$-speed $20(1 + \frac{1}{\epsilon})^2$-competitive algorithm.

Note that for each job j, we only process one copy of j. Hence, the results hold even if the jobs are non-checkpointable.

5. REFERENCES

[1] S. Albers. Energy-efficient algorithms. Communications of the ACM, 53(5):86–96, 2010.

[2] N. Bansal, A. Blum, S. Chawla, and K. Dhamdhere. Scheduling for flow-time with admission control. In Proc. ESA, pages 43–54, 2003.

[3] N. Bansal, H. L. Chan, and K. Pruhs. Speed scaling with an arbitrary power function. In Proc. SODA, pages 693–701, 2009.

[4] N. Bansal and K. Dhamdhere. Minimizing weighted flow time. ACM Transactions on Algorithms, 3(4):39, 2007.

[5] H. L. Chan, J. Edmonds, T. W. Lam, L. K. Lee, A. Marchetti-Spaccamela, and K. Pruhs. Nonclairvoyant speed scaling for flow and energy. Algorithmica, 61(3):507–517, 2011.

[6] H. L. Chan, J. Edmonds, and K. Pruhs. Speed scaling of processes with arbitrary speedup curves on a multiprocessor. In Proc. SPAA, pages 1–10, 2009.

[7] S. H. Chan, T. W. Lam, and L. K. Lee. Non-clairvoyant speed scaling for weighted flow time. In *Proc. ESA*, pages 23–35, 2010.

[8] S. H. Chan, T. W. Lam, and L. K. Lee. Scheduling for weighted flow time and energy with rejection penalty. In *Proc. STACS*, pages 392–403, 2011.

[9] J. Edmonds. Scheduling in the dark. *Theor. Comput. Sci.*, 235(1):109–141, 2000.

[10] J. Edmonds and K. Pruhs. Scalably scheduling processes with arbitrary speedup curves. In *Proc. SODA*, pages 685–692, 2009.

[11] B. Kalyanasundaram and K. Pruhs. Speed is as powerful as clairvoyance. *Journal of the ACM*, 47(4):617–643, 2000.

[12] R. Motwani, S. Phillips, and E. Torng. Nonclairvoyant scheduling. *Theor. Comput. Sci.*, 130(1):17–47, 1994.

[13] F. Yao, A. Demers, and S. Shenker. A scheduling model for reduced CPU energy. In *Proc. FOCS*, pages 374–382, 1995.

[14] J. Zhu, H. L. Chan and T. W. Lam. Non-clairvoyant weighted flow time scheduling on different multi-processor models. To appear in *Proc. WAOA*, 2011.

Appendix A: Lemma 5 for Multi-processor Setting

In this appendix, we consider $m > 1$ processors and prove Lemma 5 for the multi-processor setting. Recall that $j_1, j_2, \ldots, j_{n_a(t)}$ are the active jobs in MultiRAW at time t arranged in increasing order of arrival times, and $h(j_i) = \sum_{k=1}^{i} w(j_i)$. As mentioned in Section 4, $\Phi(t) = \gamma \sum_{i=1}^{n_a(t)} f(\frac{h(j_i)}{m}) \cdot x(j_i, t)$, where $\gamma = \frac{1}{\beta(1+\epsilon)}$ and $f(h) = h/Q(h)$.

Lemma 5. *At any time t without discrete events, $\frac{d\Phi}{dt} \leq \frac{1-2\beta}{\beta} \cdot \max\{w_a(t), w_o(t)\} - \frac{1}{\beta^2}(1-\beta)\phi(t)$.*

PROOF. We consider $\frac{d\Phi}{dt}$ as a combined effect due to the action of MultiRAW and OFF. Let $\frac{d\Phi_a}{dt}$ and $\frac{d\Phi_o}{dt}$ be the rate of change of Φ due to MultiRAW and OFF, respectively. Then $\frac{d\Phi}{dt} = \frac{d\Phi_a}{dt} + \frac{d\Phi_o}{dt}$. Note that OFF is an offline algorithm on a single processor with maximum speed $m \cdot T$, which at any time t, follows the speed $m \cdot Q(\frac{w_o(t)}{m})$, where $w_o(t)$ is the total weight of active jobs in LLB'.

Consider the schedule of MultiRAW. For each active job j in MultiRAW, if $j \in L(t) \subseteq R(t)$, j is an unsaturated job, $x(j,t) > 0$ and $h(j) \geq (1-\beta)w_a(t)$. By Lemma 10, MultiRAW processes j at a rate $(1+\epsilon)\frac{w'(j,t)}{\beta w_a(t)} \cdot m \cdot Q(\frac{w_a(t)}{m})$. Hence, for each term $\gamma \cdot f(\frac{h(j)}{m}) \cdot x(j,t)$ where $j \in L(t)$, the term is decreasing at a rate at least

$$
\begin{aligned}
&\gamma \cdot \frac{h(j)/m}{Q(h(j)/m)} \cdot (1+\epsilon)\frac{w'(j,t)}{\beta w_a(t)} \cdot m \cdot Q(\frac{w_a(t)}{m}) \\
\geq\; &\gamma \cdot \frac{(1-\beta)w_a(t)/m}{Q((1-\beta)w_a(t)/m)} \cdot (1+\epsilon)\frac{w'(j,t)}{\beta w_a(t)} \cdot m \cdot Q(\frac{w_a(t)}{m}) \\
\geq\; &\gamma \frac{1-\beta}{\beta}(1+\epsilon)w'(j,t) = \frac{1-\beta}{\beta^2}w'(j,t)
\end{aligned}
$$

where the first inequality comes from that $f(h) = h/Q(h)$ is increasing with h, and the second inequality comes from that Q is increasing. For each job $j \notin L(t)$, the term $\gamma \cdot f(\frac{h(j)}{m}) \cdot x(j,t)$ is non-increasing. Hence, $\frac{d\Phi_a}{dt} \leq -\frac{1-\beta}{\beta^2} \sum_{j \in L(t)} w'(j,t) = -\frac{1-\beta}{\beta^2}\phi(t)$.

The processing rate of an unsaturated job j in OFF is at most its speed on the single processor, which is $s_o = m \cdot Q(\frac{w_o(t)}{m})$. Thus, the worst case (in which $\frac{d\Phi_o}{dt}$ is the largest) occurs when OFF processes the job with maximum $h(j)$, which equals $w_a(t)$, using all

its speed s_o. Then $\frac{d\Phi_o}{dt} \leq \gamma \cdot f(\frac{w_a(t)}{m}) \cdot s_o = \gamma \frac{w_a(t)/m}{Q(w_a(t)/m)} \cdot m \cdot Q(w_o(t)/m)$. If $w_a(t) \geq w_o(t)$, $Q(w_a(t)/m) \geq Q(w_o(t)/m)$ and $\frac{d\Phi_o}{dt} \leq \gamma w_a(t)$. Otherwise, $w_a(t) < w_o(t)$, since f is non-decreasing, $f(\frac{w_a(t)}{m}) \leq f(\frac{w_o(t)}{m})$. Hence, $\frac{d\Phi_o}{dt} \leq \gamma f(\frac{w_o(t)}{m})s_o = \gamma w_o(t)$. Combining these two cases, we obtain that $\frac{d\Phi_o}{dt} \leq \gamma \cdot \max\{w_a(t), w_o(t)\}$. Finally, notice that $\beta = \frac{\epsilon}{2(1+\epsilon)}$ and $\frac{1}{1+\epsilon} = 1-2\beta$. Hence, $\gamma \max\{w_a(t), w_o(t)\} = \frac{1}{\beta(1+\epsilon)}\max\{w_a(t), w_o(t)\} = \frac{1-2\beta}{\beta}\max\{w_a(t), w_o(t)\}$ and the lemma follows. $\square$

Appendix B: Offline Schedule Transformation

This appendix shows the following lemma on the performance of LLB' that transforms OPT (which minimizes weighted flow plus energy on m processors) to an offline algorithm LLB' on a single processor with maximum speed $m \cdot T$, which at any time t, follows the speed $m \cdot Q(\frac{w_b(t)}{m})$, where $w_b(t)$ is the total weight of active jobs in LLB'.

LEMMA 15. *The weighted flow of LLB' is at most the weighted flow plus energy of OPT.*

Before proving Lemma 15, we first restate the algorithm LLB' given in Section 4.

Algorithm LLB'. Consider any time t. Let $n_b(t)$ be the number of active jobs in LLB'. For any job j, let $p_b(j, t)$ and $p_o(j, t)$ be the work done on j up to time t by LLB' and OPT, respectively. Furthermore, let $d(j, t) = p_o(j, t) - p_b(j, t)$. We say a job j is *lagging* at time t if $d(j, t) > 0$. Let $y(j)$ be the latest time when j has become lagging; if j is non-lagging, let $y(j) = t$. We denote the active jobs in LLB' at time t as $j_1, j_2, \ldots, j_{n_b(t)}$, arranged in increasing order of $y(j_i)$, i.e., $y(j_1) \leq y(j_2) \leq \cdots \leq y(j_{n_b(t)})$. Let ℓ be the number of lagging jobs ($0 \leq \ell \leq n_b(t)$). Let s_o be the total speed of the m processors in OPT at time t. Let $s_x \leq s_o$ be the total speed OPT assigns to all jobs j with $d(j, t) = 0$. LLB' sets its speed $s_b = m \cdot Q(\frac{w_b(t)}{m})$, and focuses on the job j_a defined to be j_ℓ if $\ell > 0$, and $j_{n_b(t)}$ otherwise. Details are as follows:

1. If OPT is not running any job j_i with $d(j_i, t) = 0$, then LLB' runs j_a with speed s_b.
2. If OPT is processing some jobs j_i with $d(j_i, t) = 0$, but $s_x \leq s_b$ (i.e., LLB' has enough speed to prevent all of them from becoming lagging), then LLB' follows OPT's speed on each of those jobs and runs j_a with the remaining speed $s_b - s_x$.
3. Otherwise ($s_b < s_x$), LLB' follows OPT's speed for each of those jobs j_i, in descending order of the index i, until there is some job j which LLB' cannot follow OPT's total speed on j. LLB' then assigns all of its remaining speed to j.

Note that any job phase has a speed-up function Γ satisfying $\Gamma(y) = y$ for $y \in (0, 1]$. Therefore, LLB' using a single processor with maximum speed $m \cdot T$ can guarantee all its speed to be fully utilized to process the jobs and no speed would be wasted.

To prove Lemma 15, we exploit potential functions. Let F_b be the total weighted flow of LLB', and let F_o and E_o be the total weighted flow and energy of OPT, respectively. For any time t, let $F_b(t)$ be the total weighted flow incurred up to time t by LLB'. Define $F_o(t)$ and $E_o(t)$ similarly. We derive a potential function $\Phi(t)$ that satisfies the following three conditions:

- *Boundary condition*: $\Phi = 0$ before the first job arrives and after all jobs are finished.
- *Discrete event condition*: Φ does not increase when a job arrives, or is completed by LLB' or OPT, or when a lagging job is changed to non-lagging or vice versa.

- *Running condition*: At any other time t, $\frac{dF_b(t)}{dt} + \frac{d\Phi(t)}{dt} \leq \frac{dF_o(t)}{dt} + \frac{dE_o(t)}{dt}$.

Integrating these conditions over time, we can conclude that $F_b \leq F_o + E_o$; Lemma 15 follows.

Potential function $\Phi(t)$. Consider any time t. Recall that the active jobs in LLB$'$ are denoted as $j_1 \ldots j_{n_b(t)}$. Define the coefficient c_i of j_i to be $\sum_{k=1}^{i} w(j_k)$. The potential function $\Phi(t)$ is defined as follows.

$$\Phi(t) = \sum_{i=1}^{n_b(t)} f(c_i) \cdot \max(d(j_i, t), 0)$$

where $f(x) = P'(P^{-1}(\frac{x}{m}))$. Note that P' is the first derivative of P. Since P is convex, P' is non-decreasing, which together with that $P^{-1}(x)$ is non-decreasing, implies that $P'(P^{-1}(x))$ is also non-decreasing. Therefore, $f(x) = P'(P^{-1}(\frac{x}{m}))$ is a non-decreasing function of x.

The boundary condition is obvious. Now we check the discrete event condition. Recall that ℓ is the number of lagging jobs. When a job j arrives at time t, we have $d(j,t) = 0$, $y(j) = t$ and the coefficients of all lagging jobs of LLB$'$ remain the same, so Φ does not change. When OPT completes a job or LLB$'$ completes a non-lagging job, Φ does not change. When LLB$'$ completes a lagging job or a lagging job changes to non-lagging at time t, that job must be j_ℓ and $d(j_\ell, t) \leq 0$. The coefficients of other lagging jobs stay the same, so Φ does not change. When one or more job(s) changes from non-lagging to lagging, those jobs must have the largest index among all lagging jobs and their $d(j,t)$'s are all 0. The coefficients of other lagging jobs stay the same, so Φ does not change.

It remains to check the running condition. Consider any time t without discrete events. Recall that s_b is the current speed of LLB$'$, and s_o is the current total processor speed of OPT. Let $w_o(t)$ be the total weight of active jobs in OPT. Then, $\frac{dF_b}{dt} = w_b(t)$ and $\frac{dF_o}{dt} = w_o(t)$. Since P is convex, the energy usage of the m processors in OPT is $\frac{dE_o}{dt} \geq m \cdot P(\frac{s_o}{m})$. If all active jobs in LLB$'$ are non-lagging, i.e., $d(j_i, t) \leq 0$ for all $1 \leq i \leq n_b(t)$, then these jobs are also active in OPT and hence $w_o(t) \geq w_b(t)$. In this case, Φ remains zero and thus $\frac{d\Phi(t)}{dt} = 0$. Then the running condition follows easily since $\frac{dF_b(t)}{dt} = w_b(t) \leq w_o(t) \leq \frac{dF_o(t)}{dt} + \frac{dE_o(t)}{dt}$. Henceforth, we assume at least one active job in LLB$'$ is lagging, i.e., $\ell > 0$.

We define a real number $\beta \leq 1$ such that $\beta w_b(t) = c_\ell$, which is the total weight of lagging jobs. Then the rate of change of Φ can be bounded easily (Lemma 16). More interestingly, we can also show that at any time t, $Q(\beta w_b(t)) \leq m \cdot T$ (Lemma 17).

LEMMA 16. $\frac{d\Phi(t)}{dt} \leq f(\beta w_b(t)) \cdot (-s_b + s_o)$.

PROOF. We consider how Φ changes in an infinitesimal amount of time (from time t to $t + dt$) where no job arrives, or completes, or changes from lagging to non-lagging or vice versa. Recall that s_x is OPT's total speed on jobs j_i with $d(j_i, t) = 0$. Then, OPT's total speed on jobs $j_{i'}$ with $d(j_{i'}, t) \neq 0$ is $s_o - s_x$.

In the definition of LLB$'$, if Case 3 happens at t, some jobs including job j become lagging, which corresponds to a discrete event condition. Right after t, j become the new j_a and LLB$'$ will follow Case 1 or Case 2. Thus, it suffices to consider Cases 1 and 2 for the running condition.

Consider each job j_i with $d(j_i, t) = 0$. By Cases 1 and 2 in the definition of LLB$'$, either both LLB$'$ and OPT are not working on j_i, or they are running j_i with the same speed (totaling to s_x for all such j_i's). Therefore, $d(j_i, t)$ remains 0 and the processing of j_i does not affect the value of Φ.

Now consider other jobs j_i with $d(j_i, t) \neq 0$. Recall that LLB$'$ is running j_ℓ with the remaining speed $s_b - s_x$. Since LLB$'$ is using

a single processor with maximum speed $m \cdot T$, j_ℓ is also processed by LLB$'$ at a rate of $s_b - s_x$. Consider the processing of OPT. The worst case that causes the largest increase in $\frac{d\Phi}{dt}$ is that OPT is also using all its remaining speed $s_o - s_x$ to run j_ℓ. It is because any job j_k with $k > \ell$ is non-lagging and OPT cannot increase Φ by processing j_k. Also, OPT cannot increase Φ by processing a job that is not active in LLB$'$. In this case, $d(j_\ell, t)$ changes at a rate of at most $-(s_b - s_x) + (s_o - s_x) = (-s_b + s_o)$. Therefore, Φ changes at rate at most $f(c_\ell) \cdot (-s_b + s_o) = f(\beta w_b(t)) \cdot (-s_b + s_o)$. $\square$

LEMMA 17. *At any time t, we have $P^{-1}(\frac{\beta w_b(t)}{m}) \leq T$.*

PROOF. We will prove $\frac{\beta w_b(t)}{m} \leq P(T)$; then the lemma follows by taking P^{-1} on both sides of the inequality. Consider the current time t. If $\frac{w_b(t)}{m} \leq P(T)$, then $\frac{\beta w_b(t)}{m} \leq \frac{w_b(t)}{m} \leq P(T)$. If $\frac{w_b(t)}{m} > P(T)$, let t_0 be the last time before t where $\frac{w_b(t)}{m} \leq P(T)$. Then the total weight of lagging jobs at t_0 is at most $m \cdot P(T)$. At any time after t_0, LLB$'$'s speed is $m \cdot T$. Since the total speed of OPT is also at most $m \cdot T$, by the definition of LLB$'$, for each job arrived after t_0, LLB$'$'s progress is at least OPT's progress. Hence, those new jobs cannot be lagging. Furthermore, Case 3 in the definition of LLB$'$ does not occur, and thus the total weight of lagging jobs cannot increase after t_0 and remains at most $m \cdot P(T)$ at time t. In other words, $\beta w_b(t) \leq m \cdot P(T)$, i.e., $\frac{\beta w_b(t)}{m} \leq P(T)$. $\square$

We are now ready to prove the running condition, which together with the boundary and discrete event conditions, implies Lemma 15.

LEMMA 18. *At any time t without discrete events, $\frac{dF_b(t)}{dt} + \frac{d\Phi(t)}{dt} \leq \frac{dF_o(t)}{dt} + \frac{dE_o(t)}{dt}$.*

PROOF. Recall that j_ℓ is the lagging job with the largest index, and $j_{\ell+1}, \ldots, j_{n_a}$ are non-lagging and must also be active jobs in OPT. The total weight of these jobs is $w_b(t) - \beta w_b(t) = (1 - \beta)w_b(t)$, so $w_o(t) \geq (1-\beta)w_b(t)$. Also recall that $\frac{dF_b(t)}{dt} = w_b(t)$ and $\frac{dF_o(t)}{dt} + \frac{dE_o(t)}{dt} \geq w_o(t) + m \cdot P(\frac{s_o}{m}) \geq (1 - \beta)w_b(t) + m \cdot P(\frac{s_o}{m})$. We note a fact (given in [3]) that for any real $x \geq 0$, $P'(P^{-1}(x)) \cdot s_o \leq P^{-1}(x) \cdot P'(P^{-1}(x)) + P(s_o) - x$. Lemma 16, together with this fact, gives

$\frac{dF_b(t)}{dt} + \frac{d\Phi(t)}{dt}$

$\leq w_b(t) + P'(P^{-1}(\frac{\beta w_b(t)}{m})) \cdot (-s_b + s_o)$

$\leq w_b(t) + (-s_b)P'(P^{-1}(\frac{\beta w_b(t)}{m})) + m \cdot P'(P^{-1}(\frac{\beta w_b(t)}{m}))(\frac{s_o}{m})$

$\leq w_b(t) + (-s_b)P'(P^{-1}(\frac{\beta w_b(t)}{m})) +$
$\quad m \cdot (P^{-1}(\frac{\beta w_b(t)}{m}) \cdot P'(P^{-1}(\frac{\beta w_b(t)}{m})) + P(\frac{s_o}{m}) - \frac{\beta w_b(t)}{m})$

$\leq w_b(t) - \beta w_b(t) + m \cdot P(\frac{s_o}{m}) +$
$\quad P'(P^{-1}(\frac{\beta w_b(t)}{m})) \cdot (-s_b + m \cdot P^{-1}(\frac{\beta w_b(t)}{m}))$.

Since $s_b = m \cdot Q(\frac{w_b(t)}{m})$, where $Q(y) = \min(P^{-1}(y), T)$, we have $s_b = m \cdot \min(P^{-1}(\frac{w_b(t)}{m}), T)$. By Lemma 17, $s_b \geq m \cdot \min(P^{-1}(\frac{w_b(t)}{m}), P^{-1}(\frac{\beta w_b(t)}{m})) = m \cdot P^{-1}(\frac{\beta w_b(t)}{m})$. Thus, the last term of the above inequality is at most 0, and hence $\frac{dF_b(t)}{dt} + \frac{d\Phi(t)}{dt} \leq (1 - \beta)w_b(t) + m \cdot P(\frac{s_o}{m}) \leq \frac{dF_o(t)}{dt} + \frac{dE_o(t)}{dt}$. $\square$

Near-Optimal Scheduling Mechanisms for Deadline-Sensitive Jobs in Large Computing Clusters

[Extended Abstract]

Navendu Jain
Microsoft Research
Redmond, WA
navendu@microsoft.com

Ishai Menache
Microsoft Research
Redmond, WA
ishai@microsoft.com

Joseph (Seffi) Naor [*]
CS Department, Technion
Haifa, Israel
naor@cs.technion.ac.il

Jonathan Yaniv
CS Department, Technion
Haifa, Israel
jyaniv@cs.technion.ac.il

ABSTRACT

We consider a market-based resource allocation model for batch jobs in cloud computing clusters. In our model, we incorporate the importance of the due date of a job rather than the number of servers allocated to it at any given time. Each batch job is characterized by the work volume of total computing units (e.g., CPU hours) along with a bound on maximum degree of parallelism. Users specify, along with these job characteristics, their desired due date and a value for finishing the job by its deadline. Given this specification, the primary goal is to determine the *scheduling* of cloud computing instances under capacity constraints in order to maximize the social welfare (i.e., sum of values gained by allocated users). Our main result is a new $\left(\frac{C}{C-k} \cdot \frac{s}{s-1}\right)$-approximation algorithm for this objective, where C denotes cloud capacity, k is the maximal bound on parallelized execution (in practical settings, $k \ll C$) and s is the slackness on the job completion time i.e., the minimal ratio between a specified deadline and the earliest finish time of a job. Our algorithm is based on utilizing dual fitting arguments over a strengthened linear program to the problem.

Based on the new approximation algorithm, we construct truthful allocation and pricing mechanisms, in which reporting the job true value and properties (deadline, work volume and the parallelism bound) is a dominant strategy for all users. To that end, we provide a general framework for transforming allocation algorithms into truthful mechanisms in domains of single-value and multi-properties. We then show that the basic mechanism can be extended under proper Bayesian assumptions to the objective of maximizing revenues, which is important for public clouds. We empirically evaluate the benefits of our approach through simulations on data-center job traces, and show that the revenues obtained under our mechanism are comparable with an *ideal* fixed-price mechanism,

[*]Work supported in part by the Technion-Micorsoft Electronic Commerce Research Center, and by ISF grant 954/11.

Permission to make digital or hard copies of all or part of this work for personal or classroom use is granted without fee provided that copies are not made or distributed for profit or commercial advantage and that copies bear this notice and the full citation on the first page. To copy otherwise, to republish, to post on servers or to redistribute to lists, requires prior specific permission and/or a fee.
SPAA'12, June 25–27, 2012, Pittsburgh, Pennsylvania, USA.
Copyright 2012 ACM 978-1-4503-1213-4/12/06 ...$10.00.

which sets an on-demand price using oracle knowledge of users' valuations. Finally, we discuss how our model can be extended to accommodate uncertainties in job work volumes, which is a practical challenge in cloud settings.

Categories and Subject Descriptors

F.2.2 [**Analysis of Algorithms and Problem Complexity**]: Nonnumerical Algorithms and Problems—*sequencing and scheduling*; K.6.2 [**Management of Computing and Information Systems**]: Installation Management—*pricing and resource allocation*

General Terms

Algorithms

Keywords

Resource Allocation, Scheduling Algorithms, Economic Models, Truthful Mechanisms, Cloud Computing

1. INTRODUCTION

1.1 Background and motivation

Batch processing applications have become a significant fraction of computing workload across both public and private clouds. Examples include MapReduce/DryadLINQ jobs, web search index update, monte carlo simulations, eScience applications and data analytics. The primary challenge for many of these applications is to meet the service level agreements (SLA) on their job completion deadline. For instance, financial firms run large batch jobs to analyze daily stock trades and need the results to develop trading strategies before market opens the next day. Similarly, job completion time is critical for web search because even a small fraction of stale results can lead to a significant loss in revenue through a reduction in purchases, search queries, or advertisement click-through rates. The second challenge is concurrently *scheduling* multiple jobs with each job requiring a large number of CPU units, under the cloud capacity constraints.

Currently, cloud providers offer three pricing schemes to users: (i) *on-demand* instances, where a user pays a fixed price for a virtual machine (VM) per unit time (e.g., an hour) and can acquire or release VMs on demand, (ii) *spot-instances*, where users bid for spot instances and get allocation when the spot market price falls below their bid, and (iii) *reservation* pricing where users pay a flat fee for long term reservation (e.g., 1-3 years) of instances and a discounted price during actual use. Despite their simplicity, these approaches have several shortcomings for batch computing. First, they offer only *best-effort* execution without any guarantees on the job completion time. However, the financial firm in the above example requires SLA on the finish time rather than how VMs are allocated over time. Further, given capacity constraints, the cloud may not even be able to meet large resource requirements under unpredictable demand. Second, current resource allocation mechanisms do not differentiate jobs based on their importance/priority e.g., financial applications have (and are willing to pay for) strict job deadlines while scientific jobs are likely willing to trade a bounded delay for lower costs. As a result, cloud systems lose the opportunity to increase profits (e.g., by prioritizing jobs with strict SLA), improve utilization (e.g., by running low priority jobs at night), or both. Finally, existing schemes do not have in-built *incentives* to prevent fluctuations between high and low resource utilization. Perhaps the most desired goal of cloud operators is to keep all their resources constantly utilized.

In this paper we consider an alternative approach to resource allocation in cloud computing clusters based on an offline scheduling problem of multiple batch jobs called the *bounded flexible scheduling* problem. In this model, we explicitly incorporate the importance of the completion time of a batch job to its owner, rather than the number of instances allocated to the job at any given time. Each batch job is characterized by the work volume (or distribution thereof) of total computing units (e.g., CPU hours) along with a bound on the maximum degree of parallelism. Users report, along with these characteristics, the job deadline and a value for finishing the job by its deadline. The goal is to decide a scheduling of cloud resources under capacity constraints to optimize a *value-integrated* objective function, such as the social welfare (i.e., sum of values gained by users with resource allocations, especially relevant for private clouds). We also focus on the design of economic mechanisms, in which a public cloud charges users based on the job parameters mentioned above. While current pricing schemes do not charge based on deadlines, this work aims to advocate the merits of incorporating deadline-based pricing schemes. This scheduling model raises fundamental questions in mechanism design, as users may try to game the system by misreporting their values or other job parameters to increase their utility. To address these challenges, our proposed solutions incentivize users to report truthfully.

1.2 Related work

The bounded flexible scheduling problem was first considered in our prior work [13], which proposed the first algorithm for the social welfare objective with a $\left(1+\frac{C}{C-k}\right)\left(1+\varepsilon\right)$-approximation factor. The algorithm, designed for general user valuation functions, served as the basis for designing a truthful-in-expectation mechanism where reporting valuations truthfully maximized the expected utility for each user. However, it had three key *practical* shortcomings. First, from the mechanism design perspective, job work volume and parallelism bounds are assumed to be truthfully reported and hence it was only necessary to guarantee truthfulness with respect to values and deadlines. Second, to guarantee truthfulness, the proposed mechanism risks low utilization with at least half of the resources unutilized. Further, the solution cannot be extended to deal with uncertainties in work volume (we use the terms work volume and job demand interchangeably). Finally, the solution requires solving a linear program which might be computationally expensive to run frequently for a large number of jobs, as common in the cloud.

Scheduling Problems. Scheduling problems have been extensively studied in operations research and computer science (see [7] for an extensive study). Of specific relevance to our work is [15], which considers the problem of preemptively allocating jobs on a single server to maximize the social welfare. Lawler gives an optimal solution in pseudo-polynomial time via dynamic programming to this problem. However, his algorithm cannot be extended to the case where jobs have parallelization limits. Our model significantly extends the basic job interval scheduling problem studied by [4, 5]. The best known approximation factor for this problem is 2. A more general version, in which every interval is given with a width, has also been studied by [19, 4].

Mechanism Design. Mechanism design is a subfield of economic theory which has received much recent attention from computer scientists, commencing with the seminal paper of Nisan and Ronen [17] (see also [18] for a survey book). In its algorithmic aspect, the goal is to design computationally efficient choice mechanisms, such as resource allocation, while optimizing an objective function (e.g., social welfare, revenue). The difficulty of algorithmic mechanism design is that unlike classic algorithmic design, participants act *rationally* in a game theoretic sense and may deviate in order to maximize their personal utilities. Since participants' preferences are usually kept private from the mechanism, we search for efficient mechanisms that implement certain strategic properties to *incentivize* users to truthfully report their preferences, while attempting to optimize an objective function.

Truthful mechanisms in single-value domains have been completely characterized by [2]. An allocation rule can implement a truthful mechanism if and only if it is monotone. For allocation rules implementing truthful mechanisms, there is a unique pricing rule implementing it in which unallocated users are charged 0. Myerson, in his celebrated paper [16], first shown this result for single item auctions under Bayesian settings. Compared to single-parameter domains, much less is known about the characterization of implementable allocation rules for multi-parameter problems. Rochet [20] gave an equivalent property to monotonicity called *cyclic monotonicity*, which is a necessary and sufficient condition for truthfulness. Yet, it is unclear how to use this property to easily construct truthful mechanisms from it and only few successful efforts are known (for example, [14]). Saks and Yu [21] showed that for deterministic settings, cyclic monotonicity is equivalent to a simpler property called *weak monotonicity*, which conditions only on cycles of length 2 (see also [3]). However, this result is not valid for randomized mechanisms [6].

Our work is much related to research on algorithmic mechanism design for scheduling problems. We note that most papers in the area mainly focus on minimizing the makespan (see, e.g., [14, 2]). Of specific relevance to our work is a recent paper by Feige and Tennenholtz [10] that provides an impossibility result for designing constant-factor approximation mechanisms when users' demands are uncertain. Our paper confronts demand uncertainties by restricting the deadlines that users may request as a function of certain job characteristics.

1.3 Our contributions

This paper makes the following contributions.

Modeling. We propose a flexible resource allocation framework for scheduling batch jobs with deadlines. In particular, the model comprises an urgency parameter s which given a job work volume and parallelism bound determines the earliest deadline that the job owner can request. This parameter enables cloud the flexibility in scheduling jobs thereby yielding higher profits and improved performance over existing approaches.

Near-optimal and computationally-efficient scheduling. We design a new $\left(\frac{C}{C-k} \cdot \frac{s}{s-1}\right)$-approximation algorithm for the optimal social welfare, where k is the maximal parallelism bounds over all jobs, and C is the cloud capacity. Note that the approximation factor approaches one under the (plausible) assumption that $k \ll C$, and s is sufficiently large. The approximation algorithm is semi-greedy - it considers the jobs one by one, and to accommodate a new job it is allowed to make certain changes to the allocation of previously allocated jobs. To analyze the algorithm, we formulate the problem as a linear program with strengthened constraints which are somewhat reminiscent of knapsack constraints [9]. We then apply the technique of *dual fitting* to prove the approximation factor. The algorithm is specifically designed to maintain unique properties, which are realized under clever dual fitting arguments. Thus, each allocation step (of a job) goes hand in hand with the construction of a feasible dual solution, such that its cost is later bounded by sophisticated charging techniques.

Full incentive compatibility. The proposed scheduling algorithm is incentive compatible with respect to *all* job parameters (value, deadline, work volume and parallelism bound). This property allows achieving the same approximation bound for both the social welfare mechanism design and the revenue maximization problem (the latter, under standard Bayesian assumptions).

Empirical study. We perform experiments with job traces taken from a large cloud provider. Our simulation study provides a surprising result: The mechanism we propose generates higher revenue than an ideal fixed-price mechanism, which has full knowledge of the private values and deadlines of users.

Dealing with demand uncertainties. We propose a new model to handle cases where job volumes are stochastic, adapt the scheduling algorithm and provide performance bounds.

2. THE MODEL

We consider a single cloud provider (or simply, the cloud), which allocates resources (CPUs) to jobs over time. Specifically, the time horizon is divided into T time slots $\mathcal{T} = \{1, 2, \ldots, T\}$. For example, in a cloud computing setting, each slot t represents an actual time interval of one hour. The cloud has a fixed capacity of C, given in CPU time units. This paper focuses on an offline setting, where all jobs that wish to be served until time T arrive to the system at time 0 and can be executed immediately.

There are n users (clients), each of them owning a single job that needs to be executed. We use the terms jobs, users and clients interchangeably. Every job is associated with a type profile $\tau_j = (v_j, d_j, D_j, k_j)$ representing the job parameters, fully described hereupon. Every user has a value $v_j \in \mathbb{R}^+$ representing the worth of a successful execution of its job, i.e., its job being fully executed before the *deadline* d_j. The size of each job j, also referred to as the *demand* of the job, is given by $D_j \in \mathbb{R}^+$ (in CPU time units). The cloud provider can *flexibly* allocate resources to jobs, that is, the amount of resources allocated to a job can change over time. For instance, a job may even be preempted and continued later on. However, each job has an upper bound k_j on the number of resources it may receive in a time slot. This bound stays fixed throughout the whole time horizon $\mathcal{T}$. Formally, an *allocation* of a job j is a function $y_j : [1, d_j] \to [0, k_j]$ representing the number of CPU units job j receives per time slot, which completes the job without violating the job parallelism bound k_j. We assume that the maximal parallelism bound $k \triangleq \max_j \{k_j\}$ is much smaller than the capacity C. A solution to the problem is a set $y = (y_1, \ldots, y_n)$ of allocations satisfying capacity constraints. The objective of an allocation algorithm is to maximize the *social welfare*, which is the

sum of values of jobs completed before their deadline. We emphasize that partial execution of a job does not yield partial value.

Let $len_j = \lceil D_j/k_j \rceil$ denote the minimal length (or duration) of a complete allocation of resources to job j. We assume that the cloud will consider scheduling a job only if its deadline satisfies $d_j \geq s \cdot len_j$, where s is a *slackness* (or urgency) parameter advertised by the cloud. We refer to this condition as the *slackness condition*. Intuitively, the slackness condition gives the cloud the time margins to schedule jobs. In the extreme case where $s = 1$, the cloud may be required to allocate a job the maximal amount of resources until termination, leaving no scheduling flexibility.

3. SCHEDULING ALGORITHMS

In this section we construct a new approximation algorithm for the bounded flexible scheduling problem called GreedyRTL, which obtains a $\left(\frac{C}{C-k} \cdot \frac{s}{s-1}\right)$-approximation to the optimal social welfare. We start off by considering in Section 3.2 a simple greedy algorithm, as follows. Sort the jobs in non-increasing order of their marginal values (i.e., their value-demand ratio). Then, allocate them one-by-one (if possible), according to the sorted order, where a job is scheduled depending on the remaining resources. Henceforth, we assume that the jobs are numbered $1, 2, \ldots, n$ such that $v_1/D_1 \geq v_2/D_2 \geq \cdots \geq v_n/D_n$. To analyze the performance of this simple algorithm, we formulate the bounded flexible scheduling problem as a linear program (Section 3.1). The proofs of performance rely on a *dual fitting* argument. We construct a feasible solution to the dual linear program at cost proportional to the total value gained by the greedy algorithm. Since the cost of a feasible solution to the dual program is an upper bound to the optimal solution, we obtain the approximation factor.

To obtain the near-optimal approximation factor, we develop a single-job allocation rule (Section 3.3) called AllocateRTL(j). The AllocateRTL(j) rule, when applied, will allocate resources to job j, possibly reallocating previously scheduled jobs $i < j$. Our allocation rule will maintain a property we define called β-consistency. This property allows us to improve the feasible solution to the dual program, significantly reducing its cost.

3.1 Preliminaries

We begin by introducing the primal and dual linear programs. Let $y_j(t)$ denote the amount of CPU hours dedicated to the execution of job j in a time slot t, $t \leq d_j$. We consider a relaxed linear programming formulation (P) of the bounded flexible scheduling problem, suggested by [13]:

$$\max \quad \sum_{j=1}^{n} \frac{v_j}{D_j} \sum_{t \leq d_j} y_j(t)$$

$$\text{s.t.} \quad \sum_{t \leq d_j} y_j(t) \leq D_j \qquad \forall j \qquad (1)$$

$$\sum_{j:t \leq d_j} y_j(t) \leq C \qquad \forall t \qquad (2)$$

$$y_j(t) - \frac{k_j}{D_j} \sum_{t' \leq d_j} y_j(t') \leq 0 \qquad \forall j, t \leq d_j \qquad (3)$$

$$y_j(t) \geq 0 \qquad \forall j, t \leq d_j \qquad (4)$$

Note that in the relaxed linear program, a job can be *fractionally* allocated, under constraints (1)–(3). Constraints (1)–(2) are job demand and capacity constraints, whereas the set of constraints in (3) is a strengthened version of the natural parallelism bound constraints of the form $y_j(t) \leq k_j$. This set of strengthened constraints, formulated by [13], is related to *knapsack cover* constraints

[9] and is used to decrease the integrality gap of the relaxed linear program.

In the corresponding dual program (D) we have a cover constraint for each job j and time slot $t \leq d_j$:

$$\min \quad \sum_{j=1}^{n} D_j \alpha_j + \sum_{t=1}^{T} C\,\beta(t)$$

$$\text{s.t.} \quad \alpha_j + \beta(t) + \pi_j(t) - \frac{k_j}{D_j} \sum_{t' \leq d_j} \pi_j(t') \geq \frac{v_j}{D_j} \qquad \forall j, t \leq d_j \tag{5}$$

$$\alpha_j, \beta(t), \pi_j(t) \geq 0 \qquad\qquad\qquad \forall j, t \tag{6}$$

Before we describe our approximation algorithms, we give some definitions and notations that we will use later on. Given an allocation y_j, we denote by $s(y_j) = \min\{t : y_j(t) > 0\}$ and by $e(y_j) = \max\{t : y_j(t) > 0\}$ the *start time* and *completion time* of allocation y_j, which are the first an last time slots in which resources are allocated to user j, respectively. Given a solution consisting of allocations y_j, we define $W(t) = \sum_{j=1}^{n} y_j(t)$ to be the total *workload* at time t and $\bar{W}(t) = C - W(t)$ to be the amount of available resources at time t. A time slot is *saturated* if $\bar{W}(t) < k$ and *unsaturated* otherwise. Finally, given a time slot t, we define:

$$R(t) = \max\left\{ t' \geq t : \forall t'' \in (t, t'], \bar{W}(t) < k \right\}. \tag{7}$$

Intuitively, if there are saturated time slots adjacent to t to the right, $R(t)$ is the rightmost timeslot out of the saturated block to the right of t. Otherwise, $R(t) = t$.

3.2   A Simple Greedy Algorithm

The first algorithm we construct is called the SimpleGreedy algorithm, which serves as the basis for the GreedyRTL algorithm. Recall that the jobs are sorted in non-increasing order of their marginal values v_j/D_j. The algorithm (see Algorithm 1) works as follows. We initialize an empty solution $y \leftarrow 0$ and go over the jobs in their sorted order. For every job j in this order we check whether we can fully allocate D_j free resource units, meeting the deadline d_j, and without violating the parallelism bound k_j. Formally, a job j can be scheduled successfully if $\sum_{t \leq d_j} \min\{\bar{W}(t), k_j\} \geq D_j$, where $\bar{W}(t)$ is the amount of available resources in time slot t. If so, we schedule job j by allocating resources arbitrarily (without violating capacity constraints and the parallelism bound). Otherwise, job j is not scheduled. We note that the job allocation phase

---

Algorithm 1: SimpleGreedy

Input: n jobs with $type_j = (v_j, d_j, D_j, k_j)$.
Output: A feasible allocation of resources to jobs.
1 **begin**
2   initialize: $y \leftarrow 0, \alpha \leftarrow 0, \beta \leftarrow 0, \pi \leftarrow 0, charge \leftarrow 0$
3   sort jobs in non-increasing order of value/demand ratio: $v_1/D_1 \geq v_2/D_2 \geq \cdots \geq v_n/D_n$
4   **for** $(j = 1 \dots n)$ **do**
         // If job j can be allocated
5   **if** $\left(\sum_{t \leq d_j} \min\{\bar{W}(t), k_j\} \geq D_j \right)$ **then**
6   **Allocate**(j)
7   **else**
8   **if** $(\beta(d_j) = 0)$ **then**
9   β-**cover**(j)

Algorithm 2: Allocate(j)

Input: Job j to be allocated.
1 **begin**
2   set $\{y_j(t)\}$ arbitrarily to complete job j without violating capacity/parallelism constraints.
3      $\alpha_j \leftarrow v_j/D_j$

---

of SimpleGreedy may seem somewhat too permitting, however, we will be able to give a good bound on the total value gained by the algorithm. Later on, we present a more sophisticated allocation rule, replacing the arbitrary assignment of resources, that will further improve the bound.

Analysis.

To bound the total value gained by SimpleGreedy, we construct a feasible solution (α, β, π) to the dual program. Recall the dual constraint (5). For every job j, we must cover using the dual variables every time slot $t \leq d_j$ by an amount of at least v_j/D_j. Initially, we set all dual variables to be 0. For allocated jobs j, we set $\alpha_j = v_j/D_j$. This covers all the dual constraints associated with j, since the variable α_j is common to all of them. Note that the cost added to the dual objective function is exactly $D_j \alpha_j = v_j$.

Dual constraints of unallocated jobs will be covered by the $\beta(t)$ variables. Note that the variable $\beta(t)$ appears in all of the dual constraints associated with t. By setting $\beta(t)$ we are able to cover (or at least partially cover) other dual constraints. We will maintain three useful properties regarding the $\beta(t)$ variables:

1. A variable $\beta(t)$ is always set to be a marginal value v_j/D_j of an unallocated job.

2. Once a variable $\beta(t)$ has been set, it remains unchanged throughout the rest of the algorithm.

3. The $\beta(t)$ variables are monotonically non-increasing in t.

We prove property 3 in Lemma 3.1, yet for now assume that it is given. Consider the moment where SimpleGreedy decides not to allocate a job j. By property 1, every time slot t with $\beta(t) > 0$ has been set before to be the marginal value (i.e., v_i/D_i) of some job i considered earlier. By the order SimpleGreedy considers jobs, we have $\beta(t) \geq v_j/D_j$. Now, consider two cases: If $\beta(d_j) > 0$, then by property 3 all the $\beta(t)$ variables for $t \leq d_j$ have been set to values larger than v_j/D_j. By property 2, they remain so until the end of the algorithm. Otherwise, $\beta(d_j) = 0$. Let $t_{cov} = \min\{t \mid \beta(t) = 0\}$ be the first time slot in which the $\beta(t)$ variable is currently set to 0. By arguments similar to the ones used in the previous case, all of the dual constraints associated with time slots $t < t_{cov}$ are covered by variables $\beta(t) \geq v_j/D_j$. Thus, it remains to cover the remaining dual constraints of job j in the interval $[t_{cov}, d_j]$. To do so, we apply a method called β-cover(j) (Algorithm 3). The β-cover(j) method sets all of the unset $\beta(t)$ variables up to time d_j to be v_j/D_j, in order to cover the remaining unsatisfied constraints of j. In fact, β-cover keeps setting $\beta(t) = v_j/D_j$ for every $d_j \leq t \leq R(d_j)$, that is, we keep setting $\beta(t)$ variables of saturated time slots $t \geq d_j$ until we reach an unsaturated time slot. We note that in the context of the SimpleGreedy algorithm, it is enough to cover the constraints up to time d_j. However, covering the $\beta(t)$ up to $R(d_j)$ instead of d_j will be useful in the next subsection. Thus to simplify arguments later on we introduce this step here. One can simplify the analysis of the SimpleGreedy algorithm by replacing $R(d_j)$ with d_j. It remains to prove Lemma 3.1, based on the β-cover step.

Algorithm 3: β-cover(j)

Input: Unallocated job j.

1 begin
2 $t_{cov} \leftarrow \min\{t : \beta(t) = 0\}$
3   **for** ($t = t_{cov} \ldots R(d_j)$) **do**
4 $\lfloor\; \beta(t) \leftarrow v_j/D_j$
5   **for** ($t = 1 \ldots R(d_j)$) **do**
6   **for** ($i = 1 \ldots n$) **do**
7   **if** ($y_i(t) > 0 \wedge charge_i(t) = 0$) **then**
8 $\lfloor\; charge_i(t) \leftarrow \left[\frac{C}{C-k} \cdot \frac{s}{s-1}\right] \cdot \frac{v_j}{D_j} \cdot y_i(t)$

CLAIM 3.1. *At the end of every call to β-cover(j), $\beta(t)$ is monotonically non-increasing in t. Moreover, for every unallocated job j, $\beta(t) \geq v_j/D_j$ for every $t \leq d_j$.*

PROOF. By induction. Initially, $\forall t, \beta(t) = 0$ and the claim trivially holds. Consider a call to β-cover(j) and let j' be the last unallocated job for which β-cover(j') was called. By the order through which the greedy algorithm considers jobs, $v_{j'}/D_{j'} \geq v_j/D_j$. Define $t_{cov} = \min\{t \mid \beta(t) = 0\}$. The claim holds since β-cover sets $\beta(t)$ to be v_j/D_j in the range $t \in [t_{cov}, R(d_j)]$ and since $d_j \leq R(d_j)$ by the definition of $R(\cdot)$. $\square$

COROLLARY 3.2. *At the end of the SimpleGreedy algorithm, (α, β, π) is a feasible solution to the dual program.*

It now remains to bound the total cost of the dual solution constructed by SimpleGreedy. Let S denote the set of jobs fully allocated by SimpleGreedy. The cost of covering the dual constraints associated with allocated jobs is exactly $\sum_{j=1}^{n} D_j \alpha_j = \sum_{j \in S} v_j$. To bound the remaining cost of $\sum_t C\beta(t)$, we use a charging argument: We charge allocated jobs for the $\beta(t)$ variables, such that the total amount charged exceeds $\sum_t C\beta(t)$, and then bound the total amount charged. Specifically, let $charge_i(t)$ be the amount charged from job i in time slot t. We will charge job i at time t an amount proportional to $y_i(t)$, the number of resources it received at time t. Every such pair (i, t) will be charged only once, according to the following rule: whenever β-cover(j) is called on an unallocated job j, we charge from every uncharged pair (i, t):

$$charge_i(t) \leftarrow \left[\frac{C}{C-k} \cdot \frac{s}{s-1}\right] \cdot \frac{v_j}{D_j} \cdot y_i(t). \quad (8)$$

By the order SimpleGreedy considers jobs, when job i is charged during a call to β-cover(j), we have $v_i/D_i \geq v_j/D_j$. Therefore, $charge_i(t) \geq \left(\frac{C}{C-k} \cdot \frac{s}{s-1}\right) \cdot v_i/D_i \cdot y_i(t)$. The total amount charged from all jobs satisfies:

$$\sum_{i \in S} \sum_{t \leq d_i} charge_i(t) \leq \left[\frac{C}{C-k} \cdot \frac{s}{s-1}\right] \sum_{i=1}^{n} \sum_{t \leq d_i} \frac{v_i}{D_i} \cdot y_i(t)$$

$$= \left[\frac{C}{C-k} \cdot \frac{s}{s-1}\right] \cdot \sum_{i \in S} v_i. \quad (9)$$

Before continuing, we note that it is possible to use similar charging arguments to prove this bound, however the form used here will be useful in the next section, when analyzing the performance of the GreedyRTL algorithm. It remains to show that total amount charged from jobs is an upper bound to $\sum_t C\beta(t)$. Define E_j to be the set of unsaturated time slots (i.e., $W(t) \geq k$) up to time $R(d_j)$ during the call to β-cover(j).

LEMMA 3.3. *After every call to β-cover(j):*

$$\sum_{i=1}^{n} \sum_{\substack{t \leq d_i: \\ W(t) < k}} charge_i(t) - \sum_{t=1}^{T} C\beta(t) \geq$$

$$C \cdot \frac{v_j}{D_j} \cdot \frac{s}{s-1} \cdot \left[\frac{R(d_j)}{s} - |E_j|\right]. \quad (10)$$

PROOF. By Induction. Initially, both sides are 0, thus the claim trivially holds. Let j' be the last unallocated job for which β-cover(j') was called and assume that the claim holds after the call to β-cover(j'). Note that saturated time slots cannot become unsaturated. Between the two calls, the left hand side (LHS) of the inequality is updated as follows:

- $R(d_j) - R(d_{j'}) - |E_j \setminus E_{j'}|$ new saturated time slots in the interval $(R(d_{j'}), R(d_j)]$ are included in the LHS. Since every active job i in such a time slot t is either being charged or has been charged before, the amount $charge_i(t)$ charged from job i at time t is at least $\left(\frac{C}{C-k} \cdot \frac{s}{s-1}\right) \cdot y_i(t) \cdot v_j/D_j$. Therefore, for each such t the leftmost expression of LHS increases by at least:

$$\frac{C}{C-k} \cdot \frac{s}{s-1} \cdot \sum_{i=1}^{j-1} y_i(t) \cdot \frac{v_j}{D_j} \geq C \cdot \frac{s}{s-1} \cdot \frac{v_j}{D_j},$$

with the inequality following since t is saturated. The cost of setting $\beta(t) = v_j/D_j$ for a time slot t is $C \cdot v_j/D_j$. Thus, LHS increases by at least:

$$\left(R(d_j) - R(d_{j'}) - |E_j \setminus E_{j'}|\right) \cdot C \cdot \left(\frac{1}{s-1}\right) \cdot \frac{v_j}{D_j}.$$

- $|E_{j'} \setminus E_j|$ time slots in the interval $[1, R(d_{j'})]$ became saturated. Since $\beta(t)$ has been already set for such time slots t, the LHS increases by at least:

$$|E_{j'} \setminus E_j| \cdot C \cdot \left(\frac{s}{s-1}\right) \cdot \frac{v_j}{D_j}.$$

- $|E_j \setminus E_{j'}|$ unsaturated time slots have been covered at cost:

$$|E_j \setminus E_{j'}| \cdot C \cdot \frac{v_j}{D_j}.$$

By applying the inductive assumption on the value of LHS before the call to β-cover(j) and rearranging terms, we have:

$$\text{LHS} \geq C \cdot \frac{v_{j'}}{D_{j'}} \cdot \frac{s}{s-1} \cdot \left[\frac{R(d_{j'})}{s} - |E_{j'}|\right] +$$

$$C \cdot \frac{v_j}{D_j} \cdot \left[\frac{R(d_j) - R(d_{j'})}{s-1} - \frac{|E_j \setminus E_{j'}|}{s-1}\right] +$$

$$C \cdot \frac{v_j}{D_j} \cdot \left[\frac{s}{s-1} \cdot |E_{j'} \setminus E_j| - |E_j \setminus E_{j'}|\right]$$

$$\geq C \cdot \frac{v_j}{D_j} \cdot \left[\frac{R(d_j)}{s-1} - \frac{s}{s-1}|E_j|\right] +$$

$$C \cdot \frac{v_j}{D_j} \cdot \frac{s}{s-1} \cdot [|E_j| - |E_{j'}| - |E_j \setminus E_{j'}| + |E_{j'} \setminus E_j|]$$

$$= C \cdot \frac{v_j}{D_j} \cdot \frac{s}{s-1} \cdot \left[\frac{R(d_j)}{s} - |E_j|\right],$$

since $|E_j| - |E_{j'}| = |E_j \setminus E_{j'}| - |E_{j'} \setminus E_j|$. $\square$

THEOREM 3.4. *SimpleGreedy gives a $\left(1 + \frac{C}{C-k} \cdot \frac{s}{s-1}\right)$ approximation to the optimal social welfare.*

Algorithm 4: GreedyRTL

> **Input**: n jobs with $type_j = (v_j, d_j, D_j, k_j)$.
> **Output**: A feasible allocation of resources to jobs.
> **1 begin**
> **2**   execute SimpleGreedy, replace Allocate(j) with: **AllocateRTL(j)**
> **3**   **foreach** *charged job j* **do**
> **4**   call α-**correct**(j)

Algorithm 5: AllocateRTL(j)

> **Input**: Job j to be allocated.
> **1 begin**
> **2** $t \leftarrow d_j$
> **3**   **while** *j has not been fully allocated* **do**
> **4** $\Delta \leftarrow \min \left\{ k_j, D_j - \sum_{t'=t+1}^{d_j} y_j(t') \right\}$
> **5**   **while** $(\bar{W}(t) < \Delta)$ **do**
> **6** $t' \leftarrow$ closest unsaturated time slot earlier than t
> **7**   **if** $(\beta(t') > 0$ or no such t' exists) **then**
> **8**   jump to line 14
> **9**   let j' be a job such that $y_{j'}(t) > y_{j'}(t')$
> **10**   **while** $(\bar{W}(t) < \Delta \wedge y_{j'}(t) > y_{j'}(t'))$ **do**
> **11**   inc. $y_{j'}(t)$ and dec. $y_{j'}(t')$ simultaneously.
> **12** $y_j(t) \leftarrow \Delta$
> **13** $t \leftarrow t - 1$
> **14**   **while** *j has not been fully allocated* **do**
> **15** $y_j(t) \leftarrow \min \left\{ k_j, \bar{W}(t), D_j - \sum_{t'=t+1}^{d_j} y_j(t') \right\}$
> **16** $t \leftarrow t - 1$

PROOF. Denote by S the set of jobs allocated by SimpleGreedy. Let j be the last job for which β-cover has been called. Since j was not allocated, we must have $|E_j| < len_j$, otherwise j could have been allocated. By the slackness assumption and since by definition, $d_j \leq R(d_j)$, we have $s \cdot |E_j| < s \cdot len_j \leq d_j \leq R(d_j)$. By Lemma 3.3 and by (9), the dual cost of the dual solution constructed by SimpleGreedy is at most $\left(1 + \frac{C}{C-k} \cdot \frac{s}{s-1}\right) \cdot \sum_{j \in S} v_j$. $\square$

3.3 The GreedyRTL Algorithm

The GreedyRTL algorithm presented in this subsection is similar in nature to the SimpleGreedy algorithm. GreedyRTL (Algorithm 4) will also sort the jobs according to their marginal values and decide whether to allocate a job using the same decision rule (if it is possible to fully allocate the job using unused resources). The main difference between the two algorithms is the allocation rule of a single job. SimpleGreedy allowed any arbitrary allocation of resources to jobs that were taken to the solution, whereas for GreedyRTL we construct a specific single-job allocation rule called AllocateRTL (Algorithm 5). Unlike the former case, AllocateRTL may also choose to reallocate previously scheduled jobs, to be described later.

Before beginning, we give some intuition behind the suggested algorithm. Our goal will be to reduce the dual cost associated with allocated jobs j, which consists of $D_j \alpha_j$ and $charge_j(t)$ for every t. Consider some monotonically non-increasing vector β and ignore for now the π variables. To satisfy the dual constraints of an allocated job j, we must set α_j to be $v_j/D_j - \beta(d_j)$, since β is monotonically non-increasing. We would like the charged values $charge_j(t)$ to be as low as possible, preferably proportional to $D_j\beta(d_j)$. Ideally, we would want all of the jobs to be *aligned to the right*. Formally speaking, in an allocation aligned to the right, we allocate k_j resource units to j in every time slot, starting from the job deadline d_j moving towards earlier time slots. The last time slot in which we allocate resources to j will not necessarily receive k_j resource units, only the remaining amount of resources needed to complete the job[1]. Yet, even if allocations took this ideal form, this would still not necessarily mean that we could construct a dual solution of low cost. To do so, we need to incorporate the dual variables $\pi_j(t)$ into our dual solution.

The AllocateRTL rule will maintain an invariant over all job allocations. Specifically, all of the job allocations will satisfy a property throughout the execution of GreedyRTL called β-consistency, which we define next in spirit of the above discussion. To define the β-consistency property, we first need the following definition:

DEFINITION 1. *The* breakpoint $bp(y_j)$ *of an allocation y_j of job j is defined as:*

$$bp(y_j) = \max \left(\{s(y_j)\} \cup \{t \mid y_j(t) < k_j\} \right). \quad (11)$$

---

[1] When D_j and k_j are integers, this amount equals $D_j \bmod k_j$.

The breakpoint $bp(y_j)$ is essentially the first time slot t, starting from the deadline moving towards earlier time slots, such that $y_j(t)$ does not coincide with the ideal aligned-to-right form of allocation. If such a time slot does not exist, we define $bp(y_j) = s(y_j)$.

DEFINITION 2. *An allocation y_j is called β-consistent if for every time slot t, $s(y_j) < t \leq bp(y_j)$, either t is saturated or $\beta(t) > 0$.*

The AllocateRTL(j) rule allocates job j as follows. First, we initialize an empty allocation $y_j = 0$. We begin at the deadline $t = d_j$ and move towards earlier time slots (hence the name Right-To-Left). In every time slot t, the algorithm will attempt to allocate $\Delta = \min\{k_j, D_j - \sum_{t \leq d_j} y_j(t)\}$ resource units to job j. That is, give job j either the maximal amount of resources k_j it can get at time t, or the remaining unallocated portion, so that eventually y_j will be β-consistent. If $\bar{W}(t) \geq \Delta$, we allocate Δ resource units to j and continue allocating resources to j in an earlier time slot. Otherwise, if $\bar{W}(t) < \Delta$ (specifically, t is saturated since $\Delta \leq k$), we attempt to free resources at time t by moving existing jobs to earlier time slots. AllocateRTL searches for the first unsaturated time slot to the left of t, denoted by t'. Notice that if $\beta(t') > 0$ then y_j will definitely be β-consistent, and therefore we can allocate the remaining portion of j arbitrarily in the interval $[1, t]$ (for the sake of consistency, we will keep allocating j from right to left, giving j in each time slot the maximal amount of resources it can get). Otherwise, the key idea is that there must be a job j' with $y_{j'}(t) > y_{j'}(t')$, since t is saturated and t' is unsaturated. As long as this condition holds, we increase $y_{j'}(t)$ in expense of $y_j(t)$, until either (i) $\bar{W}(t) = \Delta$, in which case we set $y_j(t) = \Delta$ and continue, or (ii) $y_{j'}(t) = y_{j'}(t')$, and then we keep repeating this process. It is easy to see that this operation does not violate the parallelism bound of j', since we do not continue this process if equality is reached, nor change the completion time of j'.

Analysis.

We begin our analysis by making two important observations that delimit the reallocations made by AllocateRTL. Using these observations, we prove that all of the allocations are β-consistent throughout the execution of GreedyRTL (Claim 3.7).

Algorithm 6: α-correct(j)

Input: Allocated job j.

1 **begin**
2    $\alpha(j) \leftarrow \frac{v_j}{D_j} - \beta(bp(y_j))$
3   **for** $(t = (bp(y_j) + 1) \ldots d_j)$ **do**
4      $\pi_j(t) \leftarrow \beta(bp(y_j)) - \beta(t)$
5      $\alpha_j \leftarrow \alpha_j + \frac{k_j}{D_j} \cdot (\beta(bp(y_j)) - \beta(t))$

CLAIM 3.5. *For every t, the total workload $W(t)$ does not decrease after a call to AllocateRTL(j). Specifically, GreedyRTL does not turn a satisfied time slot into an unsatisfied one.*

PROOF. The only stage of the algorithm in which we decrease the total workload $W(t)$ for some time slot t is when we cannot allocate Δ resource units during a call to AllocateRTL. Since we decrease $W(t)$ up to the point where $W(t) = C - \Delta$ and then allocate Δ resource units to j, time slot t becomes full. Specifically, saturated time slots remain saturated throughout the algorithm. $\square$

CLAIM 3.6. *Let j be an uncharged job such that the allocation y_j is β-consistent. If j is charged by the algorithm, then from that point the allocation y_j remains fixed.*

PROOF. Let j' be the first (unallocated) job for which the call to β-cover(j') charges j. In order for the allocation y_j to be changed by the algorithm, the following must hold: there must be two time slots $t' < t$, as observed by the AllocateRTL algorithm, such that: (1) $y_j(t) > y_j(t')$ (2) $\beta(t') = 0$. By the monotonicity of β we also know that $\beta(t) = 0$.

It suffices to show that after the call to β-cover(j') it holds that $\beta(bp(y_j)) > 0$. If so, by the monotonicity of β, $bp(t') < t' < t$ implying $y_j(t) = y_j(t') = k_j$, therefore AllocateRTL would not have changed y_j. At the end of the call to β-cover(j') we must have $s(y_j) \leq R(d_{j'})$, otherwise j wouldn't have been charged. Moreover, by the definition of $R(\cdot)$ and since y_j is β-consistent, we have $bp(y_j) \leq R(d_{j'})$. Therefore, after the call to β-cover(j'), $\beta(bp(y_j))$ is at least $v_{j'}/D_{j'} > 0$, as desired. $\square$

CLAIM 3.7. *The GreedyRTL algorithm maintains the following invariant throughout its execution: All of the allocations matching allocated jobs are β-consistent.*

PROOF. By Induction. Initially, the claim trivially holds. Assume that all existing allocations are β-consistent and consider a call to AllocateRTL(j). Recall that by Claim 3.5 saturated time slots remain saturated, and that variables $\beta(t) > 0$ are never unset. If at the end of the call $bp(y_j) = s(y_j)$ then the allocation is trivially β-consistent. Otherwise, consider the point where $t = bp(y_j)$. From this point on, AllocateRTL may allocate job j arbitrarily (specifically, we jump to line 14) since we cannot find an unsaturated time slot t' to the left of t with $\beta(t') = 0$. Therefore, y_j is β-consistent.

Now, consider an allocation $y_{j'}$ of an allocated job j' modified by the AllocateRTL rule, and denote by $\tilde{y}_{j'}$ the resulting modified allocation. As in claim 3.6, there must be two time slots $t' < t$ such that: (1) $y_{j'}(t) > y_{j'}(t')$ (2) $\beta(t') = \beta(t) = 0$. Notice first that $t' \leq bp(y_{j'})$, otherwise $y_{j'}(t') = k_j$ and then we wouldn't have modified $y_{j'}$. Second, by the choice of t', all time slots in the interval $(t', t]$ are either saturated or have a non-zero β value. By the β-consistency property of y_j, the same condition holds for the interval $(s(y_j), bp(y_j)]$. Thus, we have (1)

$s(\tilde{y}_{j'}) = \min \{s(y_j), t'\}$ (2) $bp(\tilde{y}_{j'}) = \max \{bp(y_{j'}), t\}$, since if $t > bp(y_{j'})$ we decrease $y_{j'}(t)$ below k_j. Combining (1) and (2) with the previous observations prove that $\tilde{y}_{j'}$ is β-consistent, since $[s(y_{j'}), bp(y_{j'})] = (s(y_j), bp(y_j)] \cup (t', t]$. $\square$

It remains to show how to set the dual variables α_j, $\pi_j(t)$ for a job j allocated according to a β-consistent allocation y_j. First, notice the following: by setting a variable $\pi_j(t)$ to be some value ε, we incur a loss of $(k_j/D_j) \cdot \varepsilon$ in all of the dual constraints associated with job j. We will cover this loss by increasing α_j accordingly. For every allocated job, we apply a method called α-**correct**(j) (Algorithm 3) to set the dual variables of job j. Initially, all of these variables are set to 0. We start by setting $\pi_j(t) = \beta(bp(y_j)) - \beta(t)$ for time slots $bp(y_j) < t \leq d_j$, and increase α_j accordingly to cover the loss incurred from setting the $\pi_j(t)$ variables. Now, all dual constraints are covered by at least $\beta(bp(y_j))$. To finish, we increase α_j by $v_j/D_j - \beta(bp(y_j))$. The following theorem proves the solution we constructed is feasible and bounds its total cost compared to the total value gained by GreedyRTL, completing the analysis.

THEOREM 3.8. *The GreedyRTL algorithm gives a $\left(\frac{C}{C-k} \cdot \frac{s}{s-1} \right)$-approximation to the optimal social welfare.*

PROOF. First we show that the dual solution (α, β, π) that is constructed by GreedyRTL is feasible, and then we bound its cost. Recall the dual constraint matching job j and time slot $t \leq d_j$:

$$\alpha_j + \beta(t) + \pi_j(t) - \frac{k_j}{D_j} \cdot \sum_{t' \leq d_j} \pi_j(t') \geq \frac{v_j}{D_j}.$$

For an unallocated job, by the way β-cover sets the $\beta(t)$ variables and since $\alpha_j = \pi_j(t) = 0$ for every time slot t, all of the dual constraints associated with j are satisfied. Now consider an uncharged job j. Here, we set $\alpha_j = v_j/D_j$ and $\pi_j(t) = 0$ for every time slot t, thus feasibility in this case follows since $\beta(t) \geq 0$ for every t.

Finally, consider a charged job j. To satisfy the dual constraints of j, we follow the routine α-correct(j) (Algorithm 6). Initially, we set $\alpha_j = (v_j/D_j - \beta(bp(y_j))$ to cover all of the constraints up to $bp(y_j)$ (by the monotonicity of β). To cover the remaining constraints, we use the $\pi_j(t)$ variables. First notice that whenever a variable $\pi_j(t)$ is set to some value ε, every time slot (including t) incurs a "punishment" of $-k_j/D_j \cdot \varepsilon$. To balance this, the routine α-correct increases α_j by $k_j/D_j \cdot \varepsilon$ (line 5). To conclude, for each $t \in (bp(y_j), d_j]$ we set $\pi_j(t)$ such that $\beta(t) + \pi_j(t) = \beta(bp(y_j))$ and correct α_j accordingly. By arguments similar to ones used in the previous case, we cover the remaining dual constraints.

We now bound the cost of the dual solution (α, β, π). Notice that unallocated jobs do not contribute to the dual objective function, since they are not charged and their α value is 0. By Claim 3.6, once an allocated job is charged for the first time, its allocation becomes fixed and is not modified by GreedyRTL. Therefore, we can apply Lemma 3.3 and bound the total dual cost by:

$$\sum_j D_j \alpha_j + \sum_{j=1}^{n} \sum_{\substack{t \leq d_i: \\ W(t) < k}} charge_i(t) \leq$$

$$\leq \sum_j D_j \alpha_j + \sum_{j=1}^{n} \sum_{t \leq d_j} charge_i(t) \quad (12)$$

Consider an allocated job j. If j has not been charged, the dual cost inflicted by it is exactly $D_j \alpha_j = v_j$. Otherwise, the first payment $D_j \alpha_j$ set by α-correct(j) equals to:

$$D_j \cdot \left[\frac{v_j}{D_j} - \beta(bp(y_j)) + \sum_{t=bp(y_j)+1}^{d_j} \frac{k_j}{D_j} \cdot (\beta(bp(y_j)) - \beta(t)) \right]$$

$$= v_j - \sum_{t \le bp(y_j)} y_j(t)\, \beta(bp(y_j)) - \sum_{t=bp(y_j)+1}^{d_j} k_j\, \beta(t). \quad (13)$$

The last inequality follows since y_j is β-consistent by Claim 3.7.

We now bound the total amount charged from j. Let j' be the first job for which the call to β-cover(j) charges j, and let y_j be the allocation of j at that point. By Claim 3.6, the allocation y_j remains fixed henceforth. Notice that $bp(y_j) \le R(d_{j'})$, since according to the definition of $bp(y_j)$, once β-cover(j') charges j, all of the time slots in $[s(y_j), bp(y_j)]$ are saturated, thus $R(d_{j'})$ is no earlier than $bp(y_j)$. Therefore, every time slot $t \le bp(y_j)$ is charged according to the marginal cost $v_{j'}/D_{j'}$ of j' and specifically, this cost is at most $\beta(bp(y_j))$ by the feasibility of the dual solution. The total amount $\sum_{t \le d_j} charge_j(t)$ charged from j equals to:

$$\left(\frac{C}{C-k} \cdot \frac{s}{s-1} \right) \cdot \left[\sum_{t \le bp(y_j)} \beta(bp(y_j))\, y_j(t) + \sum_{t=bp(y_j)+1}^{d_j} \beta(t)\, y_j(t) \right] \quad (14)$$

Moreover, we know that for any time slot t for which j is charged, $\beta(t) \le v_j/D_j$, by the order GreedyRTL considers jobs and since $\beta(t)$ is always set to be a marginal cost of an unallocated job succeeding j in the greedy order. Combining this observation along with (13) and (14) gives us:

$$D_j \alpha_j + \sum_{t \le d_j} charge_j(t) \le \left(\frac{C}{C-k} \cdot \frac{s}{s-1} \right) \cdot v_j.$$

The theorem follows by summing these inequalities over all jobs allocated by GreedyRTL. $\square$

4. TRUTHFUL MECHANISMS

In the previous section we constructed algorithms that allocate cloud resources to scheduled jobs, while ignoring the *incentives* issue, namely how to make sure that users report their true value v_j, as well as job properties (e.g., deadline, demand and parallelism bound). In this section we present a general framework for designing incentive compatible (*truthful*) allocation and pricing mechanisms, in single-value multi-property domains. The framework requires extending well-known results for single-parameter settings, where the private information held by each user consists of a single scalar. While extensions to multi-parameters auctions do exist (see, e.g., [8] and references therein), we provide here a general framework for truthfulness, which covers our model as special case.

4.1 Preliminaries

A *mechanism* $\mathcal{M} = (f, p)$ consists of an allocation rule f and a pricing rule p_j for every user j. Every user is associated with a private true type $\tau_j = \langle v_j, \mathcal{P}_j \rangle$, where $\mathcal{P}_j = \langle \rho_j^1, \rho_j^2, \dots, \rho_j^m \rangle$ is a set of m properties of the job (specific to our context, $\mathcal{P}_j = \langle d_j, D_j, k_j \rangle$), and $v_j \in \mathbb{R}^+$ represents (as before) the value gained by user j if its job is successfully completed, i.e., fully allocated according to the requested properties. Users report a bid type b_j to the cloud, which may differ from their true type τ_j. The mechanism,

given a reported bid vector $b = (b_1, b_2, \dots b_n)$, allocates the jobs according to $f(b)$ and charges a non-negative payment $p_j(b)$ from user j. We define $f_j(b \mid \mathcal{P}_j)$ to be a binary function that returns 1 if and only if the job of user j has fully completed with respect to the job properties $\mathcal{P}_j$[2]. We assume allocation functions f are *rational*, that is, if user j submitted a bid type of $b_j = \langle v_j', \mathcal{P}_j' \rangle$ and $f_j(b) = 1$, then the allocation user j receives complies with $\mathcal{P}_j'$, e.g., meets a deadline or a job demand request specified in $\mathcal{P}_j'$. Every user strives to maximize its *utility* u_j, defined to be the value it gains from the allocation f minus the payment it is charged:

$$u_j(b) = v_j f_j(b \mid \mathcal{P}_j) - p_j(b). \quad (15)$$

One desired property of mechanisms is that reporting the true valuation function of users is a dominant strategy. Given some vector x, let x_{-j} denote the vector x without its j-th entry. Specifically, τ_{-j} denotes a vector of valuation functions of all players except for j. Let (τ_j, τ_{-j}) denote the concatenated vector of τ_j and τ_{-j}. A mechanism is said to be *incentive compatible* (IC) or *truthful* if for every user j and for every choice of τ_{-j}, truth-telling is a dominant strategy, i.e., maximizes their utility:

$$\forall j \quad \forall b_j, \tau_{-j} \quad u_j(\tau_j, \tau_{-j}) \ge u_j(b_j, \tau_{-j}). \quad (16)$$

Apart from incentive compatibility, we would like to construct rational mechanisms, in which users do not lose by participating in the mechanism. A mechanism is *individually rational (IR)* if users do not receive negative utility when reporting their true valuation functions.

4.2 A Sufficient Condition for Truthfulness

In order to construct truthful mechanisms based on the algorithms presented in Section 3, we extend known results for single-value domains [2, 12] to the case in which users also hold private job properties. For user j, we shorten notation by omitting the term b_{-j}. For example, we write $f_j(v_j', \mathcal{P}_j' \mid \mathcal{P}_j)$ instead of $f_j((v_j', \mathcal{P}_j'), b_{-j} \mid \mathcal{P}_j)$. We first define two conditions on allocation rules called value-monotonicity and property-monotonicity, and prove that they are sufficient for truthfulness for any binary rational f.

DEFINITION 3. *An allocation function f is* value-monotonic *if for every user j, $\mathcal{P}_j'$ and b_{-j}, the function $f_j(v_j', \mathcal{P}_j' \mid \mathcal{P}_j)$ is monotonically non-decreasing in v. That is, for every $v_j', v_j'', v_j' \le v_j''$:*

$$f_j(v_j', \mathcal{P}_j' \mid \mathcal{P}_j) \le f_j(v_j'', \mathcal{P}_j' \mid \mathcal{P}_j). \quad (17)$$

DEFINITION 4. *An allocation function f is* property-monotonic *if for every user j, b_{-j}, $\mathcal{P}_j$, $\mathcal{P}_j'$ the following condition holds: If there is some value v for which $f_j(v, \mathcal{P}_j' \mid \mathcal{P}_j) = 1$, then:*

$$\forall s \le v \quad f_j(s, \mathcal{P}_j' \mid \mathcal{P}_j) \le f_j(s, \mathcal{P}_j \mid \mathcal{P}_j). \quad (18)$$

THEOREM 4.1. *If a binary allocation rule f for a single-value multi-property problem satisfies value-monotonicity and property-monotonicity and is rational, then the mechanism $\mathcal{M} = (f, p)$ that sets prices for every user j with true type $\tau_j = \langle v_j, \mathcal{P}_j \rangle$ according to:*

$$p_j(v_j', \mathcal{P}_j') = v_j' f_j(v_j', \mathcal{P}_j' \mid \mathcal{P}_j') - \int_0^{v_j'} f_j(s, \mathcal{P}_j' \mid \mathcal{P}_j')\, ds. \quad (19)$$

is truthful and individually rational.

---

[2]A job is fully completed with respect to $\mathcal{P}_j$ if according to the solution $f(b)$ job j receives D_j resource units before the deadline d_j, without violating the parallel execution bound k_j.

Notice that for binary monotone allocation functions f, the payment charged from each allocated user in (19) is actually the minimal value bid that would have guaranteed the job being scheduled.

PROOF. Let j be a user with $\tau_j = \langle v_j, \mathcal{P}_j \rangle$ and let $\tau_j = \langle v_j', \mathcal{P}_j' \rangle$ be an alternative type bid. To prove that $\mathcal{M}$ is truthful, we must show that $u_j(v_j, \mathcal{P}_j) \geq u_j(v_j', \mathcal{P}_j')$. First, notice that by the value-monotonicity of f, the payment set in (19) is always non-negative, since $f_j(s, \mathcal{P}_j' \mid \mathcal{P}_j') \leq f_j(v_j', \mathcal{P}_j' \mid \mathcal{P}_j')$ for every $s \leq v_j'$. By the definition of u_j and since payments are set according to (19):

$$u_j(v_j, \mathcal{P}_j) = \int_0^{v_j} f_j(s, \mathcal{P}_j \mid \mathcal{P}_j) ds \qquad (20)$$

$$u_j(v_j', \mathcal{P}_j') = v_j f_j(v_j', \mathcal{P}_j' \mid \mathcal{P}_j') - $$
$$- \left[v_j' f_j(v_j', \mathcal{P}_j' \mid \mathcal{P}_j') - \int_0^{v_j'} f_j(s, \mathcal{P}_j' \mid \mathcal{P}_j') ds \right]. \quad (21)$$

Note that (20) implies that $\mathcal{M}$ is individually rational, since the utility of a truthful user is non-negative. To conclude, we must show that $u_j(v_j, \mathcal{P}_j) \geq u_j(v_j', \mathcal{P}_j')$. Consider two cases. First, if $f_j(v_j', \mathcal{P}_j' \mid \mathcal{P}_j) = 0$, then since payments are non-negative, $u_j(v_j', \mathcal{P}_j') \leq 0$ and the required condition holds since $\mathcal{M}$ is individually rational.

The second case happens when $f_j(v_j', \mathcal{P}_j' \mid \mathcal{P}_j) = 1$, implying the following. First, by property-monotonicity we have:

$$\forall s \leq v_j', \quad f_j(s, \mathcal{P}_j' \mid \mathcal{P}_j') \leq f_j(s, \mathcal{P}_j \mid \mathcal{P}_j). \qquad (22)$$

Second, since f is rational, it implies that $f_j(v_j', \mathcal{P}_j \mid \mathcal{P}_j') = 1$. By the previous claim and since f is value-monotone, for every value $s \geq v_j'$ we have $f_j(s, \mathcal{P}_j \mid \mathcal{P}_j) = 1$. From here we conclude that for every s, $f_j(s, \mathcal{P}_j' \mid \mathcal{P}_j') \leq f_j(s, \mathcal{P}_j \mid \mathcal{P}_j)$. After applying this inequality to (20) and combining it with (21) we get:

$$u_j(v_j, \mathcal{P}_j) - u_j(v_j', \mathcal{P}_j') =$$
$$= \int_{v_j'}^{v_j} f_j(s, \mathcal{P}_j' \mid \mathcal{P}_j') ds - (v_j - v_j') f_j(v_j', \mathcal{P}_j' \mid \mathcal{P}_j'). \qquad (23)$$

Consider the case where $v_j' \leq v_j$. By value-monotonicity, for every $s \in [v_j', v_j]$ we have $f_j(s, \mathcal{P}_j' \mid \mathcal{P}_j') \geq f_j(v_j', \mathcal{P}_j \mid \mathcal{P}_j)$. Therefore, (23) is non-negative as required. The case where $v_j' \geq v_j$ is symmetric, interchanging the roles of v_j' and v_j. □

4.3 Profit Maximization in Bayesian Settings

The objective of profit maximizing is of course significant for public commercial clouds. When assuming no a-priori knowledge on clients' private valuation functions, it is well known that a truthful mechanism might charge very low payments from clients to ensure truthfulness, yielding low revenues. Thus, following a standard approach in game-theory, we consider a *Bayesian* setting, in which each user's value v_j is assumed to be drawn from a distribution with a probability density function g_j, which is common knowledge. We denote by G_j the respective cumulative distribution function (cdf). Job properties are assumed, as before, to be private information with no additional distribution information.

The goal of the mechanism in the current context is to maximize the optimal expected profit, with the expectation taken over the random draws of clients' values. For single-value domains, it is well known that the problem of maximizing profits can be reduced to the problem of maximizing social welfare over virtual values; this

basic property is due to celebrated work by Myerson [16], and has been extended in different contexts (see [18]). To formally state the result, we first need the following definitions.

DEFINITION 5. *The* revenue curve *associated with client j is defined as $R_j(q) = q \cdot G_j^{-1}(1 - q)$. The* ironed virtual valuation function *$\bar{\phi}_j$ of j is defined as: $\bar{\phi}_j(v) = \frac{d}{dq}\left[ConcaveHull\left(R_j(\cdot) \right) \right]$ for $q = 1 - G_j(v)$.*

That is, $\bar{\phi}_j(v)$ the derivative of the concave hull of $R(\cdot)$. Note that $\bar{\phi}_j(\cdot)$ is monotonically non-decreasing. Thus, if a single-value allocation rule f^{sv} is value-monotone, then so is $f^{sv}\left(\bar{\phi}(\cdot) \right)$.

THEOREM 4.2 ([16, 18]). *For any single-value truthful mechanism $\mathcal{M}^{sv}$ that gives an α-approximation to the optimal social surplus, the mechanism $\mathcal{M}^{sv}(\bar{\phi}(\cdot))$ gives an α-approximation to the optimal expected profit.*

For our purposes, we prove that this reduction due to Myerson extends to domains of single-value and multi-properties. Formally,

THEOREM 4.3. *Let f be a binary allocation rule for a single-value multi-property problem, such that f is rational, satisfies value-monotonicity and property-monotonicity, and guarantees an α approximation factor to the optimal social welfare. Let $f_{\bar{\phi}}$ be an allocation rule that replaces every type $\langle v_j, \mathcal{P}_j \rangle$ with $\langle \bar{\phi}_j(v_j), \mathcal{P}_j \rangle$ and calls f. Then, the mechanism $M_{\bar{\phi}}$ with allocation rule $f_{\bar{\phi}}$ that charges payments according to (19), with respect to $f_{\bar{\phi}}$, is truthful, and is an α-approximation to the optimal expected profit under Bayesian assumptions.*

PROOF. Consider the set properties $\mathcal{P}_j$ as fixed, making f a single-value allocation rule. By the characterization theorem of single-value allocation functions [2], since f is value-monotone, the mechanism $\mathcal{M} = (f, p)$ with p set as in (19) is truthful. By Theorem 4.2, the mechanism $\mathcal{M}_{\bar{\phi}}$ gives an α-approximation to the optimal expected profit.

It remains to show that $f_{\bar{\phi}}$ admits a truthful mechanism. Notice that since $\bar{\phi}_j$ is monotone for every j, $f_{\bar{\phi}}$ is value-monotone. Moreover, the property-monotonicity and rationality of f directly implies the property-monotonicity and rationality of $f_{\bar{\phi}}$ (since these properties are defined over any value v_j, specifically $\bar{\phi}_j(v_j)$), and therefore we can apply Theorem 4.1. □

4.4 Truthfulness of GreedyRTL

We return to the GreedyRTL algorithm and prove that it satisfies the sufficient conditions for truthfulness presented in Section 4.2: value-monotonicity, property-monotonicity and rationality. Rationality follows since if GreedyRTL schedules a job j, the allocation it receives always complies with the reported property set $\mathcal{P}_j$. We now prove the remaining two monotonicity conditions.

CLAIM 4.4. *GreedyRTL is value-monotone.*

PROOF. Let $\mathcal{P}_j = \langle d_j, D_j, k_j \rangle$ be the property set a user j. Fix the types τ_{-j} of all users apart from j and let $v_j' \leq v_j''$ be two values. It is enough to show that if $f_j(v_j'', \mathcal{P}_j \mid \mathcal{P}_j) = 0$ then $f_j(v_j', \mathcal{P}_j \mid \mathcal{P}_j) = 0$. By the order GreedyRTL goes over the jobs, user j will be considered earlier when reporting v_j''. Consider the two executions of GreedyRTL matching the two values. Notice that both executions are identical up to the point where j is handled by GreedyRTL when reporting v_j''. If j cannot be allocated when reporting v_j'', by Claim 3.5 the amount of available resources in every time slot will only keep decreasing, thus j will not be allocated when reporting v_j'. □

CLAIM 4.5. *GreedyRTL is property-monotone.*

PROOF. For a user j, fix the types τ_{-j} reported by other users and let $\mathcal{P}_j = \langle d_j, D_j, k_j \rangle$ and $\mathcal{P}'_j = \langle d'_j, D'_j, k'_j \rangle$ be two property sets for user j. Assume that there is a value v'_j for which it holds that $f_j(v'_j, \mathcal{P}'_j \mid \mathcal{P}_j) = 1$. Now, let $s \le v'_j$. We need to show that if $f_j(s, \mathcal{P}'_j \mid \mathcal{P}_j) = 1$ then $f_j(s, \mathcal{P}_j \mid \mathcal{P}_j) = 1$. Since the job of user j is fully completed under $\mathcal{P}'_j$, we have $D_j \le D'_j$. Specifically, user j will have a higher priority in the sorted list of jobs when reporting $\mathcal{P}_j$. By Claim 3.5, the are more available resources in every time slot t for allocating j when reporting $\mathcal{P}_j$ instead of $\mathcal{P}'_j$.

Out of all 4 possibilities, the most complicated one to prove is the case where $d'_j \ge d_j$ and $k'_j \ge k_j$. If j reports an earlier deadline or a smaller parallelism bound, it only makes it more difficult for GreedyRTL to allocate j. Thus, we prove the complicated case (the three other cases will hold by similar arguments). Notice the following: once a job j is allocated by GreedyRTL, any later call to AllocateRTL(j') will not change the completion time of job j. This is true since in case $y_j(t)$ is decreased for some t, at the same time $y_j(t')$ is increased for some t', stopping once they are equal (if not earlier). Therefore, for us to have $f_j(v'_j, \mathcal{P}'_j \mid \mathcal{P}_j) = 1$, job j must not have been allocated after d_j when reporting a type of $\langle v'_j, \mathcal{P}'_j \rangle$. By Claim 3.5, this is also true when reporting $s \le v'_j$. Thus, we can assume without loss of generality that $d'_j = d_j$.

Now, denote by y'_j the allocation set to job j at the end of the call to GreedyRTL when reporting $\langle v'_j, \mathcal{P}'_j \rangle$. Under the assumption that $f_j(v'_j, \mathcal{P}'_j \mid \mathcal{P}_j) = 1$, the maximal entry in y'_j is at most k_j. By the way AllocateRTL modifies allocations, every resource unit occupied by y'_j was available when j was initially allocated by GreedyRTL. Thus, when reporting $\langle v_j, \mathcal{P}_j \rangle$, since j will be considered earlier by GreedyRTL, it will also be possible to allocate j. This concludes the proof. □

This leads to the main result of this section.

COROLLARY 4.6. *GreedyRTL implements a truthful mechanism obtaining a $\left(\frac{C}{C-k} \cdot \frac{s}{s-1} \right)$-approximation to the optimal social welfare. Moreover, if the value v_j of every user is drawn from a known distribution G_j, then GreedyRTL applied on virtual values $\bar{\phi}_j(v_j)$ implements a (Bayesian) incentive compatible mechanism obtaining a $\left(\frac{C}{C-k} \cdot \frac{s}{s-1} \right)$-approximation to the optimal expected profit.*

5. EMPIRICAL STUDY

In this section, we describe some of the experiments we carried out to further evaluate the benefits of our scheduling framework. Our simulation framework utilizes empirical job traces of a large batch computing cluster. Further details of the simulation setup can be found in Appendix A.

5.1 Resource utilization

High utilization is certainly one of the main goals in the area of cloud computing (see, e.g., [11]). The main practical drawback of the solution given in [13] is that on average, more than half of the resources remain unallocated. Without considering incentives, utilization could be practically improved by adding unscheduled jobs to the solution in a greedy manner, whenever possible. Yet, it is unclear how to improve utilization under the framework of [13] without affecting the truthfulness of the mechanism. In our first experiment, we compare the average utilization under GreedyRTL and the allocation mechanism of [13]. Since the maximum possible utilization level generally depends on the job characteristics, we compare the algorithm to an upper on the utilization, denoted OPT^*_{Util}. Specifically, OPT^*_{util} is obtained by solving the relaxed linear program (P) with the marginal value of each job set to one

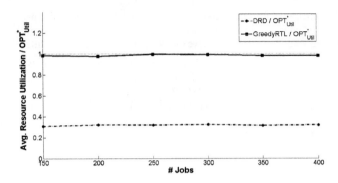

Figure 1: Average resource utilization (over time) compared to the Decompose-Randomly-Draw (DRD) mechanism of [13]. Results show that GreedyRTL utilizes nearly all of the cloud resources.

(equivalently, we set $v_j := D_j$). Figure 1 shows that GreedyRTL reaches a utilization level which is very close to OPT^*_{Util} (within 2% thereof), while the mechanism of [13] achieves around 35% of the upper bound on utilization. The results are consistent regardless of the number of jobs that we consider. The utilization results not only provide an explanation to the social welfare improvements we obtain, but also stand on their own – given the significance of achieving high utilization in large cloud clusters.

5.2 Revenue Maximization

In the next experiment, we evaluate the potential of our approach in terms of revenue maximization. In particular, we examine the revenues of our mechanism against an idealized mechanism which we term the *Optimal Fixed Price (OFP)* mechanism. A fixed price mechanism is a mechanism that charges a fixed price q per server CPU hour, regardless of the job identity. Given that the mechanism charges a fixed price q, it would only schedule a job j with non-negative net utility, namely, $v_j \ge q \cdot D_j$. To focus the comparison solely on the revenue dimension, the fixed price mechanisms uses the same allocation algorithm as the GreedyRTL mechanism, with the value of each job set to $q \cdot D_j$ (equivalently, the marginal value of each job is q) in order to maximize revenues. The *optimal fixed price (OFP)* mechanism charges a price q^*, which is the unit price that maximizes the revenues of the allocation algorithm. Since q^* must be of the form v_j/D_j for some job j (if not, then q^* can be increased without changing the allocation of jobs, thus increasing revenues), we can effectively determine q^* by repeating the allocation algorithm for n different prices $\{v_j/D_j\}_{j=1}^n$, and setting q^* to be the revenue-maximizing price among this set.

We emphasize that OFP is an *ideal* mechanism, since we assume it has *full* knowledge of the private values of users (and other job parameters). That is, users are assumed to be truthful, although the mechanism does not guarantee that. Recall that our GreedyRTL algorithm is guaranteed to obtain a near-optimal factor of the optimal revenues when we assume Bayesian knowledge on the user valuations (cf. Section 4). Note that the Bayesian assumption is weaker than having full knowledge on the values. To stretch-test GreedyRTL, we do not assume even that for our experiments. That is, for the revenue experiment, we take a worst case scenario in which the algorithm has no knowledge on value distributions, and simply maximizes social welfare by setting incentive compatible prices. We examine the revenues generated under the objective of social welfare, revenues that can be obviously improved when statistical knowledge on evaluations is available. Figure 2 depicts the

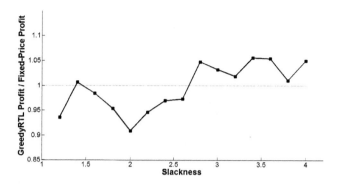

Figure 2: Revenue ratio between GreedyRTL and OFP, compared against different input slackness values (1.2–4). The truthful GreedyRTL mechanism is nearly as good as an ideal optimal fixed-price mechanism. For this experiment, we overload the system such that the total demand exceeds the cloud capacity, so that truthful pricing is strictly positive. Results are averaged over 20 runs.

ratio of revenues between GreedyRTL and OFP as a function of the slackness parameter s. Surprisingly, despite the fact that OFP has significant value information that GreedyRTL is not assume to have, that GreedyRTL achieves most of the revenues of OFP for small values of s, and outperforms it for larger values of s.

6. EXTENSION: COPING WITH DEMAND UNCERTAINTIES

Up until now, we have assumed that the job work volume (or demand) D_j is a deterministic quantity. However, it turns out to be a restrictive assumption in many applications as the exact volume is either unknown, predicted using prior executions, or often overestimated. Further, the demand might be sensitive to stochastic fluctuations, especially in jobs where some tasks have dependencies on the completion of other tasks (see, e.g., [1] and references therein). From a theoretical perspective, these demand uncertainties introduce new challenges for mechanism design and impossibility results can indeed be shown ([10]). In this section we discuss how to address demand uncertainties while maintaining the benefits of our scheduling framework. We present below one plausible model, however a comprehensive study of alternatives to address this challenge is beyond the scope of this paper.

Demand Uncertainty Model. To incorporate demand uncertainties, we extend the basic model we used for both jobs and the cloud. In particular, we consider a more general job model, where the demand of each job j is drawn from a distribution $\mathcal{D}_j$. The distribution has a finite support over $\left(0, D_j^{\mathbb{E}}(1+\delta)\right]$, where $D_j^{\mathbb{E}} \equiv \mathbb{E}\left[\mathcal{D}_j\right]$ is the *expected* volume, and δ is a positive parameter. For simplicity, this distribution is assumed to be common knowledge. The cases where $\mathcal{D}_j$ doesn't meet this assumption may be handled using a repeated auction framework, however, it is beyond the scope of this paper. From the cloud provider's side, we assume that the cloud is able to generate additional resources on-demand. We note that providing these additional resources might increase the operation cost of the cloud, hence in practice the cloud may charge the users an additional fee; however, we do not consider this aspect here for simplicity.

Algorithmic Solution. We propose the following modified mechanism.. Jobs are scheduled via the original offline GreedyRTL allocation rule using their expected work volume as input. If the

job does not complete after utilizing $D_j^{\mathbb{E}}$ resource units, it is allocated additional resources. To accommodate demand uncertainties, the offline allocation rule should guarantee that a job exceeding its initial estimate may still be completed before the deadline, taking into account the parallelism bounds. To that end, jobs are scheduled according to deadlines which are set earlier than their true deadlines, leaving an empty gap per job in which additional resources can be generated to fully complete the job. Specifically, the offline allocation rule will schedule jobs according deadlines $d_j' = \lfloor d_j(1 - \delta/s) \rfloor$ earlier than the original deadlines d_j. Note that in the remaining $\lceil d_j(\delta/s) \rceil$ time slots, the cloud can allocate at least $D_j\delta$ resource units, since $d_j \geq s \cdot len_j = s \cdot \lceil D_j/k_j \rceil$, as required. However, a job that exceeding the multiplicative bound of $(1 + \delta)$ cannot be guaranteed completion by its deadline. We prove that the decrease in total value of the modified GreedyRTL is relatively small. To obtain this result, we use the dual solution (α, β, π) constructed in Section 3.3 to bound the gap between the value gained by the modified mechanism and the optimal social welfare (with respect to the original deadlines).

THEOREM 6.1. *Let RTL' denote the social welfare obtained by the modified GreedyRTL algorithm, and let OPT denote the optimal social welfare (with original deadlines). Then, $RTL' \geq \left(1 - \frac{\delta}{s} - \frac{1}{T}\right)\left(\frac{C-k}{C}\frac{s-1}{s}\right)OPT$.*

PROOF. (SKETCH). Denote by (α', β', π') the dual solution constructed by GreedyRTL matching reported deadlines d_j'. To bound the gap between RTL' and OPT, we construct a feasible solution (α, β, π) to the dual program matching the original deadlines d_j. Notice that the difference between the two dual programs are the additional cover inequalities $t \in (d_j', d_j]$ that need to be covered. Intuitively, we "stretch" the dual vectors β, π_j towards later time slots, by a stretch factor of $\left(1 - \frac{\delta}{s} - \frac{1}{T}\right)^{-1}$, which is a bound on the ratio $d_j/d_{j'}$, and obtain a feasible dual solution to the dual program matching the original deadlines d_j. The increased dual cost is a result of the dual solution being stretched. □

7. REFERENCES

[1] Ganesh Ananthanarayanan, Srikanth Kandula, Albert G. Greenberg, Ion Stoica, Yi Lu, Bikas Saha, and Edward Harris. Reining in the outliers in map-reduce clusters using mantri. In *OSDI*, pages 1–16. USENIX Association, 2010.

[2] Aaron Archer and Éva Tardos. Truthful mechanisms for one-parameter agents. In *FOCS*, pages 482–491, 2001.

[3] Aaron Archer and Robert Kleinberg. Characterizing truthful mechanisms with convex type spaces. *SIGecom Exchanges*, 7(3), 2008.

[4] Amotz Bar-Noy, Reuven Bar-Yehuda, Ari Freund, Joseph Naor, and Baruch Schieber. A unified approach to approximating resource allocation and scheduling. *Journal of the ACM (JACM)*, 48:1069–1090, 2001.

[5] Amotz Bar-Noy, Sudipto Guha, Joseph Naor, and Baruch Schieber. Approximating the throughput of multiple machines in real-time scheduling. *SIAM Journal of Computing*, 31(2):331–352, 2001.

[6] Sushil Bikhchandani, Shurojit Chatterji, Ron Lavi, Ahuva Muálem, Noam Nisam, and Arunava Sen. Weak monotonicity characterizes deterministic dominant strategy implementations. *Econometrica*, 74:1109–1132, 2006.

[7] Peter Brucker. *Scheduling Algorithms*. Springer, 4th edition, 2004.

[8] Yang Cai, Constantinos Daskalakis, and S. Matthew Weinberg. On optimal multidimensional mechanism design. *ACM SIGecom Exchanges*, 10(2):29–33, 2011.

[9] Robert D. Carr, Lisa K. Fleischer, Vitus J. Leung, and Cynthia A. Phillips. Strengthening integrality gaps for capacitated network design and covering problems. In *SODA*, pages 106–115, 2000.

[10] Uriel Feige and Moshe Tennenholtz. Mechanism design with uncertain inputs: (to err is human, to forgive divine). pages 549–558, 2011.

[11] Albert G. Greenberg, James R. Hamilton, David A. Maltz, and Parveen Patel. The cost of a cloud: research problems in data center networks. *ACM SIGCOMM Computer Communication Review*, 39(1):68–73, 2008.

[12] Mohammad Taghi Hajiaghayi, Robert Kleinberg, Mohammad Mahdian, and David C. Parkes. Online auctions with re-usable goods. pages 165–174, 2005.

[13] Navendu Jain, Ishai Menache, Joseph Naor, and Jonathan Yaniv. A truthful mechanism for value-based scheduling in cloud computing. In *SAGT*, pages 178–189, 2011.

[14] Ron Lavi and Chaitanya Swamy. Truthful mechanism design for multi-dimensional scheduling via cycle monotonicity. In *EC*, 2007.

[15] Eugene L. Lawler. A dynamic programming algorithm for preemptive scheduling of a single machine to minimize the number of late jobs. *Annals of Operation Research*, 26:125–133, 1991.

[16] Roger Myerson. Optimal auction design. In *Mathematics of Operations Research*, volume 6, pages 58–73, 1981.

[17] Noam Nisan and Amir Ronen. Algorithmic mechanism design. In *STOC*, 1999.

[18] Noam Nisan, Tim Roughgarden, Éva Tardos, and Vijay V. Vazirani. *Algorithmic game theory*. Cambridge University Press, 2007.

[19] Cynthia A. Phillips, R. N. Uma, and Joel Wein. Off-line admission control for general scheduling problems. In *SODA*, pages 879–888, 2000.

[20] Jean Charles Rochet. A necessary and sufficient condition for rationalizability in a quasi-linear context. *Journal of Mathematical Economics*, 16(2):191–200, 1987.

[21] Michael Saks and Lan Yu. Weak monotonicity suffices for truthfulness on convex domains. In *EC*, pages 286–293, 2005.

APPENDIX

A. SIMULATION SETUP

Our simulations evaluate the performance of the mechanisms over a set of 415 jobs, taken from empirical job traces of a large batch computing cluster. The original workload consists of MapReduce jobs, comprising multiple phases with the constraint that phase $i + 1$ can only start after phase i has finished. The available information includes the runtime of the job ($totTime$), the overall amount of consumed CPU hours ($totCPUHours$), the total number of servers allocated to it ($totServers$), the number of phases ($numPhases$) and the maximum number of servers allocated to a job per phase ($maxServersPerPhase$). Since our model is not a MapReduce model, we had to adjust the raw data that was available to us, while preserving the workload characteristics. We describe below the details of the simulation choices we made.

Demand D_j. We took the $totCPUHours$ field to represent the demand of the job.

Parallelism bound k_j. Since the cloud capacity is given in units of server hours per time slot, the parallelism bound must be given in server CPU hour units as well. The data available to us does not contain information on the actual running time per job of each of servers allocated to it. Therefore, we gave the following estimated parallelism bound: We calculated the average length of a phase ($totTime/numPhases$) and averaged the maximal servers per phase ($maxServersPerPhase$) over the average length of the phase. To translate servers into CPU hours, we took the average amount of CPU hours per server to be the total amount of CPU hours ($totCPUHours$) divided by the total number of servers ($totServers$):

$$k_j = \frac{maxServersPerPhase}{(totTime/numPhases)} \cdot \frac{totCPUHours}{totServers}.$$

Values v_j **and deadlines** d_j. Our job traces do not contain any information regarding job deadlines nor any indication on the value of the job. Hence, we synthetically generate them as follows. The deadline is set according the effective length of the job, defined as $len_j = \lceil D_j/k_j \rceil$, multiplied by the slackness parameter s. The value of the job is uniformly drawn from $[0, 1]$.

Cloud parameters C, T. The cloud capacity is set according to the total demand, so that the total demand would exceed the total amount of available resources. T is set according to the maximal deadline.

Hedonic Clustering Games

[Extended Abstract]

Moran Feldman
CS Dept., Technion
Haifa, Israel
moranfe@cs.technion.ac.il

Liane Lewin-Eytan
IBM Haifa Research Lab.
Haifa, Israel
lianel@il.ibm.com

Joseph (Seffi) Naor*
CS Dept., Technion
Haifa, Israel
naor@cs.technion.ac.il

ABSTRACT

Clustering, the partitioning of objects with respect to a similarity measure, has been extensively studied as a global optimization problem. We investigate clustering from a game theoretic approach, and consider the class of *hedonic clustering games*. Here, a *self organized* clustering is obtained via decisions made by independent players, corresponding to the elements clustered. Being a hedonic setting, the utility of each player is determined by the identity of the other members of her cluster. This class of games seems to be quite robust, as it fits with rather different, yet commonly used, clustering criteria. Specifically, we investigate hedonic clustering games in two different models: *fixed clustering*, which subdivides into k-median and k-center, and *correlation clustering*. We provide a thorough and non-trivial analysis of these games, characterizing Nash equilibria, and proving upper and lower bounds on the price of anarchy and price of stability. For fixed clustering we focus on the existence of a Nash equilibrium, as it is a rather non-trivial issue in this setting. We study it both for general metrics and special cases, such as line and tree metrics. In the correlation clustering model, we study both minimization and maximization variants, and provide almost tight bounds on both price of anarchy and price of stability.

Categories and Subject Descriptors

C.2.4 [**Computer Systems Organization**]: Computer-Communication Networks—*Distributed Systems*

General Terms

Theory, Performance

Keywords

Clustering Games, Hedonic Games, Price of Anarchy, Price of Stability

*Work supported in part by the Technion-Micorsoft Electronic Commerce Research Center and by ISF grant 954/11.

Permission to make digital or hard copies of all or part of this work for personal or classroom use is granted without fee provided that copies are not made or distributed for profit or commercial advantage and that copies bear this notice and the full citation on the first page. To copy otherwise, to republish, to post on servers or to redistribute to lists, requires prior specific permission and/or a fee.
SPAA'12, June 25–27, 2012, Pittsburgh, Pennsylvania, USA.
Copyright 2012 ACM 978-1-4503-1213-4/12/06 ...$10.00.

1. INTRODUCTION

Clustering is the partitioning of objects or elements with respect to a similarity measure. The greater is the similarity of elements belonging to a cluster, or the distance between elements belonging to different clusters, the "better" is the clustering. Clustering has been extensively treated as a global optimization problem, employing a variety of optimization methods. We adopt here a novel game theoretic approach, and consider a setting in which a *self organized* clustering is obtained from decisions taken by independent players. We assume that the players correspond to the elements clustered, and their goal is to maximize their own utility functions. From the perspective of a single player, the quality, or the utility of a clustering, depends on the player's similarity to elements in her own cluster and perhaps on dissimilarity to elements in other clusters.

Our clustering games belong to the well known class of *hedonic* games, introduced in the Economics literature as a model of coalition formation. In a hedonic game, the utility of a player is solely determined by the identity of the players belonging to her coalition, and is independent of the partition of the other players into coalitions. Hedonic games were first introduced and analyzed by [11] in the context of cooperative games, and were motivated by situations in which individuals carry out joint activities as coalitions. Examples of such situations are individuals organizing themselves in groups for consumption or production purposes, or individuals relying upon local communities for the provisioning of public goods. Thus, hedonic games can be used to model settings arising in a wide variety of social, economic, and political problems, ranging from communication and trade to legislative voting. See [7] for a discussion of several real-life situations fitting the hedonic model. The notion of stability in hedonic games has been investigated both from cooperative, as well as non-cooperative, aspects [3, 7, 5]. The non-cooperative framework makes sense in environments lacking a social planner, or if the cost of coordinating movements is high. We note that most work on hedonic games has mainly focused on the existence of stable coalition partitions, whether core stable or individually stable, and on the complexity of finding such outcomes.

We investigate non-cooperative hedonic clustering games, in which elements are independent selfish players. Each player joins a group maximizing her utility, and the resulting clustering is the outcome of the choices of all players. We present a case study of two different well-known clustering models, with commonly used utility functions. The first model is *fixed clustering*, in which the number of clusters is fixed, and each cluster has a *centroid* whose position is determined by the identity of the cluster members. A player's utility depends on the location of the *centroid* of her cluster. The second model is *correlation clustering*, in which a player's utility depends on her similarity to other elements in her cluster as well as on her dissimilarity to elements in other clusters. In general, various settings in which players form clusters, and then each cluster provides a public good, or a service from a set of available alternatives, is captured by hedonic clustering games. Following are two motivating examples coming from different application areas.

In an ad-hoc (or sensor) network there is a large number of *autonomous devices* which are spread over a geographic area and wish to communicate with each other. In order to establish communication, devices invest transmission power which depends on the physical distance between them. Power is a critical resource for battery-limited devices, and thus the goal of each device is to minimize its transmission power and save on battery time. Fixed clustering is a proven method for enhancing energy efficiency and lifetime of large ad-hoc networks, and has been extensively studied in this context [1, 2]. Proposed clustering protocols organize the devices in data aggregation clusters to reduce network traffic. Each cluster has a center that receives data from other devices in the cluster, and sends it beyond the cluster limits, possibly after aggregating the received data and reducing its volume. A device will then join a cluster having the closest center to minimize the power needed for transmission, thus leading to a game-theoretic setting. We note that clustering in ad-hoc networks has been studied from a game-theoretic perspective in [19], yet their game definition is completely different from ours.

In online web advertising, publishers wish to join advertising services. Publishers are partitioned into clusters, and each cluster provides a different type of advertising service to its members. The type of service a cluster offers is derived from the attributes of its members, where possible attributes are, *e.g.*, fields of specialization, geographical area, organization size, types of product and annual budget. Publishers join or leave a cluster depending on the advertising service that the cluster offers and on the attributes of its members. For example, a new and relatively small business would prefer not to be coupled with a well-known large company specializing in a similar field. Thus, the utility of each player (publisher) depends on her similarity to the cluster, *i.e.*, how close are her advertising needs to the service provided by the cluster, and on her dissimilarity to players in other clusters (in the latter case, small and large businesses would be considered dissimilar). This is precisely the type of utility captured by correlation clustering.

Despite extensive work on clustering, not much work has been done from a game theoretic perspective, and we believe that this work contributes in that direction. We emphasize that the focus of our paper is not on a specific setting, but rather on the study of the general game theoretic framework in the context of hedonic clustering games.

1.1 Our Model

Our clustering problems are defined on a set of n points lying in a metric space with a distance function $d(\cdot, \cdot)$. The points correspond to selfish, non-cooperative, players (or users) moving between clusters at will. Players within a cluster are provided a service depending on the set of play-

ers belonging to it. A player achieves a utility from being a member of a cluster, and will naturally join the one maximizing her utility (or minimizing her cost). The notion of *social welfare* (or *social cost*) corresponds to the overall utility achieved by the system (or overall cost). The strategies of a player in a clustering game correspond to the set of clusters to which she can belong. Every choice of strategies by the players partitions them into clusters, and is called a *clustering configuration*. A Nash equilibrium[1] of the clustering game corresponds to a clustering configuration in which no user can unilaterally increase her utility (reduce her cost) by changing clusters. We investigate the clustering game in two different models: *fixed clustering* and *correlation clustering*.

Fixed Clustering.

In a fixed clustering game, the number of clusters is known beforehand and is denoted by k. Each cluster C has a *centroid*, $c(C)$, defined to be the element minimizing the cost of the cluster. We consider two well-known definitions in the clustering literature, known as *k-median* and *k-center*. In the k-median clustering problem, the cost of a cluster is defined as the sum of distances between all members of the cluster and its centroid. The centroid is thus defined as $c(C) = \arg\min_{u \in C} \left\{ \sum_{v \in C} d(u, v) \right\}$. In the k-center clustering problem, the cost of a cluster is defined by its radius, *i.e.*, the maximum distance between an element in the cluster and its center. Hence, the centroid is $c(C) = \arg\min_{u \in C} \left\{ \max_{v \in C} d(u, v) \right\}$. We note that in both models the choice of a centroid might not be unique, and therefore a tie-breaking rule is needed. We elaborate on this issue later on.

In both models, the strategy space of a player is defined by the k clusters. Each player v chooses the cluster C that minimizes her distance to the centroid $c(C^{+v})$, where C^{+v} denotes the cluster C with the addition of player v. Note that following v's addition to C, the centroid of C might change, *i.e.*, it might be that $c(C) \neq c(C^{+v})$. For k-median, the social cost is defined to be the sum of costs of all the clusters, whereas for k-center the social cost is defined to be the maximum cost of a cluster.

In fixed clustering, the service offered by a cluster is represented by its centroid. The example of ad-hoc networks fits this model, since the centroid is the node to which transmissions within a cluster are sent, and transmission costs depend on the distances to the centroid.

Correlation Clustering.

In settings where only the relationship among objects is known, correlation clustering is a natural approach. Unlike most clustering formulations, specifying the number of clusters as a separate parameter is not necessary. We assume that the similarity metric is captured by a distance metric $d(\cdot, \cdot) \in [0, 1]$. If $d(u, v) \approx 0$, then u and v are very similar, and if $d(u, v) = 1$, then they are highly distinctive, unrelated elements. Each element v has a weight w_v denoting its "measure of influence" on other elements. Elements wish to be clustered with similar elements of high weight, and to be partitioned away from unrelated elements of high weight. Since the number of clusters is not fixed, the possible strate-

---

[1]We consider in this paper only pure Nash equilibria.

gies of a player are either to join an existing cluster, or to create a new cluster and become its sole member.

Given an element v, denote by C_v its cluster in a given configuration. Typically, two variants are studied in correlation clustering. In the *minimization variant*, the objective of each element v is to minimize its cost $\sum_{u \in C_v} w_u \cdot d(u,v) + \sum_{u \notin C_v} w_u \cdot (1 - d(u,v))$, *i.e.*, an element pays for being in a cluster with unrelated nodes of high weight, and for being partitioned away from similar elements of high weight. The *social cost* is defined as the sum of the costs paid by all elements. In the *maximization* variant, the objective of each node is to maximize its utility $\sum_{u \in C_v} w_u \cdot (1 - d(u,v)) + \sum_{u \notin C_v} w_u \cdot d(u,v)$, *i.e.*, an element achieves utility from being in a cluster with similar nodes of high weight and from being partitioned away from unrelated nodes of high weight. Again, the *social welfare* is the sum of the utilities achieved by all elements.

Correlation clustering essentially models scenarios in which the objective is to either minimize the difference or maximize the similarity among objects within clusters. This type of clustering depends on the relationship among elements. The advertising example fits this model if distances between objects represent willingness to be clients of the same advertising service, and weights represent market influence.

1.2 Our Contribution

We provide a thorough and non-trivial analysis of hedonic clustering games under several models, characterizing Nash equilibria, and proving upper and lower bounds on price of anarchy and price of stability[2]. Our study covers a broad subclass of hedonic games which seems to lack previous investigation from a game theoretic perspective. This subclass captures clustering as a self organizing process governed by game theoretic considerations. We note that it is important to study clustering games in several models, since it is a diverse subject, and cannot be captured by a single framework [6]. Our models seem to have quite a robust definition, as they fit well with rather different, yet commonly used, clustering criteria.

The first clustering model we consider is fixed clustering. For a general metric, we show that Nash equilibrium does not necessarily exist. Clearly, imposing high enough penalties on players for changing the location of a centroid (when moving to a different cluster) would guarantee the existence of Nash equilibrium for both k-median and k-center models. We prove that setting the penalty to be equal to the distance traveled by the centroid suffices. This choice of penalty is very natural, and can be thought of as a fee imposed by a cluster on nodes joining it, in order to cover the incurred expenses. This choice of penalty also resembles the way costs are determined by the VCG mechanism [16].

Since Nash equilibrium does not necessarily exist in general, we study the fixed clustering game in specific metrics, *i.e.*, tree and line metrics. The strict definition of hedonic games requires that the members of a cluster uniquely determine the location of its centroid. To achieve that one needs to specify some (possibly arbitrary) static tie-breaking rules. However, there exist instances for which no Nash equi-

librium exists under any choice of a static tie-breaking rule, even for line metrics. We circumvent this issue by using tie-breaking rules that are *history dependent*; when the choice of a centroid is not unique, it depends on the previous states of the system.[3] In this respect, our work on fixed clustering deviates from the class of hedonic games. However, we emphasize that even if fixed clustering games were strictly hedonic, our results would not have followed from existing literature.

The proof of existence of Nash equilibrium in a tree metric for the k-median model is rather involved and non-trivial. It is based on a characterization of a centroid, definition of a potential function, and a judiciously chosen schedule of moves of players resulting in equilibrium. We note that for the k-center model, the proof of existence of Nash equilibrium under tree metrics requires allowing centroids to be located in an arbitrary location between the two end points of an edge. We believe that this relaxation is not necessary (as is the case for line metric), but we have not managed to prove that. For both the k-median and k-center models, we show that the price of stability is 1, while the price of anarchy is unbounded.

Going back to the example of ad-hoc networks, from a designer's perspective, our work implies that simple greedy-like algorithms are sufficient for reaching Nash equilibrium, and thus the devices do not need to run more sophisticated protocols.

The second clustering model we consider is correlation clustering, for which we obtain results for both minimization and maximization variants. This model is closely related to additively-separable hedonic games [13], and techniques used for this class of games can be extended to show that Nash equilibria always exist for correlation clustering games, but finding them is PLS-complete.

Our main results for correlation clustering games are lower and upper bounds on both the price of anarchy and price of stability. The bounds are proved by characterizing the distance between nodes belonging to the same cluster vs. the distance between nodes belonging to different clusters. The specific bounds are:

- In the special case of equal node weight, the price of stability is 1 for both the minimization and maximization variants. For arbitrary weights, the price of stability is strictly larger than 1.

- For the minimization variant, an upper bound on the price of anarchy is $O(n^2)$ and the corresponding lower bound is $n - 1$. For the special case of equal nodes weight, the lower bound still holds, and there is an improved upper bound of $n-1$ on the price of anarchy.

- For the maximization variant, the price of anarchy is $\Theta(\sqrt{n})$. This bound holds even if all nodes have equal weight and the metric is a tree metric. In case of a line metric, the price of anarchy is $\Theta(n^{1/3})$, even for equal nodes weight.

For both the fixed clustering and correlation clustering models, an intriguing question is what kind of mechanisms can be used to reduce the price of anarchy. We make a first

---

[2]Price of stability is defined as the ratio between the social value of the *best* Nash equilibrium and the social optimal solution, while price of anarchy is defined as the ratio between the social value of the *worst* Nash equilibrium and the social optimal solution.

[3]The history of the system is one of the parameters for our tie-breaking rules. For a one-shot game, these rules reduce to static tie-breaking rules.

step in this direction by showing that the price of anarchy of the maximization variant of correlation clustering can be bounded by k (for $k \geq 2$) by limiting the game to k clusters. Moreover, if all node weights are equal, this constraint can be removed after the game reaches a Nash equilibrium, and the price of anarchy still remains at most k.

Previous work.

Clustering is a vast area of research with abundant results, and therefore we mention only a few, directly related, results. Fixed clustering is the classic approach to clustering data and the goal of the optimization problem is to find a partitioning of the nodes to k clusters, such that the cost is minimized. The k-center problem was considered by Gonzalez [14], who gave the first 2-approximation algorithm (see also the 2-approximation algorithm of [17].) For the k-median problem, the first constant factor algorithm was given by [8]. The approximation factor has since been improved in a sequence of papers (see, *e.g.*, [23]). We note that in case of a tree metric, k-median can be solved optimally in polynomial time [22].

Correlation clustering was first defined by [4]. They considered the version where the edges of a complete graph are labelled as either "+" (similar) or "-" (different), and the goal is to find a partition of the nodes into clusters that agrees as much as possible with the edge labels. They considered both maximizing agreements and minimizing disagreements, obtaining a constant factor approximation for the former and a PTAS for the latter. These results were generalized for real-valued edge weights; [10, 12, 9] obtained a logarithmic approximation algorithm for the minimization version and [9] obtained a constant (greater than 1/2) factor approximation for the maximization version.

From game-theoretic perspectives, in addition to being a hedonic game, our correlation clustering game falls into a class known as *polymatrix games*, introduced by Yanovskaya [24]. Few other games that fall into both classes were also considered. We mention only those that are most closely related to our model. Hoefer [18] considered a game called "MaxAgree" which is equivalent to the maximization variant of our correlation clustering game with equal node weights and a limit ℓ on the number of possible clusters. For this game [18] shows that best response dynamics converge in polynomial time to Nash equilibrium (which does not seem likely in our model), and gives bounds on the price of anarchy. Another example is the game version of Max-Cut, considered by multiple works, *e.g.*, [18, 15], and, in a sense, is the inverse of our model.

A different game theoretic representation of clustering is given by [20, 21], however, their approach is completely different from ours.

2. FIXED CLUSTERING

In this section we consider the fixed clustering game in which the number of clusters is known beforehand, and is denoted by k. We investigate both the k-median and k-center variants of this model. In both variants, given the set of nodes in a cluster, the choice of a centroid may not be unique. As already mentioned, in order to fit perfectly into the hedonic model, a static tie-breaking rule for choosing a unique centroid is required. However, such tie breaking rules may have a negative impact on our results, as demonstrated by Theorem 2.1.

THEOREM 2.1. *With (static) tie breaking rules, there may not exist Nash equilibrium for both the k-median and k-center variants, even for line metrics with three nodes.*

We circumvent this issue by analyzing game dynamics that allow tie-breaking rules which are *history dependent*. Initially, an arbitrary static tie breaking rule R is used. (Rule R also applies to a one shot game.) During the dynamics, whenever a player performs a move and changes her strategy, each centroid remains at the same node if it is still a valid location for a centroid; otherwise, the static tie breaking rule R is used to relocate it. The use of a history dependent rule implies that the cost observed by a player does not solely depend on the identity of the other players in her cluster, but also on the history of the game. We can thus consider the fixed clustering model as a hedonic game with an additional attribute.

Due to space limitations, most proofs of this section are omitted.

2.1 The k-Median Model

In the k-median model, the cost of a cluster C is defined as the sum of the distances between all members of the cluster and its centroid, and the centroid $c(C)$ is defined as the node minimizing the cost of the cluster, that is, $c(C) = \min_{u \in C} \left\{ \sum_{v \in C} d(u, v) \right\}$. We denote by $D(u, C)$ the sum of distances between u and the other nodes in C. Thus, $c(C) = \min_{u \in C} D(u, C)$. For ease of notation, we denote by $D(C)$ the cost of a cluster C, that is, $D(C) = D(c(C), C)$.

The cost of a node v in the k-median clustering game is defined as its distance from the centroid of its cluster, $d(v, c(C_v))$. A clustering configuration of the k-median clustering game is a Nash equilibrium if no player can reduce its cost by choosing a different cluster, assuming the other players stay in their cluster. We assume a node v changes its strategy from cluster C_1 to C_2 only in case it strictly decreases its distance to the center, that is $d(v, c(C_1)) > d(v, c(C_2^{+v}))$. As mentioned, we assume that following a move performed by a player, the centroid of a cluster will not change its location unless forced (*i.e.*, only in case the sum of distances of the points from the new location of the centroid is strictly lower than from its previous location).

We first consider the general metric case, and prove that Nash equilibrium does not necessarily exist. Moreover, we show that this is the case even if centroids are allowed to be located at any location along edges, rather than only at a node of their own cluster. Then, we notice that by imposing a high enough penalty on a node whose move to a cluster changes the location of its centroid, Nash equilibrium is guaranteed to exist. Moreover, we show that it is enough to set the penalty to be equal to the distance traveled by the centroid. Motivated by these results, we study the game in line and tree metrics, and show that in these cases Nash equilibrium always exists, with no further assumptions such as penalties. Note that the existence of Nash equilibrium in the line case is implied by our result for the tree case. Still, we consider line metrics separately, since we can show that best response dynamics converge to equilibrium.

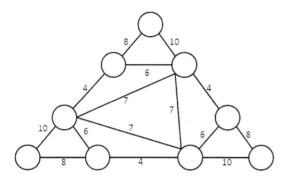

Figure 1: Graph with no Nash equilibrium (assuming two clusters).

2.1.1 The General Metric Case

For a general metric, there is no guarantee that a Nash equilibrium exists. Figure 1 displays a graph representing a metric having no Nash equilibria, assuming there are two clusters. The numbers on the edges of the graph represent the distances. The proof that no Nash equilibrium exists for this graph is done via a case analysis, showing that any selection of two nodes to be the centroids of the clusters results in a configuration where either a cluster has a non optimal centroid choice, or there is a node wishing to deviate.

A natural way to try to guarantee the existence of a Nash equilibrium is by allowing the centroid of a cluster to be located at any location along an edge of the graph. Formally, every edge (u, v) and $\lambda \in [0, 1]$ represents a possible location for a centroid. The distance of this centroid from a node w is $\min\{d(u, w) + \lambda \cdot d(u, v), d(v, w) + (1 - \lambda) \cdot d(u, v)\}$. The centroid of the cluster is placed at the location minimizing the sum of distances from the nodes of the cluster. Unfortunately, this generalization fails to guarantee the existence of a Nash equilibrium. The graph in Figure 1 represents a counter example for this case as well. In order to establish the counter example based on this graph, we use the notation of weak Nash equilibria.

Our original definition of Nash equilibrium states that a centroid will not change location unless forced. If the centroid is forced to change location, it might have multiple locations to which it can move. The choice among these possible new locations is based on some arbitrary tie breaking rule. On the other hand, a configuration is said to be in *weak Nash equilibrium* if there is no node u wishing to deviate to any cluster $C \neq C_u$, given that following u's deviation, C's centroid will move to the location farthest away from u among its possible locations. In other words, if there are multiple possible locations for the centroid of C after u's move, then the centroid will move to the worst location from the point of view of u. Moreover, this move occurs even if the original location of the centroid is still a possible location for it.

Clearly, every Nash equilibrium is also a weak Nash equilibrium, though the reverse is not necessarily true. We can show that the graph in Figure 1 allows no weak Nash equilibria with two clusters; and therefore, it also does not allow any Nash equilibria (assuming two clusters). The proof is established by case analysis, and is based on Theorem 2.2, where we show that it is sufficient to consider only half integral locations on edges as optional placements for centroids.

THEOREM 2.2. *An instance of the k-median clustering game with integral edge distances has a weak Nash equilibrium if and only if it has a weak Nash equilibrium configuration in which centroids are placed in half integral locations on edges.*

In order to guarantee the existence of Nash equilibrium, we add a rule penalizing a node whose move to a cluster C changes the location of the centroid of C. That is, the cost of a node u performing an improvement move will consist of two values:

- The distance from the updated centroid of the new cluster, $d(u, c(C^{+u}))$.

- A cost equal to the distance between the original and new centroids of C, $d(c(C), c(C^{+u}))$.

Intuitively, one can think of this choice of a penalty as a fee imposed by a cluster on nodes joining it, in order to cover the incurred expenses. Note that the total cost of the nodes in the cluster deserted by u can only decrease.

LEMMA 2.3. *Under the above penalties, a node u will only deviate from cluster C_1 to cluster C_2 if its distance from the original location of the centroid $c(C_2)$ is shorter than its distance from $c(C_1)$.*

Lemma 2.3 implies that the above penalizing rule prevents a node from deviating unless the deviation results in an improved social value. Since the social value cannot improve forever, the game must converge to Nash equilibrium. The following theorem formalizes this argument.

THEOREM 2.4. *Under the above penalties, every best response move strictly decreases the social cost. Hence, there always exists Nash equilibrium, and it is guaranteed to be reached by best response dynamics.*

COROLLARY 2.5. *Under the above penalties, the price of stability is 1.*

PROOF. By Theorem 2.4, the social cost is guaranteed to decrease with every best response move. Thus, the optimal solution must be a Nash equilibrium. □

Note that Nash equilibrium in the setting without penalties is also valid with penalties (as penalties can only decrease the benefit of a move). The price of anarchy for this case is unbounded, as shown next.

THEOREM 2.6. *The price of anarchy of the k-median clustering game is unbounded, even for a line metric.*

PROOF. Consider a line with three nodes at locations 0, 1 and M, for some large M, and assume $k = 2$. There are two clusters $\{0\}$ and $\{1, M\}$, and the centroid of the second cluster is the node 1. Clearly this is a Nash equilibrium, since the only node which is not a centroid will gain nothing by deviating. However, the cost of this equilibrium is M. On the other hand, the optimal solution has the following two clusters: $\{0, 1\}$ and $\{M\}$, yielding a cost of 1. The price of anarchy of this instance is thus M. □

2.1.2 The Line Metric Case

We prove that if players are nodes on a line, Nash equilibrium always exists (without penalties, and allowing a centroid to be placed only at a node). We begin by characterizing the centroid of a cluster on a line.

LEMMA 2.7. *The centroid of a cluster on a line is a median[4] of all nodes in the cluster.*

In case the number of nodes in a cluster is odd, there exists a single median node. Thus, this node is the single optional centroid node, and divides the other nodes in the cluster to right and left sets where each set contains $(m-1)/2$ nodes. In case the number of nodes in a cluster is even, there are two optional centroid nodes. These are two consecutive nodes on the line, each dividing the nodes to right and left sets such that one of the sets contains $\lceil \frac{m-1}{2} \rceil$ nodes and the other set contains $\lfloor \frac{m-1}{2} \rfloor$ nodes.

Given a clustering configuration $\mathcal{F}$, we define a potential function Φ, and show that it strictly decreases with each strategy change performed by a player. We assume a player changes her strategy only if it strictly decreases her distance to the center. The potential function is equal to the social cost function, that is

$$\Phi(\mathcal{F}) = \sum_{i=1}^{k} \sum_{v \in C_i} d(v, c(C_i)) . \qquad (1)$$

The following lemma is proved using the characterization of the centroid given by Lemma 2.7.

LEMMA 2.8. *The potential function Φ strictly decreases during the clustering game's natural dynamics.*

As the strategy space of all nodes is finite, the potential function will decrease following each move performed by a node until reaching a local (or global) minimum, corresponding to Nash equilibrium.

COROLLARY 2.9. *Nash equilibrium always exists for the k-median clustering game on a line.*

2.1.3 The Tree Metric Case

We assume here that the distances are defined by a tree metric, and the players are exactly the nodes of the tree. We prove that in this case, a Nash equilibrium always exists. First, we characterize the centroid node of a cluster for the tree case. To this end we define the *median node of a tree* as follows.

DEFINITION 2.10. *Given a tree T with $|V|$ nodes, a node $v^* \in T$ is called a median node if its removal partitions T into connected components of size at most $\lceil \frac{|V|-1}{2} \rceil$ each.*

The following lemma is well known.

LEMMA 2.11. *There are at most 2 median nodes in a tree.*

In order to define the relation between a median and the centroid of a cluster, we use the next definition.

DEFINITION 2.12. *A cluster C has the closure property if all nodes on each path between two nodes of C belong to C as well.*

LEMMA 2.13. *The centroid of a cluster with the closure property in a tree is a median node of the cluster.*

---

[4]A median node of a cluster is a cluster node for which the number of cluster nodes to its left and to its right differ by at most 1.

In order to prove that the k-median clustering game always has a Nash equilibrium, we use the potential function of Equation (1), and describe a schedule that converges to equilibrium. Unlike the line metric case, we cannot simply use the potential function for each improvement move performed by a node, since the closure property can easily be violated by a best response move. Instead, we need to define a set of moves that keep the closure property, allowing us to use the median characterization of centroids, and that are guaranteed to strictly decrease the potential function.

We describe the convergence schedule. It consists of iterations, where each iteration starts and ends with a clustering configuration in which all clusters have the closure property. We call such a configuration a *closed configuration*. Starting from a closed configuration, consider a node v in cluster C_1 wishing to move to cluster C_2. All nodes on the path between v and $c(C_2)$, denoted by $\delta(v, c(C_2))$, are either already in C_2 or wish to move to C_2 as well (if there are other clusters with equal distance to centroid, we choose C_2). This follows since nodes in $\delta(v, c(C_2))$ are closer than v is to $c(C_2^{+v})$. Note that the center of C_2 will be in the same way given that any node of $\delta(v, c(C_2))$ moves to C_2. In addition, if there is a node $w \in \delta(v, c(C_2))$ having a better cluster C_m such that $d(w, c(C_m^{+w})) < d(w, c(C_2^{+w}))$, then the same holds for v as well since: $d(v, c(C_m^{+v})) \leq d(w, c(C_m^{+w})) + d(w, v) < d(w, c(C_2^{+w})) + d(w, v) = d(v, C_2^{+v})$.

Thus, when starting a new iteration of the schedule, we choose a node u adjacent to C_2, and make it perform a best response move from C_1 to C_2 (we call this move "first best response"). Following this move, there are two options. In case C_1^{-u} remains connected, then it still has the closure property, and we can select a new first best response (assuming we did not reach Nash equilibrium). Otherwise, C_1^{-u} contains multiple connected components, and there is a component C_1' containing the centroid of C_1^{-u}. Let C_1'' denote $C_1^{-u} - C_1'$, *i.e.*, C_1'' contains all nodes of C_1 except for the node that made the first best response (u) and the nodes of the connected component containing C_1^{-u}'s centroid (that is, C_1'). Next, we move all nodes of C_1'' to cluster C_2, and finish the iteration. Note that beside the "first best response" move, all other moves in the iteration need not be best response moves.

Both C_1' and $C_2 \cup \{u\} \cup C_1''$ are closed clusters. No other cluster is affected by the iteration, hence, by the end of the iteration, we get back to a closed configuration. We are now ready to use our potential function, and show that it strictly decreases with each iteration of the above schedule. We conceptually divide the iteration into three steps, and show that none of them can increase the potential function, and at least one of them strictly decreases it. The three steps are as follows.

1. The first best response move made by u, including the possible relocation of the clusters' centroids.

2. The move of the nodes of C_1'' to C_2, assuming the clusters' centroids are not allowed to move.

3. A possible move of the clusters' centroids to new locations (following the move of the nodes of C_1'').

LEMMA 2.14. *In step 1 of the iteration, the potential function P strictly decreases.*

PROOF. We consider a node u moving from C_1 to C_2, and show that the sum of distances from all nodes in C_1^{-u} and

C_2^{+u} to their respective centers decreases. This is clearly true for u (the distance strictly decreases since u had an incentive to move) as well as for C_1^{-u} (as the centroid of C_1^{-u} is relocated in order to minimize its total distance from the cluster's nodes). As for C_2, observe that it has the closure property by the above schedule, hence Lemma 2.13 applies. We consider two cases. Let $Q_1, \ldots, Q_m$ denote the connected components in C_2 formed after the removal of $c(C_2)$.

1. Node u joins a connected component Q_j of size at most $\left\lceil \frac{|C_2|}{2} \right\rceil - 1$ in C_2. Then, after it joins C_2, $c(C_2)$ remains a median node of C_2^{+u} and thus the centroid remains at the same location.

2. Node u joins a connected component Q_j of size $\left\lceil \frac{|C_2|}{2} \right\rceil$ in C_2. This can occur if $|C_2|$ is even, and then $\left\lceil \frac{|C_2|}{2} \right\rceil = \left\lceil \frac{|C_2|-1}{2} \right\rceil$ and Q_j is a maximal connected component. In this case, there are two optional centroids (median nodes) in C_2, that is $c(C_2)$ and $v_{in}(Q_j)$ (the entry point to the connected component Q_j). Clearly, $D(c(C_2), C_2) = D(v_{in}(Q_j), C_2)$. Now, after v joins Q_j, the centroid is forced to move to $v_{in}(Q_j)$, but the total distance of the vertices in C_2 from their centroid remains unchanged. $\square$

LEMMA 2.15. *In steps 2 and 3 of the iteration, the potential function P cannot increase.*

COROLLARY 2.16. *The potential function P strictly decreases in each iteration of the above schedule.*

As the strategy space of all players is finite, the potential function decreases following each iteration performed by the schedule, until reaching a local minimum (or global), corresponding to Nash equilibrium.

COROLLARY 2.17. *Nash equilibrium always exists for the k-median clustering game in a tree.*

We consider only dynamics of closed configurations. The next lemma states that it is not restrictive.

LEMMA 2.18. *For any configuration of the clustering game on a tree, there always exists a closed configuration which is at least as good with respect to the social cost.*

As the potential function of the game is equal to the objective function, an optimal k-clustering closed configuration for the k-median model is also in Nash equilibrium (no move can further decrease the global minimum point of the objective function). Moreover, following Lemma 2.18, the cost of such a configuration is equal to the cost of an optimal configuration. We thus get the following corollary.

COROLLARY 2.19. *The price of stability of the clustering game in a tree is 1.*

Note that since a constant-approximation for the k-median problem (or even an optimal one for tree metrics) can be computed in polynomial time, a Nash equilibrium with a price of anarchy $O(1)$ can be guaranteed by setting the initial configuration to be such an approximate solution, converting it to a closed configuration, and then scheduling the moves as described above until reaching equilibrium. Since the cost of the clustering configuration strictly decreases along the process, it will reach Nash equilibrium with price of anarchy $O(1)$.

2.2 The k-Center Model

In the k-center model, the cost of a cluster C is defined by its radius, which is the maximal distance between its centroid and a node of the cluster. The centroid $c(C)$ is defined as the node minimizing the cost of the cluster, that is, $c(C) = \min_{u \in C} \left\{ \max_{v \in C} d(u, v) \right\}$. The cost of a node v in the k-center clustering game is defined as its distance from the centroid of its cluster, $d(v, c(C_v))$. A clustering configuration of the k-center clustering game is in Nash equilibrium if no user can reduce its cost by choosing a different cluster, assuming the other users stay in their individual clusters.

We first consider the case of a line metric, and prove that Nash equilibrium always exists. Then, we turn to tree metrics, and guarantee the existence of Nash equilibrium in case centroids can be placed anywhere along edges. Finally, we consider general metrics, and prove that Nash equilibrium does not necessarily exist, even if centroids are allowed to be placed at any location along edges. We note that by imposing a high enough penalty on a node whose move affects the location of the target cluster's centroid, existence of Nash equilibrium is guaranteed. We further show that setting the penalty to be equal to the distance traveled by the centroid is enough. As for the price of anarchy, we show it is unbounded in all settings considered.

2.2.1 The Line and Tree Metric Cases

THEOREM 2.20. *Nash equilibrium always exists for the k-center clustering game on a line.*

We suspect that Nash equilibrium also always exists in tree metrics, and best response dynamics are guaranteed to reach it. However, we manage to prove this only in case the centroid of a cluster is allowed to be placed at any location along an edge (rather than only at a node). Formally, every edge (u, v) and $\lambda \in [0, 1]$ represent a possible location for a centroid. The distance of this centroid from a node w is $\min\{d(u, w) + \lambda \cdot d(u, v), d(v, w) + (1 - \lambda) \cdot d(u, v)\}$. The centroid of the cluster is placed at the location minimizing the maximum distance from a node of the cluster. Note that the centroid could be located at a node which does not belong to its cluster, however, the configuration may be stable only if this node is also the centroid of its own cluster.

LEMMA 2.21. *In case centroids are allowed to be placed on edges, the centroid of a cluster is always located in the middle of its diameter (since we are dealing with a tree metric, all diameters share their middle point).*

The following theorem is proved using the characterization of the centroid given by Lemma 2.21.

THEOREM 2.22. *In case centroids are allowed to be on edges, Nash equilibrium always exists for tree metrics and it is guaranteed to be reached by best response dynamics.*

THEOREM 2.23. *In case centroids are allowed to be on edges, the price of anarchy of the k-center clustering game remains unbounded, even for the case of a line metric.*

2.2.2 The General Metric Case

Similarly to the k-median model, Nash equilibrium might not exist for the case of a general metric. Figure 2 represents

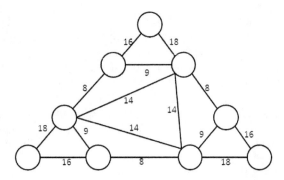

Figure 2: Graph with no Nash equilibria (assuming two clusters).

an instance that does not have a Nash equilibrium, assuming there are two clusters. The numbers on the edges of the graph represent the distances. The proof that no Nash equilibrium exists for this graph is established similarly as for the graph in Figure 1.

One can try, again, the trick that worked for tree metrics, *i.e.*, allow the centroid of a cluster to be located at any location along an edge of the graph. Unfortunately, this generalization fails to guarantee the existence of Nash equilibrium in this case. The graph in Figure 2 represents a counter example for this case as well. The proof is established by case analysis and is based on Theorem 2.24, where we show that in Nash equilibrium centroids can be placed only in half integral locations on edges.

THEOREM 2.24. *In any Nash Equilibrium configuration of the k-center clustering game with integral edge distances, centroids must be placed in half integral locations on edges.*

In order to guarantee the existence of Nash equilibrium, we add to the game a rule penalizing a node whose move to a cluster C changes the location of the centroid of C. That is, the cost of a node u performing an improvement move will consist of two values:

- The distance from the updated centroid of the new cluster, $d(u, c(C^{+u}))$.

- A cost equal to the distance between the original and new centroids of C, $d(c(C), c(C^{+u}))$.

THEOREM 2.25. *Under the above penalties, there is always a Nash equilibrium solution, and it is guaranteed to be reached by best response dynamics.*

3. CORRELATION CLUSTERING

In this section we consider the clustering game in the correlation clustering model. We investigate both minimization and maximization variants. In the minimization variant, a clustering configuration of the correlation clustering game is in Nash equilibrium if no user can unilaterally reduce its cost $\sum_{u \in C_v} w_u \cdot d(u, v) + \sum_{u \notin C_v} w_u \cdot (1 - d(u, v))$ by choosing a different cluster (respectively, in the maximization variant, a user cannot increase its profit $\sum_{u \in C_v} w_u \cdot (1 - d(u, v)) + \sum_{u \notin C_v} w_u \cdot d(u, v)$). For ease of notation, given a cluster C, we denote the total weight of its nodes by $w(C)$. We denote by V the set of elements, and by E the set of all pairs of

elements (E is the set of edges in a complete graph having V as the set of nodes). Due to space limitations, most proofs of this section are omitted from this extended abstract.

The following lemma shows that the two variants are closely related.

LEMMA 3.1. *A configuration of the game is in Nash equilibrium for the minimization variant if and only if it is in Nash equilibrium for the maximization variant.*

Correlation clustering is a hedonic game and it is closely related to the class of additively-separable hedonic games [7]. It can be shown that for every correlation clustering game, there exists an additively-separable hedonic game with the same set of Nash equilibria. However, the reverse is not true, i.e., additively-separable hedonic games strictly generalize correlation clustering games. We omit the details.

Another interesting subclass of additively-separable hedonic games are symmetric additively-sparable hedonic games [7]. A potential function argument shows that every symmetric additively-sparable hedonic game has a Nash equilibrium, but finding it is PLS-hard [13]. Although these results do not extend immediately to correlation clustering games, their techniques can be used for this type of games as well. The next two theorems follow from the use of these techniques.

THEOREM 3.2. *There always exists Nash equilibrium for the correlation clustering game. Moreover, best response dynamics of this game always converge to a Nash equilibrium.*

THEOREM 3.3. *Computing Nash equilibrium in the correlation clustering game is PLS-Complete.*

In the rest of this section we focus on the price of stability and price of anarchy of correlation clustering games. Unlike the set of Nash equilibria, these values are different for each of the game classes mentioned above, and therefore, we cannot use the relations between our model and these classes to derive results in this context. We begin with several observations on the price of stability.

LEMMA 3.4. *In the special case where all elements have an identical weight w, the price of stability is 1.*

PROOF. In the case of identical weights, the potential function Φ from the proof of Theorem 3.2 can be rewritten as

$$\Phi(\mathcal{F}) = w^2 \sum_{v \in V} \left(\sum_{u \in C_v} d(u, v) + \sum_{u \notin C_v} (1 - d(v, u)) \right) .$$

Note that given a clustering configuration $\mathcal{F}$, the value of the potential function is identical to the value of the social objective function up to a multiplicative factor of w. This implies that any best response move performed by a player will strictly decrease the social objective value. Thus, an optimal clustering configuration is also a Nash equilibrium, as no player can further reduce its cost. The proof for the maximization variant follows directly from Lemma 3.1. □

In the case of arbitrary weights of elements, the price of stability differs between the minimization and maximization variants and can be strictly larger than 1, as shown in the following example. Consider the graph depicted in Figure 3.

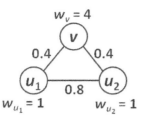

Figure 3: Graph with price on stability greater than 1.

Table 1: Price of stability

Variant	Nash Equilibrium	Optimal Configuration	Price of Stability
Minimum	5.6	5.4	≈ 1.037
Maximum	6.4	6.6	1.03125

The similarity between any two nodes appears on the edge between them, and the weight of a node appears next to it.

It is easy to verify that Nash equilibrium in this graph only occurs when all nodes share a single cluster. However, the optimal configuration is when v shares a cluster with either u_1 or u_2, and the third node is in a different cluster. Table 1 presents the price of stability provided by this example for both variants.

We now turn to analyze the price of anarchy. Despite the close relationship between the minimization and maximization variants of the game, the results obtained for their price of anarchy are quite different, as shown in the next sections. Before turning to analyzing each variant, we present general properties of Nash equilibrium which are later used for establishing the bounds on the price of anarchy for both game variants.

Properties of Nash Equilibria.
We prove two lemmata bounding distances in Nash equilibria.

LEMMA 3.5. *Consider two nodes u and v. If there exists a Nash equilibrium where u and v share a common cluster C, then $d(u,v) \leq 1 - \frac{w_u + w_v}{2w(C)}$.*

LEMMA 3.6. *Consider two nodes u and v. If there exists a Nash equilibrium where u and v belong to two different clusters C_u and C_v, then $d(u,v) \geq \frac{w_u + w_v}{2(w(C_u) + w(C_v))}$.*

3.1 Price of Anarchy - Minimization Variant

We present an upper bound of $O(n^2)$ and a lower bound of $(n-1)$ on the price of anarchy of the minimization variant of the correlation clustering game. We begin with the special case of equal weights and then proceed to arbitrary weights. The next definition is used in the sequel.

DEFINITION 3.7. *Given a clustering configuration, an edge e is of one of two types: either it is an internal edge within a single cluster, or it is an external edge between two different clusters.*

THEOREM 3.8. *If all nodes have the same weight w, price of anarchy is at most $n - 1$.*

PROOF. Without loss of generality, assume $w = 1$. Let $\mathcal{E}$ be a Nash equilibrium of the game, and let $\mathcal{O}$ be an optimal solution. In order to evaluate the contribution of an edge $e = (u, v)$ (of distance $d(u, v)$) to the total cost of $\mathcal{E}$ and $\mathcal{O}$, there are four cases to be considered.

- e is an internal edge in $\mathcal{E}$ and $\mathcal{O}$. Then, e contributes a cost of $2d(u, v)$ to both $\mathcal{E}$ and $\mathcal{O}$.

- e is an external edge in $\mathcal{E}$ and $\mathcal{O}$. Then, e contributes a cost of $2(1 - d(u, v))$ to both $\mathcal{E}$ and $\mathcal{O}$.

- e is an internal edge within cluster C in $\mathcal{E}$, but is an external edge in $\mathcal{O}$. Since e is an edge within C in a Nash equilibrium, Lemma 3.5 implies that $d(u, v) \leq 1 - 2/2w(C) \leq 1 - 1/n$. Therefore, the cost contribution of e to $\mathcal{E}$ is $2d(u, v) \leq 2(1 - 1/n)$. On the other hand, the cost contribution of e to $\mathcal{O}$ is $2(1 - d(u, v)) \geq 2/n$. Thus, the ratio between the cost contribution of e to $\mathcal{E}$ and its contribution to $\mathcal{O}$ is at most $\frac{2(1 - 1/n)}{2/n} = n - 1$.

- e is an external edge between two clusters C_1 and C_2 in $\mathcal{E}$, but is an internal edge in $\mathcal{O}$. Since e is an edge between clusters in a Nash equilibrium, Lemma 3.6 implies that $d(u, v) \geq 2/(2w(C_1) + 2w(C_2)) \geq 1/n$. Therefore the cost contribution of e to $\mathcal{E}$ is $2(1 - d(u, v)) \leq 2(1 - 1/n)$. On the other hand, the cost contribution of e to $\mathcal{O}$ is $2d(u, v) \geq 2/n$. Thus, the ratio between the cost contribution of e to $\mathcal{E}$ and its contribution to $\mathcal{O}$ is again at most $n - 1$.

It follows that the cost contribution of all edges to the cost of $\mathcal{E}$ is at most $n - 1$ times their contribution to the cost of $\mathcal{O}$, completing the proof. □

For general weights we are only able to prove a weaker result.

THEOREM 3.9. *The price of anarchy of the minimization variant of the correlation clustering game is $O(n^2)$.*

The following theorem establishes a lower bound of $(n-1)$ on the price of anarchy of the minimization variant. Note that it matches the upper bound for the special case of equal node weights.

THEOREM 3.10. *The price of anarchy of the minimization variant is at least $n-1$. This holds even when all nodes have the same weight and the metric is a line metric.*

PROOF. We show an instance in which the price of anarchy is at least $n-1$. Assume the weight of all nodes is 1. Let A and B be two disjoint sets of $n/2$ nodes. The distances between the nodes are defined as follows:

$$d(u, v) = \begin{cases} 0 & u, v \in A \text{ or } u, v \in B \\ 1/n & \text{otherwise} \end{cases}$$

This distance function is a special case of a line metric. Consider a clustering in which the nodes of A form one cluster and the nodes of B form another one. We show that this clustering is in Nash equilibrium. Due to symmetry, it suffices to show that a node $u \in A$ does not have an incentive to deviate. The cost of u under the current clustering is $(n/2 - 1) \cdot 0 + n/2 \cdot (1 - 1/n) = (n - 1)/2$. Node u has two deviation options. The first one is to move to the cluster of B which yields the same cost of $(n/2 - 1) \cdot 1 + n/2 \cdot 1/n = n/2 - 1 + 1/2 = (n-1)/2$. The other option is to form a new cluster, which increases the cost to $(n/2-1) \cdot 1 + n/2 \cdot (1 - 1/n) = n/2 - 1 + n/2 - 0.5 = n - 1.5$. Hence, the clustering is in Nash equilibrium. The social cost of the clustering solution is $n(n-1)/2$. On the other hand, the cost of the configuration in which all nodes belong to a single cluster is: $n \cdot [(n/2 - 1) \cdot 0 + n/2 \cdot 1/n] = n/2$. Thus, the price of anarchy of this game instance is at least $\frac{n(n-1)/2}{n/2} = n - 1$. $\square$

3.2 Price of Anarchy - Maximization Variant

In this section we provide tight bounds on the price of anarchy of the maximization variant of correlation clustering for general metrics and line metrics.

THEOREM 3.11. *The price of anarchy of the maximization variant is $O(\sqrt{n})$.*

The proof of Theorem 3.11 proceeds as follows. We first note that an upper bound on the maximum social welfare (total profit) is $(n-1) \cdot w(V)$. Then, we establish a lower bound of $\Omega(\sqrt{n}) \cdot w(V)$ on the total profit of any Nash equilibrium solution.

THEOREM 3.12. *The price of anarchy of the maximization variant is $\Omega(\sqrt{n})$. This bound holds even if all nodes have the same weight and the metric is a tree metric.*

THEOREM 3.13. *The price of anarchy of the maximization variant in the case of a line metric is $\Theta(n^{1/3})$. Moreover, this bound is tight even if all nodes have unit weight.*

3.2.1 Bounding the Price of Anarchy

We suggest a method for bounding the price of anarchy (at the cost of making slight modifications to the rules).

LEMMA 3.14. *If only k clusters are allowed (for $k \geq 2$), then the price of anarchy is at most k^{-1}.*

COROLLARY 3.15. *Consider the case in which all nodes have equal weight, and best response dynamics is executed by first allowing it to reach Nash equilibrium in which nodes are limited to $k \geq 2$ clusters, and then it is allowed to continue till it finds a true Nash equilibrium. Then, the resulting Nash equilibrium has value of at least k^{-1} times the optimal social value.*

PROOF. By Lemma 3.14, the Nash equilibrium reached while the nodes are limited to k clusters has social value of at least OPT/k, where OPT is the optimal social value. Moreover, the proof of Lemma 3.14 actully shows that the social value of this Nash equilibrium is also at least W/k, where W is the maximal social value possible for any configuration (with any number of clusters). Using ideas similar to the proof of Lemma 3.4, we get that the social value cannot decrease by best response dynamics. Hence, the social value of the final Nash equilibrium is at least as large as the social value of the initial Nash equilibrium. $\square$

Acknowledgements

We thank Ari Freund, Yossi Richter, and Elad Yom-Tov for helpful discussions. Special thanks go to Adam Kalai, Ronny Lempel, and Nir Ailon for fruitful comments on our work.

4. REFERENCES

[1] A. Abbasi and M. Younis. A survey on clustering algorithms for wireless sensor networks. *Computer Communications*, 30(14-15):2826–2841, June 2007.

[2] S. Bandyopadhyay and E.J. Coyle. An energy efficient hierarchical clustering algorithm for wireless sensor networks. In *Proceedings of INFOCOM*, pages 1713–1723. March 2003.

[3] S. Banerjee, H. Konishi and T. Sonmez. Core in a Simple Coalition Formation Game. *Social Choice and Welfare*, 18(1):135–153, 2001.

[4] N. Bansal, A. Blum, S. and Chawla. Correlation clustering. *Machine Learning J.*, 56(1-3):86–113, 2004.

[5] F. Bloch and E. Diamantoudi. Noncooperative formation of coalitions in hedonic games. *International Journal of Game Theory*, 40(2):263–280, 2010.

[6] A. Blum. Thoughts on clustering. In *NIPS Workshop on Clustering Theory*, 2009.

[7] A. Bogomolnaia and M.O. Jackson. The stability of hedonic coalition structures. *Games and Economic Behavior*, 38(2):201–230, 2002.

[8] M. Charikar, S. Guha, E. Tardos and D. Shmoys. A constant factor approximation algorithm for the k-median problem. In *Proceedings of STOC*, pages 1–10. ACM, 1999.

[9] M. Charikar, V. Guruswami and A. Wirth. Clustering with qualitative information. In *Proceedings of FOCS*, pages 524–533. IEEE Computer Society, 2003.

[10] E. Demaine and N. Immorlica. Correlation clustering with partial information. In *Proceedings of APPROX*, pages 71–80. Springer, 2003.

[11] J.H. Dreze and J. Greenberg. Hedonic coalitions: Optimality and stability. *Econometrica*, 48(4):987–1003, 1980.

[12] D. Emanuel and A. Fiat. Correlation clustering – Minimizing disagreements on arbitrary weighted graphs. In *Proceedings of ESA*, pages 208–220. Springer, 2003.

[13] M. Gairing and R. Savani. Computing Stable Outcomes in Hedonic Games. *Lecture Notes in Computer Science*, 10:174–185, 2010.

[14] T. F. Gonzalez. Clustering to minimize the maximum intercluster distance. *Theoretical Computer Science*, 38:293–306, 1985.

[15] L. Gourvès and J. Monnot. On Strong Equilibria in the Max Cut Game. In *Proceedings of WINE*, pages 608–615. 2009.

[16] T. Groves. Incentives in teams. *Econometrica*, 41(4):617–631, 1973.

[17] D. S. Hochbaum and D. B. Shmoys. A best possible heuristic for the k-center problem. *Mathematics of Operations Research*, 10:180–184, 1985.

[18] M. Hoefer. Cost Sharing and Clustering under Distributed Competition. Ph.D. Thesis, Universität Konstanz, 2007.

[19] G. Koltsidas and F. N. Pavlidou. A game theoretic approach to clustering of ad-hoc and sensor networks. *Telecommunication Systems*, 47(1-2):81–93, June 2011.

[20] M. Pelillo. What is a cluster? perspectives from game theory. In *NIPS Workshop on Clustering Theory*, 2009.

[21] S. R. Bulò. A game-theoretic framework for similarity-based data clustering. Ph.D. Thesis, Università Ca' Foscari di Venezia, 2009.

[22] A. Tamir. An $O(pn^2)$ algorithm for the p-median and related problems on tree graphs. *Operations Research Letters*, 19(2):59-64, August 1996.

[23] V. Vazirani. Approximation Algorithms. Springer Verlag, 2001.

[24] E. B. Yanovskaya. Equilibrium points in polymatrix games. (in Russion) *Litovskii Matematicheskii Sbornik*, 8:381–384, 1968.

Enforcing Efficient Equilibria in Network Design Games via Subsidies[*]

John Augustine
Department of Computer
Science and Engineering
Indian Institute of Technology
Madras, Chennai, India

Ioannis Caragiannis
Department of Computer
Engineering and Informatics
University of Patras & CTI,
Greece

Angelo Fanelli
School of Physical and
Mathematical Sciences
Nanyang Technological
University, Singapore

Christos Kalaitzis
Department of Computer
Engineering and Informatics
University of Patras & CTI,
Greece

ABSTRACT

The efficient design of networks has been an important engineering task that involves challenging combinatorial optimization problems. Typically, a network designer has to select among several alternatives which links to establish so that the resulting network satisfies a given set of connectivity requirements and the cost of establishing the network links is as low as possible. The MINIMUM SPANNING TREE problem, which is well-understood, is a nice example.

In this paper, we consider the natural scenario in which the connectivity requirements are posed by selfish users who have agreed to share the cost of the network to be established according to a well-defined rule. The design proposed by the network designer should now be consistent not only with the connectivity requirements but also with the selfishness of the users. Essentially, the users are players in a so-called network design game and the network designer has to propose a design that is an equilibrium for this game. As it is usually the case when selfishness comes into play, such equilibria may be suboptimal. In this paper, we consider the following question: can the network designer enforce particular designs as equilibria or guarantee that efficient designs are consistent with users' selfishness by appropriately subsidizing some of the network links? In an attempt to understand this question, we formulate corresponding optimization problems and present positive and negative results.

[*]This work was partially supported by the grant NRF-RF2009-08 "Algorithmic aspects of coalitional games" and by the EC-funded STREP project EULER.

Permission to make digital or hard copies of all or part of this work for personal or classroom use is granted without fee provided that copies are not made or distributed for profit or commercial advantage and that copies bear this notice and the full citation on the first page. To copy otherwise, to republish, to post on servers or to redistribute to lists, requires prior specific permission and/or a fee.
SPAA'12, June 25–27, 2012, Pittsburgh, Pennsylvania, USA.
Copyright 2012 ACM 978-1-4503-1213-4/12/06 ...$10.00.

Categories and Subject Descriptors

F.2 [**Theory of Computation**]: Analysis of Algorithms and Problem Complexity; J.4 [**Computer Applications**]: Social and Behavioral Sciences—*Economics*

General Terms

Algorithms, Theory, Economics

Keywords

Network design games, equilibria, subsidies

1. INTRODUCTION

Network design is a rich class of combinatorial optimization problems that model important engineering questions arising in modern networks. In an ideal scenario, a network designer that acts on behalf of a central authority is given an edge-weighted graph representing the potential links between nodes and their operation cost, and connectivity requirements between the nodes. The objective of the network designer is to compute a subgraph (the network to be established) of minimum cost that satisfies all connectivity requirements. Depending on the structure of the connectivity requirements, this definition leads to many optimization problems ranging from problems that are well-understood and efficiently solvable such as the MINIMUM SPANNING TREE to problems whose optimal solutions are even hard to approximate.

In this paper, we consider the scenario in which users are selfish and have agreed to a well-defined rule according to which they will share the cost of the network to be established. The connectivity requirements are now posed by the users; each user wishes to connect two specific nodes. A design should satisfy each connectivity requirement through a path connecting these two nodes in the established network. According to the particular cost sharing rule we consider, the corresponding user will then share the cost of each link in her path with the other users that use this link. Even though the network designer can still resort to the rich toolset of network design algorithms in order to propose a network of reasonable cost, this approach neglects the selfish behavior of the users. A user may not be satisfied with the current design since a different path that satisfies her connectivity requirement may cost her less. Then, she could unilaterally propose an alternative path that possibly includes links that were not in the proposal of the network designer. Other users could also act similarly and these negotiations compute the network to be established in a chaotic manner. The role of the network designer is almost canceled and, furthermore, it is not clear when the selfish users will reach an agreement (if they ever do) and, even if they do, whether this agreement will be really beneficial for the users as a whole, i.e., whether the total (or social) cost of the established network will be reasonable. So, the goal of the network designer is to propose a design (i.e., a network and, subsequently, a path to each user and an associated cost) that not only meets the connectivity requirements of the users but is also consistent with their selfish nature. Furthermore, the design should be efficient, i.e., the network to be established should have reasonable social cost. Essentially, the users are engaged as players in a non-cooperative strategic game, called a *network design game*, and the role of the network designer is to propose an efficient design that is an equilibrium of this game.

Typically, efficiency is not an easy goal when selfishness comes into play. This leads to the following question which falls within one of the main lines of research in *Algorithmic Game Theory*: how is the social cost affected by selfish behavior? The notion of the *price of anarchy* [13, 17] can quantify this relation. Expressed in the context of a network design game, it would be defined as the ratio of the social cost of the worst possible Nash equilibrium over the social cost of an optimal design. Hence, it is pessimistic in nature and (as its name suggests) provides a worst-case guarantee for conditions of total anarchy. Instead, the notion of the *price of stability* that was introduced by Anshelevich *et al.* [2] is optimistic in nature and quantifies how easy the job of the network designer is. It is defined as the ratio of the social cost of the best equilibrium over the cost of the optimal design and essentially answers the following question: what is the best one can hope from a design given that the players are selfish?

Unfortunately, the price of stability can be large which would mean that every design that is consistent with selfishness has high social cost. The central authority could then intervene in order to mitigate the impact of selfishness. One solution that seems natural would be to contribute to the social cost of the network to be established by partially subsidizing some of the links. According to this scenario, the network designer has to compute a design and decide which links in the established network should be subsidized by the central authority. The users will then share the unsubsidized portion of the cost of the network links they use. Essentially, they will be involved in a new network design game and the goal of the network designer should be to guarantee that the design and the subsidies computed induce an equilibrium for this new game. The problem becomes non-trivial when the central authority runs on a limited budget. What is the best design the network designer can guarantee given this budget? Alternatively, what is the minimum amount of subsidies sufficient in order to achieve a given social cost? Can optimality be achieved? Can the corresponding designs be computed efficiently?

Problem statement. In an attempt to understand these questions, we introduce and study two related optimization problems. In STABLE NETWORK ENFORCEMENT (SNE), we are given a network design game on a graph together with a particular target network T, and we wish to compute the minimum amount of subsidies that have to be put on the links of T so that the design is acceptable to the users. In STABLE NETWORK DESIGN (SND), we are given a particular budget together with the input game, and we wish to compute a network T that satisfies the connectivity requirements and to assign an amount of subsidies to the links of T within the stipulated budget so that the design is acceptable to the users. The objective is to minimize the social cost of T. Besides the standard version of both problems, we also consider their *all-or-nothing* version in which a link can either be fully subsidized or not subsidized at all; this version captures restrictions that may arise in practice, e.g., when partially subsidizing network links is logistically infeasible.

Even though some of our results apply to general network design games, our emphasis is on a special class of network design games, called *broadcast games*. In such a game, there is a special node in the input graph called the *root*. There is one player associated with each distinct non-root node and her connectivity requirement is a path from her associated node to the root. A nice property of such games is that an optimal design is the solution of the MINIMUM SPANNING TREE problem on the input graph and can be computed efficiently. Even in this seemingly simple case, as we will see, selfish behavior imposes challenging restrictions. Hence, broadcast games showcase the difficulties in solving SNE and SND that are due to selfishness.

Related work. Strategic games that arise from network design scenarios have received much attention in the *Algorithmic Game Theory* literature. The first related paper is probably [3]. The particular network design games that we consider in the current paper were introduced by Anshelevich *et al.* in [2]. An important observation made there is that network design games admit a potential function that was proposed by Rosenthal [18] for a broader class of games called congestion games. Using Rosenthal's potential and a simple but elegant argument, Anshelevich *et al.* [2] proved that the price of stability is at most $\mathcal{H}_n$, the n-th harmonic number, where n is the number of players. The $\mathcal{H}_n$ bound is known to be tight for directed networks only. For undirected networks, better bounds on the price of stability of $O(\log \log n)$ for broadcast games and $O(\log n / \log \log n)$ for generalizations known as multicast games are presented in [14] and [12], respectively. Still, the best lower bounds are only constant (e.g., see [5]). The papers [8] and [7] provide bounds on the quality of equilibria reached when players enter a multicast game one by one and play their best response and then (when all players have arrived) they concurrently play until an equilibrium is reached.

Another intriguing question is related to the complexity of computing equilibria in such games. In general, the problem was recently proved to be PLS-hard [20]. The corresponding hardness reduction does not apply to multicast or broadcast games. Unfortunately, the classical approach of minimizing the potential function that has been proved useful in the case of network congestion games [11] cannot be applied to multicast games; the authors of [8] prove that minimizing Rosenthal's potential function is NP-hard. Furthermore, in multicast games, computing an equilibrium of minimum social cost is NP-hard [20]. Approximate equilibria is the subject of [1].

Monetary incentives in strategic games have been considered in many different contexts. Most of the work in *Mechanism Design* (see [16] for an introduction) uses such incentives to motivate players to act truthfully. The (non-exhaustive) list also includes their use in *Cooperative Game Theory* in order to encourage coalitions of players reach stability [4] and as a means to stabilize normal form games [15]. However, the particular use of monetary incentives in the current paper is substantially different and aims at improving the performance of the system the game represents. In this direction, other tools such as taxes [10], Stackelberg strategies [19], and coordination mechanisms [9] have also been considered recently. An approach that is closer to ours has been followed in [6] where subsidies are used in multicast games; unlike our approach, the subsidies are collected as taxes from the players in order to guarantee efficient worst-case equilibria.

Overview of results and roadmap. In this paper we present the following results. First, we observe that SNE can be solved in polynomial time using linear programming; this observation applies to general instances of SNE. For instances of SNE with broadcast games, we present a much simpler LP in which the number of variables and constraints is linear and quadratic in the number of players, respectively. On the other hand, SND is proved to be NP-hard even for broadcast instances. In particular, detecting whether a minimum spanning tree can be enforced as an equilibrium without using any subsidies is NP-hard. This result implies that detecting whether the price of stability of a given broadcast game is 1 or not is NP-hard. In this direction, we have a stronger result: approximating the price of stability of a broadcast game is APX-hard. The last two statements significantly extend the NP-hardness result of [20] and indicate that, besides the rough estimates provided by the known bounds on the price of stability which hold for a broad class of games, the estimate the network designer can make about the most efficient designs of a particular broadcast game will also be rough. These results are presented in Section 3.

Next, we consider broadcast instances of SNE and the question of how much subsidies are sufficient and necessary in order to enforce a given minimum spanning tree as an equilibrium. We show that this can be done using a percentage of 37% of the weight of the minimum spanning tree as subsidies. The proof has two main components. First, we show how to prove this upper bound by decomposing the game into subgames with a significantly simpler structure than the original one. Second, in order to compute the subsidies in each subgame, we use a virtual approximation of the cost experienced by the players on the links of the network. We also demonstrate that our upper bound is tight: an amount of 37% of the minimum spanning tree weight as subsidies may be necessary for some simple instances. These results are presented in Section 4.

Surprisingly, in contrast to the standard case, we prove that the all-or-nothing version of SNE is hard to approximate within any factor even when restricted to instances with broadcast games. The corresponding proof is long and technically involved and indicates that the only approximation guarantee should bound the amount of subsidies as a constant fraction of the weight of the minimum spanning tree. Interestingly, we prove that significantly more subsidies may be necessary compared to the standard version of SNE. In particular, there are broadcast instances which re-

quire a percentage of 61% of the weight of the minimum spanning tree as subsidies in order to enforce it as an equilibrium. These results are presented in Section 5.

We begin with preliminary definitions and notation in Section 2 and conclude with interesting open problems in Section 6. Due to lack of space, some proofs have been omitted.

2. DEFINITIONS AND NOTATION

A *network design game* consists of an edge-weighted undirected graph $G = (V, E, w)$, a set N of n players, and a source-destination pair of nodes (s_i, t_i) for each player i. Each player wishes to connect her source to her destination and, in order to do this, she can select as a strategy any path T_i connecting s_i to t_i in G. The tuple $T = (T_1, T_2, ..., T_n)$ that consists of the strategies of the players (with one strategy per player) is called a *state*. We say that player i uses edge a in T if her strategy T_i contains a. With some abuse in notation, we also denote by T the set of edges included in strategies $T_1, T_2, ..., T_n$ as well as the subgraph of G induced by these edges. We say that an edge $a \in E$ is *established* if at least one player uses edge a. Consider such an edge a and let $n_a(T)$ be the number of players whose strategies in T contain a. Throughout the paper, we also use the notation $n_a^i(T)$ to denote whether player i uses edge a ($n_a^i(T) = 1$) or not ($n_a^i(T) = 0$). Each player i in N experiences a cost of $\text{cost}_i(T) = \sum_{a \in T_i} \frac{w_a}{n_a(T)}$, i.e., the weight of each established edge is shared as cost among the players using it.

The state T is called a (*pure Nash*) *equilibrium* if no player has an incentive to unilaterally deviate from T in order to decrease her cost, i.e., for each player i and possible strategy T_i' that connects the source-destination pair (s_i, t_i) in G, it holds that $\text{cost}_i(T) \leq \text{cost}_i(T_{-i}, T_i')$. The notation T_{-i}, T_i' denotes the state in which player i uses strategy T_i' and the remaining players use their strategies in T. Throughout the paper, we denote by $\text{wgt}(A)$ the total weight of the set of edges A in G, i.e., $\text{wgt}(A) = \sum_{a \in A} w_a$. The quality of a state is measured by the total weight of the established edges. Since the weight of each established edge is shared as cost among the players that use it, the quality of a state coincides with the total cost experienced by all players, i.e., $\text{wgt}(T) = \sum_i \text{cost}_i(T)$. The *price of stability* of a network design game is simply the ratio of the weight of the edges established in the best equilibrium over the optimal cost among all states of the game.

Given an edge-weighted graph $G = (V, E, w)$, a *subsidy assignment* b is a function that assigns a subsidy $b_a \in [0, w_a]$ to each edge $a \in E$. The cost of a subsidy assignment is simply the sum of the subsidies on all edges of G, i.e., $\sum_{a \in E} b_a$. We use the term *all-or-nothing* to refer to subsidies that are constrained so that $b_a \in \{0, w_a\}$ for each edge $a \in E$. Given a set of edges A in G, we use the notation $b(A)$ in order to refer to the total amount of subsidies assigned to the edges of A in the subsidy assignment b, i.e., $b(A) = \sum_{a \in A} b_a$. We refer to $b(E)$ as the cost of the subsidy assignment b. Given a network design game on a graph G and a subsidy assignment b on the edges of G, we use the term *extension* of the original game with subsidies b in order to refer to the network design game on graph G (with the same players and strategy sets as in the original game) with the only difference being that the cost of a player at a state T is now $\text{cost}_i(T; b) = \sum_{a \in T_i} \frac{w_a - b_a}{n_a(T)}$. When a particular state T is an equilibrium of the extension of the original game with subsidies b, we say that the subsidy assignment b *enforces* T as an equilibrium in the extension of the original game.

An instance of the STABLE NETWORK DESIGN problem (SND) consists of a network design game on a graph G, a budget B, and a positive number K. The question is whether there exists a subsidy assignment b of cost at most B on the edges of G so that a subgraph of G of total weight at most K is an equilibrium for the extension of the original game with subsidies b. An instance of the STABLE NETWORK ENFORCEMENT problem (SNE) consists of a network design game on a graph G, a budget B, and a state T. The question is whether there exists a subsidy assignment of cost at most B on the edges of G so that b enforces T as an equilibrium on the extension of the original game with subsidies b. Note that the subsidy assignment does not need to put any subsidies to edges not in T. In the integral versions of SNE and SND, the subsidy assignment in question is all-or-nothing. Of course, optimization versions of the above problems are natural. For example, in an optimization version of SNE, we are given the network design game on a graph G and a state T, and we require the subsidy assignment in question to be of minimum cost.

Broadcast games are special cases of network design games. In a broadcast game, the graph G has exactly $n + 1$ nodes; all players have the same destination node, which is called the *root* and is denoted by r, and distinct non-root nodes as sources. In such games, we refer to a player with a source node u as the player associated with node u (and use u to identify the player). Clearly, any state T in such a game spans all nodes of G and a minimum spanning tree is a state that minimizes the total cost experienced by the players. Given any spanning tree T and a non-root node u, we denote by T_u the path from u to r in T. In broadcast games, we mostly consider equilibria that are spanning trees.

3. THE COMPLEXITY OF SNE AND SND

We begin the presentation of our results with the following observation.

THEOREM 1. STABLE NETWORK ENFORCEMENT *is in P.*

This theorem applies to general instances of SNE and follows by expressing the problem using linear programming; the corresponding LPs have a large number of variables or constraints. A more detailed discussion will appear in the final version. In the following, we present a much simpler LP that applies to broadcast instances.

Given a broadcast game on an edge-weighted graph $G = (V, E, w)$ (with a root node r and n non-root nodes) and a spanning tree T of G, our LP solves the optimization version of the problem by computing a subsidy assignment b of minimum cost so that T is an equilibrium in the extension of the original game with subsidies b. The subsidies in question are the variables of the LP. We remark that, even though we only need to use variables for the subsidies on the edges of T, we assume that b_a is defined for each edge a of E in order to simplify the presentation; it should be clear that, in any optimal solution of the linear program below, $b_a = 0$ for each edge $a \in E \setminus T$. The variables are constrained so that $b_a \in [0, w_a]$. There are extra constraints that require that no player associated with a node u has an incentive to change her strategy in T and use an edge (u, v) that does not belong to T and the path from v to r in T. The corresponding LP is:

$$\min \quad \sum_{a \in E} b_a \qquad (1)$$

$$\text{s.t.} \quad \forall u \in V \setminus \{r\}, v \in V \text{ such that } (u,v) \in E \setminus T,$$

$$\sum_{a \in T_u} \frac{w_a - b_a}{n_a(T)} \leq w_{(u,v)} + \sum_{a \in T_v} \frac{w_a - b_a}{n_a(T) + 1 - n_a^u(T)}$$

$$\forall a \in E, 0 \leq b_a \leq w_a$$

The above LP has n variables and $O(|E|)$ constraints. Observe that the first set of constraints just requires that the players have no incentive to deviate to very specific paths. Hence, the correctness of the LP (i.e., its equivalence with the optimization version of SNE) is not obvious and is given by the following lemma; the proof is omitted.

LEMMA 2. *Consider an instance of* STABLE NETWORK ENFORCEMENT *consisting of a broadcast game on a graph G and a state T. A subsidy assignment b enforces T as an equilibrium in the extension of the broadcast game in G if and only if the constraints of LP (1) are satisfied.*

Next, we prove that the restriction of SND to broadcast instances is NP-hard. The hardness proof uses instances of SND with budget equal to zero with target equilibrium weight equal to the weight of the minimum spanning tree. In our reduction, there are many different minimum spanning trees but it is hard to detect whether there is one that is an equilibrium in the corresponding broadcast game.

THEOREM 3. *Given an instance of* STABLE NETWORK DESIGN *consisting of a broadcast game on a graph G, budget B, and a positive number K, it is NP-hard to decide whether there exists a subsidy assignment b of cost at most B so that the extension of the game with subsidies b has a tree of weight at most K as an equilibrium. Moreover, it is NP-hard even when B is set to zero.*

We will first describe a gadget that is used in the proof of Theorem 3; we call it the Bypass gadget of capacity κ. The gadget is shown in Figure 1. Let ℓ be the minimum positive integer such that $\mathcal{H}_{\kappa+\ell} - \mathcal{H}_\kappa > 1$. The Bypass gadget consists of a root node r connected to one end of a path of ℓ nodes formed with edges of unit weight. We call this the *basic path* of the Bypass gadget. The node c on the far end of the path from r is called the *connector node*. There is an edge from c to r of weight $\mathcal{H}_{\kappa+\ell} - \mathcal{H}_\kappa$, which we call the *bypass edge*.

Suppose this gadget is connected to a subgraph S of β nodes as shown in Figure 1. For the moment, we are not concerned with how the nodes in S are connected to each other. Consider the instance of SNE consisting of the broadcast game on the graph G of Figure 1, budget $B = 0$, and let T be a minimum spanning tree of G. Note that T does not include the bypass edge; it includes all edges in the basic path from c to r instead.

LEMMA 4. *If $\beta < \kappa$, then the player associated with node c has an incentive to deviate from her strategy in T and use the bypass edge. Otherwise, no player associated with a node in the basic path has any incentive to deviate from T.*

PROOF. Regardless of how the players associated with nodes in the subgraph S are routed, since S is connected to the Bypass gadget through node c, there are $\beta + 1$ players

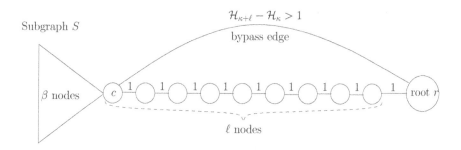

Figure 1: The Bypass gadget with capacity κ.

that need to use a path from c to r. Let us focus on the player associated with node c. If she and all the β players from S take the basic path, then her cost will be $\sum_{i=1}^{\ell} \frac{1}{\beta+i} = \mathcal{H}_{\beta+\ell} - \mathcal{H}_{\beta}$. If $\beta < \kappa$, then $\mathcal{H}_{\kappa+\ell} - \mathcal{H}_{\kappa} < \mathcal{H}_{\beta+\ell} - \mathcal{H}_{\beta}$, and therefore, the player associated with node c has an incentive to deviate to the bypass edge. On the other hand, if $\beta \geq \kappa$, then $\mathcal{H}_{\kappa+\ell} - \mathcal{H}_{\kappa} \geq \mathcal{H}_{\beta+\ell} - \mathcal{H}_{\beta}$ and any player associated with a node in the basic path experiences a cost of at most $\mathcal{H}_{\beta+\ell} - \mathcal{H}_{\beta}$ in T. Hence, no such player has an incentive to deviate from T. $\square$

PROOF OF THEOREM 3. We show that the problem is NP-hard even when we consider the special case where $B = 0$ and K equals the weight of the minimum spanning tree of the input graph G. In other words, given a broadcast game on a graph G with root node r, we ask: does this game have a minimum spanning tree of G as an equilibrium? We use a reduction from BIN PACKING.

We use a stricter form of BIN PACKING defined as follows. We are given a set of n items indexed by $i \in \{1, 2, \ldots, n\}$. The size of each item i is a positive even integer denoted by s_i. Since bin packing is strongly NP-hard, we assume that s_i is bounded by a polynomial in n. We are also given a set of k bins indexed by $j \in \{1, 2, \ldots, k\}$, each of even integer capacity C, which we assume to be at least as large as $\max_i s_i$. We furthermore assume that $\sum_{i=1}^{n} s_i = kC$. We ask whether each item can be allocated to one of the k bins so that the total size of items in each bin is exactly C. Our definition of BIN PACKING is somewhat stricter than the conventional definition in which the capacity of bins and the size of the items is not restricted to be even and bins are not required to be filled to the brim. However, we note that it is quite straightforward to see that this restricted version of the problem can be reduced from the conventional version by first adding a suitable number of unit-sized items and then doubling the size of all items and the capacity of all bins. The number of additional items is upper-bounded by the total capacity of the bins. Therefore, our restriction of BIN PACKING is also strongly NP-hard.

Given a restricted instance of BIN PACKING, we now construct an instance of SNE as follows. For each item i of size s_i, we create a star graph with one center node which we denote by x_i and $s_i - 1$ leaves. The edges connecting the leaves to the center node of the star have zero weight. Let X be the set of center nodes. For each bin j, construct a Bypass gadget with capacity $\kappa = C$. Again, let ℓ be the number of unit-weight edges in the basic path of each Bypass gadget. Recall that ℓ is the minimum positive integer such that $\mathcal{H}_{C+\ell} - \mathcal{H}_C > 1$; this implies that ℓ is linear in C. We denote the connector node in the gadget corresponding

to bin j by c_j. Let χ be the set of all connector nodes. We connect sets χ and X by a complete bipartite edge set with edges having weight $2(\mathcal{H}_{C+\ell} - \mathcal{H}_C)$. Observe that any minimum spanning tree of G consists of the $k\ell$ unit-weight edges in the Bypass gadgets, the zero-weight edges connecting the leaves to their star center, and n edges that connect nodes of χ to nodes of X so that each node of X is connected to exactly one node of χ. We set K to be the weight of the minimum spanning tree, i.e., $K = k\ell + 2n(\mathcal{H}_{C+\ell} - \mathcal{H}_C)$.

We claim that a minimum spanning tree T_{ne} of G is an equilibrium for the broadcast game on G if and only if the BIN PACKING instance has a solution. We prove this claim in both directions.

Let T_{ne} be a minimum spanning tree that is an equilibrium. Let $\beta_j + 1$ be the number of nodes in the subtree of T_{ne} rooted at c_j. From Lemma 4, we know that since T_{ne} is an equilibrium, for all j, it holds that $\beta_j \geq C$. However, we also know from the properties of the BIN PACKING instance and the construction of graph G that $\sum_{j=1}^{k} \beta_j = \sum_{i=1}^{n} s_i = kC$. Clearly, it follows that for all j, we have $\beta_j = C$. Therefore, the allocation of item i to bin j whenever x_i is connected to c_j will lead to a solution for the BIN PACKING instance since the total size of these items is exactly $\beta_j = C$.

To show the other direction, let us suppose that we have a solution to the BIN PACKING instance. We construct a minimum spanning tree T_{ne} as follows. T_{ne} contains the edges from the leaves to the corresponding star center, the basic paths from the connector nodes to the root node r, and the edge (x_i, c_j) for each item i that is allocated to bin j. Note that, for $j = 1, \ldots, k$, the number of nodes in the subtree of T_{ne} rooted at c_j is exactly C. So, any player associated with a node in a basic path experiences a cost of at most $\mathcal{H}_{C+\ell} - \mathcal{H}_C$ in T_{ne}. Furthermore, observe that each edge of T_{ne} between nodes of χ and X is used by at least two players in T_{ne}. So, any player associated with a node in a star experiences a cost of at least $2(\mathcal{H}_{C+\ell} - \mathcal{H}_C)$. Hence, no player has an incentive to deviate to a path that includes a node of χ that she does not use in T_{ne}. Any such path would include an edge of weight $2(\mathcal{H}_{C+\ell} - \mathcal{H}_C)$ between a node in χ and a node in X that is used only by that player. So, for each j, the C players associated with nodes in the subtree of c_j in T_{ne} have no incentive to deviate to a path that does not use node c_j. By Lemma 4, player c_j (and, consequently, all players that have node c_j in their path to r in T_{ne}) has no incentive to deviate to the bypass edge connecting c_j to r. This holds for any other node in the basic path of a Bypass gadget as well. Therefore, it follows that T_{ne} is an equilibrium. $\square$

Note that the proof of Theorem 3 essentially implies that deciding whether the price of stability of a given broadcast

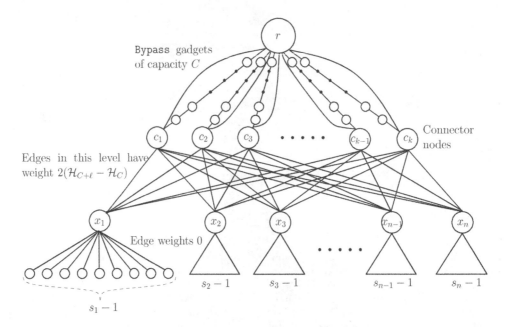

Figure 2: The graph G constructed from an instance of BIN PACKING.

game is 1 or not is NP-hard. The next statement (proof omitted) provides an even stronger negative result. It implies that given instances of SND consisting of a broadcast game on a graph G and a budget B, it is NP-hard to approximate within a factor better than $571/570$ the minimum weight among all equilibria in any extension of the original game with subsidies of cost at most B.

THEOREM 5. *Approximating the price of stability of a broadcast game within a factor better than $571/570$ is NP-hard.*

4. BOUNDS ON THE AMOUNT OF SUBSIDIES

In this section, we provide tight bounds on the amount of subsidies sufficient in order to enforce a minimum spanning tree as an equilibrium in the extension of the original broadcast game. The result is expressed as a constant fraction of the weight of the minimum spanning tree. We first prove our upper bound which is more involved. The proof uses two key ideas: first, the input SNE instance is appropriately decomposed into subinstances of SNE which have a significantly simpler structure. Our decomposition is such that the desired bound has to be proved for the subinstances; in order to do so, we use a second idea and exploit a virtual cost function that upper-bounds the actual cost experienced by the players in the extension of the game (in the subinstances) with subsidies. The main property of this virtual cost function that simplifies the analysis considerably is that the total amount of subsidies necessary depends only on the weight of the tree (and not on its structure).

THEOREM 6. *Given an instance of* STABLE NETWORK ENFORCEMENT *consisting of a broadcast game on a graph G and a minimum spanning tree T of G, there is a subsidy assignment b of cost at most $\mathtt{wgt}(T)/e$ that enforces T as an equilibrium of the extension of the game with subsidies b, where e is the basis of the natural logarithm.*

PROOF. We decompose the graph G into copies G^1, G^2, ..., G^k so that the following properties hold:

- G^j has the same set of nodes and set of edges with G.

- The edge weights in G^j belong to $\{0, c_j\}$ for some $c_j > 0$.

- If the weight of an edge a in G^j is non-zero, then the weight of a is non-zero in each of the copies $G^1, ..., G^{j-1}$ of G.

- The weight of each edge in G is equal to the sum of its weights in the copies of G.

The decomposition proceeds as follows. Let c_1 be the minimum non-zero weight among the edges of G. We construct a copy G^1 of G (i.e., with the same set of nodes and set of edges) and with edge weights equal to zero if the corresponding edge of G has zero weight and equal to c_1 otherwise. Then, we decrease each non-zero edge weight by c_1 in G and proceed in the same way with the definition of the edge weights in the copy G^2, and so on. We denote by k the number of copies of G that have some edge of non-zero weight. Note that c_k may be infinite if G contains edges of infinite weight, but k is upper bounded by the number of edges in G. Clearly, the weight of an edge in the original graph is the sum of its weights in the copies of G.

We denote by T^j the spanning tree of G^j that has the same set of edges with T. We first observe that T^j is a minimum spanning tree of G^j. Assume that this is not the case; then, there must be an edge a_1 with zero weight in G^j that does not belong to T^j such that some edge a_2 of the edges of T^j with which a_1 forms a cycle has non-zero weight c_j. By the definition of our decomposition phase, this implies that a_2 has higher weight than a_1 in G. This means that we could remove a_2 from T and include a_1 in order to obtain a spanning tree with strictly smaller weight, i.e., T would not be a minimum spanning tree.

Now, in order to compute the desired subsidy assignment that enforces T as an equilibrium in the extension of the broadcast game in G, we will exploit appropriate subsidy assignments for the broadcast games in each copy of G. We have the following lemma; its proof exploits a virtual cost function in order to compute the subsidy assignment b^j.

LEMMA 7. *Let $c_j > 0$. Consider a broadcast game on a graph G^j whose edges have weights in $\{0, c_j\}$ and let T^j be a minimum spanning tree of G^j. Then, there is a subsidy assignment b^j of cost at most $\mathtt{wgt}(T^j)/e$ that enforces T^j as an equilibrium in the extension of the game with subsidies b^j.*

PROOF. We call edges of weight 0 and c_j *light* and *heavy* edges, respectively. We also call a player associated with a node v a *light* player if the weight of the edge connecting v to its parent in T^j is zero; otherwise, we call v a *heavy* player. We denote by m_a the number of heavy players which use edge a. Clearly, $m_a \leq n_a(T^j)$.

We will introduce a *virtual cost* associated with each edge of T^j in order to upper-bound the contribution of the edge to the real cost experienced by each player that uses the edge in T^j in the extension of the game with subsidies. In particular, given subsidies y_a assigned to the heavy edge a with $y_a \in [0, c_j]$, we define the virtual cost of edge a as $\mathtt{vc}(a, y_a) = c_j \ln \frac{m_a}{m_a - 1 + y_a/c_j}$. The virtual cost of a light edge is always zero. The next claim follows by the definition of the virtual cost.

CLAIM 8. *For any heavy edge a with subsidies y_a, it holds that $\mathtt{vc}(a, y_a) \geq \frac{c_j - y_a}{n_a(T^j)}$.*

DEFINITION 9. *Consider a path q in T^j and a subsidy assignment y on the edges of T^j. We say that y is such that subsidies are packed on the least crowded heavy edges of q if $y_a < c_j$ for a heavy edge a implies that $y_{a'} = 0$ for every heavy edge a' of q with $m_{a'} > m_a$.*

We extend the notation of virtual cost so that $\mathtt{vc}(q, b^j)$ denotes the sum of the virtual cost of the edges of a path q in T^j under the subsidy assignment b^j. The following claim follows by the definitions and will be very useful later.

CLAIM 10. *Consider a path q and denote by q' the set of heavy edges of q and a subsidy assignment y. If $\cup_{a \in q'}\{m_a\}$ consists of the $|q'|$ consecutive integers $t - |q'| + 1, t - |q'| + 2, ..., t$, then the virtual cost of path q when subsidies are packed on its least crowded heavy edges is $\mathtt{vc}(q, y) = c_j \ln \frac{t}{t - |q'| + y(q)/c_j}$.*

PROOF. Recall that the only edges that contribute to the virtual cost of q are the heavy edges in q'. If $y(q) = 0$ (i.e., no subsidies are put on the edges of q'), the virtual cost is

$$
\begin{aligned}
\mathtt{vc}(q, y) &= \sum_{a \in q'} \mathtt{vc}(a, y_a) \\
&= \sum_{a \in q'} c_j \ln \frac{m_a}{m_a - 1 + y_a/c_j} \\
&= \sum_{i = t - |q'| + 1}^{t} c_j \ln \frac{i}{i - 1} \\
&= c_j \ln \frac{t}{t - |q'| + y(q)/c_j}.
\end{aligned}
$$

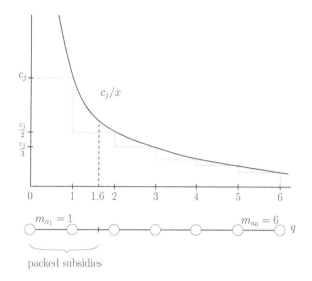

Figure 3: **A visualization of the virtual cost in a path q, with 6 heavy edges and $\cup_{a \in q}\{m_a\} = \{1, 2, ..., 6\}$, when subsidies are packed on its less crowded edges. The leftmost edge and a fraction of 60% of the second leftmost one have been subsidized. The virtual cost $\ln \frac{6}{1.6}$ (see Claim 10) is the area to the right of the dashed line that is below the black line. The real cost experienced by the player associated with the far left node is the area to the right of the dashed line that is below the grey line.**

The first two equalities follow by the definition of the virtual cost, the third one follows since $\cup_{a \in q'}\{m_a\} = \{t - |q'| + 1, t - |q'| + 2, ..., t\}$ and $y_a = 0$, and the last one is obvious.

We now consider the case $y(q) > 0$. Since subsidies are packed on the least crowded heavy edges of q, there must be a heavy edge $a \in q'$ such that $y_a > 0$ so that $y_{a'} = 0$ for each heavy edge a' with $m_{a'} > m_a$ and $y_{a''} = c_j$ for each heavy edge a'' with $m_{a''} < m_a$. Let $q'_1 = \{a' \in q' : y_{a'} = 0\}$ and $q'_2 = q' \setminus (q'_1 \cup \{a\})$. Observe that the edges of q'_2 and the light edges of q do not contribute to the virtual cost of q. Hence,

$$
\begin{aligned}
\mathtt{vc}(q, y) &= \sum_{a' \in q'_1} \mathtt{vc}(a', y_{a'}) + \mathtt{vc}(a, y_a) \\
&= \sum_{a' \in q'_1} c_j \ln \frac{m_{a'}}{m_{a'} - 1} + c_j \ln \frac{m_a}{m_a - 1 + y_a/c_j} \\
&= c_j \sum_{i = t - |q'_1| + 1}^{t} \ln \frac{i}{i - 1} + c_j \ln \frac{t - |q'_1|}{t - |q'_1| - 1 + y_a/c_j} \\
&= c_j \ln \frac{t}{t - |q'_1| - 1 + y_a/c_j} \\
&= c_j \ln \frac{t}{t - |q'| + y(q)/c_j}.
\end{aligned}
$$

The first two equalities follow by the definition of the virtual cost, the third one follows since the definition of q'_1 implies that $\cup_{a' \in q'_1}\{m_{a'}\} = \{t - |q'_1| + 1, t - |q'_1| + 2, ..., t\}$ and $m_a = t - |q'_1|$, the fourth equality is obvious, and the last one follows since $y(q) = y_a + |q'_2| c_j$ and $|q'| = |q'_1| + |q'_2| + 1$. □

Figure 3 provides a visualization of the virtual cost in a

283

path when subsidies are packed on its less crowded heavy edges.

Now, we compute the subsidy assignment b^j that assigns no subsidies to the light edges and subsidies to the heavy edges of T^j as follows. Denote by L the set of leaf-nodes of T^j such that the path T_u^j connecting such a leaf-node u to the root node r in T^j contains at least one heavy edge. For each leaf-node u of L, we pack subsidies to the least crowded heavy edges of T_u^j so that the virtual cost on the path T_u^j is exactly c_j. In particular, let S be the set of edges of T^j defined as follows. Denote by $p(v)$ the parent of node v in T^j. A heavy edge $(v, p(v))$ belongs to S if $\mathrm{vc}(T_{p(v)}^j, 0) < c_j$ and $\mathrm{vc}(T_v^j, 0) \geq c_j$. Observe that the set S disconnects the leaves of L from the root node. Indeed, if this was not the case, there would be a heavy edge that is used by exactly one heavy player and is not assigned any subsidies; by the definition of the virtual cost, its virtual cost would be infinite. All heavy edges that are on the side of the partition together with the root node are assigned zero subsidies; the heavy edges on the other side of the partition are assigned subsidies of c_j and do not contribute to the virtual cost of the paths they belong to. An edge $a = (v, p(v))$ of S is assigned subsidies b_a^j with

$$b_a^j = c_j \left(1 - m_a \left(1 - \exp \left(\frac{\mathrm{vc}(T_{p(v)}^j, 0)}{c_j} - 1 \right) \right) \right).$$

This definition implies that $\mathrm{vc}(T_{p(v)}^j, 0) + \mathrm{vc}(a, b_a^j) = c_j$. In this way, we guarantee that the virtual cost of any path to the root node r is at most c_j if it contains at least one heavy edge and zero otherwise.

We will now show that, given the subsidies we have assigned to the edges of T^j, no player has an incentive to deviate from her path to the root in T^j. Consider the player associated with a node u and recall that the definition of subsidies and Claim 8 guarantee that the cost experienced by the player when she uses T_u^j is at most c_j. Let q_u be a path from u to r in G^j that is different than T_u^j and consider the edges of q_u that do not belong to T^j (since $q_u \neq T_u^j$ there is at least one such edge). If any such edge has weight c_j, this means that, by deviating to q_u, the player associated with node u would experience a cost of at least c_j and, hence, has no incentive to do so. So, in the following we assume that the edges of q_u that do not belong to T^j have zero weight. Now, consider the subgraph H of G^j induced by the edges in the paths T_u^j and q_u. Let C be a cycle of H. It consists of edges of T^j and edges not belonging to T^j that have zero weight. This implies that all edges in C have zero weight, otherwise we could replace an edge of C that belongs to T^j (and has non-zero weight) with an edge of C that does not belong to T (which has zero weight) and obtain a spanning tree of G^j with strictly smaller weight than T^j; this would contradict the assumption that T^j is a minimum spanning tree of G^j. So, all edges of T_u^j that are contained in a cycle of H have zero weight. The remaining edges of T_u^j are also used by q_u. We conclude that the total cost experienced by the player associated with node u is the same no matter whether she uses path T_u^j or q_u and, hence, she has no incentive to deviate from path T_u^j to q_u.

We will now show that the total amount of subsidies put on the edges of T^j in this way is exactly $\mathrm{wgt}(T^j)/e$. In order to show this, we will show that the total amount of subsidies put on the edges of T^j equals the total amount of subsidies

put by the same procedure on the edges of another tree $\bar{T}$ that consists of a single path from the root that spans all the nodes and has the same number of heavy edges as the original one. As an intermediate step, consider two edges $g_1 = (v_1, p(v_1))$ and $g_2 = (v_2, p(v_2))$ of S such that the least common ancestor u of nodes v_1 and v_2 in T^j has the largest depth. We denote by h_1 and h_2 the number of heavy edges in the subtrees of v_1 and v_2, respectively, and by q_1 and q_2 the paths connecting u to v_1 and v_2 in T^j, respectively. Also, denote by q_1' (resp. q_2') the subset of q_1 (resp. q_2) consisting of heavy edges. Assume that the virtual cost of the path in T^j from r to u is ℓ for some $\ell \in [0, c_j)$; then, the virtual cost of the paths q_1 and q_2 is exactly $c_j - \ell$. Denote by $b_{g_1}^j$ and $b_{g_2}^j$ the subsidies assigned to edges g_1 and g_2 by the above procedure, respectively. Since the edges g_1 and g_2 are selected so that their least common ancestor u has the largest depth, the edges in the path q_1 are not used by any heavy player different than those in the subtree of T^j rooted at v_1. Similarly, the edges in the path q_2 are not used by any heavy player other than those in the subtree of T^j rooted at v_2. Hence, both paths q_1 and q_2 satisfy the condition of Claim 10 above in the sense that $\cup_{a \in q_1'} \{m_a\} = \{h_1+1, h_1+2, ..., h_1+|q_1'|\}$ and $\cup_{a \in q_2'} \{m_a\} = \{h_2+1, h_2+2, ..., h_2+|q_2'|\}$, respectively. Hence, we can express the virtual cost of paths q_1 and q_2 as

$$\mathrm{vc}(q_1, b^j) = c_j \ln \frac{h_1 + |q_1'|}{h_1 + b_{g_1}^j / c_j} = c_j - \ell$$

and

$$\mathrm{vc}(q_2, b^j) = c_j \ln \frac{h_2 + |q_2'|}{h_2 + b_{g_2}^j / c_j} = c_j - \ell,$$

respectively. Equivalently, we have $h_1 + |q_1'| = \exp(1 - \ell/c_j)(h_1 + b_{g_1}^j/c_j)$ and $h_2 + |q_2'| = \exp(1 - \ell/c_j)(h_2 + b_{g_2}^j/c_j)$. By summing these last two equalities, we obtain that $h_1 + h_2 + |q_1'| + |q_2'| = \exp(1 - \ell/c_j)(h_1 + h_2 + (b_{g_1}^j + b_{g_2}^j)/c_j)$ which implies

$$c_j \ln \frac{h_1 + h_2 + |q_1'| + |q_2'|}{h_1 + h_2 + (b_{g_1}^j + b_{g_2}^j)/c_j} = c_j - \ell. \qquad (2)$$

Now, consider the following transformation of T^j to another tree T'. The only change is performed in the paths q_1, q_2 and all subtrees of their nodes besides node u. We replace all these edges in T^j with a path q originating from u and spanning all the nodes in q_1 and q_2 and their subtrees so that exactly $h_1 + h_2 + |q_1'| + |q_2'|$ heavy edges are used. Let q' be the set of heavy edges in q. We pack a total amount $c_j(h_1 + h_2) + b_{g_1}^j + b_{g_2}^j$ of subsidies (i.e., the same total amount of subsidies used in the heavy edges of q_1, q_2 and in the subtrees of nodes v_1 and v_2 in T^j) on the least crowded heavy edges of path q while the assignment of subsidies on the other heavy edges of T' is the same as in the corresponding edges in T^j. Now, the path q satisfies the condition of the Claim 10 above in the sense that $\cup_{a \in q'} \{m_a\} = \{1, ..., h_1 + h_2 + |q_1'| + |q_2'|\}$. Hence, the virtual cost of path q when a total amount $c_j(h_1 + h_2) + b_{g_1}^j + b_{g_2}^j$ of subsidies is packed on its least crowded heavy edges is the one at the left hand side of equality (2) and is exactly $c_j - \ell$ while the virtual cost of the path from the root to u in T' is not affected by our transformation (the number of heavy players in the subtree of node u stays the same after the transformation) and is equal to ℓ. Hence, we have transformed T^j to T' so that the same total amount of subsidies is used and guarantees that any path from the root to a node has virtual cost at most c_j. By executing the same transformation in T' repeatedly, we end up with a tree $\bar{T}$ which consists of a path $\bar{q}$ spanning all the nodes and has the same number of heavy edges as the original tree T^j (and, obviously, the same total weight). Let $\bar{q}'$ be the set of heavy edges in $\bar{q}$. The transformation guarantees that by packing the original total amount of subsidies on the least crowded heavy edges of $\bar{q}$, we have that its virtual cost is exactly c_j. Also, note that $\cup_{a \in \bar{q}'} \{m_a\} = \{1, 2, ..., |\bar{q}'|\}$ and, by Claim 10, the virtual cost of path $\bar{q}$ when a total amount $b(T^j)$ of subsidies is packed on its least crowded heavy edges is $c_j \ln \frac{|\bar{q}'|c_j}{b(T^j)} = c_j$. This implies that the total amount of subsidies in the original tree is $b(T^j) = |\bar{q}'|c_j/e = \mathtt{wgt}(T^j)/e$. $\square$

Now, for each copy G^j of G, we use the procedure in the proof of Lemma 7 to compute a subsidy assignment b^j so that the tree T^j is an equilibrium for the extension of the broadcast game on the graph G^j with subsidies b^j. For the original game on the graph G, we assign an amount of $b_a = \sum_{j=1}^{k} b_a^j$ as subsidies to edge a (i.e., equal to the total amount of subsidies assigned to a for each copy of G). By the properties of our decomposition and Lemma 7, the total amount of subsidies is $\sum_{j=1}^{k} \mathtt{wgt}(T^j)/e = \mathtt{wgt}(T)/e$.

It remains to show that T is an equilibrium for the original broadcast game. Consider a node u of G and let q_u be any path connecting u with r in G. The cost experienced by the player associated with node u in T is

$$
\begin{aligned}
\mathtt{cost}_u(T; b) &= \sum_{a \in T_u} \frac{w_a - b_a}{n_a(T)} = \sum_{a \in T_u} \sum_{j=1}^{k} \frac{w_a^j - b_a^j}{n_a(T^j)} \\
&= \sum_{j=1}^{k} \sum_{a \in T_u} \frac{w_a^j - b_a^j}{n_a(T^j)} \\
&\leq \sum_{j=1}^{k} \sum_{a \in q_u} \frac{w_a^j - b_a^j}{n_a(T^j) + 1 - n_a^u(T^j)} \\
&= \sum_{a \in q_u} \frac{w_a - b_a}{n_a(T_{-u}, q_u)} \\
&= \mathtt{cost}_u(T_{-u}, q_u; b),
\end{aligned}
$$

i.e., not larger than the cost she would experience by deviating to path q_u; this implies that T is indeed enforced as an equilibrium in the extension of the broadcast game on G with the particular subsidies. The equalities follow by the definition of the cost experienced by the player associated with node u, or the definition of our decomposition, or due to the exchange of sums. The inequality follows since, by Lemma 7, T^j is enforced as an equilibrium in the extension of the broadcast game in G^j with subsidies b^j. $\square$

We now present our lower bound.

THEOREM 11. *For every $\epsilon > 0$, there exist a broadcast game on a graph G and a minimum spanning tree T of G such that the cost of any subsidy assignment that enforces T as equilibrium of the extension of the broadcast game with subsidies is at least $(1/e - \epsilon)\mathtt{wgt}(T)$.*

PROOF. Consider the graph G which consists of a cycle with $n + 1$ edges of unit weight that span the root node r and the n nodes which are associated with the players. Let

$a = (r, u)$ be an edge incident to the root node r and let T be the path that contains all edges of G besides a. Clearly, T is a minimum spanning tree of G. Now, in order to satisfy that the player associated with node u has no incentive to deviate from her strategy in T and use edge a instead, we have to put subsidies on some of the edges of the path T. The maximum decrease in the cost of the player associated with node u is obtained when subsidies are packed on the least crowded edges of T (i.e., on the edges of T that are further from the root); equivalently, the minimum amount of subsidies necessary in order to decrease the cost of this player to 1 is obtained when subsidies are packed on the least crowded edges of T. Let k be the number of edges that are subsidized. Since the player associated with node u has no incentive to deviate, the cost of $\mathcal{H}_n - \mathcal{H}_k$ she experiences at the $n - k$ edges on which we do not put subsidies is at most 1 while the total amount of subsidies is at least $k - 1$. Using the inequality $x \geq \ln(1 + x)$ for $x \geq 0$, we obtain $1 \geq \mathcal{H}_n - \mathcal{H}_k = \sum_{t=k+1}^{n} \frac{1}{t} \geq \sum_{t=k+1}^{n} \ln \frac{t+1}{t} = \ln \frac{n+1}{k+1}$ which implies that that the total amount of subsidies is at least $k - 1 \geq \frac{n+1}{e} - 2$. The weight of T is n and the bound follows by selecting n to be sufficiently large. $\square$

5. ALL-OR-NOTHING SUBSIDIES

In this section, we consider the all-or-nothing version of SNE. Interestingly, in contrast to the standard version, we prove that its optimization version is hard to approximate within any factor.

THEOREM 12. *Given an instance of all-or-nothing STA-BLE NETWORK ENFORCEMENT consisting of a broadcast game on a graph G and a minimum spanning tree T of G, approximating (within any factor) the minimum cost over all-or-nothing subsidy assignments that enforce T as an equilibrium in the extension of the broadcast game is NP-hard.*

The proof of Theorem 12 is omitted. Theorem 12 probably indicates that the only approximation guarantee we should hope for all-or-nothing SNE is to bound the amount of subsidies as a constant fraction of the weight of an optimal design. The next statement implies that significantly more subsidies may be necessary compared to the standard version of SNE in order to enforce a minimum spanning tree as an equilibrium.

THEOREM 13. *For every $\epsilon > 0$, there exist a broadcast game on a graph G and a minimum spanning tree T of G such that the cost of any all-or-nothing subsidy assignment that enforces T as an equilibrium in the extension of the broadcast game is at least $\left(\frac{e}{2e-1} - \epsilon\right) \mathtt{wgt}(T)$.*

PROOF. We define a graph G with $n + 1$ nodes $r, v_1, ..., v_n$ which has the path $\langle r, v_1, v_2, ..., v_n \rangle$ as minimum spanning tree. Let $x = (n - n/e + 1)^{-1}$. Edges (r, v_1) and (v_i, v_{i+1}) for $i = 1, ..., n - 2$ have weight x. Edge (v_{n-1}, v_n) has weight 1. The graph contains two additional edges: edge (r, v_{n-1}) has weight x and edge (r, v_n) has weight 1. If we do not put subsidies on the edge (v_{n-1}, v_n), then we have to put subsidies on each of the remaining edges in the path in order to guarantee that the player associated with node v_n has no incentive to use the direct edge (v_n, r), i.e., a total amount of $(n - 1)x$ as subsidies. If we put subsidies on the edge (v_{n-1}, v_n), we still have to guarantee that the player associated with node v_{n-1} has no incentive to deviate to the direct edge (v_{n-1}, r). Using the same reasoning as in the proof of Theorem 11, we will need an amount of at least $(n/e-2)x$ as subsidies on the edges of the path $\langle r, v_1, v_2, ..., v_{n-1}\rangle$, for a total of $1 + (n/c - 2)x$. By the definition of x, we have that the amount of subsidies is at least $\frac{n-1}{n-n/e+1}$ in both cases while the total weight of T is $\frac{2n-n/e}{n-n/e+1}$. The bound follows by selecting n to be sufficiently large. $\square$

6. OPEN PROBLEMS

Our work has revealed several open questions. Concerning the particular results obtained, it is interesting to design a combinatorial algorithm for SNE which, on input a graph G and a minimum spanning tree T on G, enforces T as an equilibrium on the corresponding broadcast game using minimum subsidies. Lemma 2 may be helpful in this direction. For the integral version of SNE, we have left open the question whether it is always possible to enforce a given minimum spanning tree as an equilibrium in a broadcast game using all-or-nothing subsidies of cost strictly smaller than the weight of a minimum spanning tree. Given our negative result in Theorem 12, this is probably the only approximation that makes sense. It is tempting to conjecture that our lower bound is tight, i.e., there is an algorithm that always uses a fraction of at most $\frac{e}{2e-1} \approx 61\%$ of the weight of the minimum spanning tree as subsidies in order to do so.

Approximating SND would also be interesting. Given the known hardness statements (e.g., [20]) or the lack of positive results concerning the complexity of computing equilibria, this is a far more challenging goal. A concrete question for SND instances consisting of broadcast games could be the following: can we compute in polynomial time an equilibrium tree using subsidies of cost at most an α fraction of the weight of the minimum spanning tree? Our results (Theorems 1 and 6) indicate that the answer is clearly positive if $\alpha \geq 1/e$. Is this also possible if α is an arbitrarily small constant? Definitely, more general instances of SND (e.g., involving multicast games) are challenging as well. Finally, variations of SNE and SND that consider deviations of coalitions of players (as opposed to unilateral deviations), players with different demands, or different cost sharing protocols deserve investigation.

Acknowledgments. We thank Edith Elkind, Ning Chen, Nick Gravin, and Alex Skopalik for helpful discussions.

7. REFERENCES

[1] S. Albers and P. Lenzner. On approximate Nash equilibria in network design. In *Proceedings of the 6th International Workshop on Internet and Network Economics (WINE)*, LNCS 6484, pp. 14–25, 2010.

[2] E. Anshelevich, A. Dasgupta, J. M. Kleinberg, E. Tardos, T. Wexler, and T. Roughgarden. The price of stability for network design with fair cost allocation. *SIAM Journal on Computing*, 38(4): 1602–1623, 2008.

[3] E. Anshelevich, A. Dasgupta, E. Tardos, and T. Wexler. Near-optimal network design with selfish agents. *Theory of Computing*, 4(1): 77–109, 2008.

[4] Y. Bachrach, E. Elkind, R. Meir, D. V. Pasechnik, M. Zuckerman, J. Rothe, and J. S. Rosenschein. The cost of stability in coalitional games. In *Proceedings of the 2nd International Symposium on Algorithmic Game Theory (SAGT)*, LNCS 5814, pp. 122–134, 2009.

[5] V. Bilò, I. Caragiannis, A. Fanelli, and G. Monaco. Improved lower bounds on the price of stability of undirected network design games. In *Proceedings of the 3rd International Symposium on Algorithmic Game Theory (SAGT)*, LNCS 6386, pp. 90–101, 2010.

[6] N. Buchbinder, L. Lewin-Eytan, J. Naor, and A. Orda. Non-cooperative cost sharing games via subsidies. *Theory of Computing Systems*, 47(1): 15–37, 2010.

[7] M. Charikar, H. J. Karloff, C. Mathieu, J. Naor, and M. E. Saks. Online multicast with egalitarian cost sharing. In *Proceedings of the 20th Annual ACM Symposium on Parallelism in Algorithms and Architectures (SPAA)*, pp. 70–76, 2008.

[8] C. Chekuri, J. Chuzhoy, L. Lewin-Eytan, J. Naor, and A. Orda. Non-cooperative multicast and facility location games. *IEEE Journal on Selected Areas in Communications*, 25(6): 1193–1206, 2007.

[9] G. Christodoulou, E. Koutsoupias, and A. Nanavati. Coordination mechanisms. *Theoretical Computer Science*, 410(36): 3327–3336, 2009.

[10] R. Cole, Y. Dodis, and T. Roughgarden. How much can taxes help selfish routing? *Journal of Computer and System Sciences*, 72(3): 444–467, 2006.

[11] A. Fabrikant, C. H. Papadimitriou, and K. Talwar. The complexity of pure Nash equilibria. In *Proceedings of the 36th Annual ACM Symposium on Theory of Computing (STOC)*, pp. 604–612, 2004.

[12] A. Fiat, H. Kaplan, M. Levy, S. Olonetsky, and R. Shabo. On the price of stability for designing undirected networks with fair cost allocations. In *Proceedings of the 33rd International Colloquium on Automata, Languages and Programming (ICALP)*, LNCS 4051, Part I, pp. 608–618, 2006.

[13] E. Koutsoupias and C. Papadimitriou. Worst-case equilibria. In *Proceedings of the 16th International Symposium on Theoretical Aspects of Computer Science (STACS)*, LNCS 1563, pp. 404–413, 1999.

[14] J. Li. An $O(\log n/\log \log n)$ upper bound on the price of stability for undirected Shapley network design games. *Information Processing Letters*, 109(15): 876–878, 2009.

[15] D. Monderer and M. Tennenholtz. K-Implementation. *Journal of Artificial Intelligence Research*, 21: 37–62, 2004.

[16] N. Nisan. Introduction to mechanism design (for computer scientists). Chapter 9 in *Algorithmic Game Theory*, Cambridge University Press, pp. 209–241, 2007.

[17] C. H. Papadimitriou. Algorithms, games and the internet. In *Proceedings of the 33rd Annual ACM Symposium on Theory of Computing (STOC)*, pp. 749–753, 2001.

[18] R. Rosenthal. A class of games possessing pure-strategy Nash equilibria. *International Journal of Game Theory*, 2: 65–67, 1973.

[19] T. Roughgarden. Stackelberg scheduling strategies. *SIAM Journal on Computing*, 33(2): 332–350, 2004.

[20] V. Syrgkanis. The complexity of equilibria in cost sharing games. In *Proceedings of the 6th International Workshop on Internet and Network Economics (WINE)*, LNCS 6484, pp. 366–377, 2010.

Memory-Mapping Support for Reducer Hyperobjects

I-Ting Angelina Lee [*]
MIT CSAIL

32 Vassar Street
Cambridge, MA 02139 USA
angelee@csail.mit.edu

Aamir Shafi [†]
National University of
Sciences and Technology
Sector H-12
Islamabad, Pakistan
aamir.shafi@seecs.edu.pk

Charles E. Leiserson
MIT CSAIL

32 Vassar Street
Cambridge, MA 02139 USA
cel@mit.edu

ABSTRACT

Reducer hyperobjects (reducers) provide a linguistic abstraction for dynamic multithreading that allows different branches of a parallel program to maintain coordinated local views of the same non-local variable. In this paper, we investigate how *thread-local memory mapping (TLMM)* can be used to improve the performance of reducers. Existing concurrency platforms that support reducer hyperobjects, such as Intel Cilk Plus and Cilk++, take a hypermap approach in which a hash table is used to map reducer objects to their local views. The overhead of the hash table is costly — roughly 12× overhead compared to a normal L1-cache memory access on an AMD Opteron 8354. We replaced the Intel Cilk Plus runtime system with our own Cilk-M runtime system which uses TLMM to implement a reducer mechanism that supports a reducer lookup using only two memory accesses and a predictable branch, which is roughly a 3× overhead compared to an ordinary L1-cache memory access. An empirical evaluation shows that the Cilk-M memory-mapping approach is close to 4× faster than the Cilk Plus hypermap approach. Furthermore, the memory-mapping approach admits better locality than the hypermap approach during parallel execution, which allows an application using reducers to scale better.

Categories and Subject Descriptors

D.1.3 [**Software**]: Programming Techniques—*Concurrent programming*; D.3.3 [**Software**]: Language Constructs and Features—*Concurrent programming structures*.

General Terms

Design, Experimentation, Performance.

This work was supported in part by the National Science Foundation under Grant CNS-1017058. Aamir Shafi was funded in part by a Fulbright grant during his visit at MIT.

[*]I-Ting Angelina Lee is currently affiliated with Intel Labs, Hillsboro, OR.

[†]Aamir Shafi is currently an Assistant Professor at NUST SEECS and was a Visiting Fulbright Scholar at MIT during the course of this research.

Permission to make digital or hard copies of all or part of this work for personal or classroom use is granted without fee provided that copies are not made or distributed for profit or commercial advantage and that copies bear this notice and the full citation on the first page. To copy otherwise, to republish, to post on servers or to redistribute to lists, requires prior specific permission and/or a fee.
SPAA'12, June 25–27, 2012, Pittsburgh, Pennsylvania, USA.
Copyright 2012 ACM 978-1-4503-1213-4/12/06 ...$10.00.

Keywords

Cilk, dynamic multithreading, memory mapping, reducers, reducer hyperobjects, task parallelism, thread-local memory mapping (TLMM), work stealing.

1. INTRODUCTION

Reducer hyperobjects (or *reducers* for short) [12] have been shown to be a useful linguistic mechanism to avoid determinacy races [11] (also referred as *general races* [28]) in dynamic multi-threaded programs. Reducers allow different logical branches of a parallel computation to maintain coordinated local views of the same nonlocal variable. Whenever a reducer is updated — typically using an associative operator — the *worker* thread on which the update occurs maps the reducer access to its local view and performs the update on that local view. As the computation proceeds, the various views are judiciously *reduced* (combined) by the runtime system using an associative *reduce* operator to produce a final value.

Although existing reducer mechanisms are generally faster than other solutions for updating nonlocal variables, such as locking and atomic-update, they are still relatively slow. Concurrency platforms that support reducers, specifically Intel's Cilk Plus [19] and Cilk++ [25], implement the reducer mechanism using a *hypermap approach* in which each worker employs a thread-local hash table to map reducers to their local views. Since every access to a reducer requires a hash-table lookup, operations on reducers are relatively costly — about 12× overhead compared to an ordinary L1-cache memory access on an AMD Opteron 8354. In this paper, we investigate a *memory-mapping approach* for supporting reducers, which leverages the virtual-address translation provided by the underlying hardware to yield a close to 4× faster access time.

A memory-mapping reducer mechanism must address four key questions:

1. What operating-system support is required to allow the virtual-memory hardware to map reducers to their local views?
2. How can a variety of reducers with different types, sizes, and life spans be handled?
3. How should a worker's local views be organized in a compact fashion to allow both constant-time lookups and efficient sequencing during reductions?
4. Can a worker efficiently gain access to another worker's local views without extra memory mapping?

Our memory-mapping approach answers each of these questions using simple and efficient strategies.

1. The operating-system support employs *thread-local memory mapping (TLMM)* [23]. TLMM enables the virtual-memory

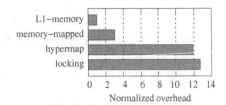

Figure 1: The relative overhead for ordinary L1-cache memory accesses, memory-mapped reducers, hypermap reducers, and locking. Each value is calculated by the normalizing the average execution time of the microbenchmark for the given category by the average execution time of the microbenchmark that performs L1-cache memory accesses.

hardware to map the same virtual address to different views in the different worker threads, allowing reducer lookups to occur without the overhead of hashing.

2. The thread-local region of the virtual-memory address space only holds pointers to local views and not the local views themselves. This *thread-local indirection* strategy allows a variety of reducers with different types, sizes, and life spans to be handled.

3. A *sparse accumulator (SPA)* data structure [14] is used to organize the worker-local views. The SPA data structure has a compact representation that allows both constant-time random access to elements and sequencing through elements stored in the data structure efficiently.

4. By combining the thread-local indirection and the use of the SPA data structure, a worker can efficiently transfer a view to another worker. This support for efficient *view transferal* allows workers to perform reductions without extra memory mapping.

We implemented our memory-mapping strategy by modifying Cilk-M [23], a Cilk runtime system that employs TLMM to manage the "cactus stack," to make it a plug-in replacement for Intel's Cilk Plus runtime system. That is, we modified the Cilk-M runtime system to replace the native Cilk runtime system shipped with Intel's C++ compiler by making Cilk-M conform to the Intel Cilk Plus Application Binary Interface (ABI) [17]. We then implemented the memory-mapping strategy in the Cilk-M runtime system and compared it on code compiled by the Intel compiler to Cilk Plus's hypermap strategy.

Figure 1 graphs the overheads of ordinary accesses, memory-mapped reducer lookups, and hypermap reducer lookups on a simple microbenchmark that performs additions on four memory locations in a tight `for` loop, executed on a single processor. The memory locations are declared to be `volatile` to preclude the compiler from optimizing the memory accesses into register accesses. Thus, the microbenchmark measures the overhead of L1-cache memory accesses. For the memory-mapped and hypermap reducers, one reducer per memory location is used. The figure also includes for comparison the overhead of locking — one `pthread_spin_lock` per memory location is employed, where the microbenchmark performs lock and unlock around the memory updates on the corresponding locks. The microbenchmark was run on a AMD Opteron processor 8354 with 4 quad-core 2 GHz CPU's with a total of 8 GBytes of memory and installed with Linux 2.6.32. As the figure shows, a memory-mapped reducer lookup is only about $3\times$ slower than an ordinary L1-cache memory access and almost $4\times$ faster than the hypermap approach (and as we shall see in Section 8, the differences between the two increases with the number of reducers). The overhead of locking is similar but slightly worse than the overhead of a hypermap reducer lookup.

A memory-mapped reducer admits a lookup operation that can be performed using only two memory accesses and a predictable

```
1   bool has_property(Node *n);
2   std::list<Node *> l;
3   // ...
4   void walk(Node *n) {
5       if(n) {
6           if(has_property(n))
7               l.push_back(n);
8           cilk_spawn walk(n->left);
9           walk(n->right);
10          cilk_sync;
11      }
12  }
```

(a)

```
1   bool has_property(Node *n);
2   list_append_reducer<Node *> l;
3   // ...
4   void walk(Node *n) {
5       if(n) {
6           if(has_property(n))
7               l->push_back(n);
8           cilk_spawn walk(n->left);
9           walk(n->right);
10          cilk_sync;
11      }
12  }
```

(b)

Figure 2: (a) An incorrect parallel code to walk a binary tree and create a list of all nodes that satisfy a given property. The code contains a race on the list `l`. (b) A correct parallelization of the code shown in Figure 2(a) using a reducer hyperobject.

branch, which is more efficient than a hypermap reducer. An unexpected byproduct of the memory-mapping approach is that it provides greater locality than the hypermap approach, which leads to more scalable performance.

The rest of the paper is organized as follows. Section 2 provides the necessary background on reducer semantics, which includes the linguistic model for dynamic multithreading and the reducer interface and guarantees. Section 3 reviews the hypermap approach to support the reducer mechanism. Sections 4, 5, 6, and 7 describe our design and implementation of the memory-mapped reducers, where each section addresses one of the four questions we mentioned above in details. Section 8 presents the empirical evaluation of the memory-mapped reducers by comparing it to the hypermap reducers. Section 9 summarizes related work. Lastly, Section 10 offers some concluding remarks.

2. CILK LINGUISTICS

This section reviews Cilk's linguistic model for dynamic multithreading in general and reducer hyperobjects in particular using the Cilk Plus [19] formulation. The results reported in this article should apply to other dynamic-multithreading[1] concurrency platforms — including MIT Cilk [13], Cilk++ [25], Cilk Plus , Fortress [2], Habanero [4, 9], Hood [7], Java Fork/Join Framework [21], OpenMP 3.0 [29], Task Parallel Library (TPL) [24], Threading Building Blocks (TBB) [31], and X10 [10] — but to our knowledge, Cilk++ and Cilk Plus are the only platforms that currently support reducers.

The dynamic multithreading support in Cilk Plus [19] augments serial C/C++ code with two principal keywords: `cilk_spawn` and `cilk_sync`.[2] The term dynamic multithreading alludes to the fact

---

[1] Sometimes called *task parallelism*.

[2] Cilk Plus also includes a `cilk_for` keyword, which provides the parallel counterpart of a **for** loop, allowing all iterations of the loop to operate in parallel. We omit it here, since the Cilk Plus compiler simply "desugars" the `cilk_for` into code containing `cilk_spawn` and `cilk_sync` that

that these keywords expose the *logical* parallelism of the computation without mentioning the number of processors on which the computation should run. The underlying runtime system efficiently schedules the computation across available worker threads, which serve as processor surrogates, in a manner that respects the logical parallelism specified by the programmer.

We shall illustrate how these keywords work using an example. The code in Figure 2(a) walks a binary tree in preorder fashion to create a list of all nodes that satisfy a given property. The code checks and appends the current node onto an output list if the node satisfies the given property and subsequently walks the node's left and right children. The code is parallelized to walk the left and right children in parallel, which is achieved by preceding the call to walk the left child in line 8 with the `cilk_spawn` keyword. When a function invocation is preceded by the keyword `cilk_spawn`, the function is *spawned*, and the scheduler may continue to execute the continuation of the caller in parallel with the spawned subroutine without waiting for it to return. Thus, in this example, the walk of the left child may execute in parallel with the continuation of the parent, which invokes the call to walk the right child (line 9).

The complement of `cilk_spawn` is the keyword `cilk_sync`, which acts as a local barrier and joins together the parallelism forked by `cilk_spawn`. The underlying runtime system ensures that statements after a `cilk_sync` are not executed until all functions spawned before the `cilk_sync` statement have completed and returned. Thus in this example, a `cilk_sync` statement is inserted at line 10 to ensure that the function does not return until the walk of the left and right children are done. This parallelization is incorrect, however, since it contains a *determinacy race* [11] (also referred a as *general race* [28]) on the list l, because the logically parallel subcomputations — the walks of the left and right subtrees — may potentially access the list in parallel.

Reducer hyperobjects (or *reducers* for short) [12] provide a linguistic mechanism to avoid such determinacy races in dynamically multithreaded computations. Figure 2(b) shows a correct parallelization of the `walk` function using a reducer. The code simply declares l in line 2 to be a reducer with a *reduce operation* that performs list append. By declaring list l to be a reducer, parallel accesses to l are coordinated by the runtime system, and the resulting output list produced by the code is identical to the result produced by a serial execution.

In order for a reducer to produce a deterministic output, the reduce operation must be associative. More precisely, a reducer is defined in terms of an algebraic *monoid*: a triple $(T, \otimes, e)$, where T is a set and $\otimes$ is an binary associative operation over T with the identity e. Example monoids include $(\mathbf{Z}, +, 0)$ (addition on integers), $(\{\text{TRUE}, \text{FALSE}\}, \wedge, \text{TRUE})$ (logical AND on Booleans), and list append with the empty list as the identity, as in the example. The Cilk Plus runtime coordinates concurrent accesses to a reducer, guaranteeing that the output is the always the same as in a serial execution, as long as its reduce operation is associative.

3. SUPPORT FOR HYPERMAP REDUCERS

This section overviews the implementation of the Cilk++ [25] and Cilk Plus [19] reducer mechanism, which is based on hypermaps. Support for reducers was first proposed in [12] and implemented in Cilk++. The implementation in Cilk Plus closely follows that in Cilk++. This section summarizes the runtime support relevant for comparing the hypermap approach to the memory-mapping approach. We refer interested readers to the original article [12] for full details on the hypermap approach.

Support for reducers in Cilk Plus is implemented as a C++ template library. The user invokes functions in the runtime system, and the runtime system calls back to user-defined functions according to an agreed-upon API [18]. The type of a reducer is dictated by the monoid it implements and the type of data set that the monoid operates on. The reducer library implements the monoid interface and provides two important operations that the runtime invokes: IDENTITY, which creates an identity view for a given reducer, and REDUCE, which implements the binary associative operator that reduces two views. A user can override these operations to define her own reducer types.

During parallel execution, accesses to a reducer hyperobject cause the runtime to generate and maintain multiple views for the given reducer, thereby allowing each worker to operate on its own local view. A reducer is distinctly different from the notion of *thread-local storage* (or *TLS*) [33], however. Unlike TLS, a worker may create and operate on multiple local views for a given reducer throughout execution. New identity views for a given reducer may be created whenever there is parallelism, because the runtime must ensure that updates performed on a single view retain serial semantics. In that sense, a local view is associated with a particular execution context but not with a particular worker. Consequently, a hypermap that contains local views is not permanently affixed to a particular worker, but rather to the execution context.

To see how local views are created and maintained, we first review how a work-stealing scheduler operates. In Cilk Plus (as well as in Cilk-M), the runtime creates a *frame* for every instance of a *Cilk* function that can spawn, which provides storage for bookkeeping data needed by the runtime. Whenever a worker encounters a `cilk_spawn`, it invokes the child and suspends the parent, pushing the parent frame onto the bottom of its *deque* (double-ended queue), so as to allow the parent frame to be stolen. When the child returns, it pops the bottom of the deque and resumes the parent frame. Pushing and popping frames from the bottom of the deque is the common case, and it mirrors precisely the behavior of a serial execution.

The worker's behavior departs from the serial execution if it runs out of work. This situation can arise, for example, when the code executed by the worker encounters a `cilk_sync` and children of the current frame have not returned. In this case the worker becomes a *thief*, and it attempts to steal the topmost (oldest) frame from a randomly chosen *victim* worker. If the steal is *successful*, the worker resumes the stolen frame. Another situation where a worker runs out of work occurs if it returns from a spawned child to discover that its deque is empty (the parent has been stolen). In this case, it checks whether the parent is stalled at a `cilk_sync` and if this child is the last child to return. If so, it performs a *joining steal* and resumes the parent function, passing the `cilk_sync` at which the parent was stalled. Otherwise, the worker engages in random work-stealing as in the case when a `cilk_sync` was encountered.

A worker's behavior precisely mimics the serial execution between successful steals. Logical parallelism morphs into true parallelism when a thief steals and resumes a function (the continuation of the parent after a spawn). Whenever a Cilk function is stolen, its frame is *promoted* into a *full frame*, which contains additional bookkeeping data to handle the true parallelism created, including hypermaps that contain local views. Specifically, each full frame may contain up to 3 hypermaps — the *user hypermap*, *left-child hypermap*, and *right-sibling hypermap* — each of which respec-

---

recursively subdivides the iteration space to execute in parallel. Cilk Plus also includes support for vector operations, which are not relevant to the discussion here.

tively contains local views generated from computations associated with the given frame, its leftmost child, and its right sibling.

During parallel execution, a worker performs reducer-related operations on the user hypermap stored in the full frame sitting on top of its deque (since everything below the full frame mirrors the serial execution). The hypermap maps reducers to their corresponding local views on which the worker operates. Specifically, the address of a reducer is used as a key to hash the local view. Whenever a full frame is stolen, its original user hypermap is left with its child executing on the victim, and an empty user hypermap is created on the thief. When a worker encounters a reducer declaration, it creates a reducer hyperobject if one does not yet exist, and it inserts a key-value pair into its hypermap. The key is the address of the reducer, and the value is the initial identity view, referred to as the *leftmost view*. When a reducer goes out of scope, at which point its leftmost view should reflect all updates, the worker removes the key-value pair from its hypermap. Finally, whenever the worker encounters an access to a reducer in the user code, the worker performs a lookup in its hypermap and returns the corresponding local view. If nothing is found in the hypermap (the user hypermap starts out empty when the frame is first promoted), the worker creates and inserts an identity view into the hypermap and returns the identity.

The other two hypermaps are placeholders. They store the accumulated values of the frame's terminated right siblings and terminated children, respectively. Whenever a frame is promoted, an additional set of local views may be created to accumulate updates from the computation associated with the full frame. These views are eventually reduced either with views from the worker's left sibling or parent in an appropriate order consistent with a serial execution. When a frame F_1 executing on W_1 terminates (i.e., returns), however, its sibling or parent F_2 may still be running, executed by another worker W_2. To avoid interfering with W_2 executing F_2, W_1 simply deposits its set of local views stored in F_1's user hypermap into F_2's left-child or right-sibling hypermap placeholder, depending on the relation between F_1 and F_2. We refer to the process of one worker depositing its local views into a frame running on another worker as *view transferal*, which more generally, refers to the process of transferring ownership of local views from one worker to another.

Similarly, before W_1 can perform view transferal from F_1 to F_2, it may find a second set of local views stored in F_1's left-child or right-sibling hypermap placeholders. If so, W_1 must reduce the two sets of views together — iterate through each view from one hypermap, look up the corresponding view in another hypermap, and reduce the two views into a single view. This process is referred as the *hypermerge* process. Worker W_1 performs hypermerges until it has only one set of local views left to deposit. We omit details on how the runtime maintains the correct orders of reduction and refer readers to [12].

4. THREAD-LOCAL MEMORY MAPPING

This section describes thread-local memory mapping (TLMM) [22, 23], which Cilk-M uses to cause the virtual-memory hardware to map reducers to local views. TLMM provides an efficient and flexible way for a thread to map certain regions of virtual memory independently from other threads while still sharing most of its virtual-memory address space. This section reviews the functionality that the TLMM mechanism provides and how we implemented it in a Linux operating system.

Cilk-M's memory-mapping reducer mechanism employs the virtual-address hardware to map accesses to a given reducer to different local views depending on the worker performing the access. Different workers must be able to map different physical pages

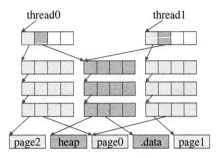

Figure 3: Example of a x86 64-bit page-table configuration for two threads on TLMM-Linux. The portion of the data structure dealing with the TLMM region is shaded light grey, and the remainder corresponding to the shared region is shaded dark grey. In the TLMM region, thread0 maps page2 first and then page0, whereas thread1 maps page1 first and then page0. The pages associated with the heap and the data segments are shared between the two threads.

within the same virtual address range so that the same global virtual address can map to different views for different workers. Given that a dynamic-multithreaded program typically executes on a shared-memory system, part of the address space must be shared to allow workers to communicate with each other and enable parallel branches of the user program to share data on the heap. In other words, this memory-mapping approach requires part of the virtual address space to be *private*, in which workers can map independently with different physical pages, while the rest being *shared*, in which different workers can share data allocated on the heap as usual.

By default, a traditional operating system does not provide such mixed sharing mode — either nothing is shared (each process has its own virtual-address space, and no two processes share the same virtual-address space), or everything is shared (all threads within a given process share the process's entire virtual-address space). TLMM designates a region, referred to as the *TLMM region*, of a process's virtual-address space as private. This special TLMM region occupies the same virtual-address range for each worker, but each worker may map different physical pages to the TLMM region. The rest of the virtual-address space is shared among workers in the process as usual.

Cilk-M's TLMM mechanism [22, 23] was originally developed to enable a work-stealing runtime system to maintain a "cactus-stack" abstraction, thereby allowing arbitrary calling between parallel and serial code. To implement TLMM, we modified the Linux kernel, producing a kernel version we call *TLMM-Linux*. The existing implementation is for Linux kernel 2.6.32 running on x86 64-bit CPU's, such as the AMD Opteron and Intel Xeon.

Figure 3 illustrates the design. TLMM-Linux assigns a unique root page directory to each thread in a process. The x86 64-bit page tables have four levels, and the page directories at each level contain 512 entries. One entry of the root-page directory is reserved for the TLMM region, which corresponds to 512 GBytes of virtual-address space, and the rest of the entries correspond to the shared region. Threads in TLMM-Linux share page directories that correspond to shared region. Therefore, the TLMM-Linux virtual-memory manager must synchronize the entries in each thread's root page directory but populate the shared lower-level page directories only once.

The TLMM mechanism provides a low-level virtual-memory interface organized around allocating and mapping physical pages. We omit the descriptions of its interface and refer interested readers to [23] for details. For the purpose of our discussion, simply note that the TLMM interface provides a way for workers to "name" a physical page using a *page descriptor*, which is analogous to a file descriptor and accessible by all workers. The system call `sys_pmap` allows a worker to map its TLMM region with particular physical pages specified by an array of page descriptors. Thus, a worker can share its TLMM region with another worker by publicizing the page descriptors corresponding to the physical pages mapped in its TLMM region.

The TLMM mechanism supports the following system calls, which provides a low-level virtual-memory interface organized around allocating and mapping physical pages. `sys_palloc` allocates a physical page and returns its page descriptor. A page descriptor is analogous to a file descriptor, which "names" a physical page and can be accessed by any thread in the process. `sys_pfree` frees a page descriptor and its associated physical page. To control the physical-page mappings in a thread's TLMM region, the thread calls `sys_pmap`, specifying an array of page descriptors to map, as well as a base address in the TLMM region at which to begin mapping the descriptors. `sys_pmap` steps through the array of page descriptors, mapping physical pages for each descriptor to subsequent page-aligned virtual addresses, to produce a continuous virtual-address mapping that starts at the base address. A special page-descriptor value `PD_NULL` indicates that a virtual-address mapping should be removed.

We added the memory-mapping reducer mechanism to Cilk-M, which now utilizes the TLMM region for both the cactus stack and memory-mapped reducers. Since a stack naturally grows downward, and the use of space for reducers is akin to the use of heap space, at system start-up, the TLMM region is divided into two parts: the cactus stack is allocated at the highest TLMM address possible, growing downwards, and the space reserved for reducers starts at the lowest TLMM address possible, growing upwards. The two parts can grow as much as needed, since in a 64-bit address space, as a practical matter, the two ends will never meet.

5. THREAD-LOCAL INDIRECTION

This section describes how Cilk-M's memory-mapping strategy for implementing reducers exploits a level of indirection so that the reducer mechanism can handle a variety of reducers with different types, sizes, and life spans. We describe the problems that arise for a naive approach in which the TLMM region directly holds reducer views. We then describe how thread-local indirection solves these problems without unduly complicating the runtime system.

We first examine a seemingly straightforward approach for leveraging TLMM to implement reducers. In this scheme, whenever a reducer is declared, the runtime system allocates the reducer at a virtual address in the TLMM region that is globally agreed upon by all workers. The runtime system instructs each worker to map the physical page containing its own local view at that virtual address. Thus, accesses to the reducer by a worker operate directly on the worker's local view.

Although this approach seems straightforward, it fails to address two practical issues. First, the overhead of mapping can be great due to fragmentation arising from allocations and deallocations of reducers in the TLMM region. Second, performing a hypermerge of views in TLMM regions is complicated and may incur heavy mapping overhead. We discuss each of these issues in turn.

Regarding the first issue, if views are allocated within a TLMM region, the runtime system must manage the storage in the region separately from its normal heap allocator. Since reducers can be allocated and deallocated throughout program execution, the TLMM region can become fragmented with live reducer hyperobjects scattered across the region. Consequently, when a worker maps in physical pages associated with a different worker's TLMM region, as must occur for a hypermerge, multiple physical pages may need

to be mapped in, each requiring two kernel crossings (from user mode to kernel mode and back). Even though the remapping overhead can be amortized against steals (and the Cilk-M runtime already performs a `sys_pmap` call upon a successful steal to maintain the cactus stack), if the number of `sys_pmap` calls is too great, the kernel crossing overhead can become a scalability bottleneck, outweighing the benefit of replacing the hash-table lookups of the hypermap approach with virtual address translations.

The second issue involves the problem of performing hypermerges. Consider a hypermerge of the local views in two workers W_1 and W_2, and suppose that W_1 is performing the hypermerge. To perform a monoid operation on a given pair of views, both views must be mapped into the same address space. Consequently, at least one of the views cannot be mapped to its appropriate location in the TLMM region, and the code to reduce them with the monoid operation must take that into account. For example, if W_2's view contains a pointer, W_1 would need to determine whether the pointer was to another of W_2's views or to shared memory. If the former, it would need to perform an additional address translation. This "pointer swizzling" could be done when W_1 maps W_2's views into its address space, but it requires compiler support to determine which locations are pointers, as well as adding a level of complexity to the hypermerge process.

Since "any problem in computing can be solved by adding another level of indirection,"[3], we shall employ *thread-local indirection*. The idea is to use the TLMM region to store pointers to local views which themselves are kept in shared memory visible to all workers. When a reducer is allocated, a memory location is reserved in the TLMM region to hold a pointer to its local view. If no view has yet been created, the pointer is null. Accessing a reducer simply requires the worker to check whether the pointer is null, and if not, dereference it, which is done by the virtual-address translation provided by the hardware. In essence, the memory-mapping reducer mechanism replaces the use of hypermaps with the use of the TLMM region.

The two problems that plague the naive scheme are solved by thread-local indirection. The TLMM region contains a small, compact set of pointers, all of uniform size, which precludes internal fragmentation. The storage management of reducers is simple and avoids pointer swizzling. The TLMM region requires only a simple scalable[4] memory allocator for single-word objects (the pointers). Since local views are stored in shared memory, the job of handling them is conveniently delegated to the ordinary heap allocator. The residual problem of managing the storage for the pointers in the TLMM region is addressed in Section 6.

Thread-local indirection also solves the problem of one worker gaining access to the views of another worker in order to perform hypermerge. Since the local views are allocated in shared memory, a worker performing the hypermerge can readily access the local views of a different worker. The residual problem of determining which local views to merge is part of the view-transferal protocol, addressed in Section 7.

6. ORGANIZATION OF WORKER-LOCAL VIEWS

This section describes how Cilk-M organizes a worker's local views in a compact fashion. Recall that after a steal, the thief resuming the stolen frame starts with an empty set of views, and

---

[3]Quotation attributed to David Wheeler in [20].
[4]To be scalable, Cilk-M memory allocator for the TLMM region allocates a local pool per worker and occasionally rebalances the fixed-size slots among local pools when necessary in the manner of Hoard [5].

whenever the thief accesses a reducer for the first time, a new identity view is created lazily. Once a local view has been created, subsequent accesses to the reducer return the local view. Moreover, during a hypermerge, a worker sequences through two sets of local views to perform the requisite monoid operations. This section shows how a worker's local views can be organized compactly using a "sparse accumulator (SPA)" data structure [14] to support these activities efficiently. Specifically, we show the following:

- Given (the address of) a reducer hyperobject, how to support a constant-time *lookup* of the local view of the reducer.

- How to *sequence* through all of a worker's local views during a hypermerge in linear time and *reset* the set of local views to the empty set.

A traditional SPA consists of two arrays:[5] an array of values, and an array containing an unordered "log" of the indices of the nonzero elements. The data structure is initialized to an array of zeros at start-up time. When an element is set to a nonzero value, its index is recorded in the log, incrementing the count of elements in the SPA (which also determines the location of the end of the log). Sequencing is accomplished in linear time by walking through the log and accessing each element in turn.

Cilk-M implements the SPA idea by arranging the pointers to local views in a *SPA map* within a worker's TLMM region. A SPA map is allocated on a per-page basis, using 4096-byte pages on x86 64-bit architectures. Each SPA map contains the following fields:

- a *view array* of 248 elements, where each element is a pair of 8-byte pointers to a local view and its monoid,

- a *log array* of 120 bytes containing 1-byte indices of the valid elements in the view array,

- the 4-byte number of valid elements in the view array, and

- the 4-byte number of logs in the log array.

Cilk-M maintains the invariant that empty elements in the view array are represented with a pair of null pointers. Whenever a new reducer is allocated, a 16-byte slot in the view array is allocated, storing pointers to the executing worker's local view and to the monoid. When a reducer goes out of scope and is destroyed, the 16-byte slot is recycled. The simple memory allocation for the TLMM region described in Section 5 keeps track of whether a slot is assigned or not. Since a SPA map is allocated in a worker's TLMM region, the virtual address of an assigned 16-byte slot represents the same reducer for every worker throughout the life span of the reducer and is stored as a member field `tlmm_addr` in the reducer object.

A reducer lookup can be performed in constant time, requiring only two memory accesses and a predictable branch. A lookup entails accessing `tlmm_addr` in the reducer (first memory access), dereferencing `tlmm_addr` to get the pointer to a worker's local view (second memory access), and checking whether the pointer is valid (predictable branch). The common case is that the `tlmm_addr` contains a valid local view, since a lookup on an empty view occurs at most once per reducer per steal. As we shall see in Section 7, however, a worker resets its SPA map by filling it with zeros between successful steals. If the worker does not have a valid view for the corresponding reducer, the `tlmm_addr` simply contains zeros.

Sequencing through the views can be performed in linear time. Since a worker knows exactly where a log array within a page starts and how many logs are in the log array, it can efficiently sequence through valid elements in the view array according to the indices stored in the log array. The Cilk-M runtime stores pointers to a

local view and the reducer monoid side-by-side in the view array, thereby allowing easy access to the monoid interface during the hypermerge process. In designing the SPA map for Cilk-M, we explicitly chose to have a 2 : 1 size ratio between the view array and the log array. Once the number of logs exceed the length of the log array, the Cilk-M runtime stops keeping track of logs. The rationale is that if the number of logs in a SPA map exceeds the length of its log array, the cost of sequencing through the entire view array, rather than just the valid entries, can be amortized against the cost of inserting views into the SPA map.

7. VIEW TRANSFERAL

This section describes how a worker in Cilk-M can efficiently gain access to another worker's local views and perform view transferal efficiently. The Cilk-M runtime system includes an efficient view-transferal protocol that does not require extra memory mapping. This section brings all the pieces together and presents the complete picture of how the memory-mapping reducer mechanism works.

In the hypermap approach, view transferal simply involves switching a few pointers. Suppose that worker W_1 is executing a full frame F_1 that is returning. The worker simply deposits its local views into another frame F_2 executing on worker W_2 that is either F_1's left sibling or parent, at the appropriate hypermap placeholder. In the memory-mapping approach, more steps are involved. In particular, even though all local views are allocated in the shared region, their addresses are only known to W_1, the worker who allocated them. Thus, W_1 must *publish* pointers to its local views, making them available in a shared region.

There are two straightforward strategies for W_1 to publish its local views. The first is the *mapping strategy*: worker W_1 leaves a set of page descriptors in frame F_2 corresponding to the SPA maps in its TLMM region, which W_2 then maps into its TLMM region to perform the hypermerge. The second strategy is the *copying strategy*: W_1 copies those pointers from its TLMM region into a shared region. Cilk-M employs the copying strategy, because the number of reducers used in a program is generally small, and thus the overhead of memory mapping greatly outweighs the cost of copying a few pointers.

For W_1 to publish its local views, whose references are stored in the *private SPA maps* in its TLMM regions, W_1 simply allocates the same number of *public SPA maps* in the shared region and *transfers* views from the private SPA maps to the public ones. As W_1 sequences through valid indices in a view array to copy from a private SPA map to a public one, it simultaneously zeros out those valid indices in the private SPA map. When all transfers are complete, the public SPA maps contain all the references to W_1's local views, and the private SPA maps are all empty (the view array contains all zeros). Zeroing out W_1's private SPA maps is important, since W_1 must engage in work-stealing next, and the empty private SPA maps ensure that the stolen frame is resumed on a worker with an empty set of local views.

Since a worker must maintain space for public SPA maps throughout its execution, Cilk-M explicitly configures SPA maps to be compact and allocated on a per-page basis. Each SPA map holds up to 248 views, making it unlikely that many SPA maps are ever needed. Recall from Section 6 that the Cilk-M runtime system maintains the invariant that an entry in a view array contains either a pair of valid pointers or a pair of null pointers indicating that the entry is empty. A newly allocated (recycled) SPA map is empty.[6]

---

[5]For some applications, a third array is used to indicate which array elements are valid, but for our application, invalidity can be indicated by a special value in the value array.

[6]To be precise, only the number of logs and the view array must contain zeros.

Name	Description
add-n	Summing 1 to x into n add-reducers in parallel
min-n	Processing x random values in parallel to find the min and accumulate the results in n min-reducers
max-n	Processing x random values in parallel to find the max and accumulate the results in n max-reducers

Figure 4: The three microbenchmarks for evaluating lookup operations. For each microbenchmark, the value x is chosen according to the value of n so that roughly the same number of lookup operations are performed.

The fact that a SPA map is allocated on the per-page basis allows the Cilk-M runtime system to recycle empty SPA maps easily by maintaining memory pools[7] of empty pages solely for allocating SPA maps.

In the memory-mapping approach, a frame contains placeholders to SPA maps, instead of to hypermaps, so that worker W_1 in our scenario can deposit the populated public SPA maps into F_2 without interrupting worker W_2. Similarly, a hypermerge involves two sets of SPA maps instead of hypermaps. When W_2 is ready to perform the hypermerge, it always sequences through the map that contains fewer view pointers and reduces them with the reduce operation into the map that contains more view pointers. After the hypermerge, one set of SPA maps contain pointers to the reduced views, whereas the other set (assuming they are public) are all empty and can be recycled. Similar to the transfer operation, when W_2 performs the hypermerge, as it sequences through the set with fewer views, it zeros out the valid views, thereby maintaining the invariant that only empty SPA maps are recycled.

View transferal in the memory-mapping approach incurs higher overhead than that in the hypermap approach, but this overhead can be amortized against steals, since view transferals are necessary only if a steal occurs. As Section 8 shows, even with the overhead from view transferal, the memory-mapping approach performs better than the hypermap approach and incurs less total overhead during parallel execution.

8. AN EMPIRICAL EVALUATION OF MEMORY-MAPPED REDUCERS

This section compares the memory-mapping approach for implementing reducers used by Cilk-M to the hypermap approach used by Cilk Plus. We quantify the overheads of the two systems incurred during serial and parallel executions on three simple synthetic microbenchmarks and one application benchmark. Our experimental results show that memory-mapped reducers not only admit more efficient lookups than hypermap reducers, they also incur less overhead overall during parallel executions, despite the additional costs of view transferal.

General setup. We compared the two approaches using a few microbenchmarks that employ reducers included in the Cilk Plus reducer library, as well as one application benchmark. Figure 4 describes the microbenchmarks, all of which are synthetic, which perform lookup operations repeatedly with simple REDUCER operations that perform addition, finding the minimum, and finding the maximum. The value n in the name of the microbenchmark dictates the number of reducers used, which is determined at compile-time. The value x is an input parameter chosen so that a given microbenchmark with different n performs 1024 million lookup operations, or 2048 million lookup operations in the case of the reduce

overhead study.[8] The application benchmark is a parallel breath-first search program [26] called PBFS.

All benchmarks were compiled using the Cilk Plus compiler version 12.0.0 with -O2 optimization. The experiments were run on an AMD Opteron 8354 system with 4 quad-core 2 GHz CPU's having a total of 8 GBytes of memory. Each core on a chip has a 64-KByte private L1-data-cache, a 512-KByte private L2-cache, and a 2-MByte shared L3-cache.

Performance evaluation using microbenchmarks

Figure 5 shows the microbenchmark execution times for a set of tests with varying numbers of reducers running on the native Cilk Plus runtime system and the Cilk-M 1.0 runtime system. Figure 5(a) shows the execution times running on a single processor, whereas Figure 5(b) shows them for 16 processors. Each data point is the average of 10 runs with a standard deviation of less than 5%. Across all microbenchmarks, the memory-mapped reducers in Cilk-M consistently outperform the hypermap reducers in Cilk Plus, executing about 4–9 times faster for serial executions, and 3–9 times faster for parallel executions.

One interesting thing to note is that, every instance of min-n (for different n) took longer to execute than its corresponding counterpart of max-n on both runtime systems. At first glance, the two microbenchmarks min-n and max-n ought to perform similarly given that the same number of comparisons are executed in both microbenchmarks. That is not the case, however — due the to artifact of how reducer min and max libraries are implemented, more updates are performed on a given view in the execution of min-n than that in the execution of max-n for the same n. Thus, min-n took longer execution time than max-n.

Lookup overhead. Figure 6 presents the lookup overheads of Cilk-M 1.0 and Cilk Plus on add-n with varying n. The overhead data was obtained as follows. First, we ran the add-n with x iterations on a single processor. Then, we ran a similar program called add-base-n, which replaces the accesses to reducers with accesses to a simple array, also running x iterations. Since hypermerges and reduce operations do not take place when executing on a single processor, add-base-n essentially performs the same operations as add-n minus the lookup operations. Figure 6 shows the difference in the execution times of add-n and add-base-n with varying n. Each data point takes the average of 10 runs with a standard deviation of less than 2% for Cilk-M and less than 12% for Cilk Plus.

The lookup overhead in Cilk-M stays fairly constant independent of n, but the lookup overhead in Cilk Plus varies significantly. This discrepancy can be understood by observing that a lookup operation in Cilk-M translates into two memory accesses and a branch irrespective of the value of n, whereas a lookup operation in Cilk Plus translates into a hash-table lookup whose time depends on how many items the hashed bucket happens to contain, as well as whether it triggers a hash-table expansion.

The reduce overhead during parallel execution. Besides the lookup overhead, we also studied the other overheads incurred by reducers during parallel executions. We refer to the overheads incurred only during parallel executions as the ***reduce overhead***, which includes overheads in performing hypermerges, creating views, and inserting views into a hypermap in Cilk Plus or a SPA map in Cilk-M. For Cilk-M, this overhead also includes view transferal. For both systems, additional lookups are performed during

---

[7]The pools for allocating SPA maps are structured like the rest of the pools for the internal memory allocator managed by the runtime. Every worker owns its own local pool, and a global pool is used to rebalance the memory distribution between local pools in the manner of Hoard [5].

[8]In the case of the reduce overhead study, we configured the microbenchmark to perform more lookup operations to prolong the execution time, because the runtime overhead measured in this study constitutes only a small part of the overall execution time.

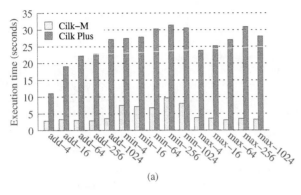

(a)

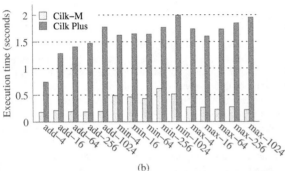

(b)

Figure 5: Execution times for microbenchmarks with varying numbers of reducers using Cilk-M and Cilk Plus, running on (a) a single processor and (b) on 16 processors, respectively.

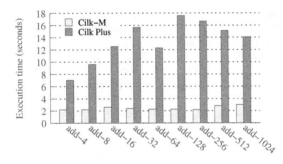

Figure 6: Reducer lookup overhead of Cilk-M and Cilk Plus running the microbenchmark using add reducers on a single processor. A single cluster in the x-axis shows the overheads for both systems for a given n, and the y-axis shows the overheads in execution time in seconds.

a hypermerge, and they are considered as part of the overhead as well.

Figure 7 compares the reduce overhead of the two systems. The data was collected by running add-n with varying n on 16 processors for both systems and instrumenting the various sources of reduce overhead directly inside the runtime system code. In order to instrument the Cilk Plus runtime, we obtained the open-source version of the Cilk Plus runtime, which was released with ports of the Cilk Plus language extensions to the C and C++ front-ends of gcc-4.7 [3]. We downloaded only the source code for the runtime system (revision 181962), inserted instrumentation code, and made it a plug-in replacement for the Cilk Plus runtime released with the official Intel Cilk Plus compiler version 12.0.0. This open-source runtime system is a complete runtime source to support the Linux operating system [3], and its performance seems comparable to the runtime released with the compiler. Given the high variation in the reduce overhead when memory latency plays a role, the data

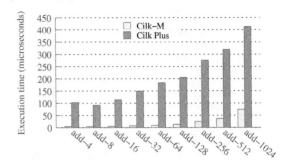

Figure 7: Comparison of the reduce overheads of Cilk-M and Cilk Plus running add-n on 16 processors. A single cluster in the x-axis shows the overheads for both system for a given n, and the y-axis shows the reduce overheads in milliseconds.

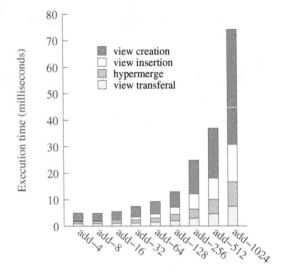

Figure 8: The breakdown of the reduce overhead in Cilk-M for add-n on 16 processors with varying n.

represents the average of 100 runs. Since the reduce overhead is correlated with the number of (successful) steals, we also verified that in these runs, the average numbers of steals for the two systems are comparable.

As can be seen in Figure 7, the reduce overhead in Cilk Plus is much higher than that in Cilk-M. Moreover, the discrepancy increases with n, which makes sense, because a higher n means more views are created, inserted, and must be reduced during hypermerges. The overhead in Cilk Plus also grows much faster than that in Cilk-M. It turns out that the Cilk Plus runtime spends much more time on view insertions (inserting newly created identity views into a hypermap), which dominates the reduce overhead, especially as n increases. Thus, Cilk Plus incurs a much higher reduce overhead, even though the Cilk-M runtime has the additional overhead of view transferal. In contrast, Cilk-M spends much less time on view insertions than Cilk Plus. A view insertion in Cilk-M involves writing to one memory location in a worker's TLMM region, whereas in Cilk Plus, it involves inserting into a hash table. Moreover, a SPA map in Cilk-M stores views much more compactly than does a hypermap, which helps in terms of locality during a hypermerge.

Figure 8 breaks down the reduce overhead for Cilk-M. Overhead is attributed to four activities: view creation, view insertion, view transferal, and hypermerge, which includes the time to execute the monoid operation. As can be seen from the figure, the overhead due

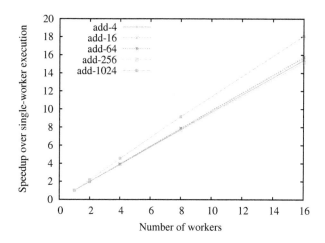

Figure 9: Speedups of `add-n` executing on Cilk-M with 1, 2, 4, 8, and 16 processors. The x-axis shows P, the number of processors used. The y-axis is the speedup, calculated by dividing the execution time running on a single processor with the execution time running on P processors.

to view transferal grows rather slowly as n increases, demonstrating that the SPA map allows efficient sequencing. Furthermore, the dominating overhead turns out to be view creations, showing that the design choices made in the memory-mapping approach do indeed minimize overhead.

Figure 9 shows the speedups for `add-n` when executing on 1, 2, 4, 8, and 16 workers. To simplify the presentation, only five different n values are shown — 4, 16, 64, 256, and 1024. As can be seen from Figure 9, despite the reduce overhead during parallel executions, the scalability is not affected. All instances of `add-n` (with different n) have good speedups with `add-1024` having superlinear speedup. As mentioned earlier, the reduce overhead is correlated with the number of successful steals and can be amortized against steals. As long as the application has ample parallelism and that the number of reducers used is "reasonable,"[9] as in the case of `add-n`, scalability of the application will not be affected by the reduce overhead.

Performance evaluation using PBFS

We evaluated the two runtime systems on a parallel breath-first search application called PBFS [26]. Given an input graph $G(V, E)$ and a starting node v_0, the PBFS algorithm finds the shortest distance between v_0 and every other node in V. The algorithm explores the graph "layer-by-layer," alternating between two "bag" data structures for insertion. As the program explores the nodes stored in one bag, all of which belong to a common layer, it inserts newly discovered nodes from the next layer into another bag. The bags are declared to be reducers to allow parallel insertion.

Figure 10(a) shows the relative execution time between Cilk-M and Cilk Plus on a single processor and on 16 processors. Since the work and span of a PBFS computation depend on the input graph, we evaluated the relative performance with 8 input graphs whose characteristics are shown in Figure 10(b). These input graphs are the same ones used in [26] to evaluate the algorithm. For each data point, we measured the mean of 10 runs, which has a standard deviation of less than 1%. Figure 10(a) shows the mean for Cilk-M normalized by the mean for Cilk Plus.

For single-processor executions, the two systems performed

---

[9]It is possible to write an application to use large number of reducers in such a way that the reduce overhead dominates the total work in the computation. In such case, the reduce overhead will affect scalability. This topic is investigated in more detail in further work by Lee [22, Ch. 5].

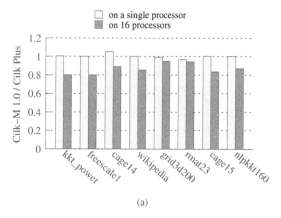

(a)

Name	$\|V\|$	$\|E\|$	D	# of lookups
`kkt_power`	2.05M	12.76M	31	1027
`freescale1`	3.43M	17.1M	128	1748
`cage14`	1.51M	27.1M	43	766
`wikipedia`	2.4M	41.9M	460	1631
`grid3d200`	8M	55.8M	598	4323
`rmat23`	2.3M	77.9M	8	71269
`cage15`	5.15M	99.2M	50	2547
`nlpkkt160`	8.35M	225.4M	163	4174

(b)

Figure 10: (a) The relative execution time of Cilk-M to that of Cilk Plus running PBFS on a single processor and on 16 processors. Each value is calculated by normalizing the execution time of the application on Cilk-M with the execution time on Cilk Plus. (b) The characteristics of the input graphs for parallel breath-first search. The vertex and edge counts listed correspond to the number of vertices and edges.

comparably, with Cilk-M being slightly slower. Since the number of lookups in PBFS is extremely small relative to the input size, the lookups constitute a tiny fraction of the overall work (measured by the size of the input graph). Thus, it is not surprising that the two systems perform comparably for serial executions. On the other hand, Cilk-M performs noticeably better during parallel executions, which is consistent with the results from the microbenchmarks. Since the reduce overhead in Cilk-M is much smaller than that in Cilk Plus, PBFS scales better.

9. RELATED WORK

Traditional virtual-memory mechanisms have been described in the literature to support various linguistic abstractions. This section summarizes this work and describes how each uses a virtual-memory mechanism to implement its respective linguistic abstraction.

Abadi et al. [1] describes how one can efficiently support "strong atomicity" in a software transactional memory (STM) [32] system using a traditional virtual-memory mechanism supported by standard hardware. An STM system implements **strong atomicity** [8] if the system detects conflicts between transactions as well as conflicts between a transaction and a **normal** memory access performed outside of a transaction. Supporting strong atomicity may incur significant overhead, however, if the system must also keep track of every normal memory access. To avoid such overhead, Abadi et al. propose an alternative approach to leverage the page protection mechanism provided by the virtual-memory hardware, mapping the heap space twice, one for normal accesses and one for transactional accesses. When a page is being read or written to by a transaction, the system revokes certain access permissions on its corresponding mapping allocated for normal accesses, thereby detecting potential conflicts at the page granularity.

Berger et al. [6] propose Grace, a runtime system that eliminates concurrency errors and guarantees deterministic executions for multithreaded computations based on fork-join parallelism. Grace employs a *threads-as-processes* paradigm, where a thread seen by a user program running on Grace is in fact implemented as a process. Since processes do not share virtual address space, this paradigm enables different processes in Grace to map the shared regions (i.e., global variables and heap) with different access permissions, thereby detecting potential currency errors such as races, deadlocks, and atomicity violations at the page granularity. Updates to the shared regions are buffered (via copy-on-write mappings) and committed at "logical thread boundaries" in a deterministic order only when the updates do not cause a "conflict" with existing values. Upon a successful commit, updates are reflected in shared mappings and become globally visible.

Liu et al. [27] present Dthreads, which has the same goal as Grace, to prevent concurrency errors and enforce deterministic executions on multithreaded computations. The Dthreads runtime system adopts the same threads-as-processes paradigm as Grace and leverages the virtual memory mechanism similarly. Dthreads differs from Grace in three ways, however. First, Dthreads supports most general-purpose multithreaded programs, whereas Grace supports only fork-join parallelism. Second, Dthreads supports the full synchronization primitives implemented by POSIX threads [16], whereas Grace does not. Finally, Dthreads resolves "conflicts" among threads deterministically using a last-writer-wins protocol, whereas Grace executes parallel branches speculatively and must roll back upon conflict detection. Consequently, Dthreads enables better performance than Grace.

Finally, Pyla and Varadarajan [30] describe Sammati, a language-independent runtime system that provides automatic deadlock detection and recovery. Like the aforementioned works, Sammati employs the same threads-as-processes paradigm and leverages the virtual-memory hardware to allow processes to employ different accesses permissions on address space allocated for shared memory. Unlike the other work, Sammati focuses on automatic deadlock detection and recovery but not on deterministic executions. Thus, Sammati does not enforce a deterministic ordering in when updates are committed. Moreover, the system assumes that the program is written correctly — even though Sammati can detect races involving two writes to the same location, it cannot detect races involving a read and a write.

Like the Cilk-M research described here, each of these three studies describes how virtual-memory hardware can support a particular linguistic mechanism. One distinct difference between these studies and Cilk-M's memory-mapped reducers is that they employ traditional virtual-memory mechanisms supported by existing operating systems, whereas Cilk-M utilizes thread-local memory mapping (TLMM), which enables each thread to map part of the virtual address range independently while preserves sharing in the rest of the address space.

10. CONCLUSION

Recently, concurrency platforms have begun to offer high-level "memory abstractions" to support common patterns of parallel-programming. A *memory abstraction* [22] is an abstraction layer between the program execution and the memory that provides a different "view" of a memory location depending on the execution context in which the memory access is made. For instance, *transactional memory* [15] is a type of memory abstraction — memory accesses dynamically enclosed by an `atomic` block appear to occur atomically. Arguably, the Grace [6] and Dthreads [27] systems described in Section 9 are also examples of memory abstractions — every memory access is buffered and eventually committed (i.e., becomes globally visible) in some deterministic order. The cactus-stack mechanism implemented in Cilk-M [22, 23] provides another example of a memory abstraction. Reducer hyperobjects are yet another memory abstraction for dynamic multithreading.

This paper has laid out a new way of implementing reducers, namely, through use of the TLMM mechanism. As demonstrated in Section 8, experimental results show that the memory-mapping approach admits an efficient implementation. Interestingly, it appears that TLMM can be used to implement Grace and Dthreads with lower runtime overhead, which suggests that the TLMM mechanism may provide a general way for building memory abstractions.

With the proliferation of multicore architectures, the computing field must move from writing serially executing software to parallel software in order to unlock the computational power provided by modern hardware. Writing parallel programs, however, gives rise to a new set of challenges in how programs interact with memory, such as how to properly synchronize concurrent accesses to shared memory. We believe that investigating memory abstractions is a fruitful path. Memory abstractions ease the task of parallel programming, directly by mitigating the complexity of synchronization, and indirectly by enabling concurrency platforms that utilize resources more efficiently.

Acknowledgments

Thanks to Matteo Frigo for tips and insights on the reducers implementation in Cilk++. Thanks to Pablo Halpern of Intel, one of the original designers of reducers and a Cilk Plus developer, for helpful discussions on the implementation of reducers in Cilk Plus. Thanks to the Cilk team at Intel and the Supertech Research Group at MIT CSAIL for their support.

11. REFERENCES

[1] Martín Abadi, Tim Harris, and Mojtaba Mehrara. Transactional memory with strong atomicity using off-the-shelf memory protection hardware. In *Proceedings of the 14th ACM SIGPLAN Symposium on Principles and Practice of Parallel Programming*, PPoPP '09, pages 185–196, Raleigh, NC, USA, 2009. ACM.

[2] Eric Allen, David Chase, Joe Hallett, Victor Luchangco, Jan-Willem Maessen, Sukyoung Ryu, Guy L. Steele Jr., and Sam Tobin-Hochstadt. *The Fortress Language Specification Version 1.0*. Sun Microsystems, Inc., March 2008.

[3] Balaji Ayer. Intel® Cilk™ Plus is now available in open-source and for GCC 4.7! http://www.cilkplus.org, 2011. The source code for the compiler and its associated runtime is available at http://gcc.gnu.org/svn/gcc/branches/cilkplus.

[4] Rajkishore Barik, Zoran Budimlić, Vincent Cavè, Sanjay Chatterjee, Yi Guo, David Peixotto, Raghavan Raman, Jun Shirako, Sağnak Taşırlar, Yonghong Yan, Yisheng Zhao, and Vivek Sarkar. The habanero multicore software research project. In *Proceeding of the 24th ACM SIGPLAN Conference on Object-Oriented Programming Systems Languages and Applications (OOPSLA)*, OOPSLA '09, pages 735–736, Orlando, Florida, USA, 2009. ACM.

[5] Emery D. Berger, Kathryn S. McKinley, Robert D. Blumofe, and Paul R. Wilson. Hoard: A scalable memory allocator for multithreaded applications. In *Proceedings of the 19th International Conference on Architectural Support for Programming Languages and Operating Systems (ASPLOS-LX)*, pages 117–128, Cambridge, MA, November 2000.

[6] Emery D. Berger, Ting Yang, Tongping Liu, and Gene Novark. Grace: Safe multithreaded programming for c/c++. In *Proceedings of the 24th ACM SIGPLAN conference on Object Oriented Programming Systems Languages and Applications*, OOPSLA '09, pages 81–96, Orlando, Florida, USA, 2009. ACM.

[7] Robert D. Blumofe and Dionisios Papadopoulos. Hood: A user-level threads library for multiprogrammed multiprocessors. Technical Report, University of Texas at Austin, 1999.

[8] Colin Blundell, E Christopher Lewis, and Milo M. K. Martin. Deconstructing transactional semantics: The subtleties of atomicity. In *Workshop on Duplicating, Deconstructing, and Debunking (WDDD)*, June 2005.

[9] Vincent Cavé, Jisheng Zhao, Jun Shirako, and Vivek Sarkar. Habenero-Java: the new adventures of old X10. In *PPPJ*. ACM, 2011.

[10] Philippe Charles, Christian Grothoff, Vijay Saraswat, Christopher Donawa, Allan Kielstra, Kemal Ebcioglu, Christoph von Praun, and Vivek Sarkar. X10: An object-oriented approach to non-uniform cluster computing. In *Proceedings of the 20th Annual ACM SIGPLAN Conference on Object-Oriented Programming, Systems, Languages, and Applications*, pages 519–538, New York, NY, USA, 2005.

[11] Mingdong Feng and Charles E. Leiserson. Efficient detection of determinacy races in Cilk programs. In *Proceedings of the Ninth Annual ACM Symposium on Parallel Algorithms and Architectures (SPAA)*, pages 1–11, Newport, Rhode Island, June 1997.

[12] Matteo Frigo, Pablo Halpern, Charles E. Leiserson, and Stephen Lewin-Berlin. Reducers and other Cilk++ hyperobjects. In *Proceedings of the Twenty-First Annual ACM Symposium on Parallelism in Algorithms and Architectures*, pages 79–90, Calgary, Canada, August 2009. Won Best Paper award.

[13] Matteo Frigo, Charles E. Leiserson, and Keith H. Randall. The implementation of the Cilk-5 multithreaded language. In *Proceedings of the ACM SIGPLAN '98 Conference on Programming Language Design and Implementation*, pages 212–223, Montreal, Quebec, Canada, June 1998. Proceedings published ACM SIGPLAN Notices, Vol. 33, No. 5, May, 1998.

[14] John R. Gilbert, Cleve Moler, and Robert Schreiber. Sparse matrices in MATLAB: Design and implementation. *SIAM J. Matrix Anal. Appl*, 13:333–356, 1992.

[15] Maurice Herlihy and J. Eliot B. Moss. Transactional memory: Architectural support for lock-free data structures. In *Proceedings of the 20th International Conference on Computer Architecture. (Also published as ACM SIGARCH Computer Architecture News, Volume 21, Issue 2, May 1993.)*, pages 289–300, San Diego, California, 1993.

[16] Institute of Electrical and Electronic Engineers. Information technology — Portable Operating System Interface (POSIX) — Part 1: System application program interface (API) [C language]. IEEE Standard 1003.1, 1996 Edition.

[17] Intel Corporation. *Intel® Cilk™ Plus Application Binary Interface Specification*, 2010. Revision: 0.9.

[18] Intel Corporation. *C++ and C interfaces for Cilk reducer hyperobjects*. Intel Corporation, 2011. Intel® C++ Compiler 12.0: `reducer.h` Header File.

[19] Intel Corporation. *Intel® Cilk™ Plus Language Specification*, 2011. Revision: 1.1.

[20] Butler Lampson, Martín Abadi, Michael Burrows, and Edward Wobber. Authentication in distributed systems: theory and practice. *ACM Trans. Comput. Syst.*, 10:265–310, November 1992.

[21] Doug Lea. A Java fork/join framework. In *Proceedings of the ACM 2000 Conference on Java Grande*, pages 36–43. ACM, 2000.

[22] I-Ting Angelina Lee. *Memory Abstractions for Parallel Programming*. PhD thesis, Massachusetts Institute of Technology Department of Electrical Engineering and Computer Science, June 2012. To be submitted in February 2012.

[23] I-Ting Angelina Lee, Silas Boyd-Wickizer, Zhiyi Huang, and Charles E. Leiserson. Using memory mapping to support cactus stacks in work-stealing runtime systems. In *PACT '10: Proceedings of the 19th International Conference on Parallel Architectures and Compilation Techniques*, pages 411–420, Vienna, Austria, September 2010. ACM.

[24] Daan Leijen and Judd Hall. Optimize managed code for multi-core machines. *MSDN Magazine*, 2007. Available from http://msdn.microsoft.com/magazine/.

[25] Charles E. Leiserson. The Cilk++ concurrency platform. *Journal of Supercomputing*, 51(3):244–257, March 2010.

[26] Charles E. Leiserson and Tao B. Schardl. A work-efficient parallel breadth-first search algorithm (or how to cope with the nondeterminism of reducers). In *Proceedings of the 22nd ACM Symposium on Parallelism in Algorithms and Architectures (SPAA)*, pages 303–314, June 2010.

[27] Tongping Liu, Charlie Curtsinger, and Emery D. Berger. Dthreads: Efficient deterministic multithreading. In *Proceedings of the Twenty-Third ACM Symposium on Operating Systems Principles*, SOSP '11, pages 327–336, Cascais, Portugal, 2011. ACM.

[28] Robert H. B. Netzer and Barton P. Miller. What are race conditions? *ACM Letters on Programming Languages and Systems*, 1(1):74–88, March 1992.

[29] OpenMP application program interface, version 3.0. OpenMP specification, May 2008.

[30] Hari K. Pyla and Srinidhi Varadarajan. Avoiding deadlock avoidance. In *Proceedings of the 19th International Conference on Parallel Architectures and Compilation Techniques*, PACT '10, pages 75–86, Vienna, Austria, 2010. ACM.

[31] James Reinders. *Intel Threading Building Blocks: Outfitting C++ for Multi-core Processor Parallelism*. O'Reilly Media, Inc., 2007.

[32] Nir Shavit and Dan Touitou. Software transactional memory. In *Proceedings of the 14th Annual ACM Symposium on Principles of Distributed Computing (PODC)*, pages 204–213, Ottowa, Ontario, Canada, August 1995.

[33] D. Stein and D. Shah. Implementing lightweight threads. In *USENIX '92*, pages 1–9, 1992.

On the Cost of Composing Shared-Memory Algorithms

Dan Alistarh
EPFL
dan.alistarh@epfl.ch

Rachid Guerraoui
EPFL
rachid.guerraoui@epfl.ch

Petr Kuznetsov
TU-Berlin/Telekom Innovation
Labs
petr.kuznetsov@tu-
berlin.de

Giuliano Losa
EPFL
giuliano.losa@epfl.ch

ABSTRACT

Decades of research in distributed computing have led to a variety of perspectives on what it means for a concurrent algorithm to be efficient, depending on model assumptions, progress guarantees, and complexity metrics. It is therefore natural to ask whether one could compose algorithms that perform efficiently under different conditions, so that the composition preserves the performance of the original components when their conditions are met.

In this paper, we evaluate the cost of composing shared-memory algorithms. First, we formally define the notion of *safely composable* algorithms and we show that every sequential type has a safely composable implementation, as long as enough state is transferred between modules. Since such generic implementations are inherently expensive, we present a more general light-weight specification that allows the designer to transfer very little state between modules, by taking advantage of the semantics of the implemented object. Using this framework, we implement a composed long-lived test-and-set object, with the property that each of its modules is asymptotically optimal with respect to the progress condition it ensures, while the entire implementation only uses objects with consensus number at most two. Thus, we show that the overhead of composition can be negligible in the case of some important shared-memory abstractions.

Keywords

Composition, Modularity, Complexity, Consensus, Test-and-Set

Categories and Subject Descriptors

D.1.3 [**Programming Techniques**]: Concurrent Programming—*Distributed Programming*

1. INTRODUCTION

Designing correct and efficient concurrent algorithms is a major challenge. There seems to be an agreement on what it means for a concurrent data structure to be correct [14, 15]; on the other hand, the situation is more complex when it comes to efficiency. Decades of research have led to a variety of algorithms designed for different models, providing different progress guarantees, and optimized for different complexity measures. It is hard to believe that we shall eventually agree on the *right* model of concurrent systems, the most beneficial progress condition, or the most important complexity criterion. All these depend on the evolving hardware specifics of modern multiprocessors or on unpredictable user computing demands.

To anticipate these uncertainties, it is tempting to look for *composable* solutions. The idea is that algorithms optimized for different complexity metrics and progress conditions could be composed to obtain new algorithms that maintain the properties of their components under a combination of the original model assumptions. Ideally, such a composed algorithm would have the ability to *adapt* to changing environment conditions, e.g. high contention, asynchrony, or failures, while maintaining correctness in all executions.

We focus on composing algorithms providing various *progress guarantees*. Thus, a composable algorithm is allowed to *abort* whenever the condition under which it is expected to make progress is violated. In case the currently employed algorithm aborts, the composition is free to switch to an algorithm that makes progress under a different set of assumptions. The resulting implementation has to guarantee correctness, regardless of the way it jumps between its underlying components. We call this property *safe composition*. Respectively, algorithms that allow such composition are called *safely composable*. Safely composable algorithms are appealing since they have the advantage of being able to optimize for the common case, while always guaranteeing correctness. Another advantage of such implementations is that they can be designed and analyzed in a modular way.

In this paper, we evaluate safely composable algorithms in terms of computational power and complexity cost, for implementations that guarantee progress in the absence of interval contention [2] or step contention [6]. First, we present a composable universal construction that allows for implementing any sequential type. Since such generic implementations are inherently expensive, we present an alternative light-weight specification that allows the designer to transfer very little state between modules, by taking advantage of the semantics of the implemented object. Using this framework, we implement a composed long-lived test-and-set object, with the property that each of its modules is asymptotically optimal with respect to its progress condition, while the entire implementation only uses objects with consensus number at most two. Thus, we show that the overhead of composition, both in terms of step and space complexity and computational power of underlying objects, can be made negligible for some shared-memory abstractions.

Permission to make digital or hard copies of all or part of this work for personal or classroom use is granted without fee provided that copies are not made or distributed for profit or commercial advantage and that copies bear this notice and the full citation on the first page. To copy otherwise, to republish, to post on servers or to redistribute to lists, requires prior specific permission and/or a fee.
SPAA'12, June 25–27, 2012, Pittsburgh, Pennsylvania, USA.
Copyright 2012 ACM 978-1-4503-1213-4/12/06 ...$10.00.

Our safely composable universal construction allows us to build and compose shared-memory implementations guaranteeing progress under different conditions. The construction extends the consensus-based algorithm of Herlihy [14] by using safely composable consensus objects: when such an object aborts, it provides the information about the "state" of the object being implemented that is used for the initialization of the next safely composable consensus object. For a generic object, this information is represented as a *history*, i.e. a sequence of operation requests that were previously submitted to the object. These histories do not have to be consistent across processes: only prefixes of *committed* (i.e., executed) operations must be consistent. A similar idea was used in [12, 20] to build an efficient abortable Byzantine fault-tolerant replicated state machine (Abstract) in message-passing systems.

A *light-weight* version of safely composable shared-memory implementations can be adapted and optimized to the object being implemented. When a safely composable implementation of the object aborts, it provides some *object-specific* information about the "state" of the object. This information is then used to initialize the next safely composable algorithm.

A natural correctness condition is that any safely composable object should be linearizable, when restricted to invocations and committed responses. Intuitively, there is a sharp trade-off between the amount of information transferred between the modules and the correctness of the composition: in particular, if too little information is transferred, the composed algorithm may no longer be linearizable. Our specification of a safely composable object deals with this issue in two ways: first, we ensure that all the values returned can be mapped to a matching set of histories of requests, which have to verify a series of consistency conditions. Second, we allow a module to restrict the possible interpretations of input values that it accepts.

The resulting specification (Section 5) has two key properties: first, the composition of any two safely composable modules is itself safely composable. Second, any safely composable module taken on its own is linearizable. These two properties greatly simplify the design and proof of composed algorithms. Finding an object specification that is both safe (guaranteeing correct composition) and general (allowing objects that export little state) is one of our main technical contributions.

We use our framework to build a speculative test-and-set (TAS) object that only uses registers in executions where there is low contention, and may revert to stronger hardware primitives in contended executions. The algorithm is built from two independent modules: the first module has constant step complexity, and ensures progress in the absence of step contention (i.e. it is obstruction-free). The second module reverts to a hardware implementation of the object and is therefore wait-free. The algorithm switches *forward* to a more contention-resilient module when contention is detected, and can also switch *back*, using the reset mechanism, to a more efficient speculative module if the algorithm is currently employing the expensive hardware object. The implementation is also *long-lived*, since the object can be reset once it has been won.

Our TAS algorithm is of independent interest for two reasons. First, the obstruction-free module shows that TAS can be implemented in constant time and space in the absence of interval contention, whereas the best known bound for obstruction-free consensus is linear [6]. A simple modification of our algorithm (described in the Appendix) yields the first *solo-fast* [6] TAS algorithm with constant step complexity for uncontended operations. Second, the entire algorithm can be seen as a simple efficient version of a *biased lock* [9], that uses only registers as long as a single process is using it, and reverts to the hardware implementation only un-der step contention, as opposed to interval contention for previous implementations [9, 19].

Our constructions have several implications concerning the cost of safe composition in shared memory. First, our speculative TAS implementation is wait-free, and results from the composition of two modules. One might expect that moving from a module that may abort to one that always makes progress would require consensus, since, intuitively, the processes need to "agree" on the value returned from a safely composable module before executing a wait-free one. Thus, the consensus number [14] of the resulting implementation should be n. We find that this is not necessarily the case. In particular, we show that if the semantic of the implemented object is known, the algorithm can speculate using only registers and a hardware implementation of the object, avoiding consensus. In particular, our composed TAS algorithm only uses objects with consensus number at most *two*.

Second, the step complexity overhead induced by composition is considerable in the case of generic implementations, since each process has to essentially obtain a snapshot of all previously performed requests. But if the semantics of the implemented object is known, as is the case of our TAS implementation, we show that the overhead of composition can be brought down to a small constant number of steps. In fact, our implementation is optimal in terms of fence complexity [7]. Therefore, safe composition does not have to imply an increase in time complexity.

Overall, this paper describes a novel framework for shared-memory composition. We present a TAS implementation that combines lightweight components, that only make progress under the absence of step contention, with a hardware TAS objects at *no cost*, either in the computational power of base objects or in step complexity. Is this possible for any object? If not, can we categorize objects based on the *cost* of their safely composable implementations, such as the power of the underlying model, complexity, or the amount state that must be transferred between the components? These are interesting directions for future research.

Roadmap. In Section 2 we present an overview of related work. Our model definitions are presented in Section 3. In Section 4 we describe a composable universal construction based on Abstract. We then present our light-weight framework for composable objects in Section 5, and showcase it by building a speculative test-and-set implementation. In the Appendix, we give abortable variants of shared-memory consensus algorithms. Due to space limitations, we only present sketches for some of the proofs. Detailed versions can be found in the full version of this paper [5].

2. RELATED WORK

Composing safe distributed algorithms optimized for the common case has been used to obtain efficient solutions to fundamental problems such as consensus [8, 10], Byzantine agreement [11, 12], mutual exclusion [17], or renaming [4].

In shared-memory, composition has either been used implicitly, by combining a fast-path algorithm with a (slower) wait-free one in an ad-hoc manner [6, 18], or explicitly, by requiring an algorithm to return an *abort* indication before a second algorithm can be called [3, 6]. Implicit solutions have focused on consensus implementations: Luchangco et al. [18] presented consensus and compare-and-swap implementations with constant step complexity in executions with no interval contention, that revert to hardware primitives otherwise; Attiya et al. [6] showed a consensus implementation with $O(n)$ step complexity in the absence of step contention, that reverts to hardware compare-and-swap otherwise, and an $\Omega(\log n)$ lower bound for the fast path of such implementations, for perturbable objects. Attiya et al. [6] also study consensus with *fails*, when a process may abort the current execution explicitly; however, their requirements on the abort condition are strictly stronger than the ones of safely composable implementations in Section 5. (For example, any instance of consensus with fails is shown to have consensus number 2, while a safely composable consensus implementation may have consensus number 1.) In this paper, we study the cost of composing such algorithms in a more general way–in particular, we analyze algorithms

that can be designed an proved independently, whose composition is always correct.

Aguilera et al. [3] define *abortable* and *query-abortable* shared-memory objects, that may return an *abort* indication under contention; if queried, these objects return the last operation of the querying process that caused a state transition and its response. The authors also introduce efficient universal constructions for such objects. Our safely composable objects always return a value together with the indication. However, this value may not be consistent with the object's actual state, and may be caused by another process's operation, therefore the two definitions are incomparable. Interestingly, reference [3] shows that abortable objects do not compose if their progress is based on step contention. Intuitively, this is because, the correctness properties of abortable objects of [3] allow an aborted operation to take effect *after* it aborts. In contrast, our definition ensures safe composition, irrespective of the progress predicate. Finally, reference [13] investigates formal specifications for composition, and their implications for the scalability of software verification. Our specification of a safely composable object can be seen as a generalization of the speculative framework given in that paper.

3. PRELIMINARIES

Model. We consider the standard wait-free asynchronous shared memory model with n processes, $n-1$ of which may fail by crashing. Processes communicate through multiple-writer-multiple-reader atomic registers. Any register R exports atomic read and write operations, with standard semantics.

Objects, Algorithms and Executions. We define an object as a quadruple $(\mathcal{Q}, s, \mathcal{I}, \mathcal{R}, \Delta)$, where $\mathcal{Q}$ is a set of states, s is a starting state, $\mathcal{I}$ is a set of requests, $\mathcal{R}$ is a set of responses, and $\Delta \subseteq \mathcal{Q} \times \mathcal{I} \times \mathcal{Q} \times \mathcal{R}$ is the *sequential specification* of the object [6]. We assume that object types are non-trivial, i.e., all these sets are non-empty. A *history* is defined as a sequence of inputs (elements of $\mathcal{I}$) that contains no duplicates. (For simplicity, we assume that each request has a unique identifier.)

For example, the (one-shot) *test-and-set* object has initial state 0, and is accessed by a test-and-set operation. The operation atomically reads the value of the test-and-set and sets it to 1. We say that the unique process that returns 0 from the test-and-set is the *winner*, while the processes that return 1 are *losers*.

To implement an object, processes follow an algorithm. Given a process and an input in the set $\mathcal{I}$, an algorithm determines a sequence of steps whose execution establish an output in $\mathcal{O}$. The steps taken may be either local steps or shared memory reads and writes. A process repeatedly chooses an arbitrary input and executes the sequence of steps described by the algorithm until it determines an output. When a process chooses an input m, we say the it *invokes* m. When it determines an output r, we say that it *commits* r. We say that an algorithm implements an object if and only if all the sequence of invocations and commits, ordered according to their real-time occurrences, that can possibly be observed in the system are linearizable [15].

We are interested in algorithms composed of a sequence of clearly separated modules. A module is similar to an algorithm, but it can be initialized and it can abort instead of committing. Two modules are composed by using the aborts of the first module as initialization values for the second module. A process starts by running the first module in the sequence of modules that compose the algorithm. Given an input, the first module determines a sequence of steps whose execution establish either an output or a *switch value* ranging over the set $\mathcal{V}$. If an output is committed, then a new input is invoked, as before. But, when a process determines a switch value v, we say that it *aborts* with the switch value v.

As for the first module, the second module determines the steps to be followed to either commit or abort an input. However it also determines a sequence of steps to execute given an input and a switch value. When a process running the first module aborts with the switch value v, the process executes the sequence of steps determined by the second module given its last input and the switch value v. In general, a process repeatedly chooses an input and executes the steps determined by its current module, until it aborts and switches to the next module.

We will be interested in properties of the sequence of aborts, invocations and commits, ordered according to their real-time occurrences, observed in the system. We call such sequences *traces*.

Let $\mathcal{V}$ be the set of *switch values*. We denote by $\mathcal{T}$ the set of tuples consisting of a request and a switch value, and we call such tuples *switch tokens*. A request m may be invoked as is or together with a proposed switch value $v \in \mathcal{V}$ for the object. In the first case an invocation is denoted by the tuple (invoke, m) and in the second case by (init, m, v). In an invocation, the purpose of the switch value is to initialize the current module of the object.

A reply may be of the form (commit, m, r) where m is the request being responded to and r is a response in $\mathcal{R}$ or (abort, m, v) where m is the request being responded to and v is a switch value in $\mathcal{V}$. In an abort response, the purpose of the switch value is to initialize a new module of the object.

Progress Conditions. Algorithms that ensure safety and progress in all executions are called *wait-free*. We will also consider implementations that ensure safety in all executions, but may not make progress if two or more processes access the implementation concurrently; we call such algorithms *contention-free*, as they ensure progress in the absence of *interval contention*. Also, we consider algorithms that guarantee that a process makes progress as long as no other process takes steps concurrently. Such algorithms are called *obstruction-free*, and they make progress in the absence of *step contention*. For more precise definitions of these progress conditions, please see [6].

4. A COMPOSABLE UNIVERSAL CONSTRUCTION

In this section, we consider implementing generic shared-memory objects in a composable way. We show that any sequential type can be implemented using only registers in executions when there is no step contention, and reverting to stronger compare-and-swap primitives otherwise. More precisely, we describe a composable universal construction, following the structure of an abortable replicated state machine (Abstract), introduced in [20] in the context of Byzantine fault-tolerant algorithms. "Light-weight" implementations that adapt to the semantics of the object are discussed in Section 5.

4.1 Definition and Properties

We introduce the definition and properties of a composable universal construction, given as an Abstract [12, 20]. An Abstract encapsulates the specification of a state machine that may abort. We begin by recalling the definition and properties of an Abstract, as given in [20].

DEFINITION 1 (ABSTRACT, [20]). *An* Abstract *exports one operation* Invoke(m, h), *that issues request m with initial history h. An* Abstract *exports two indications that may be returned to the client:* Commit(m, h), *and* Abort(m, h). *We say that the process or operation commits (resp. aborts) the request m with history h, where a history h is a sequence of requests that the process can use to compute a reply (resp., to recover). If the process commits (resp., aborts) m with history h, we refer to h as the commit history (resp., abort history).*

Abstract *ensures the following properties on its traces.*

1. *(Termination) If a correct process invokes a request m, then it eventually commits or aborts m with history h, and h contains m.*
2. *(Commit Order) Let h and h′ be any two commit histories. Then either h is a strict prefix of h′ or vice-versa.*
3. *(Abort Ordering) Every commit history is a prefix of every abort history.*
4. *(Validity) In every commit/abort history h, no request appears twice and every request was invoked by some process before the current operation returns.*
5. *(Non-Triviality) If a correct process invokes a request m and some predicate NT is satisfied, the process commits m. We say that the* Abstract *guarantees progress under predicate NT.*
6. *(Init Ordering) Any common prefix of init histories is a prefix of any commit or abort history.*

In short, an Abstract returns histories that represent the ordering of process requests. (For simplicity, we assume that every request has a unique identifier.) In case of a commit, this ordering is definitive and the result of the call is uniquely determined by the order of the requests in the history. In the case of an abort, we require that every abort history contains every commit history as its (non-strict) prefix. Thus, effectively, no request invoked after an abort can be committed.

Note that the above definition and properties hold for any system model. In this paper, we consider shared memory implementations. Thus, the non-triviality predicate NT for our implementations will be expressed in terms of different notions of contention in shared memory.

We will consider multiple Abstract instances composed to achieve wait-free object implementations whose performance may change depending on the adversarial setting. Intuitively, the *composition* of two Abstract instances A and B is an algorithm that first calls Abstract A, returning with history h if the call returns (commit, h); otherwise, if the call returns (abort, h), it calls Abstract B with initial history h. The central property of this framework is that its instances are inherently *composable*, i.e., the composition of any two Abstract instances generates a third Abstract instance.

THEOREM 1 (COMPOSITION, [20]). *The composition of any two* Abstract *instances is an* Abstract *instance.*

4.2 The Universal Construction

We build a universal construction following the Abstract specification. The construction is based on Herlihy's classic universal construction [14], replacing wait-free consensus with consensus instances that may abort in the presence of contention.

More precisely, an *abortable* consensus instance returns either a commit or an abort indication, together with a decision value v (in case of abort, the instance returns an empty value $\perp$). The instance guarantees to commit as long as a progress predicate NT holds. In the Appendix, we present abortable consensus algorithms ensuring progress in the absence of interval contention (SplitConsensus) and in the absence of step contention (AbortableBakery), which only use read-write atomic registers. These are abortable variants of algorithms already present in the literature [6, 18], respectively.

Description. Processes share an array of abortable consensus instances $Cons$ ensuring progress as long as predicate NT holds, an atomic register $Aborted$, a snapshot object $Reqs$, where process p_i adds its requests in component $Reqs[i]$, and an atomic counter C, used to assign timestamps to process requests. Each process maintains a list $lProp$ of proposed requests and a list $lPerf$ of performed requests. The process runs in parallel an instance of the universal construction and a task checkAbort that checks whether the $Aborted$ register has been set to true.

As long as the abortable consensus instances do not return an abort indication, the construction proceeds exactly as Herlihy's universal construction, using the $Cons$ vector to agree on the requests to be performed on each process' local copy of the object, and incrementing the counter C for each new request. On the other hand, if a process receives abort from a consensus instance $Cons[\ell]$ or reads $Aborted =$ true in the checkAbort task, then the process first sets the $Aborted$ register to true (in case the register is not already set), and reads $count$, the value of the counter C, to get the length of the abort history.

Then the process proceeds to compute a valid abort history. It starts from an empty history and appends, in order, all requests that have been decided in the $Cons$ vector, from 1 to $count$, irrespective of whether the requests have been committed or aborted. For consensus instances in $Cons$ to which it has not participated, the process can get a decision value by proposing $\perp$. Following this procedure, the process obtains an abort history of length at most $count$.

For initializing a new instance of the universal construction, each process proposes, in order, the requests in its (abort) history to the $Cons$ list of the new instance. The process then proceeds to execute the new instance as described above. (Note that a process may abort during this initialization step.)

Progress predicate. The above construction guarantees to commit requests as long as the progress predicate NT of the abortable consensus implementation holds. (This predicate could be the absence of interval contention, or the absence of step contention.) It follows that, given such a consensus algorithm, the construction verifies the properties of an Abstract with progress predicate NT.

LEMMA 1. *Given an abortable consensus algorithm A that always commits as long as predicate NT holds, the above construction is an* Abstract *with progress predicate NT.*

Contention-free, obstruction-free and wait-free variants. In the Appendix, we present abortable consensus algorithms that ensure progress in the absence of interval contention (SplitConsensus) and in the absence of step contention (AbortableBakery), which only use read-write atomic registers. Lemma 1 implies that these algorithms generate universal constructions with the corresponding progress predicates. It is easy to see that if the abortable consensus algorithm is replaced by a wait-free consensus algorithm we obtain a wait-free composable universal construction that never aborts. The composition of these three Abstracts is an Abstract that never aborts, and only uses registers in executions with no interval or step contention. Note that the *commit ordering* property of Abstract implies that the composition generates linearizable implementations for generic objects. We formalize this as follows.

PROPOSITION 1. *Every sequential type has an* Abstract *implementation, using only registers in the absence of interval or step contention, and employing compare-and-swap otherwise.*

Complexity Cost. On the other hand, the composition of generic object implementations comes at a price. Any wait-free universal Abstract implementation must have linear space and step complexity [16]. Moreover, we notice that *any* wait-free Abstract implementation of a non-trivial sequential type solves consensus, even if the original object has lower consensus number. This follows easily, since we can use the commit histories to reach a decision value among n processes: the process with the first committed request in the commit histories imposes its proposal value on the consensus object.

PROPOSITION 2. *Every* Abstract *implementation of a non-trivial sequential type guaranteeing wait-free progress solves wait-free consensus.*

In the next section, we examine how to avoid this cost.

5. SAFELY COMPOSABLE OBJECTS

5.1 Definitions

Given the definitions in Section 3, let $\mathcal{O} = (\mathcal{Q}, s, \mathcal{I}, \mathcal{R}, \Delta)$ be an object and $\mathcal{H}$ be the set of all possible histories (recall that a history is a sequence of requests in $\mathcal{I}$ that contains no duplicates). The definition of a safely composable algorithm takes two parameters: a set of switch values $\mathcal{V}$ and a *constraint* function $M : 2^{\mathcal{T}} \to 2^{\mathcal{H}}$, mapping every set of switch tokens into the set of possible histories that it encodes. (Recall that $\mathcal{T}$ denotes the set of switch tokens, i.e. pairs consisting of a request and a switch value.) Intuitively, a constraint function puts restrictions on the allowed interpretations of a given set of init or abort tokens.

Let β be the function from histories to responses of $\mathcal{O}$ such that $\beta(h)$ is the last response obtained by applying h sequentially to $\mathcal{O}$. Given a history h and a requests m appearing in h, we define $\beta(h, m)$ as the response matching m in h.

Given a set I of requests, we define the equivalence relation $\equiv_I$ such that $h_1 \equiv_I h_2$ iff (i) both h_1 and h_2 contain all the requests in I, (ii) for all $h \in \mathcal{H}$, $\beta(h_1 h) = \beta(h_2 h)$, and (iii) for all requests $m \in I$, $\beta(h_1, m) = \beta(h_2, m)$. Intuitively, two histories composed of requests in I are equivalent if they "appear" the same (return the same responses) in all possible extensions.

Given a set of switch tokens T, we define $requests(T)$ as the set of requests found in the token in T and we define $eq(T, M)$ as the set of equivalence classes of the relation $\equiv_{requests(T)}$ partitioning the set $M(T)$. Given a history h we denote by $[h]_{T,M}$ the equivalence class of h according to $\equiv_{requests(T)}$ in $M(T)$.

Let τ be a trace of O, as defined in Section 3. Let an *index* be a position in a trace. An index i of τ might be either an *invoke, commit, abort,* or *init* index, depending on the event appearing at i in τ. Let $Ind(\tau)$ be the set of all indices in τ. Given a commit index i, let $response(i)$ be the response appearing at i. Let $inits(\tau)$ be the set of switch tokens found in the init requests of τ and $aborts(\tau)$ be the set of switch tokens found in the abort replies of τ.

An *interpretation* ϕ is a function $\phi : Ind(\tau) \to \mathcal{H}$. We denote by ϕ_τ the trace obtained from trace τ by replacing every commit or switch value appearing in τ at index i with $\phi(i)$. A trace τ is *valid* with respect to a mapping $M : 2^{\mathcal{T}} \to 2^{\mathcal{H}}$ iff $M(inits(\tau)) \neq \emptyset$.

An interpretation ϕ is *valid* with respect to trace τ, mapping M, and history $h_{abort} \in M(aborts(\tau))$ iff:

1. There exists $h_{init} \in M(inits(\tau))$ such that for every init index $i \in \tau$, $\phi(i) = h_{init}$.
2. For every abort index $i \in \tau$, $\phi(i) = h_{abort}$.
3. For every commit index $i \in \tau$, we have that $\beta(\phi(i)) = response(i)$.
4. ϕ_τ is a trace that satisfies the properties of an Abstract from Definition 1.

Intuitively, a valid interpretation ϕ for τ produces a trace ϕ_τ by replacing every commit value or switch value appearing at index i in τ with a history h so that the invocation, init events, commit and abort responses are globally consistent.

If ϕ is valid w.r.t. τ, M, and h_{abort}, we denote by $init(\phi, \tau)$ the unique history h such that for all init index i of τ, $\phi(i) = h$. Similarly we denote by $abort(\phi, \tau)$ the unique history h such that for all abort index i of τ, $\phi(i) = h$.

DEFINITION 2 (SAFE COMPOSITION). *An algorithm A is a safely composable implementation of an object $\mathcal{O}$ with respect to a set of switch values $\mathcal{V}$ and a constraint function M iff for every trace τ of A that is valid w.r.t. M and for every equivalence class $e \in eq(aborts(\tau), M)$, there exists a history $h_{abort} \in e$ and an interpretation ϕ that is valid with respect to τ, M, and h_{abort}. If $eq(aborts(\tau), M) = \emptyset$, then ϕ has to be valid with respect to τ, M, and the empty history $\perp$.*

5.2 Properties

The key property of this specification is that the composition of any two safely composable objects is also a safely composable object. (Recall that, intuitively, the composition of A and B runs algorithm B using A's outputs as inputs.) The proof of this result illustrates a trade-off between the strength of the specification and the difficulty of proving correctness of the composition: the more general the specification, the harder it is to prove that the composition is correct.

THEOREM 2 (COMPOSITION). *Let A and B be two algorithms that are safely composable implementations of an object O with respect to a set of switch values $\mathcal{V}$ and a constraint function $\mathcal{M}$. Then the composition of A and B is a safely composable implementation of object O with respect to $\mathcal{V}$ and $\mathcal{M}$.*

PROOF. We begin the proof by stating a couple of auxiliary results.

LEMMA 2. *For all set V of switch values, the relation $\equiv_V$ is a right congruence w.r.t. history concatenation. In other words, for all set V of switch values, if $h_1 \equiv_V h_2$ then for all history h, $h_1 h \equiv_V h_2 h$.*

This lemma is straightforward from the definition of $\equiv_V$. It means that we cannot distinguish whether history h_1 or history h_2 was executed if we only look at subsequent responses. This fact in crucial in the proof of the next lemma.

Consider now an arbitrary trace τ and suppose that ϕ is an interpretation of τ such that ϕ_τ satisfies the properties of Abstract, all init indexes are mapped to the same history, and all abort indexes are mapped to the same history. By the definition of Abstract, we know that for all init, commit, or abort indexes i of τ, there exists a history h_i such that $\phi(i) = init(\phi, \tau) h_i$. Given a history h, let $subst(\phi, h)$ be the interpretation of τ such that for all init, commit, or abort indexes i of τ, $subst(\phi, h)(i) = h h_i$. Intuitively, $subst(\phi, h)$ is obtained by replacing, in every history $\phi(i)$, the longest common prefix of init histories in ϕ_τ ($init(\phi, \tau)$) with the history h.

LEMMA 3. *Consider a trace τ and suppose that ϕ is a valid interpretation of τ with respect to a constraint function M and a history h_{abort}. Let $h_{init} = init(\phi, \tau)$. Then for all histories $h'_{init} \in M(inits(\tau))$ related to h_{init} (i.e. such that $h'_{init} \in [h_{init}]_{inits(\tau),M}$), there exists a history $h'_{abort} \in M(aborts(\tau))$ related to h_{abort} (i.e. such that $h'_{aborts} \in [h_{abort}]_{aborts(\tau)),M}$) and an interpretation ϕ' such that $init(\phi', \tau) = h'_{init}$ and the interpretation ϕ' is valid w.r.t τ, M, and h'_{abort}.*

Intuitively, the lemma implies that interpretations of safely composable objects compose: in particular, every valid interpretation of abort histories of A can be used to interpret the init histories of B.

PROOF. Let $\phi' = subst(\phi, h'_{init})$ and $h'_{abort} = abort(\phi', \tau)$. Since ϕ is an interpretation of τ such that ϕ_τ satisfies the properties of Abstract, ϕ' and h'_{abort} are well defined. Moreover we claim that ϕ' is valid w.r.t τ, M, and h'_{abort}:

- $h'_{init} \in M(inits(\tau))$ by definition and we trivially have that $init(\phi', \tau) = h'_{init}$.

- We trivially have that that for all abort index i, $\phi'(i) = h'_{abort}$.

- Lemma 2 implies that $\beta(\phi'(i)) = \beta(\phi(i)) = response(i)$.

- $\phi'(\tau)$ is a trace of Abstract because, given any history h, the four properties of Abstract are left invariant by substituting h, in every history, for the longest common prefix of init histories.

Hence ϕ' is valid w.r.t. τ, M, and h'_{abort}.

It remains to show that $h'_{abort} \in [h_{abort}]_{aborts(\tau),M}$. By Lemma 2 we have that $h'_{abort} \in [h_{abort}]_{inits(\tau),M}$. Hence we know that (ii) for all $h \in \mathcal{H}$, $\beta(h'_{abort}h) = \beta(h_{abort}h)$.

Moreover because $\phi'(\tau)$ is a trace of Abstract, Validity holds of $\phi'(\tau)$. Hence (i) for all request m in $aborts(\tau)$, $m \in h'_{abort}$. By definition of h'_{abort}, we know that there exists h such that $h_{abort} = h_{init}h$ and $h'_{abort} = h'_{init}h$. We now consider two cases: Suppose $m \in h'_{init}$. By Validity we have that $m \in requests(inits(\tau))$. Then because $h'_{init} \in [h_{init}]_{inits(\tau),M}$ we have that $\beta(h_{abort}, m) = \beta(h'_{abort}, m)$. Suppose $m \in h$. Since $h'_{init} \in [h_{init}]_{inits(\tau),M}$ we have that for all h', $\beta(h_{init'}h') = \beta(h_{init}h')$. Hence (iii) $\beta(h_{init'}h, m) = \beta(h_{init}h, m)$. From (i), (ii), and (iii) we have that $h'_{abort} \in [h_{abort}]_{aborts(\tau),M}$. □

Returning to the proof of the Theorem, consider a trace τ of the composition of A and B that is valid w.r.t. M and let τ_A be the projection of τ onto the events of A and τ_B be the projection of τ onto the events of B. Consider an equivalence class $e \in eq(aborts(\tau_B), M)$. We show below that there exists $h \in e$ and an interpretation that is valid w.r.t. τ, M, and h.

First observe that since τ is valid w.r.t. M, then τ_A is valid w.r.t. M too. Thus, because A is a safely composable implementation of O w.r.t. $\mathcal{V}$ and $\mathcal{M}$, τ_B is valid w.r.t. $\mathcal{M}$. Hence, because B is a safely composable implementation of object O with respect to $\mathcal{V}$ and $\mathcal{M}$, we know that there exists a history $h^B_{abort} \in e$ and an interpretation ϕ_B of τ_B such that ϕ_B is valid with respect to τ_B, M, and h^B_{abort}.

Let $h^B_{init} = init(\phi_B, \tau_B)$, i.e. the history such that for all init index i of τ_B, $\phi_B(i) = h^B_{init}$. Observe that $h^B_{init} \in M(inits(\tau_B)) = M(aborts(\tau_A))$. Consider $e' = [h^B_{init}]_{inits(\tau_B),M}$, which is the equivalence class of h^B_{init} w.r.t. $\equiv_{inits(\tau_B)}$ in $M(inits(\tau_B))$. Because A is a safely composable implementation of object O with respect to $\mathcal{V}$ and $\mathcal{M}$, we know that there exists a history $h^A_{abort} \in e'$ and an interpretation ϕ_A of τ_A such that ϕ_A is valid with respect to τ_A, M, and h^A_{abort}.

Since $h^A_{abort} \in [h^B_{init}]_{inits(\tau_B),M}$, by Lemma 3 we obtain a history $h^{B'}_{abort} \in [h^B_{abort}]_{aborts(\tau_B),M} = e$ and an interpretation ϕ'_B that is valid w.r.t. τ_B, M, and $h^{B'}_{abort}$, and such that $init(\phi'_B, \tau_B) = h^A_{abort} = abort(\phi_A, \tau_A)$. Let ϕ be the interpretation of τ such that if i is an index of τ_A, then $\phi(i) = \phi_A(i)$ and else $\phi(i) = \phi'_B(i)$. Since ϕ_A and ϕ'_B coincide on the abort indices of τ_A (or equivalently on the init indices of τ_B), we have by the Abstract composition theorem that ϕ_τ is a trace of Abstract. Moreover since ϕ_A and ϕ'_B are valid w.r.t. τ_A and τ_B we have that for all commit index i, $\beta(\phi(i)) = response(i)$. Finally we have by validity of $\phi_A(\tau_A)$ and $\phi_B(\tau_B)$ that for every init index $i \in \tau$, $\phi(i) = init(\phi_A, \tau_A)$, and that for every abort index i in τ, $\phi(i) = h^{B'}_{abort}$.

In conclusion we obtained the interpretation ϕ which is valid w.r.t. τ, M, and $h^{B'}_{abort}$. With the fact that $h^{B'}_{abort} \in e$ this proves our goal.

Another property that follows from this specification is that any safely composable object which is not initialized by a previous module is linearizable. This follows since a valid interpretation ϕ of τ satisfies the Abstract Commit Order and Validity properties. It was proved in [13] that any trace satisfying these properties is linearizable.

THEOREM 3 (LINEARIZATION). *Consider a safely composable implementation A of object O with respect to a set of switch values $\mathcal{V}$ and a mapping $\mathcal{M}$. Consider a trace τ of A that contains no init requests. Then then projection of τ onto invoke and commit events is linearizable.*

Note that Abstract is a safely composable implementation of a generic object which responds to invocations with its full execution history. This can be seen by taking a constraint function M that maps a set of histories to their longest common prefix and by observing that in this case, the interpretation that associates to init requests the longest common prefix of all inits, to the abort request the longest common prefix of the abort requests, and to the responses the history contained in the response, is a valid interpretation.

6. A SPECULATIVE TEST-AND-SET ALGORITHM

We now present a speculative long-lived test-and-set implementation. The construction is based on two modules, composed to obtain a wait-free linearizable test-and-set (please see Figure 1 for an illustration). The first module, A1, uses only registers and has constant step complexity, ensuring progress in the absence of *step contention*. The second module A2 is essentially a hardware implementation of test-and-set. We consider an implementation where the two modules are composed in the increasing order of progress condition strength: a process first tries to execute the obstruction-free module; if this module aborts (because of contention), then it tries to execute the wait-free module A2. Upon a reset operation, the calling process also reverts the algorithm to an instance of the obstruction-free module A1, thus the module returns to speculative mode in case it was using the hardware implementation. We now describe each module in more detail.

6.1 The Obstruction-Free Module

In the first module, described in Algorithm 1, processes share four atomic registers: *aborted*, initially false, V, initially 0, and P

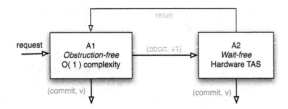

Figure 1: The structure of the test-and-set algorithm.

```
1  Shared:
2  Registers P and S, initially ⊥, register aborted, initially false,
     register V, initially 0
3  procedure A1-test-and-set( val )ᵢ
4    if aborted = true then
5      if V.read() = 0 then return (abort, W)
6      else return (abort, L)
7    if V.read() = 1 or val = L then
8      return (commit, loser)
9    if P ≠ ⊥ then return (commit, loser)
10   P ← i
11   if S ≠ ⊥ then return (commit, loser)
12   S ← i
13   if P = i then
14     V ← 1
15     if aborted = false then
16       return (commit, winner)
17     else return (abort, W)
18   else
19     aborted ← true
20     val ← V
21     if val = 1 then
22       return (commit, loser)
23     return (abort, W)
```

Algorithm 1: The obstruction-free module.

and S, initially $\perp$. The *aborted* register indicates whether the current instance has been aborted, whereas V holds the current value of the object. Registers P and S are used to indicate whether other processes are taking steps in the current execution. In short, we ensure that each process either reaches a winner/loser decision in the absence of interval contention, or that the process detects interval contention, and aborts.

More precisely, processes first check the value of the *aborted* register. If it has been set to true, then the process aborts with state W, if the V register has not been set, or with state L, dropping from contention, if V has been set. Otherwise, if *aborted* = false, competing processes race to write their value to both registers P and S, in order. If one of these registers has already been written by another process, then the current process can safely commit loser (lines 9 and 11). Otherwise, the process checks if its identifier is still the value in P (line 12). If this holds, then we are certain that the process is the only one in this state. Next, the process sets the register V to 1, modifying the value of the object (line 14). This step will cause other processes to subsequently return loser. Finally, it checks whether the instance has been aborted by another process. If not, then the process returns winner. Otherwise, the process will abort with state W, signifying that the object has not yet been won (line 17). On the other hand, if register P's value is no longer i, then interval contention occurred. In this case, the process either returns loser, if V has already been set to 1 by a concurrent process, or it aborts with state W if V is still 0 (lines 18–23).

Analysis. We show that A1 is a correct safely composable object, whose progress predicate is the absence of step contention. It is easy to see that the algorithm has constant time and space complexity. The main technical point in the proof is mapping algorithm traces to Abstract histories. We start by defining the set of input values $\mathcal{V}$ and the mapping M with respect to which A1 is safely composable. In short, $\mathcal{V}$ is the set of abort values W and L, while M maps any set of replies into a set of possible histories that all start with the same request that returned W, and contain all the requests that caused the replies.

DEFINITION 3. *We define the set* $\mathcal{V} = \{W, L\}$. *Then the mapping* $M : 2^{\mathcal{T}} \to 2^{\mathcal{H}}$ *is defined as follows. Consider a set of replies* $S = \{(r_1, v_1), \ldots, (r_\ell, v_\ell)\}$. *If S contains a reply with value* $v_i = W$, *then* $M(S) := \{h \in \mathcal{H} \mid (\exists i \in \{1, \ldots, \ell\}$ *such that* $v_i = W$ *and* $\mathsf{head}(h) = r_i)$ *and* $(\forall j \in \{1, \ldots, \ell\}.r_j \in h)\}$.

Otherwise, $M(S)$ contains histories that start with an arbitrary request r not in S, and contain all requests in S, i.e. $M(S) := \{h \in \mathcal{H} \mid (h \neq \perp$ *and* $\mathsf{head}(h) \in \mathcal{R}\backslash S)$ *and* $(\forall j \in \{1, \ldots, \ell\}, r_j \in h)\}$.

Next, we prove that module A1 is safely composable with respect this definition.

LEMMA 4 (OBSTRUCTION-FREE MODULE). *The module* A1 *in Figure 1 is a safely composable test-and-set implementation with respect to the sets* $\mathcal{V}$ *and* M *from Definition 3.*

PROOF. The proof is structured as follows: we first prove invariants on the algorithm A1, after which we use these invariants to build the mapping to an Abstract required by the definition of a safely composable object.

The following invariants hold in every execution of A1 (their proof can be found in the full version of this paper [5]):

1. At most one process may execute lines 14-17. Also, at most one process may commit winner in A1.
2. If a process commits winner, then no process aborts with W in A1.
3. In every execution, there exists at least one process p such that 1) p either a) crashes, or b) commits winner, or c) aborts with W, *and* 2) p's request is invoked before any operation commits loser.
4. No operation that aborts with W may start after an operation commits loser.
5. All operations that start after an operation aborts will abort. All operations that start after an operation aborts with L abort with L.

We now consider a trace τ of A1 that is consistent with the mapping M, i.e. that $M(inits(\tau)) \neq \emptyset$. In particular, this implies that the trace τ is non-empty. We will consider arbitrary equivalence classes of histories $e \in eq(M(aborts(\tau)))$. For each e, we show that there exists a history $h_{abort} \in e$ and an interpretation ϕ of events in τ such that ϕ is valid with respect to τ, M, and h_{abort}.

We build h_{abort} as follows. Let A be the set of requests in τ that either commit winner or abort with W. If this set is empty, then, by Invariant 3, there exists a process p that crashes, whose operation started before any operation commits loser. If A is empty, then we add the corresponding request to A, so that A is now non-empty. Next, we define the set B to contain all the requests in τ that committed loser. Finally, we define the set C to contain all the requests in τ that aborted with L. We order requests in sets B and C, respectively, based on the linearization order when reading register *aborted* in line 3. Notice that, by Invariants 4 and 5, we obtain that the concatenation, in order, of requests in sets A, B, and C respects the order of non-overlapping operations. The only ordering which is not fixed at this point is that on members of the set A of requests.

Therefore, consider an arbitrary equivalence class e from the set $eq(M(aborts(\tau)))$. We consider three cases. First, if $aborts(\tau)$ contains no requests, then all the requests committed in τ. In this case, e is trivial, h_{abort} is empty, and the set A is a singleton. To the request in A we append all requests in B, ordered as described above, to obtain history h. For each committed request r we define $\phi(r)$ as the prefix of h that ends with r. It is clear that $\beta(\phi(r)) = response(r)$ for all requests r. We also assign history h to any $init$ requests in τ. It then follows that the resulting trace ϕ_τ satisfies the Abstract properties.

Hence we can assume that $aborts(\tau)$ is not empty. If $aborts(\tau)$ contains no requests that aborted with W, then, by Definition 3, $M(aborts(\tau))$ is the set of histories starting with any request $r \notin aborts(\tau)$ that contain each request in $aborts(\tau)$. All such histories are in the same equivalence class with respect to $\equiv_{aborts(\tau)}$, therefore there exists only one possible choice for e. On the other hand, since there are no requests aborting with W, the set A is a singleton. We build the history h_{abort} by concatenating the sets A, B, and C. Since, by definition, the request in A is not in $aborts(\tau)$, we obtain that $h_{abort} \in e$ as required. To build ϕ, we associate h_{abort} to each aborting and $init$ request; to every committed request r, we associate the prefix of h_{abort} up to r. The resulting mapping ϕ verifies the Abstract properties.

Finally, we consider the case where $aborts(\tau)$ contains at least one request aborting with W. Let S be the set of these requests. By Definition 3, for each request $r \in S$, there exists an equivalence class $e_r \in eq(M(aborts(\tau)))$ with the property that each history in e_r starts with request r. In order to build the history h_{abort} for each such class, first notice that in trace τ the set A must *equal* the set S, by Invariant 2. Hence, given an equivalence class e_r for $r \in S$, we place r first in h_{abort}, after which we place the rest of the requests in S (in the linearization order when reading register $aborted$ on line 3), then requests in B and in C, in the order described above. Clearly, $h_{abort} \in e_r$. To build ϕ, we associate h_{abort} to each aborting and $init$ request; to every committed request r, we associate the prefix of h_{abort} up to r. It is straightforward to check that the resulting mapping verifies the Abstract properties.

Thus, we have verified the safely composable properties in each case, and therefore module A1 is a safely composable implementation of test-and-set under $\mathcal{V}$ and M. $\square$

6.2 The Wait-Free Module

The wait-free module A2, whose pseudocode is given in Algorithm 2, uses a hardware test-and-set T, whose value is initially 0. Participating processes entering the module with $val = \mathsf{L}$ automatically return loser; every other participant calls T, and commits the value obtained. We prove that this module is also safely composable. The proof is a simplified version of Lemma 4.

LEMMA 5 (WAIT-FREE MODULE). *The module* A2 *in Figure 2 is a safely composable test-and-set implementation with respect to the sets $\mathcal{V}$ and M given in Definition 3.*

PROOF SKETCH. We consider an arbitrary trace τ of A2. Since τ is valid w.r.t. M, τ must be non-empty. Since the module A2 never aborts requests, it follows that $aborts(\tau) = \emptyset$, therefore the history h_{abort} is empty. Therefore the only requirement is to find a valid interpretation ϕ. It is straightforward that this interpretation is given by the linearization order at the test-and-set object T, after

```
1  Shared: An array TAS[] of speculative test-and-set objects
2  A register Count, initially 0

3  procedure reset( )ᵢ
4    if crtWinner = true then
5    |  Count ← Count.read() + 1
6    |  crtWinner ← false
7    return

8  procedure test-and-set( )ᵢ
9    c ← Count.read()
10   (res, val) ← TAS[c].A1.test-and-set(⊥)
11   if res = abort then
12   |  (res, val) ← TAS[c].A2.test-and-set(val)
13   if val = winner then
14   |  crtWinner ← true
15   return val

16  Shared: Test-and-set object T
17  procedure A2-test-and-set( val )ᵢ
18    if val = L then return (commit, loser)
19    return (commit, T.test-and-set())
```

Algorithm 2: The resettable test-and-set object.

which we append requests with $val = \mathsf{L}$, respecting the order of non-overlapping operations. $\square$

6.3 Composing and Resetting the Modules

Composing the modules. The above modules have the property that they can be composed in any order to yield a linearizable implementation (in particular, module A1 can also be composed with itself). In this extended abstract, we consider A1 composed with A2, as in Figure 1. The composition yields a linearizable wait-free test-and-set object that uses only registers in the absence of step contention, as we show in Lemma 7.

Resetting the Object. The reset mechanism reverts the object to 0 once it has been set, and is also used to revert to a speculative module from the more expensive wait-free module. Practically, this mechanism ensures the *back edge* in the diagram from Figure 1.

The procedure, whose pseudocode is in Algorithm 2, works as follows: we use an array $TAS[]$ of wait-free test-and-set objects, each implemented using A1 and A2 and a shared register $Count$, which will be used as a counter. Since the test-and-set is well formed, only the current winner may reset the object [1]. When the winner calls reset, it increments the value of $Count$ by one. Each process wishing to participate in the test-and-set first reads the value of $Count$, and then participates in $TAS[Count]$, accessing each of the modules in this wait-free implementation if necessary. We note that a similar construction was used by Afek et al. [1] to obtain multi-use randomized test-and-set from single-writer registers.

6.4 Proof of Correctness

We first prove that a request may abort from A1 only in the presence of step contention.

LEMMA 6 (PROGRESS). *The algorithm* A1 *never aborts in the absence of step contention.*

PROOF. There are three possibilities for a process p to abort: either on line 17, or on line 23, or on lines 5–6. If p aborts on line 23, then the presence of step contention is straightforward: there must exist another process q that wrote to register P *after* p wrote to P. On the other hand, if p aborts on line 17, then there must exist a process q *concurrent* with p that sets the register *aborted* to true. While such a process q must exist, it is not immediate that q takes a step during p's execution. Assume for contradiction that q takes no steps during p's execution, in particular that it wrote to the *aborted* register *before p invoked its request*. In this case, however, the register P cannot equal $\perp$ during p's execution, therefore p will never reach line 17, a contradiction. Finally, if the process aborts on lines 5 or 6, then necessarily another process q wrote to the register *aborted*. It follows that process q experienced step contention, as required. $\square$

We conclude with the proof of correctness of the long-lived implementation given in Algorithm 2. We first prove that the composition of A1 and A2 is a linearizable one-shot test-and-set: from Lemma 4 and Lemma 5 plus Theorem 2, we get that the composition is safely composable. By Theorem 3, the composition is linearizable, since no request ever aborts from the composition. Second, we prove that the long-lived version can be linearized starting from the single-use linearizations.

THEOREM 4. *The composition of modules* A1 *and* A2 *given in Algorithm 2 is a correct wait-free linearizable long-lived test-and-set implementation, which uses only registers and ensures constant step complexity in obstruction-free executions.*

PROOF. First, notice that we can put together Lemma 4, Lemma 5, Theorem 2, and Theorem 3 to obtain the following result.

LEMMA 7. *The composition of modules* A1 *and* A2 *in lines 9-15 of Figure 2 is a linearizable one-shot test-and-set.*

Given this Lemma, consider an arbitrary trace of the long-lived algorithm. For each index i in the array $TAS[]$, let Op_i be the operations invoked on $TAS[i]$. From Lemma 7, we know that, for any i, we can linearize the operations in $idOp_i$ (the reset operation is simply added to the linearization order given by the Lemma) to obtain a history h_i of requests. We will then obtain a linearization order for the long-lived object by concatenating the linearization orders h_i in increasing index order. The resulting history respects the consistency requirements since it is valid on each object, and respects the order of non-overlapping operations because the register $Count$ is atomic. The second claim follows immediately from Lemma 6. $\square$

7. CONCLUSIONS AND FUTURE WORK

We have presented a framework for building safely composable shared memory algorithms, and analyzed the cost of composing such algorithms. Our results suggest that this cost is negligible when expressed in terms of step complexity or computational power, if the implementation may take advantage of the semantics of the implemented object. Our framework provides a simple way to design and prove the correctness of speculative concurrent algorithms. One direction for future work would be to apply our framework to implementations of more complex objects, such as queues or fetch-and-increment registers, and to see whether it can yield practical algorithms.

8. REFERENCES

[1] Yehuda Afek, Eli Gafni, John Tromp, and Paul M. B. Vitányi. Wait-free test-and-set (extended abstract). In *WDAG '92*, pages 85–94, London, UK, 1992. Springer-Verlag.

[2] Yehuda Afek, Gideon Stupp, and Dan Touitou. Long lived adaptive splitter and applications. *Distributed Computing*, 15(2):67–86, 2002.

[3] Marcos K. Aguilera, Svend Frolund, Vassos Hadzilacos, Stephanie L. Horn, and Sam Toueg. Abortable and query-abortable objects and their efficient implementation. In *PODC '07*, pages 23–32, New York, NY, USA, 2007. ACM.

[4] Dan Alistarh, Seth Gilbert, Rachid Guerraoui, and Corentin Travers. Generating fast indulgent algorithms. In *ICDCN'11*, pages 41–52, Berlin, Heidelberg, 2011. Springer-Verlag.

[5] Dan Alistarh, Rachid Guerraoui, Petr Kuznetsov, and Giuliano Losa. On the complexity of composing shared-memory algorithms. Technical report, EPFL, 2012.

[6] Hagit Attiya, Rachid Guerraoui, Danny Hendler, and Petr Kuznetsov. The complexity of obstruction-free implementations. *J. ACM*, 56:24:1–24:33, July 2009.

[7] Hagit Attiya, Rachid Guerraoui, Danny Hendler, Petr Kuznetsov, Maged M. Michael, and Martin T. Vechev. Laws of order: expensive synchronization in concurrent algorithms cannot be eliminated. In *POPL*, pages 487–498, 2011.

[8] Romain Boichat, Partha Dutta, Svend Frølund, and Rachid Guerraoui. Deconstructing paxos. *SIGACT News*, 34:47–67, March 2003.

[9] David Dice, Mark Moir, and William Scherer. Quickly reacquirable locks. Technical report, Sun Microsystems, 2003.

[10] Partha Dutta and Rachid Guerraoui. The inherent price of indulgence. In *PODC '02*, pages 88–97, New York, NY, USA, 2002. ACM.

[11] Oded Goldreich and Erez Petrank. The best of both worlds: Guaranteeing termination in fast randomized byzantine agreement protocols. *Inf. Process. Lett.*, 36(1):45–49, 1990.

[12] Rachid Guerraoui, Nikola Knežević, Vivien Quéma, and Marko Vukolić. The next 700 bft protocols. In *EuroSys '10*, pages 363–376, New York, NY, USA, 2010. ACM.

[13] Rachid Guerraoui, Viktor Kuncak, and Giuliano Losa. Speculative linearizability. Technical report, EPFL, 2011. Accepted for publication at PLDI 2012, available at http://lara.epfl.ch/w/slin.

[14] Maurice Herlihy. Wait-free synchronization. *ACM Transactions on Programming Languages and Systems*, 13(1):123–149, January 1991.

[15] Maurice P. Herlihy and Jeannette M. Wing. Linearizability: a correctness condition for concurrent objects. *ACM Trans. Program. Lang. Syst.*, 12(3):463–492, 1990.

[16] Prasad Jayanti. A lower bound on the local time complexity of universal constructions. In *PODC*, pages 183–192, 1998.

[17] Prasad Jayanti. Adaptive and efficient abortable mutual exclusion. In *PODC*, pages 295–304, 2003.

[18] Victor Luchangco, Mark Moir, and Nir Shavit. On the uncontended complexity of consensus. In *Proc. of the 17th International Conference on Distributed Computing*, pages 45–59, 2003.

[19] Nalini Vasudevan, Kedar S. Namjoshi, and Stephen A. Edwards. Simple and fast biased locks. In *PACT '10*, pages 65–74, New York, NY, USA, 2010. ACM.

[20] Marko Vukolic. *Abstractions for asynchronous distributed computing with malicious players*. PhD thesis, EPFL, 2008.

APPENDIX

A. ALGORITHMS FOR ABORTABLE CONSENSUS

The SplitConsensus **Algorithm.** The propose procedure contains

```
 1  Shared: S, a splitter object, V, C, D, registers, initially ⊥
 2  procedure init( old )_i
 3      (ind, res) ← propose(old)
 4      return (ind, res)
 5  procedure propose( v )_i
 6      if splitter.get() = stop then
 7          if V ≠ ⊥ then
 8              if C = false then return (commit, V)
 9              else return (abort, V)
10          V ← v
11          if C = false then
12              splitter.reset()
13              return (commit, v)
14      else
15          C = true
16          ret ← V
17          return (abort, ret)
18  procedure SplitConsensus( old, v )_i
19      (ind, res) ← init(old)
20      if ind = abort then return (abort, old)
21      else
22          if res = ⊥ then return propose(v)
23          else return (commit, res)
```

Algorithm 3: The SplitConsensus Algorithm.

```
 1  Shared:
 2      Registers (A_i), (B_i), i ∈ {1, n}, initially ⊥
 3      Register Quit, initially false, and Dec, initially ⊥
 4  procedure propose( input_i )_i
 5      V ← collect A_i
 6      k_i ← minimal k such that the registers A_i contain no values
          with timestamp > k,
 7      and no different values with timestamp k
 8      if ∃(k_i, v) ∈ V then v_i ← v
 9      else
10          V' ← collect B_i
11          if V' ≠ ∅ then v_i ← u ∈ V with highest timestamp in
              V'
12          else v_i ← input_i
13      A_i ← (k_i, v_i)
14      V ← collect A_i
15      if there are no timestamps larger than k_i and no values other
          than v_i with timestamp k_i in V then
16          B_i ← (k_i, v_i)
17          V ← collect A_i
18          if there are no timestamps larger than k_i and no values
              other than v_i with timestamp k_i in V then
19              if Quit = false then
20                  Dec = v_i
21                  return (commit, v_i)
22      Quit ← true
23      return (abort, Dec)
24  procedure init( old )_i
25      (ind, res) ← propose(old)
26      return (ind, res)
27  procedure AbortableBakery( old, v )_i
28      (ind, res) ← init(old)
29      if ind = abort then return (abort, old)
30      else
31          if res = ⊥ then return propose(v)
32          else return (commit, res)
```

Algorithm 4: The AbortableBakery consensus algorithm.

the main body of the consensus protocol, first given in [18]. Each process proposes a value and receives commit/abort indication, together with a tentative decision value. If the indication is commit, then processes agree on the tentative value; if the indication is abort, agreement is not guaranteed.

Processes share a splitter object S and atomic registers V, which holds the tentative decided value, and C, a boolean flag signaling contention. See Algorithm 3 for the pseudocode. Each process first accesses the splitter S. If the process successfully acquires the splitter, i.e. returns stop from it, then it proceeds to read the shared value V. If V has already been updated, then the process returns (commit, V) or (abort, V), respectively, depending on whether contention has been detected by reading the flag C or not.

If the register V has not been updated by other processes, then the process updates it with its initial value v. If the contention flag C is false, then the process resets the splitter object and returns a commit to its initial value v. Otherwise, if contention is detected or the process cannot acquire the splitter, it sets the contention flag C to true, and aborts with the current value of the shared value V.

In order to compose several instances of consensus protocols, we introduce a wrapper SplitConsensus function around the propose procedure. This allows the process to suggest, besides its proposal value v for the consensus object, a value old for the object that it may have inherited from another instance of abortable consensus. (If this is the first invocation of a consensus protocol by the process, or if no value is inherited, then the process has $old = ⊥$.)

The AbortableBakery Algorithm. We focus on the description of the propose procedure, since the wrapper is identical to the previous algorithm. The algorithm is an abortable variant of the solo-fast consensus algorithm presented in [6]. Processes share register arrays (A_i) and (B_i) with $i ∈ \{1, \dots, n\}$, initially ⊥. Process p_j is assigned registers A_j and B_j. Each process tries to impose its input value as the decision by associating it with the highest timestamp in the arrays (A_i) and (B_i). The process will always succeed if there is no step contention; otherwise, it may abort.

Each process p_i first performs a collect on the (A_i) array. The local variable k_i is the minimal value k such that the registers A_i contain no values with timestamp larger than k, and no distinct

values with timestamp k. If such a timestamp exists in (A_i), then p_i sets its estimate to the associated value v. Otherwise, process p_i collects the contents of the array (B_i). If the collect is not empty, then it sets its estimate v_i to the value in V' with largest timestamp. If the collect is empty, then p_i keeps its input value as its estimate.

Next, the process writes its current (k_i, v_i) combination in its slot in (A_i), and collects the contents of the array. If there are no timestamps larger than k_i and no values other than v_i with timestamp k_i in the collect, then the process writes (k_i, v_i) in B_i. The process then checks again whether any process wrote a timestamp larger than k_i or a value other than v_i with timestamp k_i in A_i. Otherwise, the process sets the decision value to v_i and returns it. If any of the previous checks fails, then the process has experienced step contention and aborts by setting the $Quit$ register to true, and returns an abort indication together with the current value of the Dec register.

B. SOLO-FAST TEST-AND-SET

The algorithm composed of modules A1 and A2 can be transformed into a solo-fast algorithm by removing the code in the if clause on line 3 of module A1. The resulting algorithm has the property that a process uses the hardware object only when itself encountering step contention, whereas in the current version a process may abort if *another* process experiences step contention. Given this modification, the composed algorithm remains correct, but the proof that A1 is a safely composable object becomes more involved.

Greedy Sequential Maximal Independent Set and Matching are Parallel on Average

Guy E. Blelloch
Carnegie Mellon University
guyb@cs.cmu.edu

Jeremy T. Fineman
Georgetown University
jfineman@cs.georgetown.edu

Julian Shun
Carnegie Mellon University
jshun@cs.cmu.edu

ABSTRACT

The greedy sequential algorithm for maximal independent set (MIS) loops over the vertices in an arbitrary order adding a vertex to the resulting set if and only if no previous neighboring vertex has been added. In this loop, as in many sequential loops, each iterate will only depend on a subset of the previous iterates (i.e. knowing that any one of a vertex's previous neighbors is in the MIS, or knowing that it has no previous neighbors, is sufficient to decide its fate one way or the other). This leads to a dependence structure among the iterates. If this structure is shallow then running the iterates in parallel while respecting the dependencies can lead to an efficient parallel implementation mimicking the sequential algorithm.

In this paper, we show that for any graph, and for a random ordering of the vertices, the dependence length of the sequential greedy MIS algorithm is polylogarithmic ($O(\log^2 n)$ with high probability). Our results extend previous results that show polylogarithmic bounds only for random graphs. We show similar results for greedy maximal matching (MM). For both problems we describe simple linear-work parallel algorithms based on the approach. The algorithms allow for a smooth tradeoff between more parallelism and reduced work, but always return the same result as the sequential greedy algorithms. We present experimental results that demonstrate efficiency and the tradeoff between work and parallelism.

Categories and Subject Descriptors: F.2 [Analysis of Algorithms and Problem Complexity]: General

Keywords: Parallel algorithms, maximal independent set, maximal matching

1. INTRODUCTION

The *maximal independent set* (MIS) problem is given an undirected graph $G = (V, E)$ to return a subset $U \subseteq V$ such that no vertices in U are neighbors of each other (independent set), and all vertices in $V \setminus U$ have a neighbor in U (maximal). The MIS is a fundamental problem in parallel algorithms with many applications [17]. For example if the vertices represent tasks and each

edge represents the constraint that two tasks cannot run in parallel, the MIS finds a maximal set of tasks to run in parallel. Parallel algorithms for the problem have been well studied [16, 17, 1, 12, 9, 11, 10, 7, 4]. Luby's randomized algorithm [17], for example, runs in $O(\log |V|)$ time on $O(|E|)$ processors of a CRCW PRAM and can be converted to run in linear work. The problem, however, is that on a modest number of processors it is very hard for these parallel algorithms to outperform the very simple and fast sequential greedy algorithm. Furthermore the parallel algorithms give different results than the sequential algorithm. This can be undesirable in a context where one wants to choose between the algorithms based on platform but wants deterministic answers.

In this paper we show that, perhaps surprisingly, a trivial parallelization of the sequential greedy algorithm is in fact highly parallel (polylogarithmic depth) when the order of vertices is randomized. In particular, removing a vertex as soon as an earlier neighbor is added to the MIS, or adding it to the MIS as soon as no earlier neighbors remain gives a parallel linear-work algorithm. The MIS returned by the sequential greedy algorithm, and hence also its parallelization, is referred to as the ***lexicographically first*** MIS [6]. In a general undirected graph and an arbitrary ordering, the problem of finding a lexicographically first MIS is P-complete [6, 13], meaning that it is unlikely that any efficient low-depth parallel algorithm exists for this problem.[1] Moreover, it is even P-complete to approximate the size of the lexicographically first MIS [13]. Our results show that for any graph and for the vast majority of orderings the lexicographically first MIS has polylogarithmic depth.

Beyond theoretical interest the result has important practical implications. Firstly it allows for a very simple and efficient parallel implementation of MIS that can trade off work with depth. Given an ordering of the vertices each step of the implementation processes a prefix of the vertices in parallel, instead of processing all vertices. Using smaller prefixes reduces parallelism but also reduces redundant work. In the limit, a prefix of size one yields the sequential algorithm with no redundant work. We show that for appropriately sized prefixes the algorithm does linear work and has polylogarithmic depth. The second implication is that once an ordering is fixed, the approach guarantees the same result whether run in parallel or sequentially or, in fact, run using any schedule of the iterations that respects the dependences. Such determinism can be an important property of parallel algorithms [3, 2].

Our results generalize the work of Coppersmith et al. [7] (CRT) and Calkin and Frieze [4] (CF). CRT provide a greedy parallel algorithm for finding a lexicographically first MIS for a random graph $G_{n,p}$, $0 \le p \le 1$, where there are n vertices and the probabil-

Permission to make digital or hard copies of all or part of this work for personal or classroom use is granted without fee provided that copies are not made or distributed for profit or commercial advantage and that copies bear this notice and the full citation on the first page. To copy otherwise, to republish, to post on servers or to redistribute to lists, requires prior specific permission and/or a fee.
SPAA'12, June 25–27, 2012, Pittsburgh, Pennsylvania, USA.
Copyright 2012 ACM 978-1-4503-1213-4/12/06 ...$10.00.

---

[1]Cook [6] shows this for the problem of finding the lexicographically first maximal clique, which is equivalent to finding the MIS on the complement graph.

ity that an edge exists between any two vertices is p. It runs in $O(\log^2 n/\log\log n)$ expected depth on a linear number of processors. CF give a tighter analysis showing that this algorithm runs in $O(\log n)$ expected depth. They rely heavily on the fact that edges in a random graph are uncorrelated, which is not the case for general graphs, and hence their results do not extend to our context. We however use a similar approach of analyzing prefixes of the sequential ordering.

The **maximal matching** (MM) problem is given an undirected graph $G = (V, E)$ to return a subset $E' \subseteq E$ such that no edges in E' share an endpoint, and all edges in $E \setminus E'$ have a neighboring edge in E'. The MM of G can be solved by finding an MIS of its line graph (the graph representing adjacencies of edges in G), but the line graph can be asymptotically larger than G. Instead, the efficient (linear time) sequential greedy algorithm goes through the edges in an arbitrary order adding an edge if no adjacent edge has already been added. As with MIS this algorithm is naturally parallelized by adding in parallel all edges that have no earlier neighboring edges. Our results for MIS directly imply that this algorithm has polylogarithmic depth for random edge orderings with high probability. We also show that with appropriate prefix sizes the algorithm does linear work. Previous results have shown polylogarithmic depth and linear-work algorithms for the MM problem [15, 14] but as with MIS, our approach returns the same result as the sequential algorithm and leads to very efficient code.

We implemented versions of our algorithms as well as Luby's algorithm and ran experiments on a parallel shared-memory machine with 32 cores. Our experiments show that achieving work-efficiency is indeed important for good performance, and more specifically show how the choice of prefix size affects total work performed, parallelism, and overall running time. With a careful choice of prefix size, our algorithms achieve good speed-up (9–23x on 32 cores) and require only a modest number of processors to outperform optimized sequential implementations. Our efficient implementation of Luby's algorithm requires many more processors to outperform its sequential counterpart. On large input graphs, our prefix-based MIS algorithm is 3–8 times faster than our optimized implementation of Luby's algorithm, since our prefix-based algorithm performs less work in practice.

2. NOTATION AND PRELIMINARIES

Throughout the paper, we use n and m to refer to the number of vertices and edges, respectively, in the graph. For a graph $G = (V, E)$ we use $N(V)$ to denote the set of all neighbors of vertices in V, and $N(E)$ to denote the neighboring edges of E (ones that share a vertex). A maximal independent set $U \subset V$ is thus one that satisfies $N(U) \cap U = \emptyset$ and $N(U) \cup U = V$, and a maximal matching E' is one that satisfies $N(E') \cap E' = \emptyset$ and $N(E') \cup E' = E$. We use $N(v)$ as a shorthand for $N(\{v\})$ when v is a single vertex. We use $G[U]$ to denote the **vertex-induced subgraph** of G by vertex set U, i.e., $G[U]$ contains all vertices in U along with edges of G with both endpoints in U. We use $G[E']$ to denote the **edge-induced subgraph** of G, i.e., $G[E']$ contains all edges E' along with the incident vertices of G.

In this paper, we use the concurrent-read concurrent-write (CRCW) parallel random access machine (PRAM) model for analyzing algorithms. We assume both the arbitrary and priority write versions, where a priority write here means that the minimum (or maximum) value written concurrently is recorded. Our results are stated in the work-depth model where work is equal to the number of operations (equivalently the product of the time and processors) and depth is equal to the number of time steps.

3. MAXIMAL INDEPENDENT SET

The sequential algorithm for computing the MIS of a graph is a simple greedy algorithm, shown in Algorithm 1. In addition to a graph G the algorithm takes an arbitrary total ordering on the vertices π. We also refer to π as priorities on the vertices. The algorithm adds the first remaining vertex v according to π to the MIS and then removes v and all of v's neighbors from the graph, repeating until the graph is empty. The MIS returned by this sequential algorithm is defined as the lexicographically first MIS for G according to π.

Algorithm 1 Sequential greedy algorithm for MIS

1: **procedure** SEQUENTIALGREEDYMIS($G = (V, E), \pi$)
2:    **if** $|V| = 0$ **then return** $\emptyset$
3:    **else**
4:       let v be the first vertex in V by the ordering π
5:       $V' = V \setminus (v \cup N(v))$
6:       **return** $v \cup$ SEQUENTIALGREEDYMIS($G[V'], \pi$)

Algorithm 2 Parallel greedy algorithm for MIS

1: **procedure** PARALLELGREEDYMIS($G = (V, E), \pi$)
2:    **if** $|V| = 0$ **then return** $\emptyset$
3:    **else**
4:       let W be the set of vertices in V with no earlier
5:          neighbors (based on π)
6:       $V' = V \setminus (W \cup N(W))$
7:       **return** $W \cup$ PARALLELGREEDYMIS($G[V'], \pi$)

By allowing vertices to be added to the MIS as soon as they have no higher-priority neighbor, we get the parallel Algorithm 2. It is not difficult to see that this algorithm returns the same MIS as the sequential algorithm. A simple proof proceeds by induction on vertices in order. (A vertex v may only be resolved when all of its earlier neighbors have been classified. If its earlier neighbors match the sequential algorithm, then it does too.) Naturally, the parallel algorithm may (and should, if there is to be any speedup) accept some vertices into the MIS at an earlier time than the sequential algorithm, but the final set produced is the same.

We also note that if Algorithm 2 regenerates the ordering π randomly on each recursive call then the algorithm is effectively the same as Luby's Algorithm A [17]. It is the fact that we use a single permutation throughout that makes Algorithm 2 more difficult to analyze.

The priority DAG

A perhaps more intuitive way to view this algorithm is in terms of a directed acyclic graph (DAG) over the input vertices where edges are directed from higher priority to lower priority endpoints based on π. We call this DAG the **priority DAG**. We refer to each recursive call of Algorithm 2 as a **step**. Each step adds the roots[2] of the priority DAG to the MIS and removes them and their children from the priority DAG. This process continues until no vertices remain. We define the number of iterations to remove all vertices from the priority DAG (equivalently, the number of recursive calls in Algorithm 2) as its **dependence length**. The dependence length is upper bounded by the longest directed path in the priority DAG, but in general could be significantly less. Indeed for a complete graph the longest directed path in the priority DAG is (n), but the dependence length is $O(1)$.

---

[2] We use the term "root" to refer to those nodes in a DAG with no incoming edges.

The main goal of this section is to show that the dependence length is polylogarithmic for most orderings π. Instead of arguing this fact directly, we consider priority DAGs induced by subsets of vertices and show that these have small longest paths and hence small dependence length. Aggregating across all sub-DAGs gives an upper bound on the total dependence length.

Analysis via a modified parallel algorithm

Analyzing the depth of Algorithm 2 directly seems difficult as once some vertices are removed, the ordering among the set of remaining vertices may not be uniformly random. Rather than analyzing the algorithm directly, we preserve sufficient independence over priorities by adopting an analysis framework similar to [7, 4]. Specifically, for the purpose of analysis, we consider a more restricted, less parallel algorithm given by Algorithm 3.

Algorithm 3 Modified parallel greedy algorithm for MIS

1: **procedure** MODIFIEDPARALLELMIS($G = (V, E), \pi$)
2:   **if** $|V| = 0$ **then return** $\emptyset$
3:   **else**
4:     choose prefix-size parameter δ
5:     let $P = P(V, \pi, \delta)$ be the vertices in the prefix
6:     $W \leftarrow$ PARALLELGREEDYMIS($G[P], \pi$)
7:     $V' \leftarrow V \setminus (P \cup N(W))$
8:     **return** $W \cup$ MODIFIEDPARALLELMIS($G[V'], \pi$)

Algorithm 3 differs from Algorithm 2 in that it considers only a prefix of the remaining vertices rather than considering all vertices in parallel. This modification may cause some vertices to be processed later than they would in Algorithm 2, which can only *increase* the total number of steps of the algorithm when the steps are summed across all calls to Algorithm 2. We will show that Algorithm 3 has a polylogarithmic number of steps, and hence Algorithm 2 also does.

We refer to each iteration (recursive call) of Algorithm 3 as a **round**. For an ordered set V of vertices and fraction $0 < \delta \leq 1$, we define the δ-**prefix** of V, denoted by $P(V, \pi, \delta)$, to be the subset of vertices corresponding to the $\delta |V|$ earliest in the ordering π. During each round, the algorithm selects the δ-prefix of remaining vertices for some value of δ to be discussed later. An MIS is then computed on the vertices in the prefix using Algorithm 2, ignoring the rest of the graph. When the call to Algorithm 2 finishes, all vertices in the prefix have been processed and either belong to the MIS or have a neighbor in the MIS. All neighbors of these newly discovered MIS vertices and their incident edges are removed from the graph to complete the round.

The advantage of analyzing Algorithm 3 instead of Algorithm 2 is that at the beginning of each round, the ordering among remaining vertices is still uniform, as the removal of a vertex outside of the prefix is independent of its position (priority) among vertices outside of the prefix. The goal of the analysis is then to argue that a) the number of steps in each parallel round is small, and b) the number of rounds is small. The latter can be accomplished directly by selecting prefixes that are "large enough," and constructively using a small number of rounds. Larger prefixes increase the number of steps within each round, however, so some care must be taken in tuning the prefix sizes.

Our analysis assumes that the graph is arbitrary (i.e., adversarial), but that the ordering on vertices is random. In contrast, the previous analysis in this style [7, 4] assume that the underlying graph is random, a fact that is exploited to show that the number of steps within each round is small. Our analysis, on the other hand, must cope with nonuniformity on the permutations of (sub)prefixes as the prefix is processed with Algorithm 2.

Reducing vertex degrees

A significant difficulty in analyzing the number of steps of a single round of Algorithm 3 (i.e., the execution of Algorithm 2 on a prefix) is that the steps of Algorithm 2 are not independent given a single random permutation that is not regenerated after each iteration. The dependence, however, arises partly due to vertices of drastically different degree, and can be bounded by considering only vertices of nearly the same degree during each round.

Let Δ be the *a priori* maximum degree in the graph. We will select prefix sizes so that after the ith round, all remaining vertices have degree at most $\Delta/2^i$ with high probability[3]. After $\log \Delta < \log n$ rounds, all vertices have degree 0, and thus can be removed in a single step. Bounding the number of steps in each round to $O(\log n)$ then implies that Algorithm 3 has $O(\log^2 n)$ total steps, and hence so does Algorithm 2.

The following lemma and corollary state that after processing the first $(n \log(n)/d)$ vertices, all remaining vertices have degree at most d.

LEMMA 3.1. *Suppose that the ordering on vertices is uniformly random, and consider the (ℓ/d)-prefix for any positive ℓ and $d \leq n$. If a lexicographically first MIS of the prefix and all of its neighbors are removed from G, then all remaining vertices have degree at most d with probability at least $1 - n/e^\ell$.*

PROOF. Consider the following sequential process, equivalent to the sequential Algorithm 1 (in this proof we will refer to a recursive call of Algorithm 1 as a step). The process consists of $n\ell/d$ steps. Initially, all vertices are **live**. Vertices become **dead** either when they are added to the MIS or when a neighbor is added to the MIS. During each step, randomly select a vertex v, without replacement. The selected vertex may be live or dead. If v is live, it has no earlier neighbors in the MIS. Add v to the MIS, after which v and all of its neighbors become dead. If v is already dead, do nothing. Since vertices are selected in a random order, this process is equivalent to choosing a permutation first then processing the prefix.

Consider any vertex u not in the prefix. We will show that by the end of this sequential process, u is unlikely to have more than d live neighbors. (Specifically, during each step that it has d neighbors, it is likely to become dead; thus, if it remains live, it is unlikely to have many neighbors.) Consider the ith step of the sequential process. If either u is dead or u has fewer than d live neighbors, then u alone cannot violate the property stated in the lemma. Suppose instead that u has at least d live neighbors. Then the probability that the ith step selects one of these neighbors is at least $d/(n - i) > d/n$. If the live neighbor is selected, that neighbor is added to the MIS and u becomes dead. The probability that u remains live during this step is thus at most $1 - d/n$. Since each step selects the next vertex uniformly at random, the probability that no step selects any of the d neighbors of u is at most $(1 - d/n)^{\delta n}$, where $\delta = \ell/d$. This failure probability is at most $((1 - d/n)^{n/d})^\ell < (1/e)^\ell$. Taking a union bound over all vertices completes the proof. □

COROLLARY 3.2. *Setting $\delta = (2^i \log(n)/\Delta)$ for the ith round of Algorithm 3, all remaining vertices after the ith round have degree at most $\Delta/2^i$, with high probability.*

---
[3]We use "with high probability" (w.h.p.) to mean probability at least $1 - 1/n^c$ for any constant c, affecting the constants in order notation.

PROOF. This follows from Lemma 3.1 with ℓ (log n) and d $\Delta/2^i$. $\square$

Bounding the number of steps in each round

To bound the dependence length of each prefix in Algorithm 3, we compute an upper bound on the length of the longest path in the priority DAG induced by the prefix, as this path length provides an upper bound on the dependence length.

The following lemma implies that as long as the prefix is not too large with respect to the maximum degree in the graph, then the longest path in the priority DAG of the prefix has length $O(\log n)$.

LEMMA 3.3. *Suppose that all vertices in a graph have degree at most d, and consider a randomly ordered δ-prefix. For any ℓ and r with $\ell \geq r \geq 1$, if $\delta < r/d$, then the longest path in the priority DAG has length $O(\ell)$ with probability at least $1 - n(r/\ell)^\ell$.*

PROOF. Consider an arbitrary set of k positions in the prefix—there are $\binom{\delta n}{k}$ of these, where n is the number of vertices in the graph.[4] Label these positions from lowest to highest $(x_1, \ldots, x_k)$. To have a directed path in these positions, there must be an edge between x_i and x_{i+1} for $1 \leq i < k$. Having the prefix be randomly ordered is equivalent to first selecting a random vertex for position x_1, then x_2, then x_3, and so on. The probability of an edge existing between x_1 and x_2 is at most $d/(n-1)$, as x_1 has at most d neighbors and there are $n-1$ other vertices remaining to sample from. The probability of an edge between x_2 and x_3 then becomes at most $d/(n-2)$. (In fact, the numerator should be $d-1$ as x_2 already has an edge to x_1, but rounding up here only weakens the bound.) In general, the probability of an edge existing between x_i and x_{i+1} is at most $d/(n-i)$, as x_i may have d other neighbors and $n-i$ nodes remain in the graph. The probability increases with each edge in the path since once $x_1, \ldots, x_i$ have been fixed, we may know, for example, that x_i has no edges to $x_1, \ldots, x_{i-2}$. Multiplying the k probabilities together gives us the probability of a directed path from x_1 to x_k, which we round up to $(d/(n-k))^{k-1}$.

Taking a union bound over all $\binom{\delta n}{k}$ sets of k positions (i.e., over all length-k paths through the prefix) gives us probability at most

$$\binom{\delta n}{k} \left(\frac{d}{n-k}\right)^{k-1} \leq n \left(\frac{e\delta n}{k}\right)^k \left(\frac{d}{n-k}\right)^k$$
$$n \left(\frac{e\delta nd}{k(n-k)}\right)^k \leq n \left(\frac{2e\delta d}{k}\right)^k$$

Where the last step holds for $k \leq n/2$. Setting k $4e\ell$ and $\delta < r/d$ gives a probability of at most $n(r/\ell)^\ell$ of having a path of length $4e\ell$ or longer. Note that if we have $4e\ell > n/2$, violating the assumption that $k \leq n/2$, then n $O(\ell)$, and hence the claim holds trivially. $\square$

COROLLARY 3.4. *Suppose that all vertices in a graph have degree at most d, and consider a randomly ordered prefix. For an $O(\log(n)/d)$-prefix or smaller, the longest path in the priority DAG has length $O(\log n)$ w.h.p. For a $(1/d)$-prefix or smaller, the longest path has length $O(\log n/\log\log n)$ w.h.p.*

PROOF. For the first claim, apply Lemma 3.3 with r $\log n$ and ℓ $4\log n$. For the second claim, use r 1 and ℓ $6\log n/\log\log n$. $\square$

---

[4]The number of vertices n here refers to those that have not been processed yet. The bound holds whether or not this number accounts for the fact that some vertices may be "removed" from the graph out of order, as the n will cancel with another term that also has the same dependence.

Note that we want our bounds to hold with high probability with respect to the original graph, so the $\log n$ in this corollary should be treated as a constant across the execution of the algorithm.

Parallel greedy MIS has low dependence length

We now combine the number $\log n$ of rounds with the $O(\log n)$ steps per round to prove the following theorem on the number of steps in Algorithm 2.

THEOREM 3.5. *For a random ordering on vertices, where Δ is the maximum vertex degree, the dependence length of the priority DAG is $O(\log \Delta \log n)$ $O(\log^2 n)$ w.h.p. Equivalently, Algorithm 2 requires $O(\log^2 n)$ iterations w.h.p.*

PROOF. We first bound the number of rounds of Algorithm 3, choosing δ $c2^i \log(n)/\Delta$ in the ith round, for some constant c and constant $\log n$ (i.e., n here means the original number of vertices). Corollary 3.2 says that with high probability, vertex degrees decrease in each round. Assuming this event occurs (i.e., vertex degree is $d < \Delta/2^i$), Corollary 3.4 says that with high probability, the number of steps per round is $O(\log n)$. Taking a union bound across any of these events failing says that every round decreases the degree sufficiently and thus the number of rounds required is $O(\log n)$ w.h.p. We then multiply the number of steps in each round by the number of rounds to get the theorem bound. Since Algorithm 3 only delays processing vertices as compared to Algorithm 2, it follows that this bound on steps also applies to Algorithm 2. $\square$

4. LINEAR WORK MIS ALGORITHMS

While Algorithm 2 has low depth a naïve implementation will require $O(m)$ work on each step to process all edges and vertices and therefore a total $O(m \log^2 n)$ work. Here we describe two linear-work versions. The first is a smarter implementation of Algorithm 2 that directly traverses the priority DAG only doing work on the roots and their neighbors on each step—and therefore every edge is only processed once. The algorithm therefore does linear work and has computation depth that is proportional to the dependence length. The second follows the form of Algorithm 3, only processing prefixes of appropriate size. It has the advantage that it is particularly easy to implement. We use this second algorithm for our experiments.

Linear work through maintaining root sets

The idea of the linear-work implementation of Algorithm 2 is to explicitly keep on each step of the algorithm the set of roots of the remaining priority DAG, e.g., as an array. With this set it is easy to identify the neighbors in parallel and remove them, but it is trickier to identify the new root set for the next step. One way to identify them would be to keep a count for each vertex of the number of neighbors with higher priorities (parents in the priority DAG), decrement the counts whenever a parent is removed, and add a vertex to the root set when its count goes to zero. The decrement, however, needs to be done in parallel since many parents might be removed simultaneously. Such decrementing is hard to do work-efficiently when only some vertices are being decremented. Instead we note that the algorithm only needs to identify which vertices have at least one edge removed on the step and then check each of these to see if all their edges have been removed. We refer to a ***mis-Check*** on a vertex as the operation of checking if it has any higher priority neighbors remaining. We assume the neighbors of a vertex have been pre-partitioned into their parents (higher priorities) and children (lower priorities), and that edges are deleted lazily—i.e. deleting a vertex just marks it as deleted without removing it from the adjacency lists of its neighbors.

LEMMA 4.1. *For a graph with m edges and n vertices where vertices are marked as deleted over time, any set of l misCheck operations can be done in $O(l + m)$ total work, and any set of misCheck operations in $O(\log n)$ depth.*

PROOF. The pointers to parents are kept as an array (with a pointer to the start of the array). A vertex can be checked by examining the parents in order. If a parent is marked as deleted we remove the edge by incrementing the pointer to the array start and charging the cost to that edge. If it is not, the misCheck completes and we charge the cost to the check. Therefore the total we charge across all operations is $l + m$, each of which does constant work. Processing the parents in order would require linear depth, so we instead use a doubling scheme: first examine one parent, then the next two, then the next four, etc. This completes once we find one that is not deleted and we charge all work to the previous ones that were deleted, and the work can be at most twice the number of deleted edges thus guaranteeing linear work. The doubling scheme requires $O(\log n)$ steps each step requires $O(1)$ depth, hence the overall depth is $O(\log n)$. □

LEMMA 4.2. *Algorithm 2 can be implemented on a CRCW PRAM in $O(m)$ total work and $O(\log^3 n)$ depth w.h.p.*

PROOF. The implementation works by keeping the roots in an array, and on each step marking the roots and its neighbors as deleted, and then using misCheck on the neighbors' neighbors to determine which ones belong in the root array for the next step. The total number of checks is at most m, so the total work spent on checks is $O(m)$. After the misCheck's all vertices with no previous vertex remaining are added to the root set for the next step. Some care needs to be taken to avoid duplicates in the root array since multiple neighbors might check the same vertex. Duplicates can be avoided, however, by having the neighbor write its identifier into the checked vertex using an arbitrary concurrent write, and whichever write succeeds is responsible for adding the vertex to the new root array. Each iteration can be implemented in $O(\log n)$ depth, required for the checks and for packing the successful checks into a new root set. Multiplying by the $O(\log^2 n)$ iterations gives an overall depth of $O(\log^3 n)$ w.h.p. Every vertex and its edges are visited once when removing them, and the total work on checks is $O(m)$, so the overall work is $O(m)$. □

Linear work through smaller prefixes

The naïve algorithm has high work because it processes every vertex and edge in every iteration. Intuitively, if we process small-enough prefixes (as in Algorithm 3) instead of the entire graph, there should be less wasted work. Indeed, a prefix of size 1 yields the sequential algorithm with $O(m)$ work but $\Omega(n)$ depth. There is some tradeoff here—increasing the prefix size increases the work but also increases the parallelism. This section formalizes this intuition and describes a highly parallel algorithm that has linear work.

To bound the work, we bound the number of edges operated on while considering a prefix. For any prefix $P \subseteq V$ with respect to permutation π, we define **internal edges** of P to be the edges in the sub-DAG induced by P, i.e., those edges that connect vertices in P. We call all other edges incident on P **external edges**. The internal edges may be processed multiple times, but external edges are processed only once.

The following lemma states that small prefixes have few internal edges. We will use this lemma to bound the work incurred by processing edges. The important feature to note is that for very small prefixes, i.e., $\delta < k/d$ with $k \quad o(1)$ and d denoting the maximum degree in the graph, the number of internal edges in the prefix is sublinear in the size of the prefix, so we can afford to process those edges multiple times.

LEMMA 4.3. *Suppose that all vertices in a graph have degree at most d, and consider a randomly ordered δ-prefix P. If $\delta < k/d$, then the expected number of internal edges in the prefix is at most $O(k |P|)$.*

PROOF. Consider a vertex in P. Each of its neighbors joins the prefix with probability $< k/d$, so the expected number of neighbors is at most k. Summing over all vertices in P gives the bound. □

The following related lemma states that for small prefixes, most vertices have no incoming edges and can be removed immediately. We will use this lemma to bound the work incurred by processing vertices, even those that may have already been added to the MIS or implicitly removed from the graph.

LEMMA 4.4. *Suppose that all vertices in a graph have degree at most d, and consider a randomly ordered δ-prefix P. If $\delta \le k/d$, then the expected number of vertices in P with at least 1 internal edge is at most $O(k |P|)$.*

PROOF. Let X_E be the random variable denoting the number of internal edges in the prefix, and let X_V be the random variable denoting the number of vertices in the prefix with at least 1 internal edge. Since an edge touches (only) two vertices, we have $X_V \le 2X_E$. It follows that $E[X_V] \le 2E[X_E]$, and hence $E[X_V] \quad O(k |P|)$ from Lemma 4.3. □

The preceding lemmas indicate that small-enough prefixes are very sparse. Choosing $k \quad 1/\log n$, for example, the expected size of the subgraph induced by a prefix P is $O(|P|/\log n)$, and hence it can be processed $O(\log n)$ times without exceeding linear work. This fact suggests the following theorem. The implementation given in the theorem is relatively simple. The prefix sizes can be determined *a priori*, and the status of vertices can be updated lazily (i.e., when the vertex is processed). Moreover, each vertex and edge is only densely packed into a new array once, with other operations being done in place on the original vertex list.

THEOREM 4.5. *Algorithm 3 can be implemented to run in expected $O(n + m)$ work and $O(\log^4 n)$ depth on a common CRCW PRAM. The depth bound holds w.h.p.*

PROOF. This implementation updates vertex status (entering the MIS or removed due to a neighbor) only when that vertex is part of a prefix.

Let Δ be the *a priori* maximum vertex degree of the graph. Group the rounds into $O(\log n)$ *superrounds*, with superround i corresponding to an $O(\log(n)/d)$-prefix where $d \quad \Delta/2^i$. Corollary 3.2 states that all superrounds reduce the maximum degree sufficiently, w.h.p. This prefix, however, may be too dense, so we divide each superround into $\log^2 n$ rounds, each operating on a $O(1/d \log n)$-prefix P. To implement a round, first process all external edges of P to remove those vertices with higher-priority MIS neighbors. Then accept any remaining vertices with no internal edges into the MIS. These preceding steps are performed on the original vertex/edge lists, processing edges incident on the prefix a constant number of times. Let $P' \subseteq P$ be the set of prefix vertices that remain at this point. Use prefix sums to count the number of internal edges for each vertex (which can be determined by comparing priorities), and densely pack $G[P']$ into new arrays. This packing has $O(\log n)$ depth and linear work. Finally, process the induced subgraph $G[P']$ using a naïve implementation of Algorithm 2, which has depth $O(D)$ and work equal to $O(|G[P']| \cdot D)$, where D is the dependence length of P'. From Corollary 3.4, $D \in O(\log n)$ with high probability. Combining this with expected prefix size of $E[|G[P']|] \in O(|P|/\log n)$ from Lemmas 4.3 and 4.4 yields expected $O(|P|)$ work for processing the prefix. Summing across all prefixes implies a total of $O(n)$ expected work for Algorithm 2 calls plus $O(m)$ work in the worst case for processing external edges. Multiplying the $O(\log n)$ prefix depth across all $O(\log^3 n)$ rounds completes the proof for depth. □

5. MAXIMAL MATCHING

One way to implement maximal matching (MM) is to reduce it to MIS by replacing each edge with a vertex, and creating an edge between all adjacent edges in the original graph. This reduction, however, can significantly increase the number of edges in the graph and therefore may not take work that is linear in the size of the original graph. Instead a standard greedy sequential algorithm is used to process the edges in an arbitrary order and include the edge in the MM if and only if no neighboring edge on either side has already been added. As with the vertices in the greedy MIS algorithms, edges can be processed out of order when they don't have any earlier neighboring edges. This idea leads to Algorithm 4 where π is now an ordering of the edges.

Algorithm 4 Parallel greedy algorithm for MM

1: **procedure** PARALLELGREEDYMM($G = (V, E), \pi$)
2:     **if** $|E| = 0$ **then return** $\emptyset$
3:     **else**
4:         let W be the set of edges in E with no adjacent
5:            edges with higher priority by π
6:         $E' = E \setminus (W \cup N(W))$
7:         **return** $W \cup$ PARALLELGREEDYMM($G[E'], \pi$)

LEMMA 5.1. *For a random ordering on edges, the number of rounds of Algorithm 4 is $O(\log^2 m)$ w.h.p.*

PROOF. This follows directly from the reduction to MIS described above. In particular an edge is added or deleted in Algorithm 4 exactly on the same step it would be for the corresponding MIS graph in Algorithm 2. Therefore Lemma 3.5 applies. □

As we did for MIS in the previous section, we now describe two linear-work algorithms for maximal matching, the first of which maintains the set of roots in the priority DAG and the second of which processes prefixes of the vertices in priority order. The second algorithm is easier to implement and is the version we used for our experiments.

Linear work through maintaining root sets

As with the algorithm used in Lemma 4.2 we can maintain on each round an array of roots (edges that have no neighboring edges with higher priority) and use them to both delete edges and generate the root set for the next round. However, we cannot afford to look at all the neighbors' neighbors. Instead we maintain for each vertex an array of its incident edges sorted by priority. This list is maintained lazily such that deleting an edge only marks it as deleted and does

not immediately remove it from its two incident vertices. We say an edge is **ready** if it has no remaining neighboring edges with higher priority. We use an **mmCheck** procedure on a vertex to determine if any incident edge is ready and identify the edge if so—a vertex can have at most one ready incident edge. The mmChecks do not happen in parallel with edge deletions.

LEMMA 5.2. *For a graph with m edges and n vertices where edges are marked as deleted over time, any set of l mmCheck operations can be done in $O(l+m)$ total work, and any set of mmCheck operations in $O(\log m)$ depth.*

PROOF. The mmCheck is partitioned into two phases. The first identifies the highest priority incident edge that remains, and the second checks if that edge is also the highest priority on its other endpoint and returns it if so. The first phase can be done by scanning the edges in priority order removing those that have been deleted and stopping when the first non-deleted edge is found. As in Lemma 4.1 this can be done in parallel using doubling in $O(\log m)$ depth, and the work can be charged either to a deleted edge, which is removed, or the check itself. The total work is therefore $O(l + m)$. The second phase can similarly use doubling to see if the highest priority edge is also the highest priority on the other side. □

LEMMA 5.3. *For a random ordering on the edges, Algorithm 4 can be implemented on a CRCW PRAM in $O(m)$ total work and $O(\log^3 m)$ depth with high probability.*

PROOF. Since the edge priorities are selected at random, the initial sort to order the edges incident on each vertex can be done in $O(m)$ work and within our depth bounds w.h.p. using bucket sorting [8]. Initially the set of ready edges are selected by using an mmCheck on all edges. On each step of Algorithm 4 we delete the set of ready edges and their neighbors (by marking them), and then check all vertices incident on the far end of each of the deleted neighboring edges. This returns the new set of ready edges in $O(\log m)$ depth. Redundant edges can easily be removed. Thus the depth per step is $O(\log m)$ and by Lemma 5.1 the total depth is $O(\log^3 m)$. Every edge is deleted once and the total number of checks is $O(m)$, so the total work is $O(m)$. □

Linear work through prefixes

Algorithm 5 is the prefix-based algorithm for maximal matching (the analogue of Algorithm 3). To obtain a linear-work maximal matching algorithm, we use Algorithm 5 with a prefix-size parameter $\delta = 1/d_e$, where d_e is the maximum number of neighboring edges any edge in G has. Each call to Algorithm 4 in line 6 of Algorithm 5 proceeds in steps. We assume the edges are pre-sorted by priority (for random priorities they can be sorted in linear work and within our depth bounds with bucket sorting [8]).

Algorithm 5 Modified parallel greedy algorithm for MM

1: **procedure** MODIFIEDPARALLELMM($G = (V, E), \pi$)
2:     **if** $|V| = 0$ **then return** $\emptyset$
3:     **else**
4:         choose prefix-size parameter δ
5:         let $P = P(E, \pi, \delta)$ be the edges in the prefix
6:         $W = $ PARALLELGREEDYMM($G[P], \pi$)
7:         $E' = E \setminus (P \cup N(W))$
8:         **return** $W \cup$ MODIFIEDPARALLELMM($G[E'], \pi$)

In each step, first every edge in the prefix does a priority write to its two endpoints (attempting to record its rank in the permutation), and after all writes are performed, every edge checks whether

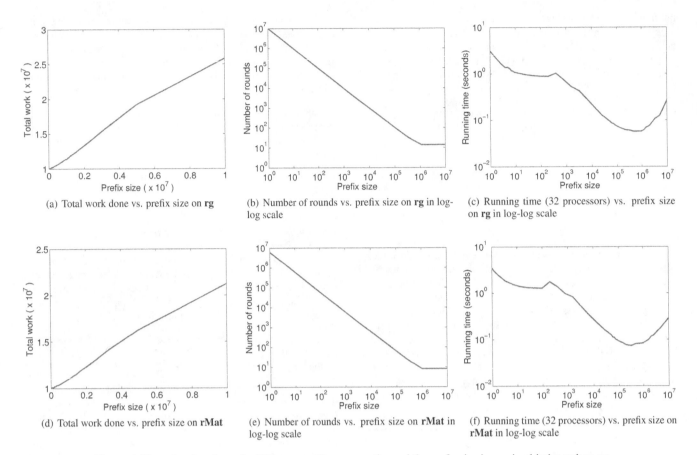

(a) Total work done vs. prefix size on **rg**

(b) Number of rounds vs. prefix size on **rg** in log-log scale

(c) Running time (32 processors) vs. prefix size on **rg** in log-log scale

(d) Total work done vs. prefix size on **rMat**

(e) Number of rounds vs. prefix size on **rMat** in log-log scale

(f) Running time (32 processors) vs. prefix size on **rMat** in log-log scale

Figure 1. Plots showing the tradeoff between various properties and the prefix size in maximal independent set.

it won on (its value was written to) both endpoints. Since edges are sorted by priority the highest priority edge incident on each vertex wins. If an edge wins on both sides, then it adds itself to the maximal matching and deletes all of its neighboring edges (by packing). Each edge does constant work per step for writing and checking. The packing takes work proportional to the remaining size of the prefix. It remains to show that the expected number of times an edge in the prefix is processed is constant.

Consider the priority DAG on the δ-prefix off E, where a node in the priority DAG corresponds to an edge in G, and a directed edge exists in the priority DAG from E_i to E_j if and only if E_i is adjacent to E_j in G and E_i has a higher priority than E_j. Note that this priority DAG is not explicitly constructed. Define the **height** of a node v_e in the priority DAG to be the length of the longest incoming path to v_e. The height of v_e is an upper bound on the number of iterations of processing the priority DAG required until v_e is either added to the MM or deleted.

THEOREM 5.4. *For a* $(1/d_e)$*-prefix, the expected height of any node (corresponding to an edge in G) in the priority DAG is $O(1)$.*

PROOF. For a given node v_e, we compute the expected length of a directed path ending at v_e. For there to be a length k path to v_e, there must be k positions $p_1, \ldots, p_k$ (listed in priority order) before v_e's position, p_e, in the prefix such that there exists a directed edge from p_k to p_e and for all $1 < i < k$, a directed edge from p_i to p_{i+1}. Using an argument similar to the one used in the proof of Lemma 3.3, the probability of this particular path existing is at most $(d_e/(m-k))^k$. The number of positions appearing before p_e

in the prefix is at most the size of the prefix itself. So summing over all possible choices of k positions, we have that the probability of a directed path from the root to some node being length k is

$$\binom{\delta m}{k}(d_e/(m-k))^k \leq (me/kd_e)^k(d_e/(m-k))^k$$

$$\leq (me/k(m-k))^k$$

Now we compute the expected length of a path from the root node by summing over all possible lengths. This expectation is upper bounded by

$$\sum_{k=1}^{\delta m} k(me/k(m-k))^k$$

$$\leq \left[\sum_{k=0}^{m/2} k(me/k(m-m/2))^k\right] + mPr(k > m/2)$$

$$\leq \left[\sum_{k=0}^{\infty} k(2e/k)^k\right] + o(1)$$

$$O(1)$$

To obtain the last inequality we apply Lemma 3.3, giving $Pr(k > m/2)$ $O(1/m^c)$ for $c > 1$. We then obtain the desired bound by using the formula $\sum_{k=0}^{\infty} k(x^k)/k!$ xe^x. □

LEMMA 5.5. *Given a graph with m edges, n vertices, and a random permutation on the edges π, Algorithm 5 can be imple-*

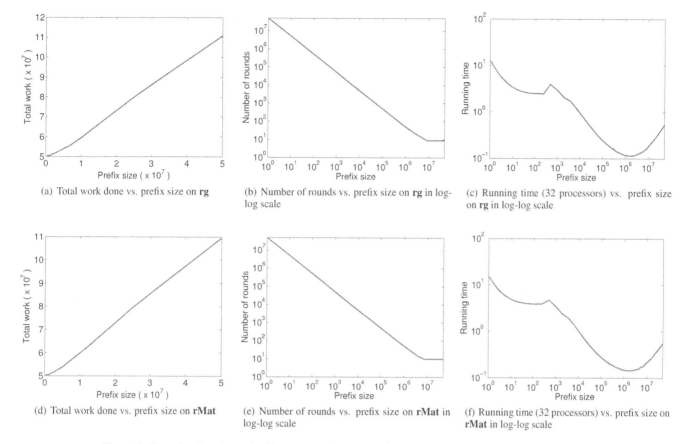

(a) Total work done vs. prefix size on **rg**

(b) Number of rounds vs. prefix size on **rg** in log-log scale

(c) Running time (32 processors) vs. prefix size on **rg** in log-log scale

(d) Total work done vs. prefix size on **rMat**

(e) Number of rounds vs. prefix size on **rMat** in log-log scale

(f) Running time (32 processors) vs. prefix size on **rMat** in log-log scale

Figure 2. Plots showing the tradeoff between various properties and the prefix size in maximal matching.

mented on a CRCW PRAM using a priority write in $O(m)$ total work in expectation and $O(\log^4 m / \log \log m)$ depth w.h.p.

PROOF. As in the proof of Theorem 4.5, group the rounds into $O(\log m)$ superrounds. Here we divide each superround into just $\log m$ rounds, each operating on a $O(1/d_e)$-prefix. It follows from Lemma 3.1 that the algorithm has $O(\log^2 m)$ rounds w.h.p, as d_e decreases by a constant factor in each superround. In each round, each step of Algorithm 4 processes the top level (root nodes) of the priority DAG. Once an edge gets processed as a root of the priority DAG or gets deleted by another edge, it will not be processed again in the algorithm. Since the expected height of an edge in the priority DAG is $O(1)$, it will be processed a constant number of times in expectation (each time doing a constant amount of work), and contributes a constant amount of work to the packing cost. Hence the total work is linear in expectation.

For a given round, the packing per step requires $O(\log |P|)$ depth where $|P|$ is the remaining size of the prefix. By Corollary 3.4, there are at most $O(\log m / \log \log m)$ steps w.h.p. Therefore, each round requires $O(\log^2 m / \log \log m)$ depth and the algorithm has an overall depth of $O(\log^4 m / \log \log m)$ w.h.p. □

6. EXPERIMENTS

We performed experiments of our algorithms using varying prefix sizes, and show how prefix size affects work, parallelism, and overall running time. We also compare the performance of our prefix-based algorithms with sequential implementations and additionally for MIS we compare with our implementation of Luby's algorithm.

Setup. We ran our experiments on a 32-core (hyperthreaded) machine with 4×2.26GHZ Intel 8-core X7560 Nehalem Processors, a 1066MHz bus, and 64GB of main memory. The parallel programs were compiled using the `cilk++` compiler (build 8503) with the `-O2` flag. The sequential programs were compiled using `g++` 4.4.1 with the `-O2` flag. For each prefix size, thread count and input, the reported time is the median time over three trials.

Input Graph	Size		
Random local graph (rg)	n	$10^7, m$	5×10^7
rMat graph (rMat)	n	$2^{24}, m$	5×10^7
3D grid (3D)	n	$10^7, m$	2×10^7

Table 1. Input Graphs

Inputs. Our input graphs and their sizes are listed in Table 1. The random local graph was generated such that probability of an edge existing between two vertices is inversely proportional to their distance in the vertex array. The rMat graph has a power-law distribution of degrees and was generated according to the procedure described in [5], with parameters a 0.5, b 0.1, c 0.1 and d 0.3. The 3D grid graph consists of vertices on a grid in a 3-dimensional space, where each vertex has edges to its 6 nearest neighbors (2 in each dimension).

Implementation. Our implementation of the prefix-based MIS and MM algorithms differ slightly from the ones with good theoretical guarantees described in the previous sections, but we found that these implementations work better in practice. Firstly, our pre-

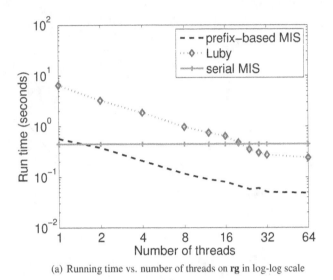

(a) Running time vs. number of threads on **rg** in log-log scale

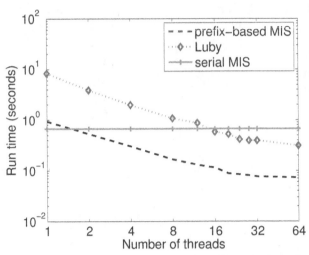

(b) Running time vs. number of threads on **rMat** in log-log scale

Figure 3. Plots showing the running time vs. number of threads for the different MIS algorithms on a 32-core machine (with hyper-threading). For the prefix-based algorithm, we used a prefix size of $n/50$.

fix size is fixed throughout the algorithm. Secondly, we do not process each prefix to completion but instead process each particular prefix only once, and move the iterates which still need to be processed into the next prefix (the number of new iterates in the next prefix is equal to the difference between the prefix size and the number of iterates which still need to be processed from the current prefix). For MIS, each time we process a prefix, there are 3 possible outcomes for each vertex in the prefix: 1) the vertex joins the MIS and is deleted because it has the highest priority among all of its neighbors; 2) the vertex is deleted because at least one of its neighbors is already in the MIS; or 3) the vertex is undecided and is moved to the next prefix. For MM, each time we process a prefix we proceed in 2 phases: In the first phase, each edge in the prefix checks whether or not either of its endpoints have been matched, and if not, the edge does a priority-write to each of its two endpoints; in the second phase, each edge checks whether its priority-writes were successful on both of its endpoints, and if so joins the MM and marks its endpoints as matched. Successful edges from the second phase and edges which discovered during the first phase that it had an endpoint already matched are deleted. Our prefix-based implementations are based on a more general concept of *deterministic reservations*, introduced in [2]. Pseudocode for the MIS implementation can be found in [2], and actual code can be found at http://www.cs.cmu.edu/~pbbs.

Input Graph	Serial MIS	Prefix-based MIS (1)	Prefix-based MIS (32h)	Luby (1)	Luby (32h)
rg	0.455	0.57	0.059	6.49	0.245
rMat	0.677	0.939	0.073	8.33	0.313
3D	0.393	0.519	0.051	4.18	0.161

Table 2. Running times (in seconds) of the various MIS algorithms on different input graphs on a 32-core machine with hyperthreading using one thread (1) and all threads (32h).

Results. For both MIS and MM, we observe that, as expected, increasing the prefix size increases both the total work performed (Figures 1(a), 1(d), 2(a) and 2(d)) and the parallelism, which is esti-

Input Graph	Serial MM	Prefix-based MM (1)	Prefix-based MM (32h)
rg	1.04	2.24	0.135
rMat	1.41	3.51	0.155
3D	0.792	1.8	0.11

Table 3. Running times (in seconds) of the various MM algorithms on different input graphs on a 32-core machine with hyperthreading using one thread (1) and all threads (32h).

mated by the number of rounds of the outer loop (selecting prefixes) the algorithm takes to complete (Figures 1(b), 1(e), 2(b) and 2(e)). As expected, the total work performed and the number of rounds taken by a sequential implementation are both equal to the input size. By examining the graphs of running time vs. prefix size (Figures 1(c), 1(f), 2(c) and 2(f)) we see that there is some optimal prefix size between 1 (fully sequential) and the input size (fully parallel). In the running time vs. prefix size graphs, there is a small bump when the prefix-to-input size ratio is between 10^{-6} and 10^{-4} corresponding to the point when the for-loop in our implementation transitions from sequential to parallel (we used a grain size of 256).

We also compare our prefix-based algorithms to optimized sequential implementations, and additionally for MIS we compare with our optimized implementation of Luby's algorithm. We implemented several versions of Luby's algorithm and report the times for the fastest one. Our prefix-based MIS implementation, using the optimal prefix size obtained from experiments (see Figures 1(c) and 1(f)), is 3–8 times faster than Luby's algorithm (shown in Figures 3(a) and 3(b)) which processes the entire remaining graph (and generates new priorities) in each round. This improvement demonstrates that our prefix-based approach, although sacrificing some parallelism, leads to less overall work and lower running time. When using more than 2 processors, our prefix-based implementation of MIS outperforms the serial version, while our implementation of Luby's algorithm requires 16 or more processors to outperform the serial version. The prefix-based algorithm achieves 9–13x speedup on 32 processors. For MM, our prefix-based algorithm outperforms the corresponding serial implementation with 4

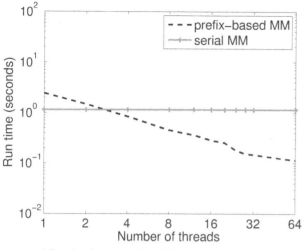

(a) Running time vs. number of threads on **rg** in log-log scale

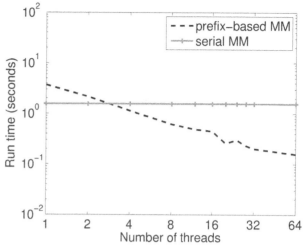

(b) Running time vs. number of threads on **rMat** in log-log scale

Figure 4. Plots showing the running time vs. number of threads for the different MM algorithms on a 32-core machine (with hyper-threading). For the prefix-based algorithm, we used a prefix size of $m/50$.

or more processors and achieves 16–23x speedup on 32 processors (Figures 4(a) and 4(b)). We note that since the serial MIS and MM algorithms are so simple, it is not easy for a parallel implementation to outperform the corresponding serial implementation.

7. CONCLUSION

We have shown that the "sequential" greedy algorithms for MIS and MM have polylogarithmic depth, for randomly ordered inputs (vertices for MIS and edges for MM). This gives random lexico-graphically first solutions for both of these problems, and in addition has important practical implications such as giving faster implementations and guaranteeing determinism. Our prefix-based approach leads to a smooth tradeoff between parallelism and total work and by selecting a good prefix size, we show experimentally that our algorithms achieve good speedup and outperform their serial counterparts using only a modest number of processors.

Open questions include whether the dependence length of our algorithms can be improved to $O(\log n)$ and whether our approach can be applied to sequential greedy algorithms for other problems.

Acknowledgements. This work is partially funded by the National Science Foundation under Grant number 1019343 to the Computing Research Association for the CIFellows Project and Grant number CCF-1018188, and by gifts from Intel and IBM.

References

[1] Noga Alon, László Babai, and Alon Itai. A fast and simple randomized parallel algorithm for the maximal independent set problem. *J. Algorithms*, 7:567–583, December 1986.

[2] Guy E. Blelloch, Jeremy T. Fineman, Phillip B. Gibbons, and Julian Shun. Internally deterministic parallel algorithms can be fast. In *Proceedings of Principles and Practice of Parallel Programming*, pages 181–192, 2012.

[3] Robert L. Bocchino, Vikram S. Adve, Sarita V. Adve, and Marc Snir. Parallel programming must be deterministic by default. In *Usenix HotPar*, 2009.

[4] Neil J. Calkin and Alan M. Frieze. Probabilistic analysis of a parallel algorithm for finding maximal independent sets. *Random Struct. Algorithms*, 1(1):39–50, 1990.

[5] Deepayan Chakrabarti, Yiping Zhan, and Christos Faloutsos. R-MAT: A recursive model for graph mining. In *SIAM SDM*, 2004.

[6] Stephen A. Cook. A taxonomy of problems with fast parallel algorithms. *Inf. Control*, 64:2–22, March 1985.

[7] Don Coppersmith, Prabhakar Raghavan, and Martin Tompa. Parallel graph algorithms that are efficient on average. *Inf. Comput.*, 81:318–333, June 1989.

[8] Thomas H. Cormen, Charles E. Leiserson, Ronald L. Rivest, and Clifford Stein. *Introduction to Algorithms (3. ed.)*. MIT Press, 2009.

[9] Andrew V. Goldberg, Serge A. Plotkin, and Gregory E. Shannon. Parallel symmetry-breaking in sparse graphs. In *SIAM J. Disc. Math*, pages 315–324, 1987.

[10] Mark Goldberg and Thomas Spencer. Constructing a maximal independent set in parallel. *SIAM Journal on Discrete Mathematics*, 2:322–328, August 1989.

[11] Mark Goldberg and Thomas Spencer. A new parallel algorithm for the maximal independent set problem. *SIAM Journal on Computing*, 18:419–427, April 1989.

[12] Mark K. Goldberg. Parallel algorithms for three graph problems. *Congressus Numerantium*, 54:111–121, 1986.

[13] Raymond Greenlaw, James H. Hoover, and Walter L. Ruzzo. *Limits to Parallel Computation: P-Completeness Theory*. Oxford University Press, USA, April 1995.

[14] Amos Israeli and A. Itai. A fast and simple randomized parallel algorithm for maximal matching. *Inf. Process. Lett.*, 22:77–80, February 1986.

[15] Amos Israeli and Y. Shiloach. An improved parallel algorithm for maximal matching. *Inf. Process. Lett.*, 22:57–60, February 1986.

[16] Richard M. Karp and Avi Wigderson. A fast parallel algorithm for the maximal independent set problem. In *STOC*, 1984.

[17] Michael Luby. A simple parallel algorithm for the maximal independent set problem. *SIAM J. Comput.*, 15:1036–1055, November 1986.

Efficient Computation of Distance Sketches in Distributed Networks

Atish Das Sarma
eBay Research Labs
San Jose, CA, USA
atish.dassarma@gmail.com

Michael Dinitz[*]
Weizmann Institute of Science
Rehovot, Israel
mdinitz@cs.cmu.edu

Gopal Pandurangan[†]
Nanyang Technological
University, Singapore
& Brown University, USA
gopalpandurangan@gmail.com

ABSTRACT

Distance computation (e.g., computing shortest paths) is one of the most fundamental primitives used in communication networks. The cost of effectively and accurately computing pairwise network distances can become prohibitive in large-scale networks such as the Internet and Peer-to-Peer (P2P) networks. To negotiate the rising need for very efficient distance computation at scales never imagined before, approximation techniques for numerous variants of this question have recently received significant attention in the literature. Several different areas of theoretical research have emerged centered around this problem, such as metric embeddings, distance labelings, spanners, and distance oracles. The goal is to preprocess the graph and store a *small* amount of information such that whenever a query for any pairwise distance is issued, the distance can be well approximated (i.e., with small *stretch*) very quickly in an online fashion. Specifically, the pre-processing (usually) involves storing a small *sketch* with each node, such that at query time only the sketches of the concerned nodes need to be looked up to compute the approximate distance.

Techniques derived from metric embeddings have been considered extensively by the networking community, usually under the name of *network coordinate systems*. On the other hand, while the computation of distance oracles has received considerable attention in the context of web graphs and social networks, there has been little work towards similar algorithms within the networking community. In this paper, we present the first theoretical study of distance sketches derived from distance oracles in a distributed network. We first present a fast distributed algorithm for computing approximate distance sketches, based on a distributed implementation of the distance oracle scheme of [Thorup-Zwick, JACM 2005]. We also show how to modify this basic construction to achieve different tradeoffs between the number of pairs for which the distance estimate is accurate, the size of the sketches, and the time and message complexity necessary to compute them. These tradeoffs can then be combined to give an efficient construction of small sketches with provable average-case as well as worst-case performance. Our algorithms use only small-sized messages and hence are suitable for bandwidth-constrained networks, and can be used in various networking applications such as topology discovery and construction, token management, load balancing, monitoring overlays, and several other problems in distributed algorithms.

Categories and Subject Descriptors

C.2.4 [**Computer-Communication Networks**]: Distributed Systems

General Terms

Algorithms, Theory

Keywords

Distance sketches, Distributed computing

[*]Work supported in part by an Israel Science Foundation grant #452/08, a US-Israel BSF grant #2010418, and by a Minerva grant.

[†]Research supported in part by the following grants: Nanyang Technological University grant M58110000, Singapore Ministry of Education (MOE) Academic Research Fund (AcRF) Tier 2 grant MOE2010-T2-2-082, and a grant from the United States-Israel Binational Science Foundation (BSF).

Permission to make digital or hard copies of all or part of this work for personal or classroom use is granted without fee provided that copies are not made or distributed for profit or commercial advantage and that copies bear this notice and the full citation on the first page. To copy otherwise, to republish, to post on servers or to redistribute to lists, requires prior specific permission and/or a fee.
SPAA'12, June 25–27, 2012, Pittsburgh, Pennsylvania, USA.
Copyright 2012 ACM 978-1-4503-1213-4/12/06 ...$10.00.

1. INTRODUCTION

A fundamental operation on large networks is finding shortest paths between pairs of nodes, or at least finding the lengths of these shortest paths. This problem is not only a common building block in many algorithms, but is also a meaningful operation in its own right. In a distributed network such as a large peer to peer network, this may be useful in search, topology discovery, overlay creation, and basic node to node communication. However, given the large size of these networks, computing shortest path distances can, if done naively, require a significant amount of both time and network resources. As we would like to make distance queries in real time with minimal latency, it becomes important to use small amounts of resources per distance query.

One approach to handle online distance requests is to perform a one-time offline or centralized computation. A straightforward brute force solution would be to compute the shortest paths between all pairs of nodes offline and to store the distances locally in the nodes. Once this has been accomplished, answering a shortest-path query online can be done with no communication overhead; however, the local space requirement is quadratic in the number of nodes in the graph (or linear if only shortest paths from the node are stored). For a large network containing millions of nodes, this is simply infeasible. An alternative, more practical approach is to store some auxiliary information with each node that can facilitate a quick distance computation online in real time. This auxiliary information is then used in the online computation that is performed for every request or query. One can view this auxiliary information as a *sketch* of the neighborhood structure of a node that is stored with each node. Simply retrieving the sketches of the two nodes should be sufficient to estimate the distance between them. Three properties are crucial for this purpose: first, these sketches should be reasonably small in size so that they can be stored with each node and accessed for any node at run time. Second, there needs to be a simple algorithm that, given the sketches of two nodes, can estimate the distance between them quickly. And third, even though the computation of the sketches is an offline computation, this cost also needs to be accounted for (as the distance information or network itself changes frequently, and this would require altering the sketches periodically).

Sketches for the specific purpose of distance computation in communication networks have been referred to as *distance labelings* (by the more theoretical literature) and as *network coordinate systems* (by the more applied literature). There has been a significant amount of work from a more theoretical point of view on the fundamental tradeoff between the size of the sketches and the accuracy of the distance estimates they give (see e.g. Thorup and Zwick [29], Gavoille et al. [11], Katz et al. [15], and Cohen et al. [5]). However, all of these papers assumed a *centralized* computation of sketches, so are of limited utility in real distributed systems. In the networking community there has also been much work on constructing good network coordinate systems, including seminal work such as the Vivaldi system [8] and the Meridian system [30]. While this line of work has resulted in almost fully functioning systems with efficient distributed algorithms, the theoretical underpinning of such systems is lacking; most of them can easily be shown to exhibit poor behavior in pathological instances. The main exception to this is Meridian, which has a significant theoretical component. However, it assumes that the underlying metric space is "low-dimensional", and it is easy to construct high-dimensional instances on which Meridian does poorly.

We attempt to move the theoretical line of research slightly closer to practice by designing efficient distributed algorithms for computing accurate distance sketches. We give algorithms with bounded round and message complexity in a standard model of distributed computation (the CONGEST model [26]) that compute sketches that give distances estimates provably close to the actual distances. In particular, we engineer a distributed version of the seminal centralized algorithm of Thorup and Zwick [29]. Their algorithm computes sketches that allow us to approximate distances within a factor $2k - 1$ (this value is known as the *stretch*) by using sketches of size $\tilde{O}(k \cdot n^{1/k})$, for any integer $k \geq 1$. Up to the factor of k in the size, this is known to be a tight tradeoff in the worst case assuming a famous conjecture by Erdős [29]. Note that this achieves its minimum size at $k = \log n$, giving an $O(\log n)$-factor approximation to the distances using

sketches of size $O(\log^2 n)$. We further extend these results to give a distributed algorithm based on the centralized algorithms of Chan et al. [4] that computes sketches with the same worst-case stretch and almost the same size, but with provably better *average* stretch. To the best of our knowledge, this is the first theoretical analysis of distributed algorithms for computing distance sketches. Our work can also be viewed as an efficient computation of local node-centric views of the global topology, which may be of independent interest for numerous different applications (cf. Section 2.1).

1.1 Our Contributions

Our main contributions are new distributed algorithms for various types of distance sketches. Most of the actual sketches have been described in previous work (namely [29] and [4]), but we are the first to show that they can be efficiently constructed in a distributed network. While we formally define the model and problem in Section 2.2, at a high level we assume a synchronous distributed network in which in a single communication "round" every node can send a message of up to $O(\log n)$ bits (or 1 word) to each of its neighbors. Every edge has a nonnegative weight associated with it, and the distance between two nodes is the total weight of the shortest path (with respect to weights) between them. We begin in Section 3 by giving a distributed algorithm that constructs Thorup-Zwick distance sketches [29] efficiently:

THEOREM 1.1. *For any integer $k \geq 1$, there is a distributed algorithm that takes $O(kn^{1/k}S \log n)$ rounds after which with high probability every node has a sketch of size at most $O(kn^{1/k} \log n)$ words that provides approximate distances up to a factor of $2k - 1$.*

The value S in this theorem is known as the *shortest-path diameter* [18], and is (informally) the maximum over all $\binom{n}{2}$ shortest paths (where "short" is determined by weight) of the number of hops on the path. (In an unweighted network, S is the same as the network diameter D, hence S can be thought of as a generalization of D in a weighted network). Note that this is essentially a lower bound on any distance computation.

In Section 4 we show how to extend the techniques of Chan, Dinitz, and Gupta [4] and combine them with the techniques of Section 3 to give sketches with "slack". Informally, a sketch has ϵ-slack if the stretch factor (i.e. the distance approximation guarantee) only holds for a $(1 - \epsilon)$-fraction of the pairs, rather than all pairs. While this is a weaker guarantee, since some pairs have no bound on the accuracy of the distance estimate at all, both the size of the sketches and the time needed to construct them become much smaller. For example, when ϵ is a constant (even a small constant) we can construct constant stretch sketches in only $O(S \log^2 n)$ rounds.

THEOREM 1.2. *For any value $\epsilon > 0$ and integer $1 \leq k \leq O(\log \frac{1}{\epsilon})$, there is a distributed sketching algorithm that with high probability gives sketches with stretch $8k - 1$ with ϵ-slack that have size at most $O(k \left(\frac{1}{\epsilon} \log n\right)^{1/k} \log n)$ words and completes in at most $O\left(kS \left(\frac{1}{\epsilon} \log n\right)^{1/k} \log n\right)$ rounds.*

Finally, in Section 4.1 we extend the slack techniques further by combining a hierarchy of sketches with different slack parameters. This allows us to efficiently construct sketches with the same worst-case stretch as in Theorem 1.1 (with $k = O(\log n)$) but with average stretch only $O(1)$:

THEOREM 1.3. *There is a distributed sketching algorithm that gives sketches of size at most $O(\log^4 n)$ with $O(\log n)$-stretch and $O(1)$ average stretch that completes in at most $O(S \log^4 n)$ rounds.*

2. RELATED WORK AND MODEL

2.1 Applications and Related Works

Applications of approximate distance computations in distributed networks include token management [13, 7], load balancing [14], small-world routing [19], and search [6, 12, 22]. Several other areas of distributed computing also use distance computations in a crucial way; some examples are information propagation and gathering [3, 16], network topology construction [12, 20, 21], monitoring overlays [23], group communication in ad-hoc network [9], gathering and dissemination of information over a network [2], and peer-to-peer membership management [10, 31].

The most concrete application of our algorithms is to quickly computing approximate shortest path distances in networks, i.e. the normal application of network coordinate systems. In particular, in weighted networks, after using our algorithms to preprocess the network and create distance sketches we can compute the approximate distance between any two nodes in at most $O(D)$ times the size of the sketch rounds (where D, the hop-diameter, is the maximum over all pairs of nodes of the minimum number of hops between the nodes) by simply exchanging the sketches of the two nodes. On the other hand, note that any distance computation without using preprocessing (say, Dijkstra's algorithm, Bellman-Ford, or even a simple network ping to obtain the round-trip time) will take at least $\Omega(S)$ rounds, where S is the shortest path diameter. This is less than ideal since S can be as large as n, the number of nodes in the networks, whereas D, the hop-diameter can be, and typically is, much smaller. Therefore our sketches yield improved algorithms for pairwise weighted-distance computations. Moreover, in networks such as P2P networks and overlay networks, using our algorithms a node can compute distances (number of hops in the overlay) in *constant* times size of sketch rounds if it simply knows the IP address of the other node: it can directly contact the other node using its IP address and ask for its sketch. Thus these sketch techniques can be very relevant and applicable even for unweighted distance computations.

Probably the closest results to ours are from the theory behind Meridian [30], which is based on a modification of the "ring-of-neighbors" theoretical framework developed by Slivkins [27, 28] to prove theoretical bounds. However, there are some substantial differences. For one, the bounds given by these papers (including [30]) are limited to special types of metric spaces: those with either bounded doubling dimension or bounded growth. Our bounds hold for all (weighted) graphs (with, of course, weaker guarantees on the stretch). Furthermore, the distributed framework used by Slivkins is significantly different from the standard CONGEST model of distributed computation that we use, and is based on being able to work in the metric completion of the graph. This means, for example, that the algorithms in [28] have the ability to send a unit-size packet between *any* two nodes

in $O(1)$ time (and the algorithms do in fact make strong use of this ability).

2.2 Model and Notation

We model a communication network as a weighted, undirected, connected n-node graph $G = (V, E)$. Every node has limited initial knowledge. Specifically, assume that each node is associated with a distinct identity number (e.g., its IP address). At the beginning of the computation, each node v accepts as input its own identity number and the identity numbers of its neighbors in G. The node may also accept some additional inputs as specified by the problem at hand. The nodes are allowed to communicate through the edges of the graph G. We assume that the communication occurs in synchronous *rounds*. We will use only small-sized messages. In particular, in each round, each node v is allowed to send a message of size $O(\log n)$ through each edge $e = (v, u)$ that is adjacent to v. The message will arrive at u at the end of the current round. We also assume that all edge weights are at most polynomial in n, and thus in a single round a distance or node ID can be sent through each edge. A *word* is a block of $O(\log n)$ bits that is sufficient to store either a node ID or a network distance.

This is a widely used standard model to study distributed algorithms (called the *CONGEST model*, e.g., see [26, 25]) and captures the bandwidth constraints inherent in real-world computer networks. Many classical network algorithms have been studied in this model, including algorithms for shortest paths (Bellman-Ford, Dijsktra), minimum spanning trees, etc. Our algorithms can be easily generalized if B bits are allowed (for any pre-specified parameter B) to be sent through each edge in a round. Typically, as assumed here, $B = O(\log n)$, which is number of bits needed to send a node id in an n-node network. We assume that n (or some constant factor estimate of n) is common knowledge among nodes in the network.

Every edge in the network has some nonnegative weight associated with it, and the distance between two nodes is the minimum, over all paths between the nodes, of the sum of the weights of the edges on the path. In other words, the normal shortest-path distance with edge weights. We let $d(u, v)$ denote this distance for all $u, v \in V$. For a set $A \subseteq V$ and a node $u \in V$, we define the distance from the node to the set to be $d(u, A) = \min\{d(u, a) : a \in A\}$. For a node $u \in V$ and real number $r \in \mathbb{R}^{\geq 0}$, the *ball* around u of radius r is defined to be the nodes within distance r of u, namely $B(u, r) = \{v \in V : d(u, v) \leq r\}$.

The *hop-diameter* D of G is defined to be the maximum over all pairs u, v in V of the number of hops between u and v. In other words, its the maximum over all pairs of the distance between u and v but where distance is computed assuming that all edge weights are 1, rather than their actual weights. The *shortest-path diameter* S of G is slightly more complicated to define. For $u, v \in V$, let $\mathcal{P}_{u,v}$ be the set of simple paths between u and v with total weight equal to $d(u, v)$ (by the definition of $d(u, v)$ there is at least one such path). Let $h(u, v)$ be the minimum, over all paths in $P \in \mathcal{P}_{u,v}$, of the number of hops in P (i.e. the number of edges). Then $S = \max_{u,v \in V} h(u, v)$. It is easy to see that $D \leq S$ and in general, any method of computing the distance from u to v must use at least S rounds (or else the shortest path will not be discovered).

3. DISTRIBUTED SKETCHES

We are concerned with the problem of constructing a distance labeling scheme in a distributed manner. Given an input (weighted) graph $G = (V, E)$, we want a distributed algorithm so that at termination every node $u \in V$ knows a small label (or sketch) $L(u)$ with the property that we can (quickly) compute an approximation to the distance between u and v just from $L(u)$ and $L(v)$. Since the requirement of sketch sizes and latency in distance computation may vary from application to application, typically one would like a trade-off between the distance approximation and these parameters.

3.1 Thorup-Zwick Construction

The famous algorithm for constructing distance sketches in a centralized manner is Thorup-Zwick [29], which works as follows. They first create a hierarchy of node sets: $A_0 = V$, and for $1 \leq i \leq k - 1$, we get A_i by randomly sampling every vertex in A_{i-1} with probability $n^{-1/k}$, i.e. every vertex in A_{i-1} is included in A_i with probability $n^{-1/k}$. We set $A_k = \emptyset$ and $d(u, A_k) = \infty$ by definition.

Let $p_i(u)$ be the vertex in A_i with minimum distance from u. Let $B_i(u) = \{w \in A_i : d(u, w) < d(u, A_{i+1})\}$, and let $B(u) = \cup_{i=0}^{k-1} B_i(u)$ (for now we will assume that all distances are distinct; this can be made without loss of generality by breaking ties consistently through processor IDs or some other method). $B(u)$ is called the *bunch* of u. The label $L(u)$ of u consists of all nodes $\{p_i(u)\}_{i=0}^{k-1}$ and $B(u)$, as well as the distances to all of these nodes. Thorup and Zwick showed that these labels are enough to approximately compute the distance, and that these labels are small. We give sketches of these proofs for completeness.

LEMMA 3.1 ([29]). *For all $u \in V$, the expected size of $L(u)$ is at most $O(kn^{1/k})$ words.*

PROOF. We prove that the expected size of $B_i(u)$ is at most $n^{1/k}$ for every $0 \leq i \leq k - 1$, which clearly implies the lemma via linearity of expectation. Suppose that we have already made the random decisions that define levels $A_0, \ldots, A_i$, and now for each $v \in A_i$ we flip the coin to see if it is also in A_{i+1}. If we flip these coins in order of distance from u (this is just in the analysis; the algorithm can flip the coins simultaneously or in arbitrary order) then the size of $B_i(u)$ is just the number of coins we flip before we see a heads, where the probability of flipping a heads is $n^{-1/k}$. In expectation this is $n^{1/k}$. □

LEMMA 3.2 ([29]). *Given $L(u)$ and $L(v)$ for some $u, v \in V$, we can compute a distance estimate $d'(u, v)$ with $d(u, v) \leq d'(u, v) \leq (2k - 1)d(u, v)$ in time $O(k)$.*

PROOF. For each $0 \leq i \leq k - 1$, we check whether $p_i(u) \in B_i(v)$ or $p_i(v) \in B_i(u)$. Let i^* be the first level at which at least one of these events occurs. Note that i^* is well-defined and is at most $k - 1$, since by definition $p_{k-1}(u) \in B_{k-1}(v)$ and $p_{k-1}(v) \in B_{k-1}(u)$. If the first condition is true then we return distance estimate $d'(u, v) = d(u, p_{i^*}(u)) + d(v, p_{i^*}(u))$, and if the second condition is true then we return $d'(u, v) = d(u, p_{i^*}(v)) + d(v, p_{i^*}(v))$. Note that the necessary distances are in the labels as part of $B_{i^*}(u)$ and $B_{i^*}(v)$, so we can indeed compute this from $L(u)$ and $L(v)$.

We first prove by induction that $d(u, p_i(u)) \leq i \cdot d(u, v)$ and $d(v, p_i(v)) \leq i \cdot d(u, v)$ for all $i \leq i^*$. In the base case, when

$i = 0$, both inequalities are true by definition. For the inductive step, let $1 \leq i \leq i^*$. Since $i \leq i^*$ we know that $i - 1 < i^*$, so $p_{i-1}(u) \notin B_{i-1}(v)$ and $p_{i-1}(v) \notin B_{i-1}(u)$. This implies that $d(v, p_i(v)) \leq d(v, p_{i-1}(u)) \leq d(v, u) + d(u, p_{i-1}(u)) \leq d(u, v) + (i - 1)d(u, v) = i \cdot d(u, v)$, where the first inequality is from $i - 1 < i^*$, the second is from the triangle inequality, and the third is from the inductive hypothesis. Similarly, we get that and $d(u, p_i(u)) \leq i \cdot d(u, v)$.

Now suppose without loss of generality that $p_{i^*}(v) \in B_{i^*}(u)$ (if the roles are reversed we can just switch the names of u and v). Then our distance estimate is $d'(u, v) = d(u, p_{i^*}(v)) + d(v, p_{i^*}(v)) \leq d(u, v) + 2d(v, p_{i^*}(v)) \leq d(u, v) + 2i^* d(u, v) = (2i^* + 1)d(u, v)$, where the first inequality is from the triangle inequality and the second is from our previous inductive proof. Since $i^* \leq k - 1$, this gives a stretch bound of $2k - 1$ as claimed. □

3.2 Distributed Algorithm

The natural question is whether we can construct these labels in a distributed manner. For a vertex $v \in A_i \setminus A_{i+1}$, let $C(v) = \{w \in V : d(w, v) < d(w, A_{i+1})\}$. This is called the *cluster* of v. Note that the clusters are the inverse of the bunches: $u \in C(v)$ if and only if $v \in B(u)$. So we will construct a distributed algorithm in which every vertex u knows exactly which clusters it is in and its distance from the centers of those clusters, and thus is able to construct its label. Also, it's easy to see that the clusters are connected: if $u \in C(v)$ then obviously any vertex w on the shortest path from u to v is also in $C(v)$.

The distributed protocol is as follows: we first divide into k phases, where in phase i we deal with clusters from vertices in $A_i \setminus A_{i+1}$. However, we run the phases from top to bottom – we first do phase $k - 1$, then phase $k - 2$, down to phase 0. In phase i the goal is for every node $u \in V$ to know for every node $v \in V$ whether $u \in C(v)$, and if so, its distance to v. Thus every node u will know $B_i(u)$ at the end of phase i. We will give an upper bound on the length of each phase with respect to n and S, so if every node knows both n and S they can all start each phase together by waiting until the upper bound is met. For now we will make the assumption that every node knows S (the shortest path diameter), thus solving the issue of synchronizing the beginning of the phases, but we will show in Section 3.3 how to remove this assumption.

Let us first consider phase $k - 1$, i.e. the first phase that is run. This phase is especially simple, since $B_{k-1}(u) = A_{k-1}$ for every node u. So at the end of this phase we simply want every node to know all of the nodes in A_{k-1} and its distances to all of them. This is known as the *k-Source Shortest Paths Problem*, and can be done in $O(|A_{k-1}|S)$ rounds by running distributed Bellman-Ford from each node in A_{k-1} simultaneously [25]. In particular, for a fixed source $v \in A_{k-1}$ every node $u \in V$ runs the following protocol: initially, u guesses that its distance to v is $d'(u, v) = \infty$. If it hears a message from a neighbor w that contains a distance $a(w)$, then it checks if $d(u, w) + a(w) < d'(u, v)$. If so, then it updates $d'(u, v)$ to $d(u, w) + a(w)$ and sends to all its neighbors a message that contains the new $d'(u, v)$. This algorithm is given in detail as Algorithm 1.

In this description we assume that there is one source v that is known to all nodes, but this clearly is not necessary. With multiple unknown sources each message could also contain the ID of the source and each node u could

Algorithm 1: Basic Bellman-Ford for u

Initialization: $d' = \infty$

1 For each neighbor w of u, get message $a(w)$
2 $z \leftarrow \min_{w \in N(u)} \{a(w) + d(u,w)\}$
3 **if** $z < d'$ **then**
4 $\quad\big|\quad$ $d' \leftarrow z$
5 $\quad\big\lfloor\quad$ Send message d' to all neighbors

---

keep track of its guesses $d'(u,\cdot)$ for every source that it has seen at least one message from. The standard analysis of Bellman-Ford (see e.g. [25]) gives the following lemmas:

LEMMA 3.3. *At the end of phase $k-1$, every node $u \in V$ knows which vertices are in A_{k-1} as well as $d(u,v)$ for all $v \in A_{k-1}$.*

LEMMA 3.4. *Phase $k-1$ uses at most $O(|A_{k-1}|S)$ rounds.*

To handle phase i, we will assume inductively that $B_{i+1}(u)$ is known to u at the start of phase i, as well as the distance from u to every node in $B_{i+1}(u)$. In particular, we will assume that u knows its distance to the *closest* node in A_{i+1}, i.e. $d(u, A_{i+1})$. In phase i we will simply use a modified version of Bellman-Ford in which the sources are $A_i \setminus A_{i+1}$, but node u only "participates" in the algorithm for sources $v \in A_i \setminus A_{i+1}$ when it gets a message that implies that $d(u,v) < d(u, A_{i+1})$, i.e. that $v \in B_i(u)$. To handle the multiple sources, each node u will maintain for every possible source $v \in V$ an outgoing message queue, which will only ever have a 0 or 1 message in it. u just does round-robin scheduling among the nonempty queues, sending the current message to all neighbors and removing it from the queue. To simplify the code, we will assume without loss of generality that $V = \{0, 1, \ldots, n-1\}$ (this assumption is only used to simplify the round-robin scheduler, and can easily be removed). This algorithm is given as Algorithm 2.

LEMMA 3.5. *At the end of phase i, every node $u \in V$ knows $B_i(u)$ and its distance to all nodes in $B_i(u)$.*

PROOF. We prove this by induction on the phase. The base case is phase $k-1$, which is satisfied by Lemma 3.3. Now consider some phase $i \geq 0$. Let $v \in A_i \setminus A_{i+1}$ – we will show by induction on the hop count of the shortest path that all nodes $u \in C(v)$ find out their distance to v. If $u \in C(v)$ is adjacent to v via a shortest path, then obviously after the first round it will know its distance to v. If $u \in C(v)$ is not adjacent to v via a shortest path, then by induction the next hop on the shortest path from u to v finds out its correct distance to v, and thus will forward the announcement to u. Thus at the end of phase i every node $u \in C(v)$ knows its distance from v, and since this holds for every $v \in A_i \setminus A_{i+1}$ we have that every $u \in V$ knows its distance to all nodes in $B_i(u)$. $\square$

Before we prove the time and message complexity bounds, we give a lemma that extends the expected size analysis of [29] to give explicit tail bounds on the probability that the construction is large:

LEMMA 3.6. *For every $i \in \{0, \ldots, k-1\}$ and every $u \in V$, the probability that $|B_i(u)| > O(n^{1/k} \ln n)$ is at most $1/n^3$.*

Algorithm 2: Modified Bellman-Ford for node u in phase i

---

1 Initialization:
2 **foreach** $v \in V \setminus \{u\}$ **do**
3 $\quad\big|\quad$ $d'(v) \leftarrow \infty$
4 $\quad\big|\quad$ $q(v) \leftarrow 0$
5 $\quad\big\lfloor\quad$ $i \leftarrow 0$

6 In the first round:
7 **if** $u \in A_i \setminus A_{i+1}$ **then**
8 $\quad\big\lfloor\quad$ Send message $\langle u, 0 \rangle$ to all neighbors

9 In each round:
$\quad$ // Receive and process new messages
10 **foreach** $w \in N(u)$ **do**
11 $\quad\big|\quad$ Get message $m(w) = \langle v_w, a_w \rangle$
12 $\quad\big|\quad$ **if** $a_w + d(u,w) < d(u, A_{i+1}) \wedge a_w + d(u,w) < d'(v_w)$ **then**
13 $\quad\big|\quad\big|\quad$ $d'(v_w) \leftarrow a_w + d(u,w)$
14 $\quad\big|\quad\big\lfloor\quad$ $q(v_w) \leftarrow 1$
$\quad$ // Send message from next nonempty queue
15 $i' \leftarrow i$
16 $i \leftarrow (i+1)\%n$
17 **while** $q(i) == 0 \wedge i \neq i'$ **do** $i \leftarrow (i+1)\%n$
18 **if** $q(i) == 1$ **then**
19 $\quad\big|\quad$ Send message $\langle i, d'(i) \rangle$ to all neighbors
20 $\quad\big\lfloor\quad$ $q(i) \leftarrow 0$

PROOF. If $|B_i(u)| > 3n^{1/k} \ln n$ then the closest $3n^{1/k} \ln n$ nodes in A_i to u must all decide not to be part of A_{i+1}. Since the probability that any particular node in A_i joins A_{i+1} is $n^{-1/k}$, the probability that this happens is at most $(1 - n^{-1/k})^{3n^{1/k} \ln n} \leq e^{-3 \ln n} = 1/n^3$. $\square$

We can now bound the time and message complexity of each phase:

LEMMA 3.7. *Each phase takes $O(n^{1/k} S \log n)$ rounds (with high probability).*

PROOF. Let $v \in A_i \setminus A_{i+1}$. Intuitively, if v were the only vertex in $A_i \setminus A_{i+1}$, then in phase i the algorithm devolves into distributed Bellman-Ford in which the only vertices that ever forward messages are vertices in $C(v)$. This would clearly take $O(S)$ rounds. In the general case, each vertex u only participates in $O(|B_i(u)|) = O(n^{1/k} \log n)$ of these shortest path algorithms, so each "round" of the original algorithm can be split up into $O(n^{1/k} \log n)$ rounds to accommodate all of the different sources. Thus the total time taken is $O(n^{1/k} S \log n)$ as claimed.

To prove this formally, let $u \in V$ and $v \in A_i \setminus A_{i+1}$, with $v \in B_i(u)$. Let $v = v_0, v_1, \ldots, v_{\ell-1} = u$ be a shortest path from v to u with the fewest number of hops. Thus $\ell \leq S$. We prove by induction that v_j receives a message $\langle v, d(v_{j-1}, v) \rangle$ at time at most $O(n^{1/k} j \log n)$, which clearly implies the lemma. For the base case, in the first round v sends out the message $\langle v, 0 \rangle$ to its neighbors, so v_1 receives the correct message at time $1 \leq n^{1/k} \log n$. For the inductive step, consider node v_j. We know by induction that v_{j-1} received a message $\langle v, d(v_{j-2}, v) \rangle$ at time at most $t = O(n^{1/k} (j-1) \log n)$. If v_{j-1} already knew this distance from v, then it also already sent a message (or put one in the queue) informing its neighbors (v_j in particular) about this. Otherwise, v_{j-1} puts a message in its outgoing queue at time t. Since the nonempty queues are processed in a round-robin manner, and by Lemma 3.6 at most $O(n^{1/k} \log n)$ queues are ever nonempty throughout the phase, v_{j-1} sends a message $\langle v, d(v_{j-1}v)\rangle$ at time at most $t + O(n^{1/k} \log n) = O(n^{1/k} j \log n)$, as claimed. $\square$

Lemmas 3.1, 3.5, and 3.7 obviously imply the following theorem:

THEOREM 3.8. *For any $k \geq 1$, there is a distributed sketching algorithm that takes $O(kn^{1/k}S \log n)$ rounds, after which with high probability every node has a sketch of size at most $O(kn^{1/k} \log n)$ words (and expected size $O(kn^{1/k})$ words) that provides approximate distances with stretch $2k-1$.*

3.3 Termination Detection

We now show how to remove the assumption that every node knows S. Note that we do not show how to satisfy this assumption, i.e. we do not give an algorithm that computes S and distributes it to all nodes. Rather, we show how to detect when a phase has terminated, and thus when a new phase should start. We use basically the same termination detection algorithm as the one used by Khan et al. [17], just adapted to our context.

At the very beginning of the algorithm, even before phase $k-1$, we run a leader election algorithm to designate some arbitrary vertex r as the *leader*, and then build a breadth-first search (BFS) tree T out of r so that every node knows its parent in the tree as well as its children. This can be done in $O(D) \leq O(S)$ rounds and $O(|E| \log n)$ messages [17].

At the beginning of phase i, the leader r sends a message to all nodes (along T) telling them when they should start phase i, so they all begin together. We say that a node u is *complete* if either $u \notin A_i \backslash A_{i+1}$ or every vertex in $C(u)$ knows its distance to u (we will see later how to use echo messages to know when this is the case). So initially the only complete nodes are the ones not in $A_i \backslash A_{i+1}$. Any such node that is also a leaf in T immediately sends a COMPLETE message to its parent in the tree. Throughout the phase, when any node has heard COMPLETE messages from all of its children in T and is itself complete, it sends a COMPLETE message to its parent.

Now suppose that when running phase i, some node u gets a message $m(w) = \langle v_w, a_w \rangle$ from a neighbor w. There are two reasons that this message might not result in a new message added to the send queue: if $a_w + d(u,w) \geq d(u, A_{i+1})$ (v_w has not yet been shown to be in $B_i(u)$), or if $a_w + d(u,w) \geq d'(v_w)$ (u already knows a shorter path to v_w). Furthermore, even if $m(w)$ does result in a new message added to the send queue, it might get superseded by a new message added to the queue with an updated value of $d'(v_w)$ before the value based on $m(w)$ can be sent. All three of these conditions can be tracked by u, so for each message m that u receives (say from neighbor w) it keeps track of whether or not it sends out a new message based on m. If it does not (one of the two conditions failed, or it was superseded), then it sends an ECHO message back to w, together with a copy of the message. If u does send out a new message based on m, then when it has received ECHO messages for m from all of its neighbors (except for w) it sends an ECHO message to w together with a copy of m.

It is easy to see inductively that when a node u sends a message m, it will also know via ECHO messages when m has ceased to propagate in the network since all of its neighbors will have ECHO'd it back to u. So if $u \in A_i \backslash A_{i+1}$, and thus only sends out one message that has first coordinate u, it will know when this message has stopped propagating, which clearly implies that every node $v \in V$ that is in $C(u)$ knows its correct distance to u (as well as the fact that $u \in B_i(v)$). At this point u is complete, so once it has received COMPLETE messages from all of its children in T it will send a COMPLETE message to its parent.

Once r has received COMPLETE messages from all of its children (and is itself complete) the phase is over. So r starts the next phase by sending a START message to all nodes using the T, and the next phase begins.

It is easy to see that the ECHOs only double the number of messages and rounds, since any message sent along an edge corresponds to exactly one ECHO sent back the other way. Electing a leader and building a BFS tree take only a negligible number of messages and rounds compared to the bounds of Theorem 3.8. Each node sends only one COMPLETE message, so there are at most $O(n)$ COMPLETE messages which is tiny compared to the bound in Theorem 3.8, and the number of extra rounds due to COMPLETE messages is clearly only $O(D)$. Thus even with the extra termination detection, the bounds of Theorem 3.8 still hold.

4. SKETCHES WITH SLACK

Let $u, v \in V$. We say that v is ϵ-*far* from u if $|\{w : d(u,w) < d(u,v)\}| \geq \epsilon n$, i.e. if v is not one of the ϵn closest nodes to u. Given a labeling $L(u)$ for each $u \in V$, we say that it has stretch $2k-1$ and ϵ-*slack* if the distance that we compute for u and v given $L(u)$ and $L(v)$ is at least $d(u,v)$ and at most $(2k-1)d(u,v)$ for all $u, v \in V$ where v is ϵ-far from u. Labelings with slack were previously studied by Chan, Dinitz, and Gupta [4] and Abraham, Bartal, Chan, Dhamdhere, Gupta, Kleinberg, Neiman, and Slivkins [1]. The main technique of Chan et al. was the use of a new type of net they called a *density net*. For each $u \in V$, let $R(u, \epsilon) = \inf\{r : |B(u,r)| \geq \epsilon n\}$ be the minimum distance necessary for the ball around u to contain at least ϵn points, and let $B^\epsilon(u) = B(u, R(u, \epsilon))$ be this ball. We give a definition of density net that is slightly modified from [4] in order to make it easier to work with in a distributed context.

DEFINITION 4.1. *A set of vertices $N \subseteq V$ is an ϵ-density net if:*

1. *For all $u \in V$, there is a vertex $v \in N$ such that $d(u,v) \leq R(u, \epsilon)$, and*

2. *$|N| \leq \frac{10}{\epsilon} \ln n$.*

Chan et al. give a centralized algorithm that computes an ϵ-density net in polynomial time for any ϵ. Their density nets are somewhat different, in that they contain only $1/\epsilon$ nodes but the closest net node to u is only guaranteed to be within $2R(u, \epsilon)$ instead of $R(u, \epsilon)$. We modify these values in order to give a distributed construction, and in fact with these modifications it is trivial to build density nets via random sampling.

LEMMA 4.2. *There is a distributed algorithm that, with high probability, constructs an ϵ-density net in constant time.*

PROOF. The algorithm is simple: every vertex independently chooses to be in N with probability $\frac{5 \ln n}{\epsilon n}$. The expected size of N is clearly $\frac{5 \ln n}{\epsilon}$, and by a simple Chernoff bound (see e.g. [24]) we have that the probability that $|N| > \frac{10 \ln n}{\epsilon}$ is at most $e^{-(20 \ln n)/(3\epsilon)} \leq 1/n^{6/\epsilon}$, so the second constraint is satisfied with high probability.

For the first constraint, that for every vertex u there is some vertex $v \in B^\epsilon(u) \cap N$, we split into two cases depending on ϵ. If $\epsilon \leq \frac{5 \ln n}{n}$, then every node has probability 1 of being in N, so the condition is trivially satisfied. Otherwise we have $\epsilon > \frac{5 \ln n}{n}$, so for every u we have $|B^\epsilon(u)| \geq 5 \ln n$ and the expected size of $B^\epsilon(u) \cap N$ is exactly $5 \ln n$. Using a similar Chernoff bound (but from the other direction) gives us that the probability that $|B^\epsilon(u) \cap N|$ is less than 1 is at most $e^{-(25 \ln n)/8} \leq 1/n^3$. Now we can just take a union bound over all u to get that the first constraint is satisfied with high probability. $\square$

Using this construction, we can efficiently construct short sketches with ϵ-slack:

THEOREM 4.3. There is a distributed algorithm that uses at most $O(S \frac{1}{\epsilon} \log n)$ rounds so that at the end of the algorithm, every node has a sketch of size at most $O(\frac{1}{\epsilon} \log n)$ words with stretch at most 3 and ϵ-slack.

PROOF. The algorithm first uses Lemma 4.2 to construct an ϵ-density net N. It is easy to see that the closest net points to u and v are a good approximation to the distance between u and v. In particular, suppose that v is ϵ-far from u, let u' be the closest node in N to u, and let v' be the closest node in N to v. Then $d(u, u') \leq R(u, \epsilon) \leq d(u, v)$ by the definition of ϵ-far and ϵ-density nets, $d(v, u') \leq d(v, u) + d(u, u') \leq 2d(u, v)$, and thus $d(u, u') + d(v, u') \leq 3d(u, v)$. This means that if every vertex keeps as its sketch its distance from all nodes in N, we will have sketches with ϵ-uniform slack and stretch 3 (to compute an approximation to $d(u, v)$ we can just consider use $\min_{w \in N} \{d(u, w) + d(w, v)\}$, which we can compute from the two sketches). The size of these sketches is clearly $O(|N|) = O(\frac{1}{\epsilon} \log n)$, since for every node in N we just need to store its ID and its distance.

It just remains to show how to compute these sketches efficiently. But this is simple, since it is exactly the k-Source Shortest Paths problem where the sources are the nodes in N. So we simply run the k-source version of Distributed Bellman-Ford, which gives the claimed time and message complexity bounds. $\square$

We can get a different tradeoff by applying Thorup and Zwick to the density net itself, instead of simply having every node remember its distance to all net nodes. This is essentially what is done in the slack labeling schemes of Chan et al. [4], just with slightly different parameters and constructions (since they were able to use centralized constructions). In particular, suppose that we manage to use Thorup-Zwick on the net, so the distances between net points are preserved up to stretch $2k - 1$. Then these sketches would have size at most $O(k|N|^{1/k} \log n) = O(k (\frac{1}{\epsilon} \log n)^{1/k} \log n)$. For each $u \in V$, let $u' \in N$ be the closest node in the density net to u. We let the sketch of u be the identity of u', the distance between u and u', and the Thorup-Zwick label of u'. We call this the (ϵ, k)-CDG sketch. Clearly this sketch has size $O(k (\frac{1}{\epsilon} \log n)^{1/k} \log n)$. Let $u, v \in V$ such that v is ϵ-far from u. Our estimate of the distance

will be $d(u, u') + d''(u', v') + d(v', v)$, where $d''(u', u') \leq (2k - 1)d(u', v')$ is the approximate distance given by the Thorup-Zwick labels. This can obviously be computed given the sketches for u and v. To bound the stretch, we simply use the definition of density nets, the triangle inequality, and the fact that v is ϵ-far from u. This gives us a distance estimate $d'(u, v)$ with

$$
\begin{aligned}
d'(u, v) &= d(u, u') + d''(u', v') + d(v', v) \\
&\leq d(u, u') + (2k-1)d(u', v') + d(v', v) \\
&\leq d(u, v) + (2k-1)(d(u', u) + d(u, v) + d(v, v')) \\
&\quad + 2d(u, v) \\
&\leq 3d(u, v) + (2k-1)(4d(u, v)) \\
&= (8k - 1)d(u, v)
\end{aligned}
$$

This gives the basic lemma about these sketches, which was proved by [4] (modulo our modifications to density nets):

LEMMA 4.4 ([4]). For any $\epsilon > 0$ and $1 \leq k \leq O(\log \frac{1}{\epsilon})$, with high probability the (ϵ, k)-CDG sketch has size at most $O(k (\frac{1}{\epsilon} \log n)^{1/k} \log n)$ words and $(8k - 1)$-stretch with ϵ-slack.

It remains to show how to construct (ϵ, k)-CDG sketches in a distributed manner, which boils down to modifying the algorithm of Theorem 3.8 to work with the density net rather than with the full point set (this is trivial in a centralized setting since we can just consider the metric completion).

LEMMA 4.5. For any $\epsilon > 0$ and $1 \leq k \leq O(\frac{1}{\epsilon})$, there is a distributed algorithm so that after $O\left(kS \left(\frac{1}{\epsilon} \log n\right)^{1/k} \log n\right)$ rounds every node knows its (ϵ, k)-CDG sketch.

PROOF. We first apply Lemma 4.2 to construct the ϵ-density net N. We now want every node u to know its closest net node u' and its distance from u'. This can be done via a single use of Distributed Bellman-Ford, where we just imagine a "super node" consisting of all of N. This takes $O(S)$ rounds.

Now we need to run Thorup-Zwick on N. But this is easy to do, since we just modify the A_i sets to be subsets of N instead of V and change the sampling probability from $n^{-1/k}$ to $\left(\frac{10}{\epsilon} \ln n\right)^{-1/k}$. Note that for every node $u \in V$ the bunch $B_i(u)$ is still well defined, and with high probability has size at most $O\left(\left(\frac{1}{\epsilon} \log n\right)^{1/k} \log n\right)$ (via an argument analogous to Lemma 3.6). This means that we can run Algorithm 2 using these new A_i sets and every node will know their Thorup-Zwick sketch for these A_i sets. In particular, the nodes in N will have a sketch that is exactly equal to the sketch they would have if we ran Algorithm 2 on the metric completion of N, rather than on G. It is easy to see that Lemma 3.7 still applies but with $n^{1/k} \log n$ (the upper bound on the size of each $B_i(u)$) changed to $O\left(\left(\frac{1}{\epsilon} \log n\right)^{1/k} \log n\right)$, so each phase takes $O\left(S \left(\frac{1}{\epsilon} \log n\right)^{1/k} \log n\right)$ rounds. Since there are k phases, this gives the desired complexity bound.

As before, this assumes that every node knows S in order to synchronize the phases. However, we can remove this assumption by using the termination detection algorithm of Section 3.3. This at most doubles the number of rounds and adds an extra $O(D)$ rounds, which is negligible. $\square$

THEOREM 4.6. *For any $\epsilon > 0$ and integer value $1 \leq k \leq O(\log \frac{1}{\epsilon})$, there is a distributed sketching algorithm that completes in at most $O\left(kS\left(\frac{1}{\epsilon}\log n\right)^{1/k}\log n\right)$ rounds, after which with high probability every node has a sketch of size at most $O(k\left(\frac{1}{\epsilon}\log n\right)^{1/k}\log n)$ words that provides approximate distances with stretch $8k-1$ and ϵ-slack.*

PROOF. Implied by Lemmas 4.4 and 4.5. □

4.1 Gracefully Degrading Sketches and Average Stretch

We now show how to use Theorem 4.6 to construct sketches with bounded *average* stretch, as well as bounded worst-case stretch. Formally, suppose that we have a weighted graph $G = (V, E)$ that induces the metric d and a sketching algorithm that allows us to compute distance estimates d' with the property that $d'(u, v) \geq d(u, v)$ for all $u, v \in V$. The *average stretch* of the sketching algorithm is defined to be $(1/\binom{n}{2})\sum_{\{u,v\}\in\binom{V}{2}}\frac{d'(u,v)}{d(u,v)}$.

In fact, we will prove a stronger statement, that there are good distributed algorithms for computing *gracefully degrading* sketches. A sketching algorithm is gracefully degrading with $f(\epsilon)$ stretch if for every $\epsilon \in (0, 1)$ it is a sketch with stretch $f(\epsilon)$ and ϵ-slack. In other words, instead of specifying ϵ ahead of time (as in the slack constructions) we need a single sketch that works simultaneously for every ϵ. It is easy to see that when f is $O(\log \frac{1}{\epsilon})$, gracefully degrading sketches provide the desired average and worst-case stretch bounds (this was implicit in Chan et al. [4], but they only formally showed this for their specific gracefully-degrading construction, which is slightly different than ours):

LEMMA 4.7. *Any gracefully degrading sketching algorithm with $O(\log \frac{1}{\epsilon})$ stretch has stretch at most $O(\log n)$ and average stretch at most $O(1)$.*

PROOF. The bound on the worst-case stretch is immediate by setting $\epsilon = \frac{1}{2n}$. With this setting of ϵ, every two points are ϵ-far from each other, and thus the stretch bound of $O(\log \frac{1}{\epsilon}) = O(\log n)$ holds for all pairs.

To bound the average stretch, for each $1 \leq i \leq \log n$ and vertex $u \in V$ let $A(u, i) = B^{1/2^{i-1}}(u) \cap (V \setminus B^{1/2^i}(u))$. In other words, $A(u, i)$ is the set of points that are outside the smallest ball around u containing at least $n/2^i$ points, but inside the smallest ball around u containing at least $n/2^{i-1}$ points. So $|A(u, i)| = n/2^i$. We can bound the stretch between u and any node in $A(u, i)$ by $O(i)$, since when we set $\epsilon = 1/2^i$ we have a stretch bound of $O(\log \frac{1}{\epsilon}) = O(i)$ for the nodes in $A(u, i)$. Then the average stretch is at most

$$\frac{1}{\binom{n}{2}}\sum_{\{u,v\}\in\binom{V}{2}}\frac{d'(u,v)}{d(u,v)} \leq \frac{1}{n(n-1)}\sum_{u\in V}\sum_{v\neq u}\frac{d'(u,v)}{d(u,v)}$$

$$\leq \frac{1}{n(n-1)}\sum_{u\in V}\sum_{i=1}^{\log n}\sum_{v\in A(u,i)}\frac{d'(u,v)}{d(u,v)}$$

$$\leq \frac{1}{n(n-1)}\sum_{u\in V}\sum_{i=1}^{\log n}O(i\cdot\frac{n}{2^i})$$

$$\leq \frac{1}{n(n-1)}\sum_{u\in V}O(n)$$

$$\leq O(1),$$

proving the lemma. □

This lemma reduces the problem of constructing sketches with good average stretch to the problem of constructing gracefully degrading sketches. But this turns out to be simple, given Theorem 4.6. The intuition behind gracefully degrading sketches is that they work simultaneously for every slack parameter ϵ, so to create them we simply use $O(\log n)$ different sketches with slack, one for each power of 2 between $1/n$ and 1.

THEOREM 4.8. *There is a distributed gracefully degrading sketching algorithm that gives sketches of size at most $O(\log^4 n)$ words with $O(\log \frac{1}{\epsilon})$-stretch that completes in at most $O(S\log^4 n)$ rounds.*

PROOF. Our construction is simple: for every $1 \leq i \leq \log n$ we use Theorem 4.6 with slack $\epsilon_i = \frac{1}{2^i}$ and stretch $k = O(\log \frac{1}{\epsilon_i}) = O(\log 2^i)$. The sketch remembered by a node is just the union of these $O(\log n)$ sketches. Given the sketches for two different vertices u and v where v is ϵ-far from u, we can compute the $O(\log n)$ different distance estimates and take the minimum of them as our estimate.

To see that this is gracefully degrading with stretch at most $O(\log \frac{1}{\epsilon})$, first note that all of the $O(\log n)$ estimates are at least as large as $d(u, v)$, so we just need to show that at least one of the estimates is at most $O(\log \frac{1}{\epsilon})d(u, v)$. Let ϵ_i be ϵ rounded down to the nearest power of $1/2$. Then v is obviously ϵ_i-far from u, so the estimate for the ϵ_i-sketch will provide an estimate of at most $O(\log \frac{1}{\epsilon_i})d(u, v) = O(\log \frac{1}{\epsilon})d(u, v)$.

Theorem 4.6, when specialized to the case of $k = O(\log \frac{1}{\epsilon})$, completes in at most $O(S\log \frac{1}{\epsilon}\log^2 n)$ rounds and provides sketches of size $O(\log \frac{1}{\epsilon}\log^2 n)$. Since we just run each of the $O(\log n)$ instantiations of the theorem back to back, the total number of rounds is at most $O(S\log^2 n)\sum_{i=1}^{\log n}\log 2^i = O(S\log^4 n)$ and the size is at most $O(\log^4 n)$. Note that we can handle determination detection for each of these as usual, based on Section 3.3. □

Together with Lemma 4.7, this gives the following corollary:

COROLLARY 4.9. *There is a distributed sketching algorithm that give sketches of size at most $O(\log^4 n)$ with at most $O(\log n)$-stretch and $O(1)$ average stretch that completes in at most $O(S\log^4 n)$ rounds.*

Note that, when compared to our sketch from Theorem 3.8 with $O(\log n)$ stretch, we pay only an extra $O(\log^2 n)$ factor in the size of the sketch as well as the number of rounds, and in return we are able to achieve constant average stretch.

5. CONCLUSIONS

In this paper we initiated the study from a theoretical point of view of distributed algorithms for computing distance sketches in a network. We showed that the Thorup-Zwick distance sketches [29], which provide an almost optimal tradeoff between the size of the sketches and their accuracy, can be computed efficiently in a distributed setting, where our notion of efficiency is the standard definition of the number of rounds in the CONGEST model. Combining this distributed algorithm with centralized techniques of Chan et al. [4], that we were also able to turn into efficient distributed algorithms, yielded a combined construction with the same worst-case stretch as the smallest version of Thorup-Zwick, but much better average stretch. This required only a polylogarithmic cost in the size of the sketches and the time necessary to construct them. These results are a first step towards making the theoretical work on distance sketches more practical, by moving from a centralized setting to a distributed setting. It would be interesting in the future to weaken the distributed model even further, by working in failure-prone and asynchronous settings, in the hope of eventually getting practical distance sketches with provable performance guarantees.

6. REFERENCES

[1] I. Abraham, Y. Bartal, T.-H. H. Chan, K. D. Dhamdhere, A. Gupta, J. Kleinberg, O. Neiman, and A. Slivkins. Metric embeddings with relaxed guarantees. In *Proceedings of the 46th Annual IEEE Symposium on Foundations of Computer Science*, FOCS '05, pages 83–100, Washington, DC, USA, 2005. IEEE Computer Society.

[2] R. Aleliunas, R. M. Karp, R. J. Lipton, L. Lovász, and C. Rackoff. Random walks, universal traversal sequences, and the complexity of maze problems. In *FOCS*, pages 218–223, 1979.

[3] A. R. Bharambe, M. Agrawal, and S. Seshan. Mercury: supporting scalable multi-attribute range queries. In *SIGCOMM*, pages 353–366, 2004.

[4] T.-H. H. Chan, M. Dinitz, and A. Gupta. Spanners with slack. In *Proceedings of the 14th European Symposium on Algorithms*, pages 196–207, 2006.

[5] R. Cohen, P. Fraigniaud, D. Ilcinkas, A. Korman, and D. Peleg. Labeling schemes for tree representation. *Algorithmica*, 53(1):1–15, 2009.

[6] B. F. Cooper. Quickly routing searches without having to move content. In *IPTPS*, pages 163–172, 2005.

[7] D. Coppersmith, P. Tetali, and P. Winkler. Collisions among random walks on a graph. *SIAM J. Discret. Math.*, 6(3):363–374, 1993.

[8] F. Dabek, R. Cox, F. Kaashoek, and R. Morris. Vivaldi: A decentralized network coordinate system. In *Proceedings of the ACM SIGCOMM '04 Conference*, Portland, Oregon, August 2004.

[9] S. Dolev, E. Schiller, and J. L. Welch. Random walk for self-stabilizing group communication in ad hoc networks. *IEEE Trans. Mob. Comput.*, 5(7):893–905, 2006. also in PODC'02.

[10] A. J. Ganesh, A.-M. Kermarrec, and L. Massoulié. Peer-to-peer membership management for gossip-based protocols. *IEEE Trans. Comput.*, 52(2):139–149, 2003.

[11] C. Gavoille, D. Peleg, S. Pérennes, and R. Raz. Distance labeling in graphs. *J. Algorithms*, 53(1):85–112, 2004.

[12] C. Gkantsidis, M. Mihail, and A. Saberi. Hybrid search schemes for unstructured peer-to-peer networks. In *INFOCOM*, pages 1526–1537, 2005.

[13] A. Israeli and M. Jalfon. Token management schemes and random walks yield self-stabilizing mutual exclusion. In *PODC*, pages 119–131, 1990.

[14] D. R. Karger and M. Ruhl. Simple efficient load balancing algorithms for peer-to-peer systems. In *SPAA*, pages 36–43, 2004.

[15] M. Katz, N. A. Katz, A. Korman, and D. Peleg. Labeling schemes for flow and connectivity. *SIAM J. Comput.*, 34(1):23–40, 2004.

[16] D. Kempe, J. M. Kleinberg, and A. J. Demers. Spatial gossip and resource location protocols. In *STOC*, pages 163–172, 2001.

[17] M. Khan, F. Kuhn, D. Malkhi, G. Pandurangan, and K. Talwar. Efficient distributed approximation algorithms via probabilistic tree embeddings. In *Proc. 27th ACM Symp. on Principles of Distributed Computing (PODC)*, 2008. Journal version: *Distributed Computing*, 2012.

[18] M. Khan and G. Pandurangan. A fast distributed approximation algorithm for minimum spanning trees. *Distributed Computing*, 20:391–402, 2008.

[19] J. M. Kleinberg. The small-world phenomenon: an algorithm perspective. In *STOC*, pages 163–170, 2000.

[20] C. Law and K.-Y. Siu. Distributed construction of random expander networks. In *INFOCOM*, 2003.

[21] D. Loguinov, A. Kumar, V. Rai, and S. Ganesh. Graph-theoretic analysis of structured peer-to-peer systems: routing distances and fault resilience. In *SIGCOMM*, pages 395–406, 2003.

[22] Q. Lv, P. Cao, E. Cohen, K. Li, and S. Shenker. Search and replication in unstructured peer-to-peer networks. In *ICS*, pages 84–95, 2002.

[23] R. Morales and I. Gupta. Avmon: Optimal and scalable discovery of consistent availability monitoring overlays for distributed systems. In *ICDCS*, page 55, 2007.

[24] R. Motwani and P. Raghavan. *Randomized algorithms*. Cambridge University Press, New York, NY, USA, 1995.

[25] G. Pandurangan and M. Khan. Theory of communication networks. In *Algorithms and Theory of Computation Handbook, Second Edition*. CRC Press, 2009.

[26] D. Peleg. *Distributed computing: a locality-sensitive approach*. Society for Industrial and Applied Mathematics, Philadelphia, PA, USA, 2000.

[27] A. Slivkins. Distance estimation and object location via rings of neighbors. In *Proceedings of the twenty-fourth annual ACM symposium on Principles of distributed computing*, PODC '05, pages 41–50, New York, NY, USA, 2005. ACM.

[28] A. Slivkins. Towards fast decentralized construction of locality-aware overlay networks. In *Proceedings of the twenty-sixth annual ACM symposium on Principles of distributed computing*, PODC '07, pages 89–98, New York, NY, USA, 2007. ACM.

[29] M. Thorup and U. Zwick. Approximate distance oracles. *J. ACM*, 52(1):1–24, 2005.

[30] B. Wong, A. Slivkins, and E. G. Sirer. Meridian: a lightweight network location service without virtual coordinates. In *Proceedings of the 2005 conference on Applications, technologies, architectures, and protocols for computer communications*, SIGCOMM '05, pages 85–96, New York, NY, USA, 2005. ACM.

[31] M. Zhong, K. Shen, and J. I. Seiferas. Non-uniform random membership management in peer-to-peer networks. In *INFOCOM*, pages 1151–1161, 2005.

Scheduling in Wireless Networks with Rayleigh-Fading Interference

Johannes Dams[*]
RWTH Aachen University
Dept. of Computer Science
52056 Aachen, Germany
dams
@cs.rwth-aachen.de

Martin Hoefer[*]
RWTH Aachen University
Dept. of Computer Science
52056 Aachen, Germany
mhoefer
@cs.rwth-aachen.de

Thomas Kesselheim[†]
RWTH Aachen University
Dept. of Computer Science
52056 Aachen, Germany
kesselheim
@cs.rwth-aachen.de

ABSTRACT

We study algorithms for wireless spectrum access of n communication requests when interference conditions are given by the Rayleigh-fading model. This model extends the recently popular deterministic interference model based on the signal-to-interference-plus-noise ratio (SINR) using stochastic propagation to address fading effects observed in reality. We consider worst-case approximation guarantees for the two standard problems of capacity maximization (maximize the expected number of successful transmissions in a single slot) and latency minimization (minimize the expected number of slots until all transmissions were successful). Our main result is a generic reduction of Rayleigh fading to the deterministic SINR model. It allows to apply existing algorithms for the non-fading model in the Rayleigh-fading scenario while losing only a factor of $O(\log^* n)$ in the approximation guarantee. This way, we obtain the first approximation guarantees for Rayleigh fading and, more fundamentally, show that non-trivial stochastic fading effects can be successfully handled using existing and future techniques for the non-fading model. Using a more detailed argument, a similar result applies even for distributed and game-theoretic capacity maximization approaches. For example, it allows to show that regret learning yields an $O(\log^* n)$-approximation with uniform power assignments. Our analytical treatment is supported by simulations illustrating the performance of regret learning and, more generally, the relationship between both models.

Categories and Subject Descriptors

C.2.1 [**Computer-Communication Networks**]: Network Architecture and Design—*Wireless Communication, Distributed Networks*; F.2.2 [**Analysis of Algorithms and**

[*]Supported by DFG grant Ho 3831/3-1.
[†]Supported by DFG through UMIC Research Centre at RWTH Aachen University.

Permission to make digital or hard copies of all or part of this work for personal or classroom use is granted without fee provided that copies are not made or distributed for profit or commercial advantage and that copies bear this notice and the full citation on the first page. To copy otherwise, to republish, to post on servers or to redistribute to lists, requires prior specific permission and/or a fee.
SPAA'12, June 25–27, 2012, Pittsburgh, Pennsylvania, USA.
Copyright 2012 ACM 978-1-4503-1213-4/12/06 ...$10.00.

Problem Complexity]: Non Numerical Algorithms and Problems

General Terms

Algorithms, Theory

Keywords

wireless network, transmission scheduling, SINR, Rayleigh fading

1. INTRODUCTION

Effective communication in wireless networks depends on successful reception in the presence of interference and noise, which have to be modeled realistically. Since the seminal work of Moscibroda and Wattenhofer [18], attention shifted from simple graph-based interference models to a more realistic model using SINR. This resulted in a variety of nontrivial insights into the algorithmic challenges and limitations of request scheduling [5, 11].

While the SINR model represents a significant improvement over previous approaches, it still uses a limited view of signal propagation. The main assumption is that any signal transmitted at power level p is always received after distance d with strength p/d^α, for some $\alpha > 0$. In contrast, in reality signal propagation is by no means deterministic. For instance, the SINR model does not account for short-term fluctuations such as fading. There exist advanced models using stochastic approaches that take fading effects into account. Most prominently, in the Rayleigh-fading model, signal strength is modeled by an exponentially distributed random variable with mean p/d^α. Stochastic propagation represents a major technical complication in the definition of interference models, and this may be a reason that – up to our knowledge – there are no general algorithmic results for request scheduling in this model or even for a direct comparison between the non-fading and Rayleigh-fading model.

In this paper, we examine the relationship between the non-fading SINR model and the Rayleigh-fading model. Our first main result is a fundamental relation between the models for instances of the same topology. It is based on a detailed analysis of the success probability in the Rayleigh-fading model, and it turns out to allow a surprisingly simple handling of the complicated stochastic propagation. This allows us to transfer existing algorithms and their performance bounds in the SINR model to the Rayleigh-fading model.

Our second main result uses a more detailed reduction to show that a similar result applies even for distributed capacity maximization via distributed regret-learning techniques. As the considered sequences generalize Nash equilibria, this result transfers the respective game-theoretic studies [1]. Our analytical results are supported by simulations illustrating the performance of regret learning and, more generally, the relationship between both models.

On a more fundamental level, our results highlight the inherent robustness of the techniques and bounds derived for the non-fading SINR model. The rather direct adaptation of existing algorithms to Rayleigh fading raises the hope that algorithms and their analyses can also be applied accordingly to interference models capturing further realistic properties.

1.1 Our Contribution

For a set of n communication requests in the non-fading model, we consider the two prominent problems of *capacity maximization* (maximizing the number of simultaneously successful requests in a single slot) and *latency minimization* (minimizing the number of slots such that every request has been successful at least once). In the Rayleigh-fading model, interference becomes stochastic, and thus capacity maximization becomes maximizing the expected number of successful requests in a single slot. Similarly, in latency minimization we strive to minimize the expected number of slots until every request has been successful at least once. In this sense, we adapt a similar perspective as in worst-case analysis of randomized algorithms – we strive to bound the expected performance of the algorithms in an arbitrary (worst-case) topology.

Our first main result characterizes the success probability of a request in the Rayleigh model. This probability is never 0, and thus requests can still be successful if in the non-fading model this is completely impossible (e.g., due to extremely large noise). For a meaningful comparison in terms of approximation factors, we thus focus on interference-dominated scenarios with reasonable noise conditions (for a formal definition see below). Under these conditions, we show in Section 3 that for every set of successful requests with respect to the non-fading model, in the Rayleigh model in expectation a constant fraction of these requests remains successful. Hence, we can use algorithms for capacity optimization in the non-fading model and lose only a constant factor when translating the output to Rayleigh fading. To bound approximation factors, however, we have to relate this to the Rayleigh-fading optimum, i.e., the maximum expected number of successful requests for any subset of transmitting requests. Here we show in Section 5 that this expected number can only be a factor of $O(\log^* n)$ larger than the maximum number of successful requests in the non-fading model. This allows to use existing algorithms and their bounds to derive approximation factors in the Rayleigh-fading model. For capacity maximization, we show, e.g., an $O(\log^* n)$-approximation with power control based on [14] and with distance-based power assignments based on [13]. For latency minimization similar arguments can be applied for algorithms that use repeated single-slot success maximization [7] or ALOHA-style protocols [15] in the non-fading model. For instance, we obtain an $O(\log^* n \cdot \log n)$-approximation for uniform power assignments based on [7]. The algorithms for latency minimization

allow to directly apply multi-hop scheduling techniques as in [6, 15, 14]. The transformation does not modify transmission powers or depend on metrical properties of the distances. Thus, the respective properties of the algorithms and also the lower bounds, e.g., on power control [5, 11] are preserved.

In Section 6 we consider distributed approaches for capacity maximization, namely regret-learning algorithms [4]. Here we are not able to plug in the results for the non-fading model in a similar black-box fashion. Instead, we have to argue in a more detailed way to show that for uniform power assignments the expected number of successful requests is only a constant factor smaller than the size of the non-fading optimum. The bound is again completed using previous arguments, and we obtain a $O(\log^* n)$-factor with respect to the Rayleigh-fading optimum. Note that $\log^* n$ is essentially "almost constant", however, deriving a (provable) constant bound remains open.

Finally, we conduct a number of experiments that highlight the relation between the two models and the performance of regret learning. In particular, we observe that with probabilistic spectrum access, the curve for success probability in the Rayleigh-fading model can be seen as a smoothed variant of the success curve in the non-fading model. We observe that the non-fading model predicts more success if total interference is small, while Rayleigh fading allows more requests to become successful if interference is large. Regret-learning algorithms show fast convergence and good performance in both models, and the number of successful requests predicted by the non-fading model is somewhat larger.

1.2 Related Work

In a seminal paper, Gupta and Kumar [9] study the capacity of a wireless peer-to-peer network with a random topology based on non-fading SINR constraints. This brought about a lot of further work in randomly distributed networks [8, 21, 3]. Similar studies have been carried out for the case of regular topologies [20, 22]. Partly, this kind of research has also been generalized to networks with fading channels. For example, Liu and Haenggi [17] consider the capacity of square, triangle, hexagon, and random networks under Rayleigh-fading interference. More often Rayleigh fading is only used to model effects of noise, and interference inside the network itself is neglected [19, 10]. This represents an orthogonal approach because we concentrate on the particular problem of coordinating simultaneous transmissions. To the best of our knowledge, a direct comparision between the non-fading and Rayleigh-fading model like it is done in this paper has not been discussed in literature yet.

Real-world networks are typically neither random nor regular. This motivates the study of arbitrary topologies, as first done by Moscibroda and Wattenhofer [18]. Following this work, approximation algorithms in the non-fading SINR world were treated quite intensively, especially for the pure scheduling problems. Important milestones for capacity maximization are constant-factor approximations for uniform transmission powers [7]. A more sophisticated approach is selecting powers based on the distance between the sender and the respective receiver [13]. For uniform power assignments also a distributed algorithm has been developed [4] that uses regret learning. For latency minimization a distributed, ALOHA-like protocol has been analyzed [15, 12].

It yields an approximation factor of $O(\log n)$ with high probability.

The probably most natural extensions are the combined problems of scheduling and power control. This is, power levels are not fixed but have to be selected by the algorithm. This offers an additional freedom to the optimal solution as well. Using uniform transmission powers yields an $O(\log \Delta)$-approximation factor [1]. Here, Δ denotes the ratio of the maximal and the minimal distance between a sender and the respective receiver. One gets $O(\log \log \Delta + \log n)$-approximations when using square-root power assignments [11], i.e. a link of length d is assigned a transmission power proportional to $\sqrt{d^\alpha}$. The given approximation factors have been shown to be asymptotically almost optimal when restricting to these power assignments. However, for non-oblivious power assignments even a constant-factor approximation exists [14].

2. FORMAL MODEL DEFINITION

We assume that our network consists of n possible communication links $(s_1, r_1), \ldots, (s_n, r_n)$, each consisting of a sender and the respective receiver. In general, we do not make any assumptions on the geometry or distribution of the network nodes.

For the propagation, we consider Rayleigh-fading channels. This is, if a signal is transmitted by sender s_j, it is received by receiver r_i at a strength of $S_{j,i}$, which is a random variable. $S_{j,i}$ is exponentially distributed with mean $\bar{S}_{j,i}$. As usual, we assume this stochastic process to be independent for different (j, i) and from timeslot to timeslot.

The receiver r_i can successfully decode the signal transmitted by its sender s_i, if the SINR is above a certain theshold β, this is

$$\frac{S_{i,i}}{\sum_{j \neq i} S_{j,i} + \nu} \geq \beta .$$

Here, $\nu \geq 0$ is a constant denoting ambient noise.

We compare this channel model to the standard non-fading propagation model. Here, the received signal strength is always (deterministically) $\bar{S}_{j,i}$. As one can easily see, this comparison might not be fair. In the case of very low transmission powers, the mean received signal strength is already exceeded by the noise. Therefore, the transmission cannot be successful at all in the non-fading model, even in the absence of interference. In the Rayleigh-fading model in contrast, a small success probability remains. Therefore, as we focus on the impact of interference, we assume that $\bar{S}_{i,i}$ is always a constant factor higher than $\beta\nu$. To simplify notation, this factor is assumed to be 2, i.e. $\bar{S}_{i,i} \geq 2\beta\nu$.

When considering approximation algorithms in the non-fading model, it is usually very important that the signal strengths $\bar{S}_{j,i}$ are not arbitrary but determined by certain model parameters. That is for example $\bar{S}_{j,i} = p_j/d(s_j, r_i)^\alpha$ where p_j is the transmission power and $d(s_j, r_i)$ the distance between s_j and r_i. In contrast, our connection between Rayleigh-fading and non-fading models shown below applies in a more general scenario, without any assumptions on the values of the (expected) signal strength $\bar{S}_{j,i}$ – except non-negativity and the relation to noise as detailed in the paragraph above. In particular, this implies that our reduction between the models holds for arbitrary power assignments, path-loss exponents, requests located in metric spaces, etc. For proving bounded approximation factors, however, algorithms for the non-fading model usually rely heavily on $\bar{S}_{j,i}$ being characterized by these parameters. Consequently, our "black-box" translation of these algorithms and their approximation factors also applies only to instances of the Rayleigh model that have expected values $\bar{S}_{j,i}$ with the same characteristics.

3. SUCCESS PROBABILITY

In this section, we consider the following situation under Rayleigh-fading constraints. Assuming each sender s_i transmits with probability q_i, we bound the probability of a successful reception that we refer to as $Q_i(q_1, \ldots, q_n)$. Fortunately, in contrast to the non-fading model, the success probability can be given in a closed-form expression.

THEOREM 1. *The probability that receiver r_i can successfully receive the signal from s_i is*

$$Q_i(q_1, \ldots, q_n) = q_i \cdot \exp\left(-\frac{\beta\nu}{\bar{S}_{i,i}}\right) \prod_{j \neq i} \left(1 - \frac{\beta q_j}{\beta + \bar{S}_{i,i}/\bar{S}_{j,i}}\right) .$$

The proof of this expression is mainly due to Liu and Haenggi [17]; it can be found the appendix. The expression has the advantage of being an exact probability. However, in order to compare the probability to the one in the non-fading channel model, we need upper and lower bounds.

LEMMA 2. *The success probability for link i is at least*

$$Q_i(q_1, \ldots, q_n) \geq q_i \cdot \exp\left(-\frac{\beta}{\bar{S}_{i,i}}\left(\nu + \sum_{j \neq i} \bar{S}_{j,i} q_j\right)\right) .$$

The success probability for link i is at most

$$Q_i(q_1, \ldots, q_n) \leq q_i \cdot \exp\left(-\frac{\beta}{2\bar{S}_{i,i}}\left(\nu + \sum_{j \neq i} \bar{S}_{j,i} q_j\right)\right) .$$

PROOF. The proof of this lemma is based on the following observation concerning the exponential function.

OBSERVATION 3. *For all $x \in (0, 1]$, $q \in [0, 1]$, we have*

$$\exp(-xq) \leq 1 - \frac{q}{\frac{1}{x} + 1} \leq \exp\left(-\frac{1}{2}xq\right) .$$

PROOF. We show the first inequality using the fact that $\exp(y) \geq 1 + y$ for all $y \in \mathbb{R}$. Setting $y = xq$ yields

$$\exp(-xq) = \frac{1}{\exp(xq)} \leq \frac{1}{1 + xq} = 1 - \frac{q}{\frac{1}{x} + q} \leq 1 - \frac{q}{\frac{1}{x} + 1} .$$

Setting $y = -\frac{q}{\frac{1}{x}+1}$, we get

$$1 - \frac{q}{\frac{1}{x} + 1} \leq \exp\left(-\frac{q}{\frac{1}{x} + 1}\right) = \exp\left(-\frac{xq}{1 + x}\right) .$$

Furthermore, we have for all $x \in (0, 1]$ that $\frac{x}{x+1} \geq \frac{1}{2}x$. This yields the second bound. $\square$

Setting now $q = q_j$ and $x = \beta\bar{S}_{j,i}/\bar{S}_{i,i}$ in this observation, we get

$$\exp\left(-\beta\frac{\bar{S}_{j,i}}{\bar{S}_{i,i}}q_j\right) \leq 1 - \frac{\beta q_j}{\beta + \bar{S}_{i,i}/\bar{S}_{j,i}} \leq \exp\left(-\frac{1}{2}\beta\frac{\bar{S}_{j,i}}{\bar{S}_{i,i}}q_j\right) .$$

Theorem 1 now yields the claim. $\square$

As a first result, this gives us the following relation between the success probability in the Rayleigh-fading channel compared to the one in the non-fading channel.

COROLLARY 4. *If a set $S \subseteq [n]$ is feasible in the non-fading channel model, setting $q_i = 1$ for all $i \in S$ and $q_i = 0$ for all $i \notin S$, we have $Q_i(q_1, \ldots, q_n) \geq 1/e$ for all $i \in S$.*

If $q_i \in \{0, 1\}$ for all $i \in [n]$ and the Rayleigh success probability is at least $1/\sqrt{e}$ for each link, the set of all links with $q_i = 1$ is feasible in the non-fading channel model.

4. TRANSFORMING SCHEDULING ALGORITHMS

The bounds given in the previous section immediately allow us to estimate the performance of algorithms for the non-fading model in a Rayleigh-fading environment after some minor modifications.

In particular, we can take an arbitrary approximation algorithm for capacity maximization. This might be one of the constant-factor approximations for the setting with uniform transmission powers [7] or monotone transmission powers [13], or even for the case in which the algorithm has to choose the transmission power itself [14]. In any case, a set of links is returned that is feasible in the non-fading model. Making exactly these links transmit with probability 1 (without changes of the transmission powers), Corollary 4 yields that each of them will be successful with probability at least $1/e$. In terms of our objective function "capacity" this means that we are at most a $1/e$-factor worse in expectation. In combination, this means that the resulting algorithm will compute transmission probabilities yielding an expected capacity that is at most a constant factor worse than the optimally achievable capacity in the non-fading model. However, it remains to show that the theoretical optimum in the Rayleigh-fading model cannot be much better than the one in the non-fading model. This will be carried out in Section 5.

Existing approximation algorithms to minimize latency can in general be divided into two classes. On the one hand, there are many algorithms actually attempting to maximize the utilization of the first time slot and then apply this procedure recursively on the remaining links. For these kinds of algorithms and analyses exactly the same argumentation as for capacity maximization can be applied. On the other hand, ALOHA-style protocols have been proposed. Here, in each time slot, each link is assigned a (small) transmission probability, which we assume to be smaller than $1/2$. If it is successful, the sender stops transmitting, otherwise it continues running the algorithm. In order to transform such algorithms to the Rayleigh-fading model, we let each (randomized) step be executed 4 times. This yields a success probability that is at least as large as in the non-fading model. If p is the success probability in the non-fading model, Corollary 4 yields the Rayleigh-fading success probability is at least $p \cdot 1/e$. In 4 independent repeats the probability of at least one success is therefore at least $1 - (1 - p/e)^4$. This is at least p if the transmission probability (and therefore the success probability) is at most $1/2$.

For multi-hop scheduling algorithms [15, 14], the single-hop transformations mentioned above can directly be generalized. Here, in fact, the resulting multi-hop schedule can also be considered as a concatenation of single-hop schedules. Transforming each of them in the described way, we still only lose constant factors.

5. TRANSFORMING THE RAYLEIGH-FADING OPTIMUM

The performance of all algorithms constructed in Section 4 were measured in terms of the value of the optimal solution in the non-fading model. However, in order to derive approximation guarantees for the Rayleigh-fading model, the value of the computed solution has to be compared within the Rayleigh-fading model. Here, the optimal solution could potentially be much better than the non-fading one. In this section, we give a possibly surprising result that this indeed cannot happen in an interference-dominated environment. To be more precise, we take an arbitrary assignment of transmission probabilities. In the Rayleigh-fading model this yields a particular success probability for each link. We then simulate this single transmission with $O(\log^* n)$ independent steps in the non-fading model. In the end, for each link the success probability is at least as large as in the single Rayleigh-fading step.

This yields that for both considered scheduling problems, the Rayleigh-fading optimum can be at most an $O(\log^* n)$-factor better than the non-fading optimum. For capacity maximization this holds because we find $O(\log^* n)$ sets that are all feasible in the non-fading sense. In expectation, their summed value is at least as large as the one of the Rayleigh-fading optimum. This means that the best one can be at most an $O(\log^* n)$ factor worse.

When considering latency minimization under Rayleigh-fading conditions, the optimum should rather be considered as an algorithm itself that assigns transmission probabilities in each step. This assignment may arbitrarily depend on previous successes and may be computed using arbitrary computation power. However, our theorem shows for this case that even the perfect algorithm computes schedules that are at most an $O(\log^* n)$ factor shorter than the non-fading optimum, because we could replace each timeslot by the described simulation, increasing the schedule length by a factor of at most $O(\log^* n)$.

THEOREM 5. *For each assignment of transmission probabilities $q_1, \ldots, q_n$ there is a simulation using $O(\log^* n)$-steps such that the non-fading success probability in these steps is at least $Q_i(q_1, \ldots, q_n)$ for each link i.*

PROOF. We define $(b_k)_{k \in \mathbb{N}}$ recursively by setting $b_0 = 1/4$, $b_{k+1} = \exp(b_k/2)$. The simulation works as follows. For each $k \geq 0$ with $b_k < n$, we let each sender transmit with probability $q_i^{(k)} := q_i/4b_k$ for 19 times independently at random.

Algorithm 1: Formal description of the simulation.

1 $k := 0, b_0 := 1/4$;
2 **while** $b_k < n$ **do**
3   **for** 19 *times* **do**
4   ⌊ transmit with probability $q_i^{(k)} := q_i/4b_k$;
5 $b_{k+1} := \exp(b_k/2), k := k + 1$;

Consider an arbitrary $i \in [n]$. We claim: The probability of success during the $O(\log^* n)$ repeats in the non-fading model is at least $Q_i(q_1, \ldots, q_n)$.

We set $A = \sum_{j \neq i} \min \left\{ 1, \beta_i \bar{S}_{j,i} / \bar{S}_{i,i} \right\} \cdot q_j$. Observe that $0 \leq A \leq n$. In order to bound the success probability, we only take the kth iteration of the *while* loop into account where $b_k \leq \exp(A/2) \leq \exp(b_k/2)$. We will show that in this iteration, the probability of a successful transmission in the non-fading model is at least as large as the original one in the Rayleigh-fading model. Using Lemma 2, we observe the probability of success in the Rayleigh-fading model is at most $\frac{q_i}{e^{A/2}} \leq \frac{q_i}{b_k}$.

Let us first consider a single one of the 19 independent iterations. Let X_j be a 0/1 random variable indicating if sender s_j transmits in this iteration. By definition $\mathbf{E}[X_j] = q_j^{(k)}$. Furthermore, set $Z = \sum_{j \neq i} \min\{1, \beta_i \bar{S}_{j,i}/\bar{S}_{i,i}\} \cdot X_j$.

To make the transmission successful in the non-fading model, we have to have $X_i = 1$ and $\bar{S}_{i,i} \geq \beta_i(\sum_{j \neq i} \bar{S}_{j,i} X_j + \nu)$. To bound the probability of the latter event, we use the assumption that $\bar{S}_{i,i} \geq 2\beta_i \nu$. Therefore it suffices to have $Z < 1/2$, allowing to estimate the probability of this event by Markov's inequality using

$$\mathbf{Pr}\left[Z \geq \frac{1}{2}\right] \leq 2\mathbf{E}[Z] = 2\sum_{j \neq i} \min\left\{1, \beta_i \frac{\bar{S}_{j,i}}{\bar{S}_{i,i}}\right\} \mathbf{E}[X_j]$$

$$= 2\sum_{j \neq i} \min\left\{1, \beta_i \frac{\bar{S}_{j,i}}{\bar{S}_{i,i}}\right\} \cdot \frac{q_j}{4b_k} \leq 2\frac{A}{4b_k} .$$

For the remaining considerations, we distinguish between the two cases $k = 0$ and $k \geq 1$.

In the case $k \geq 1$, we use the fact that $A \leq b_k$ to get that the success probability in the non-fading model in a single iteration is at least

$$q_i^{(k)} \cdot \left(1 - 2\frac{A}{4b_k}\right) \geq \frac{q_i^{(k)}}{2} = \frac{q_i}{8b_k} .$$

We use now the facts that $k \geq 1$ and therefore $b_k \geq \exp(1/8)$ and furthermore that for all $0 \leq x \leq \exp(-1/8)$ we have $1 - (1 - x/8)^{19} \geq x$. This yields that in 19 independent repeats, we get a total success probability of at least

$$1 - \left(1 - \frac{q_i}{8b_k}\right)^{19} \geq \frac{q_i}{b_k} \geq q_i \exp\left(-\frac{A}{2}\right) .$$

As we have already seen, the success probability in the Rayleigh-fading model is at most $q_i \exp(-A/2)$.

For the case $k = 0$, we use that the probability that the transmission is not successful within a single iteration of the inner loop is at most $q_i(1-2A)$. This is, the probability that at least one of the 19 independent repeats is successful is at least $1 - (1 - q_i(1-2A))^{19} \geq q_i \exp(-A/2)$ for all $0 \leq q_i \leq 1$ because $A \leq 1/4$. $\square$

Taking this theorem into account, we see that we lose at most an $O(\log^* n)$ factor in all approximation guarantees of non-fading algorithms. In particular, the constant-factor capacity-maximization algorithms of the non-fading case provide without any further modification $O(\log^* n)$ approximations in the Rayleigh-fading case.

6. REGRET LEARNING FOR CAPACITY MAXIMIZATION

Another very useful approach to solve capacity maximization was presented by Dinitz [4]. This approach provides a distributed way to solve the problem based on regret-learning techniques. The idea behind regret-learning algorithms is that the algorithm gets feedback in terms of utility depending on the chosen actions of all users and chooses its next action according to this feedback. In the model introduced by Dinitz each user i has in each step the option to attempt a transmission or not. This is, his actions q_i are to send ($q_i = 1$) or not to send ($q_i = 0$). When sending a user gets a utility of 1 for being successful and -1 for not being successful. Not sending at all yields a utility of 0.

For this model, Ásgeirsson and Mitra [2] showed that in the non-fading model the average number of successful transmissions converges to the optimum up to a constant factor. Unfortunately, due to the sequential computation, our transformation cannot be applied here. However, we are able to prove a similar result showing that the expected number of successful transmissions converges to the non-fading optimum up to a constant factor.

Generally, in regret learning, a sequence of action vectors is computed in a decentralized way. In each step, every user i decides which action a_i to take. Depending on his own choice and the one of the other users, he gets a utility $u_i(a_1, \ldots, a_n)$. The choice which action to choose then depends on the history of utilities experienced before. The *external regret* is defined as the difference between the utility of the best single action in hindsight and the summed utility experienced by the algorithm.

DEFINITION 1. *The external regret of user i at time T given a sequence of action vectors $a^{(1)}, \ldots, a^{(T)}$ is*

$$\max_{a_i' \in A_i} \sum_{t=1}^{T} u_i(a_1^{(t)}, \ldots, a_i', \ldots, a_n^{(t)}) - \sum_{t=1}^{T} u_i(a^{(t)}) ,$$

where A_i is the set of possible actions of user i.

So the user regrets what he might have won by switching to one single action for all time steps instead of using the algorithm. An algorithm has the no-regret property if the average regret per time step converges to 0 for the number of time steps T going to ∞. One famous such algorithm is Randomized Weighted Majority due to Littlestone and Warmuth [16]. For this class of algorithms we prove the following theorem.

THEOREM 6. *Consider a sequence $q^{(1)}, \ldots, q^{(t)}$ of action vectors such that each user has regret at most $\epsilon \cdot T$. Then the average number of successful transmissions is in $\Omega(\text{OPT} - \epsilon n)$, for OPT being the size of the largest feasible set in the non-fading model under uniform transmission powers.*

Theorem 6 directly follows from Lemma 7 and Lemma 8, which we will prove in the remaining part of this section. Note that this theorem together with Theorem 5 yields a factor of $O(\log^* n)$ in comparison to the Rayleigh-fading optimum. Our analysis extends the one for the non-fading case by Ásgeirsson and Mitra [2] which in some parts relies on Dinitz [4]. The results from [2] also show the $F = \Omega(\text{OPT})$ bound for regret learning in the non-fading channel. This highlights the close relationship between the models.

In the Rayleigh-fading model, the utility function itself is stochastic and therefore hard to deal with. In addition, no-regret algorithms must use internal randomization, thus we consider expected utilities and the expected regret here. We adapt the utility function from Dinitz for an analysis in expectation. It depends on the success probability $Q_i(q_1, \ldots, q_n)$ of link i. Formally, we define the utility of user i to be

$$u_i(q_1, \ldots, q_n) = \begin{cases} 0 & \text{if } q_i = 0, \\ 2 \cdot Q_i(q_1, \ldots, q_n) - 1 & \text{if } q_i = 1. \end{cases}$$

In the following, we consider a sequence $q^{(1)}, \ldots, q^{(T)}$ that exhibits external regret $\epsilon \cdot T$ for each user $i = 1, \ldots, n$. We define $f_i = \frac{1}{T} \sum_t q_i^{(t)}$ as the fraction of time steps the user chooses $q_i = 1$. Let $F = \sum_i f_i$. We define x_i to be the average success probability per time step with $x_i = \frac{1}{T} \sum_t Q_i^{(t)} \left(q_1^{(t)}, \ldots, q_n^{(t)} \right)$, and we set $X = \sum_i x_i$.

We examine such sequences and at first bound the average number of successful transmissions. It turns out that for ϵ approaching 0 half of the transmissions are successful in the long run. Besides this result, we will show that the average number of transmitting nodes F is in $\Omega(\text{OPT})$. This together shows that the average number of successful transmissions X is in $\Omega(\text{OPT})$.

LEMMA 7. $X \leq F \leq 2X + \epsilon n$

PROOF. The first inequality follows by definition. For the second inequality, we use the fact that for each user i the regret is at most ϵ. Therefore, always using action $q_i = 0$ can increase the average utility per step by at most ϵ. Formally this means $2 \cdot x_i - f_i \geq -\epsilon$. Taking the sum over all i, we get $2X - F \geq -\epsilon n$. This yields $F \leq 2X + \epsilon n$. □

We have shown a bound for the average number of successful transmissions that depends on the average number of transmitting nodes F. This allows us next to see that F is in $\Omega(\text{OPT})$.

LEMMA 8. *Let OPT denote the size of the largest feasible set in the non-fading model under uniform transmission powers, then $F = \Omega(\text{OPT})$.*

PROOF. In the following $a(j, i)$ denotes the affectance of link j on link i for uniform powers with

$$a(j, i) = \min \left\{ 1, \frac{\beta \cdot \frac{d(s_i, r_i)^\alpha}{d(s_j, r_i)^\alpha}}{1 - \beta \cdot \nu \cdot d(s_i, r_i)^\alpha} \right\} .$$

We will denote the summed affectance from other links on link i by

$$a^{(t)}(i) = \sum_{\substack{j \in [n] \\ q_j^{(t)} = 1}} a(j, i) .$$

Let p_i be the fraction of steps in which $a^{(t)}(i) \leq \frac{1}{2}$ and let $\hat{a}(i) = \frac{1}{T} \sum_t a^{(t)}(i)$.

We define the sets $\text{OPT}' = \left\{ i \in \text{OPT} : f_i < \frac{1}{2} - \epsilon \right\}$ and $\text{OPT}'' = \left\{ i \in \text{OPT}' : \sum_{j \in \text{OPT}'} a(i, j) \leq 2 \right\}$. So all links in OPT'' attempt to transmit in less than a $\frac{1}{2} - \epsilon$ fraction of the time and affect others doing so by at most 2.

If $|\text{OPT} \setminus \text{OPT}'| > |\text{OPT}|/2$, then F would be at least $\left(\frac{1}{2} - \epsilon \right) \cdot |\text{OPT} \setminus \text{OPT}'|$ and therefore in $\Omega(\text{OPT})$.

So we consider $|\text{OPT}'| \geq |\text{OPT}|/2$ for the rest of the proof. Using [2, Lemma 8], we see $|\text{OPT}''| \geq |\text{OPT}|/4$. Therefore, it is sufficient to show $F = \Omega(|\text{OPT}''|)$ and so we just need to consider links $i \in \text{OPT}''$.

We consider the utility gain for link i by switching to action $q_i = 1$ throughout every step. In an f_i fraction of the

steps nothing changes. In at least a $p_i - f_i$ fraction of the steps, link i could have been successful but did not transmit in the original sequence. As the affectance is at most $\frac{1}{2}$, we conclude from Lemma 2 that the success probability in these steps is at least $\exp(-\frac{1}{2})$. For the remaining steps, we estimate the probability simply by 0. Therefore, the utility gain is at least $(p_i - f_i) \cdot 2 \exp(-\frac{1}{2}) - (1 - f_i) \leq \epsilon$.

This yields for all $i \in \text{OPT}''$ and $\epsilon \leq 0.04$ that

$$\begin{aligned} p_i &\leq f_i + \frac{\epsilon + 1 - f_i}{2 \exp(-\frac{1}{2})} \\ &\leq \frac{1}{2} \left(1 + \frac{\exp(\frac{1}{2})}{2} \right) + \frac{\epsilon \cdot \exp(\frac{1}{2})}{2} \leq \frac{19}{20} , \end{aligned}$$

because $f_i \leq \frac{1}{2}$. For $\hat{a}(i)$, we now get by definition of q_i

$$\hat{a}(i) \geq q_i \cdot 0 + (1 - q_i) \cdot \frac{1}{2} \geq \frac{1}{20} \cdot \frac{1}{2} = \frac{1}{40} .$$

Hence, we have

$$\hat{a}(i) = \sum_{j \in [n]} f_j a(j, i) \geq \frac{1}{40} \quad \text{for all } i \in \text{OPT}''.$$

Taking the sum of all resulting inequalities, we get

$$\sum_{i \in \text{OPT}''} \sum_{j \in [n]} f_j a(j, i) \geq \frac{|\text{OPT}''|}{40}$$

or, equivalently,

$$\sum_{j \in [n]} f_j \left(\sum_{i \in \text{OPT}''} a(j, i) \right) \geq \frac{|\text{OPT}''|}{40} .$$

With [2, Lemma 11] we have that $\sum_{i \in \text{OPT}''} a(j, i) = O(1)$ for all $j \in [n]$ and hence

$$\sum_{j \in [n]} f_j = \Omega(|\text{OPT}''|) . \quad \square$$

Due to Lemma 7 and 8, for any no-regret algorithm the number of successful transmissions needs to converge to a constant fraction of the non-fading optimum. This proves Theorem 6.

7. SIMULATION RESULTS

In the sections before, we showed a close relation between the Rayleigh-fading and the non-fading models in theory. While bounds are given asymptotically for worst-case instances, our theoretical results can also be verified in simulations.

In particular, we consider the performance of an ALOHA-like protocol and the no-regret capacity-maximization algorithm. Simulations are carried out on random networks constructed by randomly placing receivers on a 1000×1000 plane. Each corresponding sender is placed by choosing the angle and the distance to the receiver uniformly at random from a fixed interval. This way, a minimal and a maximal distance between sender and receiver can be specified.

Comparing the Rayleigh-fading and the non-fading model the simulations show that the number of successful transmissions under uniform powers behave similarly when the sending probabilities are chosen uniformly, see Figure 1. The simulation was done over 40 different networks with 100 links each and 25 different seeds for the randomizer to determine which links transmit. The SINR parameters were

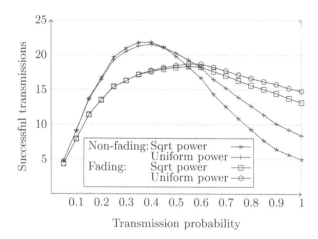

Figure 1: Number of successful transmissions for different transmission probabilities under square-root and uniform power assignment and under the Rayleigh-fading and non-fading SINR model.

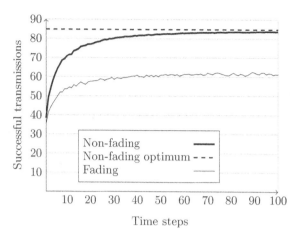

Figure 2: Number of successful transmissions under the Rayleigh-fading and non-fading model when applying a no-regret algorithm.

set to $\beta = 2.5$, $\alpha = 2.2$, and $\nu = 4 \cdot 10^{-7}$. The power for the uniform power assignment and the power from which the square-root power assignment scales was set to 2. For the Rayleigh-fading channel we additionally used 10 different seeds to determine whether a transmission is successful. The distance between a sender and the corresponding receiver was chosen between 20 and 40.

Figure 1 shows the number of successful transmissions averaged over all those runs. Neither the Rayleigh-fading model nor the non-fading model always predicts more success than the other one. The Rayleigh probability distribution leads to a smoothed curve compared to the non-fading model. This is due to the fact that even when the SINR constraint is not fulfilled in the non-fading model, the success probability in the Rayleigh-fading model still remains positive. On the other hand, when a transmission is definitely successful in the non-fading SINR model there is some probability for being not successful in the Rayleigh-fading model. The general characteristics of the curves are the same and show that the Rayleigh-fading and the non-fading model behave alike.

Choosing the optimal set of sending links under uniform powers, we reach on average 49.75 successful transmissions in those networks.

The similarity can also be seen when taking a look at no-regret algorithms. Here we analyzed a version of the Randomized Weighted Majority Algorithm of Littlestone and Warmuth [16]. The weights are initialized with 1 and multiplied by $(1 - \eta)^{l_i}$ in every time step, where l_i is the loss of not sending ($i = 0$) or sending ($i = 1$). The loss for sending and not being received is 1 and the loss of not sending at all is 0.5. In all other cases the loss is 0. These losses correspond to the utility function used in Section 6. The factor η starts with $\sqrt{0.5}$ and is multiplied by $\sqrt{0.5}$ every time the number of time steps is increased above the next power of 2.

For the simulation shown in Figure 2 we used different networks with 200 links, distances between 0 and 100, $\beta = 0.5$, $\alpha = 2.1$, and $\nu = 0$. The other settings remained as before.

The results behave in the same way as observed by Ásgeirsson and Mitra [2] in their simulations. The Rayleigh-fading model shows more fluctuations due to its stochastic nature. We can also see that the no-regret algorithm converges quite quickly near the optimum of the non-fading model. The number of time steps needed for convergence depends on the specific instance, but a good performance can already be seen after 30 to 40 timesteps.

8. DISCUSSION AND OPEN PROBLEMS

In this paper we showed that from an algorithmic point of view, the non-fading and the Rayleigh-fading model behave similarly in theory as well as in simulations. We regard this as a promising result because it indicates that existing results on approximation algorithms within non-fading models seem to apply more generally. Turning to a different, more realistic scenario does not create a fundamentally new situation as was the case when shifting from graph-based interference models to SINR-based ones.

Future research could take two different directions from this point. On the one hand, it could focus on the similarities, e.g., by improving the obtained bounds. Considering a particular situation, the $O(\log^* n)$-factor in Theorem 5 might be reduced to a constant, which we were not able to prove in general. Futhermore, the similarities could be exploited to take the best of the two worlds, in order to derive more sophisticated, hopefully distributed algorithms. On the other hand, also the differences could be taken into account. For example, the regret-learning simulation in the Rayleigh-fading model reaches a smaller capacity. It would be interesting to see if this is a general effect of the stochastic model or under which conditions this behavior can be observed.

9. REFERENCES

[1] Matthew Andrews and Michael Dinitz. Maximizing capacity in arbitrary wireless networks in the sinr model: Complexity and game theory. In *Proceedings of the 28th Conference of the IEEE Communications Society (INFOCOM)*, 2009.

[2] Eyjolfur Ingi Asgeirsson and Pradipta Mitra. On a game theoretic approach to capacity maximization in wireless networks. In *Proceedings of the 30th Conference of the IEEE Communications Society (INFOCOM)*, 2011.

[3] S. De, C. Qiao, D.A. Pados, and M. Chatterjee. Topological and MAI constraints on the performance of wireless CDMA sensor networks. In *Proceedings of the 23rd Conference of the IEEE Communications Society (INFOCOM)*, volume 1, pages 4 vol. (xxxv+2866), march 2004.

[4] Michael Dinitz. Distributed algorithms for approximating wireless network capacity. In *Proceedings of the 29th Conference of the IEEE Communications Society (INFOCOM)*, pages 1397–1405, 2010.

[5] Alexander Fanghänel, Thomas Kesselheim, Harald Räcke, and Berthold Vöcking. Oblivious interference scheduling. In *Proceedings of the 28th ACM symposium on Principles of distributed computing (PODC)*, pages 220–229, 2009.

[6] Alexander Fanghänel, Thomas Kesselheim, and Berthold Vöcking. Improved algorithms for latency minimization in wireless networks. *Theoretical Computer Science*, 412(24):2657 – 2667, 2011.

[7] Olga Goussevskaia, Roger Wattenhofer, Magnús M. Halldórsson, and Emo Welzl. Capacity of arbitrary wireless networks. In *Proceedings of the 28th Conference of the IEEE Communications Society (INFOCOM)*, pages 1872–1880, 2009.

[8] Matthias Grossglauser and David N. C. Tse. Mobility increases the capacity of ad hoc wireless networks. *IEEE/ACM Trans. Netw.*, 10:477–486, August 2002.

[9] P. Gupta and P.R. Kumar. The capacity of wireless networks. *Information Theory, IEEE Transactions on*, 46(2):388 –404, mar 2000.

[10] M. Haenggi. On routing in random rayleigh fading networks. *Wireless Communications, IEEE Transactions on*, 4(4):1553 – 1562, july 2005.

[11] Magnús M. Halldórsson. Wireless scheduling with power control. In *Proceedings of the 17th annual European Symposium on Algorithms (ESA)*, pages 361–372, 2009.

[12] Magnús M. Halldórsson and Pradipta Mitra. Nearly optimal bounds for distributed wireless scheduling in the sinr model. In *Proceedings of the 38th International EATCS Colloquium on Automata, Languages and Programming (ICALP)*, pages 625–636, 2011.

[13] Magnús M. Halldórsson and Pradipta Mitra. Wireless capacity with oblivious power in general metrics. In *Proceedings of the 22nd ACM-SIAM Symposium on Discrete Algorithms (SODA)*, pages 1538–1548, 2011.

[14] Thomas Kesselheim. A constant-factor approximation for wireless capacity maximization with power control in the SINR model. In *Proceedings of the 22nd ACM-SIAM Symposium on Discrete Algorithms (SODA)*, pages 1549–1559, 2011.

[15] Thomas Kesselheim and Berthold Vöcking. Distributed contention resolution in wireless networks. In *Proceedings of the 24th International Symposium on DIStributed Computing*, pages 163–178, 2010.

[16] Nick Littlestone and Manfred K. Warmuth. The weighted majority algorithm. *Information and Computation*, 108(2):212–261, 1994.

[17] Xiaowen Liu and Martin Haenggi. Throughput analysis of fading sensor networks with regular and random topologies. *EURASIP J. Wirel. Commun. Netw.*, 5(4):554–564, 2005.

[18] Thomas Moscibroda and Roger Wattenhofer. The complexity of connectivity in wireless networks. In *Proceedings of the 25th Conference of the IEEE Communications Society (INFOCOM)*, pages 1–13, 2006.

[19] J. Roberts and T. Healy. Packet radio performance over slow rayleigh fading channels. *Communications, IEEE Transactions on*, 28(2):279 – 286, feb 1980.

[20] J. Silvester and L. Kleinrock. On the capacity of multihop slotted aloha networks with regular structure. *Communications, IEEE Transactions on*, 31(8):974 – 982, aug 1983.

[21] S. Toumpis and A.J. Goldsmith. Capacity regions for wireless ad hoc networks. *Wireless Communications, IEEE Transactions on*, 2(4):736 – 748, july 2003.

[22] Liang-Liang Xie and P.R. Kumar. A network information theory for wireless communication: scaling laws and optimal operation. *Information Theory, IEEE Transactions on*, 50(5):748 – 767, may 2004.

APPENDIX

A. PROOF OF THEOREM 1

PROOF. Two events have to occur for successful transmission. On the one hand, sender s_i has to decide to transmit. By definition this probability is q_i. On the other hand, the SINR for the transmission must be large enough. For the latter event, Liu and Haenggi [17] derived a formula, which can be generalized to our model as follows.

The cumulated interference our transmission is exposed to is given by $I_i = \sum_{j \neq i} S_{j,i} \cdot X_j$, where X_j denotes the 0/1 random variable whether sender s_j makes a transmission attempt. The transmission is successful if $S_{i,i} \geq \beta(I_i + \nu)$. Fixing I_i, we can use the fact that $S_{i,i}$ is expontially distributed to get

$$\mathbf{Pr}\left[S_{i,i} \geq \beta(I_i + \nu) \mid I_i = x\right] = \exp\left(-\frac{\beta(x + \nu)}{\bar{S}_{i,i}}\right) .$$

Taking the expectation over I_i, we get

$$
\begin{aligned}
&\mathbf{Pr}\left[S_{i,i} \geq \beta(I_i + \nu)\right] \\
&= \mathbf{E}\left[\exp\left(-\frac{\beta(I_i + \nu)}{\bar{S}_{i,i}}\right)\right] \\
&= \mathbf{E}\left[\exp\left(-\frac{\beta(\sum_{j \neq i} S_{j,i} \cdot X_j + \nu)}{\bar{S}_{i,i}}\right)\right] \\
&= \exp\left(-\frac{\beta \cdot \nu}{\bar{S}_{i,i}}\right) \mathbf{E}\left[\prod_{j \neq i} \exp\left(-\frac{\beta \cdot S_{j,i} \cdot X_j}{\bar{S}_{i,i}}\right)\right] \\
&= \exp\left(-\frac{\beta \cdot \nu}{\bar{S}_{i,i}}\right) \prod_{j \neq i} \mathbf{E}\left[\exp\left(-\frac{\beta \cdot S_{j,i} \cdot X_j}{\bar{S}_{i,i}}\right)\right]
\end{aligned}
$$

Since $S_{j,i}$ and X_j are independent, we have

$$\mathbf{E}\left[\exp\left(-\frac{\beta \cdot S_{j,i} \cdot X_j}{\bar{S}_{i,i}}\right)\right]$$
$$= q_j \cdot \mathbf{E}\left[\exp\left(-\frac{\beta \cdot S_{j,i}}{\bar{S}_{i,i}}\right)\right] + (1 - q_j) \ .$$

Using now the fact that $S_{j,i}$ is exponentially distributed, we get

$$\mathbf{E}\left[\exp\left(-\frac{\beta \cdot S_{j,i}}{\bar{S}_{i,i}}\right)\right]$$
$$= \int_0^\infty \frac{1}{\bar{S}_{j,i}} \exp\left(-\frac{x}{\bar{S}_{j,i}}\right) \cdot \exp\left(-\frac{\beta \cdot x}{\bar{S}_{i,i}}\right) dx$$
$$= \frac{1}{1 + \beta \frac{\bar{S}_{j,i}}{\bar{S}_{i,i}}} \ .$$

This yields that $\mathbf{Pr}\left[S_{i,i} \geq \beta(I_i + \nu)\right]$ is

$$\exp\left(-\frac{\beta \cdot \nu}{\bar{S}_{i,i}}\right) \prod_{j \neq i} \left(q_j \cdot \frac{1}{1 + \beta \frac{\bar{S}_{j,i}}{\bar{S}_{i,i}}} + (1 - q_j) \right) \ ,$$

yielding the claim. $\square$

Author Index

www.ingramcontent.com/pod-product-compliance
Lightning Source LLC
Chambersburg PA
CBHW080152060326
40689CB00018B/3945